Adaptive

THE **ADAPTIVE** READING EXPERIENCE
DESIGNED TO TRANSFORM THE WAY STUDENTS READ

> More students earn **A's** and **B's** when they use McGraw-Hill Education **Adaptive** products.

SmartBook®

Proven to help students improve grades and study more efficiently, SmartBook contains the same content within the print book, but actively tailors that content to the needs of the individual. SmartBook's adaptive technology provides precise, personalized instruction on what the student should do next, guiding the student to master and remember key concepts, targeting gaps in knowledge and offering customized feedback, and driving the student toward comprehension and retention of the subject matter. Available on tablets, SmartBook puts learning at the student's fingertips—anywhere, anytime.

> Over **8 billion questions** have been answered, making McGraw-Hill Education products more intelligent, reliable, and precise.

www.mheducation.com

STUDENTS WANT

SMARTBOOK®

95% of students reported **SmartBook** to be a more effective way of reading material.

100% of students want to use the Practice Quiz feature available within **SmartBook** to help them study.

100% of students reported having reliable access to off-campus wifi.

90% of students say they would purchase **SmartBook** over print alone.

95% of students reported that **SmartBook** would impact their study skills in a positive way.

*Findings based on 2015 focus group results administered by McGraw-Hill Education

sociology

in modules

sociology
in modules

fourth edition

Richard T. Schaefer

DEPAUL UNIVERSITY

McGraw Hill Education

SOCIOLOGY IN MODULES, FOURTH EDITION

Published by McGraw-Hill Education, 2 Penn Plaza, New York, NY 10121. Copyright © 2018 by McGraw-Hill Education. All rights reserved. Printed in the United States of America. Previous editions © 2016, 2013, and 2011. No part of this publication may be reproduced or distributed in any form or by any means, or stored in a database or retrieval system, without the prior written consent of McGraw-Hill Education, including, but not limited to, in any network or other electronic storage or transmission, or broadcast for distance learning.

Some ancillaries, including electronic and print components, may not be available to customers outside the United States.

This book is printed on acid-free paper.

2 3 4 5 6 7 8 9 LMN 21 20 19 18

ISBN 978-1-259-70271-6
MHID 1-259-70271-5

Chief Product Officer, SVP Products & Markets: *G. Scott Virkler*
Vice President, General Manager, Products & Markets: *Michael Ryan*
Vice President, Content Design & Delivery: *Betsy Whalen*
Managing Director: *Gina Boedecker*
Director, Product Development: *Meghan Campbell*
Lead Product Developer: *Rhona Robbin*
Marketing Manager: *Kaitlyn Lombardo*
Market Development Manager: *Stacy Ruel*
Digital Product Analyst: *Susan Pierre-Louis*
Digital Product Developer: *Briana Porco*
Director, Content Design & Delivery: *Terri Schiesl*
Program Manager: *Marianne Musni*
Content Project Managers: *Katie Klochan, Sandra Schnee, Susan Trentacosti*
Buyer: *Laura M. Fuller*
Design: *Jessica Cuevas*
Content Licensing Specialists: *Ann Marie Jannette, Lori Slattery*
Cover Image: *© RyanJLane/iStock/Getty Images Plus/Getty Images*
Compositor: *SPi Global*
Printer: *LSC Communications*

All credits appearing on page or at the end of the book are considered to be an extension of the copyright page. About the author photo: Courtesy of Richard Schaefer. Contents chapter photos: 1: © Cathy Yeulet/123RF; 2: © RosaIreneBetancourt 3/Alamy Stock Photo; 3: © F. Poelking/age footstock; 4: © Blend Images-KidStock/Brand X Pictures/Getty Images RF; 5: © Caia Image/Glow Images RF; 6: © Franziska Krug/German Select/Getty Images; 7: © Frederick J. Brown/AFP/Getty Images; 8: © PeerPoint/Alamy; 9: © Stockbyte/Getty Images; 10: © RosaIreneBetancourt 3/Alamy; 11: © Thinkstock/Index Stock RF; 12: © Monkey Business Images/Shutterstock RF; 13: © Jeff Greenberg/The Image Works; 14: © Martin Shields/Alamy Stock Photo; 15: © Jacob Silberberg/Panos Pictures; 16: © Jim West /Image Works; 17: © Imaginechina/Corbis; 18: © Agencja Fotograficzna Caro/Alamy

Library of Congress Control Number: 2016059020

dedication

To my grandchildren, Matilda and Reuben. May they enjoy exploring life's possibilities.

about the author

Richard T. Schaefer Professor, DePaul University
BA Northwestern University; MA, PhD University of Chicago

Growing up in Chicago at a time when neighborhoods were going through transitions in ethnic and racial composition, Richard T. Schaefer found himself increasingly intrigued by what was happening, how people were reacting, and how these changes were affecting neighborhoods and people's jobs. His interest in social issues caused him to gravitate to sociology courses at Northwestern University, where he eventually received a BA in sociology.

"Originally as an undergraduate I thought I would go on to law school and become a lawyer. But after taking a few sociology courses, I found myself wanting to learn more about what sociologists studied, and fascinated by the kinds of questions they raised." This fascination led him to obtain his MA and PhD in sociology from the University of Chicago. Dr. Schaefer's continuing interest in race relations led him to write his master's thesis on the membership of the Ku Klux Klan and his doctoral thesis on racial prejudice and race relations in Great Britain.

Dr. Schaefer went on to become a professor of sociology at DePaul University in Chicago. In 2004 he was named to the Vincent DePaul professorship in recognition of his undergraduate teaching and scholarship. He has taught introductory sociology for over 35 years to students in colleges, adult education programs, nursing programs, and even a maximum-security prison. Dr. Schaefer's love of teaching is apparent in his interaction with his students. "I find myself constantly learning from the students who are in my classes and from reading what they write. Their insights into the material we read or current events that we discuss often become part of future course material and sometimes even find their way into my writing."

Dr. Schaefer is the author of *Sociology: A Brief Introduction*, 12th edition (McGraw-Hill, 2017), *Sociology*, 13th edition (McGraw-Hill, 2012), *Sociology in Modules*, 4th edition (McGraw-Hill, 2018), *Sociology Matters*, 6th edition (McGraw-Hill, 2014), and, with Robert Feldman, *Sociology and Your Life with P.O.W.E.R. Learning* (McGraw-Hill, 2016). He is also the author of *Racial and Ethnic Groups*, now in its 14th edition (2014), *Racial and Ethnic Diversity in the USA*, 1st edition, (2014), and *Race and Ethnicity in the United States*, 7th edition (2013), all published by Pearson. Together with William Zellner he coauthored the 9th edition of *Extraordinary Groups* (Waveland Press, 2015). Dr. Schaefer served as the general editor of the three-volume *Encyclopedia of Race, Ethnicity, and Society,* published by Sage in 2008. These books have been translated into Chinese, Japanese, Portuguese, and Spanish, as well as adapted for use in Canadian colleges.

Dr. Schaefer's articles and book reviews have appeared in many journals, including *American Journal of Sociology; Phylon: A Review of Race and Culture; Contemporary Sociology; Sociology and Social Research; Sociological Quarterly;* and *Teaching Sociology.* He served as president of the Midwest Sociological Society in 1994–1995.

Dr. Schaefer's advice to students is to "look at the material and make connections to your own life and experiences. Sociology will make you a more attentive observer of how people in groups interact and function. It will also make you more aware of people's different needs and interests—and perhaps more ready to work for the common good, while still recognizing the individuality of each person."

brief contents

contents

**4 Socialization and the
Life Course 76**

**5 Social Interaction,
Groups, and Social
Structure 97**

6 The Mass Media 127

chapter opening excerpts

Every chapter in this textbook begins with an excerpt from one of the works listed here. These excerpts convey the excitement and relevance of sociological inquiry and draw readers into the subject matter of each chapter.

boxed features

Sociology in the Global Community

Our Wired World

Sociology on Campus

Taking Sociology to Work

social policy sections

maps

tracking sociological perspectives tables

summing up tables

Modules Work for Instructors & Students

Modules allow you to assign the content you want in the order you prefer, and the format promotes student learning and success by presenting content in small, manageable chunks.

create

Create, Because Customization Matters.

Finally you have the ability to customize your introductory Sociology course materials to align with your course goals.

- Prefer to cover Deviance in the first few weeks of class? **No problem.** Just click and rearrange the modules.
- Want additional coverage on Family Relationships? **Easy.** Just search our database to find the best content for your students.
- Don't cover Research Methods in your course? **Simple.** Just omit those modules.

You can also upload your syllabus or any other content you have written to tailor your McGraw-Hill Sociology materials just how you want them, in a snap. Register today at **www.mcgrawhillcreate.com** and craft your course resources to match the way you teach!

Why Does Sociology Matter?

Whether you're a first-time student, someone who is returning to the classroom, or even an instructor leading a discussion, you've probably thought about that question. Sociologists examine society, from small-scale interactions to the broadest social changes, which can be daunting for any student to take in. *Sociology: A Brief Introduction,* 12th Edition, bridges the essential sociological theories, research, and concepts and the everyday realities we all experience. The program highlights the distinctive ways in which sociologists explore human social behavior—and how their research findings can be used to help students think critically about the broader principles that guide their lives. In doing so, it helps students begin to think sociologically, using what they have learned to evaluate human interactions and institutions independently.

What do a police officer, a nurse, and a local business owner need to know about the community that they serve? It turns out quite a lot. And *Sociology: A Brief Introduction* is poised to give students the tools they need to take sociology with them as they pursue their studies and their careers, and as they get involved in their communities and the world at large. Its emphasis on real-world applications enables students to see the relevance of sociological concepts to contemporary issues and events as well as students' everyday lives. In addition, the digital tools in Connect foster student preparedness for a more productive and engaging experience in class and better grades on exams.

Help Your Students Succeed with Connect

Connect® is a digital teaching and learning environment that improves performance over a variety of critical outcomes; it is easy to use; and it is proven effective. Connect includes assignable and assessable quizzes, exercises, and interactive activities, all associated with learning objectives for *Sociology: A Brief Introduction,* 12th Edition. Videos, interactive assessments, links to news articles about current issues with accompanying questions ("News-Flash"), and scenario-based activities engage students and add real-world perspective to the introductory sociology course. In addition, printable, exportable reports show how well each student or section is performing on each course segment.

Put students first with Connect's new, intuitive mobile interface, which gives students and instructors flexible, convenient, anytime-anywhere access to all components of the Connect platform. It provides seamless integration of learning tools and places the most important priorities up front in a new "to-do" list with a calendar view across all Connect courses. Enjoy on-the-go access with the new mobile interface designed for optimal use of tablet functionality.

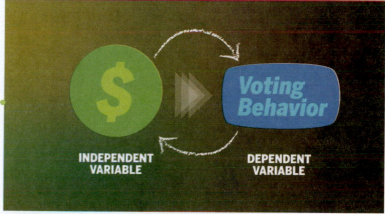

Provide a Smarter Text and Better Value with SmartBook

Mc Graw Hill Education | SMARTBOOK™

Available within Connect, **SmartBook®** makes study time as productive and efficient as possible by identifying and closing knowledge gaps. SmartBook is powered by the proven **LearnSmart®** engine, which identifies what an individual student knows and doesn't know based on the student's confidence level, responses to questions and other factors. It then provides focused help through targeted learning resources (including videos, animations, and other interactive activities).

SmartBook builds an optimal, personalized learning path for each student, so students spend less time on concepts they already understand and more time on those they don't. As a student engages with SmartBook, the reading experience continuously adapts by highlighting the most impactful content a student needs to learn at that moment in time. This ensures that every minute spent with SmartBook is returned to the student as the most value-added minute possible. The result? More confidence, better grades, and greater success.

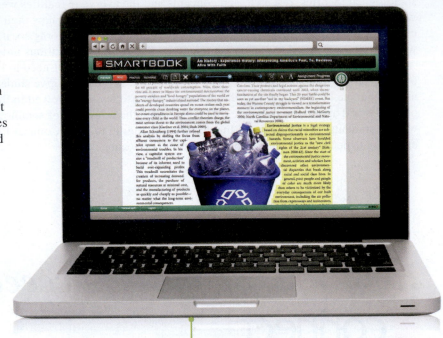

Access Performance Data Just in Time

Mc Graw Hill Education | connect INSIGHT™

Connect Insight® is Connect's new one-of-a-kind visual analytics dashboard, now available for both instructors and students, that provides at-a-glance information regarding student performance, which is immediately actionable. By presenting assignment, assessment, and topical performance results, together with a time metric that is easily visible for aggregate or individual results, Connect Insight gives the user the ability to take a just-in-time approach to teaching and learning, which was never before available. Connect Insight presents data that empowers students and helps instructors improve class performance in a way that is efficient and effective.

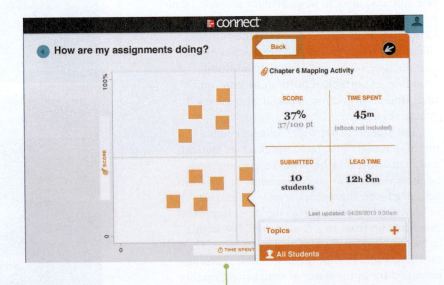

What's New

Chapter 1: Understanding Sociology

- Expanded introduction of the term *sociological imagination*
- Thinking Critically question in Module 1
- Updated coverage of sociological study of post-Katrina New Orleans
- Key term treatment of *mesosociology* and *global sociology*
- Updated table, "Major Sociological Perspectives"
- Updated research data throughout section on "Applied and Clinical Sociology"
- Updated figure, "Occupations of First-Year Sociology Majors"
- Added Taking Sociology with You question

Chapter 2: Sociological Research

- Updated figures, "Educational Level and Household Income in the United States," "Impact of a College Education on Income," and "Changing Attitudes toward the Legalization of Marijuana
- Research Today box, "Visual Sociology," with key term treatment of *visual sociology* and *applied sociology*
- Inclusion of transgender issues in section on "Queer Theory and Methodology"
- Added Thinking Critically question in section on "Queer Theory and Methodology"
- Expanded discussion of portrayal of gender in movies in "Social Policy: Studying Human Sexuality" section
- Added Taking Sociology with You question

Chapter 3: Culture

- Updated figure, "Counties with High Child Marriage Rates"
- Added photo to "Role of Language" section
- Updated data in section on values and in figure, "Life Goals of First-Year College Students"
- Added figure, "Values: Acceptance of Non-Marital Cohabitation"

Chapter 4: Socialization and the Life Course

- Opening excerpt, *The Wolfpack*, based on interview with filmmaker Crystal Moselle
- Photo of Marine basic training to illustrate concept of total institution
- Added Taking Sociology with You question

Chapter 5: Social Interaction, Groups, and Social Structure

- Enhanced discussion and new examples in section on "Ascribed and Achieved Status"

- Photo of Denali to illustrate role conflict
- Photo from *Survivor: Cambodia* to illustrate coalition building
- Thinking Critically question in Module 16
- Discussion of how gender influences ascribed status within formal organizations elaborated with new research
- Discussion of "flat" hierarchies in section Module 19
- Our Wired World box, "Becoming Social in a *Gesellschaft*"
- Coverage of 2015 U.S. labor rulings in Social Policy feature

Chapter 6: The Mass Media

- Chapter-opening photo emphasizing worldwide reach of Western media
- Enhanced discussion of conferral of status through social media
- Let's Discuss question in box, "Inside the Bubble: Internet Search Filters"
- Enhanced discussion of dominant ideology in the media and expanded Use Your Sociological Imagination question
- Enhanced discussion of feminist research and perspectives on media
- Our Wired World box, "Can Cell Phones Solve the Refugee Crisis?"

Chapter 7: Deviance, Crime, and Social Control

- Enhanced discussion of solitary confinement in Module 23
- Research Today box, "Debtor's Jails in the Twenty-First Century"
- Thinking Critically question in Module 23
- Sociology on Campus box, "Packing Firearms on Campus"
- Social Policy feature, "The Death Penalty in the U.S. and Worldwide"
- Enhanced discussion about public perceptions of violent crime in Module 25
- Figure 25-1, "Reported Hate Crimes by Category," updated and revised to reflect new category of Gender

Chapter 8: Stratification and Social Mobility in the United States

- More comprehensive definition of *income*
- Chapter-opening excerpt from Federal Reserve chair Janet Yellen's remarks about income and social inequality
- Research Today box, "The Shrinking Middle Class"
- Research Today box, "Taxes as Opportunity"
- Figure, "The Distribution of Family Wealth in the United States"
- Figure, "U.S. Minimum Wage Adjusted for Inflation, 1950–2015"
- Sociology on Campus box, "Student Debt"

Revised figures, "Current Higher Education Graduation Rates, Selected Countries," "Tuition and Room and Board Costs, 1963–2013," "Mapping Life Nationwide: Average Salary for Teachers," "College Campuses by Race and Ethnicity: Then, Now, and in the Future," and "Mapping Life Nationwide: Charter Schools"

Chapter 15: Religion

- Figure, "Religious Affiliation 2010–2050"
- Discussion of impact of the Internet on religion
- Updated discussion of religious observances in public schools

Chapter 16: Government and the Economy

- Section on the sharing economy
- Discussion of recent political trends in the United States
- Research Today box, "The Latino Political Voice," with figure, "Latino Participation in Presidential Elections, 1988–2012"
- Discussion of criticism of pluralist model of American politics
- Discussion of growing importance of online politicking
- Enhanced discussion of the influence of the elite and of money on politics
- Figure, "Global Terrorism Index"
- Discussion of terrorism and labeling theory
- Updated figures, "World's Largest Economies," "Voter Turnout Worldwide," "Women in National Legislatures, Selected Countries," and "Mapping Life Worldwide: Global Peace Index"
- Taking Sociology with You question about the sharing economy

Chapter 17: Health, Population, and the Environment

- Discussion of interactionist perspective on provider-patient relationship, with emphasis on role of class and race and on the role of technology
- Discussion of stigma associated with illness, with emphasis on electronic patient records
- Discussion of trend toward jailing of the mentally ill
- Updated Taking Sociology to Work box about director of programs focusing on children's health and health in Africa
- Figure, "The Environment versus Energy Production"
- Updated discussion of China's new two-child policy
- Sociology in the Global Community box, "Environmental Refugees"
- Discussion of 2015 Paris environmental summit
- Updated figures, "Infant Mortality Rates in Selected Countries," "AIDS by the Numbers Worldwide," "Mapping Life

Nationwide: Percentage without Health Insurance," "Total Health Care Expenditures in the United States, 1970–2020 (Projected)," and "Use of Complementary and Alternative Medicine"
- Taking Sociology with You question about effects of lack of health insurance

Chapter 18: Social Movements and Social Change

- Chapter-opening excerpt from *Social Movements and New Technology* by Victoria Carty
- Figures, "Declining Drive-Ins 1954–2012," "Walking to Work 1960–2012," "The Changing U.S. Economy," and "Estimated Global Sale of Industrial Robots, 2010–2018"
- Discussion of the importance of gender in understanding social movements
- Enhanced discussion of role of social media in developing social movements
- Example of vested interests
- Example of culture lag
- Discussion of women's role in migration of families
- Updated figures, "Internet Users by World Region," "Internet Penetration by World Region," and "Internet's Top Ten Languages"
- Thinking Critically question about the effects of technological innovation on society

Teaching Resources

Instructor's Manual. The Instructor's Manual includes detailed chapter outlines and chapter summaries; learning objectives; a chapter-by-chapter bulleted list of new content; key terms; essay questions; and critical thinking questions.

PowerPoint Slides. The PowerPoint Slides include bulleted lecture points, figures, and maps. They can be used as is or modified to meet the instructor's individual needs.

Test Bank. The Test Bank includes multiple-choice, true-false, and essay questions for every chapter. TestGen software allows the instructor to create customized exams using either publisher-supplied test items or the instructor's own questions.

These instructor resources can be accessed through the Library tab in Connect.

Take Sociology with You

Sociology in Modules highlights the distinctive ways in which sociologists examine human social behavior, as well as the ways in which research findings contribute to our understanding of society. In doing so, it helps students to think like sociologists and to apply sociological theories and concepts to human interactions and institutions. In other words, *Sociology in Modules* gives students the tools they need to take sociology with them when they graduate from college, begin to pursue careers, and become involved in their communities and the world at large.

 Thinking Critically: These questions, appearing at the end of each module, prompt students to review and reflect on the content.

 Sociology on Campus: These boxes apply a sociological perspective to issues of immediate interest to students.

 Use Your Sociological Imagination: These short, thought-provoking exercises encourage students to apply the sociological concepts they have learned to the world around them.

 Taking Sociology with You: These critical thinking questions and reflection prompts at the end of each chapter encourage students to apply the material they have just read to their daily lives.

 Taking Sociology to Work: These boxes underscore the value of an undergraduate or community college degree in sociology by profiling individuals who studied sociology and now use its principles in their work.

 Research Today: These boxes present new sociological findings on topics such as sports, social networks, and transracial adoption.

 Careers in Sociology: This appendix to Chapter 1 presents career options for students who have their undergraduate degree in sociology and explains how this degree can be an asset in a wide variety of occupations.

 Our Wired World: These boxes describe the Internet's effect on social activities such as lying, love, and politicking.

 Sociology in the Global Community: These boxes provide a global perspective on topics such as stratification, marriage, and the women's movement.

 Social Policy Sections: The end-of-chapter social policy sections apply sociological concepts and theories to important social issues currently being debated by policymakers and the general public.

 Maps: Mapping Life Nationwide and Mapping Life Worldwide maps show social trends in the United States as well as in the global community.

 **Campus**

McGraw-Hill Campus is a first-of-its-kind institutional service that provides faculty with true, single sign-on access to all of McGraw-Hill's course content, digital tools, and other high-quality learning resources from any learning management system (LMS). This innovative offering allows secure, deep integration and seamless access to any of our course solutions, including McGraw-Hill Connect, McGraw-Hill LearnSmart, McGraw-Hill Create, and Tegrity. **McGraw-Hill Campus** covers our entire content library, including eBooks, assessment tools, presentation slides, and multimedia content, among other resources. This open and unlimited service allows faculty to quickly prepare for class, create tests or quizzes, develop lecture material, integrate interactive content, and much more.

Acknowledgments

Since 2010, Elaine Silverstein has played a most significant role in the development of my introductory sociology books. Fortunately for me, in this Fourth Edition, Elaine has once again been responsible for the smooth integration of all changes and updates.

For over 30 years, I have enjoyed and benefited from the friendship and sage professional counsel of Rhona Robbin. Fortunately, she has continued to contribute to the Fourth Edition in her capacity as managing development editor. I would also like to acknowledge my 10-year working relationship with Gina Boedeker in a number of roles, most recently as managing director, Higher Education Group.

I deeply appreciate the contributions made by all those who assisted me in making this edition even better than the last. I received strong support and encouragement from Kaitlyn Lombardo, marketing manager; Marianne Musni, program manager; Susan Trentacosti, lead content project manager; Katie Klochan, senior content project manager; Briana Porco, senior product developer; Jessica Cuevas, designer; Peter de Lissovoy, copyeditor; and Susan Pierre-Louis, digital product analyst.

This edition continues to reflect the many insightful suggestions made by reviewers of the previous editions as well as hardcover and brief paperback editions. Earlier editions also benefited from the creative ideas of Betty Morgan, Thom Holmes, and Jinny Joyner.

As is evident from these acknowledgments, the preparation of a textbook is truly a collaborative effort. The most valuable member of this effort continues to be my wife, Sandy. She provides the support so necessary in my creative and scholarly activities.

I have had the good fortune to introduce students to sociology for many years. These students have been enormously helpful in spurring on my sociological imagination. In ways I can fully appreciate but cannot fully acknowledge, their questions in class and queries in the hallway have found their way into this work.

Richard T. Schaefer
www.schaefersociology.net
schaeferrt@aol.com

Academic Reviewers

This project has benefited from constructive and thorough evaluations provided by sociologists from both two-year and four-year institutions.

Bethany Johnson, *Gordon College*
Brent Ur, *Blinn College, Bryan*
Candace Warner, *Columbia State Community College*
Candy Pettus, *Orange Coast College*
Carla Newman, *El Paso Community College, Valle Verde*
Cathy Blair, *Minnesota West Community and Technical College*
David Schjott, *Northwest Florida State College*
Denise Shuster, *Owens Community College*
Douglas O'Neill, *South Dakota State University*
Erin K. Anderson, *Washington College*
Frank Stanford, *Blinn College, Bryan*
Gerald Titchener, *Des Moines Area Community College*
Glen Tolle, *Blinn College, Bryan*
Jay Vargas, *Minnesota West Community and Technical College*
Jennifer Altman, *Middlesex County College*
Jessica Halperin, *Metropolitan Community College, Maple Woods*
Joan Luxenburg, *University of Central Oklahoma*
Jonathan Treas, *Wichita State University*
Joseph LoSasso, *Triton College*
Judith Brake, *Ozarks Technical Community College*
Keith Kerr, *Quinnipiac University*

Kelly Champion, *Kishwaukee College*

Khalilah N. Hanan, *Indiana University Purdue University— Fort Wayne*

Kimberly Harris Boyd, *Germanna Community College*

Lucia Rodriguez, *El Paso Community College, Valle Verde*

Lynette Osborne, *The University of Texas, Austin*

Marshall Botkin, *Frederick Community College*

Matthew Cazessus, *Greenville Technical College*

Megan G. Swindal, *University of Alabama*

Michelle Bentz, *Central Community College, Columbus*

Monica Sosa, *Tarrant County College, Southeast*

Ray Muhammad, *Triton College*

Rhonda Eichler-Johnson, *Holmes Community College*

Richard Deutsch, *John A Logan College*

Rose Hunte, *Metro Community College, Fort Omaha*

Shonda Whetstone, *Blinn College, Bryan*

Stacey L. Callaway, *Rowan University*

Susan R. Cody, *Georgia Perimeter College*

Trish Ramirez, *El Paso Community College, Valle Verde*

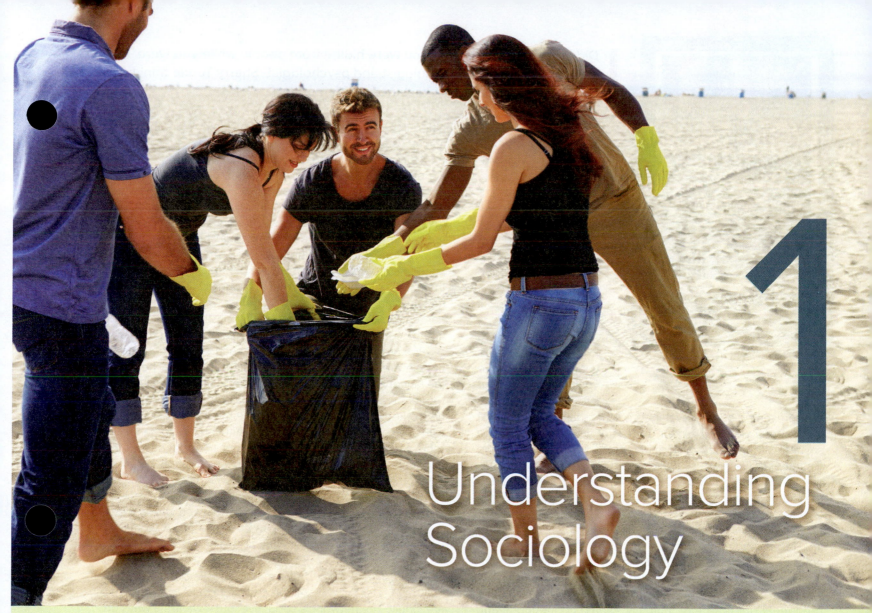

1

Understanding Sociology

© Cathy Yeulet/123RF

One of the things sociologists study is how people organize themselves into groups to perform tasks necessary to society. In California, volunteers pick up debris for eventual recycling.

1

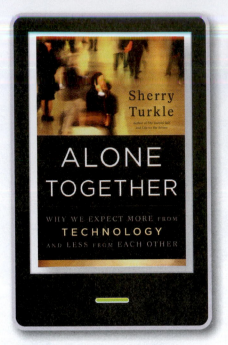

© Ira C. Roberts/Chad Enterprises Corporation

Did you ever suspect that you were hiding from people while you were online with them? MIT sociologist and psychologist Sherry Turkle thinks that the web may actually distance us from others.

"Technology proposes itself as the architect of our intimacies. These days, it suggests substitutions that put the real on the run. The advertising for Second Life, a virtual world where you get to build an avatar, a house, a family, and a social life, basically says, "Finally, a place to love your body, love your friends, and love your life." In Second Life, a lot of people, as represented by their avatars, are richer than they are in first life and a lot younger, thinner, and better dressed. And we are smitten with the idea of sociable robots, which most people first meet in the guise of artificial pets. Zhu Zhu pet hamsters, the "it" toy of the 2009–2010 holiday season, are presented as "better" than any real pet could be. We are told they are lovable and responsive, don't require cleanup, and will never die.

Technology is seductive when what it offers meets our human vulnerabilities. And as it turns out, we are very vulnerable indeed. We are lonely but fearful of intimacy. Digital connections and the sociable robot may offer the illusion of companionship without the demands of friendship. Our networked life allows us to hide from each other, even as we are tethered to each other. We'd rather text than talk.

From the start, people used interactive and reactive computers to reflect on the self and think about the difference between machines and people. Were intelligent machines alive? If not, why not?

Computers no longer wait for humans to project meaning onto them. Now, sociable robots meet our gaze, speak to us, and learn to recognize us. They ask us to take care of them; in response, we imagine that they might care for us in return. Indeed, among the most talked about robotic designs are in the area of care and companionship. And Microsoft demonstrates a virtual human, Milo, that recognizes the people it interacts with and whose personality is sculpted by them. Tellingly, in the video that introduces Milo to the public, a young man begins by playing games with Milo in a virtual garden; by the end of the demonstration, things have heated up—he confides in Milo after being told off by his parents.

We are challenged to ask what such things augur. Some people are looking for robots to clean rugs and help with the laundry. Others hope for a mechanical bride. As sociable robots propose themselves as substitutes for people, new networked devices offer us machine-mediated relationships with each other, another kind of substitution. We romance the robot and become inseparable from our smartphones. As this happens, we remake ourselves and our relationships with each other through our new intimacy with machines. People talk about web access on their BlackBerries as "the place for hope" in life, the place where loneliness can be defeated. A woman in her late sixties describes her new iPhone: "It's like having a little Times Square in my pocketbook. All lights. All the people I could meet." People are lonely. The network is seductive. But if we are always on, we may deny ourselves the rewards of solitude. "

Digital connections and the sociable robot may offer the illusion of companionship without the demands of friendship.

(*Turkle 2011*:1–3) Quotation from Sherry Turkle. Alone Together: Why We Expect More from Technology and Less from Each Other. NY: Basic Books. Copyright © 2012. Reprinted by permission of Basic Books, a member of The Perseus Books Group.

Think about your life before you owned a cell phone: How did you connect with others then? How do you connect with them now? In this excerpt from *Alone Together: Why We Expect More from Technology and Less from Each Other*, Sherry Turkle writes that modern technology—especially communications technology—is changing the way we relate to others. Today, our digital communications devices tend to preoccupy us, often burying us in a deluge of information, both audio and video. Yet in the end, they cannot substitute for the ties that bind, the face-to-face relationships that hold family and friends together. Ironically, in an effort to dig out from the communications overflow, we are constantly seeking new networking gadgets (Turkle 2011:280).

We've come a long way from the days when home entertainment meant black-and-white television, and "reaching out" involved a land-line telephone and voice messages. Today, we not only carry the telephone with us; we use it to watch television and movies delivered over the Internet. Social life is being impacted by and carried out through an object we hold in our hand.

As a field of study, sociology is extremely broad in scope. You will see throughout this book the range of topics sociologists investigate—from suicide to TV viewing habits, from Amish society to global economic patterns, from peer pressure to genetic engineering. Sociology looks at how others influence our behavior; how major social institutions like the government, religion, and the economy affect us; and how we ourselves affect other individuals, groups, and even organizations.

How did sociology develop? In what ways does it differ from other social sciences? These modules will explore the nature of sociology as both a field of inquiry and an exercise of the "sociological imagination." In Module 1, we'll look at the discipline as a science and consider its relationship to other social sciences. In Modules 2 and 3, we'll meet four pioneering thinkers—Émile Durkheim, Max Weber, Karl Marx, and W. E. B. DuBois—and examine the theoretical perspectives that grew out of their work. In Module 4, we'll note some of the practical applications for sociological theory and research. Finally, we'll see how sociology helps us to develop a sociological imagination. For those students interested in exploring career opportunities in sociology, the chapter closes with a special appendix.

MODULE 1 | What Is Sociology?

"What has sociology got to do with me or with my life?" As a student, you might well have asked this question when you signed up for your introductory sociology course. To answer it, consider these points: Are you influenced by what you see on television? Do you use the Internet? Did you vote in the last election? Are you familiar with binge drinking on campus? Do you use alternative medicine? These are just a few of the everyday life situations described in this book that sociology can shed light on. But as the opening excerpt indicates, sociology also looks at large social issues. We use sociology to investigate why thousands of jobs have moved from the United States to developing nations, what social forces promote prejudice, what leads someone to join a social movement and work for social change, how access to computer technology can reduce social inequality, and why relationships between men and women in Seattle differ from those in Singapore.

Sociology is, simply, the scientific study of social behavior and human groups. It focuses on social relationships; how those relationships influence people's behavior; and how societies, the sum total of those relationships, develop and change.

● The Sociological Imagination

In attempting to understand social behavior, sociologists rely on a particular type of critical thinking. A leading sociologist, C. Wright Mills, described such thinking as the **sociological imagination**—an awareness of the relationship between an individual and the wider society, both today and in the past (Mills [1959] 2000a). This awareness allows all of us (not just sociologists) to comprehend the links between our immediate, personal social settings and the remote, impersonal social world that surrounds and helps to shape us.

A key element in the sociological imagination is the ability to view one's own society as an outsider would, rather than only from the perspective of personal experiences and cultural biases. Consider something as simple as sporting events. On college campuses in the United States, thousands of students cheer well-trained football players. In parts of South America and the Caribbean, spectators gather around two cages, each holding a finch. The covers are lifted, and the owner of the first bird to sing 50 songs wins a trophy, a cash prize, and great prestige. In speed singing as in football, eager spectators debate the merits of their favorites and bet on the outcome of the events. Yet what is considered a normal sporting event in one part of the world is considered unusual in another part (Rueb 2015).

The sociological imagination allows us to go beyond personal experiences and observations to understand broader public issues. Divorce, for example, is unquestionably a personal hardship for a the partners who split apart. However, C. Wright Mills advocated using the sociological imagination to view divorce not as simply an individual's personal problem but rather as a societal concern. Using this perspective, we can see that an increase in the divorce rate actually redefines a major social institution—the family. Today's households frequently include stepparents and half-siblings whose parents have divorced and remarried. Through the complexities of the blended family, this private concern becomes a public issue that affects schools, government agencies, businesses, and religious institutions.

The sociological imagination is an empowering tool. It allows us to look beyond a limited understanding of human behavior to see the world and its people in a new way and through a broader lens than we might otherwise use. It may be as simple as understanding why a roommate prefers country music to hip-hop, or it may open up a whole different way of understanding other populations in the world. For example, in the aftermath of the terrorist attacks on the United States on September 11, 2001, many citizens wanted to understand how Muslims throughout the world perceived their country, and why. From time to time this textbook will offer you the chance to exercise your sociological imagination in a variety of situations.

💡 use your **sociological imagination**

You are walking down the street in your city or hometown. In looking around you, you can't help noticing that half or more of the people you see are overweight. How do you explain your observation? If you were C. Wright Mills, how do you think you would explain it?

● Sociology and the Social Sciences

Is sociology a science? The term **science** refers to the body of knowledge obtained by methods based on systematic observation. Just like other scientific disciplines, sociology involves the

© James Marshall/The Image Works

Sociology is the scientific study of social behavior and human groups.

Because humans are social animals, sociologists examine our social relationships scientifically. The range of the relationships they investigate is vast, as the current list of sections in the American Sociological Association suggests (Table 1-1).

Let's consider how different social scientists might study the impact of the Great Recession that began in 2008. Historians would stress the pattern of long-term fluctuations in world markets. Economists would discuss the roles played by government, the private sector, and the world monetary system. Psychologists would study individual cases of emotional stress among workers, investors, and business owners. And political scientists would study the degree of cooperation among nations—or lack of it—in seeking economic solutions.

What approach would sociologists take? They might note a change in marital patterns in the United States. Since the recession began, the median age of first marriage has risen to 28.7 years for men and 26.7 years for women. Sociologists might also observe that today, fewer people are making that trip to the altar than in the past. If the U.S. marriage rate had remained the same as it was in 2006, about 4 million more Americans would have married by 2010.

Similarly, sociologists might evaluate the recession's impact on education. In the United States, private school enrollment from elementary through high school declined from 13.6 percent in 2006 to 12.8 percent in 2010 as families cut back on nonessential expenditures. Sociologists might even consider the recession's effect on environmental actions, such as carpooling. In all but one of the 50 largest metropolitan areas in the United States (New Orleans), the percentage of working people aged 16 to 64 dropped significantly during the recession. When friends and co-workers are laid off, carpools shrink and more people end up driving to work alone (El Nasser and Overberg 2011).

Sociologists would take a similar approach to studying episodes of extreme violence. In April 2007, just as college students were beginning to focus on the impending end of the semester, tragedy struck on the campus of Virginia Tech. In a two-hour shooting spree, a mentally disturbed senior armed with semiautomatic weapons killed a total of 32 students and faculty at Virginia's largest university. Observers struggled to describe the events and place them in some social context. For sociologists in particular, the event raised numerous issues and topics for study, including the media's role in describing the attacks, the presence of violence in our educational institutions, the debate over gun-ownership laws, the inadequacy of the nation's mental health care system, and the stereotyping and stigmatization of people who suffer from mental illness.

organized, systematic study of phenomena (in this case, human behavior) in order to enhance understanding. All scientists, whether studying mushrooms or murderers, attempt to collect precise information through methods of study that are as objective as possible. They rely on careful recording of observations and accumulation of data.

Of course, there is a great difference between sociology and physics, between psychology and astronomy. For this reason, the sciences are commonly divided into natural and social sciences. **Natural science** is the study of the physical features of nature and the ways in which they interact and change. Astronomy, biology, chemistry, geology, and physics are all natural sciences. **Social science** is the study of the social features of humans and the ways in which they interact and change. The social sciences include sociology, anthropology, economics, history, psychology, and political science.

These social science disciplines have a common focus on the social behavior of people, yet each has a particular orientation. Anthropologists usually study past cultures and preindustrial societies that continue today, as well as the origins of humans. Economists explore the ways in which people produce and exchange goods and services, along with money and other resources. Historians are concerned with the peoples and events of the past and their significance for us today. Political scientists study international relations, the workings of government, and the exercise of power and authority. Psychologists investigate personality and individual behavior. So what do *sociologists* focus on? They study the influence that society has on people's attitudes and behavior and the ways in which people interact and shape society.

TABLE 1-1 SECTIONS OF THE AMERICAN SOCIOLOGICAL ASSOCIATION

Aging and the Life Course	Emotions	Organizations, Occupations, and Work
Alcohol, Drugs, and Tobacco	Environment and Technology	Peace, War, and Social Conflict
Altruism, Morality, and Social Solidarity	Ethnomethodology and Conversation Analysis	Political Economy of the World-System
Animals and Society	Evolution, Biology, and Society	Political Sociology
Asia and Asian America	Family	Population
Body and Embodiment	Global and Transnational Sociology	Race, Gender, and Class
Children and Youth	History of Sociology	Racial and Ethnic Minorities
Collective Behavior and Social Movements	Human Rights	Rationality and Society
Communication, Information Technologies, and Media	International Migration	Religion
Community and Urban Sociology	Inequality, Poverty, and Mobility	Science, Knowledge, and Technology
Comparative and Historical Sociology	Labor and Labor Movements	Sex and Gender
Consumers and Consumption	Latino/a Sociology	Sexualities
Crime, Law, and Deviance	Law	Social Psychology
Culture	Marxist Sociology	Sociological Practice and Public Sociology
Development	Mathematical Sociology	Teaching and Learning
Disability and Society	Medical Sociology	Theory
Economic Sociology	Mental Health	
Education	Methodology	

The range of sociological issues is very broad. For example, sociologists who belong to the Animals and Society section of the ASA may study the animal rights movement; those who belong to the Sexualities section may study global sex workers or the gay, bisexual, and transgender movements. Economic sociologists may investigate globalization or consumerism, among many other topics.

Source: American Sociological Association 2016.

Besides doing research, sociologists have a long history of advising government agencies on how to respond to disasters. Certainly the poverty of the Gulf Coast region complicated the challenge of evacuating New Orleans in 2005. With Hurricane Katrina bearing down on the Gulf Coast, thousands of poor inner-city residents had no automobiles or other available means of escaping the storm. Added to that difficulty was the high incidence of disability in the area. New Orleans ranked second among the nation's 70 largest cities in the proportion of people over age 65 who are disabled—56 percent. Moving wheelchair-bound residents to safety requires specially equipped vehicles, to say nothing of handicap-accessible accommodations in public shelters. Clearly, officials must consider these factors in developing evacuation plans (Bureau of the Census 2005b).

Sociological analysis of the disaster did not end when the floodwaters receded. Long before residents of New Orleans staged a massive anticrime rally at City Hall in 2007, researchers were analyzing resettlement patterns in the city. They noted that returning residents often faced bleak job prospects. Yet families who had stayed away for that reason often had trouble enrolling their children in schools unprepared for an influx of evacuees. Faced with a choice between the need to work and the need to return their children to school, some displaced families risked sending their older children home alone.

In the ten years since Katrina, crime has dropped significantly by many measures—the murder rate is the lowest in 40 years.

© Justin Sullivan/Getty Images

As the nation struggled to recover from a deep and lengthy recession, recently laid-off workers jostled the long-term unemployed at a crowded job fair in San Francisco. Sociologists use a variety of approaches to assess the full impact of economic change on society.

But the crime rate is still high compared to that of other cities. The majority of people feel that their neighborhoods do not have enough police presence, and over a quarter are "very worried" that they will become a crime victim. Less progress is seen in addressing crime than in repairing the levees or improving medical facilities (Hamel et al. 2015).

Throughout this textbook, you will see how sociologists develop theories and conduct research to study and better understand societies. And you will be encouraged to use your sociological imagination to examine the United States (and other societies) from the viewpoint of a respectful but questioning outsider.

Sociology and Common Sense

Sociology focuses on the study of human behavior. Yet we all have experience with human behavior and at least some knowledge of it. All of us might well have theories about why people become homeless, for example. Our theories and opinions typically come from common sense—that is, from our experiences and conversations, from what we read, from what we see on television, and so forth.

In our daily lives, we rely on common sense to get us through many unfamiliar situations. However, this commonsense knowledge, while sometimes accurate, is not always reliable, because it rests on commonly held beliefs rather than on systematic analysis of facts. It was once considered common sense to accept that the earth was flat—a view rightly questioned by Pythagoras and Aristotle. Incorrect commonsense notions are not just a part of the distant past; they remain with us today.

Contrary to the common notion that women tend to be chatty compared to men, for instance, researchers have found little difference between the sexes in terms of their talkativeness. Over a five-year period they placed unobtrusive microphones on 396 college students in various fields, at campuses in Mexico as well as the United States. They found that both men and women spoke about 16,000 words per day (Mehl et al. 2007).

Similarly, common sense tells us that today, violent crime holds communities on the border between the United States and Mexico in a kind of death grip, creating an atmosphere of lawlessness reminiscent of the old Wild West. Based on televised news stories and on concerns expressed by elected officials throughout the southwestern United States, this assertion may sound reasonable; however, it is not true. Although some communities in Mexico have fallen under the control of drug cartels, the story is different on the U.S. side of the border. All available crime data—including murder, extortion, robbery, and kidnapping rates, whether reported or documented in victim surveys—show that in the hundred-mile-deep border area stretching from San Diego to Brownsville, Texas, crime rates are significantly lower than in similar U.S. cities outside the area. Furthermore, the crime rate has been dropping faster near the border than in other similar-size U.S. communities for at least the last 15 years (Gillum 2011; Gomez et al. 2011).

Like other social scientists, sociologists do not accept something as a fact because "everyone knows it." Instead, each piece of information must be tested and recorded, then analyzed in relation to other data. Sociologists rely on scientific studies in order to describe and understand a social environment. At times, the findings of sociologists may seem like common sense, because they deal with familiar facets of everyday life. The difference is that such findings have been *tested* by researchers. Common sense now tells us that the earth is round, but this particular commonsense notion is based on centuries of scientific work that began with the breakthroughs made by Pythagoras and Aristotle.

What Is Sociological Theory?

Why do people commit suicide? One traditional commonsense answer is that people inherit the desire to kill themselves. Another view is that sunspots drive people to take their lives. These explanations may not seem especially convincing to contemporary researchers, but they represent beliefs widely held as recently as 1900.

Sociologists are not particularly interested in why any one individual commits suicide; they are more concerned with identifying the social forces that systematically cause some people to take their own lives. In order to undertake this research, sociologists develop a theory that offers a general explanation of suicidal behavior.

We can think of theories as attempts to explain events, forces, materials, ideas, or behavior in a comprehensive manner. In sociology, a **theory** is a set of statements that seeks to explain problems, actions, or behavior. An effective theory may have both explanatory and predictive power. That is, it can help us to see the relationships among seemingly isolated phenomena, as well as to understand how one type of change in an environment leads to other changes.

The World Health Organization (2010) estimates that almost a million people die from suicide every year. More than a hundred years ago, a sociologist tried to look at suicide data scientifically. Émile Durkheim ([1897] 1951) developed a highly original theory about the relationship between suicide and social factors. Durkheim was primarily concerned not with the personalities of individual suicide victims, but rather with suicide rates and how they varied from country to country. As a result, when he looked at the number of reported suicides in France, England, and Denmark in 1869, he also noted the total population of each country in order to determine the rate of suicide in each nation. He found that whereas England had only 67 reported suicides per million inhabitants, France had 135 per million and Denmark had 277 per million. The question then became "Why did Denmark have a comparatively high rate of reported suicide?"

Durkheim went much deeper into his investigation of suicide rates. The result was his landmark work *Suicide,* published in 1897. Durkheim refused to accept unproved explanations regarding suicide, including the beliefs that inherited tendencies or cosmic forces caused such deaths. Instead, he focused on social factors, such as the cohesiveness or lack of cohesiveness of religious, social, and occupational groups.

Durkheim's research suggested that suicide, although it is a solitary act, is related to group life. He found that people without religious affiliations had a higher suicide rate than those who were affiliated; the unmarried had much higher rates than married people; and soldiers had a higher rate than civilians. In addition, there seemed to be higher rates of suicide in times of peace than in times of war and revolution, and in times of economic instability and recession rather than in times of prosperity. Durkheim concluded that the suicide rates of a society reflected the extent to which people were or were not integrated into the group life of the society.

Émile Durkheim, like many other social scientists, developed a theory to explain how individual behavior can be understood within a social context. He pointed out the influence of groups and societal forces on what had always been viewed as a highly personal act. Clearly, Durkheim offered a more *scientific* explanation for the causes of suicide than that of inherited tendencies or sunspots. His theory has predictive power, since it suggests that suicide rates will rise or fall in conjunction with certain social and economic changes.

Of course, a theory—even the best of theories—is not a final statement about human behavior. Durkheim's theory of suicide is no exception. Sociologists continue to examine factors that contribute to differences in suicide rates around the world and to a particular society's rate of suicide. In Las Vegas, for example, sociologists have observed that the chances of dying by suicide are strikingly high—twice as high as in the United States as a whole. Noting Durkheim's emphasis on the relationship between suicide and social isolation, researchers have suggested that Las Vegas's rapid growth and constant influx of tourists have undermined the community's sense of permanence, even among longtime residents. Although gambling—or more accurately, losing while gambling—may seem a likely precipitating factor in suicides there, careful study of the data has allowed researchers to dismiss that explanation. What happens in Vegas may stay in Vegas, but the sense of community cohesiveness that the rest of the country enjoys may be lacking (Wray et al. 2008, 2011).

© Getty Images/Digital Vision RF

MODULE 1 | Recap and Review

Summary

Sociology is the scientific study of social behavior and human groups. In this module, we examine the nature of sociological theory and the work of some of the founders of the discipline.

1. The **sociological imagination** is an awareness of the relationship between an individual and the wider society. It is based on the ability to view our own society as an outsider might, rather than from the perspective of our limited experiences and cultural biases.

2. In contrast to other **social sciences**, sociology emphasizes the influence that groups can have on people's behavior and attitudes and the ways in which people shape society.

3. Knowledge that relies on common sense is not always reliable. Sociologists must test and analyze each piece of information they use.

4. Sociologists employ **theories** to examine relationships between observations or data that may seem completely unrelated.

Thinking Critically

1. How might sociology approach an issue such as gun-ownership laws differently from the way economics or political science would study the same issue?

2. What aspects of the social and work environment in a fast-food restaurant would be of particular interest to a sociologist? How would the sociological imagination help in analyzing the topic?

3. Think about the sociologists profiled in this module, Mills and Durkheim. Whose work seems most relevant to today's social problems? Why did you choose that thinker, and which social problems were you thinking of?

Key Terms

Natural science

Science

Social science

Sociological imagination

Sociology

Theory

People have always been curious about sociological matters—how we get along with others, what we do for a living, whom we select as our leaders. Philosophers and religious authorities of ancient and medieval societies made countless observations about human behavior. They did not test or verify those observations scientifically; nevertheless, their observations often became the foundation for moral codes. Several of these early social philosophers correctly predicted that a systematic study of human behavior would emerge one day. Beginning in the 19th century, European theorists made pioneering contributions to the development of a science of human behavior.

Early Thinkers

Auguste Comte

The 19th century was an unsettling time in France. The French monarchy had been deposed in the revolution of 1789, and Napoleon had suffered defeat in his effort to conquer Europe. Amid this chaos, philosophers considered how society might be improved. Auguste Comte (1798–1857), credited with being the most influential of the philosophers of the early 1800s, believed that a theoretical science of society and a systematic investigation of behavior were needed to improve society. He coined the term *sociology* to apply to the science of human behavior.

Writing in the 1800s, Comte feared that the excesses of the French Revolution had permanently impaired France's stability. Yet he hoped that the systematic study of social behavior would eventually lead to more rational human interactions. In Comte's hierarchy of the sciences, sociology was at the top. He called it the "queen," and its practitioners "scientist-priests." This French theorist did not simply give sociology its name; he presented a rather ambitious challenge to the fledgling discipline.

Harriet Martineau

Scholars learned of Comte's works largely through translations by the English sociologist Harriet Martineau (1802–1876). But Martineau was a pathbreaker in her own right: she offered insightful observations of the customs and social practices of both her native Britain and the United States. Martineau's book *Society in America* ([1837] 1962) examined religion, politics, child rearing, and immigration in the young nation. It gave special attention to social class distinctions and to such factors as gender and race. Martineau ([1838] 1989) also wrote the first book on sociological methods.

Martineau's writings emphasized the impact that the economy, law, trade, health, and population could have on social problems. She spoke out in favor of the rights of women, the emancipation of slaves, and religious tolerance. Later in life, deafness did not keep her from being an activist. In Martineau's ([1837] 1962) view, intellectuals and scholars should not simply offer observations of social conditions; they should *act* on their

© Spencer Arnold/Getty Images

Harriet Martineau, an early pioneer of sociology who studied social behavior both in her native England and in the United States. Martineau proposed some of the methods still used by sociologists, including systematic observation.

convictions in a manner that will benefit society. That is why Martineau conducted research on the nature of female employment and pointed to the need for further investigation of the issue (Deegan 2003; Hill and Hoecker-Drysdale 2001).

Herbert Spencer

Another important early contributor to the discipline of sociology was Herbert Spencer (1820–1903). A relatively prosperous Victorian Englishman, Spencer (unlike Martineau) did not feel compelled to correct or improve society; instead, he merely hoped to understand it better. Drawing on Charles Darwin's study *On the Origin of Species,* Spencer applied the concept of evolution of the species to societies in order to explain how they change, or evolve, over time. Similarly, he adapted Darwin's evolutionary view of the "survival of the fittest" by arguing that it is "natural" that some people are rich while others are poor.

Spencer's approach to societal change was extremely popular in his lifetime. Unlike Comte, Spencer suggested that since societies are bound to change eventually, one need not be highly critical of present social arrangements or work actively for social change. This viewpoint appealed to many influential people in England and the United States who had a vested interest in the status quo and were suspicious of social thinkers who endorsed change.

Émile Durkheim

Émile Durkheim made many pioneering contributions to sociology, including his important theoretical work on suicide. The son of a rabbi, Durkheim (1858–1917) was educated in both France and Germany. He established an impressive academic reputation and was appointed one of the first professors of sociology in France. Above all, Durkheim will be remembered for his insistence that behavior must be understood within a larger social context, not just in individualistic terms.

To give one example of this emphasis, Durkheim ([1912] 2001) developed a fundamental thesis to help explain all forms of society. Through intensive study of the Arunta, an Australian tribe, he focused on the functions that religion performed and underscored the role of group life in defining what we consider to be religion. Durkheim concluded that like other forms of group behavior, religion reinforces a group's solidarity.

Another of Durkheim's main interests was the consequences of work in modern societies. In his view, the growing division of labor in industrial societies, as workers became much more specialized in their tasks, led to what he called "anomie." **Anomie** refers to the loss of direction felt in a society when social control of individual behavior has become ineffective. Often, the state of anomie occurs during a time of profound social change, when people have lost their sense of purpose or direction. In a period of anomie, people are so confused and unable to cope with the new social environment that they may resort to suicide.

Durkheim was concerned about the dangers that alienation, loneliness, and isolation might pose for modern industrial societies. He shared Comte's belief that sociology should provide direction for social change. As a result, he advocated the creation of new social groups—mediators between the individual's family and the state—that would provide a sense of belonging for members of huge, impersonal societies. Unions would be an example of such groups.

Like many other sociologists, Durkheim did not limit his interests to one aspect of social behavior. Later in this book we will consider his thinking on crime and punishment, religion, and the workplace. Few sociologists have had such a dramatic impact on so many different areas within the discipline.

use to measure weight or temperature. To fully comprehend behavior, we must learn the subjective meanings people attach to their actions—how they themselves view and explain their behavior.

For example, suppose that a sociologist was studying the social ranking of individuals in a fraternity. Weber would expect the researcher to employ *verstehen* to determine the significance of the fraternity's social hierarchy for its members. The researcher might examine the effects of athleticism or grades or social skills or seniority on standing within the fraternity. He or she would seek to learn how the fraternity members relate to other members of higher or lower status. While investigating these questions, the researcher would take into account people's emotions, thoughts, beliefs, and attitudes (L. Coser 1977).

We also owe credit to Weber for a key conceptual tool: the ideal type. An **ideal type** is a construct or model for evaluating specific cases. In his works, Weber identified various characteristics of bureaucracy as an ideal type (discussed in detail in Chapter 5). In presenting this model of bureaucracy, Weber was not describing any particular organization, nor was he using the term *ideal* in a way that suggested a positive evaluation. Instead, his purpose was to provide a useful standard for measuring how bureaucratic an actual organization is (Gerth and Mills 1958). Later in this book, we will use the concept of *ideal type* to study the family, religion, authority, and economic systems, as well as to analyze bureaucracy.

Although their professional careers coincided, Émile Durkheim and Max Weber never met and probably were unaware of each other's existence, let alone ideas. Such was not true of the work of Karl Marx. Durkheim's thinking about the impact of the division of labor in industrial societies was related to Marx's writings, while Weber's concern for a value-free, objective sociology was a direct response to Marx's deeply held convictions. Thus, it is not surprising that Karl Marx is viewed as a major figure in the development of sociology, as well as several other social sciences (Figure 2-1).

● Max Weber

Another important early theorist was Max Weber (pronounced VAY-ber). Born in Germany, Weber (1864–1920) studied legal and economic history, but gradually developed an interest in sociology. Eventually, he became a professor at various German universities. Weber taught his students that they should employ *verstehen* (pronounced fair-SHTAY-en), the German word for "understanding" or "insight," in their intellectual work. He pointed out that we cannot analyze our social behavior by the same type of objective criteria we

© lithian/123RF

● Karl Marx

Karl Marx (1818–1883) shared with Durkheim and Weber a dual interest in abstract philosophical issues and the concrete reality of everyday life. Unlike them, however, Marx was so critical of existing institutions that a conventional academic career was impossible. He spent most of his life in exile from his native Germany.

Marx's personal life was a difficult struggle. When a paper he had written was suppressed, he fled to France. In Paris, he met Friedrich Engels (1820–1895), with whom he formed a lifelong friendship. The two lived at a time when European and North

FIGURE 2-1 **Contributors to Sociology**

© Bettman/Contributor/Getty Images

© Hulton Archive/Getty Images

© Alfredo Dagli Orti/Corbis

© Everett Collection Historical/Alamy

	Émile Durkheim 1858–1917	**Max Weber 1864–1920**	**Karl Marx 1818–1883**	**W. E. B. DuBois 1868–1963**
Academic training	Philosophy	Law, economics, history, philosophy	Philosophy, law	Sociology
Key works	1893—*The Division of Labor in Society* 1897—*Suicide: A Study in Sociology* 1912—*Elementary Forms of Religious Life*	1904–1905—*The Protestant Ethic and the Spirit of Capitalism* 1921—*Economy and Society*	1848—*The Communist Manifesto* 1867—*Das Kapital*	1899—*The Philadelphia Negro* 1903—*The Negro Church* 1903—*Souls of Black Folk*

Source: Developed by author.

American economic life was increasingly dominated by the factory rather than the farm.

While in London in 1847, Marx and Engels attended secret meetings of an illegal coalition of labor unions known as the Communist League. The following year they prepared a platform called *The Communist Manifesto,* in which they argued that the masses of people with no resources other than their labor (whom they referred to as the *proletariat*) should unite to fight for the overthrow of capitalist societies. In the words of Marx and Engels:

> The history of all hitherto existing society is the history of class struggles. . . . The proletarians have nothing to lose but their chains. They have a world to win. WORKING MEN OF ALL COUNTRIES, UNITE! (Tucker 1978:473, 500).

After completing *The Communist Manifesto,* Marx returned to Germany, only to be expelled. He then moved to England, where he continued to write books and essays. Marx lived there in extreme poverty; he pawned most of his possessions, and several of his children died of malnutrition and disease. Marx clearly was an outsider in British society, a fact that may well have influenced his view of Western cultures.

In Marx's analysis, society was fundamentally divided between two classes that clashed in pursuit of their own interests. When he examined the industrial societies of his time, such as Germany, England, and the United States, he saw the factory as the center of conflict between the exploiters (the owners of the means of production) and the exploited (the workers). Marx viewed these relationships in systematic terms; that is, he believed that a system of economic, social, and political relationships maintained the power and dominance of the owners over the workers. Consequently, Marx and Engels argued that the working class should overthrow the existing class system. Marx's

influence on contemporary thinking has been dramatic. His writings inspired those who would later lead communist revolutions in Russia, China, Cuba, Vietnam, and elsewhere.

Even apart from the political revolutions that his work fostered, Marx's significance is profound. Marx emphasized the *group* identifications and associations that influence an *individual's* place in society. This area of study is the major focus of contemporary sociology. Throughout this textbook, we will consider how membership in a particular gender classification, age group, racial group, or economic class affects a person's attitudes and behavior. In an important sense, we can trace this way of understanding society back to the pioneering work of Karl Marx.

W. E. B. DuBois

Marx's work encouraged sociologists to view society through the eyes of those segments of the population that rarely influence decision making. In the United States, some early African American sociologists, including W. E. B. DuBois (1868–1963), conducted research that they hoped would assist in the struggle for a racially egalitarian society. DuBois (pronounced doo-BOYSS) believed that knowledge was essential in combating prejudice and achieving tolerance and justice. Sociologists, he contended, needed to draw on scientific principles to study social problems such as those experienced by Blacks in the United States. To separate opinion from fact, he advocated research on the lives of African Americans. Through his in-depth studies of urban life, both White and Black, in cities such as Philadelphia and Atlanta, DuBois ([1899] 1995) made a major contribution to sociology.

Like Durkheim and Weber, DuBois saw the importance of religion to society. However, he tended to focus on religion at the community level and on the role of the church in the lives of its members ([1903] 2003). DuBois had little patience with theorists such as Herbert Spencer, who seemed content with the status quo. He believed that the granting of full political rights to Blacks was essential to their social and economic progress.

Through what became known as the Atlanta Sociological Laboratory, DuBois also promoted groundbreaking research by other scholars. While investigating religion, crime, and race relations, these colleagues trained their students in sociological research. The extensive interviews conducted by students in Atlanta still enrich our understanding of human behavior (Earl Wright II 2012).

Because many of his ideas challenged the status quo, DuBois did not always find a receptive audience within either the government or the academic world. As a result, he became increasingly involved with organizations whose members questioned the established social order. In 1909 he helped to found the National Association for the Advancement of Colored People, better known today as the NAACP (Wortham 2008).

DuBois's insights have been lasting. In 1897 he coined the term **double consciousness** to refer to the division of an individual's identity into two or more social realities. He used the term to describe the experience of being Black in White America. African Americans have held the most powerful offices in the nation, including President of the United States. Yet for millions of African Americans, the reality of being Black in the United States typically is not one of power (DuBois [1903] 1961).

Twentieth-Century Developments

Sociology today builds on the firm foundation developed by Émile Durkheim, Max Weber, Karl Marx, and W. E. B. DuBois. However, the field certainly has not remained stagnant over the past hundred years. While Europeans have continued to make contributions to the discipline, sociologists from throughout the world and especially the United States have advanced sociological theory and research. Their new insights have helped us to better understand the workings of society.

Charles Horton Cooley

Charles Horton Cooley (1864–1929) was typical of the sociologists who came to prominence in the early 1900s. Born in Ann Arbor, Michigan, Cooley received his graduate training in economics but later became a sociology professor at the University of Michigan. Like other early sociologists, he had become interested in this new discipline while pursuing a related area of study.

Cooley shared the desire of Durkheim, Weber, and Marx to learn more about society. But to do so effectively, he preferred to use the sociological perspective to look first at smaller units—intimate, face-to-face groups such as families, gangs, and friendship networks. He saw these groups as the seedbeds of society,

in the sense that they shape people's ideals, beliefs, values, and social nature. Cooley's work increased our understanding of groups of relatively small size.

Jane Addams

In the early 1900s, many leading sociologists in the United States saw themselves as social reformers dedicated to systematically studying and then improving a corrupt society. They were genuinely concerned about the lives of immigrants in the nation's growing cities, whether those immigrants came from overseas or from the rural American South. Early female sociologists, in particular, often took active roles in poor urban areas as leaders of community centers known as *settlement houses*. For example, Jane Addams (1860–1935), a member of the American Sociological Society, co-founded the famous Chicago settlement house called Hull House.

Addams and other pioneering female sociologists commonly combined intellectual inquiry, social service work, and political activism—all with the goal of assisting the underprivileged and creating a more egalitarian society. For example, working with the Black journalist and educator Ida Wells-Barnett, Addams successfully prevented racial segregation in the Chicago public

© Jane Addams Hull-House Photographic Collection/Special Collections/University of Illinois at Chicago Library

Jane Addams (right) was an early pioneer both in sociology and in the settlement house movement. She was also an activist for many causes, including the worldwide campaign for peace.

schools. Addams's efforts to establish a juvenile court system and a women's trade union reveal the practical focus of her work (Addams 1910, 1930; Deegan 1991; Lengermann and Niebrugge-Brantley 1998).

By the middle of the 20th century, however, the focus of the discipline had shifted. Sociologists for the most part restricted themselves to theorizing and gathering information; the aim of transforming society was left to social workers and activists. This shift away from social reform was accompanied by a growing commitment to scientific methods of research and to value-free interpretation of data. Not all sociologists were happy with this emphasis. A new organization, the Society for the Study of Social Problems, was created in 1950 to deal more directly with social inequality and other social problems.

Robert Merton

Sociologist Robert Merton (1910–2003) made an important contribution to the discipline by successfully combining theory and research. Born to Slavic immigrant parents in Philadelphia, Merton won a scholarship to Temple University. He continued his studies at Harvard, where he acquired his lifelong interest in sociology. Merton's teaching career was based at Columbia University.

Merton (1968) produced a theory that is one of the most frequently cited explanations of deviant behavior. He noted different ways in which people attempt to achieve success in life. In his view, some may deviate from the socially approved goal of accumulating material goods or the socially accepted means of achieving that goal. For example, in Merton's classification scheme, *innovators* are people who accept the goal of pursuing material wealth but use illegal means to do so, including robbery, burglary, and extortion. Although Merton based his explanation of crime on individual behavior that has been influenced by society's approved goals and means, it has wider applications. His theory helps to account for the high crime rates among the nation's poor, who may see no hope of advancing themselves through traditional roads to success. Module 24 discusses Merton's theory in greater detail.

Merton also emphasized that sociology should strive to bring together the *macro-level* and *micro-level* approaches to the study of society. **Macrosociology** concentrates on large-scale phenomena or entire civilizations. Harriet Martineau's study of religion and politics in the United States is an example of macro-level research. More recently, macrosociologists have examined international crime rates (see Module 25) and the stereotype of Asian Americans as a "model minority" (see Module 33). In contrast, **microsociology** stresses the study of small groups, often through experimental means. Sociological research on the micro level has included studies of how divorced men and women disengage from significant social roles (see Module 10) and of how a teacher's expectations can affect a student's academic performance (see Module 42).

While Merton intended to be inclusive of all research, over the past 50 years sociologists have identified two additional levels of research, *mesosociology* and *global sociology*. **Mesosociology** is an intermediate level of analysis embracing study of formal organizations and social movements. Max Weber's analysis of bureaucracies (see Module 19) and the study of environmentalism (see Module 56) illustrate mesosociology. **Global sociology** makes comparisons among nations, typically using entire societies as the units of analysis. Émile Durkheim's cross-cultural study of suicide is an example of global sociology, as is the study of international crime rates (Smelser, 1997).

Pierre Bourdieu

Increasingly, scholars in the United States have been drawing on the insights of sociologists in other countries. The ideas of the French sociologist Pierre Bourdieu (1930–2002) have found a broad following in North America and elsewhere. As a young man, Bourdieu did fieldwork in Algeria during its struggle for independence from France. Today, scholars study Bourdieu's research techniques as well as his conclusions.

Bourdieu wrote about how capital in its many forms sustains individuals and families from one generation to the next. To Bourdieu, *capital* included not just material goods, but cultural and social assets. **Cultural capital** refers to noneconomic goods, such as family background and education, which are reflected in a knowledge of language and the arts. Not necessarily book knowledge, cultural capital refers to the kind of education that is valued by the socially elite. Though a knowledge of Chinese cuisine is culture, for example, it is not the prestigious kind of culture that is valued by the elite. In the United States, immigrants—especially those who arrived in large numbers and settled in ethnic enclaves—have generally taken two or three generations to develop the same level of cultural capital enjoyed by more established groups.

In comparison, **social capital** refers to the collective benefit of social networks, which are built on reciprocal trust. Much has been written about the importance of family and friendship networks in providing people with an opportunity to advance. Social bonds and capital have great value in health happiness, educational achievement, and economic success. In his emphasis on cultural and social capital, Bourdieu's work extends the insights of early social thinkers such as Marx and Weber (Bourdieu and Passeron 1990; Poder 2011; Putnam 2015:207).

Today sociology reflects the diverse contributions of earlier theorists. As sociologists approach such topics as divorce, drug addiction, and religious cults, they can draw on the theoretical insights of the discipline's pioneers. A careful reader can hear Comte, Durkheim, Weber, Marx, DuBois, Cooley, Addams, and many others speaking through the pages of current research. Sociology has also broadened beyond the intellectual confines of North America and Europe. Contributions to the discipline now come from sociologists studying and researching human behavior in other parts of the world. In describing the work of these sociologists, it is helpful to examine a number of influential *theoretical perspectives,* also known as *approaches* or *views.*

Summary

The thinkers who founded the discipline of sociology and developed it in the 19th and 20th centuries were reacting to the social world in which they lived.

1. Nineteenth-century thinkers who contributed sociological insights included Auguste Comte, a French philosopher; Harriet Martineau, an English sociologist; and Herbert Spencer, an English scholar.

2. Other important figures in the development of sociology were Émile Durkheim, who pioneered work on suicide; Max Weber, who taught the need for insight in intellectual work; Karl Marx, who emphasized the importance of the economy and social conflict; and W. E. B. DuBois, who advocated for the usefulness of basic research in combating prejudice and fostering racial tolerance and justice.

3. In the 20th century, the discipline of sociology was indebted to the U.S. sociologists Charles Horton Cooley and Robert Merton, as well as to the French sociologist Pierre Bourdieu.

4. **Macrosociology** concentrates on large-scale phenomena or entire civilizations; **microsociology** stresses the study of small groups. *Mesosociology* is an intermediate level of analysis that focuses on formal organizations and social movements. *Global sociology* compares nations or entire societies.

Thinking Critically

1. Consider the work of early sociologists such as Comte and Martineau. What social problems were they reacting to? To what extent have those problems been rectified today?

2. How is 19th-century industrialization related to the development of sociological thought?

3. What are some examples of social and cultural capital that you possess?

Key Terms

Anomie

Cultural capital

Double consciousness

Global sociology

Ideal type

Macrosociology

Mesosociology

Microsociology

Social capital

Verstehen

Sociologists view society in different ways. Some see the world basically as a stable and ongoing entity. They are impressed with the endurance of the family, organized religion, and other social institutions. Other sociologists see society as composed of many groups in conflict, competing for scarce resources. To still other sociologists, the most fascinating aspects of the social world are the everyday, routine interactions among individuals that we sometimes take for granted. These three views, the ones most widely used by sociologists, are the functionalist, conflict, and interactionist perspectives. Together, these approaches will provide an introductory look at the discipline.

● Functionalist Perspective

Think of society as a living organism in which each part of the organism contributes to its survival. This view is the **functionalist perspective**, which emphasizes the way in which the parts of a society are structured to maintain its stability. In examining any aspect of society, then, functionalists emphasize the contribution that it makes to overall social stability.

Talcott Parsons (1902–1979), a Harvard University sociologist, was a key figure in the development of functionalist theory. Parsons was greatly influenced by the work of Émile Durkheim, Max Weber, and other European sociologists. For more than four decades, he dominated sociology in the United States with his advocacy of functionalism. Parsons saw any society as a vast network of connected parts, each of which helps to maintain the system as a whole. His approach, carried forward by German sociologist Niklas Luhmann (1927–1998), holds that if an aspect of social life does not contribute to a society's stability or survival—if it does not serve some identifiably useful function or promote value consensus among members of society—it will not be passed on from one generation to the next (Joas and Knöbl 2009; Knudsen 2010).

Let's examine an example of the functionalist perspective. Many Americans have difficulty understanding the Hindu prohibition against slaughtering cows (specifically, zebu). Cattle browse unhindered through Indian street markets, helping themselves to oranges and mangoes while people bargain for the little food they can afford. What explains this devotion to the cow in the face of human deprivation—a devotion that appears to be dysfunctional?

The simple explanation is that cow worship is highly functional in Indian society, according to economists, agronomists, and social scientists who have studied the matter. Cows perform two essential tasks: plowing the fields and producing milk. If eating beef were permitted, hungry families might be tempted to slaughter their cows for immediate consumption, leaving themselves without a means of cultivation. Cows also produce dung, which doubles as a fertilizer and a fuel for cooking. Finally, cow meat sustains the neediest group in society, the *Dalit,* or untouchables, who sometimes resort to eating beef in secrecy. If eating beef were socially acceptable, higher-status Indians would no doubt bid up its price, placing it beyond the reach of the hungriest.

Manifest and Latent Functions

A college catalog typically states various functions of the institution. It may inform you, for example, that the university intends to "offer each student a broad education in classical and contemporary thought, in the humanities, in the sciences, and in the arts." However, it would be quite a surprise to find a catalog that declared, "This university was founded in 1895 to assist people in finding a marriage partner." No college catalog will declare this as the purpose of the university. Yet societal institutions serve many functions, some of them quite subtle. The university, in fact, *does* facilitate mate selection.

Robert Merton (1968) made an important distinction between manifest and latent functions. **Manifest functions** of institutions are open, stated, and conscious functions. They involve the intended, recognized consequences of an aspect of society, such as the university's role in certifying academic competence and excellence. In contrast, **latent functions** are unconscious or unintended functions that may reflect hidden purposes of an institution. One latent function of universities is to hold down unemployment. Another is to serve as a meeting ground for people seeking marital partners.

Dysfunctions

Functionalists acknowledge that not all parts of a society contribute to its stability all the time. A **dysfunction** refers to an element or process of a society that may actually disrupt the social system or reduce its stability.

We view many dysfunctional behavior patterns, such as homicide, as undesirable. Yet we should not automatically interpret them in this way. The evaluation of a dysfunction depends on one's own values, or as the saying goes, on "where you sit." For example, the official view in prisons in the United States is that inmate gangs should be eradicated because they are dysfunctional to smooth operations. Yet some guards have come to view prison gangs as a functional part of their jobs. The danger posed by gangs creates a "threat to security," requiring increased surveillance and more overtime work for guards, as well as requests for special staffing to address gang problems (G. Scott 2001).

● Conflict Perspective

Where functionalists see stability and consensus, conflict sociologists see a social world in continual struggle. The **conflict perspective** assumes that social behavior is best understood in terms of tension between groups over power or the allocation of resources, including housing, money, access to services, and political representation. The tension between competing groups need not be violent; it can take the form of labor negotiations, party politics, competition between religious groups for new members, or disputes over the federal budget.

Throughout most of the 1900s, the functionalist perspective had the upper hand in sociology in the United States. However, the conflict approach has become increasingly persuasive since the late 1960s. The widespread social unrest resulting from battles over civil rights, bitter divisions over the war in Vietnam, the rise of the feminist and gay liberation movements, the Watergate political scandal, urban riots, confrontations at abortion clinics, and shrinking economic prospects for the middle class have offered support for the conflict approach—the view that our social world is characterized by continual struggle between competing groups. Currently, the discipline of sociology accepts conflict theory as one valid way to gain insight into a society.

The Marxist View

As we saw earlier, Karl Marx viewed struggle between social classes as inevitable, given the exploitation of workers that he perceived under capitalism. Expanding on Marx's work, sociologists and other social scientists have come to see conflict not merely as a class phenomenon but as a part of everyday life in

© John Lund/Tiffany Schoepp/Blend Images/Corbis RF

Functionalists would see the family, as shown here in Panama City, Panama, as important to contributing to the stability of the society.

© Elmer Martinez/AFP/Getty Images

Sociologists who take the Marxist view ask "Who benefits, who suffers, and who dominates?" What might these tattoos suggest to a Marxist theorist?

all societies. In studying any culture, organization, or social group, sociologists want to know who benefits, who suffers, and who dominates at the expense of others. They are concerned with the conflicts between women and men, parents and children, cities and suburbs, Whites and Blacks, to name only a few. Conflict theorists are interested in how society's institutions—including the family, government, religion, education, and the media—may help to maintain the privileges of some groups and keep others in a subservient position. Their emphasis on social change and the redistribution of resources makes conflict theorists more radical and activist than functionalists (Dahrendorf 1959).

© Photo Researchers, Inc./Science Source

Ida Wells-Barnett explored what it meant to be female and Black in the United States. Her work established her as one of the earliest feminist theorists.

The Feminist Perspective

Sociologists began embracing the feminist perspective only in the 1970s, although it has a long tradition in many other disciplines.

The **feminist perspective** sees inequity in gender as central to all behavior and organization. Because it focuses clearly on one aspect of inequality, it is often allied with the conflict perspective. Proponents of the feminist view tend to focus on the macro level, just as conflict theorists do. Drawing on the work of Marx and Engels, contemporary feminist theorists often view women's subordination as inherent in capitalist societies. Some radical feminist theorists, however, view the oppression of women as inevitable in *all* male-dominated societies, whether capitalist, socialist, or communist.

An early example of this perspective (long before the label came into use by sociologists) can be seen in the life and writings of Ida Wells-Barnett (1862–1931). Following her groundbreaking publications in the 1890s on the practice of lynching Black Americans, she became an advocate in the women's rights campaign, especially the struggle to win the vote for women. Like feminist theorists who succeeded her, Wells-Barnett used her analysis of society as a means of resisting oppression. In her case, she researched what it meant to be Black, a woman in the United States, and a Black woman in the United States (Giddings 2008; Wells-Barnett 1970).

A more recent contribution that continues to spark discussion is the notion of the *intersectionalities,* or the interlocking matrix of domination. In all societies, privilege or lack of privilege is determined by multiple social factors, such as gender, age, race, sexual orientation, and religion. Patricia Hill Collins (2000), among other feminist theorists, drew attention that these interlocking factors, demonstrating that it is not just wealth that influences how we navigate our daily lives in any society.

Queer Theory

Traditionally, sociologists and other researchers have assumed that men and women are heterosexual. They either ignored other sexual identifications or treated them as abnormal. Yet as French social theorist Michel Foucault (1978) has pointed out, what is regarded as normal or even acceptable human sexuality varies dramatically from one culture to another, as well as from one time period to another. Today, in *queer theory,* sociologists have moved beyond narrow assumptions to study sexuality in all its forms.

Historically, the word *queer* was used in a derogatory manner, to stigmatize a person or behavior. Beginning in the early 1970s, however, gay and lesbian activists began to use the word as a term of empowerment. They dismissed the notion of heterosexuality as the only normal form of sexuality, along with the belief that people must be either heterosexual or homosexual. Instead, they recognized multiple sexual identities, including bisexuality. **Queer theory** is the study of society from the perspective of a broad spectrum of sexual identities, including heterosexuality, homosexuality, and bisexuality.

Queer theorist Eve Sedgwick (1990) argues that any analysis of society is incomplete if it does not include the spectrum of sexual identities that people embrace. Consider, for example, the reelection of President Obama in 2012. Political scientists have often noted the overwhelming support the president received from African Americans, Latinos, and women voters. Yet most have ignored the huge support—76 percent—that the president enjoyed among gay, lesbian, and bisexual voters. In comparison, heterosexual voters split evenly (49 percent to 49 percent nationwide) between Obama and his opponent, Mitt Romney. In the three battleground states of Florida, Ohio, and Virginia, support from gay, lesbian, and bisexual voters alone was enough to put Obama over the top. If Romney had carried just 51 percent of the gay, lesbian, and bisexual vote nationwide, he would have become the next president of the United States (Gates 2012).

use your **sociological imagination**

You are a sociologist who takes the conflict perspective. How would you interpret the practice of prostitution? How would your view of prostitution differ if you took the functionalist perspective? The feminist perspective? The perspective of queer theory?

■ Interactionist Perspective

Workers interacting on the job, encounters in public places like bus stops and parks, behavior in small groups—all these aspects of microsociology catch the attention of interactionists. Whereas functionalist and conflict theorists both analyze large-scale, society-wide patterns of behavior, theorists who take the **interactionist perspective** generalize about everyday forms of social interaction in order to explain society as a whole.

Today, given concern over traffic congestion and commuting costs, interactionists have begun to study a form of commuter behavior called "slugging." To avoid driving to work, commuters gather at certain preappointed places to seek rides from complete strangers. When a driver pulls into the parking area or vacant lot and announces his destination, the first slug in line who is headed for that destination jumps in. Rules of etiquette have emerged to smooth the social interaction between driver and passenger: neither the driver nor the passenger may eat or smoke; the slug may not adjust the windows or radio or talk on a cell phone. The presence of the slugs, who get a free ride, may allow the driver to use special lanes reserved for high-occupancy vehicles (SlugLines.com 2016).

Interactionism (also referred to as *symbolic interactionism*) is a sociological framework in which human beings are viewed as living in a world of meaningful objects. Those "objects" may include material things, actions, other people, relationships, and even symbols. Interactionists see symbols as an especially important part of human communication (thus the term *symbolic interactionism*). Symbols have a shared social meaning that is understood by all members of a society. In the United States, for example, a salute symbolizes respect, while a clenched fist signifies defiance. Another culture might use different gestures to convey a feeling of respect or defiance. These types of symbolic interaction are classified as forms of **nonverbal communication**,

which can include many other gestures, facial expressions, and postures (Masuda et al. 2008).

Manipulation of symbols can be seen in dress codes. Schools frown on students who wear clothes displaying messages that appear to endorse violence or drug and alcohol consumption. Businesses stipulate the attire employees are allowed to wear on the job in order to impress their customers or clients. In 2005, the National Basketball Association (NBA) adopted a new dress code for the athletes who play professional basketball—one that involved not the uniforms they wear on court, but the clothes they wear off court on league business. The code requires "business casual attire" when players are representing the league. Indoor sunglasses, chains, and sleeveless shirts are specifically banned (Crowe and Herman 2005:A23).

While the functionalist and conflict approaches were initiated in Europe, interactionism developed first in the United States. George Herbert Mead (1863–1931) is widely regarded as the founder of the interactionist perspective. Mead taught at the University of Chicago from 1893 until his death. As his teachings have become better known, sociologists have expressed greater interest in the interactionist perspective. Many have moved away from what may have been an excessive preoccupation with the macro (large-scale) level of social behavior and have redirected their attention toward behavior that occurs on the micro (small-scale) level.

Erving Goffman (1922–1982) popularized a particular type of interactionist method known as the **dramaturgical approach**, in which people are seen as theatrical performers. The dramaturgist compares everyday life to the setting of the theater and stage. Just as actors project certain images, all of us seek to present particular features of our personalities while we hide other features. Thus, in a class, we may feel the need to project a serious image; at a party, we may want to look relaxed and friendly.

■ The Sociological Approach

Which perspective should a sociologist use in studying human behavior? Functionalist? Conflict? Interactionist? Feminist? Queer theorist? We simply cannot squeeze all sociological thinking into four or five theoretical categories—or even 10, if we include several other productive approaches. However, by studying the three major frameworks, we can better grasp how sociologists seek to explore social behavior. Table 3-1 summarizes these three broad approaches to sociological study.

Although no one approach is correct by itself, and sociologists draw on all of them for various purposes, many sociologists tend to favor one particular perspective over others. A sociologist's theoretical orientation influences his or her approach to a research problem in important ways—including the choice of what to study, how to study it, and what questions to pose (or not to pose). Box 3-1 shows how researchers would study sports from different sociological perspectives.

Whatever the purpose of sociologists' work, their research will always be guided by their theoretical viewpoints. For example, sociologist Elijah Anderson (1990) embraces both the interactionist perspective and the groundbreaking work of

TABLE 3-1 MAJOR SOCIOLOGICAL PERSPECTIVES

	Functionalist	Conflict	Interactionist
View of Society	Stable, well integrated	Characterized by tension and struggle between groups	Active in influencing and affecting everyday social interaction
Level of Analysis Emphasized	Macro Meso Global	Macro Meso Global	Micro, as a way of understanding the larger social phenomena
Key Concepts	Manifest functions Latent functions Dysfunctions	Inequality Capitalism Stratification	Symbols Nonverbal communication Face-to-face interaction
View of the Individual	People are socialized to perform societal functions	People are shaped by power, coercion, and authority	People manipulate symbols and create their social worlds through interaction
View of the Social Order	Maintained through cooperation and consensus	Maintained through force and coercion	Maintained by shared understanding of everyday behavior
View of Social Change	Predictable, reinforcing	Change takes place all the time and may have positive consequences	Reflected in people's social positions and their communications with others
Example	Public punishments reinforce the social order	Laws reinforce the positions of those in power	People respect laws or disobey them based on their own past experience
Proponents	Émile Durkheim Talcott Parsons Robert Merton	Karl Marx W. E. B. DuBois Ida Wells-Barnett	George Herbert Mead Charles Horton Cooley Erving Goffman

Research Today

BOX 3-1

Looking at Sports from Five Sociological Perspectives

We watch sports. Talk sports. Spend money on sports. Some of us live and breathe sports. Because sports occupy much of our time and directly or indirectly consume and generate a great deal of money, it should not be surprising that sports have sociological components that can be analyzed from various theoretical perspectives. In this section we will look at sports from five major sociological perspectives.

Functionalist View

In examining any aspect of society, functionalists emphasize the contribution it makes to overall social stability. Functionalists regard sports as an almost religious institution that uses ritual and ceremony to reinforce the common values of a society. For example:

- Sports socialize young people into such values as competition and patriotism.
- Sports help to maintain people's physical well-being.
- Sports serve as a safety valve for both participants and spectators, who are allowed to shed tension and aggressive energy in a socially acceptable way.
- Sports bring together members of a community (who support local athletes

and teams) or even a nation (during World Cup matches and the Olympics) and promote an overall feeling of unity and social solidarity.

Conflict View

Conflict theorists argue that the social order is based on coercion and exploitation. They emphasize that sports reflect and even exacerbate many of the divisions of society:

- Sports are a form of big business in which profits are more important than the health and safety of the workers (athletes).
- Sports perpetuate the false idea that success can be achieved simply through hard work, while failure should be blamed on the individual alone (rather than on injustices in the larger social system).
- Professional athletes' behavior can promote violence and the use of performance-enhancing drugs.
- Communities divert scarce resources to subsidize the construction of professional sports facilities.

© Eugene Tanner/AP Images

Professional golfer Stacy Lewis won $1.9 million in 2015, making her the third most successful woman on the pro golf circuit that year. Among men, her winnings would have put her in 49th place.

—*Continued*

- Sports maintain the subordinate role of Blacks and Latinos, who toil as athletes but are less visible in supervisory positions as coaches, managers, and owners.
- Team logos and mascots (like the Washington Redskins) disparage American Indians.

Feminist View

Feminist theorists consider how watching or participating in sports reinforces the roles that men and women play in the larger society:

- Although sports generally promote fitness and health, they may also have an adverse effect on participants' health. Men are more likely to resort to illegal steroid use (among bodybuilders and baseball players, for example); women, to excessive dieting (among gymnasts and figure skaters, for example).
- Gender expectations encourage female athletes to be passive and gentle, qualities that do not support the emphasis on competitiveness in sports. As a result, women find it difficult to enter sports traditionally dominated by men, such as Indy or NASCAR.
- Although professional women athletes' earnings are increasing, they typically trail those of male athletes.

Queer Theory

Proponents of queer theory emphasize the ways in which sports promote heterosexuality as the only acceptable sexual identity for athletes:

- Coaches and players routinely use slurs based on negative stereotypes

> Despite their differences, functionalists, conflict theorists, feminists, queer theorists, and interactionists would all agree that there is much more to sports than exercise or recreation.

of homosexuals to stigmatize athletes whose performance is inadequate.
- As a group, professional athletes are highly reluctant to display any sexual identity other than heterosexuality in public, for fear of damaging their careers and losing their fans and commercial sponsors.
- Parents who are not heterosexual encounter hostility when they try to register their children for sports or scouting programs, and are often rejected from coaching and other support roles.

Interactionist View

In studying the social order, interactionists are especially interested in shared understandings of everyday behavior. Interactionists examine sports on the micro level by focusing on how day-to-day social behavior is shaped by the distinctive norms, values, and demands of the world of sports:

- Sports often heighten parent–child involvement; they may lead to parental expectations for participation, and sometimes unrealistically, for success.

- Participation in sports builds the friendship networks that permeate everyday life.
- Despite class, racial, and religious differences, teammates may work together harmoniously and may even abandon common stereotypes and prejudices.
- Relationships in the sports world are defined by people's social positions as players, coaches, and referees—as well as by the high or low status that individuals hold as a result of their performances and reputations.

Despite their differences, functionalists, conflict theorists, feminists, queer theorists, and interactionists would all agree that there is much more to sports than exercise or recreation. They would also agree that sports and other popular forms of culture are worthy subjects of serious study by sociologists.

LET'S DISCUSS

1. Have you experienced or witnessed discrimination in sports based on gender, race, or sexual identity? If so, how did you react? Has the representation of Blacks, women, or gays on teams been controversial on your campus? In what ways?
2. Which of the five sociological perspectives seems most useful to you in analyzing sports? Why?

Sources: Acosta and Carpenter 2001; Eitzen 2009; Fine 1987; Sefiha 2012; Sharp et al. 2013; Young 2004; Zirin 2008.

W. E. B. DuBois. For 14 years Anderson conducted fieldwork in Philadelphia, where he studied the interactions of Black and White residents who lived in adjoining neighborhoods. In particular, he was interested in their public behavior, including their eye contact—or lack of it—as they passed one another on the street. Anderson's research tells us much about the everyday social interactions of Blacks and Whites in the United States, but it does not explain the larger issues behind those interactions. Like theories, research results illuminate one part of the stage, leaving other parts in relative darkness.

MODULE 3 | Recap and Review

Summary

Sociologists make use of five major perspectives, all of which offer unique insights into the same issues.

1. The **functionalist perspective** emphasizes the way in which the parts of a society are structured to maintain its stability.
2. The **conflict perspective** assumes that social behavior is best understood in terms of conflict or tension between competing groups.
3. The **interactionist perspective** is concerned primarily with fundamental or everyday forms of interaction,

18 ■ Understanding Sociology

including symbols and other types of **nonverbal communication**.

4. The **feminist view**, which is often allied with the conflict perspective, sees inequity in gender as central to all behavior and organization.

5. **Queer theory** stresses that to fully understand society, scholars must study it from the perspectives of a range of sexual identities, rather than exclusively from a "normal" heterosexual point of view.

Thinking Critically

1. Describe an aspect of contemporary society that you consider to be a dysfunction.

2. Describe a symbol or object that has particular meaning on your campus.

3. Relate the toys on display in your local store to issues of race, class, and gender.

Key Terms

Conflict perspective

Dramaturgical approach

Dysfunction

Feminist perspective

Functionalist perspective

Interactionist perspective

Latent function

Manifest function

Nonverbal communication

Queer theory

MODULE 4 | Taking Sociology with You

You've seen how sociologists employ the major sociological perspectives in their research. How does sociology relate to *you,* your own studies, and your own career? In this section you'll learn about *applied* and *clinical sociology,* two growing fields that allow sociology majors and those with advanced degrees in sociology to apply what they have learned to real-world settings. You'll also see how to develop your sociological imagination, one of the keys to thinking like a sociologist. See the appendix at the end of this chapter for more information on careers in sociology.

Applied and Clinical Sociology

Many early sociologists—notably, Jane Addams, W. E. B. DuBois, and George Herbert Mead—were strong advocates for social reform. They wanted their theories and findings to be relevant to policymakers and to people's lives in general. For instance, Mead was the treasurer of Hull House, where he applied his theory to improving the lives of those who were powerless (especially immigrants). He also served on committees dealing with Chicago's labor problems and public education. DuBois led the Atlanta Sociological Laboratory from 1895 to 1924, supporting scholars in their applied research on business, criminal justice, health care, and philanthropy (Earl Wright II 2012).

Today, **applied sociology** is the use of the discipline of sociology with the specific intent of yielding practical applications for human behavior and organizations. By extension, Michael Burawoy (2005), in his presidential address to the American Sociological Association, endorsed what he called *public sociology,* encouraging scholars to engage a broader audience in bringing about positive outcomes. In effect, the applied sociologist reaches out to others and joins them in their efforts to better society.

Often, the goal of applied or public sociology is to assist in resolving a social problem. For example, in the past 50 years, eight presidents of the United States have established commissions to delve into major societal concerns facing our nation. Sociologists are often asked to apply their expertise to studying such issues as violence, pornography, crime, immigration, and population. In Europe, both academic and government research departments are offering increasing financial support for applied studies.

One example of applied sociology is the growing interest in learning more about local communities. Since its founding in 1994, the Northeast Florida Center for Community Initiatives (CCI), based at the University of North Florida in Jacksonville, has conducted several community studies, including a homeless census and survey, an analysis of the economic impact of the arts in Jacksonville, and a long-term survey of the effects of Hurricane Katrina. Typical of applied sociology, these outreach efforts are collaborative, involving faculty, undergraduate and graduate students, volunteers, and community residents (Center for Community Initiatives 2014).

Another of CCI's applications of sociology, the Magnolia Project, is based in a storefront clinic in an underprivileged area of Jacksonville. Part of the federal Healthy Start initiative, which aims to decrease high infant mortality rates, the project serves women of childbearing age who have little or no regular access to health care. CCI's responsibilities include (1) interviewing and surveying key community participants, (2) coordinating data collection by the project's staff, (3) analyzing data, and (4) preparing progress reports for funding agencies and community partners. Through June 2014, not a single infant death had occurred among the 662 participants in the program (Center for Community Initiatives 2014).

© Ian Hooton/SPL/Alamy RF

The Center for Community Initiatives' Magnolia Project, an example of applied sociology, aims to decrease high rates of infant mortality.

Growing interest in applied sociology has led to such specializations as *medical sociology* and *environmental sociology*. The former includes research on how health care professionals and patients deal with disease. To give one example, medical sociologists have studied the social impact of the AIDS crisis on families, friends, and communities (see Chapter 15). Environmental sociologists examine the relationship between human societies and the physical environment. One focus of their work is the issue of "environmental justice" (see Chapter 15), raised when researchers and community activists found that hazardous waste dumps are especially likely to be situated in poor and minority neighborhoods (M. Martin 1996).

The growing popularity of applied sociology has led to the rise of the specialty of clinical sociology. Louis Wirth (1931) wrote about clinical sociology more than 85 years ago, but the term itself has become popular only in recent years. While applied sociology may simply evaluate social issues, **clinical sociology** is dedicated to facilitating change by altering social relationships (as in family therapy) or restructuring social institutions (as in the reorganization of a medical center).

Applied sociologists generally leave it to policymakers to act on their evaluations. In contrast, clinical sociologists take direct responsibility for implementation and view those with whom they work as their clients. This specialty has become increasingly attractive to graduate students in sociology because it offers an opportunity to apply intellectual learning in a practical way. A shrinking job market in the academic world has made such alternative career routes appealing.

Applied and clinical sociology can be contrasted with **basic sociology** (also called *pure sociology*), which seeks a more profound knowledge of the fundamental aspects of social phenomena. This type of research is not necessarily meant to generate specific applications, although such ideas may result once findings are analyzed. When Durkheim studied suicide rates, he was not primarily interested in discovering a way to eliminate suicide. In this sense, his research was an example of basic rather than applied sociology.

Developing a Sociological Imagination

In this book, we will be illustrating the sociological imagination in several different ways—by showing theory in practice and in current research; by noting the ways in which electronic devices and apps are changing our social behavior; by thinking globally; by exploring the significance of social inequality; by speaking across race, gender, and religious boundaries; and by highlighting social policy throughout the world.

Theory in Practice

We will illustrate how the major sociological perspectives can be helpful in understanding today's issues, from capital punishment to abortion. Sociologists do not necessarily declare, "Here I am using functionalism," but their research and approaches do tend to draw on one or more theoretical frameworks, as will become clear in the pages to follow.

Research Today

Sociologists actively investigate a variety of issues and social behavior. We have already seen that research can shed light on the social factors that affect suicide rates. Sociological research often plays a direct role in improving people's lives, as in the case of increasing the participation of African Americans in diabetes testing. Throughout the rest of the book, the research performed by sociologists and other social scientists will shed light on group behavior of all types.

Our Wired World

"What is the news today?" For many people, "the news" means the latest comments, pictures, and videos posted online by friends and acquaintances. For some, such up-to-the-minute connectivity has become addictive. During the superstorm that hit New

Jersey and New York in October 2012, more than a few people missed their wireless connections more than they did their electrical service.

Throughout this book we will frequently touch on our ever-expanding wired world. The impact of these changes was the focus of Sherry Turkle's attention in the opening excerpt of this chapter. More and more, the electronic gadgets and applications we now depend on for almost everything in our lives are altering our social behavior.

Thinking Globally

Whatever their theoretical perspective or research techniques, sociologists recognize that social behavior must be viewed in a global context. **Globalization** is the worldwide integration of government policies, cultures, social movements, and financial markets through trade and the exchange of ideas. Although public discussion of globalization is relatively recent, intellectuals have been pondering both its negative and positive social consequences for a long time. Karl Marx and Friedrich Engels warned in *The Communist Manifesto* (written in 1848) of a world market that would lead to production in distant lands, sweeping away existing working relationships.

Today, developments outside a country are as likely to influence people's lives as changes at home. For example, though much of the world was already in recession by September 2001, the terrorist attacks on New York and Washington, D.C., caused an immediate economic decline, not just in the United States, but throughout the world. One example of the massive global impact was the downturn in international tourism, which lasted for at least two years. The effects have been felt by people far removed from the United States, including African game wardens and Asian taxi drivers.

Some observers draw attention to the manner in which nations either admit or turn away migrants, often basing such decisions more on their assets, race, or religion than on the human rights merits of the individual cases. Another aspect of the world landscape is how multinational corporations are allowed to expand communications technology, particularly the Internet and satellite transmission of the mass media. Others view it more critically, as a process that allows multinational corporations to expand unchecked. We examine the impact of globalization on our daily lives and on societies throughout the world in Box 4-1 and throughout this book (Fiss and Hirsch 2005).

The Significance of Social Inequality

Who holds power? Who doesn't? Who has prestige? Who lacks it? Perhaps the major theme of analysis in sociology today is **social inequality**, a condition in which members of society have differing amounts of wealth, prestige, or power. For example, the disparity between what coffee bean pickers in developing nations are paid and the price you pay for a cup of coffee underscores global inequality (see Box 4-1). And the impact of Hurricane Katrina on residents of the Gulf Coast drew attention to social inequality in the United States. Predictably, the people who were hit the hardest by the massive storm were the poor, who had the greatest difficulty evacuating before the storm and have had the most difficulty recovering from it.

Some sociologists, in seeking to understand the effects of inequality, have made the case for social justice. W. E. B. DuBois ([1940] 1968:418) noted that the greatest power in the land is not "thought or ethics, but wealth." As we have seen, the contributions of Karl Marx, Jane Addams, and Ida Wells-Barnett also stressed this belief in the overarching significance of social inequality, and by extension, social justice. In this book, social inequality will be the central focus of Chapters 8 and 9, and sociologists' work on inequality will be highlighted throughout.

A TOAST... HERE'S TO GLOBALISM!

HERE'S TO SKYROCKETING SALES AND SOARING PROFITS!

HERE'S TO CHEAP LABOR AND HIGHER STOCK PRICES!...

THIS CHAMPAGNE WASN'T MADE IN CHINA, WAS IT?

08-15-07
MORIN
The Miami Herald

© Jim Morin/Miami Herald/Morintoons Syndicate.

Today, both the positive and negative aspects of globalization are receiving increased scrutiny from sociologists.

Speaking across Race, Gender, and Religious Boundaries

Sociologists include both men and women, who come from a variety of ethnic, national, and religious origins. In their work, sociologists seek to draw conclusions that speak to all people—not just the affluent or powerful. Doing so is not always easy. Insights into how a corporation can increase its profits tend to attract more attention and financial support than do, say, the merits of a needle exchange program for low-income inner-city residents. Yet today more than ever, sociology seeks to better understand the experiences of all people.

Sociologists have noted, for example, that the huge tsunami that hit South Asia

Your Morning Cup of Coffee

When you drink a cup of coffee, do you give much thought to where the coffee beans came from, or do you think more about the pleasure you get from the popular beverage? Coffee certainly is popular—as an import, it is second only to petroleum, the most traded commodity in the world.

Although the coffee trade has been globalized, the customs of coffee drinking still vary from place to place. Starbucks now has 21,000 locations in 65 countries. Managers find that in European countries, where the coffeehouse culture originated, 80 percent of customers sit down to drink their coffee. Europeans want to get to know their baristas, so in 2012 Starbucks introduced nametags. In the United States, by contrast, 80 percent of Starbucks customers leave the store immediately, taking their coffee with them.

Today, the coffee trade relies on the exploitation of cheap labor. Coffee is a labor-intensive crop: there is little that technology can do to ease the coffee picker's burden. The typical coffee picker works in a developing nation near the equator,

© John Foxx/Imagestate Media/Imagestate RF

receiving for a day's wages an amount that matches the price of a single cup of coffee

> The typical coffee picker works in a developing nation near the equator, receiving for a day's wages an amount that matches the price of a single cup of coffee in North America.

in North America. In the 1940s, advocacy groups began to promote the sale of certified *fair trade coffee,* which gives a living wage to those who harvest the crop, allowing them to become economically self-sufficient. Similar movements have begun to promote fair trade in the global clothing industry, reported on by Kelsey Timmerman in his book *Where Am I Wearing?*

Ecological activists have drawn attention to what they see as the coffee industry's contribution to the trend toward climate change. The need to make room for more coffee fields, they charge, has encouraged the destruction of rain forests. The same criticism can be aimed at much of the consumption in industrial nations. Of all the products that emerge from developing nations, however, few have as singular a place in many people's daily ritual as that morning cup of joe. The drink in your hand is your tangible link to rural workers in some of the poorest areas of the world.

LET'S DISCUSS

1. Do you enjoy coffee? Would you willingly pay more for a cup of coffee if you knew that the worker who picked the beans would benefit from the higher price?

2. The coffee trade has been blamed for perpetuating social inequality and global warming. Can you think of any positive effects of the coffee trade? Who benefits most from this economic activity?

Sources: Alderman 2012; Cole & Brown 2014; Ritzer 2015; Timmerman 2009.

---

in 2004 affected men and women differently. When the waves hit, mothers and grandmothers were at home with the children; men were outside working, where they were more likely to become aware of the impending disaster. Moreover, most of the men knew how to swim, a survival skill that women in these traditional societies usually do not learn. As a result, many more men than women survived the catastrophe—about 10 men for every 1 woman. In one Indonesian village typical of the disaster area, 97 of 1,300 people survived; only 4 were women. The impact of this gender imbalance will be felt for some time, given women's primary role as caregivers for children and the elderly (BBC News 2005).

Social Policy throughout the World

One important way we can use a sociological imagination is to enhance our understanding of current social issues throughout the world. Beginning with Chapter 2, each chapter will conclude with a discussion of a contemporary social policy issue. In some cases we will examine a specific issue facing national governments. For example, government funding of child care centers will be discussed in Chapter 4, Socialization and the Life Course; global immigration in Chapter 10, Racial and Ethnic Inequality;

and religion in the schools in Chapter 15, Religion. These Social Policy sections will demonstrate how fundamental sociological concepts can enhance our critical thinking skills and help us to better understand current public policy debates taking place around the world.

In addition, sociology has been used to evaluate the success of programs or the impact of changes brought about by policymakers and political activists. For example, Chapter 9, Global Inequality, includes a discussion of research on the effectiveness of welfare programs. Such discussions underscore the many practical applications of sociological theory and research.

Sociologists expect the next quarter century to be perhaps the most exciting and critical period in the history of the discipline. That is because of a growing recognition—both in the United States and around the world—that current social problems must be addressed before their magnitude overwhelms human societies. We can expect sociologists to play an increasing role in government by researching and developing public policy alternatives. It seems only natural for this textbook to focus on the connection between the work of sociologists and the difficult questions confronting policymakers and people in the United States and around the world.

Summary

Studying sociology allows you many ways to exercise your sociological imagination.

1. **Applied** and **clinical sociology** use the discipline of sociology to solve practical problems in human behavior and organizations. In contrast, **basic sociology** is sociological inquiry that seeks only a deeper knowledge of the fundamental aspects of human phenomena.

2. This textbook makes use of the sociological imagination by showing theory in practice and in current research: by thinking globally; by focusing on the significance of social inequality; by speaking across racial, gender, and religious boundaries; and by highlighting social policy around the world.

Thinking Critically

1. What issues facing your local community would you like to address with applied sociological research? Do you see any global connections to these issues?

2. In what specific ways does globalization affect your everyday life? Do you think the impact of globalization is primarily positive or negative?

Key Terms

Applied sociology

Basic sociology

Clinical sociology

Globalization

Social inequality

Appendix Careers in Sociology

For the past two decades the number of U.S. college students who have graduated with a degree in sociology has risen steadily. In this appendix we'll consider some of the options these students have after completing their education.

How do students first learn about the sociological perspective on society? Some may take a sociology course in high school. Others may study sociology at community college, where 40 percent of all college students in the United States are enrolled. Indeed, many future sociology majors first develop their sociological imaginations at a community college.

An undergraduate degree in sociology doesn't just serve as excellent preparation for future graduate work in sociology. It also provides a strong liberal arts background for entry-level positions in business, social services, foundations, community organizations, not-for-profit groups, law enforcement, and many government jobs. A number of fields—among them marketing, public relations, and broadcasting—now require investigative skills and an understanding of the diverse groups found in today's multiethnic and multinational environment. Moreover, a sociology degree requires accomplishment in oral and written communication, interpersonal skills, problem solving, and critical thinking—all job-related skills that may give sociology graduates an advantage over those who pursue more technical degrees.

Consequently, while few occupations specifically require an undergraduate degree in sociology, such academic training can be an important asset in entering a wide range of occupations. To emphasize this point, a number of chapters in this book highlight a real-life professional who describes how the study of sociology has helped in his or her career. For example, in Module 20 a Taking Sociology to Work box explains how a college graduate uses her training in sociology as a social media manager for nonprofit organizations. And in Module 48, another Taking Sociology to Work box shows how a recent graduate uses the skill set he acquired as a sociology major in his role as a government analyst.

Figure A-1 summarizes the sources of employment for those with BA or BS degrees in sociology. It shows that fields including nonprofit organizations, education, business, and government offer major career opportunities for sociology graduates. Undergraduates who know where their career interests lie are well advised to enroll in sociology courses and specialties best suited to those interests. For example, students hoping to become health planners would take a class in medical sociology; students seeking employment as social science research assistants would focus on courses in statistics and methods. Internships, such as placements at city planning agencies and survey research organizations, afford another way for sociology students to prepare for careers. Studies show that students who choose an internship placement have less trouble finding jobs, obtain better jobs, and enjoy greater job satisfaction than students without internship placements. Finally, students should expect to change fields during their first five years of employment after graduation—for example, from sales and marketing to management (American Sociological Association 2013; Salem and Grabarek 1986).

Many college students view social work as the field most closely associated with sociology. Traditionally, social workers received their undergraduate training in sociology and allied fields such as psychology and counseling. After some practical experience, social workers would generally seek a master's degree in social work (MSW) to be considered for supervisory or administrative positions. Today,

FIGURE A-1 Occupations of Graduating Sociology Majors

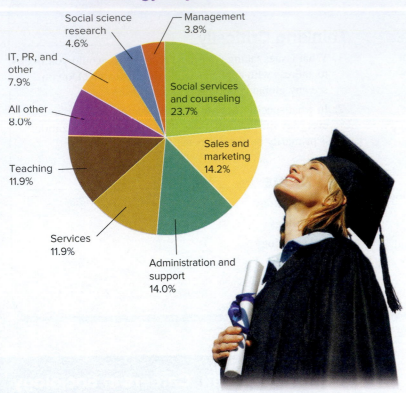

- Social science research 4.6%
- Management 3.8%
- IT, PR, and other 7.9%
- All other 8.0%
- Social services and counseling 23.7%
- Teaching 11.9%
- Sales and marketing 14.2%
- Services 11.9%
- Administration and support 14.0%

Note: Based on a national survey of current occupation in 2013 of 759 graduates with a sociology major in the Class of 2012.
Source: Spalter-Roth et al. 2013: Table 2. *Photo:* © Stockbyte/PunchStock RF

however, some students choose (where it is available) to pursue a bachelor's degree in social work (BSW). This degree prepares graduates for direct service positions, such as caseworker or group worker.

Many students continue their sociological training beyond the bachelor's degree. More than 250 universities in the United States have graduate programs in sociology that offer PhD and/or master's degrees. These programs differ greatly in their areas of specialization, course requirements, costs, and the research and teaching opportunities available to graduate students. About 71 percent of the graduates are women (American Sociological Association 2005; National Center for Education Statistics 2012).

Higher education is an important source of employment for sociologists with graduate degrees. Recently, 85 percent of recent PhD recipients in sociology have sought employment in colleges and universities. These sociologists teach not only majors who are committed to the discipline but also students hoping to become doctors, nurses, lawyers, police officers, and so forth (National Science Foundation 2011).

Sociologists who teach in colleges and universities may use their knowledge and training to influence public policy. For example, sociologist Andrew Cherlin (2003) has commented on the debate over proposed federal funding to promote marriage among welfare recipients. Citing the results of two of his studies, Cherlin questioned the potential effectiveness of such a policy in strengthening low-income families. Because many single mothers choose to marry someone other than the father of their children—sometimes for good reason—their children often grow up in stepfamilies. Cherlin's research shows that children who are raised in stepfamilies are no better off than those in single-parent families. He sees government efforts to promote marriage as a politically motivated attempt to foster traditional social values in a society that has become increasingly diverse.

For sociology graduates who are interested in academic careers, the road to a PhD (or doctorate) can be long and difficult. This degree symbolizes competence in original research; each candidate must prepare a book-length study known as a dissertation. Typically, a doctoral student in sociology will engage in four to seven years of intensive work, including the time required to complete the dissertation. Yet even this effort is no guarantee of a job as a sociology professor.

The good news is that over the next 10 years, the demand for instructors is expected to increase because of high rates of retirement among faculty from the baby boom generation, as well as the anticipated slow but steady growth in the college student population in the United States. Nonetheless, anyone who launches an academic career must be prepared for considerable uncertainty and competition in the college job market (American Sociological Association 2013).

Of course, not all people who work as sociologists teach or hold doctoral degrees. Take government, for example. The Census Bureau relies on people with sociological training to interpret data for other government agencies and the general public. Virtually every agency depends on survey research—a field in which sociology students can specialize—in order to assess everything from community needs to the morale of the agency's workers. In addition, people with sociological training can put their academic knowledge to effective use in probation and parole, health sciences, community development, and recreational services. Some people working in government or private industry have a master's degree (MA or MS) in sociology; others have a bachelor's degree (BA or BS).

Currently, about 15 percent of the members of the American Sociological Association use their sociological skills outside the academic world, whether in social service agencies or in marketing positions for business firms. Increasing numbers of sociologists

© Aleksei Ivanov/123RF

One year after graduation, one out of four sociology majors were employed in the social services as counselors, child advocates, forensic interviewers, program directors, or caseworkers.

with graduate degrees are employed by businesses, industry, hospitals, and nonprofit organizations. Studies show that many sociology graduates are making career changes from social service areas to business and commerce. For an undergraduate major, sociology is excellent preparation for employment in many parts of the business world (Spalter-Roth et al. 2013).

Whether you take a few courses in sociology or complete a degree, you will benefit from the critical thinking skills developed in this discipline. Sociologists emphasize the value of being able to analyze, interpret, and function within a variety of working situations—an asset in virtually any career. Moreover, given rapid technological change and the expanding global economy, all of us will need to adapt to substantial social change, even in our own careers. Sociology provides a rich conceptual framework that can serve as a foundation for flexible career development and assist you in taking advantage of new employment opportunities.

Mastering This Chapter

© Cathy Yeulet/123RF

taking sociology with you

1. Research! Time your daily activities. How much time do you spend communicating with others via electronic media, compared to speaking with them directly? How many different people do you converse with in person and how many via digital devices?

2. In what ways were you or your family affected by the recession that began in 2008? Did the widespread loss of jobs and homes make you and others more aware of the problem of homelessness? Similarly, how were you, your family, or your community affected by the subsequent upturn in the job market?

3. Consider some group or organization that you participate in. Using Robert Merton's concepts, list its manifest and latent functions.

4. What specific issues could be best studied using a meso level of analysis? Which are best approached through global sociology?

key terms

Anomie The loss of direction felt in a society when social control of individual behavior has become ineffective.

Applied sociology The use of the discipline of sociology with the specific intent of yielding practical applications for human behavior and organizations.

Basic sociology Sociological inquiry conducted with the objective of gaining a more profound knowledge of the fundamental aspects of social phenomena. Also known as *pure sociology*.

Clinical sociology The use of the discipline of sociology with the specific intent of altering social relationships or restructuring social institutions.

Conflict perspective A sociological approach that assumes that social behavior is best understood in terms of tension between groups over power or the allocation of resources, including housing, money, access to services, and political representation.

Cultural capital Noneconomic goods, such as family background and education, which are reflected in a knowledge of language and the arts.

Double consciousness The division of an individual's identity into two or more social realities.

Dramaturgical approach A view of social interaction in which people are seen as theatrical performers.

Dysfunction An element or process of a society that may disrupt the social system or reduce its stability.

Feminist perspective A sociological approach that views inequity in gender as central to all behavior and organization.

Functionalist perspective A sociological approach that emphasizes the way in which the parts of a society are structured to maintain its stability.

Global sociology A level of sociological analysis that makes comparisons between entire nations, using entire societies as units of analysis.

Globalization The worldwide integration of government policies, cultures, social movements, and financial markets through trade and the exchange of ideas.

Ideal type A construct or model for evaluating specific cases.

Interactionist perspective A sociological approach that generalizes about everyday forms of social interaction in order to explain society as a whole.

Latent function An unconscious or unintended function that may reflect hidden purposes.

Macrosociology Sociological investigation that concentrates on large-scale phenomena or entire civilizations.

Manifest function An open, stated, and conscious function.

Mesosociology An intermediate level of sociological analysis that focuses on formal organizations and social movements.

Microsociology Sociological investigation that stresses the study of small groups, often through experimental means.

Natural science The study of the physical features of nature and the ways in which they interact and change.

Nonverbal communication The sending of messages through the use of gestures, facial expressions, and postures.

Queer theory The study of society from the perspective of a broad spectrum of sexual identities, including heterosexuality, homosexuality, and bisexuality.

Science The body of knowledge obtained by methods based on systematic observation.

Social capital The collective benefit of social networks, which are built on reciprocal trust.

Social inequality A condition in which members of society have differing amounts of wealth, prestige, or power.

Social science The study of the social features of humans and the ways in which they interact and change.

Sociological imagination An awareness of the relationship between an individual and the wider society, both today and in the past.

Sociology The scientific study of social behavior and human groups.

Theory In sociology, a set of statements that seeks to explain problems, actions, or behavior.

Verstehen The German word for "understanding" or "insight"; used to stress the need for sociologists to take into account the subjective meanings people attach to their actions.

self-quiz

Read each question carefully and then select the best answer.

1. Sociology is
   a. very narrow in scope.
   b. concerned with what one individual does or does not do.
   c. the systematic study of social behavior and human groups.
   d. an awareness of the relationship between an individual and the wider society.

2. Which of the following thinkers introduced the concept of the sociological imagination?
   a. Émile Durkheim
   b. Max Weber
   c. Karl Marx
   d. C. Wright Mills

3. Émile Durkheim's research on suicide suggested that
   a. people with religious affiliations had a higher suicide rate than those who were unaffiliated.
   b. suicide rates seemed to be higher in times of peace than in times of war and revolution.
   c. civilians were more likely to take their lives than soldiers.
   d. suicide is a solitary act, unrelated to group life.

4. Max Weber taught his students that they should employ which of the following in their intellectual work?
   a. anomie
   b. *verstehen*
   c. the sociological imagination
   d. microsociology

5. Robert Merton's contributions to sociology include
   a. successfully combining theory and research.
   b. producing a theory that is one of the most frequently cited explanations of deviant behavior.
   c. an attempt to bring macro-level and micro-level analyses together.
   d. all of the above

6. Which sociologist made a major contribution to society through his in-depth studies of urban life, including both Blacks and Whites?
   a. W. E. B. DuBois
   b. Robert Merton
   c. Auguste Comte
   d. Charles Horton Cooley

7. In the late 19th century, before the term "feminist view" was even coined, the ideas behind this major theoretical approach appeared in the writings of
   a. Karl Marx.
   b. Ida Wells-Barnett.
   c. Charles Horton Cooley.
   d. Pierre Bourdieu.

8. Thinking of society as a living organism in which each part of the organism contributes to its survival is a reflection of which theoretical perspective?
   a. the functionalist perspective
   b. the conflict perspective
   c. the feminist perspective
   d. the interactionist perspective

9. Karl Marx's view of the struggle between social classes inspired the contemporary
   a. functionalist perspective.
   b. conflict perspective.
   c. interactionist perspective.
   d. dramaturgical approach.

10. Erving Goffman's dramaturgical approach, which postulates that people present certain aspects of their personalities while obscuring other aspects, is a derivative of what major theoretical perspective?
    a. the functionalist perspective
    b. the conflict perspective
    c. the feminist perspective
    d. the interactionist perspective

11. While the findings of sociologists may at times seem like common sense, they differ because they rest on _____ analysis of facts.

12. Within sociology, a(n) _____ is a set of statements that seeks to explain problems, actions, or behavior.

13. In _____ _____'s hierarchy of the sciences, sociology was the "queen," and its practitioners were "scientist-priests."

14. In *Society in America,* originally published in 1837, English scholar _____ _____ examined religion, politics, child rearing, and immigration in the young nation.

15. _____ _____ adapted Charles Darwin's evolutionary view of the "survival of the fittest" by arguing that it is "natural" that some people are rich while others are poor.

16. Sociologist Max Weber coined the term _____ _____ in referring to a construct or model that serves as a measuring rod against which actual cases can be evaluated.

17. In *The Communist Manifesto,* _____ _____ and _____ _____ argued that the masses of people who have no resources other than their labor (the proletariat) should unite to fight for the overthrow of capitalist societies.

18. _____ _____ , an early female sociologist, cofounded the famous Chicago settlement house called Hull House and also tried to establish a juvenile court system.

19. The university's role in certifying academic competence and excellence is an example of a(n) _____ function.

20. The _____ _____ draws on the work of Karl Marx and Friedrich Engels in that it often views women's subordination as inherent in capitalist societies.

Answers

1. (c); 2. (d); 3. (b); 4. (b); 5. (d); 6. (a); 7. (b); 8. (a); 9. (b); 10. (d); 11. systematic; 12. theory; 13. Auguste Comte; 14. Harriet Martineau; 15. Herbert Spencer; 16. ideal type; 17. Karl Marx, Friedrich Engels; 18. Jane Addams; 19. manifest; 20. feminist view

2 Sociological Research

© RosalreneBetancourt 3/Alamy

On a busy street in Toronto, a researcher interviews a man about his views on contemporary social issues. Surveys are just one of the methods sociologists use to collect data.

MODULE 5 What Is the Scientific Method?

MODULE 6 Major Research Designs

MODULE 7 Ethics of Research

MODULE 8 Developments of Methodology

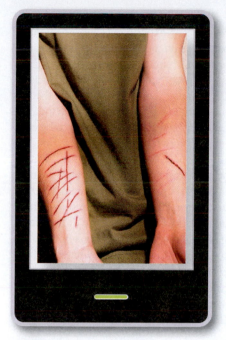

© Peter Dazeley/Getty Images

Did you ever wonder how researchers study behaviors that are private and personal?

Sociologists Patricia Adler and Peter Adler went on the Internet to study people who injure themselves. Read on to see what they learned.

" Self-injury has existed for nearly all of recorded history. Although it has been defined and regarded in various ways over time, its rise in the 1990s and early 2000s has taken a specific, although contested, form and meaning. We focus in this book on the deliberate, nonsuicidal destruction of one's own body tissue, incorporating practices such as self-cutting, burning, branding, scratching, picking at skin.

Our goal here is to discuss the form of this latest incarnation of self-injury, now often regarded as a typical behavior among adolescents, describing and analyzing it through the voices and from the perspective of those who practice it.

Many self-injurers were driven to this behavior by nothing more serious than the minor stresses typically associated with normal adolescence. People cited upsets with their friends, romantic relationships, and family members as having led them to self-injury. Mike was a scruffy-looking college student who always wore a stocking cap. He started cutting and burning himself between the ages of 12 and 14. When he was in high school Mike's girlfriend broke up with him, leaving him devastated. He reflected, "Yeah, I thought every relationship was the end of the world. I kept getting further and further depressed, and I just needed

Mike was a scruffy-looking college student who always wore a stocking cap. He started cutting and burning himself between the ages of 12 and 14.

something to where I could vent and rage without having any outward signs so that anybody could tell anything was wrong." He turned to cutting to assuage his feelings of sadness.

Over the years that we were actively involved in the self-injury cyber world, it took several twists and turns. The earliest of the sites we discovered probably originated during the late 1990s. At that time, most sites were privately owned and unmonitored. Participants often used the term *self-mutilation,* and it was not uncommon to find graphic details and pictures of injuries. Sites had names such as "bleed me," "ruin your life," "bioetchings," "bleeding to ease the pain," "cut it out," and "gallery of pain." Their main purpose, it appeared, was to offer fellowship to self-harmers so they would know they were not alone.

Over the course of our research we also collected tens of thousands (in the range of 30,000–40,000) of Internet messages and emails, including those posted publicly and those written to and by us. In 2006 we enlisted the aid of three student coders to help us sort and analyze the emails and postings from the Internet groups. At this time we were working on one paper, and the students helped us find posts and emails pertinent to our specific focus. We repeated this process again in 2008 with ten more student coders, expanding the project greatly. Each student took one set of emails we had collected from a group, board, or chat room and poured [*sic*] through the years of postings we had assembled. We divided the students into groups of five and met with each group biweekly. At each session the students submitted notes and memos about the material they had scanned, and we brainstormed for sociological codes, categories, concepts, trends, and patterns. "

(P. Adler and P. Adler 2011:1, 43, 44, 54–55)

I n this excerpt from Patricia A. Adler and Peter Adler's book *The Tender Cut: Inside the Hidden World of Self-Injury,* the authors describe their extensive research on a little-known behavior and its social underpinnings. Over a six-year period, the Adlers conducted lengthy, emotionally intense interviews with self-injurers, becoming friends with many. They met others in virtual space, through Internet-based support groups and web postings. "Rather than remaining strictly detached from our subjects, we became involved in their lives, helping them and giving voice to their experiences and beliefs," the Adlers admit (2007:542; 2011).

The Adlers' work on self-injury reflects all three major sociological approaches. For self-injurers, who rarely come into contact

with others like themselves, the Internet functions as a meeting place, a refuge from their self-imposed social isolation. As conflict theorists would point out, their unconventional behavior marginalizes them, preventing them from receiving assistance even when they would welcome it. Interactionists would recognize the critical nature of self-injurers' interpersonal contacts, in person and often online. And feminist and queer theorists would look for gender or sexual orientation differences in self-injurers' behavior.

Though many people would like to ignore the phenomenon of self-injury, believing that those who practice it will eventually "grow out of it," the Adlers' research allows us to consider it intelligently and scientifically, within the social context. Self-injurers, the Adlers found, are a diverse group, whose behavior is carefully planned and considered. Surprisingly, members often begin to injure themselves in the company of others rather than in secret. They have recently begun to coalesce as a subculture (2007:559–560).

Effective sociological research can be quite thought-provoking. It may suggest many new questions that require further study, such as why we make assumptions about people who engage in atypical behaviors like self-injury. In some cases, rather than raising additional questions, a study will simply confirm previous beliefs and findings. Sociological research can also have practical applications. For instance, research results that disconfirm accepted beliefs about marriage and the family may lead to changes in public policy.

These modules will examine the research process used in conducting sociological studies. How do sociologists go about setting up a research project? How do they ensure that the results of the research are reliable and accurate? Can they carry out their research without violating the rights of those they study?

We will look first at the steps that make up the scientific method used in research. Then we will look at various techniques commonly used in sociological research, such as experiments, observations, and surveys. We will pay particular attention to the ethical challenges sociologists face in studying human behavior, and to the debate raised by Max Weber's call for "value neutrality" in social science research. We will also examine feminists' and queer theorists' methodologies and the role technology plays in research today.

Though sociological researchers can study almost any subject, in this chapter we will concentrate on two in particular. The first is the relationship of education to income, which we will use as an example in the section on the scientific method. The second is the controversial subject of human sexual behavior. Like self-injury, sexual behavior is private and personal, and therefore hard to study. The Social Policy section that closes Module 8 describes the difficulties and challenges of researching closely guarded sexual behaviors.

Whatever the area of sociological inquiry and whatever the perspective of the sociologist—whether functionalist, conflict, feminist, queer theorist, interactionist, or any other—there is one crucial requirement: imaginative, responsible research that meets the highest scientific and ethical standards.

MODULE 5 | What Is the Scientific Method?

Like all of us, sociologists are interested in the central questions of our time: Is the family falling apart? Why is there so much crime in the United States? Can the world feed a growing population? Such issues concern most people, whether or not they have academic training. However, unlike the typical citizen, the sociologist has a commitment to use the **scientific method** in studying society. The scientific method is a systematic, organized series of steps that ensures maximum objectivity and consistency in researching a problem.

Many of us will never actually conduct scientific research. Why, then, is it important that we understand the scientific method? The answer is that it plays a major role in the workings of our society. Residents of the United States are constantly bombarded with "facts" or "data." A television news report informs us that "one in every two marriages in this country now ends in divorce," yet as Module 41 will show, that assertion is based on misleading statistics. Almost daily, advertisers cite supposedly scientific studies to prove that their products are superior. Such claims may be accurate or exaggerated. We can better evaluate such information—and will not be fooled so easily—if we are familiar with the standards of scientific research.

These standards are quite stringent, and they demand as strict adherence as possible. The scientific method requires precise preparation in developing research. Otherwise, the research data collected may not prove accurate. Sociologists and other researchers follow five basic steps in the scientific method: (1) defining the problem, (2) reviewing the literature, (3) formulating the hypothesis, (4) selecting the research design and then collecting and analyzing data, and (5) developing the conclusion (Figure 5-1). After reaching the conclusion, researchers write a report on their study. Often the report will begin with an *executive summary* of the

FIGURE 5-1 **The Scientific Method**

The scientific method allows sociologists to objectively and logically evaluate the data they collect. Their findings can suggest ideas for further sociological research.

method they followed and their conclusion. In the sections that follow, we'll use an actual example to illustrate the scientific method.

Defining the Problem

Does it "pay" to go to college? Some people make great sacrifices and work hard to get a college education. Parents borrow money for their children's tuition. Students work part-time jobs or even take full-time positions while attending evening or weekend classes. Does it pay off? Are there monetary returns for getting that degree?

The first step in any research project is to state as clearly as possible what you hope to investigate—that is, *define the problem.* In this instance, we are interested in knowing how schooling relates to income. We want to find out the earnings of people with different levels of formal schooling.

Early on, any social science researcher must develop an operational definition of each concept being studied. An **operational definition** is an explanation of an abstract concept that is specific enough to allow a researcher to assess the concept. For example, a sociologist interested in status might use membership in exclusive social clubs as an operational definition of status. Someone studying prejudice might consider a person's unwillingness to hire or work with members of minority groups as an operational definition of prejudice. In our example, we need to develop two operational definitions—education and earnings—in order to study whether it pays to get an advanced educational degree. We'll define *education* as the number of years of schooling a person has achieved and *earnings* as the income a person reports having received in the past year.

© Jason Lindsey/Alamy

It seems reasonable that these graduates of Fort Bethold Community College on the Fort Bethold Reservation, North Dakota, will earn more income than high school graduates. How would you go about testing that hypothesis?

Reviewing the Literature

By conducting a *review of the literature*—examining relevant scholarly studies and information—researchers refine the problem under study, clarify possible techniques to be used in collecting data, and eliminate or reduce avoidable mistakes. In our example, we would examine information about the salaries for different occupations. We would see if jobs that require more academic training are better rewarded. It would also be appropriate to review other studies on the relationship between education and income.

The review of the literature would soon tell us that many factors besides years of schooling influence earning potential. For example, we would learn that the children of rich parents are more likely to go to college than those of poor parents, so we might consider the possibility that rich parents may later help their children to secure better-paying jobs.

We might also look at macro-level data, such as state-by-state comparisons of income and educational levels. In one macro-level study based on census data, researchers found that in states whose residents have a relatively high level of education, household income levels are high as well (Figure 5-2). This finding suggests that schooling may well be related to income, though it does not speak to the micro-level relationship we are interested in. That is, we want to know whether *individuals* who are well educated are also well paid.

Formulating the Hypothesis

After reviewing earlier research and drawing on the contributions of sociological theorists, the researchers may then *formulate the hypothesis.* A **hypothesis** is a speculative statement about the relationship between two or more factors known as variables. Income, religion, occupation, and gender can all serve as variables in a study. We can define a **variable** as a measurable trait or characteristic that is subject to change under different conditions.

Researchers who formulate a hypothesis generally must suggest how one aspect of human behavior influences or affects another. The variable hypothesized to cause or influence another is called the **independent variable.** The other variable is termed the **dependent variable** because its action *depends* on the influence of the independent variable. In other words, the researcher believes that the independent variable predicts or causes change in the dependent variable. For example, a researcher in sociology might anticipate that the availability of affordable housing (the independent variable, *x*) affects the level of homelessness in a community (the dependent variable, *y*).

Our hypothesis is that the higher one's educational degree, the more money one will earn. The independent variable that is to be measured is the level of education. The variable that is thought to depend on it—income—must also be measured.

Identifying independent and dependent variables is a critical step in clarifying cause-and-effect relationships. As shown in Figure 5-3, **causal logic** involves the relationship between a condition or variable and a particular consequence, with one leading to the other. For instance, being less integrated into society may be directly related to, or produce a greater likelihood of, suicide. Similarly, the time students spend reviewing material for a quiz may be directly related to, or produce a greater likelihood of, getting a high score on the quiz.

A **correlation** exists when a change in one variable coincides with a change in the other. Correlations are an indication that causality *may* be present; they do not necessarily indicate causation. For example, data indicate that people who prefer

FIGURE 5-2 **Educational Level and Household Income in the United States**

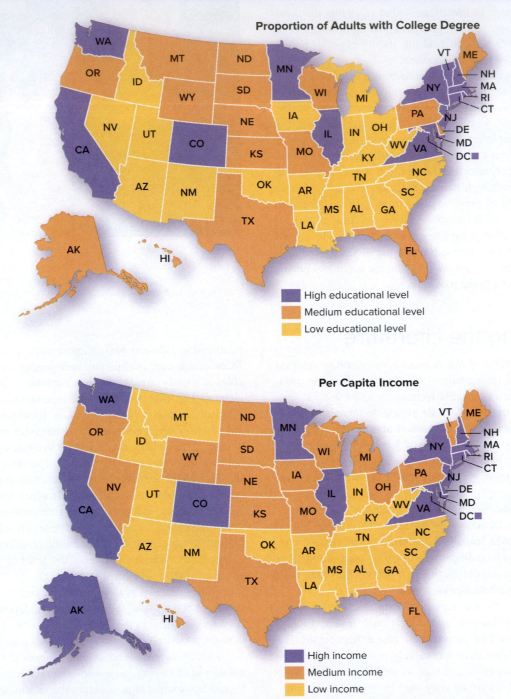

Proportion of Adults with College Degree

■ High educational level
■ Medium educational level
■ Low educational level

Per Capita Income

■ High income
■ Medium income
■ Low income

Notes: Cutoffs for high/medium and medium/low educational levels in 2011–13 were 30.7 percent and 26.3 percent of the population over age 25 with a college degree, respectively; median for the entire nation was 29.1 percent. Cutoffs for high/medium and medium/low per capita income levels in 2011–2013 were $29,000 and $25,300, respectively; national per capita median income was $27,884.
Source: American Community Survey in Bureau of the Census 2014a: Table S0201.

to watch televised news programs are less knowledgeable than those who read newspapers and newsmagazines. This correlation between people's relative knowledge and their choice of news media seems to make sense, because it agrees with the common belief that television dumbs down information. But the correlation between the two variables is actually caused by a third variable, people's relative ability to comprehend large amounts of information. People with poor reading skills are much more likely than others to get their news from television, while those who are more educated or skilled turn more often to the print

FIGURE 5-3 Causal Logic

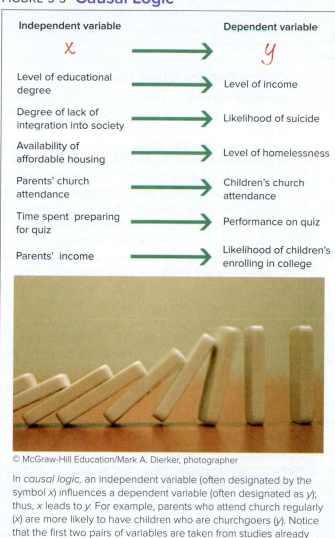

Independent variable		Dependent variable
x	→	y
Level of educational degree	→	Level of income
Degree of lack of integration into society	→	Likelihood of suicide
Availability of affordable housing	→	Level of homelessness
Parents' church attendance	→	Children's church attendance
Time spent preparing for quiz	→	Performance on quiz
Parents' income	→	Likelihood of children's enrolling in college

© McGraw-Hill Education/Mark A. Dierker, photographer

In *causal logic,* an independent variable (often designated by the symbol *x*) influences a dependent variable (often designated as *y*); thus, *x* leads to *y.* For example, parents who attend church regularly (*x*) are more likely to have children who are churchgoers (*y*). Notice that the first two pairs of variables are taken from studies already described in this textbook.

media. Though television viewing is *correlated* with lower news comprehension, then, it does not *cause* it. Sociologists seek to identify the *causal* link between variables; the suspected causal link is generally described in the hypothesis (Neuman 2009).

Collecting and Analyzing Data

How do you test a hypothesis to determine if it is supported or refuted? You need to collect information, using one of the research designs described later in the chapter. The research design guides the researcher in collecting and analyzing data.

Selecting the Sample

In most studies, social scientists must carefully select what is known as a sample. A **sample** is a selection from a larger population that is statistically representative of that population. There are many kinds of samples, but the one social scientists use most

frequently is the random sample. In a **random sample**, every member of an entire population being studied has the same chance of being selected. Thus, if researchers want to examine opinions of people from a complete listing of neighborhood residences, they might use a computer to randomly select addresses from the listing. The results would constitute a random sample. The advantage of using specialized sampling techniques is that sociologists do not need to question everyone in a population (Igo 2007).

In some cases, the subjects researchers want to study are hard to identify, either because their activities are clandestine or because lists of such people are not readily available. How do researchers create a sample of illegal drug users, for instance, or of women whose husbands are at least 10 years younger than they are? In such cases, researchers employ what are called *snowball* or *convenience samples*—that is, they recruit participants through word of mouth or by posting notices on the Internet. With the help of special statistical techniques, researchers can draw conclusions from such nonrandom samples.

It is all too easy to confuse the careful scientific techniques used in representative sampling with the many *nonscientific* polls that receive much more media attention. For example, website viewers are often encouraged to register their views on headline news or political contests. Such polls reflect nothing more than the views of those who happened to visit the website and took the time, perhaps at some cost, to register their opinions. These data do not necessarily reflect (and indeed may distort) the views of the broader population. Not everyone has access to a computer on a regular basis, or the means and/or inclination to register their opinions. Even when these techniques include answers from tens of thousands of people, they will be far less accurate than a carefully selected representative sample of 1,500 respondents.

For the purposes of our research example, we will use information collected in the American Community Survey conducted by the Bureau of the Census. Each year, the Census Bureau surveys approximately 77,000 households across the United States. Technicians at the bureau then use the data to estimate the nation's entire population.

Ensuring Validity and Reliability

The scientific method requires that research results be both valid and reliable. **Validity** refers to the degree to which a measure or scale truly reflects the phenomenon under study. A valid measure of income depends on the gathering of accurate data. Various studies show that people are reasonably accurate in reporting how much money they earned in the most recent year. If a question is written unclearly, however, the resulting data might not be accurate. For example, respondents to an unclear question about income might report their parents' or spouse's income instead of their own.

Reliability refers to the extent to which a measure produces consistent results. Some people may not disclose accurate information, but most do. In the American Community Survey, about 98 percent of the households that researchers approach participate in the survey. The Census Bureau checks their responses against those of similar households, to ensure that the data do not

FIGURE 5-4 Impact of a College Education on Income

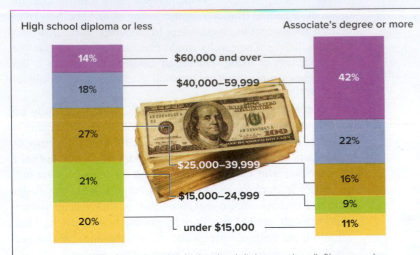

High school diploma or less		Associate's degree or more
14%	**$60,000 and over**	42%
18%	**$40,000–59,999**	22%
27%		16%
	$25,000–39,999	
21%		9%
	$15,000–24,999	
20%	**under $15,000**	11%

Forty-one percent of people with a high school diploma or less (left) earn under $25,000 per year, while only 32 percent earn $40,000 or more. In contrast, only 20 percent of those with an associate's degree or higher (right) earn less than $25,000, while 64 percent earn $40,000 or more.

Source: Author's analysis of DeNavas-Walt and Proctor. 2015: PINC-03. Only people with earnings included.
Photo: © Tom Grill/Corbis RF

differ significantly from other known responses. The Bureau also checks their responses for reliability, since more and more data are being collected online (American Community Survey 2013b).

Developing the Conclusion

Scientific studies, including those conducted by sociologists, do not aim to answer all the questions that can be raised about a particular subject. Therefore, the conclusion of a research study represents both an end and a beginning. Although it terminates a specific phase of the investigation, it should also generate ideas for future study.

Supporting Hypotheses

In our example, we find that the data support our hypothesis: people with more formal schooling *do* earn more money than others. Those with a high school diploma earn more than those who failed to complete high school, but those with an associate's degree earn more than high school graduates. The relationship continues through more advanced levels of schooling, so that those with graduate degrees earn the most.

The relationship is not perfect, however. Some people who drop out of high school end up with high incomes, and some with advanced degrees earn modest incomes, as shown in Figure 5-4. A successful entrepreneur, for example, might not have much formal schooling, while the holder of a doctorate may choose to work for a low-paying nonprofit institution. Sociologists are interested in both the general pattern that emerges from their data and exceptions to the pattern.

Sociological studies do not always generate data that support the original hypothesis. Many times, a hypothesis is refuted,

and researchers must reformulate their conclusions. Unexpected results may also lead sociologists to reexamine their methodology and make changes in the research design.

Controlling for Other Factors

A **control variable** is a factor that is held constant to test the relative impact of an independent variable. For example, if researchers wanted to know how adults in the United States feel about restrictions on smoking in public places, they would probably attempt to use a respondent's smoking behavior as a control variable. That is, how do smokers versus nonsmokers feel about smoking in public places? The researchers would compile separate statistics on how smokers and non-smokers feel about antismoking regulations.

Our study of the influence of education on income suggests that not everyone enjoys equal educational opportunities, a disparity that is one of the causes of social inequality. Since education affects a person's income, we may wish to call on the conflict perspective to explore this topic further. What impact does a person's race or gender have? Is a woman with a college degree likely to earn as much as a man with similar schooling? Later in this textbook we will consider these other factors and variables. That is, we will examine the impact that education has on income while controlling for variables such as gender and race.

© Martin Novak/Alamy RF

How would researchers study our attitudes toward people who smoke cigarettes in public? They would likely use respondents' past smoking behavior as a control variable. In that case, they might hypothesize that respondents who smoke may be more tolerant of smoking in public than respondents who don't smoke. Another interesting question would be whether people who have quit smoking feel differently about lighting up in public than other nonsmokers. What do you think?

In Summary: The Scientific Method

Let us briefly summarize the process of the scientific method through a review of the example. We *defined a problem* (the question of whether it pays to get a higher educational degree).

We *reviewed the literature* (other studies of the relationship between education and income) and *formulated a hypothesis* (the higher one's educational degree, the more money one will earn). We *collected and analyzed the data,* making sure the sample was representative and the data were valid and reliable. Finally, we *developed the conclusion:* the data do support our hypothesis about the influence of education on income.

MODULE 5 | Recap and Review

Summary

Sociologists are committed to the use of the **scientific method** in their research efforts. In this module we examine the basic principles of the scientific method.

1. There are five basic steps in the scientific method: define the problem, review the literature, formulate a hypothesis, collect and analyze data, and develop the conclusion.

2. Whenever researchers wish to study abstract concepts, such as intelligence or prejudice, they must develop workable **operational definitions**.

3. A **hypothesis** states a possible relationship between two or more **variables**.

4. By using a sample, sociologists avoid having to test everyone in a population.

5. According to the scientific method, research results must possess both **validity** and **reliability**.

Thinking Critically

1. What might be the effects of a college education on society as a whole? Think of some potential effects on the family, government, and the economy.

2. Suppose that two researchers used different operational definitions for the same term. Could both researchers' results be reliable and valid? Explain your answer.

Key Terms

Causal logic

Control variable

Correlation

Dependent variable

Hypothesis

Independent variable

Operational definition

Random sample

Reliability

Sample

Scientific method

Validity

Variable

MODULE 6 | Major Research Designs

An important aspect of sociological research is deciding *how* to collect the data. A **research design** is a detailed plan or method for obtaining data scientifically. Selection of a research design is often based on the theories and hypotheses the researcher starts with (Merton 1948). The choice requires creativity and ingenuity, because it directly influences both the cost of the project and the amount of time needed to collect the data. Research designs that sociologists regularly use to generate data include surveys, ethnography, experiments, and existing sources.

Surveys

Almost all of us have responded to surveys of one kind or another. We may have been asked what kind of detergent we use, which presidential candidate we intend to vote for, or what our favorite television program is. A **survey** is a study, generally in the form of an interview or questionnaire, that provides researchers with information about how people think and act. As anyone who watches the news during presidential campaigns knows, surveys have become a staple of political life.

When you think of surveys, you may recall seeing online polls that offer instant results. Although such polls can be highly interesting, they reflect only the opinions of those who visit the website and choose to respond online. As we have seen, a survey

Surveying Cell Phone Users

"Can you hear me now?" This question, familiar to cell phone callers everywhere, could be used to characterize a debate among researchers in sociology. Until recently, calling people on the telephone was a common way for survey takers to reach a broad range of people. Though not everyone owns a telephone—particularly not low-income people—researchers managed to account for that relatively small portion of the population in other ways.

However, the fact that many people now have a cell phone but no landline presents a serious methodological problem to scholars who depend on surveys and public opinion polling. As of 2015, 44 percent of households in the United States could be reached only by cell phone, and the proportion was rising. Among those under 30, the abandonment of landlines was nearly three times as common. These cell phone subscribers are more likely than others to be male and to earn a modest income.

Scholars are reluctant to rely only on landline-based surveys. They are concerned about the potential for misleading results, such as underestimates of the prevalence of health problems. For example, 38 percent of cell phone—only households have a binge drinker, compared to only 17 percent of landline households. And 28 percent of cell phone—only households do not have health insurance, compared to 14 percent of landline households.

> As of 2015, 44 percent of households in the United States could be reached only by cell phone, and the proportion was rising.

Unfortunately, surveying cell phone users has its own problems. In general, cell phone users are more likely than landline users to screen incoming calls or ignore them. And studies show that because cell phone users often take calls while they are involved in other activities, they are much more likely to break off a call midsurvey than someone who is speaking on a landline. Thus, it takes an average of nine calls to a working cell phone number to complete one survey, compared to five calls to a working landline number. Furthermore, federal law requires that calls to cell phones be hand-dialed; the use of automatic dialers, a standard tool of survey firms, is illegal. Survey takers have also found that calling cell phone numbers means they will reach a higher proportion of nonadults than when calling landline numbers. Finally, there are some ethical issues involved in randomly dialing cell phone users, who may be driving a motor vehicle or operating dangerous machinery when they answer.

Researchers are taking steps to stay abreast of technological change. For example, they are making allowances for people who communicate without any kind of telephone, using their personal computers and the Internet. And by drawing on historical data that suggest what kinds of people tend to adopt other wireless technologies, researchers are projecting which people are likely to abandon their landlines in the near future.

LET'S DISCUSS

1. Are you a cell phone—only user? If so, do you generally accept calls from unknown numbers? Aside from underestimating certain health problems and distorting the degree of support for certain politicians, what other problems might result from excluding cell phone—only users from survey research?

2. Apply what you have just learned to the task of surveying Internet users. Which of the problems that arise during telephone surveys might also arise during Internet surveys? Might Internet surveys involve some unique problems?

Sources: Blumberg and Luke 2007; Burger 2015; David Brown 2009; Goldman 2012; Harrisinteractive 2008; Keeter and Kennedy 2006; Lavrakas et al. 2007.

---

must be based on precise, representative sampling if it is to genuinely reflect a broad range of the population. In our wired world, more and more people can be reached only through their cell phones. Box 6-1 describes the challenges of conducting a public opinion survey on a cell phone.

Web-based surveys are becoming attractive options because the costs are so low once the questionnaire is developed. But are these anonymous Internet responses accurate? They can be quite valid. One such example is a 2009 study that used an audience of more than 1 million residents in the United States that had opted in through Internet advertising and direct mail contacts. Using this database, researchers carefully developed a sample representative of the general population and asked sensitive questions about racial stereotypes. The responses closely match the results obtained when similar questions were asked in face-to-face

© Kevin Dodge/Blend Images/AgeFotostock RF

interviews conducted in different national samples at about the same time. Comparisons like these are encouraging for the future of web-based surveys (Simmons and Bobo 2015).

In preparing to conduct a survey, sociologists must not only develop representative samples; they must also exercise great care in the wording of questions. An effective survey question must be simple and clear enough for people to understand. It must also be specific enough so that there are no problems in interpreting the results. Open-ended questions ("What do you think of the programming on educational television?") must be carefully phrased to solicit the type of information desired. Surveys can be indispensable sources of information, but only if the sampling is done properly and the questions are worded accurately and without bias.

In wording questions, researchers must also pay careful attention to changes in society. In December 2010, officials at the Bureau of Labor Statistics recognized the effects of an extended recession by changing a decades-old practice. In the past, multiple-choice questions about how long a respondent had been unemployed had ended with a maximum of "99 weeks or over." By the end of 2010, joblessness had become so chronic that the bureau increased the number of choices, ending with "up to 5 years."

There are two main forms of the survey: the **interview**, in which a researcher obtains information through face-to-face, phone, or online questioning, and the **questionnaire**, in which the researcher uses a printed or written form to obtain information from a respondent. Each of these has its own advantages. An interviewer can obtain a higher response rate, because people find it more difficult to turn down a personal request for an interview than to throw away a written questionnaire. In addition, a skillful interviewer can go beyond written questions and probe for a subject's underlying feelings and reasons. Patricia and Peter Adler conducted 139 in-depth interviews for their book on the sensitive subject of self-injury (see the chapter-opening excerpt). On the other hand, questionnaires have the advantage of being cheaper, especially in large samples.

Why do people have sex? A straightforward question, but until recently it was rarely investigated scientifically, despite its significance to public health, marital counseling, and criminology. To find the answer, researchers interviewed nearly 2,000 undergraduates at the University of Texas at Austin. In developing the question for the interview, they first asked a random sample of 400 students to list all the reasons why they had ever had sex. The explanations were highly diverse, ranging from "I was drunk" to "I wanted to feel closer to God." The team then asked another sample of 1,500 students to rate the importance of each of the 287 reasons given by the first group. Table 6-1 ranks the results. Nearly every reason was rated most important by at least some respondents. Though there were some gender differences in the replies, there was significant consensus between men and women on the top 10 reasons (Meston and Buss 2007).

Studies have shown that the characteristics of the interviewer have an impact on survey data. For example, female interviewers tend to receive more feminist responses from female subjects than do male interviewers, and Black interviewers tend to receive more detailed responses about race-related issues from Black subjects than do White interviewers. The possible impact of gender and race indicates again how much care social research requires (D. W. Davis and Silver 2003).

The survey is an example of **quantitative research**, which collects and reports data primarily in numerical form. Most of the survey research discussed so far in this book has been quantitative. While this type of research can make use of large samples, it can't offer great depth and detail on a topic. That is why researchers also make use of **qualitative research**, which relies on what is seen in field and naturalistic settings, and often focuses on small groups and communities rather than on large groups or whole nations. The most common form of qualitative research is ethnography, or observation, which we consider next. Throughout this book you will find examples of both quantitative and qualitative research, since both are used widely. Some sociologists prefer one type of research to the other, but we learn most when we draw on many different research designs and do not limit ourselves to a particular type of research.

Ethnography

Investigators often collect information or test hypotheses through firsthand studies. **Ethnography** is the study of an entire social setting through extended systematic fieldwork. **Observation**, or direct participation in closely watching a group or organization, is the basic technique of ethnography. However, ethnographic research also includes the collection of historical information and the conduct of in-person interviews. Although ethnography may seem a relatively informal method compared to surveys or experiments, ethnographic researchers are careful to take detailed notes while observing their subjects.

In some cases, the sociologist actually joins a group for a period, to get an accurate sense of how it operates. This approach is called *participant observation*. In Barbara Ehrenreich's widely read book *Nickel and Dimed: On (Not) Getting By in America*, the author was a participant observer. Disguising herself as a divorced, middle-aged housewife without a college degree, Ehrenreich set out to see what life was like for low-wage workers. Her book chronicles her own and others' experiences trying to make ends meet on a minimum wage (Ehrenreich 2001).

During the late 1930s, in a classic example of participant–observation research, William F. Whyte moved into a low-income Italian neighborhood in Boston. For nearly four years he was a member of the social circle of "corner boys" that he describes in *Street Corner Society*. Whyte revealed his identity to these men and joined in their conversations, bowling, and other leisure-time activities. His goal was to gain greater insight into the community that these men had established. As Whyte (1981:303) listened to Doc, the leader of the group, he "learned the answers to questions I would not even have had the sense to ask if I had been getting my information solely on an interviewing basis." Whyte's work was especially valuable, since at the time the academic world had little direct knowledge of the poor, and tended to rely for information on the records of social service agencies, hospitals, and courts (P. Adler et al. 1992).

The initial challenge that Whyte faced—and that every participant observer encounters—was to gain acceptance into an unfamiliar group. It is no simple matter for a college-trained

TABLE **6-1**   **TOP REASONS WHY MEN AND WOMEN HAD SEX**

Reason	Men	Women
I was attracted to the person	1	1
It feels good	2	3
I wanted to experience the physical pleasure	3	2
It's fun	4	8
I wanted to show my affection to the person	5	4
I was sexually aroused and wanted the release	6	6
I was "horny"	7	7
I wanted to express my love for the person	8	5
I wanted to achieve an orgasm	9	14
I wanted to please my partner	10	11
I realized I was in love	17	9
I was "in the heat of the moment"	13	10

Source: Meston and Buss 2007:506.

BOX 6-2

Research Today

Visual Sociology

As a discipline, sociology relies on the scientific observation of human behavior, whether directly or through data gathered in surveys, experiments, and existing sources. Increasingly, however, sociologists also recognize visual documents as a significant research tool. **Visual sociology** is the use of photographs, film, and video to study society. Sociologist Howard Becker drew attention to the importance of images in his influential essay "Photography and Sociology." For over three decades the International Visual Sociology Association has encouraged scholarship in visual sociology, not only by sociologists but also by anthropologists, communications scholars, and psychologists.

Although the term *visual sociology* is relatively new, the roots of visual research methods go deep. As Becker (1974:3) reminds us, "Photography and sociology have approximately the same birth date," in the 1830s. Early sociological works made use of photographs and other visuals, such as maps, not merely as illustrations but as the basis of research. The hardships of the American civil war, conflicts between Native Americans and U.S. Cavalry, and the Crimean War were all analyzed using early photographs. In the 20th century, scholars assessed the toll of the Great Depression in

> Photography and sociology have approximately the same birth date, in the 1830s.

the United States by looking at photographs assembled by the Farm Security Administration. At the time, however, such studies did not receive much acceptance by sociologists. Until recently, only numerical data were deemed appropriate for study.

Today the value of visuals in comprehending social behavior is easy to understand. For generations, music was shared and promoted through the radio. Then music videos transformed popular music. MTV launched in 1981 with the Buggles video "Video Killed the Radio Star," followed by Pat Benatar's "You Better Run," which suggested the changes that were about to occur in the music industry. Now scholars study these videos as extensively as they do the music and lyrics of pop music.

Visual sociology includes the conscious creation of a visual record through documentary films or photography. Sociologist Charles Suchar studied gentrification by photographing commercial and residential areas over time and then analyzing the

record to note how neighborhoods had changed. The photographs became the basis for interviews with residents and merchants about the details they revealed and the concerns they suggested, such as the desire for privacy and the need for security. Photographic records can also be useful in comparative studies. Imagine what sociologists might learn by contrasting images of a suburban barbecue and an Amish community raising a barn. In both cases, images would be treated as data, not merely as instructional aids.

Today, visual sociology is proving useful in **applied sociology,** the use of the discipline of sociology to yield practical applications for human behavior and organizations. In England, public health researchers photographed neighborhoods where illegal drug use was common. The images, which showed addicts injecting themselves in parks and public toilets, helped to identify unsafe areas where discarded needles and syringes littered the ground. Although the visuals were not necessary to the research, they proved invaluable in the researchers' effort to convince social services and law enforcement agencies that intervention was needed.

In short, the uses of visual sociology are as wide as the discipline of sociology itself. Technological innovations such as the Internet, social media, and 3D copiers will only continue to expand the field.

Source: Timothy H. O'Sullivan/Library of Congress Prints and Photographs Division [LC-B8184-7964-A]

Photographs and other visual images improve our understanding of events that affect social behavior. This scene from a Civil War battlefield suggests the utter devastation visited on society by that war.

© Urbanmyth/Alamy Stock Photo

Asking residents to describe photographs helps to call attention to details that are often overlooked, such as an emphasis on security.

LET'S DISCUSS

1. Choose an image or series of images from reality TV or social media and discuss it from a sociological perspective. What can you learn from it? What sociological concepts can you relate to it?

2. Might some images be misinterpreted by researchers? Give an example. How might scholars guard against such misinterpretation?

Sources: Becker 1974; Goffman 1979; J. Grady 2007; Harper 1988; Parker and Coomber 2009; Stryker and Wood 1973 [1935-43]; Suchar 1997; International Visual Sociology Association 2016.

sociologist to win the trust of a religious cult, a youth gang, a poor Appalachian community, or a circle of skid row residents. It requires a great deal of patience and an accepting, nonthreatening type of personality on the part of the observer.

Ethnographic research poses other complex challenges for the investigator. Sociologists must be able to fully understand what they are observing. In a sense, then, researchers must learn to see

the world as the group sees it in order to fully comprehend the events taking place around them. This raises a delicate issue. If the research is to be successful, the observer cannot allow the close associations or even friendships that inevitably develop to influence the subjects' behavior or the conclusions of the study. Even while working hard to gain acceptance from the group being studied, the participant observer *must* maintain some degree of detachment.

Experiments

When sociologists want to study a possible cause-and-effect relationship, they may conduct experiments. An **experiment** is an artificially created situation that allows a researcher to manipulate variables.

In the classic method of conducting an experiment, two groups of people are selected and matched for similar characteristics, such as age or education. The researchers then assign the subjects to one of two groups: the experimental or the control group. The **experimental group** is exposed to an independent variable; the **control group** is not. Thus, if scientists were testing a new type of antibiotic, they would administer the drug to an experimental group but not to a control group.

In some experiments, just as in observation research, the presence of a social scientist or other observer may affect the behavior of the people being studied. Sociologists have used the term **Hawthorne effect** to refer to the unintended influence that observers of experiments can have on their subjects. The term originated as the result of an experiment conducted at the Hawthorne plant of the Western Electric Company during the 1920s and 1930s. Researchers found that *every* change they made in working conditions—even reduced lighting—seemed to have a positive effect on workers' productivity. They concluded that workers had made a special effort to impress their observers. Though the carefully constructed study did identify some causes for changes in the workers' behavior that did not have to do with their being observed, the term *Hawthorne effect* has become synonymous with a placebo or guinea pig effect (Franke and Kaul 1978).

© Carnegie Mellon University

Carnegie Mellon University's Data Truck lets researchers go where their subjects are—from nightclubs to marathon races. Equipped with the latest technology, the truck allows social scientists to enter the responses to their community surveys into their databases on-site. It also gives them access to online social networks in the area, and even lets them videotape street activity.

Use of Existing Sources

Sociologists do not necessarily need to collect new data in order to conduct research and test hypotheses. The term **secondary analysis** refers to a variety of research techniques that make use of previously collected and publicly accessible information and data. Generally, in conducting secondary analysis, researchers use data in ways that were unintended by the initial collectors of information. For example, census data are compiled for specific uses by the federal government but are also valuable to marketing specialists in locating everything from bicycle stores to nursing homes.

Sociologists consider secondary analysis to be *nonreactive*— that is, it does not influence people's behavior. For example, Émile Durkheim's statistical analysis of suicide neither increased nor decreased human self-destruction. Researchers, then, can avoid the Hawthorne effect by using secondary analysis.

There is one inherent problem, however: the researcher who relies on data collected by someone else may not find exactly what is needed. Social scientists who are studying family violence can use statistics from police and social service agencies on *reported* cases of spouse abuse and child abuse, but how many cases are not reported? Government bodies have no precise data on *all* cases of abuse.

Many social scientists find it useful to study cultural, economic, and political documents, including newspapers, periodicals, radio and television tapes, the Internet, scripts, diaries, songs, folklore, and legal papers (Table 6-2). In examining these

Summing Up

TABLE **6-2** **EXISTING SOURCES USED IN SOCIOLOGICAL RESEARCH**

Most Frequently Used Sources

Census data

Crime statistics

Birth, death, marriage, divorce, and health statistics

Other Sources

Newspapers and periodicals

Personal journals, diaries, e-mail, and letters

Records and archival material of religious organizations, corporations, and other organizations

Transcripts of radio programs

Motion pictures and television programs

Web pages, blogs, and chat rooms

Song lyrics

Scientific records (such as patent applications)

Speeches of public figures (such as politicians)

Votes cast in elections or by elected officials on specific legislative proposals

Attendance records for public events

Videos of social protests and rallies

Literature, including folklore

Source: Developed by author.

TABLE **6-3**   MAJOR RESEARCH DESIGNS

Summing Up

Method	Examples	Advantages	Limitations
Survey	Questionnaires Interviews	Yields information about specific issues	Can be expensive and time-consuming
Ethnography	Observation	Yields detailed information about specific groups or organizations	Involves months if not years of labor-intensive data
Experiment	Deliberate manipulation of people's social behavior	Yields direct measures of people's behavior	Ethical limitations on the degree to which subjects' behavior can be manipulated
Existing sources/Secondary analysis	Analysis of census or health data	Cost-efficiency	Limited to data collected for some other purpose

sources, researchers employ a technique known as **content analysis**, which is the systematic coding and objective recording of data, guided by some rationale.

Content analysis can be revealing. Following a recent increase in devastating hurricanes, floods, and prolonged droughts, many people have expressed the need to educate future generations about climate change. To assess children's awareness of the environment, sociologists conducted a content analysis of award-winning picture books over the last 70 years. Their work revealed a noticeable *decline* in depictions of the natural environment and animals. Today, when children's books do address environmental events, they are more likely to portray volcanic eruptions than floods or bad weather. Even when books about urban areas show smokestacks emitting huge quantities of black smoke, the story line does not identify air pollution as a problem (J. Williams et al. 2012).

Content analysis can also document what we suspect is happening as well as reveal surprising trends. A 2015 study analyzed coverage of women's sports on the Los Angeles local television market as well as on ESPN over 25 years. Despite the tremendous increase in women's participation in sports over the last quarter century, content analysis revealed that only 3.2 percent of airtime was devoted to women's sports; further, this represented a decline from the levels back in 1989. ESPN's heavily watched SportCenter consistently devotes 2 percent of airtime to women; of this, 82 percent represents coverage of basketball (Cooky et al. 2015).

Table 6-3 summarizes the major research designs, along with their advantages and limitations.

 use your **sociological imagination**

Imagine you are a legislator or government policymaker working on a complex social problem. What might happen if you were to base your decision on faulty research?

MODULE **6** | **Recap and Review**

Summary

In this module we focus on **research designs**, or the types of plans sociologists use to collect data.

1. Sociologists use four major research designs: surveys, observation, experiments, and existing sources.

2. The two principal forms of **survey** research are the **interview** and the **questionnaire**.

3. **Ethnography** allows sociologists to study certain behaviors and communities that cannot be investigated through other research methods. **Visual sociology** is an important tool for ethnographers.

4. When sociologists wish to study a cause-and-effect relationship, they may conduct an **experiment**.

5. Sociologists may also make use of existing sources in **secondary analysis** and **content analysis**.

Thinking Critically

1. How would you set up an experiment to measure the effect of playing video games on school-age children's grades?

2. Suppose your sociology instructor has asked you to study homelessness in your community. Which research technique would you find most useful? How would you use that technique?

Key Terms

Applied sociology

Content analysis

Control group

MODULE 7 | Ethics of Research

A biochemist cannot inject a drug into a human being unless it has been thoroughly tested and the subject agrees to the shot. To do otherwise would be both unethical and illegal. Sociologists, too, must abide by certain specific standards in conducting research, called a **code of ethics**. The professional society of the discipline, the American Sociological Association (ASA), first published the society's *Code of Ethics* in 1971 and reviewed it most recently in 1997. It puts forth the following basic principles:

1. Maintain objectivity and integrity in research.

2. Respect the subject's right to privacy and dignity.

3. Protect subjects from personal harm.

4. Preserve confidentiality.

5. Seek informed consent when data are collected from research participants or when behavior occurs in a private context.

6. Acknowledge research collaboration and assistance.

7. Disclose all sources of financial support. (American Sociological Association 1999)

These basic principles probably seem clear-cut. How could they lead to any disagreement or controversy? Yet many delicate ethical questions cannot be resolved simply by reading these seven principles. For example, should a sociologist who is engaged in participant–observation research always protect the confidentiality of subjects? What if the subjects are members of a religious cult allegedly involved in unethical and possibly illegal activities? What if the sociologist is interviewing political activists and is questioned by government authorities about the research?

Because most sociological research uses *people* as sources of information—as respondents to survey questions, subjects of ethnography, or participants in experiments—these sorts of questions are important. In all cases, sociologists need to be certain they are not invading their subjects' privacy. Generally, they do so by assuring anonymity to subjects and by guaranteeing the confidentiality of personal information. In addition, research proposals that involve human subjects must now be overseen by a review board, whose members seek to ensure that subjects are not placed at an unreasonable level of risk. If necessary, the board may ask researchers to revise their research designs to conform to the code of ethics.

We can appreciate the seriousness of the ethical problems researchers confront by considering the experience of sociologist Rik Scarce, described in the next section. Scarce's vow to protect his subjects' confidentiality got him into considerable trouble with the law.

Confidentiality

Like journalists, sociologists occasionally find themselves subject to questions from law enforcement authorities because of knowledge they have gained in the course of their work. This uncomfortable situation raises profound ethical questions.

In May 1993, Rik Scarce, a doctoral candidate in sociology at Washington State University, was jailed for contempt of court. Scarce had declined to tell a federal grand jury what he knew—or even whether he knew anything—about a 1991 raid on a university research laboratory by animal rights activists. At the time, Scarce was conducting research for a book about environmental protesters and knew at least one suspect in the break-in. Curiously, although he was chastised by a federal judge, Scarce won respect from fellow prison inmates, who regarded him as a man who "wouldn't snitch" (Monaghan 1993:A8).

The American Sociological Association supported Scarce's position when he appealed his sentence. Scarce maintained his silence. Ultimately the judge ruled that nothing would be gained by further incarceration, and Scarce was released after serving 159 days in jail. In January 1994, the U.S. Supreme Court declined to hear Scarce's case on appeal. The Court's failure to consider his case led Scarce (2005) to argue that federal legislation is needed to clarify the right of scholars and members of the press to preserve the confidentiality of those they interview.

Conflict of Interest

Sometimes disclosing all the sources of funding for a study, as required in principle 7 of the ASA's *Code of Ethics,* is not a sufficient guarantee of ethical conduct. Especially in the case of both corporate and government funding, money given ostensibly for the support of basic research may come with strings attached. Accepting funds from a private organization or even a government agency that stands to benefit from a study's results can call into question a researcher's objectivity and integrity (principle 1). The controversy surrounding the involvement of social scientists in the U.S. Army's Human Terrain System is one example of this conflict of interest.

Another example is the Exxon Corporation's support for research on jury verdicts. In 1989, the Exxon oil tanker *Valdez* hit a reef off the coast of Alaska, spilling more than 11 million

Taking Sociology to Work

Dave Eberbach, *Associate Director, Iowa Institute for Community Alliances*

Courtesy of
Dave Eberbach

Dave Eberbach is a people person who has been working with computers most of his career. In 1994 he was hired as a research coordinator by the United Way of Central Iowa. In that position he helped to create and implement Iowa's Homeless Management Information System (HMIS), which coordinates data on housing and homeless service providers. Eberbach also collaborated with the Human Service Planning Alliance to create and maintain a "data warehouse" of social statistics from diverse sources. As a research coordinator, he found that the data helped him to identify small pockets of poverty that were generally hidden in state and county statistics.

Today, Eberbach works at the Iowa Institute for Community Alliances, a small nonprofit organization that offers computerized client management and on-site program monitoring to homeless and housing service providers. As Associate Director, Eberbach oversees a staff of seven and meets with clients who are working to improve service delivery to vulnerable people. "As fewer resources are being spent on social programs, it has been imperative to make sure that the focus of programs is on client success, not maintaining systems," he explains.

Eberbach went to Grinnell College, where he took a variety of social science courses before settling on sociology as a major. While there, he benefited from the presence of several visiting professors, who exposed him to a variety of racial and cultural perspectives. He found that his personal acquaintance with them complemented the concepts he was learning in his sociology classes. Today, Eberbach draws on his college experiences in his work, which brings him into contact with a diverse group of people.

As a student, Eberbach recalls, he never thought he would use statistics in his career, and didn't work very hard in the course. "As it turned out," he says, "I use it nearly every day. Understanding data and statistics and being able to explain numbers to others has been very important in my job." The reverse has also been true, however: having a background in sociology has been helpful to him in systems design. "Understanding that systems need to work for a variety of groups of people, not just folks that grew up like I did," he explains, has been very helpful. "The world is not a computer problem or a math problem to be solved," he continues, "but rather a complex environment where groups of people continually bump into one another."

LET'S DISCUSS

1. Do you know what you want to be doing 10 years from now? If so, how might a knowledge of statistics help you in your future occupation?

2. What kinds of statistics, specifically, might you find in the Human Service Planning Alliance's data warehouse? Where would they come from?

gallons of oil into Prince William Sound. Five years later a federal court ordered Exxon to pay $5.3 billion in damages for the accident. Exxon appealed the verdict and began approaching legal scholars, sociologists, and psychologists who might be willing to study jury deliberations. The corporation's objective was to develop academic support for its lawyers' contention that the punitive judgments in such cases result from faulty deliberations and do not have a deterrent effect.

Some scholars have questioned the propriety of accepting funds under these circumstances, even if the source is disclosed. In at least one case, an Exxon employee explicitly told a sociologist that the corporation offers financial support to scholars who have shown the tendency to express views similar to its own. An argument can also be made that Exxon was attempting to set scholars' research agendas with its huge war chest. Rather than funding studies on the improvement of cleanup technologies or the assignment of long-term environmental costs, Exxon chose to shift scientists' attention to the validity of the legal awards in environmental cases.

The scholars who accepted Exxon's support deny that it influenced their work or changed their conclusions. Some received support from other sources as well, such as the National Science Foundation and Harvard University's Olin Center for Law, Economics, and Business. Many of their findings were published in respected academic journals after review by a jury of peers. Still, at least one researcher who participated in the studies refused monetary support from Exxon to avoid even the suggestion of a conflict of interest.

© John Gaps III/AP Images

A floating containment barrier (or boom) encircles the Exxon oil tanker *Valdez* after it was grounded on a reef off the coast of Alaska. Exxon was found negligent in the environmental disaster and was ordered to pay $5.3 billion for the cleanup. On appeal, the company managed to reduce the damages to $500 million based on academic research that it had funded—research that some scholars believe involved a conflict of interest.

Exxon has spent roughly $1 million on the research, and at least one compilation of studies congenial to the corporation's point of view has been published. As ethical considerations require, the academics who conducted the studies disclosed Exxon's role in funding them. Nevertheless, the investment appears to have paid off. In 2006, drawing on these studies, Exxon's lawyers succeeded in persuading an appeals court to reduce the corporation's legal damages from $5.3 to $2.5 billion. In 2008 Exxon appealed that judgment to the Supreme Court, which further reduced the damages to $500 million. The final award, which is to be shared by about 32,000 plaintiffs, will result in payments of about $15,000 to each person (Freudenburg 2005; Liptak 2008).

Value Neutrality

The ethical considerations of sociologists lie not only in the methods they use and the funding they accept, but also in the way they interpret their results. Max Weber ([1904] 1949) recognized that personal values would influence the questions that sociologists select for research. In his view, that was perfectly acceptable, but under no conditions could a researcher allow his or her personal feelings to influence the *interpretation* of data. In Weber's phrase, sociologists must practice **value neutrality** in their research.

As part of this neutrality, investigators have an ethical obligation to accept research findings even when the data run counter to their personal views, to theoretically based explanations, or to widely accepted beliefs. For example, Émile Durkheim challenged popular conceptions when he reported that social (rather than supernatural) forces were an important factor in suicide.

Although some sociologists believe that neutrality is impossible, ignoring the issue would be irresponsible. Let's consider what might happen if researchers brought their own biases to the investigation. A person investigating the impact of intercollegiate sports on alumni contributions, for example, might focus only on the highly visible revenue-generating sports of football and basketball and neglect the so-called minor sports, such as tennis or soccer, which are more likely to involve women athletes. Despite the early work of W. E. B. DuBois and Jane Addams, sociologists still need to be reminded that the discipline often fails to adequately consider all people's social behavior.

In her book *The Death of White Sociology* (1973), Joyce Ladner called attention to the tendency of mainstream sociology to treat the lives of African Americans as a social problem. More recently, feminist sociologist Shulamit Reinharz (1992) has argued that sociological research should be not only inclusive but also open to bringing about social change and to drawing on relevant research by nonsociologists. Both Ladner and Reinharz maintain that researchers should always analyze whether women's unequal social status has affected their studies in any way. For example, one might broaden the study of the impact of education on income to consider the implications of the unequal pay status of men and women. The issue of value neutrality does not mean that sociologists can't have opinions, but it does mean that they must work to overcome any biases, however unintentional, that they may bring to their analysis of research.

Sociologist Peter Rossi (1987) admits to having liberal inclinations that direct him to certain fields of study. Yet in line with Weber's view of value neutrality, Rossi's commitment to rigorous research methods and objective interpretation of data has sometimes led him to controversial findings that are not necessarily supportive of his liberal values. For example, his measure of the extent of homelessness in Chicago in the mid-1980s fell far below the estimates of the Chicago Coalition for the Homeless. Coalition members bitterly attacked Rossi for hampering their social reform efforts by minimizing the extent of homelessness. Rossi (1987:79) concluded that "in the short term, good social research will often be greeted as a betrayal of one or another side to a particular controversy."

MODULE 7 | **Recap and Review**

Summary

Sociologists must abide by certain ethical principles when conducting research.

1. The **Code of Ethics** of the American Sociological Association calls for objectivity and integrity in research, confidentiality, and disclosure of all sources of financial support.

2. Max Weber urged sociologists to practice value neutrality in their research by ensuring that their personal feelings do not influence their interpretation of data.

Thinking Critically

1. If you were planning to do research on human sexuality, which of the seven principles in the ASA's Code of Ethics would particularly concern you? What ethical problems might arise in such a study, and how would you attempt to prevent them?

2. Why did Max Weber specify the need for neutrality in the interpretation of data? Is complete value neutrality possible in sociological research? To what extent should researchers try to overcome their own biases?

Key Terms

Code of ethics

Value neutrality

The feminist perspective has had a great impact on the current generation of social researchers. How might this perspective influence research? Although researchers must be objective, their theoretical orientation may influence the questions they ask—or just as important, the questions they fail to ask. Until recently, for example, researchers frequently studied work and the family separately. Yet feminist theorists see the two spheres of activity as being closely integrated. Similarly, work and leisure, paid and unpaid domestic work may be seen not as two separate spheres, but as two sides of the same coin.

Recently, feminist scholars have become interested in self-injury, a practice described at the beginning of this chapter. Research shows that 85 percent of self-injurers are female; feminist researchers seek to explain why women predominate in this population. Rather than treat the behavior as a medical disorder, they note that society encourages women much more than men to attend to their bodies through hair removal, skin treatments, and depigmentation. Given this heightened attention to the female body, feminists suggest that specific instances of victimization can lead women to self-injure. They also seek to better understand male self-injurers, and are testing the hypothesis that among men, self-injury is a manifestation of hypermasculinity in the tolerance of pain (P. Adler and Adler 2011:25–27, 35–36).

The feminist perspective has also had an impact on global research. To feminist theorists, the traditional distinction between industrial nations and developing nations overlooks the close relationship between these two supposedly separate worlds. Feminist theorists have called for more research on the special role that immigrant women play in maintaining their households; on the use of domestic workers from less developed nations by households in industrial nations; and on the global trafficking of sex workers (Cheng 2003; Cooper et al. 2007; Sprague 2005).

© Winston George/Alamy

Feminist theorists see the global trafficking of sex workers as a sign of the close relationship between the supposedly separate worlds of industrial nations and dependent developing nations.

Feminist researchers tend to involve and consult their subjects more than other researchers, and they are more oriented toward seeking change, raising the public consciousness, and influencing policy. They are particularly open to a multidisciplinary approach, such as making use of historical evidence or legal studies (T. Baker 1999; Lofland 1975; Reinharz 1992).

Queer Theory and Methodology

If researchers wish to generalize about society, their findings must be representative of all people. Over the last generation, feminist theorists have insisted that women deserve as much attention from researchers as men. Similarly, exponents of queer theory ask whether researchers consider gays and lesbians in their studies, or simply assume that the generalizations they make apply to everyone, whether heterosexual, gay, or transgender.

According to the National Bureau of Economic Research, most research significantly underreports the proportion of gays and lesbians in the population; it also underestimates the percentage of people who hold anti-gay views. The bureau suggests using a "veiled reporting" technique, in which respondents are asked whether they consider themselves to be heterosexual in the context of other much less sensitive questions, such as "Did you spend a lot of time playing video games as a child?" In one study, when respondents were asked about their sexual orientation within a group of such questions, 19 percent of them reported that they were nonheterosexual; when the question was asked more directly, the proportion was 11 percent (Coffman et al. 2013).

This study suggests that if researchers want to generalize about *both* heterosexuals and homosexuals, they should be extremely careful in wording questions about respondents' sexual orientation—compared even to other sensitive topics, such as political and religious affiliations.

The Data-Rich Future

Advances in technology have affected all aspects of our lives, and sociological research is no exception. Massive increases in available data have allowed sociologists to undertake research that was virtually impossible just a decade ago. In the recent past, only people with grants or major institutional support could work easily with large amounts of data. Now anyone with a computer can access huge amounts of data and learn more about social behavior.

Across the United States, cities and towns of all sizes receive and record citizens' complaints. Sometimes those complaints are acted on; sometimes, for a variety of reasons, they are merely recorded into a database. In Boston, researchers found a treasure trove of data on housing complaints, covering everything from poor heating and chronic dampness to the presence of pests, such as bedbugs. Hundreds of thousands of calls had been recorded

FIGURE 8-1 **Seeing Boston's Housing Issues**

Housing Issues in Boston

Highest

Lowest

More and more data are available to researchers. Boston scholars identified a link between citizen requests for city services and housing conditions. The areas with darker color registered more complaints and had lower-quality housing overall.

Source: Based on citizen complaints data summarized in Boston Area Research Initiative 2013.

along with specific addresses, allowing researchers to compare housing conditions from one neighborhood to another.

Researchers soon realized that the data could be mapped to show the relative seriousness of the city's housing problems at a glance. Figure 8-1 presents a map of Boston's neighborhoods, color-coded based on the distribution of requests for city services made over a more than two-year period. The darker the color, the greater the number of complaints. As the team noted, the data are not an exact indication of "problem housing areas," because

homeowners are much more likely than renters to call for government assistance, regardless of their income. Conversely, problems often go unreported in neighborhoods where renters dominate, whether tenants are rich or poor (O'Brien et al. 2013; Scharfenberg 2013).

In foreign countries, data are sometimes as available as they are in the United States. From 2009 through fall 2013, countries around the world experienced intense bursts of influenza. How did medical researchers track the virus's spread

BOX 8-1

Our Wired World

Lying for Love Online

Today, about 40 million people seek love online, and according to one estimate, 21 percent of heterosexual couples and 61 percent of same-sex couples meet online. But do these people tell the truth in their online postings? Not always, and not often.

Data gathered from online dating sites like Match.com, OkCupid, and Yahoo reveal both truthfulness and deception in people's online postings:

- In their profiles, people often describe an idealized self—for example, "I rock climb."
- Women typically describe themselves as 8.5 pounds heavier than they really are; men, as 2 pounds lighter.
- Men are more likely than women to say they are younger, taller, and wealthier than they really are.
- Less attractive people often post enhanced or retouched photos.
- Women post photos that are an average of 1.5 years old; men post photos that are 6 months old.
- Men are more likely than women to lie about their occupation, education, and relationship status.

Although much of the time these deceptions may be small, their widespread nature has made them an almost expected part of

© Purestock/SuperStock RF

© Peathegee Inc/Blend Images/Getty Images

> Men are more likely than women to say they are younger, taller, and wealthier than they really are.

the game. In one study, a man who posted a five-year-old photograph said he looked the "same" now except that he had a beard. In another case, a woman saw no problem in listing her occupation as "marketing" rather than retail sales. After all, she explained, "it's not like me saying I'm a janitor, and then lying and saying that I'm a CEO." That, she concluded, would be unacceptable.

Little wonder that research shows daters like the personalities they meet online better than the ones they meet in person.

LET'S DISCUSS

1. Have you tried using an online dating service? If so, were you truthful in describing yourself online? Did the people you were matched with turn out to be truthful?

2. Why do you think online daters engage in deception if they are hoping eventually to meet someone face-to-face?

Sources: N. Ellison et al. 2012; R. Epstein 2009; Gelles 2011; Rosenbloom 2011; Toma et al. 2008; Toma and Hancock 2010.

---

across a nation, much less the world? Epidemiologists typically rely on reports that originate in doctors' offices and are funneled through government agencies. Data collection is a time-consuming process, with many days passing between the detection of symptoms and the publication of official statistics. However, public health researchers may have found a way to track contagious diseases using Google. By monitoring the topics people search for and compensating for the relative access to computers in different countries (high in Sweden and low in Nigeria, for example), they can monitor the spread of disease almost in real time. Although their first efforts at online data tracking overestimated the outbreak, their accuracy improves with each passing year (Dukić et al. 2011; D. Lazer et al. 2014).

Similarly, in the past sociologists had to rely on victims' complaints or police reports to understand crime patterns. Now they are beginning to access real-time, geocoded (that is, location-specific) incident reports. These new data will offer sociologists much more information, which they can interpret and relate to other aspects of the social environment (G. King 2011). Box 8-1 describes some new opportunities the Internet offers to researchers

who study dating and mate selection (and who once were confined to surveying undergraduates).

One ethical concern raised by all these data involves individual privacy. Sociologists now have access to information about people's real estate transactions, campaign contributions, online product purchases, and even travel along tollways. What steps should they take to protect the privacy of the individuals whose data they are using? This is not an academic question. Today, 87 percent of the people in the United States can be personally identified given only their gender, date of birth, and ZIP code (G. King 2011; Conley et al. 2015).

We have seen that researchers rely on a number of tools, from time-tested observational research and use of existing sources to the latest in computer technologies. The Social Policy section that follows at the end of this module will describe researchers' efforts to survey the general population about a controversial aspect of social behavior: human sexuality. This investigation was complicated by its potential social policy implications. Because in the real world sociological research can have far-reaching consequences for public policy and public welfare, each of the following chapters in this book will close with a Social Policy section.

How can researchers study human sexual behavior? Neuroscientists Ogi Ogas and Sai Gaddam (2011) studied millions of web searches, websites, and videos related to sex. They found women and men differ decidedly in their preferences, but very little (if any) distinction between heterosexuals and homosexuals, other than their sexual orientation. This type of research has significant limitations, however. Ogas and Gaddam could not distinguish between online fantasies and rational desires, or between a single search and one of many repeated searches by the same person. Nevertheless, this cyber study is a step forward in the effort to understand human sexual behavior (Bartlett 2011).

Looking at the Issue

In this age of devastating sexually transmitted diseases, there is no time more important to increase our scientific understanding of human sexuality. As we will see, however, this is a difficult topic to research, not only because of privacy concerns but because of all the preconceptions, myths, and beliefs people bring to the subject of sexuality. Many people actively oppose research on human sexuality. How does one carry out scientific research on such a controversial and personal topic?

There is little question that we live in a highly sexualized society. The mass media continually bombard us with sexual ideas and images. However, as a study released in 2015 reveals, it is women rather than men who are disproportionately sexualized, particularly in motion pictures. A content analysis of the characters in top box-office films of 2014 showed that women are much more likely than men to be shown in sexy attire, with some degree of nudity, or specifically referred to as "attractive" (see Figure 8-2).

FIGURE 8-2 **Women More Sexualized Than Men in Top Films**

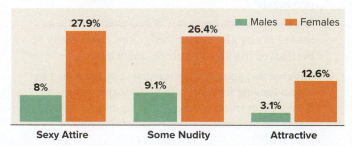

Note: Data based on analysis of 4,100 speaking or named characters in the top-grossing films released in 2014.
Source: Smith et al. 2015.

Applying Sociology

Sociologists have little reliable national data on patterns of sexual behavior in the United States. Until the 1990s, the only comprehensive study of sexual behavior was the famous two-volume *Kinsey Report,* prepared in the 1940s (Kinsey et al. 1948, 1953; see also Igo 2007). Although the *Kinsey Report* is still widely quoted, the volunteers interviewed for the report were not representative of the nation's adult population.

In part, we lack reliable data on patterns of sexual behavior because it is difficult for researchers to obtain accurate information about this sensitive subject. Moreover, until AIDS emerged in the 1980s, there was little scientific demand for data on sexual behavior, except for specific concerns such as contraception. And even though the AIDS crisis has reached dramatic proportions, government funding for studies of sexual behavior is still controversial and therefore difficult to obtain.

The controversy surrounding research on human sexual behavior raises the issue of value neutrality, which becomes especially delicate when one considers the relationship of sociology to the government. The federal government has become the major source of funding for sociological research. Yet Max Weber urged that sociology remain an autonomous discipline and not become unduly influenced by any one segment of society. According to Weber's ideal of value neutrality, sociologists must remain free to reveal information that is embarrassing to the government, or for that matter, supportive of government institutions.

Initiating Policy

In 1987 the National Institute of Child Health and Human Development sought proposals for a national survey of sexual behavior. Sociologists responded with various plans that a review panel of scientists approved for funding. However, in 1991, the U.S. Senate voted to forbid funding any survey of adult sexual practices. Despite the vote, sociologists developed the National Health and Social Life Survey (NHSLS) to better understand the sexual practices of adults in the United States. The researchers raised $1.6 million of *private* funding to make their study possible (Laumann et al. 1994a, 1994b).

The authors of the NHSLS believe that their research is important. They argue that data from their survey allow interest groups to more easily address public policy issues such as AIDS, sexual harassment, welfare reform, sex discrimination, abortion, teenage pregnancy, and family planning. Moreover, the research findings help to counter some commonsense notions. For instance, contrary to the popular beliefs that

—*Continued*

FIGURE 8-3 Median Age of First Sex

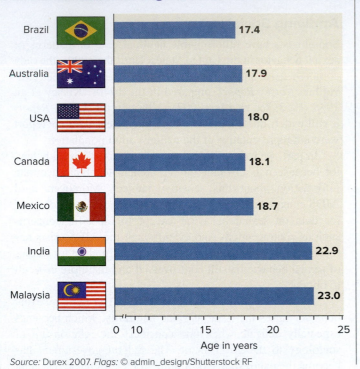

Source: Durex 2007. *Flags:* © admin_design/Shutterstock RF

women regularly use abortion for birth control and that poor teens are the most likely socioeconomic group to have abortions, researchers found that three-fourths of all abortions are the first for the woman, and that well-educated and affluent women are more likely to have abortions than poor teens (Sweet 2001).

The usefulness of the NHSLS in addressing public policy issues has proved itself. As Figure 8-3 shows, scholars around the world are now studying human sexual behavior, in an effort to reduce the occurrence of HIV/AIDS.

TAKE THE ISSUE WITH YOU

1. Do you see any merit in the position of those who oppose government funding for research on sexual behavior? Explain your reasoning.

2. Exactly how could the results of research on human sexual behavior be used to control sexually transmitted diseases?

3. Compare the issue of value neutrality in government-funded research to the same issue in corporate-funded research. Are concerns about conflict of interest more or less serious in regard to government funding?

MODULE 8 | Recap and Review

Summary

Feminist theory and technological change have had important impacts on sociological research.

1. The feminist perspective has affected the questions sociologists ask, what groups they choose to study, the methods they use, and how globalization influences research.

2. Technology plays an important role in sociological research, whether it be a computer database or information obtained from the Internet.

3. Despite failure to obtain government funding, researchers developed the National Health and Social Life Survey (NHSLS) to better understand the sexual practices of adults in the United States.

Thinking Critically

1. Even if women are represented in a study, could the researcher's gender influence the data that are collected? If so, how? How might the problem be prevented?

2. Male sociologists once overlooked women in their studies of city life. What other groups could easily be overlooked in today's research, and why?

3. Suppose that you are a sociologist. You are trying to obtain funding for a study of adult sexual behavior from a government source. What arguments would you make to convince the government to fund your study?

In their effort to better understand social behavior, sociologists rely heavily on numbers and statistics. For example, how have attitudes toward the legalization of marijuana changed over the past 50 years? A quick look at the results of 16 national surveys shows that support for legalization of the drug has increased (Figure A-2), to the point that the most recent survey shows almost majority support for legalization.

Recent legislation on the state level has complicated the task of assessing public opinion on this issue. Some states have passed initiatives legalizing the possession of small amounts of marijuana, even though possession remains illegal under the federal Controlled Substances Act. Researchers now must track how public opinion differs from the national trend in states where marijuana use is both tolerated and legal.

FIGURE A-2 **Changing Attitudes toward the Legalization of Marijuana**

Do you think the use of marijuana should be made legal, or not?

No, illegal: 84% (1969), 81% (1972), 78% (1973), 66% (1977), 70% (1979/1980), 73% (1985), 73% (1995), 64%/62% (2000/2001), 64% (2003), 60% (2005), 54% (2009), 50% (2012), 51%/50% (2013/2014)

Yes, legal: 12% (1969), 15%/16% (1972/1973), 28% (1977), 25% (1979/1980), 23% (1985), 25% (1995), 31% (2001), 34% (2003), 36% (2005), 44% (2009), 48% (2012), 47% (2013/2014)

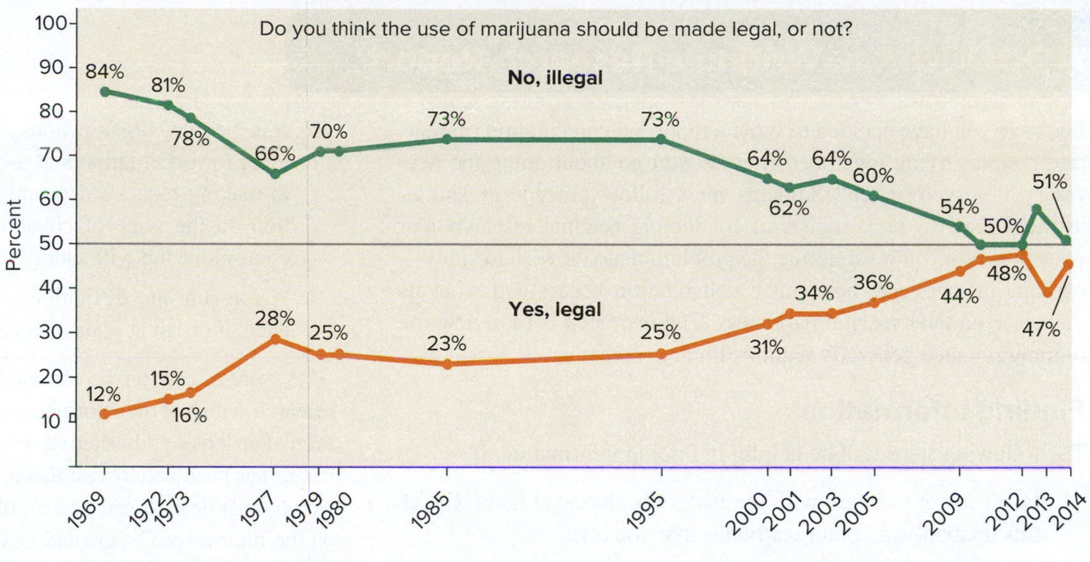

Source: Gallup 2014; see Jones and Saad. 2014.

Using Statistics

The most common summary measures used by sociologists are percentages, means, modes, and medians. A **percentage** is a portion of 100. Use of percentages allows us to compare groups of different sizes. For example, if we were comparing financial contributors to a town's Baptist and Roman Catholic churches, the absolute numbers of contributors in each group could be misleading if there were many more Baptists than Catholics in the town. By using percentages, we could obtain a more meaningful comparison, showing the proportion of persons in each group who contribute to churches.

The **mean**, or *average,* is a number calculated by adding a series of values and then dividing by the number of values. For example, to find the mean of the numbers 5, 19, and 27, we would add them together (for a total of 51), divide by the number of values (3), and discover that the mean is 17.

The **mode** is the single most common value in a series of scores. Suppose we were looking at the following scores on a 10-point quiz:

10 10 9 9 8 8 7 7 7 6 5

The mode—the most frequent score on the quiz—is 7. While the mode is easier to identify than other summary measures, it tells sociologists little about all the other values. Hence, you will find much less use of the mode in this book than of the mean and the median.

The **median** is the midpoint or number that divides a series of values into two groups of equal numbers of values. For the quiz just discussed, the median, or central value, is 8. The mean, or average, would be 86 (the sum of all scores) divided by 11 (the total number of scores), or 7.8.

Some of these statistics may seem confusing at first. But think how difficult it is to comb through an endless list of numbers to identify a pattern or central tendency. Percentages, means, modes, and medians are essential time-savers in sociological research and analysis.

Reading Graphs

Tables and figures (that is, graphs) allow social scientists to display data and develop their conclusions more easily. In December 2014, the Gallup poll interviewed 1,017 people in the United States age 18 and over, by both cell phone and landlines. Each respondent was asked, "Do you think the use of marijuana should be made legal, or not?" Without some type of summary, there is no way that analysts could examine the hundreds of individual responses to this question and reach firm conclusions. One type of summary sociologists use, a **cross-tabulation**, shows the relationship between two or more variables. Through the cross-tabulations presented graphically in Figure A-3, we can quickly

FIGURE A-3 **People Who Favor Legalization of Marijuana by Political Affiliation and Age**

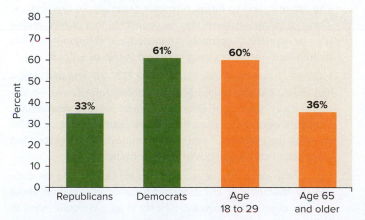

Republicans 33%, Democrats 61%, Age 18 to 29 60%, Age 65 and older 36%

Source: Gallup 2012; see Newport 2012.

see that older people are less likely to favor the legalization of marijuana than younger people, and that Republicans are less supportive of legalization than Democrats.

Graphs, like tables, can be quite useful to sociologists. And illustrations are often easier for the general public to understand, whether in newspapers or in PowerPoint presentations. Still, as with all data, we need to be careful how they are presented.

Appendix II Writing a Research Report

Let's say you have decided to write a report on cohabitation (unmarried couples living together). How do you go about doing the necessary library research? Students must follow procedures similar to those used by sociologists in conducting original research. For your first step you must define the problem that you wish to study—perhaps in this case, how much cohabitation occurs and what its impact is on later marital happiness. The next step is to review the literature, which generally requires library research.

Finding Information

The following steps will be helpful in finding information:

1. Don't forget to begin with the materials closest at hand. Check this textbook and other textbooks that you own.

2. Use the library's online catalog. Computerized library systems now access not only the college library's collection but also books and magazines from other libraries, available through interlibrary loans. These systems allow you to search for books by author or title. You can use title searches to locate books by subject as well. For example, if you search the title base for the keyword *cohabitation,* you will learn where books with that word in the title are located in the library's stacks. Near those books will be other works on cohabitation, which may not happen to have that word in the title. You may also want to search other, related keywords, such as *unmarried couples.*

3. Investigate using computerized periodical indexes, if they are available in your library. *Sociological Abstracts* online covers most sociological writing since 1952. In 2016, a search of just this one database found exactly 2,673 documents having either *cohabitation* or *unmarried couples* as keywords. Some dealt with laws about cohabitation, while others focused on trends in other countries. If you limited your topic to same-sex couples, you would find 159 citations. Other electronic databases cover general-interest periodicals (*Time, Ms., National Review, The Atlantic,* and so forth), reference materials, or newspapers. These electronic systems may be connected to a printer, allowing you to produce a printout complete with bibliographic information, and sometimes even complete copies of articles.

4. Examine government documents. The U.S. government, states and cities, and the United Nations publish information on virtually every subject of interest to social science researchers. Publications of the Census Bureau, for example, include tables showing the number of unmarried couples living together and some social characteristics of those households.

5. Use newspapers. Major newspapers publish annual or even weekly indexes that are useful in locating information about specific events or issues. LexisNexis is an electronic index to U.S. and international newspapers.

6. Ask people, organizations, and agencies concerned with the topic for information and assistance. Be as specific as possible in making requests. You might receive very different information on the issue of cohabitation from talking with marriage counselors and with clergy from different religions.

7. If you run into difficulties, consult the instructor or the reference librarian at your college library.

A word of caution: be extremely careful in using the Internet to do research. Much of the information on the Internet is simply incorrect—even if it looks authoritative, is accompanied by impressive graphics, or has been widely circulated. Unlike the information in a library, which must be screened by a highly qualified librarian, "information" on the Internet can be created and posted by anyone with a computer. Check the sources for the information and note the web page sponsor. Is the author qualified to write on the subject? Is the author even identified? Is the web page sponsor likely to be biased? Whenever possible, try to confirm what you have read on the Internet through a well-known, reputable source or organization. If the accuracy of the information could be affected by how old it is, check the date on which the page or article was created or updated. Used intelligently, the Internet is a wonderful tool that offers students access to many of the reliable print sources noted earlier, including government documents and newspaper archives extending back over a century.

Writing the Report

Once you have completed all your research, you can begin writing the report. Here are a few tips:

- Be sure the topic you have chosen is not too broad. You must be able to cover it adequately in a reasonable amount of time and a reasonable number of pages.

- Develop an outline for your report. You should have an introduction and a conclusion that relate to each other, and the discussion should proceed logically throughout the paper. Use headings within the paper if they will improve clarity and organization.

- Do not leave all the writing until the last minute. It is best to write a rough draft, let it sit for a few days, and then take a fresh look before beginning revisions.

- If possible, read your paper aloud. Doing so may be helpful in locating sections or phrases that don't make sense.

Remember that you *must* cite all information you have obtained from other sources, including the Internet. Plagiarism is a serious academic offense, for which the penalties are severe. If you use an author's exact words, it is essential that you place them in quotation marks. Even if you reworked someone else's ideas, you must indicate the source of those ideas.

Mastering This Chapter

taking sociology with you

1. Think about a job you are interested in. How can you see yourself using research techniques—surveys, observation, experiments, or existing sources—in that occupation?

2. How can a sociologist genuinely maintain value neutrality while studying a group that he or she finds repugnant (for example, a White supremacist organization, a satanic cult, or a group of convicted rapists)?

3. Choose an aspect of your day-to-day environment that could be studied using the techniques of visual sociology. How would you design a research study using these techniques?

key terms

Applied sociology The use of the discipline of sociology to yield practical applications for human behavior and organizations.

Causal logic The relationship between a condition or variable and a particular consequence, with one leading to the other.

Code of ethics The standards of acceptable behavior developed by and for members of a profession.

Content analysis The systematic coding and objective recording of data, guided by some rationale.

Control group The subjects in an experiment who are not introduced to the independent variable by the researcher.

Control variable A factor that is held constant to test the relative impact of an independent variable.

Correlation A relationship between two variables in which a change in one coincides with a change in the other.

Cross-tabulation A table or matrix that shows the relationship between two or more variables.

Dependent variable The variable in a causal relationship that is subject to the influence of another variable.

Ethnography The study of an entire social setting through extended systematic fieldwork.

Experiment An artificially created situation that allows a researcher to manipulate variables.

Experimental group The subjects in an experiment who are exposed to an independent variable introduced by a researcher.

Hawthorne effect The unintended influence that observers of experiments can have on their subjects.

Hypothesis A speculative statement about the relationship between two or more variables.

Independent variable The variable in a causal relationship that causes or influences a change in another variable.

Interview A face-to-face, phone, or online questioning of a respondent to obtain desired information.

Mean A number calculated by adding a series of values and then dividing by the number of values.

Median The midpoint or number that divides a series of values into two groups of equal numbers of values.

Mode The single most common value in a series of scores.

Observation A research technique in which an investigator collects information through direct participation, by closely watching a group or community.

Operational definition An explanation of an abstract concept that is specific enough to allow a researcher to assess the concept.

Percentage A portion of 100.

Qualitative research Research that relies on what is seen in field or naturalistic settings more than on statistical data.

Quantitative research Research that collects and reports data primarily in numerical form.

Questionnaire A printed or written form used to obtain information from a respondent.

Random sample A sample for which every member of an entire population has the same chance of being selected.

Reliability The extent to which a measure produces consistent results.

Research design A detailed plan or method for obtaining data scientifically.

Sample A selection from a larger population that is statistically representative of that population.

Scientific method A systematic, organized series of steps that ensures maximum objectivity and consistency in researching a problem.

Secondary analysis A variety of research techniques that make use of previously collected and publicly accessible information and data.

Survey A study, generally in the form of an interview or questionnaire, that provides researchers with information about how people think and act.

Validity The degree to which a measure or scale truly reflects the phenomenon under study.

Value neutrality Max Weber's term for objectivity of sociologists in the interpretation of data.

Variable A measurable trait or characteristic that is subject to change under different conditions.

Visual sociology The use of photographs, film, and video to study society.

Read each question carefully and then select the best answer.

1. The first step in any sociological research project is to
   a. collect data.
   b. define the problem.
   c. review previous research.
   d. formulate a hypothesis.

2. An explanation of an abstract concept that is specific enough to allow a researcher to measure the concept is a(n)
   a. hypothesis.
   b. correlation.
   c. operational definition.
   d. variable.

3. The variable hypothesized to cause or influence another is called the
   a. dependent variable.
   b. hypothetical variable.
   c. correlation variable.
   d. independent variable.

4. A correlation exists when
   a. one variable causes something to occur in another variable.
   b. two or more variables are causally related.
   c. a change in one variable coincides with a change in another variable.
   d. a negative relationship exists between two variables.

5. Through which type of research technique does a sociologist ensure that data are statistically representative of the population being studied?
   a. sampling
   b. experiments
   c. ethnography
   d. control variables

6. In order to obtain a random sample, a researcher might
   a. administer a questionnaire to every fifth woman who enters a business office.
   b. examine the attitudes of residents of a city by interviewing every 20th name in the city's telephone book.
   c. study the attitudes of registered Democratic voters by choosing every 10th name found on a city's list of registered Democrats.
   d. do all of the above.

7. A researcher can obtain a higher response rate by using which type of survey?
   a. an interview
   b. a questionnaire
   c. representative samples
   d. ethnographic techniques

8. In the 1930s, William F. Whyte moved into a low-income Italian neighborhood in Boston. For nearly four years, he was a member of the social circle of "corner boys" that he describes in *Street Corner Society*. His goal was to gain greater insight into the community established by these men. What type of research technique did Whyte use?
   a. experiment
   b. survey
   c. secondary analysis
   d. participant observation

9. When sociologists want to study a possible cause-and-effect relationship, they may engage in what kind of research technique?
   a. ethnography
   b. survey research
   c. secondary analysis
   d. experiment

10. Émile Durkheim's statistical analysis of suicide was an example of what kind of research technique?
    a. ethnography
    b. observation research
    c. secondary analysis
    d. experimental research

11. Unlike the typical citizen, the sociologist has a commitment to use the _____ method in studying society.

12. A(n) _____ is a speculative statement about the relationship between two or more factors known as variables.

13. _____ refers to the degree to which a measure or scale truly reflects the phenomenon under study.

14. In order to obtain data scientifically, researchers need to select a research _____.

15. If scientists were testing a new type of toothpaste in an experimental setting, they would administer the toothpaste to a(n) _____ group, but not to a(n) _____ group.

16. The term _____ refers to the unintended influence that observers of experiments can have on their subjects.

17. Using census data in a way unintended by its initial collectors would be an example of _____.

18. Using _____, researchers conducted a study of gender-stereotyped behavior in children's picture books.

19. The American Sociological Association's *Code of* _____ requires sociologists to maintain objectivity and integrity and to preserve the confidentiality of their subjects.

20. As part of their commitment to _____ neutrality, investigators have an ethical obligation to accept research findings even when the data run counter to their personal views or to widely accepted beliefs.

3
Culture

© F. Poelking/age fotostock

In Kenya, Maasai tribesmen ride bicycles through Masai Mara National Park. Shared learned behavior—what we call culture—can move across international borders to become part of other societies.

53

© Corbis RF

" Nacirema culture is characterized by a highly developed market economy which has evolved in a rich natural habitat. While much of the people's time is devoted to economic pursuits, a large part of the fruits of these labors and a considerable portion of the day are spent in ritual activity. The focus of this activity is the human body, the appearance and health of which loom as a dominant concern in the ethos of the people. While such a concern is certainly not unusual, its ceremonial aspects and associated philosophy are unique.

The fundamental belief underlying the whole system appears to be that the human body is ugly and that its natural tendency is to debility and disease. Incarcerated in such a body, man's only hope is to avert these characteristics through the use of the powerful influences of ritual and ceremony. Every household has one or more shrines devoted to this purpose. The more powerful individuals in the society have several shrines in their houses and, in fact, the opulence of a house is often referred to in terms of the number of such ritual centers it possesses. Most houses are of wattle and daub construction, but the shrine rooms of the more wealthy are walled with stone. Poorer families imitate the rich by applying pottery plaques to their shrine walls.

The focal point of the shrine is a box or chest which is built into the wall. In this chest are kept the many charms and magical potions without which no native believes he could live.

While each family has at least one such shrine, the rituals associated with it are not family ceremonies but are private and secret. The rites are normally only discussed with children, and then only during the period when they are being initiated into these mysteries. I was able, however, to establish sufficient rapport with the natives to examine these shrines and to have the rituals described to me.

The focal point of the shrine is a box or chest which is built into the wall. In this chest are kept the many charms and magical potions without which no native believes he could live. These preparations are secured from a variety of specialized practitioners. The most powerful of these are the medicine men, whose assistance must be rewarded with substantial gifts. However, the medicine men do not provide the curative potions for their clients, but decide what the ingredients should be and then write them down in an ancient and secret language. This writing is understood only by the medicine men and by the herbalists who, for another gift, provide the required charm.

The charm is not disposed of after it has served its purpose, but is placed in the charm-box of the household shrine. As these magical materials are specific for certain ills, and the real or imagined maladies of the people are many, the charm-box is usually full to overflowing. The magical packets are so numerous that people forget what their purposes were and fear to use them again. While the natives are very vague on this point, we can only assume that the idea in retaining all the old magical materials is that their presence in the charm-box, before which the body rituals are conducted, will in some way protect the worshipper. "

(Miner 1956:503–504) Quotation from Horace Miner. 1956. "Body Ritual among the Nacirema." American Anthropologist, vol. 58 (3), 1956, pp. 503–504.

n this excerpt from his journal article "Body Ritual among the Nacirema," Horace Miner casts an anthropologist's observant eye on the intriguing rituals of an exotic culture. If some aspects of this culture seem familiar to you, you are right, for what Miner is describing is actually the culture of the United States ("Nacirema" is "American" spelled backward). The "shrine" Miner writes of is the bathroom; he correctly informs us that in this culture, one measure of wealth is how many bathrooms one's home has. In their bathroom rituals, he goes on, the Nacirema use charms and magical potions (beauty products and prescription drugs) obtained from specialized practitioners (such as hair stylists), herbalists (pharmacists), and medicine men (physicians). Using our sociological imaginations, we could update Miner's description of the Nacirema's charms, written in 1956, by adding tooth whiteners, anti-aging creams, Waterpiks, and hair gel.

When we step back and examine a culture thoughtfully and objectively, whether it is our own culture in disguise or another less familiar to us, we learn something new about society. Take Fiji, an island in the Pacific where a robust, nicely rounded body has always been the ideal for both men and women. This is a society in which traditionally, "You've gained weight" has been considered a compliment, and "Your legs are skinny," an insult. Yet a recent study shows that for the first time, eating disorders have been showing up among young people in Fiji. What has happened to change their body image? Since the introduction of cable television in 1995, many Fiji islanders, especially young women, have begun to emulate not their mothers and aunts, but the small-waisted stars of television programs still airing there, like *Gossip Girl* and *Modern Family*. Studying culture in places like Fiji, then, sheds light on our society as well (A. Becker 2007; Fiji TV 2012).

In these four modules we will see just how basic the study of culture is to sociology. Our discussion will focus both on general cultural practices found in all societies and on the wide variations that can distinguish one society from another. We will define and explore the major aspects of culture, including language, norms, sanctions, and values. We will see how cultures develop a dominant ideology, and how functionalist and conflict theorists view culture. And we'll study the development of culture around the world, including the cultural effects of globalization. Finally, in the Social Policy section, we will look at the conflicts in cultural values that underlie current debates over bilingualism.

MODULE 9 | What Is Culture?

Culture is the totality of learned, socially transmitted customs, knowledge, material objects, and behavior. It includes the ideas, values, and artifacts (for example, DVDs, comic books, and birth control devices) of groups of people. Patriotic attachment to the flag of the United States is an aspect of culture, as is a national passion for the tango in Argentina.

Sometimes people refer to a particular person as "very cultured" or to a city as having "lots of culture." That use of the term *culture* is different from our use in this textbook. In sociological terms, culture does not refer solely to the fine arts and refined intellectual taste. It consists of *all* objects and ideas within a society, including slang words, ice-cream cones, and rock music. Sociologists consider both a portrait by Rembrandt and the work of graffiti spray painters to be aspects of culture. A tribe that cultivates soil by hand has just as much culture as a people that relies on computer-operated machinery. Each people has a distinctive culture with its own characteristic ways of gathering and preparing food, constructing homes, structuring the family, and promoting standards of right and wrong.

The fact that you share a similar culture with others helps to define the group or society to which you belong. A fairly large number of people are said to constitute a **society** when they live in the same territory, are relatively independent of people outside their area, and participate in a common culture. Metropolitan Los Angeles is more populous than at least 150 nations, yet sociologists do not consider it a society in its own right. Rather, they see it as part of—and dependent on—the larger society of the United States.

A society is the largest form of human group. It consists of people who share a common heritage and culture. Members of the society learn this culture and transmit it from one generation to the next. They even preserve their distinctive culture through literature, art, video recordings, and other means of expression.

Sociologists have long recognized the many ways in which culture influences human behavior. Through what has been termed a tool kit of habits, skills, and styles, people of a common culture construct their acquisition of knowledge, their interactions with kinfolk, their entrance into the job market—in short, the way in which they live. If it were not for the social transmission of culture, each generation would have to reinvent television, not to mention the wheel (Swidler 1986).

Having a common culture also simplifies many day-to-day interactions. For example, when you buy an airline ticket, you know you don't have to bring along hundreds of dollars in cash. You can pay with a credit card. When you are part of a society, you take for granted many small (as well as more important) cultural patterns. You assume that theaters will provide seats for the audience, that physicians will not disclose confidential information, and that parents will be careful when crossing the street with young children. All these assumptions reflect basic values, beliefs, and customs of the culture of the United States.

Today, when text, sound, and video can be transmitted around the world instantaneously, some aspects of culture transcend national borders. The German philosopher Theodor Adorno and others have spoken of the worldwide **culture industry** that

Source: Heikki Siltala/Flickr/CCBY 2.0

Play ball! Baseball in Finland is not the same game we know in North America. The pitcher (center of photo, in orange) stands next to the batter and throws the ball up to be hit. If successful, the batter runs to first base (where we would expect third base to be). Surveys show that baseball is the second most popular sport (after ice hockey) among men and the most popular among women. Introduced in 1907, baseball evolved very differently in Finland than in the United States, but in both countries it is a vital part of the culture.

standardizes the goods and services demanded by consumers. Adorno contends that globally, the primary effect of popular culture is to limit people's choices. Yet others have shown that the culture industry's influence does not always permeate international borders. Sometimes the culture industry is embraced; at other times, soundly rejected (Adorno [1971] 1991:98–106; Horkheimer and Adorno [1944] 2002).

Cultural Universals

All societies have developed certain common practices and beliefs, known as **cultural universals.** Many cultural universals are, in fact, adaptations to meet essential human needs, such as the need for food, shelter, and clothing. Polish-born anthropologist George Murdock (1945:124) compiled a list of cultural universals, including athletic sports, cooking, dancing, visiting, personal names, marriage, medicine, religious ritual, funeral ceremonies, sexual restrictions, and trade.

The cultural practices Murdock listed may be universal, but the manner in which they are expressed varies from culture to culture. For example, one society may let its members choose their marriage partners; another may encourage marriages arranged by the parents.

Not only does the expression of cultural universals vary from one society to another; within a society, it may also change dramatically over time. Each generation, and each year for that matter, most human cultures change and expand.

Ethnocentrism

Many everyday statements reflect our attitude that our culture is best. We use terms such as *underdeveloped, backward,* and *primitive* to refer to other societies. What "we" believe is a religion; what "they" believe is superstition and mythology.

It is tempting to evaluate the practices of other cultures on the basis of our perspectives. Sociologist William Graham Sumner (1906) coined the term **ethnocentrism** to refer to the tendency to assume that one's own culture and way of life represent the norm or are superior to all others. The ethnocentric person sees his or her group as the center or defining point of culture and views all other cultures as deviations from what is "normal." Westerners who think cattle are to be used for food might look down on India's Hindu religion and culture, which view the cow as sacred. Or people in one culture may dismiss as unthinkable the mate selection or child-rearing practices of another culture. In sum, our view of the world is dramatically influenced by the society in which we were raised.

Ethnocentrism is hardly limited to citizens of the United States. Visitors from many African cultures are surprised at the disrespect that children in the United States show their parents. People from India may be repelled by our practice of living in the same household with dogs and cats. Many Islamic fundamentalists view the United States as corrupt, decadent, and doomed to destruction. All these people may feel comforted by membership in cultures that in their view are superior to ours.

Cultural Relativism

While ethnocentrism means evaluating foreign cultures using the familiar culture of the observer as a standard of correct behavior, **cultural relativism** means viewing people's behavior from the perspective of their own culture. It places a priority on understanding other cultures, rather than dismissing them as "strange" or "exotic." Unlike ethnocentrists, cultural relativists employ the kind of value neutrality in scientific study that Max Weber saw as so important.

Cultural relativism stresses that different social contexts give rise to different norms and values. Thus, we must examine practices such as polygamy, bullfighting, and monarchy within the particular contexts of the cultures in which they are found. Although cultural relativism does not suggest that we must unquestioningly accept every cultural variation, it does require a serious and unbiased effort to evaluate norms, values, and customs in light of their distinctive culture.

Consider the practice of children marrying adults. Most people in North America cannot fathom the idea of a 12-year-old girl marrying. The custom is common in West Africa and South Asia. Should the United States respect such marriages? The apparent answer is no. In 2006 the U.S. government spent $623 million to discourage the practice in many of the countries with the highest child-marriage rates (Figure 9-1).

From the perspective of cultural relativism, we might ask whether one society should spend its resources to dictate the norms of another. However, federal officials have defended the government's actions. They contend that child marriage deprives girls of education, threatens their health, and weakens public health efforts to combat HIV/AIDS (Jain and Kurz 2007; B. Slavin 2007).

Sociobiology and Culture

While sociology emphasizes diversity and change in the expression of culture, another school of thought, sociobiology, stresses the universal aspects of culture. **Sociobiology** is the systematic study of how biology affects human social behavior. Sociobiologists assert that many of the cultural traits humans display, such as the almost universal expectation that women will be nurturers and men will be providers, are not learned but are rooted in our genetic makeup.

Sociobiology is founded on the naturalist Charles Darwin's (1859) theory of evolution. In traveling the world, Darwin had noted small variations in species—in the shape of a bird's beak, for example—from one location to another. He theorized that over hundreds of generations, random variations in genetic makeup had helped certain members of a species to survive in a particular environment. A bird with a differently shaped beak might have been better at gathering seeds than other birds, for instance. In reproducing, these lucky individuals had passed on their advantageous genes to succeeding generations. Eventually, given their advantage in survival, individuals with the variation began to outnumber other members of the species. The species was slowly adapting to its environment. Darwin called this process of adaptation to the environment through random genetic variation *natural selection.*

FIGURE 9-1 **Countries with High Child Marriage Rates**

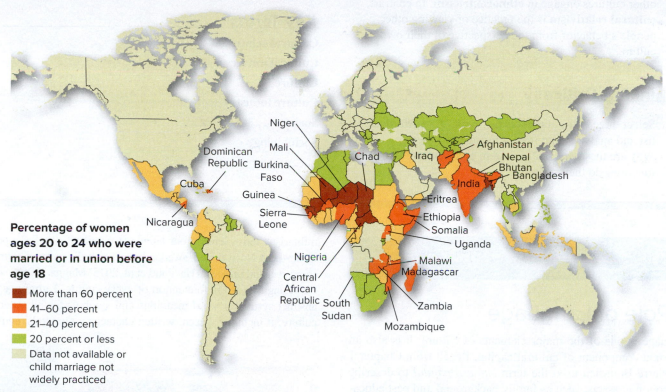

Percentage of women ages 20 to 24 who were married or in union before age 18

- More than 60 percent
- 41–60 percent
- 21–40 percent
- 20 percent or less
- Data not available or child marriage not widely practiced

Note: Data are the most recent available, ranging from 2005 to 2013.
Source: UNICEF 2014.
In 24 countries, 40 percent or more of the women under 18 are married.

Sociobiologists apply Darwin's principle of natural selection to the study of social behavior. They assume that particular forms of behavior become genetically linked to a species if they contribute to its fitness to survive (van den Berghe 1978). In its extreme form, sociobiology suggests that *all* behavior is the result of genetic or biological factors, and that social interactions play no role in shaping people's conduct.

Sociobiologists do not seek to describe individual behavior on the level of "Why is Fred more aggressive than Jim?" Rather, they focus on how human nature is affected by the genetic composition of a *group* of people who share certain characteristics (such as men or women, or members of isolated tribal bands). In general, sociobiologists have stressed the basic genetic heritage that *all* humans share and have shown little interest in speculating

about alleged differences between racial groups or nationalities. A few researchers have tried to trace specific behaviors, like criminal activity, to certain genetic markers, but those markers are not deterministic. Family cohesiveness, peer group behavior, and other social factors can override genetic influences on behavior (Guo et al. 2008; E. Wilson 1975, 1978).

Certainly most social scientists agree that there is a biological basis for social behavior. However, regardless of their theoretical position, most sociologists would likewise agree that people's behavior, not their genetic structure, defines social reality. Conflict theorists fear that the sociobiological approach could be used as an argument against efforts to assist disadvantaged people, such as schoolchildren who are not competing successfully (Freese 2008; Machalek and Martin 2010; E. Wilson 2000).

MODULE 9 | Recap and Review

Summary

Culture is the totality of learned, socially transmitted customs, knowledge, material objects, and behavior. This module examines the social practices common to all cultures.

1. A shared culture helps to define the group or **society** to which we belong.

2. Anthropologist George Murdock compiled a list of **cultural universals**, or common practices found in

every culture, including marriage, sports, cooking, medicine, and sexual restrictions.

3. People who assume their own culture is superior to other cultures engage in **ethnocentricism**. In contrast, **cultural relativism** is the practice of viewing other people's behavior from the perspective of their own culture.

Thinking Critically

1. Select three cultural universals from George Murdock's list and analyze them from a functionalist perspective. Why are these practices found in every culture? What functions do they serve?

2. What are some problems with looking at social behavior from a sociobiological point of view? What are some benefits? How useful do you find this perspective?

Key Terms

Cultural relativism

Cultural universal

Culture

Culture industry

Society

Sociobiology

Role of Language

Language is one of the major elements of culture. It is also an important component of cultural capital. Recall from Chapter 1 that Pierre Bourdieu used the term *cultural capital* to describe noneconomic assets, such as family background and past educational investments, which are reflected in a person's knowledge of language and the arts.

Members of a society generally share a common language, which facilitates day-to-day exchanges with others. When you ask a hardware store clerk for a flashlight, you don't need to draw a picture of the instrument. You share the same cultural term for a small, portable, battery-operated light. However, if you were in England and needed this item, you would have to ask for an electric torch. Of course, even within the same society, a term can have a number of different meanings. In the United States, *pot* signifies both a container that is used for cooking and an intoxicating drug. In this section we will examine the cultural influence of language, which includes both the written and spoken word and nonverbal communication.

Language: Written and Spoken

Seven thousand languages are spoken in the world today—many more than the number of countries. For the speakers of each one, whether they number 2,000 or 200 million, language is fundamental to their shared culture.

The English language, for example, makes extensive use of words dealing with war. We speak of "conquering" space, "fighting" the "battle" of the budget, "waging war" on drugs, making a "killing" on the stock market, and "bombing" an examination; something monumental or great is "the bomb." An observer from an entirely different culture could gauge the importance that war and the military have had in our lives simply by recognizing the prominence that

militaristic terms have in our language. Similarly, the Sami people of northern Norway and Sweden have a rich diversity of terms for snow, ice, and reindeer (Haviland et al. 2015; Magga 2006).

Language is the foundation of every culture. **Language** is an abstract system of word meanings and symbols for all aspects of culture. It includes speech, written characters, numerals, symbols,

Courtesy of the Oneida Indian Nation

A native speaker trains instructors from the Oneida Nation of New York in the Berlitz method of language teaching. As of 2012, there were 527 speakers of the Oneida language. Many Native American tribes are taking similar steps to recover their seldom used languages, realizing that language is the essential foundation of any culture.

and nonverbal gestures and expressions. Because language is the foundation of every culture, the ability to speak other languages is crucial to intercultural relations. Throughout the Cold War era, beginning in the 1950s and continuing well into the 1970s, the U.S. government encouraged the study of Russian by developing special language schools for diplomats and military advisers who dealt with the Soviet Union. And following September 11, 2001, the nation recognized how few skilled translators it had for Arabic and other languages spoken in Muslim countries. Language quickly became a key not only to tracking potential terrorists, but also to building diplomatic bridges with Muslim countries willing to help in the war against terrorism.

Language does more than simply describe reality; it also serves to *shape* the reality of a culture. For example, most people in the United States cannot easily make the verbal distinctions concerning snow and ice that are possible in the Sami culture. As a result, they are less likely to notice such differences.

The **Sapir-Whorf hypothesis,** named for two linguists, describes the role of language in shaping our interpretation of reality. According to Sapir and Whorf, because people can conceptualize the world only through language, language *precedes* thought. Thus, the word symbols and grammar of a language organize the world for us. The Sapir-Whorf hypothesis also holds that language is not a given. Rather, it is culturally determined, and it encourages a distinctive interpretation of reality by focusing our attention on certain phenomena (Sapir 1929).

For decades, the Navajo have referred to cancer as *lood doo na'dziihii.* Now, through a project funded by the National Cancer Institute, the tribal college is seeking to change the phrase. Why? Literally, the phrase means "the sore that does not heal," and health educators are concerned that tribal members who have been diagnosed with cancer view it as a death sentence. Their effort to change the Navajo language, not easy in itself, is complicated by the Navajo belief that to talk about the disease is to bring it on one's people (Fonseca 2008).

Similarly, feminist theorists have noted that gender-related language can reflect—although in itself it does not determine—the traditional acceptance of men and women in certain occupations. Each time we use a term such as *mailman, policeman,* or *fireman,* we are implying (especially to young children) that these occupations can be filled only by males. Yet many women work as *mail carriers, police officers,* and *firefighters*—a fact that is being increasingly recognized and legitimized through the use of such nonsexist language.

Language can shape how we see, taste, smell, feel, and hear. It also influences the way we think about the people, ideas, and objects around us. Language communicates a culture's most important norms, values, and sanctions. That's why the decline of an old language or the introduction of a new one is such a sensitive issue in many parts of the world (see the Social Policy section at the end of this chapter).

Interaction increasingly takes place via mobile devices rather than face to face. Social scientists are beginning to

© Allan Shoemake/Getty Images RF

As texting replaces face-to-face communication in many circumstances, sociologists are beginning to investigate how texting varies in different societies and cultures.

investigate how language used in texting varies in different societies and cultures. For example, in much of Africa, small farmers use texting for the vital task of checking commodity prices. You probably use texting to perform a wide range of communication tasks.

Nonverbal Communication

If you don't like the way a meeting is going, you might suddenly sit back, fold your arms, and turn down the corners of your mouth. When you see a friend in tears, you may give a quick hug. After winning a big game, you probably high-five your teammates. These are all examples of *nonverbal communication,* the use of gestures, facial expressions, and other visual images to communicate.

We are not born with these expressions. We learn them, just as we learn other forms of language, from people who share our same culture. This statement is as true for the basic expressions of happiness and sadness as it is for more complex emotions, such as shame or distress (Fridlund et al. 1987).

Like other forms of language, nonverbal communication is not the same in all cultures. For example, sociological research done at the micro level documents that people from various cultures differ in the degree to which they touch others during the course of normal social interactions. Even experienced travelers are sometimes caught off guard by these differences. In Saudi Arabia, a middle-aged man may want to hold hands with a partner after closing a business deal. In Egypt, men walk hand in hand in the street; in cafés, they fall asleep while lounging in each other's arms. These gestures, which would shock an American businessman, are considered compliments in those cultures. The meaning of hand signals is another form of nonverbal communication that can differ from one culture to the next. In Australia, the thumbs-up sign is considered rude (Passero 2002; Vaughan 2007).

A related form of communication is the use of symbols to convey meaning to others. **Symbols** are the gestures, objects, and words that form the basis of human communication. The thumbs-up gesture, a gold star sticker, and the smiley face in an e-mail are all symbols. Often deceptively simple, many symbols are rich in meaning and may not convey the same meaning in all social contexts. Around someone's neck, for example, a cross can symbolize religious reverence; over a grave site, a belief in everlasting life; or set in flames, racial hatred. Box 10-1 describes the delicate task of designing an appropriate symbol for the 9/11 memorial at New York's former World Trade Center—one that would have meaning for everyone who lost loved ones there, regardless of nationality or religious faith.

Sociology in the Global Community

BOX 10-1

Symbolizing 9/11

On September 11, 2001, the World Trade Center's twin towers took only minutes to collapse. Nearly a decade later, the creator of the memorial to those lost that day was still perfecting the site plan. Thirty-four-year-old architect Michael Arad, the man who submitted the winning design, had drawn two sunken squares, measuring an acre each, in the footprints left by the collapsed towers. His design, "Reflecting Absence," places each empty square in a reflecting pool surrounded by cascading water. Today, as visitors to the massive memorial stand at the edge of the site, they are struck by both the sound of the thundering water and the absence of life.

The memorial does not encompass the entire area destroyed in the attack, as some had wanted. In one of the great commercial capitals of the world, economic forces demanded that some part of the property produce income. Others had argued against constructing a memorial of any kind on what they regarded as hallowed ground. "Don't build on my sister's grave," one of them pleaded. They too had to compromise. On all sides of the eight-acre memorial site, new high rises have been and continue to be built. When construction is finished, the site will also accommodate a new underground transit hub.

Originally, the architect's plans called for the 2,982 victims of the attack to be listed elsewhere on the site. Today, in a revised plan, the names are displayed prominently along the sides of the reflecting pool. Arad had suggested that they be placed randomly, to symbolize the "haphazard brutality of life." Survivors objected, perhaps because they worried about locating their loved ones' names. In a compromise, the names were chiseled into the bronze walls of the memorial in groups that Arad calls "meaningful adjacencies": friends and co-workers; fellow passengers on the two downed aircraft, arranged by seat number; and first responders, grouped by their agencies or

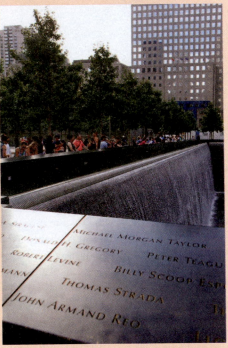

© Erica Simone Leeds RF

> Numerous small monuments and simple *plaques* grace intersections throughout metropolitan New York, particularly those that had a direct line of sight to the twin towers.

fire companies. Suggestions that would give first responders special recognition were set aside. The list includes victims of the simultaneous attack on the Pentagon in Washington,

D.C., and passengers on the flight headed for the White House, who were attempting to thwart the attack when the plane crashed in a field in Pennsylvania. The six people who perished in the 1993 truck bombing at the World Trade Center are also memorialized.

Also at Ground Zero is the National September 11 Memorial Museum, which opened with great anticipation as well as criticism. Some objected to showing pictures of the 19 hijackers, on the grounds that this would symbolically honor them. Others objected to images that would seem to objectify the victims. Unusual for a museum, recording studios were installed to allow visitors to record where they were on 9/11, remember the victims, or respond to the exhibits.

Away from Ground Zero, symbols of 9/11 abound. Numerous small monuments and simple plaques grace intersections throughout metropolitan New York, particularly those that had a direct line of sight to the twin towers. In hundreds of cities worldwide, scraps of steel from the twisted buildings and remnants of destroyed emergency vehicles have been incorporated into memorials. And the USS *New York*, whose bow was forged from seven and a half tons of steel debris salvaged from the towers, has served as a working symbol of 9/11 since its commissioning in 2009.

LET'S DISCUSS

1. What does the 9/11 memorial symbolize to you? Explain the meaning of the cascading water, the reflecting pools, and the empty footprints. What does the placement of the victims' names suggest?

2. If you were designing a 9/11 memorial, what symbol or symbols would you incorporate? Use your sociological imagination to predict how various groups would respond to your design.

Sources: Blais and Rasic 2011; Cohen 2012; Kennicott 2011; Needham 2011.

Norms and Values

"Wash your hands before dinner." "Thou shalt not kill." "Respect your elders." All societies have ways of encouraging and enforcing what they view as appropriate behavior while discouraging and punishing what they consider to be inappropriate behavior. They also have a collective idea of what is good and desirable in life—or not. In this section we will learn to distinguish between the closely related concepts of norms and values.

Norms

Norms are the established standards of behavior maintained by a society. For a norm to become significant, it must be widely shared and understood. For example, in movie theaters in the United States, we typically expect that people will be quiet while the film is shown. Of course, the application of this norm can vary, depending on the particular film and type of audience. People who are viewing a serious artistic film will be more likely to insist on the norm of silence than those who are watching a slapstick comedy or horror movie.

One persistent social norm in contemporary society is that of heterosexuality. As sociologists, and queer theorists especially, note, children are socialized to accept this norm from a very young age. Overwhelmingly, parents describe adult romantic relationships to their children exclusively as heterosexual relationships. That is not necessarily because they consider same-sex relationships unacceptable, but more likely because they see heterosexuality as the norm in marital partnerships. According to a national survey of mothers of three- to six-year-olds, one in five mothers teaches her young children that homosexuality is wrong. The same survey showed that parenting reflects the dominant ideology, in which homosexuality is treated as a rare exception. Most parents assume that their children are heterosexual; only one in four has even considered whether his or her child might grow up to be gay or lesbian (K. Martin 2009).

Types of Norms

Sociologists distinguish between norms in two ways. First, norms are classified as either formal or informal. **Formal norms** generally have been written down and specify strict punishments for violators. In the United States, we often formalize norms into laws, which are very precise in defining proper and improper behavior. Sociologist Donald Black (1995) has termed **law** "governmental social control," meaning that laws are formal norms enforced by the state. Laws are just one example of formal norms. Parking restrictions and the rules of a football or basketball game are also considered formal norms.

In contrast, **informal norms** are generally understood but not precisely recorded. Standards of proper dress are a common example of informal norms. Our society has no specific punishment, or *sanction,* for a person who shows up at school or work wearing inappropriate clothing. Laughter is usually the most likely response.

Norms are also classified by their relative importance to society. When classified in this way, they are known as *mores* and *folkways.* **Mores** (pronounced *"mor*-ays") are norms deemed highly necessary to the welfare of a society, often because they embody the most cherished principles of a people. Each society demands obedience to its mores; violation can lead to severe penalties. Thus, the United States has strong mores against murder, treason, and child abuse, which have been institutionalized into formal norms.

Folkways are norms governing everyday behavior. Folkways play an important role in shaping the daily behavior of members of a culture. Society is less likely to formalize folkways than mores, and their violation raises comparatively little concern. For example, walking up a down escalator in a department store challenges our standards of appropriate behavior, but it will not result in a fine or a jail sentence.

 use your **sociological imagination**

You are a high school principal. What norms would you want to govern the students' behavior? How might those norms differ from norms appropriate for college students?

Norms and Sanctions

Suppose a football coach sends a 12th player onto the field. Imagine a college graduate showing up in shorts for a job interview at a large bank. Or consider a driver who neglects to put money in a parking meter. These people have violated widely shared and understood norms. So what happens? In each of these situations, the person will receive sanctions if his or her behavior is detected.

Sanctions are penalties and rewards for conduct concerning a social norm. Note that the concept of *reward* is included in this definition. Conformity to a norm can lead to *positive sanctions* such as a pay raise, a medal, a word of gratitude, or a pat on the back. Failure to conform can lead to *negative sanctions* such as fines, threats, imprisonment, and stares of contempt.

Table 10-1 summarizes the relationship between norms and sanctions. As you can see, the sanctions that are associated with formal norms (which are written down and codified) tend to be formal as well. If a college football coach sends too many players onto the field, the team will be penalized 15 yards. The driver who fails to put money in the parking meter will receive a ticket and have to pay a fine. But sanctions for violations of informal norms can vary. The college graduate who goes to the bank interview in shorts will probably lose any chance of getting the job; on the other hand, he or she might be so brilliant that bank officials will overlook the unconventional attire.

The entire fabric of norms and sanctions in a culture reflects that culture's values and priorities. The most cherished values will be most heavily sanctioned; matters regarded as less critical will carry light and informal sanctions.

Acceptance of Norms

People do not follow norms, whether formal or informal, in all situations. In some cases, they can evade a norm because they know it is weakly enforced. It is illegal for U.S. teenagers to drink

TABLE **10-1** NORMS AND SANCTIONS

Norms	Sanctions	
	Positive	Negative
Formal	Salary bonus	Demotion
	Testimonial dinner	Firing from a job
	Medal	Jail sentence
	Diploma	Expulsion
Informal	Smile	Frown
	Compliment	Humiliation
	Cheers	Bullying

alcoholic beverages, yet drinking by minors is common throughout the nation. (In fact, teenage alcoholism is a serious social problem.)

In some instances, behavior that appears to violate society's norms may actually represent adherence to the norms of a particular group. Teenage drinkers are conforming to the standards of their peer group when they violate norms that condemn underage drinking. Similarly, business executives who use shady accounting techniques may be responding to a corporate culture that demands the maximization of profits at any cost, including the deception of investors and government regulatory agencies.

Norms are violated in some instances because one norm conflicts with another. For example, suppose that you live in an apartment building and one night hear the screams of the woman next door, who is being beaten by her husband. If you decide to intervene by ringing their doorbell or calling the police, you are violating the norm of minding your own business, while following the norm of assisting a victim of violence.

Acceptance of norms is subject to change as the political, economic, and social conditions of a culture are transformed. Until the 1960s, for example, formal norms throughout much of the United States prohibited the marriage of people from different racial groups. Over the past half century, however, such legal prohibitions were cast aside. The process of change can be seen today in the increasing acceptance of single parents and growing support for the legalization of marriage between same-sex couples.

When circumstances require the sudden violation of long-standing cultural norms, the change can upset an entire population. In Iraq, where Muslim custom strictly forbids touching by strangers for men and especially for women, the war that began in 2003 brought numerous daily violations of the norm. Outside important mosques, government offices, and other facilities likely to be targeted by terrorists, visitors

Woman and girl: © i love images/Alamy RF; *Bride and groom:* © liquidlibrary/PictureQuest RF

had to be patted down and have their bags searched by Iraqi security guards. To reduce the discomfort caused by the procedure, women were searched by female guards and men by male guards. Despite that concession, and the fact that many Iraqis admitted or even insisted on the need for such measures, people still winced at the invasion of their personal privacy. In reaction to the searches, Iraqi women began to limit the contents of the bags they carried or simply to leave them at home (Rubin 2003).

Values

Though we each have a personal set of values—which may include caring or fitness or success in business—we also share a general set of values as members of a society. Cultural **values** are these collective conceptions of what is considered good, desirable, and proper—or bad, undesirable, and improper—in a culture. They indicate what people in a given culture prefer as well as what they find important and morally right (or wrong). Values may be specific, such as honoring one's parents and owning a home, or they may be more general, such as health, love, and democracy. Of course, the members of a society do not uniformly share its values. Angry political debates and billboards promoting conflicting causes tell us that much.

Values influence people's behavior and serve as criteria for evaluating the actions of others. The values, norms, and sanctions of a culture are often directly related. For example, if a culture places a high value on the institution of marriage, it may have norms (and strict sanctions) that prohibit the act of adultery or make divorce difficult. If a culture views private property as a basic value, it will probably have stiff laws against theft and vandalism.

The values of a culture may change, but most remain relatively stable during any one person's lifetime. Socially shared, intensely felt values are a fundamental part of our lives in the United States. Sociologist Robin Williams (1970) has offered a list of basic values. It includes achievement, efficiency, material comfort, nationalism, equality, and the supremacy of science and reason over faith. Obviously, not all 321 million people in this country agree on all these values, but such a list serves as a starting point in defining the national character.

Each year nearly 142,000 full-time, newly entering students at nearly 200 of the nation's four-year colleges fill out a questionnaire about their values. Because this survey focuses on an array of issues, beliefs, and life goals, it is commonly cited as a barometer of the nation's values. The respondents are asked what values are personally important to them. Over the past half century, the value of "being very well-off financially" has shown the strongest gain in popularity; the proportion of first-year college students who endorse this value as "essential" or "very important" rose from 42 percent in 1966 to 82 percent in 2015 (Figure 10-1).

During the 1980s and 1990s, support for values having to do with money, power, and status grew. At the same time, support for certain values having to do with social awareness and altruism, such as "helping others," declined. According to the 2015 nationwide survey, only 44 percent of first-year college students stated that "influencing social values" was an "essential" or "very important" goal. The proportion of students for whom "helping to promote racial understanding" was an essential or very important goal reached a record high of 46 percent in 1992, then leveled off at 41.2 percent in 2015. Like other aspects of culture, such as language and norms, a nation's values are not necessarily fixed.

Whether the slogan is "Think Green" or "Reduce Your Carbon Footprint," students have been exposed to values associated with environmentalism. How many of them accept those values? Poll results over the past 50 years show fluctuations, with a high of nearly 46 percent of students indicating a desire to become involved in cleaning up the environment. By the 1980s, however, student support for embracing this objective had dropped to around 20 percent or even lower (see Figure 10-2). Even with recent attention to climate change, the proportion remains level at only 28.8 percent of first-year students in 2015.

Recently, cheating has become a hot issue on college campuses. Professors who take advantage of computerized services that can identify plagiarism, such as the search engine Google, have been shocked to learn that many of the papers their students hand in are plagiarized in whole or in part. Box 10-2 examines the shift in values that underlies this decline in academic integrity.

Values can also differ in subtle ways not just among individuals and groups, but from one culture to another. For example, in Japan, young children spend long hours working with tutors, preparing for entrance exams required for admission to selective schools. No stigma is attached to these services, known as "cram schools"; in fact, they are highly valued. Yet in South Korea, people have begun to complain that cram schools give affluent students an unfair advantage. Since 2008, the South Korean government has regulated the after-school tutoring industry, limiting its hours and imposing fees on the schools. Some think this policy has lowered their society's expectations of students, describing it as an attempt to make South Koreans "more American" (Ramstad 2011; Ripley 2011).

Another example of cultural differences in values is

FIGURE 10-1 Life Goals of First-Year College Students in the United States, 1966–2015

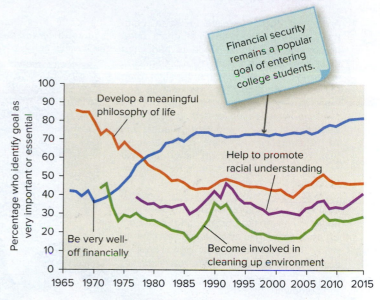

Sources: Pryor et al. 2007; Eagan et al. 2016.

public opinion regarding the treatment of different racial and ethnic groups. As Figure 10-2 shows, opinion on the acceptability of premarital cohabitation varies dramatically from one country to another.

FIGURE 10-2 Values: Acceptance of Nonmarital Cohabitation

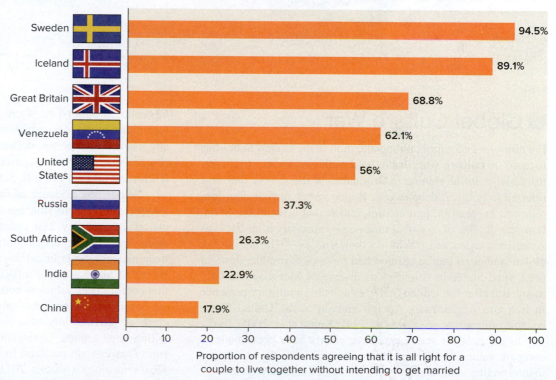

Sweden	94.5%
Iceland	89.1%
Great Britain	68.8%
Venezuela	62.1%
United States	56%
Russia	37.3%
South Africa	26.3%
India	22.9%
China	17.9%

Proportion of respondents agreeing that it is all right for a couple to live together without intending to get married

Source: International Survey Social Programme 2014:42. *Flags:* © admin_design/Shutterstock RF

A Culture of Cheating?

A Harvard teaching assistant noticed something strange while grading students' take-home exams. Several students had cited the same obscure event in 1912. Curiously, all had responded to another question using the same wording. The assistant looked more closely. Eventually, Harvard launched a formal investigation of 125 students suspected of plagiarism and illicit collaboration. At the same time, in New York City more than 70 students at a high school for high achievers were caught sharing test information using their cell phones.

Now that students do their research online, the temptation to cut and paste passages from website postings and pass them off as one's own is apparently irresistible to many. In 2012, 51 percent of high school students admitted cheating on a test, and 75 percent of them copied homework.

Research suggests that the proportion of students who cheat is even higher among college students. According to the International Center for Academic Integrity, 68 percent of undergraduates and 43 percent of graduate students admit to cheating on tests and written assignments. Students not only cut passages from the Internet and paste

them into their papers without citing the source; they share questions and answers on exams, collaborate on assignments they are supposed to do independently, and even falsify the results of their laboratory experiments.

To address what they consider an alarming trend, many colleges are rewriting or adopting new academic honor codes. Observers contend that the increase in student cheating reflects widely publicized instances of cheating in public life, which have served to create an alternative set of values in which the end justifies the means. When young people see sports heroes, authors, entertainers, and corporate executives exposed for cheating in one form or another, the message seems to be "Cheating is okay, as long as you don't get caught."

> According to the International Center for Academic Integrity, 68 percent of undergraduates admit to cheating on tests or written assignments.

© Eric Audras/PhotoAlto Agency RF Collections/Getty Images RF

LET'S DISCUSS

1. Do you know anyone who has engaged in Internet plagiarism? What about cheating on tests or falsifying laboratory results? If so, how did the person justify these forms of dishonesty?

2. Even if cheaters aren't caught, what negative effects does their academic dishonesty have on them? What effects does it have on students who are honest? Could an entire college or university suffer from students' dishonesty?

Sources: Argetsinger and Krim 2002; Bartlett 2009; International Center for Academic Integrity 2016; Sarah Glazer 2013; R. Thomas 2003; Toppo 2011; Zernike 2002.

Global Culture War

For almost a generation, public attention in the United States has focused on **culture war,** or the polarization of society over controversial cultural elements. Originally, in the 1990s, the term referred to political debates over heated issues such as abortion, religious expression, gun control, and sexual orientation. Soon, however, it took on a global meaning—especially after 9/11, as Americans wondered, "Why do they hate us?" Through 2000, global studies of public opinion had reported favorable views of the United States in countries as diverse as Morocco and Germany. But after the United States established a military presence in Iraq and Afghanistan, foreign opinion of the United States became quite negative (J. Hunter 1991; Kohut et al. 2005, 2007).

In the past 30 years, extensive efforts have been made to compare values in different nations, recognizing the challenges in interpreting value concepts in a similar manner across cultures. Psychologist Shalom Schwartz has measured values in more than

60 countries. Around the world, certain values are widely shared, including benevolence, which is defined as "forgiveness and loyalty." In contrast, power, defined as "control or dominance over people and resources," is a value that is endorsed much less often (Hitlin and Piliavin 2004; S. Schwartz and Bardi 2001).

Despite this evidence of shared values, some scholars have interpreted the terrorism, genocide, wars, and military occupations of the early 21st century as a "clash of civilizations." According to this thesis, cultural and religious identities, rather than national or political loyalties, are becoming the prime source of international conflict. Critics of this thesis point out that conflict over values is nothing new; only our ability to create havoc and violence has grown. Furthermore, speaking of a clash of "civilizations" disguises the sharp divisions that exist within large groups. Christianity, for example, runs the gamut from Quaker-style pacifism to certain elements of the Ku Klux Klan's ideology (Brooks 2011; Huntington 1993; Said 2001; Schrad 2014).

TABLE 10-2 SOCIOLOGICAL PERSPECTIVES ON CULTURE

Tracking Sociological Perspectives

	Functionalist Perspective	Conflict Perspective	Feminist Perspective	Interactionist Perspective
Norms	Reinforce societal standards	Reinforce patterns of dominance	Reinforce roles of men and women	Are maintained through face-to-face interaction
Values	Are collective conceptions of what is good	May perpetuate social inequality	May perpetuate men's dominance	Are defined and redefined through social interaction
Culture and Society	Culture reflects a society's strong central values	Culture reflects a society's dominant ideology	Culture reflects society's view of men and women	A society's core culture is perpetuated through daily social interactions
Cultural Variation	Subcultures serve the interests of subgroups	Countercultures question the dominant social order; ethnocentrism devalues groups	Cultural relativism respects variations in the way men and women are viewed in different societies	Customs and traditions are transmitted through intergroup contact and through the media

Sociological Perspectives on Culture

Functionalist and conflict theorists agree that culture and society are mutually supportive, but for different reasons. Functionalists maintain that social stability requires a consensus and the support of society's members; strong central values and common norms provide that support. This view of culture became popular in sociology beginning in the 1950s. It was borrowed from British anthropologists who saw cultural traits as a stabilizing element in a culture. From a functionalist perspective, a cultural trait or practice will persist if it performs functions that society seems to need or contributes to overall social stability and consensus.

Conflict theorists agree that a common culture may exist, but they argue that it serves to maintain the privileges of certain groups. Moreover, while protecting their self-interest, powerful groups may keep others in a subservient position. The term **dominant ideology** describes the set of cultural beliefs and practices that helps to maintain powerful social, economic, and political interests. This concept was first used by Hungarian Marxist Georg Lukacs (1923) and Italian Marxist Antonio Gramsci (1929), but it did not gain an audience in the United States until the early 1970s. In Karl Marx's view, a capitalist society has a dominant ideology that serves the interests of the ruling class.

From a conflict perspective, the dominant ideology has major social significance. Not only do a society's most powerful groups and institutions control wealth and property; even more important, they control the means of producing beliefs about reality through religion, education, and the media. Feminists would also argue that if all a society's most important institutions tell women they should be subservient to men, that dominant ideology will help to control women and keep them in a subordinate position.

A growing number of social scientists believe that it is not easy to identify a core culture in the United States. For support, they point to the lack of consensus on national values, the diffusion of cultural traits, the diversity within our culture, and the changing views of young people (look again at Figure 10-2). Instead, they suggest that the core culture provides the tools that people of all persuasions need to develop strategies for social change. Still, there is no denying that certain expressions of values have greater influence than others, even in as complex a society as the United States (Swidler 1986).

Table 10-2 summarizes the major sociological perspectives on culture.

MODULE 10 | Recap and Review

Summary

This module discusses the major elements that all cultures share: language, norms, and values.

1. **Language** includes speech, written characters, numerals, and **symbols**, as well as gestures and other forms of nonverbal communication. Language both describes culture and shapes it.

2. Sociologists distinguish between **norms** in two ways, classifying them as **formal** or **informal** and as **mores** or **folkways**.

3. The formal norms of a culture will carry the heaviest **sanctions**; informal norms will carry light sanctions.

4. The **dominant ideology** of a culture is the set of cultural beliefs and practices that help to maintain powerful social, economic, and political interests.

Thinking Critically

1. In the United States, is the norm of heterosexuality a formal norm or an informal norm? Would you categorize it with mores or folkways? Explain your reasoning.

2. Do you believe that the world is experiencing a clash of civilizations rather than of nations, as some scholars assert? Why or why not?

3. Look around your campus. Do the people you see suggest that the United States has a core culture with a dominant ideology, or a diverse culture with differing values and ideologies? What about the city or town where your college or university is located—does it suggest the same conclusion?

Key Terms

Culture war

Dominant ideology

Folkway

Formal norm

Informal norm

Language

Law

Mores

Norm

Sanction

Sapir-Whorf hypothesis

Symbol

Value

MODULE 11 | Development of Culture around the World

Today, despite the preference most of us have for our own way of life, powerful forces link us to others around the world. Thus, students in the United States may study the novels of Leo Tolstoy, the art of Pablo Picasso, or the films of Ang Lee. They may listen to pop music from Nigeria or South Korea, or follow the progress of social movements in Iran, Egypt, or Syria via satellite TV and social media. In this section we will examine two of the social processes that make these global links possible: innovation and the diffusion of culture through globalization and technology.

Innovation

The process of introducing a new idea or object to a culture is known as **innovation.** Innovation interests sociologists because of the social consequences of introducing something new. There are two forms of innovation: discovery and invention. **Discovery** involves making known or sharing the existence of an aspect of reality. The finding of the structure of the DNA molecule and the identification of a new moon of Saturn are both acts of discovery. A significant factor in the process of discovery is the sharing of newfound knowledge with others. In contrast, an **invention** results when existing cultural items are combined into a form that did not exist before. The bow and arrow, the automobile, and the television are all examples of inventions, as are Protestantism and democracy.

 use your **sociological imagination**

If you grew up in your parents' generation—without computers, e-mail, and smartphones—how would your daily life differ from the one you lead today?

Globalization, Diffusion, and Technology

The emergence of Starbucks, the worldwide chain of coffeehouses, is just one illustration of the rapidly escalating trend toward globalization (see Chapter 1). While people in Asia are beginning to enjoy coffee, people in North America have discovered sushi, which has evolved from a once-exotic dish in the United States to a mainstream food commonly found in supermarket refrigerators. Yet its move across the Pacific has changed the delicacy. Americans tend to treat sushi as a take-out or menu item. The authentic way to eat sushi is to sit at a bar and engage the chef in conversation about the day's catch.

More and more cultural expressions and practices are crossing national borders and affecting the traditions and customs of the societies exposed to them. Sociologists use the term **diffusion** to refer to the process by which a cultural item spreads from group to group or society to society. Diffusion can occur through a variety of means, among them exploration, military conquest, missionary work, and the influence of the mass media, tourism, the Internet (Box 11-1), and the fast-food restaurant.

Sociologist George Ritzer coined the term *McDonaldization of society* to describe how the principles of fast-food restaurants, developed in the United States, have come to dominate more and more sectors of societies throughout the world. For example, hair salons and medical clinics now take walk-ins. In Hong Kong, sex selection clinics offer a menu of items, from fertility enhancement to methods of increasing the likelihood of having a child of the desired sex. And religious groups—from evangelical preachers on local stations or websites to priests at the Vatican Television Center—use marketing techniques similar to those that are used to sell Happy Meals.

McDonaldization is associated with the melding of cultures, through which we see more and more similarities in cultural expression. In Japan, for example, African entrepreneurs have found a thriving market for hip-hop fashions popularized by teens in the United States. Similarly, the familiar Golden Arches of McDonald's can be seen around the world. Yet corporations

BOX 11-1

Sociology in the Global Community

Life in the Global Village

Imagine a "borderless world" in which culture, trade, commerce, money, and even people move freely from one place to another. Popular culture is widely shared, whether it be Japanese sushi or U.S. running shoes, and the English speaker who answers questions over the telephone about your credit card account is as likely to be in India or Ireland as in the United States. In this world, even the sovereignty of nations is at risk, challenged by political movements and ideologies that span nations.

What caused this great wave of cultural diffusion? First, sociologists take note of advances in communications technology. Satellite TV, cell phones, the Internet, and the like allow information to flow freely across the world, linking global markets. Consumers can view videos on handheld devices and surf the Internet on their phones, shopping online at Amazon.com, eBay, and other commercial websites from cars, airports, and cafeterias. Second, corporations in the industrial nations have become multinational, with both factories and markets in developing countries. Business leaders welcome the opportunity to sell consumer goods in populous countries such as China. Third, these multinational firms have cooperated with global financial institutions, organizations, and governments to promote free trade—unrestricted or lightly restricted commerce across national borders.

> Even *Pirates of the Caribbean* movies and Lady Gaga may be seen as threats to native cultures.

Globalization is not universally welcomed. Many critics see the dominance of "businesses without borders" as benefiting the rich, particularly the very wealthy in industrial countries, at the expense of the poor in less developed nations. They consider globalization to be a successor to the imperialism and colonialism that oppressed Third World nations for centuries.

Another criticism of globalization comes from people who feel overwhelmed by global culture. Embedded in the concept of globalization is the notion of the cultural domination of developing nations by more affluent nations. Simply put, people lose their traditional values and begin to identify with the culture of dominant nations. They may discard or neglect their native languages and dress as they attempt to copy the icons of mass-market entertainment and fashion. Even *Pirates of the Caribbean* movies and Lady Gaga may be seen as

threats to native cultures, if they dominate the media at the expense of local art forms. As Sembene Ousmane, one of Africa's most prominent writers and filmmakers, noted, "[Today] we are more familiar with European fairy tales than with our own traditional stories" (World Development Forum 1990:4).

Globalization has its positive side, too. Many developing nations are taking their place in the world of commerce and bringing in much needed income. The communications revolution helps people to stay connected and gives them access to knowledge that can improve living standards and even save lives.

LET'S DISCUSS

1. How are you affected by globalization? Which aspects of globalization do you find advantageous and which objectionable?

2. How would you feel if the customs and traditions you grew up with were replaced by the culture or values of another country? How might you try to protect your culture?

Sources: Dodds 2000; Giddens 1991; Hirst and Thompson 1996; D. Martin et al. 2006; Ritzer and Dean 2015; Sernau 2001; Tedeschi 2006.

---

like McDonald's have had to make some adjustments of their own. Until 2001, McDonald's ran its *overseas* operations from corporate headquarters in suburban Chicago.

After a few false starts, executives at McDonald's recognized the need to develop the restaurant's menus and marketing strategies overseas, relying on advice from local people. Now, at over 3,700 restaurants in Japan, customers can enjoy the Mega Tamago Burger—beef, bacon, and fried egg with special sauces. In India, patrons who don't eat beef can order a vegetarian McAloo Tikki potato burger. Because some strict vegetarians in India refuse to eat among nonvegetarians, in 2013 McDonald's began opening vegetarian-only restaurants there (Gasparro and Jargon 2012; Ritzer 2015).

Technology in its many forms has increased the speed of cultural diffusion and broadened the distribution of cultural elements. Sociologist Gerhard Lenski has defined **technology** as "cultural information about the ways in which the material resources of the environment may be used to satisfy human needs and desires" (Nolan and Lenski 2015:415). Today's technological developments no longer await publication in journals with limited circulation. Press conferences, often carried simultaneously on the Internet, trumpet the new developments.

© Frank Zeller/AFP/Getty Images

Members of Big Toe Crew, a Vietnamese hip-hop group, rehearse for a performance. Through tourism and the mass media, music and dance spread from one culture to another in a process called diffusion.

Technology not only accelerates the diffusion of scientific innovations but also transmits culture. The English language and North American culture dominate the Internet and World Wide Web. Such control, or at least dominance, of technology influences the direction of cultural diffusion. For example, websites cover even the most superficial aspects of U.S. culture but offer little information about the pressing issues faced by citizens of other nations. People all over the world find it easier to visit electronic chat rooms about the latest reality TV shows than to learn about their own governments' policies on day care or infant nutrition.

Sociologist William F. Ogburn (1922) made a useful distinction between the elements of *material* and *nonmaterial culture*. **Material culture** refers to the physical or technological aspects of our daily lives, including food, houses, factories, and raw materials. **Nonmaterial culture** refers to ways of using material objects, as well as to customs, beliefs, philosophies, governments, and patterns of communication. Generally, the nonmaterial culture is more resistant to change than the material culture. Consequently, Ogburn introduced the term **culture lag** to refer to the period of maladjustment when the nonmaterial culture is still struggling to adapt to new material conditions. For example, in 2010, manufacturers introduced electronic cigarettes, battery-powered tubes that turn nicotine-laced liquid into a vapor mist. The innovation soon had officials at airlines (which ban smoking) and the Food and Drug Administration scrambling to respond to the latest technology (Kesmodel and Yadron 2010; Swidler 1986).

Resistance to technological change can lead not only to culture lag, but to some real questions of cultural survival (Box 11-2).

© Robert Laberge/Getty Images

When a society's nonmaterial culture (its values and laws) does not keep pace with rapid changes in its material culture, people experience an awkward period of maladjustment called culture lag. The transition to nuclear power generation that began in the second half of the 20th century brought widespread protests against the new technology, as well as serious accidents that government officials were poorly prepared to deal with. Tensions over the controversial technology have not run as high in some countries as in others, however. France, where this nuclear power plant is situated, generates 78 percent of all its electricity through nuclear power. The technology is not as controversial there as in the United States and Canada, which generate less than 20 percent of their electricity through nuclear reaction.

Sociology in the Global Community

BOX 11-2

Cultural Survival in Brazil

When the first Portuguese ships landed on the coast of what we now know as Brazil, more than 2 million people inhabited the vast, mineral-rich land. The natives lived in small, isolated settlements, spoke a variety of languages, and embraced many different cultural traditions.

Today, over five centuries later, Brazil's population has grown to more than 192 million, only about 650,000 of whom are indigenous peoples descended from the original inhabitants. Over 200 different indigenous groups have survived, living a life tied closely to the land and the rivers, just as their ancestors did. But over the past two generations, their numbers have dwindled as booms in mining, logging, oil drilling, and agriculture have encroached on their land and their settlements.

Many indigenous groups were once nomads, moving around from one hunting or fishing ground to another. Now they are hemmed in on the reservations the government confined them to, surrounded by huge farms or ranches whose owners deny their

right to live off the land. State officials may insist that laws restrict the development of indigenous lands, but indigenous peoples tell a different story. In Mato Grosso, a heavily forested state near the Amazon River, loggers have been clear-cutting the land at a rate that alarms the Bororo, an indigenous group that has lived in the area for centuries. According to one elder, the Bororo are now confined to six small reservations of about 500 square miles—much

less than the area officially granted them in the 19th century.

In the face of dwindling resources, indigenous groups like the Bororo struggle to maintain their culture. Though the tribe still observes the traditional initiation rites for adolescent boys, members are finding it difficult to continue their hunting and fishing rituals, given the scarcity of game and fish in the area. Pesticides in the runoff from nearby farms have poisoned the water they fish and bathe in, threatening both their health and their culture's survival.

> In Mato Grosso, a heavily forested state near the Amazon River, loggers have been clear-cutting the land at a rate that alarms the Bororo.

LET'S DISCUSS

1. Compare the frontier in Brazil today to the American West in the 1800s. What similarities do you see?

2. What does society lose when indigenous cultures die?

Sources: Brazier and Hamed 2007; H. Chu 2005; Survival International 2016.

Summary

In this module we examine the ways in which culture changes and spreads.

1. Human culture is constantly expanding through the process of **innovation**, which includes both **discovery** and **invention**.

2. **Diffusion** —the spread of cultural items from one place to another—has fostered globalization. Still, people resist ideas that seem too foreign, as well as those they perceive as threatening to their own values and beliefs.

Thinking Critically

1. Name one culturally significant discovery and one culturally significant invention that occurred in your lifetime. Explain how these innovations have changed your culture.

2. Describe one positive example and one negative of McDonaldization that you have experienced.

Key Terms

Culture lag

Diffusion

Discovery

Innovation

Invention

Material culture

Nonmaterial culture

Technology

MODULE 12 | Cultural Variation

Despite the presence of cultural universals such as courtship and religion, great diversity exists among the world's many cultures. Inuit tribes in northern Canada, dressed in fur for the hunt, share little with farmers in southeast Asia, who dress lightly for work in their hot, humid rice paddies. Cultures adapt to meet specific circumstances, such as climate, level of technology, population, and geography.

Even *within* a single nation, certain segments of the populace develop cultural patterns that differ from the patterns of the dominant society— thus the difficulty of identifying a core culture in the United States, where regional differences fuel culture wars between conservatives and liberals. Moreover, in every region, specific communities tend to band together to form their own culture within a culture, called a *subculture*.

■ Subcultures

Rodeo riders, residents of a retirement community, workers on an offshore oil rig—all are examples of what sociologists refer to as *subcultures*. A **subculture** is a segment of society that shares a distinctive pattern of customs, rules, and traditions that differs from the pattern of the larger society. The existence of many subcultures is characteristic of complex societies such as the United States.

Members of a subculture participate in the dominant culture while engaging in unique and distinctive forms of behavior.

© Christine Pemberton/The Image Works

Employees of an international call center in India socialize after their shift has ended. Call center employees, whose odd working hours isolate them from others, tend to form tight-knit subcultures.

Frequently, a subculture will develop an **argot,** or specialized language that distinguishes it from the wider society. Athletes who play *parkour,* an extreme sport that combines forward running with fence leaping and the vaulting of walls, water barriers, and even moving cars, speak an argot they devised especially to describe their feats. Parkour runners talk about doing *King Kong vaults*—diving arms first over a wall or grocery cart and landing in a standing position. They may follow this maneuver with a *tic tac*—kicking off a wall to overcome some kind of obstacle (Kidder 2012).

Such argot allows insiders—the members of the subculture—to understand words with special meanings. It also establishes patterns of communication that outsiders can't understand. Sociologists associated with the interactionist perspective emphasize that language and symbols offer a powerful way for a subculture to feel cohesive and maintain its identity.

In India, a new subculture has developed among employees at the international call centers established by multinational corporations. To serve customers in the United States and Europe, the young men and women who work there must be fluent speakers of English. But the corporations that employ them demand more than proficiency in a foreign language; they expect their Indian employees to adopt Western values and work habits, including the grueling pace U.S. workers take for granted.

In effect, workers at these call centers live in a state of virtual migration—not quite in India, but not in the United States, either. Significantly, call centers allow employees to take the day off only on U.S. holidays, like Labor Day and Thanksgiving—not on Indian holidays like Diwali, the Hindu festival of lights. While most Indian families are home celebrating, call center employees see only each other; when they have the day off, no one else is free to socialize with them. As a result, these employees have formed a tight-knit subculture based on hard work and a taste for Western luxury goods and leisure-time pursuits (Rowe et al. 2013).

Another shared characteristic among some employees at Indian call centers is their contempt for the callers they serve. In performing their monotonous, repetitive job day after day, hundreds of thousands of these workers have come to see the faceless Americans they deal with as slow, often rude customers. Such shared understandings underpin this emerging subculture (Bhagat 2007; Gentleman 2006; Patel 2010).

Countercultures

By the end of the 1960s, an extensive subculture had emerged in the United States, composed of young people turned off by a society they believed was too materialistic and technological. The group included primarily political radicals and hippies who had dropped out of mainstream social institutions. These young men and women rejected the pressure to accumulate cars, homes, and an endless array of material goods. Instead, they expressed a desire to live in a culture based on more humanistic values, such as sharing, love, and coexistence with the environment. As a political force, this subculture opposed the United States' involvement in the war in Vietnam and encouraged draft resistance (Flacks 1971; Roszak 1969).

When a subculture conspicuously and deliberately opposes certain aspects of the larger culture, it is known as a **counterculture.** Countercultures typically thrive among the young, who have the least investment in the existing culture. In most cases, a 20-year-old can adjust to new cultural standards more easily than someone who has spent 60 years following the patterns of the dominant culture (Zellner 1995).

In the last decade, counterterrorism experts have become concerned about the growth of ultraconservative militia groups in the United States. Secretive and well armed, members of these countercultural groups tend to be antigovernment, and they often tolerate racism in their midst. Watchdogs estimate that 1,274 antigovernment groups are operating in the United States today (Southern Poverty Law Center 2015).

Culture Shock

Ever stepped out the door on your first day in a foreign country and felt weak in the knees? Anyone who feels disoriented, uncertain, out of place, or even fearful when immersed in an unfamiliar culture may be experiencing **culture shock.** This unsettling experience may even be mutual—the visitor's cultural habits may shock members of the host culture. Imagine, for

© Tyler Cacek/Redux Pictures

Members of the militia group Ohio Defense Force engage in paramilitary exercises, imagining they are destroying a threatening Muslim stronghold in the United States. Ultraconservative militia groups are a form of counterculture.

example, that you are traveling in Japan. You know that you should remove your shoes and leave them at the door when you visit someone's home. However, there are many more customs that you are unfamiliar with. During a visit with one family, as you enter the bathroom, you see several pairs of identical slippers. Thinking they are for guests, you put on a pair and rejoin your host, who reacts with horror. Unwittingly, you have worn a pair of toilet slippers into the living room (McLane 2013).

All of us, to some extent, take for granted the cultural practices of our society. As a result, it can be surprising and even disturbing to realize that other cultures do not follow our way of life.

The fact is, customs that seem strange to us may be considered normal and proper in other cultures, which may see our social practices as odd.

 use your **sociological imagination**

You arrive in a developing African country as a Peace Corps volunteer. What aspects of a very different culture do you think would be the hardest to adjust to? Explain. What might the citizens of that country find shocking about your culture?

social
policy and Culture | Bilingualism

Looking at the Issue

The staff in the emergency room is unprepared. Although the issue is not a medical one, the doctors and nurses do not understand the patient's complaints, nor can they communicate effectively with her companion. This type of incident, which occurs frequently, can have serious consequences. According to a study of two large pediatric emergency departments in Massachusetts, even when the second language is a common one like Spanish, interpreting errors can lead to clinically significant mistakes in 22 percent of such cases. In other words, language errors put patients at risk (Flores et al. 2012).

How can we learn to work and live effectively when Americans speak so many different languages? Throughout the world, not just emergency rooms but schools and other institutions must deal with people who speak many languages. **Bilingualism** refers to the use of two languages in a particular setting, such as the workplace or schoolroom, treating each language as equally legitimate. Thus, a teacher of bilingual education may instruct children in their native language while gradually introducing them to the language of the host society. If the curriculum is also bicultural, children will learn about the mores and folkways of both the dominant culture and the subculture.

To what degree should schools in the United States present the curriculum in a language other than English? This issue has prompted a great deal of debate among educators and policymakers. According to the Bureau of the Census, 61 million U.S. residents over age five—that's about 21 percent of the population—spoke a language other than English as their primary language at home (Figure 12-1). Indeed, 29 other languages are each spoken by at least 200,000 U.S. residents (C. Ryan 2013).

This segment of the population is expected to increase modestly by 2020. For example, the proportion of older Hispanics who speak Spanish is expected to hold steady or increase slightly. However, younger Hispanics—those under 45—will be less likely than their elders to speak Spanish. A similar trend is expected for speakers of European and Asian languages: many elders will continue to speak a second language, while the younger generation will tend to favor English.

This trend toward linguistic diversity is expected to continue into the foreseeable future. Even as the children and grandchildren of immigrants adopt English as their first language, a significant proportion of the U.S. population will continue to speak a language other than English (Ortman and Shin 2011).

Do bilingual programs help the children of these families to learn English? It is difficult to reach firm conclusions, because bilingual programs in general vary so widely in their quality and approach. They differ in the length of the transition to English and in how long they allow students to remain in bilingual classrooms. Moreover, results have been mixed. In the years since California effectively dismantled its bilingual education program, reading and math scores of students with limited English proficiency rose dramatically, especially in the lower grades. Yet a major overview of 17 studies, done at Johns Hopkins University, found that students who are offered lessons in both English and their home languages make better progress than similar students who are taught only in English (R. Slavin and Cheung 2003).

Applying Sociology

For a long time, people in the United States demanded conformity to a single language. This demand coincided with the functionalist view that language serves to unify members of

—*Continued*

MAPPING LIFE NATIONWIDE

FIGURE 12-1 **Percentage of People who Speak a Language other than English at Home, by State**

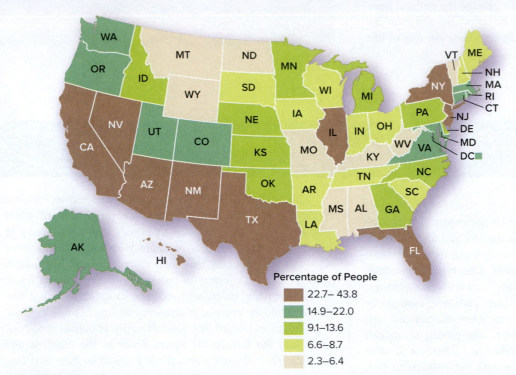

Percentage of People

- 22.7– 43.8
- 14.9–22.0
- 9.1–13.6
- 6.6–8.7
- 2.3–6.4

Note: Data drawn from the 2011 American Community Survey of people five years and over. National average was 20.8 percent.
Source: From C. Ryan. 2013.

foreign influence wherever it occurs, especially in our schools. It does not take into account that success in bilingual education may actually have beneficial results, such as decreasing the number of high school dropouts and increasing the number of Hispanics in colleges and universities.

Initiating Policy

Bilingualism has policy implications largely in two areas: efforts to maintain language purity and programs to enhance bilingual education. Nations vary dramatically in their tolerance for a variety of languages. China continues to tighten its cultural control over Tibet by extending instruction of Mandarin, a Chinese dialect, from high school into the elementary schools there, which will now be bilingual along with Tibetan. In contrast, nearby Singapore establishes English as the medium of instruction but allows students to take their mother tongue as a second language, be it Chinese, Malay, or Tamil.

One bilingual hot spot is Québec, the French-speaking province of Canada. The Québécois, as they are known, represent 83 percent of the province's population, but only 25 percent of Canada's total population. A law implemented in 1978 mandated education in French for all Québec's children except those whose parents or siblings had learned English elsewhere in Canada. While special laws like this one have advanced French in the province, dissatisfied Québécois have tried to form their own separate country. In 1995, the people of Québec indicated their preference of remaining united with Canada by only the narrowest of margins (50.5 percent). Language and language-related cultural areas both unify and divide this nation of 33 million people (*The Economist* 2005b; R. Schaefer 2014).

Policymakers in the United States have been somewhat ambivalent in dealing with the issue of bilingualism. In 1965, the Elementary and Secondary Education Act (ESEA)

a society. Little respect was granted to immigrants' cultural traditions; a young person would often be teased about his or her "funny" name, accent, or style of dress.

Recent decades have seen challenges to this pattern of forced obedience to the dominant ideology. Beginning in the 1960s, active movements for Black pride and ethnic pride insisted that people regard the traditions of all racial and ethnic subcultures as legitimate and important. Conflict theorists explain this development as a case of subordinated language minorities seeking opportunities for self-expression. Partly as a result of these challenges, people began to view bilingualism as an asset. It seemed to provide a sensitive way of assisting millions of non-English-speaking people in the United States to *learn* English in order to function more effectively within the society.

The perspective of conflict theory also helps us to understand some of the attacks on bilingual programs. Many of them stem from an ethnocentric point of view, which holds that any deviation from the majority is bad. This attitude tends to be expressed by those who wish to stamp out

provided for bilingual, bicultural education. In the 1970s, the federal government took an active role in establishing the proper form for bilingual programs. However, more recently, federal policy has been less supportive of bilingualism, and local school districts have been forced to provide an increased share of funding for their bilingual programs. Yet bilingual programs are an expense that many communities and states are unwilling to pay for and are quick to cut back. In 1998, voters in California approved a proposition that all but eliminated bilingual education: it requires instruction in English for 1.4 million children who are not fluent in the language.

In the United States, repeated efforts have been made to introduce a constitutional amendment declaring English as the nation's official language. As of 2016, 31 states had declared English their official language—an action that is now more symbolic than legislative in its significance.

Public concern over a potential decline in the use of English appears to be overblown. In reality, most immigrants and their offspring quickly become fluent in English and abandon their mother tongue. Nevertheless, many people are impatient with those immigrants who continue to use their mother tongue. The release in 2006 of *"Nuestro Himno,"* the Spanish-language version of the "Star-Spangled Banner," produced a strong public reaction: 69 percent of those who were surveyed on the topic said the anthem should be sung only in English. In reaction against the Spanish version, at least one congressman defiantly sang the national anthem in English—with incorrect lyrics. And the proprietor of a restaurant in Philadelphia posted signs advising patrons that he would accept orders for his famous steak sandwiches only in English. Throughout the year, passions ran high as policymakers debated how much support to afford people who speak other languages (J. Carroll 2006; U.S. English 2016).

In the end, the immigrant's experience is not only about learning a new language. It is about learning a whole new culture—a new totality of socially transmitted customs, knowledge, material objects, and behavior (Viramontes 2007).

TAKE THE ISSUE WITH YOU

1. Have you attended a school with students for whom English is a second language? If so, can you identify the presence of different cultures or subcultures?

2. The ultimate goal of both English-only and bilingual programs is for foreign-born students to become proficient in English. In what ways is this goal functional? Analyze the goal of such programs from the conflict and interactionist perspectives.

3. Besides bilingualism, can you think of another issue that has become controversial recently because of a clash of cultures? If so, analyze the issue from a sociological point of view.

MODULE **12** | **Recap and Review**

Summary

Each human culture has unique characteristics that evolve to meet specific circumstances of climate, geography, technological development, and population.

1. A **subculture** is a small culture that exists within a larger, dominant culture. **Countercultures** are subcultures that deliberately oppose aspects of the larger culture.

2. A person who becomes immersed in an unfamiliar culture may experience **culture shock**.

3. The social policy of **bilingualism** calls for the use of two or more languages, treating each as equally legitimate. It is supported by those who want to ease the transition of non-native-language speakers into a host society, but opposed by those who adhere to a single cultural tradition and language.

Thinking Critically

1. To what subcultures do you belong? How do they function in relation to the larger society?

2. Why do people experience culture shock? What does this phenomenon reveal about the role of culture and of everyday customs?

Key Terms

Argot

Bilingualism

Counterculture

Culture shock

Subculture

Mastering This Chapter

© F. Poelking/age fotostock

taking sociology with you

1. Locate ethnocentrism. For two days, bearing in mind what sociologists mean by *ethnocentrism,* systematically record the places where you see or hear evidence of it.

2. Study popular culture. For two days, record whatever evidence of the dominant culture you see on the Internet or in literature, music, movies, theater, television programs, and sporting events.

3. Document a subculture. For two days, record the norms, values, sanctions, and argot evident in a subculture you are familiar with.

key terms

Argot Specialized language used by members of a group or subculture.

Bilingualism The use of two languages in a particular setting, such as the workplace or schoolroom, treating each language as equally legitimate.

Counterculture A subculture that deliberately opposes certain aspects of the larger culture.

Cultural relativism The viewing of people's behavior from the perspective of their own culture.

Cultural universal A common practice or belief found in every culture.

Culture The totality of learned, socially transmitted customs, knowledge, material objects, and behavior.

Culture industry The worldwide media industry that standardizes the goods and services demanded by consumers.

Culture lag A period of maladjustment when the nonmaterial culture is still struggling to adapt to new material conditions.

Culture shock The feeling of surprise and disorientation that people experience when they encounter cultural practices that are different from their own.

Culture war The polarization of society over controversial cultural elements.

Diffusion The process by which a cultural item spreads from group to group or society to society.

Discovery The process of making known or sharing the existence of an aspect of reality.

Dominant ideology A set of cultural beliefs and practices that helps to maintain powerful social, economic, and political interests.

Ethnocentrism The tendency to assume that one's own culture and way of life represent the norm or are superior to all others.

Folkway A norm governing everyday behavior whose violation raises comparatively little concern.

Formal norm A norm that has been written down and that specifies strict punishments for violators.

Informal norm A norm that is generally understood but not precisely recorded.

Innovation The process of introducing a new idea or object to a culture through discovery or invention.

Invention The combination of existing cultural items into a form that did not exist before.

Language An abstract system of word meanings and symbols for all aspects of culture; includes gestures and other nonverbal communication.

Law Governmental social control.

Material culture The physical or technological aspects of our daily lives.

Mores Norms deemed highly necessary to the welfare of a society.

Nonmaterial culture Ways of using material objects, as well as customs, beliefs, philosophies, governments, and patterns of communication.

Norm An established standard of behavior maintained by a society.

Sanction A penalty or reward for conduct concerning a social norm.

Sapir-Whorf hypothesis A hypothesis concerning the role of language in shaping our interpretation of reality. It holds that language is culturally determined.

Society A fairly large number of people who live in the same territory, are relatively independent of people outside their area, and participate in a common culture.

Sociobiology The systematic study of how biology affects human social behavior.

Subculture A segment of society that shares a distinctive pattern of customs, rules, and traditions that differs from the pattern of the larger society.

Symbol A gesture, object, or word that forms the basis of human communication.

Technology Cultural information about the ways in which the material resources of the environment may be used to satisfy human needs and desires.

Value A collective conception of what is considered good, desirable, and proper—or bad, undesirable, and improper—in a culture.

Read each question carefully and then select the best answer.

1. Which of the following is an aspect of culture?
   a. a comic book
   b. patriotic attachment to the flag of the United States
   c. slang words
   d. all of the above

2. People's adaptations to meet the needs for food, shelter, and clothing are examples of what George Murdock referred to as
   a. norms.
   b. folkways.
   c. cultural universals.
   d. cultural practices.

3. What term do sociologists use to refer to the process by which a cultural item spreads from group to group or society to society?
   a. diffusion
   b. globalization
   c. innovation
   d. cultural relativism

4. The appearance of Starbucks coffeehouses in China is a sign of what aspect of culture?
   a. innovation
   b. globalization
   c. diffusion
   d. cultural relativism

5. Which of the following statements is true according to the Sapir-Whorf hypothesis?
   a. Language simply describes reality.
   b. Language does not transmit stereotypes related to race.
   c. Language precedes thought.
   d. Language is not an example of a cultural universal.

6. Which of the following statements about norms is correct?
   a. People do not follow norms in all situations. In some cases, they evade a norm because they know it is weakly enforced.
   b. In some instances, behavior that appears to violate society's norms may actually represent adherence to the norms of a particular group.
   c. Norms are violated in some instances because one norm conflicts with another.
   d. all of the above

7. Which of the following statements about values is correct?
   a. Values never change.
   b. The values of a culture may change, but most remain relatively stable during any one person's lifetime.
   c. Values are constantly changing; sociologists view them as being very unstable.
   d. all of the above

8. Which of the following terms describes the set of cultural beliefs and practices that help to maintain powerful social, economic, and political interests?
   a. mores
   b. dominant ideology
   c. consensus
   d. values

9. Terrorist groups are examples of
   a. cultural universals.
   b. subcultures.
   c. countercultures.
   d. dominant ideologies.

10. What is the term used when one places a priority on understanding other cultures, rather than dismissing them as "strange" or "exotic"?
    a. ethnocentrism
    b. culture shock
    c. cultural relativism
    d. cultural value

11. _____ are gestures, objects, and/or words that form the basis of human communication.

12. _____ is the process of introducing a new idea or object to a culture.

13. The bow and arrow, the automobile, and the television are all examples of _____.

14. Sociologists associated with the _____ perspective emphasize that language and symbols offer a powerful way for a subculture to maintain its identity.

15. "Put on some clean clothes for dinner" and "Thou shalt not kill" are both examples of _____ found in U.S. culture.

16. The United States has strong _____ against murder, treason, and other forms of abuse that have been institutionalized into formal norms.

17. From a(n) _____ perspective, the dominant ideology has major social significance. Not only do a society's most powerful groups and institutions control wealth and property; more important, they control the means of production.

18. Countercultures (for example, hippies) are typically popular among the _____, who have the least investment in the existing culture.

19. A person experiences _____ _____ when he or she feels disoriented, uncertain, out of place, even fearful when immersed in an unfamiliar culture.

20. From the _____ perspective, subcultures are evidence that differences can exist within a common culture.

Answers

1 (d); 2 (c); 3 (a); 4 (b); 5 (c); 6 (d); 7 (b); 8 (b); 9 (c); 10 (c); 11 Symbols; 12 Innovation; 13 inventions; 14 interactionist; 15 norms; 16 mores; 17 conflict; 18 young; 19 culture shock; 20 functionalist

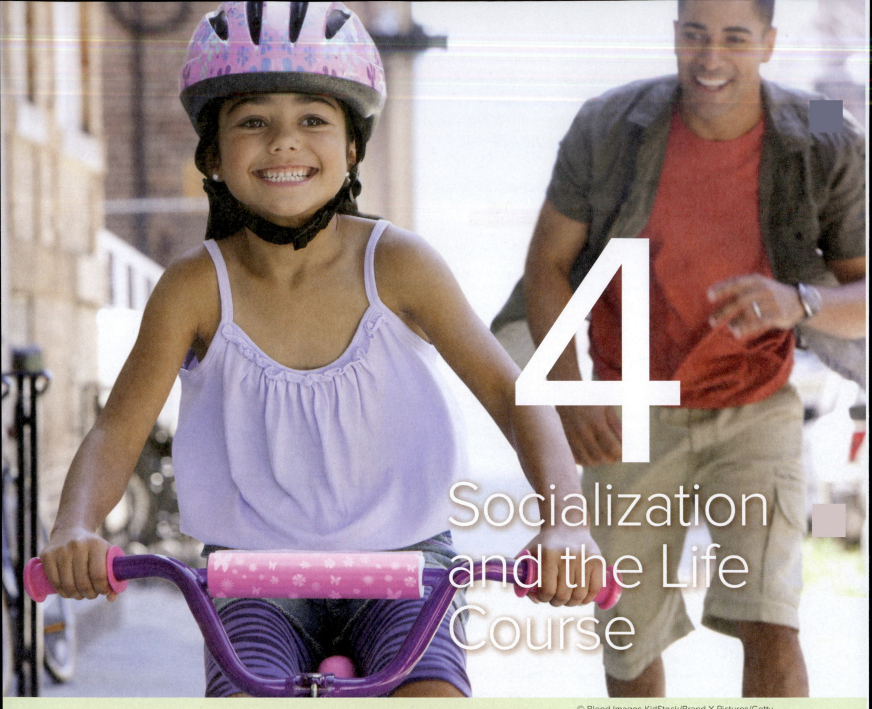

4

Socialization and the Life Course

© Blend Images-KidStock/Brand X Pictures/Getty Images RF

A father teaches his daughter to ride a bike. Around the world, the family is the most important agent of socialization.

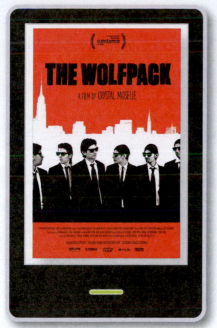

© Moviestore collection Ltd/Alamy Stock Photo

What would it be like to grow up in a family that isolates itself from society? What would it be like to break away from such an upbringing and discover the outside world for the first time?

Filmmaker Crystal Moselle documented the efforts of the six Angulo brothers, who grew up confined in a small apartment on Manhattan's Lower East Side, to discover the social world outside their family. Her documentary, *The Wolfpack*, attempted to simultaneously capture the excitement of the brothers' discoveries while suggesting the issues of abuse and confinement that arise from their extraordinary upbringing.

" It was serendipitous that I met these boys the first week they started going out into the world. It almost felt as if I had discovered a long lost tribe, except it was not from the edges of the world but from the streets of Manhattan. I was moved by their openness, resilience, and sense of humor, and I formed a trust with them that could never be duplicated. I have been by their side as they experienced the outside world for the first time . . . It has been an incredible journey for all of us, and it is strange to think that this story could never be told the same way again, with the same sense of innocence and discovery. Their minds and perceptions have already incorporated the rest of the outside world.

About five years ago, I was cruising down First Avenue in the East Village and these kids with long hair ran past me, weaving through the crowd. I counted one, two, three of them . . . then three more. . . . I asked where they were from and they said 'Delancy Street.' They mentioned how they were not supposed to talk to strangers but wondered what I did for a living. When I told them that I was a filmmaker, they got really excited, exclaiming, 'We are interested in getting into the business of filmmaking.' We made a time to meet so I could show them some cameras.

This was the start of our friendship. I started filming them here and there while teaching them and encouraging their film endeavors. About 4 months in, I was able to come into their home. This is when I realized there was a deeper story and continued from there—we shot for almost 5 years.

When I came into these boys' lives there was nothing that alarmed me about the situation. They seemed stable, well cared for and educated by their parents (especially their mother). If I had come one year earlier things may have been different. Also, at the point I came into the story the boys had started their rebellion against their father and the power in the household had shifted. They did not seem to need or desire for me to intervene.

What I did do was to encourage them to explore their interest in filmmaking, by helping them to get internships and introduce them to people in the film industry.

Susanne [the boys' mother] feels like a different person to me now. When we first met she was more submissive and reserved. I think her children's step towards freedom and socialization really helped her stand up for her own rights as well. It's a process but she is well on the right path to gaining her own independence.

Their dad brought both classic and cult movies to them. They liked the violent, horrific, morally complicated films the best. As they read more about movies they started to request specific films.

The boys first saw *Pulp Fiction* on television, and this started their Quentin Tarantino obsession. It opened their eyes to film outside the realms of the standard Hollywood films they were used to watching. Since films were their world, they started to interpret these looks into their wardrobe. Their personal style is directly related to their favorite characters from their favorite movies. A lot of their early costumes were from clothing their dad would find on the street and at Salvation Army, which they would re-work by hand into specific costumes. For example, they'd tape blue Nike swooshes on tennis shoes to look like Marty McFly's, or cut up a woman's rain coat and sew it into the shape of Mad Max's leather biker vest. "

It almost felt as if I had discovered a long lost tribe, except it was not from the edges of the world but from the streets of Manhattan.

Source: Magnolia Pictures 2015:3,9–11.

n this excerpt from an interview with Crystal Moselle, director of *The Wolfpack*, we appreciate the incredible variety of experiences that people have in coming to terms with the world around them. Moselle describes the strangeness of the six teenage brothers who grew up in isolation from all social contact except that with their immediate family. As we will see throughout this chapter, children are typically exposed to a gradually widening circle of social contacts. As their social horizons widen, they learn more and more about how to behave in their society and how to engage with different kinds of people. The Angulo brothers, in contrast, were never exposed to this widening circle, so everything they learned about the world outside their own family came from movies and TV.

Hollywood movies became the brothers' window to the world. They acted out scenes and painstakingly transcribed, word for word on an old typewriter, movies such as *Reservoir Dogs* and *The Dark Knight*. After years of isolation, the boys, acting with a desire for independence typical of the teenage years, finally ventured out, directly disobeying their father's commands.

How much of a person's personality is shaped by culture, as opposed to inborn traits? In what ways does socialization continue throughout the life course? Who are the most powerful agents of socialization? In these modules we will examine the role of socialization in human development. We will begin by analyzing the interaction of heredity with environmental factors. Then we will explore how people develop perceptions, feelings, and beliefs about themselves. We will pay particular attention to important agents of socialization, including the family, schools, peers, the media and technology, the workplace, and religion. As we will see, socialization is a process that spans the entire life course. In the Social Policy section that closes the chapter, we will focus on the socialization experience of group child care for young children.

MODULE 13 | The Role of Socialization

Sociologists, in general, are interested in the patterns of behavior and attitudes that emerge throughout the life course, from infancy to old age. These patterns are part of the lifelong process of **socialization**, in which people learn the attitudes, values, and behaviors appropriate for members of a particular culture. Socialization occurs through human interactions that begin in infancy and continue through retirement. We learn a great deal from those people most important in our lives—immediate family members, best friends, and teachers. But we also learn from people we see on the street, on television, on the Internet, and in films and magazines. From a microsociological perspective, socialization helps us to discover how to behave "properly" and what to expect from others if we follow (or challenge) society's norms and values. From a macrosociological perspective, socialization provides for the transmission of a culture from one generation to the next, to ensure the long-term continuity of a society.

Socialization also shapes our self-images. For example, in the United States, a person who is viewed as "too heavy" or "too short" does not conform to the ideal cultural standard of physical attractiveness. This kind of unfavorable evaluation can significantly influence the person's self-esteem. In this sense, socialization experiences can help to shape our personalities. In everyday speech, the term **personality** is used to refer to a person's typical patterns of attitudes, needs, characteristics, and behavior.

What makes us who we are? Is it the genes we are born with, or the environment in which we grow up? Researchers have traditionally clashed over the relative importance of biological inheritance and environmental factors in human development—a conflict called the *nature versus nurture* (or *heredity versus environment*) debate. Today, most social scientists have moved beyond this debate, acknowledging instead the *interaction* of these variables in shaping human development. However, we can better appreciate how heredity and environmental factors interact and influence the socialization process if we first examine situations in which one factor operates almost entirely without the other (Homans 1979).

Social Environment: The Impact of Isolation

Some viewers may have found the story of the Angulo brothers difficult to believe, but social scientists have encountered similar cases. The two cases that follow describe the documented effects of extreme social isolation and neglect.

Extreme Isolation: Isabelle

The dramatic story of a child called Isabelle was all too real. For the first six years of her life, Isabelle lived in almost total seclusion in a darkened room. She had little contact with other people, with the exception of her mother, who could neither speak nor hear. Isabelle's mother's parents had been so deeply ashamed of Isabelle's illegitimate birth that they kept her hidden away from the world. Ohio authorities finally discovered the child in 1938, when Isabelle's mother escaped from her parents' home, taking her daughter with her.

When she was discovered at age six, Isabelle could not speak; she could merely make various croaking sounds. Her only communications with her mother were simple gestures. Isabelle had been largely deprived of the typical interactions and socialization experiences of childhood. Since she had seen few people, she showed a strong fear of strangers and reacted almost like a wild animal when confronted with an unfamiliar person. As she became accustomed to seeing certain individuals, her reaction changed to one of extreme apathy. At first, observers believed that Isabelle was deaf, but she soon began to react to nearby sounds. On tests of maturity, she scored at the level of an infant rather than a six-year-old.

Specialists developed a systematic training program to help Isabelle adapt to human relationships and socialization. After a few days of training, she made her first attempt to verbalize. Although she started slowly, Isabelle quickly passed through six years of development. In a little over two months she was speaking in complete sentences. Nine months later she could identify both words and sentences. Before Isabelle reached age nine, she was ready to attend school with other children. By age 14 she was in sixth grade, doing well in school, and emotionally well adjusted.

Yet without an opportunity to experience socialization in her first six years, Isabelle had been hardly human in the social sense when she was first discovered. Her inability to communicate at the time of her discovery—despite her physical and cognitive potential to learn—and her remarkable progress over the next few years underscore the impact of socialization on human development (K. Davis 1947:435-437).

The scientists involved with Isabelle's case concluded that all children need socialization in the form of love, care, and affection. Absent that kind of attention, humans cannot learn to speak and interact with others as expected. This need for positive social interaction does not end with childhood; it continues throughout the life span.

Unfortunately, other children who have been locked away or severely neglected have not fared so well as Isabelle. In many instances, the consequences of their social isolation have proved much more damaging.

Extreme Neglect: Romanian Orphans

Isabelle's experience is important to researchers because there are only a few cases of children who were reared in total isolation. However, there are many cases of children raised in extremely neglectful social circumstances. In the 1990s, public attention focused on infants and young children who grew up in orphanages in the formerly communist countries of Eastern Europe. In Romanian orphanages, babies once lay in their cribs for 18 to 20 hours a day, curled against their feeding bottles, receiving little care from adults. This minimal attention continued for the first five years of their lives. Many of them grew up fearful of human contact, and prone to unpredictable antisocial behavior. As recently as 2004, some 32,000 Romanian children were institutionalized in this manner.

This situation came to light as families in North America and Europe began to adopt thousands of the orphans. For about 20 percent of those adopted, adjustment problems were so dramatic that the adopting families suffered guilty fears of being ill-fit parents. Many of them have asked for assistance in dealing with the children. Slowly, efforts are being made to introduce the deprived youngsters to feelings of attachment and socialization that they have never experienced before (Groza et al. 1999; S. Craig Smith 2006).

In 2001, Romania bowed to pressure and placed a moratorium on international adoptions. The state took steps to reunite orphans with their birth families, place them with adoptive families in Romania, or settle them in small group homes. With supervision from attentive caregivers and specialists, the once-abandoned children have made remarkable progress. UNICEF is now using the program as a model for other nations that are dealing with such children. Worldwide, an estimated 2 million children are

© Thomas Coex/AFP/Getty Images

In Romania, special programs emphasizing social interaction have helped orphans to overcome years of social isolation.

living in institutional care (Aslanian 2006; Bahrampour 2014; *The Economist* 2013a; Ironside 2011; UNICEF 2009).

As with Isabelle, the Romanian orphans underscored the significance of the social environment in a child's development. Increasingly, researchers are emphasizing the importance of the earliest socialization experiences for all children, including those who grow up in more normal environments. We know now that it is not enough to care for an infant's physical needs; parents must also concern themselves with their children's social development. If, for example, children are discouraged from having friends even as toddlers, they will miss out on experiences with peers that are critical to their socialization and emotional growth.

Primate Studies

Studies of animals raised in isolation also support the importance of socialization in development. Harry Harlow (1971), a researcher at the primate laboratory of the University of Wisconsin, conducted tests with rhesus monkeys that had been raised away from their mothers and away from contact with other monkeys. As was the case with Isabelle, the rhesus monkeys raised in isolation were fearful and easily frightened. They did not mate, and the females who were artificially inseminated became abusive mothers. Apparently, isolation had had a damaging effect on the monkeys.

A creative aspect of Harlow's experimentation was his use of "artificial mothers." In one such experiment, Harlow presented monkeys raised in isolation with two substitute mothers—one cloth-covered replica and one covered with wire that had the ability to offer milk. Monkey after monkey went to the wire mother for the life-giving milk, yet spent much more time clinging to the more motherlike cloth model. It appears that the infant monkeys developed greater social attachments from their need for warmth, comfort, and intimacy than from their need for milk.

While these studies may seem to suggest that heredity can be dismissed as a factor in the social development of humans and animals, studies of twins reveal a fascinating interplay between heredity and environment.

The Influence of Heredity

Identical twins Oskar Stohr and Jack Yufe were separated soon after their birth and raised on different continents, in very different cultural settings. Oskar was reared as a strict Catholic by his maternal grandmother in the Sudetenland of Czechoslovakia. As a member of the Hitler Youth movement in Nazi Germany, he learned to hate Jews. In contrast, his brother Jack was reared in Trinidad by the twins' Jewish father. Jack joined an Israeli kibbutz (a collective settlement) at age 17 and later served in the Israeli army. When the twins were reunited in middle age, however, some startling similarities emerged: They both wore wire-rimmed glasses and mustaches. They both liked spicy foods and sweet liqueurs, were absentminded, flushed the toilet before using it, stored rubber bands on their wrists, and dipped buttered toast in their coffee (Holden 1980).

The twins also differed in many important respects: Jack was a workaholic; Oskar enjoyed leisure-time activities. Oskar was a traditionalist who was domineering toward women; Jack was a political liberal who was much more accepting of feminism. Finally, Jack was extremely proud of being Jewish, whereas Oskar never mentioned his Jewish heritage (Holden 1987).

Oskar and Jack are prime examples of the interplay of heredity and environment. For a number of years, the Minnesota Twin Family Study has been following 137 sets of identical twins reared apart to determine what similarities, if any, they show in personality traits, behavior, and intelligence. Preliminary results from the available twin studies indicate that *both* genetic factors *and* socialization experiences are influential in human development. Certain characteristics, such as temperaments, voice patterns, and nervous habits, appear to be strikingly similar even in twins reared apart, suggesting that these qualities may be linked to hereditary causes. However, identical twins reared apart differ far more in their attitudes, values, chosen mates, and even drinking habits; these qualities, it would seem, are influenced by environmental factors. In examining clusters of personality traits among such twins, researchers have found marked similarities in their tendency toward leadership or dominance, but significant differences in their need for intimacy, comfort, and assistance.

Researchers have also been impressed with the similar scores on intelligence tests of twins reared apart in *roughly similar* social settings. Most of the identical twins register scores even closer than those that would be expected if the same person took a test twice. At the same time, however, identical twins

© encrier/Getty Images RF

Despite the striking physical resemblance between these identical twins relaxing in Paris, there are undoubtedly many differences between them. Research points to some behavioral similarities between twins, but little beyond the likenesses found among nontwin siblings.

© Saleh Al-Obeidi/AFP/Getty Images

Socialization can be negative as well as positive. When the very young come to view harmful behaviors like smoking or illegal drug use as "normal," socialization is negative. In Yemen, these child soldiers have learned to use an automatic weapon.

We need to be cautious in reviewing studies of twin pairs and other relevant research. Widely broadcast findings have often been based on preliminary analysis of extremely small samples. For example, one study (not involving twin pairs) was frequently cited as confirming genetic links with behavior. Yet the researchers had to retract their conclusions after they increased the sample and reclassified two of the original cases. After those changes, the initial findings were no longer valid.

Critics add that studies of twin pairs have not provided satisfactory information concerning the extent to which separated identical twins may have had contact with each other, even though they were raised apart. Such interactions—especially if they were extensive—could call into question the validity of the twin studies. As this debate continues, we can certainly anticipate numerous efforts to replicate the research and clarify the interplay between heredity and environmental factors in human development (Horgan 1993; Plomin 1989).

brought up in *dramatically different* social environments score quite differently on intelligence tests—a finding that supports the impact of socialization on human development (Segal 2012).

MODULE 13 | Recap and Review

Summary

Socialization is the process through which people learn the attitudes, values, and actions appropriate for members of a particular culture.

1. Socialization affects the overall cultural practices of a society; it also shapes the images we hold of ourselves.

2. Heredity and environmental factors interact in influencing the socialization process.

Thinking Critically

1. What might be some ethical concerns regarding research on the influences of heredity and environment?

2. What are some social policy implications of research on the effects of early socialization experiences?

Key Terms

Personality

Socialization

We all have various perceptions, feelings, and beliefs about who we are and what we are like. How do we come to develop them? Do they change as we age?

We were not born with these understandings. Building on the work of George Herbert Mead (1964b), sociologists recognize that our concept of who we are, the *self,* emerges as we interact with others. The **self** is a distinct identity that sets us apart from others. It is not a static phenomenon, but continues to develop and change throughout our lives.

Sociologists and psychologists alike have expressed interest in how the individual develops and modifies the sense of self as a result of social interaction. The work of sociologists Charles Horton Cooley and George Herbert Mead, pioneers of the interactionist approach, has been especially useful in furthering our understanding of these important issues.

Sociological Approaches to the Self

Cooley: Looking-Glass Self

In the early 1900s, Charles Horton Cooley advanced the belief that we learn who we are by interacting with others. Our view of ourselves, then, comes not only from direct contemplation of our personal qualities but also from our impressions of how others perceive us. Cooley used the phrase **looking-glass self** to emphasize that the self is the product of our social interactions.

The process of developing a self-identity or self-concept has three phases. First, we imagine how we present ourselves to others—to relatives, friends, even strangers on the street. Then we imagine how others evaluate us (attractive, intelligent, shy, or strange). Finally, we develop some sort of feeling about ourselves, such as respect or shame, as a result of these impressions (Cooley 1902; Michael C. Howard 1989).

A subtle but critical aspect of Cooley's looking-glass self is that the self results from an individual's "imagination" of how others view him or her. As a result, we can develop self-identities based on *incorrect* perceptions of how others see us. A student may react strongly to a teacher's criticism and decide (wrongly) that the instructor views the student as stupid. This misperception may be converted into a negative self-identity through the following process: (1) the teacher criticized me, (2) the teacher must think that I'm stupid, (3) I *am* stupid. Yet self-identities are also subject to change. If the student receives an A at the end of the course, he or she will probably no longer feel stupid.

Mead: Stages of the Self

George Herbert Mead continued Cooley's exploration of interactionist theory. Mead (1934, 1964a) developed a useful model of the process by which the self emerges, defined by three distinct stages: the preparatory stage, the play stage, and the game stage.

The Preparatory Stage During the *preparatory stage,* children merely imitate the people around them, especially family members with whom they continually interact. Thus, a small child will bang on a piece of wood while a parent is engaged in carpentry work, or will try to throw a ball if an older sibling is doing so nearby.

As they grow older, children become more adept at using symbols, including the gestures and words that form the basis of human communication. By interacting with relatives and friends, as well as by watching cartoons on television and looking at picture books, children in the preparatory stage begin to understand symbols. They will continue to use this form of communication throughout their lives.

The Play Stage Mead was among the first to analyze the relationship of symbols to socialization. As children develop skill in communicating through symbols, they gradually become more aware of social relationships. As a result, during the *play stage,* they begin to pretend to be other people. Just as an actor "becomes" a character, a child becomes a doctor, parent, superhero, or ship captain.

Mead, in fact, noted that an important aspect of the play stage is role-playing. **Role taking** is the process of mentally assuming the perspective of another and responding from that imagined viewpoint. For example, through this process a young child will gradually learn when it is best to ask a parent for favors. If the parent usually comes home from work in a bad mood, the child will wait until after dinner, when the parent is more relaxed and approachable.

The Game Stage In Mead's third stage, the *game stage,* the child of about age eight or nine no longer just plays roles but begins to consider several tasks and relationships simultaneously. At this point in development, children grasp not only their own social positions but also those of others around them—just as in a football game the players must understand their own and everyone else's positions. Consider a girl or boy who is part of a Scout troop out on a weekend hike in the mountains. The child must understand what he or she is expected to do but must also recognize the responsibilities of other Scouts as well as the leaders. This is the final stage of development under Mead's model: the child can now respond to numerous members of the social environment.

Mead uses the term **generalized other** to refer to the attitudes, viewpoints, and expectations of society as a whole that a child takes into account in his or her behavior. Simply put, this concept suggests that when an individual acts, he or she takes into account an entire group of people. For example, a child will not act courteously merely to please a particular parent. Rather, the child comes to understand that courtesy is a widespread social value endorsed by parents, teachers, and religious leaders.

Table 14-1 summarizes the three stages of the self outlined by George Herbert Mead.

Mead: Theory of the Self

Mead is best known for his theory of the self. According to Mead (1964b), the self begins at a privileged, central position in a person's world. Young children picture themselves as the focus of

TABLE **14-1** **MEAD'S STAGES OF THE SELF**

Summing Up

Stage	Self Present?	Definition	Example
Preparation	No	Child imitates the actions of others.	When adults laugh and smile, child laughs and smiles.
Play	Developing	Child takes the role of a single other, as if he or she were the other.	Child first takes the role of doctor, then the role of patient.
Game	Yes	Child considers the roles of two or more others simultaneously.	In game of hide-and-seek, child takes into account the roles of both hider and seeker.

everything around them and find it difficult to consider the perspectives of others. For example, when shown a mountain scene and asked to describe what an observer on the opposite side of the mountain might see (such as a lake or hikers), young children describe only objects visible from their vantage point. This childhood tendency to place ourselves at the center of events never entirely disappears. Many people with a fear of flying automatically assume that if any plane goes down, it will be the one they are on. And who reads the horoscope section in the paper without looking at their own horoscope first? Why else do we buy lottery tickets, if we do not imagine ourselves winning?

Nonetheless, as people mature, the self changes and begins to reflect greater concern about the reactions of others. Parents, friends, co-workers, coaches, and teachers are often among those who play a major role in shaping a person's self. The term **significant others** is used to refer to those individuals who are most important in the development of the self. Many young people, for example, find themselves drawn to the same kind of work their parents engage in (H. Sullivan [1953] 1968).

use your **sociological imagination**

How do you view yourself as you interact with others around you? How do you think you formed this view of yourself?

Goffman: Presentation of the Self

How do we manage our "self"? How do we display to others who we are? Erving Goffman, a sociologist associated with the interactionist perspective, suggested that many of our daily activities involve attempts to convey impressions of who we are. His observations help us to understand the sometimes subtle yet critical ways in which we learn to present ourselves socially. They also offer concrete examples of this aspect of socialization.

Early in life, the individual learns to slant his or her presentation of the self in order to create distinctive appearances and satisfy particular audiences. Goffman (1959) referred to this altering of the presentation of the self as **impression management**. Box 14-1 describes an everyday example of this concept—the way students behave after receiving their exam grades.

In analyzing such everyday social interactions, Goffman makes so many explicit parallels to the theater that his view has been termed the **dramaturgical approach**. According to this

perspective, people resemble performers in action. For example, a clerk may try to appear busier than he or she actually is if a supervisor happens to be watching. A customer in a singles' bar may try to look as if he or she is waiting for a particular person to arrive.

Goffman (1959) also drew attention to another aspect of the self, **face-work**. How often do you initiate some kind of face-saving behavior when you feel embarrassed or rejected? In response to a rejection at the singles' bar, a person may engage in face-work by saying, "There really isn't an interesting person in this entire crowd." We feel the need to maintain a proper image of the self if we are to continue social interaction.

Face-work is a necessity for those who are unemployed. In an economic downturn like the recent recession, unemployment affects people of all social classes, many of whom are unaccustomed to being jobless. A recent ethnographic study found the newly unemployed redefining what it means to be out of work. They were focusing more than in the past on what they were accomplishing, and had begun to value volunteer work more since they had become volunteers themselves. Participants in this study engaged in both impression management and face-work (Garrett-Peters 2009).

Goffman's work on the self represents a logical progression of sociological studies begun by Cooley and Mead on how

Cartoon © Scott Arthur Masear. Reprinted by permission of www.CartoonStock.com.

People judge us by our appearance, attire, body language, demeanor, and mannerisms. Knowing that they do, most of us alter the way we present ourselves to others, a strategy that Goffman called impression management.

Impression Management by Students

When you and fellow classmates get an exam back, you probably react differently depending on the grades each of you earned. This distinction is part of *impression management.* Researchers have found that students' reactions differ depending on the grades that others received, compared to their own. These encounters can be divided into three categories: those in which all students earned high grades (Ace–Ace encounters); those between Aces and students who received low or failing grades (Ace–Bomber encounters); and those between students who all got low grades (Bomber–Bomber encounters).

Ace–Ace encounters occur in a rather open atmosphere, because there is comfort in sharing a high mark with another high achiever. It is even acceptable to violate the norm of modesty and brag when among other Aces, since as one student admitted, "It's much easier to admit a high mark to someone who has done better than you, or at least as well."

Ace–Bomber encounters are often sensitive. Bombers generally attempt to avoid such exchanges, because "you . . . emerge

> When forced into interactions with Aces, Bombers work to appear gracious and congratulatory.

looking like the dumb one" or "feel like you are lazy or unreliable." When forced into interactions with Aces, Bombers work to appear gracious and congratulatory. For their part, Aces offer sympathy and support to the dissatisfied Bombers and even rationalize their own "lucky" high scores. To help Bombers save face, Aces may emphasize the difficulty and unfairness of the examination.

Bomber–Bomber encounters tend to be closed, reflecting the group effort to wall off the feared disdain of others. Yet within the safety of these encounters, Bombers openly share their disappointment and engage in expressions of

mutual self-pity that they themselves call "pity parties." They devise face-saving excuses for their poor performance, such as "I wasn't feeling well all week" or "I had four exams and two papers due that week."

Of course, grade comparisons are not the only occasion when students engage in impression management. Another study has shown that students' perceptions of how often fellow students work out can also influence their social encounters. In athletic terms, a bomber would be someone who doesn't work out; an ace would be someone who works hard at physical fitness.

LET'S DISCUSS

1. How do you react to those who have received higher or lower grades than you? Do you engage in impression management? How would you like others to react to your grade?

2. What social norms govern students' impression management strategies?

Sources: Albas and Albas 1988, 1996; Austin 2009; M. Mack 2003.

---

personality is acquired through socialization and how we manage the presentation of the self to others. Cooley stressed the process by which we create a self; Mead focused on how the self develops as we learn to interact with others; Goffman emphasized the ways in which we consciously create images of ourselves for others.

● Psychological Approaches to the Self

Psychologists have shared the interest of Cooley, Mead, and other sociologists in the development of the self. Early work in psychology, such as that of Sigmund Freud (1856–1939), stressed the role of inborn drives—among them the drive for sexual gratification—in channeling human behavior. More recently, psychologists such as Jean Piaget have emphasized the stages through which human development progresses.

Like Charles Horton Cooley and George Herbert Mead, Freud believed that the self is a social product, and that aspects of one's personality are influenced by other people (especially one's parents). However, unlike Cooley and Mead, he suggested that the self has components that work in opposition to each other. According to Freud, our natural impulsive instincts are in constant conflict with societal constraints. Part of us seeks limitless pleasure, while another part favors rational behavior. By interacting with others, we learn the expectations of society and then select

behavior most appropriate to our culture. (Of course, as Freud was well aware, we sometimes distort reality and behave irrationally.)

Research on newborn babies by the Swiss child psychologist Jean Piaget (1896–1980) has underscored the importance of social interactions in developing a sense of self. Piaget found that newborns have no self in the sense of a looking-glass image. Ironically, though, they are quite self-centered; they demand that all attention be directed toward them. Newborns have not yet separated themselves from the universe of which they are a part. For these babies, the phrase "you and me" has no meaning; they understand only "me." However, as they mature, children are gradually socialized into social relationships, even within their rather self-centered world.

In his well-known **cognitive theory of development**, Piaget (1954) identified four stages in the development of children's thought processes. In the first, or *sensorimotor,* stage, young children use their senses to make discoveries. For example, through touching they discover that their hands are actually a part of themselves. During the second, or *preoperational,* stage, children begin to use words and symbols to distinguish objects and ideas. The milestone in the third, or *concrete operational,* stage is that children engage in more logical thinking. They learn that even when a formless lump of clay is shaped into a snake, it is still the same clay. In the fourth, or *formal operational,* stage, adolescents become capable of sophisticated abstract thought and can deal logically with ideas and values.

TABLE 14-2 THEORETICAL APPROACHES TO DEVELOPMENT OF THE SELF

Tracking Sociological Perspectives

Scholar	Key Concepts and Contributions	Major Points of Theory
Charles Horton Cooley 1864–1929 sociologist (USA)	Looking-glass self	Stages of development not distinct; feelings toward ourselves developed through interaction with others
George Herbert Mead 1863–1931 sociologist (USA)	The self Generalized other	Three distinct stages of development; self develops as children grasp the roles of others in their lives
Erving Goffman 1922–1982 sociologist (USA)	Impression management Dramaturgical approach Face-work	Self developed through the impressions we convey to others and to groups
Sigmund Freud 1856–1939 psychotherapist (Austria)	Psychoanalysis	Self influenced by parents and by inborn drives, such as the drive for sexual gratification
Jean Piaget 1896–1980 child psychologist (Switzerland)	Cognitive theory of development	Four stages of cognitive development

According to Piaget, social interaction is the key to development. As children grow older, they pay increasing attention to how other people think and why they act in particular ways. In order to develop a distinct personality, each of us needs opportunities to interact with others. As we saw earlier, Isabelle was deprived of the chance for normal social interactions, and the consequences were severe (Kitchener 1991).

We have seen that a number of thinkers considered social interaction the key to the development of an individual's sense of self. As is generally true, we can best understand this topic by drawing on a variety of theory and research. Table 14-2 summarizes the rich literature, both sociological and psychological, on the development of the self.

Socialization throughout the Life Course

The Life Course

Among the Kota people of the Congo in Africa, adolescents paint themselves blue. Mexican American girls go on a daylong religious retreat before dancing the night away. Egyptian mothers step over their newborn infants seven times, and graduating students at the Naval Academy throw their hats in the air. These are all ways of celebrating **rites of passage**, or rituals that mark a symbolic transition from one social position to another. Rites of passage are ways of validating and or dramatizing changes in a person's status. They may mark a separation, as in a graduation ceremony, or an incorporation, as in an initiation into an organization (Van Gennep [1909] 1960).

Rites of passage are a worldwide social phenomenon. The Kota rite marks the passage to adulthood. The color blue, viewed as the color of death, symbolizes the death of childhood. Hispanic girls celebrate reaching womanhood with a *quinceañera* ceremony at age 15. In the Cuban American community of Miami, the popularity of the *quinceañera* supports a network of party planners, caterers, dress designers, and the Miss Quinceañera Latina pageant. For thousands of years, Egyptian mothers have welcomed their newborns to the world in the Soboa ceremony by stepping over the seven-day-old infant seven times.

These specific ceremonies mark stages of development in the life course. They indicate that the process of socialization continues through all stages of the life cycle. In fact, some researchers have chosen to concentrate on socialization as a lifelong process. Sociologists and other social scientists who take such a **life course approach** look closely at the social factors that influence people throughout their lives, from birth to death,

© Paul Chesley/Getty Images

A young Apache woman undergoes a mudding ceremony traditionally used in rites of passage, such as puberty and in some cases weddings.

including gender and income. They recognize that biological changes mold but do not dictate human behavior.

Several life events mark the passage to adulthood, including marriage and the birth of a first child. Of course, these turning points vary from one society or even one generation to the next. In the United States, the key event seems to be the completion of formal schooling. However, educational completion is not as clearly defined today as it was a generation or two ago. More and more people are taking full-time jobs while finishing their schooling, or returning to school to obtain a professional certificate or advanced degree. Similarly, the milestones associated with leaving home, finding a stable job, and establishing a long-term personal relationship do not now occur at specific ages (Silva 2012; T. Smith 2003).

One result of these overlapping steps to independence is that in the United States, unlike some other societies, there is no clear dividing line between adolescence and adulthood. Nowadays, few young people finish school, get married, and leave home at about the same age, clearly establishing their transition to adulthood. The terms *youthhood, emerging adulthood,* and *not quite adult* have been coined to describe the prolonged ambiguous status that young people in their 20s experience (Côté 2000; Settersten and Ray 2011; Christian Smith 2007).

 use your **sociological imagination**

Why do you think the end of formal schooling is the most important milestone of adulthood today? What about marriage, full-time employment, or financial independence from parents or guardians? Which milestone do you think is the most important?

Anticipatory Socialization and Resocialization

The development of a social self is literally a lifelong transformation that begins in the crib and continues as one prepares for death. Two types of socialization occur at many points throughout the life course: anticipatory socialization and resocialization.

Anticipatory socialization refers to processes of socialization in which a person rehearses for future positions, occupations, and social relationships. A culture can function more efficiently and smoothly if members become acquainted with the norms, values, and behavior associated with a social position before actually assuming that status. Preparation for many aspects of adult life begins with anticipatory socialization during childhood and adolescence, and continues throughout our lives as we prepare for new responsibilities.

You can see the process of anticipatory socialization take place when high school students start to consider what colleges they may attend. Traditionally, this task meant looking at publications received in the mail or making campus visits. However, with new technology, more and more students are using the web to begin their college experience. Colleges are investing more time and money in developing attractive websites through which students can take virtual campus tours and hear audio clips of everything from the college anthem to a sample zoology lecture.

Occasionally, assuming a new social or occupational position requires us to *unlearn* an established orientation. **Resocialization** refers to the process of discarding former behavior patterns and accepting new ones as part of a transition in one's life. Often resocialization occurs during an explicit effort to transform an individual, as happens in reform schools, therapy groups, prisons, religious conversion settings, and political indoctrination camps. The process of resocialization typically involves considerable stress for the individual—much more so than socialization in general, or even anticipatory socialization (Gecas 2004).

Resocialization is particularly effective when it occurs within a total institution. Erving Goffman (1961) coined the term **total institution** to refer to an institution that regulates all aspects of a person's life under a single authority, such as a prison, the military, a mental hospital, or a convent. Because the total institution is generally cut off from the rest of society, it provides for all the needs of its members. Quite literally, the crew of a merchant vessel at sea becomes part of a total institution. So elaborate are its requirements, so all-encompassing its activities, a total institution often represents a miniature society.

Goffman (1961) identified four common traits of total institutions:

- All aspects of life are conducted in the same place under the control of a single authority.
- Any activities within the institution are conducted in the company of others in the same circumstances—for example, army recruits or novices in a convent.

Source: Cpl. Benjamin E. Woodle, United States Marine Corps

Marine recruits undergoing grueling basic training at Parris Island, South Carolina. The military is an example of what sociologists call a total institution.

- The authorities devise rules and schedule activities without consulting the participants.
- All aspects of life within a total institution are designed to fulfill the purpose of the organization. Thus, all activities in a monastery might be centered on prayer and communion with God (Davies 1989; P. Rose et al. 1979).

People often lose their individuality within total institutions. For example, a person entering prison may experience the humiliation of a **degradation ceremony** as he or she is stripped of clothing, jewelry, and other personal possessions. From this point on, scheduled daily routines allow for little or no personal initiative. The individual becomes secondary and rather invisible in the overbearing social environment (Garfinkel 1956).

MODULE 14 | Recap and Review

Summary

This module examines sociological and psychological views of the development of the self.

1. In the early 1900s, Charles Horton Cooley advanced the belief that we learn who we are by interacting with others, a phenomenon he called the **looking-glass self**.

2. George Herbert Mead, best known for his theory of the **self**, proposed that as people mature, their selves begin to reflect their concern about reactions from others, both generalized others and significant others.

3. Erving Goffman has shown that in many of our daily activities, we try to convey distinct impressions of who we are, a process he called **impression management**.

4. According to Jean Piaget's cognitive theory of development, social interaction is the key to psychological development.

5. Socialization proceeds throughout the life course. Some societies mark stages of development with formal **rites of passage**. In the culture of the United States, significant events such as marriage and parenthood serve to change a person's status.

Thinking Critically

1. Use Erving Goffman's dramaturgical approach to describe impression management among members of one of the following groups: athletes, college instructors, parents, physicians, or politicians.

2. What are some similarities between Mead's stages of the self and Piaget's cognitive development stages? What are some differences?

Key Terms

Anticipatory socialization

Cognitive theory of development

Degradation ceremony

Dramaturgical approach

Face-work

Generalized other

Impression management

Life course approach

Looking-glass self

Resocialization

Rite of passage

Role taking

Self

Significant other

Total institution

MODULE 15 | Agents of Socialization

As we have seen, the culture of the United States is defined by rather gradual movements from one stage of socialization to the next. The continuing and lifelong socialization process involves many different social forces that influence our lives and alter our self-images.

The family is the most important agent of socialization in the United States, especially for children. In this chapter, we'll also discuss six other agents of socialization: the school, the peer group, the mass media and technology, the workplace, religion, and the state.

Family

The lifelong process of learning begins shortly after birth. Since newborns can hear, see, smell, taste, and feel heat, cold, and pain, they are constantly orienting themselves to the surrounding world. Human beings, especially family members, constitute an important part of their social environment. People minister to the baby's needs by feeding, cleaning, carrying, and comforting the baby.

All families engage in socialization, but the way that Amish families encourage their children to accept their community's subculture is particularly striking. Box 15-1 describes their tolerance for the period of rebellion known as *rum springa*, during which Amish children flirt with the adolescent subculture of mainstream American society.

BOX 15-1

Research Today

Rum Springa: Raising Children Amish Style

All families face challenges raising their children, but what if your parents expected you not to dance, listen to music, watch television, or access the Internet? This is the challenge faced by Amish teens and their parents, who embrace a lifestyle of the mid-1800s. Amish youths—boys in particular—often rebel against their parents' strict morals by getting drunk, behaving disrespectfully, and indulging in "worldly" activities, such as buying a car. At times even the girls may become involved, to their families' dismay. As one scholar puts it, "The rowdiness of Amish youth is an embarrassment to church leaders and a stigma in the larger community" (Kraybill 2001:138).

Yet the strong pull of mainstream American culture has led Amish parents to routinize, almost to accept, some of their children's worldly activities. They expect adolescents to test their subculture's boundaries during a period of discovery called *rum springa,* a German term meaning "running around." A common occurrence during which young people attend barn dances and break social norms that forbid drinking, smoking, and driving cars, *rum springa* is definitely not supported by the Amish religion.

Parents often react to these escapades by looking the other way, sometimes literally. If they hear radio music coming from the barn, or a motorcycle driving onto their property in the middle of the night, they don't retaliate by punishing their offspring. Instead, they pretend not to notice, secure in the knowledge that Amish children almost always return to the community's traditional values. Indeed, despite the flirtation with popular culture and modern technology that is common during the *rum springa,* the vast majority of Amish youths do return to the Amish community and become baptized. Scholars report that 85 to 90 percent of Amish children accept the faith as young adults.

To mainstream Americans, this little known and understood subculture became

© Lee Snider Photo Images/Shutterstock

> All families face challenges raising their children, but what if your parents expected you not to dance, listen to music, watch television, or access the Internet?

a source of entertainment when in 2004, UPN aired a 10-week reality program called *Amish in the City.* In the series, five Amish youths allegedly on *rum springa* moved in with six worldly wise young adults in Los Angeles. On behalf of the Amish community, some critics called the series exploitative,

a sign of how vulnerable the Amish are. No similar series would be developed on the rebellion of Muslim or Orthodox Jewish youths, they charged.

LET'S DISCUSS

1. Do you or anyone you know come from a subculture that rejects mainstream American culture? If so, describe the community's norms and values. How do they resemble and how do they differ from Amish norms and values?

2. Why do you think so many Amish youths return to their families' way of life after rebelling against it?

Sources: Kraybill 2001; R. Schaefer and Zellner 2015; Shachtman 2006; Stevick 2007; Weinraub 2004.

In the United States, social development also includes exposure to cultural assumptions regarding gender and race. Black parents, for example, have learned that children as young as age two can absorb negative messages about Blacks in children's books, toys, and television shows—all of which are designed primarily for White consumers. At the same time, Black children are exposed more often than others to the inner-city youth gang culture. Because most Blacks, even those who are middle class, live near very poor neighborhoods, their children are susceptible to these influences, despite their parents' strong family values (Linn and Poussaint 1999; Pattillo-McCoy 1999).

The term **gender role** refers to expectations regarding the proper behavior, attitudes, and activities of males and females. For example, we traditionally think of "toughness" as masculine—and desirable only in men—while we view "tenderness" as feminine. Other cultures do not necessarily assign these qualities to each gender in the way that our culture does. The existence of gender roles does not imply that inevitably, males and females will assume certain roles, nor does it imply that those roles are quite distinct from one another. Rather, gender roles emphasize the fact that males and females are not genetically predetermined to occupy certain roles.

As the primary agents of childhood socialization, parents play a critical role in guiding children into those gender roles deemed appropriate in a society. Other adults, older siblings, the mass media, and religious and educational institutions also have a noticeable impact on a child's socialization into feminine and masculine norms. A culture or subculture may require that one sex or the other take primary responsibility for the socialization of children, economic support of the family, or religious or intellectual leadership. In some societies, girls are socialized mainly by their mothers and boys by their fathers—an arrangement that may prevent girls from learning critical survival skills. In South Asia, fathers teach their sons to swim to prepare them for a life as fishermen; girls typically do not learn to swim. When a deadly tsunami hit the coast of South Asia in 2004, many more men survived than women.

© Michel Renaudeau/age fotostock

A daughter learns how to weave fabric from her mother in Guatemala. The family is the most important agent of socialization.

School

Like the family, schools have an explicit mandate to socialize people in the United States—especially children—into the norms and values of our culture.

As conflict theorists Samuel Bowles and Herbert Gintis ([1976] 2011) have observed, schools in this country foster competition through built-in systems of reward and punishment, such as grades and evaluations by teachers. Consequently, a child who is experiencing difficulty trying to learn a new skill can sometimes come to feel stupid and unsuccessful. However, as the self matures, children become capable of increasingly realistic assessments of their intellectual, physical, and social abilities.

Functionalists point out that schools, as agents of socialization, fulfill the function of teaching children the values and customs of the larger society. Conflict theorists agree, but add that schools can reinforce the divisive aspects of society, especially those of social class. For example, higher education in the United States is costly despite the existence of financial aid programs. Students from affluent backgrounds therefore have an advantage in gaining access to universities and professional training. At the same time, less affluent young people may never receive the preparation that would qualify them for the best-paying and most prestigious jobs.

Peer Group

As a child grows older, the family becomes somewhat less important in social development. Instead, peer groups increasingly assume the role of Mead's significant others. Within the peer group, young people associate with others who are approximately their age, and who often enjoy a similar social status (Giordano 2003).

We can see how important peer groups are to young people when their social lives are strained by war or disaster. In Syria, social groupings have been torn apart by civil war, invasion, and bombings. In 2012, Fatmeh described her life as that of a typical teenager whose daily routine was all about school, classes, friends, and homework. Three years later, at age 15, she was living in a makeshift shelter in Lebanon. When she left Syria, she still hoped to continue her studies in Lebanon and become a language teacher, but that is unlikely to happen, because her whole family must do farm work seven days a week to maintain their meager life. Her only connection beyond her immediate family is her cellphone, which allows her to keep up with news about Syria and to hear songs about her homeland. Fatmeh says she still has "very small hope" that someday she will be able to return to school and eventually go to college. "Very small, small hope," she says (Beaubien and Davis 2015).

Gender differences are noteworthy among adolescents. Boys and girls are socialized by their parents, peers, and the media to identify many of the same paths to popularity, but to different degrees. Table 15-1 compares male and female college students' reports of how girls and boys they knew became popular in high school. The two groups named many of the same paths to popularity but gave them a different order of importance. While neither men nor women named sexual activity, drug use, or alcohol use as one of the top five paths, college men were much more likely than women to mention those behaviors as a means to becoming popular, for both boys and girls.

Mass Media and Technology

In the past century, media innovations—radio, motion pictures, recorded music, television, and the Internet—have become important agents of socialization. The question is no longer whether young people are plugged in, but how they use these resources.

TABLE 15-1 HIGH SCHOOL POPULARITY

What makes high school girls popular?		What makes high school boys popular?	
According to college men:	According to college women:	According to college men:	According to college women:
1. Physical attractiveness	1. Grades/intelligence	1. Participation in sports	1. Participation in sports
2. Grades/intelligence	2. Participation in sports	2. Grades/intelligence	2. Grades/intelligence
3. Participation in sports	3. General sociability	3. Popularity with girls	3. General sociability
4. General sociability	4. Physical attractiveness	4. General sociability	4. Physical attractiveness
5. Popularity with boys	5. Clothes	5. Car	5. School clubs/government

Note: Students at the following universities were asked in which ways adolescents in their high schools had gained prestige with their peers: Cornell University, Louisiana State University, Southeastern Louisiana University, State University of New York at Albany, State University of New York at Stony Brook, University of Georgia, and University of New Hampshire.
Source: Suitor et al. 2001:445.

Today, 95 percent of those aged 12 to 17 are on the Internet. No surprise there, but 91 percent of them post photos identifying themselves by name. Ninety-two percent use their real names, and 82 percent post their birth dates on social media. Increasingly, then, socialization occurs online. The age at which young people go online has also been dropping, prompting concern about the potential for media abuse at an earlier and earlier age. Over the last decade, the American Academy of Pediatrics began by publishing concerns about teen use of the Internet. Recently, the organization published guidelines for the 90 percent of *infants* who use the Internet—via their parents, of course (American Academy of Pediatrics 2011, 2013; Madden et al. 2013).

The media, however, are not always a negative socializing influence. Television programs and even commercials can introduce young people to unfamiliar lifestyles and cultures. Not only do children in the United States learn about life in "faraway lands," but inner-city children learn about the lives of farm children, and vice versa. The same thing happens in other countries.

© Jake Lyell/Alamy

In Soroti, Uganda, a woman makes a quick telephone call. Cell phones play a critical role in communications and commerce in developing countries, where other ways of connecting are less available or more expensive.

Sociologists and other social scientists have begun to consider the impact of technology on socialization. They are particularly interested in the online friendship networks, like Facebook and Twitter. To assess the importance of social media in our daily lives, they typically begin by studying how we use them. In a novel approach, some researchers have asked what would happen if we stopped using social media: see Box 15-2.

Not just in industrial nations, but in Africa and other developing areas, people have been socialized into relying on new communications technologies. Not long ago, if Zadhe Iyombe wanted to talk to his mother, he had to make an eight-day trip from the capital city of Kinshasa up the Congo River by boat to the rural town where he was born. Now both he and his mother have access to a cell phone, and they send text messages to each other daily. Iyombe and his mother are not atypical. Although cell phones aren't cheap, 51 percent of people in low-income nations have them, compared to 4 percent who have a computer at home (World Bank 2015a: Tables 5.11, 5.12).

That said, not all new communications technologies are widely available in developing nations. For example, many people in these countries cannot afford broadband Internet service. In terms of their relative income, broadband service is 40 times more expensive to people in developing countries than it is to the typical person in an industrialized nation (International Telecommunication Union 2012).

● Workplace

Learning to behave appropriately in an occupation is a fundamental aspect of human socialization. It used to be that going to work began with the end of our formal schooling, but that is no longer the case, at least not in the United States. More and more young people work today, and not just for a parent or relative. Adolescents generally seek jobs in order to make spending money; 80 percent of high school seniors say that little or none of what they earn goes to family expenses. These teens rarely look on their employment as a means of exploring vocational interests or getting on-the-job training.

Taking Sociology to Work

Rakefet Avramovitz, *Program Administrator, Child Care Law Center*

Courtesy of Rakefet Avramovitz

Rakefet Avramovitz has been working at the Child Care Law Center in San Francisco since 2003. The center uses legal tools to foster the development of quality, affordable child care, with the goal of expanding child care options, particularly for low-income families. As a support person for the center's attorneys, she manages grants, oversees the center's publications, and sets up conferences and training sessions.

Avramovitz graduated from Dickinson College in 2000. She first became interested in sociology when she took a social analysis course. Though she enjoyed her qualitative courses most, she found her quantitative courses fun, "in that we got to do surveys of people on campus. I've always enjoyed fieldwork," she notes. Avramovitz's most memorable course was one that gave her the opportunity to interact with migrant farmworkers for an entire semester. "I learned ethnography and how to work with people of different cultures. It changed my life," she says.

Avramovitz finds that the skills she learned in her sociology courses are a great help to her on the job. "Sociology taught me how to work with people . . . and how to think critically. It taught me how to listen and find the stories that people are telling," she explains. Before joining the Child Care Law Center, Avramovitz worked as a counselor for women who were facing difficult issues. "My background in ethnography helped me to talk to these women and listen effectively," she notes. "I was able to help many women by understanding and being able to express their needs to the attorneys we worked with."

Avramovitz is enthusiastic about her work and her ability to make a difference in other people's lives. Maybe that is why she looks forward to summer at the center, when the staff welcomes several law students as interns. "It is really neat to see people learn and get jazzed about child care issues," she says.

LET'S DISCUSS

1. What might be some of the broad, long-term effects of the center's work to expand child care options? Explain.

2. Besides the law, what other professions might benefit from the skills a sociology major has to offer?

Some observers feel that the increasing number of teenagers who are working earlier in life and for longer hours are finding the workplace almost as important an agent of socialization as school. In fact, a number of educators complain that student time at work is adversely affecting schoolwork. The level of teenage employment in the United States is the highest among industrial countries, which may provide one explanation for why U.S. high school students lag behind those in other countries on international achievement tests.

Socialization in the workplace changes when it involves a more permanent shift from an after-school job to full-time employment. Occupational socialization can be most intense during the transition from school to job, but it continues throughout one's work history. Technological advances may alter the requirements of the position and necessitate some degree of resocialization. Today, men and women change occupations, employers, or places of work many times during their adult years. For example, the typical worker spends about four years with an employer. Occupational socialization continues, then, throughout a person's years in the labor market (Bialik 2010).

College students today recognize that occupational socialization is not socialization into one lifetime occupation. They anticipate going through a number of jobs. The Bureau of Labor Statistics (2015a) has found that from ages 18 to 48, the typical person has held 12 jobs, but nearly half of these jobs are held between ages 18 and 24. This high rate of turnover in employment applies to both men and women, and to those with a college degree as well as those with a high school diploma.

Religion and the State

Increasingly, social scientists are recognizing the importance of both religion and government ("the state") as agents of socialization, because of their impact on the life course. Traditionally, family members have served as the primary caregivers in our culture, but in the 20th century, the family's protective function was steadily transferred to outside agencies such as hospitals, mental health clinics, and child care centers. Many of these agencies are run by groups affiliated with certain religions or by the state.

Both organized religion and government have impacted the life course by reinstituting some of the rites of passage once observed in agricultural communities and early industrial societies. For example, religious organizations stipulate certain traditional rites that may bring together all the members of an extended family, even if they never meet for any other reason. And government regulations stipulate the ages at which a person may drive a car, drink alcohol, vote in elections, marry without parental permission, work overtime, and retire. These regulations do not constitute strict rites of passage: most 18-year-olds choose not to vote, and most people choose their age of retirement without reference to government dictates.

In the Social Policy section that follows, we will see that government is under pressure to become a provider of child care, which would give it a new and direct role in the socialization of infants and young children.

Unplugging the Media: What Happens?

What happens when a college campus goes media-free for a whole day? Beginning in 2010, researchers at the University of Maryland and in Salzburg, Austria, challenged students to abstain from all media for 24 hours. By the end of 2013, almost 1,000 students from a dozen colleges on five continents had accepted the challenge. After their media-free day was over, students were asked to report their successes and failures in going without social media. Together, they wrote almost half a million words.

As the accompanying figure shows, there were some differences among countries in how students felt about their day without media. "Alienation" and "distress" were common responses across the 10 participating nations. Although students had volunteered for the project and understood that their abstinence was only temporary, they found the experience extremely difficult. To give up media even for 24 hours, they said, was virtually impossible.

"For people in the modern society," said one student in China, "communication [media] is as important as breath." Without media, said another student from Slovakia, "I felt as though everything I knew was taken away from me and that I was being tortured." A student in Mexico moaned, "I feel that not even the sun can warm me." Others reported that they felt unbearably constrained, almost "paralyzed." "What really bothered me and made me feel 'tied down' was the inability to do what I wanted when I wanted it," said a student in Lebanon.

> Although students had volunteered for the project and understood that their abstinence was only temporary, they found the experience extremely difficult.

Not all responses were negative; a minority of students (from a low of 16 percent in Argentina to a high of 36 percent in Uganda) mentioned some benefits. As one Chinese student observed, "I invited my fellows to play badminton and enjoy the sunshine in our beautiful campus, chatting, laughing, eating, drinking, wandering, etc." And a British student concluded, "I have legs, which I now believe are underestimated as a social tool, as they allowed me to go and see people and communicate with them wirelessly." In effect, the unplugged students undertook more face-to-face socialization than usual.

Researchers concluded that going without media for a day made students more aware of the media, both the benefits and limitations. Students discovered that they were unable to go about their daily lives without the media. The "addiction" that many reported prompted some to confess a need to curb their media use—although most doubted they would have much success doing so.

LET'S DISCUSS

1. Could you go without media for a day? Get together with a group of friends or classmates and try going media-free for 24 hours; then share your reactions.

2. How well did students in the United States react to a media-free day compared to those in other countries? What might explain the differences?

Sources: Moeller et al. 2012; World Unplugged 2013. World Unplugged 2013 is the source of all student quotations. Quotations from "Addiction Grid" and "Benefits of Unplugging." The world UNPLUGGED. Copyright © 2011 Susan D. Moeller. All rights reserved.

RESPONSES TO A DAY WITHOUT MEDIA

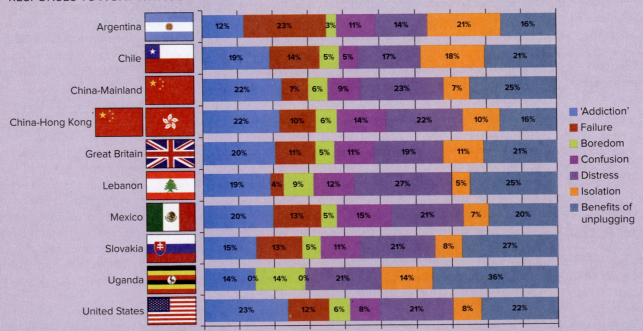

Bar chart of emotions expressed by students attending university in participating countries. The world UNPLUGGED. Copyright © 2011 Susan D. Moeller. All rights reserved. Reprinted by permission. *Flags:* © admin_design/Shutterstock RF

social
policy and socialization |
Child Care around the World

Child care programs are not just babysitting services; they have an enormous influence on the development of young children—an influence that has been growing with the movement of more and more women into the paid labor force. The rise in single-parent families, increased job opportunities for women, and the need for additional family income have all propelled mothers of young children into the working world. Who should care for the children of working parents during working hours?

Looking at the Issue

Preschoolers typically are not cared for by their parents. Eighty-eight percent of employed mothers depend on others to care for their children, and 30 percent of mothers who aren't employed have regular care arrangements. In fact, children under age five are more likely to be cared for on a daily basis by their grandparents or other relatives than by their parents. Over a third of them are cared for by nonrelatives in nursery schools, Head Start programs, day care centers, family day care, and other arrangements (Bureau of the Census 2015b).

Researchers have found that high-quality child care centers do not adversely affect the socialization of children; in fact, good day care benefits children. The value of preschool programs was documented in a series of studies conducted in the United States. Researchers found no significant differences in infants who had received extensive nonmaternal care compared with those who had been cared for solely by their mothers. They also reported that more and more infants in the United States are being placed in child care outside the home, and that overall, the quality of those arrangements is better than has been found in previous studies. It is difficult, however, to generalize about child care, since there is so much variability among day care providers, and even among government policies from one state to another (Campbell et al. 2014; NICHD 2007).

Few people in the United States or elsewhere can afford the luxury of having a parent stay at home, or of paying for high-quality live-in child care. For millions of mothers and fathers, finding the right kind of child care is a challenge both to parenting and to the pocketbook. At present, the federal government supports child care through subsidized programs, which target low-income families, and income tax credits, which benefit families with moderate incomes. The annual expenditure to assist low-income parents is about $12 billion; the expenditure to support parents with moderate incomes is $58 billion. Unfortunately, collectively these programs fall far short of meeting the needs of low-income families in the United States, where child care costs are the third highest among industrial countries (Cushing-Daniels and Zedlewski 2008; Hamm and Martin 2015).

Courtesy, Communicare, Perth, Australia

Children play at the Communicare day care center in Perth, Australia. The Australian government subsidizes children's attendance at day care and afterschool programs from birth to age 12.

Applying Sociology

Studies that assess the quality of child care outside the home reflect the micro level of analysis and the interest of interactionists in the impact of face-to-face interaction. These studies also explore macro-level implications for the functioning of social institutions like the family. Some of the issues surrounding day care have also been of interest to those who take the conflict perspective.

In the United States, high-quality day care is not equally available to all families. Parents in affluent communities have an easier time finding day care than those in poor or working-class communities. Finding *affordable* child care is also a problem. Viewed from a conflict perspective, child care costs are an especially serious burden for lower-class families. The poorest families spend 25 percent of their income for preschool child care, whereas families who are *not*

—*Continued*

poor pay only 6 percent or less of their income. Despite these problems, subsidized child care has steadily declined over the last decade.

Feminist theorists echo the concern of conflict theorists that high-quality child care receives little government support because it is regarded as "merely a way to let women work." Nearly all child care workers (97 percent) are women; many find themselves in low-status, minimum-wage jobs. Typically, food servers, messengers, and gas station attendants make more money than the 1.3 million child care workers in the United States, whose average annual salary of $19,510 (or $9.38 per hour) puts them right at the poverty level for a family of three (Bureau of Labor Statistics 2014b; Proctor et al. 2016:43).

Initiating Policy

Policies regarding child care outside the home vary throughout the world. Most developing nations do not have the economic base to provide subsidized child care. Thus, working mothers rely largely on relatives or take their children to work. In the comparatively wealthy industrialized countries of western Europe, government provides child care as a basic service, at little or no expense to parents. But even those countries with tax-subsidized programs occasionally fall short of the need for high-quality child care.

When policymakers decide that child care is desirable, they must determine the degree to which taxpayers should subsidize it. In Sweden and Denmark, one-half to two-thirds of preschoolers are in government-subsidized child care full-time. In the United States, annual fees for full-time child care of a four-year-old range from an average of $3,397 in Mississippi to an average of $12,781 in Massachusetts (Immervoll and Barber 2005; Child Care Aware 2015).

Japan is facing a special dilemma. Traditionally, married women and certainly married mothers did not remain in the labor force. Although this social pattern is slowly changing, the availability of day care has not kept pace. Many Japanese policymakers have difficulty recognizing the need for day care. "Is your work so important that you must put your baby in child-care?" they ask. "Why are you being so self-centered?" Little wonder that a single private day care center in Japan recently had a waiting list of 25,000 children (Tabuchi 2013:A9).

We have a long way to go in making high-quality child care more affordable and accessible, not just in the United States but throughout the world as well. In an attempt to reduce government spending, many European countries reduced subsidies. Indeed, 53 percent of women report that they either do not work or are forced to work part-time because child care is too expensive. Another 25 percent are unable to locate child care services. Increasingly European parents, like those in the United States, are forced to cobble together child care out of after-school programs and informal care with friends and relatives (Janta 2014).

TAKE THE ISSUE WITH YOU

1. Were you ever in a day care program? If so, do you recall the experience as good or bad? In general, do you think it is desirable to expose young children to the socializing influence of day care?

2. In the view of conflict theorists, child care receives little government support because it is "merely a way to let women work." Can you think of other explanations?

3. Should the costs of day care programs be paid by government, by the private sector, or entirely by parents?

MODULE 15 | Recap and Review

Summary

Important agents of socialization include the family, schools, peer groups, the mass media, the workplace, religious institutions, and the state.

1. As the primary agents of socialization, parents play a critical role in guiding children into those **gender roles** deemed appropriate in a society.

2. Like the family, schools in the United States have an explicit mandate to socialize people—especially children—into the norms and values of our culture.

3. Peer groups and the mass media, especially television and the Internet, are important agents of socialization for adolescents.

4. Socialization in the workplace begins with part-time employment while we are in school and continues as we work full-time and change jobs throughout our lives.

5. Religion and the state shape the socialization process by regulating the life course and influencing our views of appropriate behaviors at particular ages.

6. As more and more mothers of young children have entered the labor market, the demand for child care has increased dramatically, posing policy questions for many nations around the world.

Thinking Critically

1. How would functionalist and conflict theorists differ in their analysis of socialization by the mass media?

2. What sanctions limit participation in social networking? Describe the rules you have observed that limit the way people access and use online social networks. What are the purposes of such sanctions?

Key Terms

Gender role

Mastering This Chapter

© Blend Images-KidStock/Getty Images RF

taking sociology with you

1 For two days, keep a record of your use of the mass media—television, the Internet, and so on—including what you watched, read, or communicated and your reasons for doing so. Then take the role of a sociologist and ask how you might have been socialized by the media you used. What norms and values were you exposed to, and how did they affect you?

2 Interview a person who has recently changed jobs. Ask about the process of resocialization required

by the new job. Was the job change voluntary or involuntary, and how did it affect the person's adjustment? Which of the concepts you learned in this chapter seem relevant to the experience?

3 Which role transitions have you experienced in the past three years, and which do you anticipate in the next three years? How do you think these transitions affect the way you work? the way you interact with others?

key terms

Anticipatory socialization Processes of socialization in which a person rehearses for future positions, occupations, and social relationships.

Cognitive theory of development The theory that children's thought progresses through four stages of development.

Degradation ceremony An aspect of the socialization process within some total institutions, in which people are subjected to humiliating rituals.

Dramaturgical approach A view of social interaction in which people are seen as theatrical performers.

Face-work The efforts people make to maintain the proper image and avoid public embarrassment.

Gender role Expectations regarding the proper behavior, attitudes, and activities of males and females.

Generalized other The attitudes, viewpoints, and expectations of society as a whole that a child takes into account in his or her behavior.

Impression management The altering of the presentation of the self in order to create distinctive appearances and satisfy particular audiences.

Life course approach A research orientation in which sociologists and other social scientists look closely at the social factors that influence people throughout their lives, from birth to death.

Looking-glass self A concept that emphasizes the self as the product of our social interactions.

Personality A person's typical patterns of attitudes, needs, characteristics, and behavior.

Resocialization The process of discarding former behavior patterns and accepting new ones as part of a transition in one's life.

Rite of passage A ritual marking the symbolic transition from one social position to another.

Role taking The process of mentally assuming the perspective of another and responding from that imagined viewpoint.

Self A distinct identity that sets us apart from others.

Significant other An individual who is most important in the development of the self, such as a parent, friend, or teacher.

Socialization The lifelong process in which people learn the attitudes, values, and behaviors appropriate for members of a particular culture.

Total institution An institution that regulates all aspects of a person's life under a single authority, such as a prison, the military, a mental hospital, or a convent.

Read each question carefully and then select the best answer.

1. Which of the following social scientists used the phrase *looking-glass self* to emphasize that the self is the product of our social interactions with other people?
   a. George Herbert Mead
   b. Charles Horton Cooley
   c. Erving Goffman
   d. Jean Piaget

2. In what he called the *play stage* of socialization, George Herbert Mead asserted that people mentally assume the perspectives of others, thereby enabling them to respond from that imagined viewpoint. This process is referred to as
   a. role taking.
   b. the generalized other.
   c. the significant other.
   d. impression management.

3. George Herbert Mead is best known for his theory of what?
   a. presentation of the self
   b. cognitive development
   c. the self
   d. impression management

4. Suppose a clerk tries to appear busier than he or she actually is when a supervisor happens to be watching. Erving Goffman would study this behavior from what approach?
   a. functionalist
   b. conflict
   c. psychological
   d. interactionist

5. According to child psychologist Jean Piaget's cognitive theory of development, children begin to use words and symbols to distinguish objects and ideas during which stage in the development of the thought process?
   a. the sensorimotor stage
   b. the preoperational stage
   c. the concrete operational stage
   d. the formal operational stage

6. On the first day of basic training in the army, recruits' civilian clothes are replaced by army "greens," their hair is shaved, they lose their privacy, and they find that they must use communal bathrooms. All these humiliating activities are part of
   a. becoming a significant other.
   b. impression management.
   c. a degradation ceremony.
   d. face-work.

7. Which social institution is considered to be the most important agent of socialization in the United States, especially for children?
   a. the family
   b. the school
   c. the peer group
   d. the mass media

8. The term *gender role* refers to
   a. the biological fact that we are male or female.
   b. a role that is given to us by a teacher.
   c. a role that is given to us in a play.
   d. expectations regarding the proper behavior, attitudes, and activities of males and females.

9. Which sociological perspective emphasizes that schools in the United States foster competition through built-in systems of reward and punishment?
   a. the functionalist perspective
   b. the conflict perspective
   c. the interactionist perspective
   d. the psychological perspective

10. Which of the following statements about teenagers in Syria is true?
    a. They have lost much of their peer group due to death and relocation.
    b. They have lost peers who have joined fundamentalist groups.
    c. They attempt to stay in contact with their pre-war group through social media.
    d. all of the above

11. _____ is the term used by sociologists in referring to the lifelong process whereby people learn the attitudes, values, and behaviors appropriate for members of a particular culture.

12. In everyday speech, the term _____ is used to refer to a person's typical patterns of attitudes, needs, characteristics, and behavior.

13. Studies of twins raised apart suggest that both _____ and _____ influence human development.

14. A _____ _____ is an individual such as a parent, friend, or teacher who is most important in the development of the self.

15. Early work in _____, such as that by Sigmund Freud, stressed the role of inborn drives—among them the drive for sexual gratification—in channeling human behavior.

16. The Swiss psychologist Jean Piaget developed the _____ theory of development.

17. Preparation for many aspects of adult life begins with _____ socialization during childhood and adolescence and continues throughout our lives as we prepare for new responsibilities.

18. Resocialization is particularly effective when it occurs within a(n) _____ institution.

19. The _____ perspective emphasizes the role of schools in teaching the values and customs of the larger society.

20. As children grow older, the family becomes less important in social development, while _____ groups become more important.

Answers

1 (b); 2 (c); 3 (d); 4 (c); 5 (a); 6 (c); 7 (a); 8 (d); 9 (d); 10 (c); 11 socialization; 12 personality; 13 heredity, environment; 14 significant other; 15 psychology; 16 cognitive; 17 anticipatory; 18 total; 19 functionalist; 20 peer

5

Social Interaction, Groups, and Social Structure

© Caia Image/Glow Images RF

Groups of different sizes help individuals to navigate through the larger social world, including both informal interactions and complex social organizations.

Courtesy of Phil Zimbardo, Stanford University

If you were a prison guard, would you mistreat the inmates?

To answer this question, social psychologist Philip Zimbardo created a mock prison and enlisted college students to serve as the inmates and guards.

"The quiet of a summer Sunday morning in Palo Alto, California, was shattered by a screeching squad car siren as police swept through the city picking up college students in a surprise mass arrest. Each suspect was charged with a felony; warned of his constitutional rights; spread-eagled against the car; searched, handcuffed, and carted off in the back seat of the squad car to the police station for booking.

After being fingerprinted and having identification forms prepared for his 'jacket' (central information file), each prisoner was left isolated in a detention cell to wonder what he had done to get himself into this mess. After a while, he was blindfolded and transported to the 'Stanford County Prison.' Here he began the induction process of becoming a prisoner— stripped naked, skin searched, deloused, and issued a uniform, bedding, soap, and towel. By late afternoon when nine such arrests had been completed, these youthful 'first offenders' sat in dazed silence on the cots in their barren cells. These men were part of a very unusual kind of prison, an experimental or mock prison, created by social psychologists for the purpose of intensively studying the effects of imprisonment upon volunteer research subjects. When we planned our two-week-long simulation of prison life, we were primarily concerned about understanding the process by which people adapt to the novel and alien environment in which those called 'prisoners' lose their liberty, civil rights, independence, and privacy, while those called 'guards' gain social power by accepting the responsibility for controlling and managing the lives of their dependent charges. . . .

Our final sample of participants (10 prisoners and 11 guards) were selected from over 75 volunteers recruited through ads in the city and campus newspapers. . . . Half were randomly assigned to role-play being guards, the others to be prisoners. Thus, there were no measurable differences between the guards and the prisoners at the start of this experiment. . . .

At the end of only six days we had to close down our mock prison because what we saw was frightening. It was no longer apparent to most of the subjects (or to us) where reality ended and their roles began. The majority had indeed become prisoners or guards, no longer able to clearly differentiate between role-playing and self. There were dramatic changes in virtually every aspect of their behavior, thinking, and feeling. In less than a week the experience of imprisonment undid (temporarily) a lifetime of learning: human values were suspended; self-concepts were challenged; and the ugliest, most base, pathological side of human nature surfaced. We were horrified because we saw some boys (guards) treat others as if they were despicable animals, taking pleasure in cruelty, while other boys (prisoners) became servile, dehumanized robots who thought only of escape, of their own individual survival, and of their mounting hatred for the guards."

(Zimbardo 1972:4); Quotation from Philip G. Zimbardo, et al. 1974. "The Psychology of Imprisonment: Privation, Power, and Pathology." In Z. Rubin (ed.), Doing Unto Others: Explorations in Social Behavior, pp. 61–63. Used by permission of Philip G. Zimbardo, Inc.

> *The quiet of a summer Sunday morning in Palo Alto, California, was shattered by a screeching squad car siren as police swept through the city picking up college students in a surprise mass arrest.*

I n this study, directed and described by author Philip Zimbardo, college students adopted the patterns of social interaction expected of guards and prisoners when they were placed in a mock prison. Sociologists use the term *social interaction* to refer to the ways in which people respond to one another, whether face-to-face or over the telephone or on the computer. In the mock prison, social interactions between guards and prisoners were highly impersonal. The guards addressed the prisoners by number rather than name, and they wore reflective sunglasses that made eye contact impossible.

As in many real-life prisons, the simulated prison at Stanford University had a social structure in which guards held virtually total control over prisoners. The term *social structure* refers to the way in which a society is organized into predictable relationships. The social structure of Zimbardo's mock prison influenced how the guards and prisoners interacted. Zimbardo and his colleagues (2009:516) note that it was a real prison "in the minds of the jailers and their captives." His simulated prison experiment, first conducted more than 30 years ago, has subsequently been repeated (with similar findings) both in the United States and in other countries.

In these modules we will study social structure and its effect on our social interactions. What determines a person's status in society? How do our social roles affect our social interactions? What is the place of social institutions such as the family, religion, and government in our social structure? How can we better understand and manage large organizations such as multinational corporations? We'll begin by considering how social interactions shape the way we view the world around us. Next, we'll focus on the five basic elements of social structure: statuses, social roles,

groups, social networks, and social institutions such as the family, religion, government, and the mass media. We'll see that functionalists, conflict theorists, and interactionists approach social institutions quite differently. Finally, we'll compare our modern social structure with simpler forms, using typologies developed by Émile Durkheim, Ferdinand Tönnies, and Gerhard Lenski. The Social Policy section at the end of the chapter focuses on the changing role of labor unions.

<table>
<tr><td>M O D U L E</td><td>16</td><td>Social Interaction
and Social Structure</td></tr>
</table>

Zimbardo's experiment took on new relevance in 2004, in the wake of shocking revelations of prisoner abuse at the U.S.-run Abu Ghraib military facility in Iraq. Graphic "trophy photos" showed U.S. soldiers humiliating naked Iraqi prisoners and threatening to attack them with police dogs. The structure of the wartime prison, coupled with intense pressure on military intelligence officers to secure information regarding terrorist plots, contributed to the breakdown in the guards' behavior. But Zimbardo himself noted that the guards' depraved conduct could have been predicted simply on the basis of his research. So strong was public reaction to the Abu Ghraib scandal that in 2009, during his first week in office, President Barack Obama declared that henceforth interrogators would use only noncoercive methods for questioning suspected terrorists (Ratnesar 2011; Zimbardo 2015).

Social Interaction and Reality

The two concepts of social interaction and social structure are central to sociological study. They are closely related to socialization, the process through which people learn the attitudes, values, and behaviors appropriate to their culture. When the students in Zimbardo's experiment entered the mock prison, they began a process of resocialization. In that process, they adjusted to a new social structure and learned new rules for social interaction.

When someone in a crowd shoves you, do you automatically push back? Or do you consider the circumstances of the incident and the attitude of the instigator before you react? Chances are you do the latter. According to sociologist Herbert Blumer (1969:79), the distinctive characteristic of **social interaction** among people is that "human beings interpret or 'define' each other's actions instead of merely reacting to each other's actions." In other words, our response to someone's behavior is based on the *meaning* we attach to his or her actions. Reality is shaped by our perceptions, evaluations, and definitions.

These meanings typically reflect the norms and values of the dominant culture and our socialization experiences within that culture. As interactionists emphasize, the meanings that we attach to people's behavior are shaped by our interactions with them and with the larger society. Social reality is literally constructed from our social interactions (Berger and Luckmann 1966).

How do we define our social reality? Consider something as simple as how we regard tattoos. At one time, most of us in the United States considered tattoos weird or kooky. We associated them with fringe countercultural groups, such as punk rockers, biker gangs, and skinheads. Among many people, a tattoo elicited an automatic negative response. Now, however, so many people have tattoos—including society's trendsetters and major sports figures—and the ritual of getting a tattoo has become so legitimized, that mainstream culture regards tattoos differently. At this point, as a result of increased social interaction with tattooed people, tattoos look perfectly at home to us in a number of settings.

The nature of social interaction and what constitutes reality varies across cultures. In Western societies, with their emphasis on romantic love, couples see marriage as a relationship as well as a social status. From Valentine's Day flowers to more informal, everyday gestures, professions of love are an expected part of marriage.

In Japan, however, marriage is considered more a social status than a relationship. Although many or most Japanese couples undoubtedly do love each other, saying "I love you" does not come easily to them, especially not to husbands. Nor do most husbands call their wives by name (they prefer "Mother") or look them in the eyes. In 2006, in an effort to change these restrictive customs, some Japanese men formed the Devoted Husband Organization, which has been sponsoring a new holiday, Beloved Wives Day. In 2008, this group organized an event called Shout Your Love from the Middle of a Cabbage Patch Day. Dozens of men stood in a cabbage patch north of Tokyo and shouted, "I love you!" to their wives, some of whom had never heard their husbands say those words. In another rare gesture, husbands pledged to be home by 8 p.m. that day (Japan Aisaika Organization 2012; Kambayashi 2008).

© CMCD/Getty Images RF

The ability to define social reality reflects a group's power within a society. In fact, one of the most crucial aspects of the relationship between dominant and subordinate groups is the ability of the dominant or majority group to define a society's values. Sociologist William I. Thomas (1923), an early critic of theories of racial and gender differences, recognized that the "definition of the situation" could mold the thinking and personality of the individual. Writing from an interactionist perspective, Thomas observed that people respond not only to the objective features of a person or situation but also to the *meaning* that person or situation has for them. For example, in Philip Zimbardo's mock prison experiment, student "guards" and "prisoners" accepted the definition of the situation (including the traditional roles and behavior associated with being a guard or prisoner) and acted accordingly.

As we have seen throughout the past 60 years—first in the civil rights movement of the 1950s and 1960s and since then among such groups as women, the elderly, gays and lesbians, and people with disabilities—an important aspect of the process of social change involves redefining or reconstructing social reality. Members of subordinate groups challenge traditional definitions and begin to perceive and experience reality in a new way.

Elements of Social Structure

All social interaction takes place within a **social structure**, including those interactions that redefine social reality. For purposes of study, we can break down any social structure into five elements: statuses, social roles, groups, social networks, and social institutions. These elements make up social structure just as a foundation, walls, and ceilings make up a building's structure.

Statuses

We normally think of a person's *status* as having to do with influence, wealth, and fame. However, sociologists use the term **status** to refer to any of the full range of socially defined positions within a large group or society, from the lowest to the highest. Within our society, a person can occupy the status of president of the United States, fruit picker, son or daughter, violinist, teenager, resident of Minneapolis, dental technician, or neighbor. A person can hold a number of statuses at the same time.

Ascribed and Achieved Status Sociologists view some statuses as *ascribed* and others as *achieved* (Figure 16-1). An **ascribed status** is assigned to a person by society without regard for the person's unique talents or characteristics. Generally, the assignment takes place at birth; thus, a person's racial background, gender, and age are all considered ascribed statuses. Though these characteristics are biological in origin, they are significant mainly because of the *social* meanings they have in our culture. Conflict theorists are especially interested in ascribed statuses, since they often confer privileges or reflect a person's membership in a subordinate group (Linton 1936).

In most cases, we can do little to change an ascribed status, but we can attempt to change the traditional constraints associated with it. For example, the Gray Panthers—an activist political group founded in 1971 to work for the rights of older people—have tried to modify society's negative and confining stereotypes of the elderly. As a result of their work and that of other groups supporting older citizens, the ascribed status of "senior citizen" is no longer as difficult for millions of older people.

An ascribed status does not necessarily have the same social meaning in every society. In a cross-cultural study, sociologist Gary Huang (1988) confirmed the long-held view that respect for the elderly is an important cultural norm in China. In many cases, the prefix "old" is used respectfully: calling someone "old teacher" or "old person" is like calling a judge in the United States "your honor." Huang points out that positive age-seniority language distinctions are uncommon in the United States; consequently, we view the term *old man* as more of an insult than a celebration of seniority and wisdom.

Unlike ascribed statuses, an **achieved status** comes to us largely through our own efforts. Both "computer programmer" and "prison guard" are achieved statuses, as are "lawyer," "pianist," "sorority member," "convict," and "social worker." We must do something to acquire an achieved status—go to school, learn a skill, establish a friendship, invent a new product. But as we will see in the next section, our ascribed status heavily influences our achieved status.

Before we continue, consider the complexity of a status. *First,* ascribed status heavily influences achieved status. Being male, for example, would decrease the likelihood that a person would be encouraged to consider a career in child care. *Second,* a given status may or may not be desirable. Your

FIGURE 16-1 **Social Statuses**

Ascribed statuses

Daughter
20 years old
Latina
Female
Sister
Me
Classmate
Student
Roommate
Teammate
Employee
Friend

Achieved statuses

Source: Developed by author. *Photo:* © Lew Robertson/Getty Images RF

family background, an ascribed status, can place you in a positive or negative position. An achieved status—criminal or hero—can also be desirable or not. *Third,* some statuses can be either achieved or ascribed, depending upon the individual's circumstances. Consider religion—it is an ascribed status if a person carries on the family's faith, but it is an achieved status if he or she settles on a religion after exploring a variety of belief systems (Foladare 1969).

Master Status Each person holds many different and sometimes conflicting statuses; some may connote higher social position and some, lower position. How, then, do others view one's overall social position? According to sociologist Everett Hughes (1945), societies deal with inconsistencies by agreeing that certain statuses are more important than others. A **master status** is a status that dominates other statuses and thereby determines a person's general position in society. For example, Arthur Ashe, who died of AIDS in 1993, had a remarkable career as a tennis star, but at the end of his life, his status as a well-known personality with AIDS may have outweighed his statuses as a retired athlete, author, and political activist. Throughout the world, many people with disabilities find that their status as disabled receives undue weight, overshadowing their actual ability to perform successfully in meaningful employment (Box 16-1).

Our society gives such importance to race and gender that they often dominate our lives. These ascribed statuses frequently influence our achieved status. The Black activist Malcolm X (1925–1965), an eloquent and controversial advocate of Black power and Black pride during the early 1960s, recalled that his feelings and perspectives changed dramatically in middle school. Elected class president and finishing near the top of his class academically, he had developed a positive outlook. However, his teachers, all of them White, discouraged him from taking more challenging courses, which they felt were not appropriate for Black students. When his eighth-grade English teacher, a White man, advised him that his goal of becoming a lawyer was not realistic, and encouraged him instead to become a carpenter, Malcolm X concluded that his being a Black man (ascribed status) was an obstacle to his dream of becoming a lawyer (achieved status). In the United States, the ascribed statuses of race and gender can function as master statuses that have an important impact on one's potential to achieve a desired professional and social status (Malcolm X [1964] 1999:37; Marable 2011:36–38).

Social Roles

What Are Social Roles? Throughout our lives, we acquire what sociologists call social roles. A **social role** is a set of expectations for people who occupy a given social position or status. Thus, in the United States, we expect that cab drivers will know how to get around a city, that receptionists will be reliable in handling phone messages, and that police officers will take action if they see a citizen being threatened. With each

© ZUMA Press, Inc./Alamy

Ascribed status may intersect with a person's achieved status. This woman's achieved status as a low-income worker, combined with her minority ethnic status, contrast sharply with the high status of her customer.

distinctive social status—whether ascribed or achieved—come particular role expectations. However, actual performance varies from individual to individual. One secretary may assume extensive administrative responsibilities, while another may focus on clerical duties. Similarly, in Philip Zimbardo's mock prison experiment, some students were brutal and sadistic guards; others were not.

Roles are a significant component of social structure. Viewed from a functionalist perspective, roles contribute to a society's stability by enabling members to anticipate the behavior of others and to pattern their actions accordingly. Yet social roles can also be dysfunctional if they restrict people's interactions and relationships. If we view a person *only* as a "police officer" or "supervisor," it will be difficult to relate to him or her as a friend or neighbor.

Role Conflict Imagine the delicate situation of a woman who has worked for a decade on an assembly line in an electrical plant, and has recently been named supervisor of her unit. How is this woman expected to relate to her longtime friends and co-workers? Should she still go out to lunch with them, as she has done almost daily for years? Is it her responsibility to recommend the firing of an old friend who cannot keep up with the demands of the assembly line?

Role conflict occurs when incompatible expectations arise from two or more social positions held by the same person. Fulfillment of the roles associated with one status may directly violate the roles linked to a second status. In the example just given, the newly promoted supervisor will most likely experience a sharp conflict between her social and occupational roles. Such role conflicts call for important ethical choices. The new supervisor will have to make a difficult decision about how much allegiance she owes her friend and how much she owes her employers, who have given her supervisory responsibilities.

BOX 16-1

Research Today

Disability as a Master Status

Throughout history and around the world, people with disabilities have been subjected to cruel and inhuman treatment. For example, in the 20th century, the disabled were frequently viewed as subhuman creatures who were a menace to society. In Japan more than 16,000 women with disabilities were involuntarily sterilized with government approval from 1945 to 1995. Sweden apologized for the same action taken against 62,000 of its citizens in the 1970s.

Such blatantly hostile treatment of people with disabilities has given way to a *medical model,* in which the disabled are viewed as chronic patients. Increasingly, however, people concerned with the rights of the disabled have criticized this model as well. In their view, it is the unnecessary and discriminatory barriers present in the environment—both physical and attitudinal—that stand in the way of people with disabilities, more than any biological limitations. Applying a *civil rights model,* activists emphasize that those with disabilities face widespread prejudice, discrimination, and segregation. For example, most voting places are inaccessible to wheelchair users and fail to provide ballots that can be used by those unable to read print.

Drawing on the earlier work of Erving Goffman, contemporary sociologists have suggested that society attaches a stigma to many forms of disability, a stigma that leads to prejudicial treatment. People with disabilities frequently observe that the nondisabled see them only as blind, wheelchair users, and so forth, rather than as complex human beings with individual strengths and weaknesses, whose blindness or use of a wheelchair is merely one aspect of their lives.

Although discrimination against the disabled occurs around the world, attitudes are changing. The African nation of Botswana has plans to assist its disabled, most of whom live in rural areas and need special services for mobility and economic development. In many countries, disability rights activists are targeting issues essential to overcoming this master status and becoming a full citizen, including employment, housing, education, and access to public buildings.

> In Japan more than 16,000 women with disabilities were involuntarily sterilized with government approval from 1945 to 1995.

© Image Source/PunchStock RF

LET'S DISCUSS

1. Does your campus present barriers to disabled students? If so, what kinds of barriers—physical, attitudinal, or both? Describe some of them.

2. Why do you think nondisabled people see disability as the most important characteristic of a disabled person? What can be done to help people see beyond the wheel-chair and the Seeing Eye dog?

Sources: Albrecht 2004; Goffman 1963; Murphy 1997; *Newsday* 1997; R. Schaefer 2015; J. Shapiro 1993.

Another type of role conflict occurs when individuals move into occupations that are not common among people with their ascribed status. Male preschool teachers and female police officers experience this type of role conflict. In the latter case, female officers must strive to reconcile their workplace role in law enforcement with the societal view of a woman's role, which does not embrace many skills needed in police work. And while female police officers encounter sexual harassment, as women do throughout the labor force, they must also deal with the "code of silence," an informal norm that precludes their implicating fellow officers in wrongdoing (Fletcher 1995; S. Martin 1994).

 use your **sociological imagination**

If you were a male nurse, what aspects of role conflict might you experience? Now imagine you are a professional boxer and a woman. What conflicting role expectations might that involve? In both cases, how well do you think you would handle role conflict?

Role Strain Role conflict describes the situation of a person dealing with the challenge of occupying two social positions simultaneously. However, even a single position can cause problems. Sociologists use the term **role strain** to describe the difficulty that arises when the same social position imposes conflicting demands and expectations.

People who belong to minority cultures may experience role strain while working in the mainstream culture. Criminologist Larry Gould (2002) interviewed officers of the Navajo Nation Police Department about their relations with conventional law enforcement officials, such as sheriffs and FBI agents. Besides enforcing the law, Navajo Nation officers practice an alternative form of justice known as Peacemaking, in which they seek reconciliation between the parties to a crime. The officers expressed great confidence in Peacemaking, but worried that if they did not make arrests, other law enforcement officials would think they were too soft, or "just taking care of their own." Regardless of the strength of their ties to traditional Navajo ways, all felt the strain of being considered "too Navajo" or "not Navajo enough."

Role Exit Often, when we think of assuming a social role, we focus on the preparation and anticipatory socialization a person

© Mimotito/Digital Vision RF

In 2015, President Barack Obama issued an order to change the name of the nation's tallest peak, Mount McKinley, back to Denali, its original Athabascan name. Alaska's elected officials had been asking for this change for over 40 years. Republicans protested the decision as yet another example of the President sidestepping Congress. Senator Lisa Murkowski (R-Alaska), praised the decision, thus resolving her role conflict by siding with her state rather than her party.

© Valentino Photography/Shutterstock RF

According to sociologist Helen Rose Fuchs Ebaugh, role exit is a four-stage process. Is this transgender person in the first or the fourth stage of changing genders?

undergoes for that role. Such is true if a person is about to become an attorney, a chef, a spouse, or a parent. Yet until recently, social scientists have given little attention to the adjustments involved in *leaving* social roles.

Sociologist Helen Rose Fuchs Ebaugh (1988) developed the term **role exit** to describe the process of disengagement from a role that is central to one's self-identity in order to establish a new role and identity. Drawing on interviews with 185 people—among them ex-convicts, divorced men and women, recovering alcoholics, ex-nuns, former doctors, retirees, and transsexuals—Ebaugh (herself an ex-nun) studied the process of voluntarily exiting from significant social roles.

Ebaugh has offered a four-stage model of role exit. The first stage begins with *doubt.* The person experiences frustration, burnout, or simply unhappiness with an accustomed status and the roles associated with the social position. The second stage involves a *search for alternatives.* A person who is unhappy with his or her career may take a leave of absence; an unhappily married couple may begin what they see as a temporary separation.

The third stage of role exit is the *action stage* or *departure.* Ebaugh found that the vast majority of her respondents could identify a clear turning point that made them feel it was essential to take final action and leave their jobs, end their marriages, or engage in another type of role exit. Twenty percent of respondents saw their role exit as a gradual, evolutionary process that had no single turning point.

The fourth stage of role exit involves the *creation of a new identity.* Some young people participate in role exit when they make the transition to college. They leave behind the role of offspring living at home and take on the role of somewhat independent college students living with peers in a dorm. Sociologist Ira Silver (1996) has studied the central role that material objects play in this transition. The objects students choose to leave at home (like stuffed animals and dolls) are associated

with their prior identities. They may remain deeply attached to those objects, but do not want them to be seen as part of their new identities at college. The objects they bring with them symbolize how they now see themselves and how they wish to be perceived. iPhones and wall posters, for example, are calculated to say, "This is me."

Groups

In sociological terms, a **group** is any number of people with similar norms, values, and expectations who interact with one another on a regular basis. The members of a women's basketball team, a hospital's business office, a synagogue, or a symphony orchestra constitute a group. However, the residents of a suburb would not be considered a group, since they rarely interact with one another at one time.

Groups play a vital part in a society's social structure. Much of our social interaction takes place within groups and is influenced by their norms and sanctions. Being a teenager or a retired person takes on special meanings when we interact within groups designed for people with that particular status. The expectations associated with many social roles, including those accompanying the statuses of brother, sister, and student, become more clearly defined in the context of a group.

Social Networks and Obesity

Over the past two generations, obesity has become a public health problem in the United States. To explain the trend toward excess weight, researchers have focused on Americans' nutritional practices, as well as on their genetic tendencies. Another variable that contributes to obesity, less obvious than diet and heredity, is social networking.

The people we network with have a powerful effect on our behavior, for better or worse, and that effect includes our health. Researchers identified networking as a factor in the course of a long-term heart health survey, during which they tracked the weight of 12,067 respondents. At the same time, they mapped the social networks that respondents belonged to. Over the three decades since the survey began, they have noted that weight gain in one person is often associated with weight gain in his or her friends, siblings, spouse, and neighbors. In fact, a person's chances of becoming obese increased by 57 percent if a friend became

> Weight gain in one person is often associated with weight gain in his or her friends, siblings, spouse, and neighbors.

overweight during the same period. This association, they found, was attributable solely to selectivity in the choice of friends—that is, to people of a certain weight seeking out others of roughly the same weight.

This study shows that social networks do influence the way people behave. More important, the results suggest that networking could be exploited to spread positive health behaviors—for example, by recruiting friends to participate in a person's weight-loss

plan. Other possibilities include persuading friends to wear pedometers and share data on the distance they walk, or to compete with one another in active video games, like Nintendo Wii Fit or Microsoft Kinect. Through a similar approach, health practitioners could include social networking in efforts to control smoking, drinking, and drug abuse.

LET'S DISCUSS

1. Have you ever tried to lose weight, and if so, did your cluster of friends and family help or hinder you? In your experience, do people who are overweight tend to cluster in separate groups from those of normal weight?

2. Besides public health campaigns, what applications can you think of for research on social networking?

Sources: Christakis and Fowler 2007, 2009; Haas et al. 2010; Harmon 2011; Li et al. 2013.

Social Networks

Groups do not merely serve to define other elements of the social structure, such as roles and statuses; they also link the individual with the larger society. We all belong to a number of different groups, and through our acquaintances make connections with people in different social circles. These connections are known as a **social network**—a series of social relationships that links a person directly to others, and through them indirectly to still more people. Social networks are one of the five basic elements of social structure.

Broadly speaking, social networks encompass all the routine social interaction we have with other individuals. Traditionally, researchers have limited their network studies to face-to-face contacts and phone conversations, although recently they have begun to study interaction through all types of new media. We should be careful, however, not to equate social media like Instagram with social networks, which include a much broader spectrum of social interaction.

Social networks can center on virtually any activity, from sharing job information to exchanging news and gossip, or even sharing sex. In the mid-1990s, sociologists studied romantic relationships at a high school with about 1,000 students. They found that about 61 percent of the girls had been sexually active over the past 18 months. Among the sexually active respondents, the researchers counted only 63 steady couples, or pairs with no other partners. A much larger group of 288 students—almost a third of the sample—was involved in a free-flowing network of relationships (Bearman et al. 2004).

This research on high schoolers' sexual activity, an example of applied sociology, has clear implications for public health. Box 16-2 describes a similar but longer-term study in which public health officials used network analysis to curb obesity.

Involvement in social networks—commonly known as *networking*—is especially valuable in finding employment. Albert Einstein was successful in finding a job only when a classmate's father put him in touch with his future employer. These kinds of contacts—even those that are weak and distant—can be crucial in establishing social networks and facilitating the transmission of information.

During the recent economic downturn, electronic social networks have served a new purpose, encouraging the jobless. Websites and chat rooms that cannot locate jobs for those who have been thrown out of work concentrate instead on helping them to stick together, support one another, and maintain a positive attitude. For the unemployed, online conversations with friends or even strangers in the same predicament can be an invaluable morale booster (R. Scherer 2010b).

Research indicates, however, that both in person and online, not everyone participates equally in social networks. Women and racial and ethnic minorities are at a disadvantage when seeking new and better job opportunities or social contacts (Trimble and Kmec 2011).

Social Institutions

The mass media, the government, the economy, the family, and the health care system are all examples of social institutions found in our society. **Social institutions** are organized patterns of beliefs and behavior centered on basic social needs, such as replacing personnel (the family) and preserving order (the government).

A close look at social institutions gives sociologists insight into the structure of a society. Consider religion, for example. The institution of religion adapts to the segment of society that it serves. Church work has very different meanings for ministers who serve a skid row area and those who serve a suburban middle-class community. Religious leaders assigned to a skid row mission will focus on tending to the ill and providing food and shelter. In contrast, clergy in affluent suburbs will be occupied with counseling those considering marriage and divorce, arranging youth activities, and overseeing cultural events.

Functionalist Perspective One way to understand social institutions is to see how they fulfill essential functions. Anthropologists and sociologists have identified five major tasks, or functional prerequisites, that a society or relatively permanent group must accomplish if it is to survive:

1. *Replacing personnel.* Any group or society must replace personnel when they die, leave, or become incapacitated. This task is accomplished through such means as immigration, annexation of neighboring groups, conversion of followers, or sexual reproduction. The Shakers, a religious sect that came to the United States in 1774, are a conspicuous example of a group that has *failed* to replace personnel. Their religious beliefs commit the Shakers to celibacy; to survive, the group must recruit new members. At first, the Shakers proved quite successful in attracting members, reaching a peak of about 6,000 members in the United States during the 1840s. As of 2015, however, the only Shaker community left in this country was a farm in Maine with three members—one man and two women (Ribisi-Braley 2015; Schaefer and Zellner 2015).

2. *Teaching new recruits.* No group or society can survive if many of its members reject the group's established behavior and responsibilities. Thus, finding or producing new members is not sufficient; the group or society must also encourage recruits to learn and accept its values and customs. Such learning can take place formally, within schools (where learning is a manifest function), or informally, through interaction in peer groups (where learning is a latent function).

3. *Producing and distributing goods and services.* Any relatively permanent group or society must provide and distribute desired goods and services to its members. Each society establishes a set of rules for the allocation of financial and other resources. The group must satisfy the needs of most members to some extent, or it will risk the possibility of discontent and ultimately disorder.

4. *Preserving order.* Throughout the world, indigenous and aboriginal peoples have struggled to protect themselves from outside invaders, with varying degrees of success. Failure to preserve order and defend against conquest leads to the death not only of a people, but of a culture as well.

5. *Providing and maintaining a sense of purpose.* In order to fulfill the first four requirements, people must feel motivated to continue as members of a group or society. Patriotism, tribal identities, religious values, or personal moral codes can help people to develop and maintain such a sense of purpose. Whatever the motivator, in any society there remains one common and critical reality: if an individual does not have a sense of purpose, he or she has little reason to contribute to a society's survival.

This list of functional prerequisites does not specify *how* a society and its corresponding social institutions will perform each task. For example, one society may protect itself from external attack by amassing a frightening arsenal of weaponry, while another may make determined efforts to remain neutral in world politics and to promote cooperative relationships with its neighbors. No matter what its particular strategy, any society or relatively permanent group must attempt to satisfy all these functional prerequisites for survival. If it fails on even one condition, the society runs the risk of extinction (Aberle et al. 1950; R. Mack and Bradford 1979).

Conflict Perspective Conflict theorists do not agree with the functionalist approach to social institutions. Although proponents of both perspectives agree that social institutions are organized to meet basic social needs, conflict theorists object to the idea that the outcome is necessarily efficient and desirable.

From a conflict perspective, the present organization of social institutions is no accident. Major institutions, such as education, help to maintain the privileges of the most powerful individuals and groups within a society, while contributing to the powerlessness of others. To give one example, public schools in the United States are financed largely through property taxes. This arrangement allows more affluent areas to provide their children with better-equipped schools and better-paid teachers than low-income areas can afford. As a result, children from prosperous communities are better prepared to compete academically than children from impoverished communities. The structure of the nation's educational system permits and even promotes such unequal treatment of schoolchildren.

Conflict theorists argue that social institutions such as education have an inherently conservative nature. Without question, it has been difficult to implement educational reforms that promote equal opportunity—whether bilingual education, school desegregation, or mainstreaming of students with disabilities. From a functionalist perspective, social change can be dysfunctional, since it often leads to instability. However, from a conflict view, why should we preserve the existing social structure if it is unfair and discriminatory?

Social institutions also operate in gendered and racist environments, as conflict theorists, as well as feminists and interactionists, have pointed out. In schools, offices, and government institutions, assumptions about what people can do reflect the sexism and racism of the larger society. For instance, many people assume that women cannot make tough decisions—even those in the top echelons of corporate management. Others assume that all Black students at elite colleges represent affirmative action admissions. Inequality based on gender, economic status, race, and ethnicity thrives in such an environment—to which we might add discrimination based on age, physical disability, and sexual

TABLE 16-1 SOCIOLOGICAL PERSPECTIVES ON SOCIAL INSTITUTIONS

Tracking Sociological Perspectives

Perspective	Role of Social Institutions	Focus
Functionalist	Meeting basic social needs	Essential functions
Conflict	Meeting basic social needs	Maintenance of privileges and inequality
Interactionist	Fostering everyday behavior	Influence of the roles and statuses we accept

orientation. The truth of this assertion can be seen in routine decisions by employers on how to advertise jobs, as well as whether to provide fringe benefits such as child care and parental leave.

Interactionist Perspective Social institutions affect our everyday behavior, whether we are driving down the street or waiting in a long shopping line. Sociologist Mitchell Duneier (1994a, 1994b) studied the social behavior of the word processors, all women, who work in the service center of a large Chicago law firm. Duneier was interested in the informal social norms that emerged in this work environment and the rich social network these female employees created.

The Network Center, as it is called, is a single, windowless room in a large office building where the law firm occupies seven floors. The center is staffed by two shifts of word processors, who work either from 4:00 p.m. to midnight or from midnight to 8:00 a.m. Each word processor works in a cubicle with just enough room for her keyboard, terminal, printer, and telephone. Work assignments for the word processors are placed in a central basket and then completed according to precise procedures.

At first glance, we might think that these women labor with little social contact, apart from limited breaks and occasional conversations with their supervisor. However, drawing on the interactionist perspective, Duneier learned that despite working in a large office, these women find private moments to talk (often in the halls or outside the washroom) and share a critical view of the law firm's attorneys and day-shift secretaries. Indeed, the word processors routinely suggest that their assignments represent work that the "lazy" secretaries should have completed during the normal workday. Duneier (1994b) tells of one word processor who resented the lawyers' superior attitude and pointedly refused to recognize or speak with any attorney who would not address her by name.

Interactionist theorists emphasize that our social behavior is conditioned by the roles and statuses we accept, the groups to which we belong, and the institutions within which we function. For example, the social roles associated with being a judge occur within the larger context of the criminal justice system. The status of judge stands in relation to other statuses, such as attorney, plaintiff, defendant, and witness, as well as to the social institution of government. Although courts and jails have great symbolic importance, the judicial system derives its continued significance from the roles people carry out in social interactions (Berger and Luckmann 1966).

Table 16-1 summarizes the three major sociological perspectives on social institutions.

MODULE 16 | Recap and Review

Summary

Social interaction refers to the ways in which people respond to one another. **Social structure** refers to the way in which a society is organized into predictable relationships. This module examines the five basic elements of social structure: **statuses**, **social roles**, **groups**, **social networks**, and **social institutions**.

1. People shape their social reality based on what they learn through social interactions. Social change comes from redefining or reconstructing social reality.

2. An **ascribed status** is generally assigned to a person at birth, whereas an **achieved status** is attained largely through one's own effort. Some ascribed statuses, such as race and gender, can function as **master statuses** that affect one's potential to achieve a certain professional or social status.

3. With each distinctive status—whether ascribed or achieved—comes a particular social role, the set of expectations for people who occupy that status.

4. Much of our social behavior takes place in groups.

5. Social institutions fulfill essential functions, such as replacing personnel, training new recruits, and preserving order. The mass media, the government, the economy, the family, and the health care system are all examples of social institutions.

6. Social networks form linkages between individuals and groups and can center on virtually any activity.

Thinking Critically

1. Think back over the events of the past few days. Identify two occasions on which different people defined the same social reality differently.

2. Describe a specific master status and explain how it was established. Is it a negative status? If so, how would a person overcome it?

MODULE 17 | Social Structure in Global Perspective

Modern societies are complex, especially compared to earlier social arrangements. Sociologists Émile Durkheim, Ferdinand Tönnies, and Gerhard Lenski developed ways to contrast modern societies with simpler forms of social structure.

Durkheim's Mechanical and Organic Solidarity

In his *Division of Labor* ([1893] 1933), Durkheim argued that social structure depends on the division of labor in a society—in other words, on the manner in which tasks are performed. Thus, a task such as providing food can be carried out almost totally by one individual, or it can be divided among many people. The latter pattern is typical of modern societies, in which the cultivation, processing, distribution, and retailing of a single food item are performed by literally hundreds of people.

In societies in which there is minimal division of labor, a collective consciousness develops that emphasizes group solidarity. Durkheim termed this collective frame of mind **mechanical solidarity,** implying that all individuals perform the same tasks. In this type of society, no one needs to ask, "What do your parents do?" since all are engaged in similar work. Each person prepares food, hunts, makes clothing, builds homes, and so forth. Because people have few options regarding what to do with their lives, there is little concern for individual needs. Instead, the group is the dominating force in society. Both social interaction and negotiation are based on close, intimate, face-to-face social contacts. Since there is little specialization, there are few social roles.

As societies become more advanced technologically, they rely on greater division of labor, so that no individual can go it alone. Dependence on others becomes essential for group survival. In Durkheim's terms, mechanical solidarity is replaced by **organic solidarity,** a collective consciousness resting on the need a society's members have for one another. Durkheim chose the term *organic solidarity* because in his view, individuals become interdependent in much the same way as organs of the human body.

Tönnies's *Gemeinschaft* and *Gesellschaft*

Ferdinand Tönnies (1855–1936) was appalled by the rise of an industrial city in his native Germany during the late 1800s. In his view, the city marked a dramatic change from the ideal of a close-knit community, which Tönnies termed a *Gemeinschaft,* to that of an impersonal mass society, known as a *Gesellschaft* (Tönnies [1887] 1988).

The *Gemeinschaft* (pronounced guh-mine-shoft) is typical of rural life. It is a small community in which people have similar backgrounds and life experiences. Virtually everyone knows one another, and social interactions are intimate and familiar, almost as among kinfolk. In this community there is a commitment to the larger social group and a sense of togetherness among members. People relate to others in a personal way, not just as "clerk" or "manager." With this personal interaction comes little privacy, however: we know too much about everyone.

Social control in the *Gemeinschaft* is maintained through informal means such as moral persuasion, gossip, and even gestures. These techniques work effectively because people genuinely care how others feel about them. Social change is relatively

"I'd like to think of you as a person, David, but it's my job to think of you as personnel."

Cartoon © Dean Vietor/The New Yorker Collection/The Cartoon Bank.

In a *Gesellschaft,* people are likely to relate to one another in terms of their roles rather than their relationships.

Becoming Social in a *Gesellschaft*

Back in 2014, journalist Federico Bastiani and his wife Laurel decided to find a way to eliminate the emptiness they were feeling in their lives. The couple had been living on Bologna, Italy's, heavily residential Via Fondazza for three years but Federico's work schedule had prevented them from making friends. Because of their social isolation, the couple could not set up play dates for their 20-month-old son, Matteo. "We could hear other children around us," says Federico, "but we couldn't just knock on doors to ask kids to come out and play with Matteo."

The couple regularly saw the same people but they never really interacted with them, nor did they see other people seeking out neighbors. Clearly they were living in the kind of impersonal social environment that characterizes *Gesellschaft*.

Federico decided to create a Facebook page for the neighborhood. He publicized the electronic meeting place the old-fashioned way by printing out 50 flyers and putting them up in communal spaces and along the street. "Basically, I explained my problem, and how eager we as a family were to socialize with others."

Within a couple of weeks the Facebook page had 93 followers who lived in the area. The expanding Via Fondazza group finally decided to give the project a name, "Social Street," the first of its kind in Italy, with its own website.

Word spread online and in the media about this Social Street, and within a few months there were 160 social street projects in Italy. Today Social Street has spread worldwide to Australia, Chile, Croatia, India, and Portugal.

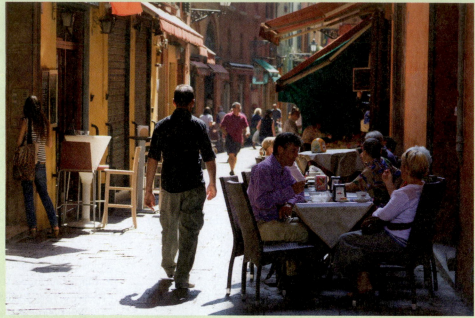

© Ken Welsh/Photolibrary/Getty Images

> Online connecting is usually associated with people remaining inside and by themselves. Social Street, in contrast, promotes face-to-face interaction.

Online connecting is usually associated with people remaining inside and by themselves. Social Street, in contrast, promotes face-to-face interaction. It will be interesting to follow the spread of Social Street as it continues to promote interpersonal interaction, even if the means it uses is more often viewed as making people isolated in today's world.

LET'S DISCUSS

1. Which aspects of a *Gesellschaft* community make it hard to form social contacts?

2. Why do you think the Facebook page was so successful?

Sources: Camponeschi and Warner 2015; Tarricone 2014.

---

limited in the *Gemeinschaft;* the lives of members of one generation may be quite similar to those of their grandparents.

In contrast, the **Gesellschaft** (pronounced guh-zell-shoft) is an ideal community that is characteristic of modern urban life. In this community most people are strangers who feel little in common with other residents. Relationships are governed by social roles that grow out of immediate tasks, such as purchasing a product or arranging a business meeting. Self-interest dominates, and there is little consensus concerning values or commitment to the group. As a result, social control must rest on more formal techniques, such as laws and legally defined punishments. Social

change is an important aspect of life in the *Gesellschaft;* it can be strikingly evident even within a single generation.

As Box 17-1 shows, people have taken to social media to overcome the lack of community in societies characterized by *Gesellschaft*.

Table 17-1 summarizes the differences between the *Gemeinschaft* and the *Gesellschaft*. Sociologists have used these terms to compare social structures that stress close relationships with those that emphasize less personal ties. It is easy to view the *Gemeinschaft* with nostalgia, as a far better way of life than the rat race of contemporary existence. However, the more intimate relationships

TABLE 17-1 COMPARISON OF THE *GEMEINSCHAFT* AND *GESELLSCHAFT*

Gemeinschaft	Gesellschaft
Rural life typifies this form.	Urban life typifies this form.
People share a feeling of community that results from their similar backgrounds and life experiences.	People have little sense of commonality. Their differences appear more striking than their similarities.
Social interactions are intimate and familiar.	Social interactions are likely to be impersonal and task-specific.
People maintain a spirit of cooperation and unity of will.	Self-interest dominates.
Tasks and personal relationships cannot be separated.	The task being performed is paramount; relationships are subordinate.
People place little emphasis on individual privacy.	Privacy is valued.
Informal social control predominates.	Formal social control is evident.
People are not very tolerant of deviance.	People are more tolerant of deviance.
Emphasis is on ascribed statuses.	Emphasis is on achieved statuses.
Social change is relatively limited.	Social change is very evident, even within a generation.

of the *Gemeinschaft* come at a price. The prejudice and discrimination found there can be quite confining; ascribed statuses such as family background often outweigh a person's unique talents and achievements. In addition, the *Gemeinschaft* tends to distrust individuals who seek to be creative or just to be different.

Lenski's Sociocultural Evolution Approach

Sociologist Gerhard Lenski (1924–2015) took a very different view of society and social structure. Rather than distinguishing between two opposite types of society, as Tönnies did, Lenski saw human societies as undergoing a process of change characterized by a dominant pattern known as **sociocultural evolution.** This term refers to long-term social trends resulting from the interplay of continuity, innovation, and selection (Nolan and Lenski 2015:415).

In Lenski's view, a society's level of technology is critical to the way it is organized. Lenski defined **technology** as "cultural information about the ways in which the material resources of the environment may be used to satisfy human needs and desires" (Nolan and Lenski 2015:415). The available technology does not completely define the form that a particular society and its social structure take. Nevertheless, a low level of technology may limit the degree to which a society can depend on such things as irrigation or complex machinery. As technology advances, Lenski wrote, a community evolves from a preindustrial to an industrial and finally a postindustrial society.

Preindustrial Societies

How does a preindustrial society organize its economy? If we know that, we can categorize the society. The first type of preindustrial society to emerge in human history was the **hunting-and-gathering society,** in which people simply rely on whatever foods and fibers are readily available. Technology in such societies is

minimal. Organized into groups, people move constantly in search of food. There is little division of labor into specialized tasks.

Hunting-and-gathering societies are composed of small, widely dispersed groups. Each group consists almost entirely of people who are related to one another. As a result, kinship ties are

© Mike Goldwater/Alamy

Preindustrial societies still exist in some remote areas. These indigenous people are from the Envira region of the Amazon rain forest, in Brazil.

the source of authority and influence, and the social institution of the family takes on a particularly important role. Tönnies would certainly view such societies as examples of the *Gemeinschaft*.

Social differentiation within the hunting-and-gathering society is based on ascribed statuses such as gender, age, and family background. Since resources are scarce, there is relatively little inequality in terms of material goods. By the close of the 20th century, hunting-and-gathering societies had virtually disappeared (Nolan and Lenski 2015).

Horticultural societies, in which people plant seeds and crops rather than merely subsist on available foods, emerged about 12,000 years ago. Members of horticultural societies are much less nomadic than hunters and gatherers. They place greater emphasis on the production of tools and household objects. Yet technology remains rather limited in these societies, whose members cultivate crops with the aid of digging sticks or hoes (Wilford 1997).

The last stage of preindustrial development is the **agrarian society**, which emerged about 5,000 years ago. As in horticultural societies, members of agrarian societies engage primarily in the production of food. However, technological innovations such as the plow allow farmers to dramatically increase their crop yields. They can cultivate the same fields over generations, allowing the emergence of larger settlements.

The agrarian society continues to rely on the physical power of humans and animals (as opposed to mechanical power). Nevertheless, its social structure has more carefully defined roles than that of horticultural societies. Individuals focus on specialized tasks, such as the repair of fishing nets or blacksmithing. As human settlements become more established and stable, social institutions become more elaborate and property rights more important. The comparative permanence and greater surpluses of an agrarian society allow members to create artifacts such as statues, public monuments, and art objects and to pass them on from one generation to the next.

Table 17-2 summarizes Lenski's three stages of sociocultural evolution, as well as the stages that follow, described next.

Industrial Societies

Although the Industrial Revolution did not topple monarchs, it produced changes every bit as significant as those resulting from political revolutions. The Industrial Revolution, which took place largely in England during the period 1760 to 1830, was a scientific revolution focused on the application of nonanimal (mechanical) sources of power to labor tasks. An **industrial society** is a society that depends on mechanization to produce its goods and services. Industrial societies rely on new inventions that facilitate agricultural and industrial production, and on new sources of energy, such as steam.

As the Industrial Revolution proceeded, a new form of social structure emerged. Many societies underwent an irrevocable shift from an agrarian-oriented economy to an industrial base. No longer did an individual or a family typically make an entire product. Instead, specialization of tasks and manufacturing of goods became increasingly common. Workers, generally men but also women and even children, left their family homesteads to work in central locations such as factories.

Postindustrial and Postmodern Societies

When Lenski first proposed the sociocultural evolutionary approach in the 1960s, he paid relatively little attention to how maturing industrialized societies may change with the emergence of even more advanced forms of technology. More recently, he and other sociologists have studied the significant changes in the occupational structure of industrial societies as they shift from manufacturing to service economies. In the 1970s, sociologist Daniel Bell wrote about the technologically advanced **postindustrial society,** whose economic system is engaged primarily in the processing and control of information. The main output of a postindustrial society is services rather than manufactured goods. Large numbers of people become involved in occupations devoted to the teaching, generation, or dissemination of ideas. Jobs in fields such as advertising, public relations, human resources, and computer information systems would be typical of a postindustrial society (D. Bell [1973] 1999).

Bell views the transition from industrial to postindustrial society as a positive development. He sees a general decline in organized working-class groups and a rise in interest groups concerned with national issues such as health, education, and the environment. Bell's outlook is functionalist, because he portrays the postindustrial society as basically consensual. As organizations and interest groups engage in an open and competitive process of decision making, Bell believes, the level of conflict between diverse groups will diminish, strengthening social stability.

Conflict theorists take issue with Bell's functionalist analysis of the postindustrial society. For example, Michael Harrington

TABLE 17-2   STAGES OF SOCIOCULTURAL EVOLUTION

Summing Up

Societal Type	First Appearance	Characteristics
Hunting-and-gathering	Beginning of human life	Nomadic; reliance on readily available food and fibers
Horticultural	About 12,000 years ago	More settled; development of agriculture and limited technology
Agrarian	About 5,000 years ago	Larger, more stable settlements; improved technology and increased crop yields
Industrial	1760–1850	Reliance on mechanical power and new sources of energy; centralized workplaces; economic interdependence; formal education
Postindustrial	1960s	Reliance on services, especially the processing and control of information; expanded middle class
Postmodern	Latter 1970s	High technology; mass consumption of consumer goods and media images; cross-cultural integration

Disney World: A Postmodern Theme Park

In the late 1970s, scholars began writing about the postmodern society and its preoccupation with consumer goods and media images. Walt Disney World is a living example of this type of society. Over 134 million people visit a Disney theme park each year. In fact, Disney operates the eight most visited amusement parks in the world. On three different continents, the Magic Kingdom funnels newly arrived visitors through a quaint-looking Main Street, where Cinderella's Castle beckons to children of all ages.

Behind the Main Street façade, one finds endless opportunities to shop. In heavily air-conditioned stores, visitors can indulge in buying sprees that typify the postmodern preoccupation with consumer goods. Later, at the exits from popular attractions, visitors encounter more shopping opportunities, tailored to what they have just seen. This practice of piggy-backing shops on exhibits is now duplicated in prestigious museums throughout the world, where shops are located just outside special exhibitions of real art and authentic treasures.

The French sociologist Jean Baudrillard (1929–2007) coined the term **hyperconsumerism** to refer to the practice of buying more than we need or want, and often more than we can afford, under such circumstances. Of course, one need not walk down Main Street in Orlando to engage in hyperconsumerism. Advertising permeates the modern world, whether we are on foot or online, tempting us to engage in unnecessary purchases out of a desire that approaches greed. Consumption is so important in the postmodern world that it has become a means of self-identification. Today, conversations are more likely to start with "Where did

Courtesy of Peter Schaefer

In the postmodern world, time-space is often compressed. Clutching a toy version of a fictional bear from the 1920s (Winnie-the-Pooh), a young visitor to Disney World reserves a ticket for a trip to New Orleans in the 1850s (the Pirates of the Caribbean attraction). In the meantime, she will travel through the 1930s in one continuous boat ride on the Congo, Zambezi, Amazon, and Irrawaddy rivers (the Jungle Cruise attraction).

> Behind the Main Street façade, one finds endless opportunities to shop.

you get that stroller?" or "Who are you wearing?" than with any reference to the social issues that plague the postmodern world.

Another essential element of postmodernism, *globalism,* is on display at Disney World, where cultural elements have been stripped of any foreign trappings. Here, Cinderella and Snow White are not figures taken from German folklore, but "Disney characters." Similarly, Belle from *Beauty and the Beast* has largely lost her 18th-century French roots, and Pinocchio is no longer recognizable as an Italian.

Nearby, Epcot's World Showcase takes the opposite approach, offering museum-like re-creations of specific cultures. Here one finds no evidence of cultural diffusion or globalization—no Starbucks in Epcot's China, no Dunkin' Donuts in Great Britain, no hip-hop in Japan. Instead, a representation of a Mayan temple is flanked by a replica of a medieval Norwegian wooden-stave church and a re-creation of the Temple of Heaven in Beijing. Visitors stroll through a managed reality that is both an ideal and a simplified rendering of 10 different cultures, compressed in time-space.

Postmodernism is on display everywhere, not just in the theme park. It can be seen in the information-driven, consumer-oriented global society we all inhabit. Whether we like it or not, new technologies and the digital transmission of culture are constantly disengaging us from a particular time or place, facilitating our hyperconsumerism.

LET'S DISCUSS

1. In just the last 24 hours, what evidence of hyperconsumerism have you witnessed?
2. How often do you find yourself moving seamlessly across time or space, in one way or another?

Sources: Baudrillard [1970] 1998; Boje 1995; Brannigan 1992; Bryman 1995; Fjellman 1992; L. Klein 1994; Kratz and Karp 1993; Scoville 2010; Themed Entertainment Association 2015.

(1980), who alerted the nation to the problems of the poor in his book *The Other America,* questioned the significance that Bell attached to the growing class of white-collar workers. Harrington conceded that scientists, engineers, and economists are involved in important political and economic decisions, but he disagreed with Bell's claim that they have a free hand in decision making, independent of the interests of the rich. Harrington followed in the tradition of Marx by arguing that conflict between social classes will continue in the postindustrial society.

Sociologists have gone beyond discussion of the postindustrial society to the ideal of the postmodern society. A **postmodern society** is a technologically sophisticated society that is preoccupied with consumer goods and media images (Lemert 2013). Such societies consume goods and information on a mass scale. Postmodern theorists take a global perspective, noting the ways that culture crosses national boundaries. For example, residents of the United States may listen to reggae music from Jamaica, eat sushi and other Japanese foods, and wear clogs from Sweden. And online social networks know no national boundaries. Box 17-2 describes one of the fixtures of the postmodern society, the theme park.

The emphasis of postmodern theorists is on observing and describing newly emerging cultural forms and patterns of social interaction. Within sociology, the postmodern view offers support for integrating the insights of various theoretical perspectives—functionalism, conflict theory, feminist theory, and interactionism—while incorporating other contemporary approaches. Feminist sociologists argue optimistically that with its indifference to hierarchies and distinctions, the postmodern society will discard traditional values of male dominance in favor of gender equality. Yet others contend that despite new technologies, postindustrial and postmodern societies can be expected to display the same problems of inequality that plague industrial societies (Denzin 2004; Smart 1990; B. Turner 1990; van Vucht Tijssen 1990).

Durkheim, Tönnies, and Lenski present three visions of society's social structure. While they differ, each is useful, and this textbook will draw on all three. The sociocultural evolutionary approach emphasizes a historical perspective. It does not picture different types of social structure coexisting within the same society. Consequently, one would not expect a single society to include hunters and gatherers along with a postmodern culture. In contrast, Durkheim's and Tönnies's theories allow for the existence of different types of community—such as a

Gemeinschaft and a Gesellschaft—in the same society. Thus, a rural New Hampshire community located 100 miles from Boston can be linked to the city by modern information technology. The main difference between these two theories is a matter of emphasis. While Tönnies emphasized the overriding concern in each type of community—one's own self-interest or the well-being of the larger society—Durkheim emphasized the division (or lack of division) of labor.

The work of these three thinkers reminds us that a major focus of sociology has been to identify changes in social structure and the consequences for human behavior. At the macro level, we see society shifting to more advanced forms of technology. The social structure becomes increasingly complex, and new social institutions emerge to assume some functions that once were performed by the family. On the micro level, these changes affect the nature of social interactions. Each individual takes on multiple social roles, and people come to rely more on social networks and less on kinship ties. As the social structure becomes more complex, people's relationships become more impersonal, transient, and fragmented.

MODULE 17 | Recap and Review

Summary

Sociologists have developed classification systems that help us contrast complex modern societies with simpler forms of social structure.

1. Émile Durkheim thought that social structure depends on the division of labor in a society. According to Durkheim, societies with minimal division of labor have a collective consciousness called **mechanical solidarity**. Those with greater division of labor show an interdependence called **organic solidarity**.

2. Ferdinand Tönnies distinguished the close-knit community of *Gemeinschaft* from the impersonal mass society known as *Gesellschaft*.

3. Gerhard Lenski thinks that a society's social structure changes as its culture and technology become more sophisticated, a process he calls **sociocultural evolution**.

Thinking Critically

1. According to Lenski, technology is the key to sociocultural evolution. What social factors are most likely to influence whether a society's culture evolves to a new stage of sociocultural evolution?

2. How are Durkheim's and Tönnies's classifications similar? How are they different?

3. Describe any personal experiences you have had with a nonindustrial, or developing, society. If you have not had that kind of experience, how do you think you would prepare for it?

Key Terms

Agrarian society

Gemeinschaft

Gesellschaft

Horticultural society

Hunting-and-gathering society

Hyperconsumerism

Industrial society

Mechanical solidarity

Organic solidarity

Postindustrial society

Postmodern society

Sociocultural evolution

Technology

Most of us use the term *group* loosely to describe any collection of individuals, whether three strangers sharing an elevator or hundreds attending a rock concert. However, in sociological terms a **group** is any number of people with similar norms, values, and expectations who interact with one another on a regular basis. A college sorority or fraternity, a dance company, a tenant association, and a chess club are each considered a group. The important point is that members of a group share some sense of belonging. This characteristic distinguishes groups from mere *aggregates* of people, such as passengers who happen to be together on an airplane flight, or from *categories* of people, such as those who share a common feature (such as being retired) but otherwise do not act together.

Consider the case of a college singing group. It has agreed-on values and social norms. All members want to improve their singing skills and schedule lots of performances. In addition, like many groups, the singing ensemble has both a formal and an informal structure. The members meet regularly to rehearse; they choose leaders to run the rehearsals and manage their affairs. At the same time, some group members may take on unofficial leadership roles by coaching new members in singing techniques and performing skills.

The groups we interact with also play an important role in our daily lives, sometimes in unexpected ways. Émile Durkheim ([1893] 1933) noted how a heinous crime can shock us, eliciting a communal response that serves to protect us in the future. In April 2007, a senior at Virginia Tech fired nearly 300 rounds of ammunition at two locations on campus, killing 32 people and wounding 17 others. Sociologists James Hawdon and John Ryan (2011) of Virginia Tech conducted three web-based surveys of the students and faculty, the first of them nine days after the shooting and the last of them 10 months later. They found that people who joined in with established, ongoing group activities that were specific to the tragedy did not necessarily find relief or a sense of solidarity with other members of the community. More critical to people's recovery was continued participation in clubs and friendship groups in the weeks following the tragedy. Group solidarity does make a difference.

Types of Groups

Sociologists have made a number of useful distinctions between types of groups—primary and secondary groups, in-groups and out-groups, reference groups, and coalitions.

Primary and Secondary Groups

Charles Horton Cooley (1902) coined the term **primary group** to refer to a small group characterized by intimate, face-to-face association and cooperation. The members of a street gang constitute a primary group; so do members of a family living in the same household, as do a group of "sisters" in a college sorority.

TABLE **18-1** COMPARISON OF PRIMARY AND SECONDARY GROUPS

Primary Group	Secondary Group
Generally small	Usually large
Relatively long period of interaction	Relatively short duration, often temporary
Intimate, face-to-face association	Little social intimacy or mutual understanding
Some emotional depth to relationships	Relationships generally superficial
Cooperative, friendly	More formal and impersonal

Primary groups play a pivotal role both in the socialization process and in the development of roles and statuses. Indeed, primary groups can be instrumental in a person's day-to-day existence. When we find ourselves identifying closely with a group, it is probably a primary group.

We also participate in many groups that are not characterized by close bonds of friendship, such as large college classes and business associations. The term **secondary group** refers to a formal, impersonal group in which there is little social intimacy or mutual understanding (Table 18-1). Secondary groups often emerge in the workplace among those who share special

© Pat Tuson/Alamy

A pizza delivery crew is an example of a *secondary group*—a formal, impersonal group in which there is little social intimacy or mutual understanding. While waiting for the next delivery, members of this crew in Surrey, England, will become well enough acquainted to distinguish those who see the job as temporary from those who view it as permanent. They will learn who looks forward to deliveries in perceived high-risk areas and who does not. They may even spend time together after work, joking or boasting about their exploits on the job, but their friendships typically will not develop beyond that point.

Taking Sociology to Work

Sarah Levy, *Owner, S. Levy Foods*

Sarah Levy didn't know anything about sociology when she entered Northwestern University, but she knew that someday she wanted to start a bakery. After graduating from Northwestern with a major in sociology, she enrolled in Chicago's French Pastry School and spent some time interning at local bakeries and restaurants. A year later she started her own bakery in her mother's kitchen. Today Sarah owns and manages S. Levy Foods, which operates food concessions at airports in New York, Sacramento, Phoenix, and San Diego.

Like many small-business owners, Sarah does anything and everything in a typical workweek, from consulting to blogging ("Simply Sweet") and serving as brand ambassador for Callebut chocolate, Karo, and Fleischmann's yeast. She is also the dining editor for *Today's Chicago Woman* magazine. A gifted publicist, Sarah once participated in a Food Network challenge that involved baking a three-foot animated dinosaur cake. Through Sarah's

Courtesy of Sarah Levy

Pastries & Candies, a bricks-and-mortar store she once owned in downtown Chicago, she contributed to several charities, including Meals on Wheels, Common Threads, and For the Love of Chocolate Foundation.

Sarah saw the connection between business and sociology in her introductory

sociology course, in which she used this textbook. Learning about how people interact, she says, has broadened her horizons and taught her how to step back and analyze a situation from a sociological perspective. "In my job, I am constantly interacting with people—employees, customers, vendors," she explains. "I think one of my greatest strengths is my ability to get along with people from all sorts of backgrounds, and make everyone get along with each other and work together towards the same goal."

LET'S DISCUSS

1. Have you ever thought of starting your own business? If so, what do you think the key to your success might be?

2. Would business have been a more practical major for Sarah? Why or why not?

---

understandings about their occupation. The distinction between primary and secondary groups is not always clear-cut, however. Some social clubs may become so large and impersonal that they no longer function as primary groups.

In-Groups and Out-Groups

A group can hold special meaning for members because of its relationship to other groups. For example, people in one group sometimes feel antagonistic toward or threatened by another group, especially if that group is perceived as being different, either culturally or racially. To identify these "we" and "they" feelings, sociologists use two terms first employed by William Graham Sumner (1906): *in-group* and *out-group*.

An **in-group** can be defined as any group or category to which people feel they belong. Simply put, it comprises everyone who is regarded as "we" or "us." The in-group may be as narrow as a teenage clique or as broad as an entire society. The very existence of an in-group implies that there is an out-group that is viewed as "they" or "them." An **out-group** is a group or category to which people feel they do *not* belong.

In-group members typically feel distinct and superior, seeing themselves as better than people in the out-group. Proper behavior for the in-group is simultaneously viewed as unacceptable behavior for the out-group. This double standard enhances the sense of superiority. Sociologist Robert Merton (1968) described this process as the conversion of "in-group virtues" into "out-group vices." We can see this differential standard operating in worldwide discussions of terrorism. When a group or a nation takes aggressive actions, it usually justifies them as necessary, even if civilians are hurt or killed. Opponents are quick to label

such actions with the emotion-laden term of *terrorist* and appeal to the world community for condemnation. Yet these same people may themselves retaliate with actions that hurt civilians, which the first group will then condemn.

 use your **sociological imagination**

Try putting yourself in the shoes of an out-group member. What does your in-group look like from that perspective?

Conflict between in-groups and out-groups can turn violent on a personal as well as a political level. In 1999 two disaffected students at Columbine High School in Littleton, Colorado, launched an attack on the school that left 15 students and teachers dead, including themselves. The gunmen, members of an out-group that other students referred to as the Trenchcoat Mafia, apparently resented taunting by an in-group referred to as the Jocks. Similar episodes have occurred in schools across the nation, where rejected adolescents, overwhelmed by personal and family problems, peer group pressure, academic responsibilities, or media images of violence, have struck out against more popular classmates.

Reference Groups

Both primary groups and in-groups can dramatically influence the way an individual thinks and behaves. Sociologists call any group that individuals use as a standard for evaluating themselves and their own behavior a **reference group.** For example, a high school student who aspires to join a social circle of hip-hop music devotees will pattern his or her behavior after that of the group. The student will begin dressing like these peers, listening to the same downloads and DVDs, and hanging out at the same stores and clubs.

Reference groups have two basic purposes. They serve a normative function by setting and enforcing standards of conduct and belief. The high school student who wants the approval of the hip-hop crowd will have to follow the group's dictates, at least to some extent. Reference groups also perform a comparison function by serving as a standard against which people can measure themselves and others. An actor will evaluate himself or herself against a reference group composed of others in the acting profession (Merton and Kitt 1950).

Reference groups may help the process of anticipatory socialization. For example, a college student majoring in finance may read the *Wall Street Journal,* study the annual reports of corporations, and listen to midday stock market news on the radio. Such a student is using financial experts as a reference group to which he or she aspires.

Often, two or more reference groups influence us at the same time. Our family members, neighbors, and co-workers all shape different aspects of our self-evaluation. In addition, reference group attachments change during the life cycle. A corporate executive who quits the rat race at age 45 to become a social worker will find new reference groups to use as standards for evaluation. We shift reference groups as we take on different statuses during our lives.

© Stan Honda/Getty Images

At a powwow, a drum circle breathes spirit into an ancient tribal tradition. These accomplished ceremonial musicians may serve as a reference group for onlookers who want to know more about drumming.

use your **sociological imagination**

Describe an experience you have had with coalition building, or one that you have read about—perhaps in politics. Was the coalition effective? What problems did the members need to overcome?

Coalitions

As groups grow larger, coalitions begin to develop. A **coalition** is a temporary or permanent alliance geared toward a common goal. Coalitions can be broad-based or narrow and can take on many different objectives. Sociologist William Julius Wilson (1999) has described community-based organizations in Texas that include Whites and Latinos, working class and affluent, who have banded together to work for improved sidewalks, better drainage systems, and comprehensive street paving. Out of this type of coalition building, Wilson hopes, will emerge better interracial understanding.

Some coalitions are intentionally short-lived. For example, short-term coalition building is a key to success in popular TV programs like *Survivor.* In the program's first season, *Survivor: Borneo,* broadcast in 2000, the four members of the "Tagi alliance" banded together to vote fellow castaways off the island. The political world is also the scene of many temporary coalitions. For example, in 1997 big tobacco companies joined with antismoking groups to draw up a settlement for reimbursing states for tobacco-related medical costs. Soon after the settlement was announced the coalition members returned to their decades-long fight against each other (Pear 1997).

© Monty Brinton/CBS Photo Archive/Getty Images

Can you outwit, outplay, outlast your competition? Maybe a coalition can help. In *Survivor: Cambodia—Second Chance,* coalition building continued to be a key to success in the long-running television series, now in its 33rd season.

Summary

Much of our social behavior takes place in **groups**.

1. When we find ourselves identifying closely with a group, it is probably a **primary group**. A **secondary group** is more formal and impersonal.

2. People tend to see the world in terms of **in-groups** and **out-groups**, a perception often fostered by the very groups to which they belong.

3. **Reference groups** set and enforce standards of conduct and serve as a source of comparison for people's evaluations of themselves and others.

4. Interactionist researchers have noted that groups allow **coalitions** to form and serve as links to social networks and their vast resources.

Thinking Critically

1. Describe an example of coalition building you have experienced or read about (perhaps in the political realm). Was the coalition effective? What problems had to be overcome?

2. Think of a primary and a secondary group to which you belong. Under what circumstances might the primary group become a secondary group, or the secondary group become a primary group?

Key Terms

Coalition

Group

In-group

Out-group

Primary group

Reference group

Secondary group

M O D U L E 19 | **Understanding Organizations**

Formal Organizations and Bureaucracies

As contemporary societies have shifted to more advanced forms of technology and their social structures have become more complex, our lives have become increasingly dominated by large secondary groups referred to as *formal organizations*. A **formal organization** is a group designed for a special purpose and structured for maximum efficiency. The U.S. Postal Service, McDonald's, and the Boston Pops orchestra are examples of formal organizations. Though organizations vary in their size, specificity of goals, and degree of efficiency, they are all structured to facilitate the management of large-scale operations. They also have a bureaucratic form of organization, described in the next section.

In our society, formal organizations fulfill an enormous variety of personal and societal needs, shaping the lives of every one of us. In fact, formal organizations have become such a dominant force that we must create organizations to supervise other organizations, such as the Securities and Exchange Commission (SEC) to regulate brokerage companies. Although it sounds more exciting to say that we live in the "computer age" than to say that we live in the "age of formal organization," the latter is probably a more accurate description (Azumi and Hage 1972; Etzioni 1964).

Ascribed statuses such as gender, race, and ethnicity can influence how we see ourselves within formal organizations. For example, a study followed the careers of nearly 4,000 women and men who entered the bar in 2000 and found that among full-time lawyers, women earned an average of $6,000 less per year than men who were at the same stage of the profession. The discrepancy held even after considering type of firm, specialization within law, and work history (whether the lawyer had taken family leave, for example).

This consistent gender wage inequality appeared to stem from a devaluation of women and their work within legal organizations. Regrettably, women lawyers operating in this work culture may come to perceive themselves as worth less and entitled to less, which in turn creates further gendered compensatory practices. For example, over time, women and men record billable hours differently: men bill for every snippet of conversation, while women bill more selectively. This pattern of organizational culture, which perpetuates salary differences and ultimately discourages women from being as tough as men at salary negotiation, has been documented in a variety of occupations (Dinovitzer et al. 2009; Sandberg 2015).

Characteristics of a Bureaucracy

A **bureaucracy** is a component of formal organization that uses rules and hierarchical ranking to achieve efficiency. Rows of desks staffed by seemingly faceless people, endless lines and forms, impossibly complex language, and frustrating encounters with red tape—all these unpleasant images have combined to make *bureaucracy* a dirty word and an easy target in political campaigns. As a result, few people want to identify their occupation as "bureaucrat," despite the fact that all of us perform various bureaucratic tasks. In an industrial society, elements of bureaucracy enter into almost every occupation.

Max Weber ([1913–1922] 1947) first directed researchers to the significance of bureaucratic structure. In an important sociological advance, Weber emphasized the basic similarity of structure and process found in the otherwise dissimilar enterprises of religion, government, education, and business. Weber saw bureaucracy as a form of organization quite different from the family-run business. For analytical purposes, he developed an ideal type of bureaucracy that would reflect the most characteristic aspects of all human organizations. By **ideal type** Weber meant a construct or model for evaluating specific cases. In actuality, perfect bureaucracies do not exist; no real-world organization corresponds exactly to Weber's ideal type.

Weber proposed that whether the purpose is to run a church, a corporation, or an army, the ideal bureaucracy displays five basic characteristics. A discussion of those characteristics, as well as the dysfunctions of a bureaucracy, follows.

1. **Division of labor.** Specialized experts perform specific tasks. In your college bureaucracy, the admissions officer does not do the job of registrar; the guidance counselor does not see to the maintenance of buildings. By working at a specific task, people are more likely to become highly skilled and carry out a job with maximum efficiency. This emphasis on specialization is so basic a part of our lives that we may not realize it is a fairly recent development in Western culture.

The downside of division of labor is that the fragmentation of work into smaller and smaller tasks can divide workers and remove any connection they might feel to the overall objective of the bureaucracy. In *The Communist Manifesto* (written in 1848), Karl Marx and Friedrich Engels charged that the capitalist system reduces workers to a mere "appendage of the machine" (Tucker 1978). Such a work arrangement, they wrote, produces extreme **alienation**—a condition of estrangement or dissociation from the surrounding society. According to both Marx and conflict theorists, restricting workers to very small tasks also weakens their job security, since new employees can easily be trained to replace them.

Although division of labor has certainly enhanced the performance of many complex bureaucracies, in some

© Dinodia Images/Alamy RF

Being an accountant in a large corporation may be a relatively high-paying occupation. In Marxist terms, however, accountants are vulnerable to alienation, since they are far removed from the product or service that the corporation creates.

cases it can lead to **trained incapacity;** that is, workers become so specialized that they develop blind spots and fail to notice obvious problems. Even worse, they may not care about what is happening in the next department. This failure to communicate within a corporation across divisions has been termed the "silo effect." Some observers believe that such developments have caused workers in the United States to become less productive on the job (Tett 2015; Veblen 1914).

In some cases, the bureaucratic division of labor can have tragic results. In the wake of the coordinated attacks on the World Trade Center and the Pentagon on September 11, 2001, Americans wondered aloud how the FBI and CIA could have failed to detect the terrorists' elaborately planned operation. The problem, in part, turned out to be the division of labor between the FBI, which focuses on domestic matters, and the CIA, which operates overseas. Officials at these intelligence-gathering organizations, both of which are huge bureaucracies, are well known for jealously guarding information from one another. They were unwilling or unable to see and communicate beyond their own "silo." Subsequent investigations revealed that they knew about Osama bin Laden and his Al-Qaeda terrorist network in the early 1990s. Unfortunately, five federal agencies—the CIA, FBI, National Security Agency, Defense Intelligence Agency, and National Reconnaissance Office—failed to share their leads on the network. Although the hijacking of the four commercial airliners used in the massive attacks may not have been preventable, the bureaucratic division of labor definitely hindered efforts to defend against terrorism, undermining U.S. national security.

2. **Hierarchy of authority.** Bureaucracies follow the principle of hierarchy; that is, each position is under the supervision of a higher authority. A president

© Brand X Pictures/PunchStock RF

heads a college bureaucracy; he or she selects members of the administration, who in turn hire their own staff. In the Roman Catholic Church, the pope is the supreme authority; under him are cardinals, bishops, and so forth.

3. **Written rules and regulations.** What if your sociology professor gave your classmate an A for having such a friendly smile? You might think that wasn't fair, that it was against the rules. Through written rules and regulations, bureaucracies generally offer employees clear standards for an adequate (or exceptional) performance. In addition, procedures provide a valuable sense of continuity in a bureaucracy. Individual workers will come and go, but the structure and past records of the organization give it a life of its own that outlives the services of any one bureaucrat.

Of course, rules and regulations can overshadow the larger goals of an organization to the point that they become dysfunctional. What if a domestic abuse counselor failed to listen to an injured woman because she had no valid proof of U.S. citizenship? If blindly applied, rules no longer serve as a means to achieving an objective, but instead become important (and perhaps too important) in their own right. Robert Merton (1968) used the term **goal displacement** to refer to overzealous conformity to official regulations.

4. **Impersonality.** Max Weber wrote that in a bureaucracy, work is carried out *sine ira et studio,* "without hatred or passion." Bureaucratic norms dictate that officials perform their duties without giving personal consideration to people as individuals. Although this norm is intended to guarantee equal treatment for each person, it also contributes to the often cold and uncaring feeling associated with modern organizations. We typically think of big government and big business when we think of impersonal bureaucracies. In some cases, the impersonality that is associated with a bureaucracy can have tragic results. More frequently, bureaucratic impersonality produces frustration and disaffection. Today, even small firms filter callers with electronic menus.

5. **Employment based on technical qualifications.** Within the ideal bureaucracy, hiring is based on technical qualifications rather than on favoritism, and performance is measured against specific standards. Written personnel policies dictate who gets promoted, and people often have a right to appeal if they believe that particular rules have been violated. Such procedures protect bureaucrats against arbitrary dismissal, provide a measure of security, and encourage loyalty to the organization.

Although ideally, any bureaucracy will value technical and professional competence, personnel decisions do not always follow that ideal pattern. Dysfunctions within bureaucracy have become well publicized, particularly because of the work of Laurence J. Peter. According to the **Peter principle,** every employee within a hierarchy tends to rise to his or her level of incompetence (Peter and Hull 1969). This hypothesis, which has not been directly or systematically tested, reflects a possible dysfunctional outcome of advancement on the basis of merit. Talented people receive promotion after promotion, until sadly, some of them finally achieve positions that they cannot handle with their usual competence.

Table 19-1 summarizes the five characteristics of bureaucracy. These characteristics, developed by Max Weber a century ago, describe an ideal type rather than an actual bureaucracy. Not every formal organization will possess all five of Weber's characteristics. In fact, wide variation exists among actual bureaucratic organizations.

 use your sociological imagination

Your school or workplace suddenly ceases to exhibit one of the five characteristics of bureaucracy. Which characteristic is it, and what are the consequences?

Bureaucracy pervades modern life; through McDonaldization, it has reached new heights. As Box 19-1 shows, the McDonald's organization provides an excellent illustration of Weber's concept of bureaucracy (Ritzer 2015).

TABLE 19-1   CHARACTERISTICS OF A BUREAUCRACY   Summing Up

	Positive Consequence	Negative Consequence For the Individual	For the Organization
Division of labor	Produces efficiency in a large-scale corporation	Produces trained incapacity	Produces a narrow perspective
Hierarchy of authority	Clarifies who is in command	Deprives employees of a voice in decision making	Permits concealment of mistakes
Written rules and regulations	Let workers know what is expected of them	Stifle initiative and imagination	Lead to goal displacement
Impersonality	Reduces bias	Contributes to feelings of alienation	Discourages loyalty to company
Employment based on technical qualifications	Discourages favoritism and reduces petty rivalries	Discourages ambition to improve oneself elsewhere	Fosters Peter principle

Robot photo: © Mark Evans/E+/Getty Images RF

BOX 19-1

Sociology in the Global Community

McDonald's and the Worldwide Bureaucratization of Society

In his book *The McDonaldization of Society,* sociologist George Ritzer notes the enormous influence of a well-known fast-food organization on modern-day culture and social life.

Not surprisingly, Max Weber's five characteristics of bureaucracy are apparent in McDonald's restaurants, as well as in the global corporation behind them. Food preparation and order-taking reflect a painstaking *division of labor,* implemented by a *hierarchy of authority* that stretches from the food workers up to the store operator, and ultimately to the corporate board of directors. Store operators learn McDonald's *written rules and regulations,* which govern even the amount of ketchup or mustard placed on a hamburger, at McDonald's Hamburger University. Little bonding occurs between servers and customers, creating a pervasive sense of *impersonality.* The emphasis on efficiency is partly to blame for this characteristic. Because McDonald's French fry machines lift the fries out of the hot oil automatically, for example, employees cannot meet a customer request for "crispy" fries. Finally, employees are expected to have specific *technical qualifications,* although most of the skills they need to perform routine tasks can be learned in a brief training period.

McDonaldization is the process by which the principles of bureaucratization have increasingly shaped organizations worldwide. Its real significance is that it is not confined to the food-service industry or to coffee shops like Starbucks. Worldwide, McDonald's brand of predictability, efficiency, and dependence on nonhuman technology have become customary in a number of services, ranging from medical care to wedding planning to education.

Even sporting events reflect the influence of bureaucratization. Around the world, stadiums are becoming increasingly similar, both physically and in the way they present the sport to spectators. All seats offer spectators an unrestricted view, and a big screen guarantees them access to instant replays, which fans have become accustomed to seeing at home and in sports bars. Scores,

© Look Die Bildagentur der Fotografen GmbH/Alamy
Believe it or not, you are aboard a cruise ship! Giving consumers no surprises and highly predictable experiences are hallmarks of McDonaldization. Ironically, many people today spend large amounts of money to travel to distant ports on cruise ships only to have minimal, if any, exposure to foreign culture or people.

> Worldwide, McDonald's brand of predictability, efficiency, and dependence on nonhuman technology have become customary in a number of services, ranging from medical care to wedding planning to education.

player statistics, and attendance figures are updated automatically by computer and displayed on an automated scoreboard or fed to people's smartphones. Spectator enthusiasm is manufactured through digital displays urging applause or rhythmic chanting. And

of course, the merchandising of teams' and even players' names and images is highly controlled.

McDonald's reliance on the five characteristics of bureaucracy is not revolutionary. What is new is the bureaucratization of services and life events that once were highly individualized, at times even spontaneous. More and more, society itself is undergoing McDonaldization.

LET'S DISCUSS

1. What features of fast-food restaurants do you appreciate? Do you have any complaints about them?

2. Analyze life at your college using Weber's model of bureaucracy. What elements of McDonaldization do you see? Do you wish life were less McDonaldized?

Sources: Ormond 2005; Ritzer 2015.

Bureaucratization as a Process

Have you ever had to speak to 10 or 12 individuals in a corporation or government agency just to find out which official has jurisdiction over a particular problem? Ever been transferred from one department to another until you finally hung up in disgust? Sociologists have used the term **bureaucratization** to refer to the process by which a group, organization, or social movement becomes increasingly bureaucratic.

Normally, we think of bureaucratization in terms of large organizations. But bureaucratization also takes place within small-group settings. Sociologist Jennifer Bickman Mendez (1998) studied domestic houseworkers employed in central California by a nationwide franchise. She found that housekeeping tasks were minutely defined, to the point that employees had to follow 22 written steps for cleaning a bathroom. Complaints and special requests went not to the workers, but to an office-based manager.

Bureaucratization is not limited to Western industrial societies. In 2012, Xi Jinping became general secretary of China's Communist Party, the nation's highest office. In his first public address, Jinping pledged to end the party's "undue emphasis on formalities and bureaucracy" in order to deliver a "better life" for the Chinese people (I. Johnson 2012:A19; Malcolm Moore 2012).

Oligarchy: Rule by a Few

Conflict theorists have examined the bureaucratization of social movements. The German sociologist Robert Michels (1915) studied socialist parties and labor unions in Europe before World War I and found that such organizations were becoming increasingly bureaucratic. The emerging leaders of the organizations—even some of the most radical—had a vested interest in clinging to power. If they lost their leadership posts, they would have to return to full-time work as manual laborers.

Through his research, Michels originated the idea of the **iron law of oligarchy,** which describes how even a democratic organization will eventually develop into a bureaucracy ruled by a few, called an oligarchy. Why do oligarchies emerge? People who achieve leadership roles usually have the skills, knowledge, or charismatic appeal (as Weber noted) to direct, if not control, others. Michels argued that the rank and file of a movement or organization look to leaders for direction and thereby reinforce the process of rule by a few. In addition, members of an oligarchy are strongly motivated to maintain their leadership roles, privileges, and power.

© Andre J. Jackson/MCT/Newscom

Menlo Innovations of Ann Arbor, Michigan, a software design and development company, operates without managers: employees basically supervise themselves. Menlo is relatively small, but such "flat" hierarchies are attracting interest from researchers in organizational development.

🟧 Bureaucracy and Organizational Culture

How does bureaucratization affect the average individual who works in an organization? The early theorists of formal organizations tended to neglect this question. Max Weber, for example, focused on the management personnel in bureaucracies, but had little to say about workers in industry or clerks in government agencies.

According to the **classical theory** of formal organizations, or **scientific management approach,** workers are motivated almost entirely by economic rewards. This theory stresses that only the physical constraints on workers limit their productivity.

Therefore, workers may be treated as a resource, much like the machines that began to replace them in the 20th century. Under the scientific management approach, management attempts to achieve maximum work efficiency through scientific planning, established performance standards, and careful supervision of workers and production. Planning involves efficiency studies but not studies of workers' attitudes or job satisfaction.

Not until workers organized unions—and forced management to recognize that they were not objects—did theorists of formal organizations begin to revise the classical approach. Social scientists became aware that along with management and administrators, informal groups of workers have an important impact on organizations. An alternative way of considering bureaucratic dynamics, the **human relations approach,** emphasizes the role of people, communication, and participation in a bureaucracy. This type of analysis reflects the interest of interactionist theorists in small-group behavior. Unlike planning under the scientific management approach, planning based on the human relations approach focuses on workers' feelings, frustrations, and emotional need for job satisfaction.

The gradual move away from a sole focus on the physical aspects of getting the job done—and toward the concerns and needs of workers—led advocates of the human relations approach to stress the less formal aspects of bureaucratic structure. Informal groups and social networks within organizations develop partly as a result of people's ability to create more direct forms of communication than under the formal structure. Charles Page (1946) used the term *bureaucracy's other face* to refer to the unofficial activities and interactions that are such a basic part of daily organizational life.

Today, research on formal organizations is following new avenues. Among them are

- The recent arrival of a small number of women and minority group members in high-level management.

- In large corporations, the decision-making role of groups that lie outside the top ranks of leadership.

- The development of bossless offices with flat or horizontal hierarchies, where middle managers are eliminated and employees increasingly supervise themselves.

- The loss of fixed boundaries in organizations that have outsourced key functions.

- The role of the Internet in influencing business and consumer preferences.

Though research on organizations still embraces Max Weber's insights, then, it has gone well beyond them (Hamm 2007; Hutson 2014; Kleiner 2003; W. Scott and Davis 2007).

social policy and socialization | The State of the Unions Worldwide

How many people do you know who belong to a labor union? Chances are you can name a lot fewer people than someone could 50 years ago. In 1954 unions represented 39 percent of workers in the private sector of the U.S. economy; in 2014 they represented only 11.1 percent—the lowest share in more than 70 years. As Figure 19-1 shows, the decline in unionization is common to virtually all industrial nations. What has happened to diminish the importance of organized labor? Can workers be represented adequately without strong unions?

Looking at the Issue

Labor unions consist of organized workers who share either the same skill (as in electronics) or the same employer (as in the case of postal employees). Unions began to emerge during the Industrial Revolution in England, in the 1700s. Groups of workers banded together to extract concessions from employers (for example, safer working conditions, a shorter workweek) and to protect their positions.

Historically, labor unions have engaged in restrictive practices that are regarded today as discriminatory. They frequently tried to protect their jobs by limiting entry to their occupation based on gender, race, ethnicity, citizenship, age, and sometimes rather arbitrary measures of skill levels. Today we see less of this protection of special interests. In selected industries, unions now play a vital role in keeping Blacks' wages competitive with those of Whites (Rosenfeld and Klegkamp 2012).

The power of labor unions varies widely from country to country. In some countries, such as Britain and Mexico, unions play a key role in the foundation of governments. In others, such as Japan and Korea, their role in politics is very limited, and their ability to influence even the private sector is relatively weak. In the United States, unions can sometimes have a significant influence on employers and elected officials, but their effect varies dramatically by type of industry and even region of the country (S. Zimmerman 2008b).

Few people today would dispute the fact that union membership is declining. Among the reasons for the decline are the following:

1. **Changes in the type of industry.** Manufacturing jobs, the traditional heart of the labor union, have declined, giving way to postindustrial service jobs.

FIGURE 19-1 Labor Union Membership Worldwide

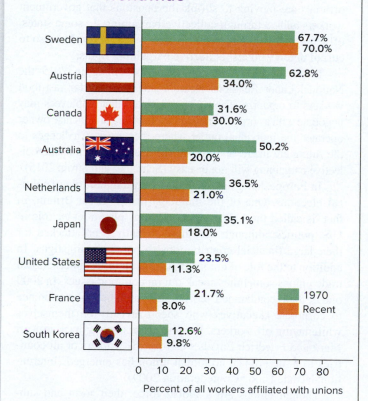

Percent of all workers affiliated with unions

Legend: 1970, Recent

Note: Recent data from 2009–2013, except for Austria (2008) and the United States (2014).
Sources: Bureau of Labor Statistics 2015b; New Unionism Network 2011; Unionwiki 2015; Visser 2006:45. *Flags:* © admin_design/Shutterstock RF

—*Continued*

2. **Growth in part-time jobs.** Between 1982 and 1998 the number of temporary jobs in the United States rose 577 percent, while total employment increased only 41 percent. Only in 2000 did laws governing collective bargaining allow temporary workers to join a union.

3. **The legal system.** The United States has not made it particularly easy for unions to organize and bargain, and some government measures have made it more difficult. A dramatic example was President Ronald Reagan's firing of 11,000 air traffic controllers in 1981, when their union threatened they would walk off the job while seeking a new contract.

4. **Globalization.** The threat of jobs leaving the country has undercut the ability of union leaders to organize workers at home. Some say that labor union demands for wage increases and additional benefits have themselves spurred the exodus of jobs to developing nations, where wages are significantly lower and unions are virtually nonexistent.

5. **Employer offensives.** Increasingly hostile employers have taken court action to block unions' efforts to represent their members.

Around the world, the economic downturn that began in 2008 has had special consequences for labor unions. Like nonunion workers, many union members lost their jobs in the recession; others saw their contracts renegotiated. As part of the $17.4 billion auto bailout legislation passed by the U.S. Congress in 2008, the United Auto Workers (UAW) accepted a nearly 20 percent pay cut. This and other rollbacks of benefits were largely accepted by U.S. unions, but in Europe, thousands of workers turned out in protest. Although some union leaders in the United States expect the hardship caused by the economic slowdown to raise union membership, how well unions will be able to represent their members through tough times remains to be seen (S. Greenhouse 2008a, 2009).

Applying Sociology

Both Marxists and functionalists would view unions as a logical response to the emergence of impersonal, large-scale, formal, and often alienating organizations. This view certainly characterized the growth of unions in major manufacturing industries with a sharp division of labor. However, as manufacturing has declined, unions have had to look elsewhere for growth.

Worldwide, today's labor unions bear little resemblance to those early unions organized spontaneously by exploited workers. In line with Robert Michels's iron law of oligarchy, unions have become increasingly bureaucratized under a sometimes self-serving leadership. Conflict theorists would point out that the longer union leaders are in office, the less responsive they are to the needs and demands of the rank and file, and the more concerned with maintaining their own positions and power. Yet research shows that under certain circumstances, union leadership can change significantly. Smaller unions are vulnerable to changes in leadership, as are

unions whose membership shifts in composition from predominantly White to African American or Latino.

Sociologists have linked the recent decline in private-sector union membership to a widening gap between hourly workers' wages and managerial and executive compensation. As union membership declined—and with it the unions' bargaining power—employers began to offer union workers less attractive pay packages. Eventually, the trend spread to nonunionized companies in the same industries, which typically strive to match union compensation in order to be competitive. In these businesses, employers no longer feel a need to raise wages to attract employees (Western and Rosenfeld 2011).

Initiating Policy

U.S. law grants workers the right to self-organize via unions. However, the United States is unique among industrial democracies in allowing employers to actively oppose their employees' decision to organize. The recent economic recession has compounded employers' opposition to unions and is even threatening workers' rights in established unions. Today, state and local governments across the United States are facing significant budget deficits. In an effort to cut costs, many elected officials are moving to shrink the pensions that government workers gained through collective bargaining. In some states, officials want not only to reduce retirees' benefits, but also to curtail union workers' collective bargaining rights.

In an unusual pro-union trend, beginning in 2015 the National Labor Relations Board made it easier for fast-food workers to organize. The ruling stipulated that employees may negotiate with a corporate headquarters even if a franchise owner operates the individual outlet where they work. Challenges to the ruling are likely, and even if the change is permanent, collective bargaining will not be easy (Schreiber and Strom 2015).

In Europe, labor unions tend to play a major role in political elections. One of the major parties in Great Britain, in fact, is called the Labour Party. Unions play a lesser role in U.S. politics, although they have recently been attacked for their large financial contributions to political campaigns. In addition to the role of unions in national politics, international trade unions sometimes speak out on common issues. In 2009 one of them condemned "corporate grand theft"—a reference to corporate executives who spend lavishly on themselves while laying off workers. Despite efforts dating back to Karl Marx and Friedrich Engels's call for the workers of all countries to unite (1847), no global union has emerged (International Trade Union Confederation 2009).

Though unions are a global force, their form and substance varies from country to country. In China, where there is only one political party, the government ordered Walmart's 31,000 workers to unionize, over the corporation's objections.

—Continued

Chinese unions are controlled by the Communist Party, whose membership has declined as the party's pervasive control has weakened. Nevertheless, these unions are more likely to listen to the government than independent unions, which listen to the workers who are their members (E. Wang 2013; Zhang 2009).

TAKE THE ISSUE WITH YOU

1. What unions are represented on your college campus? Have you been aware of union activity? Has there been any opposition to the unions on the part of the administration?

2. Why should employees who provide essential public services, such as nurses, teachers, and police officers, be allowed to organize into a union? What impact does union membership have on their representation if they cannot strike?

3. Should state and local officials be allowed to reduce government workers' retirement benefits and take away their right to collective bargaining?

MODULE 19 | **Recap and Review**

Summary

As societies become larger and more complex, daily life is increasingly dominated by large **formal organizations**.

1. Max Weber argued that in its **ideal form**, a **bureaucracy** has five basic characteristics: division of labor, hierarchical authority, written rules and regulations, impersonality, and employment based on technical qualifications. Carefully constructed bureaucratic policies can be either undermined or redefined by an organization's informal structure.

2. The **scientific management** approach to management considers workers to be economic resources. In contrast, the **human relations approach** emphasizes the role of people, communications, and participation.

Thinking Critically

1. What are some of the benefits and drawbacks of large formal organizations?

2. Recall a job that you once held. First, analyze the workplace using classical theory (the scientific management approach). Then analyze it using the human relations approach. Which approach do you find more useful in understanding that workplace?

Key Terms

Alienation

Bureaucracy

Bureaucratization

Classical theory

Formal organization

Goal displacement

Human relations approach

Ideal type

Iron law of oligarchy

Labor union

McDonaldization

Peter principle

Scientific management approach

Trained incapacity

Mastering This Chapter

© Caia Image/Glow Images RF

taking sociology with you

1 Interview a professional in a field of your choice. What role conflicts does a professional in that field commonly experience? What guidance does the profession's code of conduct offer regarding such conflicts?

2 Talk with two or three business students or businesspeople about the bureaucratization of business. On balance, do they see

bureaucratization as a positive or negative trend? What bureaucratic dysfunctions are common in business, and how do managers attempt to counteract them?

3 Speak with some members of a labor union. What work issues are important to them? What changes have they seen in unions and in the workplace since they began working?

key terms

Achieved status A social position that a person attains largely through his or her own efforts.

Agrarian society The most technologically advanced form of preindustrial society. Members engage primarily in the production of food, but increase their crop yields through technological innovations such as the plow.

Alienation A condition of estrangement or dissociation from the surrounding society.

Ascribed status A social position assigned to a person by society without regard for the person's unique talents or characteristics.

Bureaucracy A component of formal organization that uses rules and hierarchical ranking to achieve efficiency.

Bureaucratization The process by which a group, organization, or social movement becomes increasingly bureaucratic.

Classical theory An approach to the study of formal organizations that views workers as being motivated almost entirely by economic rewards.

Coalition A temporary or permanent alliance geared toward a common goal.

Formal organization A group designed for a special purpose and structured for maximum efficiency.

Gemeinschaft A close-knit community, often found in rural areas, in which strong personal bonds unite members.

Gesellschaft A community, often urban, that is large and impersonal, with little commitment to the group or consensus on values.

Goal displacement Overzealous conformity to official regulations of a bureaucracy.

Group Any number of people with similar norms, values, and expectations who interact with one another on a regular basis.

Horticultural society A preindustrial society in which people plant seeds and crops rather than merely subsist on available foods.

Human relations approach An approach to the study of formal organizations that emphasizes the role of people, communication, and participation in a bureaucracy and tends to focus on the informal structure of the organization.

Hunting-and-gathering society A preindustrial society in which people rely on whatever foods and fibers are readily available in order to survive.

Hyperconsumerism The practice of buying more than we need or want, and often more than we can afford; a preoccupation of postmodern consumers.

Ideal type A construct or model for evaluating specific cases.

Industrial society A society that depends on mechanization to produce its goods and services.

In-group Any group or category to which people feel they belong.

Iron law of oligarchy A principle of organizational life under which even a democratic organization will eventually develop into a bureaucracy ruled by a few individuals.

Labor union Organized workers who share either the same skill or the same employer.

Master status A status that dominates other statuses and thereby determines a person's general position in society.

McDonaldization The process by which the principles of bureaucratization have increasingly shaped organizations worldwide.

Mechanical solidarity A collective consciousness that emphasizes group solidarity, characteristic of societies with minimal division of labor.

Organic solidarity A collective consciousness that rests on mutual interdependence, characteristic of societies with a complex division of labor.

Out-group A group or category to which people feel they do not belong.

Peter principle A principle of organizational life according to which every employee within a hierarchy tends to rise to his or her level of incompetence.

Postindustrial society A society whose economic system is engaged primarily in the processing and control of information.

Postmodern society A technologically sophisticated society that is preoccupied with consumer goods and media images.

Primary group A small group characterized by intimate, face-to-face association and cooperation.

Reference group Any group that individuals use as a standard for evaluating themselves and their own behavior.

Role conflict The situation that occurs when incompatible expectations arise from two or more social positions held by the same person.

Role exit The process of disengagement from a role that is central to one's self-identity in order to establish a new role and identity.

Role strain The difficulty that arises when the same social position imposes conflicting demands and expectations.

Scientific management approach Another name for the classical theory of formal organizations.

Secondary group A formal, impersonal group in which there is little social intimacy or mutual understanding.

Social institution An organized pattern of beliefs and behavior centered on basic social needs.

Social interaction The ways in which people respond to one another.

Social network A series of social relationships that links a person directly to others, and through them indirectly to still more people.

Social role A set of expectations for people who occupy a given social position or status.

Social structure The way in which a society is organized into predictable relationships.

Sociocultural evolution Long-term social trends resulting from the interplay of continuity, innovation, and selection.

Status A term used by sociologists to refer to any of the full range of socially defined positions within a large group or society.

Technology Cultural information about the ways in which the material resources of the environment may be used to satisfy human needs and desires.

Trained incapacity The tendency of workers in a bureaucracy to become so specialized that they develop blind spots and fail to notice obvious problems.

self-quiz

Read each question carefully and then select the best answer.

1. In the United States, we expect that cab drivers will know how to get around a city. This expectation is an example of which of the following?
   a. role conflict
   b. role strain
   c. social role
   d. master status

2. What occurs when incompatible expectations arise from two or more social positions held by the same person?
   a. role conflict
   b. role strain
   c. role exit
   d. both a and b

3. In sociological terms, what do we call any number of people with similar norms, values, and expectations who interact with one another on a regular basis?
   a. a category
   b. a group
   c. an aggregate
   d. a society

4. The Shakers, a religious sect that came to the United States in 1774, has seen their group's membership diminish significantly due to their inability to
   a. teach new recruits.
   b. preserve order.
   c. replace personnel.
   d. provide and maintain a sense of purpose.

5. Which sociological perspective argues that the present organization of social institutions is no accident?
   a. the functionalist perspective
   b. the conflict perspective
   c. the interactionist perspective
   d. the global perspective

6. The U.S. Postal Service, the Boston Pops orchestra, and the college or university in which you are currently enrolled as a student are all examples of
   a. primary groups.
   b. reference groups.
   c. formal organizations.
   d. triads.

7. One positive consequence of bureaucracy is that it reduces bias. Reduction of bias results from which characteristic of a bureaucracy?
   a. impersonality
   b. hierarchy of authority
   c. written rules and regulations
   d. employment based on technical qualifications

8. According to the Peter principle,
   a. all bureaucracies are notoriously inefficient.
   b. if something *can* go wrong, it *will*.
   c. every employee within a hierarchy tends to rise to his or her level of incompetence.
   d. all line workers get burned in the end.

9. Social control in what Ferdinand Tönnies termed a *Gemeinschaft* community is maintained through all but which of the following means?
   a. moral persuasion
   b. gossip
   c. legally defined punishment
   d. gestures

10. Sociologist Daniel Bell uses which of the following terms to refer to a society whose economic system is engaged primarily in the processing and control of information?
    a. postmodern
    b. horticultural
    c. industrial
    d. postindustrial

11. The term _____ _____ refers to the way in which a society is organized into predictable relationships.

12. The African American activist Malcolm X wrote in his autobiography that his position as a Black man, a(n) _____ status, was an obstacle to his dream of becoming a lawyer, a(n) _____ status.

13. Sociologist Helen Rose Fuchs Ebaugh developed the term _____ _____ to describe the process of disengagement from a role that is central to one's self-identity in order to establish a new role and identity.

14. _____ groups often emerge in the workplace among those who share special understandings about their occupation.

15. In many cases, people model their behavior after groups to which they may not belong. These groups are called _____ groups.

16. In studying the social behavior of word processors in a Chicago law firm, sociologist Mitchell Duneier drew on the _____ perspective.

17. Max Weber developed a(n) _____ _____ bureaucracy, which reflects the most characteristic aspects of all human organizations.

18. According to Émile Durkheim, societies with a minimal division of labor are characterized by _____ solidarity, while societies with a complex division of labor are characterized by _____ solidarity.

19. In Gerhard Lenski's theory of sociocultural evolution, a society's level of _____ is critical to the way it is organized.

20. A(n) _____ society is a technologically sophisticated society that is preoccupied with consumer goods and media images.

© Franziska Krug/German Select/Getty Images

Mass media cross boundaries and cultures. Here people in Berlin, Germany, go to take in *Star Wars: The Force Awakens*.

6

The Mass Media

© Fabrice Lerouge/age fotostock RF

Think about the media you use today. How many of those media existed five years ago?

Lynne Gross is amazed by the rapid change that is occurring in the mass media.

"You would be hard-pressed in modern American society to find someone who does not interact with electronic media on a daily basis—someone who does not surf the Internet, watch TV, listen to the radio, download music to an iPod, go to a movie, play a video game, send an email, or talk on a smartphone. In fact, many people in this age of multitasking interact with several media at the same time. They watch a movie downloaded from the Internet while playing a video game and texting a friend.

In addition, everyone has opinions that relate to media. Our opinions decide whether a movie or a TV series is a hit or a dud. . . . We argue about the media's coverage of political candidates. We talk about the tactics used in the commercials and the sex and violence seen on TV and heard in radio song lyrics. We worry about the predators on the Internet and whether or not our cell phones will cause cancer.

The media are constantly changing. Not very long ago there was no Internet, no iPad, no Twitter. Within the past few decades, a number of technologies that were highly touted have gone by the wayside—subscription TV, VCRs, teletext. The way people used electronic media and how they perceived the media were quite different 10 years ago from what they are today.

Here are some things that were not available at the beginning of the 21st century: iPod, iTunes, iPhone, iPad, Xbox, hotspots, YouTube, Hulu, Skype, Facebook, and Twitter. The technological innovation that has occurred since 2000 has been a blur. Each month seems to bring faster computer speeds and greater storage capacities that expand capabilities of the Internet, portable platforms, and video games. Traditional media such as radio, television, and movies were separate for many years. But these new inventions now incorporate material from all of them—as well as from newspapers, magazines, the record business, the telephone industry, and many other media entities.

The interactive capabilities of the Internet, portable platforms, and video games have taken media in a new direction. Previous media forms were basically one way—producers of content distributed to the public, most of whom simply listened to or watched the material passively. Now anyone can be a producer, distributing to those who click on their site or download their information. When people interact with Internet-based media, whether for shopping, texting, emailing, or any of many other activities, they are in an active stage that involves thinking and doing. The Internet did not start out that way, however. It had humble beginnings and then took hold in ways no one had originally envisioned."

Now anyone can be a producer, distributing to those who click on their site or download their information.

(L. Gross 2013:2–3, 27–28)

In this excerpt from her book *Electronic Media,* Gross sketches the rapid transition from old-fashioned technologies to the new interactive technologies. That transition has profoundly changed the ways people use media. Once the only media available to us—radio, television, the Internet—were a one-way experience, from the producer to the audience. Today, anyone can become a producer and distribute content to others.

And that's not all: the lines between various media are blurring. Today we use the telephone not just to talk with others, but to watch television and movies. Both television and the Internet are examples of the *mass media,* which embrace print and electronic means of communication that carry messages to widespread audiences. Print media include newspapers, magazines, and books; electronic media include radio, satellite radio, television, motion pictures, and the Internet. Advertising, which falls into both categories, is also a form of mass media.

Why are the media so influential? Who benefits from media influence, and why? How do we maintain cultural and ethical standards in the face of negative media images? In these modules we will consider the ways sociology helps us to answer these questions. First we will look at how proponents of the various sociological perspectives view the media. Then we will examine who makes up the media's audience, not just at home but around the world. The chapter closes with a Social Policy section on the right to privacy in a digital age.

The social impact of the **mass media** is obvious. Consider a few examples. TV dinners were invented to accommodate the millions of couch potatoes who can't bear to miss their favorite television programs. Today, you can watch that program whenever you want, and screen time has gone well beyond television viewing to include time spent on smartphones. Candidates for political office use social media to get their message out to voters and rely on media consultants to project a winning image. World leaders use all forms of media for political advantage, whether to gain territory or to bid on hosting the Olympics. And in parts of Africa and Asia, AIDS education projects owe much of their success to media campaigns.

Few aspects of society are as central as the mass media. Through the media we expand our understanding of people and events beyond what we experience in person. The media inform us about different cultures and lifestyles and about the latest forms of technology. For sociologists, the key questions about mass media are how they affect our social institutions and how they influence our social behavior.

The social impact of the mass media has become so huge, in fact, that scholars have begun to speak of *cultural convergence*. The term **cultural convergence** refers to the flow of content across multiple media, and the accompanying migration of media audiences. As you watch a video, for example, you wonder what the star of the show is doing at the moment, and turn to the Internet. Later, while texting your best friend, you tell her what you learned, accompanied by a Google Earth map showing the celebrity's location. Using Photoshop, you may even include the star's image next to your own, post the photo on your Facebook page, and then tweet your friends to create a caption. Media convergence is not orchestrated by the media, sophisticated though they may be. You initiate it, using techniques you likely learned by interacting with others, either face-to-face or through the media (Jenkins 2006).

Over the past decade, new technologies have made new forms of mass media available to U.S. households. These new technologies have changed people's viewing and listening habits. People spend a lot of time with the media, more and more of it on the Internet. Media consumers have moved away from television and toward digital images downloaded to their computers and portable devices. Increasingly, they learn not just about the famous but about ordinary people by viewing their Facebook or Snapchat pages or by keeping in touch with their friends via instant messaging or Twitter.

How do people's viewing and listening habits affect their social behavior? In the following sections we'll use the four major sociological perspectives to examine the impact of the mass media and changes in their usage patterns.

Functionalist Perspective

One obvious function of the mass media is to entertain. Except for clearly identified news or educational programming, we often think the explicit purpose of the mass media is to occupy our leisure time—from newspaper comics and online gaming to the latest music releases on the Internet. While that is true, the media have other important functions. They also socialize us, enforce social norms, confer status, and promote consumption. An important dysfunction of the mass media is that they may act as a narcotic, desensitizing us to distressing events (Lazarsfeld and Merton 1948; C. Wright 1986).

Agent of Socialization

The media increase social cohesion by presenting a common, more or less standardized view of culture through mass communication. Early in the twentieth century, sociologist Robert Park (1922) studied how newspapers helped immigrants to the United States adjust to their environment by changing their customary habits and teaching them the opinions of people in their new home country. Unquestionably, the mass media play a significant role in providing a collective experience for members of society. Think about how the mass media bring together members of a community or even a nation by broadcasting important events and ceremonies (such as inaugurations, press conferences, parades, state funerals, and the Olympics) and by covering disasters.

Which media outlets did people turn to in the aftermath of the September 11, 2001, tragedy? Television, radio, and the telephone were the primary means by which people in the United States bonded. But the Internet also played a prominent role. About half of all Internet users—more than 5 million

Source: https://twitter.com/pccs_va

Since 2010, the Pope's twitter feed has gone out in nine languages, including Latin, to over 20 million followers.

people—received some kind of news about the attacks online (D. Miller and Darlington 2002).

Today, the news media have moved further online. Afghans of all political persuasions now connect with the Muslim community overseas to gain both social and financial support. In the realm of popular culture, a spontaneous global sharing of reactions to Michael Jackson's sudden death in 2009 crashed the websites for Google, the *Los Angeles Times,* TMZ celebrity news, Perez Hilton's blog, and Twitter (Rawlinson and Hunt 2009; Shane 2010).

Some are concerned about the media's socialization function, however. For instance, many people worry about the effect of using television as a babysitter and the impact of violent video games on children's behavior. Some people adopt a blame-the-media mentality, holding the media accountable for anything that goes wrong, especially with young people. Yet the media also have positive effects on young people. For young and even not-so-young adults, for example, a new sort of tribalism is emerging online, in which communities develop around common interests or shared identities (Tyrene Adams and Smith 2008; American Academy of Pediatrics 2013).

Enforcer of Social Norms

The media often reaffirm proper behavior by showing what happens to people who act in a way that violates societal expectations. These messages are conveyed when the bad guy gets clobbered in cartoons or is thrown in jail on *CSI.* Yet the media also sometimes glorify disapproved behavior, whether it is physical violence, disrespect to a teacher, or drug use.

The media also play a critical role in human sexuality. For example, programs have been created to persuade teens not to send nude images of themselves to others. Such images often go viral (that is, spread across the Internet) and may be used to harass teens and their parents. To define normative behavior regarding these images, one organization has launched a "That's not cool" campaign, complete with stalker messages that can be e-mailed to those who misuse such images. The widespread dissemination of compromising images that were meant to be shared only among close friends is just one aspect of the social phenomenon called *cyberbullying* (Hinduja and Patchin 2015).

Conferral of Status

The mass media confer status on people, organizations, and public issues. Whether it is an issue like homelessness or a celebrity like Kim Kardashian, they single out one from thousands of other similarly placed issues or people to become significant. Table 20-1 shows how often certain public figures are prominently featured on magazine covers and the online searches for celebrity information. Obviously, *People* magazine alone was not responsible for making Princess Diana into a worldwide figure, but collectively, all the media outlets created attention that the Princess did not welcome.

Another way the media confer celebrity status on individuals is by publishing information about the frequency of Internet searches. Some newspapers and websites carry regularly updated lists of the most heavily researched individuals and topics of the

week. This changes dramatically over time: none of the Google top 10 people searches were in the top 10 the year before.

With innovations in mass media, conferral of status can come in many ways, including through social media outlets. For example, Kim Kardashian West has over 26 million "likes" on Facebook and more than 50 million followers on Instagram. Her celebrity appearances online take place 24/7: they do not await the publication of a weekly magazine. And on social media, unlike traditional media, celebrities can respond with their own "likes," comments, and retweets to keep their status alive and interactive (Seetharaman 2015).

 use your **sociological imagination**

You are browsing through media outlets. Are you more likely than not to go to an outlet based on the person being featured? What kind of image would attract you?

Promotion of Consumption

Postmodern societies are characterized by **hyperconsumerism,** a term coined by the French sociologist Jean Baudrillard (1929–2007) to refer to the practice of buying more than we need or want, and often more than we can afford. The media certainly promote this behavior pattern. Twenty thousand commercials a year—that is the number the average child in the United States watches on television alone, not to mention other media platforms.

Young people cannot escape commercial messages. They show up on high school scoreboards, at rock concerts, and as banners on web pages. They also surface in the form of *product placement.* Product placement is nothing new. In 1951 *The*

© Tribune Content Agency LLC/Alamy Stock Photo

Product placement ("brand casting") is an increasingly important source of revenue for media and entertainment outlets. Here racecar driver Danica Patrick displays a number of brand logos, some of which have little to do with her sport.

TABLE 20-1 STATUS CONFERRED BY THE MEDIA

© dpa picture alliance/Alamy Stock Photo

© Rex Features/AP Images

© Vince Bucci/Getty Images

© Michael Ochs Archives/Stringer/Getty Images

© Ferdaus Shamim/WireImage/Getty Images

Google Rank/Person/Searches in 2015	People Rank/Person/Times on Cover	Ebony Rank/Person/Times on Cover	Rolling Stone Rank/Person/Times on Cover	IMDb Rank/Person
1. Lamar Odom	1. Princess Diana (54)	1. Janet Jackson (18)	1. John Lennon (31)	1. Johnny Depp
2. Caitlyn Jenner	2. Jennifer Aniston (43)	2. Halle Berry (17)	2. Mick Jagger (30)	2. Brad Pitt
3. Rhonda Rousey	3. Julia Roberts (35)	2. Michael Jackson (17)	3. Paul McCartney (29)	3. Angelina Jolie
4. Donald Trump	4. Brad Pitt (33)	4. Muhammad Ali (16)	4. Bob Dylan (25)	4. Natalie Portman
5. Tony Stewart	5. Prince William (29)	4. Whitney Houston (16)	5. Bruce Springsteen (24)	5. Pamela Anderson
6. Ruby Rose	5. Demi Moore (24)	6. Beyoncé (11)	6. Bono (23)	6. Tom Cruise
7. Charles Sheen	7. Angelina Jolie (23)	6. Denzel Washington (11)	7. Keith Richards (21)	7. Orlando Bloom
8. Brian Williams	8. Britney Spears (19)	6. Diahann Carroll (11)	7. Madonna (21)	8. Jennifer Lawrence
9. Adele	9. Michael Jackson (17)	6. Lena Horne (11)	8. George Harrison (19)	9. Robert Pattinson
10. Josh Duggar	9. Elizabeth Taylor (17)	6. Sidney Poitier (11)	9. Jimi Hendrix (18)	10. Leonardo DiCaprio

Source: Author's content analysis of primary cover subject for the full run of the periodicals beginning on the following dates: *People,* March 4, 1974; *Ebony,* November 1945; and *Rolling Stone,* September 1967; ending February 4, 2016. When a periodical runs multiple covers, each version is counted. In case of ties in ranking, the person on the more recent cover is listed first. Google rank based on *Google Trends. Top Charts 2015,* accessed February 4, 2016; IMDb rank based on cumulative 1990–2015 page views by more than 250 million unique viewers per month at IMDB.com.

African Queen prominently displayed Gordon's Gin aboard the boat carrying Katharine Hepburn and Humphrey Bogart. However, commercial promotion has become far more common today: the 2015 blockbuster movie *Jurassic World* featured characters swilling Starbucks lattes, sporting Beats by Dr. Dre, and driving around in a Mercedes SUV. Moreover, advertisers are attempting to develop brand or logo loyalty at younger and younger ages (Buckingham 2007; Rodman 2011:395; *The Week* 2015).

Using advertising to develop a brand name with global appeal is an especially powerful way to encourage consumption. U.S. corporations have been particularly successful in creating global brands. An analysis of the 100 most successful brands worldwide, each of which derives at least a third of its earnings outside the home country, shows that 57 of them originated in the United States; 43 others come from 14 different countries (Figure 20-1).

Media advertising has several clear functions: it supports the economy, provides information about products, and underwrites the cost of media. In some cases, advertising becomes part of the entertainment. A national survey showed that 51 percent of viewers watch the Super Bowl primarily for the commercials, and one-third of online conversations about the Super Bowl the day of and the day after the event are driven by Super Bowl advertising. Yet advertising's functions are related to dysfunctions. Media advertising contributes to a consumer culture that creates needs and raises unrealistic expectations of what is required to be happy or satisfied. Moreover, because the media depend heavily on advertising revenue, advertisers can influence media content (Carey and Gelles 2010; Nielsen Company 2010).

 use your **sociological imagination**

You are a news junkie. Where do you gather your facts or information—from newspapers, tabloids, magazines, TV newscasts, blogs, or the Internet? Why did you choose that medium?

Dysfunction: The Narcotizing Effect

In addition to the functions just noted, the media perform a *dysfunction.* Sociologists Paul Lazarsfeld and Robert Merton (1948) created the term **narcotizing dysfunction** to refer to the phenomenon in which the media provide such massive amounts of coverage that the audience becomes numb and fails to act on the information, regardless of how compelling the issue. Interested citizens may take in the information but make no decision or take no action.

Consider how often the media initiate a great outpouring of philanthropic support in response to natural disasters or family crises. But then what happens? Research shows that as time

FIGURE 20-1 Branding the Globe

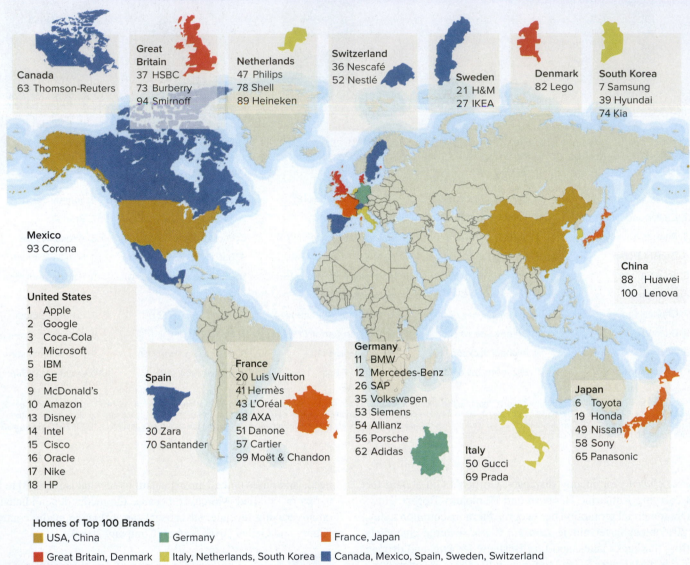

Canada
63 Thomson-Reuters

Great Britain
37 HSBC
73 Burberry
94 Smirnoff

Netherlands
47 Philips
78 Shell
89 Heineken

Switzerland
36 Nescafé
52 Nestlé

Sweden
21 H&M
27 IKEA

Denmark
82 Lego

South Korea
7 Samsung
39 Hyundai
74 Kia

Mexico
93 Corona

China
88 Huawei
100 Lenova

United States
1 Apple
2 Google
3 Coca-Cola
4 Microsoft
5 IBM
8 GE
9 McDonald's
10 Amazon
13 Disney
14 Intel
15 Cisco
16 Oracle
17 Nike
18 HP

Spain
30 Zara
70 Santander

France
20 Luis Vuitton
41 Hermès
43 L'Oréal
48 AXA
51 Danone
57 Cartier
99 Moët & Chandon

Germany
11 BMW
12 Mercedes-Benz
26 SAP
35 Volkswagen
53 Siemens
54 Allianz
56 Porsche
62 Adidas

Italy
50 Gucci
69 Prada

Japan
6 Toyota
19 Honda
49 Nissan
58 Sony
65 Panasonic

Homes of Top 100 Brands

■ USA, China	■ Germany	■ France, Japan
■ Great Britain, Denmark	■ Italy, Netherlands, South Korea	■ Canada, Mexico, Spain, Sweden, Switzerland

Note: Map shows the top 100 brands in the world in 2015 by country of ownership, except for the United States, for which only brands in the top 20 are shown. The United States has a total of 57 of the 100 leading brands.
Source: Based on Interbrand 2015.

Based on revenue and name recognition, these are the brands that dominate the global marketplace. Just 15 nations account for all the top 100 brands.

passes, viewer fatigue sets in. The mass media audience becomes numb, desensitized to the suffering, and may even conclude that a solution to the crisis has been found (Baran and Davis 2015).

The media's narcotizing dysfunction was identified 70 years ago, when just a few homes had television—well before the advent of electronic media. At that time, the dysfunction went largely unnoticed, but today commentators often point out the ill effects of addiction to screen time, especially among young people. Street crime, explicit sex, war, and HIV/AIDS apparently are such overwhelming topics that some in the audience may feel they have acted—or at the very least learned all they need to know—simply through social media.

Conflict Perspective

Conflict theorists emphasize that the media reflect and even exacerbate many of the divisions in our society and world, including those based on gender, race, ethnicity, and social class. They point in particular to the media's ability to decide what is transmitted, through a process called *gatekeeping*. Conflict theorists also stress the way interest groups monitor media content; the way powerful groups transmit society's dominant ideology through the mass media; and the technological gap between the haves and have-nots, which limits people's access to the Internet.

Gatekeeping

What story pops up when you turn on your smartphone? What motion picture plays on three screens rather than one at the local cineplex? What picture isn't released at all? Behind these decisions are powerful figures—publishers, editors, and other media moguls.

The mass media constitute a form of big business in which profits are generally more important than the quality of the programming. Within the mass media, a relatively small number of people control what eventually reaches the audience through **gatekeeping.** This term describes how material must travel through a series of gates (or checkpoints) before reaching the public. Thus, a select few decide what images to bring to a broad audience. In many countries the government plays a gatekeeping role. Even the champions of Internet freedom, who pride themselves on allowing people to pass freely through the gate, may quickly channel them in certain directions (see Box 20-1).

Gatekeeping, which prevails in all kinds of media, is not a new concept. The term was coined by a journalism scholar in the 1940s to refer to the way that small-town newspaper editors control which events receive public attention. As sociologist C. Wright Mills ([1956] 2000b) observed, the real power of the media is that they can control what is being presented. In the recording industry, gatekeepers may reject a popular local band because it competes with a group already on their label. Even if the band is recorded, radio programmers may reject the music because it does not fit the station's sound. Television programmers may keep a pilot for a new TV series off the air because they believe it does not appeal to the target audience (which is sometimes determined by advertising sponsors). Similar decisions are made by gatekeepers in the publishing industry.

In 2016 the list of twenty acting Oscar nominees was again all White and non-Hispanic, leading many critics to mount an ##oscarssowhite movement online. Yet this disproportionately White picture of mass media is hardly limited to top actors, leading conflict theorists to point out that media gatekeepers do not even come close to resembling the audiences for which they provide content. By 2014, the majority of people under age 18 in the United States belonged to racial and ethnic minorities. Yet consider the 2016 analysis that looked at the people who exercise the most influence over what books are published, what news gets covered, which motion pictures are produced, what television programs ever make it on air, or what music is produced: 94 of the 102 key gatekeepers who hold such positions are White non-Hispanics (Colby and Ortman 2015; Park et al. 2016).

Gatekeeping is not as dominant in at least one form of mass media, the Internet. You can send virtually any message to an electronic bulletin board, and create a web page or blog to advance any argument, including one that insists the earth is flat. The Internet is a means of quickly disseminating information (or misinformation) without going through any significant gatekeeping process.

© traveler1116/iStock/Getty Images RF

In 2015 a shooter killed nine people in an African American church in South Carolina's capitol of Charleston. The gunman's online presence displayed racist language and the Confederate battle flag. In the wake of the massacre, lawmakers voted to bring down the flag shown here from the Capitol grounds, and many retailers, including eBay, discontinued online sales of this symbol.

Nevertheless, the Internet is not totally without restrictions. In many nations, laws regulate content on issues such as gambling, pornography, and even politics. And popular Internet service providers will terminate accounts for offensive behavior. After the terrorist attacks in 2001, eBay did not allow people to sell parts of the World Trade Center via its online auction. In 2015, nine people were killed inside an African Methodist Episcopal Church in South Carolina. The shooter had posted an online racist manifesto illustrated with the Confederate flag. In the wake of the tragedy, eBay, along with other retail outlets, banned the sale of Confederate flags and their images. Despite, or maybe because of, such gatekeeping, growing numbers of people are involved in online communities.

Today, many countries try to control political dissent by restricting citizens' access to online comments unfavorable to the government. Beginning in 2011, online criticism fueled dissent in Arab countries like Egypt, Tunisia, Libya, Bahrain, and Syria. Using social media, activists in these countries encouraged their followers to demonstrate against the government at predetermined locales. To further encourage citizen engagement, activists posted cell phone videos of the protests on the Internet. In China, however, government officials marshaled the state's vast resources to mobilize an army of cyber-police, software developers, web monitors, and paid online propagandists. These cyber-soldiers watch, filter, censor, and guide Chinese Internet users in an effort to minimize online dissent (Castells 2015; *The Economist* 2013b; Preston and Stelter 2011).

Media Monitoring

The term *media monitoring* is used most often to refer to interest groups' monitoring of media content. The public reaction to the shootings at Virginia Tech in April 2007 provides one

Inside the Bubble: Internet Search Filters

Through Facebook, Classmates, and LinkedIn, the Internet allows us to reach out to those who are different from ourselves—or does it? Today, the search engines we use to navigate the Internet are personalized. Google, for example, uses as many as 57 sources of information, including location and past searches, to make calculated guesses about the sites a person might like to visit. Its searches have been personalized in this way since 2009. In 2012 Google carried the process one step further by collecting information from the websites that people "like" through social media, and then using that information to direct their web searches. Google sees this personalization of its searches as a service, one that helps people to cut through irrelevant information and quickly find what they are looking for.

Although Google's approach may at first sound convenient, critics charge that it can trap users in their own worlds, by routing them ever more narrowly in the same direction. In his book *The Filter Bubble,* online political activist Eli Pariser complains that when a search engine filters our searches, it encloses us in a kind of invisible bubble that limits what we see to what we are already familiar with. Thus, we are not likely to discover people, places, and ideas that are outside our comfort zone. Secure in our online bubble, which we may not even realize is there, we visit only safe, predictable sites.

What is wrong with that result? Given a choice, most of us go only to restaurants whose food we enjoy, read and listen to only those books and radio programs we know we like. Yet wasn't the Internet supposed to open new vistas to us? And if we are

> When a search engine filters our searches, it encloses us in a kind of invisible bubble that limits what we see to what we are already familiar with.

investigating a major news event, shouldn't we all see the same information when we search for it? Pariser describes what happened when two friends searched for the term "BP" in the spring of 2010, during the Deepwater Horizon oil rig's accidental discharge of crude oil into the Gulf of Mexico. Using the same browser, the two friends got very different results. One saw links to

information about the oil spill; the other saw links to information about BP's CEO, intended for investors.

Pariser has recently raised another concern: Because of the way the online world is filtered, many if not most people filter out truly important events. Stories or in-depth research about Afghanistan, world poverty, and the continuing refugee crisis do not get viewed much less read. Syria and policies about new policing methods must compete in the same search pool with cat pictures and Candy Crush and everything else people search for online. The solution, according to Pariser, is to figure out how to make the truly important issues more engaging and compelling.

One possibility, according to researchers at MIT and Yahoo Labs, is to include contrasting or opposing views in online searches. Although their work is just beginning, the hope is that someday, despite the technological challenges, the Internet will become less isolating and more open to different perspectives.

LET'S DISCUSS

1. How could you craft an Internet search to obtain a wider range of facts and opinions about a topic?
2. Choose a topic of interest to you and do an Internet search on it; ask several friends or classmates to do the same. Do your results differ? In what way?

Sources: Basulto 2011; Dredge 2014; Elgan 2011; Graells-Garrido et al. 2013; Pariser 2011a, 2011b; Stray 2012; Swartz 2012.

---

example. People did not need to be constant news monitors to learn of the rampage. Ever since the mass shootings at Columbine High School near Littleton, Colorado, in 1999, news outlets of every type have descended on the sites of such school shootings, offering insight into the perpetrators and their families, covering the mass expressions of grief, and following the communities' efforts to recover. Once again, though media outlets provided valuable information and quickly reassured viewers, listeners, and readers that the shooters posed no further danger, many people criticized the reality that they constructed through their coverage.

The term *media monitoring* can also be applied to government monitoring of individuals' phone calls without their knowledge. For example, the federal government has been criticized for authorizing wiretaps of U.S. citizens' telephone conversations without judicial approval. Government officials argue that the wiretaps were undertaken in the interest of national security, to monitor contacts between U.S. citizens and known terrorist groups following the terrorist attacks of September 11, 2001. But critics who take the conflict perspective, among others, are concerned by the apparent invasion of people's privacy. We will examine the right to privacy in greater detail in the Social Policy section at the end of this chapter (Gertner 2005).

What are the practical and ethical limits of media monitoring? In daily life, parents often oversee their children's online activities and scan the blogs they read—which are, of course, available for anyone to see. Most parents see such monitoring of children's media use and communications as an appropriate part of adult supervision. Yet their snooping sets an example for their children, who may use the technique for their own ends. Some media analysts have noted a growing trend among adolescents: the use of new media to learn not-so-public information about their parents (Delaney 2005).

One unanticipated benefit of government monitoring of private communications has been expedited disaster relief. As in the aftermath of Hurricane Katrina in 2005, the U.S. government turned to media monitoring following the 2010 earthquake in Haiti. At the Department of Homeland Security, employees at the National Operations Center monitored 31 social media sites for information regarding the disaster. The intelligence they gathered helped responders to locate people in need of rescue and identify areas outside Port-au-Prince where relief was necessary (Department of Homeland Security 2010).

Dominant Ideology: Constructing Reality

Conflict theorists argue that the mass media maintain the privileges of certain groups. Moreover, powerful groups may limit the media's representation of others to protect their own interests. The term **dominant ideology** describes a set of cultural beliefs and practices that helps to maintain powerful social, economic, and political interests. The media transmit messages that essentially define what we regard as the real world, even though those images frequently vary from the ones that the larger society experiences.

Mass media decision makers are overwhelmingly White, male, and wealthy. It may come as no surprise, then, that the media tend to ignore the lives and ambitions of subordinate groups, among them working-class people, African Americans, Hispanics, gays and lesbians, people with disabilities, overweight people, and older people. Worse yet, media content may create false images or stereotypes of these groups that then become accepted as accurate portrayals of reality. **Stereotypes** are unreliable generalizations about all members of a group that do not recognize individual differences within the group. Some broadcasters use stereotypes deliberately in a desperate bid for attention, with the winking approval of media executives.

Queer theorists have long studied the way the media present homosexuality. They have analyzed the frequent invisibility of homosexual characters, as well as the problematic ways in which they are made visible. From the perspective of queer theorists, significant strides have been made in the portrayal of nonheterosexuality as a normal and possible alternative to heterosexuality. Still, stigmatization of gays and lesbians persists, in the media as well as in society (Sloop 2009). A study of the top 100 motion pictures in 2014 identified 4,610 speaking parts; only 19 were lesbian, gay, or bisexual. Not one transgender character was portrayed (S. Smith et al. 2015).

Television also offers many examples of this tendency to ignore reality. How many overweight TV characters can you name? Heavyset television characters have fewer romances, talk less about sex, eat more often, and are more often the object of ridicule than their thin counterparts. Even though in real life 1 out of every 4 women is obese (30 or more pounds over a healthy body weight), only 3 out of 100 female TV characters are portrayed as obese (Hellmich 2001; J. Whyte 2010).

On the other hand, television news and other media outlets do alert people to the health implications of obesity. As with constructions of reality, whether some of this coverage is truly educational is debatable. Increasingly, the media have framed the problem not merely as an individual or personal one, but as a broad structural problem involving, for example, the manner in which food is processed and sold (Saguy and Almeling 2008).

Similarly, about 45 percent of all youths in the United States are children of color, yet few of the faces they see on television reflect their race or cultural heritage. Using content analysis, researchers revealed severe underrepresentation of Latinos, Asian Americans, and Native Americans, and a tendency to depict ethnic minorities stereotypically (e.g., overrepresentation of hyper-sexualized Latino characters and lower-class people of color). Certainly there are a very few successful minority-dominated shows, such as *Empire* and *Black-ish,* but the main characters in most TV shows—the leaders, the executives, the bosses, the decision-makers, the lovers—are not people of color (Tukachinsky et al. 2015).

Another concern about the media, from the conflict perspective, is that television distorts the political process. Until the U.S. campaign finance system is truly reformed, the candidates with the most money (often backed by powerful lobbying groups) will be able to buy exposure to voters and saturate the air with commercials attacking their opponents.

Dominant Ideology: Whose Culture?

CSI: Crime Scene Investigation (Les Experts) is a big hit in France, despite that nation's pride in its *"exception culturelle,"* which protects French film, television, and music producers from foreign competition. In Japan, *Glee* is must-watch TV, and *Columbo* reruns still garner viewers. Those are only the legally viewed hit shows. In Latin America, where illicit downloading of TV programs is common, the most popular shows include *The X-Factor, Breaking Bad, Homeland,* and *Modern Family.* In North Korea, *Desperate Housewives* is a cult hit. Although government officials and cultural purists may decry these shows' popularity, U.S. media are still widely watched and imitated. As sociologist Todd Gitlin puts it, American popular culture is something that "people love, and love to hate" (2002:177; Agence France-Presse 2013).

We risk being ethnocentric if we overstress U.S. dominance, however. For example, *Survivor, Who Wants to Be a Millionaire, Big Brother,* and *Iron Chef*—immensely popular TV programs in the United States—came from Sweden, Britain, the Netherlands, and Japan, respectively. Even *American Idol* originated in Britain as *Pop Idol,* featuring Simon Cowell. And the steamy telenovelas of Mexico and other Spanish-speaking countries owe very little of their origin to the soap operas on U.S. television. Unlike motion pictures, television is gradually moving away from U.S. domination and is now more likely to be locally produced (Bielby and Harrington 2008; Colucci 2008).

A related trend, the most novel one to date in this century, is the growth of **hyper-local media,** which refers to reporting

© Kami/Getty Images

Despite the popularity of Hollywood entertainment, media that are produced abroad for local consumption also do well. The animated series *Freej* features Muslim grandmothers who stumble on a cursed book while tackling their culture's wedding traditions. Produced in Dubai, the United Arab Emirates, for adult viewers, the series was launched in 2006.

that is highly local. What has been going on in that vacant lot down the street? Which Chinese takeout food is popular in your neighborhood? Why did all those police cars converge on Main Street the night before last? Hyper-local media answer these questions. The term was coined in 1991, to refer to the inclusion of local news on 24-hour cable news channels. (See Box 17–1, "Our Wired World: Becoming Social in a *Gesellschaft*," in Module 20.)

Today, with the development of online websites and blogs, such as patch.com, hyper-local media have become even more localized and oriented toward special interests. As a result, cultural values and media profiles are no longer defined only by nation, but by community and even by neighborhood. During the Arab Spring, for example, residents of Cairo, armed with cell phones and personal computers, provided hyper-local media coverage of street incidents in their neighborhoods—incidents that had national and international implications (Pavlik 2013).

Nations that feel a loss of identity may try to defend against the cultural invasion from foreign countries, especially the economically dominant United States. Yet as sociologists know, audiences are not necessarily passive recipients of foreign cultural messages, either in developing nations or in industrial nations. Thus, research on consumers of cultural products like television, music, and film must be placed in social context. Although people may watch and even enjoy media content, that does not mean that they will accept values that are alien to their own (Bielby and Harrington 2008).

Many developing nations have long argued for a greatly improved two-way flow of news and information between industrial nations and developing nations. They complain that news from the Third World is scant, and what news there is reflects unfavorably on the developing nations. For example, what do you know about South America? Most people in the United States will mention the two topics that dominate the news from countries south of the border: revolution and drugs. Most know little else about the continent.

To remedy this imbalance, a resolution to monitor the news and content that cross the borders of developing nations was passed by the United Nations Educational, Scientific, and Cultural Organization (UNESCO) in the 1980s. The United States has continued to oppose UNESCO plans, even though they were globally regarded as an important step toward protecting threatened cultures and media markets in developing nations.

The continuing opposition to media products from the United States is not limited to UNESCO or developing nations. South Korea places limits on how many days movie houses can show foreign motion pictures (primarily those from the United States). As programming is increasingly streamed, the European Union has sought to limit U.S.-based Netflix's "cultural dumping," which it regards as a threat to national cultural identity as well as to the European media industry (Barbière 2014; Baran 2015: 397–398).

 use your **sociological imagination**

How do your favorite media reflect U.S. culture as a whole? How do they reflect the culture of your local community? How do they reflect the cultures of the rest of the world?

The Digital Divide

Finally, as numerous studies have shown, advances in communications technology are not evenly distributed. Worldwide, low-income groups, racial and ethnic minorities, rural residents, and the citizens of developing countries have far less access than others to the latest technologies—a gap that is called the **digital divide.** People in low-income households, rural areas, and developing countries, for example, are less likely than others to have Internet access. When marginalized people do gain Internet access, they are still likely to trail the privileged. They may have dial-up service instead of broadband, or broadband instead of wireless Internet. The issue is not merely access to the Internet, but the cost and availability of broadband service. High-speed Internet connections are becoming increasingly essential for everything from completing school assignments to consulting with medical personnel and conducting business through routine financial transactions. Box 20-2 examines the global disconnect between the haves and have-nots of the information age (Robinson and Crenshaw 2010; P. Schaefer 2008).

Taking Sociology to Work

Lindsey Wallem, *Social Media Consultant*

Courtesy of Lindsey Wallem

Lindsey Wallem graduated from DePaul University with a major in sociology. She chose sociology because she wanted to help people, perhaps as a social worker for a nonprofit organization. Then, in her junior year, when her political science professor offered extra credit for work on a political campaign, Wallem's life took an unexpected turn. "I showed up at the Obama headquarters just as they were moving in to their downtown Chicago office," Wallem remembers. "I was assigned to the New Media department, using Facebook and MySpace to reach out to voters." At the time, the use of social media tools in a political campaign was groundbreaking. "It was an exciting place to be," she recalls. "I stayed on as a volunteer in New Media through the end of the campaign. When I graduated in 2008, I used that experience to pitch my social media services to nonprofits."

Today, Wallem is a social media manager for several nonprofit organizations in the Chicago area. She enjoys using her expertise in online organizing to help these worthy organizations grow. Wallem's work with a nonprofit that fights homelessness has been particularly satisfying to her. In 2010–11, her clients joined a coalition of organizations dedicated to creating more affordable housing in the city. "My role was to attend city council meetings and 'live-tweet' the proceedings for supporters who couldn't be in the room," she explains. "On the day when a version of our legislation was passed, it was an exciting task indeed!"

Wallem also teaches an online course in social media to high school students, through the Gifted LearningLinks program at Northwestern University. In the first few weeks of the course, she draws from her old textbooks to give students a brief lesson in sociological theory. Then she asks them to apply the theory to Facebook and Twitter. "For the next generation, the Internet is the new frontier," she muses. "It's pretty amazing to see the perspectives of these 'digital natives' at work."

Wallem finds that her background in sociology is quite relevant to her career. "I spend much of my workweek interacting with communities on Facebook and Twitter, building a content schedule, and looking for content to share with my audience," she explains. To measure and track the success of her social media campaigns—a necessity in online organizing—Wallem relies on her training in statistics. "Metrics in social media is more than just counting the number of 'Likes' you have," she notes. "You need to look at the data and determine what kind of story it is telling you, what your audience is like and what they need from you." Wallem also applies what she learned in her senior capstone course, Visual Sociology, which taught her to use photography or video to tell a story about a sociological trend. "I use this tactic every day on Facebook and YouTube—visuals are what grab attention and add weight to the message you are trying to convey," she says.

LET'S DISCUSS

1. Have you ever used social media to participate in an online campaign? If so, how did you participate—by donating money, for example, or attending a fundraising event?
2. How might you use social media in your own career?

Feminist Perspective

Feminists share the view of conflict theorists that the mass media stereotype and misrepresent social reality. According to this view, the media powerfully influence how we look at men and women, communicating unrealistic, stereotypical, and limiting images of the sexes.

Educators and social scientists have long noted the stereotypical portrayal of women and men in the mass media. Women are often shown as being shallow and obsessed with beauty. They are more likely than men to be presented unclothed, in danger, or even physically victimized. When women achieve newsworthy feats in fields traditionally dominated by men, such as professional sports, the media are often slow to recognize their accomplishments.

Even when female athletes are covered by the press, they are not treated equally. Communications researchers conducted a content analysis of over 200 hours of nationally televised coverage of professional golf events. The study showed that when female golfers are successful, they are more likely than male golfers to be called strong and intelligent. When they are not successful, they are more likely than men to be described as lacking in athletic ability. In contrast, male golfers receive more comments on their concentration and commitment. These findings suggest a subtle sexism, with women being portrayed as innately talented and men being portrayed as superior in mental or emotional makeup (T. Jacobs 2009).

Besides highlighting differences in media treatment, another aim of feminist research is to determine whether the media have a different impact on women than on men. For example for some time it was assumed that video gaming was a male world. However, by 2014 nearly half of gamers in the United States and Great Britain were female. Recently, researchers found that adolescent boys are almost three times as likely as adolescent girls to participate in online gaming. Clearly, this topic deserves further study (Grundberg and Hansegard 2014).

A continuing, troubling issue for feminists and society as a whole is pornography. Feminists tend to be very supportive of freedom of expression and self-determination, rights that are denied to women more often than to men. Yet pornography presents women as sex objects and seems to make viewing women that way acceptable. Nor are concerns about pornography limited to this type of objectification and imagery; some see their implicit endorsement of violence against women. The industry that creates risqué adult images for video and the Internet is largely unregulated, even putting its performers at risk.

Feminist scholars are cautiously optimistic about new media. For example, blogging represents a great potential for women who are underrepresented in the traditional media and whose freedom of self-expression is curtailed either by law or

Sociology in the Global Community

The Global Disconnect

Bogdan Ghirda, a Romanian, is paid 50 cents an hour to participate in multiplayer Internet games like City of Heroes and Star Wars. He is sitting in for someone in an industrialized country who does not want to spend days ascending to the highest levels of competition in order to compete with players who are already "well armed." This arrangement is not unusual. U.S.-based services can earn hundreds of dollars for recruiting someone in a less developed country, like Ghirda, to represent a single player in an affluent industrial country.

Meanwhile, in Africa, the resource-poor nation of Rwanda is developing its economy by encouraging investments in information and communications technologies. In 2011, through a combination of public investment and private competition among telecommunications companies, mobile phone and data transmission service in the country reached 96 percent. The challenges Rwanda faces remain immense: energy needs that are expensive to meet, a shortage of skilled computer specialists, and weak finances, to name a few. However, this nation of 11 million, with an annual per capita gross national income of just $1,530, may be able to create a stable economy based on new telecommunications technologies.

These two situations illustrate the technological disconnect between the developing and industrial nations. Around the world, developing nations lag far behind industrial nations in their access to and use of new technologies. The World Economic Forum's Networked Readiness Index (NRI), a ranking of 143 nations, shows the relative preparedness of individuals, businesses, and governments to benefit from information technologies. As the accompanying table shows, the haves of the world—countries like Singapore, Switzerland, and the United States—are network ready; the have-nots—countries like Angola, Yemen, and Haiti—are not.

> For developing nations, the consequences of the global disconnect are far more serious than an inability to surf the Net.

For developing nations, the consequences of the global disconnect are far more serious than an inability to surf the Net. Thanks to the Internet, multinational organizations can now function as a single global unit, responding instantly in real time, 24 hours a day. This new capability has fostered the emergence of what sociologist Manuel Castells calls a "global economy." But if large numbers of people—indeed, entire nations—are disconnected from the new global economy, their economic growth will remain slow and the well-being of their people will be affected negatively. Those citizens who are educated and skilled will emigrate to other labor markets, deepening the impoverishment of nations on the periphery.

NETWORKED READINESS INDEX

Top 10 Countries	Bottom 10 Countries
1. Singapore	134. Timor-Leste
2. Finland	135. Madagascar
3. Sweden	136. Yemen
4. Netherlands	137. Haiti
5. Norway	138. Mauritania
6. Switzerland	139. Myanmar
7. United States	140. Angola
8. United Kingdom	141. Burundi
9. Luxembourg	142. Guinea
10. Japan	143. Chad

LET'S DISCUSS

1. For nations on the periphery, what might be some specific social and economic consequences of the global disconnect?

2. What factors might complicate efforts to remedy the global disconnect in developing nations?

Sources: Anatale et al. 2013; Castells 2010a; Dutta et al. 2015; Kaneda and Bietsch 2015; T. Thompson 2005.

---

custom. In conservative cultures like Saudi Arabia, online media offer women the opportunity to explore lifestyles that traditional media outlets largely ignore (Webb and Lee 2012; Worth 2008).

Feminist researchers caution against assuming that what holds true for men's dominance of traditional media use is true for newer forms. Researchers, for example, have found since 2009 that women are slightly more likely to use social networking sites than men: as of 2015, 68 percent of women use these sites versus 62 percent of men (Perrin 2015).

Interactionist Perspective

Interactionists are especially interested in shared understandings of everyday behavior. These scholars examine the media on the micro level to see how they shape day-to-day social behavior. Increasingly, researchers talk about mass media in the context of *social capital,* as described by sociologist Pierre Bourdieu. **Social capital** is the collective benefit of social networks, which are built on reciprocal trust. The Internet generally, and social media in particular, offer us almost constant connectivity with others. These media increase our contact with family members, friends, and acquaintances, both those who live nearby and those who are far away. They also facilitate the development of new ties and new social networks (Bourdieu and Passerson 1990; Neves 2013).

Online social networks, in fact, have become a new way of promoting consumption. As Figure 20-2 shows, advertisers have traditionally marketed products and services through one-way spot ads, mass mailings, or billboards, whether they are promoting flat-screen televisions or public service messages like "Don't drink and drive." Now, using social networks, they can find consumers online and attempt to develop a two-way relationship with them there. Through Facebook, for example, Burger King awarded a free Whopper to anyone who would delete 10 friends. Facebook's staff was not happy with Burger King's promotion, which notified 239,906 Facebook users that they had been dropped for a burger—an action that violated the network's policy. Nevertheless, Burger

FIGURE 20-2 Marketing Online Through Social Networks

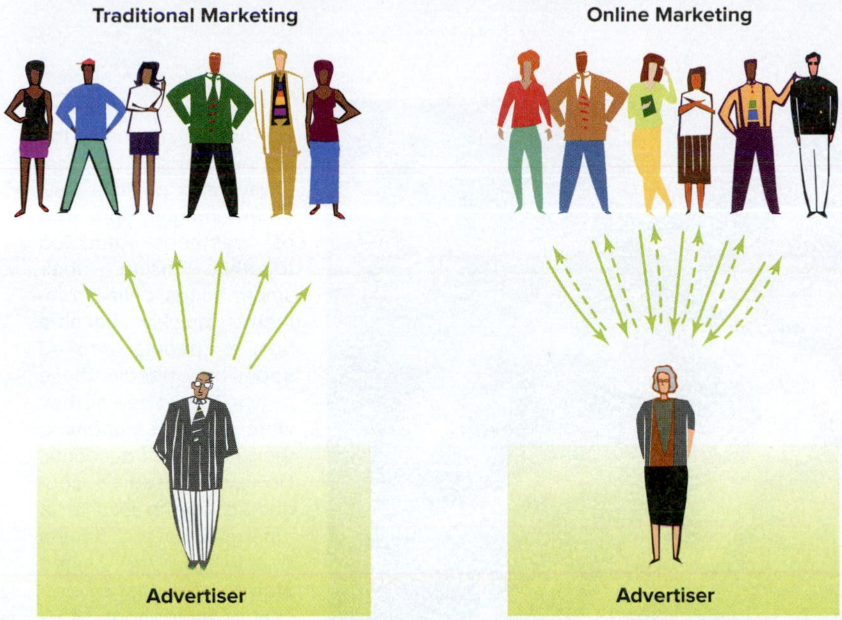

Traditional Marketing   **Online Marketing**

Advertiser   Advertiser

Traditional forms of advertising (left) allow only one-way communication, from the advertiser to the consumer. Online social networks (right) offer two-way communication, allowing advertisers to develop a relationship with consumers.

King created a vast network of consumers who enjoy Whoppers. Similarly, Kraft Foods encouraged people to post images of the Wiener-mobile on the photo site Flickr (Bacon Lovers' Talk 2009; Burger King 2009; Gaudin 2009).

Relationship marketing is not the only new use for online social networks. As Box 20-3 shows, monitoring cellphones became a potential way to track human migration during the refugee crisis that has swept across Europe.

Interactionists note, too, that friendship networks can emerge from shared viewing habits or from recollection of a cherished television series from the past. Family members and friends often gather for parties centered on the broadcasting of popular events such as the Super Bowl or the Academy Awards. And as we've seen, television often serves as a babysitter or playmate for children and even infants.

The rise of the Internet has also facilitated new forms of communication and social interaction. Grandparents can now keep up with their grandchildren via e-mail, or chat with them via Skype. Gay and lesbian teens have online resources for support and information. People can even find their lifetime partners through computer dating services.

Some troubling issues have been raised about day-to-day life on the Internet, however. What, if anything, should be done about terrorists and other extremist groups who use the Internet to exchange messages of hatred and even bomb-making recipes? What, if anything, should be done about the issue of sexual expression on the Internet? How can children be protected from it? Should "hot chat" and X-rated film clips be censored? Or should expression be completely free?

Though the Internet has created a new platform for extremists, hate groups, and pornographers, it has also given people greater control over what they see and hear. That is, the Internet allows people to manage their media exposure so as to avoid sounds, images, and ideas they do not enjoy or approve of. The legal scholar Cass Sunstein (2002) has referred to this personalized approach to news information gathering as *egocasting*. One social consequence of this trend may be a less tolerant society. If we read, see, and hear only what we know and agree with, we may be much less prepared to meet people from different backgrounds or converse with those who express new viewpoints.

Furthermore, while many people in the United States embrace the Internet, we should note that information is not evenly distributed throughout the population. The same people, by and large, who experience poor health and have few job opportunities have been left off the information highway. Figure 20-3 breaks down Internet usage by gender, age, race, income, education, and community type. Note the disparities in usage between those with high and low incomes, and between those with more and less education. The data also show a racial disparity. Though educators and politicians have touted the potential benefits to the disadvantaged, Internet usage may be reinforcing existing social-class and racial barriers.

The interactionist perspective helps us to understand one important aspect of the entire mass media system— the audience. How do we actively participate in media events? How do we construct with others the meaning of media messages? We will explore these questions in the section that follows.

Table 20-2 summarizes the various sociological perspectives on the media.

Tracking Sociological Perspectives

TABLE **20-2** SOCIOLOGICAL PERSPECTIVES ON THE MASS MEDIA

Theoretical Perspective	Emphasis
Functionalist	Socialization
	Enforcement of social norms
	Conferral of status
	Promotion of consumption
	Narcotizing effect (dysfunction)
Conflict	Gatekeeping
	Media monitoring
	Construction of reality
	Digital divide
Feminist	Misrepresentation of women
	Differential impact on women
Interactionist	Impact on social behavior
	Source of friendship networks
	Social capital

The world continues to be gripped by images of vast numbers of migrants, both economic and political refugees, making their way across the Mediterranean to Europe. The conflict in Syria was by far the biggest driver of the migration, but the ongoing violence in Afghanistan; abuses of forced labor in Eritrea; as well as grinding poverty in Iraq, Nigeria, Kosovo, Pakistan, Somalia, and Sudan also led individuals, families, and entire villages to seek new lives elsewhere.

The physical and emotional challenges to the refugees are obvious. Already traumatized before they even entered Europe, thousands died trying to cross the Mediterranean or during hazardous land crossings, which even included landmine fields that remained from previous wars. Once in Europe, they were often greeted with a less than positive reception.

Critics argued that European countries' response was more focused on securing borders than on making even short-term plans for the desperate families. Complicating the situation was the rise of nationalist parties in many receiving countries and concerns about terrorists among the large number of arrivals.

Surprisingly, cell phones may offer a solution to some of the challenges of such massive and unexpected migrations. For governments and aid groups to be able to assist migrants effectively, they need accurate and timely statistics about who the migrants are and how many are arriving. Such statistics can also counter common misperceptions that only serve to postpone an urgently needed political and humanitarian response. Without migration statistics, a country can't meaningfully plan how to allocate resources,

© Iakovos Hatzistavrou/AFP/Getty Images

> Soon it will be possible to track thousands of migrants moving from multiple countries to multiple destinations, the same way a person in Berlin can use an app to track her lost iPhone.

for instance, to assist asylum-seekers or migrants in need.

So how do cell phones figure in to this? There are now more than 7 billion mobile phone subscriptions globally, at least 5 billion of which are in developing countries. Mobile phone penetration is growing fast, particularly across Asia and Africa, as is the number of Internet users worldwide. This means that an unprecedentedly large and complex amount of data is being generated in real time, every time a call or an online payment is made, or every time people interact on social media.

The use of cell phones was observed during the refugee crisis but not always in a positive way. When images appeared of refugees huddled together using their smartphones, online comments quickly became hostile: people scoffed about how needy "these people" could be if all they were doing was updating their Facebook accounts. However, research conducted among victims of emergencies or natural disasters in the United States shows that 53 percent of smartphone users said the technology was vital to their well-being.

Soon it will be possible to track thousands of migrants moving from multiple countries to multiple destinations, the same way a person in Berlin can use an app to track her lost iPhone. Such information could be used to inform nation-states about the flow of migrants and provide them with the information they need to consider more humanitarian options.

LET'S DISCUSS

1. Have you ever used a smartphone for your own or someone else's safety during an emergency or natural disaster? What are the effects of having (or not having) this technology in such circumstances?

2. Are smartphones and other new technologies frills or vital services during emergencies? If you worked for an aid agency, how would smartphone technology help you do your job during a refugee crisis?

Sources: BBC 2015; Parke 2015; Rango 2015; Williams 2015.

FIGURE 20-3 **Who's on the Internet**

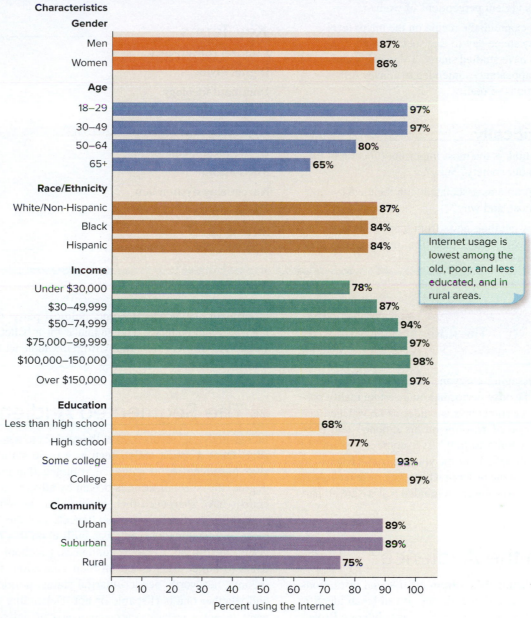

Note: Based on a national survey as of September 2015 (gender data January 9–12, 2014).
Source: Pew Research Center 2014; Rainie 2015.

MODULE 20 | **Recap and Review**

Summary

The **mass media** are print and electronic instruments of communication that carry messages to often widespread audiences. They pervade all social institutions, from entertainment to education to politics.

1. From the functionalist perspective, the media entertain, socialize, enforce social norms, confer status, and promote consumption. They can be dysfunctional to the extent that they desensitize us to serious events and issues (the **narcotizing dysfunction**).

2. Conflict theorists think the media reflect and even deepen the division in society through **gatekeeping**, or control over which material reaches the public; media monitoring, the covert observation of people's media usage and choices; and support of the **dominant ideology**, which defines reality, overwhelming local cultures.

3. Feminist theorists point out that media images of the sexes communicate unrealistic, stereotypical, limiting, and sometimes violent perceptions of women.

4. Interactionists examine the media on the micro level to see how they shape day-to-day social behavior. Interactionists have studied shared TV viewing and staged public appearances intended to convey self-serving definitions of reality.

Thinking Critically

1. What do you think is the most important function of the mass media in our society? Why?

2. Which of the problems associated with the media troubles you most, and why?

3. Americans now get their news from many different cable news networks rather than from just three national networks. What is the effect of this trend on the media's tendency to promulgate a dominant ideology?

Key Terms

Cultural convergence

Digital divide

Dominant ideology

Gatekeeping

Hyperconsumerism

Hyper-local media

Mass media

Narcotizing dysfunction

Social capital

Stereotype

MODULE 21 | The Audience

Ever felt like text-messaging everyone you know to encourage them to vote for your favorite performer on a certain reality program? Ever looked over someone's shoulder as he watched last week's episode of *Game of Thrones* on his iPhone—and been tempted to reveal the ending to him? Ever come across an old CD and tried to remember the last time you or a friend listened to one, or heard the songs in the order in which they were recorded? In this and many other ways, we are reminded that we are all part of a larger audience.

Who Is in the Audience?

The mass media are distinguished from other social institutions by the necessary presence of an audience. It can be an identifiable, finite group, such as an audience at a jazz club or a Broadway musical, or a much larger and undefined group, such as *Daredevil* viewers or readers of the same issue of *USA Today*. The audience may be a secondary group gathered in a large auditorium or a primary group, such as a family watching the latest Disney video at home.

We can look at the audience from the level of both *microsociology* and *macrosociology*. At the micro level, we might consider how audience members, interacting among themselves, respond to the media, or in the case of live performances, actually influence the performers. At the macro level, we might examine broader societal consequences of the media, such as the early childhood education delivered through programming like *Sesame Street*.

Even if an audience is spread out over a wide geographic area and members don't know one another, it is still distinctive in terms of age, gender, income, political party, formal schooling, race, and ethnicity. The audience for a ballet, for example, would likely differ substantially from the audience for alternative music.

The Segmented Audience

Increasingly, the media market themselves to a *particular* audience. Once a media outlet, such as a radio station or a magazine, has identified its audience, it targets that group. To some degree, this specialization is driven by advertising. Media specialists have sharpened their ability, through survey research, to identify particular target audiences. For the 2016 election races, political media specialists built upon this pattern by targeting specific social media audiences. Facebook allows advertisers to target users based on their education, field of study, income, net worth, gender, marital status, political affiliation, and whether one is Hispanic or not. Depending on whom you want to get a specific message, you can define the pool of recipients (Loomer 2014).

The specialized targeting of audiences has led some scholars to question the "mass" in mass media. For example, the British social psychologist Sonia Livingstone (2004) has written that the media have become so segmented, they have taken on the appearance almost of individualization. Are viewing audiences so segmented that large collective audiences are a thing of the past? That is not yet clear. Even though we seem to be living in an age of *personal* computers, large formal organizations still do transmit public messages that reach a sizable, heterogeneous, and scattered audience.

Media specialists have sharpened their ability, through survey research, to target particular audiences. During election campaigns, candidates and political action groups place advertisements in markets where surveys indicate they will find support. In the past this meant selecting television and radio programs, but more and more the effort to reach target markets focuses on social media. An estimated $1 billion was spent on online political advertising for the 2016 presidential campaign. Digital strategists use accumulated voter files to send out messages and solicit campaign contributions. Campaigns identify ad recipients by the hashtags they use on Twitter or the videos and photos they post on Snapchat. Using Facebook and Instagram, campaigns target voters by congressional district, by interest, by gender and age, and by any combination of these factors (Davies and Yadron 2016; Parker 2015).

 use your **sociological imagination**

Think about the last time you were part of an audience. Describe the performance. How similar to or different from yourself were the other audience members? What might account for whatever similarities or differences you noticed?

Audience Behavior

Sociologists have long researched how audiences interact with one another and how they share information after a media event. The role of audience members as opinion leaders particularly intrigues social researchers. An **opinion leader** is someone who influences the opinions and decisions of others through day-to-day personal contact and communication. For example, a movie or theater critic functions as an opinion leader. Sociologist Paul Lazarsfeld and his colleagues (1948) pioneered the study of opinion leaders in their research on voting behavior in the 1940s. They found that opinion leaders encourage their relatives, friends, and co-workers to think positively about a particular candidate, perhaps pushing them to listen to the politician's speeches or read the campaign literature.

Consider the audience for online news. Increasingly people gather information online rather than through other mass media such as television, print, and radio. Opinion leaders in those traditional media sources typically were columnists, "talking heads," or editorial boards. The move to online does not mean that opinion leaders do not emerge. An analysis of online discussion groups found that certain participants typically gain more attention than others and that these anonymous centers of influence can account for 40 to 60 percent of all discussion and retweets (Choi 2015)

The term "audience" may connote a passive group but this is often not the case. Protesters at political rallies or attendees who boo performers, athletes, or speakers are anything but passive. Opinion leaders may play a role here as well, by encouraging such tactics, which in turn may lead to collective action on the part of audience members (see Module 57). The activist role of the audience specifically and media in general becomes apparent in the next section as we consider the global reach of mass media (Croteau et al. 2012).

MODULE 21 | **Recap and Review**

Summary

The need for an audience distinguishes the mass media from other social institutions.

1. An audience may be small and well defined or large and amorphous. With increasing numbers of media outlets has come more and more targeting of segmented (or specialized) audiences.

2. Social researchers have studied the role of opinion leaders in influencing audiences.

Thinking Critically

1. What kind of audience is targeted by the producers of televised professional wrestling? By the creators of an animated film? By a rap group? What factors determine who makes up a particular audience?

2. Who do you consider to be your opinion leaders? Why are those individuals influential to you? Would your parents, friends, or teachers select the same opinion leaders?

Key Terms

Opinion leader

Has the rise of the electronic media created a *global village*? Canadian media theorist Marshall McLuhan predicted it would nearly 60 years ago. Today, physical distance is no longer a barrier, and instant messaging is possible across the world. The mass media have indeed created a global village. Not all countries are equally connected, as Figure 22-1 shows, but the progress has been staggering, considering that voice transmission was just beginning 120 years ago (McLuhan 1964, 1967).

Sociologist Todd Gitlin considers *global torrent* a more apt metaphor for the medias reach than *global village*. The media permeate all aspects of everyday life. Take advertising, for example. Consumer goods are marketed vigorously worldwide, from advertisements on airport baggage carriers to imprints on sandy beaches. Little wonder that people around the world develop loyalty to a brand and are as likely to sport a Nike, Coca-Cola, or Harley-Davidson logo as they are their favorite soccer or baseball insignia (Gitlin 2002; Klein 1999).

The Internet has facilitated all forms of communication. Reference materials and data banks can now be made accessible across national boundaries. Information related to international finance, marketing, trade, and manufacturing is literally just a keystroke away. We have seen the emergence of true world news outlets and the promotion of a world music that is not clearly identifiable with any single

© Noah Flanigan 2009

New technologies can create new social norms. In Gurupá, Brazil, television watching became a community social activity when three new TV owners agreed to share their sets with the community of 3,000.

FIGURE 22-1 Media Penetration in Selected Countries

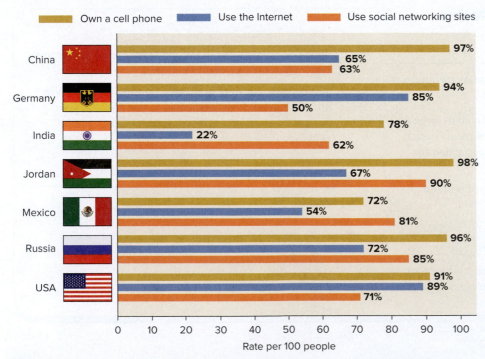

- Own a cell phone
- Use the Internet
- Use social networking sites

China: 97%, 65%, 63%
Germany: 94%, 85%, 50%
India: 78%, 22%, 62%
Jordan: 98%, 67%, 90%
Mexico: 72%, 54%, 81%
Russia: 96%, 72%, 85%
USA: 91%, 89%, 71%

Rate per 100 people

Cell phone ownership is high around the world, but in some countries outside the United States, texting is more common than calling.

Note: Data from multinational interviews by Pew Research in Spring 2015.
Source: Poushter, Jacob. 2016. *Flags:* © admin_design/Shutterstock RF

culture. Even the most future-oriented thinker would find the growth in the reach of the mass media in postindustrial and postmodern societies remarkable (Castells 2001, 2010b; Croteau and Hoynes 2006, 2014).

Although in the United States we may take television for granted, even thinking of it as an old-fashioned medium, worldwide that is not necessarily the case. In India, half of all households do not have television; in Nigeria and Bangladesh, more than 70 percent of households go without. Two technological advances are likely to change this pattern, however. First, advances in battery power now allow viewers to watch television even in areas where there is no electricity. Second, digital signal transmission permits television reception via cable or satellite.

In some developing countries, people manage to watch television even though they don't own one. Consider the town of Gurupá, in the remote Amazon area of Brazil. In 1982, the wealthiest three households in this community bought televisions. To please the rest of the town, they agreed to place their TVs near the window so that

their neighbors could watch them as well. As the TV owners proudly displayed their new status symbol, TV watching became a community social activity. The introduction of a new technology had created a new social norm (Kenny 2009; Pace 1993, 1998).

Media use can take on added importance in developing nations. Consider Kenya, a nation the size of Texas. During a recent malaria outbreak, public health researchers monitored the text messages Kenyans sent on their 15 million cell phones and used the content to map the spread of the dreaded disease. Surprisingly, they found that travelers were carrying the disease along less-traveled regional routes rather than the heavily traveled roads to and from the capital city, Nairobi. The information they gleaned proved vital to them in concentrating malaria control efforts (Wesolowski et al. 2012).

Around the world, people rely increasingly on digital media, from cell phones to the Internet. This trend has raised new concerns about the right to privacy. Should government officials have the right to monitor peoples text messages, even if they are protecting the publics health? The Social Policy section that follows examines the social implications of digital media, from censorship to criminal activity.

social policy and the Mass Media |
The Right to Privacy

"You have no privacy anyway. Get over it," the CEO of Sun Microsystems stated bluntly in 1999. A little more than a decade later, speaking at an awards ceremony, Facebook founder Mark Zuckerberg claimed that people no longer expect to have privacy, given the rise of social media. In his view, privacy is no longer a "social norm" (Carr 2010:W2; Bobbie Johnson 2010).

If there was any doubt about the effect of the new mass media on peoples privacy, it disappeared in 2013 when Edward Snowden, an IT specialist working as a contractor to the U.S. government, began leaking information about the National Security Agencys data-gathering activities. The NSA is charged with gathering intelligence on foreign security threats, both within the United States and abroad. However, Snowden revealed that in an operation code-named PRISM, agency sleuths had been secretly gathering huge amounts of information on ordinary citizens by infiltrating their accounts at some of the nations largest technology companies—Google, Apple, Microsoft, Facebook, AOL, YouTube, and Yahoo. In light of such revelations, we might ask whether any of us can expect to keep our private information private in the postmodern digital age.

Looking at the Issue

This sweeping challenge to privacy comes from **big data,** a term coined by sociologist Charles Tilly (1980) to refer to the rapid collection and analysis of enormous amounts of information by supercomputers. The accumulation of digital data has made it increasingly easy for business firms, government agencies, and even criminals to retrieve and store information about private individuals. In public places, at work, and on the Internet, surveillance devices track our every move, whether it is a keystroke or an ATM withdrawal. The information they accumulate includes everything from our buying habits to our web-surfing patterns.

© Holger Leue/Lonely Planet Images/Getty Images

A Google Street View car drives through an English town, photographing it for use with Google's online map service. Even though Google's activities occur largely on public property, people have objected to them as an invasion of privacy. Some of the images Google captures include bystanders who happen to be in the area, as well as people's backyards and even the interior of their homes, as seen through open windows and doors.

—*Continued*

So significant has big data become that corporations are regarding the aggregate data they hold, especially about consumers and their preferences, as a highly valuable asset, much like a fleet of trucks or a factory. The data must be protected but also can be used in ways about which we can only begin to speculate. For example, cable companies and other video providers could give customers summary reports of their viewing habits. Such data would tell customers which outlets they pay for and don't use and to which new channels they should subscribe. Obviously this kind of data, aggregated over many customers, becomes big data that is highly valuable to the company itself (Samuel 2015).

As technology increases its power to monitor our behavior, it raises fears of misuse for criminal or even undemocratic purposes. In short, big data may threaten not just our privacy, but our freedom from crime and censorship as well. Some obvious violations of privacy, such as identity theft—the misuse of credit card and Social Security numbers to masquerade as another person—have been well documented. Other violations involve online surveillance of dissident political groups by authoritarian regimes and the unauthorized release of classified government documents. In 2010, WikiLeaks began releasing thousands of classified U.S. foreign policy documents on its website, causing some people to condemn the action as treasonous and others to praise it as a blow against government censorship (O'Harrow 2005).

Other privacy violations are subtler, and not strictly illegal. For example, many commercial websites use "cookies" and tracking technology to monitor visitors' websurfing. Using that information, marketers can estimate a visitors age, gender, and zip code, and from that data, the persons income. They can then select advertisements that will appeal specifically to that person. So depending on who we are, or at least appear to be, one of us might see ads about weight-loss products and another, ads about travel to exotic locations.

Is this approach to online marketing just effective advertising, or is it an invasion of privacy? Because the information that marketers gather in this way can be tied to other devices a person uses, such as a cell phone or computer, some critics see online tracking as a form of fingerprinting (Angwin 2010; Angwin and Valentino-DeVries 2010a).

Applying Sociology

From a sociological point of view, the complex issues of privacy and censorship can be considered illustrations of **culture lag**, a period of maladjustment when the nonmaterial culture is still struggling to adapt to new material conditions. As usual, the material culture (technology) is changing faster than the nonmaterial culture (norms for controlling the use of technology). Too often, the result is an anything-goes approach to the use of new technologies.

Sociologists' views on the use and abuse of new technologies differ depending on their theoretical perspective. Functionalists take a generally positive view of the Internet, pointing to its manifest function of facilitating communication. From their perspective, the Internet performs the latent function of empowering people with few resources—from hate groups to special-interest organizations—to communicate with the masses.

Functionalists also note that digital surveillance can assist law enforcement agencies in preventing or detecting crimes in progress. For example, facial recognition technology can be used to identify stalkers, find lost children, or even track terrorists. Yet they admit that warrantless surveillance of people who lead mostly normal lives is dysfunctional.

In contrast, conflict theorists stress the danger that the most powerful groups in a society will use technology to violate the privacy of the less powerful.

Interactionists observe that making our web profiles and other information about ourselves publicly available may affect our future social interactions, and not necessarily for the good. One out of four college and university admissions officers reports Googling or checking out applicants' social media pages. Over a third of those gatekeepers have found something online that can hurt applicants (Belkin and Porter 2012).

Initiating Policy

Legislation regarding the surveillance of electronic communications has not always upheld citizens' right to privacy. In 1986, the federal government passed the Electronic Communications Privacy Act, which outlawed the surveillance of telephone calls except with the permission of both the U.S. attorney general and a federal judge. Telegrams, faxes, and e-mails did not receive the same degree of protection, however. In 2001, one month after the terrorist attacks of September 11, Congress passed the Patriot Act, which relaxed existing legal checks on surveillance by law enforcement officers. Federal agencies are now freer to gather data electronically, including peoples credit card receipts and banking records (Gertner 2005).

Today, most other types of online monitoring have yet to be tested in court, including the use of tracking technologies and the compilation and sale of personal profiles to merchandisers. Consistent with the concept of culture lag, privacy advocates complain that the 1986 law, which was enacted before the Internet as we know it even existed, has not kept pace with advancing technology. For example, in 2014 federal and state courts approved a total of 3,554 wiretaps using Supreme Court–approved methods that date back to 1928. However, in the same year government agencies made well over a million requests of mobile-phone companies for

—*Continued*

information on cell phone users—requests that require only a subpoena, not court approval.

Many of those requests included "tower dumps," which reveal the whereabouts of everyone in the area with a cell phone, suspects or not. Such sweeps resemble the NSAs PRISM operation in their indiscriminate nature. To date, proposed legislation has focused mainly on the consumer side of privacy. For example, in 2012 the Federal Trade Commission issued a strong call for legislation that would require companies like Google to respect Internet users' privacy by adding a "Do Not Track" (DNT) button to their browsers. As of 2016, even browsers like Firefox, which have introduced DNT technology, let each website choose whether to honor it or not (Electronic Frontier Foundation 2016).

If anything, however, people seem to be less vigilant about maintaining their privacy today than they were before the information age. Young people who have grown up browsing the Internet seem to accept the existence of the "cookies" and "spyware" they may pick up while surfing. They have become accustomed to adult surveillance of their conversation in electronic chat rooms. And many see no risk in providing personal information about themselves to strangers they meet online. It is not surprising that college professors find their students do not appreciate the political significance of their right to privacy (Turkle 2004, 2011).

The need for online privacy seems only to be increasing, however. In a new practice called *weblining,* data-gathering companies are monitoring peoples online activities not so much for merchandising purposes, but to collect negative personal information. Based on this information, collected from the websites people search or the products and people they friend, a person may be denied a job opportunity or assigned a low credit rating. Data-gathering companies also offer information on searches having to do with mental issues like bipolar disorder and anxiety, which can make it difficult for a person to secure affordable health insurance. Although weblining has not yet drawn policymakers' attention, it is sure to do so in the future (Andrews 2012).

In the near future, new technological innovations will again redefine the limits of surveillance. Sensors are being installed in more and more objects, from appliances to electronic readers, to facilitate their use. It is only a matter of time before manufacturers begin compiling big data on how we use our refrigerators and microwaves, on what we read or scan down to the sentence level. Some corporations are installing sensors on security badges, to record employees' movements and conversations.

To many people, there is a fine line between this use of big data and Big Brother, a fictional character in George

© Columbia/Photofest

George Orwell's novel *Nineteen Eighty-Four* describes a future in which all citizens suffer intensive surveillance by the government ("Big Brother"). In this poster for the 1956 motion picture version, Big Brother hovers over editor Winston Smith, played by Edmund O'Brien.

Orwells *Nineteen Eighty-Four.* Published in 1949, the novel describes a future in which the government, directed by the quasi-divine leader Big Brother, secretly scrutinizes people's every move, then manipulates their view of society and even themselves. Little wonder that in 2013, sales of *Nineteen Eighty-Four* increased 7,000 percent within a week of news about Edward Snowden's leaks (Orwell 1949; Price 2013; Silverman 2013).

TAKE THE ISSUE WITH YOU

1. How would you react if you discovered that the government was monitoring your use of the mass media?

2. If your safety were in jeopardy, would you be willing to sacrifice your privacy?

3. Which do you consider the greatest threat to society: government censorship, cybercrime, or Internet surveillance? Explain.

Summary

The media have a global reach thanks to new communications technologies, especially the Internet.

1. Some people are concerned that the media's global reach will spread unhealthy influences to other cultures.

2. The media industry is becoming more and more concentrated, creating media conglomerates. This raises concerns about how innovative and independent the media can be. In some countries, governments own and control the media.

3. The Internet is the one significant exception to the trend toward media concentration, allowing millions of people to produce their own media content.

Thinking Critically

1. Use the functionalist, conflict, and interactionist perspectives to assess the effects of global TV programming on developing countries.

2. Give one example of how individualization of the media, through the Internet, and media concentration, through journalism, films, TV, and radio, have affected your life.

Key Terms

Big data

Culture lag

Mastering This Chapter

© Franziska Krug/German Select/ Getty Images

taking sociology with you

1 For one day, categorize every media message you receive in terms of its function: Does it socialize, enforce a social norm, confer status, or promote consumption? Keep a record and tally the results. Which function was the most common? What can you conclude from the results?

2 Pick a specific audience—residents of your dorm, for example—and track their media preferences over the next day or two. Which mass media are they watching, reading, or listening to? Which media are the most popular and which the least popular? How segmented is this particular mass media audience?

3 Pick a foreign film, television program, or Internet site and study it from the point of view of a sociologist. What does it tell you about the culture that produced it?

key terms

Big data The rapid collection and analysis of enormous amounts of information by supercomputers.

Cultural convergence The flow of content across multiple media, and the accompanying migration of media audiences.

Culture lag A period of maladjustment when the nonmaterial culture is still struggling to adapt to new material conditions.

Digital divide The relative lack of access to the latest technologies among low-income groups, racial and ethnic minorities, rural residents, and the citizens of developing countries.

Dominant ideology A set of cultural beliefs and practices that helps to maintain powerful social, economic, and political interests.

Gatekeeping The process by which a relatively small number of people in the media industry control what material eventually reaches the audience.

Hyperconsumerism The practice of buying more than we need or want, and often more than we can afford; a preoccupation of postmodern consumers.

Hyper-local media Reporting that is highly local and typically Internet-based.

Mass media Print and electronic means of communication that carry messages to widespread audiences.

Narcotizing dysfunction The phenomenon in which the media provide such massive amounts of coverage that the audience becomes numb and fails to act on the information, regardless of how compelling the issue.

Opinion leader Someone who influences the opinions and decisions of others through day-to-day personal contact and communication.

Social capital The collective benefit of social networks, which are built on reciprocal trust.

Stereotype An unreliable generalization about all members of a group that does not recognize individual differences within the group.

self-quiz

Read each question carefully and then select the best answer.

1. From the functionalist perspective, the media can be dysfunctional in what way?
   a. They enforce social norms.
   b. They confer status.
   c. They desensitize us to events.
   d. They are agents of socialization.

2. Sociologist Robert Park studied how newspapers helped immigrants to the United States adjust to their environment by changing their customary habits and by teaching them the opinions held by people in their new home country. His study was conducted from which sociological perspective?
   a. the functionalist perspective
   b. the conflict perspective
   c. the interactionist perspective
   d. the dramaturgical perspective

3. There are problems inherent in the socialization function of the mass media. For example, many people worry about
   a. the effect of using the television as a babysitter.
   b. the impact of violent programming on viewer behavior.
   c. the unequal ability of all individuals to purchase televisions.
   d. both a and b

4. Media advertising has several clear functions, but it also has dysfunctions. Sociologists are concerned that
   a. it creates unrealistic expectations of what is required to be happy.
   b. it creates new consumer needs.
   c. advertisers are able to influence media content.
   d. all of the above

5. Gatekeeping, the process by which a relatively small number of people control what material reaches an audience, is largely dominant in all but which of the following media?
   a. television
   b. the Internet
   c. publishing
   d. music

6. Which sociological perspective is especially concerned with the media's ability to decide what gets transmitted through gatekeeping?
   a. the functionalist perspective
   b. the conflict perspective
   c. the interactionist perspective
   d. the dramaturgical perspective

7. Which of the following is *not* a problem feminist theorists see with media coverage?
   a. Women are underrepresented, suggesting that men are the cultural standard and that women are insignificant.
   b. Men and women are portrayed in ways that reflect and perpetuate stereotypical views of gender.
   c. Female athletes are treated differently from male athletes in television commentary.
   d. The increasing frequency of single moms in the media is providing a negative role model for women.

8. Which of the following is *not* true concerning how men and women use the Internet?
   a. Men are more likely to use the Internet daily.
   b. Women are more likely to use e-mail to maintain friendships.
   c. Men account for 100 percent of players in online sports fantasy leagues.
   d. Men are slightly more likely to have ever used the Internet than women are.

9. Sociologist Paul Lazarsfeld and his colleagues pioneered the study of
   a. the audience.
   b. opinion leaders.
   c. the media's global reach.
   d. media violence.

10. Which term refers to the relative lack of access to technology among low-income groups, racial and ethnic minorities, rural residents, and citizens of developing countries?
    a. digital divide
    b. culture lag
    c. cultural convergence
    d. narcotizing dysfunction

11. The mass media increase social cohesion by presenting a more or less standardized, common view of culture through mass communication. This statement reflects the _____ perspective.

12. Paul Lazarsfeld and Robert Merton created the term _____ _____ to refer to the phenomenon in which the media provide such massive amounts of information that the audience becomes numb and generally fails to act on the information, regardless of how compelling the issue.

13. _____ _____ is the term used to describe the set of cultural beliefs and practices that helps to maintain powerful social, economic, and political interests.

14. Sociologists blame the mass media for the creation and perpetuation of _____, or generalizations about all members of a group that do not recognize individual differences within the group.

15. The _____ perspective contends that television distorts the political process.

16. We risk being _____ if we overstress U.S. dominance and assume that other nations do not play a role in media cultural exports.

17. Both _____ and _____ theorists are troubled that the victims depicted in violent imagery are often those who are given less respect in real life: women, children, the poor, racial minorities, citizens of foreign countries, and even the physically disabled.

18. The _____ perspective examines the media on the micro level to see how they shape day-to-day social behavior.

19. From a sociological point of view, the current controversy over privacy and media censorship illustrates the concept of _____

_____.

20. Nearly 50 years ago, Canadian media theorist _____ _____ predicted that the rise of the electronic media would create a "global village."

7

Deviance, Crime, and Social Control

© Frederick J. Brown/AFP/Getty Images

What constitutes a crime? What constitues deviance? In Los Angeles, a three-day market featured cannabis farmers from throughout California selling high-quality medical marijuana.

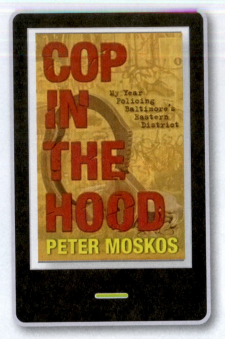

© Ira C. Roberts/Chad Enterprises Corporation

What do you think (or know) life is like in a high-crime area?

To learn about crime firsthand, sociologist Peter Moskos became a Baltimore police officer.

66 Living in Baltimore City, I was required to carry my gun both on and off duty. I never fired a shot outside of training. Only rarely was my service weapon—a charged semi-automatic nine-millimeter Glock-17 with no safety and a seventeen-round clip—pointed at somebody. But in my police duties, my gun was very routinely removed from its holster, probably every other shift. I did occasionally chase people down alleys and wrestled a few suspects. I maced one person, but did not hit anybody. As a police officer, I tried to speak softly and carry a big stick. The department issued a twenty-nine-inch straight wooden baton just for this purpose. I brought it along to all my calls.

In any account of police work, inevitably the noncriminal public, the routine, and the working folks all get short shrift. Police don't deal with a random cross-section of society, even within the areas they work. And this book reflects that. The ghetto transcends stereotypes. Families try to make it against the odds. Old women sweep the streets. People rise before dawn to go to work. On Sundays, ladies go to church wearing beautiful hats and preachers preach to the choir. But if you're looking for stereotypes, they're there. Between the vacant and abandoned buildings you'll find liquor stores, fast food, Korean corner stores, and a Jewish pawn shop. Living conditions are worse than third-world shanty towns: children in filthy apartments without plumbing or electricity, entire homes put out on eviction day, forty-five-year-old great-grand parents, junkies not raising their kids, drug dealers, and everywhere signs of violence and despair.

As a middle-class white man policing the ghetto, I should address the charge of 'exoticism', that I use poor residents for my own advantage. I plead no-contest. If you're not from the ghetto, and though it may not be politically correct to say so, the ghetto *is* exotic. One field-training officer accused me of being '*fascinated* by the ghetto'. I am. There are very few aspects of urban life that don't fascinate me. But it is not my intent to sensationalize the ghetto. This is a book about police.

If you want to read about the ghetto, good books are out there. Ghettos are diverse and encompass many cultures and classes. Some object to the very term ghetto. I use the word because it is the vernacular of police officers and many (though by no means all) of the residents. If you really want to learn about the ghetto, go there. There's probably one near you. Visit a church; walk down the street; buy something from the corner store; have a beer; eat. But most importantly, talk to people. That's how you learn. When the subject turns to drugs and crime, you'll hear a common refrain: 'It just don't make sense.'

Twenty months in Baltimore wasn't very long, but it was long enough to see five police officers killed in the line of duty. And there were other cops, friends of mine, who were hurt, shot, and lucky to live. A year after I quit the force, my friend and academy classmate became the first Baltimore police woman killed in the line of duty, dying in a car crash on the way to back up another police officer. 99

(Moskos 2008:15–17)

> *Twenty months in Baltimore wasn't very long, but it was long enough to see five police officers killed in the line of duty.*

Peter Moskos's route to becoming a sworn police officer was a bit unusual, considering that becoming one was never his goal. None of his friends were on the force, nor did he come from a family of police officers; his father was a well-known and respected sociologist. During his graduate studies, however, Moskos decided that he wanted to learn more about law enforcement. So he persuaded Baltimore's police commissioner to let him attend the police academy, as both a student and a sociologist.

On the second day of class, the commissioner was suddenly and unexpectedly ousted from office, to be replaced by a new commissioner who questioned Moskos's motives. "Why don't you want to be a cop for real?" he challenged Moskos. That was the beginning of Moskos's 20-month tour of duty with the Baltimore Police Department, during which he responded to crimes that included disorderly conduct, domestic abuse, and a 12-person shooting.

In this excerpt from his book *Cop in the Hood: My Year Policing Baltimore's Eastern District*, Moskos describes his beat as seen through the eyes of a sociologist doing an ethnographic study. Looking beyond the stereotypes, he found a diverse and vibrant community, one he would get to know by mingling with its residents. Moskos took the same approach in his study of police work, taking sociology with him to the academy, the station house, and the street.

Moskos notes that the residents he served simply could not fathom the crime that plagued their inner-city neighborhood. What does explain it? Although drug dealing, prostitution, and the sale of stolen goods are illegal activities, they provide a certain level of stability to those who live on the edge, including the homeless, drug addicts, and frightened, neglected youths. Only a thin line separates their *deviant behavior*—behavior that violates social norms, such as dropping out of school or sleeping on the street—from their illegal activities. Crime is functional in their subculture, even if it is socially unacceptable to the rest of the neighborhood.

Another example of a behavior that can be seen as either socially acceptable or socially unacceptable depending on your reference group is binge drinking. On the one hand, we can view binge drinking as *deviant,* as violating a school's standards of conduct and endangering a person's health. On the other hand, we can see it as *conforming,* or complying with peer culture. In the United States, people are socialized to have mixed feelings about both conforming and nonconforming behavior. The term *conformity* can conjure up images of mindless imitation of a peer group—whether a circle of teenagers wearing "phat pants" or a group of business executives all dressed in gray suits. Yet the same term can also suggest that an individual is cooperative, or a "team player." What about those who do not conform? They may be respected as individualists, leaders, or creative thinkers who break new ground. Or they may be labeled as "troublemakers" and "weirdos."

These modules examine the relationships among deviance and conformity, crime and social control. What is deviance, and what are its consequences? What causes crime? How does society control people's behavior, convincing us to conform to both unwritten rules and formal laws? We will begin by defining deviance and describing the stigma that is associated with it. Then we will distinguish between conformity and obedience, and examine a surprising experiment on obedience to authority. We will study the mechanisms societies use, both formal and informal, to encourage conformity and discourage deviance, paying particular attention to the law and how it reflects our social values.

Next, we will focus on theoretical explanations for deviance, including the functionalist approach employed by Émile Durkheim and Robert Merton; interactionist-based theories; labeling theory, which draws on both the interactionist and the conflict perspectives; and conflict theory. In the last part of the chapter we will focus on crime, a specific type of deviant behavior. As a form of deviance that is subject to official, written norms, crime has been a special concern of both policymakers and the public in general. We will look at various types of crime found in the United States, the ways crime is measured, and international crime rates. Finally, the Social Policy section considers the controversial topic of the death penalty.

MODULE 23 | Social Control

As we saw in Module 12, each culture, subculture, and group has distinctive norms governing appropriate behavior. Laws, dress codes, organizational bylaws, course requirements, and the rules of sports and games all express social norms.

How does a society bring about acceptance of basic norms? The term **social control** refers to the techniques and strategies for preventing deviant human behavior in any society. Social control occurs on all levels of society. In the family, we are socialized to obey our parents simply because they are our parents. Peer groups introduce us to informal norms, such as dress codes, that govern the behavior of their members. Colleges establish standards they expect of students. In bureaucratic organizations, workers encounter a formal system of rules and regulations. Finally, the government of every society legislates and enforces social norms.

Most of us respect and accept basic social norms and assume that others will do the same. Even without thinking, we obey the instructions of police officers, follow the day-to-day rules at our jobs, and move to the rear of elevators when people enter. Such behavior reflects an effective process of socialization to the dominant standards of a culture. At the same time, we are well aware that individuals, groups, and institutions *expect* us to act "properly." This expectation carries with it **sanctions,** or penalties and rewards for conduct concerning a social norm. If we fail to live up to the norm, we may face punishment through informal sanctions such as fear and ridicule or formal sanctions such as jail sentences or fines.

The challenge to effective social control is that people often receive competing messages about how to behave. While the state or government may clearly define acceptable behavior, friends or fellow employees may encourage quite different behavior patterns. Historically, legal measures aimed at blocking

© Stuart Duncan Smith/E+/Getty Images RF

Social control measures can range from facial gestures showing approval or displeasure to fines for parking violations to imprisonment and even execution for serious crimes.

discrimination based on race, religion, gender, age, and sexual orientation have been difficult to implement, because many people tacitly encourage the violation of such measures.

Functionalists maintain that people must respect social norms if any group or society is to survive. In their view, societies literally could not function if massive numbers of people defied standards of appropriate conduct. In contrast, conflict theorists contend that the successful functioning of a society will consistently benefit the powerful and work to the disadvantage of other groups. They point out that in the United States, widespread resistance to social norms was necessary to win our independence from Great Britain, to overturn the institution of slavery, to allow women to vote, to secure civil rights, and to force an end to the war in Vietnam.

Conformity and Obedience

Techniques for social control operate on both the group level and the societal level. People we think of as peers or equals influence us to act in particular ways; the same is true of people who hold authority over us or occupy awe-inspiring positions. Social psychologist Stanley Milgram (1975) made a useful distinction between these two levels of social control.

The Milgram Experiment

Milgram used the term **conformity** to mean going along with peers—individuals of our own status who have no special right to direct our behavior. In contrast, **obedience** is compliance with higher authorities in a hierarchical structure. Thus, a recruit entering military service will typically *conform* to the habits and language of other recruits and *obey* the orders of superior officers. Students will *conform* to the drinking behavior of their peers and *obey* the requests of campus security officers.

If ordered to do so, would you comply with an experimenter's instruction to administer increasingly painful electric shocks to a subject? Most people would say no; yet Milgram's research (1963, 1975) suggests that most of us *would* obey such orders. In his words (1975:xi), "Behavior that is unthinkable in an individual . . . acting on his own may be executed without hesitation when carried out under orders."

Milgram placed advertisements in New Haven, Connecticut, newspapers to recruit subjects for a learning experiment at Yale University. Participants included postal clerks, engineers, high school teachers, and laborers. They were told that the purpose of the research was to investigate the effects of punishment on learning. The experimenter, dressed in a gray technician's coat, explained that in each test, one subject would be randomly selected as the "learner," while another would function as the "teacher." However, the experiment was rigged so that the real subject would always be the teacher, while an associate of Milgram's served as the learner.

At this point, the learner's hand was strapped to an electric apparatus. The teacher was taken to an electronic "shock generator" with 30 levered switches labeled from 15 to 450 volts. Before beginning the experiment, all subjects received sample shocks of 45 volts, to convince them of the authenticity of the experiment.

The experimenter then instructed the teacher to apply shocks of increasing voltage each time the learner gave an incorrect answer on a memory test. Teachers were told that "although the shocks can be extremely painful, they cause no permanent tissue damage." In reality, the learner did not receive any shocks.

In a prearranged script, the learner deliberately gave incorrect answers and expressed pain when "shocked." For example, at 150 volts, the learner would cry out, "Get me out of here!" At 270 volts, the learner would scream in agony. When the shock reached 350 volts, the learner would fall silent. If the teacher wanted to stop the experiment, the experimenter would insist that the teacher continue, using such statements as "The experiment requires that you continue" and "You have no other choice; you *must* go on" (Milgram 1975:19–23).

Reflecting on the Milgram Experiment

The results of this unusual experiment stunned and dismayed Milgram and other social scientists. A sample of psychiatrists had predicted that virtually all subjects would refuse to shock innocent victims. In their view, only a "pathological fringe" of less than 2 percent would continue administering shocks up to the maximum level. Yet almost *two-thirds* of participants fell into the category of "obedient subjects."

Why did these subjects obey? Why were they willing to inflict seemingly painful shocks on innocent victims who had never done them any harm? There is no evidence that these subjects were

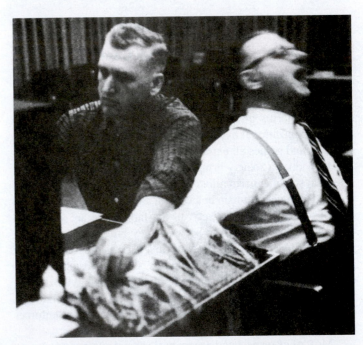

From the film *Obedience* ©1968 by Stanley Milgram. © Renewed 1993 by Alexandra Milgram. Distributed by Alexander Street Press.

In one of Stanley Milgram's experiments, the learner supposedly received an electric shock from a shock plate when he answered a question incorrectly. At the 150-volt level, the learner would demand to be released and would refuse to place his hand on the shock plate. The experimenter would then order the actual subject, the teacher, to force the hand onto the plate, as shown in the photo. Though 40 percent of the true subjects stopped complying with Milgram at this point, 30 percent did force the learner's hand onto the shock plate, despite his pretended agony.

unusually sadistic; few seemed to enjoy administering the shocks. Instead, in Milgram's view, the key to obedience was the experimenter's social role as a "scientist" and "seeker of knowledge."

Milgram pointed out that in the modern industrial world, we are accustomed to submitting to impersonal authority figures whose status is indicated by a title (professor, lieutenant, doctor) or by a uniform (the technician's coat). Because we view the authority as larger and more important than the individual, we shift responsibility for our behavior to the authority figure. Milgram's subjects frequently stated, "If it were up to me, I would not have administered shocks." They saw themselves as merely doing their duty (Milgram 1975).

From a conflict perspective, our obedience may be affected by the value we place on those whom our behavior affects. While Milgram's experiment shows that in general, people are willing to obey authority figures, other studies show that they are even more willing to obey if they feel the "victim" is deserving of punishment. Sociologist Gary Schulman (1974) re-created Milgram's experiment and found that White students were significantly more likely to shock Black learners than White learners. By a margin of 70 percent to 48 percent, they imposed more shocks on the Black learners than on the White learners.

From an interactionist perspective, one important aspect of Milgram's findings is the fact that subjects in follow-up studies were less likely to inflict the supposed shocks as they were moved physically closer to their victims. Moreover, interactionists emphasize the effect of *incrementally* administering additional dosages of 15 volts. In effect, the experimenter negotiated with the teacher and convinced the teacher to continue inflicting higher levels of punishment. It is doubtful that anywhere near the two-thirds rate of obedience would have been reached had the experimenter told the teachers to administer 450 volts immediately (Allen 1978; Katovich 1987).

Milgram launched his experimental study of obedience to better understand the involvement of Germans in the annihilation of 6 million Jews and millions of other people during World War II. In an interview conducted long after the publication of his study, he suggested that "if a system of death camps were set up in the United States of the sort we had seen in Nazi Germany, one would be able to find sufficient personnel for those camps in any medium-sized American town." Though many people questioned his remark, the revealing photos taken at Iraq's Abu Ghraib prison in 2004, showing U.S. military guards humiliating if not torturing Iraqi prisoners, recalled the experiment Milgram had done two generations earlier. Under conducive circumstances, otherwise normal people can and often do treat one another inhumanely (CBS News 1979:7–8; Hayden 2004; Zimbardo 2007a).

How willing would participants in this experiment be to shock learners today? Although many people may be skeptical of the high levels of conformity Milgram found, recent replications of his experiment confirm his findings. In 2006, using additional safeguards to protect participants' welfare, psychologist Jerry Burger (2009, 2014) repeated part of Milgram's experiment with college undergraduates. To avoid biasing the participants, Burger was careful to screen out students who had heard of Milgram's study. The results of the replication were startlingly similar to Milgram's: participants showed a high level of willingness to shock the learner, just as the participants in Milgram's experiment had almost half a century earlier. At the most comparable point in the two studies, Burger measured a rate of 70 percent full obedience—lower, but not significantly so, than the rate of 82.5 percent measured two generations earlier.

 use your **sociological imagination**

If you were a participant in Milgram's research on conformity, how far do you think you would go in carrying out orders? Do you see any ethical problem with the experimenter's manipulation of the subjects? Explain your answer.

● Informal and Formal Social Control

The sanctions that are used to encourage conformity and obedience—and to discourage violation of social norms—are carried out through both informal and formal social control. As the term implies, people use **informal social control** casually to enforce norms. Examples include smiles, laughter, a raised eyebrow, and ridicule.

© David McClain/Aurora Photos

In Singapore, a custodian removes a bit of litter from an otherwise spotless floor. Strict social controls prevail in the city-state, where the careless disposal of a cigarette butt or candy wrapper carries a $300 fine.

Box 23-1

Sociology on Campus

Binge Drinking

About 1,800 college students die each year of unintentional alcohol-related injuries. According to a study published by the Harvard School of Public Health, 44 percent of college students indulge in binge drinking (defined as at least five drinks in a row for men and four in a row for women). These numbers represent an increase from 1990s data, despite efforts on many campuses across the nation to educate students about the risks of binge drinking.

The problem is not confined to the United States—Britain, Russia, and South Africa all report regular "drink till you drop" alcoholic consumption among young people. According to a study that compared data from 22 countries, however, college students in the United States have the highest rate of drinking and driving. Nor does binge drinking begin in college. A national study found that over a 30-day period, 29 percent of high school students engaged in binge drinking.

Binge drinking on campus presents a difficult social problem. On the one hand, it can be regarded as *deviant*, violating the standards of conduct expected of those in an academic setting. In fact, Harvard researchers consider binge drinking the most serious public health hazard facing colleges. On the other hand, binge drinking represents *conformity* to the peer culture, especially in fraternities and sororities, which serve as social centers on many campuses. Most students seem to take an "everybody does it—no big deal" attitude toward the behavior.

Some colleges and universities are taking steps to make binge drinking a bit less "normal" by means of *social control*—banning kegs, closing fraternities and sororities, encouraging liquor retailers not to sell

© Steve Rubin/The Image Works

Forty-four percent of college students indulge in binge drinking.

in high volume to students, and expelling students after three alcohol-related infractions. Despite privacy laws, many schools are notifying parents whenever their underage children are caught drinking. Even with these measures, however, curbing underage drinking is a challenge.

LET'S DISCUSS

1. Why do you think most college students regard binge drinking as a normal rather than a deviant behavior?

2. Which do you think would be more effective in stopping binge drinking on your campus, informal or formal social control?

Sources: Centers for Disease Control and Prevention 2010, 2012a; McMurtrie 2014; J. Miller et al. 2007; National Center on Addiction and Substance Abuse at Columbia University 2007; Wechsler et al. 2002, 2004.

In the United States and many other cultures, adults often view spanking, slapping, or kicking children as a proper and necessary means of informal social control. Child development specialists counter that such corporal punishment is inappropriate because it teaches children to solve problems through violence. They warn that slapping and spanking can escalate into more serious forms of abuse. Yet, despite a policy statement by the American Academy of Pediatrics that corporal punishment is not effective and can indeed be harmful, 59 percent of pediatricians support the use of corporal punishment, at least in certain situations. Our culture widely accepts this form of informal social control (Chung et al. 2009).

Formal social control is carried out by authorized agents, such as police officers, judges, school administrators, employers, military officers, and managers of movie theaters. It can serve as a last resort when socialization and informal sanctions do not bring about desired behavior. Sometimes, informal social control can actually undermine formal social control, encouraging people to violate social norms. Box 23-1 examines binge drinking among college students, who receive conflicting messages about the acceptability of the behavior from sources of social control.

Historically, the death penalty has served as a significant form of social control. The threat of execution was meant as much to discourage others from committing capital crimes as it was to punish those who did. The Social Policy section at the end of this chapter discusses the sociological implications of the death penalty.

In the aftermath of September 11, 2001, new measures of social control became the norm in the United States. Some of them, such as stepped-up security and surveillance at airports

FIGURE 23-1 **The Status of Medical Marijuana**

Law and Society

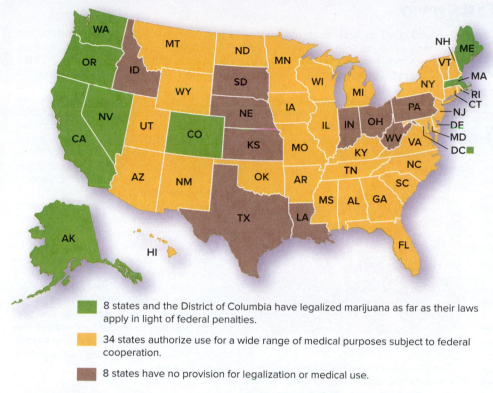

8 states and the District of Columbia have legalized marijuana as far as their laws apply in light of federal penalties.

34 states authorize use for a wide range of medical purposes subject to federal cooperation.

8 states have no provision for legalization or medical use.

Source: NORML 2016.

The actions some states have taken to legalize marijuana are largely symbolic. Federal law still prohibits doctors from writing prescriptions for marijuana, and pharmacies from distributing the substance. Although patients can still be prosecuted by the federal government for possessing or using marijuana, the Federal government stopped prosecuting medical marijuana users who comply with state laws.

Some norms are so important to a society that they are formalized into laws regarding people's behavior. **Law** may be defined as governmental social control (Black 1995). Some laws, such as the prohibition against murder, are directed at all members of society. Others, such as fishing and hunting regulations, affect particular categories of people. Still others govern the behavior of social institutions (for instance, corporate law and laws regarding the taxing of nonprofit enterprises).

Sociologists see the creation of laws as a social process. Because governments make laws in response to a perceived need for formal social control, sociologists have sought to explain how and why such a perception arises. In their view, law is not merely a static body of rules handed down from generation to generation. Rather, it reflects continually changing standards of what is right and wrong, of how violations are to be determined, and of what sanctions are to be applied (Schur 1968).

Sociologists representing varying theoretical perspectives agree that the legal order reflects the values of those in authority. Therefore, the creation of civil and criminal law can be highly controversial. Should it be against the law to employ illegal immigrants, to have an abortion, or to allow prayer in public schools? Such issues have been bitterly debated, because they require a choice among competing values. Not surprisingly, laws that are unpopular—such as the one-time prohibition of alcohol under the Eighteenth Amendment and the widespread establishment of a 55-mile-per-hour speed limit on highways—become difficult to enforce when there is no consensus supporting the norms.

One current and controversial debate over laws governing behavior is whether people should be allowed to use marijuana legally, for medical purposes. Although the majority of adults polled in national surveys support such a use, the federal government continues to regard all uses of marijuana as illegal. In 2005 the Supreme Court upheld the federal government's position. Nevertheless, eight states and the District of Columbia have legalized the use of marijuana and many more states have granted citizens the right to use marijuana for medical purposes—even if that privilege rests on dubious legal grounds (Figure 23-1).

and high-rise buildings, were highly visible to the public. The federal government has also publicly urged citizens to engage in informal social control by watching for and reporting people whose actions seem suspicious (Monahan 2011).

Many people think this kind of social control goes too far. Civil rights advocates worry that the government's request for information on suspicious activities may encourage negative stereotyping of Muslims and Arab Americans. Clearly, there is a trade-off between the benefits of surveillance and the right to privacy.

Other aspects of government social control have also undergone criticism. Solitary confinement, defined as at least 22 hours per day removed from the general prison population for at least 30 days, has become increasingly common in the United States. In 2016, at least 100,000 inmates were in solitary confinement or isolated housing in state and federal prisons on any given day. Prison officials defend the practice as necessary to managing the inmate population, while critics point to the absence of research evaluating its effectiveness or impact on the prisoners themselves. In 2016, President Obama ordered the end of solitary confinement for youths and for low-level offenders. This policy would end solitary confinement for about 10 percent of those experiencing this type of social control (Shear 2016; The Liman Program 2015).

Debtors' Jails in the Twenty-First Century

Being in jail means you have committed a crime, right? Most likely, not correct. About two-thirds of people in jails have not been convicted of a crime. They just cannot pay the bail to allow themselves to be free during the long wait to stand trial. Lack of money and jail time have a long history.

Charles Dickens is well known for writing about people living on the margins of society, whether it is Oliver Twist, a street beggar, or Bob Cratchit, the miserably paid clerk of Ebenezer Scrooge. It is easy to understand his sympathy for the downtrodden. When he was 12, his father was forced by his creditors into a debtors' prison. As was the custom, his wife, Charles, and four younger children joined him there. At age 12, Charles was regarded as old enough to support himself. His father was finally able to leave prison upon the death of a relative, whose modest estate provided enough money to cover the debts.

We can understand then, why the Eighth Amendment to the Constitution asserts that "Excessive bail shall not be required." However, over two hundred years later, an increasing number of people are concerned about the impact of bail on the accused who happened to be poor.

Nationwide, in 1990 three out of every five defendants in felony cases who were released pending trial were let go on their own recognizance or on some other condition that did not involve bail. By 2015, three out of five *were required* to post bail. A majority of those held before their trials in New York City jails in 2015 were there simply because they couldn't come up with $2,000 bail—or less, in most cases.

While $2,000 or less does not seem like a lot to avoid jail time, for members of households that have no savings and are already in debt, it is a major barrier to freedom. Annually in New York City, 45,000 indigent people—those with no savings or apparent source of income—have charges brought against them, according to a 2015 report. Only 15 percent of defendants are able to come up with the money to avoid jail.

> Defendants who can't make bail, regardless of their accused crime, are four times more likely to be sentenced to time in prison.

Besides the obvious disruptions to one's life and family, being incarcerated awaiting trial makes it more difficult to mount a defense. Defendants who can't make bail, regardless of their accused crime, are four times more likely to be sentenced to time in prison. In addition, individuals held in jail plead guilty 92 percent of the time, compared to 40 percent for those awaiting trial at home.

Legally, before demanding bail the government must show that a person is a flight risk (someone who is likely to flee the county or state to avoid prosecution). In practice the assumption of flight risk trumps the presumption of innocence. Increasingly courts also consider whether the indicted person is also likely to pose a danger to the community independent of the crime for which he or she was arrested. Research shows that from 1995 to 2010, the proportion of people out on bail who committed any misconduct gradually dropped to about 17 percent—and the vast majority of these were typically technical violations regarding court appearances. Fewer than 2 percent fail to appear for trial.

Some people feel the only sensible reform is take money out of the bail process. However, clearly that would reduce guilty pleas and leave many more cases to be tried in an already overburdened judicial system. The underlying problem is that many people, especially low-income people, are arrested for minor offenses such as failing to pay for public transit or possession of drug paraphernalia. But to convince the public and law enforcement that these types of offences should be handled differently is not a simple task.

LET'S DISCUSS

1. Do you agree with the statement that "Lack of money and jail time have a long history"? Why do the two seem to go together?

2. What are some possible solutions to the problem of poverty and jail time?

Sources: Cohen 2013; Ewing 2015; Minton and Golinelli 2014; Pinto 2015; Subramanian et al. 2015.

Socialization is the primary source of conforming and obedient behavior, including obedience to law. Generally, it is not external pressure from a peer group or authority figure that makes us go along with social norms. Rather, we have internalized such norms as valid and desirable and are committed to observing them. In a profound sense, we want to see ourselves (and to be seen) as loyal, cooperative, responsible, and respectful of others. In the United States and other societies around the world, people are socialized both to want to belong and to fear being viewed as different or deviant.

Control theory suggests that our connection to members of society leads us to systematically conform to society's norms. According to sociologist Travis Hirschi and other control theorists, our bonds to family members, friends, and peers induce us to follow the mores and folkways of our society. We give little conscious thought to whether we will be sanctioned if we fail to conform. Socialization develops our self-control so well that we don't need further pressure to obey social norms. Although control theory does not effectively explain the rationale for every conforming act, it nevertheless reminds us that while the media may focus on crime and disorder, most members of most societies conform to and obey basic norms (Brewis et al. 2011; Gottfredson and Hirschi 1990; Hirschi 1969).

Control theory focuses on societally recognized deviance and crime, which typically does not include lacking money. As we see in Box 23-2, an increasing proportion of people are in jail for their inability to pay money while they await trial.

Summary

This module examines the relationship between **conformity** and mechanisms of **social control.**

1. A society uses **social control** to encourage the acceptance of basic norms.

2. Stanley Milgram defined **conformity** as going along with one's peers; **obedience** is compliance with higher authorities in a hierarchical structure.

3. Some norms are so important to a society that they are formalized into **laws.** Socialization is a primary source of conforming and obedient behavior, including obedience to laws.

Thinking Critically

1. Think about a job you once held. How did your employer exercise social control over the employees? How did you, as an employee, use social control in relating to those around you?

2. Should youths who have been convicted of violent crimes be subject to the death penalty? Why or why not?

3. Should some illegal drugs be decriminalized? Why or why not?

Key Terms

Conformity

Control theory

Formal social control

Informal social control

Law

Obedience

Sanction

Social control

MODULE 24 | What Is Deviance?

For sociologists, the term *deviance* does not mean perversion or depravity. **Deviance** is behavior that violates the standards of conduct or expectations of a group or society. In the United States, alcoholics, compulsive gamblers, and people with mental illness would all be classified as deviants. Being late for class is categorized as a deviant act; the same is true of wearing jeans to a formal wedding. On the basis of the sociological definition, we are all deviant from time to time. Each of us violates common social norms in certain situations (Best 2004).

Is being overweight an example of deviance? In the United States and many other cultures, unrealistic standards of appearance and body image place a huge strain on people—especially women and girls—based on how they look. Journalist Naomi Wolf (1992) has used the term *beauty myth* to refer to an exaggerated ideal of beauty, beyond the reach of all but a few females, which has unfortunate consequences. In order to shed their "deviant" image and conform to unrealistic societal norms, many women and girls become consumed with adjusting their appearances. Yet what is deviant in one culture may be celebrated in another.

Deviance involves the violation of group norms, which may or may not be formalized into law. It is a comprehensive concept that includes not only criminal behavior but also many actions that are not subject to prosecution. The public official who takes a bribe has defied social norms, but so has the high school student who refuses to sit in an assigned seat or cuts class. Of course, deviation from norms is not always negative, let alone criminal. A member of an exclusive social club who speaks out against a traditional policy of not admitting women, Blacks, and Jews is deviating from the club's norms. So is a police officer who blows the whistle on corruption or brutality within the department.

From a sociological perspective, deviance is hardly objective or set in stone. Rather, it is subject to social definition within

© Koichi Kamoshida/Getty Images

In 2009, baseball fans were shocked by the revelation that like several other baseball greats, superstar Alex Rodriguez had used banned substances and lied about it. In 2013, he was suspended for 211 games, including the entire 2014 season. In the 2015 season he returned with 33 home runs, 131 hits, and a .252 batting average.

© Steven Lawton/FilmMagic/Getty Images

Deviant or normal? Television personality and recording artist Heidi Montag shocked fans in 2010 by revealing that she had undergone 10 plastic surgery procedures in a single day. Montag had already undergone breast augmentation, collagen lip injections, and rhinoplasty. Would you consider her behavior deviant?

a particular society and at a particular time. For that reason, what is considered deviant can shift from one social era to another. In most instances, those individuals and groups with the greatest status and power define what is acceptable and what is deviant. For example, despite serious medical warnings against the dangers of tobacco, made since 1964, cigarette smoking continued to be accepted for decades—in good part because of the power of tobacco farmers and cigarette manufacturers. Only after a long campaign led by public health and anticancer activists did cigarette smoking become more of a deviant activity. Today, many state and local laws limit where people can smoke.

The definition of acceptable behavior changes over time. Tattoos were long considered inappropriate for U.S. military recruits. Although the Navy lifted the ban in 2012 and the Army in 2015, tattoos must still be invisible when a soldier is uniformed and may not be racist, extremist, or vulgar.

● Deviance and Social Stigma

A person can acquire a deviant identity in many ways. Because of physical or behavioral characteristics, some people are unwillingly cast in negative social roles. Once assigned a deviant role,

they have trouble presenting a positive image to others and may even experience lowered self-esteem. Whole groups of people—for instance, "short people" or "redheads"—may be labeled in this way. The interactionist Erving Goffman coined the term **stigma** to describe the labels society uses to devalue members of certain social groups (Goffman 1963; Heckert and Best 1997).

In the aftermath of the 2012 school shooting in Newtown, Connecticut, the issue of mental illness surfaced almost immediately, amid rumors that the shooter suffered from an untreated mental disorder. In many people's eyes, such assumptions stigmatize all people with mental illness, whatever the definition of the term, as potentially violent criminals. Overwhelming evidence shows that the opposite is true, however: the vast majority of people with psychiatric disorders do *not* commit violent acts. Only 4 percent of violent crimes in the United States can be attributed to people with mental illness (R. Friedman 2012; Nocera 2012).

Stigmatization also affects people who look different from others in the eyes of their peers. Prevailing expectations about beauty and body shape may prevent people who are regarded as ugly or obese from advancing as rapidly as their abilities permit. Both overweight and anorexic people are viewed by many to be weak in character, slaves to their appetites or to media images. Because they do not conform to the beauty myth, they may be viewed as "disfigured" or "strange" in appearance, bearers of what Goffman calls a "spoiled identity." However, what constitutes disfigurement is a matter of interpretation. Of the 16 million cosmetic procedures done every year in the United States alone, many are performed on women who would be defined objectively as having a normal appearance. And while feminist sociologists have accurately noted that the beauty myth makes many women feel uncomfortable with themselves, men too lack confidence in their appearance. The number of males who choose to undergo cosmetic procedures has risen sharply in recent years (American Society of Plastic Surgeons 2016).

Often people are stigmatized for deviant behaviors they may no longer engage in. The labels "compulsive gambler," "ex-convict," "recovering alcoholic," and "ex–mental patient" can stick to a person for life. Goffman draws a useful distinction between a prestige symbol that draws attention to a positive aspect of one's identity, such as a wedding band or a badge, and a stigma symbol that discredits or debases one's identity, such as a conviction for child molestation. While stigma symbols may not always be obvious, they can become a matter of public knowledge. Starting in 1994, many states required convicted sex offenders to register with local police departments. Some communities publish the names and addresses, and in some instances even the pictures, of convicted sex offenders on the web.

While some types of deviance will stigmatize a person, other types do not carry a significant penalty. Examples of socially tolerated forms of deviance can be found in the world of high technology.

● Deviance and Technology

Technological innovations such as pagers and voicemail can redefine social interactions and the standards of behavior related to them. When the Internet was first made available to the general public, no norms or regulations governed its use. Because online communication offers a high degree of anonymity, uncivil behavior—speaking harshly of others or monopolizing chat room space—quickly became common. Online bulletin boards designed to carry items of community interest became littered with commercial advertisements. Such deviant acts are beginning to provoke calls for the establishment of formal rules for online behavior. For example, policymakers have debated whether to regulate the content of websites featuring hate speech and pornography.

Some deviant uses of technology are criminal, though not all participants see it that way. On the street, the for-profit pirating of software, motion pictures, and music has become a big business. On the Internet, the downloading of music by individual listeners, which is typically forbidden by copyright, is widely accepted. The music and motion picture industries have waged much publicized campaigns to stop these illegal uses of their products, yet among many people, no social stigma attaches to them. Deviance, then, is a complex concept. Sometimes it is trivial, sometimes profoundly harmful. Sometimes it is accepted by society and sometimes soundly rejected.

Sociological Perspectives on Deviance

Why do people violate social norms? We have seen that deviant acts are subject to both informal and formal social control. The nonconforming or disobedient person may face disapproval, loss of friends, fines, or even imprisonment. Why, then, does deviance occur?

Early explanations for behavior that deviated from societal expectations blamed supernatural causes or genetic factors (such as "bad blood" or evolutionary throwbacks to ancestors). By the 1800s, substantial research efforts were being made to identify biological factors that lead to deviance, and especially to criminal activity. Though such research was discredited in the 20th century, contemporary studies, primarily by biochemists, have sought to isolate genetic factors that suggest a likelihood of certain personality traits. Although criminality (much less deviance) is hardly a personality characteristic, researchers have focused on traits that might lead to crime, such as aggression. Of course, aggression can also lead to success in the corporate world, in professional sports, or in other walks of life.

The contemporary study of the possible biological roots of criminality is but one aspect of the larger debate over sociobiology. In general, sociologists have been critical of any emphasis on the genetic roots of crime and deviance. The limitations of current knowledge about the link between genetics and antisocial behavior have led them to draw largely on other approaches to explain deviance (Walsh 2000).

Functionalist Perspective

According to functionalists, deviance is a common part of human existence, with positive as well as negative consequences for social stability. Deviance helps to define the limits of proper behavior. Children who see one parent scold the other

for belching at the dinner table learn about approved conduct. The same is true of the driver who receives a speeding ticket, the department store cashier who is fired for yelling at a customer, and the college student who is penalized for handing in papers weeks overdue.

Durkheim's Legacy Émile Durkheim ([1895] 1964) focused his sociological investigations mainly on criminal acts, yet his conclusions have implications for all types of deviant behavior. In Durkheim's view, the punishments established within a culture (including both formal and informal mechanisms of social control) help to define acceptable behavior and thus contribute to stability. If improper acts were not sanctioned, people might stretch their standards of what constitutes appropriate conduct.

Sociologist Kai Erikson (1966) illustrated the boundary-maintenance function of deviance in his study of the Puritans of 17th-century New England. By today's standards, the Puritans placed tremendous emphasis on conventional morals. Their persecution and execution of women as witches represented a continuing attempt to define and redefine the boundaries of their community. In effect, their changing social norms created crime waves, as people whose behavior was previously acceptable suddenly faced punishment for being deviant (R. Schaefer and Zellner 2015).

Durkheim ([1897] 1951) introduced the term **anomie** into sociological literature to describe the loss of direction felt in a society when social control of individual behavior has become ineffective. Anomie is a state of normlessness that typically occurs during a period of profound social change and disorder, such as a time of economic collapse. People become more aggressive or depressed, which results in higher rates of violent crime and suicide. Since there is much less agreement on what constitutes proper behavior during times of revolution, sudden prosperity, or economic depression, conformity and obedience become less significant as social forces. It also becomes much more difficult to state exactly what constitutes deviance.

Merton's Theory of Deviance What do a mugger and a teacher have in common? Each is "working" to obtain money that can then be exchanged for desired goods. As this example illustrates, behavior that violates accepted norms (such as mugging) may be based on the same basic objectives as the behavior of people who pursue more conventional lifestyles.

On the basis of this kind of analysis, sociologist Robert Merton (1968) adapted Durkheim's notion of anomie to explain why people accept or reject the goals of a society, the socially approved means of fulfilling their aspirations, or both. Merton maintained that one important cultural goal in the United States is success, measured largely in terms of money. In addition to providing this goal for people, our society offers specific instructions on how to pursue success—go to school, work hard, do not quit, take advantage of opportunities, and so forth.

What happens to individuals in a society with a heavy emphasis on wealth as a basic symbol of success? Merton reasoned that people adapt in certain ways, either by conforming to or by deviating from such cultural expectations. His **anomie theory of deviance** posits five types of behavior or basic forms of adaptation (Table 24-1).

TABLE **24-1** MERTON'S DEVIANCE THEORY | Summing Up

Does the individual accept:	Nondeviant	Deviant			
	Conformity	Retreatism	Innovation	Ritualism	Rebellion
the goals of society, such as acquisition of wealth?	👍	👎	👍	👎	👎 👍
the use of acceptable means, such as hard work?	👍	👎	👎	👍	👎 👍

Source: Adapted by author, Richard Schaefer, from Chapter VI, "Social Structure and Anomie," in Merton 1968. *Photos: Moneybag:* © Brand X Pictures/PunchStock RF; *Time clock:* © Alamy RF

The other four types of behavior represented in Table 24-1 all involve some departure from conformity. The *retreatist* has basically retreated (or withdrawn) from both the goals and the means of society. In the United States, drug addicts and vagrants are typically portrayed as retreatists. Concern has been growing that adolescents who are addicted to alcohol will become retreatists at an early age.

In Merton's typology, the *innovator* accepts the goals of society but pursues them with means that are regarded as improper. For instance, a safecracker may steal money to buy consumer goods and expensive vacations.

The *ritualist* has abandoned the goal of material success and become compulsively committed to the institutional means. Work becomes simply a way of life rather than a means to the goal of success. An example would be the bureaucratic official who blindly applies rules and regulations without remembering the larger goals of the organization. Certainly that would be true of a welfare caseworker who refuses to assist a homeless family because their last apartment was in another district.

The final type of behavior or adaptation identified by Merton reflects people's attempts to create a *new* social structure. The *rebel* feels alienated from the dominant means and goals and may seek a dramatically different social order. Members of a revolutionary political organization, such as a militia group, can be categorized as rebels according to Merton's model.

Merton made a key contribution to the sociological understanding of deviance by pointing out that deviants such as innovators and ritualists share a great deal with conforming people. The convicted felon may hold many of the same aspirations as people with no criminal background. The theory helps us to understand deviance as a socially created behavior rather than as the result of momentary pathological impulses. However, this theory of deviance has not been applied systematically to real-world crime. Box 24-1 examines scholars' efforts to confirm the theory's validity.

Interactionist Perspective

The functionalist approach to deviance explains why rule violations continue to happen despite pressure to conform and obey. However, functionalists do not indicate how a given person comes to commit a deviant act or why on some occasions crimes do or do not occur. The emphasis on everyday behavior that is the focus of the interactionist perspective offers such an explanation: cultural transmission theory.

Cultural Transmission In the course of studying graffiti writing by gangs in Los Angeles, sociologist Susan A. Phillips (1999) discovered that the writers learned from one another. In fact, Phillips was surprised by how stable their focus was over time. She also noted how other ethnic groups built on the models of the African American and Chicano gangs, superimposing Cambodian, Chinese, or Vietnamese symbols.

Humans *learn* how to behave in social situations, whether properly or improperly. There is no natural, innate manner in which people interact with one another. These simple ideas are not disputed today, but such was not the case when sociologist Edwin Sutherland (1883–1950) first advanced the idea that an individual undergoes the same basic socialization process in learning conforming and deviant acts.

Does Crime Pay?

A driver violates the speed limit to get to a job interview on time. A financially strapped parent shoplifts goods that her family needs. These people may feel justified in violating the law because they do so to meet a reasonable objective. In Robert Merton's terms, they are *innovators*—people who violate social norms to achieve a commonly shared societal goal. Although their actions are criminal and potentially hurtful to others, from their own short-term perspective, their actions are functional.

© Stockbyte/PunchStock RF

Carried to its logical conclusion, innovation can and does become a career for some people. Yet from a purely economic point of view, even considering the fact that crime may pay is controversial, because doing so may seem to tolerate or encourage rule violation. Nothing is more controversial than the suggestion that gang-run drug deals are profitable and produce "good jobs." Although some people may see drug dealers as a cross between MBA-educated professionals and streetwise entrepreneurs, society in general does not admire these innovators.

Sociologist Sudhir Venkatesh collected detailed data on the illegal drug trade during his observation research on a Chicago street gang. Working with economist Steven Levitt,

coauthor of the best seller *Freakonomics,* to analyze the business of selling crack cocaine, he found that less than 5 percent of even the gang leaders earned $100,000 per year. The rest of the leaders and virtually all the rank and file earned less than the minimum wage. In fact, most were unpaid workers seeking to move up in the gang hierarchy. (Thus the title of a chapter in Levitt's book, "Why Do Drug Dealers Still Live with Their Moms?") As Levitt notes, the drug gang is like most corporations: the top 2 percent of workers take home most of the money.

> Less than 5 percent of even the gang leaders earned $100,000 per year. The rest of the leaders and virtually all the rank and file earned less than the minimum wage.

Why, from a sociological *and* an economic perspective, do these nonprofitable practices persist, especially considering that one in every four members of drug-oriented street gangs is eventually killed? One reason, of course, is the public's almost insatiable demand for illegal drugs. And from the drug peddler's perspective, few legitimate jobs are available to young adults in poverty-stricken areas, urban or rural. Functionally, these youths are contributing to their household incomes by dealing drugs.

Scholars see a need for further research on Merton's concept of innovation. Why, for example, do some disadvantaged groups have lower rates of reported crime than others? Why do many people who are caught in adverse circumstances reject criminal activity as a viable alternative? Merton's theory of deviance does not easily answer such questions.

LET'S DISCUSS

1. Do you know anyone who has stolen out of need? If so, did the person feel justified in stealing, or did he or she feel guilty? How long did the theft continue?

2. Economically, profit is the difference between revenues and costs. What are the costs of the illegal drug trade, both economic and social? Is this economic activity profitable for society?

Sources: Clinard and Miller 1998; Kingsbury 2008; S. Levitt and Dubner 2006; S. Levitt and Venkatesh 2000; Rosen and Venkatesh 2008; Venkatesh 2008.

Sutherland's ideas have been the dominating force in criminology. He drew on the **cultural transmission** school, which emphasizes that one learns criminal behavior by interacting with others. Such learning includes not only the techniques of lawbreaking (for example, how to break into a car quickly and quietly) but also the motives, drives, and rationalizations of the criminal. The cultural transmission approach can also be used to explain the behavior of those who habitually abuse alcohol or drugs.

Sutherland maintained that through interactions with a primary group and significant others, people acquire definitions of proper and improper behavior. He used the term **differential association** to describe the process through which exposure to attitudes *favorable* to criminal acts leads to the violation of rules. Research suggests that this view of differential association also applies to noncriminal deviant acts, such as smoking, truancy, and early sexual behavior.

Sutherland offers the example of a boy who is sociable, outgoing, and athletic and who lives in an area with a high rate of delinquency. The youth is very likely to come into contact with peers who commit acts of vandalism, fail to attend school, and so

forth, and may come to adopt such behavior. However, an introverted boy who lives in the same neighborhood may stay away from his peers and avoid delinquency. In another community, an outgoing and athletic boy may join a Little League baseball team or a scout troop because of his interactions with peers. Thus, Sutherland views improper behavior as the result of the types of groups to which one belongs and the kinds of friendships one has.

According to critics, the cultural transmission approach may explain the deviant behavior of juvenile delinquents or graffiti artists, but it fails to explain the conduct of the first-time impulsive shoplifter or the impoverished person who steals out of necessity. While it is not a precise statement of the process through which one becomes a criminal, differential association theory does direct our attention to the paramount role of social interaction in increasing a person's motivation to engage in deviant behavior (Loughran et al. 2013; Sutherland et al. 1992).

Social Disorganization Theory The social relationships that exist in a community or neighborhood affect people's behavior. Philip Zimbardo (2007a), author of the mock prison experiment described in Chapter 5, once did an experiment that demonstrated the power of communal relationships. He abandoned a car in each of two different neighborhoods, leaving its hood up and removing its hub caps. In one neighborhood, people started to strip the car for parts before Zimbardo had finished setting up a remote video camera to record their behavior. In the other neighborhood, weeks passed without the car being touched, except for a pedestrian who stopped to close the hood during a rainstorm.

What accounts for the strikingly different outcomes of Zimbardo's experiment in the two communities? According to **social disorganization theory,** increases in crime and deviance can be attributed to the absence or breakdown of communal relationships and social institutions, such as the family, school, church, and local government. This theory was developed at the University of Chicago in the early 1900s to describe the apparent disorganization that occurred as cities expanded with rapid immigration and migration from rural areas. Using the latest survey techniques, Clifford Shaw and Henry McKay literally mapped the distribution of social problems in Chicago. They found high rates of social problems in neighborhoods where buildings had deteriorated and the population had declined. Interestingly, the patterns persisted over time, despite changes in the neighborhoods' ethnic and racial composition.

This theory is not without its critics. To some, social disorganization theory seems to "blame the victim," leaving larger societal forces, such as the lack of jobs or high-quality schools, unaccountable. Critics also argue that even troubled neighborhoods have viable, healthy organizations, which persist despite the problems that surround them.

More recently, social disorganization theorists have taken to emphasizing the effect of social networks on communal bonds. These researchers acknowledge that communities are not isolated islands. Residents' bonds may be enhanced or weakened by their ties to groups outside the immediate community (Jensen 2005; Sampson and Graves 1989; Shaw and McKay 1942).

© Frank and Helena/Cultura/Getty Images

According to social disorganization theory, strong communal bonds can enhance neighborhood ties, reducing the likelihood of criminal behavior.

Labeling Perspective

The Saints and the Roughnecks were groups of high school males who were continually engaged in excessive drinking, reckless driving, truancy, petty theft, and vandalism. There the similarity ended. None of the Saints was ever arrested, but every Roughneck was frequently in trouble with police and townspeople. Why the disparity in their treatment? On the basis of observation research in their high school, sociologist William Chambliss (1973) concluded that social class played an important role in the varying fortunes of the two groups.

The Saints hid behind a facade of respectability. They came from "good families," were active in school organizations, planned on attending college, and received good grades. People generally viewed their delinquent acts as a few isolated cases of sowing wild oats. The Roughnecks had no such aura of respectability. They drove around town in beat-up cars, were generally unsuccessful in school, and aroused suspicion no matter what they did.

We can understand such discrepancies by using an approach to deviance known as **labeling theory.** Unlike Sutherland's work, labeling theory does not focus on why some individuals come to commit deviant acts. Instead, it attempts to explain why certain people (such as the Roughnecks) are *viewed* as deviants, delinquents, bad kids, losers, and criminals, whereas others whose behavior is similar (such as the Saints) are not seen in such harsh terms. Reflecting the contribution of interactionist theorists, labeling theory emphasizes how a person comes to be labeled as deviant or to accept that label. Sociologist Howard Becker ([1953] 2015; 1963:9; 1964), who popularized this approach, summed it up with this statement: "Deviant behavior is behavior that people so label."

Labeling theory is also called the **societal-reaction approach,** reminding us that it is the *response* to an act, not the behavior itself, that determines deviance. For example, studies have shown that some school personnel and therapists expand educational programs designed for learning-disabled students to include those with behavioral problems. Consequently, a "troublemaker" can be improperly labeled as "learning-disabled," and vice versa (Grattet 2011).

Labeling and Agents of Social Control Traditionally, research on deviance has focused on people who violate social norms. In contrast, labeling theory focuses on police, probation officers, psychiatrists, judges, teachers, employers, school officials, and other regulators of social control. These agents, it is argued, play a significant role in creating the deviant identity by designating certain people (and not others) as deviant. An important aspect of labeling theory is the recognition that some individuals or groups have the power to *define* labels and *apply* them to others. This view ties into the conflict perspective's emphasis on the social significance of power.

In recent years the practice of *racial profiling,* in which people are identified as criminal suspects purely on the basis of their race, has come under public scrutiny. Studies confirm the public's suspicions that in some jurisdictions, police officers are much more likely to stop Black males than White males for routine traffic violations, in the expectation of finding drugs or guns in their cars. Civil rights activists refer to these cases as DWB (Driving While Black) violations. Beginning in 2001, profiling took a new turn as people who appeared to be Arab or Muslim came under special scrutiny. (Racial profiling will be examined in more detail in Chapter 10.)

The popularity of labeling theory is reflected in the emergence of a related perspective, called social constructionism. According to the **social constructionist perspective,** deviance is the product of the culture we live in. Social constructionists focus specifically on the decision-making process that creates the deviant identity. They point out that "child abductors," "deadbeat dads," "spree killers," and "date rapists" have always been with us, but at times have become *the* major social concern of policymakers because of intensive media coverage (Liska and Messner 1999; E. R. Wright et al. 2000).

How do certain behaviors come to be viewed as a problem? Cigarette smoking, which was once regarded as a polite, gentlemanly activity, is now considered a serious health hazard, not only to the smoker but also to others nearby who don't smoke. Recently, people have become concerned about the danger, especially to children, posed by *thirdhand smoke*—smoke-related chemicals that cling to clothes and linger in rooms, cars, even elevators (Winickoff et al. 2009).

 use your **sociological imagination**

You are a teacher. What labels, freely used in education, might you attach to your students?

Conflict Perspective

Conflict theorists point out that people with power protect their interests and define deviance to suit their needs. Sociologist Richard Quinney (1974, 1979, 1980) was a leading exponent of the view that the criminal justice system serves the interests of the powerful. Crime, according to Quinney (1970), is a definition of conduct created by authorized agents of social control—such as legislators and law enforcement officers—in a politically

© David Pollack/Corbis via Getty Images

In the 1930s, the Federal Bureau of Narcotics launched a campaign to portray marijuana as a dangerous drug rather than a pleasure-inducing substance. From a conflict perspective, those in power often use such tactics to coerce others into adopting a different point of view.

organized society. He and other conflict theorists argue that lawmaking is often an attempt by the powerful to coerce others into their morality.

This theory helps to explain why our society has laws against gambling, drug use, and prostitution, many of which are violated on a massive scale. (We will examine these "victimless crimes" later in the chapter.) According to conflict theorists, criminal law does not represent a consistent application of societal values, but instead reflects competing values and interests. Thus, the U.S. criminal code outlaws marijuana because of its alleged harm to users, yet cigarettes and alcohol—both of which can be harmful to users—are sold legally almost everywhere.

In fact, conflict theorists contend that the entire criminal justice system in the United States treats suspects differently based on their racial, ethnic, or social-class background. In many cases, officials in the system use their own discretion to make biased decisions about whether to press charges or drop them, whether to set bail and how much, whether to offer parole or deny it. Researchers have found that this kind of **differential justice**—differences in the way social control is exercised over different

TABLE **24-2** SOCIOLOGICAL PERSPECTIVES ON DEVIANCE

Tracking Sociological Perspectives

Approach	Theoretical Perspective	Proponents	Emphasis
Anomie	Functionalist	Émile Durkheim Robert Merton	Adaptation to societal norms
Cultural transmission/ Differential association	Interactionist	Edwin Sutherland	Patterns learned through others
Social disorganization	Interactionist	Clifford Shaw Henry McKay	Communal relationships
Labeling/Social constructionist	Interactionist	Howard Becker William Chambliss	Societal response to acts
Conflict	Conflict	Richard Quinney	Dominance by authorized agents Discretionary justice
Feminist	Conflict/Feminist	Freda Adler Meda Chesney-Lind	Role of gender Women as victims and perpetrators

groups—puts African Americans and Latinos at a disadvantage in the justice system, both as juveniles and as adults. On average, White offenders receive shorter sentences than comparable Latino and African American offenders, even when prior arrest records and the relative severity of the crime are taken into consideration (Blow 2014a, 2014b).

The perspective advanced by conflict and labeling theorists forms quite a contrast to the functionalist approach to deviance. Functionalists see standards of deviant behavior as merely reflecting cultural norms; conflict and labeling theorists point out that the most powerful groups in a society can shape laws and standards and determine who is (or is not) prosecuted as a criminal. These groups would be unlikely to apply the label "deviant" to the corporate executive whose decisions lead to large-scale environmental pollution. In the opinion of conflict theorists, agents of social control and other powerful groups can impose their own self-serving definitions of deviance on the general public.

Feminist Perspective

Feminist criminologists such as Freda Adler and Meda Chesney-Lind have suggested that many of the existing approaches to deviance and crime were developed with only men in mind. For example, in the United States, for many years any husband who forced his wife to have sexual intercourse—without her consent and against her will—was not legally considered to have committed rape. The law defined rape as pertaining only to sexual relations between people who were not married to each other, reflecting the overwhelmingly male composition of state legislatures at the time.

It took repeated protests by feminist organizations to get changes in the criminal law defining rape. Beginning in 1993, husbands in all 50 states could be prosecuted under most circumstances for the rape of their wives. There remain alarming exceptions in at least 8 states, however. For example, the husband is exempt when he does not need to use force because his wife is asleep, unconscious, or mentally or physically impaired. These interpretations still rest on the notion that the marriage contract entitles a husband to sex (Allen 2015).

In the future, feminist scholarship can be expected to grow dramatically. Particularly on topics such as white-collar crime, drinking behavior, drug abuse, and differential sentencing rates between the genders, as well as on the fundamental question of how to define deviance, feminist scholars will have much to say.

We have seen that over the past century, sociologists have taken many different approaches in studying deviance, arousing some controversy in the process. Table 24-2 summarizes the various theoretical approaches to this topic.

MODULE **24** | **Recap and Review**

Summary

Deviant behavior is behavior that violates social norms. A wide range of behavior may be classified as deviant, and everyone violates social norms in some situations.

1. Some forms of **deviance** carry a negative social **stigma,** while other forms are more or less accepted.

2. From a functionalist point of view, deviance and its consequences help to define the limits of proper behavior.

3. Some interactionists maintain that people learn criminal behavior by interacting with others (**cultural transmission**). To them, deviance results from exposure to attitudes that are favorable to criminal acts (**differential association**).

4. Other interactionists attribute increases in crime and deviance to the absence or breakdown of communal relationships and social institutions, such as the family, school, place of worship, and local government (**social disorganization theory**).

5. An important aspect of labeling theory is the recognition that some people are viewed as deviant, while others who engage in the same behavior are not.

6. From the conflict perspective, laws and punishments are a reflection of the interests of the powerful.

7. The feminist perspective emphasizes cultural attitudes and differential economic relationships to help explain gender differences in deviance and crime.

Thinking Critically

1. Research a culture you are unfamiliar with. Do any of the customs seem deviant to you? Which of your own customs might seem deviant to members of that culture?

2. Using examples drawn from work or college life, illustrate each of Merton's five modes of individual adaptation.

3. Explain the presence of both criminals and law-abiding citizens in an inner-city neighborhood in terms of the interactionist perspective.

Key Terms

Anomie

Anomie theory of deviance

Cultural transmission

Deviance

Differential association

Differential justice

Labeling theory

Social constructionist perspective

Social disorganization theory

Societal-reaction approach

Stigma

MODULE 25 | Crime

Crime is on everyone's mind. Until recently, college campuses were viewed as havens from crime. But as Box 25-1 shows, at today's colleges and universities, there have been increased calls to allow members of the campus community to carry firearms.

Crime is a violation of criminal law for which some governmental authority applies formal penalties. It represents a deviation from formal social norms administered by the state. Laws divide crimes into various categories, depending on the severity of the offense, the age of the offender, the potential punishment, and the court that holds jurisdiction over the case.

⬤ Types of Crime

Rather than relying solely on legal categories, however, sociologists classify crimes in terms of how they are committed and how society views the offenses. In this section we will examine six types of crime differentiated by sociologists: victimless crimes, professional crime, organized crime, white-collar and technology-based crime, hate crimes, and transnational crime.

Victimless Crime

When we think of crime, we tend to think of acts that endanger people's economic or personal well-being against their will (or without their direct knowledge). In contrast, sociologists use the term **victimless crime** to describe the willing exchange among adults of widely desired but illegal goods and services, such as prostitution (Schur 1965, 1985).

Some activists are working to decriminalize many of these illegal practices. Supporters of decriminalization are troubled by the attempt to legislate a moral code for adults. In their view, prostitution, drug abuse, gambling, and other victimless crimes are impossible to prevent. The already overburdened criminal justice system should instead devote its resources to street crimes and other offenses with obvious victims.

Despite widespread use of the term *victimless crime*, however, many people object to the notion that there is no victim other than the offender in such crimes. Excessive drinking, compulsive gambling, and illegal drug use contribute to an enormous amount of personal and property damage. A person with a drinking problem may become abusive to a spouse or children; a compulsive gambler or drug user may steal to pursue his or her obsession. And feminist sociologists contend that prostitution, as well as the more disturbing aspects of pornography, reinforce the misconception that women are "toys" who can be treated as objects rather than people. According to critics of decriminalization, society must not give tacit approval to conduct that has such harmful consequences (Melissa Farley and Malarek 2008).

The controversy over decriminalization reminds us of the important insights of labeling that conflict theorists presented earlier. Underlying this debate are two questions: Who has the power to label gambling, prostitution, and public drunkenness as "crimes"? and Who has the power to label such behaviors as "victimless"? The answer is generally the state legislatures, and in some cases, the police and the courts.

Box 25-1

Sociology on Campus

Packing Firearms on Campus

The average college student's backpack probably contains notebooks, textbooks, and a laptop. What if it were legal for it to hold a gun as well? While college campuses are generally very safe, high-profile campus shootings have led to a number of changes in laws about concealed firearms on campus.

In 2007, in the wake of the mass shooting at Virginia Tech, many college officials reviewed security measures on their campuses. Administrators were reluctant to end or even limit the relative freedom of movement students enjoyed. Instead, they concentrated on improving emergency communications between campus police and students, faculty, and staff. Relying on technology to maintain social control, college leaders called for replacement of the "old" technology of e-mail with instant alerts that could be sent to cellphones via instant messaging.

Among the calls for change was the much more controversial one of allowing people to carry concealed weapons on campus. All states allow concealed weapons permits, but such provisions are strictly regulated and, until recently, have always banned weapons in schools at any level.

> In the last few years, a dozen or more state legislatures introduced bills to allow guns on campus.

In the last few years, a dozen or more state legislatures introduced bills to allow guns on campus. As of 2016, nine states permitted guns on campus (Arkansas, Colorado, Idaho, Kansas, Mississippi, Oregon, Texas, Utah, and Wisconsin). Some allow faculty and staff members to carry weapons, but not students. Others allow weapons only if a campus building lacks "adequate security." Typically, even when such laws are in effect, individual colleges have the authority to prohibit weapons from buildings they designate.

As of October 2015, 19 states had a total ban on carrying a concealed weapon on a college campus (California, Florida, Georgia, Illinois, Louisiana, Massachusetts, Michigan, Missouri, Nebraska, Nevada, New Jersey, New Mexico, New York, North Carolina, North Dakota, Ohio, South Carolina, Tennessee, and Wyoming). In the remaining 23 states, the decision to ban or allow guns on campuses is to be made by each college or university. Each institution can also stipulate that firearms may only be kept in locked cars in parking lots.

In the debates thus far, whether in legislatures or on campuses, the same arguments keep coming up. Supporters of the right to carry concealed weapons on campus argue that it's a constitutional right, an argument with which courts frequently agree, and will make campuses safe from shooters and other criminals. Opponents, who usually include administrators, faculty members, and campus law enforcement officers, claim that more firearms will increase the risk of dangerous situations.

© jabejon/E+/Getty Images RF

LET'S DISCUSS

1. Are concealed weapons allowed on your campus? What is the policy? Do you support it?

2. Is allowing guns on campus an example of social control? Why or why not?

Sources: Armed Campuses 2015; Horner 2015; Mulhere 2015; National Conference of State Legislatures 2015.

Professional Crime

Although the adage "Crime doesn't pay" is familiar, many people do make a career of illegal activities. A **professional criminal,** or *career criminal,* is a person who pursues crime as a day-to-day occupation, developing skilled techniques and enjoying a certain degree of status among other criminals. Some professional criminals specialize in burglary, safecracking, hijacking of cargo, pickpocketing, and shoplifting. Such people have acquired skills that reduce the likelihood of arrest, conviction, and imprisonment. As a result, they may have long careers in their chosen professions.

Edwin Sutherland (1937) offered pioneering insights into the behavior of professional criminals by publishing an annotated account written by a professional thief. Unlike the person who engages in crime only once or twice, professional thieves make a business of stealing. They devote

© Ingram Publishing/SuperStock RF

their entire working time to planning and executing crimes, and sometimes travel across the nation to pursue their "professional duties." Like people in regular occupations, professional thieves consult with their colleagues concerning the demands of work, becoming part of a subculture of similarly occupied individuals. They exchange information on places to burglarize, on outlets for unloading stolen goods, and on ways of securing bail bonds if arrested.

Organized Crime

A 1976 government report devotes three pages to defining the term *organized crime*. For our purposes, we will consider **organized crime** to be the work of a group that regulates relations among criminal enterprises involved in illegal activities, including prostitution, gambling, and the smuggling and sale of illegal drugs. Organized crime dominates the world of illegal business just as large corporations dominate the conventional business world. It allocates territory, sets prices for goods and services, and acts as an arbitrator in internal disputes. A secret, conspiratorial activity, it generally evades law enforcement. It takes over legitimate businesses, gains influence over labor unions, corrupts public officials, intimidates witnesses in criminal trials, and even "taxes" merchants in exchange for "protection" (National Advisory Commission on Criminal Justice 1976).

Organized crime serves as a means of upward mobility for groups of people struggling to escape poverty. Sociologist Daniel Bell (1953) used the term *ethnic succession* to describe the sequential passage of leadership from Irish Americans in the early part of the 20th century to Jewish Americans in the 1920s and then to Italian Americans in the early 1930s. Ethnic succession has become more complex, reflecting the diversity of the nation's latest immigrants. Colombian, Mexican, Russian, Chinese, Pakistani, and Nigerian immigrants are among those who have begun to play a significant role in organized crime activities (Herman 2005).

White-Collar and Technology-Based Crime

Income tax evasion, stock manipulation, consumer fraud, bribery and extraction of kickbacks, embezzlement, and misrepresentation in advertising—these are all examples of **white-collar crime,** illegal acts committed in the course of business activities, often by affluent, "respectable" people. In his 1939 presidential address to the American Sociological Association, Edwin Sutherland (1949, 1983) likened these crimes to organized crime because they are often perpetrated through occupational roles.

"KICKBACKS, EMBEZZLEMENT, PRICE-FIXING, BRIBERY... THIS IS AN EXTREMELY HIGH-CRIME AREA."

Source: Cartoon by Sidney Harris. © ScienceCartoonsPlus.com

A new type of white-collar crime has emerged in recent decades: cybercrime. **Cybercrime** is illegal activity primarily conducted through the use of computer hardware or software. Encompassed within cybercrime is cyberespionage and cyberterrorism. Cybercrime is a global problem, but the United States is victim to 80 percent of the data breaches. Because of the high-value of U.S. targets, it is estimated that this country accounts for over 90 percent of the global cost of these breaches. By 2019 the annual cost of criminal data breaches in the U.S. is estimated to reach $2 trillion (Juniper Research 2015).

When Charles Horton Cooley spoke of the self and Erving Goffman of impression management, surely neither scholar could have envisioned the insidious crime of identity theft. Each year about 7 percent of all adults find that their personal information has been misused for criminal purposes. Unfortunately, with our society's growing reliance on electronic financial transactions, assuming someone else's identity has become increasingly easy (Harrel 2015).

Identity theft does not necessarily require technology. A criminal can obtain someone's personal information by pickpocketing or by intercepting mail. However, the widespread exchange of information online has allowed criminals to access large amounts of personal information. Public awareness of the potential harm from identity theft took a giant leap in the aftermath of September 11, 2001, when investigations revealed that several hijackers had used fraudulent IDs to open bank accounts, rent apartments, and board planes. A law enacted in 2004 makes identity theft punishable by a mandatory prison sentence if it is linked to other crimes. Still, unauthorized disclosures of information, even if accidental, persist.

Sutherland (1940) coined the term *white-collar crime* in 1939 to refer to acts by individuals, but the term has been broadened more recently to include offenses by businesses and corporations as well. *Corporate crime,* or any act by a corporation that is punishable by the government, takes many forms and includes individuals, organizations, and institutions among its victims. Corporations may engage in anticompetitive behavior, environmental pollution, medical fraud, tax fraud, stock fraud and manipulation, accounting fraud, the production of unsafe goods, bribery and corruption, and health and safety violations (J. Coleman 2006).

For many years, corporate wrongdoers got off lightly in court by documenting their long history of charitable contributions and agreeing to help law enforcement officials find other white-collar criminals. Unfortunately, that is still the case. The highly visible jailing of multimedia personality Martha Stewart in 2004, as well as recent disclosures of "Wall Street greed," may lead the casual observer to think that government is cracking down on white-collar crime. An analysis of Department of Justice data shows that criminal prosecution of corporate violators fell by 29 percent between 2004 and 2014 (Transactional Records Access Clearinghouse 2015).

The leniency shown to white-collar criminals is not limited to the United States. Japan did not level a fine for insider trading on a major financial corporation until 2012. The profit from the crime was about $119,000; the penalty was $600 (Fukase and Inagaki 2012).

Even when a person is convicted of corporate crime, the verdict generally does not harm his or her reputation and career aspirations nearly so much as conviction for street crime would. Apparently, the label "white-collar criminal" does not carry the stigma of the label "felon convicted of a violent crime." Conflict theorists don't find such differential treatment surprising. They argue that the criminal justice system largely disregards the crimes of the affluent, focusing on crimes committed by the poor. Generally, if an offender holds a position of status and influence, his or her crime is treated as less serious, and the sanction is much more lenient (Simpson 2013).

Hate Crime

In contrast to other crimes, hate crimes are defined not only by the perpetrators' actions, but by the purpose of their conduct. The government considers an ordinary crime to be a **hate crime** when the offender is motivated to choose a victim based on race, religion, ethnic group, national origin, or sexual orientation, and when evidence shows that hatred prompted the offender to commit the crime. Hate crimes are sometimes referred to as *bias crimes* (Department of Justice 2008).

In 1990, Congress passed the Hate Crimes Statistics Act, which created a national mandate to identify crimes based on race, religion, ethnic group, and national origin. (Before that time, only 12 states had monitored such crimes.) Since then the act has been broadened to include disabilities, both physical and mental, and sexual orientation. In addition, some jurisdictions impose harsher sanctions (jail time or fines) for hate crimes than for other crimes. For example, if the penalty for assault is a year in jail, the penalty for an assault identified as a hate crime might be two years.

In 2016, law enforcement agencies submitted data on hate crimes to the federal government. The statistics included official reports of 5,850 hate crimes and bias-motivated offenses. As Figure 25-1 shows, race or ethnicity was the apparent motivation in 57 percent of the reports. Although vandalism and intimidation were the most common crimes, 37 percent of the incidents involved assault, rape, or murder.

The vast majority of hate crimes, although not all of them, are committed by members of the dominant group against those who are relatively powerless. One in every five racially based hate crimes is an anti-White incident. Except for the most horrific hate crimes, these offenses receive little media attention. Clearly, hostility based on race knows no boundaries.

Transnational Crime

More and more, scholars and police officials are turning their attention to **transnational crime,** or crime that occurs across multiple national borders. In the past, international crime was often limited to the clandestine shipment of goods across the border between two countries. But increasingly, crime is no more restricted by such borders than is legal commerce. Rather than concentrating on specific countries, international crime now spans the globe.

Historically, probably the most dreadful example of transnational crime has been slavery. At first, governments did not regard slavery as a crime, but merely regulated it as they would the trade in goods. In the 20th century, transnational crime grew to embrace trafficking in endangered species, drugs, and stolen art and antiquities.

Transnational crime is not exclusive of some of the other types of crime we have discussed. For example, organized criminal networks are increasingly global. Technology definitely facilitates their illegal activities, such as trafficking in child pornography. Beginning in the 1990s, the United Nations began to categorize transnational crimes; Table 25-1 lists some of the more common types.

Bilateral cooperation in the pursuit of border criminals such as smugglers has been common for many years. The first global effort to control international crime was the International Criminal Police Organization (Interpol), a cooperative network of European police forces founded to stem the movement

TABLE **25-1** **TYPES OF TRANSNATIONAL CRIME**

Bankruptcy and insurance fraud
Computer crime (treating computers as both a tool and a target of crime)
Corruption and bribery of public officials
Environmental crime
Hijacking of airplanes (skyjacking)
Illegal drug trade
Illegal money transfers (money laundering)
Illegal sales of firearms and ammunition
Infiltration of legal businesses
Intellectual property crime
Migrant smuggling
Networking of criminal organizations
Sea piracy
Terrorism
Theft of art and cultural objects
Trafficking in body parts (includes illegal organ transplants)
Trafficking in human beings (includes sex trade)

Source: Compiled and updated by the author based on Mueller 2001 and United Nations Office on Drugs and Crime 2015. *Handcuffs:* © Photodisc/Getty Images RF

FIGURE 25-1 **Reported Hate Crimes, by Category**

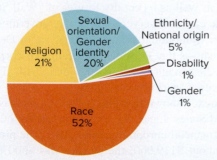

Source: Incidents reported for 2013 in 2014. Federal Bureau of Investigation 2016.

of political revolutionaries across borders. While such efforts to fight transnational crime may seem lofty—an activity with which any government should cooperate—they are complicated by sensitive legal and security issues.

Most nations that have signed protocols issued by the United Nations, including the United States, have expressed concern over potential encroachments on their national judicial systems, as well as concern over their national security. Thus, they have been reluctant to share certain types of intelligence data. The terrorist attacks of September 11, 2001, increased both the interest in combating transnational crime and sensitivity to the risks of sharing intelligence data (Deflem 2005; Felson and Kalaitzidis 2005).

 use your **sociological imagination**

As the editor of an online news service, how might you treat stories on corporate or white-collar crime differently from those on violent crime?

Crime Statistics

Crime statistics are not as accurate as social scientists would like, especially since they deal with an issue of grave concern to the people of the United States. Unfortunately, they are frequently cited as if they were completely reliable. Such data do serve as an indicator of police activity, as well as an approximate indication of the level of certain crimes. Yet it would be a mistake to interpret these data as an exact representation of the incidence of crime.

Index Crimes and Victimization Surveys

Typically, the crime data reported in the United States are based on **index crimes,** or the eight types of crime tabulated each year by the

Federal Bureau of Investigation (FBI). This category of criminal behavior generally consists of those serious offenses that people think of when they express concern about the nation's crime problem. Index crimes include murder, rape, robbery, and assault—all of which are violent crimes committed against people—as well as the property crimes of burglary, larceny-theft, motor vehicle theft, and arson (Table 25-2). The crime index is published annually by the FBI as part of the *Uniform Crime Reports.*

Obviously, many serious offenses, such as white-collar crimes, are not included in this index (although they are recorded elsewhere). In addition, the crime index is disproportionately devoted to property crimes, whereas most citizens are more worried about violent crimes. Thus, a significant decrease in the number of rapes and robberies could be overshadowed by a slightly larger increase in the number of automobiles stolen, leading to the mistaken impression that *personal* safety is more at risk than before.

The most serious limitation of official crime statistics is that they include only those crimes actually *reported* to law enforcement agencies. Because members of racial and ethnic minority groups often distrust law enforcement agencies, they may not contact the police. Feminist sociologists and others have noted that many women do not report rape or spousal abuse out of fear they will be blamed for the crime.

Partly because of these deficiencies in official statistics, the National Crime Victimization Survey was initiated in 1972. The Bureau of Justice Statistics, in compiling this annual report, seeks information from law enforcement agencies, but also interviews households across the nation and asks if they were victims of a specific set of crimes during the preceding year. In general, those who administer **victimization surveys** question ordinary people, not police officers, to determine whether they have been victims of crime.

TABLE 25-2 NATIONAL CRIME RATES AND PERCENTAGE CHANGE

Crime Index Offenses in 2014	Number Reported	Rate per 100,000 Inhabitants	Percentage Change in Rate Since 2005
Violent crime			
Murder	14,249	5	−15
Forcible rape	116,645	37	−11
Robbery	325,802	103	−27
Aggravated assault	741,291	233	−14
Total	1,165,383	366	−22
Property crime			
Burglary	1,729,806	543	−25
Larceny-theft	5,858,496	1,839	−20
Motor vehicle theft	689,527	216	−48
Total	8,299,829	2,590	−24

Notes: Arson was designated an index offense beginning in 1979; data on arson were still incomplete as of 2014. Because of rounding, the offenses may not add to totals. Beginning in 2011, the FBI broadened the definition of rape, and use of the term is being phased out. The 2014 data use the new definition; the "Change since 2005" column uses the legacy definition.

Source: Department of Justice 2014.

Unfortunately, like other crime data, victimization surveys have particular limitations. They require that victims understand what has happened to them and are willing to disclose such information to interviewers. Fraud, income tax evasion, and blackmail are examples of crimes that are unlikely to be reported in victimization studies.

Crime Trends

Crime fills the news reports on television, over the Internet, and in the newspapers. As a result, the public regards crime as a major social problem. Yet there has been a significant decline in violent crime in the United States in recent years, after many years of increases.

How much has crime declined? Consider this: the rate of crime being reported in 2014 was comparable to what it was back when gasoline cost 29 cents a gallon and the average person earned less than $6,000 a year. That was 1963.

Dramatic declines have occurred within the last decade. As Table 25-2 shows, both violent crime and property crime dropped about 23 percent in the last 10 years. Although a tragic 14,249 people were murdered in 2014, in 1991 that number was a staggering 24,700. Declines have also been registered in victimization surveys (Figure 25-2).

What explains these declines in both index crimes and victimization rates? Possible explanations include the following:

- Community-oriented policing and crime prevention programs
- New gun control laws
- A massive increase in the prison population, which at least prevents inmates from committing crimes outside prison
- New surveillance technologies
- Better residential and business security
- The decline of the crack cocaine epidemic, which soared in the late 1980s
- The aging of the population, as the number of people in their 50s increased and the number in their 20s decreased

No single explanation could account for such a marked change in crime rates. Taken together, however, these changes in public policy, public health, technology, and demographics may well explain it (Tonry 2014).

Despite the declines in crime, the general public still perceives crime to be a growing threat. Most people surveyed in each of the last thirty years have believed that there is more crime than the year before. How do we explain this perception, which is so different from reality? News media emphasizes violent crimes in the local area and, nationally, we are bombarded by coverage of highly publicized shootings at schools and workplaces (McCarthy 2015).

Feminist scholars draw our attention to one significant countertrend: the proportion of major crimes committed by women has increased. However, violent crimes committed by women, which have never been common, have declined. Despite the "mean girls" headlines in the tabloid magazines, every reliable measure shows that among women, fights, weapons possession, assaults, and violent injuries have plunged over the last decade (Males and Chesney-Lind 2010).

International Crime Rates

If developing reliable crime data is difficult in the United States, making useful cross-national comparisons is even more difficult. Nevertheless, with some care, we can offer preliminary conclusions about how crime rates differ around the world.

Beginning in the 1980s, and continuing into the 21st century, violent crimes have been much more common in the United States than in western Europe. Murders, rapes, and robberies are reported to the police at much higher rates in the United States. Yet the incidence of certain other types of crime appears to be higher elsewhere. For example, England, Ireland, Denmark, and New Zealand all have higher rates of car theft than the United States. Developing nations have significant rates of reported homicide due to civil unrest and political conflict among civilians (United Nations Office on Drugs and Crime 2015b).

A particularly worrisome development has been the rapid escalation in homicide rates in developing countries that supply drugs to industrialized countries, especially the United States. The huge profits generated by cocaine exports to North America and Europe have allowed drug gangs to arm themselves to the point of becoming illegal armies. Homicide rates in Mexico are now about twice as high as those in the United States. Honduras, Guatemala, Venezuela, and El Salvador's homicide rates are three to five times those of Mexico (Luhnow 2014).

Why are rates of violent crime generally so much higher in the United States than in western Europe? Sociologist Elliot Currie (1985, 1998) has suggested that our society places greater emphasis on individual economic achievement than other societies do. At the same time, many observers have noted that the culture of the United States has long tolerated, if not condoned, many forms of violence. Coupled with sharp disparities between poor and affluent citizens, significant unemployment, and substantial alcohol and drug abuse, these factors combine to produce a climate conducive to crime.

Another difference between the United States and other democracies is in use of the death penalty. The United States is alone among advanced democratic societies in using this extreme form of punishment (Amnesty International 2015). In the Social Policy section that follows, we'll consider the issues involved in administration of the death penalty in the United States.

FIGURE 25-2 **Victimization Rates, 1993–2014**

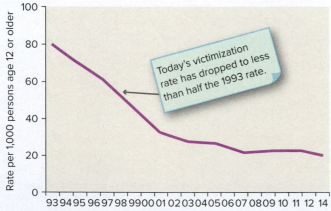

Source: Truman and Langdon 2015.

Taking Sociology to Work

Stephanie Vezzani, Special Agent, U.S. Secret Service

© Stephen Mulcahey/Alamy RF

Stephanie Vezzani wasn't sure what she wanted to major in when she entered the University of Akron, but she did know what she wanted to do with her life: she wanted a career as a crime fighter. Vezzani began as an accounting major, but switched to sociology when she discovered the department offered a special concentration in law enforcement.

Vezzani is now an agent with the U.S. Secret Service, whose twofold mission is to protect high-ranking officials and their families and to investigate financial crimes, including counterfeiting, identity theft, and computer-based attacks on the financial, banking, and telecommunications industries.

She has tackled both aspects of the job. For her, a typical week would include working on a criminal investigation in a field office or traveling around the country with a government official in need of protection.

Vezzani finds that travel is one of the most exciting aspects of her job. Over the past six years she has visited Russia, Turkey, Jordan, Vietnam, and South Korea. She also attended the 2002 Winter Olympics in Salt Lake City, where she provided protection for the athletes living in the Olympic Village. Vezzani relishes meeting people from different cultures, and of course she loves the sights she gets to see. "The architecture in St. Petersburg, Russia, was amazing," she says.

Vezzani uses her training in sociology on a daily basis, as she interviews suspects, witnesses, and victims of crime. "It is critical in the field of law enforcement to have an understanding of people's relationships and the beliefs and value systems that contribute to their decision making," she explains. "Sociology has provided me the knowledge to speak to and listen to people with different values and cultures in order to complete my job at the highest level possible."

LET'S DISCUSS

1. Besides an awareness of different beliefs, values, and cultures, what else might sociology offer to those who serve in law enforcement?

2. Law enforcement is a relatively new career option for women. What special strengths do you think a woman might bring to police work?

Social Policy and Social Control |

The Death Penalty in the United States and Worldwide

On June 11, 2001, Timothy McVeigh—the man who killed hundreds of innocent people when he bombed the federal building in Oklahoma City in 1995—was executed by the U.S. government. McVeigh was the first federal prisoner to be put to death in nearly four decades. His execution, and that of others who received the death penalty for their crimes, has raised many questions, both from supporters and from critics of capital punishment. How can the government prevent the execution of innocent men and women? Is it right to resort to a punishment that imitates the crime it seeks to condemn? Is life in prison enough of a punishment for a truly heinous crime?

Looking at the Issue

Historically, execution has been a significant form of punishment, both for deviance from social norms and for criminal behavior. In North America, the death penalty has been used for centuries to punish murder, alleged witchcraft, and a few other crimes. Yet for most of that time, little thought was given to its justification; capital punishment was simply assumed to be morally and religiously right. Today, the death penalty is still on the books in most states, where it is used to a greater or lesser extent (Figure 25-3).

In other parts of the world, serious thought has been given to the ethical implications of the ultimate penalty. Each year a few countries abolish the death penalty; about 20 nations still carry out executions. The United States ranks fourth behind China, Iraq, and Saudi Arabia (Amnesty International 2016).

Applying Sociology

Traditionally, the debate over the death penalty has focused on its appropriateness as a form of punishment and its value in deterring crime. Viewed from Émile Durkheim's functionalist perspective, sanctions against deviant acts help to reinforce society's standards of proper behavior. Supporters of capital punishment insist that fear of execution will prevent at least some criminals from committing serious offenses. Moreover, even if it does not serve as a deterrent, they still see the death penalty as justified, because they believe the worst criminals deserve to die for their crimes.

—Continued

MAPPING LIFE NATIONWIDE

FIGURE 25-3 **Executions by State Since 1976**

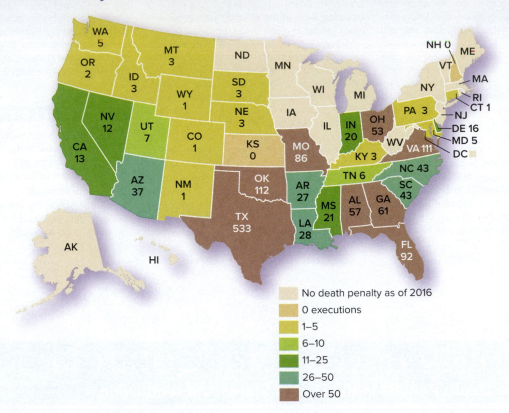

Legend:
- No death penalty as of 2016
- 0 executions
- 1–5
- 6–10
- 11–25
- 26–50
- Over 50

Notes: Number of executions carried out from January 17, 1977, to February 3, 2016, not including three federal executions. Illinois carried out 12 executions before abolishing the death penalty. Nebraska, which abolished the death penalty in 2015, had executed 3 people. The U.S. government has 61 people on death row; the military has 6. Connecticut, Maryland, and New Mexico, which still have people on death row, have abolished the death penalty for future cases.
Source: Death Penalty Information Center 2016.

The death penalty also creates some dysfunctions, however. Although many citizens are concerned that the alternative to execution, life in prison, is unnecessarily expensive, sentencing a person to death is not cheap. According to a recent analysis, in California, prosecuting death penalty cases costs $184 million more per year than prosecuting cases involving life without parole. Housing, health care, and legal representation also cost more for convicts on death row than for other inmates (Alarcón et al. 2011).

Conflict theorists counter that the persistence of social inequality in today's society puts poor people at a disadvantage in the criminal justice system. Simply put, the poor cannot afford to hire the best lawyers, but must rely instead on court-appointed attorneys, who typically are overworked and underpaid. This unequal access to legal resources may mean the difference between life and death for poor defendants. Indeed, the American Bar Association (1997) has repeatedly expressed concern about the limited defense most

defendants who face the death penalty receive. As of late 2015, DNA analysis and other new technologies had exonerated 20 death row inmates.

Another issue of crucial concern to conflict theorists and researchers is the possibility of racial discrimination. Numerous studies show that defendants are more likely to be sentenced to death if their victims were White rather than Black. About 76 percent of the victims in death penalty cases are White, even though only 50 percent of all murder victims are White. And there is some evidence that Black defendants, who constituted 42 percent of all death row inmates in 2016, are more likely to face execution than Whites in the same legal circumstance. About 60 percent of the 289 who have been exonerated for any reason, including poor legal defense, are members of minority groups. Evidence exists, too, that capital defendants receive poor legal services because of the racist attitudes of their own defense counsel. While racism is never acceptable, it is particularly devastating in the criminal justice system, where the legal process can result in an execution (Death Penalty Information Center 2016; Innocence Project 2015; Petrie and Coverdill 2010).

Initiating Policy

Many people hesitate to endorse the death penalty, yet when confronted with a horrendous crime, they feel the death penalty should be available, at least in some cases. In most people's minds, for example, Timothy McVeigh's sentence would be an appropriate use of the death penalty, although opinion on this point has fluctuated. In 2015, support for the death penalty was 61 percent—about the same level as when the question was first posed in 1937, in a national survey (Dugan 2015).

Recently, policy initiatives have moved in two different directions. In several death penalty states, legislators are considering broadening the range of offenses for which convicted criminals may be sentenced to execution. In these states, child molesters who did not murder their victims could become eligible for the death penalty, along with certain repeat offenders. The countertrend, a movement away from the death penalty, is based on doubts about whether an execution can be carried out humanely.

Legal action has been taken on behalf of those convicted to die, especially by lethal injection, which is used in virtually all death penalty jurisdictions. Concerns about lethal injection range from medical ethics (the injection must be administered by a medical technician) to the effectiveness of the technique, which sometimes takes a long time to cause death. Opponents contend that death can be excruciating. In 2008 and again in 2015, the Supreme Court ruled that lethal injections procedures were constitutional, but specified protocols for the use of chemicals, personnel training, medical supervision, and error risk that apply in all 35 states that use lethal injection (Kiener 2015).

Used by permission of Cagle Cartoons, Inc.

Attitudes toward the death penalty and how to execute are constantly changing. Back in the late 19th century, many people were horrified by botched hangings. The idea of using high-voltage electricity was suggested soon after electricity became available commercially. Famed inventor Thomas Edison advocated the use of alternating current, which he championed for such purposes. Shown above is the first electrocution, using Edison's method to execute wife-killer William Kemmler in 1890 in New York. Now, over a hundred years later, people are questioning the use of lethal injections, which were themselves introduced as more humane than the electric chair, and which largely replaced electrocutions in the 1970s.

Surprisingly, only about 20 to 40 death sentences are handed out for the more than 14,000 reported murders that occur every year. Courts continue to address the question of how this ultimate penalty can be administered in a judicially fair manner. Policymakers, however, do not seem concerned with such questions. In recent years, federal and state legislatures have declared additional crimes to be punishable by death, curtailed appeals by death row inmates, and reimbursed far fewer lawyers for their defense of condemned criminals.

Internationally, attention has focused on those nations where executions are relatively common, such as China and Iraq. Foes of the death penalty see these nations as violators of human rights. In the United States, which usually regards itself as a champion of human rights, pressure to abolish capital punishment has grown both at home and abroad.

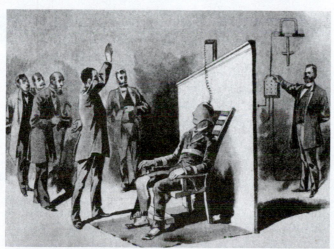

© Interfoto/Alamy

TAKE THE ISSUE WITH YOU

1. Does the death penalty deter crime? If so, why are crime rates in the United States high compared to those in other nations?

2. What is your position on the death penalty—should it be legal or should it be abolished? Explain your reasoning.

3. Should youths who have been convicted of violent crimes be subject to the death penalty? Why or why not?

Summary

Crime is deviation from formal social norms for which punishment is administered by the state.

1. Sociologists differentiate among **victimless crimes** (such as drug use and prostitution), crime committed by **professional criminals, hate crime, organized crime, white-collar crime,** and **transnational crime.**

2. Crime statistics are among the least reliable social data, partly because so many crimes are not reported to law enforcement agencies. Rates of violent crime are higher in the United States than in other Western societies, although they have been dropping.

3. The death penalty is the ultimate sanction, one that functionalists believe deters serious crime. However, it is applied disproportionately to the economically disadvantaged and to racial minorities. Worldwide, many countries have renounced the death penalty.

Thinking Critically

1. Why is it useful to sociologists to have victimization surveys in addition to reported crime data?

2. Apply at least two of the theories discussed in Module 24 to the problem of professional crime. Which theory seems to provide the best explanation?

Key Terms

Crime

Hate crime

Index crimes

Organized crime

Professional criminal

Transnational crime

Victimization survey

Victimless crime

White-collar crime

Mastering This Chapter

© Frederick J. Brown/AFP/Getty Images

taking sociology with you

1 Describe the mechanisms of social control, both formal and informal, on your campus. Which is more effective, formal or informal control?

2 Explain the presence of both criminals and law-abiding citizens in an inner-city neighborhood in terms of the interactionist perspective.

3 Pay a visit to your local courthouse and observe a trial by jury from the point of view of a sociologist. Then describe what you saw and heard using sociological concepts.

Anomie Durkheim's term for the loss of direction felt in a society when social control of individual behavior has become ineffective.

Anomie theory of deviance Robert Merton's theory of deviance as an adaptation of socially prescribed goals or of the means governing their attainment, or both.

Conformity Going along with peers—individuals of our own status who have no special right to direct our behavior.

Control theory A view of conformity and deviance that suggests that our connection to members of society leads us to systematically conform to society's norms.

Crime A violation of criminal law for which some governmental authority applies formal penalties.

Cultural transmission A school of criminology that argues that criminal behavior is learned through social interactions.

Cybercrime Illegal activity primarily conducted through the use of computer hardware or software.

Deviance Behavior that violates the standards of conduct or expectations of a group or society.

Differential association A theory of deviance that holds that violation of rules results from exposure to attitudes favorable to criminal acts.

Differential justice Differences in the way social control is exercised over different groups.

Formal social control Social control that is carried out by authorized agents, such as police officers, judges, school administrators, and employers.

Hate crime A criminal offense committed because of the offender's bias against a race, religion, ethnic group, national origin, or sexual orientation. Also referred to as *bias crime*.

Index crimes The eight types of crime tabulated each year by the FBI in the *Uniform Crime Reports:* murder, rape, robbery, assault, burglary, theft, motor vehicle theft, and arson.

Informal social control Social control that is carried out casually by ordinary people through such means as laughter, smiles, and ridicule.

Labeling theory An approach to deviance that attempts to explain why certain people are viewed as deviants while others engaged in the same behavior are not.

Law Governmental social control.

Obedience Compliance with higher authorities in a hierarchical structure.

Organized crime The work of a group that regulates relations among criminal enterprises involved in illegal activities, including prostitution, gambling, and the smuggling and sale of illegal drugs.

Professional criminal A person who pursues crime as a day-to-day occupation, developing skilled techniques and enjoying a certain degree of status among other criminals.

Sanction A penalty or reward for conduct concerning a social norm.

Social constructionist perspective An approach to deviance that emphasizes the role of culture in the creation of the deviant identity.

Social control The techniques and strategies for preventing deviant human behavior in any society.

Social disorganization theory The theory that crime and deviance are caused by the absence or breakdown of communal relationships and social institutions.

Societal-reaction approach Another name for *labeling theory*.

Stigma A label used to devalue members of certain social groups.

Transnational crime Crime that occurs across multiple national borders.

Victimization survey A questionnaire or interview given to a sample of the population to determine whether people have been victims of crime.

Victimless crime A term used by sociologists to describe the willing exchange among adults of widely desired but illegal goods and services.

White-collar crime Illegal acts committed by affluent, "respectable" individuals in the course of business activities.

self-quiz

Read each question carefully and then select the best answer.

1. Society brings about acceptance of basic norms through techniques and strategies for preventing deviant human behavior. This process is termed
   a. stigmatization.
   b. labeling.
   c. law.
   d. social control.

2. Which sociological perspective argues that people must respect social norms if any group or society is to survive?
   a. the conflict perspective
   b. the interactionist perspective
   c. the functionalist perspective
   d. the feminist perspective

3. Stanley Milgram used the word *conformity* to mean
   a. going along with peers.
   b. compliance with higher authorities in a hierarchical structure.
   c. techniques and strategies for preventing deviant human behavior in any society.
   d. penalties and rewards for conduct concerning a social norm.

4. Which sociological theory suggests that our connection to members of society leads us to conform systematically to society's norms?
   a. feminist theory
   b. control theory
   c. interactionist theory
   d. functionalist theory

5. Which of the following statements is true of deviance?
   a. Deviance is always criminal behavior.
   b. Deviance is behavior that violates the standards of conduct or expectations of a group or society.
   c. Deviance is perverse behavior.
   d. Deviance is inappropriate behavior that cuts across all cultures and social orders.

6. Which sociologist illustrated the boundary-maintenance function of deviance in his study of Puritans in 17th-century New England?
   a. Kai Erikson
   b. Émile Durkheim
   c. Robert Merton
   d. Edwin Sutherland

7. Which of the following is an example of innovation as defined in Robert Merton's anomie theory of deviance?
   a. An advocate for a new form of government initiates a blog.
   b. A bureaucrat demands higher wages.
   c. A prison guard agitates for a labor union.
   d. Rather than writing an original essay, a student copies his submission from the Internet.

8. Which sociologist first advanced the idea that an individual undergoes the same basic socialization process whether learning conforming or deviant acts?
   a. Robert Merton
   b. Edwin Sutherland
   c. Travis Hirschi
   d. William Chambliss

9. Which of the following theories contends that criminal victimization increases when communal relationships and social institutions break down?
   a. labeling theory
   b. conflict theory
   c. social disorganization theory
   d. differential association theory

10. Which of the following conducted observation research on two groups of high school males (the Saints and the Roughnecks) and concluded that social class played an important role in the varying fortunes of the two groups?
   a. Richard Quinney
   b. Edwin Sutherland
   c. Émile Durkheim
   d. William Chambliss

11. If we fail to respect and obey social norms, we may face punishment through informal or formal _____ .

12. Police officers, judges, administrators, employers, military officers, and managers of movie theaters are all instruments of _____ social control.

13. Some norms are considered so important by a society that they are formalized into _____ controlling people's behavior.

14. It is important to underscore the fact that _____ is the primary source of conformity and obedience, including obedience to law.

15. _____ is a state of normlessness that typically occurs during a period of profound social change and disorder, such as a time of economic collapse.

16. Labeling theory is also called the _____ _____ approach.

17. _____ theorists view standards of deviant behavior as merely reflecting cultural norms, whereas _____ and _____ theorists point out that the most powerful groups in a society can shape laws and standards and determine who is (or is not) prosecuted as a criminal.

18. Feminists contend that prostitution and some forms of pornography are not _____ crimes.

19. Daniel Bell used the term _____ _____ to describe the process during which leadership of organized crime was transferred from Irish Americans to Jewish Americans and later to Italian Americans and others.

20. Consumer fraud, bribery, and income tax evasion are considered _____ _____ crimes.

8 Stratification and Social Mobility in the United States

© PeerPoint/Alamy

Pedestrians pass by a homeless man panhandling for change in New York City. The United States is a society of contrasts between great wealth, modest means, and deep poverty.

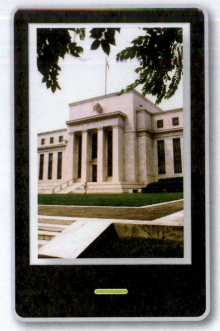

© Glow Images RF

Elected leaders such as the president and members of Congress and leaders such as Janet Yellen, Chair of the Board of Governors of the Federal Reserve Bank, have turned their attention to inequality and stratification in the United States. Yellen addressed this pressing problem in a 2014 speech.

" The distribution of income and wealth in the United States has been widening more or less steadily for several decades, to a greater extent than in most advanced countries. This trend paused during the Great Recession because of larger wealth losses for those at the top of the distribution and because increased safety-net spending helped offset some income losses for those below the top. But widening inequality resumed in the recovery, as the stock market rebounded, wage growth and the healing of the labor market have been slow, and the increase in home prices has not fully restored the housing wealth lost by the large majority of households for which it is their primary asset.

The extent of and continuing increase in inequality in the United States greatly concern me. The past several decades have seen the most sustained rise in inequality since the 19th century after more than 40 years of narrowing inequality following the Great Depression. By some estimates, income and wealth inequality are near their highest levels in the past hundred years, much higher than the average during that time span and probably higher than for much of American history before then. It is no secret that the past few decades of widening inequality can be summed up as significant income and wealth gains for those at the very top and stagnant living standards for the majority. I think it is appropriate to ask whether this trend is compatible with values rooted in our nation's history, among them the high value Americans have traditionally placed on equality of opportunity.

Some degree of inequality in income and wealth, of course, would occur even with completely equal opportunity because variations in effort, skill, and luck will produce variations in outcomes. Indeed, some variation in outcomes

The past few decades of widening inequality can be summed up as significant income and wealth gains for those at the very top and stagnant living standards for the majority.

arguably contributes to economic growth because it creates incentives to work hard, get an education, save, invest, and undertake risk. However, to the extent that opportunity itself is enhanced by access to economic resources, inequality of outcomes can exacerbate inequality of opportunity, thereby perpetuating a trend of increasing inequality. Such a link is suggested by the "Great Gatsby Curve," the finding that, among advanced economies, greater income inequality is associated with diminished intergenerational mobility. In such circumstances, society faces difficult questions of how best to fairly and justly promote equal opportunity.

In my remarks, I will review trends in income and wealth inequality over the past several decades, then identify and discuss four sources of economic opportunity in America— think of them as "building blocks" for the gains in income and wealth that most Americans hope are within reach of those who strive for them. The first two are widely recognized as important sources of opportunity: resources available for children and affordable higher education. The second two may come as more of a surprise: business ownership and inheritances. Like most sources of wealth, family ownership of businesses and inheritances are concentrated among households at the top of the distribution. But both of these are less concentrated and more broadly distributed than other forms of wealth, and there is some basis for thinking that they may also play a role in providing economic opportunities to a considerable number of families below the top.

[R]esearch about the causes and implications of inequality is ongoing, and I hope that this conference helps spur further study of economic opportunity and its effects on economic mobility. . . . I do believe that these are important questions, and I hope that further research will help answer them. "

(Yellen 2014) Quotation from Janet Yellen. 2014. "Perspectives on Inequality and Opportunity from the Survey of Consumer Finances."

r. Yellen's remarks draw attention to the serious and pervasive problem of inequality and the closely related problem of inequality of opportunity. She emphasizes the main point that we will make throughout this chapter and Chapter 9: the opportunity to advance is disproportionately available to those who already possess above average wealth and social status. We will discuss the many sociological perspectives on stratification and see that inequality is pervasive in U.S. society.

Is social inequality an inescapable part of society? How does government policy affect the life chances of the working poor? Is this country still a place where a hardworking person can move up the social ladder? These modules focus on the unequal distribution of socially valued rewards and its consequences. We will begin by examining four general systems of stratification, including the one most familiar to us, the social class system. We will examine three sociological perspectives on stratification, paying particular attention to the theories of Karl Marx and Max Weber. We'll also ask whether stratification is universal and see what sociologists, including functionalist and conflict theorists, have to say about that question.

We will see too how sociologists define social class, and examine the consequences of stratification for people's wealth and income, safety, and educational opportunities. Then we will take a close look at poverty, particularly the question of who belongs to the underclass and why. And we will confront the question of social mobility, both upward and downward. Finally, in the Social Policy section, we will examine the issue of corporate compensation—the huge salaries and bonuses that corporate executives earn even when their companies are losing money and employees are losing their jobs.

© Federal Reserve/Alamy

Dr. Janet L. Yellen, Chair of the Federal Reserve Board of Governors. The Federal Reserve's tasks, regulating the banking system and helping to keep the economy on track, greatly affect access to economic opportunity for people at all levels of the social hierarchy in the United States.

MODULE 26 | Systems of Stratification

Ever since people first began to speculate about the nature of human society, their attention has been drawn to the differences between individuals and groups within society. The term **social inequality,** which has been much in the headlines recently, describes a condition in which members of society have differing amounts of wealth, prestige, or power. Some degree of social inequality characterizes every society.

When a system of social inequality is based on a hierarchy of groups, sociologists refer to it as **stratification:** a structured ranking of entire groups of people that perpetuates unequal economic rewards and power in a society. These unequal rewards are evident not only in the distribution of wealth and income, but even in the distressing mortality rates of impoverished communities. Stratification involves the ways in which one generation passes on social inequalities to the next, producing groups of people arranged in rank order, from low to high.

Stratification is a crucial subject of sociological investigation because of its pervasive influence on human interactions and institutions. It results inevitably in social inequality, because certain groups of people stand higher in social rankings, control scarce resources, wield power, and receive special treatment. As we will see in this chapter, the consequences of stratification are evident in the unequal distribution of both income and wealth in industrial societies. The term **income** refers to salaries and wages, interest on savings, stock dividends, and rental income. In contrast, **wealth** is an inclusive term encompassing all a person's material assets, including land, stocks, and other types of property.

Sociologists consider stratification on many levels, ranging from its impact on the individual to worldwide patterns of inequality. No matter where we look, however, disparities in wealth and income are substantial. Take income and poverty patterns in the United States, for example. As the top part of Figure 26-1 shows, in some states the median household income is 75 percent higher than that in other states. And as the bottom part of the figure shows, the poverty rate in many states is twice that of other states. Later in this chapter we will address the meaning of such statistics. We'll begin our discussion here with an overview of the four basic systems of stratification. Then we'll see what sociologists have had to say on the subject of social inequality.

Look at the four general systems of stratification examined here—slavery, castes, estates, and social classes—as ideal types useful for purposes of analysis. Any stratification system may

FIGURE 26-1 The 50 States: Contrasts In Income and Poverty Levels

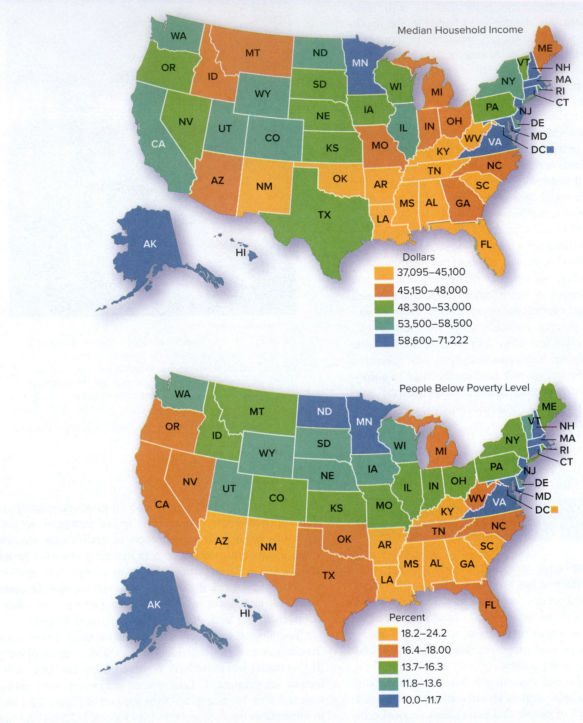

Median Household Income

Dollars
- 37,095–45,100
- 45,150–48,000
- 48,300–53,000
- 53,500–58,500
- 58,600–71,222

People Below Poverty Level

Percent
- 18.2–24.2
- 16.4–18.00
- 13.7–16.3
- 11.8–13.6
- 10.0–11.7

Note: National median household income was $52,250; national poverty rate, 14.8 percent.
Source: Bureau of the Census 2015c, 2015d.

include elements of more than one type. For example, prior to the Civil War, you could find in the southern states of the United States both social classes dividing Whites from Whites and the institutionalized enslavement of Blacks.

To understand these systems better, it may be helpful to review the distinction between *achieved status* and *ascribed*

status, explained in Module 16. **Ascribed status** is a social position assigned to a person by society without regard for the person's unique talents or characteristics. In contrast, **achieved status** is a social position that a person attains largely through his or her own efforts. The two are closely linked. The nation's most affluent families generally inherit wealth and status, while many

TABLE 26-1 HUMAN TRAFFICKING REPORT

Tier 1 Full Compliance	Tier 2 Significant Effort	Tier 2 Watch List Some Effort, But Trafficking Remains a Concern	Tier 3 Noncompliant, No Effort
Australia	Afghanistan	Burma	Algeria
Canada	Brazil	China	Belize
Chile	Colombia	Democratic Republic of Congo	Iran
Denmark	Greece	Costa Rica	Kuwait
France	India	Cuba	Libya
Germany	Iraq	Haiti	North Korea
Great Britain	Mexico	Lebanon	Russia
Norway	Philippines	Malaysia	Syria
Poland	South Africa	Saudi Arabia	Thailand
South Korea	Turkey	Sudan	Venezuela
Spain	Vietnam	Ukraine	Zimbabwe

Note: Each tier lists only a sample of all nations classified. The *Human Trafficking Report* is created by the State Department. In the report the level of compliance by the United States is considered to be "full compliance."
Source: Department of State 2015:54.

members of racial and ethnic minorities inherit disadvantaged status. Age and gender, as well, are ascribed statuses that influence a person's wealth and social position.

Four Forms of Stratification

Slavery

The most extreme form of legalized social inequality for both individuals and groups is **slavery.** What distinguishes this oppressive system of stratification is that enslaved individuals are *owned* by other people, who treat these human beings as property, just as if they were household pets or appliances.

Slavery has varied in the way it has been practiced. In ancient Greece, the main source of slaves was piracy and captives of war. Although succeeding generations could inherit slave status, it was not necessarily permanent. A person's status might change, depending on which city-state happened to triumph in a military conflict. In effect, all citizens had the potential to become slaves or receive freedom, depending on the circumstances of history. In contrast, in the United States and Latin America, where slavery was an ascribed status, racial and legal barriers prevented the freeing of slaves.

Today, the Universal Declaration of Human Rights, which is binding on all members of the United Nations, prohibits slavery in all its forms. Yet more people are enslaved today than at any point in world history. In many developing countries, bonded laborers are imprisoned in virtual lifetime employment; in some countries, human beings are owned outright. But a form of slavery also exists in Europe and the United States, where guest workers and illegal immigrants have been forced to labor for years under terrible conditions, either to pay off debts or to avoid being turned over to immigration authorities.

Both these situations are likely to involve the transnational crime of trafficking in humans. Data on human trafficking and slavery are difficult to assess since no government is voluntarily and publically going to disclose such numbers. According to the Walk Free Foundation, 29.8 million people are enslaved worldwide at any given time. The International Labour Organization places the number forced to work at any given time in the private economy at 4.5 million for sexual exploitation and 14.2 million for other forms of labor (agriculture, construction, domestic work, or manufacturing), for a total of 18.7 million people exploited globally. Whatever the estimate, clearly slavery as a form of stratification has not vanished. Indeed, for several years faith-based groups have organized under the banner of "Abolition Now" to fight trafficking (Abolition Now 2016; McCarthy 2014).

In 2000, the U.S. Congress passed the Trafficking Victims Protection Act, which established minimum standards for the elimination of human trafficking. The act requires the State Department to monitor other countries' efforts to vigorously investigate, prosecute, and convict individuals who participate in trafficking—including government officials. Each year, the department reports its findings, some of which are shown in Table 26-1. Tier 1 and Tier 2 countries are thought to be largely in compliance with the act. Tier 2 Watch countries are making efforts to comply, though trafficking remains a significant concern. Tier 3 countries are not compliant and are not making significant efforts to comply.

Castes

Castes are hereditary ranks that are usually religiously dictated and that tend to be fixed and immobile. Caste membership is an ascribed status (at birth, children automatically assume the same position as their parents). Each caste is quite sharply defined, and members are expected to marry within that caste.

The caste system is generally associated with Hinduism in India and other countries. In India there are four major castes, called *varnas*. A fifth category of outcastes, referred to as the *untouchables,* represents 16 percent of the population; its members are considered so lowly and unclean as to have no place within this stratification system. In an effort to avoid perpetuating the historical stigma these people bear, the government now refers to the untouchables as *scheduled castes.* The untouchables themselves prefer *Dalit* ("the repressed"), a term that communicates their desire to overcome their disadvantaged status.

In 1950, after gaining independence from Great Britain, India adopted a new constitution that formally outlawed the caste system. Over the past decade or two, however, urbanization and technological advances have brought more change to India's caste system than the government or politics has in more than half a century. The anonymity of city life tends to blur caste boundaries, allowing the *Dalit* to pass unrecognized in temples, schools, and places of employment. And the globalization of high technology has opened up India's social order, bringing new opportunities to those who possess the skills and ability to capitalize on them.

The term *caste* can also be applied in recent historical contexts outside India. For example, the system of stratification that characterized the southern United States from the end of the Civil War through the 1960s resembled a caste system. So did the rigid system of segregation that prevailed in the Republic of South Africa under apartheid, from 1948 through the 1990s. In both cases, race was the defining factor that placed a person in the social hierarchy.

Estates

A third type of stratification system, called *estates,* was associated with feudal societies during the Middle Ages. The **estate system,** or *feudalism,* required peasants to work land leased to them by nobles in exchange for military protection and other services. The basis for the system was the nobles' ownership of land, which was critical to their superior and privileged status. As in systems based on slavery and caste, inheritance of one's position largely defined the estate system. The nobles inherited their titles and property; the peasants were born into a subservient position within an agrarian society.

As the estate system developed, it became more differentiated. Nobles began to achieve varying degrees of authority. By the 12th century, a priesthood had emerged in most of Europe, along with classes of merchants and artisans. For the first time there were groups of people whose wealth did not depend on land ownership or agriculture. This economic change had profound social consequences as the estate system ended and a class system of stratification came into existence.

Social Classes

A **class system** is a social ranking based primarily on economic position in which achieved characteristics can influence social mobility. In contrast to slavery and caste systems, the boundaries between classes are imprecisely defined, and one can move from one stratum, or level, of society to another. Even so, class systems maintain stable stratification hierarchies and patterns of class division, and they, too, are marked by unequal distribution of wealth and power. Class standing, although it is achieved, is heavily dependent on family and ascribed factors, such as race and ethnicity.

Sociologist Daniel Rossides (1997) uses a five-class model to describe the class system of the United States: the upper class, the upper-middle class, the lower-middle class, the working class, and the lower class. Although the lines separating social classes in his model are not so sharp as the divisions between castes, members of the five classes differ significantly in ways other than just income level.

Upper and Lower Classes Rossides characterizes about 1 to 2 percent of the people of the United States as *upper class.* This group is limited to the very wealthy, who associate in exclusive clubs and social circles and exercise enormous political power through financial support of candidates and issues. In contrast, the *lower class,* consisting of approximately 20 to 25 percent of the population, disproportionately consists of Blacks, Hispanics, single mothers with dependent children, and people who cannot find regular work or must make do with low-paying work. This class lacks both wealth and income and is too weak politically to exercise significant power.

Both these classes, at opposite ends of the nation's social hierarchy, reflect the importance of ascribed status and achieved status. Ascribed statuses such as race and disability clearly influence a person's wealth and social position. People with disabilities are particularly vulnerable to unemployment, are often poorly paid, and tend to occupy the lower rungs of the occupational ladder. Regardless of their actual performance on the job, the disabled are stigmatized as not earning their keep.

© Kevin Scanlon for The New York Times/Redux

Worried about student debt or home foreclosures? Not the wealthy. The rich now spend $50,000 to $250,000 on their children's playhouses and tree houses.

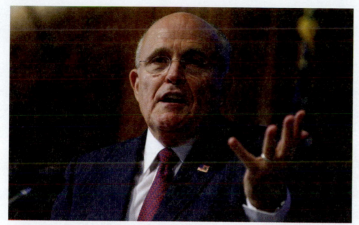
© Saul Loeb/AFP/Getty Images

© Christina Simmons/Corbis

Reactions to the Occupy Wall Street movement varied with people's socioeconomic status. "How about you occupy a job?" former New York City mayor Rudy Giuliani retorted. At the other extreme, Native American leaders observed that their lands have been occupied for five centuries.

Such are the effects of ascribed status. We will look again at the plight of the lower class when we consider poverty and welfare policies.

The economist John Kenneth Galbraith (1977:44) observed that "of all classes the rich are the most noticed and the least studied." The poor receive a good deal of attention from reporters, social activists, and policymakers seeking to alleviate their poverty, but the very affluent, who live apart from the rest of the population, are largely a mystery. Since Galbraith's comment, moreover, the residential separation of the rich has grown. The newspaper's society page may give us a peek at members of this class, but we know very little about their everyday lives. As of 2015, over 242,000 households in the United States were worth more than $10 million each. Fewer than 25 percent of these people inherited even a tenth of their money, and very few of them are celebrities (Frank 2015).

Middle Class Sandwiched between the upper and lower classes in this model are the upper-middle class, the lower-middle class, and the working class. The *upper-middle class,* about 10 to 15 percent of the population, includes professionals such as doctors, lawyers, and architects. They participate extensively in politics and take leadership roles in voluntary associations. The *lower-middle class,* about 30 to 35 percent of the population, includes less affluent professionals (such as elementary school teachers and nurses), owners of small businesses, and a sizable number of clerical workers. While not all members of the middle class hold degrees from a college, they share the goal of sending their children there. Box 26-1 describes the shrinking size of the middle class.

Working Class Rossides describes the *working class*—about 40 to 45 percent of the population—as people who hold regular manual or blue-collar jobs. Certain members of this class, such as electricians, may have higher incomes than people in the lower-middle class. Yet even if they have achieved some degree of economic security, they tend to identify with manual workers

and their long history of involvement in the labor movement of the United States.

Of the five classes, the working class is declining noticeably in size. In the economy of the United States, service and technical jobs are replacing those involved in the actual manufacturing or transportation of goods.

Class Warfare On September 17, 2011, two thousand protesters assembled in New York City, claiming to represent the vast majority of Americans. In their own words, these members of what soon became known as the Occupy Wall Street movement were "the 99 percent"—those Americans who had suffered as the wealthiest 1 percent flourished. In the next few weeks the movement, which had begun in Canada, spread across the United States to Honolulu and then throughout the world (Peralta 2011; M. Scherer 2011).

With Occupy Wall Street in the headlines, political leaders began to speak of class conflict. To some, the Occupy movement's call for a reduction in social inequality seemed a reply to the federal government's favorable tax treatment of the affluent. Before the recession began, the Bush administration had lowered the income tax rate paid by high-income filers. In 2009, the Tea Party pushed Congress to maintain that tax cut, despite a growing deficit. Others insisted that the affluent actually paid less in taxes than the average citizen, given the many loopholes—offshore bank accounts, and so on—available to them. In Congress, the suggestion that the rich should pay the same effective tax rate as other citizens was met with an angry charge of class warfare.

As we will see shortly, by any statistical measure, the gulf between the rich and everyone else in the United States has grown over the last decade—indeed, over the last 50 years. Yet people do not tend to identify with or see themselves as members of a specific social class. Still, as the rhetoric heated up during the 2012 presidential campaign, and the Occupy Wall Street movement remained visible, a growing share of the population thought they saw evidence of class conflict. In December 2011,

The Shrinking Middle Class

The cherished belief that the poor can rise to middle-class status has long been central to the United States' reputation as a land of opportunity. However, according to Lester C. Thurow, noted professor of economics and management at the Massachusetts Institute of Technology, the American middle class is disappearing. Using a widely accepted definition of a middle-class household as one whose income falls between two-thirds and double the nation's median household income (that is, between $37,674 and $113,032), only about 43 percent of American households would have been classified as middle class in 2015, compared to 80 percent in 1967.

Close analysis by Thurow indicates that of those who relinquished their middle-class status during this period, about half rose to a higher ranking in the social class system, while half dropped to a lower position. In Thurow's view, these data mean that the United States is moving toward a "bipolar income distribution." That is, a broadly based middle class is slowly being replaced by two growing groups of rich and poor.

Sociologists and other scholars have identified several factors that have contributed to the shrinking size of the middle class:

According to Lester C. Thurow, noted professor of economics and management at the Massachusetts Institute of Technology, the American middle class is disappearing.

- *Disappearing opportunities for those with little education.* Today, most jobs require formal schooling, yet less than a third of adults between ages 35 and 44 have prepared themselves with a college degree.

- *Global competition and rapid advances in technology.* These two trends, which began several decades ago, mean that workers are more easily replaced now than they were in the past. Increasingly, globalization and technological advances are affecting the more complex jobs that were once the bread and butter of middle-class workers.

- *Growing dependence on the temporary workforce.* For those workers who have no other job, temporary positions are tenuous at best, because they rarely offer health care coverage or retirement benefits.

- *The rise of new growth industries and nonunion workplaces, like fast-food restaurants.* Industries may have added employment opportunities, but they are at the lower end of the wage scale.

In response to these concerns, observers note that living standards in the United States are improving over all. Middle-class families want comfortable homes, college degrees for their children, and high-quality health care, but the cost of all these things has been growing faster than inflation. The answer, for many people, is either to go without or to work longer at multiple jobs.

© Steve Greenberg. Reprinted by permission of www.CartoonStock.com.

Today, the once broadly based middle class is on the defensive and is slowly being squeezed by two growing groups, the rich and the poor.

LET'S DISCUSS

1. Does your family belong to the middle class? If so, in what generation did your family achieve that status, and how? Are your parents struggling to maintain or achieve a middle-class lifestyle?

2. For the nation as a whole, what are the dangers of a shrinking middle class?

Sources: Blank 2010; Khan 2013; Kochhar et al. 2015; Leonhardt 2004; Proctor et al. 2016:Table 4-1; Shipler 2005; Thurow 1984; Witte 2005.

66 percent of the public (compared to 47 percent in 2009) said they perceived "strong" conflict between the rich and the poor. Younger adults, women, and African Americans were most likely to hold this view. Interestingly, personal income had little to do with such perceptions: the rich were just as likely as the poor to agree with the existence of class conflict (Archer and Orr 2011; Morin and Motel 2013; Skocpol and Williamson 2012).

By the time of the 2016 presidential campaign, specific references to Occupy Wall Street had disappeared, but the general public still showed disdain for the "1 percent." A 2015 national survey showed 63 percent of respondents perceived the distribution of money and wealth as unfair. The solution? For 52 percent of the public, it was to place heavy taxes on the rich (Newport 2015).

Sociological Perspectives on Stratification

Sociologists have hotly debated stratification and social inequality and have reached varying conclusions. No theorist stressed the significance of class for society—and for social change—more strongly than Karl Marx. Marx viewed class differentiation as the crucial determinant of social, economic, and political inequality. In contrast, Max Weber questioned Marx's emphasis on the overriding importance of the economic sector, arguing that stratification should be viewed as having many dimensions.

Karl Marx's View of Class Differentiation

Karl Marx was concerned with stratification in all types of human society, beginning with primitive agricultural tribes and continuing into feudalism. However, his main focus was on the effects of economic inequality on all aspects of 19th-century Europe. The plight of the working class made him feel that it was imperative to strive for changes in the class structure of society.

In Marx's view, social relations during any period of history depend on who controls the primary mode of economic production, such as land or factories. Differential access to scarce resources shapes the relationship between groups. Thus, under the feudal estate system, most production was agricultural, and the land was owned by the nobility. Peasants had little choice but to work according to terms dictated by those who owned the land.

Using this type of analysis, Marx examined social relations within **capitalism**—an economic system in which the means of production are held largely in private hands and the main incentive for economic activity is the accumulation of profits. Marx focused on the two classes that began to emerge as the feudal estate system declined, the bourgeoisie and the proletariat. The **bourgeoisie,** or capitalist class, owns the means of production, such as factories and machinery; the **proletariat** is the working class. In capitalist societies, the members of the bourgeoisie maximize profit in competition with other firms. In the process, they exploit workers, who must exchange their labor for subsistence wages. In Marx's view, members of each class share a distinctive culture. Marx was most interested in the culture of the proletariat, but he also examined the ideology of the bourgeoisie, through which that class justifies its dominance over workers.

According to Marx, exploitation of the proletariat will inevitably lead to the destruction of the capitalist system, because the workers will revolt. But first, the working class must develop **class consciousness**—a subjective awareness of common vested interests and the need for collective political action to bring about social change. Often, workers must overcome what Marx termed **false consciousness,** or an attitude held by members of a class that does not accurately reflect their objective position. A worker with false consciousness may adopt an individualistic viewpoint toward capitalist exploitation ("*I* am being exploited by *my* boss"). In contrast, the class-conscious worker realizes that all workers are being exploited by the bourgeoisie and have a common stake in revolution.

For Marx, class consciousness was part of a collective process in which the proletariat comes to identify the bourgeoisie as the source of its oppression. Revolutionary leaders will guide the working class in its struggle. Ultimately, the proletariat will overthrow the rule of both the bourgeoisie and the government (which Marx saw as representing the interests of capitalists) and will eliminate private ownership of the means of production. In Marx's rather utopian view, classes and oppression will cease to exist in the postrevolutionary workers' state.

How accurate were Marx's predictions? He failed to anticipate the emergence of labor unions, whose power in collective bargaining weakens the stranglehold that capitalists maintain over workers. Moreover, as contemporary conflict theorists note, he did not foresee the extent to which political liberties and relative prosperity could contribute to false consciousness. Many workers came to view themselves as individuals striving for improvement within free societies that offer substantial mobility, rather than as downtrodden members of a social class who face a collective fate. Even today, "class warfare" seems to refer more to diminished individual expectations than to a collective identity. Finally, Marx did not predict that Communist Party rule would be established and later overthrown in the former Soviet Union and throughout Eastern Europe. Still, the Marxist approach to the study of class is useful in stressing the importance of stratification as a determinant of social behavior and the fundamental separation in many societies between two distinct groups, the rich and the poor.

 use your **sociological imagination**

Have you ever been unaware of your true position in society—that is, have you experienced false consciousness? Explain.

© Aaron Black/Exactostock-1672/Superstock

An operator stands on sand on a fracking site. Karl Marx would identify such workers, who extract oil or gas from deep underground, as members of the proletariat, or working class. Even today, fracking operators must cover their own expenses and work in desolate locations with considerable dangers from exposure to chemicals. Such exploitation of the working class is a core principle of Marxist theory.

Max Weber's View of Stratification

Unlike Karl Marx, Max Weber ([1913–1922] 1947) insisted that no single characteristic (such as class) totally defines a person's position within the stratification system. Instead, writing in 1916, he identified three distinct components of stratification: class, status, and power.

Weber used the term **class** to refer to a group of people who have a similar level of wealth and income. For example, certain workers in the United States try to support their families through minimum-wage jobs. According to Weber's definition, these wage earners constitute a class because they share the same economic position and fate. Although Weber agreed with Marx on the importance of this economic dimension of stratification, he argued that the actions of individuals and groups cannot be understood *solely* in economic terms.

Weber used the term **status group** to refer to people who have the same prestige or lifestyle. An individual gains status through membership in a desirable group, such as the medical profession. But status is not the same as economic class standing. In our culture, a successful pickpocket may belong to the same income class as a college professor. Yet the thief is widely regarded as holding low status, whereas the professor holds high status.

For Weber, the third major component of stratification has a political dimension. **Power** is the ability to exercise one's will over others. In the United States, power stems from membership in particularly influential groups, such as corporate boards of directors, government bodies, and interest groups. Conflict theorists generally agree that two major sources of power—big business and government—are closely interrelated. For instance, heads of major corporations have gone on to hold powerful positions in government, and former government and military leaders now play key roles in corporations.

To summarize, in Weber's view, each of us has not one rank in society but three. Our position in a stratification system reflects some combination of class, status, and power. Each factor influences the other two, and in fact the rankings on these three dimensions often tend to coincide. John F. Kennedy came from an extremely wealthy family, attended exclusive preparatory schools, graduated from Harvard University, and went on to become president of the United States. Like Kennedy, many people from affluent backgrounds achieve impressive status and power.

Interactionist Perspective

Both Karl Marx and Max Weber looked at inequality primarily from a macrosociological perspective, considering the entire society or even the global economy. Marx did suggest the importance of a more microsociological analysis, however, when he stressed the ways in which individuals develop a true class consciousness.

Interactionists, as well as economists, have long been interested in the importance of social class in shaping a person's lifestyle. The theorist Thorstein Veblen (1857–1929) noted that those at the top of the social hierarchy typically convert part of their wealth into **conspicuous consumption**—that is, they purchase goods not to survive but to flaunt their superior wealth and social standing. For example, they may purchase more automobiles than they can reasonably use, or build homes with more rooms than they can possibly occupy. In an element of conspicuous consumption called *conspicuous leisure,* they may jet to a remote destination, staying just long enough to have dinner or view a sunset over some historic locale (Veblen [1899] 1964).

Today, conspicuous consumption has found a new outlet in the cyberworld. Users of social media can now see their friends' vacations and snazzy new cars online—an experience that can provoke what researchers call *Facebook envy*. Studies done in the United States and Germany show that even otherwise happy people can suffer envy and distress over this kind of digitally shared conspicuous consumption (Shea 2013).

At the other end of the spectrum, behavior that is judged to be typical of the lower class is subject not only to ridicule but even to legal action. Communities have, from time to time, banned trailers from people's front yards and sofas from their front porches. In some communities, it is illegal to leave a pickup truck in front of the house overnight. In others, street vendors who sell fruit, flowers, and water face restrictions meant not to serve the general public, but to protect their storefront competitors (Campo-Flores 2013).

© Gopal Chitrakar/Reuters/Corbis

With Mt. Everest in the background, a wealthy golfer plays a shot in a remote location, which he reached by helicopter. Traveling to exotic places to indulge in sports that most people play at home is an example of Thorstein Veblen's concept of conspicuous consumption, a spending pattern common to those at the very top of the social ladder.

Is Stratification Universal?

Must some members of society receive greater rewards than others? Do people need to feel socially and economically superior to others? Can social life be organized without structured inequality? These questions have been debated for centuries, especially among political activists. Utopian socialists, religious minorities, and members of recent countercultures have all attempted to establish communities that to some extent or other would abolish inequality in social relationships.

Social scientists have found that inequality exists in all societies—even the simplest. For example, when anthropologist Gunnar Landtman ([1938] 1968) studied the Kiwai Papuans of New Guinea, at first he noticed little differentiation among them. Every man in the village did the same work and lived in similar housing. However, on closer inspection, Landtman observed that certain Papuans—men who were warriors, harpooners, and sorcerers—were described as "a little more high" than others. In contrast, villagers who were female, unemployed, or unmarried were considered "down a little bit" and were barred from owning land.

Stratification is universal in that all societies maintain some form of social inequality among members. Depending on its values, a society may assign people to distinctive ranks based on their religious knowledge, skill in hunting, physical attractiveness, trading expertise, or ability to provide health care. But why has such inequality developed in human societies? And how much differentiation among people, if any, is essential?

Functionalist and conflict theorists offer contrasting explanations for the existence and necessity of social stratification. Functionalists maintain that a differential system of rewards and punishments is necessary for the efficient operation of society. Conflict theorists argue that competition for scarce resources results in significant political, economic, and social inequality.

Functionalist Perspective

Would people go to school for many years to become physicians if they could make as much money and gain as much respect working as street cleaners? Functionalists say no, which is partly why they believe that stratification is universal.

In the view of Kingsley Davis and Wilbert Moore (1945), society must distribute its members among a variety of social positions. It must make sure not only that these positions are filled but also that they are filled by people with the appropriate talents and abilities. Rewards, including money and prestige, are based on the importance of a position and the relative scarcity of qualified personnel. Yet this assessment often devalues work performed by certain segments of society, such as women's work in the home or in occupations traditionally filled by women, or low-status work in fast-food outlets.

Davis and Moore argue that stratification is universal and that social inequality is necessary so that people will be motivated to fill functionally important positions. But critics say that unequal rewards are not the only means of encouraging people to fill critical positions and occupations. Personal pleasure, intrinsic satisfaction, and value orientations also motivate people to enter particular careers. Functionalists agree, but they note that society must use some type of reward to motivate people to enter unpleasant or dangerous jobs and professions that require long training periods. This response does not address stratification systems in which status is largely inherited, such as slave or caste societies. Moreover, even if stratification is inevitable, the functionalist explanation for differential rewards does not explain the wide disparity between the rich and the poor (R. Collins 1975; Kerbo 2012).

Conflict Perspective

The writings of Karl Marx lie at the heart of conflict theory. Marx viewed history as a continuous struggle between the oppressors and the oppressed, which ultimately would culminate in an egalitarian, classless society. In terms of stratification, he argued that under capitalism, the dominant class—the bourgeoisie—manipulates the economic and political systems in order to maintain control over the exploited proletariat. Marx did not believe that stratification was inevitable, but he did see

© The History Channel/Photofest

As the reality television series *Ice Road Truckers,* now in its ninth season, suggests, long-haul truck drivers take pride in their low-prestige job. According to the conflict perspective, the cultural beliefs that form a society's dominant ideology, such as the popular image of the truck driver as hero, help the wealthy to maintain their power and control at the expense of the lower classes.

TABLE 26-2 SOCIOLOGICAL PERSPECTIVES ON SOCIAL STRATIFICATION

Tracking Sociological Perspectives

	Functionalist	Conflict	Interactionist
Purpose of social stratification	Facilitates filling of social positions	Facilitates exploitation	Influences people's lifestyles
Attitude toward social inequality	Necessary to some extent	Excessive and growing	Influences intergroup relations
Analysis of the wealthy	Talented and skilled, creating opportunities for others	Use the dominant ideology to further their own interests	Exhibit conspicuous consumption and conspicuous leisure

inequality and oppression as inherent in capitalism (E. O. Wright et al. 1982; E. O. Wright 2011).

Like Marx, contemporary conflict theorists believe that human beings are prone to conflict over scarce resources such as wealth, status, and power. However, Marx focused primarily on class conflict; more recent theorists have extended the analysis to include conflicts based on gender, race, age, and other dimensions. British sociologist Ralf Dahrendorf (1929–2009) is one of the most influential contributors to the conflict approach.

Dahrendorf (1959) has modified Marx's analysis of capitalist society to apply to modern capitalist societies. For Dahrendorf, social classes are groups of people who share common interests resulting from their authority relationships. In identifying the most powerful groups in society, he includes not only the bourgeoisie—the owners of the means of production—but also the managers of industry, legislators, the judiciary, heads of the government bureaucracy, and others. In that respect, Dahrendorf merged Marx's emphasis on class conflict with Weber's recognition that power is an important element of stratification (Cuff et al. 1990).

Conflict theorists, including Dahrendorf, contend that the powerful of today, like the bourgeoisie of Marx's time, want society to run smoothly so that they can enjoy their privileged positions. Because the status quo suits those with wealth, status, and power, they have a clear interest in preventing, minimizing, or controlling societal conflict.

One way for the powerful to maintain the status quo is to define and disseminate the society's dominant ideology. The term **dominant ideology** describes a set of cultural beliefs and practices that helps to maintain powerful social, economic, and political interests. For Marx, the dominant ideology in a capitalist society served the interests of the ruling class. From a conflict perspective, the social significance of the dominant ideology is that not only do a society's most powerful groups and institutions control wealth and property; even more important, they control the means of producing beliefs about reality through religion, education, and the media (Abercrombie et al. 1980, 1990; Robertson 1988).

The powerful, such as leaders of government, also use limited social reforms to buy off the oppressed and reduce the danger of challenges to their dominance. For example, minimum-wage laws and unemployment compensation unquestionably give some valuable assistance to needy men and women. Yet these reforms also serve to pacify those who might otherwise rebel. Of course, in the view of conflict theorists, such maneuvers can never entirely eliminate conflict, since workers will continue to demand equality, and the powerful will not give up their control of society.

Conflict theorists see stratification as a major source of societal tension and conflict. They do not agree with Davis and Moore that stratification is functional for a society or that it serves as a source of stability. Rather, conflict sociologists argue that stratification will inevitably lead to instability and social change (R. Collins 1975; L. Coser 1977).

Table 26-2 summarizes and compares the three major perspectives on social stratification.

Lenski's Viewpoint

Let's return to the question posed earlier—Is stratification universal?—and consider the sociological response. Some form of differentiation is found in every culture, from the most primitive to the most advanced industrial societies of our time. Sociologist Gerhard Lenski, in his sociocultural evolution approach, described how economic systems change as their level of technology becomes more complex, beginning with hunting and gathering and culminating eventually with industrial society.

In subsistence-based hunting-and-gathering societies, people focus on survival. While some inequality and differentiation are evident, a stratification system based on social class does not emerge because there is no real wealth to be claimed. As a society advances technologically, it becomes capable of producing a considerable surplus of goods. The emergence of surplus resources greatly expands the possibilities for inequality in status, influence, and power, allowing a well-defined, rigid social class system to develop. To minimize strikes, slowdowns, and industrial sabotage, the elites may share a portion of the economic surplus with the lower classes, but not enough to reduce their own power and privilege.

As Lenski argued, the allocation of surplus goods and services controlled by those with wealth, status, and power reinforces the social inequality that accompanies stratification systems. While this reward system may once have served the overall purposes of society, as functionalists contend, the same cannot be said for the large disparities separating the haves from the have-nots in current societies. In contemporary industrial society, the degree of social and economic inequality far exceeds what is needed to provide for goods and services (Lenski 1966; Nolan 2004; Nolan and Lenski 2015).

Lenski and others have debated whether stratification is inevitable and how it has developed. One possible way to redistribute income is by means of the tax structure, as discussed in Box 26-2.

Taxes as Opportunity

"Nothing can be said to be certain, except death and taxes." This famous aphorism is usually attributed to Ben Franklin. Even before his time and ever since, people have complained about taxes. However, taxes used to raise public funds can be constructed to rearrange a stratification system.

The first federal income tax was levied in the United States in 1861 to help pay the government's costs of the Civil War. By 1895, the Supreme Court had decided that some aspects of the income tax were unconstitutional. This led to the passage of the Sixteenth Amendment in 1916, which gave Congress the authority to impose an income tax. At that time most people paid 1 percent of their income; top earners paid up to 7 percent. Today rates start at 10 percent and top off at nearly 40 percent.

Perhaps surprisingly, 56 percent, or the majority of the population, feel that the income tax they pay is fair. And 52 percent agree with the idea that "heavy taxes on the rich" are a good way to redistribute wealth. So increasing the tax rate that very rich people pay, or removing some exemptions that benefit the very rich, would be acceptable to many people and could also reduce inequality, especially between the middle and upper class.

However, as with everything dealing with taxes, nothing is simple. Affluent people typically have considerable freedom to adjust when and how they receive income.

© Jeffrey Hamilton/Getty Images RF

Perhaps surprisingly, 56 percent, or the majority of the population, feel that the income tax they pay is fair.

Changes in tax rates can be negated if individuals come up with legal ways to be compensated that are immune from new taxes or higher rates.

At the other end of the stratification system, tax policy has been viewed as an instrument for alleviating poverty. Low-income households receive payments, rather than paying taxes, through an Earned Income Tax Credit (EITC). On the positive side, this tax credit avoids much of the social stigma associated with applying for traditional welfare checks. Typically families receive the EITC as a lump-sum payment, and they can use it to enhance economic advancement, such as by purchasing a car or making a security deposit on an apartment. Over 27 million working families receive the EITC.

Fiscal sociology, or the study of tax policy and its relationship to the stratification system, is relatively new. The redistributive effects of changing tax policy seem obvious, but wealthy individuals and their advisors can often counter changes in tax law with measures that allow them to legally escape paying more. Tax law changes also tend to have unintended consequences that may maintain inequalities or even exacerbate income differences among households.

LET'S DISCUSS

1. Do you think that high tax rates and fewer tax loopholes for the rich are a good way to alleviate inequality? Why or why not?

2. In what ways do you think that people's perceptions of the fairness of the tax system are affected by their income level?

Sources: Center on Budget and Policy Priorities 2016; Jones 2015; Martin and Prasad 2014; Newport 2016.

MODULE 26 | Recap and Review

Summary

Stratification is the structured ranking of entire groups of people that perpetuates unequal economic rewards and **power** in a society.

1. Some degree of **social inequality** characterizes all cultures.

2. Systems of social stratification include **slavery, castes, the estate system,** and social classes.

3. Karl Marx saw that differences in access to the means of production created social, economic, and political inequality, as well as two distinct classes, owners and laborers.

4. Max Weber identified three analytically distinct components of stratification: **class, status group,** and **power.**

5. Functionalists argue that stratification is necessary to motivate people to fill society's important positions. Conflict theorists see stratification as a major source of societal tension and conflict. Interactionists stress the importance of social class in determining a person's lifestyle.

Thinking Critically

1. What are the differences between slavery and caste systems? What are the similarities?

2. Give some examples of conspicuous consumption among your fellow college students. Which are obvious and which more subtle?

3. In your view, is the extent of social inequality in the United States helpful or harmful to society as a whole? Explain.

Key Terms

Achieved status

Ascribed status

Bourgeoisie

Capitalism

Caste

Class

Class consciousness

Class system

Conspicuous consumption

Dominant ideology

Estate system

False consciousness

Income

Power

Proletariat

Slavery

Social inequality

Status group

Stratification

Wealth

MODULE 27 | Stratification by Social Class

We continually assess how wealthy people are by looking at the cars they drive, the houses they live in, the clothes they wear, and so on. Yet it is not so easy to locate an individual within our social hierarchies as it would be in slavery or caste systems of stratification. To determine someone's class position, sociologists generally rely on the objective method.

Objective Method of Measuring Social Class

In the **objective method** of measuring social class, class is viewed largely as a statistical category. Researchers assign individuals to social classes on the basis of criteria such as occupation, education, income, and place of residence. The key to the objective method is that the *researcher,* rather than the person being classified, identifies an individual's class position.

The first step in using this method is to decide what indicators or causal factors will be measured objectively, whether wealth, income, education, or occupation. The prestige ranking of occupations has proved to be a useful indicator of a person's class position. For one thing, it is much easier to determine accurately than income or wealth. The term **prestige** refers to the respect and admiration that an occupation holds in a society. "My daughter, the physicist" connotes something very different from "my daughter, the waitress." Prestige is independent of the particular individual who occupies a job, a characteristic that distinguishes it from esteem. **Esteem** refers to the reputation that a specific person has earned within an occupation. Therefore, one can say that the position of president of the United States has high prestige, even though it has been occupied by people with varying degrees of esteem. A hairdresser may have the esteem of his clients, but he lacks the prestige of a corporate executive.

Table 27-1 ranks the prestige of a number of well-known occupations. In a series of national surveys, sociologists assigned prestige rankings to about 500 occupations, ranging from surgeon to panhandler. The highest possible prestige score was 100; the lowest was 0. Surgeon, physician, lawyer, dentist, and college professor were the most highly regarded occupations. Sociologists have used such data to assign prestige rankings to virtually all jobs and have found a stability in rankings from 1925 to the present. Similar studies in other countries have also developed useful prestige rankings of occupations (Nakao and Treas 1994).

Gender and Occupational Prestige

For many years, studies of social class neglected the occupations and incomes of *women* as determinants of social rank. With more than half of all married women working outside the home, this approach seems outmoded. How should we judge class or status in dual-career families—by the occupation regarded as having greater prestige, the average, or some other combination of the two? Sociologists—in particular, feminist sociologists in Great Britain—are drawing on new approaches to assess women's social class standing. One approach is to focus on the individual (rather than the family or household) as the basis for categorizing a woman's class position. Thus, a woman would be classified according to her own occupational status rather than that of her spouse (Mandel 2016; McCall 2008).

Another feminist effort to measure the contribution of women to the economy reflects a more clearly political agenda. International Women Count Network, a global grassroots feminist organization, has sought to give a monetary value to women's unpaid work. Besides providing symbolic recognition of women's role in labor, this value would also be used to calculate pension and other benefits, which are usually based on wages received. The United Nations has placed an $11 trillion price tag on unpaid labor by women, largely in child care, housework, and agriculture. Whatever the figure, the continued undercounting of many workers' contributions to a family and to an entire economy means that virtually all measures of stratification are

TABLE 27-1 PRESTIGE RANKINGS OF OCCUPATIONS

Occupation	Score	Occupation	Score
Physician	86	Bank teller	50
College professor	78	Electrician	49
Lawyer	76	Farm manager	48
Dentist	74	Insurance agent	47
Banker	72	Secretary	46
Architect	71	Mail carrier	42
Airline pilot	70	Farmer	41
Clergy	69	Correctional officer	40
Registered nurse	66	Carpenter	40
High school teacher	63	Barber	38
Legislator	61	Child care worker	36
Pharmacist	61	Hotel clerk	32
Elementary school teacher	60	Bus driver	32
Veterinarian	60	Truck driver	30
Police officer or detective	60	Salesworker (shoes)	28
Prekindergarten teacher	60	Waiter and waitress	28
Accountant	57	Cook (short-order)	28
Librarian	55	Bartender	25
Firefighter	53	Garbage collector	17
Funeral director	52	Janitor	16
Social worker	52	Newspaper vendor	15

Note: 100 is the highest and 0 the lowest possible prestige score.

Source: General Social Survey 2015 in T. Smith et al. 2015: Appendix F. *Doctors:* © ERproductions Ltd/Blend Images RF; *homeless man:* © Con Tanasiuk/Design Pics RF

in need of reform (James 2012; United Nations Economic and Social Council 2010).

Multiple Measures

Another complication in measuring social class is that advances in statistical methods and computer technology have multiplied the factors used to define class under the objective method. No longer are sociologists limited to annual income and education in evaluating a person's class position. Today, studies use as criteria the value of homes, sources of income, assets, years in present occupations, neighborhoods, and considerations regarding dual careers. Adding these variables will not necessarily paint a different picture of class differentiation in the United States, but it does allow sociologists to measure class in a more complex and multidimensional way. When researchers use multiple measures, they typically speak of **socioeconomic status (SES),** a measure of social class that is based on income, education, and occupation. To determine the socioeconomic status of a young person, such as a college student under age 25, they use *parental* income, education, and occupation.

Whatever the technique used to measure class, the sociologist is interested in real and often dramatic differences in power, privilege, and opportunity in a society. The study of stratification is a study of inequality. Nowhere is the truth of that statement more evident than in the distribution of income and wealth.

Income and Wealth

By all measures, income in the United States is distributed unevenly. Nobel Prize–winning economist Paul Samuelson has described the situation in the following words: "If we made an income pyramid out of building blocks, with each layer portraying $500 of income, the peak would be far higher than Mount Everest, but most people would be within a few feet of the ground" (Samuelson and Nordhaus 2010:324).

Recent data support Samuelson's analogy. In 2014, the median household income in the United States was $53,657. In other words, half of all households had higher incomes that year and half had lower incomes. However, this fact does not fully convey the income disparities in our society.

We can gain some insight into income inequality in the United States by looking at the relative placement of households within the income distribution. One of the most common ways of doing so is to line up all income-earning households from low to high and then break them into quintiles, or fifths. Because there are approximately 125 million households in the United States, each quintile includes an equal number of about 25 million households. This method gives us a sense of the average income within each quintile, along with the percentage of the nation's total income earned in each quintile.

As Figure 27-1 shows, looking at the population in this way reveals a significant degree of income inequality. The mean income for households in the lowest quintile is $12,457; in the top quintile, it is $202,366. If we were to move up to the highest end of the income distribution, we would find that the top 0.01 percent of taxpayers—about 15,000 households—make incomes of at least $11.5 million a year. Collectively, they control 6 percent of the nation's total income (DeNavas-Walt and Proctor 2015:40; Sloan 2009:27).

There has been a modest redistribution of income in the United States over the past 80 years, but not always to the benefit of the poor or even the middle class. From 1929 through 1970, the government's economic and tax policies shifted some income to the poor. However, in the past four decades—especially in the 1980s and in the decade from 2001 through 2010—federal tax policies favored the affluent. Moreover, while the salaries of highly skilled workers and professionals have continued to rise, the wages of less skilled workers have *decreased* when controlled for inflation.

Careful economic analysis has shown that over the past 30 years, federal and state tax policies have tended to accentuate this trend toward income inequality. During one 25-year period, the top 1 percent of income earners saw their *after tax* incomes rise 228 percent, compared to only 21 percent for households in the middle quintile. Little wonder that the middle class is shrinking (Billitteri 2009; A. Sherman 2007).

Globalization is often blamed for this growing inequality, because it has forced less skilled workers to compete with lower-paid foreign-born workers. While that is true, research suggests that the number of displaced workers who are reemployed at similarly paid or even higher-paid jobs roughly equals the number of workers whose earnings drop (S. Zimmerman 2008a).

The growing inequality in income is mirrored in increasing inequality in wealth. Consider the years between 1970 and 2015. The incomes of both the upper and lower classes increased, while the middle class's share of income declined. Gains in net worth, even with the Great Recession, have been decidedly in favor of the most wealthy. The pattern is clear: the biggest winners have been the affluent (Pew Research Center 2015d).

Indeed, wealth is distributed much more unevenly than income in the United States. A 2013 Federal Reserve Bank study showed that 3 percent of the nation's families control 54 percent of the nation's wealth (Figure 27-2). Put another way, the wealth

FIGURE 27-1 **Mean Household Income by Quintile**

Source: Data for 2015 in Proctor et al. 2016:31. *Photo:* © Stockbyte/PunchStock RF.

FIGURE 27-2 **Distribution of Family Wealth in the United States**

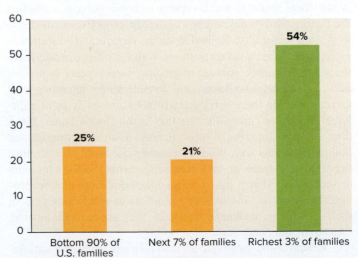

Source: Data for 2013 from Institute for Policy Studies 2015.

of the top 3 percent exceeds the collective wealth of the bottom 97 percent.

Researchers have also found a dramatic disparity in the wealth of African Americans and Hispanics compared to that of Whites. The median wealth of White households is now 10 times the median wealth of Latino households and 13 times that of Blacks. Furthermore, evidence suggests that the gap widened further between 1983 and 2013 (Kochhar 2014).

MODULE 27 | Recap and Review

Summary

One consequence of social class in the United States is that both **income** and **wealth** are distributed unevenly.

1. Sociologists use the **objective method** of measuring social class, which uses criteria such as occupation, education, and income. **Socioeconomic status (SES)** is an objective measure based on these criteria.

2. Regardless of the measure used, income inequality rose from the late 1960s to the end of the 20th century.

Thinking Critically

1. To what degree are students motivated by the prestige of their future occupations?

2. What does the pattern of income distribution in the United States tell you about your own future income? How much can you expect it to grow over the years?

Key Terms

Esteem

Objective method

Prestige

Socioeconomic status (SES)

MODULE 28 | Poverty and Social Mobility

About 11 percent of the people in the United States live below the poverty line established by the federal government. In 2015, no fewer than 43.1 million people were living in poverty. The economic correction that followed the Great Recession passed these people by. A Bureau of the Census report shows that one in five households has trouble meeting basic needs, from paying the utility bills to buying dinner (Proctor et al. 2016:31).

One contributor to the United States' high poverty rate has been the large number of workers employed at minimum wage. As Figure 28-1 shows, the federal government raised the minimum wage over the last 60 years from 75 cents in 1950 to $7.25 in 2009. But in terms of its real value, adjusted for inflation, the minimum wage has failed to keep pace with the cost of living. In fact, its real value today is *lower* than it was at any time from 1956 to 1984 (see Figure 28-1). Little wonder, then, that low-income workers can barely scrape by. In this section, we'll consider just how social scientists define *poverty*. We'll also take a closer look at the people who fall into that category, including the working poor.

Sociologists have long had an interest in the impact of substandard work on society, beginning with the writings of Karl Marx, Émile Durkheim, and Max Weber. Their interest increased with the global economic decline that began in 2008, which trapped many people in jobs they did not want or left them unemployed.

use your **sociological imagination**

Have you ever worked for the minimum wage? If so, where were you living, and who paid your basic living expenses? Could you have survived if the minimum wage had been your only source of support?

Studying Poverty

The efforts of sociologists and other social scientists to better understand poverty are complicated by the difficulty of defining it. This problem is evident even in government programs that conceive of poverty in either absolute or relative terms. **Absolute poverty** refers to a minimum level of subsistence that no family should be expected to live below.

One commonly used measure of absolute poverty is the federal government's *poverty line,* a money income figure that is adjusted annually to reflect the consumption requirements of families based on their size and composition. The poverty line serves as an official definition of which people are poor. In 2015, for example, any family of four (two adults and two children) with a combined income of $24,036 or less fell below the poverty line. This definition determines which individuals and families will be eligible for certain government benefits (Proctor et al. 2016:43).

Although by absolute standards, poverty has declined in the United States, it remains higher than in many other industrial

FIGURE 28-1 **U.S. Minimum Wage Adjusted for Inflation**

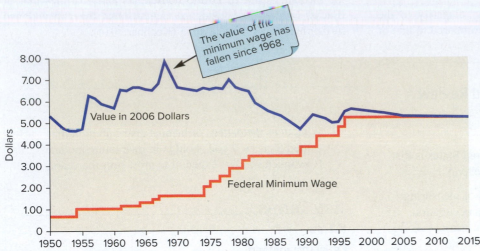

The value of the minimum wage has fallen since 1968.

Value in 2006 Dollars

Federal Minimum Wage

Note: In 2007 the federal minimum wage was raised to $5.85, with provisions for $6.55 in 2008 and $7.25 in 2009. Some states legislate different standards. As of November 2015, minimums were actually lower in two states (Georgia and Wyoming) and higher in 29 states.

Source: Author's estimate, Bureau of the Census 2005a, and Department of Labor 2015a.

In contrast, **relative poverty** is a floating standard of deprivation by which people at the bottom of a society, whatever their lifestyles, are judged to be disadvantaged *in comparison with the nation as a whole.* Therefore, even if the poor of 2016 are better off in absolute terms than the poor of the 1930s or 1960s, they are still seen as deserving of special assistance.

Debate has been growing over the accuracy of the federal government's measure of poverty, which has remained largely unchanged since 1963. If noncash benefits such as Medicare, Medicaid, tax credits, food stamps (the Supplemental Nutrition Assistance Program, or SNAP), public housing, and health care and other employer-provided fringe benefits were included, the reported poverty rate would be lower. On the other hand, if out-of-pocket medical expenses and mandatory work expenses for transportation and child care were included, the poverty rate would be higher. Furthermore, although the current poverty measure does consider family size, it does not consider a household's location, whether in a relatively expensive city like New York or in a less expensive rural area. Nor does it consider whether a householder pays rent or a mortgage installment, lives at home or with someone else.

nations. As Figure 28-2 shows, a comparatively high proportion of U.S. households is poor, meaning that they are unable to purchase basic consumer goods. If anything, this cross-national comparison understates the extent of poverty in the United States, since U.S. residents are likely to pay more for housing, health care, child care, and education than residents of other countries, where such expenses are often subsidized.

FIGURE 28-2 **Poverty in Selected Countries**

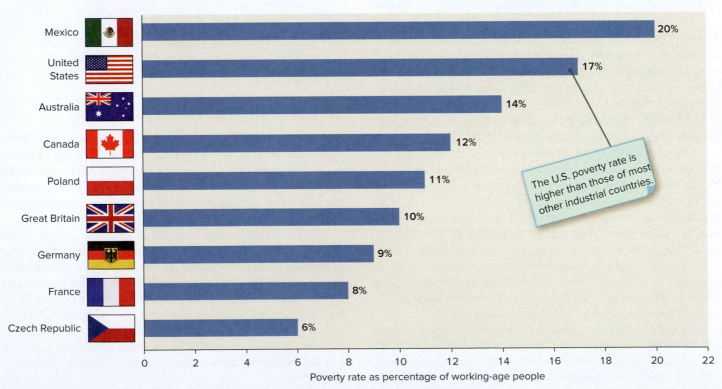

Note: Data are for 2010 or latest year reported in 2015. Poverty threshold is 50 percent of a nation's median household income.

Source: Organisation for Economic Co-Operation and Development 2015a. *Flags:* © admin_design/Shutterstock RF

TABLE 28-1   WHO ARE THE POOR IN THE UNITED STATES?

Group	Percentage of the Population of the United States	Percentage of the Poor of the United States
Age		
Under 18 years old	24%	34%
18 to 64 years old	63	56
65 years and older	13	10
Race-Ethnicity		
Whites (non-Hispanic)	63	41
Blacks	13	23
Hispanics	17	28
Asians and Pacific Islanders	5	5
Family Composition		
Married couples with both members present	72	35
Female householders	20	54
Nativity		
Native born	87	83
Foreign born (naturalized citizen)	6	5
Foreign born (not citizens)	6	12
People with Disabilities	8	10

Note: People with disabilities includes ages 18–64.
Source: Data for 2015 in Proctor et al. 2016:13.

To address some of these shortcomings, in 2010 the federal government launched a second statistic called the Supplemental Poverty Measure (SPM), which is used to estimate economic hardship. The SPM is a relative poverty measure that is based on a broad range of changing household resources and expenses. It was calculated beginning in late 2011, but does not replace the poverty line in determining a household's eligibility for benefits (Blank 2011; Short 2015).

Who Are the Poor?

Not only does the category of the poor defy any simple definition; it counters the common stereotypes about "poor people." For example, many people in the United States believe that the poor are able to work but will not. Yet 39 percent of poor adults age 18–64 *do* work outside the home—28 percent of them full time—compared to 30 percent of all adults. Such stereotypes lead to a faulty picture of the poor and mistaken notions about how to reduce poverty (Proctor et al. 2016:13).

Though many of the poor live in urban slums, a majority live outside those poverty-stricken areas. Poverty is no stranger in rural areas, from Appalachia to hard-hit farming regions to Native American reservations.

© Mark Kostich/Getty Images RF
Even if this single parent works her way up the ladder, supporting her family will still be difficult.

Table 28-1 provides additional statistical information regarding low-income people in the United States.

Feminization of Poverty

Since World War II, an increasing proportion of the poor people of the United States have been women, many of whom are divorced or never-married mothers. In 1959, female householders accounted for 26 percent of the nation's poor; by 2014, that figure had risen to 54 percent (see Table 28-1). This alarming trend, known as the **feminization of poverty,** is evident not just in the United States but around the world.

About half of all women living in poverty in the United States are in transition, coping with an economic crisis caused by the departure, disability, or death of a husband. The other half tend to be economically dependent either on the welfare system or on friends and relatives living nearby. A major factor in the feminization of poverty has been the increase in families with women as single heads of the household. Conflict theorists and other observers trace the higher rates of poverty among women to three distinct factors: the difficulty in finding affordable child care, sexual harassment, and sex discrimination in the labor market (Burns 2010).

The Underclass

In 2014, 40 percent of poor people in the United States were living in central cities. These highly visible urban residents are the focus of most government efforts to alleviate poverty. Yet according to many observers, the plight of the urban poor is growing worse, owing to the devastating interplay of inadequate education and limited employment prospects. Traditional employment opportunities in the industrial sector are largely closed to the unskilled poor. Past and present discrimination heightens these problems for those low-income urban residents who are Black or Hispanic.

Along with other social scientists, sociologist William Julius Wilson (1996, 2012a, 2012b) and his colleagues (2004) have used the term **underclass** to describe the long-term poor who lack training and skills. According to an analysis of census data, 10.3 million people live in extremely impoverished areas. Although not all of them are poor, living in such disadvantaged neighborhoods means limited educational opportunities, greater exposure to crime and health risks, reduced access to private investment, and higher prices for goods and services. About 38 percent of the population in these neighborhoods is Black, 30 percent Hispanic, and 26 percent White non-Hispanic (Bishaw 2011).

Those statistics may sound high, but they could climb higher. Some scholars are predicting that the recent economic downturn may swell the ranks of the underclass, increasing the proportion of the U.S. population that they represent. Indeed, the recession seems to have accelerated the demise of less efficient, less profitable firms. When the downturn is over, jobs will not return to declining industries.

Analyses of the poor in general reveal that they are not a static social class. The overall composition of the poor changes continually, because some individuals and families near the top edge of poverty move above the poverty level after a year or two, while others slip below it. Still, hundreds of thousands of people remain in poverty for many years at a time. Blacks and Latinos are more likely than Whites to be persistently poor. Both Latinos and Blacks are less likely than Whites to leave the welfare rolls as a result of welfare reform (Jäntti 2009; Sampson 2011).

Explaining Poverty

Why is it that poverty pervades a nation of such vast wealth? In 2013, poverty levels matched those of 50 years earlier. Sociologist Herbert Gans (1995), who has applied functionalist analysis to the existence of poverty, argues that various segments of society actually *benefit* from the existence of the poor. Gans has identified a number of social, economic, and political functions that the poor perform for society (Porter 2013):

- The presence of poor people means that society's dirty work—physically dirty or dangerous, dead-end and underpaid, undignified and menial jobs—will be performed at low cost.

- Poverty creates jobs for occupations and professions that serve the poor. It creates both legal employment (public health experts, welfare caseworkers) and illegal jobs (drug dealers, numbers runners).

- The identification and punishment of the poor as deviants upholds the legitimacy of conventional social norms and mainstream values regarding hard work, thrift, and honesty.

- Within a relatively hierarchical society, the existence of poor people guarantees the higher status of the rich. As psychologist William Ryan (1976) noted, affluent people may justify inequality (and gain a measure of satisfaction) by *blaming the victims* of poverty for their disadvantaged condition.

- Because of their lack of political power, the poor often absorb the costs of social change. Under the policy of deinstitutionalization, mental patients released from long-term hospitals have been transferred primarily to low-income communities and neighborhoods. Similarly, halfway houses for rehabilitated drug abusers, rejected by more affluent communities, often end up in poorer neighborhoods.

In Gans's view, then, poverty and the poor actually satisfy positive functions for many nonpoor groups in the United States.

Life Chances

Max Weber saw class as being closely related to people's **life chances**—that is, their opportunities to provide themselves with material goods, positive living conditions, and favorable life experiences (Gerth and Mills 1958). Life chances are reflected in measures such as housing, education, and health. Occupying a higher social class in a society improves your life chances and brings greater access to social rewards. In contrast, people in the lower social classes are forced to devote a larger proportion of their limited resources to the necessities of life. In some cases, life chances are a matter of life and death. According to a medical study published in 2011, in the United States, approximately 133,000 deaths a year can be attributed to individual poverty, and another 119,000 to income inequality. That is over a quarter million deaths per year caused by severely limited resources (Galea et al. 2011).

In times of danger, the affluent and powerful have a better chance of surviving than people of ordinary means. When the supposedly unsinkable British ocean liner *Titanic* hit an iceberg in 1912, it was not carrying enough lifeboats to accommodate all passengers. Plans had been made to evacuate only first- and second-class passengers. About 62 percent of the first-class passengers survived the disaster. Despite a rule that women and children would go first, about a third of those passengers were male. In contrast, only 25 percent of the third-class passengers survived. The first attempt to alert them to the need to abandon ship came well after other passengers had been notified. In an ironic demonstration of continuing social inequality, a luxury travel organization called Bluefish charges passengers $60,000 each to view the underwater remains of the *Titanic* from a deep-sea submersible (Butler 1998; Crouse 1999; Dickler 2011; Riding 1998).

Class position also affects people's vulnerability to natural disasters. When Hurricane Katrina hit the Gulf Coast of the United States in 2005, affluent and poor people alike became its victims. However, poor people who did not own automobiles (100,000 of them in New Orleans alone) were less able than others to evacuate in advance of the storm. The poor who survived its fury had no nest egg to draw on, and thus were more likely than others to accept relocation wherever social service agencies could place them—sometimes hundreds or thousands of miles from home. Those who were able to return are still dealing with the toxic debris left behind, in what urban scholars refer to as "churning": a family moves into a new home that replicates the social environment and conditions they abandoned (Bullard and Wright 2009; Gladwell 2015).

Wealth, status, and power may not ensure happiness, but they certainly provide additional ways of coping with problems and disappointments. For this reason, the opportunity for advancement—for social mobility—is of special significance to those on the bottom of society. Most people want the rewards and privileges that are granted to high-ranking members of a culture. What can society do to increase their social mobility? One strategy is to offer financial aid to college students from low-income families, on the theory that education lifts people out of poverty. Yet such programs are not having as great an effect as their authors once hoped (Box 28-1).

Box 28-1

Sociology on Campus

Student Debt

Today's young people have been dubbed Millennials, but a more appropriate name for them might be Generation Debt. We have seen that an important aspect of stratification is not just income but wealth, measured by the assets people hold. For increasing number of students, debt from student loans follows them for years, lowering their assets and affecting their plans not only for the present but the future. Student debt is not a rare occurrence. As of 2014, 19 percent of all households held student debt; among households where the head was under age 35, this figure was 40 percent.

Every year, millions of prospective college students and their parents struggle through the intricate and time-consuming process of applying for financial aid. Originally, financial aid programs were intended to level the playing field—to allow qualified students from all walks of life to attend college, regardless of the cost. But have those programs fulfilled their promise?

Over the past few decades, student borrowing has steadily increased. From 2000 to 2014, the outstanding federal student debt nearly quadrupled to over $1.1 trillion. At the same time, while the total number of students increased, the number of student borrowers more than doubled to reach 42 million. To complete the bleak picture, default rates among new borrowers rose to the highest levels in 20 years.

Student debt may well force students to make less than desirable career choices after leaving college. Borrowers with high amounts of debt report levels of satisfaction with their career choices around 11 percentage points lower than those who graduated from college without debt.

Another significant change in the pattern of student indebtedness is that it is higher among students of for-profit schools, which often offer extensive online courses. In 2000, only one of the 25 schools whose students owed the most federal debt was a for-profit institution; in 2014, 13 out of 25 were for-profit schools. Borrowers from those 13 schools owed almost 10 percent of all federal student loans (approximately $109 billion).

Observers agree that student indebtedness may level off, because the Great Recession most likely fueled the recent spike in loans and defaults. Despite the spiraling cost of an education, the widespread difficulty in paying for college stems from three trends. First, over the past few decades, colleges and universities have been moving away from making outright grants, such as scholarships, to deserving students, and toward low-interest student loans. Second, much of the assistance schools offer in the form of loans is not based strictly on need. Third, interest rates on federally guaranteed loans have risen steadily, increasing the burden of repayment.

© sshepard/Getty Images RF

> Statistics that show the educational level in the United States rising overall obscure the widening gap between the advantaged and the less advantaged.

The differential impact of student debt along racial and social lines is apparent. Analysis using data from three U.S. Department of Education surveys and the Federal Reserve's 2013 Survey of Consumer Finances reveals a system that is divided along class and racial lines. Because of the student debt-finance system, Black and Latino students tend to have higher loan balances. In addition, high numbers of low-income students and students of color drop out without receiving the credentials they worked for.

These trends in financial aid for higher education are closely tied to trends in social inequality. As noted earlier in this chapter, over the past half century, rather than declining, inequality in income and wealth has actually increased. In a variation on the truism that the rich tend to get richer while the poor get poorer, the rich are getting better educations and the poor are getting poorer educations. Statistics that show the educational level in the United States rising overall obscure the widening gap between the advantaged and the less advantaged.

LET'S DISCUSS

1. How important are student loans to you and your friends? Without them, would you be able to cover your college expenses?
2. What might be the impact of student loan debt on recent college graduates' career paths?

Sources: Burke 2015; Dews 2014; Huelsman 2015.

 ## use your **sociological imagination**

Imagine a society in which there are no social classes—no differences in people's wealth, income, and life chances. What would such a society be like? Would it be stable, or would its social structure change over time?

 ## Social Mobility

In the movie *Maid in Manhattan,* Jennifer Lopez plays the lead in a modern-day Cinderella story, rising from the lowly status of chambermaid in a big-city hotel to a company supervisor and the girlfriend of a well-to-do politician. The ascent of a person from a poor background to a position of prestige, power, or financial reward is an example of social mobility. Formally defined, the term **social mobility** refers to the movement of individuals or groups from one position in a society's stratification system to another. But how significant—how frequent, how dramatic—is mobility in a class society such as the United States?

Open versus Closed Stratification Systems

Sociologists use the terms *open stratification system* and *closed stratification system* to indicate the degree of social mobility in a society. An **open system** implies that the position of each individual is influenced by his or her *achieved* status. Such a system encourages competition among members of society. The United States is moving toward this ideal type as the government attempts to reduce the barriers faced by women, racial and ethnic minorities, and people born in lower social classes. Even in the midst of the economic downturn of 2008–2009, nearly 80 percent of people in the United States felt they could get ahead (Economic Mobility Project 2009).

At the other extreme of social mobility is the **closed system,** which allows little or no possibility of individual social mobility. The slavery and caste systems of stratification are examples of closed systems. In such societies, social placement is based on *ascribed* statuses, such as race or family background, which cannot be changed.

Types of Social Mobility

An elementary school teacher who becomes a police officer moves from one social position to another of the same rank. Each occupation has the same prestige ranking: 60 on a scale ranging from a low of 0 to a high of 100 (see Table 27-1). Sociologists call this kind of movement **horizontal mobility.** However, if the teacher were to become a lawyer (prestige ranking of 76), he or she would experience **vertical mobility,** the movement of an individual from one social position to another of a different rank. Vertical mobility can also involve moving *downward* in a society's stratification system, as would be the case if the teacher became a bank teller (ranking of 50). Pitirim Sorokin ([1927] 1959) was the first sociologist to distinguish between horizontal and vertical mobility. Most sociological analysis, however, focuses on vertical mobility.

One way of examining vertical social mobility is to contrast its two types, intergenerational and intragenerational mobility. **Intergenerational mobility** involves changes in the social position of children relative to their parents. Thus, a plumber whose father was a physician provides an example of downward intergenerational mobility. The celebrated movie star Leonardo DiCaprio, who was raised by a single mother in a neighborhood frequented by drug dealers and prostitutes, illustrates upward intergenerational mobility. Because education contributes significantly to upward mobility, any barrier to the pursuit of advanced degrees can definitely limit intergenerational mobility (see Box 28-1).

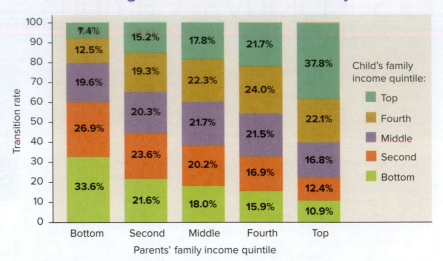

FIGURE 28-3 **Intergenerational Income Mobility**

Over a 25-year period, adult children often end up in the same income bracket as their parents. For example, as the first column shows, only 7 percent of those who begin in the bottom quintile reach the top quintile as adults; their story is one of rags to riches. By comparison, a third of the people in their quintile (33 percent) stay at the bottom, where they began.

Source: Mazumder 2008:11.

Figure 28-3 shows intergenerational mobility based on income. In 1978–1980, a national survey looked at the family income of 6,000 young people. Two decades later, in 1997–2003, researchers followed up on those young adults and their income. The results showed a strong stickiness in both the bottom and top quintiles, or fifths, of the income distribution. Just over 33 percent of those whose parents were in the bottom quintile and 37 percent of those who were in the top quintile remained in the same quintile as adults. Yet the study also showed mobility: almost 66 percent of those in the bottom quintile moved up, and over 60 percent of those at the top experienced downward mobility.

Among men born in the 1960s, this consistent intergenerational mobility resulted largely from economic growth. On average, these men earned more than their fathers did at the same age; their family incomes improved as well. However, the trend has not continued into the next generation. Currently, young men are earning less than their fathers did at the same age—about 12 percent less. Family incomes are slightly higher than in the last generation, but only because women have moved into the paid labor force to supplement their husbands' earnings. With so few women left to join the labor force, most families will need to increase their wages to raise their incomes further (Sawhill and Haskins 2009).

Intragenerational mobility involves changes in social position within a person's adult life. A woman who begins work as a teacher's aide and eventually becomes superintendent of the school district experiences upward intragenerational mobility. A man who becomes a taxicab driver after his accounting firm goes bankrupt undergoes downward intragenerational mobility.

Social Mobility in the United States

The belief in upward mobility is an important value in our society. Does that mean that the United States is indeed the land of

© Stockbyte/Getty Images RF

If this lawyer were the daughter of a car mechanic, her rise to the upper-middle class would illustrate intergenerational mobility. If she had begun as a paralegal and worked her way up the occupational ladder, her career would illustrate intragenerational mobility.

opportunity? Not unless such ascriptive characteristics as race, gender, and family background have ceased to be significant in determining one's future prospects. We can see the impact of these factors in the occupational structure.

Occupational Mobility   Two sociological studies conducted a decade apart offer insight into the degree of mobility in the nation's occupational structure. Taken together, these investigations lead to several noteworthy conclusions. First, occupational mobility (both intergenerational and intragenerational) has been common among males. Approximately 60 to 70 percent of sons are employed in higher-ranked occupations than their fathers (Blau and Duncan 1967; Featherman and Hauser 1978).

Second, although there is a great deal of mobility in the United States, much of it is minor. That is, people who reach an occupational level above or below that of their parents usually advance or fall back only one or two out of a possible eight occupational levels. Thus, the child of a laborer may become an artisan or a technician, but he or she is less likely to become a manager or professional. The odds against reaching the top are extremely high unless one begins from a relatively privileged position.

The Impact of Education   Another conclusion of both studies is that education plays a critical role in social mobility. The impact of formal schooling on adult status is even greater than that of family background (although as we have seen, family background influences the likelihood that one will receive higher education). Furthermore, education represents an important means of intergenerational mobility. A person who was born into a poor family but who graduates from college has a one in five chance of entering the top fifth of all income earners as an adult (Isaacs et al. 2008).

The impact of education on mobility has diminished somewhat in the past decade, however. An undergraduate degree—a BA or a BS—serves less as a guarantee of upward mobility now than it did in the past, simply because more and more entrants into the job market hold such a degree. Moreover, intergenerational mobility is declining, since there is no longer such a stark difference between generations. In earlier decades, many high school–educated parents successfully sent their children to college, but today's college students are increasingly likely to have college-educated parents (Greenstone et al. 2013; Sawhill and Morton 2007).

The Impact of Race and Ethnicity   Sociologists have long documented the fact that the class system is more rigid for African Americans than it is for members of other racial groups. African American men who have good jobs, for example, are less likely than White men to see their adult children attain the same status. The cumulative disadvantage of discrimination plays a significant role in the disparity between the two groups' experiences. Compared to White households, the relatively modest wealth of African American households means that adult African American children are less likely than adult White children to receive financial support from their parents. Indeed, young African American couples are much more likely than young

© Ralph Orlowski/Bloomberg/Getty Images

Mary Barra, CEO of General Motors, began her career in 1980 as a plant engineer. In 2014 she reached the top of the corporate ladder. Despite equal opportunity laws, occupational barriers still limit women's climb to the top. As of January 2014, women ran just 25 of the Fortune 500 companies; men ran the other 475.

White couples to be assisting their parents—a sacrifice that hampers their social mobility.

African American rates of upward intergenerational social mobility are lower. Based on national income data beginning in 1968 and following three generations, Black children are more likely to be born into poverty than White children, and they are less likely to escape. In fact, the majority of Black adults raised at the bottom of the stratification system remain stuck there as adults, compared to only a third of Whites. In summary, Black Americans are more likely to stay in the bottom and fall from the middle (Pew Charitable Trust 2012; Reeves and Venator 2014).

Latino social mobility shows a more mixed picture. Hispanics whose parents were both born outside the United States are substantially better off than their immigrant parents. They have higher incomes; more are college graduates and homeowners; and fewer live in poverty. The immigrants themselves often face work situations that have significantly lower prestige than what they left behind, even if their absolute incomes are higher (Nicklett and Burgard 2009; Pew Research Center 2013).

The Latino wealth and asset picture is bleaker and more resembles that of African Americans. According to one analysis, the median wealth of White non-Hispanic households is 18 times that of Hispanic households. This lopsided wealth ratio is the largest since the government first published these data in the 1980s. Continuing immigration accounts for part of the disparity: most of the new arrivals are destitute. But even the wealthiest 10 percent of Latino households have only a third as much net worth as the top 5 percent of White households (Kochhar et al. 2011).

The Impact of Gender   Studies of mobility, even more than those of class, have traditionally ignored the significance of gender, but some research findings are now available that explore the relationship between gender and mobility.

Women's employment opportunities are much more limited than men's. Moreover, according to recent research, women whose skills far exceed the jobs offered them are more likely than men to withdraw entirely from the paid labor force. Their withdrawal violates an assumption common to traditional mobility studies: that most people will aspire to upward mobility and seek to make the most of their opportunities.

In contrast to men, women have a rather large range of clerical occupations open to them. But the modest salary ranges and limited prospects for advancement many of these positions provide limit the possibility of upward mobility. Self-employment as shopkeepers, entrepreneurs, independent professionals, and the like—an important road to upward mobility for men—is more difficult for women, who find it harder to secure the necessary financing. Although sons commonly follow in the footsteps of their fathers, women are unlikely to move into their fathers' positions. Consequently, gender remains an important factor in shaping social mobility. Women in the United States (and in other parts of the world) are especially likely to be trapped in poverty, unable to rise out of their low-income status (Beller 2009; Heilman 2001).

On the positive side, though today's women lag behind men in employment, their earnings have increased faster than their mothers' did at a comparable age, so that their incomes are substantially higher. The one glaring exception to this trend is the daughters of low-income parents. Because these women typically care for children—many as single parents—and sometimes for other relatives as well, their mobility is severely restricted (Isaacs 2007b).

social
policy and Stratification | Executive Compensation

Few topics in the news today have led to such public outrage as the compensation received by top executives in the private sector. In the wake of recent corporate meltdowns, such as those involving several huge mortgage lending institutions, executive salaries and bonuses that run into the millions of dollars have begun to strike people as inappropriate. Is multimillion-dollar compensation really necessary, much less desirable, to attract talented corporate leaders?

Looking at the Issue

Over the period from 2000 to 2010, Barry Diller, CEO of Expedia, received a staggering $1.14 billion in compensation—despite the fact that the company's shares lost 22 percent of their value. Over an eight-year period, United Health's top executive, William McGuire, took home $453 million, even though the company's stockholders lost 99 percent of their investment. In defense, spokesmen for the two men claimed that their compensation reflected the stocks' solid performance during earlier periods (Thurm 2010).

Although executive pay has always been high in the United States, in recent years it has grown dramatically. The corporate executives who head private companies now earn the highest incomes in the nation. In fact, the gap between their salaries and those of average workers has widened significantly over time. In 1965, top executives earned only 24 times the average worker's pay. By 2014 CEO-to-worker compensation had reached a ratio of 303 to 1. This was not as large as it had been prior to the Great Recession, but it did show that chief executive officers recovered nicely from the economic decline and never suffered as so many rank and file workers did (Mishel and Davis 2015).

—Continued

In 2011, as the U.S. economy began to pull out of a deep, long-lasting recession, corporate executives were still earning huge salaries and bonuses, despite the fact that many workers remained jobless.

Applying Sociology

From a functionalist perspective, such generous compensation seems reasonable given the potential for gain that a talented executive brings to a corporation. Today, even a small increase in a multibillion-dollar company's performance can add hundreds of millions of dollars to its bottom line. Not surprisingly, then, competition to attract top-performing executives to a company is fierce. Not all these executives are successful all the time, however; sometimes their leadership reduces profits. Critics point out that 7 of the top 25 highly paid executives presided over companies that lost money (Frank 2010; Thurm 2010).

Conflict theorists question not only the relatively high levels of executive compensation, but also the process through which executives' pay is determined. The board of directors, which holds the responsibility for determining executives' pay, has an incentive to go along with arrangements that are favorable to top executives. Board members themselves earned an average of about $228,000 in 2009, so they have a natural desire to avoid conflict over high salaries. Furthermore, board members are often CEOs themselves or at least aspire to that role, so they have little reason to keep compensation plans more reasonable (Bebchuk and Fried 2010; Kim et al. 2015; Strauss 2011).

Taking an almost interactionist approach, sociologist Thomas DiPrete and his colleagues have observed that today, corporations must report executives' compensation relative to their peer group's compensation—that is, to the compensation received by leaders of similar businesses of similar size. Although members of such peer groups do not interact in the way that members of a primary group or even a secondary group would, they do form a social network. Thus, public comparisons of executive compensation within particular industries may influence board members' decisions, prompting them to tie executives' compensation more directly to their performance (DiPrete et al. 2010).

Initiating Policy

Although policymakers have long been concerned about executive compensation, until recently hard data have been difficult to obtain. Before 1992, corporations were required to disclose executives' pay, but not in a uniform manner. Many companies disguised the dollar amounts by literally spelling the words out in the midst of long, densely written documents. Today, the law mandates that companies publish "summary compensation tables." In 2006, reporting requirements were expanded to cover retirement packages, including the "golden parachute" clauses that protect executives who bail out of failing companies (Bebchuk and Fried 2010).

During the economic downturn that began in 2008, the value of the stock that top executives received as part of their compensation packages did decline. Yet overall, CEOs' salaries in the 500 largest corporations still rose 3 percent in 2009. In response, the White House appointed a Treasury Department official, whom reporters quickly dubbed the "pay czar," to look into executive compensation. Given the deferred stock payments, expense accounts, and other perquisites executives typically receive, the assignment was a difficult one with no lasting impact (Wagner 2011).

So has there been no policy action in the last generation? In 2015, the Securities and Exchange Commission approved a rule that requires companies to report pay-ratio levels between their chief executives and a sample of their employees across different positions, beginning in 2018. While many cheer this move toward transparency, some note that lobbyists have plenty of time to stop the rule's full implementation and accountants will find ways to maneuver around it (*New York Times* 2015).

TAKE THE ISSUE WITH YOU

1. Should corporate executives earn high salaries even when their companies lose money? Explain. How do you think functionalists would defend such a practice?

2. What do you think of the "golden parachute" clauses that allow executives to bail out of failing companies unharmed? What might be the effect of such clauses on executives' performance? On shareholders and on lower-level employees?

3. Relate the increases in executive compensation over the past half century to changes in U.S. social structure during that time. How have these changes affected you and your family?

Summary

Poverty is difficult to explain or define, although its effects are obvious and pervasive.

1. Many of those who live in poverty are full-time workers who struggle to support their families at minimum-wage jobs. The long-term poor—those who lack the training and skills to lift themselves out of poverty—form an **underclass.**

2. Functionalists find that the poor satisfy positive functions for many of the nonpoor in the United States.

3. One's **life chances**—opportunities for obtaining material goods, positive living conditions, and favorable life experiences—are related to one's social class. Occupying a high social position improves a person's life chances.

4. **Social mobility** is more likely to be found in an **open system** that emphasizes achieved status than in a **closed system** that emphasizes ascribed status. Race, gender, and family background are important factors in social mobility.

5. During the past half century, the gap between executive compensation and the average worker's pay has increased enormously. Although corporations claim that talented leaders enhance their performance, making executive pay packages well worth the money, they have gone to some trouble to disguise the expense from public scrutiny.

Thinking Critically

1. How do you identify areas of poverty in your own community or one nearby? Do you consider residents' achieved or ascribed characteristics?

2. How do people's life chances affect society as a whole?

3. Which factor—occupation, education, race and ethnicity, or gender—do you expect will have the greatest impact on your own social mobility? Explain.

Key Terms

Absolute poverty

Closed system

Feminization of poverty

Horizontal mobility

Intergenerational mobility

Intragenerational mobility

Life chances

Open system

Relative poverty

Social mobility

Underclass

Vertical mobility

Mastering This Chapter

© PeerPoint/Alamy

taking sociology with you

1 Do some research on the educational and occupational levels in the city or town where you live. Based on what you have learned, describe the social-class stratification of your community.

2 Use census data to create a map showing the median income levels and/or property values in the geographic areas surrounding your home. What patterns does it show?

3 Talk with a parent or grandparent about your family's history. What can you learn about your forebears' life chances? About their social mobility? How do you hope to fit into the story?

Absolute poverty A minimum level of subsistence that no family should be expected to live below.

Achieved status A social position that a person attains largely through his or her own efforts.

Ascribed status A social position assigned to a person by society without regard for the person's unique talents or characteristics.

Bourgeoisie Karl Marx's term for the capitalist class, comprising the owners of the means of production.

Capitalism An economic system in which the means of production are held largely in private hands and the main incentive for economic activity is the accumulation of profits.

Caste A hereditary rank, usually religiously dictated, that tends to be fixed and immobile.

Class A group of people who have a similar level of wealth and income.

Class consciousness In Karl Marx's view, a subjective awareness held by members of a class regarding their common vested interests and the need for collective political action to bring about social change.

Class system A social ranking based primarily on economic position in which achieved characteristics can influence social mobility.

Closed system A social system in which there is little or no possibility of individual social mobility.

Conspicuous consumption Purchasing goods not to survive but to flaunt one's superior wealth and social standing.

Dominant ideology A set of cultural beliefs and practices that helps to maintain powerful social, economic, and political interests.

Estate system A system of stratification under which peasants were required to work land leased to them by nobles in exchange for military protection and other services. Also known as *feudalism.*

Esteem The reputation that a specific person has earned within an occupation.

False consciousness A term used by Karl Marx to describe an attitude held by members of a class that does not accurately reflect their objective position.

Feminization of poverty A trend in which women constitute an increasing proportion of the poor people of both the United States and the world.

Horizontal mobility The movement of an individual from one social position to another of the same rank.

Income Salaries and wages, interest on savings, stock dividends, and rental income.

Intergenerational mobility Changes in the social position of children relative to their parents.

Intragenerational mobility Changes in social position within a person's adult life.

Life chances The opportunities people have to provide themselves with material goods, positive living conditions, and favorable life experiences.

Objective method A technique for measuring social class that assigns individuals to classes on the basis of criteria such as occupation, education, income, and place of residence.

Open system A social system in which the position of each individual is influenced by his or her achieved status.

Power The ability to exercise one's will over others.

Prestige The respect and admiration that an occupation holds in a society.

Proletariat Karl Marx's term for the working class in a capitalist society.

Relative poverty A floating standard of deprivation by which people at the bottom of a society, whatever their lifestyles, are judged to be disadvantaged *in comparison with the nation as a whole.*

Slavery A system of enforced servitude in which some people are owned by other people.

Social inequality A condition in which members of society have differing amounts of wealth, prestige, or power.

Social mobility Movement of individuals or groups from one position in a society's stratification system to another.

Socioeconomic status (SES) A measure of social class that is based on income, education, and occupation.

Status group People who have the same prestige or lifestyle, independent of their class positions.

Stratification A structured ranking of entire groups of people that perpetuates unequal economic rewards and power in a society.

Underclass The long-term poor who lack training and skills.

Vertical mobility The movement of an individual from one social position to another of a different rank.

Wealth An inclusive term encompassing all a person's material assets, including land, stocks, and other types of property.

Read each question carefully and then select the best answer.

1. Which of the following describes a condition in which members of a society have different amounts of wealth, prestige, or power?
   a. stratification
   b. status inconsistency
   c. slavery
   d. social inequality

2. In Karl Marx's view, the destruction of the capitalist system will occur only if the working class first develops
   a. bourgeois consciousness.
   b. false consciousness.
   c. class consciousness.
   d. caste consciousness.

3. Which of the following were viewed by Max Weber as analytically distinct components of stratification?
   a. conformity, deviance, and social control
   b. class, status, and power
   c. class, caste, and age
   d. class, prestige, and esteem

4. Which sociological perspective argues that stratification is universal and that social inequality is necessary so that people will be motivated to fill socially important positions?
   a. the functionalist perspective
   b. the conflict perspective
   c. the interactionist perspective
   d. the labeling perspective

5. British sociologist Ralf Dahrendorf viewed social classes as groups of people who share common interests resulting from their authority relationships. Dahrendorf's ideology aligns best with which theoretical perspective?
   a. the functionalist perspective
   b. the conflict perspective
   c. the interactionist perspective
   d. sociocultural evolution

6. The respect or admiration that an occupation holds in a society is referred to as
   a. status.
   b. esteem.
   c. prestige.
   d. ranking.

7. Approximately how many people in the United States live below the poverty line established by the federal government?
   a. 5 percent
   b. 10 percent
   c. 15 percent
   d. 25 percent

8. Which sociologist has applied functionalist analysis to the existence of poverty and argues that various segments of society actually benefit from the existence of the poor?
   a. Émile Durkheim
   b. Max Weber
   c. Karl Marx
   d. Herbert Gans

9. A measure of social class that is based on income, education, and occupation is known as
   a. the objective method.
   b. stratification.
   c. socioeconomic status.
   d. the open system.

10. A plumber whose father was a physician is an example of
    a. downward intergenerational mobility.
    b. upward intergenerational mobility.
    c. downward intragenerational mobility.
    d. upward intragenerational mobility.

11. _____ is the most extreme form of legalized social inequality for individuals or groups.

12. In the _____ system of stratification, or feudalism, peasants were required to work land leased to them by nobles in exchange for military protection and other services.

13. Karl Marx viewed _____ differentiation as the crucial determinant of social, economic, and political inequality.

14. _____ _____ is the term Thorstein Veblen used to describe the extravagant spending patterns of those at the top of the class hierarchy.

15. _____ poverty is the minimum level of subsistence that no family should be expected to live below.

16. _____ poverty is a floating standard of deprivation by which people at the bottom of a society, whatever their lifestyles, are judged to be disadvantaged in comparison with the nation as a whole.

17. Sociologist William Julius Wilson and other social scientists have used the term _____ to describe the long-term poor who lack training and skills.

18. Max Weber used the term _____ _____ to refer to people's opportunities to provide themselves with material goods, positive living conditions, and favorable life experiences.

19. An open class system implies that the position of each individual is influenced by the person's _____ status.

20. _____ mobility involves changes in social position within a person's adult life.

9 Global Inequality

© Stockbyte/Getty Images

A young boy scavenges for items that might be of use to his family on Smokey Mountain, a massive landfill in Manila, Philippines. Thousands pick through the rubbish despite landslides that take the lives of scavengers. About half of Manila's 11 million people live in slums.

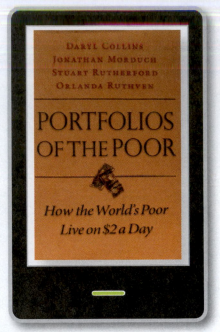

© Ira C. Roberts/Chad Enterprises Corporation

Could you live on less than $2 a day, including your rent or campus housing?

When a team of researchers asked poor people in developing countries how they spent their meager incomes, the results were surprising.

❝ To get a first sense of what the financial diaries [of the poor] reveal, consider Hamid and Khadeja. The couple married in a poor coastal village of Bangladesh where there was very little work for a poorly educated and unskilled young man like Hamid. Soon after their first child was born they gave up rural life and moved, as so many hundreds of thousands had done before them, to the capital city, Dhaka, where they settled in a slum. After spells as a cycle-rickshaw driver and construction laborer and many days of unemployment, Hamid, whose health was not good, finally got taken on as a reserve driver of a motorized rickshaw. That's what he was doing when we first met Hamid and Khadeja in late 1999, while Khadeja stayed home to run the household, raise their child, and earn a little from taking in sewing work. Home was one of a strip of small rooms with cement block walls and a tin roof, built by their landlord on illegally occupied land, with a toilet and kitchen space shared by the eight families that lived there.

In an average month they lived on the equivalent of $70, almost all of it earned by Hamid, whose income arrived in unpredictable daily amounts that varied according to whether he got work that day (he was only the reserve driver) and, if he did get work, how much business he attracted, how many hours he was allowed to keep his vehicle, and how often it broke down. A fifth of the $70 was spent on rent (not always paid on time), and much of the rest went toward the most basic necessities of life—food and the means to prepare it. By the couple's own reckoning, which our evidence agrees with, their income put them among the poor of Bangladesh, though not among the very poorest. By global standards they would fall into the bottom two-fifths of the world's income distribution tables.

An unremarkable poor household: a partly educated couple trying to stay alive, bring up a child, run a one-room home, and keep Hamid's health in shape—on an uncertain $0.78 per person per day. You wouldn't expect them to have much of a financial life. Yet the diversity of instruments in their year-end household balance sheet shows that Hamid and Khadeja, as part of their struggle to survive within their slim means, were active money managers.

Far from living hand-to-mouth, consuming every taka as soon as it arrived, Hamid and Khadeja had built up reserves in six different instruments, ranging from $2 kept at home for minor day-to-day shortfalls to $30 sent for safe-keeping to his parents, $40 lent out to a relative, and $76 in a life insurance savings policy. In addition, Hamid always made sure he had $2 in his pocket to deal with anything that might befall him on the road.

In addition to saving, borrowing, and repaying *money*, Hamid and Khadeja, like nearly all poor and some not-so-poor households, also saved, borrowed, and repaid in kind. Khadeja, sharing a crude kitchen with seven other wives, would often swap small amounts of rice or lentils or salt with her neighbors. She would keep a note of the quantities in her head, and so would her partners in these exchanges, to ensure that their transactions were fair over the long haul. Virtually all of the rural Bangladeshi households followed the well-established tradition of *musti chaul*—of keeping back one fistful of dry rice each time a meal was cooked, to hold against lean times, to have ready when a beggar called, or to donate to the mosque or temple when called on to do so. For rural respondents in India and Bangladesh, the intermediation of goods and services rather than cash was common, and included borrowing grain to be repaid after the harvest, repaying a loan with one's labor, or using labor to buy farm inputs. We recorded much of this activity. ❞

> *An unremarkable poor household: a partly educated couple trying to stay alive, bring up a child, run a one-room home, and keep Hamid's health in shape—on an uncertain $0.78 per person per day. You wouldn't expect them to have much of a financial life.*

(D.D. Collins et al. 2009:7–8, 10–11) Quotation from Daryl Collins et al. 2009. Portfolios of the Poor: How the World's Poor Live on $2 a Day. Princeton, NJ: Princeton University Press, 2009.

Nearly 1 billion people live on less than $2 a day— the widely recognized definition of poverty in the developing world (World Bank 2015d:4). To find out how these poor households survive, four researchers conducted an intensive study of 250 families in Bangladesh, India, and South Africa. Daryl Collins, Jonathan Morduch, Stuart Rutherford, and Orlanda Ruthven wanted to know how best to use *microfinance*—small lending— to assist poor families in the developing world. As explained in the book *Portfolios of the Poor: How the World's Poor Live on*

$2 a Day, rather than simply interviewing the families, Collins and her colleagues asked them to maintain financial diaries for a year. Through the diaries, the research team discovered that the families were quite adept at managing their income. Financial management, although not necessarily in currency, was a fundamental part of their lives, a skill they used every day of the year. Because the stakes were high—there is no room for error on $1 or $2 a day—these mostly uneducated people had developed surprisingly sophisticated methods for managing their resources.

In developing countries like Bangladesh, where Hamid and Khadeja live, most but not all the people are poor. Even in the poorest countries, the poor rub shoulders with the very wealthy. Inequality, then, exists within all countries, not just within the United States. On a global scale, inequality also exists *between* developing and developed nations, which is why a living allowance of $2 a day is so difficult for those of us in the developed world to comprehend. In this chapter we will consider social inequality both within developing nations and between the developing and developed worlds.

What economic and political conditions explain the divide between rich nations and poor? Within developing nations, how are wealth and income distributed, and how much opportunity does the average worker have to move up the social ladder? How do race and gender affect social mobility in these countries? In these modules we will focus on global inequality, beginning with the global divide. We will consider the impact of colonialism and neocolonialism, globalization, the rise of multinational corporations, and the trend toward modernization. Then we will focus on stratification within nations, in terms of the distribution of wealth and income as well as social mobility. Module 30 closes with a Social Policy section on welfare reform in Europe and North America.

MODULE 29 | Stratification in the World System

The Global Divide

In some parts of the world, the people who have dedicated their lives to fighting starvation refer to what they call "coping mechanisms"—ways in which the desperately poor attempt to control their hunger. Eritrean women will strap flat stones to their stomachs to lessen their hunger pangs. In Mozambique, people eat the grasshoppers that have destroyed the crops, calling them "flying shrimp." Though dirt eating is considered a pathological condition (called *pica*) among the well-fed, the world's poor eat dirt to add minerals to their diet. And in many countries, mothers have been known to boil stones in water, to convince their hungry children that supper is almost ready. As they hover over the pot, these women hope that their malnourished children will fall asleep (McNeil 2004).

Around the world, inequality is a significant determinant of human behavior, opening doors of opportunity to some and closing them to others. Indeed, disparities in life chances are so extreme that in some places, the poorest of the poor may not be aware of them. Western media images may have circled the globe, but in extremely depressed rural areas, those at the bottom of society are not likely to see them.

A few centuries ago, such vast divides in global wealth did not exist. Except for a very few rulers and landowners, everyone in the world was poor. In much of Europe, life was as difficult as it was in Asia or South America. This was true until the Industrial Revolution and rising agricultural productivity produced explosive economic growth.

The resulting rise in living standards was not evenly distributed across the world.

To gain insight into global inequality, we need to consider what poverty means in industrial countries in comparison to what it means in the rest of the world (Box 29-1).

Although the divide between industrialized and developing nations is sharp, sociologists recognize a continuum of nations, from the richest of the rich to the poorest of the poor. For example, in 2015, the average value of goods and services produced per citizen (or per capita gross national income) in the industrialized countries of the United States, the Netherlands, Switzerland, France, and Norway was more than $47,000. In at least 18 poorer countries, the value was just $2,000 or less. However, most countries fell somewhere

Used by permission of Cartoon Movement.

To reduce global poverty, wealthy industrial countries must address the problem consistently, on a long-term basis.

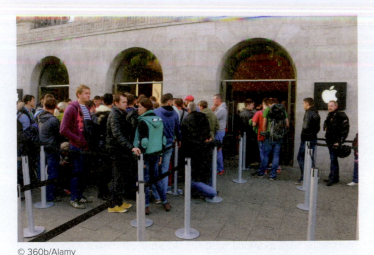

© 360b/Alamy

© Photofusion Picture Library/Alamy

What do we stand in line for? People's needs and desires differ dramatically depending on where they live. Eager customers line up outside a store in Berlin to purchase the newly released iPhone 6s; residents of Ethiopia line up to receive water.

between those extremes, as Figure 29-1 shows (Kaneda and Bietsch 2015).

Still, the contrasts are stark. Three forces discussed here are particularly responsible for the domination of the world marketplace by a few nations: the legacy of colonialism, the advent of multinational corporations, and modernization.

The Legacy of Colonialism

Colonialism occurs when a foreign power maintains political, social, economic, and cultural domination over a people for an extended period. In simple terms, it is rule by outsiders. The long reign of the British Empire over much of North America, parts

---

Sociology in the Global Community

Box 29-1

It's All Relative: Appalachian Poverty and Congolese Affluence

What does it mean to be well off? To be poor? To explore this question, the editors of the London-based publication *The Economist* compared the situations of two men living very different lives: an unemployed truck driver in the Appalachian Mountains and a physician in Congo.

Enos Banks makes his home in a forgotten pocket of rural poverty, described over 50 years ago in Michael Harrington's *The Other America*. Banks once worked for a coal-mining company, but a heart attack forced him to quit his job. In his 60s, he lives in a trailer and gets by on a little more than $500 a month in supplemental security income (SSI). Because he owns a truck, he is not eligible for food stamps.

In the other side of the world, in the Democratic Republic of Congo, Mbwebwe Kabamba earns about $100 or $200 more per month than Enos Banks. Kabamba is a surgeon and head of the emergency room at a hospital in Kinshasha, the country's capital. He supplements his hospital salary of $250 per month by performing surgery on the side. In Congo, the same income that impoverishes Enos Banks places Kabamba near the middle of his society's income distribution.

> In Congo, the same income that impoverishes Enos Banks places Kabamba near the middle of his society's income distribution.

Though Kabamba may seem better off than Banks, especially given the Congo's lower cost of living, such is not the case. Kabamba supports a family of 12, while Banks supports only himself. By U.S. standards, Kabamba's four-bedroom home, spacious compared with Banks's trailer, is overcrowded. And although Kabamba's home has a kitchen, it lacks running water, dependable electric service, and air conditioning—services most Americans take for granted. Considered wealthy in his own country, Kambamba is worse off than a poor person in the United States.

Nevertheless, Banks's poverty is real; he occupies a position close to the bottom of the social class hierarchy. In absolute terms

defined by his own society, Kabamba is not poor, even though in some ways he is less well off than Enos Banks. Relative to most of the world's population, however, both men are doing well.

LET'S DISCUSS

1. Have you ever lived in or traveled to a foreign country where income and living standards were very different from those in the United States? If so, did the contact give you a new perspective on poverty? What differences between living standards in the two societies stand out in your mind?

2. If absolute measures of poverty, such as household income, are inconsistent from one country to the next, what other measures might give a clearer picture of a person's relative well-being? Should the poverty level be the same everywhere in the world? Why or why not?

Sources: The Economist 2005a; Harrington 1962; Kaneda and Bietsch 2015.

FIGURE 29-1 Gross National Income Per Capita

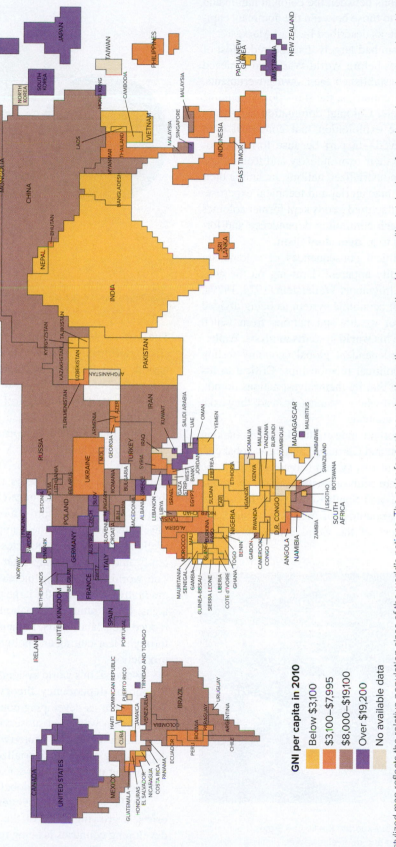

This stylized map reflects the relative population sizes of the world's nations. The color for each country shows the gross national income (the total value of goods and services produced by the nation in a given year) per capita.

Note: Country sizes and incomes based on 2010 estimates. Includes only those countries with 3 million or more people.
Sources: Haub 2010; Weeks 2012.

GNI per capita in 2010

- Below $3,100
- $3,100–$7,995
- $8,000–$19,100
- Over $19,200
- No available data

of Africa, and India was an example of colonial domination. The same can be said of French rule over Algeria, Tunisia, and other parts of North Africa. Relations between the colonial nation and colonized people are similar to those between the dominant capitalist class and the proletariat, as described by Karl Marx.

By the 1980s, colonialism had largely disappeared. Most of the nations that were colonies before World War I had achieved political independence and established their own governments. However, for many of those countries, the transition to genuine self-rule was not yet complete. Colonial domination had established patterns of economic exploitation that continued even after nationhood was achieved—in part because former colonies were unable to develop their own industry and technology. Their dependence on more industrialized nations, including their former colonial masters, for managerial and technical expertise, investment capital, and manufactured goods kept former colonies in a subservient position. Such continuing dependence and foreign domination are referred to as **neocolonialism.**

The economic and political consequences of colonialism and neocolonialism are readily apparent. Drawing on the conflict perspective, sociologist Immanuel Wallerstein (1974, 1979a, 2000, 2012) views the global economic system as being divided between nations that control wealth and nations from which resources are taken. Through his **world systems analysis,** Wallerstein has described an interdependent global economy resting on unequal economic and political relationships. Critical to his analysis is the understanding that by themselves, nations do not, nor have they ever, constituted whole systems. Instead, they exist within a larger, global social context.

In Wallerstein's view, certain industrialized nations (among them the United States, Japan, and Germany) and their global corporations dominate the *core* of this system (Figure 29-2). At the *semiperiphery* of the system are countries with marginal economic status, such as Israel, Ireland, and South Korea. Wallerstein suggests that the poor developing countries of Asia, Africa, and Latin America are on the *periphery* of the world economic system.

© Imaginechina via AP Images

Chinese workers assemble toys for export to the United States. Globalization impacts both foreign and domestic workers, limiting employment opportunities at home and worsening working conditions abroad.

FIGURE 29-2 **World Systems Analysis**

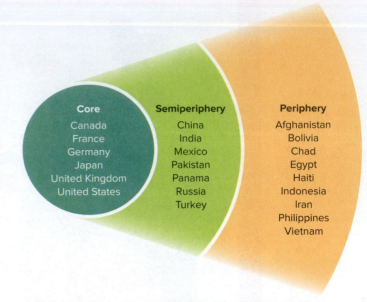

Core	Semiperiphery	Periphery
Canada	China	Afghanistan
France	India	Bolivia
Germany	Mexico	Chad
Japan	Pakistan	Egypt
United Kingdom	Panama	Haiti
United States	Russia	Indonesia
	Turkey	Iran
		Philippines
		Vietnam

Note: Figure shows only a partial listing of countries, selected by the author.

The key to Wallerstein's macro-level analysis is the exploitative relationship of *core* nations toward *noncore* nations. Core nations and their corporations control and exploit noncore nations' economies. Unlike other nations, they are relatively independent of outside control (Chase-Dunn and Grimes 1995; G. Williams 2013).

The division between core and periphery nations is significant and remarkably stable. A study by the International Monetary Fund (2000; Alvaredo 2011) found little change over the course of the past 115 years for the more than 24 economies that were studied. The only changes were Japan's movement up into the group of core nations and China's movement down toward the margins of the semiperiphery nations. Yet Immanuel Wallerstein (2012:9) speculates that the world system as we currently understand it may soon undergo unpredictable changes. The world is becoming increasingly urbanized, a trend that is gradually eliminating the large pools of low-cost workers in rural areas. In the future, core nations will have to find other ways to reduce their labor costs. Exhaustion of land and water resources through clear-cutting and pollution is also driving up the costs of production.

Wallerstein's world systems analysis is the most widely used version of **dependency theory.** According to this macro-level theory, even as developing countries make economic advances, they remain weak and subservient to core nations and corporations in an increasingly intertwined global economy. This interdependency allows industrialized nations to continue to exploit developing countries. In a sense, dependency theory applies the conflict perspective on a global scale.

In the view of world systems analysts and dependency theorists, a growing share of the human and natural resources of developing countries is being redistributed to the core industrialized nations. This redistribution happens in part because developing countries owe huge sums of money to industrialized nations as a result of foreign aid, loans, and trade deficits. The global debt crisis has intensified the Third World dependency begun under colonialism, neocolonialism, and multinational investment. International financial institutions are pressuring indebted countries to take severe measures to meet their interest payments. The result is that developing nations may be forced to devalue their currencies, freeze workers' wages, increase the privatization of industry, and reduce government services and employment.

Closely related to these problems is **globalization,** the worldwide integration of government policies, cultures, social movements, and financial markets through trade and the exchange of ideas. Because world financial markets transcend governance by conventional nation-states, international organizations such as the World Bank and the International Monetary Fund have emerged as major players in the global economy. The function of these institutions, which are heavily funded and influenced by core nations, is to encourage economic trade and development and to ensure the smooth operation of international financial markets. As such, they are seen as promoters of globalization and defenders primarily of the interests of core nations.

Critics call attention to a variety of issues, including violations of workers' rights, the destruction of the environment, the loss of cultural identity, and discrimination against minority groups in periphery nations. The impact of globalization appears to be most problematic for developing countries in Latin America and Africa. In Asia, developing nations seem to do better. Foreign investment there involves the high-tech sector, which produces more sustainable economic growth. Even there, however, globalization definitely has not reduced income disparities, either between nations or within countries (Kerbo 2006).

Some observers see globalization and its effects as the natural result of advances in communications technology, particularly the Internet and worldwide transmission of the mass media. Others view it more critically, as a process that allows multinational corporations to expand unchecked, as we will see shortly (Chase-Dunn et al. 2000; Guenther and Kasi 2015).

 use your **sociological imagination**

You are traveling through a developing country. What evidence do you see of neocolonialism and globalization?

Poverty Worldwide

In developing countries, any deterioration of the economic well-being of those who are least well off threatens their very survival. By U.S. standards, even those who are well-off in the developing world are poor (see Box 9-1). Those who are poor in developing countries are truly destitute.

How do social scientists measure global poverty? There is significant disagreement over where to draw the poverty line in the United States; adding the rest of the world

to the equation further complicates the task. Individually, many developing nations define poverty based on the minimum income a person needs to survive—an amount that typically ranges from a low of $1 a day to a high of $2 a day. Zambia defines poverty in terms of the inability to afford specific foods in a subsistence diet (Oxford Poverty and Human Development Initiative 2012).

Millennium Development Goals

In 2000 the United Nations launched the Millennium Project, whose objective was to halve extreme poverty worldwide by the year 2015. The millennium development goals targeted eight areas: poverty, education, gender equality, child mortality, maternal health, disease, the environment, and global partnership. Each goal was supported by 21 specific targets and more than 60 indicators. Although 15 years may have seemed a long time, the challenge was great. To reach the project's goal, planners estimated that industrialized nations had to set aside 0.51 percent of their *gross national income*—that is, the total value of a nation's goods and services (GNP), plus or minus income received from and sent to other nations—to aid developing countries.

At the time the Millennium Project was launched, only five countries were giving at that target rate: Denmark, Luxembourg, the Netherlands, Norway, and Sweden. Although in dollar terms the U.S. government delivers far more aid to foreign countries and multinational organizations than any other nation, the amount is not impressive considering the nation's tremendous wealth compared to other countries. In terms of the percentage of gross national income, the United States' contribution is among the lowest of the 23 most advanced industrialized countries, on a par with Japan's (Figure 29-3).

While many objectives were not achieved, a great deal of attention was given to reducing world poverty. The number of people living on less than $1.25 a day was reduced from 1.9 billion in 1990 to 836 million in 2015, narrowly missing the ambitious target of halving the proportion of people suffering from hunger. Back in 1990, it was assumed that making these advances would take a huge increase in assistance from industrial countries, which, for the most part, did not occur. Rather, selective developing countries benefited from significantly increased commodity prices sustained by rapid industrialization and urbanization of their emerging economies. China was a stellar example of this: that country alone experienced a drop of 470 million people living below $1.25 a day and accounted for almost half of the global decline in poverty. Despite the improvement, hundreds of millions of people remain in poverty or, as our chapter-opening excerpt described, have a spending pattern of $2 a day or below.

A related global concern is malnourishment, which prevents young children from receiving necessary nutrients during their first three years of life. The condition can lead to developmental problems that affect a child's quality of life through adulthood, and

© Peter Probst/Alamy

The United Nations, founded after World War II with 51 member nations, now comprises 193 countries.

can even prevent a person from contributing to economic growth. Conflict theorists see malnourishment and its developmental effects as yet another result of inequality. However, functionalists point out that for developing societies—indeed, for any society—malnourishment is not only dysfunctional; it contributes to the growth of inequality over time (Warrell 2013).

Privileged people in industrialized nations tend to assume that the world's poor lack significant assets. Yet again and again, observers from these countries have been startled to discover how far even a small amount of capital can go. Numerous microfinance programs, which involve relatively small grants or loans, have encouraged marginalized people to invest not in livestock, which may die, or jewelry, which may be stolen, but in technological improvements such as small stoves.

■ Multinational Corporations

We have seen that globalization has not necessarily improved the lives of the poor in the developing world. Another trend that

Open displays of social inequality are apparent in every nation. In Mumbai, India, billionaire Mukesh Ambani built this 27-story home for his wife and three children, complete with three helicopter pads and a 160-vehicle garage. To run the building, Ambani employs a staff of 600.
© Frederic Soltan/Corbis

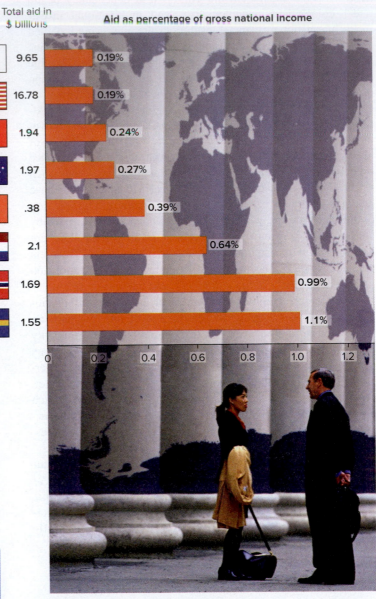

FIGURE 29-3 Foreign Aid Per Capita in Nine Countries

	Total aid in $ billions	Aid as percentage of gross national income
Japan	9.65	0.19%
USA	16.78	0.19%
Canada	1.94	0.24%
Australia	1.97	0.27%
Ireland	.38	0.39%
Netherlands	2.1	0.64%
Norway	1.69	0.99%
Sweden	1.55	1.1%

Note: Actual net development assistance in 2014.
Source: Organisation for Economic Co-Operation and Development 2015b.
Flags: © admin_design/Shutterstock RF; *photo:* © PhotoDisc Imaging/Getty Images RF

does not always serve developing countries well has been the rise of multinational corporations. Worldwide, corporate giants play a key role in neocolonialism. The term **multinational corporation** refers to commercial organizations that are headquartered in one country but do business throughout the world. Such private trade and lending relationships are not new; merchants have conducted business abroad for hundreds of years, trading gems, spices, garments, and other goods. However, today's multinational giants are not merely buying and selling overseas; they are also *producing* goods all over the world (Wallerstein 1974).

Moreover, today's "global factories" (factories throughout the developing world that are run by multinational corporations) may soon have the "global office" sitting alongside them.

FIGURE 29-4 Multinational Corporations Compared to Nations

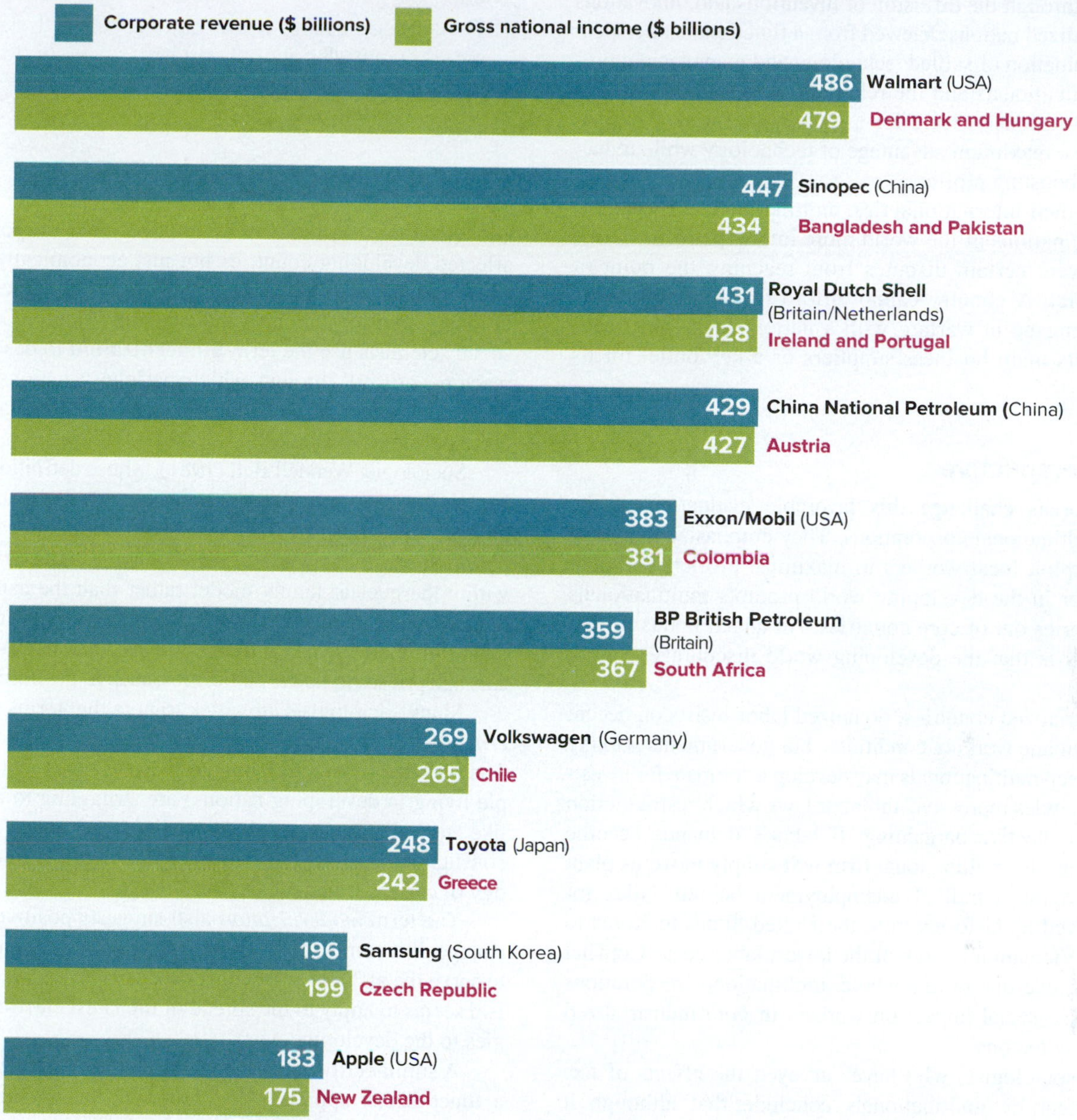

■ Corporate revenue ($ billions)　　■ Gross national income ($ billions)

486 Walmart (USA)
479 Denmark and Hungary

447 Sinopec (China)
434 Bangladesh and Pakistan

431 Royal Dutch Shell (Britain/Netherlands)
428 Ireland and Portugal

429 China National Petroleum (China)
427 Austria

383 Exxon/Mobil (USA)
381 Colombia

359 BP British Petroleum (Britain)
367 South Africa

269 Volkswagen (Germany)
265 Chile

248 Toyota (Japan)
242 Greece

196 Samsung (South Korea)
199 Czech Republic

183 Apple (USA)
175 New Zealand

Sources: Ranking prepared by author. Revenue from corporate quarterly report statements for 2014. GNI for 2014 (World Bank 2015c).

Multinationals based in core countries are beginning to establish reservation services and centers for processing data and insurance claims in periphery nations. As service industries become a more important part of the international marketplace, many companies are concluding that the low costs of overseas operations more than offset the expense of transmitting information around the world.

Do not underestimate the size of these global corporations. As Figure 29-4 shows, the total revenues of multinational businesses are on a par with the total value of goods and services exchanged in *entire nations*. Foreign sales represent an important source of profit for multinational corporations, which are constantly seeking to expand into other countries (in many cases, developing nations). The economy of the United States depends heavily on foreign commerce, much of which is conducted by multinationals. Over 12 percent of all goods and services produced in the United States relates to the export of goods to foreign countries, which supports an estimated 11 million jobs (Office of the United States Trade Representative 2016).

Functionalist and conflict theorists differ on the social and economic effects of multinational corporations, as we will see next.

Functionalist Perspective

Functionalists believe that multinational corporations can actually help the developing nations of the world. They bring jobs and industry to areas where subsistence agriculture once served as the only means of survival. Multinationals also promote rapid development through the diffusion of inventions and innovations from industrialized nations. Viewed from a functionalist perspective, the combination of skilled technology and management provided by multinationals and the relatively cheap labor available in developing nations is ideal for a global enterprise. Multinationals can take maximum advantage of technology while reducing costs and boosting profits.

Through their international ties, multinational corporations also make the nations of the world more interdependent. These ties may prevent certain disputes from reaching the point of serious conflict. A country cannot afford to sever diplomatic relations or engage in warfare with a nation that is the headquarters for its main business suppliers or a key outlet for its exports.

Conflict Perspective

Conflict theorists challenge this favorable evaluation of the impact of multinational corporations. They emphasize that multinationals exploit local workers to maximize profits. The pool of cheap labor in the developing world prompts multinationals to move factories out of core countries. An added bonus for the multinationals is that the developing world discourages strong trade unions.

In industrialized countries, organized labor insists on decent wages and humane working conditions, but governments seeking to attract or keep multinationals may develop a "climate for investment" that includes repressive antilabor laws which restrict union activity and collective bargaining. If labor's demands become too threatening, the multinational firm will simply move its plant elsewhere, leaving a trail of unemployment behind. Nike, for example, moved its factories from the United States to Korea to Indonesia to Vietnam in search of the lowest labor costs. Conflict theorists conclude that on the whole, multinational corporations have a negative social impact on workers in *both* industrialized and developing nations.

Several sociologists who have surveyed the effects of foreign investment by multinationals conclude that although it may at first contribute to a host nation's wealth, it eventually increases economic inequality within developing nations. This conclusion holds true for both income and land ownership. The upper and middle classes benefit most from economic expansion; the lower classes benefit least. As conflict theorists point out, multinationals invest in limited economic sectors and restricted regions of a nation. Although certain sectors of the host nation's economy expand, such as hotels and expensive restaurants, their very expansion appears to retard growth in agriculture and other economic sectors. Moreover, multinational corporations often buy out or force out local entrepreneurs and companies, thereby increasing economic and cultural dependence (Chase-Dunn and Grimes 1995; Kerbo 2012; Wallerstein 1979b).

© Photodisc Collection/Getty Images RF

use your **sociological imagination**

Think of something you bought recently that was made by a multinational corporation. How do you know the maker was a multinational?

Modernization

Globalization and the rise of multinational corporations have affected developing countries not just economically, but culturally. Around the world, millions of people are witnessing a revolutionary transformation of their day-to-day life. Contemporary social scientists use the term **modernization** to describe the far-reaching process through which periphery nations move from traditional or less developed institutions to those characteristic of more developed societies.

Sociologist Wendell Bell (1981), whose definition of modernization we are using, notes that modern societies tend to be urban, literate, and industrial. These societies have sophisticated transportation and media systems. Their families tend to be organized within the nuclear family model rather than the extended-family model. Thus, members of societies that undergo modernization must shift their allegiance from traditional authorities, such as parents and priests, to newer authorities, such as government officials.

Many sociologists are quick to note that terms such as *modernization* and even *development* contain an ethnocentric bias. The unstated assumption behind these terms is that "they" (people living in developing nations) are struggling to become more like "us" (people in core industrialized nations). Viewed from a conflict perspective, these terms perpetuate the dominant ideology of capitalist societies.

The term *modernization* also suggests positive change. Yet change, if it comes, often comes slowly, and when it does it tends to serve the affluent segments of industrialized nations. This truism seems to apply to the spread of the latest electronic technologies to the developing world.

A similar criticism has been made of **modernization theory,** a functionalist approach that proposes that modernization and development will gradually improve the lives of people in developing nations. According to this theory, even though nations develop at uneven rates, the development of peripheral nations will be assisted by innovations transferred from the industrialized world. Critics of modernization theory, including dependency theorists, counter that any such technology transfer only increases the dominance of core nations over developing nations and facilitates further exploitation.

When we see all the Coca-Cola and Apple signs going up in developing nations, it is easy to assume that globalization and economic change are effecting cultural change. But that is not always the case, researchers note. Distinctive cultural traditions, such as a particular religious orientation or a nationalistic identity, often persist and can soften the impact of modernization on a developing nation. Some contemporary

The commercial titled JEANS was done by Springer & Jacoby Werbung advertising agency for AGAINST CHILD LABOUR (a UNICEF campaign) in Germany. Copywriter: Sven Keitel; Art Director: Claudia Todt; Creative Director: Timm Weber/Bettina Olf

Where am I wearing? This UNICEF poster reminds affluent Western consumers that the brand-name jeans they wear may be produced by exploited workers in developing countries. In sweatshops throughout the developing world, nonunion garment workers—some of them children—labor long hours for what we would consider extremely low wages—even if for the workers in those semiperiphery countries, wages are relatively high.

sociologists emphasize that both industrialized and developing countries are "modern." Increasingly, researchers gauge modernization using a series of social indicators—among them degree of urbanization, energy use, literacy, political democracy, and use of birth control. Clearly, some of these are subjective indicators; even in industrialized nations, not everyone would agree that wider use of birth control is an example of progress (Armer and Katsillis 1992; Hedley 1992; Inglehart and Baker 2000).

Tracking Sociological Perspectives

TABLE 29-1 SOCIOLOGICAL PERSPECTIVES ON GLOBAL INEQUALITY

Approach	Sociological Perspective	Explanation
World systems analysis	Functionalist and conflict	Unequal economic and political relationships maintain sharp divisions between nations.
Dependency theory	Conflict	Industrialized nations exploit developing nations through colonialism and multinational corporations.
Modernization theory	Functionalist	Developing nations move away from traditional cultures and toward the cultures of industrialized nations.

Current modernization studies generally take a convergence perspective. Using the indicators just noted, researchers focus on how societies are moving closer together, despite traditional differences. From a conflict perspective, the modernization of developing nations often perpetuates their dependence on and continued exploitation by industrialized nations. Conflict theorists view such continuing dependence on foreign powers as an example of contemporary neocolonialism.

Table 29-1 summarizes the three major approaches to global inequality.

MODULE 29 | Recap and Review

Summary

Worldwide, stratification can be seen both in the gap between rich and poor nations and in the inequality within countries. This module examines the global divide and stratification within nations as well as the impact of **globalization, modernization,** and **multinational corporations** on developing countries.

1. Developing nations account for most of the world's population and most of its births, but they also bear the burden of most of its poverty, disease, and childhood deaths.

2. Former colonized nations are kept in a subservient position, subject to foreign domination, through the process of **neocolonialism.**

3. Drawing on the conflict perspective, Immanuel Wallerstein's **world systems analysis** views the global economic system as divided between nations that control wealth (core nations) and those from which capital is taken (periphery nations).

4. According to **dependency theory,** even as developing countries make economic advances, they remain weak and subservient to core nations and corporations in an increasingly integrated global economy.

5. **Globalization,** the worldwide integration of government policies, cultures, social movements, and financial markets through trade and the exchange of ideas, is a controversial trend that critics blame for contributing to the cultural domination of periphery nations by core nations.

6. **Multinational corporations** bring jobs and industry to developing nations, but they also tend to exploit workers in order to maximize profits.

7. Sociologists note that terms such as **modernization** and even development carry an ethnocentric bias. **Modernization theory** suggests that the development of periphery countries will be assisted by innovations transferred from the industrialized world.

Thinking Critically

1. Relate Durkheim's, Tönnies's, and Lenski's theories of social structure to the global divide that exists today. Could sociocultural evolution have something to do with the global divide?

2. Relate modernization theory to dependency theory. Do you agree with critics that modernization will increase the dominance of core nations? Why or why not?

Key Terms

Colonialism

Dependency theory

Globalization

Modernization

Modernization theory

Multinational corporation

Neocolonialism

World systems analysis

MODULE 30 — Stratification within Nations: A Comparative Perspective

At the same time that the gap between rich and poor nations is widening, so too is the gap between rich and poor citizens *within* nations. As discussed earlier, stratification in developing nations is closely related to their relatively weak and dependent position in the global economy. Local elites work hand in hand with multinational corporations and prosper from such alliances. At the same time, the economic system creates and perpetuates the exploitation of industrial and agricultural workers. That is why foreign investment in developing countries tends to increase economic inequality.

 use your sociological imagination

Imagine that the United States borders a country with a much higher standard of living. In this neighboring country, the salaries of workers with a college degree start at $120,000 a year. What is life in the United States like?

Distribution of Wealth and Income

Global inequality is staggering. Worldwide, the richest 2 percent of adults own more than 50 percent of the world's household wealth. In at least 17 nations around the world, the most affluent 10 percent of the population receives at least 40 percent of all income. Figure 30-1 compares the distribution of income in selected industrialized and developing nations (World Bank 2015c).

FIGURE 30-1 **Distribution of Income in Nine Nations**

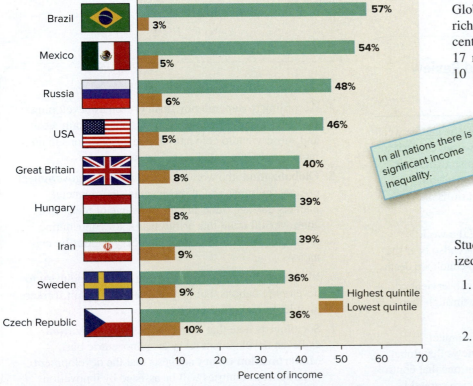

In all nations there is significant income inequality.

Highest quintile
Lowest quintile

Note: Data are considered comparable although based on statistics covering 2011 to 2013.
Source: World Bank 2015b. *Flags:* © admin_design/Shutterstock RF

Social Mobility

Mobility in Industrial Nations

Studies of intergenerational mobility in industrialized nations have found the following patterns:

1. Substantial similarities exist in the ways that parents' positions in the stratification system are transmitted to their children.

2. As in the United States, mobility opportunities in other nations have been influenced by structural factors, such as labor market changes that lead to the rise or decline of an occupational group within the social hierarchy.

3. Immigration continues to be a significant factor in shaping a society's level of intergenerational mobility.

Cross-cultural studies suggest that intergenerational mobility has been increasing over the past 50 years in most but not all countries. In particular, researchers have noted a common pattern of movement away from agriculture-based occupations. However, they are quick to point out that growth in mobility does not necessarily bring growth in equality. Indeed, despite the evidence of steady upward mobility, their studies show that the gap between the rich and the poor has grown. Over the past 30 years, poverty levels in the 30 largest industrial economies have remained relatively constant (Eurostat 2015; Organisation for Economic Co-operation and Development 2008).

Mobility in Developing Nations

Mobility patterns in industrialized countries are usually associated with both intergenerational and intragenerational mobility. However, in developing nations, macro-level social and economic changes often overshadow micro-level movement from one occupation to another. For example, there is typically a substantial wage differential between rural and urban areas, which leads to high levels of migration to the cities. Yet the urban industrial sectors of developing countries generally cannot provide sufficient employment for all those seeking work.

In large developing nations, the most socially significant mobility is the movement out of poverty. This type of mobility is difficult to measure and confirm, however, because economic trends can differ from one area of a country to another. As noted earlier in this chapter, in China, large numbers of people have moved out of poverty. However, income has not grown as rapidly in the rural areas of China as in the cities, or in some regions compared to others. In China, people who live in rural areas are basically shut out of the economic gains enjoyed by residents who live in centers of skilled labor and technology. Similarly, in India during the 1990s and through 2015, poverty declined in urban areas but may have remained static at best in rural areas. Around the world, downward social mobility is also dramatically influenced by catastrophes such as crop failure and warfare.

Despite the continuing struggles of massive numbers of people, the global economic situation is not entirely bleak. Although economists have documented the persistence of poverty around the world despite some gains, they have also noted some growth in the number of people who enjoy a middle-class lifestyle. At the beginning of the 21st century, millions of people entered the middle class in the populous nations of China, India, Russia, Brazil, and Mexico. Entrepreneurship, microfinancing, merchandising, and in some countries, a growing, relatively well-paid government sector have fostered this increase in upward social mobility (Beddoes 2012; India, Government of 2009).

In Box 30-1 we consider how people today see their opportunities for advancement. Is there a difference between the way people view this crucial question in developing and rich economies?

Gender Differences in Mobility

Women in developing countries find life especially difficult. The last two weeks of 2015 were declared by the African Women's

© Eco Images/Universal Images Group/Getty Images

In developing countries, people who hope to rise out of poverty often move from the country to the city, where employment prospects are better. The jobs available in industrialized urban areas offer perhaps the best means of upward mobility. These women work in a T-shirt factory in San José, Costa Rica.

Development Fund the "16 Days of Activism Against Gender Based Violence." This campaign was part of a global effort to organize strategies by individuals and groups to eliminate all forms of violence against women, including sexual violence, child marriages, and violence within schools (African Women's Development Fund 2015).

The challenges to girls and women are not limited to any one continent. Karuna Chanana Ahmed, an anthropologist from India who has studied women in developing nations, calls women the most exploited of oppressed people. Beginning at birth women face sex discrimination. They are commonly fed less than male children, are denied educational opportunities, and are often hospitalized only when they are critically ill. Inside or outside the home, women's work is devalued. When economies fail, as they did in Asian countries in the late 1990s, women were the first to be laid off from work (J. Anderson and Moore 1993; Kristof 1998).

Surveys show a significant degree of *female infanticide* (the killing of baby girls) in China and rural areas of India. Only one-third of Pakistan's sexually segregated schools are for women, and one-third of those schools have no buildings. In Saudi Arabia, women are prohibited from driving, walking alone in public, and socializing with men outside their families.

Only recently have researchers begun to investigate the impact of gender on the mobility patterns of developing nations. Many aspects of the development process—especially modernization in rural areas and the rural-to-urban migration just described—may result in the modification or abandonment of traditional cultural practices and even marital systems. The effects on women's social standing and mobility are not necessarily positive. As a country develops and modernizes, women's vital role in food production deteriorates, jeopardizing both their autonomy and their material well-being. Moreover, the movement of families to the cities weakens women's ties to relatives who can provide food, financial assistance, and social support (Lawson 2008; United Nations Secretary General 2014).

Box 30-1

Sociology in the Global Community

Getting Ahead Globally

Surveys of public opinion across 44 nations show some consistent views about mobility and getting ahead. A majority of people in all these countries believe that getting a good education and working hard are key to getting ahead. But in these same countries, majorities agree that the gap between the rich and the poor is a problem.

So what are the opportunities for mobility? Generally the poorer the country, the more optimistic people are that their children will grow up to be financially better off than they are themselves. As shown in the accompanying figure, adults in industrial countries are more cautious that their children will improve. For example, only 13 percent of French people believe their children will get ahead, compared to 63 percent in Senegal, a former French colony in Africa.

However, despite this optimism about their children's future, in some countries a large proportion of people see more opportunities abroad than at home. For example, 23 percent of Mexicans and 42 percent of Senegalese recommend that young people move abroad for "a good life." Yet even in nations that face massive social challenges, staying at home is heavily favored. For example 53 percent of parents in the Palestinian Territory and 66 percent in Pakistan recommend that their children stay at home.

When parents counsel young people to go abroad, it is most often to industrial coun-

FIGURE 9-3 Will Children, When They Grow Up, Be Better Off Than Their Parents?

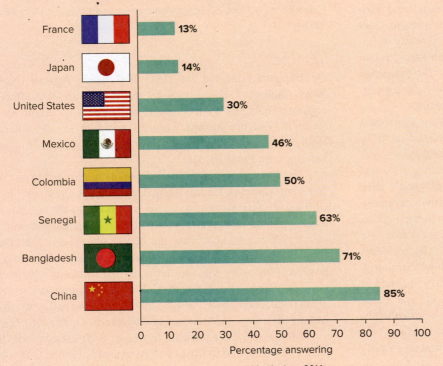

Percentage answering

> Generally the poorer the country, the more optimistic people are that their children will grow up to be financially better off than they are themselves.

tries, even though they understand the great disparity between rich and poor in those nations. Economic optimism seems to be greatest when the parents' own status is the most marginal. These findings point to the need to frame discussions of social mobility within the context of a particular society.

LET'S DISCUSS

1. Are your relatives optimistic about your economic future? Are you? On what factors do you base your opinion?
2. Why do you think people in poor countries are more optimistic about their children's futures than those in rich ones?

Note: Selected results from a 44-nation survey conducted March–June 2014.
Source: Pew Research Center 2014b:7.
Flags: © admin_design/Shutterstock RF

Sources: Banyan 2014; Pew Research Center 2014b.

In the Philippines, however, women have moved to the forefront of the indigenous peoples' struggle to protect their ancestral land from exploitation by outsiders. Having established their right to its rich minerals and forests, members of indigenous groups had begun to feud among themselves over the way in which the land's resources should be developed. Aided by the United Nations Partners in Development Programme, women volunteers established the Pan-Cordillera Women's Network for Peace and Development, a coalition of women's groups dedicated to resolving local disputes. The women mapped boundaries, prepared development plans, and negotiated more than 2,000 peace pacts among community members. They have also run in elections, campaigned against social problems, and organized residents to work together for the common good (United Nations Development Programme 2000:87; United Nations Secretary General 2014).

Studies of the distribution of wealth and income within various countries, together with cross-cultural research on mobility, consistently reveal stratification based on class, gender, and other factors within a wide range of societies.

Clearly, a worldwide view of stratification must include not only the sharp contrast *between* wealthy and impoverished nations but also the layers of hierarchy *within* industrialized nations and developing nations. In the Social Policy section that follows, we will see that even in the relatively wealthy countries of Europe and North America, significant numbers of families require assistance from the government to meet their basic needs.

social
policy and Global Inequality|
Rethinking Welfare in Europe and North America

In Pasadena, California, Denise Sims-Bowles, who has been out of work for more than three years, has sent 273 résumés to prospective employers. A victim of the deep economic recession and jobless recovery that followed the stock market crash of 2008, she has more than two decades of experience as a white-collar worker, yet she cannot find an opening. Her experience is a common one. Nationwide, the average duration of unemployment in the period ending in October 2015 was 28 weeks (Bureau of Labor Statistics 2015e).

In Barcelona, Spain, Paco Gonzalez, a former bank cashier, worries about the future. The 70-year-old once dreamed of a quiet retirement near the beach; now he fears his pension may not outlive him. The European economic crisis has pushed Spain's government to the brink, forcing officials to make difficult budget cuts (Somaskanda 2012).

In Athens, Greece, where the economic collapse was so bad that the nation had to be bailed out by the European Union, the story is even worse. Anargyros D., reluctant to give his last name, has lost everything—his father's business, his home, his personal possessions. Among men his age, the unemployment rate has more than doubled since 2008. His father is supporting him now, on a government pension that has been cut by a third. Looking broken, Anargyros says he has entertained thoughts of suicide. He is not alone. Calls to a local suicide help line have doubled in the last two years (Hay 2009; R. Scherer 2010a, 2010c; L. Thomas Jr. 2011; Wessel 2011).

These are the faces of people living on the edge. In a time of economic stress and growing need, governments in all parts of the world are searching for the right solution to welfare: How much subsidy should they provide? How much responsibility should fall on the shoulders of the poor?

Looking at the Issue

In the 1990s, an intense debate took place in the United States over the issue of welfare. Welfare programs were costly, and concern was widespread (however unfounded) that welfare payments discouraged recipients from seeking jobs. Both Democrats and Republicans vowed to "end welfare as we know it."

In late 1996, in a historic shift in federal policy, Congress passed the Personal Responsibility and Work Opportunity Reconciliation Act, ending the long-standing federal guarantee of assistance to every poor family that meets eligibility requirements. The law set a lifetime limit of five years of welfare benefits, and required all able-bodied adults to work after receiving two years of benefits (although hardship exceptions were allowed). Since then the federal government has awarded grants to the states to use as they wish in assisting poor and needy residents, presumably to permit states to experiment with ways to move people off welfare (Center on Budget and Policy Priorities 2015).

In the United States, the government safety net now falls far short of

© Pascal Saez/Alamy

In northern and western Europe, following the deep worldwide recession that began in 2008, countries with strong social safety nets were forced to cut back benefits. These civil servants in Granada, Spain, are protesting salary cutbacks.

—*Continued*

that in Europe, even after recent cutbacks there. Available data indicate that in Great Britain, 84 percent of health expenditures are paid for by the government; in Sweden, 82 percent; in Canada, 70 percent; but in the United States, only 47 percent. In fact, most industrialized nations devote higher proportions of their expenditures to housing, social security, welfare, health care, and unemployment compensation than the United States does. Even during the Great Recession, the increase in social spending in the United States was relatively modest. As U.S. economist Dean Baker declared, "We're not France" (Cauchon 2009; World Bank 2015f).

Applying Sociology

Many sociologists tend to view the debate over welfare reform in industrialized nations from a conflict perspective: the "haves" in positions of policymaking listen to the interests of other "haves," while the cries of the "have-nots" are drowned out. Critics of welfare reform believe that the nation's economic problems are unfairly blamed on welfare spending and the poor. From a conflict perspective, this backlash against welfare recipients reflects deep fears and hostility toward the nation's urban, predominantly African American and Hispanic underclass.

Those who are critical of the backlash note that "welfare scapegoating" conveniently ignores the lucrative federal handouts that go to *affluent* individuals and families. For example, while federal housing aid to the poor was cut drastically in the 1980s, tax deductions for mortgage interest and property taxes more than doubled.

Conflict theorists have noted an oft-ignored aspect of the welfare system, administrative sanctions. The law allows administrators to end welfare payments if clients fail to complete job-readiness classes, community work, or job searches. A great deal of discretion is used in applying sanctions. According to one study, Black clients are more likely to be sanctioned than White clients (Schram et al. 2009).

Those who take a conflict perspective also urge policymakers and the general public to look closely at **corporate welfare**—the tax breaks, bailouts, direct payments, and grants that the government gives to corporations—rather than looking closely at the comparatively small allowances being given to mothers and their children. Yet any suggestion to curtail such corporate welfare brings a strong response from special-interest groups that are much more powerful than any coalition on behalf of the poor. One example of corporate welfare is the huge federal bailouts given to distressed financial institutions in fall 2008 and to bankrupt automobile companies in 2009. Although the outlay of hundreds of billions of dollars was vital to the nation's economic recovery, the measure received relatively little scrutiny from Congress. Just a few months later, however, when legislation was proposed to extend the safety net for laid-off workers—unemployment compensation, food stamps, subsidized child care, assistance to the homeless, disability support, and infant nutrition—it met with loud demands for the monitoring of expenditures (DeParle 2009; Piven and Cloward 1996).

Initiating Policy

The government likes to highlight welfare-reform success stories. Though many people who once depended on tax dollars are now working and paying taxes themselves, it is much too soon to see if "workfare" will be successful. The new jobs that were generated by the booming economy of the late 1990s were an unrealistic test of the system. Prospects have faded for the hard-core jobless—people who are difficult to train or are encumbered by drug or alcohol abuse, physical disabilities, or child care needs—since that boom passed.

True, fewer people remain on the rolls since welfare reform was enacted in August 1996. By June 2015 just under 1.4 million families were still on the rolls, less than one third of the high of 5.1 million in 1994. But while those families that have left the rolls are modestly better off now, most of their breadwinners continue to hold low-paying, unskilled jobs. For them, the Great Recession that was well in place by 2009 made finding work tougher than ever. Of those adults who remain on welfare, nearly 70 percent are not in school or in welfare-to-work programs, as the law requires them to be. This group tends to face the greatest challenges—substance abuse, mental illness, or a criminal record (Bitler and Hoynes 2010; Danziger 2010; Department of Health and Human Services 2015).

European governments have encountered many of the same citizen demands as in North America: keep our taxes low, even if it means reducing services to the poor. However, nations in eastern and central Europe have faced a special challenge since the end of communism. Though governments in those nations traditionally provided an impressive array of social services, they differed from capitalist systems in several important respects. First, the communist system was premised on full employment, so there was no need to provide unemployment insurance; social services focused on the old and the disabled. Second, subsidies for housing and even utilities played an important role. With new competition from the West and tight budgets, some of these countries are beginning to realize that universal coverage is no longer affordable and must be replaced with targeted programs.

The reduction in state assistance to the unemployed is not limited to the former Soviet bloc. Even Denmark, despite its long history of social welfare programs, is feeling the pinch. Student stipends are being reduced, early retirement plans have been reduced, and the maximum time for receiving unemployment benefits has been cut in half (although it is still a generous *two years*). Yet by any standard, the European

—Continued

safety net is still significantly stronger than that of the United States (Daley 2013; Petrášová 2006).

This decline in public assistance has not escaped public attention. Erik O. Wright, 2012 president of the American Sociological Society, has observed that the Occupy Wall Street movement "is not a uniquely American event . . . it is part of a global wave of protests." Wright senses rising concern that "harsh inequalities" are becoming "increasingly illegitimate. It would appear the present trends in welfare policy are doing little to address these concerns" (E. O. Wright 2011).

MODULE 30 | Recap and Review

Summary

This module examines the effects of stratification within nations.

1. The global economic system creates and perpetuates the gap between the rich and poor in developing nations.

2. Intergenerational mobility has been increasing over the past 50 years in most but not all countries. In large developing nations, the most socially significant mobility is the movement out of poverty.

3. Gender differences in mobility exist in both developed and developing societies. Women tend to have more difficulties moving up the economic ladder at all phases of the life course.

4. In Europe and North America, countries have been forced to cut back welfare programs after a deep

recession drained their treasuries. Even Denmark, known worldwide for its social safety net, has had to cut benefits.

Thinking Critically

1. Contrast social mobility in developing and industrial nations. Do you think the differences will eventually disappear? Why or why not?

2. What social structural factors contribute to making women "the most exploited of oppressed people"?

Key Terms

Corporate welfare

Mastering This Chapter

© Stockbyte/Getty Images

taking sociology with you

1 Pick a multinational corporation whose products you are familiar with and look up its financial statements. In which countries does the corporation produce products and in which does it sell products? In which country does the corporation pay taxes? To which country do its profits flow? Why should the answers to these questions matter to you?

2 Choose a foreign country that you are interested in and do some research on social stratification in that country. How equally or unequally are wealth and income distributed there, in comparison to the United States? How extensive is social mobility? Explain the reasons for any differences in stratification.

3 Choose a European country and a developing country and do some research on their welfare systems. How do the two systems differ? How does each reflect the culture and society it serves?

key terms

Colonialism The maintenance of political, social, economic, and cultural domination over a people by a foreign power for an extended period.

Corporate welfare Tax breaks, bailouts, direct payments, and grants that the government gives to corporations.

Dependency theory An approach that contends that industrialized nations continue to exploit developing countries for their own gain.

Globalization The worldwide integration of government policies, cultures, social movements, and financial markets through trade and the exchange of ideas.

Modernization The far-reaching process through which periphery nations move from traditional or less developed institutions to those characteristic of more developed societies.

Modernization theory A functionalist approach that proposes that modernization and development will gradually improve the lives of people in developing nations.

Multinational corporation A commercial organization that is headquartered in one country but does business throughout the world.

Neocolonialism Continuing dependence of former colonies on foreign countries.

World systems analysis The global economy as an interdependent system of economically and politically unequal nations.

self-quiz

Read each question carefully and then select the best answer.

1. The maintenance of political, social, economic, and cultural domination over a people by a foreign power for an extended period is referred to as
   a. neocolonialism.
   b. government-imposed stratification.
   c. colonialism.
   d. dependency.

2. In viewing the global economic system as divided between nations that control wealth and those that are controlled and exploited, sociologist Immanuel Wallerstein draws on the
   a. functionalist perspective.
   b. conflict perspective.
   c. interactionist perspective.
   d. dramaturgical approach.

3. Which of the following nations would Immanuel Wallerstein classify as a *core* country within the world economic system?
   a. Germany
   b. South Korea
   c. Ireland
   d. Mexico

4. In reviewing the results of the United Nations Millenium Development Goals project, which nation has made the most dramatic change in reducing poverty?
   a. India
   b. China
   c. Greece
   d. United States

5. Which statement about multinational corporations is correct?
   a. They often produce goods in many nations.
   b. While large, they are not as economically big as entire countries.
   c. They are relatively new, emerging only in the last 30 years.
   d. They typically depend on domestic rather than foreign sales.

6. Which sociological perspective argues that multinational corporations can actually help the developing nations of the world?
   a. the interactionist perspective
   b. the feminist perspective
   c. the functionalist perspective
   d. the conflict perspective

7. Which of the following terms is used by contemporary social scientists to describe the far-reaching process by which peripheral nations move from traditional or less developed institutions to those characteristic of more developed societies?
   a. dependency
   b. globalization
   c. industrialization
   d. modernization

8. Which statement about inequality within nations is correct?
   a. Inequality in wealth and income are about the same.
   b. Inequality in income is much greater than inequality in wealth.
   c. Inequality in wealth is much greater than inequality in income.
   d. There is little inequality in either income or wealth.

9. In at least 17 nations around the world, the most affluent 10 percent receives at least what percentage of all income?
   a. 20 percent
   b. 30 percent
   c. 40 percent
   d. 50 percent

10. Karuna Chanana Ahmed, an anthropologist from India who has studied developing nations, calls which group the most exploited of oppressed people?
   a. children
   b. women
   c. the elderly
   d. the poor

11. Colonial domination established patterns of economic exploitation leading to former colonies remaining dependent on more industrialized nations. Such continuing dependence and foreign domination are referred to as _____.

12. According to Immanuel Wallerstein's analysis, the United States is at the _____ while neighboring Mexico is on the _____ of the world economic system.

13. Wallerstein's world systems analysis is the most widely used version of _____ theory.

14. In many developing nations, _____ is defined as the minimum income a person needs to survive, typically $1 to $2 a day.

15. _____ factories are factories found throughout the developing world that are run by multinational corporations.

16. As _____ industries become a more important part of the international marketplace, many companies have concluded that the low costs of overseas operations more than offset the expense of transmitting information around the world.

17. Viewed from a(n) _____ perspective, the combination of skilled technology and management provided by multinationals and the relatively cheap labor available in developing nations is ideal for a global enterprise.

18. Modernization theory reflects the _____ perspective.

19. In large developing nations, the most significant form of social mobility is the movement out of _____.

20. Tax breaks, bailouts, direct payments, and grants are all forms of _____ _____ .

10 Racial and Ethnic Inequality

© RosalreneBetancourt 3/Alamy

U.S. society is becoming increasingly diverse as immigrants from around the world bring their skills, languages, and cultures with them to their new home. Pictured here are new citizens reciting the Pledge of Allegiance as part of an Oath of Citizenship ceremony in Miami Beach, Florida.

Courtesy of Charles Trimble. Photo by Don Doll SJ

Have you ever been torn between fitting in and being true to who you are?

Charles Trimble has been rethinking that trade-off.

❝ I am an Iyeska, a mixed-blood—Oglala Lakota and bits of European nationalities, mostly Irish and English. Over the years we were called half-breeds, breeds, as well as various other names from both sides of our ancestry, many of them unprintable.

Iyeska in Lakota translates as "speaks white," but through the years has taken on the generic term for "mixed blood." What I write here comes from my own experiences as an Iyeska, and from what I have observed among Iyeskas I have known.

Whether or not we admit it, most of the mixed blood kids that I knew in the Indian boarding school I attended and in my home village on the Pine Ridge Reservation through the 1940s and 50s wished sometimes that we were not Indian at all. That came perhaps from seeing movies and reading books in which the white guys always won, had all the money, nice cars and girls. Indians were always the bad guys, killing innocent settlers who only wanted us dead and our land theirs. And in most towns on the reservation, the stores and other businesses were owned by whites. In reservation border towns, we often faced discrimination. In short, our futures sometimes didn't look all that promising as Indians.

So we bought into what was being pushed on us anyway: assimilation; and we acted out what was expected of us to get jobs and fit into the larger society. . . .

We need to take pride in our Indianness, no matter how thin our tribal blood quantum; but we also need to give some credit to our white or Latino or black forebears.

In the schools, there was often a sense of superiority among Iyeskas over the full-bloods, and sometimes there was tension between them. "Buck" was a common term used to describe a person who the Iyeska considered backward—mainly full-bloods. But an Iyeska didn't say it too loudly, because many of the best athletes and the toughest boys were full-bloods.

It seems to me that during our growing-up years, we used our white characteristics to our advantage in getting scholarships and employment opportunities, and now that there are more opportunities for Indians—especially from casino earnings—we want to take back our Indianness, at least in our fantasies.

Admittedly, what I have written above could be seen as cynical or even mean. I admit that the scenario applies to me to a greater or lesser degree, or I would not have written it. It is true that most Iyeskas who stayed on the reservation are very comfortable in their status, and their relations in their communities. And many Iyeskas are very serious in their search to find their roots and a culture they may feel to have been deprived of. For whatever reason they may have "returned to the blanket," some are happy in finding that special goodness and peace that can be found in traditional life.

But for many of us Iyeskas, I think that perhaps it's time to quit trying to impress white people and younger generations of Indians with fantasy stories of another life, or blaming someone else for having given up a culture that was largely peripheral to our lives anyway. We need to take pride in our Indianness, no matter how thin our tribal blood quantum; but we also need to give some credit to our White or Latino or black forebears. The inner peace of living a real life, with a true life story, is worth it. ❞

(Trimble 2008:5)

I n this excerpt from "Iyeska: Notes from Mixed-Blood Country," Charles Trimble, scholar, journalist, and former executive director of the National Congress for American Indians, recalls his childhood as a mixed-blood Indian from the Pine Ridge Reservation in South Dakota. A member of the Oglala Lakota Sioux, Trimble attended a boarding school where Native American youths were pressed to renounce their tribal heritage and adopt White culture instead. Although he went on to succeed in mainstream American society, later in life he began to question the choice he had made as a youth. "Who am I, really?" Trimble seems to ask himself in these notes.

What sense are we to make of the issues of race, ethnicity, and immigration in the 21st century? Today, members of racial and ethnic minorities still struggle with the question of whether to assimilate. As they age, many look back with regret. Too often, those who do assimilate face continued prejudice and discrimination. Like class, race and ethnicity still affect people's place and status in a stratification system, not only in this country, but throughout the world. High incomes, a good command of English, and hard-earned professional credentials do not always override racial and ethnic stereotypes or protect those who fit them from the sting of racism.

What is prejudice, and how is it institutionalized in the form of discrimination? In what ways have race and ethnicity affected the experience of immigrants from other countries? What are the fastest-growing minority groups in the United States today? In these modules we will focus on the meaning of race and ethnicity. We will begin by identifying the basic characteristics of a minority group and distinguishing between racial and ethnic groups. Then we will examine the dynamics of prejudice and discrimination. After considering four sociological perspectives on race and ethnicity, we'll take a look at common patterns of intergroup relations. The following section will describe the major racial and ethnic groups in the United States. Finally, in the Social Policy section we will explore the global refugee crisis of the early 21st century.

MODULE 31 — Minority, Racial, and Ethnic Groups

Sociologists frequently distinguish between racial and ethnic groups. The term **racial group** describes a group that is set apart from others because of physical differences that have taken on social significance. Whites, African Americans, and Asian Americans are all considered racial groups in the United States. While race does turn on physical differences, it is the culture of a particular society that constructs and attaches social significance to those differences, as we will see later. Unlike racial groups, an **ethnic group** is set apart from others primarily because of its national origin or distinctive cultural patterns. In the United States, Puerto Ricans, Jews, and Polish Americans are all categorized as ethnic groups (Table 31-1).

Minority Groups

A numerical minority is any group that makes up less than half of some larger population. The population of the United States includes thousands of numerical minorities, including television actors, green-eyed people, tax lawyers, and descendants of the Pilgrims who arrived on the *Mayflower*. However, these numerical minorities are not considered to be minorities in the sociological sense; in fact, the number of people in a group does not necessarily determine its status as a social minority (or a dominant group). When sociologists define a minority group, they are concerned primarily with the economic and political power, or powerlessness, of that group. A **minority group** is a subordinate group whose members have significantly less control or power over their own lives than the members of a dominant or majority group have over theirs.

Sociologists have identified five basic properties of a minority group: unequal treatment, physical or cultural traits, ascribed status, solidarity, and in-group marriage (Wagley and Harris 1958):

1. Members of a minority group experience unequal treatment compared to members of a dominant group. For example, the management of an apartment complex may refuse to rent to African Americans, Hispanics, or Jews. Social inequality may be created or maintained by prejudice, discrimination, segregation, or even extermination.

2. Members of a minority group share physical or cultural characteristics that distinguish them from the dominant group.

Each society arbitrarily decides which characteristics are most important in defining groups.

3. Membership in a minority (or dominant) group is not voluntary; people are born into the group. Thus, race and ethnicity are considered *ascribed* statuses.

4. Minority group members have a strong sense of group solidarity. William Graham Sumner, writing in 1906, noted that people make distinctions between members of their own group (the *in-group*) and everyone else (the *out-group*). When a group is the object of long-term prejudice and discrimination, the feeling of "us versus them" can and often does become extremely intense.

5. Members of a minority group generally marry others from the same group. A member of a dominant group is often unwilling to marry into a supposedly inferior minority group. In addition, the minority group's sense of solidarity encourages marriage within the group and discourages marriage to outsiders.

Race

Many people think of race as a series of biological classifications. However, research shows that is not a meaningful way of differentiating people. Genetically, there are no systematic differences between the races that affect people's social behavior and abilities. Instead, sociologists use the term *racial group* to refer to those minorities (and the corresponding dominant groups) who are set apart from others by obvious physical differences. But what is an "obvious" physical difference? Each society labels those differences that people consider important, while ignoring other characteristics that could serve as a basis for social differentiation.

Social Construction of Race

Because race is a social construction, the process of defining races typically benefits those who have more power and privilege than others. In the United States, we see differences in both skin color and hair color. Yet people learn informally that differences in skin color have a dramatic social and political meaning, whereas differences in hair color do not.

When observing skin color, many people in the United States tend to lump others rather casually into the traditional categories of "Black," "White," and "Asian." Subtle differences in skin color often go unnoticed. In many nations of Central America and South America, in contrast, people recognize color gradients

TABLE 31-1 RACIAL AND ETHNIC GROUPS IN THE UNITED STATES, 2014

Classification	Number in Thousands	Percentage of Total Population
Racial Groups		
Whites (non-Hispanic)	195,371	60.3
Blacks/African Americans	37,686	12.2
Native Americans, Alaskan Natives	2,247	0.7
Asian Americans	15,553	5.0
Chinese	3,347	1.1
Asian Indians	2,843	0.9
Filipinos	2,556	0.8
Vietnamese	1,548	0.5
Koreans	1,424	0.5
Japanese	763	0.2
Pacific Islanders, Native Hawaiians	1,847	0.6
Other Asian Americans	1,225	0.5
Arab Americans	1,517	0.5
Two or more races	9,009	2.9
Ethnic Groups		
White ancestry		
Germans	49,341	16.0
Irish	35,664	11.6
English	26,873	8.7
Italians	17,486	5.7
Poles	9,757	3.2
French	9,159	3.0
Scottish and Scots-Irish	9,122	3.0
Jews	6,452	2.1
Hispanics (or Latinos)	50,478	16.4
Mexican Americans	31,798	10.3
Puerto Ricans	4,624	1.5
Cubans	1,785	0.6
Salvadorans	1,648	0.5
Dominicans	1,415	0.5
Guatemalans	1,044	0.3
Other Hispanics	8,164	2.7
TOTAL (all groups)	**308,746**	

Note: All data are for 2014 except White Ancestry data, which are estimates, based on 2009-2013 5-year data. Percentages do not total 100 percent, and when subcategories are added they do not match totals in major categories because of overlap between groups (e.g., Polish American Jews or people of mixed ancestry such as Irish and Italian).

Sources: American Community Survey 2013:DP02; 2014: B02018, C03002; 2015:B03001; Asi and Beaulieu 2013; Bureau of the Census 2015e: PEPSR5H; Sheskin and Dashefsky 2015: 14.

on a continuum from light to dark skin color. Brazil has approximately 40 color groupings, while in other countries people may be described as "Mestizo Hondurans," "Mulatto Colombians," or "African Panamanians." What we see as "obvious" differences, then, are subject to each society's social definitions.

The largest racial minorities in the United States are African Americans (or Blacks), Native Americans (or American Indians), and Asian Americans (Japanese Americans, Chinese Americans, and other Asian peoples). Figure 31-1 provides information about the population of racial and ethnic groups in the United States over the past five centuries, projected through 2060.

The racial and ethnic composition of what is today the United States has been undergoing change not just for the past 50 years, but for the past 500. Five centuries ago the land was populated only by indigenous Native Americans.

Given current population patterns, it is clear that the nation's diversity will continue to increase. In 2011, for the first time ever, census data revealed that the majority of all children ages three and under are now either Hispanic or non-White. This turning point marked the beginning of a pattern in which the nation's minority population will slowly become the majority. By 2014, the majority people under age 18 in the United States belonged to racial or ethnic minority groups (Colby and Ortman 2015).

Racial definitions are crystallized through what Michael Omi and Howard Winant (2015) have called **racial formation,** a sociohistorical process in which racial categories are created, inhabited, transformed, and destroyed. In this process, those who have power define groups of people according to a racist social structure. The creation of a reservation system for Native Americans in the late 1800s, which later influenced Charles Trimble's life and work, is one example of racial formation. Federal officials combined what were distinctive tribes into a single racial group, which we refer to today as Native Americans. The extent and frequency with which peoples are subject to racial formation is such that no one escapes it.

Another example of racial formation from the 1800s was known as the "one-drop rule." If a person had even a single drop of "Black blood," that person was defined and viewed as Black, even if he or she *appeared* to be White. Clearly, race had social significance, enough so that White legislators established official standards about who was "Black" and who was "White."

The one-drop rule was a vivid example of the *social construction of race*—the process by which people come to define a group as a race based in part on physical characteristics, but also on historical, cultural, and economic factors. For example, in the 1800s, immigrant groups such as Italian and Irish Americans were not at first seen as being "White," but as foreigners who were not necessarily trustworthy. The social construction of race is an ongoing process that is subject to debate, especially in a diverse society such as the United States, where each year increasing numbers of children are born to parents of different racial backgrounds.

Recognition of Multiple Identities

In 1900, in an address to the Anti-Slavery Union in London, scholar W. E. B. DuBois predicted that "the color line" would become the foremost problem of the 20th century. DuBois, born a free Black man in 1868, had witnessed prejudice and discrimination throughout the United States. His comment was prophetic. Today, over a century later, race and ethnicity still carry enormous weight in the United States (DuBois [1900] 1969).

The color line has blurred significantly since 1900, however. Interracial marriage is no longer forbidden by law and custom. Thus, Geetha Lakshmi-narayanan, a native of Ann Arbor, Michigan, is both White and Asian Indian. Often mistaken for a Filipina or Latina, she has grown accustomed to the blunt question "What are you?" (Navarro 2005).

In the late 20th century, with immigration from Latin America rising, the fluid nature of racial formation became evident. Suddenly, people were speaking about the "Latin Americanization" of the United States, or about a biracial, Black/White society being replaced by a triracial one. In the 2010 Census, over 9 million people in the United States (or about 2.9 percent of the population) reported that they were of two or more races. Half the people classified as multiracial were under age 18, suggesting that this segment of the population will grow in the years to come. People who claimed both White and American Indian ancestry, like Charles Trimble (see the chapter-opening excerpt), were the largest group of multiracial residents (Bonilla-Silva 2004; Humes et al. 2011).

This statistical finding of millions of multiracial people obscures how individuals are often asked to handle their identity. For example, the enrollment forms for government programs typically include only a few broad racial-ethnic categories. This approach to racial categorization is part of a long history that dictates single-race identities. Still, many individuals, especially young adults, struggle against social pressure to choose a single identity, and instead openly embrace multiple heritages. Public figures, rather than hide their mixed ancestry, now flaunt it. Singer Mariah Carey celebrates her Irish American background, and President Barack Obama speaks of being born in Hawai'i to a Kenyan father and a White mother from Kansas.

💡 use your sociological imagination

Using a TV remote control, how quickly do you think you could find a television show in which all the characters share your racial or ethnic background? What about a show in which all the characters share a different background from yours—how quickly could you find one?

🟧 Ethnicity

An ethnic group, unlike a racial group, is set apart from others because of its national origin or distinctive cultural patterns. Among the ethnic groups in the United States are peoples with a Spanish-speaking background, referred to collectively as *Latinos* or *Hispanics,* such as Puerto Ricans, Mexican Americans, Cuban Americans, and other Latin Americans. Other ethnic groups in this country include Jewish, Irish, Italian, and Norwegian Americans.

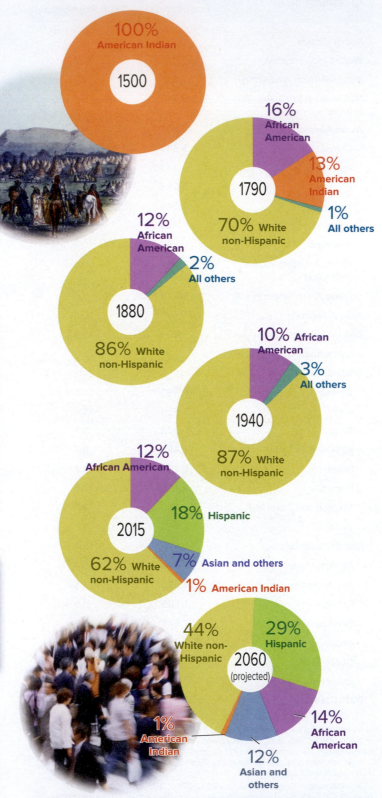

FIGURE 31-1 Racial and Ethnic Groups in the United States, 1500–2060 (Projected)

1500 — 100% American Indian

1790 — 70% White non-Hispanic; 16% African American; 13% American Indian; 1% All others

1880 — 86% White non-Hispanic; 12% African American; 2% All others

1940 — 87% White non-Hispanic; 10% African American; 3% All others

2015 — 62% White non-Hispanic; 18% Hispanic; 12% African American; 7% Asian and others; 1% American Indian

2060 (projected) — 44% White non-Hispanic; 29% Hispanic; 14% African American; 12% Asian and others; 1% American Indian

Sources: Author's estimate; Bureau of the Census 2004a, 2013b; Colby and Ortman 2015:9. *Photos: Native Americans:* Library of Congress Prints and Photographs Division [LC-USZC2-1745]; *Crowd:* © Ken Usami/Photodisc/Getty Images RF

Although these groupings are convenient, they serve to obscure differences *within* ethnic categories (as in the case of Hispanics), as well as to overlook the mixed ancestry of so many people in the United States.

Man: © Juanmonino/Getty Images RF; Woman: © Motofish Images/Corbis

Today, some children of mixed-race families identify themselves as biracial or multiracial, rejecting efforts to place them in a single racial category.

The distinction between racial and ethnic minorities is not always clear-cut. Some members of racial minorities, such as Asian Americans, may have significant cultural differences from other racial groups. At the same time, certain ethnic minorities, such as Latinos, may have obvious physical differences that set them apart from other ethnic groups in the United States.

Despite categorization problems, sociologists continue to feel that the distinction between racial groups and ethnic groups is socially significant. In most societies, including the United States, socially constructed physical differences tend to be more visible than ethnic differences. Partly as a result of this fact, stratification along racial lines is more resistant to change than stratification along ethnic lines. Over time, members of an ethnic minority can sometimes become indistinguishable from the majority—although the process may take generations and may never include all members of the group. In contrast, members of a racial minority find it much more difficult to blend in with the larger society and gain acceptance from the majority.

● Prejudice and Discrimination

Looking at the United States in the 21st century, some people wonder aloud if race and ethnicity are still relevant to social stratification. After all, African Americans have served as secretary of state, secretary of defense, chairman of the Joint Chiefs of Staff, and, most notably, president of the United States; the office of attorney general has been held by both an African American and a Hispanic. As historic as these leaders' achievements have been, however, in every case their elevation meant that they left behind a virtually all-White government department or assembly.

At the same time, college campuses across the United States have been the scene of bias-related incidents. Student-run newspapers and radio stations have ridiculed racial and ethnic minorities; threatening literature has been stuffed under the doors of minority students; graffiti endorsing the views of White supremacist organizations such as the Ku Klux Klan have been scrawled on university walls. In some cases, there have even been violent clashes between groups of White and Black students. In 2015, students staged protests, sit-ins, and hunger strikes over incidents

such as prejudiced statements by college leaders, fraternities issuing invitations to "white girls only," and human feces on bathroom walls in the form of swastikas (Hartcollis and Bidgood 2015; Miller 2015). What causes such ugly incidents?

Prejudice

Prejudice is a negative attitude toward an entire category of people, often an ethnic or racial minority. If you resent your roommate because he or she is sloppy, you are not necessarily guilty of prejudice. However, if you immediately stereotype your roommate on the basis of such characteristics as race, ethnicity, or religion, that is a form of prejudice. Prejudice tends to perpetuate false definitions of individuals and groups.

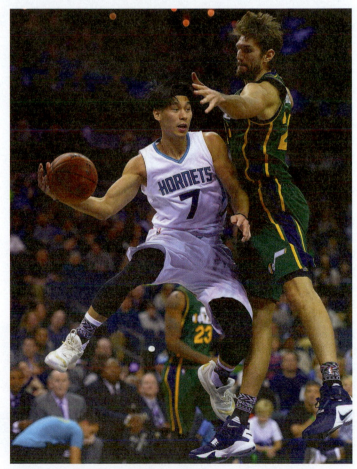

© Tribune Content Agency LLC/Alamy

Even successful members of minority groups, like Jeremy Lin, point guard for the Charlotte Hornets, are subjected to ethnic slurs. "Chink in the Armor" proclaimed a headline on ESPN's website in 2012 after Lin, who had spearheaded a multigame winning streak, had a bad night. The network later apologized for the remark.

Sometimes prejudice results from **ethnocentrism**—the tendency to assume that one's own culture and way of life represent the norm or are superior to all others. Ethnocentric people judge other cultures by the standards of their group, which leads quite easily to prejudice against cultures they view as inferior.

One important and widespread ideology that reinforces prejudice is **racism,** the belief that one race is supreme and all others are innately inferior. When racism prevails in a society, members of subordinate groups generally experience prejudice, discrimination, and exploitation. In 1990, as concern mounted about racist attacks in the United States, Congress passed the Hate Crimes Statistics Act. As a result, hate crimes are now beginning to be reported and investigated in much the same way as conventional crimes against property and people.

Prejudice is also rooted in racial and ethnic **stereotypes**—unreliable generalizations about all members of a group that do not recognize individual differences within the group. The dominant or majority group creates these stereotypes through the process of racial formation. As the interactionist William I. Thomas (1923) noted, the dominant group's "definition of the situation" is often so powerful, it can mold the individual personality. That is, people respond not only to the objective features of a situation or person, but to the *social meaning* that situation or person carries. Thus, the false images or stereotypes created by the dominant group can become real in their consequences.

Color-Blind Racism

Over the past three generations, nationwide surveys have consistently shown growing support among Whites for integration, interracial dating, and the election of minority group members to public office—including the presidency of the United States. How can this trend be explained, given the persistence of residential segregation and the commission of thousands of hate crimes every year? The answer, to some extent, is that prejudice and discriminatory attitudes are no longer expressed as freely as they once were. Often, they are couched in terms of equal opportunity.

Color-blind racism is the use of the principle of race neutrality to defend a racially unequal status quo. Proponents of race neutrality claim they believe that everyone should be treated equally. However, the way they apply the principle to government policy is anything but neutral. Proponents of this approach oppose affirmative action, public welfare assistance, and to a large extent, government-funded health insurance, all of which they see largely as favors to minority groups. Yet they do not object to practices that privilege Whites, such as college admissions criteria that give preference to the relatives of alumni. Nor do they oppose tax breaks for homeowners, most of whom are White, or government financial aid to college students, who are also disproportionately White. Though race neutrality is not based on theories of racial superiority or inferiority, then, the idea that society should be color-blind only perpetuates racial inequality.

Color-blind racism has also been referred to as "covert racism." Although its proponents rarely speak of racism, other indicators of social status, such as social class or citizenship, tend to become proxies for race. Thus, many White people can convince themselves that they are not racist—nor do they know anyone who is—and yet remain prejudiced against "welfare mothers" and "immigrants." They can conclude, mistakenly, that racial tolerance, or even racial and ethnic equality, has been achieved.

Researchers who have surveyed White attitudes toward African Americans over the past several decades have reached two inescapable conclusions. First, people's attitudes do change. In periods of social upheaval, dramatic attitudinal shifts can occur within a single generation. Second, less racial progress was made in the late 20th and early 21st centuries than in the relatively brief period of the 1950s and 1960s. Today, economically disadvantaged groups such as African Americans and Latinos have become so closely associated with urban decay, homelessness, welfare, and crime that those problems are now viewed as racial issues, even if they are not labeled as such. The tendency to *blame the victims* of these social ills complicates their resolution, especially at a time when government's ability to address social problems is limited by recession, antitax initiatives, and concern over terrorism. In short, the color line is still in place, even if more and more people refuse to acknowledge its existence (Ansell 2008; Bonilla-Silva 2014).

Discriminatory Behavior

Prejudice often leads to **discrimination,** the denial of opportunities and equal rights to individuals and groups because of prejudice or other arbitrary reasons. Say that a White corporate president with a prejudice against Asian Americans has to fill an executive position. The most qualified candidate for the job is a Vietnamese American. If the president refuses to hire this candidate and instead selects an inferior White candidate, he or she is engaging in an act of racial discrimination.

Prejudiced *attitudes* should not be equated with discriminatory *behavior*. Although the two are generally related, they are not identical; either condition can be present without the other. A prejudiced person does not always act on his or her biases. The White corporate president, for example, might choose—despite his or her stereotypes—to hire the Vietnamese American. That would be prejudice without discrimination. On the other hand, a White corporate president with a completely respectful view of Vietnamese Americans might refuse to hire them for executive posts out of fear that biased clients would take their business elsewhere. In that case, the president's action would constitute discrimination without prejudice.

A field experiment by sociologist Devah Pager, then a doctoral candidate at the University of Wisconsin–Madison, documented racial discrimination in hiring. Pager sent four polite, well-dressed young men out to look for an entry-level job in Milwaukee, Wisconsin. All were 23-year-old college students, but they presented themselves as high school graduates with similar job histories. Two of the men were Black and two were White. One Black applicant and one White applicant claimed to have served 18 months in jail for a felony conviction—possession of cocaine with intent to distribute.

As one might expect, the four men's experiences with 350 potential employers were vastly different. Predictably, the

White applicant with a purported prison record received only half as many callbacks as the other White applicant—17 percent compared to 34 percent. But as dramatic as the effect of his criminal record was, the effect of his race was more significant. Despite his prison record, he received slightly more callbacks than the Black applicant *with no criminal record* (17 percent compared to 14 percent). Race, it seems, was more of a concern to potential employers than a criminal background.

The implications of this research are not limited to any one city, such as Milwaukee. Similar studies have confirmed discriminatory handling of job applications in Chicago; New York City; Long Island, New York; San Diego; and Washington, D.C. Over time, the cumulative effect of such differential behavior by employers contributes to significant differences in income. Figure 31-2 vividly illustrates the income inequality between White men and almost everyone else (Pager 2007; Pager et al. 2009).

If race serves as a barrier, why do Asian American men earn slightly more income than White men (see Figure 31-2)? Not all Asian American men earn high incomes; indeed, some Asian American groups, such as Laotians and Vietnamese, have high levels of poverty. Nevertheless, a significant number of Asian Americans have advanced degrees that qualify them for highly paid jobs, and which raise the median income for the group as a whole. With a doctorate holder in the family, the typical Asian American or White family earns an estimated $142,000 annually (DeNavas-Walt and Proctor 2015:FINC-01).

Sometimes racial and ethnic discrimination is overt. Internet forums like Craigslist.org or Roommates.com feature classified ads that state "African Americans and Arabians tend to clash with me" or "Clean, Godly Christian men only." While antidiscrimination laws prevent such notices from being published in the newspapers, existing law has not caught up with online bigotry in hiring and renting. Internet postings can be subtly discriminatory. In 2015, landlords were stating that potential renters' use of housing vouchers (mostly issued by the government to Blacks and Latinos) is unacceptable (Liptak 2006; C. Morris 2015).

Discrimination persists even for the most educated and qualified minority group members from the best family backgrounds. Despite their talents and experiences, they sometimes encounter attitudinal or organizational bias that prevents them from reaching their full potential. The term **glass ceiling** refers to an invisible barrier that blocks the promotion of a qualified individual in a work environment because of the individual's gender, race, or ethnicity (R. Schaefer 2014).

In early 1995, the federal Glass Ceiling Commission issued the first comprehensive study of barriers to promotion in the United States. The commission found that glass ceilings continue to block women and minority group men from top management positions in the nation's industries.

FIGURE 31-2 **U.S. Median Income by Race, Ethnicity, and Gender**

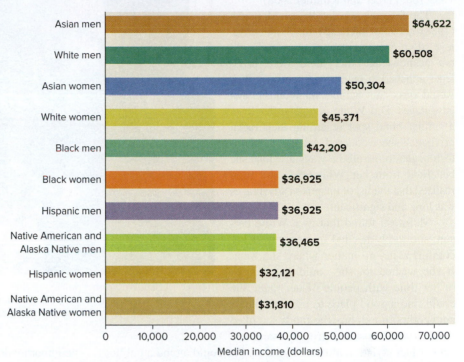

Note: Data released in 2016 for income earned in 2015. Median income is from all sources and is limited to year-round, full-time workers at least 25 years old. Data for White men and women are for non-Hispanics.
Sources: American Community Survey 2016:S2021; American Social and Economic Support 2016:PINC-03..

Income gaps remain significant, with Hispanic and Native American women needing to work two years what Asian and White men earn in one year.

 use your **sociological imagination**

How might online social networking maintain prejudice and discrimination?

The Privileges of the Dominant

One aspect of discrimination that is often overlooked is the privileges that dominant groups enjoy at the expense of others. For instance, we tend to focus more on the difficulty women have getting ahead at work and getting a hand at home than on the ease with which men manage to make their way in the world and avoid household chores. Similarly, we concentrate more on discrimination against racial and ethnic minorities than on the advantages members of the White majority enjoy. Indeed, most White people rarely think about their "Whiteness," taking their status for granted.

Sociologists and other social scientists are becoming increasingly interested in what it means to be "White," for White privilege is the other side of the proverbial coin of racial discrimination. In this context, **White privilege** refers to rights or immunities granted to people as a particular benefit or favor simply because they are White (Ferber and Kimmel 2008). This view of whiteness as a privilege echoes an observation by W. E. B. DuBois that rather than wanting fair working conditions for all laborers,

White workers had accepted the "public and psychological wage" of whiteness ([1935] 1962:700; Ferber and Kimmel 2008).

The feminist scholar Peggy McIntosh (1988) became interested in White privilege after noticing that most men would not acknowledge that there were privileges attached to being male—even if they would agree that being female had its disadvantages. Did White people suffer from a similar blind spot regarding their racial privilege? she wondered. Intrigued, McIntosh began to list all the ways in which she benefited from her Whiteness. She soon realized that the list of unspoken advantages was long and significant.

McIntosh found that as a White person, she rarely needed to step out of her comfort zone, no matter where she went. If she wished to, she could spend most of her time with people of her race. She could find a good place to live in a pleasant neighborhood, buy the foods she liked to eat from almost any grocery store, and

© Enigma/Alamy

White people are accustomed to seeing other White people in professional positions and jobs with authority and prestige. Whiteness *does* have its privileges.

get her hair styled in almost any salon. She could attend a public meeting without feeling that she did not belong, that she was different from everyone else.

McIntosh discovered, too, that her skin color opened doors for her. She could cash checks and use credit cards without suspicion, browse through stores without being shadowed by security guards. She could be seated without difficulty in a restaurant. If she asked to see the manager, she could assume he or she would be of her race. If she needed help from a doctor or a lawyer, she could get it.

McIntosh also realized that her Whiteness made the job of parenting easier. She did not need to worry about protecting her children from people who didn't like them. She could be sure that their schoolbooks would show pictures of people who looked like them, and that their history texts would describe White people's achievements. She knew that the television programs they watched would include White characters.

Finally, McIntosh had to admit that others did not constantly evaluate her in racial terms. When she appeared in public, she didn't need to worry that her clothing or behavior might reflect poorly on White people. If she was recognized for an achievement, it was seen as her achievement, not that of an entire race. And no one ever assumed that the personal opinions she voiced should be those of all White people. Because McIntosh blended in with the people around her, she wasn't always onstage.

In the wake of the Great Recession that began in the United States in 2007, researchers looked at the differential impact of home loan practices and found evidence of **redlining**, a devastating form of racial bias. African Americans, Latinos, and others fall victim to this pattern of discrimination against people trying to buy homes in minority and racially changing neighborhoods. Redlining was especially rampant in the first half of the 20th century, but evidence of its persistence still appears. Controlling for a variety of personal financial factors and home value, the researchers found that Black residents of Black neighborhood in Baltimore, Maryland, paid 5 to 11 percent more in monthly payments than comparable White residents of White neighborhoods.

It has not been just scholars who unearthed redlining in the 21st century. The federal government levied a $22 million fine on the Hudson City Savings Bank, the nation's seventh largest, whose executives had purposefully avoided Black and Latino neighborhoods, building bank branches where home loans could be offered to local residents. This was not an isolated case: In 2015 alone, fines were also applied to banks in Buffalo, Milwaukee, Providence, Rochester, and St. Louis (Rugh et al. 2015; Swarns 2015).

 use your **sociological imagination**

How often do you think people are privileged because of their race or ethnicity? How about yourself—how often are you privileged?

Institutional Discrimination

Discrimination is practiced not only by individuals in one-to-one encounters but also by institutions in their daily operations. Social scientists are particularly concerned with the ways in which structural factors such as employment, housing, health care, and government operations maintain the social significance of race and ethnicity. **Institutional discrimination** refers to the denial of opportunities and equal rights to individuals and groups

Taking Sociology to Work

Prudence Hannis, *Associate Director, First Nations Post-Secondary Institution, Odanak, Québec*

Courtesy of
Prudence Hannis

Prudence Hannis is a First Nations (Native American) woman who belongs to the Abenaki tribe. As associate director of the First Nations Post-Secondary Institution, which opened in 2011, she is helping to establish a school "built for and by First Nations." Hannis sees the new institution as a significant step toward self-determination among First Nations peoples. Historically, graduation rates have been very low among Québec's First Nations, for political, cultural, social, and economic reasons. The First Nations Post-Secondary Institution was conceived to provide the kind of support that mainstream educational institutions don't offer First Nations students, including everything from day care services to academic support.

The school also offers social-emotional support to students who may not be comfortable in an academic environment. In the social sciences, students participate in weekly sharing circles, where they learn about the root causes of high dropout rates and are encouraged to become agents of

change. In deciding to "step out of victimization," students exert a positive influence on the school, on their own future and that of generations to come, and on their peoples' relationship with mainstream society. Hannis is proud to report that in 2011, all the incoming students finished the first term (the dropout rate was zero). The next term, 19 additional students enrolled.

Before taking her current position, Hannis was a liaison officer at the National Institute of Science Research at the University of Québec, where she advised scholars wishing to do research on First Nations communities. She has also worked on women's health issues, first at the Centre of Excellence on Women's Health, Consortium Université de Montréal, and later as a researcher and community activist with Québec Native Women. Her job with Québec Native Women, she explains, was "to defend First Nations women's concerns, to be their spokesperson when needed, to analyze critical situations for our sisters, and mostly, to determine ways in which women can empower themselves, their families, and their communities."

Hannis received her BA in sociology from the University of Québec at Montréal in

2000. "I have made good use of what I have learned concerning gender inequality, social class, racial and ethnic inequality (tensions, conflict, and struggles), domination, oppression, and social exclusion," she says. "These concepts allow for a better analysis of social problems First Nations are facing (high rates of unemployment, low graduation rates, greater health risks, ghettoization)." Hannis finds her studies have also helped in her work with government agencies, allowing her to raise public awareness of issues such as violence against native women and to identify possible solutions. "I have never been hired as a 'sociologist' per se," she explains, "but the work I was given always involved sociological analysis of issues relevant to First Nations."

LET'S DISCUSS

1. What is the dropout rate at your school? What political, cultural, social, and economic conditions might contribute to that dropout rate?

2. In speaking of empowering First Nations women, what sociological perspective do you think Hannis is drawing on?

---

that results from the normal operations of a society. This kind of discrimination consistently affects certain racial and ethnic groups more than others.

The Commission on Civil Rights (1981:9–10) has identified various forms of institutional discrimination:

- Rules requiring that only English be spoken at a place of work, even when it is not a business necessity to restrict the use of other languages.

- Preferences shown by law and medical schools in the admission of children of wealthy and influential alumni, nearly all of whom are White.

- Restrictive employment-leave policies, coupled with prohibitions on part-time work, that make it difficult for the heads of single-parent families (most of whom are women) to obtain and keep jobs.

In some cases, even seemingly neutral institutional standards can have discriminatory effects. African American students at a midwestern state university protested a policy under which fraternities and sororities that wished to use campus facilities for a dance were required to pay a $150 security deposit to cover possible damages. They complained that the policy had a

discriminatory impact on minority student organizations. Campus police countered that the university's policy applied to all student groups interested in using the facilities. However, since the overwhelmingly White fraternities and sororities at the school had their own houses, which they used for dances, the policy indeed affected only the African American and other minority organizations.

Attempts have been made to eradicate or compensate for institutional discrimination. The 1960s saw the passage of many pioneering civil rights laws, including the landmark 1964 Civil Rights Act (which prohibits discrimination in public accommodations and publicly owned facilities on the basis of race, color, creed, national origin, and gender). Yet today, voting rights are still an issue in some states (Box 31-1).

For more than 40 years, affirmative action programs have been instituted to overcome past discrimination. **Affirmative action** refers to positive efforts to recruit minority group members or women for jobs, promotions, and educational opportunities. Many people resent these programs, arguing that advancing one group's cause merely shifts the discrimination to another group. By giving priority to African Americans in admissions, for example, schools may overlook more qualified

Institutional Discrimination in the Voting Booth

Eddie Lee Holloway Jr. has been voting since he was 18. Now, decades later, he is having trouble not only casting his ballot but receiving disability benefits. Because of a clerical error that was made when he was born—Eddie's birth certificate names him Eddie Junior Holloway—the state of Wisconsin will not allow him to vote. Eddie's Social Security card shows his correct name, as does an expired Illinois photo ID. His father's name, Eddie Lee Holloway, appears on his birth certificate. Still, the state government will not recognize him as a U.S. citizen. Like a lot of non-White Americans, Eddie has lost his birthright due to institutional discrimination.

How should government establish the authenticity of a person's right to vote? Today, many states have begun to require a government-issued ID bearing a photograph, presumably to prevent voter fraud. Other states will accept any photo ID (see the figure). In the past, voters usually did not need to show any kind of identification at the polls; their identity was established at the time they registered to vote.

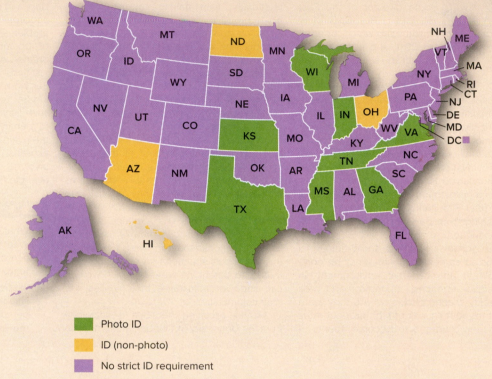

MAPPING LIFE NATIONWIDE

Voter ID Requirements

- 🟩 Photo ID
- 🟨 ID (non-photo)
- 🟪 No strict ID requirement

Source: National Conference of State Legislatures 2015.

Courts have been reluctant to uphold the new voter ID laws, for not all eligible voters can easily obtain these credentials. Such laws disproportionately disenfranchise the elderly and members of minority groups, simply because they do not have a driver's license. According to national surveys, 25 percent of African American citizens and 16 percent of Latino citizens do not have a valid government-issued photo ID, compared to 8 percent of White citizens. These findings fit the definition of institutional discrimination, in that *through the normal operations of society*—in this case, the holding of elections—people of color are more likely than others to be denied their rights. Indeed, research into who can and cannot vote suggests the existence of institutional discrimination in our national elections.

Why the sudden emphasis on establishing voters' identity? There is little evidence

> Such laws disproportionately disenfranchise the elderly and members of minority groups, simply because they do not have a driver's license.

to suggest that people have been impersonating eligible voters at the polls.

These findings are one more example of the painful underlying context of American intergroup relations and are viewed as a form of voter suppression. Institutional discrimination consistently imposes more hindrances on, and awards fewer benefits to, certain racial and ethnic groups compared to others.

LET'S DISCUSS

1. Are you a registered voter? If so, how does your local polling place verify voters' identity? Have you ever had difficulty establishing your identity on election day?

2. Why are citizens and state legislators suddenly so concerned about requiring voters to establish their identity?

Sources: ACLU 2016; Brennan Center 2013, 2016; Dade 2012; Rasmussen Reports 2013.

© Russell Lee/MPI/Getty Images

Before passage of the Civil Rights Act (1964), segregation of public accommodations was the norm throughout the South. Whites used the most up-to-date bathrooms, waiting rooms, and even drinking fountains, while Blacks ("Colored") were directed to older facilities in inferior conditions. Such separate but unequal arrangements are a blatant example of institutional discrimination.

White candidates. In many parts of the country and many sectors of the economy, affirmative action is being rolled back, even though it was never fully implemented.

Discriminatory practices continue to pervade nearly all areas of life in the United States today. In part, that is because various individuals and groups actually *benefit* from racial and ethnic discrimination in terms of money, status, and influence. Discrimination permits members of the majority to enhance their wealth, power, and prestige at the expense of others. Less qualified people get jobs and promotions simply because they are members of the dominant group. Such individuals and groups will not surrender these advantages easily. We'll turn now to a closer look at this functionalist analysis, as well as the conflict, labeling, and interactionist perspectives on race and ethnicity.

MODULE 31 | Recap and Review

Summary

The social dimensions of race and ethnicity are important factors in shaping people's lives.

1. A **racial group** is set apart from others by physical differences; an **ethnic group** is set apart primarily by national origin or cultural patterns.

2. When sociologists define a **minority group,** they are concerned primarily with the economic and political power, or powerlessness, of the group.

3. The meaning people attach to the physical differences between races gives social significance to race, producing **stereotypes.**

4. **Prejudice** often but not always leads to **discrimination.** Sometimes, through **color-blind racism,** prejudiced people try to use the principle of racial neutrality to defend a racially unequal status quo.

5. **Institutional discrimination** results from the normal operations of a society.

Thinking Critically

1. Why does the social construction of race defy the traditional notion of race as a biological category?

2. What are the implications of the differences in earning power of members of different ethnic groups?

3. Which would be more socially significant, the elimination of prejudice or the elimination of discrimination? Explain.

Key Terms

Affirmative action

Color-blind racism

Discrimination

Ethnic group

Ethnocentrism

Glass ceiling

Institutional discrimination

Minority group

Prejudice

Racial formation

Racial group

Racism

Redlining

Stereotype

White privilege

Relations among racial and ethnic groups lend themselves to analysis from four major sociological perspectives. Viewing race from the macro level, functionalists observe that racial prejudice and discrimination serve positive functions for dominant groups. Conflict theorists see the economic structure as a central factor in the exploitation of minorities. Labeling theorists note the way in which minorities are singled out for differential treatment by law enforcement officers. On the micro level, interactionist researchers stress the manner in which everyday contact between people from different racial and ethnic backgrounds contributes to tolerance or hostility.

Functionalist Perspective

What possible use could racial bigotry have? Functionalist theorists, while agreeing that racial hostility is hardly to be admired, point out that it serves positive functions for those who practice discrimination.

Anthropologist Manning Nash (1962) identified three functions of racially prejudiced beliefs for the dominant group:

1. Racist views provide a moral justification for maintaining an unequal society that routinely deprives a minority group of its rights and privileges. Southern Whites justified slavery by believing that Africans were physically and spiritually subhuman and devoid of souls.

2. Racist beliefs discourage the subordinate minority from attempting to question its lowly status, which would be to question the very foundations of society.

3. Racial myths suggest that any major societal change (such as an end to discrimination) would only bring greater poverty to the minority and lower the majority's standard of living. As a result, racial prejudice grows when a society's value system (one underlying a colonial empire or slavery, for example) is threatened.

Although racial prejudice and discrimination may serve the powerful, such unequal treatment can also be dysfunctional for a society, and even for the dominant group. Sociologist Arnold Rose (1951) outlined four dysfunctions that are associated with racism:

1. A society that practices discrimination fails to use the resources of all individuals. Discrimination limits the search for talent and leadership to the dominant group.

2. Discrimination aggravates social problems such as poverty, delinquency, and crime, and places the financial burden of alleviating those problems on the dominant group.

3. Society must invest a good deal of time and money to defend its barriers to the full participation of all members.

4. Racial prejudice and discrimination often undercut goodwill and friendly diplomatic relations between nations.

Conflict Perspective

Conflict theorists would certainly agree with Arnold Rose that racial prejudice and discrimination have many harmful consequences for society. Sociologists such as Oliver Cox, Robert Blauner, and Herbert M. Hunter have used the **exploitation theory** (or *Marxist class theory*) to explain the basis of racial subordination in the United States. Karl Marx viewed the exploitation of the lower class as a basic part of the capitalist economic system. From a Marxist point of view, racism keeps minorities in low-paying jobs, thereby supplying the capitalist ruling class with a pool of cheap labor. Moreover, by forcing racial minorities to accept low wages, capitalists can restrict the wages of all members of the proletariat. Workers from the dominant group who demand higher wages can always be replaced by minorities who have no choice but to accept low-paying jobs (Blauner 1972; Cox 1948; Hunter 2000).

The conflict view of race relations seems persuasive in a number of instances. Japanese Americans were the object of little prejudice until they began to enter jobs that brought them into competition with Whites. The movement to keep Chinese immigrants out of the United States became most fervent during the latter half of the 19th century, when Chinese and Whites fought over dwindling work opportunities. Both the enslavement of Blacks and the extermination and removal westward of Native Americans were economically motivated.

However, the exploitation theory is too limited to explain prejudice in its many forms. Not all minority groups have been exploited to the same extent. In addition, many groups (such as the Quakers and the Mormons) have been victimized by prejudice for other than economic reasons. Still, as Gordon Allport (1979:210) concludes, the exploitation theory correctly "points a sure finger at one of the factors involved in prejudice, . . . rationalized self-interest of the upper classes."

Labeling Perspective

One practice that fits both the conflict perspective and labeling theory is racial profiling. **Racial profiling** is any arbitrary action initiated by an authority based on race, ethnicity, or national origin rather than on a person's behavior. Generally, racial profiling occurs when law enforcement officers, including customs officials, airport security, and police, assume that people who fit a certain description are likely to be engaged in illegal activities. Beginning in the 1980s with the emergence of the crack cocaine market, skin color became a key characteristic in racial profiling. This practice is often based on very explicit stereotypes. For example, one federal antidrug initiative encouraged officers to look specifically for people with dreadlocks and for Latino men traveling together.

Today, authorities continue to rely on racial profiling, despite overwhelming evidence that it is misleading. A recent study showed that Blacks are still more likely than Whites to be frisked and handled with force when they are stopped. Yet Whites are more likely than Blacks to possess weapons, illegal drugs, or stolen property (Farrell and McDevitt 2010).

Research on the ineffectiveness of racial profiling, coupled with calls by minority communities to end the stigmatization, has led to growing demands to end the practice. But these efforts came to an abrupt halt after the September 11, 2001, terrorist attacks on the United States, when suspicions arose about Muslim and Arab immigrants. Foreign students from Arab countries were summoned for special questioning by authorities. Legal immigrants who were identified as Arab or Muslim were scrutinized for possible illegal activity and prosecuted for violations that authorities routinely ignored among immigrants of other ethnicities and faiths.

National surveys have found little change since 2001 in public support for profiling of Arab Americans at airports. In recent years numerous incidents between people of color and police officers, which many viewed as showing that law enforcement officers profile certain groups for mistreatment and even death, have received widespread media attention. In 2014, a national survey showed 61 percent of Whites and 88 percent of African Americans felt that police believe members of certain racial or ethnic groups are more likely than others to commit crimes (De Pento et al. 2015:Question 6; Zogby 2010).

The issue of racial profiling has become a more visible part of the national discussion in recent years. The first instance is the Black Lives Matter movement that emerged to call attention to the deaths of African Americans, especially men, at the hands of police officers. In 2012, Trayvon Martin, an unarmed 17-year-old, was shot to death by neighborhood watch coordinator George Zimmerman, in Florida. Zimmerman's acquittal was broadly viewed as a miscarriage of justice. At the same time, the increased use of cameras, either on bystanders' phones or mounted on the dashboards of police vehicles, to record police actions, created a visual record that many see as a pattern of excessive show of force.

Out of these events, as well as several other deaths of Black men at the hands of police throughout the country, emerged the Black Lives Matter protest movement. Those who defend the police counter that "all lives matter" and draw attention to the dangerous situations in which police officers often find themselves. Yet more and more photos and videos emerged in a large number of cities showing problematic police-African American encounters. Not surprisingly a 2015 national survey showed that only 8 percent of African Americans, compared to 42 percent of Whites, felt that Whites and Blacks have the same chance for fair treatment from the police.

A second area in which racial profiling has come to the forefront of debate involves the strident calls for greater scrutiny of Muslims, including Muslim Americans, in the wake of terrorist episodes by Islamic extremists. Notably, in 2015 presidential candidate Donald Trump called for a ban on all Muslims from entering the United States pending thorough background checks. A national survey of likely voters at the time showed that over one-third supported such a stance. This singling out of a group of people by virtue of religion received strong condemnation from other political leaders. The broad level of support nonetheless

© moodboard/Brand X Pictures/Getty Images RF

In U.S. retail stores, Black customers have different experiences from White customers. They are more likely than Whites to have their checks or credit cards refused and more likely to be profiled by security personnel.

underscores the persistent temptation to use profiling, whether racial or religious, as a shortcut for maintaining public safety (McCormick 2015; Marist Poll 2015: Question 7F).

Interactionist Perspective

A Hispanic woman is transferred from a job on an assembly line to a similar position working next to a White man. At first, the White man is patronizing, assuming that she must be incompetent. She is cold and resentful; even when she needs assistance, she refuses to admit it. After a week, the growing tension between the two leads to a bitter quarrel. Yet over time, each slowly comes to appreciate the other's strengths and talents. A year after they begin working together, these two workers become respectful friends. This story is an example of what interactionists call the *contact hypothesis* in action.

The **contact hypothesis** states that in cooperative circumstances, interracial contact between people of equal status will cause them to become less prejudiced and to abandon old stereotypes. People begin to see one another as individuals and discard the broad generalizations characteristic of stereotyping. Note the phrases *equal status* and *cooperative circumstances*. In the story just told, if the two workers had been competing for one vacancy as a supervisor, the racial hostility between them might have worsened (Allport 1979; Fine 2008).

As Latinos and other minorities slowly gain access to better-paying and more responsible jobs, the contact hypothesis may take on even greater significance. The trend in our society is toward increasing contact between individuals from dominant and subordinate groups. That may be one way of eliminating—or

TABLE 32-1 SOCIOLOGICAL PERSPECTIVES ON RACE AND ETHNICITY

Perspective	Emphasis
Functionalist	The dominant majority benefits from the subordination of racial minorities.
Conflict	Vested interests perpetuate racial inequality through economic exploitation.
Labeling	People are profiled and stereotyped based on their racial and ethnic identity.
Interactionist	Cooperative interracial contacts can reduce hostility.

© Gaizka Iroz/AFP/Getty Images

French police remove a member of the Roma minority who is resisting deportation to his home country. The expulsion of certain racial or ethnic groups is an extreme result of prejudice.

at least reducing—racial and ethnic stereotyping and prejudice. Another may be the establishment of interracial coalitions, an idea suggested by sociologist William Julius Wilson (1999). To work, such coalitions would obviously need to be built on an equal role for all members.

Table 32-1 summarizes the four major sociological perspectives on race. No matter what the explanation for racial and ethnic distinctions—functionalist, conflict, labeling, or interactionist—these socially constructed inequalities can have powerful consequences in the form of prejudice and discrimination. In the next section, we will see how inequality based on the ascribed characteristics of race and ethnicity can poison people's interpersonal relations, depriving whole groups of opportunities others take for granted.

Spectrum of Intergroup Relations

Racial and ethnic groups can relate to one another in a wide variety of ways, ranging from friendships and intermarriages to hostility, from behaviors that require mutual approval to behaviors imposed by the dominant group.

Genocide

One devastating pattern of intergroup relations is **genocide**—the deliberate, systematic killing of an entire people or nation. This term describes the killing of 1 million Armenians by Turkey beginning in 1915. It is most commonly applied to Nazi Germany's extermination of 6 million European Jews, as well as gays, lesbians, and the Roma ("Gypsies"), during World War II. The term *genocide* is also appropriate in describing the United States' policies toward Native Americans in the 19th century. In 1800, the Native American (or American Indian) population of the United States was about 600,000; by 1850, it had been reduced to 250,000 through warfare with the U.S. cavalry, disease, and forced relocation to inhospitable environments.

The *expulsion* of a people is another extreme means of acting out racial or ethnic prejudice. In 1979, for example, the government of Vietnam expelled nearly 1 million ethnic Chinese from the country. The action resulted partly from centuries of hostility between Vietnam and neighboring China.

More recently (beginning in 2009), France expelled over 10,000 ethnic Roma (or Gypsies) who had immigrated from their home countries of Bulgaria and Romania. The action appeared to violate the European Union's ban against targeting ethnic groups, as well as its policy of "freedom of movement" throughout the EU. In 2011, the EU withdrew the threat of legal action when the French government modified its policy to apply only to those Roma who lived in "illegal camps." However, many observers saw the concession as a thinly veiled attempt to circumvent the EU's long-standing human rights policies.

In a variation of expulsion, called *secession*, failure to resolve an ethnic or racial conflict results in the drawing of formal boundaries between the groups. In 1947, India was partitioned into two separate countries in an attempt to end violent conflict between Hindus and Muslims. The predominantly Muslim areas in the north became the new country of Pakistan; the rest of India became predominantly Hindu.

Secession, expulsion, and genocide are extreme behaviors, clustered on the negative end of what is called the Spectrum of Intergroup Relations (Figure 32-1). More typical intergroup relations follow four identifiable patterns: (1) segregation, (2) amalgamation, (3) assimilation, and (4) pluralism. Each pattern defines the dominant group's actions and the minority group's responses. Intergroup relations are rarely restricted to only one of the four patterns, although invariably one does tend to dominate. Think of these patterns primarily as ideal types.

Segregation

Separate schools, separate seating on buses and in restaurants, separate washrooms, even separate drinking fountains—these were all part of the lives of African Americans in the South when

FIGURE 32-1 Spectrum of Intergroup Relations

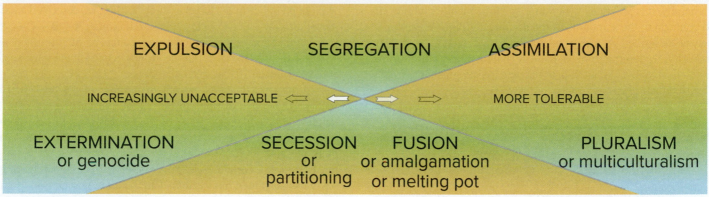

EXPULSION   SEGREGATION   ASSIMILATION

INCREASINGLY UNACCEPTABLE ⇦ ⇦ ⇨ ⇨ MORE TOLERABLE

EXTERMINATION   SECESSION   FUSION   PLURALISM
or genocide   or   or amalgamation   or multiculturalism
                      partitioning   or melting pot

Source: Prepared by author, Richard T. Schaefer.

segregation ruled early in the 20th century. **Segregation** refers to the physical separation of two groups of people in terms of residence, workplace, and social events. Generally, a dominant group imposes this pattern on a minority group. Segregation is rarely complete, however. Intergroup contact inevitably occurs, even in the most segregated societies.

From 1948 (when it received its independence) to 1990, the Republic of South Africa severely restricted the movement of Blacks and other non-Whites by means of a wide-ranging system of segregation known as **apartheid.** Apartheid even included the creation of separate homelands where Blacks were expected to live. However, decades of local resistance to apartheid, combined with international pressure, led to marked political changes in the 1990s. In 1994, a prominent Black activist, Nelson Mandela, was elected South Africa's president in the first election in which Blacks (the majority of the nation's population) were allowed to vote. Mandela had spent almost 28 years in South African prisons for his anti-apartheid activities. His election was widely viewed as the final blow to South Africa's oppressive policy of segregation.

In contrast to the enforced segregation in South Africa, the United States exemplifies an unmandated but nevertheless persistent separation of the races. In their book *American Apartheid,* sociologists Douglas Massey and Nancy Denton (1993) described segregation in U.S. cities using 1990 census data. As the book's title suggests, the racial makeup of U.S. neighborhoods resembles the rigid government-imposed segregation that prevailed for so long in South Africa.

The major change in residential segregation over the last generation has been the trend for suburban communities to become homogenous—overwhelmingly White or Black or Latino. Representative of this trend is the town of Ferguson, Missouri, a St. Louis suburb whose population changed from 25 percent Black to 65 percent Black in just 20 years. In 2015, Ferguson was rocked by police-civilian encounters

© Barbara Penoyar/Getty Images RF

and protest following the shooting death of an unarmed Black man by a White police officer. The incident drew attention to the overwhelmingly White makeup of the city's police force and government as well as giving credence to the Black Lives Matter movement and drawing attention to violence against African Americans (Lichter et al. 2015).

Amalgamation

Amalgamation happens when a majority group and a minority group combine to form a new group. Through intermarriage over several generations, various groups in society combine to form a new group. This pattern can be expressed as $A + B + C \rightarrow D$, where A, B, and C represent different groups in a society, and D signifies the end result, a unique cultural-racial group unlike any of the initial groups (W. Newman 1973).

The belief in the United States as a "melting pot" became compelling in the first part of the 20th century, particularly since that image suggested that the nation had an almost divine mission to amalgamate various groups into one people. However, in actuality, many residents were not willing to include Native Americans, Jews, African Americans, Asian Americans, and Irish Roman Catholics in the melting pot. Therefore, this pattern does not adequately describe dominant–subordinate relations in the United States. There *has* been a significant increase in interracial marriage among Whites, Blacks, Asians, and Hispanics in recent years—a trend we will examine in Module 40.

Assimilation

In India, many Hindus complain about Indian citizens who copy the traditions and customs of the British. In France, people of Arab and African origin, many of them Muslim, complain they are treated as second-class citizens—a charge that provoked riots in 2005 and again in 2012. And in the United States, some Italian Americans, Polish Americans, Hispanics, and Jews have changed their ethnic-sounding family names to names that are typically found among White Protestant families.

Assimilation is the process through which a person forsakes his or her cultural tradition to become part of a different culture. Generally, it is practiced by a minority group member who wants to conform to the standards of the dominant group. Assimilation can be described as a pattern in which A + B + C → A. The majority, A, dominates in such a way that members of minorities B and C imitate it and attempt to become indistinguishable from it (W. Newman 1973).

 use your **sociological imagination**

You have immigrated to another country with a very different culture. What steps might you take to assimilate?

A recent comparison study of immigrant groups in the United States, Canada, and Europe found that for the most part, assimilation has progressed further in the United States than in Europe, although more slowly than in Canada. In the United States, the rate of assimilation has generally been constant across groups. However, the recent recession has hampered new groups' ability to move into a broad range of jobs.

Pluralism

In a pluralistic society, a subordinate group does not have to forsake its lifestyle and traditions to avoid prejudice or discrimination. **Pluralism** is based on mutual respect for one another's

cultures among the various groups in a society. This pattern allows a minority group to express its own culture and still participate without prejudice in the larger society. Earlier, we described amalgamation as A + B + C → D, and assimilation as A + B + C → A. Using this same approach, we can conceive of pluralism as A + B + C → A + B + C. All the groups coexist in the same society (W. Newman 1973).

In the United States, pluralism is more of an ideal than a reality. There are distinct instances of pluralism—the ethnic neighborhoods in major cities, such as Koreatown, Little Tokyo, Andersonville (Swedish Americans), and Spanish Harlem—yet there are also limits to cultural freedom. To survive, a society must promote a certain consensus among its members regarding basic ideals, values, and beliefs. Thus, if a Hungarian immigrant to the United States wants to move up the occupational ladder, he or she cannot avoid learning the English language.

Switzerland exemplifies the modern pluralistic state. There, the absence of both a national language and a dominant religious faith leads to a tolerance for cultural diversity. In addition, various political devices safeguard the interests of ethnic groups in a way that has no parallel in the United States. In contrast, Great Britain has had difficulty achieving cultural pluralism in a multiracial society. East Indians, Pakistanis, and Blacks from the Caribbean and Africa experience prejudice and discrimination within the dominant White society there. Some British advocate cutting off all Asian and Black immigration, and a few even call for expulsion of those non-Whites currently living in Britain.

MODULE 32 | **Recap and Review**

Summary

Four major theoretical perspectives—functionalism, conflict theory, labeling theory, and interactionism—are useful for analyzing relations among racial and ethnic groups.

1. Functionalists point out that **discrimination** is both functional and dysfunctional for society.

2. Conflict theorists explain racial subordination through **exploitation theory.**

3. **Racial profiling** is any arbitrary action initiated by an authority based on race, ethnicity, or national origin rather than on a person's behavior. Based on false stereotypes of certain racial and ethnic groups, the practice is not an effective way to fight crime.

4. Interactionists pose the **contact hypothesis** as a means of reducing prejudice and discrimination.

5. Four patterns describe typical intergroup relations in North America and elsewhere: **amalgamation, assimilation, segregation,** and **pluralism.** Pluralism remains more of an ideal than a reality.

Thinking Critically

1. Describe an example of labeling that you are personally familiar with.

2. Give examples of amalgamation, assimilation, segregation, and pluralism that you have seen on your campus or in your workplace.

Key Terms

Amalgamation

Apartheid

Assimilation

Contact hypothesis

Exploitation theory

Genocide

Pluralism

Racial profiling

Segregation

Few societies have a more diverse population than the United States; the nation is truly a multiracial, multiethnic society. Of course, that has not always been the case. The population of what is now the United States has changed dramatically since the arrival of European settlers in the 1600s, as Figure 31-1 shows. Immigration, colonialism, and in the case of Blacks, slavery determined the racial and ethnic makeup of our present-day society.

Today, the largest racial minorities in the United States are African Americans, Native Americans, and Asian Americans. The largest ethnic groups are Latinos, Jews, and the various White ethnic groups. Figure 33-1 shows where the major racial and ethnic minorities are concentrated.

African Americans

"I am an invisible man," wrote Black author Ralph Ellison in his novel *Invisible Man* (1952:3). "I am a man of substance, of flesh and bone, fiber and liquids—and I might even be said to possess a mind. I am invisible, understand, simply because people refuse to see me."

Over six decades later, many African Americans still feel invisible. Despite their large numbers, they have long been treated as second-class citizens. Currently, by the standards of the federal government, more than 1 out of every 4 African Americans—as opposed to 1 out of every 10 White non-Hispanics—is poor (DeNavas-Walt and Proctor 2015:13).

Contemporary institutional discrimination and individual prejudice against African Americans are rooted in the history of slavery in the United States. Many other subordinate groups had little wealth and income, but as sociologist W. E. B. DuBois ([1909] 1970) and others have noted, enslaved African Americans were in an even more oppressive situation, because by law they could not own property and could not pass on the benefits of their labor to their children. Today, African Americans and sympathetic Whites are calling for *slave reparations* to compensate for the injustices of forced servitude. Reparations could include official expressions of apology from governments such as the United States, ambitious programs to improve African Americans' economic status, or even direct payments to descendants of slaves. While the economic loss caused by enslavement would easily reach trillions of dollars, the primary reason for discussing reparations tends to focus on the need and appropriateness of an apology (Coates 2014).

The end of the Civil War did not bring genuine freedom and equality for Blacks. The Southern states passed Jim Crow laws to enforce official segregation, and the Supreme Court upheld them as constitutional in 1896. In addition, Blacks faced the danger of lynching campaigns, often led by the Ku Klux Klan, during the late 1800s and early 1900s. From a conflict perspective, Whites maintained their dominance formally through legalized segregation and informally by means of vigilante terror and violence (Franklin and Higginbotham 2011).

During the 1960s, a vast civil rights movement emerged, with many competing factions and strategies for change. The Southern Christian Leadership Conference (SCLC), founded by Dr. Martin Luther King Jr., used nonviolent civil disobedience to oppose segregation. The National Association for the Advancement of Colored People (NAACP) favored use of the courts to press for equality for African Americans. But many younger Black leaders, most notably Malcolm X, turned toward an ideology of Black power. Proponents of **Black power** rejected the goal of assimilation into White middle-class society. They defended the beauty and dignity of Black and African cultures and supported the creation of Black-controlled political and economic institutions (Ture and Hamilton 1992).

MAPPING LIFE NATIONWIDE

FIGURE 33-1 **Minority Population by County**

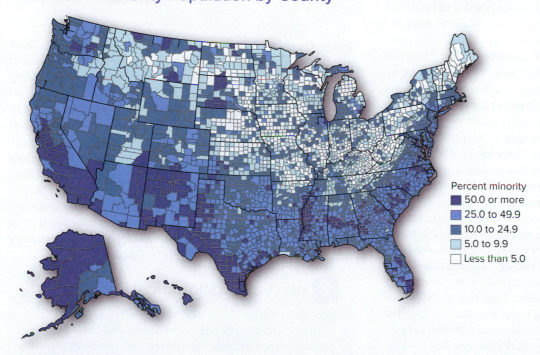

Percent minority
- 50.0 or more
- 25.0 to 49.9
- 10.0 to 24.9
- 5.0 to 9.9
- Less than 5.0

Source: Jones-Puthoff 2013: slide 5.

In four states (California, Hawai'i, New Mexico, and Texas) and the District of Columbia, as well as in about one out of every nine counties, minorities constitute the numerical majority.

Despite numerous courageous actions to achieve Black civil rights, Black and White citizens are still separate, still unequal. From birth to death, Blacks suffer in terms of their life chances. Life remains difficult for millions of poor Blacks, who must attempt to survive in ghetto areas shattered by high unemployment and abandoned housing. Today the median household income of Blacks is still 60 percent that of Whites, and the unemployment rate among Blacks is more than twice that of Whites.

Some African Americans—especially middle-class men and women—have made economic gains over the past 60 years. For example, data show that the number of African Americans in management increased nationally from 2.4 percent of the total in 1958 to 7.3 percent in 2015. Yet Blacks still represented 7 percent or less of all physicians, engineers, scientists, college professors, lawyers, and marketing managers (Bureau of Labor Statistics 2016a: Table 11).

● Native Americans

Today, about 2.2 million Native Americans represent a diverse array of cultures distinguishable by language, family organization, religion, and livelihood. The outsiders who came to the United States—European settlers—and their descendants came to know these native peoples' forefathers as "American Indians." By the time the Bureau of Indian Affairs (BIA) was organized as part of the War Department in 1824, Native American–White relations had already included more than two centuries of hostile actions that had led to the virtual elimination of native peoples (see Figure 31-1). During the 19th century, many bloody wars wiped out a significant part of the tribal population. By the end of the century, schools for Native Americans—operated by the BIA or by church missions—prohibited the practice of traditonal cultures. Yet at the same time, such schools did little to make the children effective members of White society.

Today, life remains difficult for members of the 554 tribal groups in the United States, whether they live in cities or on reservations. For example, one Native American teenager in six has attempted suicide—a rate four times higher than the rate for other teenagers. Traditionally, some Native Americans have chosen to assimilate and abandon all vestiges of their tribal cultures to escape certain forms of prejudice. However, by the 1990s, an increasing number of people in the United States were openly claiming a Native American identity. Since 1960, the federal government's count of Native Americans has tripled.

Native Americans have made some progress in redressing their past mistreatment. In 2009, the federal government settled a 13-year-old lawsuit for the recovery of lease payments due on tribal lands used by the government for oil and gas exploration and grazing. Although the $3.4 billion settlement was large, it was long overdue—some of the government's debts dated back to 1887—and from the perspective of tribal leaders, it was too little, too late. The United States is not the only country that has tried to redress the government's past actions toward indigenous peoples (see Box 33-1).

The introduction of gambling on Indian reservations has transformed the lives of some Native Americans. Native Americans got into the gaming industry in 1988, when Congress passed the

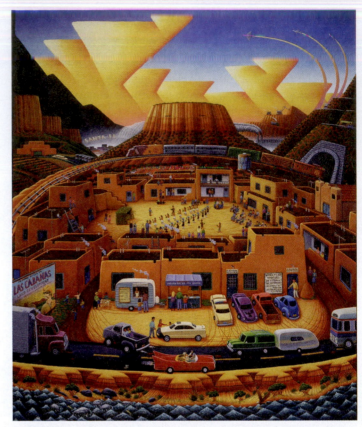

© Peabody Essex Museum, Salem, Massachusetts, USA/Bridgeman Images

Artist David Bradley, a Minnesota Chippewa, shows a Santa Fe Super Chief speeding down a track behind a tribal village that is celebrating a feast day. Tourists watch the dancers, buy fry bread, and frequent a casino (top left of the image). Note the portrayal of inroads on Native American lands: the land development billboard on the left and the bulldozer cutting into a mesa at the top right. What message does the painting convey?

Indian Gambling Regulatory Act. The law stipulates that states must negotiate agreements with tribes interested in commercial gaming; they cannot prevent tribes from engaging in gambling operations, even if state law prohibits such ventures. The income from gambling operations is not evenly distributed. About half of Native American tribes are involved in gambling ventures, and while some earn substantial revenues, it does not necessarily mean the life chances of tribal members are greatly improved. Worsening economic opportunities beyond the resort often offsets gains from casinos. For every success, there are reservations where despite casino revenue, poverty rates have actually increased. In summary, while the advent of gaming has definitely transformed Native American country, overall economic development still remains a major challenge (*The Economist* 2015a; Guedel 2014).

💡 use your **sociological imagination**

You are a Native American whose tribe is about to open a reservation-based casino. Will the casino further the assimilation of your people into mainstream society or encourage pluralism? Explain your reasoning.

Box 33-1

Sociology in the Global Community

The Aboriginal People of Australia

The indigenous, or Aboriginal, people of Australia have inhabited their home continent continuously for at least 50,000 years. Today they make up about 3 percent of Australia's total population, at about 200,000. Although their numbers are relatively small, they are highly visible in Australian society.

The cultural practices of the Aboriginal people are quite diverse, given their many clans, language groups, and communities. Except for occasional connections between kin or trading partners, these groups have little social contact. When Europeans first arrived in Australia, the diversity of Aborigines was even greater: an estimated 600 to 700 different groups spoke 200 to 250 languages as distinct from each other as French is from German. The existence of many dialects, or variants of languages that were more or less understandable to others, increased the complexity.

Like the American Indians, Australia's Aboriginal population declined dramatically following European settlement. New diseases, some of which were not life-threatening to Europeans, had a devastating effect on Aboriginal communities, which lacked immunity to them. Mistreatment under the British colonial regime, dispossession of their land, and the disruption and disintegration of their culture also overwhelmed the Aboriginal people. Decades of protests and legal efforts regarding their land rights have brought little change.

Historically, the Aboriginal people received little legal recognition from Europeans. Only in 1967 did the government of Australia extend citizenship and voting rights

to the Aboriginals, along with access to welfare and unemployment benefits. Yet it would be misleading to view the Aboriginal people as passive victims, either in colonial days or in more recent times. They have worked actively to secure their rights.

As in the United States, Whites' low regard for the Aboriginal people became the basis for an effort to stamp out their culture. From 1910 to 1970, thousands of Aboriginal children were forcibly removed from their families so they could be raised by Whites and impressed into the dominant culture. Between 10 to 30 percent of all Aboriginal children were affected by this program. Not until 2008 did the Australian government finally apologize to Aboriginals for "the Stolen Generations."

© Russotwins/Alamy

Yet despite its efforts, the homeless rate among Aboriginal people is 12 times that of the rest of the population, and the death rate is double.

> From 1910 to 1970, thousands of Aboriginal children were forcibly removed from their families so they could be raised by Whites and impressed into the dominant culture.

The government has expressed its intention to improve the Aboriginal people's living conditions and their prospects for the future.

LET'S DISCUSS

1. Try to think of a situation in your culture in which the government might forcibly remove a child from his or her family. Do you know anyone who has had such an experience? If so, what were the repercussions?

2. What kind of reasoning do you think lay behind the Australian government's forced removal of Aboriginal children from their families? In sociological terms, what actually happened?

Sources: W. Anderson 2003; Attwood 2003; Australia Bureau of Statistics 2014a, 2014b; Australian Indigenous Health Info Net 2015.

Asian Americans

Asian Americans are a diverse group, one of the fastest-growing segments of the U.S. population (up 43 percent between 2000 and 2010). Among the many groups of Americans of Asian descent are Vietnamese Americans, Chinese Americans, Japanese Americans, and Korean Americans (Figure 33-2).

Asian Americans are also economically diverse. There are rich and poor Japanese Americans, rich and poor Filipino Americans, and so forth. In fact, Southeast Asians living in the United States have the highest rate of welfare dependency of any racial or ethnic group. According to a study published in 2011, poverty rates are particularly high among the adult children of Cambodian, Hmong, and Thai immigrants to the United States. Though Asian Americans have substantially more schooling than other ethnic groups, their median income is only slightly higher than Whites' income, and their poverty rate is higher. In 2012, for

every Asian American household with an annual income of $150,000 or more, there was another earning less than $20,000 a year (DeNavas-Walt et al. 2013; Takei and Sakamoto 2011).

The fact that as a group, Asian Americans work in the same occupations as Whites suggests that they have been successful—and many have. However, there are some differences between the two groups. Asian immigrants, like other minorities and immigrants before them, are found disproportionately in low-paying service occupations. At the same time, better-educated Asian Americans are concentrated near the top in professional and managerial positions, although they rarely reach the pinnacle. Instead, they hit the glass ceiling, or try to "climb a broken ladder," as some put it.

Ironically, Asian Americans are often held up as an unqualified success story. According to popular belief, they have succeeded in adapting to mainstream U.S. culture despite past prejudice and discrimination, and without resorting to

Asian Americans: A Model Minority?

Many people suppose that Asian Americans constitute a **model**, or **ideal, minority** group. According to this belief, Asian Americans have succeeded economically, socially, and educationally despite past prejudice and discrimination, and without resorting to political and violent confrontations with Whites. Proponents of this view add that because Asian Americans have achieved success, they are no longer disadvantaged. This portrayal of Asian Americans as a model minority ignores their economic diversity. Moreover, even those Asian Americans who are clustered at the high end of the social scale face some barriers to advancement.

The dramatic success of Asian Americans in the U.S. educational system has undoubtedly contributed to the model minority stereotype. Compared with their numbers in the population as a whole, Asian Americans are greatly overrepresented in the student bodies of the most prestigious universities, public and private. Their upward mobility in schooling can be attributed in part to a strong cultural belief in the value of education, to family pressure to succeed, and to the desire to escape discrimination through academic achievement.

The resulting perception of Asian Americans as academic stars does not always work to their advantage. Asian American students who do not excel in school may face criticism from parents or teachers for their failure to conform to the "whiz kid" image. In fact, the high school dropout rate among Asian Americans is increasing rapidly. In California's

special program for low-income, academically disadvantaged students, Asian Americans make up 30 percent of the students, and their proportion of all students in the program is rising.

School districts are often concerned about the usually overlooked Asian-American segment of their student body. For example, public school officials in St. Paul, Minnesota, found that Asian Americans, the largest racial group in their schools, have impeccable attendance records and the fewest suspensions of any group. But in the important benchmark of standardized testing, those same students are falling far short of the district average in both math and in reading. School board member Chue Vue believes that

© Ariel Skelley/Getty Images RF

> The resulting perception of Asian Americans as academic stars does not always work to their advantage.

Asian-American students have been harmed by educators' presumption of the "Model Minority" stereotype.

LET'S DISCUSS

1. Are Asian Americans seen as "whiz kids" at your school? If so, how close to reality do you think that stereotype is?

2. Talk with some Asian American students about their grades and their study habits. Do they all have the same work ethic? How does your own work ethic compare to theirs?

Sources: Guillermo 2015; Takei and Sakamoto 2011; Teranishi 2010; Xu and Lee 2013.

FIGURE 33-2 **Asian American and Pacific Islander Population by Origin, 2014**

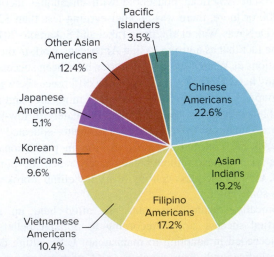

- Pacific Islanders 3.5%
- Other Asian Americans 12.4%
- Japanese Americans 5.1%
- Korean Americans 9.6%
- Vietnamese Americans 10.4%
- Filipino Americans 17.2%
- Asian Indians 19.2%
- Chinese Americans 22.6%

Sources: American Community Survey 2014: B02018; Bureau of the Census 2015e: PEPSR5H. All nationalities with more than 1 million are included.

confrontations with Whites. Box 33-2 compares this common conception with Asian Americans' actual experience.

Chinese Americans

Unlike African slaves and Native Americans, the Chinese were initially encouraged to immigrate to the United States. From 1850 to 1880, thousands of Chinese immigrated to this country, lured by job opportunities created by the discovery of gold. However, as employment possibilities decreased and competition for mining jobs grew, the Chinese became the target of a bitter campaign to limit their numbers and restrict their rights. Chinese laborers were exploited, then discarded.

In 1882, Congress enacted the Chinese Exclusion Act, which prevented Chinese immigration and even forbade Chinese in the United States to send for their families. As a result, the Chinese population declined steadily until after World War II. More recently, the descendants of the 19th-century immigrants have been joined by a new influx from Hong Kong and Taiwan. These groups may contrast sharply in their degree of assimilation, desire to live in Chinatowns, and feelings about this country's relations with the People's Republic of China.

Currently, over 3 million Chinese Americans live in the United States. Some Chinese Americans have entered lucrative occupations, yet many immigrants struggle to survive under living and working conditions that belie the model-minority stereotype. New York City's Chinatown district is filled with illegal sweatshops in which recent immigrants—many of them Chinese women—work for minimal wages. Outside of Chinatown, 23 percent of Asian Americans fall into the low-income category. At the other end of the income distribution, barely 5 percent of Chinatown's residents earn more than $100,000 a year, compared to 25 percent of Asian Americans who live elsewhere in New York City (Logan et al. 2002; Wong 2006).

Asian Indians

After Chinese Americans, the second-largest Asian American group, immigrants from India and their descendants, numbers over 2.8 million. It is difficult to generalize about Asian Indian Americans because Asian Indians are such a diverse population. India, a country of more than 1.2 billion people that is fast becoming the most populous nation in the world, is multiethnic. Perhaps because Asian Indian immigrants feel threatened by mainstream U.S. culture, religious orthodoxy is often stronger among first-generation immigrants to the United States than it is in India. New immigrants try to practice their religion just as they did in India rather than join congregations already established by other immigrant groups.

Maintaining family traditions is a major challenge for Asian Indian immigrants to the United States. Family ties remain strong despite their immigration—so much so that many Asian Indians feel more connected to their relatives in India than Americans do to relatives nearby. These *Desi* (pronounced day-see, colloquial for people who trace their ancestry to South Asia, especially India) are particularly concerned about the erosion of traditional family authority. Indian American children dress like their peers, go to fast-food restaurants, and even eat hamburgers, rejecting the vegetarian diet typical of both Hindus and many Asian Indian Muslims. Sons do not feel the extent of responsibility to the family that tradition dictates. Daughters, whose occupations and marriage partners the family could control in India, assert their right to choose their careers, and even their husbands (Rangaswamy 2005).

Filipino Americans

Filipinos are the third-largest Asian American group in the United States, with nearly 2.6 million people. For geographic reasons, social scientists consider them to be of Asian extraction, but physically and culturally this group also reflects centuries of Spanish and U.S. colonial rule, as well as the more recent U.S. military occupation.

Filipinos began immigrating to the United States as American nationals when the U.S. government gained possession of the

© Everett Collection/Alamy

Rarely does an Indian American star in, much much less write, her own television show, but Mindy Kaling of *The Mindy Project* does both. While the Asian American community largely applauded this pathbreaker when her show premiered in 2012, some criticized the show because her character dates a White guy. In response, Kaling asked why no one writes about White leads on shows who don't date outside their race. For example, on *Seinfeld*, Jerry Seinfeld's character dated over 100 women—all White (Ryan 2015).

Philippine Islands at the end of the Spanish–American War (1899). When the Philippines gained their independence in 1948, Filipinos lost their unrestricted immigration rights, although farmworkers were welcome to work in Hawai'i's pineapple groves. Aside from this exception, immigration was restricted to 50 to 100 Filipinos a year until 1965, when the Immigration Act lifted the strict quotas.

Today, a significant percentage of Filipino immigrants are well-educated professionals who work in the field of health care. Although they are a valuable human resource in the United States, their immigration has long drained the medical establishment in the Philippines. When the U.S. Immigration and Naturalization Service stopped giving preference to physicians, Filipino doctors began entering the country as nurses—a dramatic illustration of the incredible income differences between the two countries. Like other immigrant groups, Filipino Americans save much of their income and send a significant amount of money, called **remittances,** back to their extended families.

For several reasons, Filipino Americans have not coalesced in a single formal social organization, despite their numbers. Their strong loyalty to the family (*sa pamilya*) and to the church—particularly Roman Catholicism—reduces their need for a separate organization. Moreover, their diversity complicates the task of uniting the Filipino American community, which reflects the same regional, religious, and linguistic distinctions that divide their homeland. Thus, the many groups that Filipino Americans have organized tend to be club-like or fraternal in nature. Because those groups do not represent the general population of Filipino Americans, they remain largely invisible to Anglos.

Although Filipinos remain interested in events in their homeland, they also seek to become involved in broader, non-Filipino organizations and to avoid exclusive activities (McNamara and Batalova 2015; Padilla 2008).

Vietnamese Americans

Vietnamese Americans came to the United States primarily during and after the Vietnam War—especially after U.S. withdrawal from the conflict in 1975. Refugees from the communist government in Vietnam, assisted by local agencies, settled throughout the United States, tens of thousands of them in small towns. Over time, however, Vietnamese Americans have gravitated toward the larger urban areas, establishing Vietnamese restaurants and grocery stores in their ethnic enclaves there.

In 1995, the United States resumed normal diplomatic relations with Vietnam. Gradually, the *Viet Kieu,* or Vietnamese living abroad, began to return to their old country to visit, but usually not to take up permanent residence. Shuttling between two nations, Viet Kieu leave their cultural mark on both countries. Today, more than 40 years after the end of the Vietnam War, sharp differences of opinion remain among Vietnamese Americans, especially the older ones, concerning the war and the present government of Vietnam (Harris 2015; Rkasnuam and Batalova 2014).

Korean Americans

At over 1.8 million, the population of Korean Americans now exceeds that of Japanese Americans. Yet Korean Americans are often overshadowed by other groups from Asia.

Today's Korean American community is the result of three waves of immigration. The initial wave arrived between 1903 and 1910, when Korean laborers migrated to Hawai'i. The second wave followed the end of the Korean War in 1953; most of those immigrants were wives of U.S. servicemen and war orphans. The third wave, continuing to the present, has reflected the admissions priorities set up in the 1965 Immigration Act. These well-educated immigrants arrive in the United States with professional skills. Yet because of language difficulties and discrimination, many must settle at least initially for positions of lower responsibility than those they held in Korea and must suffer through a period of disenchantment. Stress, loneliness, and family strife may accompany the pain of adjustment.

In the early 1990s, the apparent friction between Korean Americans and another subordinate racial group, African Americans, attracted nationwide attention. Conflict between the two groups was dramatized in Spike Lee's 1989 movie *Do the Right Thing.* The situation stemmed from Korean Americans' position as the latest immigrant group to cater to the needs of inner-city populations abandoned by those who have moved up the economic ladder. This type of friction is not new; generations of Jewish, Italian, and Arab merchants have encountered similar hostility from what to outsiders seems an unlikely source—another oppressed minority (K. Kim 1999; Zong and Batalova 2014).

Japanese Americans

Approximately 1.4 million Japanese Americans live in the United States. As a people, they are relatively recent arrivals.

In 1880, only 148 Japanese lived in the United States, but by 1920 there were more than 110,000. Japanese immigrants—called the *Issei* (pronounced ee-say), or first generation—were usually males seeking employment opportunities. Many Whites saw them (along with Chinese immigrants) as a "yellow peril" and subjected them to prejudice and discrimination.

In 1941, the attack on Hawai'i's Pearl Harbor by Japan had severe repercussions for Japanese Americans. The federal government decreed that all Japanese Americans on the West Coast must leave their homes and report to "evacuation camps." In effect, Japanese Americans became scapegoats for the anger that other people in the United States felt concerning Japan's role in World War II. By August 1943, in an unprecedented application of guilt by virtue of ancestry, 113,000 Japanese Americans had been forced into hastily built camps. In striking contrast, only a few German Americans and Italian Americans were sent to evacuation camps (Hosokawa 1969).

In 1983, a federal commission recommended government payments to all surviving Japanese Americans who had been held in detention camps. The commission reported that the detention was motivated by "race prejudice, war hysteria, and a failure of political leadership." It added that "no documented acts of espionage, sabotage, or fifth-column activity were shown to have been committed" by Japanese Americans. In 1988, President Ronald Reagan signed the Civil Liberties Act, which required the federal government to issue individual apologies for all violations of Japanese Americans' constitutional rights, and established a $1.25 billion trust fund to pay reparations to the approximately 77,500 surviving Japanese Americans who had been interned (Department of Justice 2000).

Arab Americans

Arab Americans are immigrants, and their descendants, from the 22 nations of the Arab world. As defined by the League of Arab States, these are the nations of North Africa and what is popularly known as the Middle East, including Lebanon, Syria, Palestine, Morocco, Iraq, Saudi Arabia, and Somalia. Not all residents of those countries are Arab; for example, the Kurds, who live in northern Iraq, are not Arab. And some Arab Americans may have immigrated to the United States from non-Arab countries such as Great Britain or France, where their families have lived for generations.

The Arabic language is the single most unifying force among Arabs, although not all Arabs, and certainly not all Arab Americans, can read and speak Arabic. Moreover, the language has evolved over the centuries so that people in different parts of the Arab world speak different dialects. Still, the fact that the Koran (or Qur'an) was originally written in Arabic gives the language special importance to Muslims, just as the Torah's compilation in Hebrew gives that language special significance to Jews.

Estimates of the size of the Arab American community differ widely. Nearly 4 million people of Arab ancestry reside in the United States. Among those who identify themselves as Arab Americans, the most common country of origin is Lebanon, followed by Syria, Egypt, and Palestine. In 2000, these four countries of origin accounted for two-thirds of all Arab Americans.

© George Rose/Getty Images

In Chicago, a young Muslim woman sports an "I Love New York" T-shirt. Across the United States, racial and ethnic diversity has increased dramatically.

Their rising numbers have led to the development of Arab retail centers in several cities, including Dearborn and Detroit, Michigan; Los Angeles; Chicago; New York City; and Washington, D.C.

As a group, Arab Americans are extremely diverse. Many families have lived in the United States for several generations; others are foreign born. Their points of origin range from the metropolis of Cairo, Egypt, to the rural villages of Morocco. Despite the stereotype, most Arab Americans are *not* Muslim (Figure 33-3). Nor can Arab Americans be characterized as having a specific family type, gender role, or occupational pattern (David 2004, 2008).

In spite of this great diversity, profiling of potential terrorists at airports has put Arab and Muslim Americans under special surveillance. For years, a number of airlines and law enforcement authorities have used appearance and ethnic-sounding names to identify and take aside Arab Americans and search their belongings. After the terrorist attacks of September 2001 and more recent attacks in Europe and North America, criticism of this practice declined as concern for the public's safety mounted.

Latinos

Together, the various groups included under the general category *Latinos* represent the largest minority in the United States. There are more than 55 million Hispanics in this country, including 35 million Mexican Americans, more than 5 million Puerto

FIGURE 33-3 Arab American Religious Affiliations, 2010

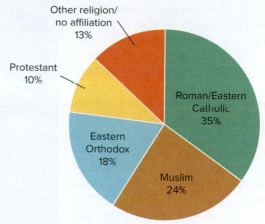

Notes: Roman/Eastern Catholic includes Roman Catholic, Maronite, and Melkite (Greek Catholic); Eastern Orthodox includes Antiochian, Syrian, Greek, and Coptic; Muslim includes Sunni, Shi'a, and Druze.
Source: Arab American Institute 2010, based on 2002 Zogby International Survey.

Ricans, and smaller numbers of Cuban Americans and people of Central and South American origin (Figure 33-4). The latter group represents the fastest-growing and most diverse segment of the Hispanic community.

According to Census Bureau data, the Latino population now outnumbers the African American population in 6 of the 10 largest metropolitan areas of the United States: New York City, Los Angeles, Chicago, Dallas–Fort Worth, Houston, and Miami–Fort Lauderdale. The rise of the Hispanic population of the United States—fueled by comparatively high birthrates and immigration levels—has Latinos beginning to flex their muscles as voters. In the 2012 presidential election, Latinos accounted for

FIGURE 33-4 Hispanic Population by Origin

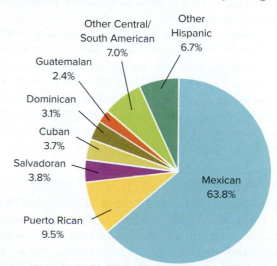

Note: "Other Hispanic" includes Spanish Americans and Latinos identified as mixed ancestry as well as other Central and South Americans not otherwise indicated by specific country.
Source: American Community Survey 2015: B03001. All nationalities with more than 1 million are named.

more than 8 percent of eligible voters. As Hispanics age and immigrants become citizens, their presence in the voting booth will be felt even more strongly (Bureau of the Census 2011a:Table 23 on page 31; Lopez 2011; Lopez and Gonzalez Barrera 2013).

The various Latino groups share a heritage of Spanish language and culture, which can cause serious problems in their assimilation. An intelligent student whose first language is Spanish may be presumed slow or even unruly by English-speaking schoolchildren, and frequently by English-speaking teachers as well. The labeling of Latino children as underachievers, as learning disabled, or as emotionally disturbed can act as a self-fulfilling prophecy for some children. Bilingual education aims at easing the educational difficulties experienced by Hispanic children and others whose first language is not English.

The educational difficulties of Latino students certainly contribute to Hispanics' generally low economic status. In 2015, about 15 percent of all Hispanic households earned less than $15,000, compared to 11 percent of White non-Hispanic households; the poverty rate was 23.6 percent for Hispanics, compared to 10.1 percent for White non-Hispanics. Although Latinos are not as affluent as White non-Hispanics, a middle class is beginning to emerge (DeNavas-Walt and Proctor 2015: 13, 25, 29).

Mexican Americans

The largest Latino population is Mexican Americans, who can be further subdivided into those descended from residents of the territories annexed after the Mexican American War of 1848 and those who have immigrated from Mexico to the United States. The opportunity for a Mexican to earn in one hour what it would take an entire day to earn in Mexico has pushed millions of legal and illegal immigrants north.

Many people view Mexican Americans as primarily an immigrant group. Since at least 2000, however, the number of Mexican Americans who were born in the United States has far exceeded those who immigrated here. Overall, Mexican Americans accounted for 42 percent of the nation's population growth in the decade 2000–2010, but the rate of growth has slowed more recently. Two-thirds of them were born here; the other third are new arrivals (Krogstad 2015).

Puerto Ricans

The second-largest segment of Latinos in the United States is Puerto Ricans. Since 1917, residents of Puerto Rico have held the status of American citizens; many have migrated to New York and other eastern cities. Unfortunately, Puerto Ricans have experienced serious poverty both in the United States and on the island. Those who live in the continental United States earn barely half the family income of Whites. As a result, many returned to the Island to take advantage of cheaper living

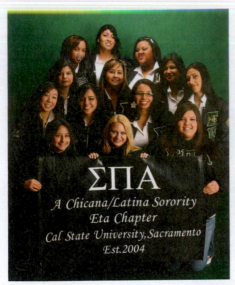

Courtesy of Sigma Pi Alpha Sorority at Sacramento State University

conditions and supportive extended families. However, in recent years the economic situation of Puerto Rico has deteriorated to the point that beginning in 2010, increasing numbers of Puerto Ricans left for the Mainland (L. Alvarez 2015).

Politically, Puerto Ricans in the United States have not been as successful as Mexican Americans in organizing for their rights. For many mainland Puerto Ricans—as for many residents of the island—the paramount political issue is the destiny of Puerto Rico itself: should it continue in its present commonwealth status, petition for admission to the United States as the 51st state, or attempt to become an independent nation? This question has divided Puerto Rico for decades and remains a central issue in Puerto Rican elections. In a 1998 referendum, voters supported a "none of the above" option, effectively favoring continuation of the commonwealth status over statehood or independence. The recent severe economic problems seemed to encourage a rise in calls for independence, encouraged by support from some of the 2016 presidential candidates (Yuhas 2015).

© The Collection of the Supreme Court of the United States/MCT/Getty Images
Sonia Sotomayor was born in the Bronx, New York, of Puerto Rican parents. In 2009 she became the first Hispanic, and one of only four women, ever to be appointed to the U.S. Supreme Court. Of the other 108 justices, 2 have been African American men and 106 have been White men.

Cuban Americans

Cuban immigration to the United States dates back as far as 1831, but it began in earnest following Fidel Castro's assumption of power in the Cuban revolution (1959). At the time it was seen as a refugee crisis, much like those described in the policy section at the end of this chapter. The first wave of 200,000 Cubans included many professionals with relatively high levels of schooling; these men and women were largely welcomed as refugees from communist tyranny. However, more recent waves of immigrants have aroused growing concern, partly because they were less likely to be skilled professionals. Throughout these waves of immigration, Cuban Americans have been encouraged to locate around the United States. Nevertheless, many continue to settle in (or return to) metropolitan Miami, Florida, with its warm climate and proximity to Cuba.

The Cuban experience in the United States has been mixed. Cuban Americans in Miami have expressed concern over what they view as the indifference of the city's Roman Catholic hierarchy. Like other Hispanics, Cuban Americans are underrepresented in leadership positions within the church. The most dramatic development in the last generation has been the improvement of relations between the Cuban and United States governments. In 2013, Cuba eased its travel restrictions, which led to a large increase in migration to the United States, primarily via Mexico. In 2015, the two countries restored diplomatic relations, allowing Cuban Americans (57 percent of whom are U.S. residents not born in the United States) to easily visit their homeland and permitting more Cubans to move to the United States (pending action to ease longstanding restrictions on legal entry from Cuba) (Krogstad 2015; Masud-Piloto 2008).

Central and South Americans

Immigrants from Central and South America are a diverse population that has not been closely studied. Indeed, most government statistics treat members of this group collectively as "other," rarely differentiating among them by nationality. Yet people from Chile and Costa Rica have little in common other than their hemisphere of origin and the Spanish language—if that. The fact is, not all Central and South Americans speak Spanish. Immigrants from Brazil, for example, speak Portuguese; immigrants from French Guyana speak French; and immigrants from Suriname speak Dutch.

Racially, many of the nations of Central and South America follow a complex classification system that recognizes a multitude of color gradients. Experience with this multiracial system does not prepare immigrants to the United States for the stark Black–White racial divide that characterizes U.S. society. Beyond their diversity in color and language, immigrants from Central and South America are differentiated by social class distinctions, religious differences, urban or rural upbringings, and dialects. Some of them may come from indigenous populations, especially in Guatemala and Belize. If so, their social identity would be separate from any national allegiance.

In short, social relations among Central and South Americans, who collectively number nearly 7 million people in the United States, defy generalization. The same can be said about their relations with other Latinos and with non-Latinos. Central and South Americans do not form, nor should they be expected to form, a cohesive group. Nor do they easily form coalitions with Cuban Americans, Mexican Americans, or Puerto Ricans.

Jewish Americans

Jews constitute about 2 percent of the population of the United States. They play a prominent role in the worldwide Jewish community, because the United States has the world's largest concentration of Jews. Like the Japanese, many Jewish immigrants came to this country and became white-collar professionals in spite of prejudice and discrimination.

Anti-Semitism—anti-Jewish prejudice—has often been vicious in the United States, although rarely so widespread and never so formalized as in Europe. In many cases, Jews have been used as scapegoats for other people's failures. Not surprisingly, Jews have not achieved equality in the United States. Despite high levels of education and professional training, they are still conspicuously absent from the top management of large corporations (except for the few firms founded by Jews). Nonetheless, a national survey in 2009 showed that one out of four people in the United States blames "the Jews" for the financial crisis. In addition, private social clubs and fraternal groups frequently continue to limit membership to Gentiles (non-Jews), a practice upheld by the Supreme Court in the 1964 case *Bell v. Maryland* (Malhotra and Margalit 2009).

© Rachel Morton/Impact/HIP/The Image Works

For practicing Jews, the Hebrew language is an important part of religious instruction. This young pupil learns the Hebrew alphabet with a Jewish teacher.

The Anti-Defamation League (ADL) of B'nai B'rith coordinates an annual tally of reported anti-Semitic incidents. Although the number has fluctuated, in 2012 the tabulation of the total reported incidents of harassment, threats, vandalism, and assaults came to 927. Some incidents were inspired and carried out by neo-Nazi skinheads—groups of young people who champion racist and anti-Semitic ideologies. Such threatening behavior only intensifies the fears of many Jewish Americans, who remember the Holocaust—the extermination of 6 million Jews by the Nazi Third Reich during World War II (Anti-Defamation League 2013).

As is true for other minorities discussed in this chapter, Jewish Americans face the choice of maintaining ties to their long religious and cultural heritage or becoming as indistinguishable as possible from Gentiles. Many Jews have tended to assimilate, as is evident from the rise in marriages between Jews and Christians. In marriages that occurred in the 1970s, more than 70 percent of Jews married Jews or people who converted to Judaism. In marriages since 1996, that proportion has dropped to 53 percent. This trend means that today, American Jews are almost as likely to marry a Gentile as a Jew. For many, religion is a nonissue—neither parent practices religious rituals. Two-thirds of the children of these Jewish–Gentile marriages are not raised as Jews. Finally, in 2005, two-thirds of Jews felt that the biggest threat to Jewish life was anti-Semitism; only one-third named intermarriage as the biggest threat (American Jewish Committee 2005; Sanua 2007).

© David L. Moore – Oregon/Alamy

White Americans often express their ethnicity with special celebrations, such as this Scandinavian Festival parade in Junction City, Oregon. Participants proudly display the flag of Denmark.

White Ethnics

A significant segment of the population of the United States is made up of White ethnics whose ancestors arrived from Europe within the last century and a half. The nation's White ethnic population includes about 49 million people who claim at least partial German ancestry, 36 million Irish Americans, 17 million Italian Americans, and 10 million Polish Americans, as well as immigrants from other European nations. Some of these people continue to live in close-knit ethnic neighborhoods, whereas others have largely assimilated and left the "old ways" behind.

Many White ethnics today identify only sporadically with their heritage. **Symbolic ethnicity** refers to an emphasis on concerns such as ethnic food or political issues rather than on deeper ties to one's ethnic heritage. It is reflected in the occasional family trip to an ethnic bakery, the celebration of a ceremonial event such as St. Joseph's Day among Italian Americans, or concern about the future of Northern Ireland among Irish Americans. Such practices are another example of the social construction of race and ethnicity. Except in cases in which new immigration reinforces old traditions, symbolic ethnicity tends to decline with each passing generation (Alba 1990; Winter 2008).

Although the White ethnic identity may be a point of pride to those who share it, they do not necessarily celebrate it at the expense of disadvantaged minorities. It is all too easy to assume that race relations are a zero-sum game in which one group gains at the expense of the other. Rather, the histories of several White ethnic groups, such as the Irish and the Italians, show that once marginalized people can rise to positions of prestige and influence (Alba 2009).

That is not to say that White ethnics and racial minorities have not been antagonistic toward one another because of economic competition—an interpretation that agrees with the conflict approach to sociology. As Blacks, Latinos, and Native Americans emerge from the lower class, they must compete with working-class Whites for jobs, housing, and educational opportunities. In times of high unemployment or inflation, any such competition can easily generate intense intergroup conflict.

In many respects, the plight of White ethnics raises the same basic issues as that of other subordinate people in the United States. How ethnic can people be—how much can they deviate from an essentially White, Anglo-Saxon, Protestant norm—before society punishes them for their willingness to be different? Our society does seem to reward people for assimilating, yet as we have seen, assimilation is no easy process. In the years to come, more and more people will face the challenge of fitting in, not only in the United States but around the world, as the flow of immigrants from one country to another continues to increase.

Immigration and Continuing Diversity

A significant segment of the population of the United States is made up of White ethnics whose ancestors arrived from Europe within the last 150 years. The United States has long had policies to determine who has preference to enter the country. Often, clear racial and ethnic biases are built into these policies. In the 1920s, U.S. policy gave preference to people from Western Europe, while making it difficult for residents of southern and eastern Europe, Asia, and Africa to enter the country.

Since the 1960s, policies in the United States have encouraged the immigration of people who have relatives here as well as of those who have needed skills. This change has significantly altered the pattern of sending nations. Previously, Europeans dominated, but for the last 40 years, immigrants have come primarily from Latin America and Asia (see Figure 33–5). This means that in the future, an ever-growing proportion of the United States will be Asian or Hispanic. To a large degree, fear and resentment of this growing racial and ethnic diversity is a key factor in opposition to immigration. Many people are very concerned that the new arrivals do not reflect how they define the nation's cultural and racial heritage.

Feeling pressure for immigration control, Congress ended a decade of debate by approving the Immigration Reform and Control Act of 1986. The act marked a historic change in the nation's immigration policy. For the first time, the hiring of illegal aliens was outlawed, and employers caught violating the law became subject to fines and even prison sentences. Just as significant a change was the extension of amnesty and legal status to many illegal immigrants already living in the United States.

More than 30 years later, the act appears to have had mixed results. Substantial numbers of illegal immigrants continue to enter the country each year; an estimated 11.3 million are present at any given time—a marked increase since 1990, when their number was estimated at close to 3.5 million. Over 62 percent have been in the United States at least 10 years and over a third live with U.S.- born children. The presence of illegal immigrants has led to a wide array of policy suggestions from massive deportations and the creation of a massive wall along the 2,000 mile Mexico-United border to a pathway to full citizenship for those illegally here meeting certain criteria after paying hefty fees (Passel and Cohn 2015).

Despite people's fears about it, immigration performs many valuable functions. For the receiving society, it alleviates labor shortages, such as exist in the fields of health care and technology in the United States. In 1998 Congress debated not whether individuals with technological skills should be allowed into the country, but just how much to increase the annual quota. For the sending nation, migration can relieve economies unable to support large numbers of people. Often overlooked is the large amounts of money immigrants send back to their home nations. According to the World Bank's estimate, globally, immigrants from developing nations send about $430 billion per year back to their home countries (World Bank 2015b).

Immigration can be dysfunctional as well. Although studies generally show that it has a positive impact on the receiving nation's economy, areas that accept high concentrations of immigrants may have difficulty meeting short-term social service needs. Furthermore, when migrants with skills or educational potential leave developing countries, their absence can be dysfunctional for those nations. No amount of money sent back home can make up for the loss of valuable human resources from poor nations.

In contrast, conflict theorists have noted how much of the debate over immigration is phrased in economic terms. The debate intensifies when the arrivals are of different racial and ethnic backgrounds from the host population. Fear and dislike of "new" ethnic groups divide countries throughout the world, as we will see in the Social Policy section, which focuses on the worldwide challenge of growing numbers of refugees.

FIGURE 33-5 **Legal Migration to the United States, 1820–2020**

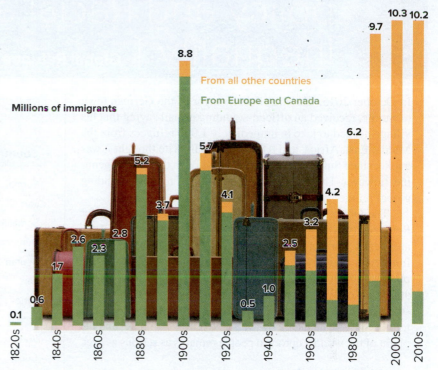

Millions of immigrants

From all other countries
From Europe and Canada

For the past five decades, the majority of immigrants to the United States have come from outside Europe and Canada.
Source: Office of Immigration Statistics 2014 and the author's estimates for projection to 2020. Photo: © pixhook/Getty Images RF

policy and Racial and Ethnic Inequality | Global Refugee Crisis

In October 2015, Christian Fabel, mayor of the German town of Sumte, received an official-sounding e-mail saying that his village needed to take in immediately 1,000 refugees from the Middle East, Africa, and Afghanistan. His wife thought it was a joke, since Sumte had a population of only 102. It was genuine, however. This is only one illustration of the long-standing global refugee crisis (Higgins 2015).

The Office of the United Nations High Commissioner for Refugees (UNHCR) was established on December 14, 1950, and began work in Geneva, Switzerland, on January 1, 1951. Initially, it was given a three-year mandate to help solve the plight of about 1 million European refugees remaining in the aftermath of World War II. After three years the agency was supposed to disband, the refugee problem resolved once and for all. Sixty years later, however, UNHCR is still here, and the plight of the world's uprooted people remains as serious as ever.

Looking at the Issue

As of late 2015, more than 60 million people worldwide were forcibly displaced as a result of conflict and persecution, the highest number since the mid-1990s. Several additional million people remain displaced because of natural disasters, although updated statistics are not available. About half of the uprooted are refugees who fled their home countries, while the other half are people who remain displaced by conflict within their own homelands—so—called "internally displaced" people. (UN High Commissioner for Refugees 2015).

Refugees are people who live outside their country of citizenship for fear of political or religious persecution. Unlike refugees, immigrants are people who choose to move not because of a direct threat of persecution or death but most often to improve their lives by finding work, going to school, reuniting with family, or some other reasons. Unlike refugees, who cannot safely return home, migrants face no such impediment. If they choose to return home, they will continue to receive the protection of their government.

The United States, insulated by distance from wars and famines throughout much of the world, has been able to be selective about which and how many refugees are welcomed. The United States resettles between 56,000 and 73,000 refugees annually and has hosted over 1 million refugees between 1990 and 2014. Table 33-1 lists the major sources of refugees to the United States.

According to the United Nations treaty on refugees, which our government ratified in 1968, countries are obliged to refrain from forcibly returning people to territories where

TABLE 33-1 TOP SOURCES OF REFUGEES TO THE UNITED STATES, 2015

Country
Burma
Iraq
Somalia
Democratic Republic of Congo
Bhutan
Iran
Syria
Eritrea
Sudan
Cuba

Source: Mossaad 2016:3.

their lives or liberty might be endangered. However, it is not always clear whether a person is fleeing for his or her personal safety or to escape poverty. Although people in the latter category may be of humanitarian interest, they do not meet the official definition of refugees and are subject to deportation.

Refugees are people who are granted the right to enter a country while still residing abroad. **Asylees** are foreigners who have already entered a nation and seek protection because of persecution or a well-founded fear of persecution. This persecution may be based on the individual's race, religion, nationality, membership in a particular social group, or political opinion.

Because asylees, by definition, are already here, they are either granted legal entry or returned to their home country. In recent years, sudden and prolonged conflicts in Africa, Asia, and the Middle East have increased by millions the numbers of people who flee their countries without first securing permission before entering neighboring countries. This became especially poignant in 2015, as millions of Syrians, Afghans, and others entered member countries of the European Union, particularly Greece and Hungary.

Applying Sociology

In many countries where refugees seek to settle, the economy is in desperate need of workers. Consequently, refugees could ultimately, even if not in the short run, function to provide a needed economic boost. The 2015 surge of refugees into

—*Continued*

Slovakian political cartoonist Marian Kamensky illustrates the mixed welcome that Middle Eastern refugees received in his home country in 2015.

Europe from Syria, Afghanistan, Iraq and other war-ravaged countries presents a striking contrast to the relatively older population of western Europe. The hundreds of thousands of predominantly young people are trying to enter a region where the population is older than in almost any other place on earth. Researchers contend that the influx of youthful refugees could be a long-term benefit to an aging Europe, renewing the supply of younger workers who are needed to support the continent's large numbers of retirees (Desilver 2015).

Conflict theorists point out that framing the issue as a "refugee crisis" may inadvertently stigmatize the refugees as the ones responsible for the problem, thus "blaming the victim" (Ryan 1976). The refugees are overwhelmingly the result, not the cause, of civil unrest, warfare, persecution, and poverty. Indeed sometimes affluent industrial countries play a role in creating the social conditions leading to the involuntary mass migrations.

Initiating Policy

Decisions to open or close a nation's borders are difficult to make. Many countries have sought to develop long-term strategies to head off refugees. These may take the form of providing international assistance to make the social conditions better in the home country or creating livable refugee camps near the origin of the exodus to facilitate movement back when the situations improve. A 2015 summit meeting in Malta with European and African leaders sought to develop a consensus about what could be done to improve life in much of Africa and head off the tens of thousands of young Africans who try to cross a treacherous desert and sea in hope of reaching brighter prospects in Europe (Sengupta 2015).

Deciding where to locate refugees within a country can be critical to both the migrants' successful transition and the host country's willingness to continue to accept refugees in the future. In the 1970s, when the United States accepted Vietnamese refugees at the end of the war there, religious organizations played a critical role in receiving immigrants. As a result, Vietnamese refugees were dispersed throughout the country. Ultimately many resettled in large cities near fellow refugees, but the initial dispersal helped remove concerns that any one area was receiving "too many."

More recently, Chicago and the Dallas-Ft. Worth metropolitan areas have received large numbers of Syrian refugees. Nongovernmental agencies assisting with refugee settlement have made a concerted effort to place refugees in more affordable medium-sized cities, and as a result, Boise, Idaho, has accepted more refugees than Los Angeles and New York City combined and Worcester, Massachusetts, has taken in more than Boston (H. Park 2015).

Despite these positive steps, people in potential receiving countries remain hostile to refugees, especially those from Middle Eastern countries. A series of terrorist attacks in France in 2015 changed Europe's migrant focus from one of compassion to one of concerns about security. The murder of over 130 civilians in Paris left many wondering, there and elsewhere, whether potential terrorists might be hiding among future refugees and asylees. Hate speech quickly spread across social media.

Within days of the Paris attacks, nearly half of the governors in the United States proclaimed that their states would not accept refugees from the Middle East, despite their lack of authority to close their borders. A national survey at the time showed that 53 percent of the public were opposed to accepting Syrian refugees. (This opposition is hardly new: in 1939, 61 percent were unwilling to accept German-Jewish refugee children, even after the Nazi government's anti-Semitic intentions were clear.) While they understand the popular appeal of such pronouncements, foreign policy specialists question the accuracy of characterizing refugees as criminals. These specialists note that one of the most powerful recruiting tools for terrorist groups is to point to a nation's generalized fear as a way to win over those alienated by the prejudice they have already felt (Sauerbrey 2015; Spiegel et al. 2015; Talev 2015; Tharoor 2015).

Unfortunately, but predictably, new foreign military campaigns will bring new refugee issues. Measured responses are needed, as are innovative ways to reduce the creation of refugees in the first place.

TAKE THE ISSUE WITH YOU

1. Did you or your family come to the United States as refugees or asylees? Explain the circumstances.

2. Is it fair to say that affluent countries play a role in creating a refugee crisis? Explain your answer.

3. Do you live, work, or study with recent refugees to the United States? Are they well accepted into your community? What kinds of prejudice and discrimination do they face?

Summary

The U.S. population is highly diverse, both racially and ethnically.

1. Contemporary prejudice and discrimination against African Americans are rooted in the history of slavery in the United States.

2. Asian Americans are commonly viewed as a **model,** or **ideal minority,** a false stereotype that is not necessarily beneficial to members of that group.

3. The various groups included under the general term *Latinos* represent the largest ethnic minority in the United States.

4. Worldwide, immigration is at an all-time high, fueling controversy not only in the United States but also in the European Union.

5. Conflict and economic turmoil in the developing world have created a continuing immigration crisis in Europe and the United States, as receiving countries struggle to absorb large numbers of **refugees** and **asylees.**

Thinking Critically

1. Mexican culture seems alive in many Mexican American communities. Native Americans routinely display their tribal identities. Why do White ethnic identities seem more elusive?

2. To what extent has U.S. society achieved pluralism? Give examples from your own experience to support your viewpoint.

3. On balance, do the functions of immigration to the United States outweigh the dysfunctions? Explain your answer.

Key Terms

Anti-Semitism

Asylees

Black power

Model, or ideal, minority

Refugee

Remittances

Symbolic ethnicity

Mastering This Chapter

© RosalreneBetancourt 3/Alamy

taking sociology with you

1 Consider one or more jobs you have had, or an occupation you aspire to. How diverse is the staff you worked with, or would work with? What about your clients or customers? Do you expect racial and ethnic diversity to play an important role in your future career?

2 Talk with an older relative about your family's past. Did your ancestors experience prejudice or discrimination because of their race or ethnicity, and if so, in what way? Did they ever use racial or ethnic slurs to refer to people of other races or ethnicities? Have your family's attitudes toward members of other groups changed over the years, and if so, why?

3 Look up the census statistics on the racial and ethnic composition of your community. What are the predominant racial and ethnic groups? How many other groups are represented? How many members of your community are immigrants, and where do they come from?

Affirmative action Positive efforts to recruit minority group members or women for jobs, promotions, and educational opportunities.

Amalgamation The process through which a majority group and a minority group combine to form a new group.

Anti-Semitism Anti-Jewish prejudice.

Apartheid A former policy of the South African government, designed to maintain the separation of Blacks and other non-Whites from the dominant Whites.

Assimilation The process through which a person forsakes his or her cultural tradition to become part of a different culture.

Asylees Foreigners who have already entered a receiving country because of persecution of a well-founded fear of persecution.

Black power A political philosophy, promoted by many younger Blacks in the 1960s, that supported the creation of Black-controlled political and economic institutions.

Color-blind racism The use of the principle of race neutrality to defend a racially unequal status quo.

Contact hypothesis An interactionist perspective which states that in cooperative circumstances, interracial contact between people of equal status will reduce prejudice.

Discrimination The denial of opportunities and equal rights to individuals and groups because of prejudice or other arbitrary reasons.

Ethnic group A group that is set apart from others primarily because of its national origin or distinctive cultural patterns.

Ethnocentrism The tendency to assume that one's own culture and way of life represent the norm or are superior to all others.

Exploitation theory A Marxist theory that views racial subordination in the United States as a manifestation of the class system inherent in capitalism.

Genocide The deliberate, systematic killing of an entire people or nation.

Glass ceiling An invisible barrier that blocks the promotion of a qualified individual in a work environment because of the individual's gender, race, or ethnicity.

Institutional discrimination The denial of opportunities and equal rights to individuals and groups that results from the normal operations of a society.

Minority group A subordinate group whose members have significantly less control or power over their own lives than the members of a dominant or majority group have over theirs.

Model, or ideal, minority A subordinate group whose members supposedly have succeeded economically, socially, and educationally despite past prejudice and discrimination, and without resorting to political and violent confrontations with Whites.

Pluralism Mutual respect for one another's cultures among the various groups in a society, which allows minorities to express their cultures without experiencing prejudice.

Prejudice A negative attitude toward an entire category of people, often an ethnic or racial minority.

Racial formation A sociohistorical process in which racial categories are created, inhabited, transformed, and destroyed.

Racial group A group that is set apart from others because of physical differences that have taken on social significance.

Racial profiling Any arbitrary action initiated by an authority based on race, ethnicity, or national origin rather than on a person's behavior.

Racism The belief that one race is supreme and all others are innately inferior.

Redlining The pattern of discrimination against people who try to buy homes in minority and racially changing neighborhoods.

Refugee People living outside their country of citizenship for fear of political or religious persecution.

Remittances The monies that immigrants return to their families of origin.

Segregation The physical separation of two groups of people in terms of residence, workplace, and social events; often imposed on a minority group by a dominant group.

Stereotype An unreliable generalization about all members of a group that does not recognize individual differences within the group.

Symbolic ethnicity An ethnic identity that emphasizes concerns such as ethnic food or political issues rather than deeper ties to one's ethnic heritage.

White privilege Rights or immunities granted to people as a particular benefit or favor simply because they are White.

Read each question carefully and then select the best answer.

1. Sociologists have identified five basic properties of a minority group. Which of the following is *not* one of those properties?
   a. unequal treatment
   b. physical traits
   c. ascribed status
   d. cultural bias

2. The largest racial minority group in the United States is
   a. Asian Americans.
   b. African Americans.
   c. Native Americans.
   d. Jewish Americans.

3. Racism is a form of which of the following?
   a. ethnocentrism
   b. discrimination
   c. prejudice
   d. both b and c

4. Suppose that a White employer refuses to hire a qualified Vietnamese American but hires an inferior White applicant. This decision is an act of
   a. prejudice.
   b. ethnocentrism.
   c. discrimination.
   d. stigmatization.

5. Suppose that a workplace requires that only English be spoken, even when it is not a business necessity to restrict the use of other languages. This requirement would be an example of
   a. prejudice.
   b. scapegoating.
   c. a self-fulfilling prophecy.
   d. institutional discrimination.

6. Working together as computer programmers for an electronics firm, a Hispanic woman and a Jewish man overcome their initial prejudices and come to appreciate each other's strengths and talents. This scenario is an example of
   a. the contact hypothesis.
   b. a self-fulfilling prophecy.
   c. amalgamation.
   d. reverse discrimination.

7. Intermarriage over several generations, resulting in various groups combining to form a new group, would be an example of
   a. amalgamation.
   b. assimilation.
   c. segregation.
   d. pluralism.

8. Alphonso D'Abruzzo changed his name to Alan Alda. His action is an example of
   a. amalgamation.
   b. assimilation.
   c. segregation.
   d. pluralism.

9. In which of the following racial or ethnic groups has one teenager in every six attempted suicide?
   a. African Americans
   b. Asian Americans
   c. Native Americans
   d. Latinos

10. Advocates of *Marxist class theory* argue that the basis for racial subordination in the United States lies within the capitalist economic system. Another representation of this point of view is reflected in which of the following theories?
   a. exploitation
   b. functionalist
   c. interactionist
   d. contact

11. Sociologists consider race and ethnicity to be _____ statuses, since people are born into racial and ethnic groups.

12. The one-drop rule was a vivid example of the social _____ of race—the process by which people come to define a group as a race based in part on physical characteristics, but also on historical, cultural, and economic factors.

13. _____ are unreliable generalizations about all members of a group that do not recognize individual differences within the group.

14. Sociologists use the term _____ to refer to a negative attitude toward an entire category of people, often an ethnic or racial minority.

15. When White Americans can use credit cards without suspicion and browse through stores without being shadowed by security guards, they are enjoying _____ _____.

16. _____ _____ refers to positive efforts to recruit minority group members or women for jobs, promotions, and educational opportunities.

17. After the Civil War, the Southern states passed "_____" _____ laws to enforce official segregation, and the Supreme Court upheld them as constitutional in 1896.

18. In the 1960s, proponents of _____ _____ rejected the goal of assimilation into White, middle-class society. They defended the beauty and dignity of Black and African cultures and supported the creation of Black-controlled political and economic institutions.

19. Asian Americans are held up as a(n) _____ or _____ minority group, supposedly because despite past suffering from prejudice and discrimination, they have succeeded economically, socially, and educationally without resorting to political and violent confrontations with Whites.

20. Mexican Americans and Puerto Ricans are parts of the larger ethnic group called _____.

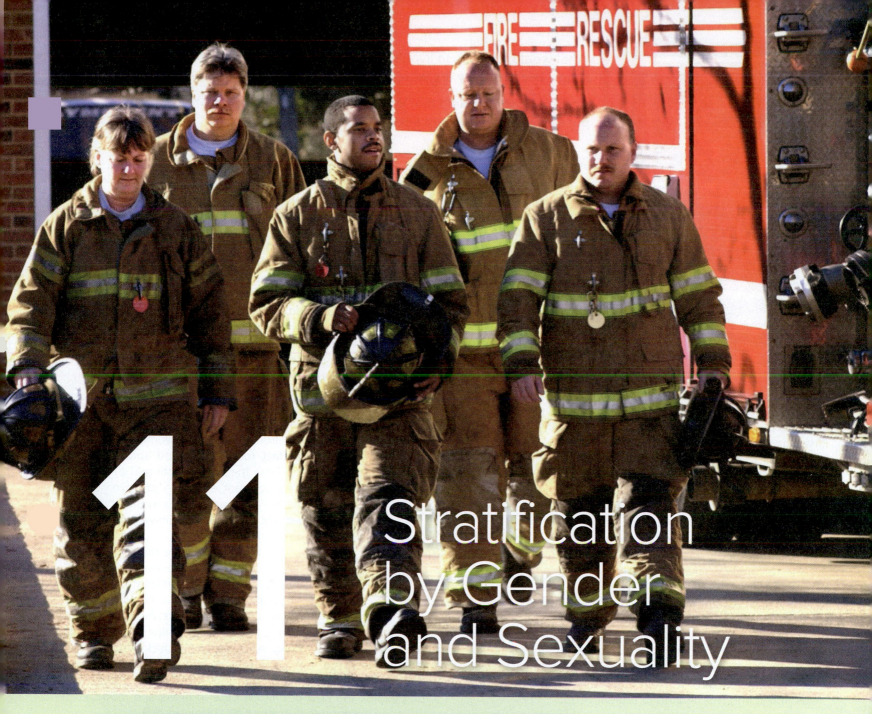

11

Stratification by Gender and Sexuality

© Thinkstock/Index Stock RF

Gender stratification exists in all societies. Around the world, most occupations are dominated by either men or women.

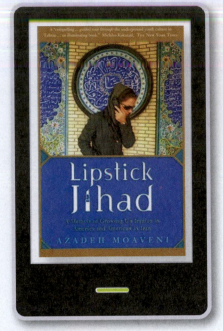

© Ira C. Roberts/Chad Enterprises Corporation

What would it be like to live in a society that restricts women's freedom, simply because they are women?

Azadeh Moaveni found that in Iran, women took every opportunity to push against government social controls.

66 Young people sought Elvis's café [in Tehran, Iran] as refuge from the relentless ugliness that pervaded most public gathering places. Even in the rainy winter, people would crowd outside in the drizzle for an hour, smoking soggy cigarettes and waiting for a table. It was the only café in Tehran designed with innovative elegance and attracted young people starved for aesthetic beauty—the artists, writers, and musicians whose sensibilities suffered acutely in a city draped with grim billboards of war martyrs.

Elvis's coffeehouse inspired imitations all over the neighborhood and then the city. In early 2000, when Celine and I first began to haunt the tiny, modern nook, it was one of a kind. By the following summer of 2001, dozens of tastefully decorated cafés dotted the city, but Elvis's remained the original. In the Gandhi shopping complex, where it was located, at least six others sprang up, and the area became center stage in a café scene of shocking permissiveness. By that time, the dress code was so relaxed that everyone buzzed with tales of "You'll never believe what I saw this girl wearing!"; the fashion spring was likened to a silent coup.

Girls dressed in every color imaginable—veils of bright emerald, violet, buttercup—and in short, coat-like tunics called *manteaus* (also known by the Farsi word *roopoosh*) that hugged their curves, Capri pants that exposed long stretches of calf, pedicured toes in delicate sandals. They sat at the tables outside, in mixed groups, alone with boyfriends,

Often, once we finished discussing work, men, and the new styles of head scarf we coveted, Celine and I would sit and people-watch. The throng of students and young professionals flirted brazenly, and the coquettish slipping of veils produced nothing less than social theater.

laughing and talking into the late evening, past eleven. For a few weeks, Tehran actually had something like nightlife in public, not just sequestered parties inside people's houses. . . .

Often, once we finished discussing work, men, and the new styles of head scarf we coveted, Celine and I would sit and people-watch. The throng of students and young professionals flirted brazenly, and the coquettish slipping of veils produced nothing less than social theater. The Tehran of the revolution was one of the most sexualized milieus I had ever encountered. Even the chat rooms, Celine informed me, were rife with erotic discussion. People really, really wanted to talk about sex. . . .

Made neurotic by the innate oppressiveness of restriction, Iranians were preoccupied with sex in the manner of dieters constantly thinking about food. The subject meant to be *unmentionable*—to which end women were forced to wear veils, sit in the back of the bus, and order hamburgers from the special "women's line" at fast food joints—had somehow become the most mentioned of all. The constant exposure to covered flesh—whether it was covered hideously, artfully, or plainly—brought to mind, well, flesh.

The relaxing of the dress code encouraged this tendency, by breathing sexuality back into public space. Women walked down the street with their elbows, necks, and feet exposed, their figures outlined in form-fitting tunics. After two decades in exile, skin was finally back. And so imaginations flared, everyone eagerly thought about and talked about sex a lot, as though they were afraid if they didn't exploit the new permissiveness in dress and mood, they might wake up to find it had disappeared. 99

Azadeh Moaveni, the author of *Lipstick Jihad,* was born in California after her parents, both Iranian, fled the political turbulence of the Iranian revolution. In 1979, Islamic religious leaders overthrew the U.S.-backed monarchy that had ruled the country for decades. Almost overnight, the country was transformed from a relatively secular, Western-oriented society into a conservative Muslim state. Women who had been accustomed to dressing much as American women did were suddenly expected to cover themselves in dark robes. Young women who had been required to attend school and serve in the armed forces were now forbidden even to appear in public without a male escort.

Though Moaveni grew up in the United States, she was conversant with her Persian cultural heritage, albeit from a distance. After graduating from college, she lived in Iran for two years, where she covered the country's affairs as a news correspondent. There she found a different society from the one her parents had fled a generation before.

The lipstick jihad she refers to in the title of her book is an allusion to the recent relaxation of the strict standards for women's dress and behavior—a change that Iranian women effected by personally defying government sanctions. (*Jihad* is the Arabic term for one's inner struggle against the forces of ungodliness [Moaveni 2005b].)

In her role as the *Guardian*'s contributor on the Middle East, Moaveni (2007, 2009) continues to observe women's lives inside the Islamic Republic of Iran. She has noted a new trend in the formerly austere capital—an appetite for high-priced designer-label fashion accessories, particularly among the young. Today, *nouveau riche* Iranians are indulging in Western-style conspicuous consumption—something their parents would never have done. Iranian housewives can be seen driving through the city in BMW SUVs, Burberry scarves showing beneath their full-length black *chadors* (coats).

Recent political changes in Iran and the beginning of more direct U.S.-Iran diplomatic contacts have led Moaveni and others to be optimistic that gender relations will improve. One of the toughest challenges is in the workforce, where women account for more than 60 percent of all college students but represent less than 20 percent of the labor force (Amos 2014; Moaveni 2005b, 2015).

How do gender roles differ from one culture to another? Are women in the United States still oppressed because of their gender? Have men's and women's positions in society changed? In these modules we will study these and other questions by looking first at how various cultures, including our own, assign women and men to particular social roles. We'll consider the complexity of human sexual behavior, both gay and straight, as well as other sexual identities. Then we will address the sociological explanations for gender stratification. We will see that around the world, women constitute an oppressed majority of the population. We'll learn that women have developed a collective consciousness of their oppression and the way in which their gender combines with other factors to create social inequality. Finally, we will close Module 36 with a Social Policy section on the controversy over a woman's right to abortion.

MODULE 34 | Social Construction of Gender

How many airline passengers do you think are startled on hearing a female captain's voice from the cockpit? What do we make of a father who announces that he will be late for work because his son has a routine medical checkup? Consciously or unconsciously, we are likely to assume that flying a commercial plane is a *man's* job and that most parental duties are, in fact, a *woman's*. Gender is such a routine part of our everyday activities that we typically take notice only when someone deviates from conventional behavior and expectations.

Although a few people begin life with an unclear sexual identity, the overwhelming majority begin with a definite sex and quickly receive societal messages about how a person of that sex should behave. In fact, virtually all societies have established social distinctions between females and males that do not inevitably result from biological differences between the sexes (such as women's reproductive capabilities).

In studying gender, sociologists are interested in the gender-role socialization that leads females and males to behave differently. In Module 15, **gender roles** were defined as expectations regarding the proper behavior, attitudes, and activities of males and females. The application of dominant gender roles leads to many forms of differentiation between women and men. Both sexes are capable of learning to cook and sew, yet most Western societies determine that women should perform those tasks. Both men and women are capable of learning to weld and to fly airplanes, but those functions are generally assigned to men.

As we will see throughout this chapter, however, social behavior does not mirror the mutual exclusivity suggested by these gender roles. Nor are gender roles independent: in real life, the way men behave influences women's behavior, and the way women behave affects men's behavior. Thus, most people do not display strictly "masculine" or "feminine" qualities all the time.

Indeed, such standards can be ambiguous. For instance, though men are supposed to be unemotional, they are allowed to become emotional when their favorite athletic team wins or loses a critical game. Yet our society still focuses on "masculine" and "feminine" qualities as if men and women must be evaluated in those terms. Despite recent inroads by women into male-dominated occupations, our construction of gender continues to define significantly different expectations for females and males.

Gender roles are evident not only in our work and behavior but also in how we react to others. We are constantly "doing gender" without realizing it. If the father mentioned earlier sits in the doctor's office with his son in the middle of a workday, he will probably receive approving glances from the receptionist and from other patients. "Isn't he a wonderful father?" runs through their minds. But if the boy's mother leaves *her* job and sits with the son in the doctor's office, she will not receive such silent applause.

We socially construct our behavior so as to create or exaggerate male/female differences. For example, men and women come in a variety of heights, sizes, and ages. Yet traditional norms regarding marriage and even casual dating tell us that in heterosexual couples, the man should be older, taller, and make more money than the woman. As we will see throughout this chapter, such social norms help to reinforce and legitimize patterns of male dominance.

Gender Roles in the United States

Gender-Role Socialization

Male babies get blue blankets; females get pink ones. Boys are expected to play with trucks, blocks, and toy soldiers; girls receive dolls and kitchen goods. Boys must be masculine—active, aggressive, tough, daring, and dominant—but girls must be feminine—soft, emotional, sweet, and submissive. These traditional gender-role patterns have been influential in the socialization of children in the United States.

TABLE 34-1 AN EXPERIMENT IN GENDER NORM VIOLATION BY COLLEGE STUDENTS

Norm If by Women	Norm If by Men
Send men flowers	Wear fingernail polish
Spit in public	Do needlepoint in public
Use men's bathroom	Throw housewares party
Buy jock strap	Cry in public
Buy/chew tobacco	Have pedicure
Talk knowledgeably about cars	Apply to babysit
Open doors for men	Shave body hair

Source: Adapted by author from Nielsen et al. 2000:287.
In an experiment testing gender-role stereotypes, sociology students were asked to behave in ways that might be regarded as violations of gender norms, and to keep notes on how others reacted. This is a sample of their choices of behavior over a seven-year period.

An important element in traditional views of proper "masculine" and "feminine" behavior is **homophobia,** fear of and prejudice against homosexuality. Homophobia contributes significantly to rigid gender-role socialization, since many people stereotypically associate male homosexuality with femininity and lesbianism with masculinity. Consequently, men and women who deviate from traditional expectations about gender roles are often presumed to be gay. Despite the advances made by the gay liberation movement, the continuing stigma attached to homosexuality in our culture places pressure on all males (whether gay or not) to exhibit only narrow masculine behavior and on all females (whether lesbian or not) to exhibit only narrow feminine behavior.

It is *adults,* of course, who play a critical role in guiding children into those gender roles deemed appropriate in a society. Parents are normally the first and most crucial agents of socialization. But other adults, older siblings, the mass media, and religious and educational institutions also exert an important influence on gender-role socialization, in the United States and elsewhere.

It is not hard to test how rigid gender-role socialization can be. Just try transgressing some gender norm—say, by smoking a cigar in public if you are female, or by carrying a purse if you are male. That was exactly the assignment given to sociology students at the University of Colorado and Luther College in Iowa. Professors asked students to behave in ways that they thought violated the norms of how a man or woman should act. The students had no trouble coming up with gender-norm transgressions (Table 34-1), and they kept careful notes on others' reactions to their behavior, ranging from amusement to disgust.

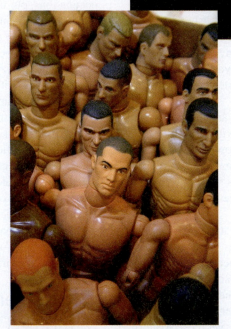

© Justin Sullivan/Getty Images

© Eric Jamison/AP Images
In our society, men and women receive different messages about the ideal body image. For women, the Miss America pageant promotes a very slim, statuesque physique. For men, "action figures" like the G.I. Joe doll promote an exaggerated muscularity typical of professional wrestlers (Angier 1998; Byrd-Bredbenner and Murray 2003).

Women's Gender Roles

How does a girl develop a feminine self-image, while a boy develops one that is masculine? In part, they do so by identifying with females and males in their families and neighborhoods and in the media. If a young girl regularly sees female television characters of all ages and body types, she is likely to grow up with a normal body image. And it will not hurt if the women she knows—her mother, sister, parents' friends, and neighbors—are comfortable with their body types, rather than constantly obsessed with their weight. In contrast, if this young girl sees only attractive actresses and models on television, her self-image will be quite different. Even if she grows up to become a well-educated professional, she may secretly regret falling short of the media stereotype—a sexy young woman in a bathing suit.

Television is far from alone in stereotyping women. Studies of children's books published in the United States in the 1940s, 1950s, and 1960s found that females were significantly underrepresented in central roles and illustrations. Virtually all female characters were portrayed as helpless, passive, incompetent, and in need of a strong male caretaker. Studies of picture books published from the 1970s through the present have found some improvement, but males still dominate the central roles. While males are portrayed as a variety of characters, females tend to be shown mostly in traditional roles, such as mother, grandmother, or volunteer, even if they also hold nontraditional roles, such as working professional.

Traditional gender roles have restricted females more severely than males. This chapter shows how women have been confined to subordinate roles in the political and economic institutions of the United States. Yet it is also true that gender roles have restricted males. A valuable area of research is to explore the ways in which women and men are represented in new media, including those created and distributed by users (Collins 2011; Etaugh 2003).

Men's Gender Roles

Stay-at-home fathers? Until recent decades such an idea was unthinkable. Yet in a 2012 nationwide survey, 22 percent of men said they preferred to stay at home and take care of the house and family. That lifestyle preference is much more common among women, however; 44 percent of women said they preferred to stay at home. But while people's conceptions of gender roles are obviously changing, the fact is that men who stay home to care for their children are still an unusual phenomenon. Among couples with a stay-at-home parent, 84 percent have mothers staying home, while 16 percent have fathers staying home (Livingstone 2014a; Saad 2012).

© Gideon Mendel/Corbis

Gender roles serve to discourage men from entering certain low-paying female-dominated occupations, such as child care. Only 5 percent of day care workers are male.

While attitudes toward parenting may be changing, studies show little change in the traditional male gender role. Men's roles are socially constructed in much the same way as women's are. Family, peers, and the media all influence how a boy or man comes to view his appropriate role in society. The male gender role, besides being antifeminine (no "sissy stuff"), includes proving one's masculinity at work and sports—often by using force in dealing with others—as well as initiating and controlling all sexual relations (Coontz 2012).

Males who do not conform to the socially constructed gender role face constant criticism and even humiliation, both from children when they are boys and from adults as men. It can be agonizing to be treated as a "chicken" or a "sissy" as a youth—particularly if such remarks come from one's father or brothers. And grown men who pursue nontraditional occupations, such as preschool teaching or nursing, must constantly deal with others' misgivings and strange looks. In one study, interviewers found that such men frequently had to alter their behavior in order to minimize others' negative reactions. One 35-year-old nurse reported that he had to claim he was "a carpenter or something like that" when he "went clubbing," because women weren't interested in getting to know a male nurse. The subjects made similar accommodations in casual exchanges with other men (Cross and Bagilhole 2002:215).

At the same time, boys who successfully adapt to cultural standards of masculinity may grow up to be inexpressive men who cannot share their feelings with others. They remain forceful and tough, but as a result they are also closed and isolated. In fact, a small but growing body of scholarship suggests that for men as well as women, traditional gender roles may be disadvantageous. In many communities across the nation, girls seem to outdo boys in high school, grabbing a disproportionate share of the leadership positions, from valedictorian to class president to yearbook editor—everything, in short, except captain of the boys' athletic teams. Their advantage continues after high school. In the 1980s, girls in the United States became more likely than boys to go to college. Since then, women have consistently accounted for 54 to 55 percent of first-year students at community colleges and four-year colleges. This trend is projected to continue through at least 2021 (Hussar and Bailey 2013:Table 30).

Aside from these disadvantages, many men find that traditional masculinity does not serve them well in the job market. The growth of a service economy over the past two generations has created a demand for skills, attitudes, and behaviors that are the antithesis of traditional masculinity. Increasingly, this sector is the place where low-skilled men must look for jobs. As a British study showed, many out-of-work men are reluctant to engage in the kind of sensitive, deferential behavior required by service sector jobs (Nixon 2009).

Women in Combat Worldwide

In 2016 over 200,000 women, or about 15 percent of the nation's active duty armed forces, served in the U.S. military. Yet these women had never been allowed to fight alongside men—at least, not officially.

For some time now, women in uniform have been serving—and dying—in supportive roles on the warfront. In 2004 Tammy Duckworth, an Army reservist, was serving as a co-pilot in Iraq when a rocket-propelled grenade took down her Black Hawk helicopter. Duckworth, who was severely injured in the attack, received the Purple Heart. She was elected to the House of Representatives in 2012 and to the Senate in 2016.

Although the Army does recognize women for their distinguished service—Duckworth was promoted to major soon after the attack—historically, the official prohibition against women serving in combat has prevented them from receiving full credit for their service. In the U.S. Army, the most desirable jobs and career paths require combat experience. Because women officially could not serve in combat positions until 2013, they have been shut out of many types of duty that might interest them. Little wonder that today, the top brass at the Pentagon is almost exclusively male.

Conflict theorists call this obstacle to women's advancement in the Army (their official exclusion from combat) the **brass ceiling.** They note that for women, second-class service in dangerous jobs is nothing new. Historically, both women and racial minorities have often served under hazardous conditions without full recognition.

In 2016, recognizing the injustice of the situation, the the U.S. military lifted the ban on women serving directly in combat with no exceptions—Rangers, Green Berets, Army infantry, Navy SEALs, Air Force parajumpers, and all other positions. From a sociological point of view, the decision can be related to past directives regarding other minority groups. Functionalists would note that historically, African Americans, Asian Americans, and gays and lesbians were excluded from combat based in part on the fear that their presence would prove dysfunctional. That is, prejudice against those groups would cause conflict in military units, which would undermine their effectiveness on the battlefield. When experience with those minority groups proved that such fears were unfounded, the Army dropped its exclusionary policies. Among women, opposition to full service can also be related to the fixed gender roles women and men have traditionally played, which reflect stereotypical images of masculinity and femininity.

Interactionists find that women feel empowered by the experience of combat.

Despite their full-fledged service, however, these women are often pushed into roles based on traditional gender expectations. In Israel, sociologist Orlee Hauser (2011) interviewed female soldiers aged 18 to 31. She found that like women in the civilian workforce, many female soldiers became the targets of sexual harassment. In active war zones, these women were more likely than men to be assigned educational or training duties, or to perform what was essentially social work. Off the battlefield, women reported being asked to choose a new carpet or bake a cake.

The United States is hardly a trailblazer in deciding to allow women in combat. Israel has assigned women to combat regularly since the late 1990s. Soviet women did served in combat during World War II, although they are not allowed to do so today in Russia. Women have served in combat positions not just in Israel, but in many other countries. Australia, Canada, China, Denmark, France, Germany, the Netherlands, and North Korea have also opened up combat to women. Although it would be incorrect to assume that the transition has been smooth—indeed, in Canada and Israel, it happened under court order—the new gender-integrated combat units are proving to be capable and effective on the battlefield.

As in other countries that have opened up combat to women, the new policy in the United States will go through a long period of implementation. At the time of the announcement, Pentagon officials stressed that the standards for combat positions would be "gender-neutral." Strength tests, such as the ability to repeatedly load 55-pound tank shells, might limit women's access to certain positions. Similarly,

© Rex Features/AP Images

In 2004 Army reservist Tammy Duckworth, who was elected to the U.S. Senate in 2016, was co-piloting a Black Hawk helicopter in Iraq when a rocket-propelled grenade hit the aircraft and severely wounded her; she lost both legs. At the time, although women in uniform often served in dangerous roles, they were officially banned from combat operations.

women would face the same qualifications as men for admission to elite units like the Navy SEALs or the Army Rangers and Green Berets. However, as with the military as a whole, it is more likely that the military culture will resist women's participation than that physical fitness will be the real barrier.

LET'S DISCUSS

1. Have you or a woman you know experienced combat? If so, describe the challenges and opportunities women faced on or near the battlefield. Do you agree that women should be allowed to serve in combat without restrictions? Explain your reasoning.

2. What do you think will be the military effect of women's presence in combat roles? Justify your position.

Sources: Ackerman 2015; Bowman 2013; Domi 2013; Llana and Eulich 2013; Mulrine 2012; Schwartz and Lubold 2015; *Time* 2015.

> Historically, both women and racial minorities have often served under hazardous conditions without official recognition.

In the past 40 years, inspired in good part by the contemporary feminist movement (examined later in the chapter), increasing numbers of men in the United States have criticized the restrictive aspects of the traditional male gender role. Some men have taken strong public positions in support of women's struggle for full equality and have even organized voluntary associations for the purpose. However, their actions have been countered by other men who feel they are unfairly penalized by laws related to alimony, child support and custody, family violence, and affirmative action (Kimmel 2008; National Organization for Men Against Sexism 2015).

Research on gender roles has shown that in fact there is no single, simple characterization of the male gender role. Australian sociologist R. W. Connell (1987, 2002, 2005) has spoken of **multiple masculinities,** meaning that men play a variety of gender roles, including a nurturing-caring role and an effeminate-gay role, in addition to their traditional gender role of dominating women. Nevertheless, society reinforces their traditional, dominating role more than any other role (McCormack 2010).

Few aspects of contemporary life dramatize contemporary gender roles more than modern warfare. Box 34-1 looks at women's roles in today's military.

© STR/EPA/Newscom

Being harassed or groped on public transit is a problem for women all over the world. In Tokyo, separate subway cars are reserved for women to protect them from sex offenses.

use your **sociological imagination**

What evidence can you see of women's changing roles over the past few generations?

Cross-Cultural Perspective

To what extent do actual biological differences between the sexes contribute to the cultural differences associated with gender? This question brings us back to the debate over "nature versus nurture." In assessing the alleged and real differences between men and women, it is useful to examine cross-cultural data.

Around the world, anthropologists have documented highly diverse constructions of gender that do not always conform to our ideals of masculinity and femininity. Beginning with the path-breaking work of Margaret Mead ([1935] 2001) and continuing through contemporary fieldwork, these scholars have shown that gender roles can vary greatly from one physical environment, economy, and political system to the next.

In any society, gender stratification requires not only individual socialization into traditional gender roles within the family, but also the promotion and support of those traditional roles by other social institutions, such as religion and education.

Moreover, even with all major institutions socializing the young into conventional gender roles, every society has women and men who resist and successfully oppose the stereotypes: strong women who become leaders or professionals, gentle men who care for children, and so forth. It seems clear that differences between the sexes are not dictated by biology. Indeed, the maintenance of traditional gender roles requires constant social controls—and those controls are not always effective.

We can see the social construction of gender roles in process in societies strained by war and social upheaval. U.S. troops were sent to Afghanistan primarily to quell terrorist operations, but also to improve women's rights in a country where social protections and the rule of law had broken down. In this patriarchal society wracked by poverty and war, Afghani women have never been secure; their appearance in public is especially dangerous. Not only is violence against women common in Afghanistan; it is seldom investigated or prosecuted, even in the most severe cases. Victims of sexual violence risk being charged with adultery if they report the crime to authorities (Organisation for Economic Co-Operation and Development 2012b).

Sociological Perspectives on Gender

Cross-cultural studies indicate that societies dominated by men are much more common than those in which women play the decisive role. Sociologists have turned to all the major theoretical perspectives to understand how and why these social distinctions are established. Each approach focuses on culture rather than biology as the primary determinant of gender differences. Yet in other respects, advocates of these sociological perspectives disagree widely.

Functionalist Perspective

Functionalists maintain that gender differentiation has contributed to overall social stability. Sociologists Talcott Parsons and Robert Bales (1955) argued that to function most effectively, the family requires adults who specialize in particular roles. They viewed the traditional gender roles as arising out of the need to establish a division of labor between marital partners.

Parsons and Bales contended that women take the expressive, emotionally supportive role and men the instrumental, practical role, with the two complementing each other. **Expressiveness** denotes concern for the maintenance of harmony and the internal emotional affairs of the family. **Instrumentality** refers to an emphasis on tasks, a focus on more distant goals, and a concern for the external relationship between one's family and other social institutions. According to this theory, women's interest in expressive goals frees men for instrumental tasks, and vice versa. Women become anchored in the family as wives, mothers, and household managers; men become anchored in the occupational world outside the home. Of course, Parsons and Bales offered this framework in the 1950s, when many more women were full-time homemakers than is true today. These theorists did not explicitly endorse traditional gender roles, but they implied that dividing tasks between spouses was functional for the family as a unit.

Given the typical socialization of women and men in the United States, the functionalist view is initially persuasive. However, it would lead us to expect girls and women who have no interest in children to nevertheless become babysitters and mothers. Similarly, males who love spending time with children might be programmed into careers in the business world. Such differentiation might harm the individual who does not fit into prescribed roles, as well as deprive society of the contributions of many talented people who feel confined by gender stereotyping. Moreover, the functionalist approach does not convincingly explain why men should be assigned categorically to the instrumental role and women to the expressive role.

Conflict Perspective

Viewed from a conflict perspective, the functionalist approach masks the underlying power relations between men and women. Parsons and Bales never explicitly presented the expressive and instrumental roles as being of unequal value to society, yet their inequality is quite evident. Although social institutions may pay lip service to women's expressive skills, men's instrumental skills are more highly rewarded, both in terms of money and prestige. Consequently, according to feminists and conflict theorists, any division of labor by gender into instrumental and expressive tasks is far from neutral in its impact on women.

Conflict theorists contend that the relationship between females and males has traditionally been one of unequal power, with men in a dominant position over women. Men may originally have become powerful in preindustrial times because their size, physical strength, and freedom from childbearing duties allowed them to dominate women physically. In contemporary societies, such considerations are not so

© Wamsteker/Bloomberg/Getty Images

Conflict theorists emphasize that men's work is uniformly valued, whereas women's work (whether unpaid labor in the home or wage labor) is devalued. This woman is removing pencils from a conveyor belt at General Pencil Co.'s factory in Jersey City, New Jersey.

important, yet cultural beliefs about the sexes are long established, as anthropologist Margaret Mead and feminist sociologist Helen Mayer Hacker (1951, 1974) both stressed. Such beliefs support a social structure that places males in controlling positions.

Conflict theorists, then, see gender differences as a reflection of the subjugation of one group (women) by another group (men). If we use an analogy to Marx's analysis of class conflict, we can say that males are like the bourgeoisie, or capitalists; they control most of the society's wealth, prestige, and power. Females are like the proletariat, or workers; they can acquire valuable resources only by following the dictates of their bosses. Men's work is uniformly valued; women's work (whether unpaid labor in the home or wage labor) is devalued.

Feminist Perspective

A significant component of the conflict approach to gender stratification draws on feminist theory. Although use of the term *feminist theory* is comparatively recent, the critique of women's position in society and culture goes back to some of the earliest works that have influenced sociology. Among the most important are Mary Wollstonecraft's *A Vindication of the Rights of Women* (originally published in 1792), John Stuart Mill's *The Subjection of Women* (originally published in 1869), and Friedrich Engels's *The Origin of the Family, Private Property, and the State* (originally published in 1884).

Engels, a close associate of Karl Marx, argued that women's subjugation coincided with the rise of private property during industrialization. Only when people moved beyond an agrarian economy could males enjoy the luxury of leisure and withhold rewards and privileges from women. Drawing on the work of Marx and Engels, many contemporary feminist theorists view women's subordination as part of the overall exploitation and injustice that they see as inherent in capitalist societies.

© Inti St. Clair/Getty Images RF

Some radical feminist theorists, however, view the oppression of women as inevitable in *all* male-dominated societies, whether they are labeled capitalist, socialist, or communist (Feuer 1989; Tuchman 1992; Tucker 1978:734–759).

Feminist sociologists would find little to disagree with in the conflict theorists' perspective, but are more likely to embrace a political agenda. Rather than be caught up in discussing progress toward gender equality over the last generation, they would draw attention to the need for greater progress. Feminists would also argue that until the 1970s, the very discussion of women and society, however well meant, was distorted by the exclusion of women from academic thought, including sociology. We have noted the many accomplishments of Jane Addams and Ida Wells-Barnett, but they generally worked outside the discipline, focusing on what we would now call applied sociology and social work. At the time, their efforts, while valued as humanitarian, were seen as unrelated to the research and conclusions being reached in academic circles, which of course were male academic circles (Andersen 2015; J. Howard 1999; Ridgeway 2011).

Intersections with Race, Class, and Other Social Factors

Contemporary feminists recognize the differential treatment of some women not only because of their gender but also because of the intersection of their race, ethnicity, and socioeconomic status. Simply put, Whites dominate these poor, non-White women because they are non-White; men dominate them because they are women; and the affluent dominate them because they are poor. The African American feminist theorist Patricia Hill Collins (2000) has termed the convergence of social forces that contributes to the subordinate status of these low-status women the **matrix of domination** (Figure 34-1).

Gender, race, and social class are not the only sources of oppression in the United States, though they profoundly affect women and people of color. Other forms of categorization and stigmatization that might be included in the matrix are sexual orientation, religion, disability, and age. If we apply the matrix to the world as a whole, we might add citizenship status or perceived colonial or neocolonial status to the list (Winant 2006).

Though feminists have addressed themselves to the needs of minority women, these women are oppressed much more by their race and ethnicity than by their gender. The question for Latinas (Hispanic women), African American women, Asian American women, and Native American women appears to be whether they should unite with their brothers against racism or challenge them for their sexism. Those who stress the importance of intersectionality emphasize the need for action across both color and social class lines. Social organizing and community activism go hand in hand with intersectionality studies. As Karl Marx stated a century and half ago, it is not enough to describe the inequality; one must work for social justice (Crenshaw 1991; Collins 2015).

The discussion of gender roles among African Americans has always provoked controversy. Advocates of Black nationalism contend that feminism only distracts women from participating fully in the African American struggle. The existence of feminist groups among Blacks, in their view, simply divides the Black community, thereby serving the dominant White majority. In contrast,

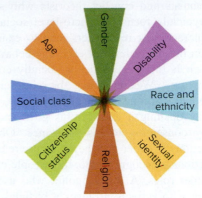

FIGURE 34-1 **Matrix of Domination**

Source: Developed by author.

The matrix of domination illustrates how several social factors, including gender, social class, and race and ethnicity, can converge to create a cumulative impact on a person's social standing.

Black feminists such as bell hooks (1994) argue that little is to be gained by accepting the gender-role divisions of the dominant society, which place women in a separate, subservient position. Though the media commonly portray Black women in a negative light—as illiterates, welfare queens, or prostitutes—Black feminists emphasize that it is not solely Whites and the White-dominated media who focus on such negative images. Black men (most recently, Black male rap artists) have also portrayed Black women in a negative way (Threadcraft 2008; Wilkins 2012).

Historically, Native Americans stand out as an exception to the patriarchal tradition in North America. At the time of the European settlers' arrival, Native American gender roles varied greatly from tribe to tribe. Southern tribes, for reasons unclear to today's scholars, were usually matriarchal and traced their descent through the mother. European missionaries, who sought to make the native peoples more like Europeans, set out to transform this arrangement, which was not entirely universal. Like members of other groups, some Native American women have resisted gender stereotypes (Lajimodiere 2013; Rose 2015).

Because sociologists have usually considered Latinas as part of either the Hispanic or feminist movements, they have ignored their distinctive experience. In the past, Latinas have been excluded from decision making in the two social institutions that most affect their daily lives: the family and the church. Particularly in the lower class, the Hispanic family suffers from the pervasive tradition of male domination. And the Catholic Church relegates women to supportive roles, while reserving the leadership positions for men (Bray 2012; M. Ortega 2015).

Prior to this chapter, much of our discussion has focused on the social effects of race and ethnicity, coupled with poverty, low incomes, and meager wealth. The matrix of domination highlights the confluence of these factors with gender discrimination, which we must include to fully understand the plight of women of color.

 use your **sociological imagination**

Which elements of the matrix of domination privilege you? Which place you at a disadvantage?

Interactionist Perspective

While functionalists and conflict theorists who study gender stratification typically focus on macro-level social forces and institutions, interactionist researchers tend to examine gender stratification on the micro level of everyday behavior. The key to this approach is the way gender is socially constructed in everyday interactions. We "do gender" by reinforcing traditionally masculine and feminine actions. For example, a man "does masculinity" by opening a door for his girlfriend; she "does femininity" by consenting to his assistance. Obviously, the social construction of gender goes beyond these relatively trivial rituals. Interactionists recognize, too, that people can challenge traditional gender roles. A female golfer who uses the men's tees and a man who actively arranges a birthday luncheon at work are redoing gender (Deutsch 2007; West and Zimmerman 1987, 2009).

One continuing subject of investigation is the role of gender in cross-sex conversations (sometimes referred to as "cross-talk"), specifically the idea that men interrupt women more than women interrupt men. Interestingly, empirical research does not clearly support this assertion. True, people in positions of authority or status—who are much more likely to be male than female—dominate interpersonal conversations. That does not necessarily mean that women per se cannot be heard, however. Future research results may deemphasize the clichéd advice

Tracking Sociological Perspectives

TABLE **34-2** SOCIOLOGICAL PERSPECTIVES ON GENDER

Theoretical Perspective	Emphasis
Functionalist	Gender differentiation contributes to social stability
Conflict	Gender inequality is rooted in the female–male power relationship
Feminist	Women's subjugation is integral to society and social structure
Interactionist	Gender distinctions and "doing gender" are reflected in people's everyday behavior

that women must speak up and focus instead on the situational structures that cast men in dominant positions. Another avenue of research will be a consideration of online gender crosstalk (Tannen 1990; Weatherall 2015).

Table 34-2 summarizes the major sociological perspectives on gender.

MODULE **34** | Recap and Review

Summary

Gender is an ascribed status that provides a basis for social differentiation. This module examines the social construction of gender and theories of stratification by gender.

1. In the United States, the social construction of gender continues to define significantly different expectations for females and males.

2. **Gender roles** show up in our work and behavior and in how we react to others. Throughout history, these roles have constricted women much more than they have men.

3. Though men may exhibit a variety of different gender roles, or **multiple masculinities**, society reinforces their traditional role of dominating women.

4. Anthropological research points to the importance of cultural conditioning in defining the social roles of males and females.

5. Functionalists maintain that sex differentiation contributes to overall social stability, but conflict theorists charge that the relationship between females and males is one of unequal power, with men dominating women. This dominance shows up in people's everyday interactions.

6. Many women experience differential treatment, not only because of their gender but because of their race,

ethnicity, and social class. This convergence of social forces is called the **matrix of domination**.

7. As an example of their micro-level approach to the study of gender stratification, interactionists have analyzed men's verbal dominance over women through conversational interruption.

Thinking Critically

1. Compare the social construction of gender with the social construction of race.

2. Which aspects of the functionalist and conflict perspectives on gender make the most sense to you? Explain.

Key Terms

Brass ceiling

Expressiveness

Gender role

Homophobia

Instrumentality

Matrix of domination

Multiple masculinities

Gender roles are an important part of how we interact in everyday life, but they do not actually define who we are or how we see ourselves. This is true even in very young children who are just beginning to interact socially with others. The relationship between gender roles and self-identity is complex. As a result, many people question their gender roles and sexual identity. And this questioning often results in controversy, no matter how liberal or industrialized the society. Box 35-1 shows that "gender neutral" can become an aspect of children's lives and education very early in life.

As we have seen, gender roles involve cultural expectations that we learn through social interaction with other members of society. And "gender neutral" does not mean that gender is meaningless or unimportant.

Gender and Human Sexuality

Related but different are gender identity and sexual identity. **Gender identity** refers to how people see themselves: as male or female or something else. This identity can be different from one's biological sex at birth, although most people develop a gender identity that conforms to that biological identity.

Sociology in the Global Community

BOX 35-1

No Gender, Please: It's Preschool!

Few schools receive as much global attention as did Egalia, a small, co-educational, state-supported preschool that opened in Stockholm, Sweden, in 2010. Egalia follows a curriculum that omits gender designations. Some of the school's practices are not unusual in today's educational environment: both boys and girls are encouraged to use cooking utensils, build with blocks, and play with dolls and trucks. Blue and pink designations are absent. But in addition, at Egalia staff members avoid using words like "him" or "her" (*han* or *hon* in Swedish). They use the gender-neutral personal pronoun, *hen,* instead, to create a more egalitarian and inclusive atmosphere. In 2015, the Swedish national encyclopedia accepted *hen* as a gender-neutral personal pronoun.

From the color and placement of toys to the choice of books, every detail has been carefully planned to make sure the children don't fall into conventional gender stereotypes. "Society expects girls to be girlie, nice and pretty and boys to be manly, rough and outgoing," says Jenny Johnsson, a 31-year-old teacher. "Egalia gives them a fantastic opportunity to be whoever they want to be."

Some parents worry things have gone too far. An obsession with obliterating gender roles, they say, could make the children confused and ill-prepared to face the world outside kindergarten. Since 1998 Swedish preschools have been mandated by law to counteract traditional gender roles and gender patterns. However, preschools often reproduce rather than counteract these gender roles and patterns. Many Swedes think that preschools are not working hard enough to counteract traditional gender roles and patterns. The government mandate is purposefully vague, so that unless a

© georgi1969/iStock/Getty Images Plus/Getty Images RF

> Since 1998 Swedish preschools have been mandated by law to counteract traditional gender roles and gender patterns. However, preschools often reproduce rather than counteract these gender roles and patterns.

school has a very committed staff, as at Egalia, traditional gender roles emerge.

Egalia works to create conditions for children to grow up free from expectations based on their gender. Consequently, criticism abounds. Anonymous threats to employees and break-ins were widely covered in the media. Some dismissed the school as an elite project that fails to address the real needs of society. Amidst charges of "gender madness," it became necessary for the head of Egalia to repeatedly stress to the media that the school is not trying to eliminate children's awareness of sex (dolls are anatomically correct, for example), or to make everyone homosexual. The latter criticism came in response to the media attention given to the children's picture books, which emphasize single parents and gay couples—no Cinderella stories here!

Praise is easy to find too. The preschool has a long waiting list. The local district showcases Egalia as a model for all its preschools and considers its gender approach a resource for educating preschool employees. Yet there is little evidence that teachers in other nearby preschools have any real knowledge about the presentation of gender roles at Egalia besides what they see in the media.

Researchers would be interested in studying the long-term impact of an Egalia-like education. Perhaps it will help eliminate gender differences, or perhaps the influence of the mass media and experiences outside the school will undercut the mission of such programs.

LET'S DISCUSS

1. Think back to your early educational experiences (day care, preschool, and kindergarten). Did they reinforce or help eliminate societal gender role stereotypes?

2. To what extent do you think preschool or education in general can change gender role stereotypes?

Sources: Lind-Valdan 2014; Noack 2015; Soffel 2011.

Sexual identity, also referred to as sexual orientation, is the self-awareness of being romantically or sexually attracted to a defined group of people. Typically, people become aware of their gender identity at a very young age, but a strong sexual identity may not emerge until well into adolescence.

Society's recognition that gender is not necessarily fixed at birth as either male or female and that individuals are not automatically heterosexual has emerged only in the last generation, perhaps, and even in the last ten years. Today, online sites routinely include or solicit descriptions of almost any kind of human sexuality. Increasing numbers of jurisdictions around the world accept same-sex marriage on equal footing with traditional heterosexual marriage. In 2014, Facebook offered, instead of the original two choices of self-designation (male or female), 50 designations that users could choose for gender identity.

Despite this recognition in social media of a broadening of sexual identities, society is only just beginning to avoid stigmatizing people who do not conform to the either/or male/female paradigm. Until recently, these individuals have occupied a lower position in the social stratification hierarchy.

© Kevin Winter/Getty Images

Lady Gaga's 2011 hit single "Born This Way" was written as an anthem to diversity and acceptance of all people, including gays and lesbians.

● Labeling and Identity

We have seen how society singles out certain groups of people by labeling them in positive or negative ways—as "good kids" or "delinquents," for example. Labeling theorists have also studied how labels are used to sanction certain sexual behaviors as "deviant."

The definition of deviant sexual behavior has varied significantly over time and in different cultures. Until 1973, the American Psychiatric Association considered homosexuality a "sociopathic personality disorder," which in effect meant that homosexuals should seek therapy. Two years later, however, the association removed homosexuality from its list of mental illnesses. Today, the organization publicly proclaims that "being gay is just as healthy as being straight." To use Goffman's term, mental health professionals have removed the *stigma* from this form of sexual expression. As a result, in the United States and many other countries, consensual sex between same-sex adults is no longer a crime (American Psychological Association 2008; Outright Action International 2015).

Despite the change in health professionals' attitudes, however, the social stigma of homosexuality lingers. As a result, many people prefer the more positive terms *gay* and *lesbian.* Others, in defiance of the stigma, have proudly adopted the pejorative term *queer* in a deliberate reaction to the ridicule they have borne because of their sexual identity. Still others maintain that constructing one's sexual identity as either homosexual or heterosexual is too limiting. Indeed, such labels ignore those who are *bisexual,* or sexually attracted to both sexes.

Placing gays and lesbians on equal footing in the stratification system with heterosexuals is just one part of reducing stratification by sex. We are only just beginning to address the disadvantages involved in other sexual identities, such as transgender.

Many people find the male and female categories either too restrictive or inaccurate descriptions of how they identify. In the United States and many other societies, we are moving toward a gender spectrum where, while many people identify themselves as either male or female, many others see themselves as somewhere between these two traditional fixed categories. One such a group is *transgender persons,* or those whose current gender identity does not match their physical identity at birth. Some transgender persons see themselves as both male and female.

© Brandon Thibodeaux/The New York Times/Redux Pictures

Many people assume that individuals who defy the traditional labels of male/female are either relatively young or the subject of tabloid media. For most transgender people this is not the case. Phyllis Frye has served as a judge in the Houston municipal courts since 2010 after a lifetime of personal and professional struggle. She transitioned from male to female in the 1970s.

Others, called *transsexuals,* may take hormones or undergo surgery in an effort to draw physically closer to their chosen gender identity. Transgender persons are sometimes confused with *transvestites,* or cross-dressers who wear the clothing of the opposite sex. Transvestites are typically men, either gay or heterosexual, who choose to wear women's clothing.

The use of these terms even in a positive or nonjudgmental way is problematic, since they still imply that human sexuality can be confined in neat, mutually exclusive categories. Moreover, the destigmatization of these labels tends to reflect the influence of the socially privileged—that is, the affluent—who

have the resources to overcome the stigma. In contrast, the traditional Native American concept of the *two spirit,* a personality that blends the masculine and the feminine, has been largely ridiculed or ignored (Gilley 2006; Wentling et al. 2008).

What does constitute sexual deviance, then? The broadening of sexual identities beyond the traditional heterosexual categories means that people may more openly express who they are sexually as well as engage in consensual relationships that in the past were considered wrong or even criminal. The answer to the question of what is deviance seems to change with each generation.

MODULE 35 | **Recap and Review**

Summary

The relationship between gender roles and self-identity is complex.

1. **Sexual identity**, also referred to as sexual orientation, is the self-awareness of being romantically or sexually attracted to a defined group of people. A strong sexual identity may not emerge until well into adolescence.

2. Society is just beginning to avoid stigmatizing people who do not conform to the either/or male/female paradigm.

3. Many people find the male and female categories either too restrictive or inaccurate descriptions of their sexual identification. The United States and many other societies are moving toward a gender spectrum.

4. *Transgender persons* are those whose current gender identity does not match their physical identity at birth.

5. The definition of deviant sexual behavior has varied significantly over time and in different cultures.

Thinking Critically

1. What are some consequences for society as a whole of recognizing that sexual identity exists along a continuum?

2. Compare the social construction of gender with the social construction of race.

Key Terms

Gender identity

Sexual identity

MODULE 36 | **Women: The Oppressed Majority**

Many people, both male and female, find it difficult to conceive of women as a subordinate and oppressed group. Yet take a look at the political structure of the United States: women remain noticeably underrepresented. Entering the 2016 election season, for example, only 6 of the nation's 50 states had a female governor (New Hampshire, New Mexico, Oklahoma, Oregon, Rhode Island, and South Carolina).

Women have made slow but steady progress in certain political arenas. In 1981, out of 535 members of Congress, there were only 21 women: 19 in the House of Representatives and 2 in the Senate. In contrast, the Congress that held office following the 2014 elections had 104 women: 84 in the House and 20 in the Senate. Yet the membership and leadership of Congress remain overwhelmingly male.

In October 1981, Sandra Day O'Connor was sworn in as the nation's first female Supreme Court justice; as of 2015, three

women sat on the Court: Ruth Bader Ginsburg, Elena Kagan, and Sonia Sotomayor. Still, among the first 44 U.S. presidencies, no woman ever served as president of the United States. The same goes for vice president and chief justice of the Supreme Court.

Sexism and Sex Discrimination

Just as African Americans are victimized by racism, women in our society are victimized by sexism. **Sexism** is the ideology that one sex is superior to the other. The term is generally used to refer to male prejudice and discrimination against women. In Module 31, we noted that Blacks can suffer from both individual acts of racism and institutional discrimination. **Institutional discrimination** was defined as the denial of opportunities and equal rights to individuals and groups that results from the normal operations of a society. In the same sense, women suffer from both individual acts of sexism (such as sexist remarks and acts of violence) and institutional sexism.

It is not simply that particular men in the United States are biased in their treatment of women. All the major institutions of our society—including the government, armed forces, large corporations, the media, universities, and the medical establishment—are controlled by men. These institutions, in their normal, day-to-day operations, often discriminate against women and perpetuate sexism. For example, if the central office of a nationwide bank sets a policy that single women are a bad risk for loans—regardless of their incomes and investments—that bank will discriminate against women in state after state. It will do so even at branches where loan officers hold no personal biases toward women, but are merely "following orders."

Our society is run by male-dominated institutions, yet with the power that flows to men come responsibility and stress. Men have higher reported rates of certain types of mental illness than women, and a greater likelihood of death due to heart attack or stroke. The pressure on men to succeed, and then to remain on top in the competitive world of work, can be especially intense. That is not to suggest that gender stratification is as damaging to men as it is to women. But it is clear that the power and privilege men enjoy are no guarantee of personal well-being.

use your **sociological imagination**

Think of organizations or institutions you belong to whose leadership positions are customarily held by men. What would those organizations be like if they were led by women?

The Status of Women Worldwide

According to a detailed overview of the status of the world's women, issued by the World Bank in 2015, a renewed gender strategy is needed to raise the bar on gender equality. Both public and private sectors need to reduce the differential constraints for poor women and men in economic spheres. In many parts of the world, women still lag far behind men in their earnings and in their ability to speak out politically (World Bank 2015c).

This critique applies to Western as well as non-Western countries. Although Westerners tend to view some societies—for example, Muslim countries—as being particularly harsh toward women, that perception is actually an overgeneralization. Muslim countries are exceedingly varied and complex and do not often fit the stereotypes created by the Western media. For a discussion of the status of Muslim women today, see Box 36-1.

Regardless of culture, however, women everywhere suffer from second-class status. It is estimated that women grow half the

world's food, but they rarely own land. They constitute one-third of the world's paid labor force, but are generally found in the lowest-paying jobs. Single-parent households headed by women, which appear to be on the rise in many nations, are typically found in the poorest sections of the population. The feminization of poverty has become a global phenomenon. As in the United States, women around the world are underrepresented politically.

Despite these challenges, women are not responding passively. They are mobilizing, individually and collectively. Given the significant underrepresentation of women in government offices and national legislatures, however, the task is difficult.

Not surprisingly, there is a link between the wealth of industrialized nations and the poverty of women in developing countries. Viewed from a conflict perspective or through the lens of Immanuel Wallerstein's world systems analysis, the economies of developing nations are controlled and exploited by industrialized countries and multinational corporations based in those countries. Much of the exploited labor in developing nations, especially in the nonindustrial sector, is performed by women. Women workers typically toil long hours for low pay, but contribute significantly to their families' incomes (UN Women 2015).

In industrialized countries, women's unequal status can be seen in the division of housework, as well as in the jobs they hold and the pay they earn. Sociologist Jan Paul Heisig analyzed gender inequality among the rich (the top decile in income) and the poor (the bottom decile) in 33 industrialized countries. Typically, poor men did more housework than rich men, but as Figure 36-1 shows, rich or poor, men did much less housework than women. The recent economic recession accentuated this unequal division

FIGURE 36-1 **Gender Inequality in Housework**

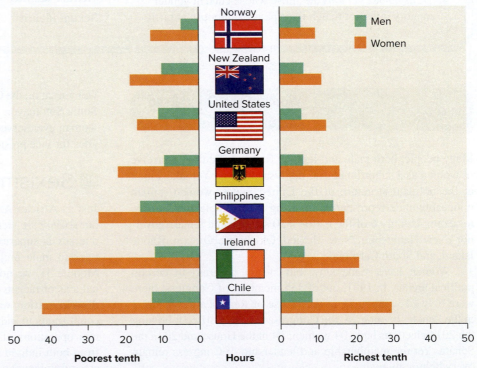

Note: Housework includes laundry, grocery shopping, dinner preparation, and care for sick family members.
Source: Adapted from Heisig 2011:84. *Flags:* © admin_design/Shutterstock RF

Around the world, rich or poor, women do much more housework than men.

BOX 36-1

Sociology in the Global Community

The Head Scarf and the Veil: Complex Symbols

The wearing of a veil or head scarf by women is common to many but not all Middle Eastern societies. All Muslims, men and women alike, are expected to cover themselves and avoid revealing clothes designed to accentuate the body's contours or emphasize its physical beauty. The Koran does permit Muslims to wear revealing garments in private, with their families or with members of the same sex.

The Prophet Muhammad recommended that women cover all of their bodies except for the face, hands, and feet. The Koran adds that a woman's headcovering should fall over the neck and upper chest. A variety of women's outer garments comply with these guidelines for modest attire; collectively, they are referred to as the *hijab*. Face veils are dictated by cultural tradition, however—not by Islam.

In effect, the veil represents a rejection of the beauty myth (see Module 24), which is so prevalent in Western societies. By covering themselves almost completely, Muslim women assure themselves and their families that their physical appearance will not play a role in their contacts outside the family. Rather, these women will be known only for their faith, their intellect, and their personalities.

The veil was politicized by modernization movements that pitted Western cultural values against traditional Islamic values. In Turkey, for instance, in the early 20th century, government officials attempted to subordinate traditional ethnic and religious influences to their nationalistic goals. Though women weren't forbidden to wear the veil, they were not allowed to veil themselves in public places like schools.

Many Muslims resented these forced social changes.

In the United States today, Muslim women select from an array of traditional garments, including a long, loose tailored coat and a loose black overgarment that is worn with a scarf or perhaps a face veil. However, they are just as apt to wear an overblouse and a long skirt or loose pants, which they can buy at local clothing stores.

> In effect, the veil represents a rejection of the beauty myth, which is so prevalent in Western societies.

In some non-Muslim countries, notably France, officials have come under fire for banning the *hijab,* or the head scarf, in public schools, as well as a full-body, face-covering robe anywhere in public. After the French law was implemented, many French Muslim women began to work at home or turned to self-employed e-trading, only further isolating them.

The custom of covering generally has not been an issue in the United States, though one 11-year-old had to go to federal court to establish her right to wear a head scarf at school in Muskogee, Oklahoma. The U.S. Department of Justice supported her lawsuit, leading to a revision in the student dress policy to accommodate religious-based clothing.

© John Birdsall/The Image Works

The head scarf—an expression of modesty, a woman's right as an individual, or a sign of oppression?

LET'S DISCUSS

1. Consider life in a society in which women wear veils. Can you see any advantages, from the woman's point of view? From the man's?

2. Do you find the Western emphasis on physical beauty oppressive? If so, in what ways?

Sources: Charrad 2011; Chrisafis 2013; Morin 2014; Selod 2008b; Zerouala 2014.

---

of housework. Obviously, being unemployed leaves both men and women with more time for household chores. However, unemployed women typically do double the amount of extra housework as unemployed men (Gough and Killewald 2011).

The Workforce of the United States

Forty years ago, the U.S. Commission on Civil Rights (1976:1) concluded that the passage in the Declaration of Independence proclaiming that "all men are created equal" has been taken too literally for too long—especially with respect to women's opportunities for employment. In this section we will see how gender bias has limited women's opportunities for employment outside

the home, at the same time that it forces them to carry a disproportionate burden inside the home.

Labor Force Participation

Women's participation in the paid labor force of the United States and other industrialized countries increased steadily throughout the 20th century and into the 21st century (Figure 36-2). Today, millions of women—married or single, with or without children, pregnant or recently having given birth—are in the labor force.

Still, women entering the job market find their options restricted in important ways. Women are *underrepresented* in occupations historically defined as "men's jobs," which often carry much greater financial rewards and prestige than women's jobs. For example, in 2015, women accounted for approximately 47 percent of the paid labor force of the United States, yet they

FIGURE 36-2 **Women's Labor Force Participation Rates, Selected Countries, 1970–2009**

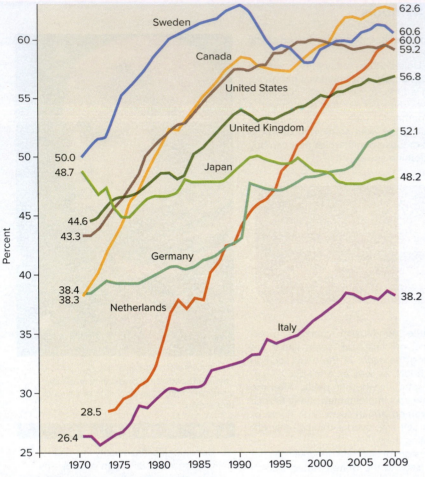

Source: Bureau of Labor Statistics 2011:13.

objective tests that show strong financial performance under gender-diverse leadership, some investors tend to balk. Small investors often sell their shares when women become corporate leaders, apparently falling for the stereotype that associates males with success. This sell pattern is not characteristic of larger investors, who have long argued that gender-diverse leadership is good for business (Dobbin and Jung 2010).

This type of inequality is not unique to the United States. Worldwide, women hold less than 1 percent of corporate managerial positions. In recognition of the underrepresentation of women on boards of directors, the Norwegian legislature established minimum quotas for the number of female board members of publicly traded companies. In response, about three-quarters of public Norwegian companies chose to become private rather than comply with the law. Despite that backlash, at least 12 other countries, including Australia, Canada, France, Italy, India, Israel, and Spain, followed with their own quota laws (Shankland 2015).

Compensation

He works. She works. Both are physicians—a high-status occupation with considerable financial rewards. He makes $140,000. She makes $88,000.

These median annual earnings for physicians in the United States, released by the Census Bureau, are typical of the results of the bureau's detailed study of occupations and income. Take financial advisors. He makes $80,000; she makes $55,000. Or physical therapists: he makes $71,000; she makes $62,000. What about bus drivers? He makes $34,000; she makes $27,000. Statisticians at the bureau looked at the median annual earnings for no fewer than 821 occupations ranging from dishwasher to chief executive. After adjusting for workers' ages, education, and work experience, they came to an unmistakable conclusion: across the board, there is a substantial gender gap in the median earnings of full-time workers.

Men do not always earn more than women for doing the same work. Researchers at the Census Bureau found two occupations out of 821 in which women typically earn about 1 percent more income than men: hazardous materials recovery and telecommunications line installation. These two occupations employed less than 1 out of every 1,000 workers the bureau studied. Forecasting analyses show no convincing evidence that the wage gap is narrowing.

What accounts for these yawning wage gaps between men and women in the same occupation? Scholars at the Census Bureau studied the following characteristics of men and women in the same occupation:

- Age and degree of formal education
- Marital status and the presence of children at home
- Specialization within the occupation (for example, family practice versus surgical practice)
- Years of work experience
- Hours worked per year

constituted only 13 percent of civil engineers, 34 percent of computer systems analysts, and 38 percent of physicians (Table 36-1).

Such occupational segregation is not unique to the United States but typical of industrial countries. In Great Britain, for example, only 6 percent of engineers are women, while 71 percent of cashiers and 88 percent of nurses are women (Office for National Statistics 2013).

Women from all groups and men from minority groups sometimes encounter attitudinal or organizational bias that prevents them from reaching their full potential. As we saw in Module 31, the term **glass ceiling** refers to an invisible barrier that blocks the promotion of a qualified individual in a work environment because of the individual's gender, race, or ethnicity. Furthermore, women and minority men confront not only a glass ceiling that limits their upward mobility, but glass walls that reduce their ability to move horizontally into fast-track jobs that lead directly up to the highest rungs on the corporate ladder. A study of the *Fortune* 500 largest corporations in the United States showed that in 2016, barely 20 percent of the seats on their boards of directors were held by women (E. Fry 2015).

When women do gain entry to corporate boards of directors, the response in the financial world is not entirely positive. Despite

TABLE 36-1 U.S. WOMEN IN SELECTED OCCUPATIONS: WOMEN AS A PERCENTAGE OF ALL WORKERS IN THE OCCUPATION

Underrepresented		Overrepresented	
Firefighters	8%	High school teachers	59%
Aircraft pilots and engineers	9	Flight attendants	75
Civil engineers	13	Travel agents	76
Police officers	14	Elementary school teachers	81
Chefs and head cooks	20	Social workers	84
Clergy	21	Bank tellers	82
Dentists	26	Librarians	83
Computer systems analysts	34	Registered nurses	89
Lawyers	35	Receptionists	91
Athletes, coaches, and umpires	36	Word processors	92
Physicians	38	Child care workers	95
Postal service mail carriers	41	Dental hygienists	96

Note: Women constitute 47 percent of the labor force age 16 and over.
Source: Data for 2015 reported in Bureau of Labor Statistics 2016a.

Taking all these factors into consideration reduced the pay gap between men and women by only 3 cents. Women still earned 80 cents for every dollar earned by men. In sum, the disparity in pay between men and women cannot be explained by pointing to women's career choices (Bureau of Labor Statistics 2013d: Table 2; Government Accountability Office 2003; Weinberg 2004, 2007).

Legally, sex discrimination in wage payments is difficult to prove. Witness the case of former Goodyear worker Lilly Ledbetter, who learned 19 years after she was hired that she was being paid less than men doing the same job. Ledbetter sued and was awarded damages, only to have the Supreme Court overturn the decision on the grounds that she made her claim more than six months after the first discriminatory paycheck was issued. Congress relaxed this restriction in 2009 (Pear 2009).

Not all the obstacles women face in the workplace originate with management. Unfortunately, many workers, both male and female, would prefer not to work for a woman (Box 36-2).

What happens to men who enter traditionally women's occupations? Research shows that the glass ceiling that women face does not appear to hamper them. Instead, men who enter traditionally female occupations are more likely than women to rise to the top. Male elementary school teachers become principals; male nurses become supervisors. The term **glass escalator** refers to this advantage men experience in occupations dominated by women. Whereas women who enter traditionally male occupations may be seen as tokens, men who move out of sex-typical jobs are likely to be advantaged.

This difference between the sexes is associated with a pay differential. A national study released in 2015 found that among full-time, year-round registered nurses, females earn $60,000 on average, compared with $70,000 for their male counterparts. Even

when specializations or higher degrees are considered, pay differences remain (Muench et al. 2015).

Social Consequences of Women's Employment

Today, many women face the challenge of trying to juggle work and family. Their situation has many social consequences. For one thing, it puts pressure on child care and financing of day care. For another, it raises questions about what responsibility male wage earners have in the household.

Who does the housework when women become productive wage earners? Studies indicate that there is a clear gender gap in the performance of housework, although it has been narrowing (see Figure 36-1). Women do more housework and spend more time on child care than men do, whether on a workday or a non-workday. Taken together, then, a woman's workday on and off the job is much longer than a man's (Yavorsky et al. 2015).

Sociologist Arlie Hochschild (1990, 2005, 2012) has used the phrase **second shift** to describe the double burden—work outside the home followed by child care and housework—that many women face and few men share equitably. Unfortunately, today's workplace is becoming a 24/7 virtual office thanks to the advent of mobile information technologies. As these devices take over what little personal time employees have left, the physical toll on women becomes even more burdensome.

What is life like for these women? On the basis of interviews with and observations of 52 couples over an eight-year period, Hochschild reports that the wives (and not their husbands) drive home from the office while planning domestic schedules and play dates for children—and then begin their second shift. Drawing on national studies, she concludes that women spend 15 fewer hours each week in leisure activities than their husbands. In a year, these women work an extra month of 24-hour days because of the second shift; over a dozen years, they work an extra year of 24-hour days. Hochschild found that the married couples she studied were fraying at the edges, and so were their careers and their marriages. With such reports in mind, many feminists have advocated greater governmental and corporate support for child care, more flexible family leave policies, and other reforms designed to ease the burden on the nation's families (Eby et al. 2010).

The greater amounts of time women put into caring for their children, and to a lesser degree into housework, take a special toll on women who are pursuing careers. In a survey published in the *Harvard Business Review,* about 40 percent of women indicated that they had voluntarily left work for months or years, compared to only 24 percent of men. As Figure 36-3 shows, women were much more likely than men to take time off for family reasons. Even women in the most prestigious professions have difficulty balancing home and work responsibilities. In the Social Policy section of Chapter 12 we will consider family leave. The absence of such a benefit has different impacts on women than on men.

Give Me a Male Boss, Please

As women increased their presence in the managerial ranks from 19.7 percent in 1972 to 51.6 percent in 2014, the desirability of having a male supervisor became a topic of casual conversation. Numerous studies suggest that compared to all the other social factors present in the workplace, the boss's gender has little effect on the nature and quality of the manager–employee relationship. However, that fact does not prevent potential workers—male or female—from preferring a male boss. National opinion polls consistently show that in general—that is, without reference to particular people—workers prefer to take orders from a man by a two-to-one margin. If anything, women are more likely than men to prefer a male supervisor.

© Stefano Lunardi/Alamy RF

> National opinion polls consistently show that in general, workers prefer to take orders from a man by a two-to-one margin.

This preference is so strong that many people are willing to accept less pay to get a male boss. Researchers at the University of Chicago's business school asked college students who were about to graduate to consider hypothetical job opportunities at consulting firms. The positions varied in terms of their starting salary, location, paid holidays, and the boss's sex.

The students' choices matched their stated preferences for salary, location, and holidays. Surprisingly, the boss's sex turned out to be a far more important variable than the other three, whether students were male or female. In a variety of scenarios describing both salary and the boss's characteristics, students chose to take a 22 percent reduction in starting salary to get a male boss. But it is not just students: a 2014 national survey indicated that 39 percent of women prefer a male boss, while 25 percent prefer a woman and 34 percent have no preference.

LET'S DISCUSS

1. Have you ever worked for a female boss? If so, were you comfortable taking orders from her? Did you notice any differences in the way your boss was treated, compared to men on her level?

2. What might explain the strong preference for a male boss? Do you expect this preference to remain stable or disappear over time? Explain.

Sources: Bureau of Labor Statistics 2015a; Bureau of Labor Statistics 2003; Caruso et al. 2009; Gibbs 2009:31; G. Powell 2010; Riffkin 2014; Whittaker 2006.

Emergence of a Collective Consciousness

Feminism is an ideology that favors equal rights for women. The feminist movement of the United States was born in upstate New York, in a town called Seneca Falls, in the summer of 1848. On July 19, the first women's rights convention began, attended by Elizabeth Cady Stanton, Lucretia Mott, and other pioneers in the struggle for women's rights. This first wave of *feminists,* as they are currently known, battled ridicule and scorn as they fought for legal and political equality for women. They were not afraid to risk controversy on behalf of their cause; in 1872, Susan B. Anthony was arrested for attempting to vote in that year's presidential election.

Ultimately, the early feminists won many victories, among them the passage and ratification of the Nineteenth Amendment to the Constitution, which granted women the right to vote in national elections beginning in 1920. But suffrage did not lead to other reforms in women's social and economic position, and in the early and middle 20th century the women's movement became a much less powerful force for social change.

The second wave of feminism in the United States emerged in the 1960s and came into full force in the 1970s. In part, the movement was inspired by three pioneering books arguing for women's rights: Simone de Beauvoir's *The Second Sex,* Betty Friedan's *The Feminine Mystique,* and Kate Millett's *Sexual Politics.* In addition, the general political activism of the 1960s led women—many of whom were working for Black civil rights or against the war in Vietnam—to reexamine their own powerlessness.

The sexism often found within even allegedly progressive and radical political circles convinced many women that they needed to establish a movement for women's liberation (Stansell 2011).

As more and more women became aware of sexist attitudes and practices, including attitudes they themselves had accepted through socialization into traditional gender roles, they began to challenge male dominance. A sense of sisterhood, much like the class consciousness that Marx hoped would emerge in the proletariat, became evident. Individual women identified their interests with those of the collectivity *women*. The women in the movement would no longer accept submissive, subordinate roles ("false consciousness" in Marxist terms).

By the 1980s, however, the movement's influence was beginning to wane. In 1998, in a provocative cover illustration, the editors of *Time* magazine asked "Is Feminism Dead?" Young women, they wrote, seemed to take women's improved status for granted, to see their mothers' struggles for equal rights as irrelevant to their own lives. Fewer women, they noted, were identifying themselves as feminists.

How do today's women perceive the movement? According to a national survey done in 2013, about 23 percent of women (and 12 percent of men) call themselves feminists. There is little reason to believe that younger women are less willing to accept the label than older women. Perhaps more telling is the fact that 32 percent of women and 42 percent of men think the term *feminist* has negative connotations.

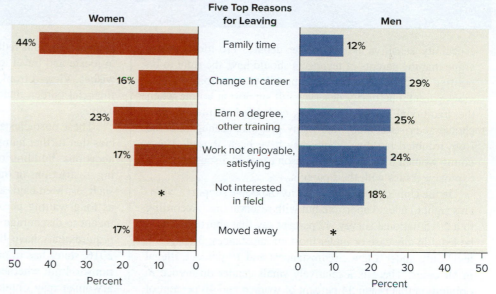

FIGURE 36-3 **Why Leave Work?**

* Not one of top 5 reasons

Note: Based on a representative Harris Interactive survey of "highly qualified" workers, defined as those with a graduate degree, a professional degree, or a high honors undergraduate degree.
Source: Adapted by author from data in Hewlett and Luce 2005.

Is feminism dead? Many feminists resent that question, because it seems to imply that all their concerns have been resolved. Today's feminists argue that they have moved beyond early criticism that the movement was too obsessed with the concerns of White middle-class women, that it marginalized African American feminists and others. Indeed, current polling shows that African American and Latino women are more likely than others to call themselves feminists. Recognizing the legal and economic victories they have made over the last 40 years, feminists are now working to improve women's lives in nonindustrial countries, where they focus on eliminating malnutrition, starvation, extreme poverty, and violence (Reger 2014; Swanson 2013).

social
policy and gender stratification
The Battle over Abortion from a Global Perspective

Few issues seem to stir as much intense conflict as abortion. A critical victory in the struggle for legalized abortion in the United States came in 1973, when the Supreme Court granted women the right to terminate pregnancies. This ruling, known as *Roe v. Wade,* was based on a woman's right to privacy. The Court's decision was generally applauded by pro-choice groups, which believe women should have the right to make their own decisions about their bodies and should have access to safe and legal abortions. It was bitterly condemned by those opposed to abortion. For these pro-life groups, abortion is a moral and often a religious issue. In their view, human life begins at the moment of conception, so that its termination through abortion is essentially an act of murder.

Looking at the Issue

The debate that has followed *Roe v. Wade* revolves around prohibiting abortion altogether, or at the very least, limiting it. In 1979, for example, Missouri required parental consent for minors wishing to obtain an abortion, and the Supreme Court upheld the law. Parental notification and consent have become

—*Continued*

especially sensitive issues in the debate. Pro-life activists argue that the parents of teenagers should have the right to be notified about—and to permit or prohibit—abortions. In their view, parental authority deserves full support at a time when the traditional nuclear family is embattled. However, pro-choice activists counter that many pregnant teenagers come from troubled families where they have been abused. These young women may have good reason to avoid discussing such explosive issues with their parents.

In the United States, the majority of people support a woman's right to a legal abortion, but with reservations. According to a 2015 national survey, 42 percent say that abortion should be legal in any case or under most circumstances; 36 percent, legal only under a few circumstances; and 19 percent, illegal in all cases. There is a relatively small gender difference in opinion on this issue: 54 percent of women and 46 percent of men identify themselves as "pro-choice" (Saad 2015).

The United States is not alone in debating abortion. Latin American countries typically have the strictest measures against the practice, but occasionally changes occur. In 2007, Mexico loosened decade-old restrictions to permit legal abortions during the first three months of a pregnancy, for any reason (M. Davis 2010).

Applying Sociology

Sociologists see gender and social class as the defining issues surrounding abortion. That is, the intense conflict over abortion reflects broader differences over women's position in society. Feminists involved in defending abortion rights typically believe that men and women are essentially similar. They support women's full participation in work outside the home and oppose all forms of sex discrimination. Feminists also claim that pregnancy and childbirth have been socially constructed by male-centered health care systems and patriarchal religious traditions. In contrast, most antiabortion activists believe that men and women are fundamentally different. In their view, men are best suited to the public world of work, while women are best suited to the demanding and crucial task of rearing children. These activists are troubled by women's growing participation in work outside the home, which they view as destructive to the family, and ultimately to society (Lorber 2005; Pollitt 2015).

Another obstacle facing the poor is access to abortion providers. In the face of vocal pro-life sentiment, fewer and fewer hospitals throughout the world are allowing physicians to perform abortions, except in extreme cases. Moreover, some doctors who work in clinics, intimidated by death threats and murders, have stopped performing abortions. For poor people in rural areas, this reduction in service makes it more difficult to locate and travel to a facility that will accommodate their wishes. Viewed from a conflict perspective, this is one more financial burden that falls especially heavily on low-income women.

These obstacles are compounded by state and local policies that further hamper the doctors and clinics that provide abortions: building requirements and bans on public funding; restrictions or outright bans on public health insurance, such as Medicaid and Obamacare. Other policies, such as long waiting periods and required ultrasound tests, are meant to discourage women from seeking abortions. These requirements have become more onerous since 2000. By 2016, states had imposed a wide variety of laws and regulations to limit whether, when, and under what circumstances a woman may obtain an abortion. For example, 18 states require an abortion to be performed in a hospital, rather than a clinic, after some specified point in the pregnancy. Eleven states restrict coverage of abortion in private health insurance plans except when the woman's life is in danger. Seventeen states mandate counseling before an abortion, and 28 states require a waiting period—usually 24 hours, but in some states as long as 72 hours (Guttmacher Institute 2016).

Initiating Policy

In 1973 the Supreme Court supported the general right to terminate a pregnancy by a narrow 5–4 majority. Although pro-life activists continue to hope for an overruling of *Roe v. Wade,* they have focused in the interim on weakening the decision through tactics such as limiting the use of fetal tissue in medical experiments and prohibiting certain late-term abortions, which they term "partial-birth" abortions. The Supreme Court continues to hear cases involving such restrictions.

What is the policy in other countries? In about two-thirds of countries, abortion is permitted when the physical or mental health of the mother is endangered, and in half of the countries when the pregnancy results from rape or incest. Only about one-third of countries permit abortion for economic or social reasons or on request.

Eighty-six percent of governments in developed regions allow abortion when the pregnancy results from rape or incest, compared with only 41 percent in developing regions. The legal grounds for abortion are the most restrictive in the least developed countries, where only 6 percent of governments permit abortion for economic and social reasons and only 4 percent allow it on request (United Nations Population Division 2014).

—Continued

MAPPING LIFE WORLDWIDE

FIGURE 36-4 **The Global Divide on Abortion**

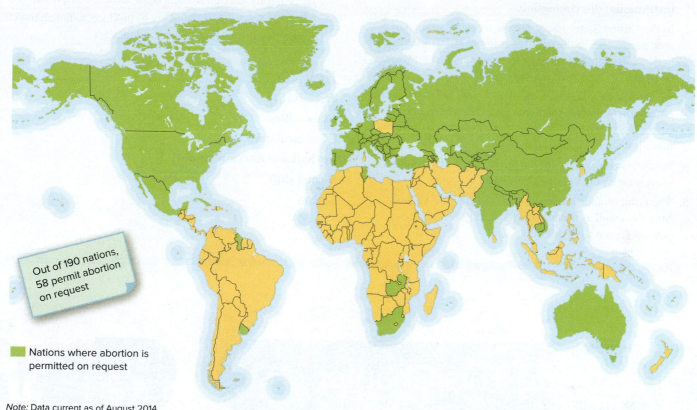

Out of 190 nations, 58 permit abortion on request

■ Nations where abortion is permitted on request

Note: Data current as of August 2014.
Source: Developed by the author based on United Nations Population Division 2014: Table 1.

The policies of the United States are intertwined with those of developing nations. From the 1980s through January 2009, members of Congress who opposed abortion successfully blocked foreign aid to countries that might use the funds to encourage abortion. Yet developing nations generally have the most restrictive abortion laws. As Figure 36-4 shows, it is primarily in Africa, Latin America, and parts of Asia that women are not allowed to terminate a pregnancy on request. As might be expected, illegal abortions are most common in those nations. An estimated quarter of the world's women live in countries where abortion is illegal or is permitted only if a woman's life is in jeopardy. Indeed, the rate of abortions in countries with legal restrictions on the procedure matches the rate in countries that permit it. Hence, 40 percent of abortions worldwide—about 16 million procedures each year—are performed illegally (P. Baker 2009; Guttmacher Institute 2008).

TAKE THE ISSUE WITH YOU

1. How easy do you think it is for a young adult woman to obtain an abortion? What do you think should be the first step she takes in considering one?

2. Do you think teenage girls should be required to get their parents' consent before having an abortion? Why or why not?

3. Under what circumstances should abortions be allowed? Explain your reasoning.

Summary

This module examines the status of women as an oppressed minority in the United States and around the world.

1. Women around the world suffer from **sexism** and **institutional discrimination.**

2. In the United States today, almost as many women as men participate in the paid labor force, but women are underrepresented in managerial positions and underpaid compared to men with the same jobs.

3. As women have taken on more and more hours of paid employment outside the home, they have been only partially successful in getting their husbands to take on more homemaking duties, including child care.

4. Many women agree with the positions of the feminist movement but reject the label *feminist*.

5. The issue of abortion has bitterly divided the United States (as well as other nations), pitting pro-choice activists against pro-life activists.

Thinking Critically

1. What are the challenges to comparing the status of women across different nations?

2. How would you argue that women have come either very far or not far enough in their labor force participation?

3. Today, is feminism more likely to produce social change or respond to social change? Explain.

Key Terms

Feminism

Glass ceiling

Glass escalator

Institutional discrimination

Second shift

Sexism

Mastering This Chapter

© Thinkstock/Index Stock RF

taking sociology with you

1 For a day or two, watch for examples of people "doing gender" on your campus. Record your sightings in a journal and compare them with those of your classmates.

2 Find out what percentage of the faculty members at your college are women. What percentage of the women have tenure, compared to the men? What percentage hold full professorships? Do the percentages vary much from one department to another, and if so, why?

3 Use your school's alumni network to get in touch with graduates who have entered the workforce. Are mothers of young children having difficulty balancing work and parenting? Do both men and women feel they have a chance to get ahead? Are both men and women well compensated?

key terms

Brass ceiling An invisible barrier that blocks the promotion of a woman in the military because of her official (not necessarily actual) exclusion from combat.

Expressiveness Concern for the maintenance of harmony and the internal emotional affairs of the family.

Feminism An ideology that favors equal rights for women.

Gender identity How people see themselves, as male or female, or something else.

Gender role Expectations regarding the proper behavior, attitudes, and activities of males and females.

Glass ceiling An invisible barrier that blocks the promotion of a qualified individual in a work environment because of the individual's gender, race, or ethnicity.

Glass escalator The advantage men experience in occupations dominated by women.

Homophobia Fear of and prejudice against homosexuality.

Institutional discrimination The denial of opportunities and equal rights to individuals and groups that results from the normal operations of a society.

Instrumentality An emphasis on tasks, a focus on more distant goals, and a concern for the external relationship between one's family and other social institutions.

Matrix of domination The cumulative impact of oppression because of race and ethnicity, gender, and social class, as well as religion, sexual orientation, disability, age, and citizenship status.

Multiple masculinities A variety of male gender roles, including nurturing-caring and effeminate-gay roles, that men may play along with their more pervasive traditional role of dominating women.

Second shift The double burden—work outside the home followed by child care and housework—that many women face and few men share equitably.

Sexism The ideology that one sex is superior to the other.

Sexual identity The self-awareness of being romantically or sexually attracted to a defined group of people. Also referred to as *sexual orientation.*

self-quiz

Read each question carefully and then select the best answer.

1. Both males and females are physically capable of learning to cook and sew, yet most Western societies determine that women should perform these tasks. This illustrates the operation of
   a. gender roles.
   b. sociobiology.
   c. homophobia.
   d. comparable worth.

2. An important element in traditional views of proper "masculine" and "feminine" behavior is fear of homosexuality. This fear, along with accompanying prejudice, is referred to as
   a. lesbianism.
   b. femme fatalism.
   c. homophobia.
   d. claustrophobia.

3. The most crucial agents of socialization in teaching gender roles in the United States are
   a. peers.
   b. teachers.
   c. media personalities.
   d. parents.

4. Research by anthropologist Margaret Mead has shown that
   a. biology is the most important factor in determining the social roles of males and females.
   b. cultural conditioning is the most important factor in determining the social roles of males and females.
   c. biology and cultural conditioning have an equal impact in determining the social roles of males and females.
   d. biology and cultural conditioning have a negligible impact in determining the social roles of males and females.

5. Which sociological perspective would acknowledge that it is not possible to change gender roles drastically without dramatic revisions in a culture's social structure?
   a. functionalist perspective
   b. conflict perspective
   c. interactionist perspective
   d. both a and b

6. The term *sexism* is generally used to refer to
   a. female prejudice and discrimination against men.
   b. male prejudice and discrimination against women.
   c. female discrimination against men and male discrimination against women equally.
   d. discrimination between members of the same sex.

7. Which of these statements is true?
   a. More boys than girls take AP exams.
   b. Women in the United States are more likely than men to attend college.
   c. Women in the United States are less likely than men to obtain doctoral degrees.
   d. all of the above

8. Which sociological perspective distinguishes between instrumental and expressive roles?
   a. functionalist perspective
   b. conflict perspective
   c. interactionist perspective
   d. labeling theory

9. Contemporary feminists recognize the differential treatment of some women not only because of their gender, but also because of their
   a. race.
   b. ethnicity.
   c. socioeconomic status.
   d. all of the above

10. The sense of sisterhood that became evident during the rise of the contemporary feminist movement resembled the Marxist concept of
    a. alienation.
    b. dialectics.
    c. class consciousness.
    d. false consciousness.

11. Talcott Parsons and Robert Bales contend that women take the _____, emotionally supportive role in the family and that men take the _____, practical role, with the two complementing each other.

12. A significant component of the _____ approach to gender stratification draws on feminist theory.

13. It is not simply that particular men in the United States are biased in their treatment of women. All the major institutions of our society—including the government, the armed forces, large corporations, the media, universities, and the medical establishment—are controlled by men. This situation is symptomatic of institutional _____.

14. Women from all groups and men from minority groups sometimes encounter attitudinal or organizational bias that prevents them from reaching their full potential. This is known as the _____ _____.

15. Sociologist Arlie Hochschild has used the phrase _____ _____ to describe the double burden that many women face and few men share equitably: work outside the home followed by child care and housework.

16. Within the general framework of their theory, _____ sociologists maintain that gender differentiation has contributed to overall social stability.

17. Through the rise of contemporary _____, women are developing a greater sense of group solidarity.

18. _____ contributes significantly to rigid gender-role socialization, since many people stereotypically associate male homosexuality with femininity and lesbianism with masculinity.

19. The term _____ _____ _____ was coined by feminist theorist Patricia Hill Collins to describe the convergence of social forces that contributes to the subordinate status of poor, non-White women.

20. The author of the pioneering argument for women's rights, *The Feminine Mystique,* was _____ _____.

Answers

1 (a); 2 (c); 3 (d); 4 (b); 5 (d); 6 (b); 7 (b); 8 (a); 9 (d); 10 (c); 11 expressive, instrumental; 12 conflict; 13 discrimination; 14 glass ceiling; 15 second shift; 16 functionalist; 17 feminism; 18 Homophobia; 19 matrix of domination; 20 Betty Friedan

12 Stratification by Age

© Monkey Business Images/Shutterstock RF

Individuals from several generations enjoy a soccer game. Age serves as a basis for social stratification, sometimes separating the old from the young more than is necessary or desirable. To a great extent, older people's quality of life, including their livelihoods, their social relationships, and their leisure pursuits, depend on society's view of aging.

MODULE 37 | Aging and Society

MODULE 38 | Aging Worldwide

MODULE 39 | Age Stratification in the United States

© Steven Day/AP Images

How do different cultures regard elderly people?

Sociologist Jill Quadagno investigated the many ways in which culture determines what it means to be elderly.

66 On January 15, 2009, Captain Chesley Sullenberger, known as Sully, became a national hero when he landed an engineless plane in the Hudson River, saving the lives of 154 passengers. It was the first time in 45 years that a major aircraft crash-landed in the water without fatalities. Sullenberger had decades of experience flying everything from a glider to a jumbo jet.

After both engines blew, Sullenberger reportedly told his 150 passengers to brace for impact because they were going down before maneuvering over a bridge and between skyscrapers to land the plane safely on the river.

He walked the length of the sinking jet twice to verify that all his passengers had got off safely before exiting himself. Sully was nearing his 60th birthday at the time of the crash. If he had not been flying that day, the outcome might well have been different. Yet as late as 2007, airline pilots were required to retire at age 60. The presumption was that older pilots are less alert and less able to act decisively than younger pilots. In this instance, however, experience clearly trumped age.

In non-Western traditional cultures, the elderly are often accorded great respect and esteem. Among the Kirghiz, for example, a small community of 2,000 people who live in the high valleys of Afghanistan, the household head, called oey *bashi,* is the most senior male, or, in the absence of a male, the most senior female. The oey *bashi* exercises complete authority over the household and represents its social relations with the community.

Traditional Chinese culture also places a high value on old age. The veneration of the old is linked to Confucian values emphasizing that the parent should treat the child with *zi,* or nurturance, and the child should treat the parent with *xiao,* meaning filial piety or absolute obedience. To be *xiao* means showing one's parents respect at all times, performing acts of ancestor worship after they die, and generating grandsons to carry on the family name.

Xiao extends beyond respect for one's own parents to include deference to all elderly people. It is accompanied by many symbolic and conventional gestures, such as speaking politely, deferring in conversation to those older than oneself, and never ridiculing or insulting the aged. It would be a shameful breach of *xiao* to neglect the needs of the elderly or to put them in a nursing home. Although women always have lower status than men, the position of a woman in Chinese culture improves as she ages, and a few old women become genuinely powerful. . . .

Singer Dean Martin was a superstar in his heyday. He was comedian Jerry Lewis's sidekick and a member of Frank Sinatra's rat pack. His Las Vegas shows were sold out months in advance. In his later years, however, he became a recluse, sitting in his mansion in Los Angeles watching old cowboy movies and refusing all interviews.

Then there's "Banana" George Blair (known for his neon-yellow wetsuit), who water skis barefoot at 40 miles per hour. At age 71, George won a place in the *Guinness Book of World Records* as the first person to water ski barefoot on all seven continents. Which lifestyle represents normal aging? 99

(Source: Quadagno 2014:47, 60, 147. Also see Amoss and Harrell 1981; Henderson 1977; Shahrani 1981.)

> *As late as 2007, airline pilots were required to retire at age 60. . . . In this instance, however, experience clearly trumped age.*

A s sociologist Jill Quadagno demonstrates in her work on social gerontology, not all old people are frail and dependent, in need of support. Many are healthy, energetic, and engaged. Unfortunately, younger people tend to stereotype the aged. Like race or gender, age is socially constructed, an ascribed status that dominates people's perceptions of others, obscuring individual differences. Rather than suggesting that a particular elderly person is no longer competent to drive, for instance, we may condemn the entire age group: "These old codgers shouldn't be allowed on the road!"

How do people's roles change as they age? What are the social implications of the growing number of elderly in the United States? In these modules we will look at the process of aging throughout the life course and around the world. After exploring various theories of the impact of aging, we will discuss the role transitions typical of the major stages in the life course. We will consider the challenges facing the "sandwich generation," middle-aged people who care for both their children and their aging parents. We will pay particular attention to the effects of prejudice and discrimination on older people, and to the rise of a political consciousness among the elderly. Finally, in the Social Policy section we will discuss the controversial issue of the right to die.

The Sherpas—a Tibetan-speaking Buddhist people in Nepal—live in a culture that idealizes old age. Almost all elderly members of the Sherpa culture own their homes, and most are in relatively good physical condition. Typically, older Sherpas value their independence and prefer not to live with their children. Among the Fulani of Africa, however, older men and women move to the edge of the family homestead. Since that is where people are buried, the elderly sleep over their own graves, for they are viewed socially as already dead. Like gender stratification, age stratification varies from culture to culture. One society may treat older people with great reverence, while another sees them as unproductive and "difficult" (M. C. Goldstein and Beall 1981; Stenning 1958; Tonkinson 1978).

Age Stratification

It is understandable that all societies have some system of age stratification that associates certain social roles with distinct periods in life. Some of this age differentiation seems inevitable; it would make little sense to send young children off to war, or to expect most older citizens to handle physically demanding tasks, such as loading freight at shipyards. However, as is the case with stratification by gender, in the United States age stratification goes far beyond the physical constraints on human beings at different ages.

"Being old" is a master status that commonly overshadows all others in the United States. Thus, the insights of labeling theory can help us in analyzing the consequences of aging. Once people have been labeled "old," the designation has a major impact on how others perceive them, and even on how they view themselves. Negative stereotypes of the elderly contribute to their position as a minority group subject to discrimination, as we will see later in the chapter.

The model of five basic properties of a minority or subordinate group (introduced in Module 31) can be applied to older people in the United States to clarify their subordinate status:

1. Older people experience unequal treatment in employment and may face prejudice and discrimination.

2. Older people share physical characteristics that distinguish them from younger people. In addition, their cultural preferences and leisure-time activities often differ from those of the rest of society.

3. Membership in this disadvantaged group is involuntary.

4. Older people have a strong sense of group solidarity, as is reflected in the growth of senior citizens' centers, retirement communities, and advocacy organizations.

5. Older people generally are married to others of comparable age.

There is one crucial difference between older people and other subordinate groups, such as racial and ethnic minorities or women: *all* of us who live long enough will eventually assume the ascribed status of an older person (Barron 1953; Levin and Levin 1980; Wagley and Harris 1958).

Sociological Perspectives on Aging

Aging is one important aspect of socialization—the lifelong process through which an individual learns the cultural norms and values of a particular society. There are no clear-cut definitions for different periods of the aging cycle in the United States. *Old age* has typically been regarded as beginning at 65, which corresponds to the retirement age for many workers, but not everyone in the United States accepts that definition. With the increase in life expectancy, writers are beginning to refer to people in their 60s as the "young old," to distinguish them from those in their 80s and beyond (the "old old").

The particular problems of the elderly have become the focus of a specialized field of research and inquiry known as gerontology. **Gerontology** is the scientific study of the sociological and psychological aspects of aging and the problems of the aged. It originated in the 1930s, as an increasing number of social scientists became aware of the plight of the elderly.

© Hill Street Studios/Blend Images RF

Extended family arrangements are important to Americans, especially Latinos. Thirty-one percent of Hispanic women age 65 and older live with their relatives, compared to 13 percent of White non-Hispanic women. Among men of the same age, the rate is 15 percent for Hispanics, compared to 6 percent for White non-Hispanics (Jacobsen et al. 2011).

Gerontologists rely heavily on sociological principles and theories to explain the impact of aging on the individual and society. They also draw on psychology, anthropology, physical education, counseling, and medicine in their study of the aging process. Two influential views of aging—disengagement theory and activity theory—can best be understood in terms of the sociological perspectives of functionalism and interactionism, respectively. The conflict perspective also contributes to our sociological understanding of aging.

use your **sociological imagination**

Time has passed, and you are now in your 70s or 80s. How does old age in your generation compare with your parents' or grandparents' experience of old age?

Functionalist Perspective

After studying elderly people in good health and relatively comfortable economic circumstances, Elaine Cumming and William Henry (1961) introduced their **disengagement theory**, which implicitly suggests that society and the aging individual mutually sever many of their relationships. In keeping with the functionalist perspective, disengagement theory emphasizes that passing social roles on from one generation to another ensures social stability.

According to this theory, the approach of death forces people to drop most of their social roles—including those of worker, volunteer, spouse, hobby enthusiast, and even reader. Younger members of society then take on these functions. The aging person, it is held, withdraws into an increasing state of inactivity while preparing for death.

Since it was first outlined five decades ago, disengagement theory has generated considerable controversy. Today, gerontologists and sociologists are more likely to see the elderly in terms of social connectedness, postretirement employment, and volunteerism. For their part, producers and retailers of electronic products are likely to see the older set as e-savvy consumers. Growth in computer and digital camera sales has been greatest in that market segment. And retirement homes have had to make room for residents who want to bowl or play tennis on Nintendo's Wii system.

Interactionist Perspective

How important is it for older people to stay actively involved, whether at a job or in other pursuits? A tragic disaster in Chicago in 1995 showed that it can be a matter of life and death. An intense heat wave lasting more than a week—with a heat index exceeding 115 degrees on two consecutive days—resulted in 733 heat-related deaths. About three-fourths of the deceased were 65 and older. Subsequent analysis showed that older people who lived alone had the highest risk of dying, suggesting that support networks for the elderly literally help to save lives. Older Hispanics and Asian Americans had lower death rates from the heat wave than other racial and ethnic groups. Their stronger social networks probably resulted in more regular contact with family members and friends (Klinenberg 2015; R. Schaefer 1998).

Often seen as an opposing approach to disengagement theory, **activity theory** suggests that those elderly people who remain active and socially involved will be best adjusted. Proponents of this perspective acknowledge that a person age 70 may not have the ability or desire to perform various social roles that he or she had at age 40. Yet they contend that old people have essentially the same need for social interaction as any other group.

The improved health of older people—sometimes overlooked by social scientists—has strengthened the arguments of activity theorists. Illness and chronic disease are no longer quite the scourge of the elderly that they once were. The recent emphasis on fitness, the availability of better medical care, greater control of infectious diseases, and the reduction of fatal strokes and heart attacks have combined to mitigate the traumas of growing old. As we saw at the beginning of the chapter, Captain Sully Sullenberger is certainly both physically and mentally fit.

Accumulating medical research also points to the importance of remaining socially involved. Among those who decline in their mental capacities later in life, deterioration is most rapid in those who withdraw from social relationships and activities. Fortunately, older people are finding new ways to remain socially engaged, as evidenced by their increasing use of the Internet, especially to keep in touch with family and friends (Clifford 2009b).

© Strauss/Curtis/Corbis RF
These "silver surfers" in California still enjoy life to the fullest, just as they did when they were young. According to activity theory, staying active and involved is healthy for the older population.

BOX 37-1

Research Today

Elderspeak

"Who did you used to be?" This comment reveals an unflattering assumption about what happens to people when they grow old. Unfortunately, such remarks are far too frequent. In fact, condescending language is so often directed at elderly people that gerontologists have come to call it *elderspeak*.

According to scholars who have done observation research in nursing homes and retirement facilities, staff in these institutions tend to relate to the elderly residents in a manner befitting infants, calling them "dear," "good girl," and "sweetie." Medical professionals may patronize elderly patients, asking "Did you understand what I said?" or cajole them with "You don't want to upset your family, do you?" Although the people who make these remarks do not regard them as derogatory, older people find the unintended insults demoralizing.

Many older people experience ageism long before they retire. They may find that past a certain age, they will not be hired or even interviewed for a job. Yet research has shown that older workers can be an asset to employers. In response to such findings, some U.S. corporations, including Home Depot, are actively recruiting retired people.

Still, many older people have difficulty finding work, often as the result of age-ism. Economist Johanna Lahey sent similar resumes for fictitious women of different ages to employers in Boston and St. Petersburg, Florida. The results were striking. In Boston, a younger worker was 42 percent more likely than an older worker to be offered an interview for an entry-level job, such as a clerical position. In St. Petersburg, the difference was 46 percent.

To determine why the older applicants had more difficulty getting an interview, Lahey tried making them look more desirable.

To prevent a 62-year-old applicant from being seen as inflexible, undependable, or out of touch, she added a certificate of completion of a recent computer course to the person's application, along with an indication of health insurance coverage. However, these "extras" had no effect on the call-back rate.

> Many older people experience ageism long before they retire. They may find that past a certain age, they will not be hired or even interviewed for a job.

This study mirrored the results of one done two decades earlier, which showed that younger applicants are significantly more welcome in the job market than older applicants. Although further research might

© Stefan Kiefer/imagebroker/Alamy

About 30 percent of older workers choose to remain on the job past the usual retirement age. Research shows they can be retrained in new technologies and are more dependable than younger workers.

be done, the pattern seems clear: ageism is entrenched in our society.

LET'S DISCUSS

1. Have you ever worked alongside an older person? If so, did that person's age affect the way he or she did the job? In what ways?

2. Are older people the only ones who experience ageism? What signs of ageism might those who are not old experience?

Sources: Austin 2013; Charness and Villeval 2009; Freudenheim 2005; Lahey 2006; Lohr 2008; Roscigno 2010; K. Williams et al. 2009.

Admittedly, many activities open to older adults involve unpaid labor, for which younger adults may receive salaries.

Unpaid elderly workers include hospital volunteers (versus aides and orderlies), drivers for charities such as the Red Cross (versus chauffeurs), tutors (as opposed to teachers), and craftspeople for charity bazaars (as opposed to carpenters and dressmakers). However, some companies have recently begun programs to hire retirees for full-time or part-time work.

Though disengagement theory suggested that older people find satisfaction in withdrawal from society, conveniently receding into the background and allowing the next generation to take over, proponents of activity theory view such withdrawal as harmful to both the elderly and society. Activity theorists focus on the potential contributions of older people to the maintenance of society. In their opinion, aging citizens will feel satisfied only when they can be useful and productive in society's terms—primarily by working for wages (Charles and Carstensen 2009; Quadagno 2014).

Another aspect of the interactionist approach to aging is how younger people interact in everyday life and in the workforce with older members of society. The result is not always positive, as we find in research described in Box 37-1, "Elderspeak."

Labeling Perspective

Just who are "the elderly"? Labeling theorists, who study the way reality is constructed through our culture and social interactions, have noted that recently, our society has begun to reconsider what makes a person old.

As early as 1975, social scientists were suggesting that old age should be defined not in terms of how old one is, but in terms of how long one can be expected to live. As life expectancy lengthens, then, the age at which one is labeled old rises. Some have suggested that the threshold of old age should begin in the last 10 or 15 years of a person's expected life. Using that definition, old age would begin at about age 70 or 75, at least for those of us who live in the United States.

Is this new definition of old age likely to be accepted? From the labeling perspective, it all depends on who you are. Understandably, many people would prefer to be considered old later rather than sooner. Those who advocate for the elderly would prefer a broader definition. For example, the AARP offers membership to anyone age 50 or older. It argues that people should begin planning for old age in their 50s, but clearly, encouraging the "young old" to join gives them strength in numbers.

The labeling of old age also differs from one culture to the next, due in part to differences in physical health and life opportunities. In relatively prosperous cultures like the United States, 70 is the new 60. But in countries whose health and social support systems have been significantly weakened over the past 20 years—Russia, for example—50 is the new 60 (Sanderson and Scherbov 2008).

Conflict Perspective

Conflict theorists have criticized both disengagement theorists and activity theorists for failing to consider the impact of social structure on aging patterns. Neither approach, they say, questions why social interaction must change or decrease in old age. In addition, they often ignore the impact of social class on the lives of elderly people.

The privileged upper class generally enjoys better health and vigor and less likelihood of dependency in old age. Affluence cannot forestall aging indefinitely, but it can soften the economic hardships people face in later years. Although pension plans, retirement packages, and insurance benefits may be developed to assist older people, those whose wealth allows them access to investment funds can generate the greatest income for their later years.

In contrast, the working class often faces greater health hazards and a greater risk of disability; aging is particularly difficult for those who suffer job-related injuries or illnesses. Working-class people also depend more heavily on Social Security benefits and private pension programs. During inflationary times, their relatively fixed incomes from these sources barely keep pace with the escalating costs of food, housing, utilities, and other necessities (Atchley and Barusch 2004).

According to the conflict approach, the treatment of older people in the United States reflects the many divisions in our society. The low status of older people is seen in prejudice and discrimination against them, in age segregation, and in unfair job practices—none of which are directly addressed by either disengagement or activity theory.

TABLE **37-1** SOCIOLOGICAL PERSPECTIVES ON AGING

Sociological Perspective	View of Aging	Social Roles	Portrayal of Elderly
Functionalist	Disengagement	Reduced	Socially isolated
Interactionist	Activity	Changed	Involved in new networks
Labeling	Socially constructed	Changing	Varies by audience
Conflict	Competition	Relatively unchanged	Victimized, organized to confront their victimization

Conflict theorists have noted, too, that in the developing world, the transition from agricultural economies to industrialization and capitalism has not always been beneficial to the elderly. As a society's production methods change, the traditionally valued role of older people tends to erode. Their wisdom is no longer relevant in the new economy.

In sum, the four perspectives considered here take different views of the elderly. Functionalists portray older people as socially isolated, with reduced social roles; interactionists see them as involved in new networks and changing social roles. Labeling theorists see old age as a life stage that is defined by society. Conflict theorists see it as a time when people are victimized and their social roles devalued. Table 37-1 summarizes these perspectives.

 use your **sociological imagination**

Have you noticed signs of second-class treatment of older people? If so, in what ways?

MODULE **37** | **Recap and Review**

Summary

Age, like gender and race, is an ascribed status that forms the basis for social differentiation.

1. Like other forms of stratification, age stratification varies from culture to culture.

2. In the United States, being old is a master status that seems to overshadow all others.

3. The particular problems of the aged have become the focus of a specialized area of research and inquiry known as **gerontology.**

4. **Disengagement theory** implies that society should help older people withdraw from their accustomed social roles. In contrast, **activity theory** suggests that the elderly person who remains active and socially involved will be better adjusted.

5. Labeling theorists note that people of the same age are labeled differently in different societies, based largely on difference in physical health, life opportunities, and life expectancy.

6. From a conflict perspective, the low status of older people is reflected in prejudice and discrimination against them and in unfair job practices.

Thinking Critically

1. Why is disengagement theory an example of functionalism?

2. Is labeling the same as stereotyping? Why or why not?

Key Terms

Activity theory

Disengagement theory

Gerontology

MODULE 38 | Aging Worldwide

Today the world's population is evenly divided between those people who are under age 28 and those who are over age 28. By the middle of the 21st century, the median age will have risen to 40. Even though the United Nations held the first world assembly on aging in 1982, few people gave much thought to this prospect of whole populations—that is, nations—growing older until the 1990s. By 2015, the world had more than 617 million people age 65 and over. They constituted 8.5 percent of the world's population. By 2050, nearly twice that proportion, or 16.7 percent of the world's population, will be over 65.

In an important sense, this trend toward the aging of the world's population represents a major success story, one that unfolded during the latter years of the 20th century. Through the efforts of national governments and international agencies, many societies have drastically reduced their incidence of disease, and with it their rate of death. As a result, these nations—particularly the industrialized countries of Europe and North America— have a high and steadily rising proportion of older members (Figure 38-1) (Fishman 2010a, 2010b; He et al. 2016).

Overall, Europe's population is older than that of any other continent. Though many European countries have long prided themselves on their generous pension programs, as the proportion of older people continues to rise,

government officials have reluctantly begun to reduce pension benefits and raise the age at which workers can receive them. Japan, too, has a relatively old population; the Japanese enjoy a life expectancy of 83 years, compared to 79 in the United States. But though four more years of life may sound like a bonus, it presents a real and growing challenge to Japanese society (see Box 38-1).

In most developing countries, people over 60 are likely to be in poorer health than their counterparts in industrialized nations. Yet few of those countries are in a position to offer extensive

FIGURE 38-1 **World's "Oldest" Countries versus the United States**

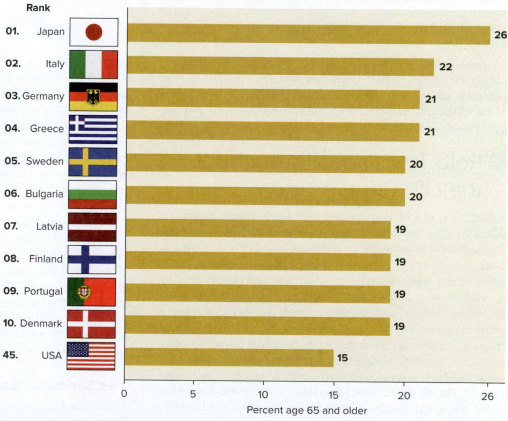

Rank		Percent age 65 and older
01.	Japan	26
02.	Italy	22
03.	Germany	21
04.	Greece	21
05.	Sweden	20
06.	Bulgaria	20
07.	Latvia	19
08.	Finland	19
09.	Portugal	19
10.	Denmark	19
45.	USA	15

Percent age 65 and older

Source: Developed by Richard Schaefer from Kaneda and Bietsch 2015. *Flags:* © admin_design/Shutterstock RF

Box 38-1

Sociology in the Global Community

Aging, Japanese Style

An electric water kettle is wired so that people in another location can determine whether it has been used in the previous 24 hours. This arrangement may seem a zany use of modern technology, but it symbolizes a change that is taking place around the globe: the growing needs of an aging population. The Japanese Welfare Network Ikebukuro Honcho installed these wired hotpots so that volunteers can monitor whether the elderly have prepared morning tea. An unused pot initiates contacts to see whether that person needs help. This technological monitoring system indicates not just the tremendous growth in Japan's elderly population, but the increasing numbers of elderly people who live alone.

Indeed, Japan is struggling to confront the challenges posed by the world's most rapidly aging population. For generations, Japanese families have lived with and cared for their aging parents and grandparents. But this tradition of living under the same roof with one's elders is fading as more and more couples and even single adults strike out on their own. Hence the need for the wired hotpots.

Compared to the United States and Canada, Japan is less well equipped to deal with this social phenomenon. Assisted living, in-home services, and nursing homes are all much less common in Japan than they are in North America.

As in the United States, research documents that the more elders connect with others and with the larger community, the more their health and quality of life improve.

One challenge many aging couples face is the "retired-husband syndrome." In their working days, most older Japanese men labored long hours in workplaces where women traditionally did not hold supervisory positions. When these men retire and begin to stay home full-time, some of them tend to treat their wives as subservient laborers. Moreover, many of them were so "married" to their jobs that they failed to develop hobbies or outside interests that might occupy them in retirement. Their wives, who have had free rein around the house all their lives, often find sharing the home with their dictatorial husbands a real challenge. Though Japanese gender roles are changing as record numbers of women enter positions of real responsibility, the senior generation is still hampered by yesterday's stereotypes.

The aging of Japan's workforce has forced government officials to reexamine the nation's policy toward immigrant workers. Although work opportunities dried up during the global economic downturn, the government does not want to lose this small group of immigrants, given Japan's looming labor shortage. So policymakers are devising programs that will allow immigrant workers to stay and will encourage their countrymen to join them when Japan's economy rebounds. Little wonder that a 21-nation study conducted in 2014 found the highest proportion of people (87 percent) in Japan agreeing that "aging is a major problem for the country" (Kochhnar 2014:1).

LET'S DISCUSS

1. What do you think caused the change in housing patterns that has resulted in so many elderly Japanese living alone? Could the change in housing patterns be related to the change in life expectancy? How?

2. How might living alone, rather than with extended family, contribute to the retired-husband syndrome noted among aging Japanese couples?

Sources: Faiola 2005, 2006; Hani 1998; Inoue et al., 2013; Kochhnar 2014; Schlesinger and Martin 2015; Shirahase 2015.

---

financial support to the elderly. Ironically, though the modernization of the developing world has brought many social and economic advances, it has undercut the traditionally high status of the elderly. In many cultures, the earning power of younger adults now exceeds that of their older relatives.

Role Transitions throughout the Life Course

Socialization is a lifelong process. We simply do not experience things the same way at different points in the life course. For example, one study found that even falling in love differs according to where we are in the life course. Young unmarried adults tend to treat love as a noncommittal game or an obsession characterized by possessiveness and dependency. People over age 50 are much more likely to see love as involving commitment, and they tend to take a practical approach to finding a partner who meets a set of rational criteria. That does not mean that romance is dead among the older generation, however. Among those age 65 and over, 39 percent are "head over heels in love," compared to only 25 percent of those ages 18 to 34. The life course, then, affects the manner in which we relate to one another (G. Anderson 2009; Montgomery and Sorell 1997).

How we move through the life course varies dramatically, depending on our personal preferences and circumstances. Some of us marry early, others late; some have children and some don't. These individual patterns are influenced by social factors such as class, race, and gender. Only in the most general terms, then, can we speak of stages or periods in the life course.

One transitional stage, identified by psychologist Daniel Levinson, begins at the time at which an individual gradually enters the adult world, perhaps by moving out of the parental home, beginning a career, or entering a marriage. The next transitional period, the midlife transition, typically begins at about age 40. Men and women often experience a stressful period of self-evaluation, commonly known as the **midlife crisis**, in which they realize that they have not achieved basic goals and ambitions and have little time left to do so. Thus, Levinson (1978, 1996) found that most adults surveyed experienced tumultuous midlife conflicts within the self and with the external world.

Not all the challenges at this time of life come from career or one's partner. In the next section we will examine a special challenge faced by a growing number of middle-aged adults: caring for two generations at once.

The Sandwich Generation

During the late 1990s social scientists focused on the **sandwich generation**—adults who simultaneously try to meet the competing needs of their parents and their children. That is, caregiving

© Rex Moreton/Bubbles Photolibrary/Alamy

This sandwich-generation mom cares for both her aging parent and her children. Increasingly, members of the baby boom generation find themselves caring for two generations at once.

goes in two directions: (1) to children, who even as young adults may still require significant direction, and (2) to aging parents, whose health and economic problems may demand intervention by their adult children. By 2010, 13 million Americans were caring for both their children and their parents.

Like the role of caring for children, the role of caring for aging parents falls disproportionately on women. Overall, women provide 66 percent of the care their parents receive, and even more as the demands of the role grow more intense and time-consuming. Increasingly, middle-aged women and younger are finding themselves on the "daughter track," as their time and attention are diverted by the needs of their aging mothers and fathers (National Alliance for Caregiving 2009).

The last major transition identified by Levinson occurs after age 60—sometimes well after that age, given advances in health care, greater longevity, and gradual acceptance within society of older people. Nonetheless, there is a point at which people transition to a different lifestyle. As we will see, this is a time of dramatic changes in people's everyday lives.

Adjusting to Retirement

Retirement is a rite of passage that marks a critical transition from one phase of a person's life to another. Typically, symbolic events are associated with this rite of passage, such as retirement gifts, a retirement party, and special moments on the last day on the job. The preretirement period itself can be emotionally charged, especially if the retiree is expected to train his or her successor (Atchley 1976).

Today, the retirement stage is complicated by economic deterioration. From 1950 to 1990, the average age at retirement in the United States declined; since then, however, it has risen. In 1992, 11.5 percent of those over age 64 were in the labor force. By 2012, the proportion had increased to 18.5 percent, and is projected to hit 23.0 percent by 2022. In that year, the proportion of people still working in their upper 70s will match the proportion of those who were working in their upper 60s in 1992. Indeed, as recently as 2012, 5 percent of women and 11 percent of men over age 75 were still working (Bureau of Labor Statistics 2013c).

A variety of factors explains this reversal in the trend toward earlier retirement. Changes in Social Security benefits, the recent economic recession, and workers' concern about maintaining their health insurance and pension benefits have all contributed. At the same time, life expectancy has increased and the quality of people's health has improved (Toossi 2012).

Phases of Retirement Gerontologist Robert Atchley (1976) has identified several phases of the retirement experience:

- *Preretirement,* a period of anticipatory socialization as the person prepares for retirement.

- *The near phase,* when the person establishes a specific departure date from his or her job.

- *The honeymoon phase,* an often euphoric period in which the person pursues activities that he or she never had time for before.

- *The disenchantment phase,* in which retirees feel a sense of letdown or even depression as they cope with their new lives, which may include illness or poverty.

- *The reorientation phase,* which involves the development of a more realistic view of retirement alternatives.

- *The stability phase,* a period in which the person has learned to deal with life after retirement in a reasonable and comfortable fashion.

- *The termination phase,* which begins when the person can no longer engage in basic, day-to-day activities such as self-care and housework.

Retirement is not a single transition, then, but rather a series of adjustments that varies from one person to another. The length and timing of each phase will differ for each individual, depending on such factors as financial status and health. A particular person will not necessarily go through all the phases identified by Atchley (Reitzes and Mutran 2006).

Some factors, such as being forced into retirement or being burdened with financial difficulties, can further complicate the retirement process. People who enter retirement involuntarily or without the necessary means may never experience the

Naturally Occurring Retirement Communities (NORCs)

With recent improvements in health care, older Americans have gained new choices in where to live. Today, rather than residing in nursing homes or planned retirement communities, many of them congregate in areas that have gradually become informal centers for senior citizens. Social scientists have dubbed such areas **naturally occurring retirement communities** (**NORCs**).

Using observation research, census data, and interviews, sociologists have developed some interesting conclusions about NORCs in the United States, which account for an estimated 17 to 25 percent of people age 65 or older. These communities can be as small as a single apartment building or as large as a neighborhood in a big city. Often, they emerge as singles and young couples move out and older people move in. Sometimes couples simply remain where they are; as they grow older, the community becomes noticeably grayer. Such has been the case in the Fort Hamilton neighborhood in Brooklyn, New York, where a third of residents are now over 55. In time, business establishments that cater to the elderly—pharmacies, medical supply outlets, small restaurants, senior citizen centers—relocate to NORCs, making them even more attractive to older citizens.

Unfortunately, residents of some of these communities are threatened by gentrification, or the takeover of low-income neighborhoods by higher-income residents. In Chicago, a high-rise building known as Ontario Place is converting to a condominium, at prices that current residents cannot afford. About half the building's occupants are Russian immigrants; most of the others are elderly or disabled people living on fixed incomes. These people are distressed not just because they will need to move, but because their community is being destroyed (Gregor 2013; Piturro 2012; Sheehan 2005).

Death and Dying

Among the role transitions that typically (but not always) come later in life is death. Until recently, death was viewed as a taboo topic in the United States. However, psychologist Elisabeth Kübler-Ross (1969), through her pioneering book *On Death and Dying*, greatly encouraged open discussion of the process of dying. Drawing on her work with 200 cancer patients, Kübler-Ross identified five stages of the experience: denial, anger, bargaining, depression, and finally acceptance.

Despite its popular appeal, the five-stage theory of dying has been challenged. Observers ofen cannot substantiate these stages. With medical advances, dying now tends to be a much longer process than it was when Kübler-Ross did her research a halfcentury ago. Moreover, research suggests that each person declines in his or her own way. Thus, one should not expect—much less counsel—a person to approach death in any particular way. Cross-culturally, the variation in approaches is even more marked. Box 38-2 describes some of the ways in which different Native American tribes acknowledge death (Okun and Nowinski 2011).

"I prefer 'Baby Boomer' rather than 'Senior Citizen'."

Source: Cartoon © Dave Carpenter. Reprinted by permission of Cartoonstock.com

honeymoon phase. In the United States, many retirees continue in the paid labor force, often taking part-time jobs to supplement their pensions. The impact of the prolonged economic downturn that began in 2008 on this pattern remains to be seen.

Like other aspects of life in the United States, the experience of retirement varies according to gender, race, and ethnicity. White males are most likely to benefit from retirement wages, as well as to have participated in a formal retirement preparation program. As a result, anticipatory socialization for retirement is most complete for White men. In contrast, members of racial and ethnic minority groups—especially African Americans—are more likely to exit the paid labor force through disability than through retirement. Because of their comparatively lower incomes and smaller savings, men and women from racial and ethnic minority groups work intermittently after retirement more often than older Whites (National Institute on Aging 1999; Quadagno 2014).

 use your **sociological imagination**

How have people close to you, such as relatives, personally handled their retirement from the labor force?

Native Americans and Death

The native peoples of North America include hundreds of distinctive cultures, as different from one another as English culture is from Turkish culture. Their practices with respect to death and dying reflect this cultural diversity. Sociologist Gerry Cox conducted ethnographic fieldwork and interviews with tribal peoples on 42 reservations throughout the United States and Canada. He found that among the Creek and some other tribes, those closest to the deceased accompany the body in the days before the burial. In other tribes, such as the Navajo, Apache, and Hopi, relatives spend little time with the body.

> Family members smudge the body with ashes immediately after death, then go with it to a funeral home for embalming.

© Richard Wong/Alamy

Among the Navajo, the taboo against speaking of death is so strong that health care providers can only approach the subject of end-of-life care with patients and family members indirectly through a poem. Written in both Navajo and English, the poem about death allows elderly patients and family members to begin a discussion about end-of-life issues.

In many cases, these practices evolved after contact with European Americans. Religious proselytizing, intermarriage, and the enforcement of colonial regulations all had an impact on cultural traditions. Among the first to experience Hispanic contact in the 16th century were the Zuni and other Pueblo peoples of present-day Arizona and New Mexico. In those cultures, burials that had once been done quickly, with little ceremony, moved onto church grounds or to graveyards consecrated by Christian ritual. At the same time, Native Americans

continued their traditional burial practices, in secret when necessary.

Among the Flathead of Montana, who converted to Roman Catholicism a century ago, traditional practices persist. Family members smudge the body with ashes immediately after death, then go with it to a funeral home for embalming. Before the body is placed in a coffin, they wash it in rose water. The Catholic funeral mass that precedes the burial includes native songs and ceremonial drums.

Today, Native Americans have won some concessions from hospitals that care for the dying. Lakota patients are allowed to have more relatives in the room than other patients. They may ask to use smoke for ceremonial purposes, even though smoking is strictly forbidden. Apaches, in contrast, prefer to die alone. Navajos may want to hold a "sing."

Native American rituals demonstrate reverence and respect for life as well as death. Despite the great diversity in their values,

beliefs, and normative behavior regarding death, one broad belief unites Native Americans: death is a natural and accepted part of the life cycle. Native Americans also share the belief that their dear ones continue to love, care for, and protect families and friends after death.

LET'S DISCUSS

1. Does your own family observe traditional cultural practices regarding death and dying, independent of formal religious ritual? If so, explain their meaning and importance to your family.

2. Apply the concepts you learned in Chapter 3 to Native American burial practices. Which of them do you find most useful in understanding these practices?

Sources: G. R. Cox 2010; Daitz 2011; S. R. Kaufman and Morgan 2005; A. C. Walker and Balk 2007.

Functionalist analysis brings to mind the cherished yet controversial concept of a "good death." One researcher described a good death among the Kaliai, a people of the South Pacific. In that culture, the dying person calls together all his relatives, settles his debts, disposes of his possessions, and then announces that it is time for him to die (Counts and Counts 2004).

The Kaliai concept of a good death has a parallel in Western societies, where people may speak of a "natural death," an "appropriate death," or "death with dignity." The practice

of **hospice care,** introduced in London, England, in 1967, is founded on this concept. Hospice workers seek to improve the quality of a dying person's last days by offering comfort and by helping the person to remain at home, or in a homelike setting at a hospital or other special facility, until the end. Currently, more than 33,000 home care and hospice programs serve over 12 million people a year in the United States through federal programs such as Medicare and Medicaid (National Association for Home Care and Hospice 2016).

© Gero Breloer/dpa/Corbis

Did you guess that this is the shop of an expert woodcarver working with an undertaker? Coffins in Ghana sometimes are quite elaborate to try to reflect status or the way the dead lived their lives.

individual efforts and social resources away from attempts to extend life. Still others argue that fatally ill older people should not just passively accept death, but should forgo further treatment in order to reduce public health care expenditures. Such issues are at the heart of current debates over the right to die and physician-assisted suicide.

Today, in many varied ways, people have broken through the historic taboos about death and are attempting to arrange certain aspects of the idealized good death. For example, bereavement practices—once highly structured—are becoming increasingly varied and therapeutic. More and more people are actively addressing the inevitability of death by making wills, leaving "living wills" (health care proxies that explain their feelings about the use of life-support equipment), donating organs, and providing instructions for family members about funerals, cremations, and burials. Given medical and technological advances and a breakthrough in open discussion and negotiation regarding death and dying, it is possible that good deaths may become a social norm in the United States.

Although the Western ideal of the good death makes the experience of dying as positive as possible, some critics fear that acceptance of the concept of a good death may direct both

MODULE 38 | Recap and Review

Summary

The industrialized nations of Europe, North America, and Asia have high and steadily rising proportions of older citizens.

1. People move through the life course in highly individual ways that vary with culture and individual circumstance. The **midlife crisis** is a stressful period of self-evaluation that many individuals experience at around age 40.

2. Adults who simultaneously care for their children and their parents belong to the **sandwich generation**.

3. Retirement is not a single transition but is rather a series of stages in itself. The experience of retirement varies because of individual factors but also because of factors related to race, gender, and ethnicity.

4. Dying is increasingly seen as the last stage of life, as people attempt to break through traditional taboos regarding death in order to achieve a good death.

Thinking Critically

1. Today, many young adults continue to live with their parents after finishing their schooling. Contrast their situation with that of the elderly who live with their children. Does society treat dependent adult children in the same way as dependent parents? Why or why not?

2. How might interactionists consider a NORC?

Key Terms

Hospice care

Midlife crisis

Naturally occurring retirement community (NORC)

Sandwich generation

The "Graying of America"

When Lenore Schaefer, a ballroom dancer, tried to get on the *Tonight Show,* she was told she was "too young": she was in her early 90s. When she turned 101, she made it. But even at that age, Lenore is no longer unusual in our society. Today, people over 100 constitute, proportionately, the country's fastest-growing age group. They are part of the increasing proportion of the population of the United States that is composed of older people (Himes 2001; Rimer 1998).

As Figure 39-1 shows, in the future, an increasing proportion of the U.S. population will be composed of older people. This trend is expected to continue well into the 21st century, as the mortality rate declines and members of the postwar baby boom age. At the same time, the "oldest old"—that is, the segment of the population representing those who are age 85 or older—will grow at an even faster rate.

Compared with the rest of the population, the elderly are more likely to be female than male. Men tend to have higher death rates than women at every age. By old age, women outnumber men by a ratio of 3 to 2. The gap widens with advancing age, so that among the oldest old, the ratio is 5 to 2.

The elderly are also more likely than others to be White: about 80 percent of the elderly are White and non-Hispanic. Although this segment of the population is becoming more racially and ethnically diverse, the higher death rates of racial and ethnic minorities, together with the continuing immigration of younger Latinos and Asians, is likely to keep it more White than the nation as a whole. Yet the overall pattern of an increasingly diversified population will show up among older Americans. As the projections in Figure 39-2 show, as the 21st century advances, non-Whites and Latinos will make up an increasing proportion of those who are 65 and over.

Finally, the elderly are more likely than the rest of the population to live in certain states. The highest proportions of older people are found in Florida, Pennsylvania, Rhode Island, Iowa, West Virginia, and Arkansas. In 2010, Florida was the state most populated by the elderly, with 17.4 percent of the population over age 65. Yet as Figure 39-3 shows, in less than 20 years, more than half the states will have an even greater proportion of elderly people than Florida does now.

The graying of the United States is a phenomenon that can no longer be ignored, either by social scientists or by government policymakers. Advocates for the elderly have spoken out on a wide range of issues. Politicians court the votes of older people, since they are the age group most likely to register and vote. In fact, in the 2012 election, 71.9 percent of people over 65 voted, compared to 41.2 percent for those under 25 (Bureau of the Census 2012b).

Wealth and Income

There is significant variation in wealth and poverty among the nation's older people. Some individuals and couples find themselves poor in part because of fixed pensions and skyrocketing health care costs (see Chapter 17, Module 53). Nevertheless, as a group, older people in the United States are neither homogeneous nor poor. The typical elderly person enjoys a standard of living that is much higher now than at any point in the nation's past. Class differences among the elderly remain evident, but tend to narrow somewhat: those older people who enjoyed middle-class incomes while younger tend to remain better off after retirement, but less so than before (D. Smith and Tillipman 2000).

To some extent, older people owe their overall improved standard of living to a greater accumulation of wealth—in the form of home ownership, private pensions, and other financial

FIGURE 39-1 **Percentage of U.S. Population in Selected Age Groups, 1970–2060**

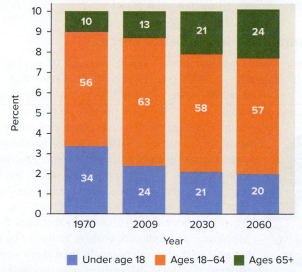

Source: Population Reference Bureau analysis of Bureau of the Census data, in Colby and Ortman 2015: Figure 5.

FIGURE 39-2 **Minority Population Age 65 and Older, 2012–2060**

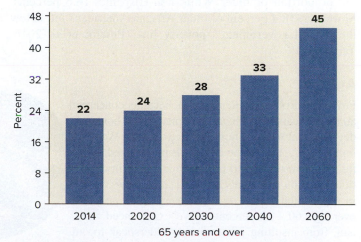

Source: Bureau of the Census in Mather et al. 2015.

FIGURE 39-3 Twenty-Eight Floridas by 2030

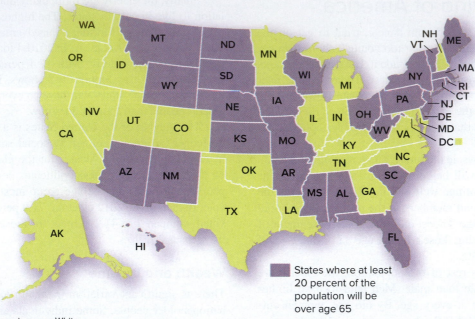

States where at least 20 percent of the population will be over age 65

Note: Minority defined as Hispanic or non-White.
Source: Bureau of the Census 2005 in Mather et al. 2015.

assets. Indeed, the median net worth of the elderly has increased by 42 percent over the past 25 years. At the extremes of poverty are those groups who were more likely to be poor at earlier points in the life cycle: female-headed households and racial and ethnic minorities.

Box 39-1 examines this cautionary tale of the improving economic status of older people but injects some information that carries a more pessimistic future outlook.

Viewed from a conflict perspective, it is not surprising that older women experience a double burden; the same is true of elderly members of racial and ethnic minorities. For example, in 2015 the proportion of older Latinos with incomes below the poverty level (17.5 percent) was much greater than the proportion of older White non-Hispanics (6.6 percent). Moreover, 18.4 percent of older African Americans fell below the federal government's poverty line (Proctor et al. 2016: Table B-2).

Ageism

Physician Robert Butler (1990) became concerned about 50 years ago when he learned that a housing development near his home in metropolitan Washington, D.C., barred the elderly. Butler coined the term **ageism** to refer to prejudice and discrimination based on a person's age. Research shows that in the United States, a large majority of people over age 60—84 percent—have experienced ageism, from insulting jokes such as elderspeak to outright disrespect (Roscigno 2010:7).

© Masterfile RF

Ageism is especially difficult for the old, because at least youthful recipients of prejudice know that in time they will be "old enough." For many, old age symbolizes disease. While physical condition does weaken with age, today's older people are in much better shape than their counterparts even one generation ago. In any event, most jobs today require little brawn. Studies also indicate that older workers are better at jobs that require personnel skills, which comprise a growing proportion of the jobs available. In what has been termed the *silver collar economy,* more companies are hiring people 65 and older because they believe these workers are reliable and productive (*The Economist* 2011d; Trumbull 2006).

Competition in the Labor Force

Although paid employment is not typical after age 65, it is becoming increasingly common (see Figure 39-4). Concerned over their pension benefits, more and more people who are healthy enough to continue working have decided to postpone their retirement. Their decision has further eroded job opportunities for younger workers, already handicapped by the highest unemployment rates in a generation. Unfortunately, some people view older workers as "job stealers"—a biased judgment similar to that directed against illegal immigrants—instead of as experienced contributors to the labor force. Moreover, unemployed workers in their 50s find that potential employers rarely give them serious consideration. These difficulties not only intensify age conflict but lead to age discrimination as well

Research Today

Box 39-1

Cautiously Good News: Declining Poverty among the Aged

One of the great economic success stories of the 20th century was the decline in poverty among the elderly. In 1959, 39 percent of all people over age 65 lived below the poverty line, but by 2014, just 10 percent did. This is a highly significant decline, and while there are plenty of exceptions—many elderly individuals are still poor—compared to the recent past, the change is remarkable. However, there is room for caution. There is concern that the trend is starting to change.

A typical American worker in the middle rung of the earnings ladder, whose career pay averages out at about $46,000 per year in today's money, would retire at age 65 with a Social Security benefit worth 39 percent of his or her career-average pay, or around $18,000 per year or $1500 per month. But here comes the caution: unless something is done to replenish Social Security's shrinking trust funds, by 2035 that worker's first pension check might amount to as little as 27.5 percent of her or his career wage (closer to $12,600 per year or $1050 per month), according to calculations published by the Social Security Administration.

> The current older cohort may be the last generation for some time to widely enjoy pension benefits supplemented by a government safety net.

The economically vulnerable situation of these older persons results from a lack of retirement income and/or employment opportunities, inadequate assets and financial management tools, limited health insurance coverage and access to key public benefits, and high levels of disability and poor health. Furthermore, these harsh circumstances disproportionately affect women, minorities, and persons living alone. One cannot underestimate the importance of Social Security and employer-sponsored employment plans in keeping older households above the poverty threshold. A study released in 2008

determined that the poverty rate for individuals age 65 and above would have increased from 9.4 percent to 44.9 percent in 2006 without Social Security.

Fewer and fewer workers nearing retirement age today have an employer-sponsored retirement plan. The current older cohort may be the last generation for some time to widely enjoy pension benefits supplemented by a government safety net. So the decline in poverty among those over 65 may end or even be reversed in the next few years.

LET'S DISCUSS

1. To what extent do the elderly people in your family rely on Social Security for their income? Do they have employer-funded pensions or other sources of regular income?

2. Do you think you will enjoy Social Security benefits when you reach retirement age? How do you think the retirement system will change by then?

Sources: AARP 2008; Bureau of the Census 2016a; Kadlec 2015; Porter 2015; Searcey and Gebeloff 2015.

(Jacobsen et al. 2011). From the 1940s through the early 1990s, the proportion of people over age 65 who were working declined steadily, and the rate dropped faster for men than for women. Since the 1990s this pattern has reversed for both men and women. In little more than a decade, the percentage of older people who are working doubled.

Even more remarkable is the shift of older workers to full-time employment. In 2002, for the first time, more older people were working full-time than part-time. This trend has continued through the recession that began in 2008. Older workers face high unemployment rates, but more and more have continued to

seek work, perhaps to offset losses to their retirement savings (see Figure 39-4).

As the baby boom generation ages, the share of workers in the 55-years-and-older age group is expected to increase dramatically, at least through 2018. Despite this trend, the participation rates of older workers are not expected to reach the working levels of those in their 40s (Bureau of Labor Statistics 2010; Toossi 2012).

The federal Age Discrimination in Employment Act (ADEA), which went into effect in 1968, was passed to protect workers who are age 40 and older from being fired because of their age and replaced with younger workers, who would presumably receive lower salaries. The Supreme Court strengthened federal protection against age discrimination in 1996, ruling unanimously that such lawsuits can be successful even if an older worker is replaced by someone who is older than 40. Consequently, firing a 65-year-old employee to make way for a 45-year-old can be construed as age discrimination.

While firing people simply because they are old violates federal law, courts have upheld the right to lay off older workers for economic reasons. Critics contend that later, the same firms hire young, cheaper workers to replace experienced older workers. When economic growth began to slow in 2008 and companies cut back on their workforces, complaints of age bias grew sharply as older workers began to suspect they were bearing a disproportionate share of the layoffs. Little wonder, then, in the wake of a bad economy, that workers are approaching their

FIGURE 39-4 **Labor Force by Age, 2004–2024**

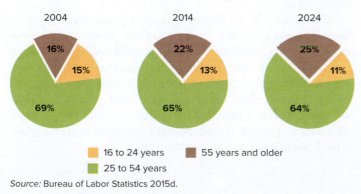

16 to 24 years		55 years and older
25 to 54 years		

Source: Bureau of Labor Statistics 2015d.

retirement warily. A national survey showed that only 14 percent of workers are confident of living comfortably in retirement, compared with 27 percent in 2007, before the recent recession (R. Helman et al. 2012:7; Roscigno 2010).

 use your **sociological imagination**

How likely are you to watch a television show that is based on older characters who spend a lot of time together? Explain.

The Elderly: Emergence of a Collective Consciousness

During the 1960s, students at colleges and universities across the country, advocating "student power," collectively demanded a role in the governance of educational institutions. In the following decade, many older people became aware that *they* were being treated as second-class citizens and turned to collective action.

The largest organization representing the nation's elderly is the AARP, founded in 1958 by a retired school principal who was having difficulty getting insurance because of age prejudice. Many of the AARP's services involve discounts and insurance for its 40 million members (43 percent of Americans age 50 and older), but the organization is also a powerful lobbying group. Recognizing that many elderly people are still gainfully employed, it has dropped its full name, American Association of *Retired* Persons (Donnelly 2007; Eggen 2009).

The potential power of the AARP is enormous. It is the third-largest voluntary association in the United States (behind only the Roman Catholic Church and the American Automobile Association), representing one out of every four registered voters in the United States. The AARP has endorsed voter registration campaigns, nursing home reforms, and pension reforms. In acknowledgment of its difficulties recruiting members of racial and ethnic minority groups, the AARP recently began a Minority Affairs Initiative. The spokeswoman for the initiative, Margaret Dixon, became the AARP's first African American president in 1996 (Birnbaum 2005).

People grow old in many different ways. Not all elderly people face the same challenges or enjoy the same resources. While the AARP lobbies to protect the elderly in general, other groups work in more specific ways. For example, the National Committee to Preserve Social Security and Medicare, founded in 1982, has successfully lobbied Congress to keep Medicare benefits for the ailing poor elderly. Other large special-interest groups represent retired federal employees, retired teachers, and retired union workers However, when AARP supported the Affordable Care Act (Obamacare), the organization lost up to 400,000 members to conservative-leaning groups seeking to be a voice of older Americans (Johannes 2014; Quadagno 2014).

Still another manifestation of the new awareness of older people is the formation of organizations for elderly homosexuals.

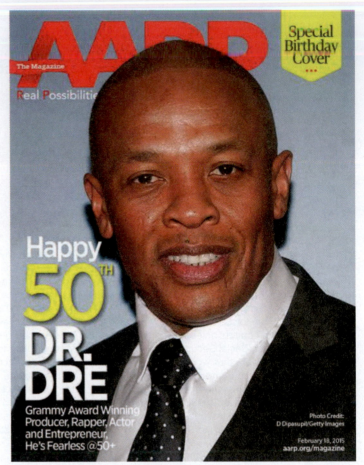

Source: American Association of Retired Persons

The AARP is a major voice for the elderly. By featuring rapper and entrepreneur Dr. Dre (born in 1965) on the cover of its widely distributed magazine, the organization is signaling a desire to represent the younger and more racially diverse members of the older generation, as well as to portray the active lives many older people lead.

One such group, Services and Advocacy for GLBT Elders (SAGE), was established in New York City in 1977 and now oversees a nationwide network of community groups, as well as affiliates in Canada and Germany. Like traditional senior citizens' groups, SAGE sponsors workshops, classes, dances, and food deliveries to the homebound. Throughout the United States, retirement homes are self-identifying themselves as seeking older lesbian, gay, bisexual and transgender couples. Some but not all of these facilities are gay-owned (C. Lehman 2012; SAGE 2016).

The elderly in the United States are better off today both financially and physically than ever before. Many of them have strong financial assets and medical care packages that will meet almost any health need. But as we have seen, a significant segment is impoverished, faced with the prospect of declining health and mounting medical bills. And some older people must now add being aged to a lifetime of disadvantage. Like people in all other stages of the life course, the aged constitute a diverse group in the United States and around the world.

On August 4, 1993, Dr. Jack Kevorkian, a retired patholo-gist, helped a 30-year-old Michigan man with Lou Gehrig's disease to commit suicide in a van. The patient died after inhaling carbon monoxide through a mask designed by Dr. Kevorkian; in doing so, he became the 17th person to commit suicide with Kevorkian's assistance. Kevorkian was openly challenging a Michigan law (aimed at him) that makes it a felony—punishable by up to four years in jail— to assist in a suicide. Since then Kevorkian has assisted in numerous other suicides, but not until he did it on television in 1998 did the charges brought against him result in his imprisonment for second-degree murder. Kevorkian completed his sentence in 2007 and died of circulatory problems in 2011.

Looking at the Issue

The issue of physician-assisted suicide is but one aspect of the larger debate in the United States and other countries over the ethics of suicide and euthanasia. The term **euthanasia** has been defined as the "act of bringing about the death of a hopelessly ill and suffering person in a relatively quick and painless way for reasons of mercy" (Council on Ethical and Judicial Affairs, American Medical Association 1992:229). This type of mercy killing reminds us of the ideal of the "good death" discussed in Module 38. The debate over euthanasia and assisted suicide often focuses on cases involv-ing older people, although it can involve younger adults with terminal and degenerative dis-eases, or even children.

National surveys show that public opinion on this contro-versial practice is divided. In 2014, 69 percent of respondents said that a physician should be legally permitted to end a patient's life if both the patient and the patient's family make such a request (McCarthy 2014).

Currently, public policy in the United States does not permit *active euthanasia* (such as a deliberate injection of lethal drugs into a terminally ill patient) or physician-assisted

suicide. Although suicide itself is no longer a crime, assisting suicide is illegal in virtually all states (see Figure 39-5). There is greater legal tolerance for *passive euthanasia* (such as discon-necting life-support equipment from a comatose patient).

Applying Sociology

Many societies are known to have practiced *senilicide*— "kill-ing of the aged"—because of extreme difficulties in provid-ing basic necessities such as food and shelter. In a study of the treatment of elderly people in 41 nonindustrialized soci-eties, Anthony Glascock (1990) found some form of "death-hastening" behavior in 21 of them. Killing of elderly people was evident in 14 of the societies; abandoning them was evi-dent in 8. Typically, death hastening occurs when older peo-ple become decrepit and are viewed as already dead. In these nonindustrialized cultures it is open and socially approved. Family members generally make the decisions, often after open consultation with those who are about to die.

Conflict theorists ask questions about the values raised by such decisions. By endorsing physician-assisted suicide,

---

MAPPING LIFE NATIONWIDE

FIGURE 39-5 **Physician-Assisted Suicide by State**

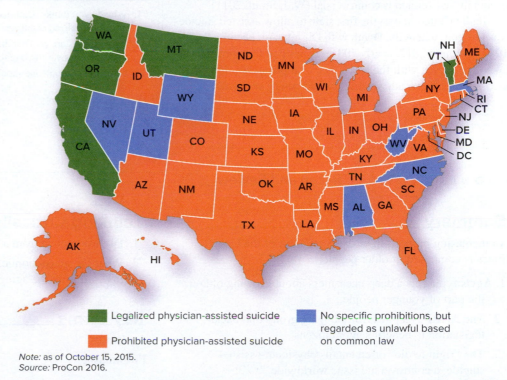

Legend:
- Legalized physician-assisted suicide (green)
- Prohibited physician-assisted suicide (orange)
- No specific prohibitions, but regarded as unlawful based on common law (blue)

Note: as of October 15, 2015.
Source: ProCon 2016.

—Continued

are we devaluing the disabled through an acceptance of their premature death? Critics note that we are all only temporarily able-bodied; disease or a speeding automobile can place any one of us among the disabled. By establishing a precedent for ending the lives of selected disabled people, we may unwittingly contribute to negative social views and labeling of all disabled people. Further reflecting the conflict perspective, gerontologist Elizabeth Markson (1992:6) argues that the "powerless, poor or undesirable are at special risk of being 'encouraged' to choose assisted death."

Despite these concerns, research to date shows little bias. In studies of physician-assisted suicide in Oregon and the Netherlands, researchers looked at how implementation of the controversial policy might affect people who were vulnerable because of their disability, age, mental health, or race and ethnicity. Overall, those people who died with a doctor's help were more likely to be socially, economically, and educationally privileged than to be particularly vulnerable (Battin et al. 2007; *The Economist* 2015b).

Initiating Policy

In the industrialized world, euthanasia is legal and widely accepted in only five countries: the Netherlands, Belgium, Switzerland, Canada, and Colombia. Switzerland allows foreigners to be euthanized. While physician-assisted suicide is accepted by the public in all three countries, the "suicide tourism" that occurs in Switzerland is controversial (W. J. Smith 2011).

In the United States, the first state to allow assisted suicide was Oregon, where the Death with Dignity Act became law in 1997. Through 2012, nearly 700 terminally ill Oregonians had taken their lives with the assistance of a physician. President George W. Bush's administration had made an unsuccessful attempt to stop the prescription of lethal drugs to terminally ill patients in Oregon. In 2006, the Supreme Court ruled 6-3 that the federal government had overstepped its authority in punishing doctors in Oregon who had helped terminally ill patients to end their lives.

Brittany Maynard was the unusual case of a person who, by doing what she felt was best for her, changed policy and perhaps rekindled a public debate. In 2014, the 29-year-old Californian was diagnosed with an inoperable malignant brain tumor. She moved with her family from California to Oregon so she could exercise the option to legally kill herself with prescribed medication. Not only her use of social media but also her age ignited debate; at the time, Oregon's typical patient seeking assisted suicide was 71. Her situation, and the fact that she was forced to move to another state, underscored the implications of the debate over physician-assisted suicide. Within a year of Brittany's death, California joined the small number of states permitting physician-assisted suicide (Bever 2014).

Advances in technology now allow us to prolong life in ways that were unimaginable decades ago. But should people be forced or expected to prolong lives that are unbearably painful, or that are in effect "lifeless"? Unfortunately, medical and technological advances cannot provide answers to these complex ethical, legal, and political questions.

TAKE THE ISSUE WITH YOU

1. Why do you think "death-hastening" behavior is common in nonindustrialized countries?

2. In what ways are conflict theory and disengagement theory relevant to the debate over the "right to die"?

3. Do you think someone should be allowed to choose to die? Why or why not?

MODULE 39 | Recap and Review

Summary

An increasing proportion of the population of the United States is composed of older people.

1. **Ageism** reflects a deep uneasiness about growing old on the part of younger people.

2. The AARP is a powerful lobbying group that backs legislation to benefit senior citizens.

3. The "right to die" often entails physician-assisted suicide, a controversial issue worldwide.

Thinking Critically

1. Discuss ageism from a conflict perspective.

2. What social, economic, and political changes are likely to result from the aging of the U.S. population?

Key Terms

Ageism

Euthanasia

Mastering This Chapter

© Monkey Business Images/
Shutterstock RF

taking sociology with you

1 Think about your grandparents: Would you describe them as active or disengaged? Do you think their social class has had an impact on the way they have aged? Explain. How well have they adjusted to retirement?

2 What public agency or organization—the senior center, council on aging—is responsible for serving seniors in your community? Visit the site and learn about the programs offered there. Then relate your findings to what you learned in this chapter.

3 Find out the percentage of people age 65 and over who live in your community. How does that percentage compare to your state or to the United States as a whole? If you can, determine whether residents in this age bracket are clustered in particular areas. Are you aware of any naturally occurring retirement communities (NORCs) where you live?

Key Terms

Activity theory An interactionist theory of aging that suggests that those elderly people who remain active and socially involved will be best adjusted.

Ageism Prejudice and discrimination based on a person's age.

Disengagement theory A functionalist theory of aging that suggests that society and the aging individual mutually sever many of their relationships.

Euthanasia The act of bringing about the death of a hopelessly ill and suffering person in a relatively quick and painless way for reasons of mercy.

Gerontology The scientific study of the sociological and psychological aspects of aging and the problems of the aged.

Hospice care Treatment of the terminally ill in their own homes, or in special hospital units or other facilities, with the goal of helping them to die easily, without pain.

Midlife crisis A stressful period of self-evaluation that begins at about age 40.

Naturally occurring retirement community (NORC) An area that has gradually become an informal center for senior citizens.

Sandwich generation The generation of adults who simultaneously try to meet the competing needs of their parents and their children.

self-quiz

Read each question carefully and then select the best answer.

1. Activity theory is associated with the
   a. functionalist perspective.
   b. conflict perspective.
   c. interactionist perspective.
   d. labeling perspective.

2. What is the one crucial difference between older people and other subordinate groups, such as racial and ethnic minorities or women?
   a. Older people do not experience unequal treatment in employment.
   b. Older people have a strong sense of group solidarity and other groups do not.
   c. All of us who live long enough will eventually assume the ascribed status of being an older person.
   d. Older people are generally married to others of comparable age and other minorities do not marry within their group.

3. Which field of study was originally developed in the 1930s as an increasing number of social scientists became aware of the plight of the elderly?
   b. sociology
   b. gerontology
   c. gerontocracy
   d. senilicide

4. Which sociological perspective is most likely to emphasize the important role of social networks in providing life satisfaction for elderly people?
   a. functionalist perspective
   b. conflict perspective
   c. interactionist perspective
   d. labeling theory

5. Elaine Cumming and William Henry introduced an explanation of the impact of aging known as
   a. disengagement theory.
   b. activity theory.
   c. labeling theory.
   d. the contact hypothesis.

6. According to psychologist Elisabeth Kübler-Ross, the first stage of the experience of dying that a person may undergo is
   a. denial.
   b. anger.
   c. depression.
   d. bargaining.

7. Which of the following statements about the elderly is correct?
   a. Being old is a master status.
   b. Once people are labeled as "old," the designation has a major impact on how others perceive them, and even on how they view themselves.
   c. Negative stereotypes of the elderly contribute to their position as a minority group subject to discrimination.
   d. all of the above

8. The text points out that the model of five basic properties of a minority or subordinate group can be applied to older people in the United States. Which of the following is not one of those basic properties?
   a. Older people experience unequal treatment in employment and may face prejudice and discrimination.
   b. Statistically, the elderly represent a majority.
   c. Membership in this group is involuntary.
   d. Older people have a strong sense of group solidarity.

9. Which of the following theories argues that elderly people have essentially the same need for social interaction as any other group and that those who remain active and socially involved will be best adjusted?
   a. conflict theory
   b. functionalist theory
   c. activity theory
   d. disengagement theory

10. According to your text, which of the following statements is true?
   a. Functionalists portray the elderly as being socially isolated, with reduced social roles.
   b. Interactionists see older people as being involved in new networks of people and in changing social roles.
   c. Conflict theorists regard older people as being victimized by social structure, with their social roles relatively unchanged but devalued.
   d. all of the above

11. The elderly are _____ regarded in the traditional Sherpa (Tibet) culture.

12. In keeping with the _____ perspective of sociology, disengagement theory emphasizes that a society's stability is ensured when social roles are passed on from one generation to another.

13. The final phase of retirement, according to Robert Atchley, is the _____ phase, which begins when the person can no longer engage in basic, day-to-day activities such as self-care and housework.

14. _____ theorists argue that both the disengagement and the activity perspectives often ignore the impact of social class in the lives of elderly people.

15. The fastest-growing age group in the United States is people over age _____.

16. _____ is the scientific study of the sociological and psychological aspects of aging and the problems of the aged. It originated in the 1930s as an increasing number of social scientists became aware of the plight of elderly people.

17. Based on a study of elderly people in good health and relatively comfortable economic circumstances, _____ theory suggests that society and the aging individual mutually sever many of their relationships.

18. During the late 1990s, social scientists focused on the _____ _____ adults who simultaneously try to meet the competing needs of their parents and their children.

19. In 2010, _____ was the state most populated by the elderly, with 17.4 percent of the population over age 65.

20. Physician Robert Butler coined the term _____ to refer to prejudice and discrimination based on a person's age.

13

The Family and Household Diversity

© Jeff Greenberg/The Image Works

In Ann Arbor, Michigan, several generations of Dulins celebrate their 18th family reunion. Despite marital strains and geographical separation, countless families come together every year to reaffirm the importance of this social institution.

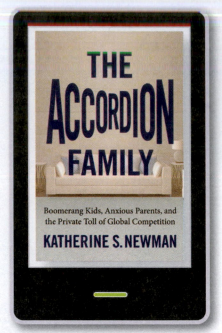
© Ira C. Roberts/Chad Enterprises Corporation

" William Rollo and his wife arrived in Newton [Massachusetts] in 1989 after having lived in Seattle, Philadelphia, and Summit, New Jersey. A Brooklyn native, William married Janet at the age of 22 and set about completing a residency in podiatry. Their eldest son, John, grew up in Newton and did well enough in high school to attend the liberal arts college Williams, one of the nation's most selective. Even so, he beat it home after graduating and has lived with his parents for several years while preparing to apply to graduate school. "A lot of my friends are living at home to save money," he explains.

Tight finances are not all that is driving John's living arrangements. The young man had choices and decided he could opt for more of the ones he wanted if he sheltered under his parents' roof. John is saving money from his job in an arts foundation for a three-week trip to Africa, where he hopes to work on a mobile health-care project in a rural region. It's a strategic choice designed to increase his chances to be accepted into Harvard University's competitive graduate program in public health.

John needs to build up his credentials if he wants to enter a school like that. To get from here to there, he needs more experience working with patients in clinics or out in the field. It takes big bucks to travel to exotic locations, and a master's degree will cost him dearly, too. In order to make good on his aspirations, John needs his parents to cover him for the short run. On his own, John could pay the rent on an apartment, especially if he had roommates. What he can't afford is to pay for both privacy *and* travel, to support

On his own, John could pay the rent on an apartment, especially if he had roommates. What he can't afford is to pay for both privacy and travel, to support himself and save for his hoped-for future.

himself *and* save for his hoped-for future. Autonomy turns out to be the lesser priority, so he has returned to the bedroom he had before he left for college, and there he stays.

John sees few drawbacks to this arrangement. His parents don't nag him or curtail his freedom. Janet wonders if they should ask him to pay rent, to bring him down to earth a bit and teach him some life skills, like budgeting. William is not so sure. He enjoys his son's company and was happy when he moved back into his old bedroom. Having a son around to talk to is a joy, particularly since John's younger brother is out of the house now, studying at the University of Vermont. That empty nest has refilled, and thank goodness, says William, rather quietly.

If John had no goals, no sense of direction, William would not be at ease with this "boomerang arrangement." Hiding in the basement playing video games would not do. Happily, that is not on John's agenda. William is glad to help his son realize his ambitions. He approves of John's career plans and doesn't really care if they don't involve making a handsome living. What really matters is that the work *means* something. It will help to remake the world, something William has not felt he could contribute to very directly in his work. Having a son who can reach a bit higher—if not financially, then morally—is an ambition worth paying for.

And it will cost this family, big time. William and Janet have invested nearly two hundred thousand dollars in John's education already. They will need to do more if John is going to become a public health specialist. They are easily looking at another fifty thousand dollars, even if John attends a local graduate program and continues to live with them. Fortunately, there are excellent options—some of the nation's finest—close by. Whatever it costs, they reason, the sacrifice is worth it. "

(*Newman 2012:xv–xvii*) Quotation from Katherine S. Newman. 2012. *The Accordion Family: Boomerang Kids, Anxious Parents, and the Private Toll of Global Competition.* Boston: Beacon Press, 2012.

In this excerpt from *The Accordion Family: Boomerang Kids, Anxious Parents, and the Private Toll of Global Competition,* sociologist Katherine S. Newman describes one of the major trends in family life today. In the United States as well as in many other countries, parenthood is being extended as single adult children remain at home, or return home after college or a brief foray into the job market. In the United States in 2015, 18 percent of men and 12 percent of women between the ages of 25 and 34 lived with their parents. Some of those adult children were still pursuing an education, but in many cases financial difficulties underlay their living arrangements. For younger job seekers, employment is often short term or low paying—not secure enough to support a separate household. And with many marriages now ending in divorce—most commonly in the first seven years—divorced sons and daughters often return to their parents, sometimes with their own children in tow (Bureau of the Census 2015e: Table AD-1).

Whether we refer to such combined households as "accordion families," as Newman does, or to the returning adult children as "boomerang kids," this trend is an example of the increasing complexity of family life. The family of today is not what it was a century ago, or even a generation ago. New roles, new gender distinctions, new child-rearing patterns have all combined to create new forms of family life. Today, for example, more and more women are taking the breadwinner's role, whether married or as a single parent. Blended families—the result of divorce and remarriage—are almost the norm. And many people are seeking intimate relationships without being married (Cherlin 2009, 2011).

The word *family* is inadequate to describe some of these arrangements, including cohabiting partners, same-sex marriages, and single-parent households. In 2011, the nation crossed a major threshold: the majority of births to women under age 30 occurred outside of marriage (Cherlin 2011; Wildsmith et al. 2011).

These modules address family and human sexuality in the United States as well as other parts of the world. As we will see,

family patterns differ from one culture to another and even within the same culture. Despite the differences, however, the family is universal—found in every culture.

What are families in different parts of the world like? How do people select their mates? When a marriage ends, how does the divorce affect the children? What are the alternatives to the nuclear family, and how prevalent are they? In this chapter we will look at the family and intimate relationships from the functionalist, conflict, interactionist, and feminist points of view. We'll examine variations in marital patterns and family life, including child rearing, paying particular attention to the increasing numbers of people in dual-income and single-parent families. We'll consider the similarities and differences between gay and straight relationships. We'll examine divorce in the United States and consider diverse lifestyles such as cohabitation and marriage without children. Finally, in the Social Policy section we'll confront the issue of family leave, comparing policies in the United States with those in other parts of the world.

MODULE 40 | Global View of the Family

Among Tibetans, a woman may be married simultaneously to more than one man, usually brothers. This system allows sons to share the limited amount of good land. Among the Betsileo of Madagascar, a man has multiple wives, each one living in a different village where he cultivates rice. Wherever he has the best rice field, that wife is considered his first or senior wife. Among the Yanomami of Brazil and Venezuela, it is considered proper to have sexual relations with your opposite-sex cousins if they are the children of your mother's brother or your father's sister. But if your opposite-sex cousins are the children of your mother's sister or your father's brother, the same practice is considered to be incest (Haviland et al. 2015; Kottak 2015).

Universal Principles

As these examples illustrate, there are many variations in the family from culture to culture. Yet the family as a social institution exists in all cultures. A **family** can be defined as a set of people related by blood, marriage or some other agreed-on relationship, or adoption, who share the primary responsibility for reproduction and caring for members of society. Moreover, certain general principles concerning its composition, kinship patterns, and authority patterns are universal.

Composition: What Is the Family?

If we were to take our information on what a family is from what we see on television, we might come up with some strange scenarios. The media do not always present a realistic view of the family. Moreover, many people still think of the family in very narrow

terms—as a married couple and their unmarried children living together. However, this is but one type of family, what sociologists refer to as a **nuclear family.** The term *nuclear family* is well chosen, since this type of family serves as the nucleus, or core, on which larger family groups are built.

Most people in the United States see the married heterosexual couple with their own children as the preferred family arrangement. Yet by 2013, only one out of five of the nation's family households fit this model. The proportion of households in the United States that is composed of married heterosexual couples with children at home has decreased steadily over the past 50 years and is expected to continue shrinking (see Figure 40-1). At the same time, the number of single-parent households has increased (American Community Survey 2015b: Table D802).

FIGURE 40-1 **Living Arrangements of Adults age 18 and over, 2014**

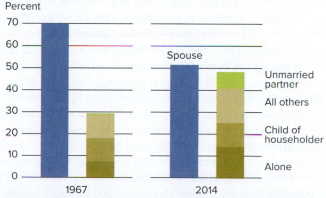

Note: "All others" includes adults who live with a parent, roommate, sibling, foster child, or grandchild.
Source: Bureau of the Census 2015d: Figure AD-3a.

A family in which relatives—such as grandparents, aunts, or uncles—live in the same home as parents and their children is known as an **extended family.** Although not common, such living arrangements do exist in the United States. The structure of the extended family offers certain advantages over that of the nuclear family. Crises such as death, divorce, and illness put less strain on family members, since more people can provide assistance and emotional support. In addition, the extended family constitutes a larger economic unit than the nuclear family. If the family is engaged in a common enterprise—a farm or a small business—the additional family members may represent the difference between prosperity and failure.

In considering these different family types, we have limited ourselves to the form of marriage that is characteristic of the United States—monogamy. The term **monogamy** describes a form of marriage in which an individual has only one partner. Until recently, the societal expectation was that the couple would be a man and a woman. Now same-sex couples are entering legal marriages. Regardless, observers, noting the high rate of divorce in the United States, have suggested that "serial monogamy" is a more accurate description of the form marriage takes in this country. In **serial monogamy,** a person may have several spouses in a lifetime, but only one spouse at a time.

Some cultures allow an individual to have several husbands or wives simultaneously. This form of marriage is known as **polygamy.** In fact, most societies throughout the world, past and present, have preferred polygamy to monogamy. According to a mid-20th century analysis of 565 societies, polygamy was preferred in more than 80 percent. While polygamy declined steadily through most of the 20th century, in at least five countries in Africa 20 percent of men still have polygamous marriages (Murdock 1949, 1957; Population Reference Bureau 1996).

There are two basic types of polygamy. According to Murdock, the most common—endorsed by the majority of cultures he sampled—is *polygyny.* **Polygyny** refers to the marriage of a man to more than one woman at the same time. The wives are often sisters, who are expected to hold similar values and have already had experience sharing a household. In polygynous societies, relatively few men actually have multiple spouses. Most individuals live in monogamous families; having multiple wives is viewed as a mark of status.

The other principal variation of polygamy is **polyandry,** in which a woman may have more than one husband at the same time. Polyandry, however, is exceedingly rare today, though it is accepted in some extremely poor societies. Like many other societies, polyandrous cultures devalue the social worth of women, since men are still seen as dominant within the household and society.

By the end of the 20th century, polygamy had been relegated to the margins of U.S. society, and to discussion of other cultures. Recently, however, it has resurfaced. As the concept of marriage is redefined to include same-sex marriage, Mormon fundamentalists and Muslims who practice polygamy have asked why it should not also embrace polygamy. Indeed, in his dissent to the Supreme Court's *Obergefell* decision, which recognized the right to same-sex marriage (discussed in detail later in the chapter), Chief Justice John Roberts raised that very possibility. However, no court has indicated even a tolerance of plural marriage (Baude 2015).

Kinship Patterns: To Whom Are We Related?

Many of us can trace our roots by looking at a family tree or by listening to elderly family members talk about their lives—and about the lives of ancestors who died long before we were born. Yet a person's lineage is more than simply a personal history; it also reflects societal patterns that govern descent. In every culture, children encounter relatives to whom they are expected to show an emotional attachment. The state of being related to others is called **kinship.** Kinship is culturally learned, however, and is not totally determined by biological or marital ties. For example, adoption creates a kinship tie that is legally acknowledged and socially accepted.

The family and the kin group are not necessarily one and the same. Whereas the family is a household unit, kin do not always live together or function as a collective body on a daily basis. Kin groups include aunts, uncles, cousins, in-laws, and so forth. In a society such as the United States, the kinship group may come together only rarely, for a wedding or funeral. However, kinship ties frequently create obligations and responsibilities. We may feel compelled to assist our kin, and we may feel free to call on them for many types of aid, including loans and babysitting.

How do we identify kinship groups? The principle of descent assigns people to kinship groups according to their relationship to a mother or father. There are three primary ways of determining descent. The United States follows the system of **bilateral descent,** which means that both sides of a person's family are regarded as equally important. For example, no higher value is given to the brothers of one's father than to the brothers of one's mother.

Most societies—according to George Murdock, 64 percent—give preference to one side of the family or the other in tracing descent. In **patrilineal descent** (from the Latin *pater,* "father"), only the father's relatives are significant in terms of property, inheritance, and emotional ties. Conversely, in societies that favor **matrilineal descent** (from the Latin *mater,* "mother"), only the mother's relatives are significant.

New forms of reproductive technology will necessitate a new way of looking at kinship. Today, a combination of biological and social processes can "create" a family member, requiring that more distinctions be made about who is related to whom.

 use your **sociological imagination**

In your family, which relatives do you have a significant relationship with? Which do you hardly ever see? Explain the reasons for the difference in relationships.

Authority Patterns: Who Rules?

Imagine that you have recently married and must begin to make decisions about the future of your new family. You and your spouse face many questions. Where will you live? How will you furnish your home? Who will do the cooking, the shopping, the cleaning? Whose friends will be invited to dinner? Each time a decision must be made, an issue is raised: Who has the power

© ImagesBazaar/Alamy RF

Although spouses in an egalitarian family may not share all their decisions, they regard themselves as equals. This pattern of authority is becoming more common in the United States.

very uncommon, emerged among Native American tribal societies and in nations in which men were absent for long periods because of warfare or food-gathering expeditions (Farr 1999).

In a third type of authority pattern, the **egalitarian family,** spouses are regarded as equals. That does not mean, however, that all decisions are shared in such families. Wives may hold authority in some spheres, husbands in others. Many sociologists believe the egalitarian family has begun to replace the patriarchal family as the social norm in the United States.

There are seemingly endless varieties that family form may take. For example, consider a group of families ruled for more than a generation by patriarchs who determined everything about family structure, including sexual expression. Such was the case of the Oneida Community, described in Box 40-1.

to make the decision? In simple terms, who rules the family? Conflict theorists examine these questions in the context of traditional gender stratification, under which men have held a dominant position over women.

Societies vary in the way power is distributed within the family. A society that expects males to dominate in all family decision making is termed a **patriarchy.** In patriarchal societies, such as Iran, the eldest male often wields the greatest power, although wives are expected to be treated with respect and kindness. An Iranian woman's status is typically defined by her relationship to a male relative, usually as a wife or daughter. In many patriarchal societies, women find it more difficult to obtain a divorce than a man does. In contrast, in a **matriarchy,** women have greater authority than men. Matriarchies, which are

● Sociological Perspectives on the Family

Do we really need the family? Over a century ago, Friedrich Engels ([1884] 1959), a colleague of Karl Marx, described the family as the ultimate source of social inequality because of its role in the transfer of power, property, and privilege. More recently, conflict theorists have argued that the family contributes to societal injustice, denies women opportunities that are extended to men, and limits freedom in sexual expression and mate selection. In contrast, the functionalist view focuses on the ways in which the family gratifies the needs of its members and contributes to social stability. The interactionist view considers the intimate, face-to-face relationships that occur in the family. And the feminist approach examines the role of the wife and mother, especially in the absence of an adult male.

Functionalist Perspective

The family performs six paramount functions, first outlined nearly 80 years ago by sociologist William F. Ogburn (Ogburn and Tibbits 1934):

1. **Reproduction.** For a society to maintain itself, it must replace dying members. In this sense, the family contributes to human survival through its function of reproduction.

2. **Protection.** In all cultures, the family assumes the ultimate responsibility for the protection and upbringing of children.

3. **Socialization.** Parents and other kin monitor a child's behavior and transmit the norms, values, and language of their culture to the child.

© Burke/Triolo Productions/Brand X/Corbis RF

An Extraordinary Patriarchy: The Oneida Community

Few groups or organizations have been so clearly defined by sex, both in terms of gender and of sexual activity, as the Oneida Community, a nineteenth-century Utopian group that lived in New York State. At its head was John Humphrey Noyes, who spread a religious doctrine of perfectionism and attempted to create a Utopian society without sin. His first followers in the 1830s were largely limited to his own family and his wife. He gradually developed a type of social organization referred to as a *commune*—a form of cooperative living where community assets are shared and individual ownership is discouraged. Communes are popularly associated with the "flower power" and hippie movements of the 1960s, but they have a long history and persist as an alternative lifestyle.

© ZAP Collection\Alamy

> Noyes's commune, called the Oneida Community for the city in New York where the group eventually settled, was extraordinary because of the members' complete dedication to Noyes and willingness to accept his and other elders' decisions about who should have sex with whom.

Noyes's commune, called the Oneida Community for the city in New York where the group eventually settled, was extraordinary because of the members' complete dedication to Noyes and willingness to accept his and other elders' decisions about who should have sex with whom. Why? The community members believed that with the help of Almighty God, as expressed through the person of John Humphrey Noyes, they were going to create a heaven on earth. The means were to be found in the principle of *ascending fellowship*—the practice of allowing older godly males, members of a special group called the Central Committee, to pick a virgin of about age fourteen for whom they were spiritually responsible. The elder males

then made decisions as to who would have sex for the purposes of producing the most biologically desirable offspring.

So this all happened in the mid-1800s in New York. Where was the law or protests? Efforts were occasionally made to prosecute Noyes and the other elders, but no one was willing to testify against them. The members of this strange fellowship, which flourished for over forty years, conformed to the larger society in many ways: there were no elopements, no orgies, no exhibitionism. Nor was there any instance of homosexuality, sadism, masochism, or any other sexual activity that would have been considered reprehensible by the standards then current. Throughout its history, the Oneida Community was more likely to face suspicion and legal action for its communal economic operations than for the nature of sexual relationships under the stern patriarchy,

Eventually the Oneida Community fell apart from within. Noyes aged and was unable to create an acceptable pattern of succession. Economically the commune prospered, even creating a nationally respected brand of silverware that flourished into the

21st century. In the mid-20th century the successors of the commune, no longer believers in the ascending fellowship and its iron-grip patriarchy, began to worry about negative publicity concerning the corporation's roots.

The Oneidas had kept diaries and detailed records of their activities, sexual as well as economic, in their effort to create a perfect society. The corporate leaders secretly destroyed these records in what has come to be termed the Burning. Oneida silverware still lives on, even if the ascending fellowship does not. However, the Oneida Community remains as an example of the diversity of family forms that people have used.

LET'S DISCUSS

1. Would a society based on free love tend to be long-lasting? What social forces would make it stay together or fall apart?
2. Was the Oneida Community a family? Why or why not?

Sources: Carden 1969; Kephart 1963; Schaefer and Zellner 2015; Wayland-Smith 2016.

---

4. **Regulation of sexual behavior.** Sexual norms are subject to change both over time (for instance, in the customs for dating) and across cultures (compare strict Saudi Arabia to the more permissive Denmark). However, whatever the time period or cultural values of a society, standards of sexual behavior are most clearly defined within the family circle.

5. **Affection and companionship.** Ideally, the family provides members with warm and intimate relationships, helping them

to feel satisfied and secure. Of course, a family member may find such rewards outside the family—from peers, in school, at work—and may even perceive the home as an unpleasant or abusive setting. Nevertheless, we expect our relatives to understand us, to care for us, and to be there for us when we need them.

6. **Provision of social status.** We inherit a social position because of the family background and reputation of our parents and siblings. The family presents the newborn child with an ascribed status based on race and ethnicity that helps to determine his or her place within society's stratification system. Moreover, family resources affect children's ability to pursue certain opportunities, such as higher education.

Traditionally, the family has fulfilled a number of other functions, such as providing religious training, education, and recreational outlets. But Ogburn argued that other social institutions have gradually assumed many of those functions. Education once took place at the family fireside; now it is the responsibility of professionals working in schools and colleges. Even the family's traditional recreational function has often been transferred to outside groups such as soccer leagues, athletic clubs, and Twitter.

Conflict Perspective

Conflict theorists view the family not as a contributor to social stability, but as a reflection of the inequality in wealth and power that is found within the larger society. Feminist and conflict theorists note that the family has traditionally legitimized and perpetuated male dominance. Throughout most of human history—and in a wide range of societies—husbands have exercised overwhelming power and authority within the family. Not until the first wave of contemporary feminism in the United States, in the mid-1800s, was there a substantial challenge to the historic status of wives and children as the legal property of husbands.

While the egalitarian family has become a more common pattern in the United States in recent decades—owing in good part to the activism of feminists beginning in the late 1960s and early 1970s—male dominance over the family has hardly disappeared. The number of fathers who are at home with their children for any reason has nearly doubled since 1989. It reached its highest point in 2010, just after the official end of the Great Recession. Since that time, the number has fallen slightly. Side by side with this trend is a continuing rapid increase in the number of fathers who do not live with the family, leaving all caretaking to the mother or other caregivers. Sociologists have found that while married men are increasing their involvement in child care, their wives still perform a disproportionate amount of it. Furthermore, for every stay-at-home dad there are five stay-at-home moms. And unfortunately, many husbands reinforce their power and control over wives and children through acts of domestic violence (Livingstone 2014a).

Conflict theorists also view the family as an economic unit that contributes to societal injustice. The family is the basis for transferring power, property, and privilege from one generation to the next. Although the United States is widely viewed as a land of opportunity, social mobility is restricted in important ways. Children inherit the privileged or less-than-privileged social and economic status of their parents (and in some cases, of earlier generations). The social class of parents significantly influences

© Don Mason/Blend Images LLC RF

Interactionists are particularly interested in the ways in which parents relate to each other and to their children. The close and loving relationship illustrated here is one of the foundations of a strong family.

children's socialization experiences and the degree of protection they receive. Thus, the socioeconomic status of a child's family will have a marked influence on his or her nutrition, health care, housing, educational opportunities, and in many respects, life chances as an adult. For this reason, conflict theorists argue that the family helps to maintain inequality.

Interactionist Perspective

Interactionists focus on the micro level of family and other intimate relationships. They are interested in how individuals interact with one another, whether they are cohabiting partners or longtime married couples. For example, in a study of both Black and White two-parent households, researchers found that when fathers are more involved with their children (reading to them, helping them with homework, or restricting their television viewing), the children have fewer behavior problems, get along better with others, and are more responsible.

Another interactionist study might examine the role of the stepparent. The increased number of single parents who remarry has sparked an interest in those who are helping to raise other people's children. Studies have found that stepmothers are more likely than stepfathers to accept the blame for bad relations with their stepchildren. Interactionists theorize that stepfathers (like most fathers) may simply be unaccustomed to interacting directly with children when the mother isn't there (Bastaits and Mortelmans 2014).

Feminist Perspective

Because "women's work" has traditionally focused on family life, feminist sociologists have taken a strong interest in the family as a social institution. Research on gender roles in child care and household chores has been extensive. Sociologists have looked particularly closely at how women's work outside the home impacts their child care and housework—duties Arlie Hochschild (1990, 2005, 2012) has referred to as the "second shift."

Today, researchers recognize that for many women, the second shift includes the care of aging parents as well.

Feminist theorists have urged social scientists and social agencies to rethink the notion that families in which no adult male is present are automatically a cause for concern, or even dysfunctional. They have also contributed to research on single women, single-parent households, and lesbian couples. In the case of single mothers, researchers have focused on the resiliency of many such households, despite economic stress. According to Velma McBride Murray and her colleagues (2001) at the University of Georgia, such studies show that among African Americans, single mothers draw heavily on kinfolk for material resources, parenting advice, and social support. Considering feminist research on the family as a whole, one researcher concluded that the family is the "source of women's strength" (V. Taylor et al. 2009).

Finally, feminists who take the interactionist perspective stress the need to investigate neglected topics in family studies. For instance, in a growing number of dual-income households, the wife earns a higher income than the husband. In 1987, in families where both wives and husbands had earnings, women earned more than men in fewer than 18 percent of the households. That proportion has steadily grown to over 29 percent by 2013 (Bureau of Labor Statistics 2015f).

Tracking Sociological Perspectives

TABLE **40-1** **SOCIOLOGICAL PERSPECTIVES ON THE FAMILY**

Theoretical Perspective	Emphasis
Functionalist	The family as a contributor to social stability
	Roles of family members
Conflict	The family as a perpetuator of inequality
	Transmission of poverty or wealth across generations
Interactionist	Relationships among family members
Feminist	The family as a perpetuator of gender roles
	Female-headed households

Table 40-1 summarizes the four major theoretical perspectives on the family.

MODULE 40 | **Recap and Review**

Summary

The family, in its many forms, is present in all human cultures.

1. Families vary from culture to culture and even within the same culture.

2. The structure of the **extended family** can offer certain advantages over that of the **nuclear family**.

3. Societies determine **kinship** by descent from both parents (**bilateral descent**), from the father only (**patrilineal descent**), or from the mother only (**matrilineal descent**).

4. Sociologists do not agree on whether the **egalitarian family** has replaced the patriarchal family in the United States.

5. William F. Ogburn outlined six basic functions of the family: reproduction, protection, socialization, regulation of sexual behavior, companionship, and the provision of social status.

6. Conflict theorists argue that male dominance of the family contributes to societal injustice and denies women opportunities. Interactionists focus on how individuals interact within the family and other intimate relationships. Feminists stress the need to broaden research on the family. Like conflict theorists, they see the family's role in socializing children as the primary source of sexism.

Thinking Critically

1. From a woman's point of view, what are the economic advantages and disadvantages of monogamous, polygamous, and polyandrous families? What are the advantages and disadvantages of each of these family situations for men?

2. How would functionalist, conflict, interactionist, and feminist theorists explain a polygamous family structure?

Key Terms

Bilateral descent	**Polyandry**
Egalitarian family	**Polygamy**
Extended family	**Polygyny**
Family	**Serial monogamy**
Kinship	
Matriarchy	
Matrilineal descent	
Monogamy	
Nuclear family	
Patriarchy	
Patrilineal descent	

Currently, over 95 percent of all men and women in the United States marry at least once during their lifetimes. Historically, the most consistent aspect of family life in this country has been the high rate of marriage. In fact, despite the high rate of divorce, there are some indications of a miniboom in marriages of late.

In this part of the chapter, we will examine various aspects of love, marriage, and parenthood in the United States and contrast them with cross-cultural examples. Though we're used to thinking of romance and mate selection as strictly a matter of individual preference, sociological analysis tells us that social institutions and distinctive cultural norms and values also play an important role.

Courtship and Mate Selection

In the past, most couples met their partners through family or friends in their neighborhood or workplace. Today, however, many couples meet on the Internet, through online dating services. Box 41-1 takes a look at this new meeting place.

Internet romance is only the latest courtship practice. In the central Asian nation of Uzbekistan and many other traditional cultures, courtship is defined largely through the interaction of two sets of parents, who arrange marriages for their children. Typically, a young Uzbekistani woman will be socialized to eagerly anticipate her marriage to a man whom she has met only once, when he is presented to her family at the time of the final inspection of her dowry. In the United States, in contrast, courtship is conducted primarily by individuals who have a romantic interest in each other. In our culture, courtship often requires these individuals to rely heavily on intricate games, gestures, and signals. Despite such differences, courtship—whether in the United States, Uzbekistan, or elsewhere—is influenced by the norms and values of the larger society (C. Williams 1995).

One unmistakable trend in mate selection is that the process appears to be taking longer today than in the past. A variety of factors, including concerns about financial security and personal independence, has contributed to this delay in marriage. Back in 1966, men were typically under age 23 and women under 21 when they were first married. In 2015, the average age was 29 for men and close to 27 years for women. Most people are now well into their 20s before they marry, both in the United States and in most other countries (Figure 41-1) (Bureau of the Census 2013b).

Aspects of Mate Selection

Many societies have explicit or unstated rules that define potential mates as acceptable or unacceptable. These norms can be distinguished in terms of endogamy and exogamy. **Endogamy** (from the Greek *endon,* "within") specifies the groups within which a spouse must be found and prohibits marriage with others. For example, in the United States, many people are expected to marry within their racial, ethnic, or religious group, and are strongly discouraged or even prohibited from marrying outside the group. Endogamy is intended to reinforce the cohesiveness of the group by suggesting to the young that they should marry someone "of their own kind."

Even in the United States, interracial and interethnic marriages are still the exception. According to a report released in 2015, among newly married White people, about 7 percent marry someone of a different race or ethnicity. Among African American people the proportion is 19 percent; among Latinos, 26 percent; and among Asian Americans, 28 percent (W. Wang 2012, 2015).

In contrast, **exogamy** (from the Greek *exo,* "outside") requires mate selection outside certain groups, usually one's family or certain kinfolk. The **incest taboo,** a social norm common to virtually all societies, prohibits sexual relationships between certain culturally specified relatives. For those of us in the United States, this taboo means that we must marry outside the nuclear

© Dominique Charriau/WireImage/Getty Images

Although most interracial couples are not as visible as Robert De Niro and Grace Hightower, such unions are becoming increasingly common and accepted. They are also blurring the definitions of race. Will the children of these couples be considered Black or White? Why do you think so?

Love Is in the Air and on the Web

I just met a girl on Facebook, like, messaged her and then met her in person. That was all. I just met her.

— HIGH SCHOOL BOY

Well, if you are really putting yourself out there, you could comment on their picture with a heart emoji.

— HIGH SCHOOL GIRL

According to a recent national survey, 1 in 10 people has used an online dating site or mobile dating app. Among online daters, 66 percent have gone out with someone they met through an online dating site; 23 percent have met a spouse or long-term partner that way. As a source of romantic partners, the Internet is second only to friends—ahead of family, workplace, and neighborhood.

Significantly, online networking is just as important to mate-seekers in their 40s and 50s as it is to those under 30. It is especially important to gays and lesbians: 61 percent of same-sex couples meet online, compared to 23 percent of heterosexual couples. Sociologists have observed that members of groups with a thin or limited market for romantic partners, such as middle-aged people or gays and lesbians, are more likely than others to see the advantage of online dating services.

The Internet dating site eHarmony claims to be the first to use a "scientific approach" to matching people, one that is based on a variety of abilities and interests. This approach is based on a concept called *homogamy.* Sharing interests is so important

to prospective mates that certain online dating services target specific segments of the population, such as pet lovers, fans of a particular sport, or members of a certain religion, nationality, or immigrant group. As in real life, online searchers typically do not seek out people of a different race. According to one study of Yahoo daters, over 71 percent of women and 53 percent of men indicate their racial preferences explicitly.

> Among online daters, 66 percent have gone out with someone they met through an online dating site; 23 percent have met a spouse or long-term partner that way.

As we might suspect, **impression management**—the altering of the presentation of the self in order to create distinctive appearances and satisfy particular audiences—is common in online dating. That is, prospective mates make a conscious attempt to present themselves in a favorable light. Compared to real-world dating, online dating services offer users more opportunity to manage their self-presentations, based on the way they answer questions about themselves. Do you want to come across as serious, athletic, or fun-loving? Then compose your answers accordingly. And

why stop there? Although not much research has been done on the topic, studies show that the majority of those who participate in online dating think that others often lie about their age, marital status, and appearance. In response, some people have gone online to check public records and search for discrepancies in the way others answer questions.

Online dating and mate selection, then, is not the same as meeting people face-to-face. Through an online dating service, a person can now meet and date complete strangers. Studies show that online daters are more apprehensive about meeting online prospects in person than they are about meeting people they don't know in the real world. At some point the two approaches may converge, however. Phone apps now allow singles to identify other singles who happen to be sitting, standing, or walking near them.

LET'S DISCUSS

1. Have you ever gone out with a person you met online? If so, did the person resemble his or her online presentation? In what ways?

2. Which method of locating other singles do you think would be more useful, going to an online dating site or using an app to locate singles near you? Explain.

Sources: Cali et al. 2013; Ortulay 2013; Paul 2014; Pew Research Center 2015a; Robnett and Feliciano 2011; J. Rosenfeld 2010; M. Rosenfeld and Thomas 2012; A. Smith and Duggan 2013.

---

family. We cannot marry our siblings, and in most states we cannot marry our first cousins.

Another factor that influences the selection of a marriage partner is **homogamy,** the conscious or unconscious tendency to select a mate with personal characteristics similar to one's own. The "like marries like" rule can be seen in couples with similar personalities and cultural interests. However, mate selection is unpredictable. Though some people may follow the homogamous pattern, others observe the "opposites attract" rule: one person is dependent and submissive—almost childishly so—while the other is dominant and controlling.

The Love Relationship

Today's generation of college students seems more likely to hook up or cruise in large packs than to engage in the romantic dating relationships of their parents' and grandparents' generations. Still, at some point in their adult lives, the great majority

of today's students will meet someone they love and enter into a long-term relationship that focuses on creating a family.

Most parents in the United States tend to value love highly as a rationale for marriage, so they encourage their children to develop intimate relationships based on love and affection. Songs, films, books, magazines, television shows, and even cartoons and comic books reinforce the theme of love. At the same time, our society expects parents and peers to help a person confine his or her search for a mate to "socially acceptable" members of the opposite sex.

Though most people in the United States take the importance of falling in love for granted, the coupling of love and marriage is by no means a cultural universal. Many of the world's cultures give priority in mate selection to factors other than romantic feelings. In societies with *arranged marriages* engineered by parents or religious authorities, economic considerations play a significant role. The newly married couple is expected to develop a feeling of love *after* the legal union is formalized, if at all (J. Lee 2013).

FIGURE 41-1 **Median Age at First Marriage in Eight Countries**

Finland — Women 30.3, Men 32.6
Canada — Women 28.4, Men 30.2
Australia — Women 27.9, Men 29.6
Brazil — Women 27.1, Men 29.5
United States — Women 27.1, Men 29.2
Poland — Women 25.6, Men 27.5
Russia — Women 22.6, Men 24.8
India — Women 17.8, Men 23.7

Age: 0 10 20 30 40 50 60

Source: United Nations Statistics Division 2013; Bureau of the Census 2015e, Table MS-2. *Flags:* © admin_design/Shutterstock RF

use your **sociological imagination**

Your parents and/or a matchmaker are going to arrange a marriage for you. What kind of mate will they select? Will your chances of having a successful marriage be better or worse than if you selected your own mate?

● Variations in Family Life and Intimate Relationships

Within the United States, social class, race, and ethnicity create variations in family life. Studying these variations will give us a more sophisticated understanding of contemporary family styles in our country.

Social Class Differences

Various studies have documented the differences in family organization among social classes in the United States. In the upper class, the emphasis is on lineage and maintenance of family position. If you are in the upper class, you are not simply a member of a nuclear family, but rather a member of a larger family tradition (think of the Rockefellers or the Kennedys). As a result,

upper-class families are quite concerned about what they see as proper training for children.

Lower-class families do not often have the luxury of worrying about the "family name"; they must first struggle to pay their bills and survive the crises often associated with a life of poverty. Such families are more likely to have only one parent at home, which creates special challenges in child care and financial management. Children from lower-class families typically assume adult responsibilities—including marriage and parenthood—at an earlier age than children from affluent homes. In part, that is because they may lack the money needed to remain in school.

Social class differences in family life are less striking today than they once were. In the past, family specialists agreed that the contrasts in child-rearing practices were pronounced. Lower-class families were found to be more authoritarian in rearing children and more inclined to use physical punishment. Middle-class families were more permissive and more restrained in punishing their children. And compared to lower-class families, middle-class families tended to schedule more of their children's time, or even to overstructure it. However, these differences may have narrowed as more and more families from all social classes turned to the same books, magazines, and even television talk shows for advice on rearing children (Kronstadt and Favreault 2008; Luster et al. 1989; J. Sherman and Harris 2012).

A marriage model is emerging that shows some distinct social class differences. Among the college-educated, both spouses are delaying marriage, which typically means that both have solid earnings and relatively stable job futures. Not surprisingly, divorce rates are relatively low among college-educated people, especially among those who married during the first decade of the 21st century, when compared to non-college-educated couples (Miller 2014; Stevenson and Wolfers 2007).

Among the poor, women often play a significant role in the economic support of the family. Men may earn low wages, may be unemployed, or may be entirely absent from the family. In 2015, 28.2 percent of all families headed by women with no husband present fell below the federal government's poverty line. In comparison, the poverty rate for married couples was only 5.4 percent. The disproportionate representation of female-headed households among the poor is a persistent and growing trend, referred to by sociologists as the *feminization of poverty* (Proctor et al. 2016:16).

Finally, in her book *The Accordion Family* (see the chapter-opening excerpt), Katherine S. Newman (2012) noted that the accordion or boomerang family differs by social class. An upper-middle-class family like the one described in the opening excerpt can afford to provide space to an adult child who is working toward an advanced degree. Less privileged families tend to hang on to their adult children for the labor or income they can contribute to the family's welfare.

Many racial and ethnic groups appear to have distinctive family characteristics. However, racial and class factors are often closely related. In examining family life among racial and ethnic minorities, keep in mind that certain patterns may result from class as well as cultural factors.

© Hill Street Studios/Blend Images/Corbis RF

Racial and Ethnic Differences

The subordinate status of racial and ethnic minorities in the United States profoundly affects their family lives. For example, the lower incomes of African Americans, Native Americans, most Hispanic groups, and selected Asian American groups make creating and maintaining successful marital unions a difficult task. The economic restructuring of the past 60 years, described by sociologist William Julius Wilson (1996, 2009) and others, has especially affected people living in inner cities and desolate rural areas, such as reservations. Furthermore, the immigration policy of the United States has complicated the successful relocation of intact families from Asia and Latin America.

The African American family suffers from many negative and inaccurate stereotypes. It is true that in a significantly higher proportion of Black than White families, no husband is present in the home (Figure 41-2). Yet Black single mothers often belong to stable, functioning kin networks, which mitigate the pressures of sexism and racism. Members of these networks—predominantly female kin such as mothers, grandmothers, and aunts—ease financial strains by sharing goods and services. In addition to these strong kinship bonds, Black family life has emphasized deep religious commitment and high aspirations for achievement (Cleek et al. 2012; DuBois [1909] 1970).

Like African Americans, Native Americans draw on family ties to cushion many of the hardships they face. On the Navajo reservation, for example, teenage parenthood is not regarded as the crisis that it is elsewhere in the United States. The Navajo trace their descent matrilineally. Traditionally, couples reside with the wife's family after marriage, allowing the grandparents to help with the child rearing. While the Navajo do not approve of teenage parenthood, the deep emotional commitment of their extended families provides a warm home environment for children, even when no father is present or involved (Dalla and Gamble 2001; John 2012).

Sociologists also have taken note of differences in family patterns among other racial and ethnic groups. For example, Mexican American men have been described as exhibiting a sense of virility, personal worth, and pride in their maleness that is called **machismo.** Mexican Americans are also described as being more familistic than many other subcultures. **Familism (or *familismo*)** refers to pride in the extended family, expressed

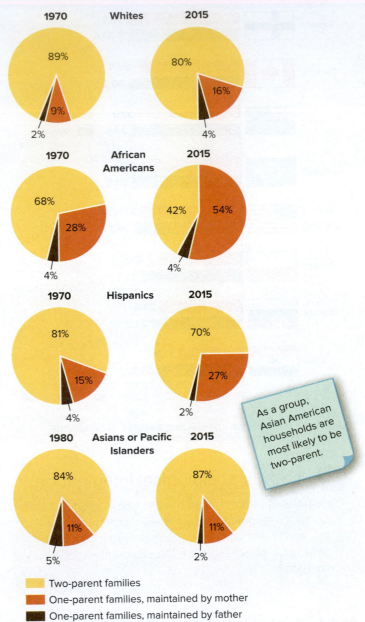

FIGURE 41-2 **Rise of Single-Parent Families in the United States, 1970–2015**

Whites
1970: 89%, 9%, 2%
2015: 80%, 16%, 4%

African Americans
1970: 68%, 28%, 4%
2015: 42%, 54%, 4%

Hispanics
1970: 81%, 15%, 4%
2015: 70%, 27%, 2%

Asians or Pacific Islanders
1980: 84%, 11%, 5%
2015: 87%, 11%, 2%

As a group, Asian American households are most likely to be two-parent.

- Two-parent families
- One-parent families, maintained by mother
- One-parent families, maintained by father

Note: Families are groups with children under 18. Early data for Asian Americans are for 1980. Hispanics can be of any race. Not included are unrelated people living together with no children present. All data exclude children who live with neither parent.
Sources: Bureau of the Census 2008a:56; 2015d:Table C3.

through the maintenance of close ties and strong obligations to kinfolk outside the immediate family. Traditionally, Mexican Americans have placed proximity to their extended families above other needs and desires.

Although familism is often seen as a positive cultural attribute, it may also have negative consequences. Sociologists who have studied the relatively low college application rates of Hispanic students have found they have a strong desire to stay at home. Even the children of college-educated parents express this preference, which diminishes the likelihood of their getting a four-year degree and dramatically reduces the possibility that they will apply to a selective college.

These family patterns are changing, however, in response to changes in Latinos' social class standing, educational achievements, and occupations. Like other Americans, career-oriented Latinos in search of a mate but short on spare time are turning to Internet sites. As Latinos and other groups assimilate into the dominant culture of the United States, their family lives take on both the positive and negative characteristics associated with White households (Hossain et al. 2015).

Child-Rearing Patterns

The Nayars of southern India acknowledge the biological role of fathers, but the mother's eldest brother is responsible for her children. In contrast, uncles play only a peripheral role in child care in the United States. Caring for children is a universal function of the family, yet the ways in which different societies assign this function to family members can vary significantly. Even within the United States, child-rearing patterns are varied. A trend that began in the 20th century and has only accelerated into the 21st century is a dramatic rearrangement of children's living situation, which began in the 1950s. Today fewer than one in five children lives in a household with a father present and working, a mother present, and no other step or custodial children present (P. Cohen 2014).

We'll take a look here at parenthood and grandparenthood, adoption, dual-income families, single-parent families, and stepfamilies.

Parenthood and Grandparenthood

The socialization of children is essential to the maintenance of any culture. Consequently, parenthood is one of the most important (and most demanding) social roles in the United States. Sociologist Alice Rossi (1968, 1984) has identified four factors that complicate the transition to parenthood and the role of socialization. First, there is little anticipatory socialization for the social role of caregiver. The normal school curriculum gives scant attention to the subjects most relevant to successful family life, such as child care and home maintenance. Second, only limited learning occurs during the period of pregnancy itself. Third, the transition to parenthood is quite abrupt. Unlike adolescence, it is not prolonged; unlike the transition to work, the duties of caregiving cannot be taken on gradually. Finally, in Rossi's view, our society lacks clear and helpful guidelines for successful parenthood. There is little consensus on how parents can produce happy and well-adjusted offspring—or even on what it means to be well adjusted. For these reasons, socialization for parenthood involves difficult challenges for most men and women in the United States.

In some homes, the full nest holds grandchildren. In the United States, about 10 percent of all children live with a grandparent. In over 15 percent of these households, no parent is present, so a grandparent truly is raising the child. Nine percent of White children, 17 percent of Black children, and 14 percent of Hispanic children lived with at least one grandparent. In about a third of these homes, no parent was present to assume responsibility for the youngsters. Special difficulties are inherent in such relationships, including legal custodial concerns, access to health care, financial issues, and emotional problems for adults and youths alike. It is not surprising that support groups such as Grandparents as Parents have emerged to provide assistance (Ellis and Simmons 2014).

Adoption

In a legal sense, **adoption** is the transfer of the legal rights, responsibilities, and privileges of parenthood to a new legal parent or parents. In many cases, these rights are transferred from a biological parent or parents (often called birth parents) to an adoptive parent or parents. Every year, about 135,000 children are adopted in the United States (Child Welfare Information 2011).

Viewed from a functionalist perspective, government has a strong interest in encouraging adoption. Policymakers, in fact, have both a humanitarian and a financial stake in the process. In theory, adoption offers a stable family environment for children who otherwise might not receive satisfactory care. Moreover, government data show that unwed mothers who keep their babies tend to be of lower socioeconomic status and often require public assistance to support their children. The government can lower its social welfare expenses, then, if children are transferred to economically self-sufficient families. From an interactionist perspective, however, adoption may require a child to adjust to a very different family environment and parental approach to child rearing.

© Lori Waselchuck/New York Times/Redux Pictures

When nine-year-old Blake Brunson shows up for a basketball game, so do his *eight* grandparents—the result of his parents' remarriages. Blended families can be very supportive to children, but what message do they send to them on the permanency of marriage?

Transracial Adoption: The Experience of Children from Korea

Caleb Littell was born in South Korea and adopted by a White couple in the United States as an infant. He joined a loving family in the predominantly White suburb of Renton, Washington, just outside Seattle. Now in his 30s, Caleb always knew that he was loved and fiercely wanted by his parents. Still, he struggled with his identity. Why did he look different from his parents? Why was he adopted? What did it mean to be Korean? These questions didn't trouble him at home, but at school and in the wider community, where he was often teased for being "Oriental" or "Asian." His White parents, whom he identified with, didn't see him as different from themselves, he reasoned, yet people outside the family did—why? Caleb wasn't just hurt; he was confused.

This story, recounted by educator Mia Tuan and sociologist Jiannbin Lee Shiao, is all too familiar to children who have experienced transracial adoption, the adoption of a non-White child by White parents or a Hispanic child by non-Hispanics. About 300,000 such children under age 16 live in the United States today. Although this type of adoption has occurred for generations, it became more common in the 1990s with the increase in international adoptions. About 85 percent of international adoptions are transracial.

Although no single case is typical, the lifelong socialization of the transracially adopted child does present some special challenges: A child's relationship to his or her parents is an ascribed status, as is ethnicity or race. Korean children who were adopted by White families find that when they move outside their protective nuclear families, their ascribed identities are immediately questioned. Sociologists and other researchers point out that their experience reflects contemporary racial and ethnic relations in the United States. That is to say,

© Purestock/Alamy RF

> Now in his 30s, Caleb always knew that he was loved and fiercely wanted by his parents. Still, he struggled with his identity.

these children find acceptance and opportunity as well as intolerance and conflict in their new home country.

Assessing the long-term success of **transracial adoption** is difficult, since the outcomes of raising children in general are complex. The researcher must separate normal parenting problems from transracial parenting problems. One common transracial parenting problem is that White parents may lack the individual experiences, and at first the resources, to transmit positive identity messages to their adopted children. For advice, parents often turn to support groups and online chat rooms. Some send their children to *heritage camps*, which have emerged over the last 30 years to immerse

children in cultural experiences reflective of their cultural background, be it African, Asian, or Hispanic. Besides offering language instruction, such camps allow children to socialize with others who were transracially adopted. The degree and quality of support from other relatives and from the surrounding community is also important to the children's adjustment.

In terms of the children's adult identity, there is no single outcome. Some choose to live in South Korea, often becoming part of a loose-knit organization of some 500 adoptees who have returned from many countries. Adult Korean American adoptees may describe themselves as "Korean American," "Caucasian, except when looking in the mirror," or "Amerasian trying to be White." Research indicates that for most adoptees, identification with Korea is weak, although it has strengthened a bit among more recent adoptees, as support structures have improved. Few of them really learn to speak the Korean language or to truly enjoy Korean food.

LET'S DISCUSS

1. As a child, did you know anyone who may have been transracially adopted? If so, did the child fit in well with his or her peers? Relate your answer to the community you grew up in.

2. Compare the experience of transracial adoption to the experience of entering a blended family. From the child's point of view, what might be the advantages and disadvantages of each? From the parents' point of view, what might be the challenges of each?

Sources: M. Jones 2015; Kreider 2011; Randolph and Holtzman 2010; Tuan and Shiao 2011.

There are two legal methods of adopting an unrelated person: the adoption may be arranged through a licensed agency, or in some states it may be arranged through a private agreement sanctioned by the courts. Adopted children may come from the United States or from abroad. In 2014, over 6,400 children entered the United States as the adopted children of U.S. citizens (Bureau of Consular Affairs 2015).

Having a new child is a major adjustment for everyone in the family; adopting a child is an even bigger adjustment. If the adopted child comes from another culture and is racially or ethnically different from the adopting family, the challenge is that much greater. Box 41-2 describes research on the adjustment that occurs when a U.S. family adopts a child from South Korea.

The 2010 earthquake in Haiti drew attention to the foreign perspective on international adoptions, which is not always positive. When well-meaning people from the United States arrived in Haiti to rescue alleged orphans and arrange for their adoption in other countries, government officials objected. Some of the children, it turned out, were not orphans; their parents were simply too poor to care for them. For the governments of overstressed developing nations, adoption can be both a solution and a problem.

Adoption is controversial not only abroad but at home as well. In some cases, those who adopt children are not married. In 1995, an important court decision in New York held that a couple does not need to be married to adopt a child. Under this ruling, unmarried heterosexual couples, lesbian couples, and gay couples can all adopt children in New York. Today, most states permit gay and lesbian couples to adopt. Significant restrictions or outright prohibitions exist in Mississippi, Nebraska, and Utah (ACLU 2015).

For every child who is adopted, many more remain the wards of state-sponsored child protective services. At any given time, around half a million children in the United States are living in foster care. Every year, about 52,000 of them are adopted; another 101,000 are eligible and waiting to be adopted (Department of Health and Human Services 2013).

Dual-Income Families

The idea of a family consisting of a wage-earning husband and a wife who stays at home has largely given way to the dual-income household. Among married people between ages 25 and 64, 96 percent of the men and 69 percent of the women were in the labor force in 2010 (Bureau of the Census 2011a:Table 597).

Why has there been such a rise in the number of dual-income couples? A major factor is economic need, coupled with a desire by both men *and* women to pursue their careers. Evidence of this

trend can be found in the rise in the number of married couples living apart for reasons other than marital discord. The 3.6 million couples who now live apart represent 1 out of every 33 marriages. More than half of them live farther than 100 miles apart, and half of those live 1,000 or more miles apart. Of course, couples living apart are nothing new; men have worked at transient jobs for generations as soldiers, truck drivers, or traveling salesmen. Now, however, the woman's job is often the one that creates the separation. The existence of such household arrangements reflects an acceptance of the egalitarian family type (Higgins et al. 2010; Holmes 2009; Silverman 2009).

Single-Parent Families

The 2004 *American Idol* winner Fantasia Barrino's song "Baby Mama" offers a tribute to young single mothers—a subject she knows about. Barrino was 17 when she became pregnant with her daughter. Though critics charged that the song sends the wrong message to teenage girls, Barrino says it is not about encouraging teens to have sex. Rather, she sees the song as an anthem for young mothers courageously trying to raise their children alone (Cherlin 2006).

In recent decades, the stigma attached to unwed mothers and other single parents has significantly diminished. **Single-parent families,** in which only one parent is present to care for the children, can hardly be viewed as a rarity in the United States. In 2015, a single parent headed about 20 percent of White families with children under 18, 30 percent of Hispanic families with children, and 58 percent of African American families with children (see Figure 41-2).

The lives of single parents and their children are not inevitably more difficult than life in a traditional nuclear family. It is as inaccurate to assume that a single-parent family is necessarily deprived as it is to assume that a two-parent family is always secure and happy. Nevertheless, life in a single-parent family can be extremely stressful, in both economic and emotional terms. A family headed by a single mother faces especially difficult problems when the mother is a teenager.

Why might low-income teenage women wish to have children and face the obvious financial difficulties of motherhood? Viewed from an interactionist perspective, these women tend to have low self-esteem and limited options; a child may provide a sense of motivation and purpose for a teenager whose economic worth in our society is limited at best. Given the barriers that many young women face because of their gender, race, ethnicity, and class, many teenagers may believe they have little to lose and much to gain by having a child.

According to a widely held stereotype, "unwed mothers" and "babies having

© Cheryl Gerber for The New York Times/Redux Pictures

Miles Harvey reads to his children via Skype. Harvey, who is happily married, lives 900 miles from his family in Chicago. He accepted a job in New Orleans for economic reasons.

babies" in the United States are predominantly African American. However, this view is not entirely accurate. African Americans account for a disproportionate share of births to unmarried women and teenagers, but the majority of all babies born to unmarried teenage mothers are born to White adolescents. Moreover, since 1980, birthrates among Black teenagers have generally declined (J. Martin et al. 2015).

Although 84 percent of single parents in the United States are mothers, the number of households headed by single fathers more than quadrupled from 1980 to 2013. Though single mothers often develop social networks, single fathers are typically more isolated. In addition, they must deal with schools and social service agencies that are more accustomed to women as custodial parents (Bureau of the Census 1981, 2013d).

 use your **sociological imagination**

What personal experience do you have with child rearing by grandparents, dual-income families, or single-parent families? Describe what you observed using sociological concepts.

Stepfamilies

Approximately 45 percent of all people in the United States will marry, divorce, and then remarry. The rising rates of divorce and remarriage have led to a noticeable increase in stepfamily relationships.

The exact nature of blended families has social significance for adults and children alike. Certainly resocialization is required when an adult becomes a stepparent or a child becomes a stepchild and stepsibling. Moreover, an important distinction must be made between first-time stepfamilies and households where there have been repeated divorces, breakups, or changes in custodial arrangements.

In evaluating the rise of stepfamilies, some observers have assumed that children would benefit from remarriage because they would be gaining a second custodial parent, and would potentially enjoy greater economic security. However, after reviewing many studies of stepfamilies, sociologist Andrew J. Cherlin (2010) concluded that children whose parents have remarried do not have higher levels of well-being than children in divorced single-parent families.

Stepparents can play valuable and unique roles in their stepchildren's lives, but their involvement does not guarantee an improvement in family life. In fact, standards may decline. Studies suggest that children raised in families with stepmothers are likely to have less health care, education, and money spent on their food than children raised by biological mothers. The measures are also negative for children raised by stepfathers, but only half as negative as in the case of stepmothers. These results don't mean that stepmothers are "evil"—it may be that the stepmother holds back out of concern for seeming too intrusive, or relies mistakenly on the biological father to carry out parental duties (Jensen and Howard 2015).

 use your **sociological imagination**

What special challenges might stepfamilies face? What advantages might they enjoy? Explain using sociological concepts.

MODULE 41 | **Recap and Review**

Summary

People select mates in a variety of ways: in some societies, marriages are arranged, while in others, people select their own mates.

1. Some societies require mates to be chosen within a certain group (**endogamy**) or outside certain groups (**exogamy**). Consciously or unconsciously, many people look for a mate with similar personal characteristics (**homogamy**).

2. In the United States, family life varies with social class, race, and ethnicity.

3. Currently, in the majority of all married couples in the United States, both husband and wife work outside the home.

4. Single-parent families account for an increasing proportion of U.S. families.

Thinking Critically

1. How do both cultural and socioeconomic factors contribute to the following trends: later age of first marriage, the increasing number of extended-family households, and the boomerang generation?

2. Explain mate selection from the functionalist and interactionist perspectives.

Key Terms

Adoption

Endogamy

Exogamy

Familism (*Familismo*)

Homogamy

Impression management

Incest taboo

Machismo

Single-parent family

Transracial adoption

Divorce

In the United States, the pattern of family life includes commitments both to marriage and to self-expression and personal growth. Needless to say, the tension between those competing commitments can undermine a marriage, working against the establishment of a lasting relationship. This approach to family life is distinctive to the United States. In some nations, such as Italy, the culture strongly supports marriage and discourages divorce. In others, such as Sweden, people treat marriage the same way as cohabitation, and both arrangements are just as lasting (Cherlin 2009).

Statistical Trends in Divorce

Just how common is divorce? Surprisingly, this is not a simple question; divorce statistics are difficult to interpret. The media frequently report that one out of every two marriages ends in divorce, but that figure is misleading. It is based on a comparison of all divorces that occur in a single year (regardless of when the couples were married) with the number of new marriages in the same year.

Marriage is showing signs of longevity. About 70 percent of marriages that began in the 1990s were still together as of late 2014. Those who married in the first decade of the 21st century are showing even more of a tendency to stay together. Given current trends, two-thirds of marriages will never end in divorce (C. Miller 2014).

In many countries, divorce began to increase in the late 1960s but then leveled off; since the late 1980s, it has declined by 30 percent. (Figure 42-1 shows the pattern in the United States.) This trend is due partly to the aging of the baby boomer population and the corresponding decline in the proportion of people of marriageable age. But it also indicates an increase in marital stability in recent years.

Getting divorced obviously does not sour people on marriage. About 57 percent of all divorced people in the United States have remarried, a level that has remained relatively steady for more than 50 years. Women are less likely than men to remarry because many retain custody of their children after a divorce, which complicates a new adult relationship (Livingston 2014b).

Some people regard the nation's high rate of remarriage as an endorsement of the institution of marriage, but it does lead to the new challenges of a kin network composed of both current and prior marital relationships. Such networks can be particularly complex if children are involved or if an ex-spouse remarries.

Most households in the United States do not consist of two parents living with their unmarried children.

Factors Associated with Divorce

Perhaps the most important factor in the increase in divorce over the past hundred years has been the greater social *acceptance* of divorce. It is no longer considered necessary to endure an unhappy marriage. More important, various religious denominations have relaxed their negative attitudes toward divorce, so that most religious leaders no longer treat it as a sin.

The growing acceptance of divorce is a worldwide phenomenon. The majority of people in a cross-national study see divorce as morally acceptable or do not even view it as a moral issue. Out of 40 nations, in just 12 do at least 40 percent of respondents find divorce unacceptable; those nations are in Latin America, Africa, and Asia. Globally, gambling and alcohol are much more likely to raise moral indignation than divorce (Poushter 2014).

In the United States, several factors have contributed to the growing social acceptance of divorce:

- Most states have adopted more liberal divorce laws in the past four decades. No-fault divorce laws, which allow a couple to end their marriage without fault on either side (by specifying adultery, for instance), accounted for an initial surge in the divorce rate after they were introduced in the 1970s, but appear to have had little effect beyond that.

FIGURE 42-1 **Trends in Marriage and Divorce in the United States, 1920–2014**

Both the divorce rate and the marriage rate have declined since 1979.

Sources: Bureau of the Census 1975:64; Centers for Disease Control and Prevention 2012b, 2015a.

- Divorce has become a more practical option in newly formed families, since families tend to have fewer children now than in the past.

- A general increase in family incomes, coupled with the availability of free legal aid to some poor people, has meant that more couples can afford costly divorce proceedings.

- As society provides greater opportunities for women, more and more wives are becoming less dependent on their husbands, both economically and emotionally. They may feel more able to leave a marriage if it seems hopeless.

Impact of Divorce on Children

Divorce may be traumatic for all involved, but it has special meaning for the more than 1 million children whose parents divorce each year. Of course, for some of these children, divorce signals the welcome end to a very dysfunctional relationship. Perhaps that is why a national study that tracked 6,332 children both before and after their parents' divorce found that their behavior did not suffer from the marital breakups. Other studies have shown greater unhappiness among children who live amid parental conflict than among children whose parents are divorced.

Still, it would be simplistic to assume that children are automatically better off following the breakup of their parents' marriage. The interests of the parents do not necessarily serve children well. Custodial arrangements can take a long time to work out and are not necessarily followed. Recent data show that about 62 percent of court-ordered child support is paid. Overwhelmingly, where only one parent has custody of children, that parent is the mother. The proportion of custodial mothers with incomes below the poverty level is 31.8 percent. Only about half as many custodial fathers live in poverty (Grall 2013; H. Kim 2011; Zi 2007).

Lesbian and Gay Relationships

Twenty-one-year-old Parke, a junior in college, grew up in a stable, loving family. A self-described fiscal conservative, he credits his parents with instilling in him a strong work ethic. Sound like an average child of an average family? The only break with traditional expectations in this case is that Parke is the son of a lesbian couple (P. Brown 2004).

The lifestyles of lesbians and gay men are varied. Some live in long-term, monogamous relationships; others live alone or with roommates. The possibility of living openly in a long-term relationship, like any opposite sex couple, expanded dramatically with the 2015 Supreme Court *Obergefell* decision. In *Obergefell vs. Jones* the court heard the case of Jim Obergefell, who had married his terminally ill

© ValaGrenier/iStock/Getty Images Plus/Getty Images RF

partner in 2011 in a state where same-sex marriage was legal. However, because the couple's home state of Ohio did not recognize same-sex marriage, his name could not be listed on his deceased spouse's death certificate. The court, in a surprising 5-4 vote, chose to go beyond ruling on the specifics of the case and declared that the Constitution guarantees the right to same-sex marriage. One national study estimated that close to 200,000 new same-sex marriages were solemnized in the four months following the decision (Jones and Gates 2015).

With marriage legalized, states and social agencies now begin to deal with another new social reality: same-sex divorce. In the short run, the issue is exceedingly complicated, because in the years before the Supreme Court decision, many gay couples traveled to jurisdictions where same-sex marriage was legal to be married and then returned to live in their home states where it was not (for example, Massachusetts began recognizing such unions back in 2004). Couples who seek divorce usually must either return to the place where they were married and reestablish legal residence or try to work through the still-undefined process in their home state. It will be many years before it is possible to identify the divorce and remarriage patterns of same-sex couples.

In addition to marriage equality, the last few years have seen dramatic changes in legal discrimination against lesbian, gay, bisexual, and transgender (LGBT) people. Although significant barriers remain, especially in family law and in publicly expressed prejudicial attitudes, progress has been made in other areas. Increasingly, businesses are seeing the benefit of hiring LGBT people. In 2012 the CIA began active recruitment in the LGBT community—a sharp departure from the past, when the CIA and other federal agencies routinely denied security clearances to gay men and women. As a result, even before the *Obergefell* decision, 92 percent of lesbian, gay, bisexual, and transgender adults felt that society had become more accepting in the past decade (G. Allen 2012; Suh 2014).

With marriage legally broadened, all the topics discussed in this chapter, from divorce to child-rearing, have expanded dramatically to encompass marriage with two women and two men. Do such households differ from each other? Do they differ from opposite-sex partnerships? Even before *Obergefell*, queer theorists argued that gays and lesbians are often understudied by researchers (although that is beginning to change). In particular, queer theorists point to the relative lack of high-quality research on LGBT households and their relationship to the larger society, not to mention non-LGBT relatives. As the campaign for same-sex marriage gains momentum, some scholars see a need to focus on gay men and lesbians who do not fit the new "gay norm," who reject the desire to create a nuclear family household. Continuing to focus on the margins of society, queer theorists argue for more attention to people of color, the working class, the poor, and immigrants in the LGBT community (Moore and Stambolis-Ruhstorfer 2013).

use your **sociological imagination**

What is the significance of legalizing same-sex marriage for the couple's relatives? For the wider society?

Diverse Lifestyles

Marriage is no longer the presumed route from adolescence to adulthood. Instead, it is treated as just one of several paths to maturity. As a result, the marriage ceremony has lost much of its social significance as a rite of passage. The nation's marriage rate has declined since 1960 because people are postponing marriage until later in life, and because more couples, including same-sex couples, are deciding to form partnerships without marriage (Haq 2011).

Cohabitation

In the United States, testing the marital waters by living together before making a commitment is a common practice among marriage-wary 20- and 30-somethings. The tremendous increase in the number of male–female couples who choose to live together without marrying, a practice called **cohabitation,** is one of the most dramatic trends of recent years.

About half of all *currently* married couples in the United States say that they lived together before marriage. This percentage is likely to increase. The number of households in the United States that are headed by unmarried opposite-sex couples has been rising steadily; in 2015 it was over 8 million. About 40 percent of cohabiting couples' households included children under age 18—nearly the same proportion as married couples' households (Bureau of the Census 2015e: Table UC3).

In much of Europe, cohabitation is so common that the general sentiment seems to be "Love, yes; marriage, maybe." In Iceland, 62 percent of all children are born to single mothers; in France, Great Britain, and Norway, about 40 percent. Government policies in these countries make few legal distinctions between married and unmarried couples or households. Perhaps as a result, partnerships between cohabiting adults are not necessarily brief or lacking in commitment. Children born to a cohabiting couple in Sweden, for example, are less likely than children born to a cohabiting couple in the United States to see their parents break up (Cherlin 2009; Lyall 2002; M. Moore 2006).

People tend to associate cohabitation with younger, childless couples. Although that stereotype may have been accurate a generation or more ago, it is not now. Since 1970, the number of unmarried couples with children has increased 12-fold.

© Amos Morgan/Getty Images RF

Periodically, legislators attempt to bolster the desirability of a lifelong commitment to marriage. In 2002, President George W. Bush backed funding for an initiative to promote marriage among those who receive public assistance. Under the Healthy Marriage and Responsible Fatherhood Initiative, the federal government created a resource center that promoted marriage-related programs. Critics charged that the effort was underfunded or an inappropriate mission for the federal government. The initiative extends grants to programs that strengthen fathers' ties with their children and partners. It has also established pilot projects to serve formerly incarcerated parents and their families, designed to provide activities that strengthen their marriages and encourage responsible parenting and economic stability (Bartlett 2014; Office of Family Assistance 2015).

Remaining Single

Looking at TV programs today, you would be justified in thinking that most households are composed of singles. Although that is not the case, it is true that more and more people in the United States are postponing entry into a first marriage. Over one out of three households with children in the United States is a single-parent household. Even so, less than 4 percent of women and men in the United States are likely to remain single throughout their lives (Bureau of the Census 2015e).

The trend toward maintaining a single lifestyle for a longer period is related to the growing economic independence of young people. This trend is especially significant for women. Freed from financial needs, women don't necessarily need to marry to enjoy a satisfying life. Divorce, late marriage, and longevity also figure into this trend.

There are many reasons why a person may choose not to marry. Some singles do not want to limit their sexual intimacy to one lifetime partner. Some men and women do not want to become highly dependent on any one person—and do not want anyone depending heavily on them. In a society that values individuality and self-fulfillment, the single lifestyle can offer certain freedoms that married couples may not enjoy. Even divorced parents may not feel the need to remarry. Andrew J. Cherlin (2009) contends that a single parent who connects with other adults, such as grandparents, to form a solid, supportive relationship for child rearing should not feel compelled to re-partner.

Nevertheless, remaining single represents a clear departure from societal expectations; indeed, it has been likened to "being single on Noah's Ark." A single adult must confront the inaccurate view that he or she is always lonely, is a workaholic, or is immature. These stereotypes help to support the traditional assumption in the United States and most other societies that to be truly happy and fulfilled, a person must get married and raise a family. To counter these societal expectations, singles have formed numerous support groups (Bryant 2016, McKeown 2015).

Marriage without Children

There has been a modest increase in childlessness in the United States. According to census data, about 16 to 17 percent of women will now complete their childbearing years without having borne any children, compared to 10 percent in 1980. As many as 20 percent of women in their 30s expect to remain childless (Biddlecom and Martin 2006; Bureau of the Census 2014c: Figure H1).

Childlessness within marriage has generally been viewed as a problem that can be solved through such means as adoption and artificial insemination. More and more couples today, however, choose not to have children and regard themselves as child-free rather than childless. They do not believe that having children automatically follows from marriage, nor do they feel that reproduction is the duty of all married couples. Childless couples have formed support groups (with names like No Kidding) and set up websites.

Economic considerations have contributed to this shift in attitudes; having children has become quite expensive. According to a government estimate made for 2012, the average middle-class family will spend $241,080 to feed, clothe, and shelter a child from birth to age 18. If the child attends college, that amount could double, depending on the college chosen. In 1960, parents spent only 2 percent of their income on child care and education; now they spend 16 percent, reflecting the rising dependence on nonfamily child care. Aware of the financial pressures, some couples are weighing the advantages of a child-free marriage (Lino 2013).

Childless couples are beginning to question current practices in the workplace. While applauding employers' efforts to provide child care and flexible work schedules, some nevertheless express concern about tolerance of employees who leave early to take children to doctors, ball games, or after-school classes. As more dual-career couples enter the paid labor force and struggle to balance career and familial responsibilities, conflicts with employees who have no children may increase (Blackstone 2014).

Family leave is an issue important to almost all the families we have considered in this chapter. All working parents, whether they are married, single, gay, or straight, struggle to find ways to care for children and for elderly and sick family members. The Social Policy section that follows considers family leave issues in the United States and throughout the world.

 use your **sociological imagination**

What would happen to our society if many more married couples suddenly decided not to have children? How would society change if cohabitation and/or singlehood became the norm?

social policy and the Family | Family Leave Worldwide

Kim Knoblauch gave birth to her first baby in the United States. The only "maternity leave" pay she received was one month's accrued vacation and sick time, and when she was ready to return to work, her job no longer existed. Because she worked for a small company, the federal requirement that her job be protected for 12 weeks did not apply.

Four years later, her husband's job had taken Knoblauch and her family to Germany, where she had a very different experience. The family was entitled to Germany's full range of maternity and postpartum benefits.

The day after baby Eva came home from the hospital, a midwife came to Knoblauch's home to weigh her, check the cord stump, and help with breastfeeding. In addition, the family was entitled to *Kindergeld,* a government allowance that helps cover the costs of child rearing. Because she had two children, Knoblauch collected about 300 euros (over $300) per month (Ramnarace 2015).

Protecting parents in the workplace has a long history worldwide. Historically policies were enacted allowing pregnant women to work, prohibiting child labor, and providing family health and life insurance. In recent generations, countries have created programs that require employers to allow new mothers to take leaves of absence. At first, most laws provided only for unpaid leave. Later paid leave was required, and finally, the benefits were extended to new fathers.

Looking at the Issue

Paid parental leave for mothers and fathers with newborns or newly adopted children is common in industrial countries. When Australia enacted its family leave law in 2010, this left the United States as the only industrialized nation that did not mandate paid family leave. The United States does not even require employers to grant unpaid leave, which would guarantee the new parents a job when they returned to work.

In the United States family leave is left to employers' discretion, including decisions about paid versus unpaid leave or even whether an employee can use accrued sick leave. This is not typical at all. Of the 185 countries surveyed by the International Labour Organization, only two provided no cash benefits for women during maternity leave—the United States and Papua New Guinea.

Worldwide, 98 nations provide a minimum of 14 weeks of maternity leave and 107 nations require some pay during a woman's leave. The trend is toward expanding the length and

—Continued

increasing the level of payment—about a 30 percent increase globally between 1994 and 2013. Paternity leave is less common but has also been increasing since 1994. Presently 80 nations guarantee paternity leave, and 71 of those include paid leave. Figures 42-2 and 42-3 compare policies in selected countries.

Applying Sociology

As noted earlier in the chapter, functionalists identify a series of paramount functions that societies provide, including socialization of children, which is particularly critical for newborns or newly adopted children. To functionalists family leave is particularly important as a means of facilitating the parent-child interaction that is crucial to socialization.

Interactionists look at family leave policy as having direct impact on everyday relations both at work and home. In the workplace the issue is how supervisors, peers, and subordinates adjust to the absence of the worker. At home, the focus would be on how family leave policies affect the household. For example, research suggests that when mothers are granted family leave, infants are more likely to be breast-fed, which lowers illness and hospitalization rates for infants and benefits women's health. Beyond these health advantages, paid maternity leave yields economic gains in terms of reduced health care costs, reduced recruitment and retraining costs, and improved long-term earnings for women (Heymann with McNeill 2013).

Conflict theorists note the inherent class bias in family leave policy. In the United States, employees who receive paid leave are a relatively small number of relatively affluent workers. The much larger group of workers in retail and service jobs are left out. Existing or proposed leave policies are often based on a worker's current job history, which favors higher-level employees. Most paid leave programs in the United States are limited to long-term, full-time employees, who are greatly advantaged over the many people, particularly women, who piece together several jobs or work part-time. Unless family leave is heavily supported by government, this portion of the work force will be unable to participate.

To seek an effective solution, one is reminded of Karl Marx and Friedrich Engels's 1847 refrain about workers of all countries uniting. Dividing family leave policies between full-time professionals and the rest of the labor force will only contribute to inequality among workers (Tucker 1978:473, 500).

Feminist scholars note that the absence of mandatory paid leave policies fails to recognize the realities of today's

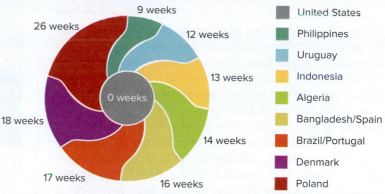

FIGURE 42-2 **Paid Maternity Leave, Selected Countries, 2013**

- United States
- Philippines
- Uruguay
- Indonesia
- Algeria
- Bangladesh/Spain
- Brazil/Portugal
- Denmark
- Poland

Source: Addati et al. 2014: 133-143, 150-166.

All countries shown, except the United States, provide full pay for the periods indicated. Some provide partial pay beyond the periods indicated.

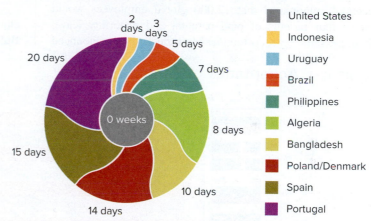

FIGURE 42-3 **Paid Paternity Leave, Selected Countries, 2013**

- United States
- Indonesia
- Uruguay
- Brazil
- Philippines
- Algeria
- Bangladesh
- Poland/Denmark
- Spain
- Portugal

Source: Addati et al. 2014: 133-143, 150-166.

All countries shown, except the United States, provide full pay for the periods indicated. Some provide partial pay beyond the periods indicated.

families, in which 70 percent of children live in households with two working adults.

Moreover, even when family leave plans exist, companies seem to stigmatize the use of these policies beyond the very limited assistance given to new mothers, especially in the United States. Feminist scholars contend that this results from a flexibility stigma. **Flexibility stigma** is the devaluation of workers who seek or are presumed to need flexible work arrangements. Research shows that women often face a tough and unfair choice: they can either be stigmatized for taking advantage of leave options or remain in precarious, low-paying jobs (Jacobs and Padavic 2015).

—Continued

Initiating Policy

The FMLA (Family and Medical Leave Act) enacted in 1993 entitles eligible employees of covered employers to take unpaid, job-protected leave for specified family and medical reasons with continuation of group health insurance coverage for up to twelve weeks. Advocates have sought unsuccessfully to expand these provisions. One such proposal is the FAMILY Act (Family and Medical Insurance Leave Act), which would provide paid leave of up to 66 percent of regular wages, with a maximum amount of $1,000 per week. Opponents question the cost of the program to the employer or the government, while supporters point to studies showing that such a policy would promote family stability, confer long-term health benefits, and lower public assistance rates. FAMILY or another proposal, the Healthy Families Act, has been introduced to Congress regularly, but as of early 2016, it had not yet even been the subject of hearings (Farrell and Glynn 2013; Healthy Families Act 2015).

As the federal government struggles to develop a mandated policy, selected private corporations continue to introduce path-breaking family friendly policies. Notably in 2015 Facebook announced that 12,000 global employees would receive four months of paid parental and maternity leave. About the same time, co-founder Mark Zuckerberg announced

© Photoshot

Facebook co-founder Mark Zuckerberg, pictured here with his wife Priscilla Chan and their newborn daughter, announced an employee benefit of four months of paid parental and maternity leave throughout his global business.

that he would take two months of parental leave when his wife, Priscilla Chan, gave birth to their first child (Zorthian 2015).

There is reason to be optimistic, as parental leave enjoys wide support worldwide, as shown in Figure 42-4. But as with most policy issues, the devil lies in the details.

FIGURE 42-4 **Acceptance of Parental Leave**

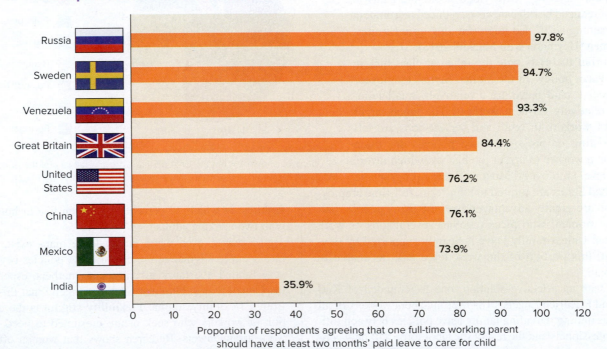

Proportion of respondents agreeing that one full-time working parent should have at least two months' paid leave to care for child

Source: International Survey Social Programme 2014:42. *Flags:* © admin_design/Shutterstock RF

Proportion of respondents agreeing that one full-time working parent should have at least two months' paid leave to care for a child.

—Continued

—Continued

While over three-quarters of Americans want paid maternity or paternity leave for at least two months, only 7 percent want the government to pay for it, while 50 percent think the cost should be borne by the government and the employer, and 37 percent said that costs should be covered by the employer alone. How this policy, one that has been found to be effective in so many other industrialized nations, can be achieved remains to be seen.

TAKE THE ISSUE WITH YOU

1. Do you know of a family that has been in a situation where a paid family leave policy would have greatly benefited them? Describe the circumstances. What benefits, if any, were available?

2. Research the family leave policies of your employer or your college or university. How could they be improved? Which employees are they designed to benefit?

3. Do you agree that family leave benefits should be mandatory? What kind of program would you design? Who do you think should pay for it?

MODULE 42 | Recap and Review

Summary

Divorce and alternatives to traditional marriage such as cohabitation now represent common choices of family style.

1. Among the factors that contribute to the rising divorce rate in the United States are greater social acceptance of divorce and the liberalization of divorce laws in many states.

2. More and more people are living together without marrying, a practice known as **cohabitation**.

3. The Supreme Court's *Obergefell* decision legalized same-sex marriage in all 50 states in 2015. As a result, gays and lesbians enjoy legal marriage equality, but many legal challenges remain.

4. Unlike many countries all over the world, the United States has no laws that mandate family leave, paid or unpaid, or any other social benefits to families with children.

Thinking Critically

1. Do you think it is correct to say that marriage has lost much of its social significance as a rite of passage? Explain your response. What are the major rites of passage into adulthood in today's society?

2. In a society that maximizes the welfare of all family members, how easy should it be for couples to divorce? How easy should it be to get married?

Key Terms

Cohabitation

Flexibility stigma

Mastering This Chapter

© Jeff Greenberg/The Image Works

taking sociology with you

1 Go online and try tracing your family roots using one of the genealogical search sites. How far back can you go? Why might certain ancestral paths be more difficult to trace than others?

2 Do some research on the divorce law in your state. Has the law changed much over the past few decades, and if so, how? From a sociological perspective, why would the law change? Explain.

key terms

Adoption In a legal sense, the transfer of the legal rights, responsibilities, and privileges of parenthood to a new legal parent or parents.

Bilateral descent A kinship system in which both sides of a person's family are regarded as equally important.

Cohabitation The practice of living together as a male–female couple without marrying.

Egalitarian family An authority pattern in which spouses are regarded as equals.

Endogamy The restriction of mate selection to people within the same group.

Exogamy The requirement that people select a mate outside certain groups.

Extended family A family in which relatives—such as grandparents, aunts, or uncles—live in the same home as parents and their children.

Familism (*Familismo*) Pride in the extended family, expressed through the maintenance of close ties and strong obligations to kinfolk outside the immediate family.

Family A set of people related by blood, marriage or some other agreed-on relationship, or adoption, who share the primary responsibility for reproduction and caring for members of society.

Flexibility stigma The devaluation of workers who seek or who are presumed to need flexible work arrangements.

Homogamy The conscious or unconscious tendency to select a mate with personal characteristics similar to one's own.

Impression management The altering of the presentation of the self in order to create distinctive appearances and satisfy particular audiences.

Incest taboo The prohibition of sexual relationships between certain culturally specified relatives.

Kinship The state of being related to others.

Machismo A sense of virility, personal worth, and pride in one's maleness.

Matriarchy A society in which women dominate in family decision making.

Matrilineal descent A kinship system in which only the mother's relatives are significant.

Monogamy A form of marriage in which an individual has only one partner.

Nuclear family A married couple and their unmarried children living together.

Patriarchy A society in which men dominate in family decision making.

Patrilineal descent A kinship system in which only the father's relatives are significant.

Polyandry A form of polygamy in which a woman may have more than one husband at the same time.

Polygamy A form of marriage in which an individual may have several husbands or wives simultaneously.

Polygyny A form of polygamy in which a man may have more than one wife at the same time.

Serial monogamy A form of marriage in which a person may have several spouses in his or her lifetime, but only one spouse at a time.

Single-parent family A family in which only one parent is present to care for the children.

Transracial adoption The adoption of a non-White child by White parents or a Hispanic child by non-Hispanics.

self-quiz

Read each question carefully and then select the best answer.

1. Alice, age seven, lives in a private home with her parents, her grandmother, and her aunt. Alice's family is an example of a(n)
   a. nuclear family.
   b. dysfunctional family.
   c. extended family.
   d. polygynous family.

2. In which form of marriage may a person have several spouses in his or her lifetime, but only one spouse at a time?
   a. serial monogamy
   b. monogamy
   c. polygamy
   d. polyandry

3. The marriage of a woman to more than one man at the same time is referred to as
   a. polygyny.
   b. monogamy.
   c. serial monogamy.
   d. polyandry.

4. Which system of descent is followed in the United States?
   a. matrilineal
   b. patrilineal
   c. bilateral
   d. unilateral

5. According to the functionalist perspective, which of the following is *not* one of the paramount functions performed by the family?
   a. mediation
   b. reproduction
   c. regulation of sexual behavior
   d. affection and companionship

6. Which norm requires mate selection outside certain groups, usually one's own family or certain kinfolk?
   a. exogamy
   b. endogamy
   c. matriarchy
   d. patriarchy

7. According to the discussion of social class differences in family life and intimate relationships, which of the following statements is true?
   a. Social class differences in family life are more striking than they once were.
   b. The upper class emphasizes lineage and maintenance of family position.
   c. Among the poor, women usually play an insignificant role in the economic support of the family.
   d. In examining family life among racial and ethnic minorities, most patterns result from cultural, but *not* class, factors.

8. One recent development in family life in the United States has been the extension of parenthood as adult children continue to live at home or return home after college. The reason for this is
   a. the rising divorce rate.
   b. high rents.
   c. financial difficulties.
   d. all of the above

9. In the United States, the *majority* of all babies born to unmarried teenage mothers are born to whom?
   a. African American adolescents
   b. White adolescents
   c. Latina adolescents
   d. Asian American adolescents

10. Which of the following factors is associated with the high divorce rate in the United States?
    a. the liberalization of divorce laws
    b. the fact that contemporary families have fewer children than earlier families did
    c. the general increase in family incomes
    d. all of the above

11. The principle of _____ assigns people to kinship groups according to their relationship to an individual's mother or father.

12. _____ emerged among Native American tribal societies, and in nations in which men were absent for long periods because of warfare or food-gathering expeditions.

13. In the view of many sociologists, the _____ family has begun to replace the patriarchal family as the social norm in the United States.

14. As _____ theorists point out, the social class of couples and their children significantly influences the socialization experiences to which the children are exposed and the protection they receive.

15. _____ focus on the micro level of family and other intimate relationships; for example, they are interested in whether people are cohabiting partners or are longtime married couples.

16. The rule of _____ specifies the groups within which a spouse must be found and prohibits marriage with others.

17. Social class differences in family life are less striking today than they once were; however, in the past, _____-class families were found to be more authoritarian in rearing children and more inclined to use physical punishment.

18. Caring for children is a(n) _____ function of the family, yet the ways in which different societies assign this function to family members can vary significantly.

19. Viewed from the _____ perspective, the government has a strong interest in encouraging adoption.

20. The rising rates of divorce and remarriage have led to a noticeable increase in _____ relationships.

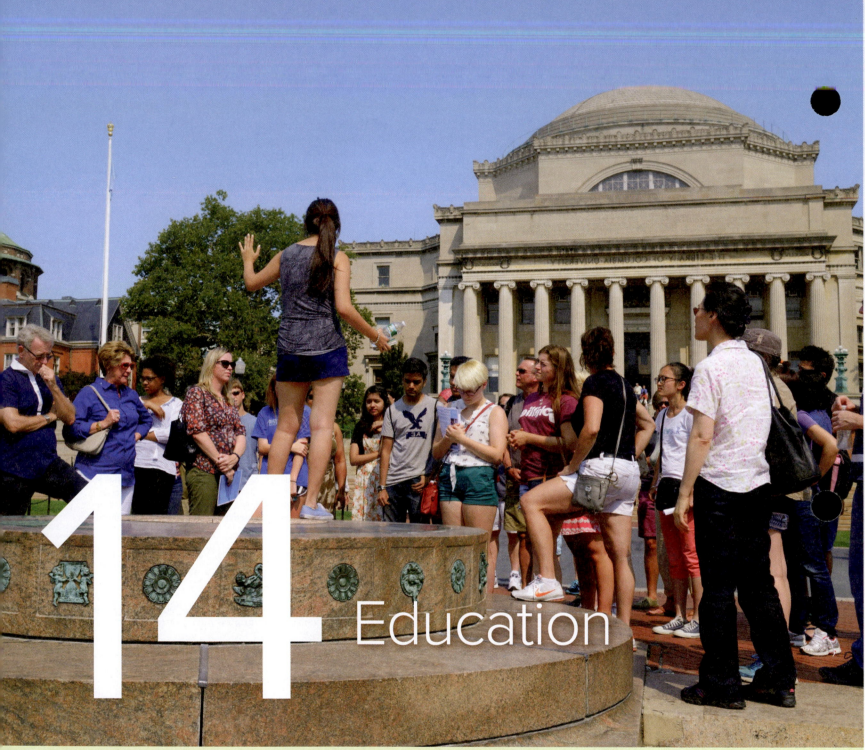

14 Education

© Martin Shields/Alamy Stock Photo

Prospective students and their parents tour the campus of Columbia University in New York City. From informal learning in the family to formal study at institutions of higher learning, education is a cultural universal.

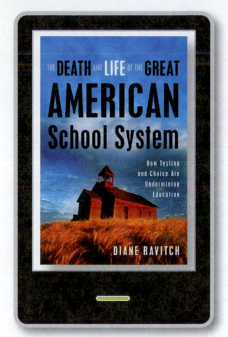

© Ira C. Roberts/Chad Enterprises Corporation

What makes a teacher great? What qualities make teaching and learning both effective and memorable?

After a long career, Diane Ravitch lost faith in the educational reforms she had once championed as a way to rescue failing schools. Searching for a better answer, she looked back on her own experience in high school, to her favorite English teacher.

❝ My favorite teacher was Mrs. Ruby Ratliff. She is the teacher I remember best, the one who influenced me most, who taught me to love literature and to write with careful attention to grammar and syntax. More than fifty years ago, she was my homeroom teacher at San Jacinto High School in Houston, and I was lucky enough to get into her English class as a senior.

Mrs. Ratliff was gruff and demanding. She did not tolerate foolishness or disruptions. She had a great reputation among students. . . . What I remember most about her was what she taught us. We studied the greatest writers of the English language. . . . We read Shakespeare, Keats, Shelley, Wordsworth, Milton, and other major English writers. Now, many years later, in times of stress or sadness, I still turn to poems that I first read in Mrs. Ratliff's class.

Mrs. Ratliff did nothing for our self-esteem. She challenged us to meet her exacting standards. I think she imagined herself bringing enlightenment to the barbarians (that was us). When you wrote something for her class, which happened with frequency, you paid close attention to proper English. Accuracy mattered. She had a red pen and she used it freely. Still, she was always sure to make a comment that encouraged us to do a better job. Clearly she had multiple goals for her students, beyond teaching literature and grammar. She was also teaching about character and personal responsibility. These are not the sorts of things that appear on any standardized test.

She loved her subject, and she enjoyed the respect the students showed her, especially since this was a large high school where students did not easily give respect to their teachers. Despite the passage of years, I still recall a class discussion of Shelley's "Ozymandias," and the close attention that

Clearly she had multiple goals for her students, beyond teaching literature and grammar. She was also teaching about character and personal responsibility. These are not the sorts of things that appear on any standardized test.

thirty usually rowdy adolescents paid to a poem about a time and a place we could barely imagine. I wonder if Mrs. Ratliff has her counterparts today, teachers who love literature and love to teach it, or whether schools favor teachers who have been trained to elicit mechanical responses from their students about "text-to-self connections," "inferencing," "visualizing," and the other formalistic behaviors so beloved by au courant pedagogues. If Mrs. Ratliff were planning to teach these days, I expect that her education professors and supervisors would warn her to get rid of that red pen, to abandon her insistence on accuracy, and to stop being so judgmental. And they would surely demand that she replace those dated poems and essays with young adult literature that teaches adolescents about the lives of other adolescents just like themselves.

I think of Mrs. Ratliff when I hear the latest proposals to improve the teaching force. Almost every day, I come across a statement by a journalist, superintendent, or economist who says we could solve all our problems in American education if we could just recruit a sufficient number of "great" teachers. I believe Mrs. Ratliff was a great teacher, but I don't think she would have been considered "great" if she had been judged by the kind of hard data that is used now. The policy experts who insist that teachers should be judged by their students' scores on standardized tests would have been frustrated by Mrs. Ratliff. Her classes never produced hard data. They didn't even produce test scores. How would the experts have measured what we learned? We never took a multiple-choice test. We wrote essays and took written tests, in which we had to explain our answers, not check a box or fill in a bubble. If she had been evaluated by the grades she gave, she would have been in deep trouble, because she did not award many A grades. An observer might have concluded that she was a very ineffective teacher who had no measurable gains to show for her work. ❞

In her book *The Death and Life of the Great American School System*, education historian Diane Ravitch laments society's failure in improving the quality of education in the United States. In recalling her favorite teacher, Ravitch questions what she sees as the current tendency to reduce the art of teaching to test cramming and relying solely on standardized tests as measures of students' performance. She is really asking the same questions that sociologists ask about education: what are its goals, and what is it supposed to accomplish, for individuals and for society as a whole?

Education is a cultural universal. As such it is an important aspect of socialization, the lifelong process of learning the attitudes, values, and behavior considered appropriate to members of a particular culture. Socialization can occur in the classroom or at home, through interactions with parents, teachers, friends, and even strangers. Exposure to books, films, television, and other forms of communication also promotes socialization. When learning is explicit and formalized—when some people consciously teach, while others adopt the role of learner—the process of socialization is called *education*. But students learn far more about their society at school than what is included in the curriculum.

What social purposes does education serve? Do public schools offer everyone a way up the socioeconomic ladder, or do they reinforce divisions among social classes? What is the "hidden curriculum" in U.S. schools? What have sociologists learned about the latest trends in education, such as competency testing? We will begin with a discussion of the four sociological perspectives on education: functionalist, conflict, feminist, and interactionist. We'll look at schools as formal organizations—as bureaucracies and subcultures of teachers and students. We'll also examine homeschooling, a movement away from institutionalized education and its much-publicized failures. Finally, in the Social Policy section we'll return to the subject of education with a discussion of charter schools.

MODULE 43 — Sociological Perspectives on Education

Besides being a major industry in the United States, **education** is the social institution that formally socializes members of our society. In the past few decades, increasing proportions of people have obtained high school diplomas, college degrees, and advanced professional degrees. Figure 43-1 shows the proportion of the college-educated population in selected countries.

Throughout the world, education has become a vast and complex social institution that prepares citizens for the roles demanded by other social institutions, such as the family, government, and the economy. The functionalist, conflict, feminist, and interactionist perspectives offer distinctive views of education as a social institution.

● Functionalist Perspective

Like other social institutions, education has both manifest (open, stated) and latent (hidden) functions. The most basic *manifest* function of education is the transmission of knowledge. Schools teach students how to read, speak foreign languages, and repair automobiles. Another important manifest function is the bestowal of status. Because many believe this function is performed inequitably, we will consider it later, in the section on the conflict view of education.

In addition to these manifest functions, schools perform a number of *latent* functions: transmitting culture, promoting social and political integration, maintaining social control, and serving as an agent of change.

Transmitting Culture

As a social institution, education performs a rather conservative function—transmitting the dominant culture. Schooling exposes each generation of young people to the existing beliefs, norms, and values of their culture. In our society, we learn respect for social control and reverence for established institutions, such as religion, the family, and the presidency. Of course, this statement is true of many other cultures as well. While schoolchildren in the United States are hearing about the accomplishments of George Washington and Abraham Lincoln, British children are hearing about the distinctive contributions of Queen Elizabeth I and Winston Churchill.

All governments shape culture through education, but some do so more forcefully than others. Beginning in 2010, the South Korean

FIGURE 43-1 **Current Higher Education Graduation Rates (BA/BS), Selected Countries**

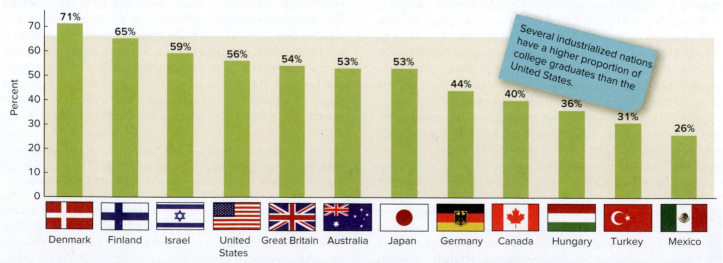

Several industrialized nations have a higher proportion of college graduates than the United States.

Country	Percent
Denmark	71%
Finland	65%
Israel	59%
United States	56%
Great Britain	54%
Australia	53%
Japan	53%
Germany	44%
Canada	40%
Hungary	36%
Turkey	31%
Mexico	26%

Note: For adults ages 25 to 64 in 2013. The percentages are estimates of the eventual proportion of the entire adult population that will attain at least a college degree, given current students' rate of degree completion.
Source: Organisation for Economic Co-Operation and Development 2015c:Table A3.1. *Flags:* © admin_design/Shutterstock RF

government required publishers to submit textbooks for approval; once approved, teachers could choose from any of the books that had been deemed satisfactory. Since then, educators and scholars have protested the intrusion. In response, the government announced that it will produce a single history textbook to be used beginning in 2017. Many are concerned that coverage of both post-Korean War dictatorships and protest movements against the government over the last three generations will be excluded. The result of presenting a single version of history remains to be seen (Borowicc 2015).

Promoting Social and Political Integration

Many institutions require students in their first year or two of college to live on campus, to foster a sense of community among diverse groups. Education serves the latent function of promoting social and political integration by transforming a population composed of diverse racial, ethnic, and religious groups into a society whose members share—to some extent—a common identity. Historically, schools in the United States have played an important role in socializing the children of immigrants into the norms, values, and beliefs of the dominant culture. From a functionalist perspective, the common identity and social integration fostered by education contribute to societal stability and consensus (J. Collins 2009; Touraine 1974).

In the past, the integrative function of education was most obvious in its emphasis on promoting a common language. Immigrant children were expected to learn English. In some instances, they were even forbidden to speak their native language on school grounds. More recently, bilingualism has been defended both for its educational value and as a means of encouraging cultural diversity. However, critics argue that bilingualism undermines the social and political integration that education has traditionally promoted.

Maintaining Social Control

In performing the manifest function of transmitting knowledge, schools go far beyond teaching skills like reading, writing, and mathematics. Like other social institutions, such as the family and religion, education prepares young people to lead productive and orderly lives as adults by introducing them to the norms, values, and sanctions of the larger society.

Through the exercise of social control, schools teach students various skills and values essential to their future positions in the labor force. They learn punctuality, discipline, scheduling, and responsible work habits, as well as how to negotiate the complexities of a bureaucratic organization. As a social institution, education reflects the interests of both the family and another social institution, the economy. Students are trained for what is ahead, whether it be the assembly line or a physician's office. In effect, then, schools serve as a transitional agent of social control, bridging the gap between parents and employers in the life cycle of most individuals (Bowles and Gintis [1976] 2011; Foley 2011).

Schools direct and even restrict students' aspirations in a manner that reflects societal values and prejudices. School administrators may allocate ample funds for athletic programs but give much less support to music, art, and dance. Teachers and guidance counselors may encourage male students to pursue

© Kim Karpeles/Alamy

Schools transmit culture in traditional ways, such as through social studies lessons, as well as in some more innovative ways. Here a mural on a school in Pilsen, a Latino neighborhood in Chicago, underscores pride in the Latino heritage of the students and their families.

careers in the sciences but steer female students into careers as early childhood teachers. Such socialization into traditional gender roles can be viewed as a form of social control.

Serving as an Agent of Change

So far, we have focused on the conservative functions of education—on its role in transmitting the existing culture, promoting social and political integration, and maintaining social control. Yet education can also stimulate or bring about desired social change. Sex education classes were introduced to public schools in response to the soaring pregnancy rate among teenagers. Affirmative action in admissions—giving priority to females or minorities—has been endorsed as a means of countering racial and sexual discrimination. And Project Head Start, an early childhood program that serves nearly one million children annually, has sought to compensate for the disadvantages in school readiness experienced by children from low-income families.

These educational programs can transform and have transformed people's lives. For example, continued formal education has had a positive effect on the income people earn; median earnings rise significantly with each step up the educational ladder. Consider the significance of those increased earnings when they stretch over an entire lifetime. Obviously, racial, ethnic, and gender differences in income are also significant. Yet as significant as those inequalities are, the best indicator of a person's lifetime earnings is still the number of years of formal schooling that person has received (see Figure 43-2) (Julian and Kominski 2011; Wessel and Banchero 2012).

Numerous sociological studies have revealed that additional years of formal schooling are also associated with openness to new ideas and liberal social and political viewpoints. Sociologist Robin Williams points out that better-educated people tend to have greater access to factual information, to hold more diverse opinions, and

© Mark Peterson/Redux Pictures

In response to a high pregnancy rate among adolescent girls, many schools now offer sex education courses that promote abstinence as well as safe sex. When schools attempt to remedy negative social trends, they are serving as an agent of social change.

to possess the ability to make subtle distinctions in analysis. Formal education stresses both the importance of qualifying statements (in place of broad generalizations) and the need at least to question (rather than simply accept) established truths and practices. The scientific method, which relies on *testing* hypotheses, reflects the questioning spirit that characterizes modern education (R. Williams et al. 1964).

■ Conflict Perspective

The functionalist perspective portrays contemporary education as a basically benign institution. For example, it argues that schools rationally sort and select students for future high-status positions, thereby meeting society's need for talented and expert personnel. In contrast, the conflict perspective views education as an instrument of elite domination. Conflict theorists point out the sharp inequalities

FIGURE 43-2 **Lifetime Earnings by Race, Gender, and Degree Level**

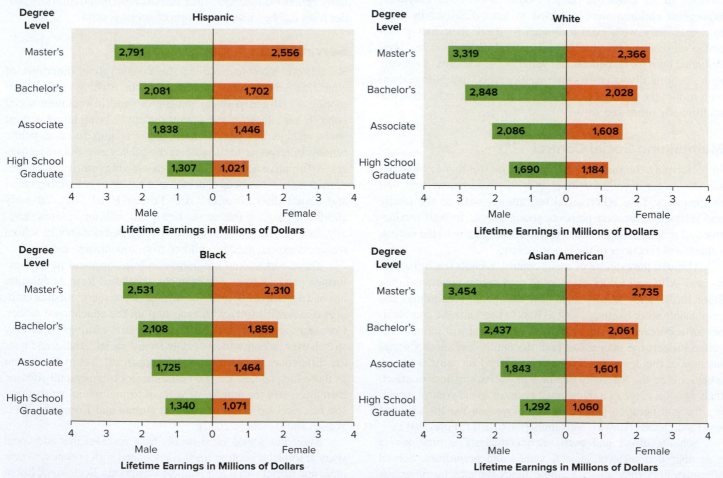

Note: Estimates for lifetime earnings for full-time, year-round workers ages 25 to 64 based on the American Community Survey for 2006–2008. Data are for Hispanics, non-Hispanic Whites, Blacks, and Asian Americans. Data points shown in thousands of dollars.
Source: Julian and Kominski 2011:6.

that exist in the educational opportunities available to different racial and ethnic groups. In 2014, the nation marked the 60th anniversary of the Supreme Court's landmark decision *Brown v. Board of Education,* which declared unconstitutional the segregation of public schools. Yet today, our schools are still characterized by racial isolation. For example, although White students account for just over half the nation's school enrollment, the typical White student attends a school where three-quarters of his or her peers are White. Fully 15 percent of Black students and 14 percent of Latino students attend what have been termed "apartheid schools," where Whites make up less than 1 percent of the enrollment. And despite the dramatic suburbanization of African American and Hispanic families in recent decades, across the nation, 80 percent of Latino students and 74 percent of Black students still attend majority non-White schools—that is, schools that are 50 to 100 percent minority (Orfield et al. 2012).

Conflict theorists also argue that the educational system socializes students into values dictated by the powerful, that schools stifle individualism and creativity in the name of maintaining order, and that the level of change they promote is relatively insignificant. From a conflict perspective, the inhibiting effects of education are particularly apparent in the "hidden curriculum" and the differential way in which status is bestowed.

The Hidden Curriculum

Schools are highly bureaucratic organizations, as we will see later. To maintain order, many teachers rely on rules and regulations. Unfortunately, the need for control and discipline can take precedence over the learning process. Teachers may focus on obedience to the rules as an end in itself, in which case students and teachers alike become victims of what Philip Jackson (1968) has called the *hidden curriculum.*

The term **hidden curriculum** refers to standards of behavior that are deemed proper by society and are taught subtly in schools. According to this curriculum, children must not speak until the teacher calls on them and must regulate their activities according to the clock or bells. In addition, they are expected to concentrate on their own work rather than to assist other students who learn more slowly. A hidden curriculum is evident in schools around the world. For example, Japanese schools offer guidance sessions that seek to improve the classroom experience and develop healthy living skills. In effect, these sessions instill values and encourage behaviors that are useful in the Japanese business world, such as self-discipline and openness to group problem solving and decision making (Okano and Tsuchiya 1999).

In a classroom that is overly focused on obedience, value is placed on pleasing the teacher and remaining quiet rather than on creative thought and academic learning. Habitual obedience to authority may result in the type of distressing behavior documented by Stanley Milgram in his classic obedience studies.

Another example of hidden curriculum, although some would argue it is not very hidden, is the marginalization in sex and relationships education in schools of anything other than heterosexual relationships. Queer theorists and others contend that young people do not receive unbiased information or, indeed, any information about lesbian, gay, and transgender lifestyles. While this is no longer the case in some school districts, others have chosen to abandon sex and relationship education altogether rather than be more inclusive in the curriculum (B. Smith 2015).

 use your sociological imagination

In what ways did the high school you attended convey the hidden curriculum of education?

Credentialism

Sixty years ago, a high school diploma was the minimum requirement for entry into the paid labor force of the United States. Today, a college diploma is virtually the bare minimum. This change reflects the process of **credentialism**—a term used to describe an increase in the lowest level of education needed to enter a field.

In recent decades, the number of occupations that are viewed as professions has risen. Credentialism is one symptom of this trend. Employers and occupational associations typically contend that such changes are a logical response to the increasing complexity of many jobs. Indeed, one study in Australia that looked at 400 occupations found such an expansion of educational certificates and titles that the jobs being obtained by graduates, especially in business, were lower level than they had been 15 years earlier. However, in many cases, employers raise the degree requirements for a position simply because all applicants have achieved the existing minimum credential (David K. Brown 2001; Hurn 1985; Karmel 2015).

Conflict theorists observe that credentialism may reinforce social inequality. Applicants from poor and minority backgrounds are especially likely to suffer from the escalation of qualifications, since they lack the financial resources needed to obtain degree after degree. In addition, upgrading of credentials serves the self-interest of the two groups most responsible for this trend. Educational institutions profit from prolonging the investment of time and money that people make by staying in school. Moreover, as C. J. Hurn (1985) has suggested, current jobholders have a stake in raising occupational requirements, since credentialism can increase the status of an occupation and lead to demands for higher pay. Max Weber anticipated this possibility as early as 1916, concluding that the "universal clamor for the creation of educational certificates in all fields makes for the formation of a privileged stratum in businesses and in offices" (Gerth and Mills 1958:240–241).

Bestowal of Status

Sociologists have long recognized that schooling is central to social stratification. Both functionalist and conflict theorists agree that education performs the important function of bestowing status. According to Kingsley Davis and Wilbert E. Moore (1945), society must distribute its members among a variety of social positions. Education can contribute to this process by sorting people into appropriate levels and courses of study that will prepare them for positions in the labor force.

As noted earlier, an increasing proportion of people in the United States are obtaining high school diplomas, college degrees, and advanced professional degrees. From a functionalist perspective, this widening bestowal of status is beneficial not only to particular recipients but to society as a whole.

Conflict theorists are far more critical of the *differential* way in which education bestows status. They stress that schools sort pupils according to their social class backgrounds. Although the educational system helps certain poor children to move into middle-class professional positions, it denies most disadvantaged children the same educational opportunities afforded to children of the affluent. In this way, schools tend to preserve social class inequalities in each new generation. Higher education in particular acts more like a sieve that sorts people out of the educated classes than a social ladder that helps all with ambition to rise (Duncan and Murnane 2014; Giroux 1988; Sacks 2007).

The status that comes with advanced training is not cheap and has been getting progressively more expensive for several decades. Over the past 50 years, average tuition and fees at community colleges have risen at a relatively modest pace that matches the inflation rate (Figure 43-3). The increases have been greater at four-year institutions. At the same time as tuition has been increasing, financial aid has become more difficult to obtain (see Box 28-2).

Even a single school can reinforce class differences by putting students in tracks. The term **tracking** refers to the practice of placing students in specific curriculum groups on the basis of their test scores and other criteria. Tracking begins very early, often in reading groups during first grade. The practice can reinforce the disadvantages that children from less affluent families may face if they haven't been exposed to reading materials, computers, and other forms of educational stimulation during their early childhood years. To ignore this connection between tracking and students' race and social class is to fundamentally misunderstand how schools perpetuate the existing social structure.

Children placed in academic tracks (with the expectation that they will attend college) typically receive text-based instruction that demands written and verbal displays of knowledge. In contrast, students in nonacademic tracks receive watered-down, slower paced instruction that aims them toward the world of work after high school. Studies of tracking show that children placed in lower tracks tend to come from low-income or one-parent households or from minority groups. The most damaging aspect of tracking is that it can become a caste system: Once students are placed into low-ability groups, they remain there and are seldom promoted to high-ability groups later on (Mehan 2015).

Conflict theorists hold that the educational inequalities produced by tracking are designed to meet the needs of modern capitalist societies. Samuel Bowles and Herbert Gintis ([1976] 2011) have argued that capitalism requires a skilled, disciplined labor force, and that the educational system of the United States is structured with that objective in mind. Citing numerous studies, they offer support for what they call the **correspondence principle.** According to this approach, schools promote the values expected of individuals in each social class and perpetuate social class divisions from one generation to the next. Thus, working-class children, assumed to be destined for subordinate positions, are likely to be placed in high school vocational and general tracks, which emphasize close supervision and compliance with authority. In contrast, young people from more affluent families are likely to be directed to college preparatory tracks, which stress leadership and decision making—the skills they are expected to need as adults (Golann 2015; McLanahan and Percheski 2008).

© Comstock/PunchStock RF

FIGURE 43-3 **Costs of Tuition, Room, and Board, 1963–2013**

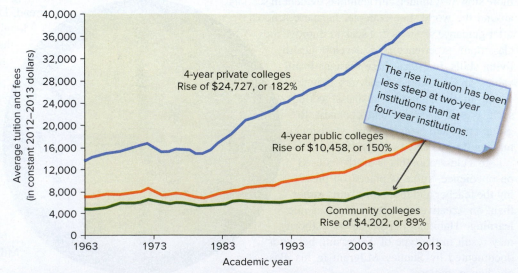

4-year private colleges
Rise of $24,727, or 182%

The rise in tuition has been less steep at two-year institutions than at four-year institutions.

4-year public colleges
Rise of $10,458, or 150%

Community colleges
Rise of $4,202, or 89%

Note: Community college data excludes private colleges. Private 4-year college data excludes for-profit colleges.
Source: National Center for Education Statistics 2015a.

Feminist Perspective

The educational system of the United States, like many other social institutions, has long been characterized by discriminatory treatment of women. In 1833, Oberlin College became the first institution of higher learning to admit female students—some 200 years after the first men's college was established. But Oberlin believed that women should aspire to become wives and mothers, not lawyers and intellectuals. In addition to attending classes, female students washed men's clothing, cared for their rooms, and served them at meals. In the 1840s, Lucy Stone, then an Oberlin undergraduate and later one of the nation's most outspoken feminist leaders, refused to write a commencement address because it would have been read to the audience by a male student.

Sexism in education shows up in many ways—in textbooks with negative stereotypes of women, counselors' pressure on female students to prepare for "women's work," and unequal funding for women's and men's athletic programs. But perhaps nowhere has educational discrimination been more evident than in the employment of teachers. The positions of university professor and college administrator, which hold relatively high status in the United States, have been generally filled by men. Public school teachers, who earn much lower salaries, have been largely female.

Women have made great strides in one area: the proportion of women who continue their schooling. As recently as 1969, twice as many men as women received college degrees; today, women outnumber men at college commencements. Moreover, women's access to graduate education and to medical, dental, and law schools has increased dramatically in the past few decades as a result of the Education Act of 1972. Box 43-1 examines the far-reaching effects of Title IX, the part of the act that concerns discrimination against women in education.

Sociology on Campus

BOX 43-1

The Debate over Title IX

Few federal policies have had such a visible effect on education as Title IX, which mandates gender equity in education in federally funded schools. Congressional amendments to the Education Act of 1972 have brought significant changes for both men and women at all levels of schooling. Title IX eliminated sex-segregated classes, prohibited sex discrimination in admissions and financial aid, and mandated that girls receive more opportunities to play sports, in proportion to their enrollment and interest.

Under this landmark legislation, to receive federal funds, a school or college must pass one of three tests. First, the numbers of male and female athletes must be proportional to the numbers of men and women enrolled at the school. Second, lacking that, the school must show a continuing history of expanding opportunities for female athletes. Or third, the school must demonstrate that the level of female participation in sports meets female students' level of interest or ability.

Today, Title IX is still one of the more controversial attempts ever made by the federal government to promote equality for all citizens. Its consequences for the funding of college athletics programs are hotly debated, while its real and lasting effects on college admissions and employment are often forgotten. Critics charge that men's

> Critics charge that men's teams have suffered from proportional funding of women's teams and athletic scholarships.

teams have suffered from proportional funding of women's teams and athletic scholarships, since schools with tight athletic budgets can expand women's sports only at the expense of men's sports. Yet from 1972, when Title IX was passed, to 2014, the number of girls participating in high school athletics jumped from 300,000 to over 3.2 million.

From the women's point of view, however, the increased funding for women's sports has benefited men in some ways. In terms of coaching and administration, men have increasingly replaced women as directors of women's sports since Title IX was passed. Today only 19 percent of collegiate women's athletic administrators are women, compared to over 90 percent in the early 1970s. No national data exists for high school sports leadership, but an analysis of Minnesota youth soccer found that only 15 percent of head coaches were women.

Sociologists caution that the social effects of sports on college campuses are not all positive. Michael A. Messner, professor of sociology at the University of Southern California, points to some troubling results of a survey by the Women's Sports Foundation. The study shows that teenage girls who play sports simply for fun have more positive body images than girls who don't play sports. But those who are "highly involved" in sports are more likely than other girls to take steroids and to become risk takers. "Everyone has tacitly agreed, it seems, to view men's sports as the standard to which women should strive to have equal access," Messner writes. He is skeptical of a system that propels a lucky few college athletes to stardom each year while leaving the majority, many of them African American, without a career or an education. Certainly that was not the kind of equal opportunity legislators envisioned when they wrote Title IX.

LET'S DISCUSS

1. Has Title IX had an effect on you personally? If so, explain. On balance, do you think the increase in women's participation in sports has been good for society as a whole?

2. How might Title IX affect the way students and the public view gender roles?

Sources: Brady 2010; Cooky and LaVoi 2012; The Economist 2013e; Messner 2002; National Federation of State High School Associations 2015; Pennington 2008; Spencer 2008; Tigay 2011.

© Photodisc/Getty Images RF

Much has been made of the superior academic achievement of girls and women. Today, researchers are beginning to examine the reasons for their comparatively strong performance in school—or to put it another way, for men's lackluster performance. Some studies suggest that men's aggressiveness, together with the fact that they do better in the workplace than women, even with less schooling, predisposes them to undervalue higher education. While the "absence of men" on many college campuses has captured headlines, it has also created a false crisis in public discourse. Few students realize their potential exclusively through formal education; other factors, such as ambition and personal talent, contribute to their success. And many students, including low-income and immigrant children, face much greater challenges than the so-called gender gap in education (Sutherland 2015).

In cultures in which traditional gender roles remain the social norm, women's education suffers appreciably. Since September 11, 2001, the growing awareness of the Taliban's repression of Afghan women has dramatized the gender disparities in education in developing nations. Research has demonstrated that women are critical to economic development and good governance, and that education is instrumental in preparing them for those roles. Educating women, especially young girls, yields high social returns by lowering birthrates and improving agricultural productivity through better management (World Bank 2016).

Interactionist Perspective

High school students know who they are—the kids who qualify for a free lunch. So stigmatized are they that in some schools, these students will buy a bit of food in the cash line or simply go without eating to avoid being labeled a "poor kid." School officials in San Francisco are so concerned about their plight that they moved to cashless cafeterias, in which everyone, rich or poor, uses a debit card (Pogash 2008).

The labeling approach suggests that if we treat people in particular ways, they may fulfill our expectations. Children who are labeled as "troublemakers" may come to view themselves as delinquents. Similarly, a dominant group's stereotyping of racial minorities may limit their opportunities to break away from expected roles.

Can the labeling process operate in the classroom? Because interactionist researchers focus on micro-level classroom dynamics, they have been particularly interested in this question. Sociologist Howard S. Becker (1952) studied public schools in low-income and affluent areas of Chicago. He noticed that administrators expected less of students from poor neighborhoods, and wondered if teachers accepted their view. A decade later, in *Pygmalion in the Classroom,* psychologist Robert Rosenthal and school principal Lenore Jacobson (1968, 1992) documented what they referred to as a **teacher-expectancy effect**—the impact that a teacher's expectations about a student's performance may have on the student's actual achievements. This effect is especially evident in the lower grades (through Grade 3).

Studies in the United States have revealed that teachers wait longer for an answer from a student they believe to be a high achiever and are more likely to give such children a second chance. In one experiment, teachers' expectations were even shown to have an impact on students' athletic achievements. Teachers obtained better athletic performance—as measured in the number of sit-ups or push-ups performed—from those students of whom they *expected* higher numbers. Despite the controversial nature of these findings, researchers continue to document the existence of the teacher-expectancy effect. Interactionists emphasize that ability alone may be less predictive of academic success than one might think (Friedrich et al. 2015; Rosenthal and Jacobson 1992:247–262).

Table 43-1 summarizes the four major theoretical perspectives on education.

© Szaijiten/Datacraft/Getty Images

In Tokyo, parents escort their daughter to an admissions interview at a highly competitive private school. Some Japanese families enroll children as young as two years of age in cram schools. Like parents in the United States, Japanese parents know that higher education bestows status.

TABLE 43-1 SOCIOLOGICAL PERSPECTIVES ON EDUCATION

Theoretical Perspective	Emphasis
Functionalist	Transmission of the dominant culture Integration of society Promotion of social norms, values, and sanctions Promotion of desirable social change
Conflict	Domination by the elite through unequal access to schooling Hidden curriculum Credentialism Bestowal of status
Interactionist	Teacher-expectancy effect
Feminist	Treatment of female students Role of women's education in economic development

[1]A few narrow plans sacrificed.

Source: A few narrow plans sacrificed.

Summary

Education is a cultural universal found in varied forms throughout the world.

1. The transmission of knowledge and bestowal of status are manifest functions of education. Among the latent functions are transmitting culture, promoting social and political integration, maintaining social control, and serving as an agent of social change.

2. In the view of conflict theorists, education serves as an instrument of elite domination by creating standards for entry into occupations, bestowing status unequally, and subordinating the role of women.

3. Although U.S. women attain higher levels of education than do men, their performance in the workplace continues to lag. In cultures that maintain traditional gender roles, education of women is critical to economic and social development.

4. Teacher expectations about a student's performance can sometimes affect the student's actual achievement.

Thinking Critically

1. How do the functions of integration and social control reinforce each other? How do they work against each other?

2. What are the functions and dysfunctions of tracking in schools? In what ways might tracking have a positive impact on the self-concepts of various students? In what ways might it have a negative impact?

Key Terms

Correspondence principle

Credentialism

Education

Hidden curriculum

Teacher-expectancy effect

Tracking

MODULE 44 | **Schools as Formal Organizations**

Nineteenth-century educators would be amazed at the scale of schools in the United States in the 21st century. The nation has about 15 million high school students today, compared to 10 million in 1961 and 5 million in 1931 (Bureau of the Census 2012c; National Center for Education Statistics 2015b).

In many respects, today's schools, when viewed as an example of a formal organization, are similar to factories, hospitals, and business firms. Like those organizations, schools do not operate autonomously; they are influenced by the market of potential students. This statement is especially true of private schools, but could have broader impact if acceptance of voucher plans and other school choice programs increases. The parallels between schools and other types of formal organizations will become more apparent as we examine the bureaucratic nature of schools, teaching as an occupation, and the student subculture (Bidwell 2001; Diehl and McFarland 2015).

● Bureaucratization of Schools

It simply is not possible for a single teacher to transmit culture and skills to children of varying ages who will enter many diverse occupations. The growing number of students being served by school systems and the greater degree of specialization required within a technologically complex society have combined to bureaucratize schools.

Max Weber noted five basic characteristics of bureaucracy, all of which are evident in the vast majority of schools, whether at the elementary, secondary, or even college level:

1. **Division of labor.** Specialized experts teach particular age levels and specific subjects. Public elementary and secondary schools now employ instructors whose sole responsibility is to work with children with learning disabilities or physical impairments.

2. **Hierarchy of authority.** Each employee of a school system is responsible to a higher authority. Teachers must report to principals and assistant principals and may also be supervised by department heads. Principals are answerable to a superintendent of schools, and the superintendent is hired and fired by a board of education.

3. **Written rules and regulations.** Teachers and administrators must conform to numerous rules and regulations in the performance of their duties. This bureaucratic trait can become dysfunctional; the time invested in completing required forms could instead be spent in preparing lessons or conferring with students.

4. **Impersonality.** As class sizes have swelled at schools and universities, it has become more difficult for teachers to give personal attention to each student. In fact, bureaucratic

norms may actually encourage teachers to treat all students in the same way, despite the fact that students have distinctive personalities and learning needs.

5. **Employment based on technical qualifications.** At least in theory, the hiring of instructors is based on professional competence and expertise. Promotions are normally dictated by written personnel policies; people who excel may be granted lifelong job security through tenure.

Functionalists take a generally positive view of the bureaucratization of education. Teachers can master the skills needed to work with a specialized clientele, since they no longer are expected to cover a broad range of instruction. The chain of command within schools is clear. Students are presumably treated in an unbiased fashion because of uniformly applied rules. Finally, security of position protects teachers from unjustified dismissal. In general, then, functionalists stress that the bureaucratization of education increases the likelihood that students, teachers, and administrators will be dealt with fairly—that is, on the basis of rational and equitable criteria.

In contrast, conflict theorists argue that the trend toward more centralized education has harmful consequences for disadvantaged people. The standardization of educational curricula, including textbooks, will generally reflect the values, interests, and lifestyles of the most powerful groups in our society, and may ignore those of racial and ethnic minorities. In addition, the disadvantaged, more so than the affluent, will find it difficult to sort through complex educational bureaucracies and to organize effective lobbying groups. Therefore, in the view of conflict theorists, low-income and minority parents will have even less influence over citywide and statewide educational administrators than they have over local school officials (Bowles and Gintis [1976] 2011; Katz 1971).

Sometimes schools can seem overwhelmingly bureaucratic, with the effect of stifling rather than nourishing intellectual

© Andy Sacks/Getty Images

Despite efforts to establish positive relationships among students and between teachers and students, many young people view their schools as impersonal institutions.

curiosity in students. This concern has led many parents and policymakers to push for school choice programs—allowing parents to choose the school that suits their children's needs, and forcing schools to compete for their "customers."

In the United States, another significant countertrend to the bureaucratization of schools is the availability of education over the Internet. Increasingly, colleges and universities are reaching out via the web, offering entire courses and even majors to students in the comfort of their homes. Online curricula provide flexibility for working students and others who may have difficulty attending conventional classes because of distance or disability. Research on this type of learning is just beginning, so the question of whether teacher–student contact can thrive online remains to be settled. Computer-mediated instruction may also have an impact on instructors' status as employees, which we will discuss next, as well as on alternative forms of education like homeschooling.

💡 use your **sociological imagination**

How would you make your school less bureaucratic? What would it be like?

🟢 Teachers: Employees and Instructors

Whether they serve as instructors of preschoolers or of graduate students, teachers are employees of formal organizations with bureaucratic structures. There is an inherent conflict in serving as a professional in a bureaucracy. The organization follows the principles of hierarchy and expects adherence to its rules, but professionalism demands the individual responsibility of the practitioner. This conflict is very real for teachers, who experience all the positive and negative consequences of working in bureaucracies.

A teacher undergoes many perplexing stresses every day. While teachers' academic assignments have become more specialized, the demands on their time remain diverse and contradictory. Conflicts arise from serving as an instructor, a disciplinarian, and an employee of a school district at the same time. In too many schools, discipline means dealing with violence (see Box 44-1). Burnout is one result of these stresses: between a quarter and a third of new teachers quit within their first three years, and as many as half leave poor urban schools in their first five years (Wallis 2008).

Given these difficulties, does teaching remain an attractive profession in the United States? In 2015, 2.4 percent of male first-year college students and 5.1 percent of women indicated that they were interested in becoming either elementary or high school teachers. These figures are dramatically lower than the 11 percent of first-year male students and 37 percent of first-year female students who held those occupational aspirations in 1966 (Egan et al. 2016; Pryor et al. 2007:122, 76).

Taking Sociology to Work

Diane Belcher Gray, *Assistant Director of Volunteer Services, New River Community College*

Courtesy of Diane Belcher Gray

Not until Diane Belcher Gray enrolled at New River Community College in Dublin, Virginia, did she realize that social work had always been part of her daily life. To this mother of two teenagers, helping people in need was something she just did, without even thinking about it.

Today, as assistant director of Volunteer Services at New River, Belcher Gray assists Partners for Success, a mentoring program that matches struggling students with people in the community who have the time and energy to help them. With the director, she recruits and trains a "talent bank" of mentors, matches the mentors with student partners, and develops support programs for students experiencing problems with child care, transportation, and other necessities. The program's goal is to develop confident and successful learners who can take charge of their own studies.

Before she moved to Volunteer Services, Belcher Gray was an administrative assistant in Workforce Development at New River, where she helped youths who lack direction and workers laid off from local factories to develop more marketable skills. In that job, she facilitated new students' transition to college, helping them to register and apply for financial aid and connecting them with professors in their fields of interest. Belcher Gray also worked directly with the administration to develop a special fast-track program for laid-off workers.

As in all human services jobs, people skills, particularly sensitivity and compassion, are of paramount importance in Belcher Gray's work. An understanding of the social and economic forces that affect the larger society is also essential. Belcher Gray credits her sociology courses with helping her to "engage where needed." "Sociology exposed me to other people's situations and the role of society in creating them," she explains. "It helped me look beyond the individual level to understand societal impacts and solutions."

Asked to advise current sociology majors, Belcher Gray says, "Drink it up, try and take it all in, relate it to the real world. Take notice of current cultural and economic conditions, understanding that when you attempt to 'fix' one part of society you must also be aware of how that will affect other parts of society."

LET'S DISCUSS

1. Have you, like Diane Belcher Gray, realized through education that something you were doing without thinking about it has helped to prepare you for employment? Explain.

2. Do some research on Dublin, Virginia, and the surrounding area. What kind of economy does this community have? Relate the layoffs the community has been experiencing to larger societal forces.

Undoubtedly, economic considerations enter into students' feelings about the attractiveness of teaching. In 2015, the average salary for all public elementary and secondary school teachers in the United States was reported at $57,379, placing teachers somewhere near the average of all the nation's wage earners. In most other industrialized countries, teachers' salaries are higher in relation to the general standard of living. Of course, teachers' salaries vary considerably from state to state (Figure 44-1), and even more from one school district to another. Nevertheless, the economic reward for teaching is minuscule compared to some career options: the CEO of a major corporation makes more money in a day than the average teacher makes in a year.

The status of any job reflects several factors, including the level of education required, financial compensation, and the respect given the occupation by society. The teaching profession (see Table 27-1) is feeling pressure in all three of these areas. First, the level of formal schooling required for teaching remains high, and the public has begun to call for new competency examinations. Second, the statistics just cited demonstrate that teachers' salaries are significantly lower than those of many professionals and skilled workers. Third, the overall prestige of the teaching profession has declined in the past decade. Many teachers have become disappointed and frustrated and have left the educational world for careers in other professions (Banchero 2014).

Signe Wilkinson Editorial Cartoon used with the permission of Signe Wilkinson, the Washington Post Writers Group and the Cartoonist Group. All rights reserved.

From preschool through high school, teachers face a variety of challenges, including preparing students for standardized tests.

Student Subcultures

An important latent function of education relates directly to student life: schools provide for students' social and recreational needs. Education helps toddlers and young children to develop interpersonal skills that are essential during adolescence and adulthood. In their high school and college years, students may

Violence in the Schools

Littleton, Colorado; Red Lake, Minnesota; Jonesboro, Arkansas; West Paducah, Kentucky; Newtown, Connecticut; Edinboro, Pennsylvania; Springfield, Oregon—these are now more than just the names of small towns and medium-size cities. They resonate with the sound of gunshots, or kids killing kids on school grounds. As a result, people no longer perceive schools to be safe havens. But how accurate is that impression?

Studies of school violence put the recent spate of school killings in perspective:

- 11 homicides of children ages 5 to 18 occurred at school during the 2011–2012 year.
- Less than 1 percent of youth homicides occur at school.
- About 9 percent of teachers report being threatened with injury or physically attacked by a student from their school.

Schools, then, are safer than neighborhoods, but people are still unnerved by the perception of an alarming rise in school violence generated by heavy media coverage of recent incidents. Some conflict theorists object to the huge outcry about recent violence in schools. After all, they note, violence in and around inner-city schools has a long history. It seems that only when middle-class White children are the victims does school violence become

a plank on the national policy agenda. When violence hits the middle class, the problem is viewed not as an extension of delinquency but a structural issue in need of legislative remedies such as gun control.

Feminists observe that virtually all the offenders in these incidents are male, and in some instances, such as the case in Jonesboro, the victims are disproportionately female. The precipitating factor in the violence is often a broken-off dating relationship—yet another example of the violence of men against women (or in this case, boys against girls).

Increasingly, efforts to prevent school violence focus on the ways in which the socialization of young people contributes to violence. For example, the American Medical Association has invested in a violence-prevention curriculum for elementary school students that teaches social skills related to anger management, impulse control, and empathy. More recently, school safety was seen as one part of broader societal concerns about violence. Today the Department of Homeland

> A child has a less than one in a million chance of being killed in school.

Security is assisting schools in "hardening" facilities against potential intruders.

Some people believe that a key ingredient in the prevention of violence, in and out of school, is greater parental supervision of and responsibility for their children. In her book *A Tribe Apart,* Patricia Hersch documents the lives of eight teens growing up in a Virginia suburb over a three-year period. Her conclusion: children need meaningful adult relationships in their lives. Former Secretary of Education Richard Riley cites studies showing that youths who feel connected to their parents and schools are less likely than others to engage in high-risk behaviors.

LET'S DISCUSS

1. Has a shooting or other violent episode ever occurred at your school? If so, how did students react? Do you feel safer at school than at home, as experts say you are?

2. What steps have administrators at your school taken to prevent violence? Have they been effective, or should other steps be taken?

Sources: Centers for Disease Control and Prevention 2015; Department of Education 2016; Department of Homeland Security 2016; Donahue et al. 1998; Hersch 1998.

---

meet future husbands and wives and establish lifelong friendships. It is important to remember that these informal aspects of schools, community colleges, and universities do not exist independently of schools' explicit educational functions. Furthermore, informal social systems can be as important as the academic system in determining students' positive and negative outcomes (Crosnoe 2011).

When people observe high schools, community colleges, or universities from the outside, students appear to constitute a cohesive, uniform group. However, the student subculture is actually quite complex and diverse. High school cliques and social groups may crop up according to race, social class, physical attractiveness, placement in courses, athletic ability, and leadership roles in the school and community. In his classic community study of "Elmtown," August B. Hollingshead (1975) found some 259 distinct cliques in a single high school. The cliques, whose average size was five, were centered on the school itself, on recreational activities, and on religious and community groups. Student cliques and subcultures can become so powerful that educators may be warned to make sure staff and teachers are not somehow recruited into one group or another (Gruenert and Whitaker 2015).

Amid these close-knit and often rigidly segregated cliques, gay, lesbian, and transgender students are particularly vulnerable.

Peer group pressure to conform is intense at this age. Although coming to terms with one's sexuality is difficult for all adolescents, it can be downright dangerous for those whose sexual identity does not conform to societal expectations.

© Andrew Holbrooke/The Image Works

Student subcultures are more diverse today than in the past. Many adults are returning to college to obtain further education, advance their careers, or change their line of work.

FIGURE 44-1 **Average Salary for Teachers**

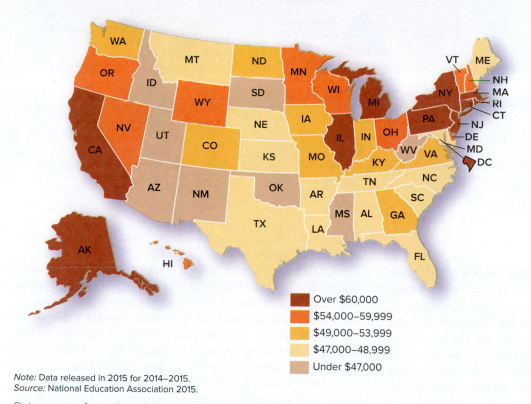

■	Over $60,000
■	$54,000–59,999
■	$49,000–53,999
■	$47,000–48,999
■	Under $47,000

Note: Data released in 2015 for 2014–2015.
Source: National Education Association 2015.

State averages for teacher salaries range from a low of $40,661 in South Dakota to a high of $77,628 in New York.

2. The *academic* subculture identifies with the intellectual concerns of the faculty and values knowledge for its own sake.

3. The *vocational* subculture is interested primarily in career prospects and views college as a means of obtaining degrees that are essential for advancement.

4. Finally, the *nonconformist* subculture is hostile to the college environment and seeks ideas that may or may not relate to academic studies. This group may find outlets through campus publications or issue-oriented groups.

Each college student is eventually exposed to these competing subcultures and must determine which (if any) seems most in line with his or her feelings and interests.

The typology used by the researchers reminds us that school is a complex social organization—almost like a community with different neighborhoods. Of course, these four subcultures are not the only ones evident on college campuses in the United States. For example, one might find subcultures of veterans from conflicts in Iraq and Afghanistan or of former full-time homemakers at community colleges and four-year commuter institutions. And as more and more students from minority groups decide to continue their formal education beyond high school, subcultures based on race and ethnicity will become more evident. As Figure 44-2 shows, college campuses are becoming increasingly diverse.

Sociologist Joe R. Feagin has studied a distinctive collegiate subculture: Black students at predominantly White universities. These students must function academically and socially within universities where there are few Black faculty members or administrators, where harassment of Blacks by campus police is common, and where curricula place little emphasis on Black contributions. Feagin (1989:11) suggests that "for minority students life at a predominantly White college or university means long-term encounters with pervasive whiteness." In Feagin's view, Black students at such institutions experience both blatant and subtle racial discrimination, which has a cumulative impact that can seriously damage the students' confidence (see also Feagin et al. 1996).

Teachers and administrators are becoming more sensitized to these issues. Perhaps more important, some schools are creating gay–straight alliances (GSAs), school-sponsored support groups that bring gay teens together with sympathetic straight peers. Begun in Los Angeles in 1984, these programs numbered nearly 3,000 nationwide in 2005; most were founded after the murder of Matthew Shepard, a gay college student, in 1998. In some districts parents have objected to these organizations, but the same court rulings that protect the right of conservative Bible groups to meet on school grounds also protect GSAs. In 2003, the gay–straight movement reached a milestone when the New York City public schools moved an in-school program for gays, bisexuals, and transgender students to a separate school. The Harvey Milk High School was named in memory of San Francisco's first openly gay city supervisor, who was assassinated in 1978 (Gay, Lesbian and Straight Education Network 2016).

We can find a similar diversity of student groups at the college level. Sociologists have identified four distinctive subcultures among college students (Clark and Trow 1966; Horowitz 1987; Sperber 2000):

1. The *collegiate* subculture focuses on having fun and socializing. These students define what constitutes a "reasonable" amount of academic work (and what amount of work is "excessive" and leads to being labeled a "grind"). Members of the collegiate subculture have little commitment to academic pursuits. Athletes often fit into this subculture.

 use your **sociological imagination**

What distinctive subcultures can you identify at your college?

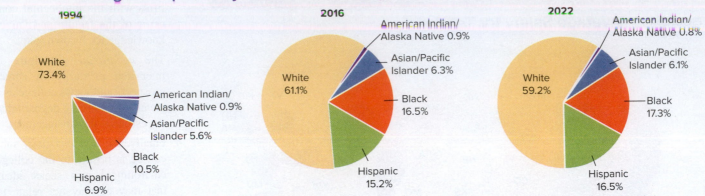

FIGURE 44-2 College Campuses by Race and Ethnicity: Then, Now, and in the Future

1994
White 73.4%
American Indian/Alaska Native 0.9%
Asian/Pacific Islander 5.6%
Black 10.5%
Hispanic 6.9%

2016
American Indian/Alaska Native 0.9%
Asian/Pacific Islander 6.3%
White 61.1%
Black 16.5%
Hispanic 15.2%

2022
American Indian/Alaska Native 0.8%
Asian/Pacific Islander 6.1%
White 59.2%
Black 17.3%
Hispanic 16.5%

Note: Percentages do not add to 100 due to rounding error. Nonresident aliens whose race/ethnicity is unknown excluded. White and Black racial categories include non-Hispanic only.
Source: Hussar and Bailey 2011:Table 29; 2014:Table 29.

Homeschooling

When most people think of school, they think of bricks and mortar and the teachers, administrators, and other employees who staff school buildings. But for an increasing number of students in the United States, home is the classroom and the teacher is a parent. About 1.7 million students are now being educated at home. That is about 3 percent of the K–12 school population. For these students, the issues of bureaucratization and social structure are less significant than they are for public school students.

In the 1800s, after the establishment of public schools, families that taught their children at home lived in isolated environments or held strict religious views that were at odds with the secular environment of public schools. But today, homeschooling is attracting a broader range of families not necessarily tied to organized religion. Poor academic quality, peer pressure, and school violence are motivating many parents to teach their children at home. In addition, some immigrants choose homeschooling as a way to ease their children's transition to a new society. For example, the growing Arab American population recently joined the movement toward homeschooling (MacFarquhar 2008; National Center for Education Statistics 2015c).

While supporters of homeschooling believe children can do just as well or better in homeschools as in public schools, critics counter that because homeschooled children are isolated from the larger community, they lose an important chance to improve their socialization skills. But proponents of homeschooling claim their children benefit from contact with others besides their own age group. They also see homeschools as a good alternative for children who suffer from attention-deficit/hyperactivity disorder (ADHD) and learning disorders (LDs). Such children often do better in smaller classes, which present fewer distractions to disturb their concentration.

Quality control is an issue in homeschooling. While homeschooling is legal in all 50 states, 12 states require no notification that a child will be homeschooled, and another 14 require notification only, with no specification of subjects taught. Other states may require parents to submit their children's curricula or test scores for professional evaluation. Despite the lack of uniform standards, a research review by the Home School Legal Defense Association (2016; Ray 2009) reports that homeschooled students score higher than others on standardized tests, in every subject and every grade.

Who are the people who are running homeschools? In general, they tend to have higher-than-average incomes and educational levels. Most are two-parent families, and their children watch less television than average—both factors that are likely to support superior educational performance. The same students, with the same support from their parents, would probably do just as well in the public schools. As research has repeatedly shown, small classes are better than big classes, and strong parental and community involvement is key (R. Cox 2003:28).

Whatever the controversy over homeschooling in the United States, it is much less serious than in some other nations. In 2010, the U.S. Immigration and Naturalization Service began granting political asylum to German families who homeschool their children, in violation of their country's constitution. German parents can be fined and imprisoned for homeschooling their children (Francis 2010).

Charter schools are another area of controversy in the educational system. In the Social Policy section that follows we consider the significance of these schools and whether parents should be able to enroll their children in them.

Discontent with public schools stretches back for decades. In the 1970s, "classrooms without walls" were supposed to open up the curriculum to students' creativity. In 2002, the No Child Left Behind initiative was supposed to guarantee that all students would learn the basics. Although test scores inched up a bit in response, critics complained that schools were becoming too test-oriented, and scores on interactive science and math tests sank compared to those in other nations. Meanwhile, the charter school movement had been gathering strength since these schools first appeared in Minnesota in 1992 (Berends 2015; K. Clark 2010).

Charter schools are experimental schools that are developed and managed by individuals, groups of parents, or an educational management organization. Although these schools are typically considered to be public schools because they are publicly financed, they are administered outside the official public school system. Their charters (legal contracts) permit them to establish their own rules, curricula, and admissions and professional standards. Within their communities, however, charter schools must still abide by prevailing standards for health, public safety, and equal opportunity (Renzulli and Roscigno 2007).

Looking at the Issue

By 2014, about 2.6 million children were enrolled in charter schools in 42 different states (Figure 44-3). Advocates of charter schools claim that they offer parents accountability for their children's education. In effect, charter schools compete with public schools, offering an alternative that was once available only to the wealthy. However, the proportion of poor children in charter schools is now comparable to that in traditional public schools. By 2011, 53 percent of charter school students were eligible for free or reduced-price lunch, compared to 50 percent of the nation's students as a whole (Berends 2015).

MAPPING LIFE NATIONWIDE

FIGURE 44-3 **Charter Schools**

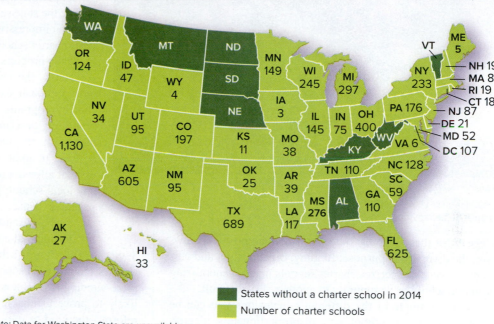

WA

OR 124

ID 47

MT

ND

MN 149

VT

ME 5

NH 19

NV 34

UT 95

WY 4

SD

WI 245

MI 297

NY 233

MA 81

RI 19

CT 18

CA 1,130

CO 197

NE

IA 3

IL 145

IN 75

OH 400

PA 176

NJ 87

DE 21

AZ 605

NM 95

KS 11

MO 38

KY

WV

VA 6

MD 52

DC 107

OK 25

AR 39

TN 110

NC 128

SC 59

AK 27

TX 689

LA 117

MS 276

AL

GA 110

HI 33

FL 625

■ States without a charter school in 2014
■ Number of charter schools

Note: Data for Washington State are unavailable.
Source: National Alliance for Public Charter Schools 2015.

Applying Sociology

Functionalists argue that charter schools meet society's need for education while serving a diverse student body. Despite criticism that charter schools are elitist institutions that serve the children of privileged White families, data show that 55 percent of the students enrolled in these schools are African American or Latino. More than a third of them qualify for free or reduced price lunches (Gabriel 2010).

Although charter schools are publicly financed, most are not unionized. From a conflict perspective, charter schools do not represent teachers' interests well and are contributing to the decline of labor unions. Partly in response to this concern, public school districts in Denver, Detroit, Milwaukee, Boston, and Minnesota have empowered teachers to create their own charter schools (Dillon 2008; Hu 2010).

Because the charter school movement is a comparatively recent one, we do not have much research on the long-term impact of charter versus noncharter schools. Of course, there is great variation within the same city much less the same state. News stories about individual charter schools and high-profile advocates like the Bill and Melinda Gates Foundation

—Continued

© Charlie Varley/Sipa USA/Newscom

The children of Lycée Français de la Nouvelle-Orléans on their first day at the new campus of their charter school.

suggest that these schools' outcomes are quite positive. However, the diversity in purpose, funding, organization, and curriculum that characterizes charter schools makes generalizing from one school or community to another very difficult.

As an example of the different conclusions that can be reached, many top school lists disproportionately identify charter schools as outperforming noncharter schools. Yet research released in 2012 shows that at least a third of charter schools do *worse* than the public schools they replaced. However, research done at Stanford University on charter schools in 26 states shows that charter school students had an equivalent of eight extra days of learning each year beyond their peers in traditional schools (CREDO 2013; Berends 2015; Lubienski and Weitzel 2012).

Initiating Policy

In the United States, unlike virtually all other industrial nations, school policy is driven at the local level. Although the federal government may encourage certain policies through public funding, and may dictate certain standards like nondiscrimination, school policy is created largely at the community level following statewide standards. Even in the absence of any specific policies, charter schools have taken their strongest hold in urban areas. More than 40 percent of schoolchildren in New Orleans, Detroit, Flint, the District of Columbia, Kansas City, and Gary, Indiana are enrolled in charter schools. In the wake of hurricane Katrina, New Orleans, after struggling for years with a "recovery school district," moved toward a charter school model. School performance, assisted by funding from sources outside the state seeking to get the city back on its feet, has been impressive. Success has not been uniform, as some charter schools were not renewed for insufficient academic progress (Bankston 2013; Khadaroo 2014).

Today, the charter school movement is not the only approach to educational reform; other school choice programs are available to families. Homeschooling, described earlier in this chapter, could be viewed as the most complete alternative to public schools. In addition, some cities offer parents vouchers that allow them, in effect, to send their children to any local school, public, private, or religious, at taxpayers' expense.

Karl Alexander (1997:17) eloquently noted in his presidential address to the Southern Sociological Society, "The charter school movement, with its 'let 1,000 flowers bloom' philosophy, is certain to yield an occasional prize-winning rose. But is . . . [this approach to school choice] likely to prove a reliable guide for broad-based, systematic reform—the kind of reform that will carry the great mass of our children closer to where we want them to be? I hardly think so." Indeed, with such diversity in learning environments found among thousands of charter schools, the jury is still out on their effectiveness. As with most educational institutions, one cannot assume quality just based on a certain structure, size, affiliation, or funding source.

TAKE THE ISSUE WITH YOU

1. Do you have any experience with educational reform, either as a student yourself or as a parent? If so, describe the changes that you witnessed. Were they successful in improving educational outcomes?

2. Which type of school choice program, if any, would you favor—homeschooling, charter schools, or school vouchers? Explain your choice.

3. Are you concerned about educational standards in the United States? If so, do you think schools should be reformed at the local level? Should the federal government become more involved in school reform?

Summary

Most schools in the United States are organized like formal organizations such as factories and hospitals.

1. Weber's five basic characteristics of bureaucracies are all evident in schools.

2. Teachers are professionals who serve as part of a bureaucracy. There is an inherent conflict in combining those two different roles.

3. Schools provide for students' social and emotional needs as well as their educational needs. Student subcultures within high schools and colleges are complex and varied.

4. Homeschooling has become a viable alternative to traditional public and private schools. In some countries homeschooling is illegal.

5. **Charter schools**—experimental schools that are developed and managed by individuals, groups of parents, or an educational management organization—are one of several recent attempts to reform the public school system in the United States. Although charter schools are popular with parents, research shows that about a third of them do worse than the public schools they replaced.

Thinking Critically

1. Select two functions of education and suggest how they could be fulfilled through homeschooling.

2. What student subcultures can you identify on your campus? Which have the highest and lowest social status? How would functionalists, conflict theorists, and interactionists view the existence of student subcultures on a college campus?

Key Terms

Charter school

Mastering This Chapter

© Martin Shields/Alamy Stock Photo

taking sociology with you

1 Attend a meeting of a local Parent Teacher Association (PTA). What issues are parents talking about? Describe their concerns using one or more sociological perspectives.

2 Make a list of the student subcultures on your campus, then describe them using the concepts you learned in Module 12. Do any of these subcultures serve as outgroups for other subcultures?

3 Does your school have a gay–straight alliance? If so, speak with one of the officers. What are members doing to reduce prejudice and foster better relations among gay and straight students? Explain their approach using sociological theory.

key terms

Charter school An experimental school that is developed and managed by individuals, groups of parents, or educational management organizations.

Correspondence principle The tendency of schools to promote the values expected of individuals in each social class and to perpetuate social class divisions from one generation to the next.

Credentialism An increase in the lowest level of education needed to enter a field.

Education A formal process of learning in which some people consciously teach, while others adopt the social role of learner.

Hidden curriculum Standards of behavior that are deemed proper by society and are taught subtly in schools.

Teacher-expectancy effect The impact that a teacher's expectations about a student's performance may have on the student's actual achievements.

Tracking The practice of placing students in specific curriculum groups on the basis of their test scores and other criteria.

self-quiz

Read each question carefully and then select the best answer.

1. Which sociological perspective emphasizes that the common identity and social integration fostered by education contribute to overall societal stability and consensus?
   a. the functionalist perspective
   b. the conflict perspective
   c. the interactionist perspective
   d. labeling theory

2. Which one of the following was introduced into school systems to promote social change?
   a. sex education classes
   b. affirmative action programs
   c. Project Head Start
   d. all of the above

3. The correspondence principle was developed by
   a. Max Weber.
   b. Karl Marx and Friedrich Engels.
   c. Samuel Bowles and Herbert Gintis.
   d. James Thurber.

4. The student subculture that is hostile to the college environment and seeks out ideas that may or may not relate to studies is called the
   a. collegiate subculture.
   b. academic subculture.
   c. vocational subculture.
   d. nonconformist subculture.

5. Most recent research on ability grouping raises questions about its
   a. effectiveness, especially for lower-achieving students.
   b. failure to improve the prospects of higher-achieving students.
   c. ability to improve the prospects of lower- and higher-achieving students.
   d. both a and b

6. The most basic *manifest* function of education is
   a. transmitting knowledge.
   b. transmitting culture.

   c. maintaining social control.
   d. serving as an agent of change.

7. Sixty years ago, a high school diploma was the minimum requirement for entry into the paid labor force of the United States. Today, a college diploma is virtually the bare minimum. This change reflects the process of
   a. tracking.
   b. credentialism.
   c. the hidden curriculum.
   d. the correspondence principle.

8. Samuel Bowles and Herbert Gintis have argued that capitalism requires a skilled, disciplined labor force and that the educational system of the United States is structured with that objective in mind. Citing numerous studies, they offer support for what they call
   a. tracking.
   b. credentialism.
   c. the correspondence principle.
   d. the teacher-expectancy effect.

9. The teacher-expectancy effect is most closely associated with
   a. the functionalist perspective.
   b. the conflict perspective.
   c. the interactionist perspective.
   d. anomie theory.

10. Sociologist Max Weber noted five basic characteristics of bureaucracy, all of which are evident in the vast majority of schools, whether at the elementary, secondary, or even college level. Which of the following is not one of them?
    a. division of labor
    b. written rules and regulations
    c. impersonality
    d. shared decision making

11. The _____ perspective stresses the importance of education in transmitting culture, maintaining social control, and promoting social change.

12. In the past, the integrative function of education was most obvious through its emphasis on promoting a common _____.

13. The _____ subculture identifies with the intellectual concerns of the faculty and values knowledge for its own sake.

14. A _____ _____ is an experimental school that is developed and managed outside the public school system.

15. Women's education tends to suffer in those cultures with traditional _____ _____.

16. Schools perform a variety of _____ functions, such as transmitting culture, promoting social and political integration, and maintaining social control.

17. Sociologist _____ _____ points out that better-educated people tend to have greater access to information, to hold more diverse opinions, and to possess the ability to make subtle distinctions in analysis.

18. The term _____ _____ refers to standards of behavior that are deemed proper by society and are taught subtly in schools. For example, children must not speak until the teacher calls on them and must regulate their activities according to the clock or the bell.

19. _____ is the practice of placing students in specific curriculum groups on the basis of their test scores and other criteria.

20. Of the four distinctive subcultures among college students discussed in the text, the _____ subculture is interested primarily in career prospects, and views college as a means of obtaining degrees that are essential for advancement.

Answers

1 (a); 2 (d); 3 (c); 4 (d); 5 (a); 6 (a); 7 (b); 8 (c); 9 (c); 10 (d); 11 functionalist; 12 language; 13 academic; 14 charter school; 15 gender roles; 16 latent; 17 Robin Williams; 18 hidden curriculum; 19 Tracking; 20 vocational

15 Religion

© Jacob Silberberg/Panos Pictures

Religion is expressed in a variety of social settings. At this Christian rock festival in New Hampshire, fans pray in response to the music.

© Ira C. Roberts/Chad Enterprises Corporation

Did you have religious toys when you were young? If so, how did you play with them, and what did you learn?

Nikki Bado-Fralick and Rebecca Sachs Norris have spent years studying religious toys and their sociological meaning.

"There are many types of religious toys: stuffed torahs; Moses, David, and Jesus and the Tomb action figures; Noah's ark collections; and Resurrection Eggs, which supplement a young child's Easter book. "Lead your kids on a fun, faith-filled Easter egg hunt this year—one that teaches them about Jesus' death and resurrection! Each egg carton is filled with a dozen colorful plastic eggs. Pop them open and find miniature symbols of the Easter story inside." One of the dozen plastic eggs contains a crown of thorns, another is empty, representing the disappearance of the body of Jesus from the tomb, and pointing to his resurrection. Muslim toys include a mosque building set, mosque jewelry cases, and a prayer practice chart. Jewish toys include dreidels, wooden Shabbat sets, toy sukkahs, and a Plush Plagues Bag that includes "all 10 Plagues!"

Religious dolls are part of this wonderland of sacred fun. There are plush and plastic talking Bible dolls, pumped-up Christian action figures, dolls designed to support a Jewish girl's religious identity and conform to religious requirements, goddess dolls designed for affluent young feminists, talking Muslim dolls that teach Arabic phrases, and "anti-Barbies"—Muslim dolls deliberately designed to compete with Barbie for the hearts and minds of young girls. There are plush Buddha and Siva dolls, and cuddly Jesus and Esther dolls as well.

Numerous card games and puzzles teach a variety of languages, including Hebrew, Arabic, and Punjabi. The Christian Book Distributors website not only offers religiously themed educational materials, they also offer nonreligious toys that appeal to parents with religious consciences who may be looking for nonviolent toys, such as a food groups toy with hand-painted pieces in four wooden crates, a pizza party game with different toppings, and a car towing game.

Not all religious toys are meant for the edification of the young. Many religious games and toys are satirical or simply products meant to be amusing enough to sell in an era where we are oversatiated with things, and any cultural phenomenon is fair game for marketing purposes. These items amuse or appall us, depending on how clever or offensive the item is, and for whom it is intended. . . .

Games and toys not only transmit cultural values but reflect them as well. . . . Games and religion have a long and complex history—they were used for divination and gambling, for this-worldly satire, and in the afterlife. Games were objects and methods used to interpret divine powers and influence supernatural forces. These religious and magical functions reflect the presence and movement of the sacred in the material world, indicators of a complex whole rather than a dualism where sacred and ordinary occupy separate realms. Contemporary religious games have their roots in ancient practices, but their flavor—their style and substance—as well as their commercial focus reveal a specifically twenty-first century American form of religiosity. "

Contemporary religious games have their roots in ancient practices, but their flavor—their style and substance—as well as their commercial focus reveal a specifically twenty-first century American form of religiosity.

(Bado-Fralick and Norris 2010:7–8, 29–30)

In this excerpt from *Toying with God: The World of Religious Games and Dolls,* Bado-Fralick and Norris consider how religiously themed toys and games reflect both popular and religious culture. Depending on their purpose and design, the authors note, as well as on the social context in which they are used, these dolls and board games can either reinforce or undermine organized religion. Their impact on the children who play with them parallels the broader influence of religion on society. Despite the much-publicized decline of organized religion over the past century, even a casual observer can see that religion still permeates our social environment. As a result, nonbelievers are influenced by believers, whether they want to be or not. Similarly, believers are influenced by nonbelievers and by those of different faiths, despite any attempts they may make to screen out other points of view.

Indeed, religion plays a major role in people's lives, and religious practices of some sort are evident in every society. That makes religion a cultural universal, along with other common practices or beliefs found in every culture, such as dancing, food preparation, the family, and personal names. At present, an estimated 4 billion people belong to the world's many religious faiths.

What social purposes does religion serve? Does religion help to hold society together or foster social change? Do public schools offer everyone a way up the socioeconomic ladder, or do they reinforce divisions among social classes? We will begin this chapter with a discussion of the sociological perspective on religion, followed by an overview of the world's major religions.

We'll explore religion's role in social integration, social support, social change, and social control. Then we'll examine three important components of religious behavior—belief, ritual, and experience—as well as the basic forms of religious organization, including new religious movements. Finally, in the Social Policy section we'll address the subject of religion in the schools.

● Durkheim and the Importance of Religion

How do sociologists study religion? The same way we study other social institutions such as education or politics. If a group believes that it is being directed by a "vision from God," sociologists do not attempt to prove or disprove the revelation. Instead, they assess the effects of the religious experience on the group. What sociologists are interested in is the social impact of religion on individuals and institutions.

Émile Durkheim was perhaps the first sociologist to recognize the critical importance of religion in human societies. He saw its appeal for the individual, but more important, he stressed the *social* impact of religion. In Durkheim's view, religion is a collective act that includes many forms of behavior in which people interact with others. As in his work on suicide, Durkheim was not so interested in the personalities of religious believers as he was in understanding religious behavior within a social context.

Durkheim defined **religion** as a "unified system of beliefs and practices relative to sacred things." In his view, religion involves a set of beliefs and practices that are uniquely the property of religion, as opposed to other social institutions and ways of thinking. Durkheim ([1893] 1933; [1912] 2001) argued that religious faiths distinguish between certain transcending events and the everyday world. He referred to those realms as the *sacred* and the *profane*.

The **sacred** encompasses elements beyond everyday life that inspire awe, respect, and even fear. People become part of the sacred realm only by completing some ritual, such as prayer or sacrifice. Because believers have faith in the sacred, they accept what they cannot understand. In contrast, the **profane** includes the ordinary and commonplace. This concept can be confusing, however, because the same object can be either sacred or profane, depending on how it is viewed. A normal dining room table is profane, but it becomes sacred to some Christians if it bears the elements of a communion. A candelabra becomes sacred to Jews if it is a menorah. For Confucians and Taoists, incense sticks are not mere decorative items, but highly valued offerings to the gods in religious ceremonies that mark the new and full moons.

When religion's influence on other social institutions in a society diminishes, the process of **secularization** is said to be under way. During this process, religion will survive in the private sphere of individual and family life (as in the case of many Native American families); it may even thrive on a personal level. But at the same time, other social institutions—such as the economy, politics, and education—maintain their own sets of norms, independent of religious guidance. Even so, religion is enormously resilient. Although specific faiths or organizations may change, their transformation does not signal the demise of religious faith. Rather, it contributes to the diversity of religious expression and organization (Christian Smith 2008, Stark 2004).

Following the direction established by Durkheim a century ago, contemporary sociologists view religion in two different ways. First, they study the norms and values of religious faiths by examining their substantive beliefs. For example, it is possible to compare the degree to which Christian faiths interpret the Bible literally, or Muslim groups follow the Qur'an (or Koran), the sacred book of Islam. At the same time, sociologists examine religion in terms of the social functions it fulfills, such as providing social support or reinforcing social norms. By exploring both the beliefs and the functions of religion, we can better understand its impact on the individual, on groups, and on society as a whole.

● Sociological Perspectives on Religion

Since religion is a cultural universal, it is not surprising that it plays a basic role in human societies. In sociological terms, it performs both manifest and latent functions. Among its *manifest* (open and stated) functions, religion defines the spiritual world and gives meaning to the divine. It provides an explanation for events that seem difficult to understand, such as what lies beyond the grave. The *latent* functions of religion are unintended, covert, or hidden. Even though the manifest function of a church service is to offer a forum for religious worship, it might at the same time fulfill a latent social function as a meeting ground for unmarried members.

Functionalists and conflict theorists both evaluate religion's impact on human societies. We'll consider a functionalist view of religion's role in integrating society, providing social support, and promoting social change, and then look at religion from the conflict and feminist perspectives, as a means of social control. Note that for the most part, religion's impact is best understood from a macro-level viewpoint that is oriented toward the larger society. Its social support function is an exception: it is best understood on the micro, or individual, level.

The Integrative Function of Religion

Émile Durkheim viewed religion as an integrative force in human society—a perspective that is reflected in functionalist thought today. Durkheim sought to answer a perplexing question: "How can human societies be held together when they are generally composed of individuals and social groups with diverse interests and aspirations?" In his view, religious bonds often transcend these personal and divisive forces. Durkheim acknowledged that religion is not the only integrative force; nationalism or patriotism may serve the same end.

How does religion provide this "societal glue"? Religion, whether it be Buddhism, Hinduism, Islam, Christianity, or Judaism, gives meaning and purpose to people's lives. It offers certain ultimate values and ends to hold in common. Although they are subjective and not always fully accepted, these values and ends help society to function as an integrated social system. For example, funerals, weddings, bar and bat mitzvahs, and confirmations serve to integrate people into larger communities by providing shared beliefs and values about the ultimate questions of life.

The integrative power of religion can be seen, too, in the role that churches, synagogues, and mosques have traditionally played and continue to play for immigrant groups in the United States. For example, Roman Catholic immigrants may settle near a parish church that offers services in their native language, such as Polish or Spanish. Similarly, Korean immigrants may join a

© Johnathan Nackstrand/AFP/Getty Images

Most of the world's religions seek to give children an appreciation of their faith, an example of an integrative function. Jewish youths who spin the dreidel, a four-sided top, during the Hanukkah holiday are recalling a tradition born before Christianity, when the children of Greek Jews who studied the Torah secretly in caves played with the tops to pass the time.

Presbyterian church that has many Korean American members and follows religious practices like those of churches in Korea. Like other religious organizations, these Roman Catholic and Presbyterian churches help to integrate immigrants into their new homeland.

In recent years, the most talked about immigrant religious group has been Muslims. Throughout the world, including the United States, Muslims are divided into a variety of sects, including Sunni and Shia (or Shiite). However, inside and outside these sects, people express their Islamic faith in many different ways, not just these two. To speak of Musims as if they were all either Sunni or Shia would be like assuming that all Christians are either Roman Catholics or Baptists.

Depending on the circumstances, Islam in the United States can be integrative by faith, ethnicity, or both. The great majority of Muslims in the United States are Sunni Muslims—literally, those who follow the *Sunnah,* or way of the Prophet. Compared to other Muslims, Sunnis tend to be more moderate in their religious orthodoxy. The Shia, who come primarily from Iraq and Iran, are the second-largest group. In sufficient numbers, these two Muslim groups will choose to worship separately, even if they must cross ethnic or linguistic lines to do so. Whatever group Muslims belong to, however, there has been a remarkable increase in the number of Islamic places of worship in the United States. Between 2000 and 2010, the number of mosques rose 74 percent (Bagby 2012; Selod 2008a).

In some instances, religious loyalties are *dysfunctional;* that is, they contribute to tension and even conflict between groups or nations. During the Second World War, the German Nazis attempted to exterminate the Jewish people; approximately 6 million European Jews were killed. In modern times, nations such as Lebanon (Muslims versus Christians), Israel (Jews versus Muslims, as well as Orthodox versus secular Jews), Northern Ireland (Roman Catholics versus Protestants), and India (Hindus versus Muslims, and more recently, Sikhs) have been torn by clashes that are in large part based on religion.

Religion and Social Support

Most of us find it difficult to accept the stressful events of life—the death of a loved one, serious injury, bankruptcy, divorce, and so forth—especially when something "senseless" happens. How can family and friends come to terms with the death of a talented college student, not even 20 years old?

Through its emphasis on the divine and the supernatural, religion allows us to "do something" about the calamities we face. In some faiths, adherents can offer sacrifices or pray to a deity in the belief that such acts will change their earthly condition. On a more basic level, religion encourages us to view our personal misfortunes as relatively unimportant in the broader perspective of human history—or even as part of an undisclosed divine purpose. Friends and relatives of the deceased college student may see his death as being "God's will," or as having some ultimate benefit that we cannot understand now. This perspective may be much more comforting than the terrifying feeling that any of us can die senselessly at any moment—and that there is no divine answer to why one person lives a long and full life, while another dies tragically at a relatively early age.

Religion and Social Change

The Weberian Thesis

When someone seems driven to work and succeed, we often attribute the Protestant work ethic to that person. The term comes from the writings of Max Weber, who carefully examined the connection between religious allegiance and capitalist development. Weber's findings appeared in his pioneering work *The Protestant Ethic and the Spirit of Capitalism* ([1904] 2011).

Weber noted that in European nations with both Protestant and Catholic citizens, an overwhelming number of business leaders, owners of capital, and skilled workers were Protestant. In his view, this fact was no mere coincidence. Weber pointed out that the followers of John Calvin (1509–1564), a leader of the Protestant Reformation, emphasized a disciplined work ethic, this-worldly concerns, and a rational orientation to life that have become known as the **Protestant ethic.** One by-product of the Protestant ethic was a drive to accumulate savings that could be used for future investment. This "spirit of capitalism," to use Weber's phrase, contrasted with the moderate work hours, leisurely work habits, and lack of ambition that Weber saw as typical of the times.

Few books on the sociology of religion have aroused as much commentary and criticism as Weber's work. It has been hailed as one of the most important theoretical works in the field and an excellent example of macro-level analysis. Like Durkheim, Weber demonstrated that religion is not solely a matter of intimate personal beliefs. He stressed that the collective nature of religion has consequences for society as a whole. Indeed, a recent analysis of historical economic data shows that the Protestant ethic was an important factor in the growth of capitalism from 1500 through 1870 (Sanderson et al. 2011).

Weber provided a convincing description of the origins of European capitalism. However, this economic system has now been adopted by non-Calvinists in many parts of the world. Studies done in the United States today show little or no difference in achievement orientation between Roman Catholics and Protestants. Apparently, the "spirit of capitalism" has emerged as a generalized cultural trait rather than a specific religious tenet (Greeley 1989).

Conflict theorists caution that Weber's theory—even if it is accepted—should not be regarded as an analysis of mature capitalism, as reflected in the rise of multinational corporations. Marxists would disagree with Weber not on the origins of capitalism, but on its future. Unlike Marx, Weber believed that capitalism could endure indefinitely as an economic system. He added, however, that the decline of religion as an overriding force in society opened the way for workers to express their discontent more vocally (R. Collins 1980).

Liberation Theology

Sometimes the clergy can be found in the forefront of social change. Many religious activists, especially in the Roman Catholic Church in Latin America, support **liberation theology**—the use of a church in a political effort to eliminate poverty, discrimination, and other forms of injustice from a secular society. Advocates of this religious movement sometimes sympathize with Marxism. Many believe that radical change, rather than economic development in itself, is the only acceptable solution to the desperation of the masses in impoverished developing countries. Activists associated with liberation theology believe that organized religion has a moral responsibility to take a strong public stand against the oppression of the poor, racial and ethnic minorities, and women (T. Cooper 2015).

The term *liberation theology* dates back to the publication in 1973 of the English translation of *A Theology of Liberation.* The book was written by a Peruvian priest, Gustavo Gutiérrez, who lived in a slum area of Lima during the early 1960s. After years of exposure to the vast poverty around him, Gutiérrez concluded that "in order to serve the poor, one had to move into political action." Eventually, politically committed Latin American theologians came under the influence of social scientists who viewed the domination of capitalism and multinational corporations as central to the hemisphere's problems. One result was a new approach to theology that built on the cultural and religious traditions of Latin America rather than on models developed in Europe and the United States (R. M. Brown 1980:23; Gutiérrez 1990).

Television scripts often poke fun at organized religion, while presenting characters who are atheists as enlightened people. A notable exception is the character Booth (left) in *Bones,* who does not hide his Roman Catholicism. Like many others who are both thoughtful and religious, Booth receives social support from his faith.

© The Star-Ledger/Jennifer Brown/The Image Works

A Protestant congregation worships at Sunday service. Although Weber traced the "spirit of capitalism" to Protestant teachings, in the United States today Protestants and Catholics share the same work ethic.

Liberation theology may be dysfunctional, however. Some Roman Catholic worshippers have come to believe that by focusing on political and governmental injustice, the clergy are no longer addressing their personal and spiritual needs. Partly as a result of such disenchantment, some Catholics in Latin America are converting to mainstream Protestant faiths or to Mormonism.

 use your **sociological imagination**

The social support that religious groups provide is suddenly withdrawn from your community. How will your life or the lives of others change? What will happen if religious groups stop pushing for social change?

● Religion and Social Control: A Conflict Perspective

Liberation theology is a relatively recent phenomenon that marks a break with the traditional role of churches. It was this traditional role that Karl Marx ([1844] 1964) opposed. In his view, religion *impeded* social change by encouraging oppressed people to focus on otherworldly concerns rather than on their immediate poverty or exploitation. Marx described religion as an opiate that was particularly harmful to oppressed peoples. He felt that religion often drugged the masses into submission by offering a consolation for their harsh lives on earth: the hope of salvation in an ideal afterlife. For example, during the period of slavery in the United States, White masters forbade Blacks to practice native African religions, while encouraging them to adopt Christianity, which taught them that obedience would lead to salvation and

eternal happiness in the hereafter. Viewed from a conflict perspective, Christianity may have pacified certain slaves and blunted the rage that often fuels rebellion.

Today, however, people around the world see religion more as a source of support through adversity than a source of oppression. In a combination of public opinion polls taken across 114 nations, 95 percent of those living in the poorest nations felt that religion was important in daily life, compared to only 47 percent of those in the wealthiest countries (Crabtree 2010).

Religion does play an important role in propping up the existing social structure. The values of religion, as already noted, tend to reinforce other social institutions and the social order as a whole. From Marx's perspective, however, religion's promotion of social stability only helps to perpetuate patterns of social inequality. According to Marx, the dominant religion reinforces the interests of those in power.

For example, contemporary Christianity reinforces traditional patterns of behavior that call for the subordination of the less powerful. The role of women in the church is an example of this uneven distribution of power. Assumptions about gender roles leave women in a subservient position both within Christian churches and at home. In fact, women find it as difficult to achieve leadership positions in many churches as they do in large corporations. A "stained glass ceiling" tends to stunt clergywomen's career development, even in the most liberal denominations.

Like Marx, conflict theorists argue that to whatever extent religion actually does influence social behavior, it reinforces existing patterns of dominance and inequality. From a Marxist perspective, religion keeps people from seeing their lives and societal conditions in political terms—for example, by obscuring the overriding significance of conflicting economic interests. Marxists suggest that by inducing a "false consciousness" among the disadvantaged, religion lessens the possibility of collective political action that could end capitalist oppression and transform society.

● Feminist Perspective

Drawing on the feminist approach, researchers and theorists have stressed the fundamental role women play in religious socialization. Most people develop their allegiance to a particular faith in their childhood, with their mothers playing a critical role in the process. Significantly, nonworshipping mothers tend to influence their children to be highly skeptical of organized religion.

However, women generally take a subordinate role in religious governance. Indeed, most faiths have a long tradition of exclusively male spiritual leadership. Furthermore, because most religions are patriarchal, they tend to reinforce men's dominance in secular as well as spiritual matters. Women do play a vital

TABLE **45-1**   SOCIOLOGICAL PERSPECTIVES
                 ON RELIGION

Tracking Sociological Perspectives

Theoretical Perspective	Emphasis
Functionalist	Religion as a source of social integration and unification
	Religion as a source of social support for individuals
Conflict	Religion as a potential obstacle to structural social change
	Religion as a potential source of structural social change (through liberation theology)
Feminist	Religion as an instrument of women's subordination, except for their role in religious socialization
Interactionist	Individual religious expression through belief, ritual, and experience

© Steve Skjold/Alamy Stock Photo

While women comprise an increasing proportion of Christian clergy in the United States, most congregations are still likely to see a man at the front of their church on any given Sunday.

role as volunteers, staff, and religious educators, but even today, religious decision making and leadership typically fall to the men. Exceptions to this rule, such as the Shakers and Christian Scientists, as well as Hinduism and Wicca, with their goddess heritages, are rare (R. Schaefer and Zellner 2015).

In the United States, women are much more likely than men to be affiliated with religion, to pray, to believe in God, to claim that religion is important in their lives, and to attend weekly worship services. Yet organized religion typically does not give them leadership roles. Nationally, women compose 21 percent of U.S. clergy, though they account for 28 percent of students enrolled in theological institutions. Women clerics typically have shorter careers than men, often in related fields that do not involve congregational leadership, such as counseling. In faiths that restrict leadership positions to men, women serve unofficially. For example, about 4 percent of Roman Catholic congregations are led by women who hold nonordained pastoral positions—a necessity in a church facing a shortage of male priests (Association of Theological Schools 2015:Table 2-12B; Bureau of Labor Statistics 2016a).

Table 45-1 summarizes the four major sociological perspectives on religion.

MODULE 45 | **Recap and Review**

Summary

Religion is a cultural universal found throughout the world in various forms.

1. Émile Durkheim stressed the social impact of religion in attempting to understand individual religious behavior within the context of the larger society.

2. Religion helps to integrate a diverse society and provides social support in time of need.

3. Max Weber saw a connection between religious allegiance and capitalistic behavior in a religious orientation he termed the **Protestant ethic.**

4. In **liberation theology,** the teachings of Christianity become the basis for political efforts to alleviate poverty and social injustice.

5. From a Marxist point of view, religion serves to reinforce the social control of those in power. It discourages collective political action, which could end capitalist oppression and transform society.

Thinking Critically

1. What objects that you regard as profane might others consider to be sacred?

2. Explain how the Weberian thesis and liberation theology promote social change.

Key Terms

Liberation theology

Profane

Protestant ethic

Religion

Sacred

Secularization

MODULE 46 | World Religions

Worldwide, tremendous diversity exists in religious beliefs and practices. Overall, about 84 percent of the world's population adheres to some religion; thus, only about 15 percent is nonreligious. This level of adherence changes over time and also varies by country and age group. In the United States today, those who are nonreligious account for about 16 percent of the population; in 1900, they accounted for a mere 1.3 percent of all Americans. And in 2015, 30 percent of incoming U.S. college students had no religious preference (or were agnostic or atheist), compared to 17 percent of their mothers (Newport 2010b; Eagan et al. 2016).

Christianity is the largest single faith in the world; the second largest is Islam (Table 46-1). Although global news events often suggest an inherent conflict between Christians and Muslims, the two faiths are similar in many ways. Both are monotheistic (based on a single deity); both include a belief in prophets, an afterlife, and a judgment day. In fact, Islam recognizes Jesus as a prophet, though not as the son of God. Both faiths impose a moral code on believers, which varies from fairly rigid proscriptions for fundamentalists to relatively relaxed guidelines for liberals.

Over the next forty years, as shown in Figure 46-1, Christians will remain the largest religious group, but Islam will grow faster than any other major world religious group. The growth of Islam is primarily due to the young age of its followers: fertility rates among Muslims are high. But another factor leading to growth is conversion, particularly in Africa. Over the same period of time, Christianity can expect to see level growth or some decline due to two similar factors: low fertility, plus the trend of people in North American and Europe to become unaffiliated with any major religion.

The followers of Islam, called *Muslims,* believe that Islam's holy scriptures were received from Allah (God) by the prophet Mohammad nearly 1,400 years ago. They see Mohammad as the last in a long line of prophets, preceded by Adam, Abraham, Moses, and Jesus. Islam is more communal in its expression than Christianity, particularly the more individualistic Protestant denominations. Consequently, in countries that are predominantly Muslim, the separation of religion and the state is not considered necessary or even desirable. In fact, Muslim governments

TABLE 46-1 MAJOR WORLD RELIGIONS

Summing Up

Faith	Current Following, in Millions (Percentage of World Population)	Primary Location of Followers Today	Founder (and Approximate Birth Date)	Important Texts (and Holy Sites)
Buddhism	516 (7.1%)	Southeast Asia, Mongolia, Tibet	Gautama Siddhartha (563 B.C.)	Triptaka (areas in Nepal)
Christianity	2,390 (33.0%)	Europe, North America, South America	Jesus (6 B.C.)	Bible (Jerusalem, Rome)
Hinduism	975 (13.5%)	India, Indian communities overseas	No specific founder (1500 B.C.)	Sruti and Smrti texts (seven sacred cities, including Vavansi)
Islam	1,674 (23.1%)	Middle East, Central Asia, North Africa, Indonesia	Muhammad (A.D. 570)	Qur'an, or Koran (Mecca, Medina, Jerusalem)
Judaism	14 (0.2%)	Israel, United States, France, Russia	Abraham (2000 B.C.)	Torah, Talmud (Jerusalem)

Sources: Author, based on C. Adams 2015 at Britannica Online; Swatos 1998. Data as of mid-2014.

FIGURE 46-1

Projected Change in Global Religious Affiliation 2010–2050

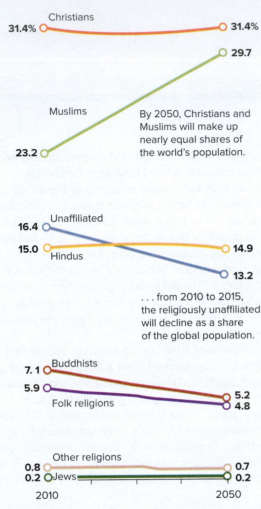

Percent of global population, 2010–2050

Christians
31.4%   31.4%

                                          29.7

Muslims   By 2050, Christians and
                           Muslims will make up
                           nearly equal shares of
23.2   the world's population.

Unaffiliated
16.4
15.0   14.9
Hindus
                                          13.2

                           ...from 2010 to 2015,
                           the religiously unaffiliated
                           will decline as a share
                           of the global population.

Buddhists
7.1
5.9   5.2
Folk religions   4.8

Other religions
0.8   0.7
0.2 Jews   0.2
2010   2050

Folk religions include African traditional religions, Chinese folk religions, Native american religions, and Australian aboriginal religions. Other religions include Baha'i faith, Taoism, Jainism, Shintoism, Sikhism, Tenrikyo, Wicca, Zoroastrianism, and many others.

Source: Pew-Templeton 2015:6.

often reinforce Islamic practices through their laws. Muslims do vary sharply in their interpretation of several traditions, some of which—such as the wearing of veils by women—are more cultural than religious in origin.

Like Christianity and Islam, Judaism is monotheistic. Jews believe that God's true nature is revealed in the Torah, which Christians know as the first five books of the Old Testament. According to these scriptures, God formed a covenant, or pact, with Abraham and Sarah, the ancestors of the tribes of Israel. Even today, observant Jews believe, this covenant holds them accountable to God's will. If they follow both the letter and spirit of the Torah, a long-awaited Messiah will one day bring paradise to earth. Although Judaism has a relatively small following compared to other major faiths, it forms the historical foundation

for both Christianity and Islam. That is why Jews revere many of the same sacred Middle Eastern sites as Christians and Muslims.

Two other major faiths developed in a different part of the world, India. The earliest, Hinduism, originated around 1500 B.C. Hinduism differs from Judaism, Christianity, and Islam in that it embraces a number of gods and minor gods, although most worshippers are devoted primarily to a single deity, such as Shiva or Vishnu. Hinduism is also distinguished by a belief in reincarnation, or the perpetual rebirth of the soul after death. Unlike Judaism, Christianity, and Islam, which are based largely on sacred texts, Hindu beliefs have been preserved mostly through oral tradition.

A second religion, Buddhism, developed in the sixth century B.C. as a reaction against Hinduism. This faith is founded on the teachings of Siddhartha (later called Buddha, or "the enlightened one"). Through meditation, followers of Buddhism strive to overcome selfish cravings for physical or material pleasures, with the goal of reaching a state of enlightenment, or nirvana. Buddhists created the first monastic orders, which are thought to be the models for monastic orders in other religions, including Christianity. Though Buddhism emerged in India, its followers were eventually driven out of that country by the Hindus. It is now found primarily in other parts of Asia. (Contemporary adherents of Buddhism in India are relatively recent converts.)

Although the differences among religions are striking, they are exceeded by variations within faiths. Consider the variations within Christianity, from relatively liberal denominations such as Presbyterians or the United Church of Christ to the more conservative Mormons and Greek Orthodox Catholics. Similar variations exist within Hinduism, Islam, and other world religions (C. Adams 2015; Swatos 1998).

 use your sociological imagination

What evidence do you see of different religions in the area surrounding your college or university? What about on campus?

Components of Religion

All religions have certain elements in common, yet those elements are expressed in the distinctive manner of each faith. These patterns of religious behavior, like other patterns of social behavior, are of great interest to sociologists—especially interactionists—because they underscore the relationship between religion and society.

Religious beliefs, religious rituals, and religious experience all help to define what is sacred and to differentiate the sacred from the profane. Let's examine these three components of religion, as seen through the eyes of interactionists.

Belief

Some people believe in life after death, in supreme beings with unlimited powers, or in supernatural forces. **Religious beliefs** are statements to which members of a particular religion adhere. These views can vary dramatically from religion to religion.

In the late 1960s, something rather remarkable took place in the expression of religious beliefs in the United States. Denominations that held to relatively liberal interpretations of religious scripture (such as the Presbyterians, Methodists, and Lutherans) declined in membership, while those that held to more conservative interpretations grew in numbers. Furthermore, in most faiths, those members who held strict views of scripture became more outspoken, questioning those who remained open to a variety of newer interpretations.

This trend toward *fundamentalism* ran counter to the secularization that was evident in the wider society. **Fundamentalism** may be defined as an emphasis on doctrinal conformity and the literal interpretation of sacred texts. The phrase "religious fundamentalism" was first applied to Protestant believers in the United States who took a literal interpretation of the Bible, but fundamentalism is found worldwide among all major religious groups, including Roman Catholicism, Islam, and Judaism. Even in relatively new faiths, some adherents contend that too much has changed. For followers of many religions, fundamentalists can be as challenging to accommodate as secularists.

Fundamentalists vary immensely in their behavior. Some stress the need to be strict in their own personal faith but take little interest in broad social issues. Others are watchful of societal actions, such as government policies, that they see as conflicting with fundamentalist doctrine.

The Adam and Eve account of creation found in Genesis, the first book of the Old Testament, is an example of a religious belief. Many people in the United States strongly adhere to this biblical explanation of creation and even insist that it be taught in public schools. These people, known as *creationists,* are worried by the secularization of society, and oppose teaching that directly or indirectly questions biblical scripture.

In general, spirituality is not as strong in industrialized nations as in developing nations. The United States is an exception to the trend toward secularization, in part because the government encourages religious expression (without explicitly supporting it) by allowing religious groups to claim charitable status, and even to receive federal aid for activities such as educational services. And although belief in God is relatively weak in formerly communist states such as Russia, surveys show a growth in spirituality in those countries over the past 10 years (Mazurczak 2014).

Ritual

Religious rituals are practices required or expected of members of a faith. Rituals usually honor the divine power (or powers) worshipped by believers; they also remind adherents of their religious duties and responsibilities. Rituals and beliefs can be interdependent; rituals generally affirm beliefs, as in a public or private statement confessing a sin. Like any social institution, religion develops distinctive norms to structure people's behavior. Moreover, sanctions are attached to religious rituals, whether rewards (bar mitzvah gifts) or penalties (expulsion from a religious institution for violation of norms).

In the United States, rituals may be quite simple, such as saying grace at a meal or observing a moment of silence to commemorate someone's death. Yet certain rituals, such as the process of canonizing a saint, are quite elaborate. Most religious rituals in our culture focus on services conducted at houses of worship. Attendance at a service, silent and spoken prayers, communion, and singing of spiritual hymns and chants are common forms of ritual behavior that generally take place in group settings. From an interactionist perspective, these rituals serve as important face-to-face encounters in which people reinforce their religious beliefs and their commitment to their faith.

For Muslims, a very important ritual is the *hajj,* a pilgrimage to the Grand Mosque in Mecca, Saudi Arabia. Every Muslim who is physically and financially able is expected to make this trip at least once. Each year 3 million pilgrims go to Mecca during the one-week period indicated by the Islamic lunar calendar. Muslims from all over the world make the *hajj,* including those in the United States, where many tours are arranged to facilitate the trip.

FIGURE 46-2 **Religious Participation in Selected Countries**

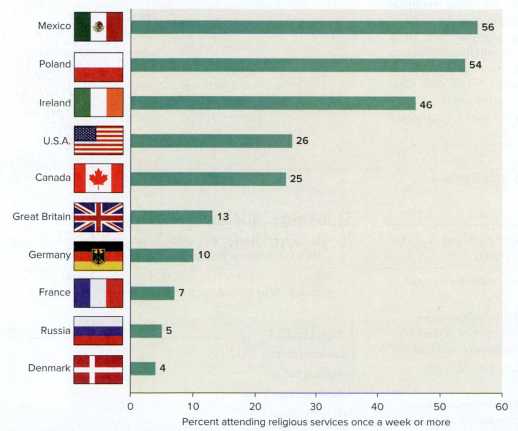

Percent attending religious services once a week or more

Mexico — 56
Poland — 54
Ireland — 46
U.S.A. — 26
Canada — 25
Great Britain — 13
Germany — 10
France — 7
Russia — 5
Denmark — 4

Note: Data are for 2006, except for Canada and Mexico, which are for 2004.
Source: Tom W. Smith 2009:28, 60, 72. *Flags:* © admin_design/Shutterstock RF

© Kazuyoshi Nomachi/HAGA/The Image Works

Pilgrims on *hajj* to the Grand Mosque in Mecca, Saudi Arabia. Islam requires all Muslims who are able to undertake this religious ritual at least once in a lifetime.

In recent decades, participation in religious rituals has tended to hold steady or decline in most countries. Figure 46-2 shows religious participation in selected countries.

Experience

In the sociological study of religion, the term **religious experience** refers to the feeling or perception of being in direct contact with the ultimate reality, such as a divine being, or of being overcome with religious emotion. A religious experience may be rather slight, such as the feeling of exaltation a person receives from hearing a choir sing Handel's "Hallelujah Chorus." But many religious experiences are more profound, such as a Muslim's experience on a *hajj*. In his autobiography, the late African American activist Malcolm X ([1964] 1999:338) wrote of his *hajj* and how deeply moved he was by the way that Muslims in Mecca came together across race and color lines. For Malcolm X, the color blindness of the Muslim world "proved to me the power of the One God."

Another profound religious experience, for many Christians, is being *born again*—that is, at a turning point in one's life, making a personal commitment to Jesus. According to a 2014 national survey, 35 percent of people in the United States claim they have had a born-again Christian experience at some time in their lives. The collective nature of religion, as emphasized by Durkheim, is evident in the way the beliefs and rituals of a particular faith can create an atmosphere either friendly or indifferent to this type of religious experience (Pew Research Center 2015b).

Table 46-2 summarizes the three components of religion.

Summing Up

TABLE 46-2 COMPONENTS OF RELIGION

Element	Definition	Examples
Belief	Statement to which members of a particular religion adhere	Creation account Sacred characters or people
Ritual	Practice required or expected of members of a faith	Worship Prayer Singing or chanting
Experience	Feeling or perception of being in direct contact with the ultimate reality (such as a divine being) or of being overcome with religious emotion	Born-again experience Communion with holy spirit

MODULE 46 | Recap and Review

Summary

Tremendous diversity exists in religious beliefs and practices, although all religions share basic components.

1. Of the world's population, 85 percent adheres to some form of religion.

2. Religious behavior is expressed through three major components: beliefs, rituals, and experience. **Religious beliefs** are statements to which all members of a faith adhere.

3. **Religious rituals** vary from the very simple to the highly complex.

4. **Religious experience**, or the feeling that one is having a direct encounter with the divine, is part of all major religions.

Thinking Critically

1. Which component of religion is easiest to measure? Which is hardest to measure? Explain.

2. What rituals—either religious or nonreligious—do you perform? Why do you perform them?

Key Terms

Fundamentalism

Religious belief

Religious experience

Religious ritual

The collective nature of religion has led to many forms of religious association. In modern societies, religion has become increasingly formalized. Specific structures such as churches and synagogues have been constructed for religious worship; individuals have been trained for occupational roles within various fields. These developments make it possible to distinguish clearly between the sacred and secular parts of one's life—a distinction that could not be made easily in earlier times, when religion was largely a family activity carried out in the home.

Four Basic Forms of Organization

Sociologists find it useful to distinguish between four basic forms of organization: the ecclesia, the denomination, the sect, and the new religious movement, or cult. We can see differences among these four forms of organization in their size, power, degree of commitment that is expected from members, and historical ties to other faiths.

Ecclesiae

An **ecclesia** (plural, *ecclesiae*) is a religious organization that claims to include most or all members of a society and is recognized as the national or official religion. Since virtually everyone belongs to the faith, membership is by birth rather than conscious decision. Examples of ecclesiae include Islam in Saudi Arabia and Buddhism in Thailand. However, significant differences exist within this category. In Saudi Arabia's Islamic regime, leaders of the ecclesia hold vast power over actions of the state. In contrast, the Lutheran Church in contemporary Sweden holds no such power over the Riksdag (parliament) or the prime minister.

Generally, ecclesiae are conservative, in that they do not challenge the leaders of a secular government. In a society with an ecclesia, the political and religious institutions often act in harmony and reinforce each other's power in their relative spheres of influence. In the modern world, ecclesiae are declining in power.

Denominations

A **denomination** is a large, organized religion that is not officially linked to the state or government. Like an ecclesia, it tends to have an explicit set of beliefs, a defined system of authority, and a generally respected position in society. Denominations claim as members large segments of a population. Generally, children accept the denomination of their parents and give little thought to membership in other faiths. Denominations also resemble ecclesiae in that they make few demands on members. However, there is a critical difference between these two forms of religious organization. Although the denomination is considered respectable and is not viewed as a challenge to the secular government, it lacks the official recognition and power held by an ecclesia (Doress and Porter 1977).

The United States is home to a large number of denominations. In good measure, this diversity is a result of our nation's immigrant heritage. Many settlers brought with them the religious commitments native to their homelands. Some Christian denominations in the United States, such as the Roman Catholics, Episcopalians, and Lutherans, are the outgrowth of ecclesiae established in Europe. New Christian denominations also emerged, including the Mormons and Christian Scientists. Within the past generation, immigrants have increased the number of Muslims, Hindus, and Buddhists living in the United States.

Although by far the largest denomination in the United States is Roman Catholicism, at least 24 other Christian faiths have 1 million or more members. Protestants collectively accounted for about 47 percent of the nation's adult population in 2014, compared to 21 percent for Roman Catholics and 2 percent for Jews. Mormons make up close to 2 percent, with about 6 million members in the United States. There are also 5 million Muslims in the United States, and large numbers of people adhere to Eastern faiths such as Buddhism (3 million) and Hinduism (1 million) (Lindner 2012; Pew Research Center 2015b).

Sects

A **sect** can be defined as a relatively small religious group that has broken away from some other religious organization to renew what it considers the original vision of the faith. Many sects, such as that led by Martin Luther during the Reformation, claim to be the "true church," because they seek to cleanse the established faith of what they regard as extraneous beliefs and rituals (Stark and Bainbridge 1985). Max Weber ([1916] 1958:114) termed the sect a "believer's church," because affiliation is based on conscious acceptance of a specific religious dogma.

Sects are fundamentally at odds with society and do not seek to become established national religions. Unlike ecclesiae and denominations, they require intensive commitments and demonstrations of belief by members. Partly owing to their outsider status, sects frequently exhibit a higher degree of religious fervor and loyalty than more established religious groups. Recruitment focuses mainly on adults, and acceptance comes through conversion.

Sects are often short-lived. Those that survive may become less antagonistic to society over time and begin to resemble denominations. In a few instances, sects have endured over several generations while remaining fairly separate from society. Sociologist J. Milton Yinger (1970:226–273) uses the term **established sect** to describe a religious group that is the outgrowth of a sect, yet remains isolated from society. Hutterites, Jehovah's Witnesses, Seventh-Day Adventists, and Amish are contemporary examples of established sects in the United States (Tracey 2012).

 use your **sociological imagination**

Choose a religious tradition other than your own. How would your religious beliefs, rituals, and experience differ if you had been raised in that tradition?

New Religious Movements or Cults

In 1997, 38 members of the Heaven's Gate cult were found dead in Southern California after a mass suicide timed to occur with the appearance of the Hale-Bopp comet. They believed the comet hid a spaceship on which they could catch a ride once they had broken free of their "bodily containers."

Partly as a result of the notoriety generated by such groups, the popular media have stigmatized the word *cult,* associating it with the occult and the use of intense and forceful conversion techniques. The stereotyping of cults as uniformly bizarre and unethical has led sociologists to abandon the term and refer instead to a *new religious movement (NRM).* While some NRMs exhibit strange behavior, many do not. They attract new members just like any other religion, and often follow teachings similar to those of established Christian denominations, though with less ritual.

Sects are difficult to distinguish from cults. A **new religious movement (NRM)** or **cult** is generally a small, secretive religious group that represents either a new religion or a major innovation of an existing faith. NRMs are similar to sects in that they tend to be small and are often viewed as less respectable than more established faiths. Unlike sects, however, NRMs normally do not result from schisms or breaks with established ecclesiae or denominations. Some cults, such as those focused on UFO sightings, may be totally unrelated to existing faiths. Even when a cult does accept certain fundamental tenets of a dominant faith—such as a belief in Jesus as divine or in Mohammad as a messenger of God—it will offer new revelations or insights to justify its claim to being a more advanced religion (Stark and Bainbridge 1979, 1985).

Like sects, NRMs may be transformed over time into other types of religious organization. An example is the Christian Science Church, which began as a new religious movement under the leadership of Mary Baker Eddy. Today, this church exhibits the characteristics of a denomination. In fact, most major religions, including Christianity, began as cults. NRMs may be in the early stages of developing into a denomination or new religion, or they may just as easily fade away through the loss of members or weak leadership (R. Schaefer and Zellner 2008, 2015).

Comparing Forms of Religious Organization

How can we determine whether a particular religious group falls into the sociological category of ecclesia, denomination, sect, or NRM? As we have seen, these types of religious organization have somewhat different relationships to society. Ecclesiae are recognized as national churches; denominations, although not officially approved by the state, are generally widely respected. In contrast, sects and NRMs are much more likely to be at odds with the larger culture.

Still, ecclesiae, denominations, and sects are best viewed as types along a continuum rather than as mutually exclusive categories. Table 47-1 summarizes some of the primary characteristics of the ideal types.

Since the United States has no ecclesiae, sociologists studying this country's religions have focused on the denomination and the sect. These religious forms have been pictured on either end of a continuum, with denominations accommodating to the secular world and sects protesting against established religions. Although NRMs also are included in the table, they lie outside the continuum, because they generally define themselves in terms of a new view of life rather than in terms of existing religious faiths. In fact, one of the most controversial NRMs, Wicca, may not fully qualify as a religion (Box 47-1).

Sociologists look at religion from an organizational perspective, which tends to stress the stability of religious adherence, but there are other ways to view religion. From an individual perspective, religion and spirituality are remarkably fluid. People often

TABLE 47-1 CHARACTERISTICS OF ECCLESIAE, DENOMINATIONS, SECTS, AND NEW RELIGIOUS MOVEMENTS

Summing Up

Characteristic	Ecclesia	Denomination	Sect	New Religious Movement (or Cult)
Size	Very large	Large	Small	Small
Wealth	Extensive	Extensive	Limited	Variable
Religious services	Formal, little participation	Formal, little participation	Informal, emotional	Variable
Doctrines	Specific, but interpretation may be tolerated	Specific, but interpretation may be tolerated	Specific, purity of doctrine emphasized	Innovative, pathbreaking
Clergy	Well-trained, full-time	Well-trained, full-time	Trained to some degree	Unspecialized
Membership	By virtue of being a member of society	By acceptance of doctrine	By acceptance of doctrine	By an emotional commitment
Relationship to the state	Recognized, closely aligned	Tolerated	Not encouraged	Ignored or challenged

Sources: Adapted from Vernon 1962; see also Chalfant et al. 1994.

Wicca: Religion or Quasi-Religion?

"I'm not a Witch," Christine O'Donnell famously declared in her 2010 campaign for the U.S. Senate. Eleven years earlier, she admitted, she had dabbled in Witchcraft. To most voters, the idea was beyond the pale. Yet today, thousands of people, both men and women, do view themselves as Witches; they practice a little-known religion called Wicca (which should not be confused with Satanism—there is no place in the Craft for devil worship).

Wicca (Anglo-Saxon for witch and wizard) is a modern form of Witchcraft, practiced for the last hundred years. The Englishman Gerald Gardner, born in 1884, drew on past rituals to found the Craft. Gardner stressed the importance of worshipping skyclad, or "clothed by the sky"—that is, naked. Being skyclad, he believed, helped a person to gain insight.

Not all Wiccans follow in Gardner's tradition. Today, Wiccan ritual takes on a dizzying variety of forms, ranging from the elementary to the highly detailed and sophisticated. A Wiccan circle or meeting can include a single heartfelt prayer or a highly complex and time-consuming ritual. Like members of more accepted religions, Wiccans observe several rituals associated with the life cycle. Parents name their children at a Wiccaning, which includes a dedication to the Goddess and the God. Contemporary Wiccans also celebrate a wedding-like ceremony called a handfasting, which is typically performed by a High Priest and/or Priestess.

Just as Wiccans' worship varies, so does their organization. Some Witches practice alone, as a solitaire; others practice in a group of similarly minded Witches, called a coven. A coven may include just 3 or 4 Witches, male and/or female, or as many as 30; members tend to come and go just as they do in a church, temple, or mosque. In a mixed coven, the assembly is often governed by a High Priest or Priestess, or by both.

Revealing one's membership in any non-traditional group is always difficult, but perhaps especially so for Wiccans, who refer to the experience as "coming out of the broom closet." Many Wiccans are young, and so must come out to their parents. Parental reactions range from cutting off contact with the Witch to wanting to learn more about the Craft. Many parents treat the religion as a "phase" in their child's spiritual journey.

Most scholars treat Wicca as a **quasi-religion**, a category that includes organizations that may see themselves as religious, but are seen by others as "sort of religious." National surveys that allow respondents to self-identify showed 8,000 Wiccans in 1990; 134,000 in 2001; and 342,000 in 2008, the latest year for which reliable national data are available. These estimates suggest

© Wes Pope KRT/Newscom

either an increase in willingness to identify as Wiccan or an absolute growth in the faithful—probably both.

> Some Witches practice alone, as a solitaire; others practice in a group of similarly minded Witches, called a coven.

LET'S DISCUSS

1. Do you know anyone who practices Wicca? If so, describe the person's practices.
2. Do you think that Wicca should be considered a religion? Why or why not?

Sources: Chase 2010; M. Howard 2009; Kosmin and Keysar 2009; Rabinovitch and Lewis 2004; R. Schaefer and Zellner 2015:347–377.

---

change their places of worship or move from one denomination to another. In many countries, including the United States, churches, temples, and mosques operate in a highly competitive market.

One sign of this fluidity is the rapid rise of still another form of religious organization, the electronic church. Facilitated by cable television and satellite transmission, *televangelists* (as they are called) direct their messages to more people—especially in the United States—than are served by all but the largest denominations. While some televangelists are affiliated with religious denominations, most give viewers the impression that they are dissociated from established faiths.

As we move well into the 21st century, scholars debate the impact of the Internet on religion. Some argue that the growth in Internet usage helps to explain the increase in the number of unaffiliated adults, as more people find websites that question long-held beliefs or simply spend large amounts of time online, leaving less time for group activities. On the other hand, religious groups worldwide are rapidly adapting to new media, though not without unevenness and ineptitude at times. Facebook, blogs, texting, and streaming are still less prevalent among organized religions than in the corporate world, but new media are nevertheless transforming the ways in which religious faiths socially interact with people and enhance their sense of religious community (Downey 2014; Thurma 2012). Religion in the schools is the subject of the Social Policy section of this chapter.

Should public schools be allowed to sponsor organized prayer in the classroom? How about Bible reading, or just a collective moment of silence? Can athletes at public schools offer up a group prayer in a team huddle? Should students be able to initiate voluntary prayers at school events? Each of these situations has been an object of great dissension among those who see a role for prayer in the schools and those who want to maintain strict separation of church and state.

Another controversy concerns the teaching of theories about the origin of humans and the universe. Mainstream scientific thinking holds that humans evolved over billions of years from one-celled organisms, and that the universe came into being 13 to 15 billion years ago as a result of a huge cosmic explosion (the big bang theory). These theories are challenged by people who hold to the biblical account of the creation of humans and the universe some 10,000 years ago—a viewpoint known as **creationism.** Creationists, many of whom are Christian fundamentalists, want their belief taught in the schools as the only one—or at the very least, as an alternative to the theory of evolution.

Looking at the Issue

The issues just described go to the heart of the First Amendment's provisions regarding religious freedom. On the one hand, the government must protect the right to practice one's religion; on the other, it cannot take any measures that would seem to establish one religion over another (separation of church and state). In the key case of *Engle v. Vitale,* the Supreme Court ruled in 1962 that the use of nondenominational prayer in New York schools was "wholly inconsistent" with the First Amendment's prohibition against government establishment of religion. In finding that organized school prayer violated the Constitution—even when no student was required to participate—the Court argued, in effect, that promoting religious observance was not a legitimate function of government or education. Subsequent Court decisions have allowed voluntary school prayer by students, but forbid school officials to sponsor any prayer or religious observance at school events.

Despite these rulings, many public schools still regularly lead their students in prayer recitations or Bible readings. Public schools and even states have mandated a moment of silence at the start of the school day, in what critics contend is a transparent attempt to get around *Engle v. Vitale* and similar legal precedents. Although legislators clearly intended to set aside time for prayer or religious thoughts when they created these "moments," to date the courts have recognized such policies as constitutional, treating them as secular rather than sacred. In 2013 Arkansas became the most recent state to mandate an opening moment of silence (Yemma 2013).

People on both sides of the debate between science and creationism invoke the name of Albert Einstein. Evolutionists emphasize the need for verifiable scientific data, like that which confirmed Einstein's groundbreaking scientific theories. Advocates of intelligent design quote the Nobel Prize–winning physicist's assertion that religion and science should coexist.

As with school prayer, the teaching of creationism has significant support among the general public. Unlike Europeans, many people in the United States seem highly skeptical of evolutionary theory, which is taught as a matter of course in science classes. In 2014, a national survey showed that 42 percent of adults believe that God created humans in their present form. (Newport 2014).

In 1987, the Supreme Court ruled that states could not compel the teaching of creationism in public schools if the primary purpose was to promote a religious viewpoint. In response, those who believe in the divine origin of life have recently advanced a concept called **intelligent design (ID),** the idea that life is so complex that it could only have been created by intelligent design. Though this concept is not based explicitly on the biblical account of creation, fundamentalists feel comfortable with it. Supporters of intelligent design consider it a more accurate account of the origin of life than Darwinism and hold that at the very least, ID should be taught as an alternative to the theory of evolution. But in 2005, in *Kitzmiller v. Dove Area School District,* a federal judge ended a Pennsylvania school district's plans to require teachers to present the concept in class. In essence, the judge found ID to be "a religious belief," a subtler but similar approach to creationism in that both find God's fingerprints in nature. The issue continues to be hotly debated and is expected to be the subject of future court cases (Clemmitt 2005; Tierney and Holley 2008).

—Continued

Applying Sociology

Supporters of school prayer and of creationism feel that strict Court rulings have forced too great a separation between what Émile Durkheim called the sacred and the profane. They insist that the use of nondenominational prayer can in no way lead to the establishment of an ecclesia in the United States. Moreover, they believe that school prayer—and the teaching of creationism—can provide the spiritual guidance and socialization that many children today do not receive from parents or regular church attendance. Many communities also believe that schools should transmit the dominant culture of the United States by encouraging prayer.

Opponents of school prayer and creationism argue that a religious majority in a community might impose viewpoints specific to its faith at the expense of religious minorities. These critics question whether school prayer can remain truly voluntary. Drawing on the interactionist perspective and small group research, they suggest that children will face enormous social pressure to conform to the beliefs and practices of the majority.

Initiating Policy

Public school education is fundamentally a local issue, so most initiatives and lobbying have taken place at the local or state level. Federal courts have taken a hard line on religion in the schools. In a decision that the Supreme Court reversed in 2004, a federal appeals court ruled that reciting the phrase "under God" during the Pledge of Allegiance that opens each school day violates the U.S. Constitution (Religion News Service 2003).

Religion–school debates show no sign of ending. The activism of religious fundamentalists in the public school system raises the question "Whose ideas and values deserve a hearing in classrooms?" Critics see this campaign as one step toward sectarian religious control of public education. They worry that at some point in the future, teachers may not be able to use books or make statements that conflict with fundamentalist interpretations of the Bible. For advocates of a liberal education and of intellectual (and religious) diversity, this is a genuinely frightening prospect (Wilgoren 2005).

TAKE THE ISSUE WITH YOU

1. Was there organized prayer in any school you attended? Was creationism part of the curriculum?

2. Do you think that promoting religious observance is a legitimate function of education?

3. How might a conflict theorist view the issue of organized school prayer?

MODULE 47 | **Recap and Review**

Summary

Religious organizations grow and evolve over time and in reaction to social changes.

1. Four basic types of religious organizations are the **ecclesia,** the **denomination,** the **sect,** and the **new religious movement**, or **cult.**

2. Advances in communication have led to a new type of church organization, the electronic church. Televangelists now preach to more people than belong to many denominations, and every day millions of people use the Internet for religious purposes.

3. Today, the question of how much religion, if any, should be permitted in U.S. public schools is a matter of intense debate.

Thinking Critically

1. What do you think attracts people to new religious movements?

2. What is the difference between a new religious movement and a quasi-religion?

Key Terms

Creationism

Denomination

Ecclesia

Established sect

Intelligent design (ID)

New religious movement (NRM) or cult

Quasi-religion

Sect

Mastering This Chapter

© Jacob Silberberg/Panos Pictures

taking sociology with you

1 Find out how many different religious groups there are at your school or in your community. How many belong to mainstream denominations? How many are fundamentalist? Are there any sects or new religious movements?

2 If your school or community has an interfaith organization, attend a meeting. What issues are the members currently dealing with? What sociological concepts are relevant to those issues?

3 How have the topics of creationism and intelligent design been considered in your education?

key terms

Creationism A literal interpretation of the Bible regarding the creation of humanity and the universe, used to argue that evolution should not be presented as established scientific fact.

Denomination A large, organized religion that is not officially linked to the state or government.

Ecclesia A religious organization that claims to include most or all members of a society and is recognized as the national or official religion.

Established sect A religious group that is the outgrowth of a sect, yet remains isolated from society.

Fundamentalism An emphasis on doctrinal conformity and the literal interpretation of sacred texts.

Intelligent design (ID) The idea that life is so complex it could only have been created by intelligent design.

Liberation theology Use of a church, primarily Roman Catholic, in a political effort to eliminate poverty, discrimination, and other forms of injustice from a secular society.

New religious movement (NRM) or **cult** A small, secretive religious group that represents either a new religion or a major innovation of an existing faith.

Profane The ordinary and commonplace elements of life, as distinguished from the sacred.

Protestant ethic Max Weber's term for the disciplined work ethic, this worldly concerns, and rational orientation to life emphasized by John Calvin and his followers.

Quasi-religion A scholarly category that includes organizations that may see themselves as religious but may be seen by others as "sort of religious."

Religion A unified system of beliefs and practices relative to sacred things.

Religious belief A statement to which members of a particular religion adhere.

Religious experience The feeling or perception of being in direct contact with the ultimate reality, such as a divine being, or of being overcome with religious emotion.

Religious ritual A practice required or expected of members of a faith.

Sacred Elements beyond everyday life that inspire awe, respect, and even fear.

Sect A relatively small religious group that has broken away from some other religious organization to renew what it considers the original vision of the faith.

Secularization The process through which religions influence on other social institutions diminishes.

self-quiz

Read each question carefully and then select the best answer.

1. Which of the following sociologists stressed the social impact of religion and was perhaps the first to recognize the critical importance of religion in human societies?
   a. Max Weber
   b. Karl Marx
   c. Émile Durkheim
   d. Talcott Parsons

2. A Roman Catholic parish church offers services in the native language of an immigrant community. This is an example of
   a. the integrative function of religion.
   b. the social support function of religion.
   c. the social control function of religion.
   d. none of the above.

3. Sociologist Max Weber pointed out that the followers of John Calvin emphasized a disciplined work ethic, this-worldly concerns, and a rational orientation to life. Collectively, this point of view has been referred to as
    a. capitalism.
    b. the Protestant ethic.
    c. the sacred.
    d. the profane.

4. The use of a church, primarily Roman Catholic, in a political effort to eliminate poverty, discrimination, and other forms of injustice evident in a secular society is referred to as
    a. creationism.
    b. ritualism.
    c. religious experience.
    d. liberation theology.

5. Many people in the United States strongly adhere to the biblical explanation of the beginning of the universe. Adherents of this point of view are known as
    a. liberationists.
    b. creationists.
    c. ritualists.
    d. experimentalists.

6. The Adam and Eve account of creation found in Genesis, the first book of the Old Testament, is an example of a religious
    a. ritual.
    b. experience.
    c. custom.
    d. belief.

7. Which of the following is not an example of an ecclesia?
    a. the Lutheran church in Sweden
    b. Islam in Saudi Arabia
    c. Buddhism in Thailand
    d. the Episcopal church in the United States

8. Religion defines the spiritual world and gives meaning to the divine. These are what functions of religion?
    a. manifest
    b. latent
    c. positive
    d. negative

9. Which sociological perspective emphasizes the integrative power of religion in human society?
    a. functionalist perspective
    b. conflict perspective
    c. interactionist perspective
    d. all of the above

10. Most Muslims in the United States are
    a. Shia.
    b. Sufi.
    c. Wahhabi.
    d. Sunni.

11. The _____ encompasses elements beyond everyday life that inspire awe, respect, and even fear, as compared to the _____, which includes the ordinary and the commonplace.

12. Wicca is an example of a(n) _____.

13. _____ is the largest single faith in the world; the second largest is _____.

14. _____ _____ are statements to which members of a particular religion adhere.

15. A(n) _____ is a religious organization that claims to include most or all members of a society and is recognized as the national or official religion.

16. Because they are _____, most religions tend to reinforce men's dominance in secular as well as spiritual matters.

17. The single largest denomination in the United States is _____ _____.

18. The big bang theory is challenged by _____, who hold to the biblical account of creation of humans and the universe.

19. Unlike ecclesiae and denominations, _____ require intensive commitments and demonstrations of belief by members.

20. A possible dysfunction of _____ _____ would be the belief that when Roman Catholics focus on political and governmental injustice, the clergy are no longer addressing people's personal and spiritual needs.

16 Government and the Economy

© Jim West/The Image Works

Citizens are becoming increasingly frustrated with the government and the economy, two major social institutions, as reflected by this protester.

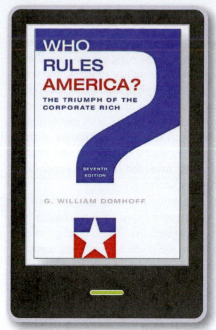

© Ira C. Roberts/Chad Enterprises Corporation

How much power do you think you have over the U.S. economy? Over the economic policies of the U.S. government?

According to sociologist G. William Domhoff, unless you belong to the corporate elite, you have no real power.

" How can the owners and managers of highly competitive corporations develop the policy unity to shape government policies? And how can large corporations have such great power in a democratic country? The step-by-step argument and evidence presented in previous chapters provide the foundation for a theory that can explain these paradoxes—a *class-domination* theory of power in the United States.

Domination means that the commands of a group or class are carried out with relatively little resistance, which is possible because that group or class has been able to establish the organizations, rules, and customs through which everyday life is conducted. Domination, in other words, is the institutionalized outcome of great distributive power ("power over"). The corporate rich are a dominant class in terms of this definition because the cumulative effect of their various distributive powers leads to a situation in which most Americans generally accept (or acquiesce in) its policies. Even when there are highly vocal complaints, the routinized ways of acting in the United States follow from the rules and regulations needed by the corporate community to continue to grow and make profits.

The overall distributive power of the dominant class is first of all based in its structural power, which falls to it by virtue of being owners and high-level executives in corporations that sell goods and services for a profit in a market economy that is fashioned in good part to benefit the sellers of goods and services, not employees or consumers. The power to invest or not invest and to hire and fire employees leads to a political context in which most elected officials try to do as much as they can to create a favorable investment climate in order to avoid being voted out of office in the event of an economic downturn. This structural power is augmented by the ability to create new policies through the policy-planning network, which it was possible for the corporate rich to develop gradually over many decades because their common economic interests and social cohesion give them enough unity to sustain such an endeavor.

But even these powers might not have been enough to generate a system of extreme class domination if the bargains and compromises embodied in the Constitution had not led unexpectedly to a two-party system in which one party was controlled by the Northern rich and the other by the Southern rich. This in turn reinforced a personality-oriented candidate-selection process that is heavily dependent on large campaign donations—now and in the nineteenth century as well. The system of party primaries is the one adaptation to this constrictive two-party system that has provided some openings for insurgent liberals and trade unionists on one side and social conservatives and libertarians on the other.

Structural power, policies generated in the policy-planning network, and control of the two parties resulted in a polity in which there is little or no organized public opinion on specific legislative issues that is independent of the limits, doubts, and obfuscations generated by the opinion-shaping network.

In addition, the fragmented and constrained system of government crafted by the Founding Fathers led to a relatively small federal government that is easily entered and influenced by wealthy and well-organized private citizens, whether through Congress, the separate departments of the executive branch, or a myriad of regulatory agencies.

Despite their lack of power, many Americans feel a sense of empowerment because they have religious freedom, freedom of expression, the right to vote, and the hope that they can make more money or rise in the class structure if they try hard enough.

Despite their lack of power, many Americans feel a sense of empowerment because they have religious freedom, freedeom of expression, the right to vote, and the hope that they can make more money or rise in the class structure if they try hard enough. Those with educational credentials and/or secure employment experience a degree of dignity and respect that allows them to hold their heads high and maintain their sense of self-regard, because elite arrogance and condescension toward average people is rarely expressed publicly. Then, too, liberals and leftists retain hope because they had success in helping to expand individual rights and freedom—for people of color, for women, and for gays and lesbians.

But individual rights and freedoms do not necessarily add up to distributive power. In the same time period between 1965 and 2000 in which individual rights and freedoms expanded, corporate power also became greater because industrial unions were decimated, the civil rights movement dissipated, and the liberal-labor alliance splintered as part of the resistance to the integration of job sites, neighborhoods, and schools. Thus, class domination actually increased in recent decades in spite of increases in individual freedom. It is therefore possible to have class domination in a society based on individualistic liberal values, as many decisions by the Supreme Court also demonstrate. "

(*Domhoff 2014a:192–194*)

n this excerpt from his book *Who Rules America? The Triumph of the Corporate Rich,* Domhoff explains how large corporations increased their power in recent decades. The general public seems to share Domhoff's assertion about who rules America: 70 percent feel that the government should do more to tame corporate power. And this view is not limited to the United States: the same sentiment was expressed by 62 percent of the people of India, 67 percent of Canadians, and 68 percent of Germans (International Trade Union Confederation 2014: Chart 23).

The unequal distribution of power in the United States, where a small group of corporate elites wields more power than the entire citizenry, is compounded by inequality of income and wealth. The same is true of the world as a whole. Shortly after *Who Rules America?* was published, the human rights organization Oxfam announced that 85 of the world's richest people own the same amount of wealth as half the world's population.

The inequality both within the United States and between the United States and other nations—between the big industrial powers and the developing world—underscores the importance of understanding our economic and political institutions. To many observers, the massive concentration of economic resources in the hands of just a few threatens our founding fathers' vision of an inclusive political and economic system. Instead of moving forward together, Americans seem increasingly split by inequality in economic and political power—a trend that will inevitably heighten social tensions.

This chapter will present a combined analysis of the economy and government. It is hard to imagine two social institutions more intertwined. Besides serving as the largest employer in the nation, government at all levels regulates commerce and entry into many occupations. At the same time, the economy generates the revenue to support government services.

We begin with a general discussion of power and authority, and specific descriptions of four major types of government in which that power and authority operates. We'll also briefly touch on war, peace, and terrorism. Next we'll see how politics works, and we'll look at two models of power in the United States. We'll then turn to a macro-level analysis of capitalism and socialism. We'll examine how the U.S. economy is changing in response to globalization. Finally, in the Social Policy section, we'll explore the effects of a financial innovation called *microfinancing* on the lives of poor people in developing countries.

MODULE 48 | Government, Power, and Authority

Power and Authority

In any society, someone or some group—whether it be a tribal chief, a dictator, or a parliament—makes important decisions about how to use resources and how to allocate goods. One cultural universal, then, is the exercise of power and authority. Inevitably, the struggle for power and authority involves **politics,** which political scientist Harold Lasswell (1936) tersely defined as "who gets what, when, and how." In their study of politics and government, sociologists are concerned with social interactions among individuals and groups and their impact on the larger political and economic order.

The social institution that is responsible for implementing and achieving society's goals is the **political system.** Each country has a unique political system that is founded on a recognized set of procedures. The political system interacts closely with the **economic system,** the social institution through which goods and services are produced, distributed, and consumed. As we will see throughout the next four modules, the political and economic systems are inextricably intertwined, and together they regulate power and authority within society.

Power

Power lies at the heart of a political system. According to Max Weber, **power** is the ability to exercise one's will over others. To put it another way, whoever can overcome the resistance of others and control their behavior is exercising power. Power relations can involve large organizations, small groups, or even people in an intimate association.

Because Weber developed his conceptualization of power in the early 1900s, he focused primarily on the nation-state and its sphere of influence. Today scholars recognize that the trend toward globalization has brought new opportunities, and with them new concentrations of power. Power is now exercised on a global as well as a national stage, as countries and multinational corporations vie to control access to resources and manage the distribution of capital (R. Schaefer 2008b; Sernau 2001).

There are three basic sources of power within any political system: force, influence, and authority. **Force** is the actual or threatened use of coercion to impose one's will on others. When leaders imprison or even execute political dissidents, they are applying force; so, too, are terrorists when they seize or bomb an embassy or assassinate a political leader.

Influence, on the other hand, refers to the exercise of power through a process of persuasion. A citizen may change his or her view of a Supreme Court nominee because of a newspaper editorial, the expert testimony of a law school dean before the Senate Judiciary Committee, or a stirring speech by a political activist at a rally. In each case, sociologists would view such efforts to persuade people as examples of influence. Now let's take a look at the third source of power, *authority.*

Types of Authority

The term **authority** refers to institutionalized power that is recognized by the people over whom it is exercised. Sociologists commonly use the term in connection with those who hold legitimate power through elected or publicly acknowledged positions. A person's authority is often limited. Thus, a referee has the authority to decide whether a penalty should be called during a football game, but has no authority over the price of tickets to the game.

Max Weber ([1913–1922] 1947) developed a classification system for authority that has become one of the most useful and frequently cited contributions of early sociology. He identified three ideal types of authority: traditional, rational-legal, and charismatic. Weber did not insist that only one type applies to a given society or organization. All can be present, but their relative importance will vary. Sociologists have found Weber's typology valuable in understanding different manifestations of legitimate power within a society.

© C Squared Studios/Getty Images RF

Traditional Authority

Until the middle of the past century, Japan was ruled by a revered emperor whose absolute power was passed down from generation to generation. In a political system based on **traditional authority,** legitimate power is conferred by custom and accepted practice. A king or queen is accepted as ruler of a nation simply by virtue of inheriting the crown; a tribal chief rules because that is the accepted practice. The ruler may be loved or hated, competent or destructive; in terms of legitimacy, that does not matter. For the traditional leader, authority rests in custom, not in personal characteristics, technical competence, or even written

law. People accept the ruler's authority because that is how things have always been done. Traditional authority is absolute when the ruler has the ability to determine laws and policies.

Rational-Legal Authority

The U.S. Constitution gives Congress and our president the authority to make and enforce laws and policies. Power made legitimate by law is known as **rational-legal authority.** Leaders derive their rational-legal authority from the written rules and regulations of political systems, such as a constitution. Generally, in societies based on rational-legal authority, leaders are thought to have specific areas of competence and authority but are not thought to be endowed with divine inspiration, as in certain societies with traditional forms of authority.

Charismatic Authority

Joan of Arc was a simple peasant girl in medieval France, yet she was able to rally the French people and lead them into major battles against English invaders. How was this possible? As Weber observed, power can be legitimized by the *charisma* of an individual. The term **charismatic authority** refers to power made legitimate by a leader's exceptional personal or emotional appeal to his or her followers.

Charisma lets a person lead or inspire without relying on set rules or traditions. In fact, charismatic authority is derived more from the beliefs of followers than from the actual qualities of leaders. So long as people perceive a charismatic leader such as Jesus, Joan of Arc, Gandhi, Malcolm X, or Martin Luther King Jr. as having qualities that set him or her apart from ordinary citizens, that leader's authority will remain secure and often unquestioned.

Observing charismatic authority from an interactionist perspective, sociologist Carl Couch (1996) points out that the growth of electronic media has facilitated the development of charismatic authority. During the 1930s and 1940s, the heads of state of the United States, Great Britain, and Germany all used radio to issue direct appeals to citizens. Now, television and the Internet allow leaders to "visit" people's homes and communicate with them.

As we noted earlier, Weber used traditional, rational-legal, and charismatic authority as ideal types. In reality, particular leaders and political systems combine elements of two or more of these forms. Presidents Franklin D. Roosevelt, John F. Kennedy, and Ronald Reagan wielded power largely through the rational-legal basis of their authority. At the same time, they were unusually charismatic leaders who commanded the personal loyalty of large numbers of citizens.

© RichardBakerFarnborough/Alamy

English billionaire Richard Branson is known for his charismatic leadership style. Founder of Virgin Group, which comprises more than 400 companies, he is currently overseeing LauncherOne, a rocket that is to take paying customers into orbit around the Earth.

Types of Government

Each society establishes a political system through which it is governed. In modern industrialized nations, these formal systems of government make a significant number of critical political decisions. We will survey five basic types of government here: monarchy, oligarchy, dictatorship, totalitarianism, and democracy.

Monarchy

A **monarchy** is a form of government headed by a single member of a royal family, usually a king, queen, or some other hereditary ruler. In earlier times, many monarchs claimed that God had granted them a divine right to rule. Typically, they governed on the basis of traditional forms of authority, sometimes accompanied by the use of force. By the beginning of the 21st century, however, monarchs held genuine governmental power in only a few nations, such as Monaco. Most monarchs now have little practical power; they serve primarily ceremonial purposes.

Oligarchy

An **oligarchy** is a form of government in which a few individuals rule. A rather old method of governing that flourished in ancient Greece and Egypt, oligarchy now often takes the form of military rule. In developing nations in Africa, Asia, and Latin America, small factions of military officers will forcibly seize power, either from legally elected regimes or from other military cliques.

Strictly speaking, the term *oligarchy* is reserved for governments that are run by a few selected individuals. However,

© Liu Xingzhe/VCG via Getty Images

North Korea has a totalitarian government whose leaders attempt to control all aspects of people's lives. Masses of people paid homage to Kim Jong-un as a great leader at the 2015 celebration of the 70th anniversary of the Worker's Party of Korea.

the People's Republic of China can be classified as an oligarchy if we stretch the meaning of the term. In China, power rests in the hands of a large but exclusive ruling *group*, the Communist Party. In a similar vein, drawing on conflict theory, one might argue that many industrialized nations of the West should be considered oligarchies (rather than democracies), since only a powerful few—leaders of big business, government, and the military—actually rule. Later in this chapter, we will examine the *elite model* of the U.S. political system in greater detail.

Dictatorship and Totalitarianism

A **dictatorship** is a government in which one person has nearly total power to make and enforce laws. Dictators rule primarily through the use of coercion, which often includes torture and executions. Typically, they *seize* power rather than being freely elected (as in a democracy) or inheriting power (as in a monarchy). Some dictators are quite charismatic and manage to achieve a certain popularity, though their supporters' enthusiasm is almost certainly tinged with fear. Other dictators are bitterly hated by the people over whom they rule.

Frequently, dictators develop such overwhelming control over people's lives that their governments are called *totalitarian*. (Monarchies and oligarchies may also achieve this type of dominance.) **Totalitarianism** involves virtually complete government control and surveillance over all aspects of a society's social and political life. Germany during Hitler's reign, the Soviet Union in the 1930s, and North Korea today are classified as totalitarian states.

Democracy

In a literal sense, **democracy** means government by the people. The word *democracy* originated in two Greek roots—*demos,* meaning "the populace" or "the common people," and *kratia,* meaning "rule." Of course, in large, populous nations such as the United States, government by the people is impractical at the national level. Americans cannot vote on every important issue that comes before Congress. Consequently, popular rule is generally maintained through **representative democracy,** a form of government in which certain individuals are selected to speak for the people.

The United States is commonly classified as a representative democracy, since the elected members of Congress and state legislatures make our laws. However, critics have questioned whether our democracy really is representative. Even today, not everyone in the United States feels included. Conspicuous among those who view themselves as excluded are Native Hawaiians (Box 48-1).

Do Congress and the state legislatures genuinely represent the masses, including minorities? Are the people of the United States legitimately self-governing, or has our government become a forum for powerful elites? We will explore these issues in Module 49.

Sovereignty in the Aloha State

The people of Hawai'i are highly diverse. Twenty-three percent of the population is White; 38 percent, Asian American; 9 percent, Hawaiian or other Pacific Islander; 9 percent, Hispanic; and 2 percent, African American. Another 19 percent of the population, including Hawai'i-born Barack Obama, declare themselves to be of two or more races. Yet Hawai'i is not a racial paradise: certain occupations and even social classes tend to be dominated by Whites, Chinese, or Japanese Americans. Nor is Hawai'i immune to intolerance, although compared to the mainland and much of the rest of the world, race relations there are more harmonious than discordant.

For one group in particular, Native Hawaiians, access to any kind of power has been severely limited for generations. Now, through the **sovereignty movement,** the indigenous people of Hawai'i are hoping to win self-government, as well as restoration of—or compensation for—1.2 million acres of ancestral lands they have lost over the last century. Their movement is comparable to efforts made by American Indian tribes in the continental United States, both in its roots and in its significance.

The sovereignty movement began in 1996, when Native Hawaiians held a referendum on the question "Shall the Hawaiian people elect delegates to propose a Native Hawaiian government?" The results indicated that 73 percent of those who voted favored such an effort. Since then, the state Office of Hawaiian Affairs has sought to create a registry of people with significant Hawaiian ancestry on the islands.

In Washington, D.C., Hawai'i's congressional delegation is seeking passage of the Native Hawaiian Government Reorganization Act, also referred to as the Akaka Bill, after late U.S. Senator Daniel Akaka. The act would give people of Hawaiian ancestry more say over the use of local resources, including land and fresh water; provide them with affordable housing; take steps to preserve their culture; and create ways for them to better express their grievances. As of 2016, the measure has not been seriously considered by Congress in several years.

Meanwhile, Native Hawaiians do what they can to create political pressure for their cause. On occasion, they form alliances with environmental groups that want to halt commercial development on the

© Marco Garcia/AP Images

An activist cuts out Hawai'i's statehood star in a symbolic action to mark the long struggle for sovereignty by Native Hawaiians.

islands. In 2008 and again in 2011, a Native Hawaiian independence group seized the royal palace in Honolulu to protest the U.S.-backed overthrow of the Hawaiian monarchy in 1893.

> For one group in particular, Native Hawaiians, access to any kind of power has been severely limited for generations.

Most recently, in 2015 the Supreme Court of Hawaii ruled in favor of sovereignty activists who blocked a massive new thirty meter telescope, costing $1.4 billion, set to be installed in the observatory on Mauna Kea, the volcanic mountain on the Big Island of Hawaii. The court recognized that the mountain holds importance to Native Hawaiians.

LET'S DISCUSS

1. From a mainstream point of view, what might be the advantages and disadvantages of extending sovereignty to an indigenous group? Discuss using sociological concepts.

2. Do some research on the legal basis for tribal sovereignty. How did American Indian tribes gain the status of separate nations?

Sources: Grant 2015; Kelleher 2011;PBS Hawaii 2015; Staton 2004; Toensing 2009; Welch 2011.

War and Peace

Conflict is a central aspect of social relations. Too often it becomes ongoing and violent, engulfing innocent bystanders as well as intentional participants. Sociologists Theodore Caplow and Louis Hicks (2002:3) have defined **war** as conflict between organizations that possess trained combat forces equipped with deadly weapons. This meaning is broader than the legal definition, which typically requires a formal declaration of hostilities.

War

Sociologists approach war in three different ways. Those who take a *global view* study how and why two or more nations become engaged in military conflict. Those who take a *nation-state view* stress the interaction of internal political, socioeconomic, and cultural forces. And those who take a *micro view* focus on the social impact of war on individuals and the groups they belong to (Kiser 1992; Wimmer 2014).

From the nation-state perspective, there is little to be said for the supposed socioeconomic benefits of war. Although armed conflicts increase government expenditures on troops and weapons, which tend to stimulate the economy, they also divert workers from civilian health and medical services. Thus, they have a negative effect on civilians' life chances, causing higher levels of civilian mortality. It is exceedingly difficult for a society to engage in armed conflict while maintaining citizens' well-being at home (Carlton-Ford 2010).

Although the decision to go to war is made by government leaders, public opinion plays a significant role in its execution. By 1971, the number of U.S. soldiers killed in Vietnam had surpassed 50,000, and antiwar sentiment was strong. Surveys done at that time showed the public was split roughly equally on the question of whether war was an appropriate way to settle differences between nations.

A major change in the composition of the U.S. military is the growing presence of women. Women now account for 15 percent of active U.S. military forces and are now in uniform, serving not just as support personnel but as a part of all combat units. The first casualty of the war in Iraq, in fact, was Private First Class Lori Piestewa, a member of the Hopi tribe and a descendant of Mexican settlers in the Southwest (see Box 34-1).

From a micro view, war can bring out the worst as well as the best in people. In 2004, graphic images of the abuse of Iraqi prisoners by U.S. soldiers at Iraq's Abu Ghraib prison shocked the world. For social scientists, the deterioration of the guards' behavior brought to mind Philip Zimbardo's mock prison experiment, done in 1971. Although the results of the experiment, highlighted in Chapter 5, have been applied primarily to civilian correctional facilities, Zimbardo's study was actually funded by the Office of Naval Research. In July 2004, the U.S. military began using a documentary film about the experiment to train military interrogators to avoid mistreatment of prisoners (Zarembo 2004a; Zimbardo 2004).

Peace

Sociologists have considered **peace** both as the absence of war and as a proactive effort to develop cooperative relations among nations. While we will focus here on international relations, we should note that the vast majority of armed conflicts occur *within* rather than between states. Often, outside powers become involved in these internal conflicts, either as supporters of particular factions or in an attempt to broker a peace accord. The countries where such conflicts occur would not be considered core nations in world systems analysis (Institute for Economics and Peace 2015a; Kriesberg 1992; D. Smith 1999).

Another way of picturing the relative peacefulness of nations around the world is the Global Peace Index (Figure 48-1). This index is based on 24 indicators, including organized internal conflict, violent crime, political instability, the potential for terrorist acts, and a nation's level of military expenditures compared to its neighbors'.

Currently, Iceland and Denmark are at the top of the index (very peaceful); Syria and Afghanistan are at the bottom (great civil unrest). The United States ranks 94 on this list of 162 nations, between Peru and Saudi Arabia. The map shows that the world contains large areas with very high levels of peace—North America and Europe for example. Yet 2.3 billion people live in the 20 least peaceful countries, while only 500 million live in the 20 most peaceful (Alford 2015).

Taking Sociology to Work

Joseph W. Drummond, *Management Analyst, U.S. Army Space and Missile Defense Command*

Courtesy of Joseph W. Drummond

When Joseph Drummond entered Morehouse College, he was planning to major in political science. But after taking an introductory sociology course, he felt that sociology gave him a clearer picture of the complexity and interconnectedness of society. "The career track that I had in mind was to enter the field of sociology as a researcher/policy maker," he explains. However, he soon ran into "a disconnect between academia and policy making," and an apparent lack of representation of sociologists at the policymaking level.

Drummond credits one of his sociology professors for steering him toward quantitative courses. "If you ever plan on having a job," the professor suggested, "make sure you have a lot of classes with quantitative analysis—for example, statistics and data analysis. These classes tell whatever company you want to work for that you have practical skills." Later, when Drummond asked his current employer why he had gotten the job he now holds, he was told that his data analysis and social statistics courses had made him competitive.

Today, Drummond works at the U.S. Army's Space and Missile Defense Command (SMDC), near Huntsville, Alabama. He began there as an intern, after responding to an e-mail from Morehouse College's career office. Drummond is now a junior analyst with a team that formulates and develops doctrine, organization, and material requirements for Army units assigned to space and missile defense. In a typical workweek, he reviews military force structure—units, battalions, and so on—and helps to implement directives from Department of the Army headquarters. "A lot of what we do is attempting to translate very high-level guidance to something that's practical," he explains.

Drummond values the support and professional development he has received from the Army, including classes on program management, data analysis, national security, and force management. An Army-sponsored Technology and Government in Your Future event emphasized the need for interns to pursue graduate studies in math and science to land the best jobs. Drummond says the real-world experience he got as an intern at SMDC not only brought classroom theory to life; it also made him more attractive to future employers.

Asked how he uses sociology in his work, Drummond replies that his academic training has helped him to look critically at problems and to think about the second- and third-order effects of a decision. Seeing society from a macro-level view is also invaluable to him. "When U.S. leadership began to realize that a 'hearts and minds' campaign means that we need to understand the social-historical context of the people whose country we're occupying, that changed the way that we did business and also impacted the way U.S. military force structure was managed," he explains. "A lot of people had problems making the connection." Finally, sociology has taught Drummond not to take things at face value. "Most problems/issues that we come across very seldom have easy fixes," he notes. "Sociology taught me that thorough analysis means leaving no stone unturned."

LET'S DISCUSS

1. Have you ever considered a career in national defense? Do you know anyone with a college degree who works in the field?

2. Why do you think quantitative analysis is such an important skill to employers? How might you use it in your career?

FIGURE 48-1 **Global Peace Index**

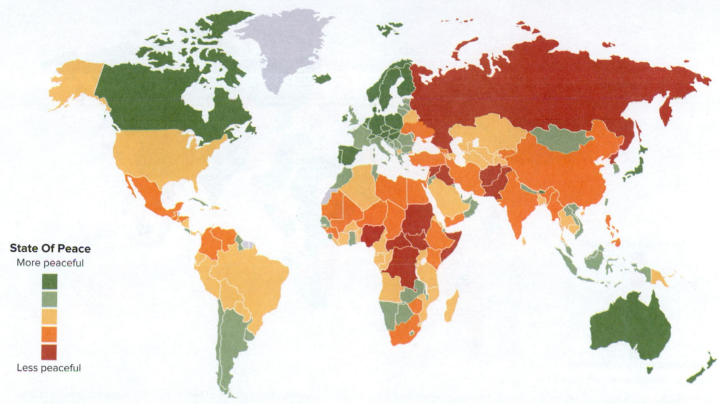

State Of Peace

More peaceful

Less peaceful

Source: Institute for Economics and Peace 2015a. From 2015 Global Peace Index.

The world's leading measure of national peacefulness, the Global Peace Index, measures peace according to 23 qualitative and quantitative indicators.

Sociologists and other social scientists who draw on sociological theory and research have tried to identify conditions that deter war. One of their findings is that international trade may act as a deterrent to armed conflict. As countries exchange goods, people, and then cultures, they become more integrated and less likely to threaten each other's security. Viewed from this perspective, not just trade but immigration and foreign exchange programs have a beneficial effect on international relations.

Another means of fostering peace is the activity of international charities and activist groups called nongovernmental organizations (NGOs). The Red Cross and Red Crescent and Doctors Without Borders donate their services wherever they are needed, without regard to nationality. In the past decade or more, these global organizations have been expanding in number, size, and scope. By sharing news of local conditions and clarifying local issues, they often prevent conflicts from escalating into violence and war. Some NGOs have initiated cease-fires, reached settlements, and even ended warfare between former adversaries.

Finally, many analysts stress that nations cannot maintain their security by threatening violence. Peace, they contend, can best be maintained by developing strong mutual security agreements between potential adversaries (Etzioni 1965; Shostak 2002).

In recent years, the United States has begun to recognize that its security can be threatened not just by nation-states, but by political groups that operate outside the bounds of legitimate authority. Indeed, terrorism is now considered the foremost threat to U.S. security.

 use your **sociological imagination**

Do you hear much discussion of how to promote worldwide peace, or do the conversations you hear focus more on ending a particular conflict? Which approach would more likely result in a positive outcome? Why?

Terrorism

Acts of terror, whether perpetrated by a few or by many people, can be a powerful political force. Formally defined, **terrorism** is the use or threat of violence against random or symbolic targets in pursuit of political aims. For terrorists, the end justifies the means. They believe the status quo is oppressive and that desperate measures are essential to end the suffering of the deprived. Convinced that working through the formal political process will not effect the desired political change, terrorists insist that illegal actions—often directed against innocent people—are needed. Ultimately, they hope to intimidate society and thereby bring about a new political order.

People sometimes remark that we have become numbed to the violence we witness, both personally and through the media. An analysis through 2014 of the direct and indirect impact of about 160,000 incidents of terrorism in 162 nations in terms of lives lost,

FIGURE 48-2 **Global Terrorism Index**

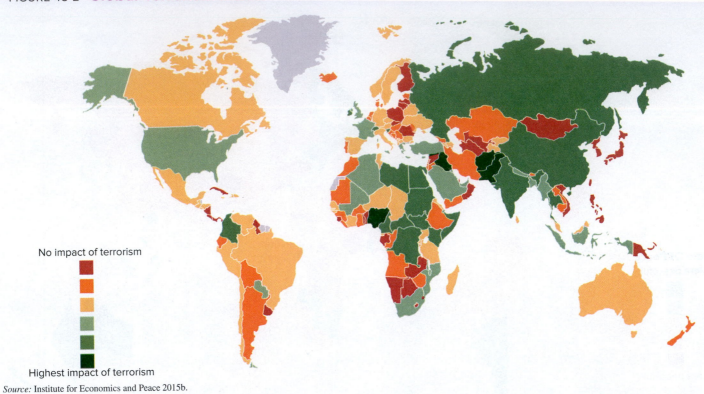

No impact of terrorism

Highest impact of terrorism

Source: Institute for Economics and Peace 2015b.

The Global Terrorism Index measures the impact of terrorism in 162 countries. To account for the lasting effects of terrorism, each country is given a score that represents a five-year weighted average.

injuries, property damage and emotional toll of the after-effects has been used to produce the Global Terrorism Index (Figure 48-2).

At the time the analysis was made, the United States ranked 35th, just below Great Britain and just ahead of Iran, in danger of terrorism. The top five countries experiencing terrorism are Iraq, Afghanistan, Nigeria, Pakistan, and Syria. Among the nations in the least danger of terrorism are countries as varied as Haiti, South Korea, and Vietnam.

An essential aspect of contemporary terrorism involves use of the media. Terrorists may wish to keep secret their individual identities, but they want their political messages and goals to receive as much publicity as possible. Drawing on Erving Goffman's dramaturgical approach, sociologist Alfred McClung Lee (1983) has likened terrorism to the theater, where certain scenes are played out in predictable fashion. Whether through calls to the media, anonymous manifestos, or other means, terrorists typically admit responsibility for and defend their violent acts.

Sociologists and others have studied the role of labeling in how behavior comes to be regarded as "terrorism." Social media allows groups labeled "terrorist," such as Boko Haram, ISIS, and al Qaeda, to define their activities as justified and the actions of nation-states against them as unlawful and evil. As labeling theory shows, the label used depends on one's point of view: recently, civil rights groups such as Black Lives Matter have questioned the limited use of the terrorist label in the United States, suggesting that in some cases it should belong to perpetrators of

anti-Black violence, including police officers. The argument, as reflected in the Black Lives Matter movement, is that terrorism is not the sole domain of terrorist groups designated by the UN Security Council (Gladstone 2015; Kampf 2014).

Since September 11, 2001, governments worldwide have renewed their efforts to fight terrorism. Although the public generally regards increased surveillance and social control as a necessary evil, these measures have nonetheless raised governance issues. For example, some citizens in the United States and elsewhere have questioned whether measures such as the USA Patriot Act of 2001 threaten civil liberties. Citizens have also complained about the heightened anxiety created by the vague alerts issued by the federal government from time to time. Worldwide, immigration and the processing of refugees have slowed to a crawl, separating families and preventing employers from filling job openings. As these efforts to combat political violence illustrate, the term *terrorism* is an apt one (R. Howard and Sawyer 2003; A. Lee 1983; R. Miller 1988).

Increasingly, governments are becoming concerned about another form of political violence, the potential for malicious cyberattacks. In an age in which computer viruses can spread worldwide through the Internet, this kind of attack could render a nation's computer systems useless, or even shut down its power plants. A few years ago, such a scenario would have been considered pulp fiction, but it is now the subject of contingency planning throughout the world (Clayton 2011).

MODULE 48 | Recap and Review

Summary

Every society must have a **political system** to allocate valued resources

1. There are three basic sources of **power** within any political system: **force, influence,** and **authority.**

2. Max Weber identified three ideal types of authority: **traditional, rational-legal,** and **charismatic.**

3. There are four basic types of government: **monarchy, oligarchy, dictatorship,** and **democracy.**

4. **War** may be defined as conflict between organizations that possess trained combat forces equipped with deadly weapons—a definition that includes conflict with terrorist organizations.

Thinking Critically

1. On your campus, what are some examples of the three types of authority?

2. Contrast the use of power in a dictatorship with its use in a democracy, as defined by Max Weber.

3. What is the greatest threat to world peace, and how would you counter it?

Key Terms

Authority	Political system
Charismatic authority	Politics
Democracy	Power
Dictatorship	Rational-legal authority
Economic system	Representative democracy
Force	Sovereignty movement
Influence	Terrorism
Monarchy	Totalitarianism
Oligarchy	Traditional authority
Peace	War

MODULE 49 | Political Behavior and Power in the United States

Citizens of the United States take for granted many aspects of their political system. They are accustomed to living in a nation with a Bill of Rights, two major political parties, elections by secret ballot, an elected president, state and local governments distinct from the national government, and so forth. Yet each society has its own ways of governing itself and making decisions. U.S. residents expect Democratic and Republican candidates to compete for public office; residents of Cuba and the People's Republic of China are accustomed to one-party rule by the Communist Party. In this section, we will examine several aspects of political behavior within the United States.

● Participation and Apathy

In theory, a representative democracy will function most effectively and fairly if an informed and active electorate communicates its views to government leaders. Unfortunately, that is hardly the case in the United States. Virtually all citizens are familiar with the basics of the political process, and many identify to some extent with a political party. About 45 percent of eligible voters *lean* toward the Democrats and 42 percent lean toward the Republicans.

Yet such numbers do not reflect two trends of the last 20 years. First, if given an opportunity, 43 percent self-identify as independent of either major party. Second, those who do identify with a major party are becoming increasingly polarized from one another. A fourth to a third of party faithful sees the other party as a "threat to the nation's well-being." An astonishing 92 percent of Republicans are to the right of (that is, more conservative than) the typical Democrat, and 94 percent of Democrats are to the left of (more liberal than) the typical Republican. Consequently, political compromise and coalition building become increasingly difficult (Jones 2015a, 2015b; Pew Research Center for the People and the Press 2014).

By the 1980s, it had become clear that many people in the United States were beginning to be turned off by political parties, politicians, and big government. The most dramatic indication of this growing alienation came from voting statistics. Today, voters of all ages and races appear to be less enthusiastic than ever about elections, even presidential contests. For example, in the presidential election of 1896, almost 80 percent of eligible voters in the United States went to the polls. Yet by the 2012 election, turnout was only 62 percent of citizens—well below the levels of the 1960s. Two years later, in the 2014 midterm election, turnout fell to 43 percent, lower than in most other nations (Figure 49-1).

In the end, political participation makes government accountable to the voters. If participation declines, government operates with less of a sense of accountability to society. This issue is most serious for the least powerful individuals and groups in the United States. Historically, voter turnout has been particularly low among members of racial and ethnic minorities. However, in post-election surveys following the 2012 presidential election, a higher proportion of African Americans than Whites reported that they actually voted.

Many more potential voters fail to register to vote. The poor—whose focus understandably is on survival—are traditionally underrepresented among voters as well. The low turnout found among these groups is explained at least in part by their common feeling of powerlessness. Yet these low statistics encourage political power brokers to continue to ignore the interests of the less affluent and the nation's minorities.

The segment of the voting population that has shown the most voter apathy is the young. Even the 2012 presidential election, held against the background of President Obama's reelection bid and continuing global economic decline, did not pique the interest of voters ages 18 to 24. Only 41.2 percent of them voted, compared to 71.9 percent of those age 65 and older.

What lies behind voter apathy among the young? The popular explanation is that people—especially young people—are alienated from the political system, turned off by the shallowness and negativity of candidates and campaigns. However, because young people do vote as they age, other explanations seem more plausible, such as the difficulty of registering or absentee voting (Bureau of the Census 2011e: Table 10; File 2013).

© Frank Micelotta/Getty Images

Race and Gender in Politics

Because politics is synonymous with power and authority, we should not be surprised that political strength is lacking in marginalized groups, such as women and racial and ethnic minorities. Nationally, women did not get the vote until 1920. Most Chinese Americans were turned away from the polls until 1926. And African Americans were disenfranchised until 1965, when national voting rights legislation was passed. Predictably, it has taken these groups some time to develop their political power and begin to exercise it effectively.

Progress toward the inclusion of minority groups in government has been slow. In 2016, 19 percent of members of Congress were women and 18 percent were members of racial and ethnic minorities. While these represented record numbers, it meant that White non-Hispanic men constituted two out of three of the nation's elected representatives.

Today, with record-high numbers of Blacks and Latinos holding elective office, many critics

FIGURE 49-1 **Voter Turnout Worldwide**

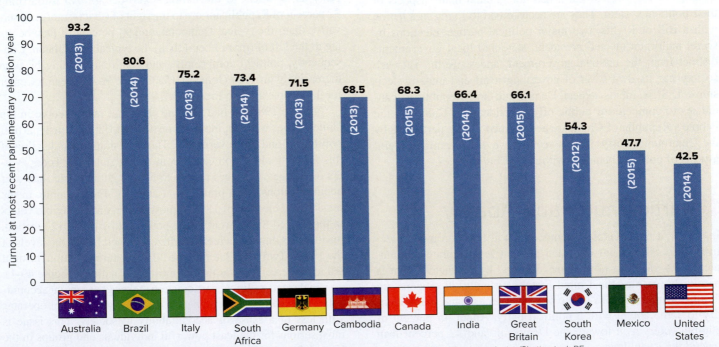

Source: International Institute for Democracy and Electoral Assistance 2015; data for Canada from Ferrera 2015. *Flags:* © admin_design/Shutterstock RF

Box 49-1

The Latino Political Voice

Until the late twentieth century, Latinos' political activity remained outside conventional electoral activities. Instead, it focused primarily on grassroots organizing over specific issues such as migrant workers' rights. But as numbers of Hispanics who were eligible to vote began to grow, they recognized their political clout over local elections and even congressional seats.

A growing Hispanic population has not necessarily meant a growing presence in the voting box. The Latino population includes many individuals who are under the legal age to vote as well as many who are not citizens. Current estimates indicate that 49 percent of Hispanics are eligible to vote, compared to 74 percent of non-Hispanics.

Yet the growing Latino presence has led Hispanic communities to anticipate that they will have greater political representation in the future. As shown in the figure below, Latino participation has grown greatly over the past 30 years and is expected to double as a proportion of the electorate by 2030.

Both major political parties have begun to recognize that Latinos are a force in the

> Both major political parties have begun to recognize that Latinos are a force in the election process, even in presidential elections.

election process, even in presidential elections. The numbers of Latinos in key swing or battleground states, such as Colorado, Florida, Michigan, Missouri, Nevada, New Mexico, Ohio, and Virginia is now sufficient to affect which party captures the state's electoral votes.

U.S. voting policy toward Latinos has been ambivalent: some laws facilitate the Hispanic vote while others tend to suppress it. On a positive note, Congress has acknowledged the multilingual background of the U.S. population by requiring local jurisdictions to provide bilingual or even multilingual ballots in voting districts where at least 5 percent of the voting-age population, or 10,000, people do not speak English. However, recent measures in some states to require voters to show government-issued IDs, may prevent many low-income Latinos from voting. As we noted in Box 31-1, it is estimated that 16 percent of Latino citizens do not have a valid government-issued photo ID.

Restrictions aside, many presidential candidates make an effort to reach out to the Hispanic community by visiting neighborhoods and issuing statements and campaign literature in Spanish. Like African Americans, many Latinos resent that political movers and shakers seem to rediscover that they exist once every four years. Latino community leaders derisively label candidates'

fascination with Latino concerns around election time as either *fiesta politics* or *Hispandering*. Between major elections, only modest efforts have been made to court Hispanic interests, except by Latino elected officials; however, this may change as Latino presence at the ballot box is felt.

Democrats, who typically capture over 60, sometimes 70, percent of the Latino vote have clearly garnered the allegiance of Hispanics with their more positive stance on immigration reform and backing of renewed diplomatic relations with Cuba. In contrast the Republicans face a difficult challenge. Many Republican leaders take an extremely anti-immigrant stance, such as "no pathway to citizenship" for those already here illegally; others tend to be more open to naturalizing illegal immigrants after they move through a series of steps. Yet it would be wrong to assume that immigration is the only issue for Latino voters, as many focus more on economic and family or social issues. On these topics Hispanic voters often find Republican candidates more persuasive than Democrats.

Republicans cannot afford to dismiss the Latino vote, and Democrats should not take it for granted. The Hispanic community's rapid growth, increasing proportions of voter registration, and growing electoral participation guarantee future efforts by politicians to gain their support

LET'S DISCUSS

1. In what ways are Latinos, as a voting group, similar to other ethnic and racial groups? In what ways are they different?

2. Read the news for a few days to determine two specific ways in which Latino issues are important to current politics, either on a national or local level.

Sources: ACLU 2015a; Brennan Center 2015; Lopez and Gonzalez-Barrera 2013; Taylor et al. 2012; Cohn 2014; Peters 2015.

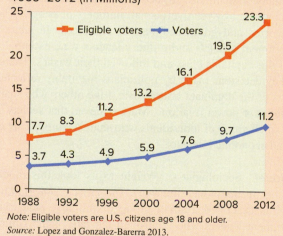

Latino Participation in Presidential Elections, 1988–2012 (in Millions)

Note: Eligible voters are U.S. citizens age 18 and older.
Source: Lopez and Gonzalez-Barerra 2013.

---

decry the fact that politicians seem to recognize minority racial and ethnic groups only at election time. In Box 49-1, we will consider the growing political voice of Hispanic Americans.

Female politicians may be enjoying more electoral success now than in the past, but there is some evidence that the media cover them differently from male politicians. A content analysis of newspaper coverage of recent gubernatorial races showed that reporters wrote more often about a female candidate's personal life, appearance, or personality than a male candidate's, and less

often about her political positions and voting record. Furthermore, when political issues were raised in newspaper articles, reporters were more likely to illustrate them with statements made by male candidates than by female candidates (Devitt 1999; Jost 2008).

Figure 49-2 shows the representation of women in selected national legislatures. While the proportion of women in national legislatures has increased in the United States and many other nations, in all but one country women still do not account for half the members of the national legislature. The African Republic

© Win McNamee/Getty Images

Minnesota Democrat Keith Ellison created quite a stir in 2007 when he became the first person to take the congressional oath of office on a Qur'an. The newly elected member of the House of Representatives, who is Muslim, thought the Qur'an would make his oath more meaningful than a Bible. Speaker of the House Nancy Pelosi (left) borrowed Thomas Jefferson's two-volume Qur'an for the occasion—a reminder that acknowledging diversity is nothing new in U.S. politics. In 2008, André Carson was elected to Congress from Indiana. He became the second Muslim member of Congress.

FIGURE 49-2 **Women in National Legislatures, Selected Countries**

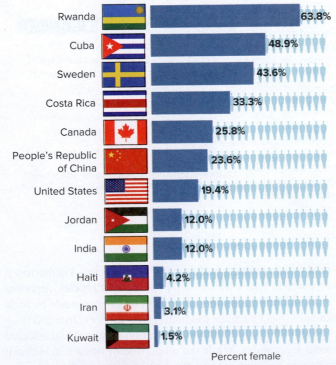

Country	Percent female
Rwanda	63.8%
Cuba	48.9%
Sweden	43.6%
Costa Rica	33.3%
Canada	25.8%
People's Republic of China	23.6%
United States	19.4%
Jordan	12.0%
India	12.0%
Haiti	4.2%
Iran	3.1%
Kuwait	1.5%

Percent female

Notes: Data are for lower legislative houses only, as of November 1, 2015; data on upper houses, such as the U.S. Senate, are not included.
Source: Inter-Parliamentary Union 2015. *Flags:* © admin_design/Shutterstock RF

of Rwanda, the exception, ranks the highest, with 63.8 percent of its legislative seats held by women. Overall, the United States ranked 84th among 190 nations in the proportion of women serving as national legislators at the end of 2015.

To remedy this situation, many countries have adopted quotas for female representatives. In some, the government sets aside a certain percentage of seats for women, usually from 14 to 30 percent. In others, political parties have decided that 20 to 40 percent of their candidates should be women. Currently 118 countries and some territories have some kind of female quota system (International Institute for Democracy and Electoral Assistance 2013).

Models of Power Structure in the United States

Who really holds power in the United States? Do "we the people" genuinely run the country through our elected representatives? Or is it true that behind the scenes, a small elite controls both the government and the economic system? It is difficult to determine the location of power in a society as complex as the United States. In exploring this critical question, social scientists have developed two basic views of our nation's power structure: the power elite and the pluralist models.

Power Elite Models

Karl Marx believed that 19th-century representative democracy was essentially a sham. He argued that industrialized societies were dominated by relatively small numbers of people who owned factories and controlled natural resources. In Marx's view, government officials and military leaders were essentially servants of this capitalist class and followed their wishes. Therefore, any key decisions made by politicians inevitably reflected the interests of the dominant bourgeoisie. Like others who share an **elite model** of power relations, Marx believed that society is ruled by a small group of individuals who share a common set of political and economic interests.

Mills's Model Sociologist C. Wright Mills took this model a step further in his pioneering work *The Power Elite* ([1956] 2000b). Mills described a small group of military, industrial, and government leaders who controlled the fate of the United States—the **power elite.** Power rested in the hands of a few, both inside and outside government.

A pyramid illustrates the power structure of the United States in Mills's model (Figure 49-3a). At the top are the corporate rich, leaders of the executive branch of government, and heads of the military (whom Mills called the "warlords"). Directly below are local opinion leaders, members of the legislative branch of government, and leaders of special-interest groups. Mills contended that these individuals and groups would basically follow the wishes of the dominant power elite. At the bottom of the pyramid are the unorganized, exploited masses.

The power elite model is in many respects similar to the work of Karl Marx. The most striking difference is that Mills believed

FIGURE 49-3 Power Elite Models

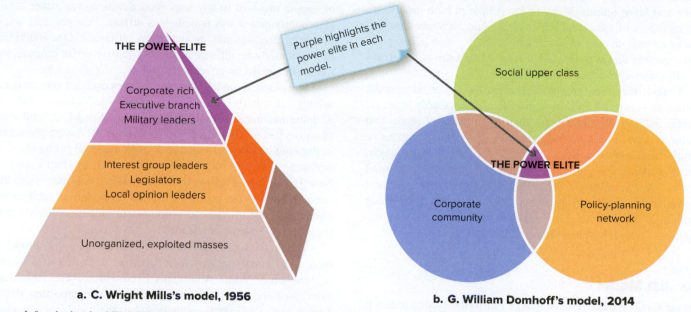

a. C. Wright Mills's model, 1956

b. G. William Domhoff's model, 2014

THE POWER ELITE

Corporate rich
Executive branch
Military leaders

Interest group leaders
Legislators
Local opinion leaders

Unorganized, exploited masses

Purple highlights the power elite in each model.

Social upper class

THE POWER ELITE

Corporate community

Policy-planning network

that the economically powerful coordinate their maneuvers with the military and political establishments to serve their common interests. He rejected Marx's belief that by itself, the economic structure of capitalism could create a ruling class. Still, the powerless masses at the bottom of Mills's power elite model certainly bring to mind Marx's portrait of the oppressed workers of the world, who have "nothing to lose but their chains."

A fundamental element in Mills's thesis is that the power elite not only includes relatively few members but also operates as a self-conscious, cohesive unit. Although not necessarily diabolical or ruthless, the elite comprises similar types of people who interact regularly with one another and have essentially the same political and economic interests. Mills's power elite is not a conspiracy, but rather a community of interest and sentiment among a small number of influential people (A. Hacker 1964).

Admittedly, Mills failed to clarify when the elite opposes protests and when it tolerates them; he also failed to provide detailed case studies that would substantiate the interrelationships among members of the power elite. Nevertheless, his challenging theories forced scholars to look more critically at the democratic political system of the United States.

In commenting on the scandals that have rocked major corporations, observers have noted that members of the business elite are closely interrelated. In a study of the members of the boards of directors of Fortune 1000 corporations, researchers found that each director can reach every other board of directors in just 3.7 steps. That is, by consulting acquaintances of acquaintances, each director can quickly reach someone who sits on each of the other 999 boards. Furthermore, the face-to-face contact directors regularly have in their board meetings makes

them a highly cohesive elite. Finally, the corporate elite is not only wealthy, powerful, and cohesive; it is also overwhelmingly White and male. However, the unity of perspective in the power elite is not infallible, as witnessed in the financial crisis of 2008. This underscores the fact that the powerful may work at cross-purposes to each other (Davis 2004; Fry 2015; Mizruchi 2010, 2013; Schaefer 2008b).

The effort to curb the power of those who influence political campaign financing received a blow in the Supreme Court's 2010 decision, *Citizens United v. Federal Election Commission*, which ended restrictions on the amount of campaign contributions by organizations, corporations, lobbyists, and individuals wishing to create their own campaign materials or to launch media advertising spots.

One outgrowth of Mills's power elite model is current research on the presence of a *global* power elite—that is, those business, political, and former military leaders who exercise influence across national borders. Because this avenue of scholarship is relatively new, there is some disagreement on the definition of the term. Must the members of the global power elite demonstrate as much consensus as the members of Mills's power elite? Or can the global power elite include such diverse voices as publisher Rupert Murdoch and former president Bill Clinton, in his role as head of the Clinton Global Initiative (L. Miller 2008; Rothkopf 2008)?

Domhoff's Model Over the past three decades, sociologist G. William Domhoff (2014a, 2014b), author of the chapter-opening excerpt, has agreed with Mills that a powerful elite runs the United States. He finds that it is still largely older, White, male, and upper class. However, Domhoff stresses the role played both by elites of the corporate community and by leaders of organizations in the policy-planning network, such as chambers of commerce and labor unions. Many of the people in both groups are also members of the social upper class. And he notes the presence of a small number of women and minority men in key positions—groups that were excluded from Mills's top echelon and are still underrepresented today.

Though the three groups in Domhoff's power elite model overlap, as Figure 49-3b shows, they do not necessarily agree on specific policies. Domhoff notes that in the electoral arena, two coalitions have exercised influence. A *corporate-conservative coalition* has played a large role in both political parties, generating support for particular candidates through direct-mail appeals. A *liberal-labor coalition* is based in unions, local environmental organizations, a segment of the minority group community, liberal churches, and the university and arts communities (Zweigenhaft and Domhoff 2006).

Pluralist Model

Several social scientists insist that power in the United States is shared more widely than the elite models indicate. In their view, a pluralist model more accurately describes the nation's political system. According to the **pluralist model,** many competing groups within the community have access to government, so that no single group is dominant.

The pluralist model suggests that a variety of groups play a significant role in decision making. Typically, pluralists make use of intensive case studies or community studies based on observation research. One of the most famous—an investigation

© Haraz Ghanbari/AP Images

Pluralism can be seen in action in the activity of lobbying groups attempting to influence public policy. The highly publicized battle over stem cell research is one example; it has pitted conservative religious groups against health advocacy groups, dividing political leaders in the process. Legislation to support the research technique had the backing of several prominent Republican lawmakers, including Senator Orrin Hatch (R-Utah), shown here with actor and activist Michael J. Fox. Nevertheless, in 2001 President George W. Bush banned federal funding of stem cell research. Eight years later President Obama lifted the restrictions.

of decision making in New Haven, Connecticut—was reported by Robert Dahl (1961). Dahl found that although the number of people involved in any important decision was rather small, community power was nonetheless diffuse. Few political actors exercised decision-making power on all issues. One individual or group might be influential in a battle over urban renewal, but have little impact on educational policy.

The pluralist model, however, has not escaped serious questioning. Domhoff (1978, 2014) reexamined Dahl's study of decision making in New Haven and argued that Dahl and other pluralists had failed to trace how local elites who were prominent in decision making belonged to a larger national ruling class. In addition, studies of community power, such as Dahl's work in New Haven, can examine decision making only on issues that become part of the political agenda. They fail to address the potential power of elites to keep certain matters entirely out of the realm of government debate.

The most significant criticism of the pluralist model is that, as originally proposed, it failed to note that it is largely a pluralism of White Americans from which racial and ethnic minorities are largely absent. Yes, there are important Black, Latino, and Asian decision makers, but their influence is overwhelmingly felt in policy areas where members of racial and ethnic minorities dominate, such as voting rights or immigration reform. Even in those areas Whites continue to play significant roles, while minorities are rarely important actors in political spheres composed primarily of Whites (Berry and Junn 2015; Pinderhughes 1987).

Historically, pluralists have stressed ways in which large numbers of people can participate in or influence governmental decision making. New communications technologies are increasing the opportunity to be heard, not just in countries such as the United States, but in developing countries the world over. One common point of the elite and pluralist perspectives stands out, however: in political systems, power is unequally distributed. All citizens may be equal in theory, yet those who are high in the nation's power structure are "more equal." Social upheaval, such as the Arab Spring uprisings of 2010-2012, creates broad political participation, but ultimately long-term decision making remains in the hands of relatively few (Freedman 2014; Ishak 2013).

Regardless of the form of government, social media and people's ability to access it has transformed political life, as Box 49-2 illustrates.

Perhaps the ultimate test of power, no matter what a nation's power structure, is the decision to go to war. Because the rank and file of any army is generally drawn from the lower classes—the least powerful groups in society—such a decision has life-and-death consequences for people far removed from the center of power. In the long run, if the general population is not convinced that war is necessary, military action is unlikely to succeed. Thus, war is a risky way in which to address conflict between nations. In the following section we will contrast war and peace as ways of addressing societal conflict, and more recently, the threat of terrorism.

Politicking Online

Until recently, citizens could exercise their political rights by voting, supporting candidates for office with their time or money, and writing an occasional letter to the local newspaper. Public rallies or protests, though not for everyone, were another way to display support for a particular politician or social issue. Then came the Internet and social media, and the possibilities for politicking broadened dramatically.

Today, social media are playing a growing part in Americans' political and civic engagement. During the 2014 midterm elections, 28 percent of registered voters used their cell phones to follow political news, and 16 percent followed specific candidates on social media. Republican-leaning and Democratic-leaning citizens are equally likely to use social media for these purposes.

Although online politicking is more common among younger people, the differences between age groups are not great. For example, 43 percent of those under age 30 seek out digital political material, compared to 22 percent of those age 50 to 64.

Research is just beginning on the effectiveness of online civic engagement. What impact, if any, does online social networking have on people's politics or political views? Over 40 percent follow political figures on social media so they can learn "political news before others." One out of four judge online information to be more reliable than the information they get from traditional news organizations. An important area for further research is whether online politicking actually persuades people to change their minds. Early analysis of Twitter use by politicians in Europe suggests that social media may

be mostly "preaching to the converted," but given the low cost of such outreach, producing any new votes, confirming supporters in their choice, and making them more likely to vote would be significant political outcomes.

Another question of interest is the effect of social media on campaign contributions. Beginning in 2012, the Federal Election Commission allowed political campaigns to accept contributions via text messages. At that point, 10 percent of all donors were already using the new method to back their candidates.

> During the 2014 midterm elections, 28 percent of registered voters used their cell phones to follow political news, and 16 percent followed specific candidates on social media.

Earlier in this chapter we noted the poor turnout of young people. Online politicking would seem to be an obvious way to increase their engagement in election politics. However, 18- to 21-year-olds are not typically included in the voter databases available to campaigns, so to receive campaign information, the young voter must contact the campaign. This will most likely become less of an issue as political campaigns become more sophisticated in locating potential voters.

Given the tendency of the Internet and social media to encourage political activity, governments have tried to suppress them. Nations frequently clamp down on online activity that opposes the central government or asserts human rights, such as the right to freedom of expression or to minority or religious views. In 2006, when a military coup overthrew the democratically elected government of Thailand, citizens lost access to websites critical of the takeover. Such actions give new meaning to the use of force as a source of power, for censorship of online content is just as much a use of force as closing down a newspaper or arresting dissidents.

Like citizens, governments also use the Internet to reach well beyond national borders. In what has been described as "public diplomacy," the U.S. State Department has taken to using Twitter abroad. In 2012, within minutes of violent attacks on U.S. embassies and consulates in the Middle East, the U.S. embassy in Cairo tweeted an emergency number to American citizens, and thanked fellow tweeters for their condolences on the murder of the ambassador to Libya.

LET'S DISCUSS

1. Do you use the Internet or social media for political purposes? If so, do those in your social network affect your political views or participation?

2. What might be some drawbacks of online political activity?

Sources: Deibert et al. 2008; *The Economist* 2012, 2014a; Smith 2014; A. Smith and Duggan 2012; Vergeer 2015.

MODULE 49 | Recap and Review

Summary

Political participation makes government accountable to citizens.

1. Both in the United States and in other countries, voters display a good deal of apathy toward the political system.

2. Women are still underrepresented in politics but are becoming more successful at winning election to public office.

3. Advocates of the **elite model** of the U.S. power structure see the nation as being ruled by a small group of individuals who share common political and economic interests (a **power elite**). Advocates of a **pluralist model** believe that power is shared more widely among conflicting groups.

MODULE 50 | Economic Systems

The sociocultural evolution approach developed by Gerhard Lenski categorizes preindustrial society according to the way in which the economy is organized. The principal types of preindustrial society, as you recall, are hunting-and-gathering societies, horticultural societies, and agrarian societies.

The *Industrial Revolution*—which took place largely in England during the period 1760 to 1830—brought about changes in the social organization of the workplace. People left their homesteads and began working in central locations such as factories. As the Industrial Revolution proceeded, a new form of social structure emerged: the **industrial society,** a society that depends on mechanization to produce its goods and services.

The scope of these large economies is massive, as Figure 50-1 shows. Over the last three centuries, industrialization has greatly increased the wealth of nations. Since 1990 China, which only began to mechanize its rural areas in the last half of the 20th century, has grown from eleventh largest economy in the world to second largest.

Two basic types of economic system distinguish contemporary industrial societies: capitalism and socialism. As described in the following sections, capitalism and socialism are ideal types of economic system. No nation precisely fits either model. Instead, each nation's economy represents a mixture of capitalism and socialism, although one type or the other is generally more useful in describing a society's economic structure.

FIGURE 50-1 World's Largest Economies

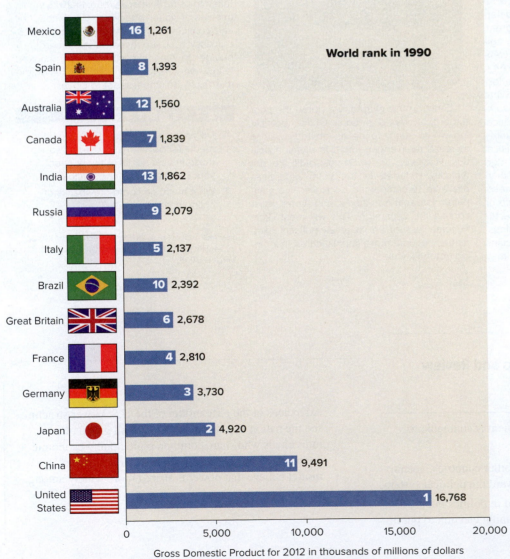

World rank in 1990

Country	Rank	GDP
Mexico	16	1,261
Spain	8	1,393
Australia	12	1,560
Canada	7	1,839
India	13	1,862
Russia	9	2,079
Italy	5	2,137
Brazil	10	2,392
Great Britain	6	2,678
France	4	2,810
Germany	3	3,730
Japan	2	4,920
China	11	9,491
United States	1	16,768

Gross Domestic Product for 2012 in thousands of millions of dollars

Sources: World Bank 2015c:Table 4-10. *Flags:* © admin_design/Shutterstock RF

Capitalism

In preindustrial societies, land was the source of virtually all wealth. The Industrial Revolution changed all that. It required that certain individuals and institutions be willing to take substantial risks to finance new inventions, machinery, and business enterprises. Eventually, bankers, industrialists, and other holders of large sums of money replaced landowners as the most powerful economic force. These people invested their funds in the hope of realizing even greater profits, and thereby became owners of property and business firms.

The transition to private ownership of business was accompanied by the emergence of the capitalist economic system. **Capitalism** is an economic system in which the means of production are held largely in private hands and the main incentive for economic activity is the accumulation of profits. In practice, capitalist systems vary in the degree to which the government regulates private ownership and economic activity (D. Rosenberg 1991).

Immediately following the Industrial Revolution, the prevailing form of capitalism was what is termed **laissez-faire** ("let them do"). Under the principle of laissez-faire, as expounded and endorsed by British economist Adam Smith (1723–1790), people could compete freely, with minimal government intervention in the economy. Business retained the right to regulate itself and operated essentially without fear of government interference (Smelser 1963).

Two centuries later, capitalism has taken on a somewhat different form. Private ownership and maximization of profits still remain the most significant characteristics of capitalist economic systems. However, in contrast to the era of laissez-faire, capitalism today features government regulation of economic relations. Without regulations, business firms can mislead consumers, endanger workers' safety, and even defraud the companies' investors—all in the pursuit of greater profits. That is why the government of a capitalist nation often monitors prices, sets safety and environmental standards for industries, protects the rights of consumers, and regulates collective bargaining between labor unions and management. Yet under capitalism as an ideal type, government rarely takes over ownership of an entire industry.

Contemporary capitalism also differs from laissez-faire in another important respect: capitalism tolerates monopolistic practices. A **monopoly** exists when a single business firm controls the market. Domination of an industry allows the firm to effectively control a commodity by dictating pricing, quality standards, and availability. Buyers have little choice but to yield to the firm's decisions; there is no other place to purchase the product or service. Monopolistic practices violate the ideal of free competition cherished by Adam Smith and other supporters of laissez-faire capitalism.

Some capitalistic nations, such as the United States, outlaw monopolies through antitrust legislation. Such laws prevent any business from taking over so much of an industry that it controls the market. The U.S. federal government allows monopolies to exist only in certain exceptional cases, such as the utility and transportation industries. Even then, regulatory agencies scrutinize these officially approved monopolies to protect the public. The protracted legal battle between the Justice Department and Microsoft, owner of the dominant operating system for personal computers, illustrates the uneasy relationship between government and private monopolies in capitalistic countries.

Conflict theorists point out that although *pure* monopolies are not a basic element of the economy of the United States, competition is still much more restricted than one might expect in what is called a *free enterprise system*. In numerous industries, a few companies largely dominate the field and keep new enterprises from entering the marketplace.

During the severe economic downturn that began in 2008, the United States moved even farther away from the laissez-faire ideal. To keep major financial institutions from going under, the federal government invested hundreds of billions of dollars in distressed banking, investment, and insurance companies. Then in 2009, the government bailed out the failing automobile industry, taking a 60 percent interest in General Motors. The Canadian government took another 12 percent.

As we have seen in earlier chapters, globalization and the rise of multinational corporations have spread the capitalistic pursuit of profits around the world. Especially in developing countries, governments are not always prepared to deal with the sudden influx of foreign capital and its effects on their economies. One particularly striking example of how unfettered capitalism can harm developing nations is found in the Democratic Republic of Congo (formerly Zaire). The Congo has significant deposits of the metal columbite-tantalite—coltan, for short—which is used in the production of electronic circuit boards. Until the market for cell phones, pagers, and laptop computers heated up, U.S. manufacturers got most of their coltan from Australia. But at the height of consumer demand, they turned to miners in the Congo to increase their supply.

Predictably, the escalating price of the metal—as much as $600 a kilogram at one point, or more than three times the average Congolese worker's yearly wages—attracted undesirable attention. Soon the neighboring countries of Rwanda, Uganda,

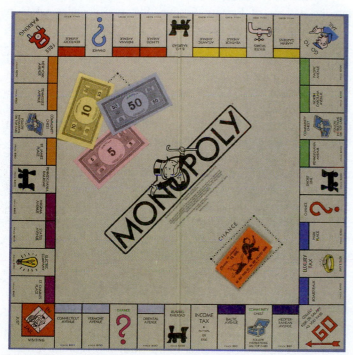

© The McGraw-Hill Companies, Inc./Mark Steinmetz, photographer

For more than a century, the board game of Monopoly has entertained millions of people around the world. In the game, players strive to dominate the fictitious economy, gleefully bankrupting other players. Ironically, Monopoly was developed to demonstrate the weaknesses of capitalist economies, such as excessive rents and the tendency for money to accumulate in the hands of a few.

© Tom Stoddart Archive/Getty Images

Workers mine for coltan with sweat and shovels. The sudden increase in demand for the metal by U.S. computer manufacturers caused incursions into the Congo by neighboring countries hungry for capital to finance a war. Too often, globalization can have unintended consequences for a nation's economy and social welfare.

and Burundi, at war with one another and desperate for resources to finance the conflict, were raiding the Congo's national parks, slashing and burning to expose the coltan beneath the forest floor. Indirectly, the sudden increase in the demand for coltan was financing war and the rape of the environment. U.S. manufacturers have since cut off their sources in the Congo in an effort to avoid abetting the destruction. But their action has only penalized legitimate miners in the impoverished country (*The Economist* 2011c; Fagge 2015).

 use your **sociological imagination**

Which aspects of capitalism do you personally appreciate? Which do you find worrisome? Explain.

Socialism

Socialist theory was refined in the writings of Karl Marx and Friedrich Engels. These European radicals were disturbed by the exploitation of the working class that emerged during the Industrial Revolution. In their view, capitalism forced large numbers of people to exchange their labor for low wages. The owners of an industry profit from the labor of workers primarily because they pay workers less than the value of the goods produced.

As an ideal type, a socialist economic system attempts to eliminate such economic exploitation. Under **socialism,** the means of production and distribution in a society are collectively rather than privately owned. The basic objective of the economic system is to meet people's needs rather than to maximize profits. Socialists reject the laissez-faire philosophy that free competition benefits the general public. Instead, they believe that the central government, acting as the representative of the people, should make basic economic decisions. Therefore, government ownership of all major industries—including steel production,

automobile manufacturing, and agriculture—is a primary feature of socialism as an ideal type.

In practice, socialist economic systems vary in the extent to which they tolerate private ownership. For example, in Great Britain, a nation with some aspects of both a socialist and a capitalist economy, passenger airline service was once concentrated in the government-owned corporation British Airways. Even before the airline was privatized in 1987, however, private airlines were allowed to compete with it.

Socialist nations differ from capitalist nations in their commitment to social service programs. For example, the U.S. government provides health care and health insurance to the elderly and poor through the Medicare and Medicaid programs. But socialist countries typically offer government-financed medical care to *all* citizens. In theory, the wealth of the people as a collectivity is used to provide health care, housing, education, and other key services to each individual and family.

Marx believed that socialist societies would eventually "wither away" and evolve into *communist* societies. As an ideal type, **communism** refers to an economic system under which all property is communally owned and no social distinctions are made on the basis of people's ability to produce. In recent decades, the Soviet Union, the People's Republic of China, Vietnam, Cuba, and nations in Eastern Europe were popularly thought of as examples of communist economic systems. However, this usage represents an incorrect application of a term with sensitive political connotations. All nations known as communist in the 20th century actually fell far short of the ideal type (Walder and Nguyen 2008).

By the early 1990s, Communist parties were no longer ruling the nations of Eastern Europe. Just two decades later, in 2015, Moscow had no fewer than 78 billionaires—the same as New York (78) and more than London (46). That same year, traditionally communist China had 45 billionaires in its capital city, Beijing, plus 64 in Hong Kong, 25 in Shenzan, and 2 in Shanghai. Also in 2015 the Shanghai Stock Exchange, with market capitalization of over $2.7 trillion, was the world's fifth largest stock exchange. Obviously capitalism has found a place in countries politically ruled by Communist parties (Chen 2015).

As we have seen, capitalism and socialism are ideal types of economic system. In reality, the economy of each industrial society—including the United States, the European Union, and Japan—includes elements of both capitalism and socialism (Table 50-1). Whatever the differences—whether a society more closely fits the ideal type of capitalism or socialism—all industrial societies rely chiefly on mechanization in the production of goods and services.

The Informal Economy

In many countries, one aspect of the economy defies description as either capitalist or socialist. In the **informal economy,** transfers of money, goods, or services take place but are not reported to the government. Examples of the informal economy include trading services with someone—say, a haircut for a computer lesson; selling goods on the street; and engaging in illegal transactions, such as gambling or drug deals. The informal economy also includes off-the-books work in landscaping, child care, and

TABLE 50-1 CHARACTERISTICS OF THE THREE MAJOR ECONOMIC SYSTEMS

Economic System	Characteristics	Contemporary Examples
Capitalism	Private ownership of the means of production Accumulation of profits the main incentive	Canada Mexico United States
Socialism	Collective ownership of the means of production Meeting people's needs the basic objective	Russia Sweden
Communism	Communal ownership of all property No social distinctions made on basis of people's ability to produce	Cuba North Korea

Note: Countries listed in column three are typical of one of the three economic systems, but not perfectly so. In practice, the economies of most countries include a mix of elements from the three major systems.

housecleaning. Participants in this type of economy avoid taxes and government regulations.

In the United States, the informal economy accounts for about 8 percent of total economic activity. In other industrialized nations it varies, from 11 percent in Great Britain to 20 percent in Spain and Portugal and 25 percent in Greece. In developing nations, the informal economy represents a much larger (40 to 60 percent) and often unmeasured part of total economic activity. Yet because this sector of the economy depends to a large extent on the labor of women, work in the informal economy is undervalued or even unrecognized the world over (T. Barnes 2009; F. Schneider 2010).

Functionalists contend that bureaucratic regulations sometimes contribute to the rise of an informal, or underground, economy. In the developing world, governments often set up burdensome business regulations that overworked bureaucrats must administer. When requests for licenses and permits pile up, delaying business projects, legitimate entrepreneurs find they need to go underground to get anything done. Despite its apparent efficiency, this type of informal economy is dysfunctional for a country's overall political and economic well-being. Since informal firms typically operate in remote locations to avoid detection, they cannot easily expand when they become profitable. And given the limited protection for their property and contractual rights, participants in the informal economy are less likely than others to save and invest their income.

Whatever the functions an informal economy may serve, it is in some respects dysfunctional for workers. Working conditions in these illegal businesses are often unsafe or dangerous, and the jobs rarely provide any benefits to those who become ill or cannot continue to work. Perhaps more significant, the longer a worker remains in the informal economy, the less likely that person is to make the transition to the formal economy. No matter how efficient or productive a worker, employers expect to see experience in the formal economy on a job application. Experience as a successful street vendor or self-employed cleaning person does not carry much weight with interviewers (Venkatesh 2006; WEIGO 2016).

MODULE 50 | Recap and Review

Summary

A society's **economic system** has an important influence on social behavior and on other social institutions.

1. With the Industrial Revolution, a new form of social structure emerged: the **industrial society.**

2. Systems of **capitalism** vary in the degree to which the government regulates private ownership and economic activity, but all emphasize the profit motive.

3. The basic objective of **socialism** is to eliminate economic exploitation and meet people's needs. Marx believed that **communism** would evolve naturally out of socialism.

4. In developing nations, the **informal** economy represents a significant part of total economic activity. Yet because this sector depends largely on women's work, it is undervalued.

Thinking Critically

1. In the United States, what factors might encourage the growth of the informal economy? Are those factors related to the country's economic system?

2. Why have so-called communist countries failed to achieve communist systems according to Marx's definition?

Key Terms

Capitalism

Communism

Industrial society

Informal economy

Laissez-faire

Monopoly

Socialism

As advocates of the power elite model point out, the trend in capitalist societies has been toward concentration of ownership by giant corporations, especially multinational ones. In the following sections we will examine four outgrowths of this trend in the United States: the changing face of the workforce, deindustrialization, the sharing economy, the temporary workforce, and offshoring. As these trends show, any change in the economy has social and political implications.

The Changing Face of the Workforce

The workforce in the United States is constantly changing. During World War II, when men were mobilized to fight abroad, women entered the workforce in large numbers. And with the rise of the civil rights movement in the 1960s, minorities found numerous job opportunities opening to them. Box 51-1 takes a closer look at the active recruitment of women and minorities into the workplace, known as *affirmative action.*

Although predictions are not always reliable, sociologists and labor specialists foresee a workforce increasingly composed of women and racial and ethnic minorities. In 1960 there were twice as many men in the labor force as women. From 1988 to 2018, however, 52 percent of new workers are expected to be women. The dynamics for minority group workers are even more dramatic, as the number of Black, Latino, and Asian American workers continues to increase at a faster rate than the number of White workers (Toossi 2009).

More and more, then, the workforce reflects the diversity of the population, as ethnic minorities enter the labor force and immigrants and their children move from marginal jobs or employment in the informal economy to positions of greater visibility and responsibility. The impact of this changing labor force is not merely statistical. A more diverse workforce means that relationships between workers are more likely to cross gender, racial, and ethnic lines. Interactionists note that people will soon find themselves supervising and being supervised by people very different from themselves.

Deindustrialization

What happens when a company decides it is more profitable to move its operations out of a long-established community to another part of the country, or out of the country altogether? People lose jobs; stores lose customers; the local government's tax base declines and it cuts services. This devastating process has occurred again and again in the past decade or so.

The term **deindustrialization** refers to the systematic, widespread withdrawal of investment in basic aspects of productivity, such as factories and plants. Giant corporations that deindustrialize are not necessarily refusing to invest in new economic opportunities. Rather, the targets and locations of investment change, and the need for labor decreases as advances in technology continue to automate production. First, companies may move their plants from the nation's central cities to the suburbs. The next step may be relocation from suburban areas of the Northeast and Midwest to the South, where labor laws place more restrictions on unions. Finally, a corporation may simply relocate *outside* the United States to a country with a lower rate of prevailing wages. General Motors, for example, decided to build a multi-billion-dollar plant in China rather than in Kansas City or even in Mexico (Lynn 2003).

Although deindustrialization often involves relocation, in some instances it takes the form of corporate restructuring, as companies seek to reduce costs in the face of growing worldwide competition. When such restructuring occurs, the impact on the bureaucratic hierarchy of formal organizations can be significant. A large corporation may choose to sell off or entirely abandon less productive divisions and to eliminate layers of management viewed as unnecessary. Wages and salaries may be frozen and benefits cut—all in the name of restructuring. Increasing reliance on automation also spells the end of work as we have known it.

The term **downsizing** was introduced in 1987 to refer to reductions taken in a company's workforce as part of deindustrialization. Viewed from a conflict perspective, the unprecedented attention given to downsizing in the mid-1990s reflected the continuing importance of social class in the United States. Conflict theorists note that job loss has long been a feature of deindustrialization among blue-collar workers. But when large numbers of middle-class managers and other white-collar employees with substantial incomes began to be laid off, suddenly the media began expressing great concern over downsizing.

The extended economic downturn that began in 2008 accelerated the processes of deindustrialization and downsizing. As the recession deepened, many plants shut down either temporarily or permanently, leaving more and more workers without jobs. With those jobs and shuttered plants went the hope of restoring or expanding heavy industry, including automobile manufacturing. The bankruptcy of Chrysler and General Motors hit the midwestern states particularly hard.

The social costs of deindustrialization and downsizing cannot be overemphasized. Plant closings lead to substantial unemployment in a community, which has a devastating impact on both the micro and macro levels. On the micro level, the unemployed person and his or her family must adjust to a loss of spending power. Painting or re-siding the house, buying health insurance or saving for retirement, even thinking about having another child must be put aside. Both marital happiness and family cohesion may suffer as a result. Although many dismissed workers eventually reenter the paid labor force, they must often accept less desirable positions with lower salaries and fewer benefits. Unemployment and underemployment are tied to many of the social problems discussed throughout this textbook, among them the need for child care and the controversy over welfare.

The Sharing Economy

Why pay a high retail price for a product or service, in a store or online, when you can buy or rent it more cheaply from a

BOX 51-1

Research Today

Affirmative Action

The term *affirmative action* first appeared in an executive order issued by President John F. Kennedy in 1961. That order called for contractors to "take affirmative action to ensure that applicants are employed, and that employees are treated during employment, without regard to their race, creed, color, or national origin." In 1967, the order was amended by President Lyndon Johnson to prohibit discrimination on the basis of sex as well, but affirmative action remained a vague concept. Currently, **affirmative action** refers to positive efforts to recruit minority group members or women for jobs, promotions, and educational opportunities.

> Critics warn against hiring and admissions quotas, complaining that they constitute a kind of "reverse discrimination" against White males.

Sociologists—especially conflict and feminist theorists—view affirmative action as a legislative attempt to reduce the inequality embedded in the social structure by increasing opportunities for groups who were deprived in the past, such as women and African Americans. Despite the clear disparity in earnings between White males and other groups, however, many people doubt that everything done in the name of affirmative action is desirable. Critics warn against hiring and admissions quotas, complaining that they constitute a kind of "reverse discrimination" against White males.

Affirmative action became a prominent issue in state and national political campaigns in 1996, when California's voters approved by a 54 to 46 percent margin the California Civil Rights Initiative. Better known as Proposition 209, this measure amended the state constitution to *prohibit* any program that gives preference to women and minorities in college admissions, hiring, promotion, or government contracts. In other words, it aimed to abolish affirmative action programs. The courts have since upheld the measure. In 1998, voters in Washington State passed a similar anti–affirmative action measure.

Colleges and universities responded with new policies designed to broaden opportunities for traditionally underrepresented minority students. However, opponents of affirmative action continue to argue in court that such actions unconstitutionally disadvantage White applicants. And colleges continue to reexamine their policies in light of the latest legal rulings.

Increasingly, critics of affirmative action are calling for color-blind policies that would end affirmative action. Presumably, such policies would allow all applicants to be judged fairly. However, opponents warn against the danger of **color-blind racism**—the use of the principle of race neutrality to defend a racially unequal status quo. Will "color-blind" policies put an end to institutional practices that now favor Whites, they ask? According to the latest data, for example, Harvard University admits 40 percent of those applicants who are children of alumni—almost all of whom are White—compared to 11 percent

Cartoon © 2003 Mike Keefe, *The Denver Post*. Used by permission of Cagle Cartoons, Inc.

The Supreme Court's many decisions on the constitutionality of affirmative action programs have made it difficult for organizations to encourage diversity without transgressing the law.

of nonalumni children. Ironically, studies show that children of alumni are far more likely than either minority students or athletes to run into trouble academically.

LET'S DISCUSS

1. Is affirmative action part of the admissions policy at the college or university you attend? If so, do you think the policy has helped to level the playing field? Might it have excluded some qualified White applicants?

2. Take a poll of your classmates. What percentage of the class supports affirmative action in hiring and college admissions? How does that group break down in terms of gender, race, and ethnicity?

Sources: Kahlenberg 2015; Massey and Mooney 2007; Pincus 2003, 2008; University of Michigan 2003.

---

stranger? This is the principle behind a range of online services that enable people to share cars (such as Uber and Lyft), accommodations (Airbnb), pet care, bicycles, household appliances and other items. **Sharing economy** refers to connecting owners of underused assets with others willing to pay to use them.

Critics argue that the sharing economy is just an extension of the temporary workforce and that most of sharing economy entrepreneurs would prefer to work for a firm with better wages, legal protection, guaranteed minimum weekly hours, and fringe benefits. They argue that it is not a coincidence that many peer-to-peer rental firms were founded between 2008 and 2010, in the midst of the Great Recession, when conventional employment opportunities tanked. Others argue that the sharing economy serves to commodify services that might otherwise have been given away for free such as offering rides or places to sleep to friends or acquaintances.

Consumers of the sharing economy are attracted to the notion that they may be saving money, and workers like the income and flexible work. However, established businesses question the quality of the services rendered. For example, taxi companies and hotel chains question the nature of their competition in this emerging online marketplace. In addition, governments are

© Age Fotostock/Superstock   © Bloomberg/Getty Images

Gutted factories like this one in Boston, Massachusetts, contrast with the glamorous corporate campus of Google Corporation in Mountain View, California. Deindustrialization and the rise of high technology have shifted the U.S. labor market, displacing many workers in the process.

beginning to regulate such services, especially when the taxes that competing businesses would pay for their income are not being paid in the sharing economy (DuPuis and Rainwater 2014; *The Week* 2014; White 2015).

The Temporary Workforce

Over the last four decades, U.S. employers have been relying more and more on the part-time workforce. The recent economic downturn and the slow recovery that followed only accelerated the trend, which began in 1970. In 2015, about 26 million of the 149 million people employed in the United States were working part time, many of them at more than one job (Bureau of Labor Statistics 2015g).

This pattern of expanding part-time work is slowly reshaping the U.S. workforce. Traditionally, businesses employed workers through good times and bad, protecting them from economic ups and downs. In numerous industries, however, that is no longer the case. Today, many part-time employees—those who work 1 to 34 hours a week—are actually temporary or seasonal employees, who work part time for part of the year. These workers typically do not enjoy benefits like health insurance, paid sick-leave, or even unemployment compensation.

Certainly some workers seek out part-time jobs, welcoming the flexibility they offer. For example, students taking college classes may prefer part-time work. For most workers, however, part-time employment is not a first choice. In response to the trend away from traditional full-time jobs, more and more workers are adopting a "free agent mentality," actively seeking work wherever and whenever they can find it instead of expecting to be hired full time. This change in attitude is related to an increase in what has been termed **precarious work**—employment that is poorly paid, and from the worker's perspective, insecure and unprotected (P. Davidson 2012).

Offshoring

U.S. firms have been outsourcing certain types of work for generations. For example, moderate-sized businesses such as furniture stores and commercial laundries have long relied on outside trucking firms to make deliveries to their customers. The trend toward **offshoring** carries this practice one step further, by transferring other types of work to foreign contractors. Now, even large companies are turning to overseas firms, many of them located in developing countries. Offshoring has become the latest tactic in the time-worn business strategy of raising profits by reducing costs.

Significantly, the transfer of work from one country to another is no longer limited to manufacturing. Office and professional jobs are being exported, too, thanks to advanced telecommunications. Table 51-1 lists those occupations most likely to be offshored.

In 2012, complaints about working conditions in Apple's factories in China called attention to the fact that the company's financial success had been built on outsourced labor. At one time, Apple manufactured its computers in the United States. Today the company still employs about 43,000 full-time workers in the United States, and another 20,000 full-time workers

TABLE **51-1** **OCCUPATIONS MOST VULNERABLE TO OFFSHORING**

Rank	Occupation
1	Computer programming
2	Data entry
3	Electrical and electronics drafting
4	Mechanical drafting
5	Computer and information science, research
6	Actuarial science
7	Mathematics
8	Statistics
9	Mathematical science (all other)
10	Film and video editing

Sources: Bureau of Labor Statistics data cited in Hira 2008; Moncarz et al. 2008.

abroad. However, Apple contracts on a short-term basis with an additional 700,000 workers who both engineer and build its products overseas. As complaints grew about Apple's offshoring, economists released estimates that in the next four years, another 375,000 well-paid jobs in information technology, human resources, and finance and merchandising would be lost to overseas competition (China Labor Watch 2015; Duhigg and Bradsher 2012; P. Davidson 2012).

Offshoring is not completely inevitable. In a recent countertrend called *reshoring,* widely reported in the media, some U.S. companies have been bringing manufacturing jobs and service centers back to the United States. General Electric, Ford, and Whirlpool are among the 200 or more companies that have already made the move. Typically, quality concerns or rising wages—notably in China—make developing countries less competitive than the home country for these companies, especially when shipping costs are factored in. Most experts agree that while reshoring is occurring on a case-by-case basis, it does not offset continued offshoring of jobs (Cohen 2015; *The Economist* 2013f; Northam 2014).

Because offshoring, like outsourcing in general, tends to improve the efficiency of business operations, it can be viewed as functional to society. Offshoring also increases economic interdependence in the production of goods and services, both in enterprises located just across town and in those located around the globe. Still, conflict theorists charge that this aspect of globalization furthers social inequality. Although moving high-tech work to developing countries does help to lower a company's costs, the impact on technical and service workers at home is clearly devastating. Certainly middle-class workers are alarmed by the trend. Because offshoring increases efficiency, economists oppose efforts to block the practice and instead recommend assistance to displaced workers.

There is a downside to offshoring for foreigners, as well. Although outsourcing is a significant source of employment for the upper-middle class in developing countries, hundreds of millions of other foreign workers have seen little to no positive impact from the trend. Thus the long-term impact of offshoring on developing nations is difficult to predict. Another practice, *microfinancing,* is having a more positive impact on the lower classes in developing nations: see the Social Policy section that follows.

 use your **sociological imagination**

Do you know anyone whose job has been transferred to a foreign country? If so, was the person able to find a comparable job in the same town, or did he or she have to relocate? How long was the person unemployed?

social policy and the Economy | Microfinancing

In India, a very small loan has made a big change in a young mother's life. Not many years ago Siyawati was dependent on what little income her husband could earn as a day laborer. Then a $212 microloan allowed her to buy a machine for making candles. Today, Siyawati's cottage venture has expanded into a factory with eight employees, and her monthly income has climbed from $42 to $425. Her increased earnings have allowed her to enroll her children in a good school—the dream of struggling parents in developing countries around the world (Glazer 2010:1).

Looking at the Issue

In some respects "microfinancing" offers a small solution to a big problem. **Microfinancing** is lending small sums of money to the poor so they can work their way out of poverty. Borrowers use the money to start small businesses in the informal economy—to buy yarn to weave into cloth, cows to produce milk, or tools, equipment, and bamboo to make stools. The products they produce are then sold in the local shops. Typically, microloans are less than $600, often as little as $20. The recipients are people who ordinarily would not be able to qualify for banking services.

Sometimes referred to as "banking the unbanked," microfinancing was the brainchild of Bangladeshi economist Muhammad Yunus (pronounced Iunus). In 1976, in the midst of a devastating famine in Bangladesh, Yunus founded the Grameen (meaning "Village") Bank, which he headed until 2011. The idea came to him when he reached into his pocket to lend money to a group of villagers who had asked him for help. Working through local halls or meeting places, the Grameen Bank has now extended 7 million microloans. The idea has spread, and has even been underwritten by over a thousand for-profit banks and multinational organizations. According to the most recent estimates, microfinancing is now reaching over 200 million families in 100 countries (Grameen Bank 2016; Microcredit Summit Exchange 2015; Yunus 2010).

Although microfinancing has benefited many families, critics charge that some lenders are taking advantage of the poor. Especially in India, the extension of microloans to financially questionable projects with little chance for success has left some borrowers in debt. At the other extreme, some lenders have reaped extraordinary profits, both for themselves and for the investment banks they have created. Proponents of microfinancing acknowledge that improvements can be made.

—*Continued*

© Farjana K. Godhuly/AFP/Getty Images

In 2006 Muhammad Yunus, founder of the Grameen Bank, was awarded the Nobel Peace Prize for his work in championing the concept of microfinancing. The small loans his bank makes to the poor, many of them women, have improved the quality of life of countless families.

The microfinance movement is not a failure, however. It has evolved to offer borrowers scholarships, low-cost health care, and even solar power. Research supports the conclusion that the poorest of the poor can and do become entrepreneurs when they can obtain credit at acceptable interest rates (Dickson 2013; Ledgerwood 2013).

Applying Sociology

Researchers who draw on the interactionist approach have shown that there is more to microfinancing than money. A study done by microfinance expert Daryl Collins and her colleagues (2009), described in the opening excerpt to Chapter 9, shows how even with modest assistance, poor people can significantly improve their circumstances through mutual support. Collins asked villagers and slum dwellers in Bangladesh, India, and South Africa to keep diaries of how they spent every penny they earned. She and her team found that most of the poor households they studied did not live hand to mouth, spending everything they earned as soon as they got it. Instead, they used financial tools that were linked to their extended families and informal social networks. They saved money, squeezed it out of creditors whenever possible, ran sophisticated savings clubs, and took advantage of microfinancing whenever it was available. Their tactics suggested new methods of fighting poverty and encouraged the development of broader microfinance programs.

An analysis of 545 quantitative data sets from 90 separate studies found that microfinancing has a positive impact on the individual entrepreneurs. In fact, the more economically challenging the environment, the greater the social impact. However, on a case-by-case basis, the impact is often modest, and those who look for major societal transformations will likely be disappointed (Banerjee 2013; Chliova et al. 2015; World Bank 2015c).

Because an estimated 83 percent of the recipients of microcredit are women, feminist theorists are especially interested in the growth of microfinancing. Women's economic status has been found to be critical to the well-being of their children, and the key to a healthy household environment. In developing countries, where women often are not treated as well as men, being entrusted with credit is particularly empowering to them. Research indicates that women recipients are more likely than men to participate in networks and collective action groups, perhaps because they must overcome resistance to women serving as economic decision makers. Another finding is that microfinance most effectively empowers women when they use the microloans for self-employment rather than share the funds with their whole household (Dickson 2013; Microcredit Summit Exchange 2015).

Drawing on world systems analysis, sociologist Marina Karides (2010) contrasts microfinancing with the Western model of economic development, in which multinational corporations based in core countries take advantage of the low wages and natural resources in periphery and semi-periphery countries. The low-wage workers employed by the multinationals rarely escape subsistence living, while the vast majority of people in core nations enjoy a comparatively high standard of living. Microfinanciers hope that in contrast, the cottage industries they help to establish will contribute to the local economies in developing countries, and ultimately to the well-being of those societies, rather than merely serve the economic interests of core nations.

—*Continued*

Some critics complain that the creation of small home-based industries reduces the demand for formal employment opportunities. Supporters of microenterprise counter that much time has passed without a significant change in job growth. Microfinancing, they claim, is the best way to create sustainable market opportunities for the poor in developing nations, even if those opportunities are much less attractive than those available in core nations.

Initiating Policy

Even supporters of microfinancing acknowledge the need to reduce overlending and monitor the success of small loans in helping borrowers to escape poverty. Some indicators suggest that many borrowers do not achieve self-sufficiency. If that is true, lenders should increase their oversight and attempt to identify best practices—that is, those types of assistance that are most effective in helping the poor. Less than a decade ago, microfinancing was hailed as the single best solution to world poverty. With modifications, it should continue to reduce hardship and suffering among the poor (Banerjee 2013; Bari 2013).

Lenders also need to work with political leaders, and vice versa, to ensure that they do not regard one another as competitors for political support from the poor. Grameen Bank seemed to survive the bitter controversy that ensued when Bangladesh ordered the dismissal in 2011 of Yunus as head of the bank on the grounds he had exceeded the nation's statutory retirement age of 60 (Yunus was 70 at the time) (Bari 2013).

Some government leaders in countries where microfinancing is a significant phenomenon have gone so far as to charge lenders with profiteering at the expense of the poor, and to take extraordinary measures for the protection of borrowers. In 2010, officials of one state in India required all loans to be approved by the government, and their eventual repayment to be made in person before a public official. To

© Adeel Halim/Bloomberg via Getty Images

At a workshop in Mumbai, India, Sharda Bhandare cuts the pieces for a pair of gloves from a towel. Microloans make such small businesses possible, and help them to become self-sustaining.

the degree that profiteering is truly a problem, some type of remedy, whether through legislation or self-monitoring, may need to be introduced. Given the cultural, political, and legal differences among nations where microfinanciers operate, the development of this type of government policy will be a major undertaking (World Bank 2015a).

TAKE THE ISSUE WITH YOU

1. Do you think microfinancing might be useful in the United States? If so, how and under what conditions?

2. Using sociological concepts, explain why some politicians might resent microfinancing programs.

3. What obstacles might prevent poor people, either in the United States or elsewhere, from improving their lives through microfinancing? Might the government have a role to play in removing those obstacles?

MODULE 51 | Recap and Review

Summary

Any change in the economy has both social and political implications.

1. In the United States, workers are coping with **deindustrialization** and **offshoring** and employers are training an increasingly diverse workforce.

2. **Affirmative action** is intended to remedy the effects of discrimination against minority groups and women. The concept is controversial, however, because some people see it as reverse discrimination against majority groups.

3. In developing countries, **microfinancing** is improving the lives of millions of poor people.

Thinking Critically

1. What are the implications of trends such as deindustrialization and offshoring on social institutions such as the family, education, and government in the United States?

2. What evidence of deindustrialization or downsizing do you see, specifically, in your own community? What broad economic shifts brought about those changes?

Key Terms

Affirmative action

Color-blind racism

Deindustrialization

Downsizing

Microfinancing

Offshoring

Precarious work

Sharing

Mastering This Chapter

© Jim West/The Image Works

taking sociology with you

1 Pick a nongovernmental organization with worldwide recognition, such as the Red Cross, Doctors Without Borders, or Amnesty International. Go online and find out how the organization works on behalf of peace. What specifically has this NGO done to prevent or stop war?

2 Investigate a sharing service such as Lyft, Uber, or Airbnb. What are the benefits and drawbacks to the worker? To the customer? What services is the company replacing?

3 If your college has a club for young Republicans or Democrats, attend one of their meetings. What issues are members interested in, and why? How are they planning to put their beliefs into action? Are they concerned about voter apathy among young people?

Key Terms

Affirmative action Positive efforts to recruit minority group members or women for jobs, promotions, and educational opportunities.

Authority Institutionalized power that is recognized by the people over whom it is exercised.

Capitalism An economic system in which the means of production are held largely in private hands and the main incentive for economic activity is the accumulation of profits.

Charismatic authority Power made legitimate by a leader's exceptional personal or emotional appeal to his or her followers.

Color-blind racism The use of the principle of race neutrality to defend a racially unequal status quo.

Communism As an ideal type, an economic system under which all property is communally owned and no social distinctions are made on the basis of people's ability to produce.

Deindustrialization The systematic, widespread withdrawal of investment in basic aspects of productivity, such as factories and plants.

Democracy In a literal sense, government by the people.

Dictatorship A government in which one person has nearly total power to make and enforce laws.

Downsizing Reductions taken in a company's workforce as part of deindustrialization.

Economic system The social institution through which goods and services are produced, distributed, and consumed.

Elite model A view of society as being ruled by a small group of individuals who share a common set of political and economic interests.

Force The actual or threatened use of coercion to impose one's will on others.

Industrial society A society that depends on mechanization to produce its goods and services.

Influence The exercise of power through a process of persuasion.

Informal economy Transfers of money, goods, or services that are not reported to the government.

Laissez-faire A form of capitalism under which people compete freely, with minimal government intervention in the economy.

Microfinancing Lending small sums of money to the poor so they can work their way out of poverty.

Monarchy A form of government headed by a single member of a royal family, usually a king, queen, or some other hereditary ruler.

Monopoly Control of a market by a single business firm.

Offshoring The transfer of work to foreign contractors.

Oligarchy A form of government in which a few individuals rule.

Peace The absence of war, or more broadly, a proactive effort to develop cooperative relations among nations.

Pluralist model A view of society in which many competing groups within the community have access to government, so that no single group is dominant.

Political system The social institution that is founded on a recognized set of procedures for implementing and achieving society's goals.

Politics In Harold Lasswell's words, "who gets what, when, and how."

Power The ability to exercise one's will over others.

Power elite A small group of military, industrial, and government leaders who control the fate of the United States.

Precarious work Employment that is poorly paid, and from the worker's perspective, insecure and unprotected.

Rational-legal authority Power made legitimate by law.

Representative democracy A form of government in which certain individuals are selected to speak for the people.

Sharing economy Connecting owners of underused assets with others willing to pay to use them.

Socialism An economic system under which the means of production and distribution are collectively owned.

Sovereignty movement The effort by the indigenous people of Hawai'i to win self-government, as well as the restoration of—or compensation for—their ancestral lands.

Terrorism The use or threat of violence against random or symbolic targets in pursuit of political aims.

Totalitarianism Virtually complete government control and surveillance over all aspects of a society's social and political life.

Traditional authority Legitimate power conferred by custom and accepted practice.

War Conflict between organizations that possess trained combat forces equipped with deadly weapons.

self-quiz

Read each question carefully and then select the best answer.

1. Which two basic types of economic system distinguish contemporary industrial societies?
   a. capitalism and communism
   b. capitalism and socialism
   c. socialism and communism
   d. capitalism and dictatorship

2. According to the discussion of capitalism in the text, which of the following statements is true?
   a. The means of production are held largely in private hands.
   b. The main incentive for economic activity is the accumulation of profits.
   c. The degree to which the government regulates private ownership and economic activity will vary.
   d. all of the above

3. G. William Domhoff's model is an example of a(n)
   a. elite theory of power.
   b. pluralist theory of power.
   c. functionalist theory of power.
   d. interactionist theory of power.

4. In terms of voter turnout, the United States typically ranks
   a. highest among all countries.
   b. highest among industrialized nations.
   c. lowest among industrialized nations.
   d. lowest among all countries.

5. What are the three basic sources of power within any political system?
   a. force, influence, and authority
   b. force, influence, and democracy
   c. force, legitimacy, and charisma
   d. influence, charisma, and bureaucracy

6. Which of the following is *not* part of the classification system of authority developed by Max Weber?
   a. traditional authority
   b. pluralist authority
   c. legal-rational authority
   d. charismatic authority

7. According to C. Wright Mills, power rests in the hands of the
   a. people.
   b. representative democracy.
   c. aristocracy.
   d. power elite.

8. The systematic, widespread withdrawal of investment in basic aspects of productivity such as factories and plants is called
   a. deindustrialization.
   b. downsizing.
   c. postindustrialization.
   d. gentrification.

9. Sociologists and labor specialists foresee a workforce increasingly composed of
   a. women.
   b. racial minorities.
   c. ethnic minorities.
   d. all of the above

10. Currently, _____ _____ refers to positive efforts to recruit minority group members or women for jobs, promotions, and educational opportunities.
    a. equal rights
    b. affirmative action
    c. work programs
    d. equal action

11. The principle of _____, as expounded and endorsed by the British economist Adam Smith, was the prevailing form of capitalism immediately following the Industrial Revolution.

12. Under _____, the means of production and distribution in a society are collectively rather than privately owned, and the basic objective of the economic system is to meet people's needs rather than to maximize profits.

13. _____ is an economic system under which all property is communally owned and no social distinctions are made based on people's ability to produce.

14. _____ theorists point out that while pure monopolies are not a basic element of the economy of the United States, competition is much more restricted than one might expect in what is called a free enterprise system.

15. Some capitalist nations, such as the United States, outlaw _____ through antitrust legislation.

16. The elite model of political power implies that the United States has a(n) _____ as its form of government.

17. Sexism has been the most serious barrier to women interested in holding public office. To remedy this situation, many countries have adopted _____ for female representatives.

18. _____ is the exercise of power through a process of persuasion.

19. The United States is commonly classified as a(n) _____ _____, because the elected members of Congress and state legislatures make our laws.

20. Advocates of the _____ model suggest that competing groups within the community have access to government, so that no single group is dominant.

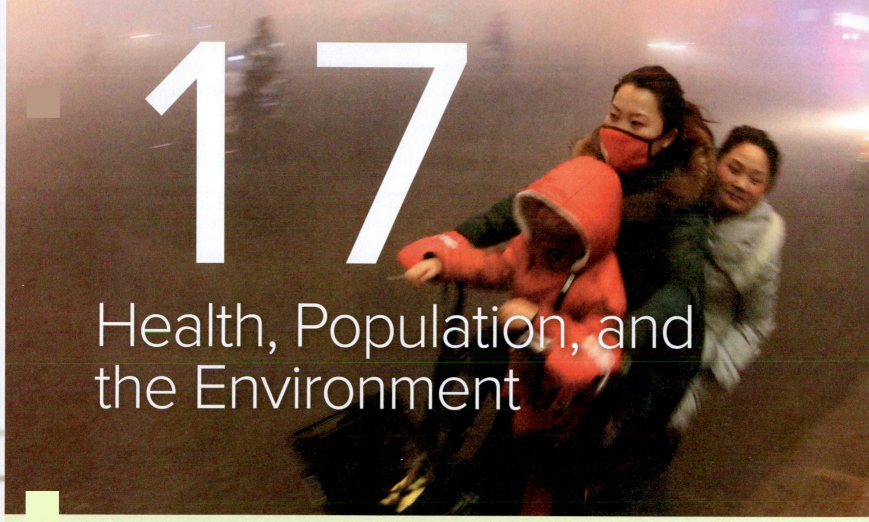

17

Health, Population, and the Environment

© Imaginechina/Corbis

In Beijing, one of the 15 largest cities in the world, cyclists drive through a street shrouded in dense smog. So dangerous is the pollution to residents that the government closes schools and factories when smog descends on the city.

© Johannes Kroemer/Getty Images

Do you remember a time when you or your parents didn't worry about the food you ate and the water you drank?

Andrew Szasz does. It was a time before the environmental movement.

66 Not that long ago, hardly a generation back, people did not worry about the food they ate. They did not worry about the water they drank or the air they breathed. It never occurred to them that eating, drinking water, satisfying basic, mundane bodily needs, might be dangerous things to do. Parents thought it was good for their kids to go outside, get some sun.

That is all changed now. People see danger everywhere. Food, water, air, sun. We cannot do without them. Sadly, we now also fear them. We suspect that the water that flows from the tap is contaminated with chemicals that can make us ill. We have learned that conventionally grown fruits and vegetables have pesticide residues and that when we eat meat from conventionally raised animals, we are probably getting a dose of antibiotics and hormones, too. Contaminants can be colorless, tasteless, and odorless, invisible to the senses, and that fact increases the feeling of vulnerability.

According to the Environmental Protection Agency (EPA), indoor air is more toxic than outdoor air. That is because many household cleaning products and many contemporary home furnishings—carpets, drapes, the fabrics that cover sofas and easy chairs, furniture made of particle board—outgas toxic volatile organic chemicals. OK, we will go outside . . . only to inhale diesel exhaust, particulates suspended in the air, molecules of toxic chemicals wafting from factory smokestacks.

Even sunshine is now considered by many a hazard. Expose yourself to too much sun and your skin will age prematurely. You risk getting skin cancer. The ozone layer has

People see danger everywhere. Food, water, air, sun. We cannot do without them. Sadly, we now also fear them.

thinned, making exposure to sunlight even more dangerous. The incidence of melanoma, the deadliest form of skin cancer, is on the rise.

The response has been swift. Everywhere one looks, Americans are buying consumer products that promise to reduce their exposure to harmful substances.

In 1975, Americans were drinking, on average, one gallon of bottled water per person per year. By 2005, the latest year for which we have data, consumption had grown to twenty-six gallons per person per year, over seven and a half billion gallons of bottled water. Bottled water used to account for only a tiny fraction of beverage consumption, inconsequential when compared to soft drinks, coffee and tea, beer, milk, and juice. Today, after enjoying years of "enviable, unending growth," bottled water has become the "superstar [of] the beverage industry." In addition, nearly half of all households use some kind of water filter in the home.

A couple of decades back, organic foods had only a tiny share of the overall food market. Organically grown foods were sold, typically, in small "health food" stores. They were hard to find, even if you wanted them. Few people did. But now, after years of 20 percent annual growth, organic food is mainstream. There are not only organic fruits and vegetables but organic breads and cereals, organic meat, fish, and dairy, organic beer, organic snack food. One can find organic foods in large, attractive, upscale chain stores, such as Whole Foods, and also increasingly in mainstream supermarkets. Safeway and Wal-Mart both sell organic foods.

Those who can afford it buy "organic" or "natural" personal hygiene products, shampoo, soap, makeup; "nontoxic" home cleaning products; clothing made of natural fibers; furniture made of real wood; and rugs made of natural fiber. There is a new ritual in America (at least in middle-class America): applying 30 SPF sunscreen to our children's exposed skin every morning before they go to school, to summer camp, or to the beach. 99

(A. Szasz 2007:1–2)

n this excerpt from *Shopping Our Way to Safety: How We Changed from Protecting the Environment to Protecting Ourselves,* sociologist Andrew Szasz links the environmental consciousness that arose from the environmental movement to a new category of products and services. Today, he notes, many people fear the everyday environmental hazards present in their immediate environment, from the tap water to the air.

Rather than work for the health of the environment as a whole, some try to quarantine themselves from these perceived threats by shopping for supposedly pure, uncontaminated food, clothing, furniture, and cleaning products.

There is little question that some people do try to shop their way to safety. However, as Szasz notes, unless their largely individual responses go beyond self-protection, they won't improve society's health. What are the many people who cannot afford to drink bottled water or move to a healthier environment supposed to do? Won't the environment eventually reach a state that will threaten everyone, no matter how much organic food they consume?

What defines a healthy environment? How is the environment connected to our health as a society? How do health and health care vary from one social class to another and from one nation to another? In this chapter, we present a sociological overview of health, illness, health care, and medicine as a social institution. We begin by examining how functionalists, conflict theorists, interactionists, and labeling theorists look at health-related issues. Then we study the distribution of diseases in a society by social class, race and ethnicity, gender, and age.

We'll look too at the evolution of the U.S. health care system. Sociologists are interested in the roles people play in the health care system and the organizations that deal with issues of health and sickness. Therefore, we will analyze the interactions among physicians, nurses, and patients; alternatives to traditional health care; the role of government in providing health care services to the needy; and the issues people with mental illness face.

The study of population is closely linked to both health and environment. In our coverage of population, we focus on patterns of birth, death, and fertility in societies at different stages of evolution. This overview of population trends leads to a discussion of migration, a major factor in population change.

Later in the chapter, we examine the environmental problems facing the world in the 21st century. We draw on the functionalist and conflict perspectives to better understand environmental issues. We'll see that it is important not to oversimplify the relationships among health, population, and the environment. Finally, in the Social Policy section, we explore the recently renewed interest in environmentalism.

MODULE 52 | Sociological Perspectives on Health and Illness

How can we define health? Imagine a continuum with health on one end and death on the other. In the preamble to its 1946 constitution, the World Health Organization defined **health** as a "state of complete physical, mental, and social well-being, and not merely the absence of disease and infirmity" (Leavell and Clark 1965:14). In this definition, the "healthy" end of the continuum represents an ideal rather than a precise condition.

Along the continuum, individuals define themselves as healthy or sick on the basis of criteria established by themselves and relatives, friends, co-workers, and medical practitioners. Health and illness, in other words, are socially constructed. They are rooted in culture and are defined by claims makers—people who describe themselves as healthy or ill—as well as by a broad range of interested parties, including health care providers, pharmaceutical firms, and even food providers (Conrad and Barker 2010).

Because health is socially constructed, we can consider how it varies in different situations or cultures. Why is it that you may consider yourself sick or well when others do not agree? Who controls definitions of health and illness in our society, and for what ends? What are the consequences of viewing yourself (or of being viewed) as ill or disabled? By drawing on four sociological perspectives—functionalism, conflict theory, interactionism, and labeling theory—we can gain greater insight into the social context that shapes definitions of health and the treatment of illness.

Functionalist Perspective

Illness entails breaks in our social interactions, both at work and at home. From a functionalist perspective, being sick must therefore be controlled, so that not too many people are released from their societal responsibilities at any one time. Functionalists contend that an overly broad definition of illness would disrupt the workings of a society.

Sickness requires that one take on a social role, if only temporarily. The **sick role** refers to societal expectations about the attitudes and behavior of a person viewed as being ill. Sociologist Talcott Parsons (1951, 1975), well known for his contributions to functionalist theory, outlined the behavior required of people who are considered sick. They are exempted from their normal, day-to-day responsibilities and generally do not suffer blame for their condition. Yet they are obligated to try to get well, which includes seeking competent professional care. This obligation arises from the common view that illness is dysfunctional, because it can undermine social stability. Attempting to get well is particularly important in the world's developing countries. Modern automated industrial societies can absorb a greater degree of illness or disability than horticultural or agrarian societies, in which the availability of workers is far more critical (Conrad and Leiter 2013).

© Paul Souders/Corbis

Health practices vary from one country to another. Unlike people in most other societies, the Japanese often wear surgical masks in public, to protect themselves from disease or pollution. The practice began in 1919, when the worldwide Spanish flu epidemic became a public health menace. Today mask wearing persists even when there is no public health threat.

According to Parsons's theory, physicians function as *gate-keepers* for the sick role. They verify a patient's condition either as "illness" or as "recovered." The ill person becomes dependent on the physician, because the latter can control valued rewards (not only treatment of illness, but also excused absences from work and school). Parsons suggests that the physician–patient relationship is somewhat like that between parent and child. Like a parent, the physician helps the patient to enter society as a full and functioning adult.

The concept of the sick role is not without criticism. First, patients' judgments regarding their own state of health may be related to their gender, age, social class, and ethnic group. For example, younger people may fail to detect warning signs of a dangerous illness, while elderly people may focus too much on the slightest physical malady. Second, the sick role may be more applicable to people who are experiencing short-term illnesses than to those with recurring, long-term illnesses. Finally, even simple factors, such as whether a person is employed, seem to affect one's willingness to assume the sick role—as does the impact of socialization into a particular occupation or activity. For example, beginning in childhood, athletes learn to define certain ailments as "sports injuries" and therefore do not regard themselves as "sick." Nonetheless, sociologists continue to rely on Parsons's model for functionalist analysis of the relationship between illness and societal expectations of the sick (Frank 2015).

 use your sociological imagination

Describe some situations you have witnessed that illustrate different definitions of the "sick role."

informal social control as occurring within families and peer groups, and formal social control as being carried out by authorized agents such as police officers, judges, school administrators, and employers. Viewed from a conflict perspective, however, medicine is not simply a "healing profession"; it is a regulating mechanism.

How does medicine manifest its social control? First, medicine has greatly expanded its domain of expertise in recent decades. Physicians now examine a wide range of issues, among them sexuality, old age, anxiety, obesity, child development, alcoholism, and drug addiction. We tolerate this expansion of the boundaries of medicine because we hope that these experts can bring new "miracle cures" to complex human problems, as they have to the control of certain infectious diseases.

In defining these new conditions, physicians determine and control the course of treatment, and even affect patients' views of themselves. Once a problem is viewed using this **medical model,** it becomes more difficult for common people to join the discussion and exert influence on decision making. It also becomes more difficult to view these issues as being shaped by social, cultural, or psychological factors, rather than simply by physical or medical factors (Caplan 1989; Conrad 2009; Zola 1972, 1983).

Second, medicine serves as an agent of social control by retaining absolute jurisdiction over many health care procedures. It has even attempted to guard its jurisdiction by placing health care professionals such as chiropractors and nurse-midwives outside the realm of acceptable medicine. Despite the fact that midwives first brought professionalism to child delivery, they have been portrayed as having invaded the "legitimate" field of obstetrics, in both the United States and Mexico. Nurse-midwives have sought licensing as a way to achieve professional respectability, but physicians continue to exert power to

● Conflict Perspective

Conflict theorists observe that the medical profession has assumed a preeminence that extends well beyond whether to excuse a student from school or an employee from work. Sociologist Eliot Freidson (1970:5) has likened the position of medicine today to that of state religions yesterday—it has an officially approved monopoly of the right to define health and illness and to treat illness. Conflict theorists use the term *medicalization of society* to refer to the growing role of medicine as a major institution of social control.

The Medicalization of Society

Social control involves techniques and strategies for regulating behavior in order to enforce the distinctive norms and values of a culture. Typically, we think of

© Hill Street Studios/Blend Images/Getty Images RF

The growing concern about obesity among the young has focused attention on their eating habits and their need for exercise. Concern about obesity is a sign of the medicalization of society.

ensure that midwifery remains a subordinate occupation (Scharnberg 2007).

Inequities in Health Care

The medicalization of society is but one concern of conflict theorists as they assess the workings of health care institutions. As we have seen throughout this textbook, in analyzing any issue, conflict theorists seek to determine who benefits, who suffers, and who dominates at the expense of others. Viewed from a conflict perspective, glaring inequities exist in health care delivery in the United States. For example, poor areas tend to be underserved because medical services concentrate where people are wealthy.

Similarly, from a global perspective, obvious inequities exist in health care delivery. Today, the United States has about 25 physicians per 10,000 people, while collectively, African nations have fewer than 1 per 10,000. This situation is only worsened by the **brain drain**—the immigration to the United States and other industrialized nations of skilled workers, professionals, and technicians who are desperately needed in their home countries. As part of this brain drain, physicians, nurses, and other health care professionals have come to the United States from developing countries such as India, Pakistan, and various African states. Conflict theorists view their emigration out of the Third World as yet another way in which the world's core industrialized nations enhance their quality of life at the expense of developing countries. One way the developing countries suffer is in lower life expectancy. In Africa and much of Latin America and Asia, life expectancy is far lower than in industrialized nations (Migration Policy Institute 2016).

Conflict theorists emphasize that inequities in health care have clear life-and-death consequences. From a conflict perspective, the dramatic differences in *infant mortality rates* around the world (Figure 52-1) reflect, at least in part, unequal distribution of health care resources based on the wealth or poverty of various nations. The **infant mortality rate** is the number of deaths of infants under 1 year old per 1,000 live births in a given year. This measure is an important indicator of a society's level of health care; it reflects prenatal nutrition, delivery procedures, and infant screening measures. Still, despite the wealth of the United States, at least 48 nations have *lower* infant mortality rates. Conflict theorists point out that unlike the United States, these countries offer some form of government-supported health care for all citizens, which typically leads to greater availability and use of prenatal care.

 use your **sociological imagination**

From a sociological point of view, what might be the greatest challenge to reducing inequities in health care?

FIGURE 52-1 **Infant Mortality Rates in Selected Countries**

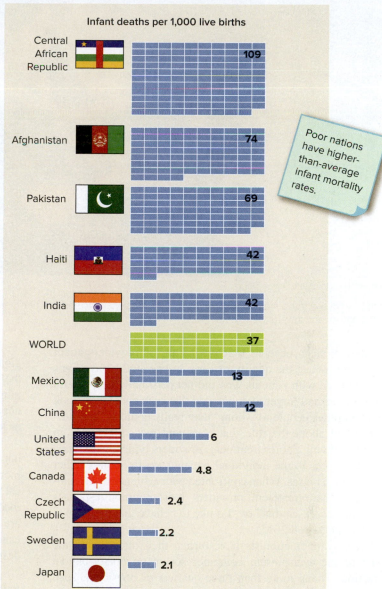

Infant deaths per 1,000 live births

Central African Republic	109
Afghanistan	74
Pakistan	69
Haiti	42
India	42
WORLD	37
Mexico	13
China	12
United States	6
Canada	4.8
Czech Republic	2.4
Sweden	2.2
Japan	2.1

Poor nations have higher-than-average infant mortality rates.

Source: Kaneda and Bietsch 2015. *Flags*: © admin_design/Shutterstock RF

Interactionist Perspective

From an interactionist point of view, patients are not passive; often, they actively seek the services of a health care practitioner. In examining health, illness, and medicine as a social institution, then, interactionists engage in micro-level study of the roles played by health care professionals and patients. Interactionists are particularly interested in how physicians learn to play their occupational role. For example, in one of his earliest works, sociologist Howard Becker took the perspective that medical education socialized students into the role of doctor as much as it transferred medical knowledge to them (H. Becker et al. 1961).

© ERproductions Ltd./Getty Images RF

With the use of electronic medical records, medical professionals increasingly turn their attention away from the patient and toward the screen.

Interactionists observe that the nature of provider-patient contact can reduce the quality of care. In one study, physicians who interacted with patients who did not personally keep health records or seemed forgetful concluded that such encounters took time from other people to whom "they really could be helpful." When asked about the role that class and race might play in patients receiving poorer treatment, providers typically assigned such differences to the individual patient's shortcomings rather than their own biases. When confronted with evidence of inequality in health care treatment, providers' most common responses were "I just can't see that" or "I'd like to believe that there isn't" (Gengler and Jarrell 2015).

Recently interactionists have turned their attention to the impact of the ever-present computer screen on doctor-patient interaction. Today more than three-quarters of physicians scan the screen for past visits and test results and enter their observations for the current visit while interacting with a patient. As a result, face-to-face interaction has been reduced by one-third. So concerned has the medical profession become about this trend that, drawing on social interaction studies, doctors are now told to review the electronic medical record before seeing the patient and to share the computer screen so the patient can become more involved in the visit (Duke et al. 2013; Reddy 2015).

Labeling Perspective

Labeling theory helps us to understand why certain people are *viewed* as deviants, "bad kids," or criminals, whereas others whose behavior is similar are not. Labeling theorists also suggest that the designation "healthy" or "ill" generally involves social definition by others. Just as police officers, judges, and other regulators of social control have the power to define certain people as criminals, health care professionals (especially physicians) have the power to define certain people as sick. Moreover, like labels that suggest nonconformity or criminality, labels that are associated with illness commonly reshape how others treat us and how we see ourselves.

A historical example illustrates perhaps the ultimate extreme in labeling social behavior as a sickness. As enslavement of Africans in the United States came under increasing attack in the 19th century, medical authorities provided new rationalizations for the oppressive practice. Noted physicians published articles stating that the skin color of Africans deviated from "healthy" white skin coloring because Africans suffered from congenital leprosy. Moreover, the continuing efforts of enslaved Africans to escape from their White masters were classified as an example of the "disease" of drapetomania (or "crazy runaways"). The prestigious *New Orleans Medical and Surgical Journal* suggested that the remedy for this "disease" was to treat slaves kindly, as one might treat children. Apparently, these medical authorities would not entertain the view that it was healthy and sane to flee slavery or join in a slave revolt (T. Szasz 2010).

A new concern about how illness can be stigmatized grows out of the dependence on electronic health records. As more and more medical records are digitized to facilitate access by medical professionals, concerns have increased over how a person's medical history may be viewed or misinterpreted if the records are improperly shared. There are a host of medical labels, from cancer survivor to diabetic, that could result in discrimination, despite laws prohibiting such practices (Stablen et al. 2015).

Similarly, labeling theorists suggest that behaviors viewed today as mental illnesses may not really be illnesses. Instead, the individual's problems arise from living in society, not from physical maladies. From this perspective, a variety of life experiences treated as illnesses today may not be illnesses at all. Premenstrual syndrome, post-traumatic stress disorders, and hyperactivity are examples of medically recognized disorders that labeling theorists would consider questionable.

Probably the most noteworthy medical example of labeling is the case of homosexuality. For years, psychiatrists classified being gay or lesbian not as a lifestyle but as a mental disorder subject to treatment. This official sanction became an early target of the growing gay and lesbian rights movement in the United States. In 1974, members of the American Psychiatric Association finally voted to drop homosexuality from the standard manual on mental disorders (Conrad 2009).

Table 52-1 summarizes four major sociological perspectives on health and illness. Although they may seem quite different, two

Taking **Sociology** to **Work**

Lola Adedokun, *Director, African Health Initiative, and Program Director, Child Well-Being Program, Doris Duke Charitable Foundation*

© Amanda Gentile

When Lola Adedokun entered Dartmouth College, she was thinking of concentrating in biology and pre-medical studies, but after taking a sociology course on racial disparities, she realized that sociology was the only subject that offered courses on topics she was passionate about. Eventually, she settled on sociology as her undergraduate major, along with a special social science major in health policy that she created herself. After completing her undergraduate degree, she began work at a consulting firm focused on tackling many of the toughest social issues facing our society. It was her early training in sociological studies that positioned her well for this job. After several years as a consultant she went on to pursue her master's degree in public health at Columbia University.

Today, Adedokun is working at one of the largest private foundations in the country, where she serves as Director of two programs, Child Well-being and African Health. Though the programs serve populations that are geographically different from one another, they both aim to respond to the fundamental social issues that serve as barriers to the overall health and well-being of children, families, and the societies in which they live. As a member of a philanthropic organization, it is her responsibility to remain abreast of the changing issues in today's society, including poverty, inequality, racism, sexism, child abuse, and mass incarceration. This means reading the news, keeping up with relevant research, and talking to community and research leaders to remain informed. With this wealth of information, she is then prepared to make responsible decisions about what grants to fund, focusing on those that are best positioned to improve lives of children and families.

Travel has been one of the high points in Adedokun's career. "It has been my privilege to be able to travel throughout the United States and around the world to gain first-hand knowledge of the growing needs of families and neighbors. I have not only learned about the needs that our grantmaking can fill, but also the creative and innovative solutions that individuals and communities have designed and led to solve their own challenges." She has had the opportunity to meet ministers of health, community organizers, research experts, and global and local leaders that have inspired her.

Asked what advice she would give to current students of sociology, Adedokun replies, "Sociology has been at the foundation of my career. It is the basic principles of sociology that continue to inform my work and allow me to achieve my goals to improve society." She continues, "It is the fundamentals of sociology that will be most relevant to any area that you choose to pursue in your future, so ask questions, debate, discuss, and argue, as the knowledge that you will pull from that will lead to some of the most important life lessons you may ever learn."

LET'S DISCUSS

1. What social issue or problem do you feel passionate about, and how can sociology help you address it?
2. Adedokun is a self-starter who created her own major and began her career as an independent consultant. Have you ever considered creating your own career path, rather than relying on large institutions to map your future? What might be the benefits of such an approach? The drawbacks?

TABLE **52-1** **SOCIOLOGICAL PERSPECTIVES ON HEALTH AND ILLNESS**

Tracking Sociological Perspectives

	Functionalist	Conflict	Interactionist	Labeling
Major emphasis	Control of the number of people who are considered sick	Overmedicalization Gross inequities in health care	Doctor–patient relationship Interaction of medical staff	Definition of illness and health
Controlling factors	Physician as gatekeeper	Medical profession Social inequities	Medical profession	Medical profession
Proponents	Talcott Parsons	Thomas Szasz Irving Zola	Howard Becker	Thomas Szasz

common themes unite them. First, any person's health or illness is more than an organic condition, since it is subject to the interpretation of others. The impact of culture, family and friends, and the medical profession means that health and illness are not purely biological occurrences, but sociological occurrences as well.

Second, since members of a society (especially industrial societies) share the same health care delivery system, health is a group and societal concern. Although health may be defined as the complete well-being of an individual, it is also the result of one's social environment, as the next section will show (Cockerham 2012).

Summary

The concept of **health** is shaped by social definitions of behavior.

1. According to Talcott Parsons's functionalist perspective, physicians function as "gatekeepers" for the **sick role,** either verifying a person's condition as "ill" or designating the person as "recovered."

2. Conflict theorists use the term *medicalization of society* to refer to medicine's growing role as a major institution of social control.

3. Labeling theorists suggest that the designation of a person as "healthy" or "ill" generally involves social definitions by others. These definitions affect how others see us and how we view ourselves.

Thinking Critically

1. Define the term "health" from the functionalist, conflict, interactionist, and labeling perspectives.

2. Describe an occasion on which people you know disagreed about a socially applied medical label. What was the label, and why did people disagree?

Key Terms

Brain drain

Health

Infant mortality rate

Labeling theory

Medical model

Sick role

MODULE 53 | **Social Epidemiology and Health Care in the United States**

Social Epidemiology and Health

Social epidemiology is the study of the distribution of disease, impairment, and general health status across a population. Initially, epidemiologists concentrated on the scientific study of epidemics, focusing on how they started and spread. Contemporary social epidemiology is much broader in scope, concerned not only with epidemics but also with nonepidemic diseases, injuries, drug addiction and alcoholism, suicide, and mental illness. Epidemiologists have taken on the new role of tracking bioterrorism. In 2001, they mobilized to trace the anthrax outbreak and prepare for any terrorist use of smallpox or other lethal microbes. Epidemiologists draw on the work of a wide variety of scientists and researchers, among them physicians, sociologists, public health officials, biologists, veterinarians, demographers, anthropologists, psychologists, and meteorologists.

Epidemiologists have found that worldwide, an estimated 37 million people were infected with HIV at the end of 2015. Women account for a growing proportion of new cases of HIV/AIDS, especially among racial and ethnic minorities. Although the spread of AIDS is stabilizing, with fewer new cases reported, the disease is not evenly distributed. Those areas that are least equipped to deal with it—the developing nations of sub-Saharan Africa—face the greatest challenge (Figure 53-1).

When disease data are presented as rates, or as the number of reports per 100,000 people, they are called **morbidity rates.** (The term **mortality rate** refers to the rate of *death* in a given population.) Sociologists find morbidity rates useful because they may reveal that a specific disease occurs more frequently in one segment of a population. As we shall see, social class, race, ethnicity, gender, and age can all affect a population's morbidity rates.

Social Class

Social class is clearly associated with differences in morbidity and mortality rates. Studies in the United States and other countries have consistently shown that people in the lower classes have higher rates of mortality, morbidity, and long-term disability than others.

Why is class linked to health? Crowded living conditions, substandard housing, poor diet, and stress all contribute to the ill health of many low-income people in the United States. In certain instances, poor education may lead to a lack of awareness of measures necessary to maintain good health. Financial strains are certainly a major factor in the health problems of less affluent people.

What is particularly troubling about social class differences is that they appear to be cumulative. Little or no health care in childhood or young adulthood is likely to mean more illness later in life. The longer that low income presents a barrier to adequate health care, the more chronic and difficult to treat illness becomes.

FIGURE 53-1 AIDS by the Numbers Worldwide

Year	New infections (children)	New HIV infections (millions)	AIDS related deaths (millions)	People accessing treatment (millions)
2001	550 000	3.4		
2002	560 000	3.3		
2003	560 000	3.1		
2004	550 000	3.0	2.3	
2005	540 000	2.9	2.3	1.3
2006	520 000	2.8	2.3	2.0
2007	480 000	2.7	2.2	2.9
2008	450 000	2.6	2.1	4.1
2009	400 000	2.6	2.0	5.3
2010	360 000	2.5	1.9	6.6
2011	330 000	2.3	1.5	9.4
2012	280 000	2.2	1.4	11.4
2013	250 000	2.1	1.3	13.0
2014	220 000	2.0	1.2	14.9

Source: UNAIDS 2013, 2015.

Another reason for the link between social class and health is that the poor—many of whom belong to racial and ethnic minorities—are less able than others to afford quality medical care. The affluent are more likely than others to have health insurance, either because they can afford it or because they have jobs that provide it. Pharmacists report that people purchase only those medications they "need the most," or buy in small quantities, such as four pills at a time. Between 2008 and 2013, the uninsured rate ranged from 14.5 percent to 15.5 percent. The percentage of the population who were uninsured dropped between 2013 and 2014 to 11.7, marking the largest decline in the uninsured rate during this period (Figure 53-2). While health insurance coverage has improved, children in households earning less than $25,000 are still half as likely to have access to any kind of insurance plan than the more affluent.

Finally, in the view of Karl Marx and contemporary conflict theorists, capitalist societies such as the United States care more about maximizing profits than they do about the health and safety of industrial workers. As a result, government agencies do not take forceful action to regulate conditions in the workplace, and workers suffer many preventable job-related injuries and illnesses. As we will see later in this chapter, research also shows that the lower classes are more vulnerable to environmental pollution than are the affluent, not only where they work but where they live.

use your sociological imagination

In what ways do the costs of health care affect the way you receive medical services?

Race and Ethnicity

The health profiles of many racial and ethnic minorities reflect the social inequality evident in the United States. The poor economic and environmental conditions of groups such as African Americans, Hispanics, and Native Americans are manifested in high morbidity and mortality rates for those groups. It is true that some diseases, such as sickle-cell anemia among Blacks, have a clear genetic basis. But in most instances, environmental factors contribute to the differential rates of disease and death.

As noted earlier, infant mortality is regarded as a primary indicator of health care. There is a significant gap in the United States between the infant mortality rates of African Americans and Whites. Generally, the rate of infant death is more than twice as high among Blacks (MacDorman and Mathews 2009).

The medical establishment is not exempt from racism. Discrimination and prejudice are often overlooked by the media, which tend to focus on the most overt forms of racism, such as hate crimes. Minorities often receive inferior medical care even when they are insured. Despite having access to care, Blacks, Latinos, and Native Americans are treated unequally as a result of racial prejudice and differences in the quality of various health care plans. Furthermore, national clinical studies have shown that even allowing for differences in income and insurance coverage, racial and ethnic minorities are less likely than other groups to receive both standard health care and life-saving treatment for conditions such as HIV infection (Centers for Disease Control and Prevention 2013; Phelan and Link 2015).

Drawing on the conflict perspective, sociologist Howard Waitzkin (1986) suggests that racial tensions also contribute to the medical problems of Blacks. In his view, the stress that results from racial prejudice and discrimination helps to explain the higher rates of hypertension found among African Americans (and Hispanics) compared to Whites. Hypertension, which affects over 41 percent of Blacks but fewer than 29 percent of non-Hispanic Whites, is believed to be a critical factor in high mortality rates from heart disease, kidney disease, and stroke found among African Americans (Gillespie and Hurvitz 2013).

Some Mexican Americans and many other Latinos adhere to cultural beliefs that make them less likely than others to use the established medical system. They may interpret their illnesses according to *curanderismo,* or traditional Latino folk medicine—a form of holistic health care and healing. *Curanderismo* influences how one approaches health care and even how

FIGURE 53-2 **Percentage without Health Insurance**

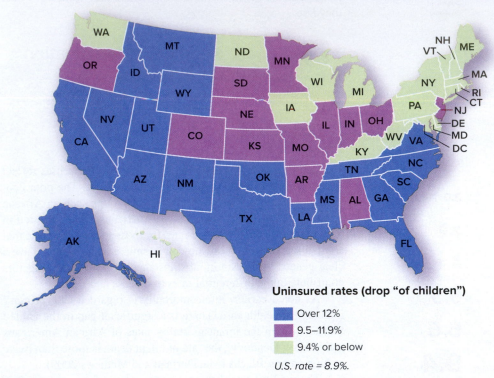

Uninsured rates (drop "of children")

- Over 12%
- 9.5–11.9%
- 9.4% or below

U.S. rate = 8.9%.

Note: In 2014, people without private or government health insurance, not covered by Medicaid, Medicare, or military health care.
Source: Smith and Medalia 2015:H106.

one defines illness. Most Hispanics probably use *curanderos,* or folk healers, infrequently, but perhaps 20 percent rely on home remedies. Some define such illnesses as *susto* (fright sickness) and *atague* (fighting attack) according to folk beliefs. Because these complaints often have biological bases, medical practitioners need to deal with them sensitively in order to diagnose and treat illnesses accurately. Moreover, it would be a mistake to blame the poor health care that Latinos receive on cultural differences. Latinos are much more likely to seek treatment for pressing medical problems at clinics and emergency rooms than they are to receive regular preventive care through a family physician (Centers for Disease Control and Prevention 2013; Hendrickson 2015).

Gender

A large body of research indicates that compared with men, women experience a higher occurrence of many illnesses, although they tend to live longer. There are some variations—for example, men are more likely to have parasitic diseases, whereas women are more likely to become diabetic—but as a group, women appear to be in poorer health than men.

The apparent inconsistency between the ill health of women and their greater longevity deserves an explanation, and researchers have advanced a theory. Women's lower rate of cigarette smoking (reducing their risk of heart disease, lung cancer,

and emphysema), lower consumption of alcohol (reducing the risk of auto accidents and cirrhosis of the liver), and lower rate of employment in dangerous occupations explain about one-third of their greater longevity than men. Moreover, some clinical studies suggest that the differences in morbidity may actually be less pronounced than the data show. Researchers argue that women are much more likely than men to seek treatment, to be diagnosed as having a disease, and thus to have their illnesses reflected in the data examined by epidemiologists.

From a conflict perspective, women have been particularly vulnerable to the medicalization of society, with everything from birth to beauty being treated in an increasingly medical context. Such medicalization may contribute to women's higher morbidity rates compared to those of men. Ironically, even though women have been especially affected by medicalization, medical researchers have often excluded them from clinical studies. Female physicians and researchers charge that sexism lies at the heart of such research practices, and insist there is a desperate need for studies of female subjects (Centers for Disease Control and Prevention 2013; Gengler and Jarrell 2015; Rieker and Bird 2000).

Age

Health is the overriding concern of the elderly. Most older people in the United States report having at least one chronic illness, but only some of those conditions are potentially life threatening or require medical care. At the same time, health problems can affect the quality of life of older people in important ways. Almost half of older people in the United States are troubled by arthritis, and many have visual or hearing impairments that can interfere with the performance of everyday tasks.

Older people are also especially vulnerable to certain mental health problems. Alzheimer's disease, the leading cause of dementia in the United States, afflicts an estimated 5.1 million people age 65 or over—that is, 11 percent of that segment of the population. While some individuals with Alzheimer's exhibit only mild symptoms, the risk of severe problems resulting from the disease rises substantially with age (Alzheimer's Association 2016).

Not surprisingly, older people in the United States (age 75 and older) are five times more likely to use health services than younger people (ages 15–24). The disproportionate use of the U.S. health care system by older people is a critical factor in all discussions about the cost of health care and possible reforms of the health care system.

In sum, to achieve greater access and reduce health disparities, federal health officials must overcome inequities that are rooted not just in age, but in social class, race and ethnicity, and gender. If that were not enough, they must also deal with a geographical disparity in health care resources.

Health Care in the United States

As the entire nation is well aware, the costs of health care have skyrocketed. (Figure 53-3). By 2000, the amount spent on health care already equaled that spent on education, defense, prisons, farm subsidies, food stamps, and foreign aid combined. By the year 2020, total expenditures for health care in the United States are expected to exceed $4.2 trillion. The implementation of the 2010 Affordable Care Act, discussed in detail later, was expected by some to control health costs. Instead, costs have continued to rise. This is spurred by several factors: the economy's recovery from the Great Recession led many people to undergo postponed procedures, the aging population consumes ever more health care, and pharmaceutical companies continue to develop high-priced specialty drugs (Armour 2015).

FIGURE 53-3 **Total Health Care Expenditures in the United States, 1960–2020 (Projected)**

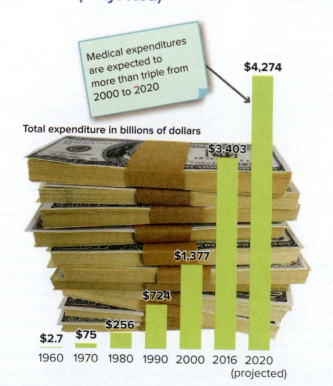

Medical expenditures are expected to more than triple from 2000 to 2020

Total expenditure in billions of dollars

$4,274
$3,403
$1,377
$724
$256
$75
$2.7

| 1960 | 1970 | 1980 | 1990 | 2000 | 2016 | 2020 (projected) |

Source: Centers for Medicare and Medicaid Services, 2015. *Photo:* © Comstock Images/Alamy RF

The health care system of the United States has moved far beyond the days when general practitioners living in a neighborhood or community typically made house calls and charged modest fees for their services. How did health care become a big business involving nationwide hospital chains and marketing campaigns? How have these changes reshaped the interactions between doctors, nurses, and patients? We will address these questions in this section.

A Historical View

Today, state licensing and medical degrees confer authority on medical professionals that is maintained from one generation to the next. However, health care in the United States has not always followed this model. The "popular health movement" of the 1830s and 1840s emphasized preventive care and what is termed "self-help." Strong criticism was voiced of "doctoring" as a paid occupation. New medical philosophies or sects established medical schools and challenged the authority and methods of traditional doctors. By the 1840s, most states had repealed medical licensing laws.

In response, through the leadership of the American Medical Association (AMA), founded in 1848, "regular" doctors attacked lay practitioners, sectarian doctors, and female physicians. Once they had institutionalized their authority through standardized programs of education and licensing, they conferred it only on those who completed their programs. The authority of the physician no longer depended on lay attitudes or on the person occupying the sick role; it was built into the structure of the medical profession and the health care system. By the 1920s, physicians controlled hospital technology, the division of labor of health personnel, and indirectly, other professional practices such as nursing and pharmacy (R. Coser 1984).

Patients have traditionally relied on medical personnel to inform them of health care issues, but increasingly they are turning to the media for health care information. Recognizing this change, pharmaceutical firms advertise their prescription drugs directly to potential customers through television and magazines. The Internet is another growing source for patient information. Medical professionals are understandably suspicious of these new sources of information.

Today, consumers get more than their health care information in new ways. Over the past decade, they have discovered a new way to access traditional medicine: going to the store (Box 53-1).

Physicians and Patients

Traditionally, physicians have held a position of dominance in their dealings with patients. The functionalist and interactionist perspectives offer a framework for understanding the professional socialization of physicians as it relates to patient care. Functionalists suggest that established physicians and medical school professors serve as mentors or role models who transmit knowledge, skills, and values to the passive learner—the medical student. Interactionists emphasize that students are molded by the medical school environment as they interact with their classmates.

Health Care, Retail Style

Greeting cards are in aisle 7; vaccinations, in aisle 4. Today, over 1,200 health clinics are located in retail stores throughout the United States, including Walgreens, CVS, and Walmart. Staffed by nurse-practitioners and nurses with advanced degrees, these in-store clinics treat a limited menu of complaints, including sore throats, ear infections, pinkeye, and noncomplicated respiratory conditions. And the nurses do write prescriptions.

What are the implications of these new clinics for traditional health care? Having a regular physician is becoming less and less common in the United States, given the the frequent changes in employment and in corporate health plans. Like it or not, the physician you see this year simply may not be available to you next year. Under these circumstances, retail medical care may not pose much of a challenge to traditional medical practices.

© Nati Harnik/AP Images

> For three acute conditions— sore throat, middle ear infection, and urinary tract infection—retail clinics delivered the same or better-quality care than traditional medical settings.

What about the quality of care offered at in-store clinics? Recently, researchers compared the care delivered in retail clinics to the care available in doctors' offices, urgent care departments, and emergency rooms. For three acute conditions—sore throat, middle ear infection, and urinary tract infection— they found that retail clinics delivered the same or better-quality care than traditional

medical settings, including preventive care during or after the first visit.

In-store clinics are another example of **McDonaldization,** the process by which the principles of bureaucratization have increasingly shaped organizations worldwide. McDonaldization offers the benefit of clearly stated services and prices, but the drawback of impersonality. Family doctors note that 40 percent of clinic patients have a family physician. Yet given the shortcomings of health care delivery in the United States, it is difficult to argue against an innovative new method of providing health care. While health care scholars often consider more time spent with a patient a good thing, the McDonaldization of health care maximizes efficiency of time on task. Little surprise,

then, that the CVS pharmacy chain calls its more than one thousand in-store medical care facilities MinuteClinics.

LET'S DISCUSS

1. Have you ever been treated at an in-store clinic? If so, were you satisfied with the care you received? What about the price you paid—was it reasonable?

2. Evaluate the emergence of clinics from a functionalist and then a conflict perspective. On balance, do you think these clinics are a benefit to society?

Sources: Hamilton 2014; Pickert 2009; RAND 2010; Ritzer 2015.

Both approaches argue that the typical training of physicians in the United States leads to rather dehumanizing physician–patient encounters. Dr. Lori Alvord, a Navajo surgeon, has observed that the patient-physician relationship is "central to the development of trust. It is a time when patients have voluntarily given control over their bodies to others, and this can be frightening. The experiences the patient has at the time of surgery are also important, and I try to make sure that our surgical environment, to the extent possible, is a positive experience" (2009).

Despite many efforts to introduce a humanistic approach to patient care into the medical school curriculum, patient overload and cost-cutting by hospitals have tended to undercut positive relations. Moreover, widespread publicity about malpractice suits and high medical costs has further strained the physician–patient relationship. Interactionists have closely examined compliance and negotiation between physician and patient. They concur with Talcott Parsons's view that the relationship is generally asymmetrical, with doctors holding a position of dominance and controlling rewards.

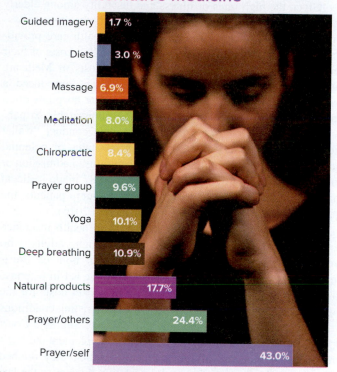

use your **sociological imagination**

If you were a patient, would you put yourself entirely in the physician's hands, or would you do some research on your own? If you were a doctor, would you want your patient checking medical information on the Internet? Explain your positions.

Alternatives to Traditional Health Care

In traditional forms of health care, people rely on physicians and hospitals for the treatment of illness. More and more adults are using additional techniques to be healthy. If a non-mainstream practice is used together with conventional medicine, it's considered *complementary*. If a non-mainstream practice is used in place of conventional medicine, it's considered *alternative*. These techniques are increasingly seen as part of preventive health practices and are sometimes even covered by health insurance.

In recent decades interest has grown in *holistic* (also spelled *wholistic*) medical principles, first developed in China. **Holistic medicine** refers to therapies in which the health care practitioner considers the person's physical, mental, emotional, and spiritual characteristics. The individual is regarded as a totality rather than a collection of interrelated organ systems. Treatment methods include massage, chiropractic medicine, acupuncture, respiratory exercises, and the use of herbs as remedies. Nutrition, exercise, and visualization may also be used to treat ailments that are generally treated through medication or hospitalization.

Practitioners of holistic medicine do not necessarily function totally outside the traditional health care system. Some have medical degrees and rely on X-rays and EKG machines for diagnostic assistance. Others who staff holistic clinics, often referred to as *wellness clinics*, reject the use of medical technology. The recent resurgence of holistic medicine comes amid widespread recognition of the value of nutrition and the dangers of over-reliance on prescription drugs (especially those used to reduce stress, such as Valium).

The medical establishment—professional organizations, research hospitals, and medical schools—has generally served as a stern protector of traditionally accepted health care techniques. However, a major breakthrough occurred in 1992 when the federal government's National Institutes of Health—the nation's major funding source for biomedical research—opened the National Center for Complementary and Integrative Health, empowered to accept grant requests. NIH-sponsored national surveys found that one in four adults in the United States had used some form of "complementary and alternative medicine" during the previous month or year. Examples included acupuncture, folk medicine, meditation, yoga, homeopathic treatments, megavitamin therapy, and chiropractic treatment. When prayer was included as an alternative or complementary form of medicine, the proportion of adults who used alternative medicine rose to over 62 percent (Figure 53-4).

On the international level, the World Health Organization (WHO) has begun to monitor the use of alternative medicine

FIGURE 53-4 Use of Complementary and Alternative Medicine

Guided imagery 1.7 %
Diets 3.0 %
Massage 6.9%
Meditation 8.0%
Chiropractic 8.4%
Prayer group 9.6%
Yoga 10.1%
Deep breathing 10.9%
Natural products 17.7%
Prayer/others 24.4%
Prayer/self 43.0%

Note: Data from 2012 survey, except for prayer data from 2002 survey. Yoga includes Tai Chi and Qi Gong. Chiropractic includes osteopathic manipulation.

Source: P. Barnes et al. 2004; Black et al. 2015. *Photo:* © MarioPonta/Alamy

around the world. According to WHO, 80 percent of people who live in the poorest countries in the world use some form of alternative medicine, from herbal treatments to the services of a faith healer. In most countries, these treatments are largely unregulated, even though some of them can be fatal. For example, kava kava, an herbal tea used in the Pacific Islands to relieve anxiety, can be toxic to the liver in concentrated form. However, other alternative treatments have been found to be effective in the treatment of serious diseases, such as malaria and sickle-cell anemia. WHO's goal is to compile a list of such practices, as well as to encourage the development of universal training programs and ethical standards for practitioners of alternative medicine. Over 80 percent of the world's population depends on herbal medicines and products for healthy living (Kunle et al. 2012; McNeil 2002).

The Role of Government

Not until the 20th century did health care receive federal aid. The first significant involvement was the 1946 Hill-Burton Act, which provided subsidies for building and improving hospitals, especially in rural areas. A far more important change came with the enactment in 1965 of two wide-ranging government assistance programs: Medicare, which is essentially a compulsory health insurance plan for the elderly, and Medicaid, which is a noncontributory federal and state insurance plan for the poor.

These programs greatly expanded federal involvement in health care financing for needy men, women, and children.

Given the high rates of illness and disability among elderly people, Medicare has had a huge impact on the health care system. Initially, Medicare simply reimbursed health care providers such as physicians and hospitals for the billed costs of their services. However, in 1983, as the overall costs of Medicare increased dramatically, the federal government introduced a price-control system. Under this system, private hospitals often transfer patients whose treatment may be unprofitable to public facilities. In fact, many private hospitals conduct "wallet biopsies"—that is, investigate the financial status of potential patients. Those judged undesirable are then refused admission or dumped. Although a federal law passed in 1987 made it illegal for any hospital receiving Medicare funds to dump patients, the practice continues (Office of Inspector General 2016).

The 2010 Affordable Care Act improved health insurance coverage for people of all ages, especially young adults, who were allowed to remain longer on their parents' policies. President Obama's administration had pushed for the act in response to several problems, including high out-of-pocket costs for the uninsured and the inability of people with preexisting conditions to get insurance. In 2012 and again in 2015 the Supreme Court upheld the federal government's authority to implement the law's provisions. Opponents of the legislation, which they dubbed "Obamacare," have vowed to seek legislative changes to the law and to make further legal challenges. Critics complain that the act is too expensive for taxpayers, and unnecessarily—perhaps even unconstitutionally—dictates citizens' health care decisions.

© John Bazemore/AP Images

Tensions ran high as the Supreme Court heard arguments on the constitutionality of controversial new federal health care legislation. These citizens are indicating their opposition to the 2010 Affordable Care Act.

MODULE 53 | Recap and Review

Summary

Social epidemiology is concerned both with epidemic and with nonepidemic diseases, injuries, drug addiction and alcoholism, suicide, and mental illness. The health care system in the United States is a complex and expensive social institution that has evolved from relatively simple roots

1. Studies consistently show that people from lower socioeconomic groups have higher rates of mortality and disability than others.

2. Racial and ethnic minorities have higher rates of morbidity and mortality than Whites.

3. Women tend to be in poorer health than men, but nevertheless they live longer.

4. Older people are especially vulnerable to mental health problems such as Alzheimer's disease, as well as to physical ailments.

5. The preeminent role of physicians in the U.S. health care system gives them a position of dominance in their dealings with nurses and patients.

6. Many people use alternative health care techniques such as **holistic medicine** and self-help groups.

Thinking Critically

1. Which is a more important factor in the adequate delivery of health care, race or gender?

2. In the United States, a nation with a world-renowned medical system, why do so many people seek alternative forms of health care?

Key Terms

Curanderismo

Holistic medicine

McDonaldization

Morbidity rate

Mortality rate

Social epidemiology

Like other illnesses, mental disorders affect not just individuals and their families, but society as a whole. In industrial economies, mental disorders are a significant cause of disability. Thus, as a British medical journal declared in connection with the Global Mental Health Summit, there can be "no health without mental health" (Prince et al. 2007).

Sadly, the words *mental illness* and *insanity* evoke dramatic and often inaccurate images of emotional problems. Though the media routinely emphasize the most violent behavior of those with emotional disturbances, mental health and mental illness can more appropriately be viewed as a continuum of human behavior. Using this definition, we can consider a person to have a mental disorder "if he or she is so disturbed that coping with routine, everyday life is difficult or impossible." The term **mental illness** should be reserved for a disorder of the brain that disrupts a person's thinking, feeling, and ability to interact with others (J. Coleman and Cressey 1980:315; National Alliance on Mental Illness 2008).

Traditionally, people in the United States have maintained a negative and suspicious view of those with mental disorders. Holding the status of "mental patient" or even "former mental patient" can have unfortunate and undeserved consequences. Voting rights are denied in some instances, acceptance for jury duty is problematic, and past emotional problems are an issue in divorce and custody cases. Moreover, content analysis of network television programs and films shows that mentally ill characters are uniformly portrayed in a demeaning and derogatory fashion; many are labeled as "criminally insane," "wackos," or "psychos." From an interactionist perspective, a key social institution is shaping social behavior by manipulating symbols and intensifying people's fears about the mentally ill (Diefenbach and West 2007).

In 2012, a tragic mass shooting at an elementary school in Newtown, Connecticut, led to renewed scrutiny of the role of mental illness in incidents of gun violence. The shooter was said to have had a mental illness, for which he apparently went untreated. As a result, some people argued that to curb gun violence, legislators should focus on mental health rather than on gun control. Unfortunately, such public debates tend to perpetuate the false assumption that people with mental illness are dangerous, furthering the *stigma* associated with their illness. The term **stigma,** coined by the interactionist Erving Goffman (1963), describes the labels society uses to devalue members of certain social groups.

A review of the available survey data shows that over time, the general public has become more sophisticated about mental illness, and perhaps a bit more open to disclosure, recognition, and response to mental health problems. Yet since 1950, people have become much more likely to associate "violence" with "mental illness," despite overwhelming evidence to the contrary. In fact, the vast majority of people with psychiatric disorders *do not* commit violent acts. Only 4 percent of violent crimes in the United States can be attributed to people with mental illness (Pescosolido and Martin 2015).

© JEP Celebrity Photos/Alamy

In 2011, actress Catherine Zeta-Jones announced that she was being treated for bipolar disorder, a condition she shares with an estimated 2 percent of the U.S. population. The stigma of mental illness is slowly diminishing as celebrities come forward to reveal they are being treated for various mental disorders.

Despite the stigmatization of mental illness, more people are seeking care and professional assistance than in the past. In the military services, the depression and post-traumatic stress that many veterans experience is receiving growing attention. And increasingly, legislators are recognizing the need to provide services for all who suffer from mental illness (Kessler et al. 2006; Tanielian 2009).

Theoretical Models of Mental Disorders

In studying mental illness, we can draw on both the medical model and a more sociological approach derived from labeling theory. Each model rests on distinctive assumptions regarding treatment of people with mental disorders.

According to the medical model, mental illness is rooted in biological causes that can be treated through medical intervention. Problems in brain structure or in the biochemical balance in the brain, sometimes due to injury and sometimes due to genetic inheritance, are thought to be at the bottom of these disorders. The U.S. Surgeon General (1999) released an exhaustive report on mental health in which he declared that the accumulated weight of scientific evidence leaves no doubt about the physical origins of mental illness.

That is not to say that social factors do not contribute to mental illness. Just as culture affects the occurrence of illness and its treatment, so too it can affect mental illness. In fact, the very definition of mental illness differs from one culture to the next. Mainstream U.S. culture, for instance, considers hallucinations highly abnormal. However, many traditional cultures view them as evidence of divine favor and confer a special status on those who experience them. As we have noted throughout this textbook, a given behavior may be viewed as normal in one society, disapproved of but tolerated in a second, and labeled as sick and heavily sanctioned in a third.

A major focus of the controversy over the medical model is the *Diagnostic and Statistical Manual of Mental Disorders (DSM)*, which came out in its fifth edition in 2013 (*DSM-5*). The *DSM*, which was introduced in 1952 by the American Psychiatric Association (APA), is intended to establish standard criteria for diagnosing mental disorders. Over time, however, the classification of various conditions has changed, seeming to undercut the notion that mental disorders are fixed medical conditions. A 1987 revision, for example, dropped the diagnosis "sexual orientation disturbance," ending the treatment of homosexuality as a curable disorder. In *DSM-5*, binge eating and some forms of hoarding have been added to the list of disorders, and bereavement has been removed as a symptom of depression.

Importantly, the *DSM* is more than an academic volume. The categories it sets forth become the basis for insurance coverage, special educational and behavioral services, and medical prescriptions, and may qualify those with a diagnosis for disability benefits. Although supporters of the *DSM* acknowledge its limitations, they stress the need for practitioners to reach a consensus on the definition and treatment of mental disorders (American Psychiatric Association 2013; Satel 2013; Scheid 2013).

In contrast to the medical model, labeling theory suggests that some behaviors that are viewed as mental illnesses may not really be illnesses. For example, the U.S. Surgeon General's report (1999:5) notes that "bereavement symptoms" of less than two months' duration do not qualify as a mental disorder, but beyond that they may be redefined. Sociologists would see this approach to bereavement as labeling by those with the power to affix labels rather than as an acknowledgment of a biological condition.

Psychiatrist Thomas Szasz ("Sahz"), in his book *The Myth of Mental Illness* (2010), advanced the view that numerous personality disorders are not diseases, but simply patterns of conduct labeled as disorders by significant others. The response to Szasz's challenging thesis was sharp: the commissioner of the New York State Department of Hygiene demanded his dismissal from his university position because Szasz did not "believe" in mental illness. But many sociologists embraced his model as a logical extension of examining individual behavior in a social context.

In sum, the medical model is persuasive because it pinpoints the causes of mental illness and offers treatment for disorders. Yet proponents of the labeling perspective maintain that mental illness is a distinctively social process, whatever other processes are involved. From a sociological perspective, the ideal approach to mental illness integrates the insights of labeling theory with those of the medical approach (Horwitz 2002; Scheid 2013).

Patterns of Care

For most of human history, those who suffered from mental disorders were deemed the responsibility of their families. Yet mental illness has been a matter of governmental concern much longer than physical illness has. That is because severe emotional disorders threaten stable social relationships and entail prolonged incapacitation. As early as the 1600s, European cities began to confine the insane in public facilities along with the poor and criminals. Prisoners, indignant at being forced to live with "lunatics," resisted this approach. The isolation of people with mental illness from others in the same facility and from the larger society soon made physicians the central and ultimate authority over their welfare.

A major policy development in caring for those with mental disorders came with the passage of the Community Mental Health Centers Act (1963). The CMHC program, as it is known, not only increased the federal

© Doug Schneider/Alamy

For generations, many thousands of people with mental illness were effectively removed from society and placed in residential facilities. The now abandoned Harlem Valley Psychiatric Center in Dover, New York, which operated from 1924 to 1993, included 80 buildings; at its peak it housed 5,000 patients.

government's involvement in the treatment of people with mental illness. It also established community-based mental health centers to treat clients on an *outpatient* basis, thereby allowing them to continue working and living at home. The program showed that outpatient treatment could be more effective than the institutionalized programs of state and county mental hospitals.

A troubling trend as state facilities for the mentally ill were closed was an increase in the number of people with mental illness who wind up in jail. About 20 to 40 percent of jail inmates have a diagnosed mental illness. The nation's largest three jails (Cook County, Illinois; Los Angeles County; and New York City) have 11,000 inmates under treatment for mental illnesses. All together the nation's 213 state psychiatric

hospitals have just four times that number. Obviously jails cannot provide the most desirable treatment programs (Fields and Phillips 2013).

The Mental Health Parity and Addiction Equity Act of 2008, which took effect in 2010, required insurers to extend comparable benefits for mental and physical health care beginning in 2014. However, true parity between mental and physical health benefits has not been achieved, because the act exempts group health insurance plans from providing comparable mental health benefits if doing so would increase premiums by 1 percent or more. Higher co-pays, deductibles, and out-of-pocket maximums also have undercut the legislation's effectiveness (Health Cost Institute 2013; Hernandez and Uggen 2012).

MODULE 54 | Recap and Review

Summary

Mental illness is a disorder of the brain that disrupts a person's thinking, feeling, and ability to interact with others.

1. Mental illness should be seen within a continuum of behavior that ranges from mental health to mental illness.

2. People with mental illness bear a **stigma** that devalues members of their social group. The false assumption that people who suffer from mental illness are violent contributes to that stigma.

3. Mental disorders may be viewed from two different perspectives, the **medical model** and the sociological model, which is based on labeling theory. In the United States, society has traditionally taken a negative, suspicious attitude toward people with mental disorders.

Thinking Critically

1. What factors perpetuate the social stigma associated with mental illness? How could that stigma be eliminated?

2. Why did the policy of deinstitutionalization result in negative outcomes for people with mental illness? How can the shortcomings of the policy be eliminated?

Key Terms

Mental illness

Stigma

MODULE 55 | Population

The study of population issues engages the attention of both natural and social scientists. The biologist explores the nature of reproduction and casts light on factors that affect **fertility**, the level of reproduction in a society. The medical pathologist examines and analyzes trends in the causes of death. Geographers, historians, and psychologists also have distinctive contributions to make to our understanding of population. Sociologists, more than these other researchers, focus on the social factors that influence population rates and trends.

In their study of population issues, sociologists are aware that the norms, values, and social patterns of a society profoundly affect various elements of population, such as fertility, mortality (the death rate), and migration. Fertility is influenced by people's age of entry into sexual unions and by their use of contraception—both of which, in turn, reflect the social and religious values that guide a particular culture. Mortality is shaped by a nation's level of nutrition, acceptance of immunization, and provisions for sanitation, as well as its general commitment to health care and health education. Migration from one country to another can depend on marital and kinship ties, the relative degree of racial and religious tolerance in various societies, and people's evaluation of their employment opportunities.

© Gianni Muratore/Alamy

An immigration officer checks the passports of passengers arriving at Palermo Airport, on the Italian island of Sicily. Population growth is a dynamic process that is affected not just by birth and death rates, but by the migration of people from one place or country to another.

Demography: The Study of Population

Demography is the scientific study of population. It draws on several components of population, including size, composition, and territorial distribution, to understand the social consequences of population change. Demographers study geographical variations and historical trends in their effort to develop population forecasts. They also analyze the structure of a population—the age, gender, race, and ethnicity of its members. A key figure in this analysis was Thomas Malthus.

Malthus's Thesis and Marx's Response

The Reverend Thomas Robert Malthus (1766–1834), who was educated at Cambridge University, spent his life teaching history and political economy. He strongly criticized two major institutions of his time—the church and slavery—yet his most significant legacy to contemporary scholars is his still-controversial Essays on the Principle of Population, published in 1798.

Essentially, Malthus held that the world's population was growing more rapidly than the available food supply. He argued that food supply increases in arithmetic progression (1, 2, 3, 4, and so on), whereas population expands by geometric progression (1, 2, 4, 8, and so on). According to his analysis, the gap between food supply and population will continue to grow over time. Even though the food supply will increase, it will not increase nearly enough to meet the needs of an expanding world population.

Malthus advocated population control to close the gap between rising population and the food supply, yet he explicitly denounced artificial means of birth control because they were not sanctioned by religion. For Malthus, one appropriate way to control population was to postpone marriage. He argued that couples must take responsibility for the number of children they choose to bear; without such restraint, the world would face widespread hunger, poverty, and misery (Mayhew 2014).

Karl Marx strongly criticized Malthus's views on population. He could not accept the Malthusian notion that rising world population, rather than capitalism, was the cause of social ills. In Marx's opinion, there was no special relationship between world population and the supply of resources (including food). If society were well ordered, increases in population would lead to greater wealth, not to hunger and misery.

Of course, Marx did not believe that capitalism operated under these ideal conditions. He maintained that capitalism devoted resources to the financing of buildings and tools rather than to the equitable distribution of food, housing, and other necessities of life. Marx's work is important to the study of population because he linked overpopulation to the unequal distribution of resources. His concern with the writings of Malthus also testifies to the importance of population in political and economic affairs.

The insights of Malthus and Marx regarding population issues have come together in what is termed the neo-Malthusian view, best exemplified by the work of Paul Ehrlich (1968; Ehrlich and Ehrlich 1990), author of *The Population Bomb*. Neo-Malthusians agree with Malthus that population growth is outstretching the world's natural resources. However, in contrast to the British theorist, they insist that birth control measures are needed to regulate population increases. Showing a Marxist bent, neo-Malthusians condemn the developed nations, which despite their low birthrates consume a disproportionately large share of world resources. While rather pessimistic about the future, these theorists stress that birth control and sensible use of resources are essential responses to rising world population (J. Tierney 1990; Weeks 2012).

Studying Population Today

The relative balance of births and deaths is no less important today than it was during the lifetime of Malthus and Marx. The suffering that Malthus spoke of is certainly a reality for many people of the world. Malnutrition accounts for 45 percent of the 6 million annual children deaths in developing countries. Warfare and large-scale

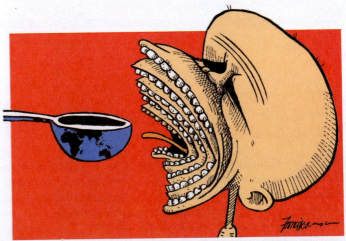

Cartoon by Manny Francisco © 2008 www.PoliticalCartoons.com. Reproduced by permission.

In this cartoon, Manny Francisco, based in the heavily populated Philippine Islands, takes a grim Malthusian view of world hunger.

migration intensify problems of population and food supply. For example, recent strife in Syria, Afghanistan, the Congo, and Iraq has caused maldistribution of food supplies, leading to regional health concerns. Combating world hunger may require reducing human births, dramatically increasing the world's food supply, or perhaps both. The study of population-related issues, then, seems to be essential (World Health Organization Media Centre 2014).

In the United States and most other countries, the census is the primary mechanism for collecting population information. A **census** is an enumeration, or counting, of a population. The Constitution of the United States requires that a census be held every 10 years to determine congressional representation. This periodic investigation is supplemented by **vital statistics**, or records of births, deaths, marriages, and divorces that are gathered through a registration system maintained by governmental units. In addition, other government surveys provide up-to-date information on commercial developments, educational trends, industrial expansion, agricultural practices, and the status of groups such as children, the elderly, racial minorities, and single parents.

In administering a nationwide census and conducting other types of research, demographers employ many skills and techniques, including questionnaires, interviews, and sampling. The precision of population projections depends on the accuracy of a series of estimates demographers must make. First, they must determine past population trends and establish a current base population. Next, birthrates and death rates must be determined, along with estimates of future fluctuations. In projecting a nation's population trends for the future, demographers must consider migration as well, since a significant number of individuals may enter and leave a country.

Elements of Demography

Demographers communicate population facts with a language derived from the basic elements of human life—birth and death. The **birthrate** (or more specifically, the crude birthrate) is the number of live births per 1,000 population in a given year. In 2015, for example, there were 13 live births per 1,000 people in the United States. The birthrate provides information on the reproductive patterns of a society.

One way demographers can project future growth in a society is to make use of the **total fertility rate (TFR)** . The TFR is the average number of children born alive to any woman, assuming that she conforms to current fertility rates. The TFR reported for the United States in 2015 was 1.9 live births per woman, compared to nearly 8 births per woman in a developing country such as Niger.

Mortality, like fertility, is measured in several different ways. The **death rate** (also known as the crude death rate) is the number of deaths per 1,000 population in a given year. In 2015, the United States had a death rate of 6.0 per 1,000 population. The infant mortality rate serves as an important indicator of a society's level of health care; it reflects prenatal nutrition, delivery procedures, and infant screening measures. The infant mortality rate also functions as a useful indicator of future population growth, since those infants who survive to adulthood will contribute to further population increases.

A general measure of health used by demographers is **life expectancy**, the median number of years a person can be

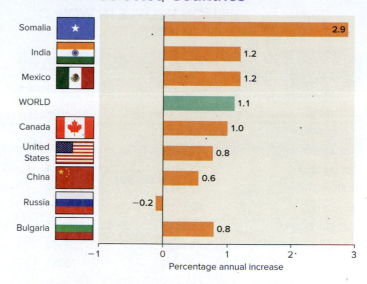

FIGURE 55-1 **Population Growth Rate in Selected Countries**

Source: United Nations Department of Economic and Social Affairs 2015.
Flags: © admin_design/Shutterstock RF

expected to live under current mortality conditions. Usually the figure is reported as life expectancy at birth. At present, Japan reports a life expectancy at birth of 83 years—slightly higher than the United States' figure of 79 years. In contrast, life expectancy at birth is as low as 44 in the African nation of Lesotho (Kaneta and Bietsch 2015).

The **growth rate** of a society is the difference between births and deaths, plus the difference between immigrants (those who enter a country to establish permanent residence) and emigrants (those who leave a country permanently) per 1,000 population. For the world as a whole, the growth rate is simply the difference between births and deaths per 1,000 population, since worldwide immigration and emigration must of necessity be equal. In 2015, the United States had a growth rate of 0.8 percent, compared to an estimated 1.1 percent for the entire world (Figure 55-1).

World Population Patterns

One important aspect of demographic work involves a study of the history of population. But how is that possible? After all, official national censuses were relatively rare before 1850. Researchers interested in early population must turn to archaeological remains, burial sites, baptismal and tax records, and oral history sources. In the next section we will see what such detective work has told us about changes in population over time.

Demographic Transition

On October 13, 1999, in a maternity clinic in Sarajevo, Bosnia-Herzegovina, Helac Fatina gave birth to a son who has been designated the 6 billionth person on this planet. Until modern times, relatively few humans lived in the world. One estimate places the global population of a million years ago at only 125,000 people. As Table 55-1 indicates, in the past 200 years the world's population has exploded (World Health Organization 2000:3).

TABLE 55-1 ESTIMATED TIME FOR EACH SUCCESSIVE INCREASE OF 1 BILLION PEOPLE IN WORLD POPULATION

Population Level	Time Taken to Reach New Population Level	Year of Attainment
First billion	Human history before 1800	1804
Second billion	123 years	1927
Third billion	32 years	1959
Fourth billion	15 years	1974
Fifth billion	13 years	1987
Sixth billion	12 years	1999
Seventh billion	12 years	2011
Eighth billion	15 years	2026
Ninth billion	16 years	2042

Sources: Bureau of the Census 2013b; Kunzig 2011:40.

FIGURE 55-2 Demographic Transition

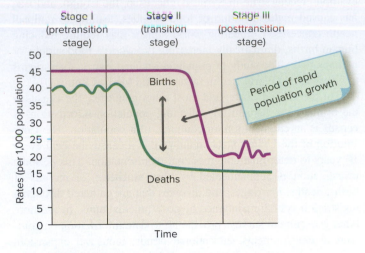

Source: Developed by the author.

Demographers use the concept of demographic transition to describe changes in birthrates and death rates that occur during a nation's development. This graph shows the pattern that took place in presently developed nations. In the first stage, both birthrates and death rates were high, so that there was little population growth. In the second stage, the birthrate remained high while the death rate declined sharply, which led to rapid population growth. By the last stage, which many developing countries have yet to enter, the birthrate had declined as well, reducing population growth.

The phenomenal growth of population in recent times can be accounted for by changing patterns in births and deaths. Beginning in the late 1700s—and continuing until the mid-1900s—death rates in northern and western Europe gradually decreased. People were beginning to live longer because of advances in food production, sanitation, nutrition, and public health care. But while death rates fell, birthrates remained high; as a result, this period of European history brought unprecedented population growth. By the late 1800s, however, the birthrates of many European countries had begun to decline, and the rate of population growth had also decreased.

The changes in birthrates and death rates that occurred in 19th-century Europe serve as an example of demographic transition. Demographers use the term **demographic transition** to describe changes in birthrates and death rates that occur during a nation's development, resulting in new patterns of vital statistics. In many nations today, we are seeing a demographic transition from high birthrates and death rates to low birthrates and death rates. As Figure 55-2 shows, this process typically takes place in three stages:

1. Pretransition stage: high birthrates and death rates with little population growth.

2. Transition stage: declining death rates—primarily the result of reductions in infant deaths—along with high to medium fertility, resulting in significant population growth.

3. Posttransition stage: low birthrates and death rates with little population growth.

The demographic transition should be regarded not as a "law of population growth," but rather as a generalization of the population history of industrial nations. This concept helps us to understand world population problems better. About two-thirds of the world's nations have yet to pass fully through the second stage of the demographic transition. Even if such nations make dramatic advances in fertility control, their populations will nevertheless increase greatly because of the large base of people already at prime childbearing age.

The pattern of demographic transition varies from nation to nation. One particularly useful distinction is the contrast between the rapid transition now occurring in developing nations—which include about two-thirds of the world's population—and that which occurred over the course of almost a century in more industrialized countries. In developing nations, the demographic transition has involved a rapid decline in death rates, with adjustments in birthrates in some nations but not in others.

Specifically, in the post–World War II period, the death rates of developing nations began a sharp decline. This revolution in "death control" was triggered by antibiotics, immunization, insecticides (such as DDT, used to strike at malaria-bearing mosquitoes), and largely successful campaigns against such fatal diseases as smallpox. Substantial medical and public health technology was imported almost overnight from more developed nations. As a result, the drop in death rates that had taken a century in Europe was telescoped into two decades in many developing countries.

Birthrates had little time to adjust. Cultural beliefs about the proper size of families could not possibly change as quickly as the falling death rates. For centuries, couples had given birth to as many as eight or more children, knowing that perhaps only two or three would survive to adulthood. Families were more willing to accept technological advances that prolonged life than to abandon fertility patterns that reflected time-honored tradition and religious training. The result was an astronomical population explosion that was well under way by the middle 1900s. By the middle 1970s, however, demographers had observed a slight decline in the growth rate of some developing nations, as family-planning efforts began to take hold (Haub 2013; R. Lee and Reher 2011).

● The Population Explosion

Often, rapid population growth is referred to in emotional terms as the "population bomb" or the "population explosion." Such striking language is not surprising, given the staggering increases in world population recorded during the 20th century (Table 55-1).

Beginning in the 1960s, governments in certain developing nations sponsored or supported campaigns to encourage family planning. In China, the government's strict one-child policy actually produced a negative growth rate in some urban areas (Box 55-1).

Yet even if family-planning efforts are successful in reducing fertility rates, the momentum toward a growing world population is well established. Developing nations face the prospect of continued population growth, since a substantial proportion of their population is approaching the childbearing years (see the population pyramid for Afghanistan at the top of Figure 55-3).

A **population pyramid** is a special type of bar chart that shows the distribution of a population by gender and age; it is generally used to illustrate the population structure of a society. As Figure 55-3 shows, a substantial portion of the population of Afghanistan consists of children under age 15, whose childbearing years are still to come. Thus, the built-in momentum for

population growth is much greater in Afghanistan (and in many other developing countries in other parts of the world) than in the United States and especially in many European nations (see the population pyramid for Italy in the middle of Figure 55-3).

Consider the population data for India, which in 2000 surpassed 1 billion residents. Sometime around 2025, India's population will exceed China's. The substantial momentum for growth that is built into India's age structure means that the nation will face a staggering increase in population in the coming decades, even if its birthrate declines sharply (Bureau of the Census 2013b).

Population growth is not a problem in all nations. Today, a handful of countries are even adopting policies that encourage growth. One such country is Japan, where the total fertility rate has fallen sharply. Nevertheless, a global perspective underscores the serious consequences that could result from continued population growth overall.

 use your **sociological imagination**

You are living in a country that is so heavily populated that basic resources such as food, water, and living space are running short. What will you do? How will you respond to the crisis if you are a government social planner? a politician? an ordinary citizen?

⊕ Sociology in the Global Community

BOX 55-1

Population Policy in China

In a residential district in Shanghai, a member of the local family-planning committee knocks on the door of a childless couple. Why, she inquires, have they not started a family? Such a question would have been unthinkable in 1979, when family-planning officials, in an attempt to avoid a looming population explosion, began resorting to sterilization to enforce the government rule of one child per family.

Then in 2015, the Communist Party dramatically announced it was replacing the one-child policy with a two-child allowance. This was seen as a way to confront two challenges: stagnating economic growth and an aging population, with a growing proportion of elderly people with fewer and fewer younger adults to look after them.

The legacy of nearly two generations of one child per family will not disappear soon. For example, in an effort to ensure that their one child would be a male capable of perpetuating the family line, many couples chose to abort female fetuses or quietly allowed female infants to die of neglect. As a result, in 2015, among children age one to four, the sex ratio (the ratio of males to females) was about 116 to 100—well above the normal rate at birth of 105 to 100.

As a result of the high sex ratio, Chinese officials worry about a future with too few women. In about 20 to 25 years, they expect, almost one-fifth of the baby boys now being born will be unable to find brides. In an attempt to reverse the situation, the government is paying the parents of daughters to speak with other parents and persuade them to raise girls.

Another legacy of the one-child policy is a shortage of caretakers for the elderly. Coupled with improvements in longevity, the generation-long decline in births has greatly increased the ratio of dependent elders to able-bodied children. The migration of young adults within China has further compromised the care of the elderly.

No other country in the world faces the prospect of caring for such a large population of seniors with so little social support.

To compound the crisis, barely one in four of China's elders receives any pension at all. No other country in the world faces the prospect of caring for such a large population of seniors with so little social support.

While the two-child policy received a lot of attention in China and globally, it remains to be seen if people will adjust their family plans, given the mixed economic outlook most households face. Unlike countries such as The United States, Australia, and Canada, China can count only on internal population growth. It does not receive immigrants who can supply a young and dynamic workforce.

LET'S DISCUSS

1. Does any government, no matter how overpopulated a country is, have a right to sterilize women who do not voluntarily limit the size of their families? Why or why not?

2. What do you think has been the most dramatic consequence of the one-child policy?

Sources: Burkitt 2015; Erlanger 2015; Greenhalgh 2008.

FIGURE 55-3 **Population Structure of Afghanistan, Italy, and the United States, 2017**

Fertility Patterns in the United States

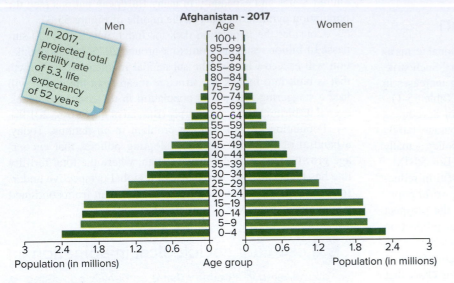

In 2017, projected total fertility rate of 5.3, life expectancy of 52 years

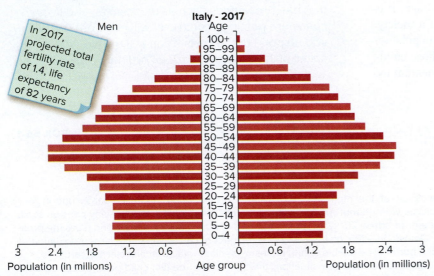

In 2017, projected total fertility rate of 1.4, life expectancy of 82 years

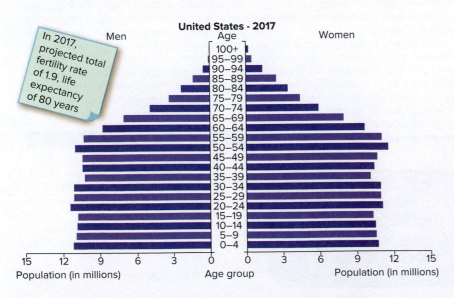

In 2017, projected total fertility rate of 1.9, life expectancy of 80 years

Source: Projections updated to 2017 as of December 2015. Bureau of the Census 2015h.

Over the past six decades, the United States and other industrial nations have passed through two different patterns of population growth—the first marked by high fertility and rapid growth (stage II in the theory of demographic transition), the second marked by declining fertility and little growth (stage III). Sociologists are keenly aware of the social impact of these fertility patterns.

The Baby Boom

The most recent period of high fertility in the United States has often been referred to as the baby boom. During World War II, large numbers of military personnel were separated from their spouses. When they returned, the annual number of births began to rise dramatically. Still, the baby boom was not a return to the large families common in the 1800s. In fact, there was only a slight increase in the proportion of couples having three or more children. Instead, the boom was the result of a striking decrease in the number of childless marriages and one-child families. Although a peak was reached in 1957, the nation maintained a relatively high birthrate of over 20 live births per 1,000 population until 1964. By 2015 the birthrate had fallen to 13 live births per 1,000 population (Bureau of the Census 1975; Kaneta and Bietsch 2015).

It would be a mistake to attribute the baby boom solely to the return home of large numbers of soldiers. High wages and general prosperity during the postwar period encouraged many married couples to purchase homes and have children. In addition, several sociologists—as well as feminist author Betty Friedan (1963)—have noted the strong societal pressure on women during the 1950s to marry and become mothers and homemakers (Bouvier 1980).

Stable Population Growth

Although the total fertility rate of the United States has remained low over the past three decades, the nation continues to grow in size because of two factors: the momentum built into our age structure by the postwar population boom and continued high rates of immigration. First, because of the upsurge of births beginning in the 1950s, there are now many more people in their childbearing years than in older age groups (in which most deaths occur). This growth of the childbearing population represents a "demographic echo" of the baby boom generation. Consequently, the number of people born each year in the United States continues to exceed the number who die.

Second, the nation allows a large number of immigrants to enter each year. Looking ahead, immigration is the main driver of population growth. Projections show that immigrants, legal and illegal, together with their children and grandchildren, will account for 85 percent of population growth between 2015 and 2065. To put it another way, if all immigration had stopped on January 1, 2015, and previous immigrants had no more children, the United States would have 114 million fewer people by 2065 (Pew Research Center 2015c).

Many countries other than the United States will not experience population growth but rather are expected to reach **zero population growth (ZPG)**. ZPG is the state of a population in which the number of births plus immigrants equals the number of deaths plus emigrants. In the recent past, although some nations have achieved ZPG, it has been relatively short-lived. Yet today, projections of population change between 2015 and 2050 indicate that 31 countries, including 22 in Europe, are showing a decline in population (Kaneta and Bietsch 2015).

What would a society with stable population growth be like? In demographic terms, it would be quite different from the United States of around 2017. There would be relatively equal numbers of people in each age group, and the median age of the population might perhaps be as high as 45 (compared to 37.2 in 2010). As a result, the population pyramid of the United States (as shown in Figure 55-3) would look more like a rectangle.

There would also be a much larger proportion of older people, especially age 75 and over. These citizens would place a greater demand on the nation's social service programs and health care institutions. In the United States today, the drop in births that began with the Great Recession of 2008, coupled with a slowdown in immigration, has created concerns about the growing gap between the working-age population that funds social programs and the senior citizens who rely on those programs (Last 2013).

On a more positive note, the economy would be less volatile under ZPG, since the number of entrants into the paid labor force would remain stable. ZPG would also lead to changes in family life. With fertility rates declining, women would devote fewer years to child rearing and to the social roles of motherhood; the proportion of married women entering the labor force would continue to rise.

Migration

Along with births and deaths, migration is one of the three factors that affect population growth or decline. The term **migration** refers to the relatively permanent movement of people, with the purpose of changing their place of residence. Migration usually describes movement over a sizable distance, rather than from one side of a city to another (Prehn 1991).

As a social phenomenon, migration is fairly complex; it results from a variety of factors. The most important tend to be economic—financial failure in the "old country" and a perception of greater economic opportunity and prosperity in the new homeland. Other factors that contribute to migration include racial and religious bigotry, dislike for prevailing political regimes, and a desire to reunite one's family. All these forces combine to *push* some individuals out of their homelands and *pull* them to areas they believe to be more attractive.

International Migration

International migration—changes of residence across national boundaries—has been a significant force in redistributing the world's population during certain periods of history. For example, the composition of the United States has been significantly altered by immigrants who came here beginning in the 19th century and continuing through the present. Their entry was encouraged or restricted by various immigration policies.

In the past decade, immigration has become a controversial issue throughout much of Europe. Western Europe in particular has become a desirable destination for individuals and families from former colonies or former communist-bloc countries who are fleeing the poverty, persecution, and warfare of their native lands. The number of immigrants and, most recently, refugees from Syria, Iraq, and Afghanistan, has been increasing at a time of widespread unemployment and housing shortages, provoking a striking rise in anti-foreign (and often openly racist) sentiment in Germany, France, the Netherlands, and other countries. The Brexit vote in June 2016, in which the British people voted to withdraw from the European Union, was considered to be largely based on anti-immigrant sentiment.

Developing countries in Asia and Africa are also encountering difficulties as thousands of displaced people seek assistance

© Mustafa Ozer/AFP/Getty Images

Refugees at this camp in Turkey are fleeing the violent conflict in Syria which began in 2011. Catastrophic conflicts such as war and terrorism often trigger massive international migrations.

and asylum. By late 2015, an estimated 60 million people worldwide were refugees or asylum seekers. Needless to say, the political and economic problems of developing nations are only intensified by such massive migration, begun under desperate conditions (UNHCR 2015).

Internal Migration

Migratory movements within societies can vary in important ways. In traditional societies, migration often represents a way of life, as people move to accommodate the changing availability of fertile soil and wild game. In industrial societies, people may relocate because of job transfers or because they believe that a particular region offers better employment opportunities or a more desirable climate.

Although nations typically have laws and policies governing movement across their borders, the same is not true of internal movement. Generally, the residents of a country are legally free to move from one locality to another. Of course, that is not the case in all nations; historically, the Republic of South Africa restricted the movement of Blacks and other non-Whites through the system of segregation known as *apartheid*.

 use your **sociological imagination**

What would happen if present patterns of migration, both internal and international, reversed themselves? How would your hometown change? What would be the effect on the nation's economy? Would your own life change?

MODULE 55 | **Recap and Review**

Summary

This module explains how population trends affect the world's communities. It covers the size, composition, and distribution of the population, as well as the means of measuring population.

1. Thomas Malthus suggested that the world's population was growing more rapidly than the available food supply, and that the gap would increase over time. Karl Marx saw capitalism, not rising population, as the real cause of social ills.

2. The primary mechanism for obtaining population information in the United States and most other countries is the **census**.

3. Roughly two-thirds of the world's nations have yet to pass fully through the second stage of **demographic transition**. Thus they continue to experience significant population growth.

4. Developing nations face the prospect of continued population growth because a substantial portion of their population is approaching childbearing age. Some developed nations have begun to stabilize their population growth.

5. The most important factors in **migration** tend to be economic—financial failure in the "old country" and a perception of greater economic opportunity elsewhere.

Thinking Critically

1. Choose a developing country and look up its population statistics. Based on those statistics, in what stage of the demographic transition would you put that country? Explain.

2. Select a social policy issue that particularly interests you. How would the size, composition, and distribution of the population influence that issue?

Key Terms

Birthrate

Census

Death rate

Demographic transition

Demography

Fertility

Growth rate

Life expectancy

Migration

Population pyramid

Total fertility rate (TFR)

Vital statistics

Zero population growth (ZPG)

We have seen that the environment people live in has a noticeable effect on their health. Those who live in stressful, overcrowded places suffer more from disease than those who do not. Likewise, people have a noticeable effect on their environment. Around the world, increases in population, together with the economic development that accompanies them, have had serious environmental consequences. We can see signs of despoliation almost everywhere: our air, our water, and our land are being polluted, whether we live in St. Louis, Mexico City, or Lagos, Nigeria.

Though environmental problems may be easy to identify, devising socially and politically acceptable solutions to them is much more difficult. In this section we will see what sociologists have to say about the trade-off between economic growth and development and its effects on the environment. In the section that follows we will look more closely at specific environmental issues.

Human Ecology

Human ecology is an area of study that is concerned with the interrelationships between people and their environment. As the environmentalist Barry Commoner (1971:39) put it, "Everything is connected to everything else." Human ecologists focus on how the physical environment shapes people's lives and on how people influence the surrounding environment.

There is no shortage of illustrations of the interconnectedness of people and their environment. For example, scientific research has linked pollutants in the physical environment to people's health and behavior. The increasing occurrence of asthma, lead poisoning, and cancer have all been tied to human alterations to the environment. Similarly, the rise in melanoma (skin cancer) diagnoses has been linked to global warming. Ecological changes in our food and diet have been related to early obesity and diabetes. And finally, global population growth has had a huge impact on the environment (see Table 55-1 in Module 55).

With its view that "everything is connected to everything else," human ecology stresses the trade-offs inherent in every decision that alters the environment. In facing the environmental challenges of the 21st century, government policymakers and environmentalists must determine how they can fulfill humans' pressing needs for food, clothing, and shelter while preserving the environment.

Conflict Perspective on the Environment

World systems analysis shows how a growing share of the human and natural resources of developing countries is being redistributed to the core industrialized nations. This process only intensifies the destruction of natural resources in poorer regions of the world. From a conflict perspective, less affluent nations are being forced to exploit their mineral deposits, forests, and fisheries in order to meet their debt obligations. The poor turn to the only means of survival available to them: they plow mountain slopes, burn plots in tropical forests, and overgraze grasslands (Pellow and Brehm 2013).

Brazil exemplifies this interplay between economic troubles and environmental destruction. Each year more than 5.7 million acres of forest are cleared for crops and livestock. The elimination of the rain forest affects worldwide weather patterns, heightening the gradual warming of the earth. These socioeconomic patterns, with their harmful environmental consequences, are evident not only in Latin America but in many regions of Africa and Asia.

Conflict theorists are well aware of the environmental implications of land use policies in the Third World, but they contend that focusing on the developing countries is ethnocentric. First, throughout most of history, developed countries have been the major source of greenhouse gas emissions. Only recently have developing nations begun to emit greenhouse gases in the same quantities as developed nations. Greenhouse gas emissions will be discussed in more detail later (Environmental Protection Agency 2012).

© Lynne Sladky/AP Images

Yes, someone is living underwater, or at least appears to be doing so. To mark the 2015 Paris summit on climate change, artist Lars Jen created an installation in which a person spent long periods in a cube-shaped aquarium to draw attention to the rising levels of the world's oceans and the out-of-control nature of climate change.

Second, the industrialized nations of North America and Europe account for only 12 percent of the world's population but are responsible for 60 percent of worldwide consumption. Who, these theorists ask, is more to blame for environmental deterioration: the poverty-stricken and "food-hungry" populations of the world or the "energy-hungry" industrialized nations? The money that residents of developed countries spend on ocean cruises each year could provide clean drinking water for everyone on the planet. Ice cream expenditures in Europe alone could be used to immunize every child in the world. Thus, conflict theorists charge, the most serious threat to the environment comes from the global consumer class (Pellow and Brehm 2013).

Allan Schnaiberg (1994) further refined this analysis by shifting the focus from affluent consumers to the capitalist system as the cause of environmental troubles. In his view, a capitalist system creates a "treadmill of production" because of its inherent need to build ever-expanding profits. This treadmill necessitates the creation of increasing demand for products, the purchase of natural resources at minimal cost, and the manufacturing of products as quickly and cheaply as possible—no matter what the long-term environmental consequences. Indeed, over a century ago, Max Weber predicted that rampant industrialism would continue until "the last ton of fossil fuel has burnt to ashes" ([1904] 2011:157).

Ecological Modernization

Critics of the human ecological and conflict models argue that they are too rooted in the past. People who take these approaches, they charge, have become bogged down in addressing existing practices. Instead, proponents of **ecological modernization** focus

© helovi/E+/Getty Images RF

Many households recycle or adjust the thermostat to save energy, but few go as far as the dwellers of the Earthship pictured here. This dwelling, part of a community in Taos, New Mexico, utilizes passive solar heat and is made of both natural and recycled materials, such as tires. The goal is minimal reliance on public utilities and fossil fuels.

on the alignment of environmentally favorable practices with economic self-interest through constant adaptation and restructuring (Gould and Lewis 2015).

Ecological modernization can occur on both the macro and micro levels. On a macro level, adaptation and restructuring can mean reintegrating industrial waste back into the production process. On a micro level, it can mean reshaping individual lifestyles, including the consumption patterns described at the start of this chapter. In a sense, those who practice ecological modernization seek to refute the oft-expressed notion that being environmentally conscious means "going back to nature" or "living off the grid." Even modest changes in production and consumption patterns, they believe, can increase environmental sustainability (York et al. 2010).

Environmental Justice

In autumn 1982, nearly 500 African Americans participated in a six-week protest against a hazardous waste landfill in North Carolina. Their protests and legal actions against the dangerous cancer-causing chemicals continued until 2004, when decontamination of the site finally began. This 20-year battle could be seen as yet another "not in my backyard" (NIMBY) event. But today, the Warren County struggle is viewed as a transformative moment in contemporary environmentalism: the beginning of the *environmental justice* movement (Bullard 1993; McGurty 2000; North Carolina Department of Environmental and Natural Resources 2008).

Environmental justice is a legal strategy based on claims that racial minorities are subjected disproportionately to environmental hazards. Some observers have heralded environmental justice as the "new civil rights of the 21st century" (Kokmen 2008:42). Since the start of the environmental justice movement, activists and scholars have discovered other environmental disparities that break along racial and social class lines. In general, poor people and people of color are much more likely than others to be victimized by the everyday consequences of our built environment, including the air pollution from expressways and incinerators.

Some people cannot safely drink their tap water even after boiling it. No, this situation did not occur in a developing nation but in Flint, Michigan, a city of over 100,000 people. In what was described as a case of environmental racism by some candidates in the 2016 general election, the city of Flint, faced with huge budget problems, decided in 2014 to save money by obtaining its water from the industrially polluted Flint River. As a result, water polluted with unsafe levels of lead and other toxic chemicals entered people's homes. The people of Flint, who are overwhelmingly Black and disproportionately poor, found their early concerns ignored or discounted as "grandstanding"

Cartoon © Steve Greenberg. Ventura County Reporter, CA. 2010. Used by permission.

Environmental justice draws attention to the fact that the poor, along with racial and ethnic minorities, are more likely than the rich to live near refineries, waste dumps, and other environmental hazards.

by government officials. Regrettably Flint is not a unique case of environmental injustice (Eligon 2016).

African Americans making $50,000 to $60,000 per year are much more likely to live in a polluted environment than White families making just $10,000. An analysis of over 600 hazardous waste treatment, storage, and disposal facilities in the United States found that non-Whites and Latinos make up 43 percent of the people who live within one mile of these dangerous sites. Skeptics often argue that minorities move near such sites because of low housing prices. However, two recent longitudinal (long-term) research studies, done over 30- and 50-year periods, found that toxic facilities tend to be located in minority communities (Ellison 2015; Mohai and Saha 2007; Mohai et al. 2009:413).

The environmental justice movement has become globalized, for several reasons. In many nations, activists have noticed similar patterns in the location of hazardous waste sites. These groups have begun to network across international borders, to share their tactics and remedies. Their unified approach is wise, because the offending corporations are often multinational entities; influencing their actions, much less prosecuting them, is difficult. As we have noted before, the global warming debate often focuses criticism on developing nations like China and India, rather than on established industrial giants with a long history of greenhouse gas emissions (Pellow and Brehm 2013).

An important aspect of the globalization of the environmental justice movement has been drawing attention to the growing number of environmental refugees, as described in Box 56-1.

Sociology in the Global Community

Box 56-1

Environmental Refugees

Three years after the Indian Ocean swallowed his home on the Bangladeshi coast, farmer Ajmad Miyah dispairs of ever settling down again. He has no land or possessions, and he survives by working other people's fields in exchange for food. "I've accepted that this is reality," the 36-year-old Miyah said. "My house will always be temporary now, like me on this Earth."

Miyah's circumstances are becoming increasingly common. Over 19 million people worldwide were driven from their homes by natural disasters in 2014, 90 percent of which were related to weather events, according to the Geneva-based Internal Displacement Monitoring Center.

As with so many other aspects of life, the environment and population are tightly linked. Famine, typhoons, rising sea levels, expanding deserts, chronic water shortages, and earthquakes, among other environmental events, lead to migration. **Environmental refugees** are people forced to leave their communities because of natural disasters, or the effects of climate change and global warming. A particularly deadly aspect of this forced movement is that overwhelmingly the migrants are vulnerable poor people who move to developing countries that are unprepared to receive them.

> The International Red Cross estimates that there are more environmental refugees fleeing natural disasters than political refugees fleeing war.

Some scholars have argued that global development inequalities, as described by world systems analysis, are one of the root causes of vulnerability to environmental changes and hazards. For example, human displacement from large development projects, such as dams, irrigation systems, and land reforms, has huge social impacts.

Movement created by environmental changes is not new. Migration has been a frequent response to climate variability and change in the past. Examples include migration from environmental hardships, such as the drying of the Great Plains in the 1930s (the Dust Bowl, as it was called), and from environmental calamities, such as Hurricane Katrina in 2005. But these environmental refugees largely remained within their own countries. Increasingly, environmental refugees must cross international borders to find a place of safety.

The International Red Cross estimates that there are more environmental refugees fleeing natural disasters than political refugees fleeing war. In ten countries affected by both conflict- and disaster-induced displacement, natural hazards displaced five times more people than armed conflict.

The prospects are not encouraging. A survey conducted in Pakistan, Nepal, India, Bangladesh, China, Vietnam, and Indonesia revealed that 68 percent of the respondents believed that their community is at medium to high risk of extreme weather events and 87 percent believed that changes in weather and the availability of food and water will significantly impact their lives.

LET'S DISCUSS

1. What environmental disasters are most likely to confront your community?

2. What does it mean to say that a person's home is temporary? What would make a person feel that way?

Sources: Daigle 2015; Ellison 2015; Environmental Justice Foundation 2015; Hunter et al. 2015; National Geographic 2015.

● Environmental Issues

Around the world, people are recognizing the need to address challenges to the environment. Yet in the United States, survey respondents do not see environmental issues as the most pressing of concerns, and they often balk at proposed solutions. Unfortunately, framing environmental issues as "problems" may prevent people from seeing environmental deterioration as the by-product of both institutional practices and their own behavior. Thus, in a 2015 global study, only 45 percent of the people in the United States felt that climate change was a very serious problem, compared to 61 percent of people in Africa and 74 percent in Latin America (Stokes et al. 2015).

We will discuss the enormous challenge of global warming in this section, along with three broad areas of environmental concern. Two of them, air and water pollution, are thought to be contributors to global warming.

Air Pollution

Worldwide, more than 1 billion people are exposed to potentially health-damaging levels of air pollution. Unfortunately, in cities around the world, residents have come to accept smog and polluted air as normal. Urban air pollution is caused primarily by emissions from automobiles and secondarily by emissions from electric power plants and heavy industries. Smog not only limits visibility; it also can lead to health problems as uncomfortable as eye irritation and as deadly as lung cancer. Such problems are especially severe in developing countries.

Although people are capable of changing their behavior, they are unwilling to make such changes permanent. During the 1984 Olympics in Los Angeles, residents were asked to carpool and stagger their work hours to relieve traffic congestion and improve the quality of the air athletes would breathe. These changes resulted in a remarkable 12 percent drop in ozone levels. But when the Olympians left, people reverted to their normal behavior and the ozone levels climbed back up. Similarly, in the 2008 Olympics, China took drastic action to ensure that Beijing's high levels of air pollution did not mar the games. Construction work in the city ceased, polluting factories and power plants closed down, and roads were swept and sprayed with water several times a day. This temporary solution hardly solved China's ongoing problem, however (A. Jacobs 2010).

On an everyday basis—that is, when cities are not holding down their emissions because of global sports events—air pollution remains a serious issue. Today, half of all people live in countries where they are exposed to dangerously high levels of air pollution, either short-term or year-round. Solutions range from community efforts to clean up power plants and enforce or strengthen air quality standards to individual actions, like driving less often or using less electricity (American Lung Association 2011).

Water Pollution

Throughout the United States, dumping of waste materials by industries and local governments has polluted streams, rivers, and lakes. Consequently, many bodies of water have become unsafe for drinking, fishing, and swimming. Around the world, pollution of the oceans is an issue of growing concern. Such pollution results regularly from waste dumping and is made worse by fuel leaks from shipping and occasional oil spills. When the oil tanker Exxon *Valdez* ran aground in Prince William Sound, Alaska, in 1989, its cargo of more than 11 million gallons of crude oil spilled into the sound and washed onto the shore, contaminating 1,285 miles of shoreline. Altogether, about 11,000 people joined in a massive cleanup effort that cost over $2 billion. Globally, oil tanker spills occur regularly. The oil spilled from BP's Deepwater Horizon oil platform in 2010 is estimated at *sixteen times* or more that of the Exxon *Valdez* (ITOPF 2006; Shapley 2010).

Less dramatic than large-scale accidents or disasters, but more common in many parts of the world, are problems with the basic water supply. The situation is worsened by heavy, widespread pollution of surface and groundwater by towns, industries, agriculture, and mining operations. In Egypt, a typical example, agricultural and industrial waste pours into the Nile. Every year about 17,000 Egyptian children die from diarrhea and dehydration after contact with the river's polluted water. Although water conditions in North America are not as deadly, from 2000 through 2014 the western United States and Canada experienced moderate to exceptional drought and an escalating demand for water (Hengeveld 2012; National Oceanic and Atmospheric Administration 2014).

Climate Change

Climate change is an observable alteration of the global atmosphere that affects natural weather patterns over several decades or longer. Periods of climate change occurred well before humans walked the earth. Recently, climate change has included rapid *global warming*.

The term **global warming** refers to the significant rise in the earth's surface temperatures that occurs when industrial gases like carbon dioxide (CO_2) turn the planet's atmosphere into a virtual greenhouse. These *greenhouse gases,* which also include methane, nitrous oxide, and ozone, trap heat in the lower atmosphere. Even one additional degree of warmth in the globe's average surface temperature can increase the likelihood of wildfires, shrinkage of rivers and lakes, expansion of deserts, and torrential downpours, including typhoons and hurricanes. Greenhouse emissions are highest in highly industrialized nations such as Germany, Russia, and Japan. However, these nations have made efforts to reduce the emission of CO_2, as shown in Figure 56-1. However, in developing nations such as China and India CO_2 emissions have greatly increased, even when population growth is taken in to consideration.

"The End of Snow?" asked a newspaper headline during the 2014 Winter Olympics. Although snow will not disappear from the earth, climatologists predict that finding suitable sites for the snow-dependent international competition will become increasingly difficult. Of the 19 cities that have hosted the Winter Olympics in the past, as few as 10 might be cold

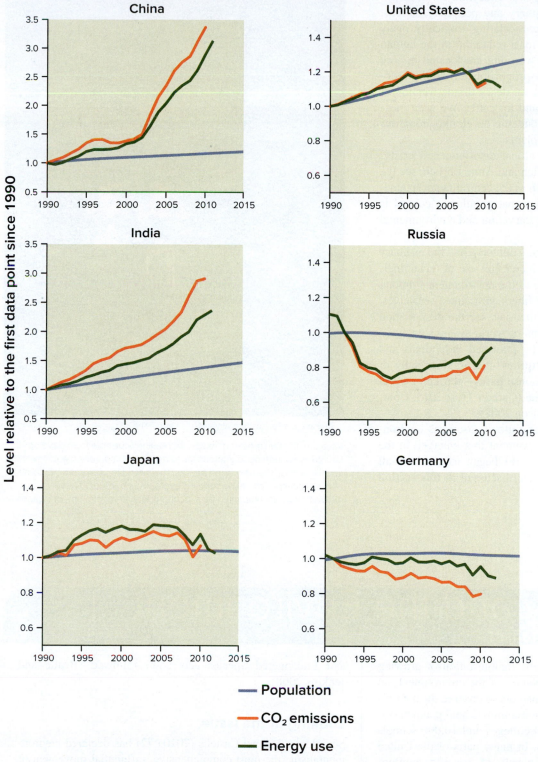

FIGURE 56-1 Change in CO₂ Emissions in Selected Countries, 1990–2015

China

United States

India

Russia

Japan

Germany

— Population

— CO₂ emissions

— Energy use

Among the world's largest emitters of CO₂, very different trends can be seen over the past 20 years.

Source: United Nations 2015.

reduced snowfall. Decline in the snowpack is now jeopardizing half of all ski resorts in the northeastern United States; if it continues, they may not be viable 30 years from now. Similar trends are threatening ski resorts in the western United States. More important, snowpack is not just for skiers; the spring runoff from melting snow is critical to maintaining water supplies (Fox 2014).

Although scientific concern over global warming has heated up, climate change remains low on policymakers' list of concerns. The problem seems abstract, and in many countries, officials think that the real impact of any action they may take depends on decisive action by other nations. The Kyoto Protocol of 1997 was intended to reduce global emissions of heat-trapped gases, which can contribute to global warming and climate change.

The Kyoto Protocols have been updated periodically, and nations have met bilaterally and collectively to reach some agreement. Most recently, under the leadership of the United Nations, 195 nations met outside of Paris in late 2015. As a result of the meeting, participants committed to lowering planet-warming greenhouse gas emissions to help stave off the most drastic effects of climate change. While still not drastic enough, according to many environmentalists, this agreement represents a major step in bringing together industrial and developing nations that are now undergoing the kind of industrialization (and pollution generation) long seen elsewhere. Significant was the agreement that richer nations should help poorer ones reduce greenhouse emissions; however, no specific amounts of assistance were determined (Davenport 2015).

enough to do so in 2050, and just 6 in 2100. For people digging out from the record snowfalls of 2014–2015, that prediction might have seemed laughable, but the global trend is toward

We can view global warming from the point of view of world systems analysis. Historically, core nations have been the major emitters of greenhouse gases. Today, however, manufacturing has moved to semi-periphery and periphery nations, where greenhouse gas emissions are escalating. Ironically, many of the forces that are now calling for a reduction in the human activity that contributes to global warming are located in core nations, which have contributed disproportionately to the problem. We want our hamburgers, but we decry the destruction of the rain forests to create grazing land for cattle. We want inexpensive clothes and toys, but we condemn developing countries for depending on coal-fired power plants.

What are the causes of this global environmental crisis? Some observers, such as Paul Ehrlich and Anne Ehrlich, see the pressure of world population growth as the central factor in environmental deterioration. They argue that population control is essential in preventing widespread starvation and environmental decay.

Barry Commoner, a biologist, counters that the primary cause of environmental ills is the increasing use of technological innovations that are destructive to the environment—among them plastics, detergents, synthetic fibers, pesticides, herbicides, and chemical fertilizers. Conflict theorists see the despoliation of the environment through the lens of world systems analysis. And interactionists stress efforts by informed individuals and groups to reduce their carbon footprint—that is, their daily or even lifetime production of greenhouse gases—through careful selection of the goods they consume (Carbon Trust 2015; Commoner 1990, 2007; Ehrlich and Ellison 2002).

The Social Policy section that follows discusses environmentalism, a widespread social movement that emerged in the 1970s as people throughout the world began to see how all the environmental problems we have discussed in this section interacted.

© Ariadne Van Zandbergen/Africa Media Online/The Image Works

Vacation in an unspoiled paradise! Increasingly, people from developed countries are turning to ecotourism as an environmentally friendly way to see the world. The new trend bridges the interests of environmentalists and businesspeople, especially in developing countries. These birdwatchers, accompanied by a local guide, are vacationing in Uganda.

Social
Policy and the Environment
Environmentalism

On April 22, 1970, in a dramatic manifestation of growing grassroots concern over preservation of the environment, an estimated 25 million people turned out to observe the nation's first Earth Day. Two thousand communities held planned celebrations, and more than 2,000 colleges and 10,000 schools hosted environmental teach-ins. In many parts of the United States, citizens marched on behalf of specific environmental causes. That same year, the activism of these early environmentalists convinced Congress to establish the Environmental Protection Agency. The Clean Air, Clean Water, and Endangered Species acts soon followed (Brulle and Jenkins 2008).

Looking at the Issue

Sociologist Manuel Castells (2010a:72) has declared environmentalism "the most comprehensive, influential movement of our time." Several social trends helped to mobilize the environmental movement. First, the activist subculture of the 1960s and early 1970s encouraged people, especially young people,

—Continued

to engage in direct action regarding social issues. Second, the dissemination of scientific knowledge about serious environmental problems like oil spills and air pollution alarmed many Americans. And third, the growing popularity of outdoor recreation increased the number of people who were concerned about the environment. In this climate of broad-based interest in environmental issues, many organizations that had once focused narrowly on the conservation of natural resources evolved into full-fledged environmental groups (Dunlap and Mertig 1991).

Today, Earth Day has been enshrined on the calendars of city councils, zoos, and museums worldwide. Environmental issues have also moved up the agenda of mainstream political parties. Increasingly, efforts to publicize environmental concerns and create support for action have moved to the Internet. Although times have changed, two beliefs continue to galvanize environmentalists: the environment is in dire need of protection, and the government must take strong action in response. Although environmentalists recognize that they must "think locally" and monitor their own carbon footprints, they also see preservation of the environment as a global challenge. They note that while significant progress has been made toward environmental protection, government regulation of the environment has been curtailed in some ways (Brulle and Jenkins 2008; Rootes 2007; Sieber et al. 2006).

The general public has a mixed reaction to environmental issues. On the one hand, many people question the scientific arguments behind the theory of climate change. On the other, many recognize that there is a trade-off between cheap energy and preserving the environment (Figure 56-2). The public seems evenly divided on the issue.

In times of economic stress, people tend to put off or ignore environmental concerns. Thus, there seems to be little public enthusiasm for the positive, forward-looking approach of ecological modernization. Not surprisingly, the political debate over the environmental movement grew more partisan between 2000 and 2012: Democrats became more sympathetic and Republicans more antagonistic (Dunlap 2010).

Today's college students show less interest in the environment than students of past decades. In 2015, 28.8 percent of first-year college students in the United States wanted to clean up the environment—down from 45.9 percent in 1972. U.S. high school students' interest in the issue does not compare favorably with that of teens in other major countries. In a 30-nation comparative study, 15-year-olds in the United States tied those in another country for 22nd place in their knowledge of environmental issues (Pryor et al. 2007, 2013).

Applying Sociology

Sociologists would be quick to stress that environmentalism is not a single movement. Today's activities often have grown out of conservation and preservation movements. Another long-term theme has been animal rights, which has addressed cruelty to pets and domesticated animals historically but now

FIGURE 56-2 **The Environment versus Energy Production**

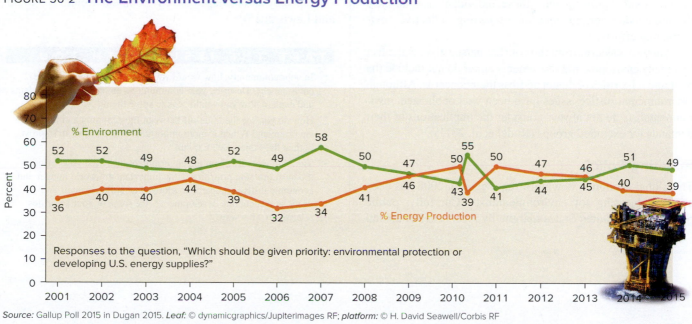

Responses to the question, "Which should be given priority: environmental protection or developing U.S. energy supplies?"

Source: Gallup Poll 2015 in Dugan 2015. *Leaf:* © dynamicgraphics/Jupiterimages RF; *platform:* © H. David Seawell/Corbis RF

—Continued

also questions the use of animals for purposes of testing or entertainment. The *ecofeminist* movement, which emerged in the 1980s, focuses on the typically male-dominated decision-making processes that have endangered our environment and the need to empower women to make these decisions. As climate change has become globally recognized as a major problem, U.S.-based organizations have become networked with like-minded activists throughout the world (Brulle 2015).

Even those who support environmentalists' goals are troubled by the fact that nationwide, the most powerful environmental organizations are predominantly White, male-dominated, and affluent. One study notes that while women are overrepresented in the environmental movement (particularly in grassroots environmental groups), men continue to hold most of the high-profile upper-management positions in mainstream national organizations. The perceived middle-class orientation of the movement is especially relevant given the class, racial, and ethnic factors associated with environmental hazards. As we saw earlier in the context of environmental justice, low-income communities and areas with significant minority populations are more likely than affluent White communities to be located near waste sites.

Viewed from a conflict perspective, the disproportionate exposure of the poor and minorities to environmental pollutants can act as a disincentive for others to take action. As Andrew Szasz (2007) noted in his book *Shopping Our Way to Safety* (see the chapter-opening excerpt), more affluent households can try to avoid exposing themselves and their children to health hazards by drinking bottled spring water, installing water and air filters in their homes, and buying organic food. Unfortunately, these individual actions have the unintended consequence of weakening collective environmental efforts.

Another concern, from the conflict perspective, is the fact that many environmental movements either do not include the poor and minorities or do not address their concerns. Although environmental justice issues have been well publicized, environmentalists do not always consider the implications of their demands for excluded groups (Rudel et al. 2011).

Initiating Policy

The global economic downturn that began in 2008 has been a mixed blessing for environmentalists. Currently, public opinion in the United States marginally favors environmental progress over energy production. The Great Recession had the side effect of reducing consumption, and as a result, energy use. The nations of the world convened in Paris in 2015 to map out a short-term and long-term strategy to combat global warming. But as has been noted, not a single fossil-fuel-burning power plant will be closed down in the immediate future as a result of the many declarations arising from that meeting.

Environmentalists are torn between two imperfect choices: applauding the steps forward (which Greenpeace did after the 2015 Paris summit), or criticizing governments for not doing more and urging followers to work locally (as Friends of the Earth International did) (Bond 2015).

The one certainty moving forward is that environmentalism is not a static, unchanging social phenomenon. One can anticipate that all groups' efforts will be informed by new scientific studies, but it is uncertain whether efforts to improve the environment will primarily center on global concerns such as climate change or on local issues.

It is likely that environmentalists, recognizing that green issues are intertwined with issues of economic growth and fairness, will seek to form coalitions with grassroots political and economic activists. Coalitions between environmentalists, business, and labor would sustain development while also addressing environmental issues. For example, such coalitions might work toward the creation of energy-efficient products and the promotion of ecotourism that financially rewards preservation of natural resources. This multipronged approach is familiar to sociologists, whose study of society shows again and again that society is shaped by and reshapes the environment around it (Gould and Lewis 2015).

TAKE THE ISSUE WITH YOU

1. In your community, how would you act locally to preserve the environment? Describe your community's environmental problems and explain how you would seek to solve them.

2. How do you see the trade-off between the economy and the environment? Which is more important? Is it possible to improve both at the same time? Explain.

3. Thinking globally about the environment, list what you consider the most pressing priorities. How important are world hunger and economic justice compared to global warming, clean air and water, and economic development? Are some of your priorities related? In what way?

MODULE 56 | Recap and Review

Summary

The **human ecology** perspective suggests that the environment serves three basic functions: it provides essential resources, serves as a waste repository, and houses our species.

1. Conflict theorists charge that the most serious threat to the environment comes from Western industrialized nations.

2. **Environmental justice** addresses the disproportionate subjection of minorities to environmental hazards.

3. Four broad areas of environmental concern include air and water pollution, global warming, and globalization. Although globalization can contribute to environmental woes, it can also have beneficial effects.

4. Environmentalism is a social movement that is dominated by wealthy White people from industrialized countries. Increasingly, however, people of all races, ethnicities, social classes, and nationalities are becoming concerned about global warming and the threat it poses to our planet's health.

Thinking Critically

1. How are the physical and human environments connected in your neighborhood or community?

2. Which issue is more significant in your local community, air or water pollution? Why?

Key Terms

Climate change

Ecological modernization

Environmental justice

Environmental refugee

Global warming

Human ecology

Mastering This Chapter

© Imaginechina/Corbis

taking sociology with you

1 Visit the emergency room of your local hospital and observe what is going on in the waiting room. How crowded is the waiting room? How many people in the room appear to be severely ill or injured? How many do not seem to have an emergency? What else can you observe about the people who are gathered there, and how might that help to explain their presence?

2 Interview at least three people you know who do not have health insurance to determine how the lack of insurance affects their health-care decisions. (If you have been uninsured, include your own experiences.)

3 Do an Internet search to locate the hazardous waste sites nearest your school or home. How many of them have been cleaned up, and at what cost? Who paid that cost? How many of these sites are still a problem?

Birthrate The number of live births per 1,000 population in a given year. Also known as *crude birthrate.*

Brain drain The immigration to the United States and other industrialized nations of skilled workers, professionals, and technicians who are desperately needed in their home countries.

Census An enumeration, or counting, of a population.

Climate change An observable alteration of the global atmosphere that affects natural weather patterns over several decades or longer.

Curanderismo Latino folk medicine, a form of holistic health care and healing.

Death rate The number of deaths per 1,000 population in a given year. Also known as the *crude death rate.*

Demographic transition The change from high birthrates and death rates to low birthrates and death rates.

Demography The scientific study of population.

Ecological modernization The alignment of environmentally favorable practices with economic self-interest through constant adaptation and restructuring.

Environmental justice A legal strategy based on claims that racial minorities are subjected disproportionately to environmental hazards.

Environmental refugee A person who has been displaced by rising seas, destructive storms, expanding deserts, water shortages, or high levels of toxic pollutants.

Fertility The level of reproduction in a society.

Global warming A significant rise in the earth's surface temperatures that occurs when industrial gases like carbon dioxide turn the planet's atmosphere into a virtual greenhouse.

Growth rate The difference between births and deaths, plus the difference between immigrants and emigrants, per 1,000 population.

Health As defined by the World Health Organization, a state of complete physical, mental, and social well-being, and not merely the absence of disease and infirmity.

Holistic medicine Therapies in which the health care practitioner considers the person's physical, mental, emotional, and spiritual characteristics.

Human ecology An area of study that is concerned with the interrelationships between people and their environment.

Infant mortality rate The number of deaths of infants under 1 year old per 1,000 live births in a given year.

Labeling theory An approach to deviance that attempts to explain why certain people are viewed as deviants while others engaged in the same behavior are not.

Life expectancy The median number of years a person can be expected to live under current mortality conditions.

McDonaldization The process by which the principles of bureaucratization have increasingly shaped organizations worldwide.

Medical model An approach in which medical experts define illness or disease, determine and control the course of treatment, and even affect patients' view of themselves.

Mental illness A disorder of the brain that disrupts a person's thinking, feeling, and ability to interact with others.

Migration The relatively permanent movement of people with the purpose of changing their place of residence.

Morbidity rate The rate of disease in a given population.

Mortality rate The rate of death in a given population.

Population pyramid A special type of bar chart that shows the distribution of a population by gender and age.

Sick role Societal expectations about the attitudes and behavior of a person viewed as being ill.

Social epidemiology The study of the distribution of disease, impairment, and general health status across a population.

Stigma A label used to devalue members of certain social groups.

Total fertility rate (TFR) The average number of children born alive to any woman, assuming that she conforms to current fertility rates.

Vital statistics Records of births, deaths, marriages, and divorces gathered through a registration system maintained by governmental units.

Zero population growth (ZPG) The state of population in which the numbers of births plus immigrants equals the number of deaths plus emigrants.

self-quiz

Read each question carefully and then select the best answer.

1. Which sociologist developed the concept of the sick role?
   a. Émile Durkheim
   b. Talcott Parsons
   c. C. Wright Mills
   d. Erving Goffman

2. Regarding health care inequities, the conflict perspective would note that
   a. physicians serve as gatekeepers for the sick role, either verifying a patient's condition as "illness" or designating the patient as "recovered."
   b. patients play an active role in health care by failing to follow a physician's advice.
   c. emigration out of the Third World by physicians is yet another way that the world's core industrialized nations enhance their quality of life at the expense of developing countries.
   d. the designation "healthy" or "ill" generally involves social definition by others.

3. Which one of the following nations has the lowest infant mortality rate?
   a. the United States
   b. India
   c. Canada
   d. Japan

4. Compared with Whites, Blacks have higher death rates from
   a. heart disease.
   b. diabetes.
   c. cancer.
   d. all of the above

5. Which theorist notes that capitalist societies, such as the United States, care more about maximizing profits than they do about the health and safety of industrial workers?
   a. Thomas Szasz
   b. Talcott Parsons
   c. Erving Goffman
   d. Karl Marx

6. Which program is essentially a compulsory health insurance plan for the elderly?
   a. Medicare
   b. Medicaid
   c. Blue Cross
   d. Healthpac

7. Which of the following is a criticism of the sick role?
   a. Patients' judgments regarding their own state of health may be related to their gender, age, social class, and ethnic group.
   b. The sick role may be more applicable to people experiencing short-term illnesses than to those with recurring long-term illnesses.
   c. Even such simple factors as whether a person is employed or not seem to affect the person's willingness to assume the sick role.
   d. all of the above

8. The final stage of the demographic transition is marked by
   a. high birthrates and high death rates.
   b. high birthrates and low death rates.
   c. low birthrates and high death rates.
   d. low birthrates and low death rates.

9. Which of the following approaches stresses the alignment of environmentally favorable practices with economic self-interest?
   a. conflict theory
   b. human ecology
   c. ecological modernization
   d. environmental justice

10. Conflict theorists would contend that blaming developing countries for the world's environmental deterioration contains an element of
    a. ethnocentrism.
    b. xenocentrism.
    c. separatism.
    d. goal displacement.

11. A _____ _____ studies the effects of social class, race and ethnicity, gender, and age on the distribution of disease, impairment, and general health across a population.

12. From a(n) _____ perspective, "being sick" must be controlled so as to ensure that not too many people are released from their societal responsibilities at any one time.

13. The immigration to the United States and other industrialized nations of skilled workers, professionals, and technicians who are desperately needed by their home countries is known as the _____ _____.

14. Traditionally, the relationship between doctors and nurses has paralleled _____ dominance of the larger society.

15. Sociologists find it useful to consider _____ rates because they reveal that a specific disease occurs more frequently among one segment of a population compared with another.

16. _____, or the scientific study of populations, draws on several components, including size, composition, and territorial distribution.

17. _____ _____ are records of births, deaths, marriages, and divorces that are gathered through a registration system maintained by governmental units.

18. The biologist _____ _____ blames environmental degradation primarily on technological innovations such as plastics and pesticides.

19. Regarding environmental problems, three broad areas of concern stand out: _____ pollution, _____ pollution, and _____ _____.

20. _____ _____ is a legal strategy based on claims that racial minorities are subjected disproportionately to environmental hazards.

18

Social Change in the Global Community

© Agencja Fotograficzna Caro/Alamy

Social change is global, its effects both obvious and subtle. In Fang, Thailand, novice Buddhist monks amuse themselves by playing computer games. Computers and the Internet also promote the Dharma—the Buddha's teachings—in ways unimaginable just a decade ago.

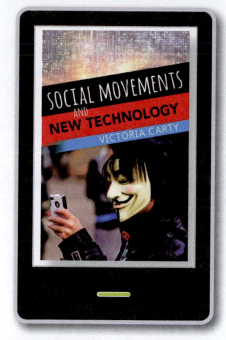

© Ira C. Roberts/Chad Enterprises Corporation

How do electronic media affect the ways you communicate with others, on an intimate level as well as throughout the wider social world?

Sociologist Victoria Carty believes that social media have had a revolutionary effect on social movements in recent years.

❝ Digital natives, millennials, Gen Y, Gen 2.0: however you label them, the generation born roughly between 1980 and 2000 has been immersed in revolutionary digital technologies since birth. For those of you who fit into this age cohort, life was experienced very differently in the 1990s, and these technological novelties have had vast repercussions at the individual and societal level. The way people communicate has fundamentally changed with the advent of new information communication technologies (ICTs), from e-mail to Snapchat. Not only can messages, photos, and videos be sent instantly, they have the potential to be spread far and wide throughout social networks—and the ramifications have been felt in all areas of society.

On a personal level, new technology has resulted in a radical shift in the way individuals view themselves and their social ties. Students of previous generations, for example, interacted in a much more limited though intimate way. Friendships and ways of communicating consisted of conversations in the cafeteria at lunch, bonding through sports or other extracurricular activities, sitting next to someone in class and passing secret notes (on paper!), or having neighborhood playmates. The main vehicle of communication was physically going to friends' houses to see whether they were free to play or using the telephone—the one or two stationary phones inside the house that the whole family shared. In sum, communication was initiated, shared, and sustained among people who knew each other personally, and it took effort on the part of the receiver and sender of information. This has changed in many ways as communication now, for many people, takes place to a great extent through digital venues, especially among youth. For example, in 2009 the average U.S. teenager, on Twitter alone, was receiving or sending more than 3,000 messages a month. In 2010 researchers at the University of Maryland conducted a study of two hundred students who were asked to abstain from using electronic media for twenty-four hours. Though everything else about their college experience was the same—they were surrounded by other students and their identity was intact—not being connected *virtually* to others horrified the participants. One student states that he had never felt so "alone and secluded from my life." Another reported, "Although I go to a school with thousands of students, the fact that I was not able to communicate with anyone via technology was almost unbearable."

Many long-standing, profitable, and dominant businesses are now obsolete as digitized industries have replaced analog ones: Polaroid declared bankruptcy with the introduction of digital cameras in 2001; iTunes replaced Tower Records as the largest music retailer in the United States, and the chain bookstore Borders, which at one point had more than 1,000 stores throughout the United States, closed after the rise of e-reading technology such as Amazon's Kindle.

Unsurprisingly, the rise of digital technology and social media also deeply affects contentious politics as well as the organization of and participation in social movements. Over the past several years, there has been an explosion of protest activity among young people around the globe as they embrace a new vision of the future and demand radical changes in the existing economic and political systems. *Time* magazine, in fact, named the protester as its Person of the Year in 2011.

Unsurprisingly, the rise of digital technology and social media also deeply affects contentious politics as well as the organization of and participation in social movements.

In essence, the media ecology can either accelerate—or, conversely, impede—serious political discussion and debate, and ultimately facilitate displays of collective behavior. With new digital technology at their disposal, social movement actors have access to innovative media outlets that help nurture a new political terrain within which they can discuss grievances, disseminate information, and collectively make demands.

There are, of course, many factors to consider when examining recent forms of collective behavior—namely, the austere economic conditions around the globe, political disenfranchisement, and a lack of accountability among political elites. The focus of this book, however, is the use of digital technology in different social movements, communities, and campaigns—from the Indignados in Europe and Mexico, to women seeking social justice, to the Arab spring in the Middle East and North Africa, to Occupy Wall Street and the DREAMers' quest for immigration reform, to the savvy digital organizing by political groups and communities in the United States. People are challenging political authorities, entrenched dictators, and political and economic systems once taken for granted. On a more micro and individual level, and particularly as it pertains to youth, individuals aided by digital technology are mobilizing to confront skyrocketing debt and current policies regarding immigration through contentious politics. ❞

(Carty 2015:1–5)

n *Social Movements and New Technology*, sociologist Victoria Carty reflects on the recent explosion in electronic media and the impact it is having on social movements worldwide. She herself had been involved in protests regarding United States involvement in the civil turmoil in Central America and later the 1990 Gulf War (Operation Desert Shield), but at the time, before the rise of social media, she understandably felt far removed from what was really going on. Even finding out where meetings or activities were being held was difficult—one had to rely on word of mouth. But as she describes, the ready availability of social media changed all that and caused protest movements themselves to evolve in new and unexpected ways.

Social change often follows the introduction of new electronic social media. *Social change* has been defined as significant alteration over time in behavior patterns and culture (W. Moore 1967). But what constitutes a "significant" alteration? Certainly the dramatic rise in formal education in the last century represents a change that has had profound social consequences. Other social changes that have had long-term and important consequences include the emergence of slavery as a system of stratification, the Industrial Revolution, and the increased participation of women in the paid labor forces of the United States and Europe.

How does social change happen? Is the process unpredictable, or can we make certain generalizations about it? How has globalization contributed to social change? In this chapter we examine the process of social change, with special emphasis on the impact of globalization. We begin with collective behavior, from rumors, fads, and fashions to social movements, behavior that can bring about genuine social change. We will see that recent advances in communications technology have allowed some social movements to circle the world. Next, we examine three theories of social change: the evolutionary, functionalist, and conflict perspectives. Then we discuss vested interests, which often attempt to block changes they see as threatening. And we recognize the influence of globalization in spreading social change around the world, noting the rapid social change that has occurred over a matter of decades in the Middle Eastern city-state of Dubai. Finally, we turn to the unanticipated social change that occurs when innovations such as new technologies sweep through society. The chapter closes with a Social Policy section on a controversial aspect of global social change, the creation of *transnationals*—immigrants with an allegiance to more than one nation.

MODULE 57 | Collective Behavior

Practically all behavior can be thought of as *collective behavior*. For sociologists, however, the term has a more distinct meaning. According to Neil Smelser (1981:431), a sociologist who specializes in this field of study, **collective behavior** is the "relatively spontaneous and unstructured behavior of a group of people who are reacting to a common influence in an ambiguous situation." Rumors are a form of collective behavior, as is public opinion—people's reactions to shared events such as wars and elections. In this module we will examine three sociological theories of collective behavior, as well as 10 different forms of collective behavior, from fads and fashions to social movements.

● Theories of Collective Behavior

In 1979, 11 rock fans died of suffocation after a crowd outside Cincinnati's Riverfront Stadium pushed to gain entrance to a concert by The Who. In 2003, 100 people died after a pyrotechnics display by Great White ignited a fire at a nightclub in West Warwick, Rhode Island. Many had watched excitedly as flames engulfed the bandstand, thinking they were part of the act. And in 2008, a healthy 34-year-old security guard was crushed to death—still standing but unable to breathe—as excited shoppers at a Walmart store in Long Island, New York, surged through the doors in quest of Black Friday bargains.

Like these incidents, collective behavior is usually unstructured and spontaneous. Its fluidity makes it more difficult for sociologists to generalize about people's behavior in such situations. Nevertheless, sociologists have developed various theoretical perspectives that can help us to study—and deal with in a constructive manner—crowds, riots, fads, and other types of collective behavior.

Emergent-Norm Perspective

Early writings on collective behavior implied that crowds are basically ungovernable. However, that is not always the case. In many situations, crowds are effectively governed by norms and procedures, including queuing, or waiting in line. We routinely encounter queues when we await service in a fast-food restaurant or bank, or when we enter or exit a movie theater or football stadium. Normally, physical barriers, such as guardrails and checkout counters, help to regulate queuing. When massive crowds are involved, ushers or security personnel may be present to assist in the orderly movement of the crowd. Nevertheless, there are times when such measures prove inadequate, as the examples just given and the one that follows demonstrate.

In December 1991, more than 5,000 people showed up early for a heavily promoted celebrity basketball game at the City College gymnasium in New York City. Seeing the size of the crowd, many of them must have realized that they could not all fit into the gym, which would accommodate only 2,730 people. As frustrated patrons waited to see which of them would be allowed in, restlessness and discontent swept through the crowd, and sporadic fights broke out.

When the doors to the gym finally opened, only 50 people at a time were allowed to enter. They then had to descend two

© Ed Betz/AP Images

Because collective behavior is often unstructured and spontaneous, it can prove deadly. So strong was the surge of shoppers when this Walmart store opened on the day after Thanksgiving, a security guard was asphyxiated.

flights of stairs and enter the gym through a single unlocked entrance—a maddeningly slow process in the overcrowded passageway. Finally, well past the game's starting time and with the arena more than full, the doors to the gym were closed. As rumors spread outside the building that the game was beginning, more than 1,000 additional fans poured through the building's entrance and headed for the stairs. Trapped between the locked gymnasium doors and those pushing down the stairs behind them, 9 young men and women died and 29 were injured through the sheer pressure of bodies pressing against walls and doors (Mollen 1992).

Sociologists Ralph Turner and Lewis Killian (1987) have offered a view of collective behavior that is helpful in assessing a tragic event like this. It begins with the assumption that a large crowd, such as a group of rock or soccer fans, is governed by expectations of proper behavior just as much as four people playing doubles tennis. But during an episode of collective behavior, a definition of what behavior is appropriate or not emerges from the crowd. Turner and Killian call this view the **emergent-norm perspective**. Like other social norms, the emergent norm reflects shared convictions held by members of the group and is enforced through sanctions. The new norm of proper behavior may arise in what seems at first to be an ambiguous situation. There is latitude for a wide range of acts within a general framework established by the emergent norm (for a critique of this perspective, see McPhail 1991).

Using the emergent-norm perspective, we can see that fans outside the charity basketball game at City College found themselves in an ambiguous situation. Normal procedures of crowd control, such as orderly queues, were rapidly dissolving. Simultaneously, a new norm was emerging: it is acceptable to push forward, even if the people in front protest. Some members of the crowd—especially those with valid tickets—may have felt that their push forward was justified as a way of ensuring that they would get to see the game. Others pushed forward simply to relieve the physical pressure of those pushing behind them. Even individuals who rejected the emergent norm may have felt

afraid to oppose it, fearing ridicule or injury. Thus, conforming behavior, which we usually associate with highly structured situations, was evident in this rather chaotic crowd, as it had been at the concerts by The Who and Great White and at Walmart's Black Friday sale. However, it would be misleading to assume that these fans acted simply as a united, collective unit in creating a dangerous situation.

The advent of social media and the real-time updates it affords can work in both positive and negative ways. Social media may be beneficial in summoning help and warning people to avoid dangerous developing situations. However, such alerts can also draw people to situations, thereby endangering themselves and thwarting efforts by first responders (Wasik 2012).

Value-Added Perspective

Neil Smelser (1962) proposed a different sociological explanation for collective behavior. He used the **value-added model** to explain how broad social conditions are transformed in a definite pattern into some form of collective behavior. This model outlines six important determinants of collective behavior: structural conduciveness, structural strain, a generalized belief, a precipitating factor, mobilization for action, and the exercise of social control.

In Smelser's view, certain elements must be present for an incident of collective behavior to take place. He used the term *structural conduciveness* to indicate that the organization of society can facilitate the emergence of conflicting interests. Structural conduciveness was evident in North Africa and the Middle East prior to the democratic uprisings that arose in the Arab world in 2011, the so-called Arab Spring. At that time, authoritarian governments responded to anti-government demonstrations with violence; in some cases, government-backed militias faced down the protesters. Social media shared the protestors' successes, which precipitated people in other nations to take collective action. Such structural conduciveness makes collective behavior possible, though not inevitable.

The second determinant of collective behavior, *structural strain,* occurs when the conduciveness of the social structure to potential conflict gives way to a perception that conflicting interests do, in fact, exist. The intense desire of many East Germans to travel to or emigrate to western European countries placed great strain on the social control exercised by the Communist Party. Such structural strain contributes to what Smelser calls a *generalized belief*—a shared view of reality that redefines social action and serves to guide behavior. The overthrow of communist rule in East Germany and other Soviet-bloc nations occurred in part as a result of a generalized belief that the communist regimes were oppressive and that popular resistance *could* lead to social change.

Smelser suggests that a specific event or incident, known as a *precipitating factor,* triggers collective behavior. The event may grow out of the social structure, but whatever its origins, it contributes to the strains and beliefs shared by a group or community. For example, in the aftermath of the 2013 acquittal of a man for the shooting death of unarmed Trayvon Martin, an African American teenager, people throughout the nation organized to bring attention to the perceived indiscriminate shooting deaths of Black youth. An activist movement using the hashtag #BlackLivesMatter surfaced and continued to gain strength with each ensuing incident that seemingly showed a Black life did not matter to law enforcement officers.

According to Smelser, the four determinants just identified are necessary for collective behavior to occur. In addition to these factors, the group must be *mobilized for action*. An extended thundershower or severe snowstorm may preclude such mobilization. People are more likely to come together on weekends than on weekdays, and in the evening rather than during the day.

The *manner in which social control is exercised*—both formally and informally—can be significant in determining whether the preceding factors will end in collective behavior. Stated simply, social control may prevent, delay, or interrupt a collective outburst. In some instances, those using social control may be guilty of misjudgments that intensify the severity of an outbreak.

Sociologists have questioned the validity of both the emergent-norm and value-added perspectives because of their imprecise definitions and the difficulty of testing them empirically. Some have criticized the emergent-norm perspective for being too vague in defining what constitutes a norm; others have challenged the value-added model for lack of specificity in defining generalized belief and structural strain. Of the two theories, the emergent-norm perspective appears to offer a more useful explanation of society-wide episodes of collective behavior, such as crazes, than the value-added approach (M. Brown and Goldin 1973; Quarantelli and Hundley 1975; K. Tierney 1980).

Smelser's value-added model, however, represents an advance over earlier theories that treated crowd behavior as being dominated by irrational, extreme impulses. The value-added approach firmly relates episodes of collective behavior to the overall social structure of a society (G. Marx 2012; for a critique, see McPhail 1991, 1994).

Assembling Perspective

A series of football victory celebrations at the University of Texas that had spilled over into the main streets of Austin came under the scrutiny of sociologists (Snow et al. 1981). Some participants had actively tried to recruit passersby for the celebrations by thrusting out open palms "to get five," or by yelling at drivers to honk their horns. In fact, encouraging further assembling became a preoccupation of the celebrators. Whenever passersby were absent, participants were relatively quiet. As we have seen, a key determinant of collective behavior is mobilization for action. How do people come together to undertake collective action?

Clark McPhail, perhaps the most prolific researcher of collective behavior in the past four decades, sees people and organizations consciously responding to one another's actions. Building on the interactionist approach, McPhail and Miller (1973) introduced the concept of the assembling process. In their **assembling perspective**, they sought to examine how and why people move from different points in space to a common location. Before the advent of new technologies, the process of assembling for collective action was slower and more deliberate than it is today, but McPhail's approach still applies.

A basic distinction has been made between two types of assemblies. **Periodic assemblies** include recurring, relatively routine gatherings of people such as work groups, college classes, and season-ticket holders in an athletic series. These assemblies are characterized by advance scheduling and recurring attendance of the majority of participants. For example, members of an introductory sociology class may gather for lectures every Monday, Wednesday, and Friday morning at 10 a.m. In contrast, **nonperiodic assemblies** include demonstrations, parades, and gatherings at the scene of fires, accidents, and arrests. Such assemblies, which often result from word-of-mouth information, are generally less formal than periodic assemblies. One example would be an organized rally held at Gallaudet University in 1988 to back a deaf person for president of the school for deaf students (McPhail 2006, 2008; D. L. Miller 2014).

These three approaches to collective behavior give us deeper insight into relatively spontaneous and unstructured situations. Although episodes of collective behavior may seem irrational to outsiders, norms emerge among the participants, and organized efforts are made to assemble at a certain time and place.

> ### use your sociological imagination
> Think about the practice of assembling to attend class or to study in the library. On a daily basis, how is this practice affected by the direct or indirect actions of your fellow students, co-workers, relatives, or teammates?

© Jewel Samad/Getty Images

Antiwar protesters rally against their nation's participation in the military intervention in Libya in 2011. According to the assembling perspective, nonperiodic assemblies like this one are relatively spontaneous, loosely organized reactions to galvanizing events.

● Forms of Collective Behavior

Did you go see the latest Ninja Turtles movie? Do you know anyone who collected Beanie Babies? Any grunge clothes or tube tops lurking in your parents' closet? These are all fads and fashions that depend on collective behavior. Using the emergent-norm, value-added, and assembling perspectives along with other aspects of sociological study, sociologists have investigated many forms of collective behavior not only fads and fashions but also crowds, disaster behavior, panics and crazes, rumors, public opinion, and social movements (covered in Module 58). In this section we will study all these forms of collective behavior.

Crowds

A **crowd** is a temporary gathering of people in close proximity who share a common focus or interest. Spectators at a baseball game, participants at a pep rally, and rioters are all examples of a crowd. Sociologists have been interested in the characteristics that are common to crowds. Of course, it can be difficult to generalize, since the nature of crowds varies dramatically. Think about how hostages on a hijacked airplane might feel, as opposed to participants in a religious revival.

Like other forms of collective behavior, crowds are not totally lacking in structure. Even during riots, participants are governed by identifiable social norms and exhibit definite patterns of behavior. In fact, crowds are no more emotional, suggestible, or destructive than any other social gathering. Sociologists Richard Berk and Howard Aldrich (1972) analyzed patterns of vandalism in 15 cities in the United States during the riots of the 1960s. They found that the stores of merchants who were perceived as exploitative were more likely to be attacked, while private homes and public agencies with positive reputations were more likely to be spared. Apparently, looters had reached a collective agreement as to what constituted a "proper" or "improper" target for destruction. Today, this type of information can be shared instantly via social media.

The emergent-norm perspective suggests that during urban rioting, a new social norm that basically condones looting is accepted, at least temporarily. The norms of respect for private property—as well as norms involving obedience to the law—are replaced by a concept of all goods being community property. All desirable items, including those behind locked doors, can be used for the "general welfare." In effect, the emergent norm allows looters to take what they regard as properly theirs—a scenario that was played out in Baghdad after the collapse of Saddam Hussein's regime in 2003. Yet not everyone participates in the free-for-all. Typically, most community residents reject the new norm, and either stand by passively or attempt to stop the wholesale theft (Couch 1968; Quarantelli and Dynes 1970; see also McPhail 1991, 2006, 2008).

Crowds have taken on new meaning in the Internet age. The term *crowdsourcing* has been coined to describe the online practice of asking Internet surfers for ideas or participation in an activity or movement. The compilation of Wikipedia, an online encyclopedia that is written and edited entirely by unrelated users, is the best-known example of crowdsourcing. Online crowds have also helped astronomers to map the galaxy, political activists to track politicians' travels, and marketers to spread the word about a new product (*The Economist* 2008b:10).

Another use for crowds in the Internet era is the **flash mob**: a group of people organized by social media to assemble suddenly in a public space, perform some collective activity, and then quickly disperse. The activity can range from inane behaviors, like jumping up and down 10 times near an intersection, to artistic expressions, such as singing in unison at a shopping mall, or even more elaborately staged events. It can also be political in nature, such as demonstrations of approval or disapproval of an organization or elected official. In 2001, in one of the first flash mobs, residents of Manila gathered to demonstrate against the president of the Philippines after receiving the text message "Go 2EDSA, Wear blck." Over a period of four days, more than a million of them converged on Eifano de los Santos Avenue ("EDSA") clothed in black. Within a few days, the military dropped their support of the president, who was facing impeachment, and allowed a new president to be named.

Flash mobs are often recorded on smartphones by passersby, who upload their video clips to YouTube, where they can be viewed by millions. In 2009 a "historic" flash mob performed "Do Re Mi" in a train station in Antwerp, Belgium, and the Internet video of the event went viral. To capitalize on the popularity of such online videos, especially among young people, some corporations have hired actors to stage flash mobs in an effort to spread their advertising messages through social media. Indeed, the supposedly spontaneous rendering of "Do Re Mi" in Antwerp was orchestrated to promote a talent search for the lead performer in a stage revival of *The Sound of Music*. More recently, Nike paid an amateur dance troop in San Francisco to stage a flash mob at the product launch for a new golf shoe.

 use your sociological imagination

Have you ever witnessed a flash mob in person or participated in one? How organized did it seem to be? Did some participants seem to give directions or cues to others?

In a deviant application of flash mobs, gangs have used social media to assemble members at a specific time and location to commit a crime, such as shoplifting, and then disperse. This type of action has become so common that law enforcement officials routinely refer to it as a *flash gang*. To anticipate such events, detectives have begun to monitor social media. In sum, like many elements of collective action, crowds and mobs can vary significantly in both their structure and their purpose (Holguin 2013).

Disaster Behavior

Newspapers, television reports, and even rumors bring word of many disasters around the world. The term **disaster** refers to a sudden or disruptive event or set of events that overtaxes a community's resources, so that outside aid is necessary. Traditionally, disasters have been catastrophes related to nature, such as earthquakes, floods, and fires. Yet in an industrial age, natural disasters have been joined by such "technological disasters" as airplane crashes, industrial explosions, nuclear power plant melt-downs, and massive chemical poisonings. However, there is no real distinction between the two types of disaster. As environmentalists have observed, human practices either contribute to or trigger natural disasters. Building in floodplains, engineering natural waterways, clear-cutting forests, and erecting rigid structures in earthquake zones all create the potential for disaster (Marshall and Picou 2008).

Disaster Research Sociologists have made enormous strides in disaster research, despite the problems inherent in this type of investigation. The work of the Disaster Research Center at the University of Delaware has been especially important. The center has teams of trained researchers prepared to leave for the site of any disaster on four hours' notice. Their field kits include identification material, recording equipment, and interview guidelines for use in various types of disasters. En route to the scene, these researchers try to become informed about the conditions they may encounter. On arrival, they establish a communication post to coordinate fieldwork and maintain contact with the center's headquarters.

© Pat Milton/AP Images

When a terrorist attack destroyed New York City's emergency command center, officials quickly set up a new one to direct the search and recovery effort. Even in times of unimaginable disaster, people respond in predictable ways.

Since its founding in 1963, the Disaster Research Center has conducted more than 700 field studies of natural and technological disasters in the United States and other nations. Its research has been used to develop effective planning in the delivery of emergency health care, the establishment and operation of rumor-control centers, the coordination of mental health services after disasters, and the implementation of disaster-preparedness and emergency-response programs. The center has also provided training and field research for graduate students, who maintain a professional commitment to disaster research and often go on to work for disaster service organizations such as the Red Cross and civil defense agencies (Disaster Research Center 2016; K. Tierney 2007).

Case Studies: Collapse of the World Trade Center and Hurricane Katrina Two devastating but very different disasters have provided fascinating case studies for researchers to examine. One was the collapse of the World Trade Center following the terrorist attack of September 11, 2001, which caused nearly three thousand deaths and billions of dollars worth of property damage. The other was the unprecedented destruction caused by Hurricane Katrina in August 2005, which left hundreds of thousands of people homeless. Sociologists who have studied such disasters have found that they are often followed by the creation of an emergency operations group, which coordinates both public services and some private-sector services, such as food distribution. Decision making becomes more centralized during these periods than it is in normal times.

Such was the case on September 11, 2001. New York City's well-designed Emergency Management Center, located in the World Trade Center, was destroyed when the building collapsed and all power at nearby City Hall was cut off. Yet within hours, both an incident command post and a new emergency operations center had been established to direct the search and recovery effort at the 16-acre site. Shortly thereafter came a victims' center, information kiosks, and an office for issuing death certificates, staffed around the clock by counselors, as well as facilities for serving meals to rescue workers. To identify potential hazards to rescuers and survey what had become a gigantic crime scene, police and public safety officials turned to computer maps and aerial photographs. They also designated places where victims could be identified, human resource functions relocated, and charitable contributions collected (Wachtendorf 2002).

Hurricane Katrina was an entirely different kind of disaster. Although unlike September 11, the storm's arrival was expected, its path of destruction was much greater, covering 90,000 square miles—an enormous area compared to the World Trade Center. In the four years since September 11, 2001, all levels of government in the United States had worked to improve their response to disasters, whatever the origin. Yet while the destruction of low-lying coastal areas in the Southeast by a catastrophic hurricane could have been anticipated, days passed before authorities managed to mount a full-scale rescue effort in response to Katrina. With streets flooded and communications knocked out, stranded residents waited on their rooftops for food, water, or a helicopter lift, wondering where the rescue teams were.

What went wrong? A monumental lack of coordination stymied government authorities. Confusion reigned among the numerous agencies involved in the effort, including the Federal Emergency Management Agency (FEMA), which had been reorganized under the authority of the Department of Homeland Security less than two years earlier; the National Guard, with a different command structure in each state; the active-duty military; and literally thousands of city, county, and state governments, each with its own sphere of authority. Amidst all this confusion, the biggest challenge facing FEMA was that in revising the nation's emergency response plan following September 11, federal officials had decided to rely on local government to manage in the first few days after a disaster. However, Katrina overwhelmed both local police and National Guard units stationed near the Gulf. In this case, the centralization of decision making that typically follows a disaster occurred over a period of days, not hours. In reviewing what happened, federal officials revised their emergency-response plan and reexamined laws governing change-of-command authority to expedite federal and military aid when necessary.

© Vincent Laforet/AP Images

A helicopter hovers over a flooded New Orleans neighborhood, searching for survivors on the rooftops. In the days that followed the storm, federal, state, and local authorities struggled to coordinate their rescue efforts, as thousands of stranded residents went without food or water.

The long-term recovery from Katrina was even more complicated than the rescue operation. In contrast to the World Trade Center's collapse, Hurricane Katrina had a disproportionately large effect on the poor, who possessed few if any resources to draw on in the emergency. Lacking a nest egg, these families had little choice in where to relocate, and they faced much more difficulty than others in finding permanent shelter and employment.

Disaster research has shown that in the wake of calamity, maintaining and restoring communications is vital not just to directing relief efforts, but to reducing survivors' anxiety. On September 11, most cell phones in Manhattan were rendered useless by the destruction of communications towers and relay stations. To contact loved ones or to plan their escape from a city clogged with emergency vehicles, people stood in line at pay phones. In the days to follow, families seeking information about their loved ones posted fliers at makeshift information centers. Following Hurricane Katrina, survivors who had been dispersed to shelters across the nation—often without knowing whether family members were alive or dead—turned to special websites to find their kin, business associates, teachers, and even pets. In the aftermath of unimaginable disaster, people and organizations responded in predictable ways (Brunsma et al. 2010).

Fads and Fashions

An almost endless list of objects and behavior patterns seems temporarily to catch the fancy of adults and children. Think about Silly Putty, Hula Hoops, the Rubik's Cube, break dancing, Mentos and Coke, speed dating, Sudoku puzzles, wristbands for a cause, and mosh pits. Fads and fashions are sudden movements toward the acceptance of some lifestyle or particular taste in clothing, music, or recreation.

Fads are temporary patterns of behavior involving large numbers of people; they spring up independently of preceding trends and do not give rise to successors. In contrast, **fashions** are pleasurable mass involvements that feature a certain amount of acceptance by society and have a line of historical continuity. Thus, punk haircuts would be considered a fashion, part of the constantly changing standards of hair length and style, whereas dancing the Macarena would be considered a fad of the mid-1990s (J. Lofland 1981, 1985).

Typically, when people think of fashions, they think of clothing styles and consumer behavior. In reality, the swiftly changing nature of consumer tastes has created an incredible burden on less developed countries. Most used clothing and even old sports caps, whether donated to charities or thrown out, over $4 billion worth globally every year, end up in periphery countries, to use Immanuel Wallerstein's term in his world systems analysis. There it is resold through stalls in street markets or, more likely, recycled into material for rags and scrap with buttons and zippers salvaged. While this creates some local businesses locally, critics point out it has virtually destroyed the textile industry in many African countries. Therefore, many developing nations are moving to ban the importing of surplus goods across their borders.

Fads and fashions allow people to identify with something different from the dominant institutions and symbols of a culture.

© Hocine Zaourar/AFP/Getty Images

A by-product of changing fashions in clothing are tons and tons of discarded clothing, as shown here in the bales of fabric in Algeria. Observers argue that the movement of donated clothing to developing nations has stifled the local textile industry in many countries that are now moving to ban such goods.

Members of a subculture can break with tradition while remaining in with a significant reference group of peers. Fads are generally short-lived and tend to be viewed with amusement or lack of interest by most nonparticipants. Fashions, in contrast, often have wider implications, because they can reflect (or give the impression of) wealth and status.

 use your **sociological imagination**

List some current fads and fashions. Now think back to when you were in elementary school. Can you name at least two fads from that time that seem to have faded away?

Panics and Crazes

Panics and crazes both represent responses to some generalized belief. A **craze** is an exciting mass involvement that lasts for a relatively long period. For example, in late 1973, a press release from a Wisconsin congressman described how the federal bureaucracy had failed to contract for enough toilet paper for government buildings. Then, on December 19, as part of his nightly monologue, *Tonight Show* host Johnny Carson suggested that it would not be strange if the entire nation experienced a shortage of toilet paper. Millions of people took his humorous comment seriously and immediately began stockpiling the item out of fear that it would soon be unavailable. Shortly thereafter, as a consequence of this craze, a shortage of toilet paper actually did occur. Its effects were felt into 1974 (Crockett 2014).

In contrast, a **panic** is a fearful arousal or collective flight based on a generalized belief that may or may not be accurate. In a panic, people commonly think there is insufficient time or inadequate means to avoid injury. Panics often occur on battlefields, in overcrowded burning buildings, or during stock market crashes. The key distinction between panics and crazes is that panics are flights *from* something, whereas crazes are movements *toward* something.

One of the most famous cases of panic in the United States was touched off by a media event: the 1938 Halloween eve radio dramatization of H. G. Wells's science fiction novel *The War of the Worlds*. This broadcast told realistically of an invasion from Mars, with interplanetary visitors landing in northern New Jersey and taking over New York City 15 minutes later. The announcer indicated at the beginning of the broadcast that the account was fictional, but about 80 percent of the listeners tuned in late. Many became frightened by what they assumed to be a news report.

Some accounts have exaggerated the extent of people's reactions to *The War of the Worlds*. One report concluded that "people all over the United States were praying, crying, fleeing frantically to escape death from the Martians." In contrast, a CBS national survey of listeners found that only 20 percent were genuinely scared by the broadcast. Although perhaps a million people *reacted* to the program, many reacted by switching to other stations to see if the "news" was being carried elsewhere. This "invasion from outer space" set off a limited panic rather than mass hysteria (Schwartz 2015).

It is often believed that people who are engaged in panics or crazes are unaware of their actions, but that is certainly not the case. As the emergent-norm perspective suggests, people take cues from one another about how to act during such forms of collective behavior. Even in the midst of an escape from a life-threatening situation, such as a fire in a crowded theater, people do not tend to run in a headlong stampede. Rather, they adjust their behavior on the basis of the perceived circumstances and the conduct of others who are assembling in a given location. To outside observers studying the events, people's decisions may seem foolish (pushing against a locked door) or suicidal (jumping from a balcony). Yet for that individual at that moment, the action may genuinely seem appropriate—or the only desperate choice available (L. Clarke 2002; Quarantelli 1957).

Rumors

Slender Man might cause nightmares, but he seems like an unlikely basis for homicide. He is a fictitious figure that emerged on a website where people create short horror stories. Created in 2009 with computer graphic techniques and a bit of a storyline alongside other fictional characters including vampires, zombies, and aliens, Slender Man was usually portrayed as a disproportionately tall, skinny man dressed in a dark suit who silently stalked his victims.

Slender Man's fan base grew, even though most people, certainly most adults, had never heard of him. In 2014, Slender

Man became very real for two 12-year-old girls in Wisconsin. They believed that he haunted a nearby woods and in a macabre effort to appease him, they brutally stabbed another girl to near death in the woods. Slender Man, a figure that existed only on the Internet, had indeed taken a victim—in a way the legendary Sasquatch, or Yeti, or Loch Ness monster could never have imagined (L. Miller 2015).

None of us is immune to hearing or starting such rumors. A **rumor** is a piece of information gathered informally that is used to interpret an ambiguous situation. Rumors serve a function by providing a group with a shared belief. As a group strives for consensus, members eliminate those rumors that are least useful or credible. Research reveals that in the workplace, rumors about what is or may be happening are usually highly accurate. Therefore, rumors can serve as a means of adapting to change. If a business is about to be taken over by another firm, rumors will usually abound as to the significance the move will have for personnel. Gradually, such rumors are either verified or discarded, but the very exchange of rumors allows people to cope with changes over which they have little control. Scary rumors probably spread the fastest, because fear induces stress and stress is reduced by sharing the fear with others. Moreover, some people enjoy provoking fear in others (Fine and DiFonzo 2011; Hutson 2015; D. E. Miller 2006).

The attack on the Pentagon and the World Trade Center produced a flurry of rumors. According to one false account, a police officer "surfed" a steel beam down 86 floors as one of the towers collapsed. Given the role of the media in covering the event, many rumors centered on them. For example, one rumor suggested that a CNN film of Palestinians dancing in the streets after the attack was actually file footage photographed during the Gulf War. In Pakistan, rumors spread that the vivid photos of the hijacked planes crashing into the World Trade Center had actually been staged.

Like these examples, rumors often reinforce people's ideologies and their suspicion of the mass media. Also unsettling was the growing presence of social media during the 2016 U.S. presidential election and, indeed, in politics throughout the world, of what came to be termed "fake news." These unfounded

rumors distracted citizens from real issues and concerns. Journalists became increasingly concerned that the general public was increasingly turned off from all news outlets, believing that no news accounts could be trusted. Like these examples, rumors often reinforce people's ideologies and their suspicion of the mass media (Fine and Ellis 2011; Mozur and Scott 2016; Slackman 2008).

Publics and Public Opinion

The least organized and most individualized form of collective behavior is the public. The term **public** refers to a dispersed group of people, not necessarily in contact with one another, who share an interest in an issue. As the term is used in the study of collective behavior, the public does not include everyone. Rather, it is a collective of people who focus on some issue, engage in discussion, agree or disagree, and sometimes dissolve when the issue has been decided (Blumer 1955, 1969; R. Turner and Killian 1987).

The term **public opinion** refers to expressions of attitudes on matters of public policy that are communicated to decision makers. The last part of this definition is particularly important. Theorists of collective behavior see no public opinion without both a public and a decision maker. In studying public opinion, we are not concerned with the formation of an *individual's* attitudes on social and political issues. Instead, we focus on the ways in which a public's attitudes are communicated to decision makers, and on the ultimate outcome of the public's attempts to influence policymaking.

Polls and surveys play a major role in assessing public opinion. Using the techniques for developing reliable questionnaire and interview schedules, survey specialists conduct studies of public opinion for business firms (market analyses), the government, the mass media (program ratings), and of course, politicians. Survey data have become extremely influential not only in preselecting the products we buy but in determining which political candidates are likely to win an election and even which potential Supreme Court nominees should be selected (Gans 2013; Manza and Brooks 2012).

Today's political polls are well-constructed surveys based on representative sampling techniques. As a result, their projections of presidential elections often fall within a few percentage points of the actual vote. In marked contrast to these polls, some surveys are downright misleading, such as those in which people are asked to text a certain number to register an opinion.

In sum, sociologists study collective behavior because it incorporates activities that we all engage in on a regular basis. Moreover, they acknowledge the crucial role that social movements can play in mobilizing discontented members of a society and initiating social change. Table 57-1 summarizes the 10 forms of collective behavior that sociologists study.

© Raoul Minsart/Superstock

"Did you hear that?" Rumors are a common type of social interaction that underscores shared understandings—even if the information they convey is incorrect. Today more and more rumors, many of them personal and highly inflammatory, are spread through the Internet.

 use your **sociological imagination**

Can you recall a time when you changed your view on some issue after hearing or reading about prevailing public opinion on that issue?

TABLE 57-1 FORMS OF COLLECTIVE BEHAVIOR

Form	Definition	Example
Crowd	Temporary gathering of people in close proximity who share a common focus or interest	Political or team rally
Disaster	Sudden or disruptive event or set of events that overtaxes a community's resources, so that outside aid is necessary	Response to a tornado, hurricane, or refinery fire
Fad	Temporary pattern of behavior that involves large numbers of people and is independent of preceding trends	Backpack zipper pulls (charms, cartoon characters, superheroes)
Fashion	Pleasurable mass involvement that has a line of historical continuity	Designer purses
Panic	Fearful arousal or collective flight based on a generalized belief that may or may not be accurate	Travel cancellations during an epidemic
Craze	Exciting mass involvement that lasts for a relatively long period	Traveling fans of a music group or sports team
Rumor	Piece of information gathered informally that is used to interpret an ambiguous situation	Fabrication of U.S. moon landings using special effects
Public	Dispersed group of people, not necessarily in contact with one another, who share an interest in an issue	Environmentalists
Public opinion	Expressions of attitudes on matters of public policy that are communicated to decision makers	Views on global warming
Social movement	Organized collective activity to bring about or resist fundamental change in an existing group or society	Gay rights movement

MODULE 57 | Recap and Review

Summary

Collective behavior is the relatively spontaneous and unstructured behavior of a group that is reacting to a common influence in an ambiguous situation.

1. The **emergent-norm perspective** suggests that new forms of behavior may emerge during an episode of collective behavior. The **value-added model** outlines six determinants of collective behavior: structural conduciveness, structural strain, generalized belief, a precipitating factor, mobilization of participants for action, and the operation of social control. The **assembling perspective** examines how and why people move from different points in space to a common location.

2. In **crowds,** people are in relatively close contact and interaction for a period and are focused on something of common interest.

3. Researchers are interested in how groups interact in times of **disaster.**

4. **Fads** are temporary patterns of behavior involving large numbers of people; **fashions** have more historical continuity than fads.

5. A **panic** is a flight *from* something, whereas a **craze** is a mass movement *toward* something.

6. A **rumor** is a piece of information that is used to interpret an ambiguous situation and provide a group with a shared belief.

7. **Publics** represent the most individualized and least organized form of collective behavior. **Public opinion** is the expression of individuals' attitudes on public policy to decision makers.

Thinking Critically

1. Describe the emergency response that followed the Boston Marathon bombings of 2013. Did the collective response to the attack illustrate the findings of disaster research? In what ways?

2. What other forms of collective behavior were evident on that day? Describe their role.

Key Terms

Assembling perspective

Collective behavior

Craze

Crowd

Disaster	Panic
Emergent-norm perspective	Periodic assembly
Fad	Public
Fashion	Public opinion
Flash mob	Rumor
Nonperiodic assembly	Value-added model

MODULE 58 | Social Movements

Although such factors as the physical environment, population, technology, and social inequality serve as sources of change, it is the *collective* effort of individuals organized into social movements that ultimately leads to change. Sociologists use the term **social movement** to refer to an organized collective activity to bring about or resist fundamental change in an existing group or society (Benford 1992). Herbert Blumer (1955:19) recognized the special importance of social movements when he defined them as "collective enterprises to establish a new order of life."

In many nations, including the United States, social movements have had a dramatic impact on the course of history and the evolution of the social structure. Consider the actions of abolitionists, suffragists, civil rights workers, activists opposed to the war in Vietnam, and Occupy Wall Street and #BlackLivesMatter protesters. Members of each social movement stepped outside traditional channels for bringing about social change, yet each had a noticeable influence on public policy. In Eastern Europe, equally dramatic collective efforts helped to topple communist regimes in a largely peaceful manner, in nations that many observers had thought were "immune" to such social change (Taylor 2016).

Though social movements imply the existence of conflict, we can also analyze their activities from a functionalist perspective. Even when they are unsuccessful, social movements contribute to the formation of public opinion. Initially, people thought the ideas of Margaret Sanger and other early advocates of birth control were radical, yet contraceptives are now widely available in the United States.

Because social movements know no borders, even nationalistic movements are deeply influenced by global events. Increasingly, social movements are taking on an international dimension from the start. Global enterprises, in particular, lend themselves to targeting through international mobilization, whether they are corporations like McDonald's or governmental bodies like the World Trade Organization. Global activism is not new, however; it began with the writing of Karl Marx, who sought to mobilize oppressed peoples in other industrialized countries. Today, activist networking is facilitated by the Internet. Participation in transnational activism is much more widespread now than in the past, and passions are quicker to ignite.

The Emergence of Social Movements

How and why do social movements emerge? Obviously, people are often discontented with the way things are. What causes them to organize at a particular moment in a collective effort to effect

© Oli Scarff/Getty Images

In 2010, protesters in London disguised themselves as characters in the movie *Avatar* to draw attention to the plight of an indigenous tribe in India. The Dongria Kondh people's way of life, the protesters charged, was threatened by a multinational corporation's plan to construct a mine on their land. The Indian government blocked the project, agreeing with protesters that it would have violated the tribe's rights.

change? Sociologists rely on two explanations for why people mobilize: the relative deprivation and resource mobilization approaches.

 use your **sociological imagination**

What social movements are most visible on your campus? In the community where you live? What do you think these groups need to do to be effective?

Relative Deprivation Approach

Those members of a society who feel most frustrated and disgruntled by social and economic conditions are not necessarily the worst off in an objective sense. Social scientists have long recognized that what is more significant is the way in which people *perceive* their situation. As Karl Marx pointed out, although the misery of the workers was important to their perception of their oppressed state, so was their position *in relation to* the capitalist ruling class (Marx and Engels [1847] 1955).

The term **relative deprivation** is defined as the conscious feeling of a negative discrepancy between legitimate expectations and present actualities (J. Wilson 1973). In other words, things aren't as good as you hoped they would be. Such a state may be characterized by scarcity rather than a complete lack of necessities (as we saw in the distinction between absolute and relative poverty in Module 28). A relatively deprived person is dissatisfied because he or she feels downtrodden relative to some appropriate reference group. Thus, blue-collar workers who live in two-family houses on small plots of land—though hardly at the bottom of the economic ladder—may nevertheless feel deprived in comparison to corporate managers and professionals who live in lavish homes in exclusive suburbs.

In addition to the feeling of relative deprivation, two other elements must be present before discontent will be channeled into a social movement. People must feel that they have a *right* to their goals, that they deserve better than what they have. At the same time, the disadvantaged group must perceive that its goals cannot be attained through conventional means. This belief may or may not be correct. Whichever is the case, the group will not mobilize into a social movement unless there is a shared perception that members can end their relative deprivation only through collective action (D. Morrison 1971).

Critics of this approach have noted that people don't need to feel deprived to be moved to act. In addition, this approach fails to explain why certain feelings of deprivation are transformed into social movements, whereas in similar situations, no collective effort is made to reshape society. Consequently, in recent years, sociologists have paid increasing attention to the forces needed to bring about the emergence of social movements (G. Martin 2015).

 use your **sociological imagination**

Why might well-off people feel deprived?

Resource Mobilization Approach

It takes more than desire to start a social movement. It helps to have money, political influence, access to the media, and personnel. The term **resource mobilization** refers to the ways in which a social movement utilizes such resources. Indeed, the success of a movement for change will depend in good part on what resources it has and how effectively it mobilizes them. In other words, recruiting adherents and marshalling resources is critical to the growth and success of social movements (D. Miller 2014).

Leadership is a central factor in the mobilization of the discontented into social movements. Often, a movement will be led by a charismatic figure, such as Dr. Martin Luther King Jr. As Max Weber described it in 1904, *charisma* is that quality of an individual that sets him or her apart from ordinary people. Of course, charisma can fade abruptly, which helps to account for the fragility of certain social movements (Morris 2000).

Many social movements are mobilized by institutional insiders. During the nationwide debate of the Obama administration's plan for health care reform in 2009, for example, health insurance companies encouraged their employees to attend the forums arranged by the White House. Managers distributed "Town Hall Tips" that included a list of concerns employees could raise and suggestions on how to make their comments as personal as possible, by talking about their own health issues (E. Walker 2010).

Why do certain individuals join a social movement while others who are in similar situations do not? Some of them are recruited to join. Karl Marx recognized the importance of recruitment when he called on workers to become *aware* of their oppressed status and to develop a class consciousness. Like theorists of the resource mobilization approach, Marx held that a social movement (specifically, the revolt of the proletariat) would require leaders to sharpen the awareness of the oppressed. They would need to help workers to overcome feelings of **false consciousness**, or attitudes that did not reflect workers' objective position, in order to organize a revolutionary movement. Similarly, one of the challenges faced by women's liberation activists of the late 1960s and early 1970s was to convince women that they were being deprived of their rights and of socially valued resources.

Gender and Social Movements

Sociologists point out that gender and sexual identities are important elements in understanding social movements. Our society has traditionally been dominated by male leaders and policymakers, and day-to-day life tends to assume that relationships are heterosexual. Further, traditional examination of the sociopolitical system tends to focus on such male-dominated corridors of power as legislatures and corporate boardrooms, to the neglect of more female-dominated domains such as households, community-based groups, and faith-based networks. While the feminist approach is changing that bias, many scholars still consider social movements only through a framing that entirely overlooks same-sex relationships.

Scholars of social movements now realize that gender can affect even the way we view organized efforts to bring about or resist change. For example, an emphasis on using rationality and cold logic to achieve goals helps to obscure the importance of passion and emotion in successful social movements. It would be difficult to find any movement—from labor battles to voting rights to animal rights—in which passion was not part of the consensus-building force. Yet calls for a more serious study of the role of emotion are frequently seen as applying only to the women's movement, because emotion is traditionally thought of as being feminine (Hurwitz and Taylor 2012).

 ## use your **sociological imagination**

Try to imagine a society without any social movements. Under what conditions could such a society exist? Would you want to live in it?

New Social Movements

Beginning in the late 1960s, European social scientists observed a change in both the composition and the targets of emerging social movements. Previously, traditional social movements had focused on economic issues, often led by labor unions or by people who shared the same occupation. However, many social movements that have become active in recent decades—including the contemporary women's movement, the peace movement, and the environmental movement—do not have the social class roots typical of the labor protests in the United States and Europe over the past century (Tilly 1993, 2004).

The term **new social movement** refers to an organized collective activity that addresses values and social identities, as well as improvements in the quality of life. These movements may be involved in developing collective identities. Many have complex agendas that go beyond a single issue, and even cross national boundaries. Educated, middle-class people are significantly represented in some of these new social movements, such as the women's movement and the movement for lesbian and gay rights. Box 58-1 describes the women's movements in South Korea and India.

New social movements generally do not view government as their ally in the struggle for a better society. While they typically do not seek to overthrow the government, they may criticize, protest, or harass public officials. Researchers have found that members of new social movements show little inclination to accept established authority, even scientific or technical authority. This characteristic is especially evident in the environmental and anti–nuclear power movements, whose activists present their own experts to counter those of government or big business (Garner 1996; Polletta and Jasper 2001; A. Scott 1990).

The environmental movement is one of many new movements with a worldwide focus (see the Social Policy section in Chapter 17). In their efforts to reduce air and water pollution, curtail global warming, and protect endangered animal species, environmental activists have realized that strong regulatory measures within a single country are not sufficient. Similarly, labor union leaders and human rights

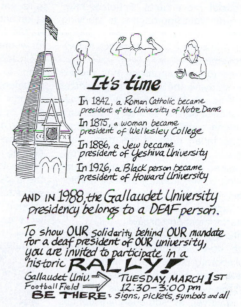

© 1995 by Gallaudet University.

Illustration: Illustration reprinted by permission of the publisher from John B. Christiansen and Sharon N. Barnartt, Deaf President Now! The 1988 Revolution at Gallaudet University. Gallaudet University Press, 1995, p. 22.

© The Washington Post/Getty Images.

Gallaudet University in Washington, D.C., is the only four-year liberal arts college for deaf students in the United States. A leaflet was distributed in 1988 as part of a successful effort by students, faculty, and alumni to force the appointment of the university's first deaf president. In 2007, after that president's retirement, students protested once again over the election process. Ultimately an experienced college administrator who was born deaf was appointed. The mobilization of resources, including leaflets, is one key to the success of a social movement.

Women's Social Movements in South Korea and India

Women have long played a significant role in social movements. Scholars have taken two different approaches to studying these movements: a macro-level, national approach and a more local approach to new social movements.

The macro-level approach has proved useful in studying the women's movement in South Korea. In 1987, a nationwide movement that included a variety of women's organizations toppled the country's long-time authoritarian ruler. In the democratic environment that followed his overthrow, women joined together in Korean Women's Association United (KWAU) to seek a voice on issues involving families, the environment, education, and sexuality, including sexual harassment and assault.

Eventually, the women's movement in South Korea became an institutionalized collaborator with the central government, even receiving government grants. Progress on women's issues has not been steady, however, as some administrations have been less friendly than others to the KWAU. To gain traction, the KWAU reached out to the United Nations in its efforts to further women's social equality, and to other international bodies, such as those seeking to curb human trafficking. One of the more visible activities of the KWAU has been to

organize the annual Women's Day activities. In recent years these have sparked a campaign and demonstrations on behalf of living wages and more employment opportunities for women.

In India, the women's social movement tends to be locally based, often in farming communities, where about 71 percent of the nation's 1.2 billion people live. As in other parts of the developing world, rural families in India are quite poor. For decades, villagers have been moving to the cities in hopes of earning a better income, only to be exploited in sweatshops and multinational factories. In the mid-1980s, 5,000 striking textile workers returned to their rural villages to mobilize support for their movement. As the strike wore on, some of those women remained

in the villages and sought work on government drought-relief projects. However, there weren't enough jobs for the villagers, much less for the striking textile workers.

This experience inspired a new social movement in rural India. With unemployment threatening an expanded population in rural villages, activists formed what came to be called the *Shoshit, Shetkari, Kashtakari, Kamgar, Mukti Sangharsh* (SSKKMS), which means "exploited peasants, toilers, workers liberation struggle." The movement's initial goal was to provide drought relief for farmers, but the deeper goal was to empower rural residents.

Indian women have also worked across social class lines. Women in the middle and upper class have become involved in movements focused on the problems of the poorest of poor women. These relatively affluent women must negotiate their way through familial disapproval. They have also had to fight being discriminated against themselves by those who look down upon such advocacy work. As social movement research has frequently shown, relatively privileged women must work against their own tendency to become controlling. Rather, they must seek to work with the poor women who are trying to overcome oppression, not merely represent them.

From workers' rights to the voting booth, from education to freedom from sexual violence, women's issues are an increasingly common feature of politics in both India and South Korea.

> From workers' rights to the voting booth, from education to freedom from sexual violence, women's issues are an increasingly common feature of politics in both India and South Korea.

©Ahn Young-joon/AP Images

The driving force behind the annual Women's Day in South Korea has been the Korean Women's Association (KWAU). The protest sign reads, "Preserve a living wage."

LET'S DISCUSS

1. What do you think might explain the differences between women's social movements and issues in South Korea and in India?

2. What would happen if "powerless" people in the United States formed a social movement of their own? Would it succeed? Why or why not?

Sources: Hur 2011; Korean Women's Association United 2010; Mee 2015; Mitra 2013; Sengupta 2009; Subramaniam 2006; Working Women's Forum 2016.

advocates cannot adequately address exploitative sweatshop conditions in a developing country if multinational corporations can simply move their factories to another country, where workers earn even less. Whereas traditional views of social movements tended to emphasize resource mobilization on a local level, new social movement theory offers a broader, global perspective on social and political activism.

Table 58-1 summarizes the sociological approaches that have contributed to social movement theory. Each has added to our understanding of the development of social movements.

TABLE 58-1 CONTRIBUTIONS TO SOCIAL MOVEMENT THEORY

Approach	Emphasis
Relative deprivation	Social movements are especially likely to arise when expectations are frustrated.
Resource mobilization	The success of social movements depends on which resources are available and how effectively they are used.
New social movement	Social movements arise when people are motivated by value issues and social identity questions.

● Communications and the Globalization of Social Movements

Today, through social media, activists can reach a large number of people around the world almost instantaneously, with relatively little effort and expense. As the chapter-opening excerpt shows, social networking allows organizers of social movements to enlist like-minded people without face-to-face contact, or even simultaneous interaction.

Moreover, television and the Internet, as contrasted with books and newspapers, often convey a false sense of intimacy reinforced by immediacy. We seem to be personally affected by the latest celebrity news. Therefore, the latest technology brings us together to act and react in an electronic global village (Della Porta and Tarrow 2005; Garner 1999).

This sense of online togetherness extends to social movements, which more and more are being mounted on the web. Through the instantaneous communication that is possible over the Internet, Mexican Zapatistas and other groups of indigenous peoples can transform their cause into an international lobbying effort, and Greenpeace organizers can link environmental activists throughout the world via video recorded on members' cell phones.

Sociologists have begun to refer to such electronic enhancement of established social movements as **computer-mediated communication** (CMC). Computer-mediated communication may be defined as communicative interaction through two or more networked devices, such as a computer or cell phone. The term applies to a variety of text-based or video interactions, including e-mails and text messages, some of which may be supported by social media. This kind of electronic communication strengthens a group's solidarity, allowing fledgling social movements to grow and develop faster than they might otherwise. Thus the face-to-face contact that once was critical to a social movement is no longer necessary. As Box 58-2 suggests, however, the legitimacy of such online movements is a matter of opinion (Castells 2010b; Niezen 2005).

The new global communications technology also helps to create enclaves of similarly minded people. Alex Steffen (2008), editor of the book *World Changing,* notes that the Internet is changing the way people relate to one another across vast distances, allowing small, focused audiences to become part of a global conversation. In doing so, they may find a common purpose. These social connections happen because of the Internet's technological structure. Websites are not autonomous and independent; they are connected by a global electronic network. One website generally lists a variety of other sites that serve as links. For example, seeking information on racism on college campuses will lead you to activist groups on specific campuses as well as to descriptions and videos of effective mobilization tactics. New developments in communications technology have clearly broadened the way we interact with one another.

💡 use your **sociological imagination**

Have you ever learned about a social movement outside the United States through social media?

© Pavel Filatov/Alamy

Rural residents of Mongolia pose outside their home with their satellite dish. In 2008 protesters rocked Mongolia's capital in anger over election fraud. Since then protesters have demanded more equitable distribution of the nation's mining wealth and drawn attention to environmental pollution. In all these protests, people from rural areas use the Internet to organize for action.

BOX 58-2

))) OUR Wired World

Organizing for Controversy via Computer-Mediated Communication

With the Arab Spring, which began in Tunisia in 2011, and the Occupy Wall Street movement, which sprang up later that year, computer-mediated communication became a social necessity. In a remarkably short period, the two tech-savvy social movements overthrew dictators and mounted mass protests in cities across the United States. What gave their new form of communication such power? Unlike more traditional forms of communication, social media can be used almost anywhere by almost anyone with a cause, from street protesters to people trying to launch a petition from home.

The widespread use of computer-mediated communication in social movements is not lost on those in authority, who monitor and sometimes seek to control citizens' access to networked communications. Around the world, government leaders worry about people using the Internet and social media to incite terrorist acts. And they have good reason. Islamic extremist websites, many of which are technologically advanced and written in English, have been garnering support for Islamic causes outside the Middle East. Ku Klux Klan websites have also been growing in number, complete with online "news shows" and streaming video.

Yet drawing the line between criminal activity and legitimate activity is not necessarily easy. A troubling example of what can

© Photodisc/Getty Images RF

happen when authorities gain unbridled control of computer-mediated communication occurred in Maryland, where a public school teacher could not figure out why she was unable to send or receive e-mails. The woman, whose first name happened to be Gay, finally learned that the school system had banned all homosexual-bisexual-transgender content. The site's filters had automatically blocked all messages bearing her name. They did, however, allow users to access anti-LGBT information.

Just as disturbing to many people are sites that promote what they see as destructive or self-destructive behavior. The Internet allows people who engage

in odd forms of vandalism, such as collecting parking meters, to network and become a virtual group. More troubling to many doctors and parents are the slick websites that encourage self-injury (see the opening to Chapter 2) or anorexia and bulimia (disorders characterized by little or no eating or by overeating and purging). Internet chat rooms for those who engage in these life-threatening behaviors are flourishing. Screen displays urge participants to "go public" by sending in for a beaded bracelet that supports their behavior.

To counteract these sites, members of the medical community have established websites to promote recovery and safe behavior. Their actions illustrate the double-edged nature of free expression. On the street or on the Internet, social movements may be seen either as promoting desirable social change or as supporting negative behaviors that many people find objectionable.

> On the street or on the Internet, social movements may be seen either as promoting desirable social change or as supporting negative behaviors that many people find objectionable.

LET'S DISCUSS

1. Have you ever been involved in a social or political movement whose legitimacy some people considered questionable? If so, what was the movement, and what were the objections to it? Did you consider the objections to be legitimate?

2. Can any social movement ever be totally free from controversy? Would you want to live in a society in which controversy is not tolerated?

Sources: Teaching Tolerance 2012; Thomasrobb.com 2007; Tibbles 2007; Whitlock 2005.

MODULE 58 | Recap and Review

Summary

Social movements are more structured than other forms of collective behavior and persist over longer periods.

1. A group will not mobilize into a social movement without a shared perception that its **relative deprivation** can be ended only through collective action.

2. The success of a social movement depends in good part on effective **resource mobilization**.

3. **New social movements** tend to focus on more than just economic issues and often cross national boundaries.

4. Advances in communications technology—especially the Internet—have had a major impact on social movements.

Thinking Critically

1. What might be some drawbacks of global communications technology?

2. What aspects of traditional gender roles explain the roles that women and men typically play in social movements?

Key Terms

Computer-mediated communication

False consciousness

New social movement

Relative deprivation

Resource mobilization

Social movement

MODULE 59 | Social Change

Theories of Social Change

We have defined **social change** as significant alteration over time in behavior patterns and culture. Social change can occur so slowly as to be almost undetectable to those it affects, but it can also happen with breathtaking rapidity. As Figure 59-1 shows, the U.S. economy has grown through rapid change in just the beginning of the 21st century. For example, we can see the rapid growth in health and social assistance jobs to the point where these are now the leading sector of employment. Meanwhile, manufacturing continues the decline it began in the last century.

Consider two changes to which you probably have not given much thought. First is the decline of drive-in movie theaters in the United States (Figure 59-2). You may have never been to a drive-in, but half a century ago they were a major entertainment destination. Now we go to a multiplex or we stream movies rather than go to a drive-in. A second example of social change is walking to work (Figure 59-3). Who does that anymore in the United States? Not many. In certain urban areas it is a bit more common—10 percent of people in New York City walk to work, 12 percent in Washington, DC, and 15 percent in Boston, but almost anywhere else, it just does not happen (McKenzie 2014).

Explanations of social change are clearly a challenge in the diverse and complex world we inhabit today. Nevertheless, theorists from several disciplines have sought to analyze social change. In some instances, they have examined historical events to arrive at a better understanding of contemporary changes. We will review three theoretical approaches to change—evolutionary, functionalist, and conflict—and then take a look at resistance to social change.

Evolutionary Theory

The pioneering work of Charles Darwin (1809–1882) in biological evolution contributed to 19th-century theories of social change. Darwin's approach stresses a continuing progression of successive life-forms. For example, human beings came at a later stage of evolution than reptiles and represent a more complex form of life. Social theorists seeking an analogy to this biological model originated **evolutionary theory**, in which society is viewed as moving in a definite direction. Early evolutionary theorists generally agreed that society was progressing inevitably toward a higher state. As might be expected, they concluded in ethnocentric fashion that their behavior and culture were more advanced than those of earlier civilizations.

Auguste Comte (1798–1857), a founder of sociology, was an evolutionary theorist of change. He saw human societies as moving forward in their thinking, from mythology to the scientific method. Similarly, Émile Durkheim ([1893] 1933) maintained that society progressed from simple to more complex forms of social organization.

Today, evolutionary theory influences sociologists in a variety of ways. For example, it has encouraged sociobiologists to investigate the behavioral links between humans and other animals. It has also influenced human ecology, the study of the interaction between communities and their environment (Maryanski et al. 2015).

Functionalist Perspective

Because functionalist sociologists focus on what *maintains* a system, not on what changes it, they might seem to offer little to the study of social change. Yet as the work of sociologist Talcott Parsons demonstrates, functionalists have made a distinctive contribution to this area of sociological investigation.

Parsons (1902–1979), a leading proponent of the functionalist perspective, viewed society as being in a natural state of equilibrium. By "equilibrium," he meant that society tends toward a state of stability or balance. Parsons would view even prolonged labor strikes or civilian riots as temporary disruptions in the status quo rather than as significant alterations in social structure. Therefore, according to his **equilibrium model**, as changes occur in one part of society, adjustments must be made in other parts. If not, society's equilibrium will be threatened and strains will occur.

Reflecting the evolutionary approach, Parsons (1966) maintained that four processes of social change are inevitable. *Differentiation* refers to the increasing complexity of social organization. The transition from medicine man to physician, nurse, and pharmacist is an illustration of differentiation in the field of health. This process is accompanied by *adaptive upgrading,* in which social institutions become more specialized in their

FIGURE 59-1 The Changing U.S. Economy, 1997–2012

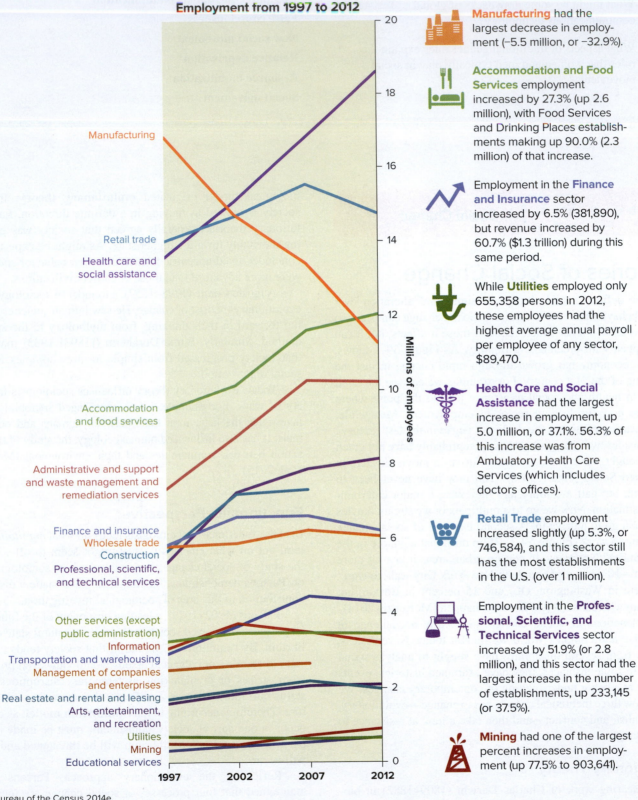

Employment from 1997 to 2012

Manufacturing had the largest decrease in employment (−5.5 million, or −32.9%).

Accommodation and Food Services employment increased by 27.3% (up 2.6 million), with Food Services and Drinking Places establishments making up 90.0% (2.3 million) of that increase.

Employment in the **Finance and Insurance** sector increased by 6.5% (381,890), but revenue increased by 60.7% ($1.3 trillion) during this same period.

While **Utilities** employed only 655,358 persons in 2012, these employees had the highest average annual payroll per employee of any sector, $89,470.

Health Care and Social Assistance had the largest increase in employment, up 5.0 million, or 37.1%. 56.3% of this increase was from Ambulatory Health Care Services (which includes doctors offices).

Retail Trade employment increased slightly (up 5.3%, or 746,584), and this sector still has the most establishments in the U.S. (over 1 million).

Employment in the **Professional, Scientific, and Technical Services** sector increased by 51.9% (or 2.8 million), and this sector had the largest increase in the number of establishments, up 233,145 (or 37.5%).

Mining had one of the largest percent increases in employment (up 77.5% to 903,641).

Source: Bureau of the Census 2014e.

FIGURE 59-2 Declining Drive-Ins, 1954–2012

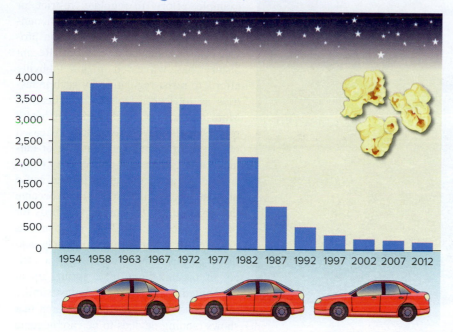

Source: Bureau Of The Census 2015i.

FIGURE 59-3 Walking to Work, 1960 to 2012

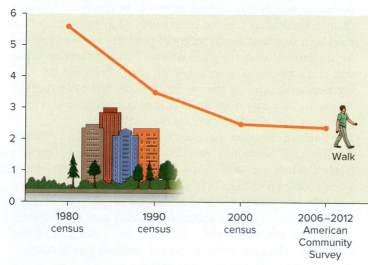

Source: Bureau of the Census 2014d.

purposes. The division of physicians into obstetricians, internists, surgeons, and so forth is an example of adaptive upgrading.

The next process Parsons identified is the *inclusion* of groups that were previously excluded because of their gender, race, ethnicity, or social class. Medical schools have practiced inclusion by admitting increasing numbers of women and African Americans. Finally, Parsons contends that societies experience *value generalization,* the development of new values that tolerate and legitimate a greater range of activities. The acceptance of preventive and alternative medicine is an example of value generalization: society has broadened its view of health care. All four processes identified by Parsons stress consensus—societal agreement on the nature of social organization and values (S. Best 2015).

Although Parsons's approach explicitly incorporates the evolutionary notion of continuing progress, the dominant theme in his model is stability. Society may change, but it remains stable through new forms of integration. For example, in place of the kinship ties that provided social cohesion in the past, people develop laws, judicial processes, and new values and belief systems.

Conflict Perspective

The functionalist perspective minimizes the importance of change. It emphasizes the persistence of social life and sees change as a means of maintaining society's equilibrium (or balance). In contrast, conflict theorists contend that social institutions and practices persist because powerful groups have the ability to maintain the status quo. Change has crucial significance, since it is needed to correct social injustices and inequalities.

Karl Marx accepted the evolutionary argument that societies develop along a particular path. However, unlike Comte and Spencer, he did not view each successive stage as an inevitable improvement over the previous one. History, according to Marx, proceeds through a series of stages, each of which exploits a class of people. Ancient society exploited slaves; the estate system of feudalism exploited serfs; modern capitalist society exploits the working class. Ultimately, through a socialist revolution led by the proletariat, human society will move toward the final stage of development: a classless communist society, or "community of free individuals," as Marx described it in 1867 in *Das Kapital* (see Bottomore and Rubel 1956:250).

As we have seen, Marx had an important influence on the development of sociology. His thinking offered insights into such institutions as the economy, the family, religion, and government. The Marxist view of social change is appealing because it does not restrict people to a passive role in responding to inevitable cycles or changes in material culture. Rather, Marxist theory offers a tool for those who wish to seize control of the historical process and gain their freedom from injustice. In contrast to functionalists' emphasis on stability, Marx argues that conflict is a normal and desirable aspect of social change. In fact, change must be encouraged as a means of eliminating social inequality.

One conflict theorist, Ralf Dahrendorf (1958), has noted that the contrast between the functionalist perspective's emphasis on stability and the conflict perspective's focus on change reflects the contradictory nature of society. Human societies are stable and long-lasting, yet they also experience serious conflict. Dahrendorf found that the functionalist and conflict perspectives were ultimately compatible, despite their many points of disagreement. Indeed, Parsons spoke of new functions that result from social change, and Marx recognized the need for change so that societies could function more equitably.

© WIN-Initiative/Getty Images

On the outskirts of Rio de Janiero, site of the 2016 Summer Olympics, a squatter settlement forms a stark contrast to the gleaming skyscrapers in the wealthy downtown area. Marxists and conflict theorists see social change as a way of overcoming the kind of social inequality evident in this photograph.

suffer in the event of social change. For example, efforts to regulate, restrict, or ban a product or service typically encounter stiff opposition from those who provide those goods and services. Recent history has witnessed major lobbying efforts to resist regulation by such industries as tobacco, alcohol, and firearms. More recently, policymakers and health professionals have advocated increased restriction if not an outright ban of tanning salons, to prevent unnecessary exposure to ultraviolet light, a proven cause of skin cancer. In 2003 Brazil became the first country to ban tanning beds for people under 18; in 2009 the ban was extended to cover all use for solely aesthetic purposes. Not surprisingly, a variety of organizations have sprung up in the United States to fight against similar restrictions and to discredit research that shows tanning devices to be carcinogenic to humans.

Tracking Sociological Perspectives

TABLE **59-1** SOCIOLOGICAL PERSPECTIVES ON SOCIAL CHANGE

Evolutionary	Social change moves society in a definite direction, frequently from simple to more complex.
Functionalist	Social change must contribute to society's stability.
	Modest adjustments must be made to accommodate social change.
Conflict	Social change can correct social injustices and inequalities.

Table 59-1 summarizes the differences between the three major perspectives on social change.

● Resistance to Social Change

Efforts to promote social change are likely to meet with resistance. In the midst of rapid scientific and technological innovations, many people are frightened by the demands of an ever-changing society. Moreover, certain individuals and groups have a stake in maintaining the existing state of affairs.

Social economist Thorstein Veblen (1857–1929) coined the term **vested interests** to refer to those people or groups who will

Economic and Cultural Factors

Economic factors play an important role in resistance to social change. For example, it can be expensive for manufacturers to meet high standards for the safety of products and workers, and for the protection of the environment. Conflict theorists argue that in a capitalist economic system, many firms are not willing to pay the price of meeting strict safety and environmental standards. They may resist social change by cutting corners or by pressuring the government to ease regulations.

Communities, too, protect their vested interests, often in the name of "protecting property values." The abbreviation *NIMBY* stands for "not in my backyard," a cry often heard when people protest landfills, prisons, nuclear power facilities, and even bike trails and group homes for people with developmental disabilities. The targeted community may not challenge the need for the facility, but may simply insist that it be located elsewhere. The "not in my backyard" attitude has become so common that it is almost impossible for policymakers to find acceptable locations for facilities such as hazardous-waste dumps (Jasper 2014).

On the world stage, what amounts to a "not on planet Earth" campaign has emerged. Members of this movement stress many issues, from profiteering to nuclear proliferation, from labor rights to the eradication of poverty and disease. Essentially an antiglobalization movement, it manifests itself at international meetings of trade ministers and heads of state.

Like economic factors, cultural factors frequently shape resistance to change. William F. Ogburn (1922) distinguished between material and nonmaterial aspects of culture. *Material culture* includes inventions, artifacts, and technology; *nonmaterial culture* encompasses ideas, norms, communications, and social organization. Ogburn pointed out that one cannot devise

© Alexander Kolomietz/123RF

The increasing use of drones has led to a variety of concerns, ranging from privacy issues to moral concerns over their use in warfare.

methods for controlling and using new technology before the introduction of a technique. Thus, nonmaterial culture typically must respond to changes in material culture. Ogburn introduced the term **culture lag** to refer to the period of maladjustment when the nonmaterial culture is still struggling to adapt to new material conditions. Aerial drones are a recent example of culture lag in action. At least fifty countries use such unmanned aircraft for military surveillance or launching air-to-ground missiles or bombs. The civilian population has embraced drones for work purposes, such as surveying agricultural land, and for recreation. Yet society has only begun to deal with the nonmaterial aspects of this technology, whether it be the moral issues of unmanned warfare or the need to restrict drones from interfering with aircraft or invading people's privacy.

In certain cases, changes in material culture can strain the relationships between social institutions. For example, new means of birth control have been developed in recent decades. Large families are no longer economically necessary, nor are they commonly endorsed by social norms. However, certain religious faiths, among them Roman Catholicism, continue to extol large families and to disapprove methods of limiting family size, such as contraception and abortion. This issue represents a lag between aspects of material culture (technology) and nonmaterial culture (religious beliefs). Conflicts may also emerge between religion and other social institutions, such as government and the educational system, over the dissemination of birth control and family-planning information.

 use your **sociological imagination**

What kind of social change do you find the hardest to accept? The easiest?

Resistance to Technology

Technology is cultural information about the ways in which the material resources of the environment may be used to satisfy human needs and desires. Technological innovations are examples of changes in material culture that often provoke resistance. The *Industrial Revolution,* which took place largely in England during the period 1760 to 1830, was a scientific revolution focused on the application of nonanimal sources of power to labor tasks. As this revolution proceeded, societies came to rely on new inventions that facilitated agricultural and industrial production and on new sources of energy, such as steam. In some industries, the introduction of power-driven machinery reduced the need for factory workers and made it easier for factory owners to cut wages.

Strong resistance to the Industrial Revolution emerged in some countries. In England, beginning in 1811, masked craft workers took extreme measures: they mounted nighttime raids on factories and destroyed some of the new machinery. The government hunted these rebels, known as **Luddites**, and ultimately banished or hung them. In a similar effort in France, angry workers threw their *sabots* (wooden shoes) into factory machinery to destroy it, giving rise to the term *sabotage.* While the resistance of the Luddites and the French workers was short-lived and unsuccessful, they have come to symbolize resistance to technology.

Are we now in the midst of a second industrial revolution, with a contemporary group of Luddites engaged in resisting? Many sociologists believe that we are living in a *postindustrial society.* It is difficult to pinpoint exactly when this era began. Generally, it is viewed as having begun in the 1950s, when for the first time the majority of workers in industrial societies became involved in services rather than in the actual manufacture of goods.

Just as the Luddites resisted the Industrial Revolution, people in many countries have resisted postindustrial technological changes. The term *neo-Luddites* refers to those who are wary of technological innovations and who question the incessant expansion of industrialization, the increasing destruction of the natural and agrarian world, and the "throw-it-away" mentality of contemporary capitalism, with its resulting pollution of the environment (Volti 2013).

A new slang term, *urban amish,* refers specifically to those who resist technological devices that have become part of our daily lives, such as smartphones. Such people insist that whatever the presumed benefits of industrial and postindustrial technology, such technology has distinctive social costs and may represent a danger to both the future of the human species and our planet (Urban Dictionary 2016).

Other people will resist a new technology simply because they find it difficult to use or because they suspect that it will complicate their lives. Both these objections are especially true of new information and media technologies. Whether it is hoverboards or FitBit, many consumers are leery of these so-called must-have items.

Summary

Social change is significant alteration over time in behavior patterns and culture, including mores and values.

1. Early advocates of the **evolutionary theory** of social change believed that society was progressing inevitably toward a higher state.

2. Talcott Parsons, a leading advocate of functionalist theory, viewed society as being in a natural state of equilibrium or balance.

3. Conflict theorists see change as having crucial significance, since it is needed to correct social injustices and inequalities.

4. In general, those with a disproportionate share of society's wealth, status, and power have a **vested interest** in preserving the status quo and will resist change.

5. The period of maladjustment when a nonmaterial culture is still struggling to adapt to new material conditions is known as **culture lag**.

Thinking Critically

1. Which perspective on social change do you find most convincing? Why?

2. Which do you think play more of a role in resistance to social change, economic or cultural factors? Why?

Key Terms

Culture lag

Equilibrium model

Evolutionary theory

Luddites

Social change

Technology

Vested interests

MODULE 60 | Global Social Change

The recent past has been a truly dramatic time in history to consider global social change. Maureen Hallinan (1997), in her presidential address to the American Sociological Association, asked those present to consider just a few of the recent events: the collapse of communism; terrorism in various parts of the world, including the United States; major regime changes and severe economic disruptions in Africa, the Middle East, and Eastern Europe; the spread of AIDS; and the computer revolution. Just a few months after her remarks came the first verification of the cloning of a complex animal, Dolly the sheep. Since then, scientists have made significant strides in treating AIDS, new pandemic diseases have emerged, scholars debate the promise and threat of artificial intelligence, and researchers have generated human embryonic stem cells.

● Anticipating Change

In this era of massive social, political, and economic change, global in scale, is it possible to predict change? Some technological changes seem obvious, but the collapse of communist governments in the former Soviet Union and Eastern Europe in the early 1990s took people by surprise. Yet prior to the Soviet collapse, sociologist Randall Collins (1986, 1995), a conflict theorist, had observed a crucial sequence of events that most observers had missed.

In seminars as far back as 1980, and in a book published in 1986, Collins had argued that Soviet expansionism had resulted in an overextension of resources, including disproportionate spending on military forces. Such an overextension will strain a regime's stability. Moreover, geopolitical theory suggests that nations in the middle of a geographic region, such as the Soviet Union, tend to fragment into smaller units over time. Collins predicted that the coincidence of social crises on several frontiers would precipitate the collapse of the Soviet Union.

And that is just what happened. In 1979, the success of the Iranian revolution had led to an upsurge of Islamic fundamentalism in nearby Afghanistan, as well as in Soviet republics with substantial Muslim populations. At the same time, resistance to communist rule was growing both throughout Eastern Europe and within the Soviet Union itself. Collins had predicted that the rise of a dissident form of communism within the Soviet Union might facilitate the breakdown of the regime. Beginning in the late 1980s, Soviet leader Mikhail Gorbachev chose not to use military power and other types of repression to crush dissidents in Eastern Europe. Instead, he offered plans for democratization and social reform of Soviet society, and seemed willing to reshape the Soviet Union into a loose federation of somewhat autonomous states. But in 1991, six republics on the western periphery declared their independence, and within months the entire Soviet Union had formally disintegrated into Russia and a number of other independent nations.

In her presidential address, Maureen Hallinan (1997) cautioned that we need to move beyond the restrictive models of social change—the linear view of evolutionary theory and the assumptions about equilibrium in the functionalist perspective. Hallinan noted that upheavals and major shifts do occur, and that sociologists must learn to predict their occurrence, as Collins did with the Soviet Union. Imagine, for example, the dramatic nonlinear social change that accompanies the transformation of a small, undeveloped principality into a major financial and communications hub called Dubai.

Social Change in Dubai

The story of Dubai, a Middle Eastern principality the size of Rhode Island, is a tale of two cities. When the Maktoum family took control of Dubai (pronounced Doo-Bye) in 1883, it was a pearl-fishing village on the Persian Gulf. But in 1966, the discovery of oil changed everything. When the state's oil reserves proved too limited to fund significant economic and social change, Dubai reinvented itself as a free-trade oasis. By 2000 it had become a tax-free information-technology hub. In less than a single generation—barely a decade—Dubai had transformed itself into what *Forbes* magazine calls the richest city in the world. This is a place that in the late 1950s had no electricity and no paved roads.

© Howard Boylan/Getty Images

© David Cannon/Getty Images

From 1990 to 2008, the area surrounding the Emirates Golf Club in Dubai changed dramatically.

Wide-eyed journalists have described Dubai's air-conditioned indoor ski run, open year-round in a country where the daytime temperature averages 92 degrees. Then there is the 162-story Burj Khalifa, which opened in 2010; at a half-mile high, it is by far the world's tallest building. At one point, so much of the city was under construction that 10 percent of the world's construction cranes were located there.

A constitutional monarchy, Dubai is no democratic utopia—there are no contested elections, and there is little public opposition to the government. Socially, however, Dubai is relatively progressive for an Arab state. Women are encouraged to work, and there is little separation of the sexes, as is common in neighboring states. Alcohol is available, speech is relatively free, and the media are largely uncensored.

The citizens of Dubai share its affluence: they receive cheap electricity, free land and water, free health care and education (including graduate study abroad), as well as an average subsidy of $55,000 per year. They pay no income or property taxes. Ironically, the government handouts that citizens enjoy mean that most have little interest in competitive work, so high-skilled positions tend to go to foreigners. The social consequences of Dubai's wealth have been less than benign, however. Environmentally, the cost of its lavish lifestyle is exorbitant. Dubai ranks at the top of the list in terms of its greenhouse gas emissions, at twice the level of the United States and triple the global average.

Another significant social problem, hidden from the investment bankers and tourists who visit Dubai, is the treatment of immigrant laborers. About 95 percent of Dubaians are foreigners from India, Pakistan, the Philippines, Sri Lanka, North Korea, Bangladesh, China, and Yemen. A million of them—seven times the number of Dubai nationals—come from India alone. These migrant laborers sold everything they owned to come to Dubai and take jobs stacking bricks, watering lawns, and cleaning floors. The pay is good relative to their home countries—$275 a month for a skilled electrician—but very poor compared to what the lowest-paid citizen of Dubai earns. At best, an immigrant must work two years just to break even.

There is little government oversight of working or living conditions in Dubai, both of which are poor. For foreign workers seeking to escape the slums in distant deserts, one-bedroom apartments rent for $1,400 per month. In 2008, fire investigators found 500 laborers living in a house built for a single family. Little wonder that late in 2009, when Dubai's economic expansion ground to a halt, foreign workers were heading home at an estimated rate of 5,000 a day.

The global economic downturn that began in 2008 was particularly savage to Dubai. Having borrowed heavily and invested not always wisely, both the government and major companies are groaning under a debt load that is heavier than even the United States' or Europe's. By 2010, however, Dubai's economy was back on the move, and by 2014, its airport had surpassed London's Heathrow as the world's busiest. In the second decade of the 21st century, the well-to-do are still flying lobster in for extravagant parties. Overworked foreign laborers, although many fewer of them remain, are still earning wages well above those available in their home countries. Political analysts note that Dubai is the most stable country in the Arab world, with a measured tolerance for outside cultural influences and an intolerance for corruption (Ali 2010; Gorney 2014; Harman 2009; Krane 2009, 2010; Mouawad 2014; Tatchell 2009).

Technology and the Future

Technological advances—the airplane, the automobile, the television, the atomic bomb, and more recently, the computer, digital media, and the cell phone—have brought striking changes to our cultures, our patterns of socialization, our social institutions, and our day-to-day social interactions. Technological innovations are, in fact, emerging and being accepted with remarkable speed (see the chapter-opening excerpt).

In the past generation alone, industrial countries have seen a major shift in consumer technologies. No longer do we buy electronic devices to last for even 10 years. Increasingly, we buy them with the expectation that within as little as 3 years, we will need to upgrade to an entirely new technology, whether it be a handheld device or a home computer. Of course, there are those people who either reject the latest gadgets or become frustrated trying to adapt to them. And then there are the "tech-no's"—people who resist the worldwide movement toward electronic networking. Those who become tech-no's are finding that it is a life choice that sets them apart from their peers, much like deciding to be "child free" (Darlin 2006; Kornblum 2007).

In the following sections, we examine various aspects of our technological future and consider their impact on social change, including the social strain they will cause. We focus in particular

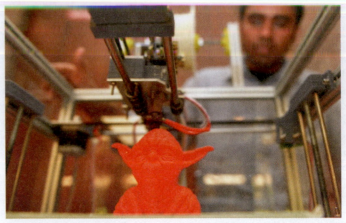

© Manjunath Kiran/AFP/Getty Images

3D printers are now widely available, although still expensive, and are used increasingly to transmit both designs and objects. This bust of a *Star Wars* character was constructed by a 3D printer in Bangalore, India, in 2014. By 2016, such printers were available to consumers at Barnes & Noble stores.

on recent developments in computer technology, electronic censorship, and biotechnology.

Computer Technology

The past decade witnessed an explosion of computer technology in the United States and around the world. Its effects were particularly noteworthy with regard to the Internet, the world's largest computer network. In 2015 the Internet reached 3.3 billion users, compared to just 50 million in 1996. Box 60-1 sketches the worldwide access to and use of the Internet.

The Internet evolved from a computer system built in 1962 by the U.S. Defense Department to enable scholars and military researchers to continue their government work even if part of the nation's communications system were destroyed by a nuclear attack. Until a generation ago, it was difficult to gain access to the Internet without holding a position at a university or a government research laboratory. Today, however, virtually anyone can reach the Internet with a cellphone or a computer. People buy and sell cars, trade stocks, auction off items, research new medical remedies, vote, and track down long-lost friends online—to mention just a few of the thousands of possibilities.

Unfortunately, not everyone can get onto the information highway, especially not the less affluent. Moreover, this pattern of inequality is global. The core nations that Immanuel Wallerstein described in his world systems analysis have a virtual monopoly on information technology; the peripheral nations of Asia, Africa, and Latin America depend on the core nations both for technology and for the information it provides. For example, North America, Europe, and a few industrialized nations in other regions possess almost all the world's *Internet hosts*—computers that are connected directly to the worldwide network.

Regardless of social class position, we have all been affected by advances in robotics developed and operated through computer technology. Digitization is transforming entire industries. Falling prices of computing, combined with increased

"We have to move - they're putting in a cell phone tower here."

Cartoon by Baloo. Copyright by © Rex F. May.

Finding a place where you can't receive a text message is getting harder and harder.

BOX 60-1

Our Wired World

The Internet's Global Profile

The old notion of an Internet accessed primarily in the United States and dominated by English-only content is passé. In fact, usage patterns are changing so fast, generalizing about global use of the Internet requires careful research and phrasing.

For example, Figure A, Internet Users by World Region, shows an Internet that is dominated by users in Asia and Europe, two relatively populous continents. However, Figure B, Internet Penetration by World Region, shows a dramatically different picture, one in which the *proportion* of people in each region who access the Internet is highest in North America. That is, numerically, most Internet users live in Asia and Europe, but the likelihood of a person being an Internet user is greatest in North America. Figure B shows dramatically low Internet use in Africa, where less than 30 percent of residents access the global network.

FIGURE A Internet Users by World Region

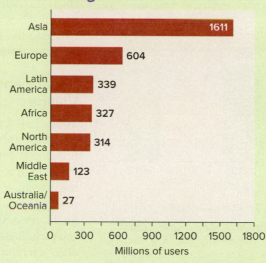

Region	Millions of users
Asia	1611
Europe	604
Latin America	339
Africa	327
North America	314
Middle East	123
Australia/Oceania	27

FIGURE B Internet Penetration by World Region

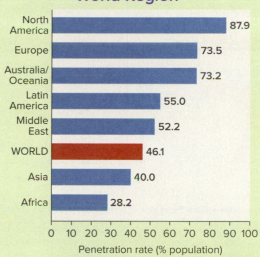

Region	Penetration rate (% population)
North America	87.9
Europe	73.5
Australia/Oceania	73.2
Latin America	55.0
Middle East	52.2
WORLD	46.1
Asia	40.0
Africa	28.2

> The old notion of an Internet accessed primarily in the United States and dominated by English-only content is passé.

FIGURE C Internet's Top 10 Languages

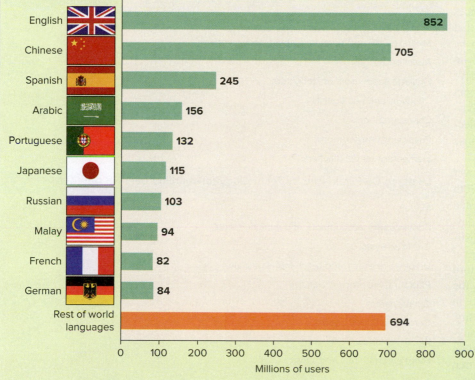

Language	Millions of users
English	852
Chinese	705
Spanish	245
Arabic	156
Portuguese	132
Japanese	115
Russian	103
Malay	94
French	82
German	84
Rest of world languages	694

Though English is still the primary language of Internet users, as Figure C shows, use of the Chinese language has become much more common. Interestingly, 91 percent of all Japanese speakers use the Internet, compared to 61 percent of all English speakers, though in absolute terms, speakers of Japanese are a significantly smaller group.

LET'S DISCUSS

1. Of the three figures shown here, which do you think presents the most sociologically significant statistics? Explain.
2. Why do you think the use of Chinese on the Internet has increased so dramatically in just a decade?

Source: All data taken from Internet World Stats 2015 as of November 15, 2015, for Figures A and B and June 30, 2015, for Figure C.

Flags: © admin_design/Shutterstock RF

FIGURE 60-1 Estimated Global Sale of Industrial Robots, 2010–2018

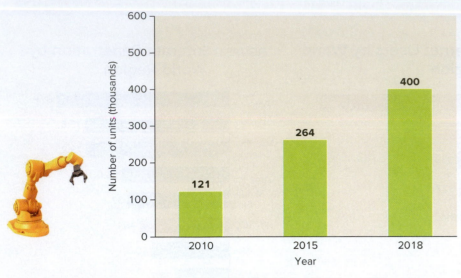

Sources: International Federation of Robotics 2015a, 2015b. *Robot:* © iLexx/Getty Images RF

Increasingly, routine jobs are done robotically. In addition to industrial robots typically used in manufacturing and delivery, service robots work in every area from surgery to window washing. The growth in use of autonomous operating devices has led to the observation that jobs are increasingly divided into two categories, lousy and lovely, with fewer and fewer ordinary jobs in between.

adaptability, has brought about an astronomical rise in the sale of robots in the industrial workplace (see Figure 60-1).

The unsettling aspect of this technological innovation is the possibility that such advances could eliminate people's jobs. Even jobs that have recently been offshored are expected to be replaced by robotic devices. Already, people who monitor the performance of digital networks have been replaced. It is anticipated that within about five years workers who field calls from bank customers or from people seeking to reset their electronic devices will be replaced by robots like those that respond to online chat lines (Moss 2016).

The concern that machines will take over people's jobs is not new; throughout the 20th century, first machines and then sophisticated robots took the place of human workers. Today, with software becoming steadily more sophisticated and affordable, the pace of technological innovation is increasing. Researchers at Oxford University looked at 702 occupations in the United States in terms of the worker's role in manipulating objects, thinking with originality, negotiating with or persuading others, and gauging others' emotions and reactions. They then used their findings to predict the likelihood that existing or foreseeable technologies could automate those 702 jobs within the next decade or two. Table 60-1 summarizes a portion of their research.

These predictions are by no means airtight; changes in many variables could affect the researchers' probability estimates. For example, even if a technology can be developed to perform a specific skill, access to cheap labor or relatively high technological costs could prevent automation of that skill. Labor organizing could also defer such an outcome. Nevertheless, around 47 percent of total U.S. employment falls into the high-risk category, in danger of being automated within the next decade or two.

Privacy and Censorship in a Global Village

Today, new technologies like robots, cars that can park themselves, and smartphones are bringing about sweeping social change. While much of that change is beneficial, there are some negative effects. Recent advances in computer technology have made it increasingly easy for business firms, government agencies, and even criminals to retrieve and store information about everything from our buying habits to our web-surfing patterns. In public places, at work,

TABLE 60-1 JOBS PROJECTED TO BE ELIMINATED BY COMPUTERIZATION

Unlikely to Be Eliminated by Technology (probability under 0.5 percent)

- Emergency management directors
- Mental health and substance abuse social workers
- Audiologists
- First-line supervisors of firefighters
- Dietitians and nutritionists
- Choreographers
- Physicians and surgeons
- Elementary school teachers

Likely to Be Eliminated by Technology (probability over 98 percent)

- Models
- Bookkeepers, accountants, and auditing clerks
- Credit analysts
- Umpires, referees, and other sports officials
- Photographic process workers
- Tax preparers
- Cargo and freight agents
- Watch repairers
- Hand embroiderers and sewers

Note: Probability that an occupation could be computerized in the next decade or two. Occupations selected from those extremely likely or unlikely to be computerized on a list of 702 U.S. occupations.
Source: Data from Appendix in Frey and Osborne 2013.

and on the Internet, surveillance devices now track our every move, be it a keystroke or an ATM withdrawal. The ever-present cell phone enables the most pervasive and sophisticated attacks on people's privacy and anonymity. In response, some people are beginning to advocate for the creation of a new agency that would respond to electronic viruses the way the CDC (Centers for Disease Control and Prevention) responds to biological threats. However, the trade-off for ensuring total privacy is to restrict the ability of law enforcement to search electronic communications for messages that reveal potential threats, whether those are theft or terrorism (Lucas 2015; Rosen 2015).

From a sociological point of view, the complex issues of privacy and censorship can be considered illustrations of culture lag. As usual, the material culture (technology) is changing faster than the nonmaterial culture (norms for controlling the use of technology). Too often, the result is an anything-goes approach to the use of new technologies.

Legislation regarding the surveillance of electronic communications has not always upheld citizens' right to privacy. In 1986, the federal government passed the Electronic Communications Privacy Act, which outlawed the surveillance of telephone calls except with the permission of both the U.S. attorney general and a federal judge. Telegrams, faxes, and e-mail did not receive the same degree of protection, however. Then in 2001, one month after the terrorist attacks of September 11, Congress passed the Patriot Act, which relaxed existing legal checks on surveillance by law enforcement officers. As a result, federal agencies are now freer to gather electronic data, including credit-card receipts and banking records. In 2005, Americans learned that the National Security Agency was covertly monitoring phone calls with the cooperation of major U.S. telecommunications companies. Since then, federal courts have ruled that wiretapping without warrants is legal (ACLU 2015b).

Sociologists' views on the use and abuse of new technologies differ depending on their theoretical perspective. Functionalists take a generally positive view of the Internet, pointing to its manifest function of facilitating communication. From their perspective, the Internet performs the latent function of empowering those with few resources—from hate groups to special-interest organizations—to communicate with the masses. Conflict theorists, in contrast, stress the danger that the most powerful groups in a society will use technology to violate the privacy of the less powerful. Indeed, officials in the People's Republic of China censor online discussion groups and web postings that criticize the government. The same abuses can occur in the United States, civil liberties advocates remind us, if citizens are not vigilant in protecting their right to privacy (Magnier 2004).

If anything, people seem to be less vigilant today about maintaining their privacy than they were before the information age. Young people who have grown up browsing the Internet seem to accept the existence of the cookies and spyware they may pick up while surfing. They have become accustomed to adult surveillance of their conversation in electronic chat rooms. Many see no risk in providing personal information about themselves to the strangers they meet online. Little wonder that college professors find their students do not appreciate the political significance of their right to privacy (Turkle 2004).

 use your sociological imagination

Do you hold strong views regarding the privacy of your electronic communications? When using a smartphone or similar device, do you ever suspect you are being watched or your actions monitored?

Biotechnology and the Gene Pool

Another field in which technological advances have spurred global social change is biotechnology. Sex selection of fetuses, genetically engineered organisms, cloning of sheep, cows, and some small animals—these have been among the significant yet controversial scientific advances in the field of biotechnology. George Ritzer's (2015) concept of McDonaldization applies to the entire area of biotechnology. Just as the fast-food concept has permeated society, no phase of life now seems exempt from therapeutic or medical intervention. In fact, sociologists view many aspects of biotechnology as an extension of the recent trend toward the medicalization of society. Through genetic manipulation, the medical profession is expanding its turf still further (Clarke et al. 2003; Human Genome Project 2016).

One notable success of biotechnology—an unintended consequence of modern warfare—has been progress in the treatment of traumatic injuries. In response to the massive numbers of soldiers who survived serious injury in Iraq and Afghanistan, military doctors and therapists have come up with electronically controlled prosthetic devices. Their innovations include artificial limbs that respond to thought-generated nerve impulses, allowing amputees to move prosthetic legs, arms, and even individual fingers. These applications of computer science to the rehabilitation of the injured will no doubt be extended to civilians.

© Andre Kudyusov/Photodisc/Alamy RF

© Trevor Snapp/Bloomberg via Getty Images

A Ugandan farmer checks the price of coffee beans on his cell phone.

One startling biotechnological advance is the possibility of altering human behavior or physical traits through genetic engineering. Fish and plant genes have already been mixed to create frost-resistant potato and tomato crops. More recently, human genes have been implanted in pigs to provide humanlike kidneys for organ transplant. William F. Ogburn probably could not have anticipated such scientific developments when he wrote of culture lag over 80 years earlier. However, advances like these or even the successful cloning of sheep illustrate again how quickly material culture can change, and how nonmaterial culture moves more slowly in absorbing such changes.

Although today's biotechnology holds itself out as totally beneficial to human beings, it is in constant need of monitoring. Biotechnological advances have raised many difficult ethical and political questions, among them the desirability of tinkering with the gene pool, which could alter our environment in unexpected and unwanted ways. In particular, controversy has been growing concerning genetically modified (GM) food, an issue that arose in Europe but has since spread to other parts of the world, including the United States. The idea behind the technology is to increase food production and make agriculture more economical. But critics use the term *Frankenfood* (as in "Frankenstein") to refer to everything from breakfast cereals made from genetically engineered grains to fresh GM tomatoes. Members of the antibiotech movement object to tampering with nature, and are concerned about the possible health effects of GM food. Supporters of genetically modified food include not just biotech companies, but those who see the technology as a way to help feed the burgeoning populations of Africa and Asia (Shuttleworth 2015).

In contrast, less expensive and controversial technologies can further agriculture where it is needed more, in the developing world. Consider cell phones. Unlike most new technologies, the majority of the world's cell phones are used in *less* developed countries. Relatively cheap and not as dependent as computers on expensive communications infrastructure, cell phones are common in the world's poorest areas. In Uganda, farmers use them to check weather forecasts and commodity prices. In South Africa, laborers use them to look for work. Researchers at the London Business School have found that in developing countries, a 10 percent increase in cell phone use is correlated with a 0.6 percent rise in GDP (Bures 2011).

While farmers in the developing world use cell phones to improve their incomes, others set out for foreign countries. The Social Policy section that follows considers *transnationals,* immigrants who travel back and forth between the developing and developed worlds, forging human rather than technological links.

social policy and globalization | Transnationals

Around the world, new communications technologies—cell phones, the Internet—have hastened the process of globalization. Yet without human capital, these innovations would not have spurred the huge increase in global trade and development that occurred over the last several decades. Who are the people behind the trend toward globalization? Often, they are people who see a business opportunity abroad and strike out on their own to take advantage of it. In the process, many of them become migrants.

To facilitate trade and investment with other countries, migrants often exploit their social connections and their familiarity with their home language and culture. In Southeast Asia, for example, Chinese migrants dominate the trade with China. Some migrants invest directly in their home countries

—*Continued*

to get the manufactured goods they sell abroad. Opportunities abound, and those with capital and good business skills can become quite wealthy (Guest 2011).

The millions of migrant laborers who leave home in search of a better life also play a role in the global economy, filling jobs where there are shortages in the labor market. Although they do not become wealthy working as landscapers or short-order cooks, they consider themselves better off than they were in the old country. Unfortunately, citizens of the host countries often react negatively to the migrants' arrival, worrying that they will take jobs away from the native-born.

Looking at the Issue

About 232 million people, or 3 percent of the world's population, were international migrants. That is more than double the number in 1970. The rest of the world's population were "stayers"—that is, people who continued to live in the countries where they were born (United Nations 2013).

Figure 60-2 shows the worldwide movement of workers with and without the legal right to immigrate. Several areas, such as the European Union, have instituted international agreements that provide for the free movement of laborers. But in most other parts of the world, immigration restrictions give foreign workers only temporary status. Despite such legal restrictions, the labor market has become an increasingly global one. Just as globalization has integrated government policies, cultures, social movements, and financial markets, it has unified what were once discrete national labor markets. So today, for example, immigrants from at least eight different countries work in one small Middle Eastern state, Dubai.

Globalization has changed the immigrant experience as well as the labor market. In generations past, immigrants read foreign language newspapers to keep in touch with events in their home countries. Today, the Internet gives them immediate access to their countries and kinfolk. In this global framework,

MAPPING LIFE WORLDWIDE

FIGURE 60-2 **Labor Migration**

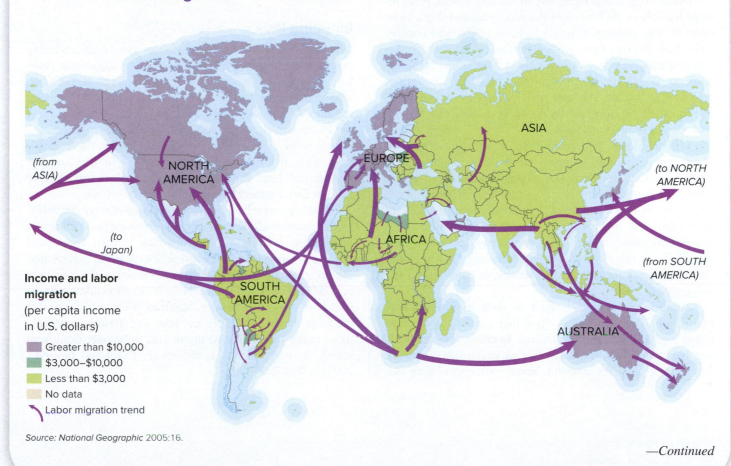

Income and labor migration

(per capita income in U.S. dollars)

- Greater than $10,000
- $3,000–$10,000
- Less than $3,000
- No data
- Labor migration trend

Source: National Geographic 2005:16.

—*Continued*

immigrants are less likely than they were in the past to think of themselves as residents of just one country. **Transnationals** are immigrants who sustain multiple social relationships that link their societies of origin with their societies of settlement.

Applying Sociology

As with other issues, sociologists differ in their opinion of transnationals, depending on their theoretical perspective. Functionalists see the free flow of immigrants, even when it is legally restricted, as one way for economies to maximize their use of human labor. Given the law of supply and demand, they note, countries with too few workers will inevitably attract laborers, while those with too many will become unattractive to residents.

Functionalists also embrace the assimilationist view of immigration, which emphasizes how people forsake their cultural tradition to become a part of their new society. The recognition that many transnationals sustain multiple relationships, including homeland connections, amends the assimilationist view, which ignores this aspect of immigrants' daily lives in the their new homes (Waldinger 2015).

Interactionists are interested in the day-to-day relationships transnationals have with the people around them, from those of their country of origin to those of the host country and fellow workers from other countries. These scholars are studying transnationals' involvement in local ethnic organizations, to see whether their membership facilitates or retards their integration into the host society. They have discovered that members of global social networks provide one another with mutual support and trust.

Transnationals also participate in social movements. Many transnationals emigrate either to a country with greater political freedom (for example, an Iranian immigrant to Great Britain) or to a nation with better work opportunities (for example, a Filipino worker in Dubai). In these situations, transnational migrants often monitor social movements that interest them via computer. They may also facilitate the growth of a social movement from a distance, by providing information, money, or both (Aunio and Staggenborg 2011).

Another question of interest to interactionists is how transnationals see themselves—how they see their own identities as well as those of their children. In effect, transnationals negotiate their identities, depending on which social network they belong to at the moment. Some sociologists note that while being a transnational can be exhilarating, it can also isolate a person, even in a city of millions. Others worry that transnationals may become so cosmopolitan that they will lose touch with their national identities (Calhoun 2003; Evergeti and Zontini 2006; Plüss 2005; Portes et al. 2008; Rajan and Sharma 2006; Tilly 2007).

Feminist theorists call attention to the way that migration has historically occurred in waves: first men moved to seek better opportunities, while women stayed behind until their husbands could afford to send for them. Women's responsibilities were to care for the household and maintain connections to the larger kinship network. In today's world of global social media, women play a critical role in maintaining communications and the flow of information across borders. Physical proximity is no longer a prerequisite for family maintenance (Herrera 2013).

Conflict theorists charge that globalization and international migration have increased the economic gulf between developed and developing nations. Through tourism and the global reach of the mass media, people in the poorer countries have become aware of the affluent lifestyle common in developed nations—and of course, many of them now aspire to it (C. L. Smith 2011).

Initiating Policy

Although connecting to two societies can be an enriching experience, transnationals face continuing adjustment problems in their new home countries. As we saw with Dubai, immigrant laborers often face difficult living and working conditions. Some sending countries, such as Indonesia and the Philippines, have created national agencies to ensure the protection of their workers abroad. Their objective is ambitious, given that funding for the agencies is limited, and diplomatic and legal challenges complicate their task (United Nations Development Programme 2009:102–104).

Another unresolved transnational issue is voter eligibility. Not all nations allow dual citizenship; even those countries that do may not allow absent nationals to vote. The United States and Great Britain are rather liberal in this regard, permitting dual citizenship and allowing émigrés to continue to vote. Mexico, in contrast, has been reluctant to allow citizens who have emigrated to vote. Mexican politicians worry that the large number of Mexicans who live abroad (especially those in the United States) might vote differently from local voters, causing different outcomes (P. Levitt and Jaworsky 2007; Sellers 2004).

—Continued

—Continued

Finally, the controversial issue of illegal immigration has yet to be settled, perhaps because of culture lag. That is, both public attitudes and government policies (nonmaterial culture) have not kept pace with, much less adjusted to, the increasing ease of migration around the globe (material culture). Though globalization has created a global labor market—one that many countries depend on, legal or illegal—the general public's attitude toward illegal immigrants remains hostile, especially in the United States.

Antagonism is by no means limited to transnationals who are in a nation illegally. A 2015 international survey found that more than 40 percent of the people in the United States, France, Poland, Greece, Spain, and Italy view immigrants as a burden to their country and are resistant to the social change that immigration brings (Krogstad 2015).

TAKE THE ISSUE WITH YOU

1. Suppose you live in an impoverished developing country and have the opportunity to earn a much higher income by immigrating to the United States. Will you do it, even if it means entering the country illegally and working long hours doing menial labor? If so, how will you justify your decision to those who condemn illegal immigration?

2. The U.S. economy depends on the cheap labor that some immigrants provide. Should immigrants receive the same social services that U.S. citizens receive? What about their children who are born in the United States (and therefore are U.S. citizens)? Explain your reasoning.

3. Globalization has increased international trade and development at the same time that it has strained nations' social service systems, as migrant workers flow toward countries offering the most extensive social protection. On balance, do you think its overall effect has been beneficial or harmful? What might be done to alleviate the harmful effects of globalization?

MODULE 60 | Recap and Review

Summary

We are living in a time of sweeping social, political, and economic change—change that occurs not just on a local or national basis but on a global scale.

1. Computer technology has made it increasingly easy for any individual, business, or government agency to retrieve more and more information about any of us, thereby infringing on our privacy.

2. Advances in biotechnology have raised difficult ethical questions about genetic engineering.

3. Dubai is a Middle Eastern state that reinvented itself as an information technology hub, in the process undergoing massive social change.

4. Globalization has increased the international migration of laborers, producing a new kind of immigrant.

Transnationals are immigrants who sustain multiple social relationships that link their societies of origin with their societies of settlement.

Thinking Critically

1. Which aspect of biotechnology do you find most promising?

2. Do you sometimes see your future more in the electronic world than in the people and places around you?

3. Overall, is technological innovation harmful or beneficial to society? Explain your answer.

Key Terms

Transnational

Mastering This Chapter

© Agencja Fotograficzna Caro/Alamy

taking sociology with you

1. Choose a social movement that you are interested in and do some research on it. If possible, visit with members of the movement in your local community. Which sociological theory fits this movement better, relative deprivation or resource mobilization? Would you describe the movement as a new social movement? What has been the role of communications in the movement?

2. Try turning off all your electronic devices—phone, laptop, and so on—for a specific period, say a day. Afterward, analyze the experiment from a sociological perspective. What functions did you lose while you were without the devices? Did you gain anything from the experience?

3. Choose a new technology that interests you and analyze it from a sociological point of view. What do you think this technology might contribute to society? What might be some negative effects of the technology? Have you noticed any resistance to it, and if so, on what grounds?

key terms

Assembling perspective A theory of collective behavior introduced by McPhail and Miller that seeks to examine how and why people move from different points in space to a common location.

Collective behavior In the view of sociologist Neil Smelser, the relatively spontaneous and unstructured behavior of a group of people who are reacting to a common influence in an ambiguous situation.

Computer-mediated communication Communicative interaction through two or more networked devices, such as a computer or cell phone. The term applies to a variety of text-based or video interactions, including e-mails, chat rooms, and text messages, some of which may be supported by social media.

Craze An exciting mass involvement that lasts for a relatively long period.

Crowd A temporary gathering of people in close proximity who share a common focus or interest.

Culture lag A period of maladjustment when the nonmaterial culture is still struggling to adapt to new material conditions.

Disaster A sudden or disruptive event or set of events that overtaxes a community's resources, so that outside aid is necessary.

Emergent-norm perspective A theory of collective behavior proposed by Turner and Killian that holds that a collective definition of appropriate or inappropriate behavior emerges during episodes of collective behavior.

Equilibrium model The functionalist view that society tends toward a state of stability or balance.

Evolutionary theory A theory of social change that holds that society is moving in a definite direction.

Fad A temporary pattern of behavior that involves large numbers of people and is independent of preceding trends.

Fashion A pleasurable mass involvement that features a certain amount of acceptance by society and has a line of historical continuity.

False consciousness A term used by Karl Marx to describe an attitude held by members of a class that does not accurately reflect their objective position.

Flash mob A group of people organized by social media to assemble suddenly in a public space, perform some collective activity, and then quickly disperse.

Luddites Rebellious craft workers in 19th-century England who destroyed new factory machinery as part of their resistance to the Industrial Revolution.

New social movement An organized collective activity that addresses values and social identities, as well as improvements in the quality of life.

Nonperiodic assembly A nonrecurring gathering of people that often results from word-of-mouth information.

Panic A fearful arousal or collective flight based on a generalized belief that may or may not be accurate.

Periodic assembly A recurring, relatively routine gathering of people, such as a college class.

Public A dispersed group of people, not necessarily in contact with one another, who share an interest in an issue.

Public opinion Expressions of attitudes on matters of public policy that are communicated to decision makers.

Relative deprivation The conscious feeling of a negative discrepancy between legitimate expectations and present actualities.

Resource mobilization The ways in which a social movement utilizes such resources as money, political influence, access to the media, and personnel.

Rumor A piece of information gathered informally that is used to interpret an ambiguous situation.

Social change Significant alteration over time in behavior patterns and culture, including norms and values.

Social movement An organized collective activity to bring about or resist fundamental change in an existing group or society.

Technology Cultural information about the ways in which the material resources of the environment may be used to satisfy human needs and desires.

Transnational An immigrant who sustains multiple social relationships that link his or her society of origin with the society of settlement.

Value-added model A theory of collective behavior proposed by Neil Smelser to explain how broad social conditions are transformed in a definite pattern into some form of collective behavior.

Vested interests Those people or groups who will suffer in the event of social change, and who have a stake in maintaining the status quo.

self-quiz

Read each question carefully and then select the best answer.

1. In sociological terms, which of the following constitute a crowd?
   a. spectators at a baseball game
   b. participants at a college pep rally
   c. urban rioters
   d. all of the above

2. The least organized and most individualized form of collective behavior is represented by
   a. rumors.
   b. publics.
   c. fashions.
   d. panics.

3. Karl Marx held that leaders of social movements must help workers overcome feelings of
   a. class consciousness.
   b. false consciousness.
   c. socialist consciousness.
   d. surplus value.

4. Organized collective activities that promote autonomy and self-determination, as well as improvements in the quality of life, are referred to as
   a. new social movements.
   b. social revolutions.
   c. resource mobilizations.
   d. crazes.

5. The text cites which of the following as a recognized definition of social change?
   a. tumultuous, revolutionary alternatives that lead to changes in leadership
   b. a significant alteration over time in behavior patterns and culture
   c. regular alteration in a consistent social frame of reference
   d. subtle alterations in any social system

6. Nineteenth-century theories of social change reflect the pioneering work in biological evolution done by
   a. Albert Einstein.
   b. Harriet Martineau.
   c. James Audubon.
   d. Charles Darwin.

7. According to Talcott Parsons's equilibrium model, during which process do social institutions become more specialized in their purposes?
   a. differentiation
   b. adaptive upgrading
   c. inclusion
   d. value generalization

8. Which of the following statements regarding Karl Marx is *not* true?
   a. Marx accepted the evolutionary argument that societies develop along a particular path.
   b. Marx believed that history proceeds through a series of stages, each of which exploits a class of people.
   c. Marx accepted Parsons's equilibrium model, which states that as changes occur in one part of society, there must be adjustments in other parts if stability is to be maintained.
   d. Marx argued that conflict is a normal and desirable aspect of social change.

9. Which of the following terms did William F. Ogburn use to refer to the period of maladjustment during which the nonmaterial culture is still struggling to adapt to new material conditions?
   a. economic shift
   b. political turmoil
   c. social change
   d. culture lag

10. Which sociological perspective sees transnationals as a way for economies to maximize their use of human labor?
    a. functionalist
    b. conflict
    c. interactionist
    d. feminist

11. _____ _____ are organized collective activities to bring about or resist fundamental change in an existing group or society.

12. A person suffering from relative deprivation is dissatisfied because he or she feels downtrodden relative to some appropriate _____ group.

13. Early evolutionary theorists concluded in a(n) _____ fashion that their own behavior and culture were more advanced than those of earlier civilizations.

14. Talcott Parsons used the term _____ to refer to the increasing complexity of social organization.

15. Social economist Thorstein Veblen coined the term _____ _____ to refer to those people or groups who will suffer in the event of social change.

16. The term _____ refers to those who are wary of technological innovations, and who question the incessant expansion of industrialization, the increasing destruction of the natural and agrarian world, and the "throw-it-away" mentality of contemporary capitalism.

17. In 2001, one month after the terrorist attacks of September 11, Congress passed the _____ Act, which relaxed existing legal checks on surveillance by law enforcement officers. Federal agencies are now free to gather data electronically, including credit card receipts and banking records.

18. The _____ is the world's largest computer network.

19. In developing countries, _____ _____ are a less expensive way of furthering agriculture than biotechnology.

20. The _____ perspective would stress the danger that the most powerful groups in a society will use technology to violate the privacy of the less powerful.

glossary

a

Absolute poverty A minimum level of subsistence that no family should be expected to live below.

Achieved status A social position that a person attains largely through his or her own efforts.

Activity theory An interactionist theory of aging that suggests that those elderly people who remain active and socially involved will be best adjusted.

Adoption In a legal sense, the transfer of the legal rights, responsibilities, and privileges of parenthood to a new legal parent or parents.

Affirmative action Positive efforts to recruit minority group members or women for jobs, promotions, and educational opportunities.

Ageism Prejudice and discrimination based on a person's age.

Agrarian society The most technologically advanced form of preindustrial society. Members engage primarily in the production of food, but increase their crop yields through technological innovations such as the plow.

Alienation A condition of estrangement or dissociation from the surrounding society.

Amalgamation The process through which a majority group and a minority group combine to form a new group.

Anomie Durkheim's term for the loss of direction felt in a society when social control of individual behavior has become ineffective.

Anomie theory of deviance Robert Merton's theory of deviance as an adaptation of socially prescribed goals or of the means governing their attainment, or both.

Anti-Semitism Anti-Jewish prejudice.

Anticipatory socialization Processes of socialization in which a person rehearses for future positions, occupations, and social relationships.

Apartheid A former policy of the South African government, designed to maintain the separation of Blacks and other non-Whites from the dominant Whites.

Applied sociology The use of the discipline of sociology with the specific intent of yielding practical applications for human behavior and organizations.

Argot Specialized language used by members of a group or subculture.

Ascribed status A social position assigned to a person by society without regard for the person's unique talents or characteristics.

Assembling perspective A theory of collective behavior introduce by McPhail and Miller that seeks to examine how and why people move from different points in space to a common location.

Assimilation The process through which a person forsakes his or her cultural tradition to become part of a different culture.

Asylees Foreigners who have already entered a host country and now seek protection because of persecution or a well-founded fear of persecution.

Authority Institutionalized power that is recognized by the people over whom it is exercised.

b

Basic sociology Sociological inquiry conducted with the objective of gaining a more profound knowledge of the fundamental aspects of social phenomena. Also known as *pure sociology*.

Big data The rapid collection and analysis of enormous amounts of information by supercomputers.

Bilateral descent A kinship system in which both sides of a person's family are regarded as equally important.

Bilingualism The use of two languages in a particular setting, such as the workplace or schoolroom, treating each language as equally legitimate.

Birthrate The number of live births per 1,000 population in a given year. Also known as the *crude birthrate*.

Black power A political philosophy, promoted by many younger Blacks in the 1960s, that supported the creation of Black-controlled political and economic institutions.

Bourgeoisie Karl Marx's term for the capitalist class, comprising the owners of the means of production.

Brain drain The immigration to the United States and other industrialized nations of skilled workers, professionals, and technicians who are desperately needed in their home countries.

Brass ceiling An invisible barrier that blocks the promotion of a woman in the military because of her official (not necessarily actual) exclusion from combat.

Bureaucracy A component of formal organization that uses rules and hierarchical ranking to achieve efficiency.

Bureaucratization The process by which a group, organization, or social movement becomes increasingly bureaucratic.

c

Capitalism An economic system in which the means of production are held largely in private hands and the main incentive for economic activity is the accumulation of profits.

Caste A hereditary rank, usually religiously dictated, that tends to be fixed and immobile.

Causal logic The relationship between a condition or variable and a particular consequence, with one leading to the other.

Census An enumeration, or counting, of a population.

Charismatic authority Max Weber's term for power made legitimate by a leader's exceptional personal or emotional appeal to his or her followers.

Charter school An experimental school that is developed and managed by individuals, groups of parents, or educational management organizations.

Class A group of people who have a similar level of wealth and income.

Class consciousness In Karl Marx's view, a subjective awareness held by members of a class regarding their common vested interests and the need for collective political action to bring about social change.

Class system A social ranking based primarily on economic position in which achieved characteristics can influence social mobility.

Classical theory An approach to the study of formal organizations that views workers as being motivated almost entirely by economic rewards.

Climate change An observable alteration of the global atmosphere that affects natural weather patterns over several decades or longer.

Clinical sociology The use of the discipline of sociology with the specific intent of altering social relationships or restructuring social institutions.

Closed system A social system in which there is little or no possibility of individual social mobility.

Coalition A temporary or permanent alliance geared toward a common goal.

Code of ethics The standards of acceptable behavior developed by and for members of a profession.

Cognitive theory of development Jean Piaget's theory that children's thought progresses through four stages of development.

Cohabitation The practice of living together as a male–female couple without marrying.

Collective behavior In the view of sociologist Neil Smelser, the relatively spontaneous and unstructured behavior or a group of people who are reacting to a common influence in an ambiguous situation.

Colonialism The maintenance of political, social, economic, and cultural domination over a people by a foreign power for an extended period.

Color-blind racism The use of the principle of race neutrality to defend a racially unequal status quo.

Communism An economic system under which all property is communally owned and no social distinctions are made on the basis of people's ability to produce.

Community A spatial or political unit of social organization that gives people a sense of belonging, based either on shared residence in a particular place or on a common identity

Computer-mediated communication Communicative interaction through two or more networked devices, such as a computer or cell phone. The term applies to a variety of text-based or video interactions, including e-mails, chat rooms, and text messages, some of which may be supported by social media.

Concentric-zone theory A theory of urban growth devised by Ernest Burgess that sees growth in terms of a series of rings radiating from the central business district.

Conflict perspective A sociological approach that assumes that social behavior is best understood in terms of tension between groups over power or the allocation of resources, including housing, money, access to services, and political representation.

Conformity Going along with peers—individuals of our own status who have no special right to direct our behavior.

Conspicuous consumption Purchasing goods not to survive but to flaunt one's superior wealth and social standing.

Contact hypothesis An interactionist perspective which states that in cooperative circumstances, interracial contact between people of equal status will reduce prejudice.

Content analysis The systematic coding and objective recording of data, guided by some rationale.

Control group The subjects in an experiment who are not introduced to the independent variable by the researcher.

Control theory A view of conformity and deviance that suggests that our connection to members of society leads us to systematically conform to society's norms.

Control variable A factor that is held constant to test the relative impact of an independent variable.

Corporate welfare Tax breaks, bailouts, direct payments, and grants that the government gives to corporations.

Correlation A relationship between two variables in which a change in one coincides with a change in the other.

Correspondence principle A term used by Bowles and Gintis to refer to the tendency of schools to promote the values expected of individuals in each social class and to perpetuate social class divisions from one generation to the next.

Counterculture A subculture that deliberately opposes certain aspects of the larger culture.

Craze An exciting mass involvement that lasts for a relatively long period.

Creationism A literal interpretation of the Bible regarding the creation of humanity and the universe, used to argue that evolution should not be presented as established scientific fact.

Credentialism An increase in the lowest level of education needed to enter a field.

Crime A violation of criminal law for which some governmental authority applies formal penalties.

Cross-tabulation A table or matrix that shows the relationship between two or more variables.

Crowd A temporary gathering of people in close proximity who share a common focus or interest.

Cultural capital Noneconomic goods, such as family background and education, which are reflected in a knowledge of language and the arts.

Cultural convergence The flow of content across multiple media, and the accompanying migration of media audiences.

Cultural relativism The viewing of people's behavior from the perspective of their own culture.

Cultural transmission A school of criminology that argues that criminal behavior is learned through social interactions.

Cultural universal A common practice or belief found in every culture.

Culture The totality of learned, socially transmitted customs, knowledge, material objects, and behavior.

Culture industry The worldwide media industry that standardizes the goods and services demanded by consumers.

Culture lag A period of maladjustment when the nonmaterial culture is still struggling to adapt to new material conditions.

Culture shock The feeling of surprise and disorientation that people experience when they encounter cultural practices that are different from their own.

Culture war The polarization of society over controversial cultural elements.

Curanderismo Latino folk medicine, a form of holistic health care and healing.

Cybercrime Illegal activity primarily conducted through the use of computer hardware or software.

d

Death rate The number of deaths per 1,000 population in a given year. Also known as the *crude death rate*.

Degradation ceremony An aspect of the socialization process within some total institutions, in which people are subjected to humiliating rituals.

Deindustrialization The systematic, widespread withdrawal of investment in basic aspects of productivity, such as factories and plants.

Democracy In a literal sense, government by the people.

Demographic transition A term used to describe the change from high birthrates and death rates to low birthrates and death rates.

Demography The scientific study of population.

Denomination A large, organized religion that is not officially linked to the state or government.

Dependency theory An approach that contends that industrialized nations continue to exploit developing countries for their own gain.

Dependent variable The variable in a causal relationship that is subject to the influence of another variable.

Deviance Behavior that violates the standards of conduct or expectations of a group or society.

Dictatorship A government in which one person has nearly total power to make and enforce laws.

Differential association A theory of deviance proposed by Edwin Sutherland that holds that violation of rules results from exposure to attitudes favorable to criminal acts.

Differential justice Differences in the way social control is exercised over different groups.

Diffusion The process by which a cultural item spreads from group to group or society to society.

Digital divide The relative lack of access to the latest technologies among low-income groups, racial and ethnic minorities, rural residents, and the citizens of developing countries.

Disaster A sudden or disruptive event or set of events that overtaxes a community's resources, so that outside aid is necessary.

Discovery The process of making known or sharing the existence of an aspect of reality.

Discrimination The denial of opportunities and equal rights to individuals and groups because of prejudice or other arbitrary reasons.

Disengagement theory A functionalist theory of aging that suggests that society and the aging individual mutually sever many of their relationships.

Dominant ideology A set of cultural beliefs and practices that helps to maintain powerful social, economic, and political interests.

Double consciousness The division of an individual's identity into two or more social realities.

Downsizing Reductions taken in a company's workforce as part of deindustrialization.

Dramaturgical approach A view of social interaction, popularized by Erving Goffman, in which people are seen as theatrical performers.

Dysfunction An element or process of a society that may disrupt the social system or reduce its stability.

e

Ecclesia A religious organization that claims to include most or all members of a society and is recognized as the national or official religion.

Ecological modernization The alignment of environmentally favorable practices with economic self-interest through constant adaptation and restructuring.

Economic system The social institution through which goods and services are produced, distributed, and consumed.

Education A formal process of learning in which some people consciously teach, while others adopt the social role of learner.

Egalitarian family An authority pattern in which spouses are regarded as equals.

Elite model A view of society as being ruled by a small group of individuals who share a common set of political and economic interests.

Emergent-norm perspective A theory of collective behavior proposed by Turner and Killian that holds that a collective definition of appropriate or inappropriate behavior emerges during episodes of collective behavior.

Endogamy The restriction of mate selection to people within the same group.

Environmental justice A legal strategy based on claims that racial minorities are subjected disproportionately to environmental hazards.

Environmental refugee A person who has been displaced by rising seas, destructive storms, expanding deserts, water shortages, or high levels of toxic pollutants.

Equilibrium model Talcott Parsons's functionalist view that society tends toward a state of stability or balance.

Established sect J. Milton Yinger's term for a religious group that is the outgrowth of a sect, yet remains isolated from society.

Estate system A system of stratification under which peasants were required to work land leased to them by nobles in exchange for military protection and other services. Also known as *feudalism*.

Esteem The reputation that a specific person has earned within an occupation.

Ethnic group A group that is set apart from others primarily because of its national origin or distinctive cultural patterns.

Ethnocentrism The tendency to assume that one's own culture and way of life represent the norm or are superior to all others.

Ethnography The study of an entire social setting through extended systematic fieldwork.

Euthanasia The act of bringing about the death of a hopelessly ill and suffering person in a relatively quick and painless way for reasons of mercy.

Evolutionary theory A theory of social change that holds that society is moving in a definite direction.

Exogamy The requirement that people select a mate outside certain groups.

Experiment An artificially created situation that allows a researcher to manipulate variables.

Experimental group The subjects in an experiment who are exposed to an independent variable introduced by a researcher.

Exploitation theory A Marxist theory that views racial subordination in the United States as a manifestation of the class system inherent in capitalism.

Expressiveness Concern for the maintenance of harmony and the internal emotional affairs of the family.

Extended family A family in which relatives—such as grandparents, aunts, or uncles—live in the same home as parents and their children.

f

Face-work A term used by Erving Goffman to refer to the efforts people make to maintain the proper image and avoid public embarrassment.

Fad A temporary pattern of behavior that involves large numbers of people and is independent of preceding trends.

False consciousness A term used by Karl Marx to describe an attitude held by members of a class that does not accurately reflect their objective position.

Familism (*Familismo*) Pride in the extended family, expressed through the maintenance of close ties and strong obligations to kinfolk outside the immediate family.

Family A set of people related by blood, marriage or some other agreed-on relationship, or adoption, who share the primary responsibility for reproduction and caring for members of society.

Fashion A pleasurable mass involvement that features a certain amount of acceptance by society and has a line of historical continuity.

Feminism An ideology that favors equal rights for women.

Feminist perspective A sociological approach that views inequity in gender as central to all behavior and organization.

Feminization of poverty A trend in which women constitute an increasing proportion of the poor people of both the United States and the world.

Fertility The level of reproduction in a society.

Flash mob A group of people organized by social media to assemble suddenly in a public space, perform some collective activity, and then quickly disperse.

Flexibility stigma The devaluation of workers who seek or who are presumed to need flexible work arrangements.

Folkway A norm governing everyday behavior whose violation raises comparatively little concern.

Force The actual or threatened use of coercion to impose one's will on others.

Formal norm A norm that has been written down and that specifies strict punishments for violators.

Formal organization A group designed for a special purpose and structured for maximum efficiency.

Formal social control Social control that is carried out by authorized agents, such as police officers, judges, school administrators, and employers.

Functionalist perspective A sociological approach that emphasizes the way in which the parts of a society are structured to maintain its stability.

Fundamentalism An emphasis on doctrinal conformity and the literal interpretation of sacred texts.

g

Gatekeeping The process by which a relatively small number of people in the media industry control what material eventually reaches the audience.

Gemeinschaft A term used by Ferdinand Tönnies to describe a close-knit community, often found in rural areas, in which strong personal bonds unite members.

Gender identity How people see themselves, as male or female, or something else.

Gender role Expectations regarding the proper behavior, attitudes, and activities of males and females.

Generalized other A term used by George Herbert Mead to refer to the attitudes, viewpoints, and expectations of society as a whole that a child takes into account in his or her behavior.

Genocide The deliberate, systematic killing of an entire people or nation.

Gentrification The resettlement of low-income city neighborhoods by prosperous families and business firms.

Gerontology The scientific study of the sociological and psychological aspects of aging and the problems of the aged.

Gesellschaft A term used by Ferdinand Tönnies to describe a community, often urban, that is large and impersonal, with little commitment to the group or consensus on values.

Glass ceiling An invisible barrier that blocks the promotion of a qualified individual in a work environment because of the individual's gender, race, or ethnicity.

Glass escalator The advantage men experience in occupations dominated by women.

Global sociology A level of sociological analysis that makes comparisons between entire nations, using entire societies as units of analysis.

Global warming A significant rise in the earth's surface temperatures that occurs when industrial gases like carbon dioxide turn the planet's atmosphere into a virtual greenhouse.

Globalization The worldwide integration of government policies, cultures, social movements, and financial markets through trade and the exchange of ideas.

Goal displacement Overzealous conformity to official regulations of a bureaucracy.

Group Any number of people with similar norms, values, and expectations who interact with one another on a regular basis.

Growth rate The difference between births and deaths, plus the difference between immigrants and emigrants, per 1,000 population.

h

Hate crime A criminal offense committed because of the offender's bias against a race, religion, ethnic group, national origin, or sexual orientation. Also referred to as *bias crime.*

Hawthorne effect The unintended influence that observers of experiments can have on their subjects.

Health As defined by the World Health Organization, a state of complete physical, mental, and social well-being, and not merely the absence of disease and infirmity.

Hidden curriculum Standards of behavior that are deemed proper by society and are taught subtly in schools.

Holistic medicine Therapies in which the health care practitioner considers the person's physical, mental, emotional, and spiritual characteristics.

Homogamy The conscious or unconscious tendency to select a mate with personal characteristics similar to one's own.

Homophobia Fear of and prejudice against homosexuality.

Horizontal mobility The movement of an individual from one social position to another of the same rank.

Horticultural society A preindustrial society in which people plant seeds and crops rather than merely subsist on available foods.

Human ecology An area of study that is concerned with the interrelationships between people and their environment.

Human relations approach An approach to the study of formal organizations that emphasizes the role of people, communication, and participation in a bureaucracy and tends to focus on the informal structure of the organization.

Hunting-and-gathering society A preindustrial society in which people rely on whatever foods and fibers are readily available in order to survive.

Hyper-local media Reporting that is highly local and typically Internet-based.

Hyperconsumerism The practice of buying more than we need or want, and often more than we can afford; a preoccupation of postmodern consumers.

Hypothesis A speculative statement about the relationship between two or more variables.

i

Ideal type A construct or model for evaluating specific cases.

Impression management A term used by Erving Goffman to refer to the altering of the presentation of the self in order to create distinctive appearances and satisfy particular audiences.

In-group Any group or category to which people feel they belong.

Incest taboo The prohibition of sexual relationships between certain culturally specified relatives.

Income Refers to salaries and wages, interest on savings, stock dividends, and rental income.

Independent variable The variable in a causal relationship that causes or influences a change in another variable.

Index crimes The eight types of crime tabulated each year by the FBI in the *Uniform Crime Reports:* murder, rape, robbery, assault, burglary, theft, motor vehicle theft, and arson.

Industrial city A relatively large city characterized by open competition, an open class system, and elaborate specialization in the manufacturing of goods.

Industrial society A society that depends on mechanization to produce its goods and services.

Infant mortality rate The number of deaths of infants under 1 year old per 1,000 live births in a given year.

Influence The exercise of power through a process of persuasion.

Informal economy Transfers of money, goods, or services that are not reported to the government.

Informal norm A norm that is generally understood but not precisely recorded.

Informal social control Social control that is carried out casually by ordinary people through such means as laughter, smiles, and ridicule.

Innovation The process of introducing a new idea or object to a culture through discovery or invention.

Institutional discrimination The denial of opportunities and equal rights to individuals and groups that results from the normal operations of a society.

Instrumentality An emphasis on tasks, a focus on more distant goals, and a concern for the external relationship between one's family and other social institutions.

Intelligent design (ID) The idea that life is so complex that it could only have been created by intelligent design.

Interactionist perspective A sociological approach that generalizes about everyday forms of social interaction in order to explain society as a whole.

Intergenerational mobility Changes in the social position of children relative to their parents.

Interview A face-to-face, phone, or online questioning of a respondent to obtain desired information.

Intragenerational mobility Changes in social position within a person's adult life.

Invention The combination of existing cultural items into a form that did not exist before.

Iron law of oligarchy A principle of organizational life developed by Robert Michels, under which even a democratic organization will eventually develop into a bureaucracy ruled by a few individuals.

k

Kinship The state of being related to others.

l

Labeling theory An approach to deviance that attempts to explain why certain people are viewed as deviants while others engaged in the same behavior are not.

Labor union Organized workers who share either the same skill or the same employer.

Laissez-faire A form of capitalism under which people compete freely, with minimal government intervention in the economy.

Language An abstract system of word meanings and symbols for all aspects of culture; includes gestures and other nonverbal communication.

Latent function An unconscious or unintended function that may reflect hidden purposes.

Law Governmental social control.

Liberation theology Use of a church, primarily Roman Catholic, in a political effort to eliminate poverty, discrimination, and other forms of injustice from a secular society.

Life chances Max Weber's term for the opportunities people have to provide themselves with material goods, positive living conditions, and favorable life experiences.

Life course approach A research orientation in which sociologists and other social scientists look closely at the social factors that influence people throughout their lives, from birth to death.

Life expectancy The median number of years a person can be expected to live under current mortality conditions.

Looking-glass self A concept used by Charles Horton Cooley that emphasizes the self as the product of our social interactions.

Luddites Rebellious craft workers in 19th-century England who destroyed new factory machinery as part of their resistance to the Industrial Revolution.

m

Machismo A sense of virility, personal worth, and pride in one's maleness.

Macrosociology Sociological investigation that concentrates on large-scale phenomena or entire civilizations.

Manifest function An open, stated, and conscious function.

Mass media Print and electronic means of communication that carry messages to widespread audiences.

Master status A status that dominates others and thereby determines a person's general position in society.

Material culture The physical or technological aspects of our daily lives.

Matriarchy A society in which women dominate in family decision making.

Matrilineal descent A kinship system in which only the mother's relatives are significant.

Matrix of domination The cumulative impact of oppression because of race and ethnicity, gender, and social class, as well as religion, sexual orientation, disability, age, and citizenship status.

McDonaldization The process by which the principles of bureaucratization have increasingly shaped organizations worldwide.

Mean A number calculated by adding a series of values and then dividing by the number of values.

Mechanical solidarity A collective consciousness that emphasizes group solidarity, characteristic of societies with minimal division of labor.

Median The midpoint or number that divides a series of values into two groups of equal numbers of values.

Medical model An approach in which medical experts define illness or disease, determine and control the course of treatment, and even affect patients' views of themselves.

Mental illness A disorder of the brain that disrupts a person's thinking, feeling, and ability to interact with others.

Mesosociology An intermediate level of sociological analysis that focuses on formal organizations and social movements.

Microfinancing Lending small sums of money to the poor so they can work their way out of poverty.

Microsociology Sociological investigation that stresses the study of small groups, often through experimental means.

Midlife crisis A stressful period of self-evaluation that begins at about age 40.

Migration The relatively permanent movement of people, with the purpose of changing their place of residence.

Minority group A subordinate group whose members have significantly less control or power over their own lives than the members of a dominant or majority group have over theirs.

Mode The single most common value in a series of scores.

Model, or ideal, minority A subordinate group whose members supposedly have succeeded economically, socially, and educationally despite past prejudice and discrimination, and without resorting to political and violent confrontations with Whites.

Modernization The far-reaching process through which periphery nations move from traditional or less developed institutions to those characteristic of more developed societies.

Modernization theory A functionalist approach that proposes that modernization and development will gradually improve the lives of people in developing nations.

Monarchy A form of government headed by a single member of a royal family, usually a king, queen, or some other hereditary ruler.

Monogamy A form of marriage in which an individual has only one partner.

Monopoly Control of a market by a single business firm.

Morbidity rate The rate of disease in a given population.

Mores Norms deemed highly necessary to the welfare of a society.

Mortality rate The rate of death in a given population.

Multinational corporation A commercial organization that is headquartered in one country but does business throughout the world.

Multiple masculinities A variety of male gender roles, including nurturing-caring and effeminate-gay roles, that men may play along with their more pervasive traditional role of dominating women.

Multiple-nuclei theory A theory of urban growth developed by Harris and Ullman that views growth as emerging from many centers of development, each of which reflects a particular urban need or activity.

n

Narcotizing dysfunction The phenomenon in which the media provide such massive amounts of coverage that the audience becomes numb and fails to act on the information, regardless of how compelling the issue.

Natural science The study of the physical features of nature and the ways in which they interact and change.

Naturally occurring retirement community (NORC) An area that has gradually become an informal center for senior citizens.

Neocolonialism Continuing dependence of former colonies on foreign countries.

New religious movement (NRM) or cult A small, secretive religious group that represents either a new religion or a major innovation of an existing faith.

New social movement An organized collective activity that addresses values and social identities, as well as improvements in the quality of life.

New urban sociology An approach to urbanization that considers the interplay of local, national, and worldwide forces and their effect on local space, with special emphasis on the impact of global economic activity.

Nonmaterial culture Ways of using material objects, as well as customs, beliefs, philosophies, governments, and patterns of communication.

Nonverbal communication The sending of messages through the use of gestures, facial expressions, and postures.

Norm An established standard of behavior maintained by a society.

Nuclear family A married couple and their unmarried children living together.

o

Obedience Compliance with higher authorities in a hierarchical structure.

Objective method A technique for measuring social class that assigns individuals to classes on the basis of criteria such as occupation, education, income, and place of residence.

Observation A research technique in which an investigator collects information through direct participation, by closely watching a group or community.

Offshoring The transfer of work to foreign contractors.

Oligarchy A form of government in which a few individuals rule.

Open system A social system in which the position of each individual is influenced by his or her achieved status.

Operational definition An explanation of an abstract concept that is specific enough to allow a researcher to assess the concept.

Opinion leader Someone who influences the opinions and decisions of others through day-to-day personal contact and communication.

Organic solidarity A collective consciousness that rests on mutual interdependence, characteristic of societies with a complex division of labor.

Organized crime The work of a group that regulates relations between criminal enterprises involved in illegal activities, including prostitution, gambling, and the smuggling and sale of illegal drugs.

Out-group A group or category to which people feel they do not belong.

p

Panic A fearful arousal or collective flight based on a generalized belief that may or may not be accurate.

Patriarchy A society in which men dominate in family decision making.

Patrilineal descent A kinship system in which only the father's relatives are significant.

Peace The absence of war, or more broadly, a proactive effort to develop cooperative relations among nations.

Percentage A portion of 100.

Personality A person's typical patterns of attitudes, needs, characteristics, and behavior.

Peter principle A principle of organizational life, originated by Laurence J. Peter, according to which every employee within a hierarchy tends to rise to his or her level of incompetence.

Pluralism Mutual respect for one another's cultures among the various groups in a society, which allows minorities to express their cultures without experiencing prejudice.

Pluralist model A view of society in which many competing groups within the community have access to government, so that no single group is dominant.

Political system The social institution that is founded on a recognized set of procedures for implementing and achieving society's goals.

Politics In Harold Lasswell's words, "who gets what, when, and how."

Polyandry A form of polygamy in which a woman may have more than one husband at the same time.

Polygamy A form of marriage in which an individual may have several husbands or wives simultaneously.

Polygyny A form of polygamy in which a man may have more than one wife at the same time.

Population pyramid A special type of bar chart that shows the distribution of a population by gender and age.

Postindustrial city A city in which global finance and the electronic flow of information dominate the economy.

Postindustrial society A society whose economic system is engaged primarily in the processing and control of information.

Postmodern society A technologically sophisticated society that is preoccupied with consumer goods and media images.

Power The ability to exercise one's will over others.

Power elite A term used by C. Wright Mills to refer to a small group of military, industrial, and government leaders who control the fate of the United States.

Precarious work Employment that is poorly paid, and from the worker's perspective, insecure and unprotected.

Preindustrial city A city of only a few thousand people that is characterized by a relatively closed class system and limited mobility

Prejudice A negative attitude toward an entire category of people, often an ethnic or racial minority.

Prestige The respect and admiration that an occupation holds in a society.

Primary group A small group characterized by intimate, face-to-face association and cooperation.

Profane The ordinary and commonplace elements of life, as distinguished from the sacred.

Professional criminal A person who pursues crime as a day-to-day occupation, developing skilled techniques and enjoying a certain degree of status among other criminals.

Proletariat Karl Marx's term for the working class in a capitalist society.

Protestant ethic Max Weber's term for the disciplined work ethic, this-worldly concerns, and rational orientation to life emphasized by John Calvin and his followers.

Public A dispersed group of people, not necessarily in contact with one another, who share an interest in an issue.

q

Qualitative research Research that relies on what is seen in field or naturalistic settings more than on statistical data.

Quantitative research Research that collects and reports data primarily in numerical form.

Quasi-religion A scholarly category that includes organizations that may see themselves as religious but may be seen by others as "sort of religious."

Queer theory The study of society from the perspective of a broad spectrum of sexual identities, including heterosexuality, homosexuality, and bisexuality.

Questionnaire A printed or written form used to obtain information from a respondent.

r

Racial formation A sociohistorical process in which racial categories are created, inhabited, transformed, and destroyed.

Racial group A group that is set apart from others because of physical differences that have taken on social significance.

Racial profiling Any arbitrary action initiated by an authority based on race, ethnicity, or national origin rather than on a person's behavior.

Racism The belief that one race is supreme and all others are innately inferior.

Random sample A sample for which every member of an entire population has the same chance of being selected.

Rational-legal authority Power made legitimate by law.

Redlining The pattern of discrimination against people trying to buy homes in minority and racially changing neighborhoods.

Reference group Any group that individuals use as a standard for evaluating themselves and their own behavior.

Refugees People living outside their country of citizenship for fear of political or religious persecution.

Relative deprivation The conscious feeling of a negative discrepancy between legitimate expectations and present actualities.

Relative poverty A floating standard of deprivation by which people at the bottom of a society, whatever their lifestyles, are judged to be disadvantaged *in comparison with the nation as a whole.*

Reliability The extent to which a measure produces consistent results.

Religion According to Émile Durkheim, a unified system of beliefs and practices relative to sacred things.

Religious belief A statement to which members of a particular religion adhere.

Religious experience The feeling or perception of being in direct contact with the ultimate reality, such as a divine being, or of being overcome with religious emotion.

Religious ritual A practice required or expected of members of a faith.

Remittances The monies that immigrants return to their families of origin.

Representative democracy A form of government in which certain individuals are selected to speak for the people.

Research design A detailed plan or method for obtaining data scientifically.

Resocialization The process of discarding former behavior patterns and accepting new ones as part of a transition in one's life.

Resource mobilization The ways in which a social movement utilizes such resources as money, political influence, access to the media, and personnel.

Rite of passage A ritual marking the symbolic transition from one social position to another.

Role conflict The situation that occurs when incompatible expectations arise from two or more social positions held by the same person.

Role exit The process of disengagement from a role that is central to one's self-identity in order to establish a new role and identity.

Role strain The difficulty that arises when the same social position imposes conflicting demands and expectations.

Role taking The process of mentally assuming the perspective of another and responding from that imagined viewpoint.

Rumor A piece of information gathered informally that is used to interpret an ambiguous situation.

S

Sacred Elements beyond everyday life that inspire awe, respect, and even fear.

Sample A selection from a larger population that is statistically representative of that population.

Sanction A penalty or reward for conduct concerning a social norm.

Sandwich generation The generation of adults who simultaneously try to meet the competing needs of their parents and their children.

Sapir-Whorf hypothesis A hypothesis concerning the role of language in shaping our interpretation of reality. It holds that language is culturally determined.

Science The body of knowledge obtained by methods based on systematic observation.

Scientific management approach Another name for the classical theory of formal organizations.

Scientific method A systematic, organized series of steps that ensures maximum objectivity and consistency in researching a problem.

Second shift The double burden—work outside the home followed by child care and housework—that many women face and few men share equitably.

Secondary analysis A variety of research techniques that make use of previously collected and publicly accessible information and data.

Secondary group A formal, impersonal group in which there is little social intimacy or mutual understanding.

Sect A relatively small religious group that has broken away from some other religious organization to renew what it considers the original vision of the faith.

Secularization The process through which religion's influence on other social institutions diminishes.

Segregation The physical separation of two groups of people in terms of residence, workplace, and social events; often imposed on a minority group by a dominant group.

Self According to George Herbert Mead, a distinct identity that sets us apart from others.

Serial monogamy A form of marriage in which a person may have several spouses in his or her lifetime, but only one spouse at a time.

Sexism The ideology that one sex is superior to the other.

Sexual identity The self-awareness of being romantically or sexually attracted to a defined group of people. Also referred to as *sexual orientation*.

Sharing economy Connecting owners of underused assets with others willing to pay to use them.

Sick role Societal expectations about the attitudes and behavior of a person viewed as being ill.

Significant other A term used by George Herbert Mead to refer to an individual who is most important in the development of the self, such as a parent, friend, or teacher.

Single-parent family A family in which only one parent is present to care for the children.

Slavery A system of enforced servitude in which some people are owned by other people.

Social capital The collective benefit of social networks, which are built on reciprocal trust.

Social change Significant alteration over time in behavior patterns and culture, including norms and values.

Social constructionist perspective An approach to deviance that emphasizes the role of culture in the creation of the deviant identity.

Social control The techniques and strategies for preventing deviant human behavior in any society.

Social disorganization theory The theory that crime and deviance are caused by the absence or breakdown of communal relationships and social institutions.

Social epidemiology The study of the distribution of disease, impairment, and general health status across a population.

Social inequality A condition in which members of society have differing amounts of wealth, prestige, or power.

Social institution An organized pattern of beliefs and behavior centered on basic social needs.

Social interaction The ways in which people respond to one another.

Social mobility Movement of individuals or groups from one position in a society's stratification system to another.

Social movement An organized collective activity to bring about or resist fundamental change in an existing group or society.

Social network A series of social relationships that links a person directly to others, and through them indirectly to still more people.

Social role A set of expectations for people who occupy a given social position or status.

Social science The study of the social features of humans and the ways in which they interact and change.

Social structure The way in which a society is organized into predictable relationships.

Socialism An economic system under which the means of production and distribution are collectively owned.

Socialization The lifelong process in which people learn the attitudes, values, and behaviors appropriate for members of a particular culture.

Societal-reaction approach Another name for *labeling theory*.

Society A fairly large number of people who live in the same territory, are relatively independent of people outside their area, and participate in a common culture.

Sociobiology The systematic study of how biology affects human social behavior.

Sociocultural evolution Long-term social trends resulting from the interplay of continuity, innovation, and selection.

Socioeconomic status (SES) A measure of social class that is based on income, education, and occupation.

Sociological imagination An awareness of the relationship between an individual and the wider society, both today and in the past.

Sociology The scientific study of social behavior and human groups.

Sovereignty movement The effort by the indigenous people of Hawai'i to win self-government, as well as the restoration of—or compensation for—their ancestral lands.

Squatter settlement An area occupied by the very poor on the fringe of a city, in which housing is constructed by the settlers themselves from discarded material.

Status A term used by sociologists to refer to any of the full range of socially defined positions within a large group or society.

Status group A term used by Max Weber to refer to people who have the same prestige or lifestyle, independent of their class positions.

Stereotype An unreliable generalization about all members of a group that does not recognize individual differences within the group.

Stigma A label used to devalue members of certain social groups.

Stratification A structured ranking of entire groups of people that perpetuates unequal economic rewards and power in a society.

Subculture A segment of society that shares a distinctive pattern of customs, rules, and traditions that differs from the pattern of the larger society.

Suburb According to the Census Bureau, any territory within a metropolitan area that is not included in the central city.

Survey A study, generally in the form of an interview or questionnaire, that provides researchers with information about how people think and act.

Symbol A gesture, object, or word that forms the basis of human communication.

Symbolic ethnicity An ethnic identity that emphasizes concerns such as ethnic food or political issues rather than deeper ties to one's ethnic heritage.

t

Teacher-expectancy effect The impact that a teacher's expectations about a student's performance may have on the student's actual achievements.

Technology Cultural information about the ways in which the material resources of the environment may be used to satisfy human needs and desires.

Terrorism The use or threat of violence against random or symbolic targets in pursuit of political aims.

Theory In sociology, a set of statements that seeks to explain problems, actions, or behavior.

Total fertility rate (TFR) The average number of children born alive to any woman, assuming that she conforms to current fertility rates.

Total institution A term coined by Erving Goffman to refer to an institution that regulates all aspects of a person's life under a single authority, such as a prison, the military, a mental hospital, or a convent.

Totalitarianism Virtually complete government control and surveillance over all aspects of a society's social and political life.

Tracking The practice of placing students in specific curriculum groups on the basis of their test scores and other criteria.

Traditional authority Legitimate power conferred by custom and accepted practice.

Trained incapacity The tendency of workers in a bureaucracy to become so specialized that they develop blind spots and fail to notice obvious problems.

Transnational An immigrant who sustains multiple social relationships that link his or her society of origin with the society of settlement.

Transnational crime Crime that occurs across multiple national borders.

Transracial adoption The adoption of a non-White child by White parents or a Hispanic child by non-Hispanics.

u

Underclass The long-term poor who lack training and skills.

Urban ecology An area of study that focuses on the interrelationships between people and their environment in urban areas.

v

Validity The degree to which a measure or scale truly reflects the phenomenon under study.

Value

Value A collective conception of what is considered good, desirable, and proper—or bad, undesirable, and improper—in a culture.

Value-added model A theory of collective behavior proposed by Neil Smelser to explain how broad social conditions are transformed in a definite pattern into some form of collective behavior.

Value neutrality Max Weber's term for objectivity of sociologists in the interpretation of data.

Variable A measurable trait or characteristic that is subject to change under different conditions.

Verstehen The German word for "understanding" or "insight"; used by Max Weber to stress the need for sociologists to take into account the subjective meanings people attach to their actions.

Vertical mobility The movement of an individual from one social position to another of a different rank.

Vested interests Veblen's term for those people or groups who will suffer in the event of social change, and who have a stake in maintaining the status quo.

Victimization survey A questionnaire or interview given to a sample of the population to determine whether people have been victims of crime.

Victimless crime A term used by sociologists to describe the willing exchange among adults of widely desired but illegal goods and services.

Visual sociology The use of photographs, film, and video to study society.

Vital statistics Records of births, deaths, marriages, and divorces gathered through a registration system maintained by governmental units.

W

War Conflict between organizations that possess trained combat forces equipped with deadly weapons.

Wealth An inclusive term encompassing all a person's material assets, including land, stocks, and other types of property.

White privilege Rights or immunities granted to people as a particular benefit or favor simply because they are White.

White-collar crime Illegal acts committed by affluent, "respectable" individuals in the course of business activities.

World systems analysis The global economy as an interdependent system of economically and politically unequal nations.

Z

Zero population growth (ZPG) The state of a population in which the number of births plus immigrants equals the number of deaths plus emigrants.

references

a

AARP. 2008. *Poverty and Aging in America: Profiles of Low-Income in the Older Population.* Washington DC: AARP.

Abercrombie, Nicholas, Bryan S. Turner, and Stephen Hill, eds. 1990. *Dominant Ideologies.* Cambridge, MA: Unwin Hyman.

———, Stephen Hill and Bryan S. Turner. 1980. *The Dominant Ideology Thesis.* London: Allen and Unwin.

Aberle, David F., A. K. Cohen, A. K. Davis, M. J. Leng, Jr., and F. N. Sutton. 1950. "The Functional Prerequisites of a Society." *Ethics* 60 (January):100–111.

Abolition Now. 2016. "About Us." Accessed February 22 at www.abolitionnow.com.

Ackerman, Elliot. 2015. "The Real Barrier for Women Marines." *New York Times,* July 18, p. A19.

ACLU. 2015. "Frank v. Walker: Fighting Voter Suppression in Wisconsin." March 26. Accessed March 1, 2016 at www.aclu.org/voting-rights/ frank-v-walker-fighting-voter-suppression- wisconsin.

———. 2015a. "Fighting Voter Suppression." Accessed November 12 at www.aclu.org.

———. 2015b. "NSA Surveillance." Accessible at www.aclu.org.

———. 2016. "Fighting Voter Suppression." Accessible at www.aclu.org.

Acosta, R. Vivian, and Linda Jean Carpenter. 2001. "Women in Intercollegiate Sport: A Longitudinal Study: 1977–1998." Pp. 302–308 in *Sport in Contemporary Society: An Anthology,* 6th ed., edited by D. Stanley Eitzen. New York: Worth.

Adams, Charles Joseph. 2015. "Classification of Religions." *Britannica Online.* 2015. May 1. Accessible at www.britannica.com.

Adams, Tyrene L., and Stephen A. Smith. 2008. *Electronic Tribes: The Virtual Worlds of Geeks, Gamas, Shamans, and Scammers.* Austin: University of Texas Press.

Addams, Jane. 1910. *Twenty Years at Hull-House.* New York: Macmillan.

———. 1930. *The Second Twenty Years at Hull-House.* New York: Macmillan.

Addati, Laura, Naomi Cassirer, and Katherine Gilchrist. 2014. *Maternity and Paternity at Work, Law and Practice Across the World.* Geneva: International Labour Office. Accessible at www.ilb.org.

Adler, Patricia A., and Peter Adler. 2007. "The Demedicalization of Self-Injury: From Psychopathology to Sociological Deviance." *Journal of Contemporary Ethnography* 36 (October):537–570.

———. 2011. *The Tender Cut: Inside the Hidden World of Self-Injury.* New York: New York University Press.

———, and John M. Johnson. 1992. "Street Corner Society Revisited."*Journal of Contemporary Ethnography* 21 (April):3–10.

Adorno, Theodor. [1971] 1991. *The Culture Industry.* London: Routledge.

African Women's Development Fund. 2015. Call for Proposals: 16 Days of Activism Against Gender Based Violence Grant (2015). August 7. Accessed December 2 at www.awdf.org.

Agence France-Presse. 2013. "World Watches American TV, Not Always Legally." September 21. Accessed November 23, 2013 at http://www. rawstory.com/rs/2013/09/21/world-watches- american-tv-not-always- legally/.

Alarcón, Arthur L., Paula M. Mitchell, Laurie L. Levenson, and James P. Gray. 2011. "Death Penalty Reform." *Loyola of Los Angeles Review* 44 (Special Issue).

Alba, Richard D. 1990. *Ethnic Identity: The Transformation of White America.* New Haven, CT: Yale University Press.

Albas, Cheryl, and Daniel Albas. 1996. "An Invitation to the Ethnographic Study of University Examination Behavior: Concepts, Methodology and Implications." *Canadian Journal of Higher Education* 26 (3):1–26.

Albas, Daniel, and Cheryl Albas. 1988. "Aces and Bombers: The Post-Exam Impression Management Strategies of Students." *Symbolic Interaction* 11 (Fall):289–302.

Albrecht, Gary L. 2004. "Disability: Sociological Perspectives." Pp. 3710–3713 in *International Encyclopedia of the Social and Behavioral Sciences,* edited by Neil J. Smelser and Paul B. Baltes. New York: Elsevier.

Alcindor, Yamiche. 2012. "Homelessness made tougher in many cities." *USA Today* (June 11), p. 2A.

Alderman, Liz. 2012. "Starbucks on the Seine." *New York Times,* March 30, pp. B1, B8.

Alexander, Karl L. 1997. "Public Schools and the Public Good." *Social Forces* 70 (September):1–30.

Alford, Cassidy. 2015. "Why Is the World Less Peaceful?" *Christian Science Monitor* (October 12): 13.

Ali, Syed. 2010. "Permanent Impermanence." *Contexts* (Spring):26–31.

Allen, Bem P. 1978. *Social Behavior: Fact and Falsehood.* Chicago: Nelson-Hall.

Allen, Greg. 2012. "Mission Diversify: CIA Begins LGBT Recruiting." December 2. Accessible at www.wbur.org.

Allen, Samantha. 2015. "Marital Rape is Semi-legal in 8 States." June 9. *The Daily Beast.* Accessible at the dailybeast.com.

Allport, Gordon. W. 1979. *The Nature of Prejudice.* 25th anniversary edition. Reading, MA: Addison-Wesley.

Alvaredo, Facundo. 2011. "Inequality over the Past Century." *Finance & Development* 48 (3):29.

Alvarez, Lizette. 2015. "Puerto Ricans Seeking New Lives Put Stamp on Central Florida." *New York Times.* August 25, pp. A1, A14.

Alvord, Lori. 2009. "Dispatches from the Cutting Edge of Healing: Surgery and Spirit." July 3. Accessible at www.religiondispatches.com.

Alzheimer's Association. 2016. *2015 Alzheimer's Disease Facts and Figures.* Accessible at www. alz.org.

American Academy of Pediatrics. 2011. "Media Use by Children Younger Than 2 Years." *Pediatrics* 128 (November):1040–1045.

———. 2013. "Children, Adolescents, and the Media." *Pediatrics* 132 (November):958–959.

American Bar Association. 1997. *Section of the Individual Rights and Responsibilities: Section of Litigation (Capital Punishment).* Chicago: Division for Policy Administration, ABA.

American Community Survey. 2011. "American Community Survey 2010." Accessible at http:// www.census.gov/acs/www/.

———. 2013. *2009–2013 American Community Survey 5-Year Estimates.* Accessible at www. census.gov.

———. 2013b. "Survey Methodology Main." Accessible at www. census.gov/acs/www/methodology/ methodology_main/.

———. 2014. *2014 American Community Survey 1-Year Estimates.* Accessible at www.census.gov.

———. 2014a. "Selected Population Profile in the United States." *2011–2013 American Community Survey 3-Year Estimates.* Accessible at census. gov.

———. 2015. *2014 American Community Survey 1-Year Estimates.* October 27. Accessible at www.census.gov.

———. 2015b. "Selected Social Characteristics in the United States 2009–2013 American Community Survey 5-Year Estimates." Accessible at www.census.gov.

———. 2016. "2015 *American Community Survey 1-Year Estimates.* Accessible at www.census.gov.

American Jewish Committee. 2005. *2005 Annual Survey of American Jewish Opinion.* New York: AJC.

American Lung Association. 2011. "State of the Air 2011." Accessed March 26, 2012 (www. stateoftheair.org).

American Psychiatric Association. 2013. *Diagnostic and Statistical Manual of Mental Disorders,* Fifth Edition (DSM-5(TM)). Arlington VA: American Psychiatric Publishing.

American Psychological Association. 2008. "Being Gay Is Just as Healthy as Being Straight." Accessed February 25 (www.apa.org).

American Social and Economic Support. 2016. *Current Population Survey (CPS) 2015 Annual Social and Economic (ASEC) Supplement.* Accessible at census.gov.

American Society of Plastic Surgeons. 2016. "Plastic Surgery Procedural Statistics." February 15. Accessible at www.plasticsurgery.org.

American Sociological Association. 1999. *Code of Ethics.* Reprinted 2008. Washington DC: ASA.

———. 2005. "Need Today's Data Yesterday." Accessed December 17 (www.asanet.org.)

———. 2013. *21st Century Careers with an Undergraduate Degree in Sociology.* Washington, DC: ASA.

———. 2016. Current Sections. Accessed January 20, 2016 (www.asanet.org/sections/list.cfm).

American Soybean Association. 2011. "World Soybean Production 2009." Accessible at www.soystats.com.

Amnesty International. 2015. "Death Sentences and Executions 2014." February 11, 2016. Accessible at amnestyusa.org.

———. 2016. "Death Sentences and Executions 2014." March 31. Accessible at amnestyusa.org.

Amos, Deborah. 2014. "Iranian Women Make a Push for Greater Opportunities." March 5. Accessible at www.wnpr.org.

Amos, Pamela, and Steven Harrell. 1981. *Other Ways of Growing Old.* Stanford, CA: Stanford University Press.

Anatale, Alex, Atsushi Yamanaka, and Didier Nkurikiyimfura. 2013. "The Metamorphosis to a Knowledge-Based Society: Rwanda." Chapter 2.2 in *The Global Information Technology Report 2013: Growth and Jobs in a Hyperconnected World,* edited by Beñat Bilbao-Osorio, Soumitra Dutta, and Bruno Lanvin. April 10. Geneva: World Economic Forum. Accessible at www.weforum.org/reports/global-information-technology-report-2013.

Andersen, Margaret. 2015. *Thinking about Women: Sociological Perspectives on Sex and Gender.* 10th ed. New York: Pearson.

Anderson, Elijah. 1990. *Streetwise: Race, Class, and Change in an Urban Community.* Chicago: University of Chicago Press.

Anderson, Gretchen. 2009. *Love, Actually: A National Survey of Adults 18 + on Love, Relationships, and Romance.* Washington, DC: AARP.

Anderson, John Ward, and Molly Moore. 1993. "The Burden of Womanhood." *Washington Post National Weekly Edition* 10 (March 22–28):6–7.

Anderson, Warwick. 2003. *The Cultivation of Whiteness: Science, Health and Racial Destiny in Australia.* New York: Perseus.

Andrews, Lori. 2012. "Facebook Is Using You." *New York Times,* February 5, Sunday Review, p. 7.

Angier, Natalie. 1998. "Drugs, Sports, Body Image and G.I. Joe." *New York Times,* December 22, pp. D1, D3.

Angwin, Julia. 2010. "The Web's New Gold Mine: Your Secrets." *Wall Street Journal,* July 31, pp. W1, W2.

———, and Jennifer Valentino-DeVries. 2010a. "Race Is On to 'Fingerprint' Phones, PCs." *Wall Street Journal,* December 1, pp. A1, A15.

Ansell, Amy E. 2008. "Color Blindness." Pp. 320–321, vol. 1, in *Encyclopedia of Race, Ethnicity, and Society,* edited by Richard T. Schaefer. Thousand Oaks, CA: Sage.

Anti-Defamation League. 2013. 2012 Audit of AntiSemitic Incidents. Accessible at http://www.adl.org.

Arab American Institute. 2010. "Demographics." Accessible at http://www.aaiusa.org.

Archer, Patrick, and Bryan Orr. 2011. "Class Identification in Review: Past Perspectives and Future Directions." *Sociology Compass* 5 (January):104–115.

Argetsinger, Amy, and Jonathan Krim. 2002. "Stopping the Music." *Washington Post National Weekly Edition* 20 (December 2):20.

Armed Campuses. 2015. "Guns on Campus: Laws for Public Colleges and Universities." Accessed October 25 at armedcampuses.org.

Armer, J. Michael, and John Katsillis. 1992. "Modernization Theory." Pp. 1299–1304, vol. 4, in *Encyclopedia of Sociology,* edited by Edgar F. Borgatta and Marie L. Borgatta. New York: Macmillan.

Armour, Stephanie. 2015. "Health Spending Picks Up." *Wall Street Journal,* December 3, p. A3.

Asi, Maryam, and Daniel Beaulieu. 2013. *Arab Households in the United States 2006–2010.* ACSBR/10-20. Accessible at www.census.gov .

Aslanian, Sasha. 2006. "Researchers Still Learning from Romanian's Orphans." NPR, September 16. Accessed September 25, 2013 at http://www.npr.org/templates/story/story.php?storyi=6089477.

Association of Theological Schools. 2015. "ATS Data Tables 2014–2015." Accessible at www.ats.edu.

Atchley, Robert C. 1976. *The Sociology of Retirement.* New York: Wiley.

Atchley, Robert C., and Amanda S. Barusch. 2004. *Social Forces and Agency: An Introduction to Social Gerontology.* 10th ed. Belmont, CA: Thomson.

Atchley, Robert. 1976. *A Guide to Federal Laws and Regulations Prohibiting Sex Discrimination.* Washington, DC: U.S. Government Printing Office.

Attwood, Bain. 2003. *Rights for Aborigines.* Crows Nest, Australia: Allen and Unwin.

Aunio, Anna-Lisa, and Suzanne Staggenborg. 2011. "Transnational Linkages and Movement Communities." *Sociology Compass* 5 (5):364–375.

Austin, Chammie. 2009. *Impression Management.* Accessed January 11, 2012 (www.education.com/reference/article/impression-management).

Austin, Karen. 2013. "Elderspeak: Babytalk Directed at Older Adults." February 6. Accessible at www.changingaging.org.

Australia Bureau of Statistics. 2014a. *Estimates and Projections, Aboriginal and Torres Strait Islander Australians, 2001 to 2026.* April 4. Accessible at www.abs.gov.au.

———. 2014b. "Information Paper: Aboriginal and Torres Strait Islander Peoples Perspectives on Homelessness, 2014." April 17. Accessible at www.abs.gov.au.

Australian Indigenous HealthInfoNet. 2015. *Overview of Australian Indigenous Health Status 2014.* Accessible at www.healthinfonet.ecu.edu.au.

Azumi, Koya, and Jerald Hage. 1972. *Organizational Systems.* Lexington, MA: Heath.

b

Bacon Lovers' Talk. 2009. "Bacon Lovers' Talk." Accessed February 4 (www.bacontalk.com/).

Bado-Fralick, Nikki and Rebecca Sachs Norris. 2010. *Toying with God: The World of Religious Games and Dolls.* Waco, TX: Baylor University Press.

Bagby, Ihsam. 2012. *The American Mosque 2011.* Washington, DC: Council on American-Islamic Relations.

Bahrampour, Tara. 2014. "Romanian Orphans Subjected to Deprivation Must Now Deal with Dysfunction." January 30. Accessible at washingtonpost.com.

Baker, Peter. 2009. "Obama Reverses Rules on U.S. Abortion Aid."*New York Times,* January 24.

Baker, Therese L. 1999. *Doing Social Research.* 3rd ed. New York: McGraw-Hill.

Banchero, Stephanie. 2014. "Young Teachers Stick Around." *Wall Street Journal,* April 8, p. A3.

Banerjee, Abhijit Vinayak. 2013. "Microcredit Under the Microscope: What Have We Learned in the Past Two Decades, and What Do We Need to Know?" *Annual Review of Economics* 5:487–519.

Bankston III, Carl I. 2013. "What New Orleans Can Teach Us." *Contexts* 12 (Summer):16–19.

Banyan, By. 2014. "The Optimistic Continent." *The Economist* (October 9). Accessible at www.economist.com.

Baran, Stanley J. 2015. *Introduction to Mass Communications: Media, Literacy, and Culture.* 8th edition. Updated Edition. New York: McGraw-Hill.

———, and Dennis K. Davis. 2015. *Mass Communication Theory: Foundations, Ferment, and Future,* 7th Edition. Belmont CA: Cengage.

Barbière, Cécile. 2014. "French Fear 'Cultural Dumping' from Netflix's EU Expansion." July 31. Accessible at www.euractiv.com.

Bari, Rashidul. 2013. "The Never-ending Trial of Muhammad Yunus." September 19. *Times of India.* Accessible at times of www.india.indiatimes.com.

Barnes, Patricia, Eve Powell-Griner, Ken McFann, and Richard L. Nation. 2004. "Complementary and Alternative Medicine Use among Adults: United States, 2002." *Advance Data from Vital and Health Statistics,* No. 343. National Center for Health Statistics. 2009. "Rise of the Shadow Economy."

Barnes, T. 2009. "Rise of the Shadow Economy." *Christian Science Monitor,* November 8, pp. 30–31.

Barron, Milton L. 1953. "Minority Group Characteristics of the Aged in American Society." *Journal of Gerontology* 8:477–482.

Bartlett, Thomas. 2009. "How the International Essay Mill Has Changed Cheating." *Chronicle of Higher Education,* March 20, pp. A1, A22–A25.

———. 2011. "A Database Named Desire: 2 Scientists Examine Online Searches for Sex."*Chronicle of Higher Education* 57 (August 12):A12.

———. 2014. "The Great Mom & Dad Experiment." *Chronicle of Higher Education* (January 24): B6-B9.

Bastaits, Kim, and Dimitri Mortelmans. 2014. "Does the Parenting of Divorced Mothers and Fathers Affect Children's Well-Being in the Same Way?" *Child Indicators Research* 7 (No. 2): 351–367.

Basulto, Dominic. 2011. "Popping the 'Supercommittee' 'Filter Bubble.'" *Washington Post* (November 3). Accessed November 11 (www.washingtonpost.com/blogs/innovations/post/popping-the-supercommittee-filter-bubble/2010/12/20glQAMfcviM_blog.html).

Battin, Margaret P., Agnes van der Heide, and Bregje D. Onwuleaka-Philipsen. 2007. "Legal Physician-Assisted Dying in Oregon and the Netherlands: Evidence Concerning the Impact on Patients in 'Vulnerable' Groups." *Journal of Medical Ethics* 33 (October): 591–597.

Baude, William. 2015. "Is Polygamy Next?" *New York Times* (July 21): A27.

Baudrillard, Jean. [1970] 1998. *The Consumers Society.* London: Sage.

BBC News. 2005. "Indonesian Village Report: January 12, 2005." Accessed January 19 (www.theworld.org).

Bearman, Peter S., James Moody, and Katherine Stovel. 2004. "Chains of Affection: The Structure of Adolescent Romantic and Sexual Networks." *American Journal of Sociology* 110 (July):44–91.

Beaubien, Jason, and Rebecca Davis. 2015. "A Teen Who Fled Syria Had High Hopes of Life in Lebanon." October 25. Accessed February 10, 2016 at npr.org.

Bebchuk, Lucian A. and Jesse M. Fried. 2010. "Tackling the Managerial Power Problem." *Pathways* (Summer): 9–12.

Becker, Anne E. 2007. "Facets of Acculturation and Their Diverse Relations to Body Shape Concerns in Fiji." *International Journal of Eating Disorders* 40 (1):42–50.

Becker, Howard S. 1952. "Social Class Variations in the Teacher-Pupil Relationship." *Journal of Educational Sociology* 25 (April):451–465.

———. 1963. *The Outsiders: Studies in the Sociology of Deviance.* New York: Free Press.

———. (ed.). 1964. *The Other Side: Perspectives on Deviance.* New York: Free Press.

———. 1974. "Photography and Sociology." *Studies in the Anthropology of Visual Communication* 1, 3–26. Accessible

at http://lucy.ukc.ac.uk/becker.html. Reproduced in *Doing Things Together: Selected Papers.* 1986. Evanston: Northwestern University Press.

———. [1953] 2015. *Becoming a Marijuana User.* Chicago: University of Chicago Press.

———, Blanche Geer, Everett C Hughes, and Anselm Strauss. 1961. *Boys in White: Student Culture in Medical School.* Chicago: University of Chicago Press.

Beddoes, Zanny Milton. 2012. "For Richer, for Poorer." *The Economist* (October 13): Special Report.

Belkin, Douglas, and Caroline Porter. 2012. "Web Profiles Haunt Students." *Wall Street Journal,* October 4, p. A3.

Bellman, Eric. 2016. "Fashion Feeds Recycling Network." June 27. *Wall Street Journal* (June 27): A1, A2.

Bell, Daniel. 1953. "Crime as an American Way of Life." *Antioch Review* 13 (Summer):131–154.

———. [1973] 1999. *The Coming of Post-Industrial Society: A Venture in Social Forecasting.* With new foreword. New York: Basic Books.

Bell, Wendell. 1981. "Modernization." Pp. 186–187 in *Encyclopedia of Sociology.* Guilford, CT: DPG Publishing.

Beller, Emily. 2009. "Bringing Intergenerational Social Mobility Research into the Twenty-first Century: Why Mothers Matter." *America Sociological Review* 74 (August):507–528.

Belz, Adam. 2011. "Farm Boom Leaves Main Street Wanting." *USA Today* (June 1), p. 6A.

Benford, Robert D. 1992. "Social Movements." Pp. 1880–1887, vol. 4, in *Encyclopedia of Sociology,* edited by Edgar F. Borgatta and Marie Borgatta. New York: Macmillan.

Berends, Mark. 2015. "Sociology and School Choice: What We Know After Two Decades of Charter Schools." *Annual Review of Sociology* 41:159–180.

Berger, Peter, and Thomas Luckmann. 1966. *The Social Construction of Reality.* New York: Doubleday.

Berk, Richard A., and Howard E. Aldrich. 1972. "Patterns of Vandalism during Civil Disorders as an Indicator of Selection of Targets." *American Sociological Review* 37(October): 533–547.

Berry, Justin A., and Jane Junn. 2015. "Silent Citizenship among Asian Americans and Latinos: Opting Out or Left Out?" *Citizenship Studies* 19 (5): 570 – 590.

Best, Joel. 2004. *Deviance: Career of a Concept.* Belmont, CA: Wadsworth Thomson.

Best, Shaun. 2015. *Talcott Parsons: Despair and Modernity.* Farnham UK: Ashgate.

Bever, Lindsey. 2014. "How Brittany Maynard may change the right-to-die debate." *Washington Post* (November 3). Accessible at www.washingtonpost.com.

Bhagat, Chetan. 2007. *One Night at the Call Centre.* London: Black Swan.

Bialik, Carol. 2010. "Seven Careers in a Lifetime? Think Twice, Researchers Say." *Wall Street Journal,* September 4, p. A6.

Biddlecom, Ann, and Steven Martin. 2006. "Childless in America." *Contexts* 5 (Fall):54.

Bidwell, Charles E. 2001. "Analyzing Schools as Organizations: Long-Term Permanence and Short-Term Change." *Sociology of Education* 74 (Extra Issue: Current of Thought: Sociology of Education at the Dawn of the 21st Century): 100–114.

Bielby, Denise D., and C. Lee Harrington. 2008. *Global TV: Exporting Television and Culture in the World Market.* New York: New York University Press.

Billitteri, Thomas, J. 2009. "Middle-Class Squeeze." *CQ Researcher* 19 (March 6):201–224.

Birnbaum, Jeffrey H. 2005. "Listen to the Wallet." *Washington Post National Weekly Edition,* April 4, p. 11.

Bishaw, Aleyayehu. 2011. "Areas with Concentrated Poverty: 2006–2010." American Community Survey Briefs. Issued December 2011 ACSBR/10-17. Accessible at http://www.census.gov/prod/2011pubs/acsbr10-17.pdf.

Bitler, Marianne, and Hilary W. Hoynes. 2010. "The State of the Safety Net in the Post-Welfare Reform Era." Paper prepared for Brooking Papers on Economic Activity, Washington, DC, September 16–20.

Black, Donald. 1995. "The Epistemology of Pure Sociology." *Law and Social Inquiry* 20 (Summer):829–870.

Black, Lindsey, Tainya Clarke, Patricia Barnes, Barbara Stussman, Richard L. Hanin. 2015. "Use of Complementary Health Approaches among Children Aged 4–17 Years in the United States: National Health Interview Survey, 2007–2012." *National Health Statistics Reports;* no 78. Hyattsville, MD: National Center for Health Statistics. 2015. Accessible at www.nccih.nih.gov.

Blackstone, Amy. 2014. "Doing Family Without Having Kids." *Sociology Compass* 6 (1): 52–62.

Blais, Allison, and Lynn Rasic. 2011. *A Place of Remembrance: Official Book of the National September 11 Memorial.* Washington, DC: National Geographic.

Blank, Rebecca M. 2010. "Middle Class in America." *Focus* 27 (Summer):1–8.

———. 2011. *Changing Inequality.* Berkeley: University of California Press.

Blau, Peter M., and Otis Dudley Duncan. 1967. *The American Occupational Structure.* New York: Wiley.

Blauner, Robert. 1972. *Racial Oppression in America.* New York: Harper and Row.

Blow, Charles M. 2014a. "Crime, Bias, and Statistics." *New York Times* (September 8): A19.

———. 2014b. "Crime and Punishment." *New York Times* (December 1): A27.

Blumberg, Stephen J., and Julian V. Luke. 2007. "Coverage Bias in Traditional Telephone Surveys of Low-Income and Young Adults."*Public Opinion Quarterly* 71 (5):734–749.

Blumer, Herbert. 1955. "Collective Behavior." Pp. 165–198 in *Principles of Sociology,* 2nd ed., edited by Alfred McClung Lee. New York: Barnes and Noble.

———. 1969. *Symbolic Interactionism: Perspective and Method.* Englewood Cliffs, N.J.: Prentice Hall.

Boje, David M. 1995. "Stories of Storytelling Organization: A Postmodern Analysis of Disney as 'Tamara-Land.'" *Academy of Management Journal* 38:997–1035.

Bond, Patrick. 2015. "Can Climate Activists' 'Movement Below' Transcend Negotiators' 'Paralysis Above'?" *Journal of World-Systems Research* 21(No. 2). Accessible at www.jwsr.otg.

Bonilla-Silva, Eduardo. 2004. "From Bi-Racial to Tri-Racial: Towards a New System of Racial Stratification in the USA." *Ethics and Racial Studies* 27 (November):931–950

Bonilla-Silva, Eduardo. 2006. *Racism without Racists.* Lanham, MD: Rowman and Littlefield.

———. 2014. *Racism without Racists.* 4th ed. New York: Rowman and Littlefield.

Borowiec, Steven. 2015. "A High School Heroine Has South Koreans Fighting over History Textbooks." *Los Angeles Times,* November 8.

Boston Area Research Initiative. 2013. "Housing Issues." Accessible at http://www.bostonarea-researchinitiative.net.

Bottomore, Tom, and Maximilien Rubel, eds. 1956. *Karl Marx: Selected Writings in Sociology and Social Philosophy.* New York: McGraw-Hill.

Bourdieu, Pierre, and Jean-Claude Passerson. 1990. *Reproduction in Education, Society and Culture.* 2nd ed. London. Sage. Originally published as La reproduction.

Bouvier, Leon F. 1980. "America's Baby Boom Generation: The Fateful Bulge." *Population Bulletin* 35 (April).

Bowles, Samuel and Herbert Gintis. [1976] 2011. *Schooling in Capitalist America: Educational Reform and the Contradictions of Economic Life.* With a new introduction by the authors. Chicago: Haymarket Books.

Bowman, Thomas. 2013. "As Qualified Men Dwindle, Military Looks for a Few Good Women." March 23. Accessible at http://www.npr.org/2013/03/25/174966070/as-qualified-men-dwindle-military-looks-for-a-few-good-women.

Brady, Erik. 2010. "Title IX Model Survey Policy to Be Rescinded." *USA Today,* April 20, p. C1.

Brannigan, Augustine. 1992. "Postmodernism." Pp. 1522–1525 in *Encyclopedia of Sociology,* vol. 3, edited by Edgar F. Borgatta and Marie L. Borgatta. New York: Macmillan.

Bray, Karen. 2012. "What's in a Name? Tracing the Development of Latina Theologies of Their Own." *Theological and Philosophical Studies* (March). Accessible at www.drew.edu.

Brazier, Chris, and Amir Hamed, eds. 2007. *The World Guide.* 11th ed: Oxford, UK: New Internationalist.

Brennan Center. 2013. *Election 2012 Laws Roundup.* Accessible at http://brennancenter.org.

———. 2015. "Voting Rights and Elections." Accessed November 12 at www.brennancenter.org.

———. 2016. "Voting Rights and Elections." Accessed February 25 at www.brennancenter.org.

Brewis, Alexandra, Amber Wutich, Ashlan Falletta-Cowden, and Isa Rodriguez-Soto. 2011. "Body Norms and Fat Stigma in Global Perspective." *Current Anthropology* 52 (April):269–276.

Brooks, David. 2011. "Huntington's Clash Revisited." *New York Times* (March 3): Op-Ed at nytimes.com.

Brown, David K. 2001. "The Social Sources of Educational Credentialism: Status Cultures, Labor Markets, and Organizations." *Sociology of Education* 74 (Extra issue):19–34.

Brown, David. 2009. "Doing a Number on Surveys."*Washington Post National Weekly Edition* 26 (January 19):37.

Brown, Michael, and Amy Goldin. 1973. *Collective Behavior: A Review and Reinterpretation of the Literature.* Pacific Palisades, CA: Goodyear.

Brown, Patricia Leigh. 2004. "For Children of Gays, Marriage Brings Joy." *New York Times,* March 19, p. A13.

Brown, Robert McAfee. 1980. *Gustavo Gutierrez.* Atlanta: John Knox.

Brown, Roger W. 1954. "Mass Phenomena." Pp. 833 -873, vol. 2, in *Handbook of Social Psychology,* edited by Gardner Lindzey. Reading, MA: Addison-Wesley.

Brulle, Robert J. 2015. "U.S. Environmental Movements." Pp. 263–292 in Kenneth A. Gould and Tammy L. Lewis (eds.). 2015. *Twenty Lessons in Environmental Sociology.* Second Ed. New York: Oxford University Press.

———, and J. Craig Jenkins. 2008. "Fixing the Bungled U.S. Environmental Movement." *Contexts* 7 (Spring):14–18.

Brunsma, David L., David Overfelt, and Steven J. Pico (eds.). 2010. *The Sociology of Katrina: Perspectives on a Modern Catastrophe.* 2nd ed. New York: Rowman and Littlefield.

Bryant, Chalandra M. 2016. "Simplifying the Complex Complicates Our Findings: Understanding Marriage, Singlehood, and Health." *Gender and Couple Relationships* 6:215–222.

Bryman, Alan. 1995. *Disney and His Worlds.* London: Routledge.

Buckingham, David. 2007. "Selling Childhood? Children and Consumer Culture." *Journal of Children and Media* 1 (1):15–24.

Bullard, Robert D. 1993. *Dumping in Dixie: Race, Class, and Environmental Quality.* 2nd ed. Boulder, CO: Westview Press.

———, and Beverly Wright. 2009. *Race, Place, and Environmental Justice after Hurricane Katrina.* Boulder, CO: Westview Press.

Burawoy, Michael. 2005. "For Public Sociology." *American Sociological Review* 70 (February): 4–28.

Bureau of Consular Affairs. 2015. FY 2014 Annual Report on Intercountry Adoption, March 2015. Washington, DC: Bureau of Consular Affairs, U.S. Department of State.

Bureau of Labor Statistics. 2003. "Women at Work: A Visual Essay." Monthly Labor Review (October):45.

———. 2010. "Record Unemployment among Older Workers Does Not Keep Them Out of the Job Market." *Issues in Labor Statistics.* Accessed May 18 at www.bls.gov/spotlight.

———. 2011. *BLS Spotlight On Statistics: Women At Work.* March. Accessible at www.bls.gov.

———. 2013c. "Labor force projections to 2022: the labor force participation rate continues to fall." *Monthly Labor Review* (December). Accessible at bls.gov.

———. 2013d. *Highlights of Women's Earnings in 2012.* October. Accessible at www.bls.gov.

———. 2014b. "Childcare Workers." January 8. Occupational Outlook Handbook. Accessible at bls.gov.

———. 2015. "Civilian labor force by age, gender, race, and ethnicity, 1994, 2004, 2014, and projected 2024." December 8. Accessible at www.bls.gov.

———. 2015a. "Number of Jobs Held, Labor Market Activity, and Earnings Growth Among the Youngest Baby Boomers: Results from a Longitudinal Survey Summary." March 31, Accessible at http://www.bls.gov/news.release/nlsoy.nr0.htm.

———. 2015b. *Union Membership--2014.* January 23. Economic News Release. Accessible at bls.gov.

———. 2015e. Table A-12. Unemployed persons by duration of unemployment. November 6. Accessible at ww.bls.gov.

———. 2015f. "Wives Who Earn More Than Their Husbands, 1987–2013." June 9. Accessible at www.bls.gov.

———. 2015g. "Table A-8. Employed persons by class of worker and part-time status." December 4. Accessible at www.bls.gov.

———. 2016a. "Labor Force Statistics from Current Population Survey." Updated February 10. Accessible at www.bls.com.

Bureau of the Census. 1975. *Historical Statistics of the United States, Colonial Times to 1970.* Washington, DC: U.S. Government Printing Office.

———. 1981. "Statistical Abstract of the United States, 1980." Accessible at www.census.gov/compendia/statlab/.

———. 2004a. *Statistical Abstract of the United States, 2004–2005.* Washington, DC: U.S. Government Printing Office.

———. 2005a. Florida, California and Texas Future Population Growth. Census Bureau Reports, CB05-52. Washington, DC: U.S. Government Printing Office.

———. 2005a. *Statistical Abstract of the United States 2006.*Washington, DC: U.S. Government Printing Office.

———. 2008a. *Statistical Abstract of the United States, 2008.* Washington, DC: U.S. Government Printing Office.

———. 2011a. *Statistical Abstract of the United States, 2012.* Washington, DC: U.S. Government Printing Office.

———. 2011e. "America's Families and Living Arrangements: 2011" November 3. Accessible at www.census.gov/newsroom/releases/archives/families_households/cb11-183.html.

———. 2012b. Table 5. Reported Voting and Registration, by Age, Sex, and Educational

Attainment: November 2012. Accessible at www.census.gov.

———. 2012c. "Graphs on Historical Voting Trends." February 15. Accessible at www.census.gov/newsroom/releases/archives/voting/cb12-tps08.html.

———. 2012e. "Annual Estimates of the Resident Population." Accessible at www.census.gov/popest/data/national/asrh/2011/index.html.

———. 2013b. "Estimated Median Age at First Marriage, by Sex: 1890 to the Present." Accessible at http://www.census.gov/hhes/families/data/marital.html.

———. 2013d. "America's Families and Living Arrangements: 2013: Children (C table series): tabC3-all." Accessible at www.census.gov.

———. 2014c. Current Population Survey Fertility Supplement. Accessible at www.census.gov.

———. 2014d. "Walking to Work." May 13. Visualizations and Infographics. Accessible at www.census.gov.

———. 2014e. "Changing U.S. Economy." May 15. Visualizations and Infographics. Accessible at www.census.gov.

———. 2015b. How do we know? Child care, an important part of life. May 12. Accessible at www.census.gov.

———. 2015c. Annual Social and Economic Supplement: Income of Households by State Ranked from Highest to Lowest Using 3-Year-Average Medians. Based on estimates as of September 15, 2015. Accessed October 30 at www/census.gov.

———. 2015d. Annual Social and Economic Supplement: 2014 Poverty Table of Contents. POV46:Poverty Status by State, Below 100% of Poverty—All Ages. Accessed October 30 at www.census.gov.

———. 2015e. Annual Estimates of the Resident Population. Accessible at www.census.gov.

———. 2015e. Living Arrangements of Adults and Families. Accessible at www.census.gov.

———. 2015h. International Data Programs. Accessible at www.census.gov.

———. 2015i. "Drive-Ins." February 10. Visualizations and Infographics. Accessible at www.census.gov.

———. 2016a. Historical Poverty Tables- People. Accessed April 25 at www.census.gov.

———. 2016b. Annual Estimates of Resident Population: April 1, 2010 to July 1, 2015. Accessible at factfinder.census.gov.

Bures, Frank. 2011. "Can You Hear Us Now?" Utne Reader (March–April):8–9, 11.

Burger King. 2009. "Whopper Sacrifice." Accessed February 4 (www.whoppersacrifice.com/).

Burger, Andrew. 2015. "Report, April 6." Accessible at www.telecompetitor.com.

Burger, Jerry M. 2009. "Replicating Milgram: Would People Still Obey Today?" American Psychologist 64 (January):1–11.

———. 2014. "Situational Features in Milgram's Experiment That Kept His Participants Shocking." Journal of Social Issues 70 (3):489–500.

Burgess, Ernest W. 1925. "The Growth of the City." Pp. 47–62 in The City, edited by Robert E. Park, Ernest W. Burgess, and Roderick D. McKenzie. Chicago: University of Chicago Press.

Burke, Allison. 2015. "5 Facts about Student Debt in the U.S." October 13. Accessible at www.brookings.com.

Burkitt, Laurie. 2015. "China's Leaders Scrap One-Child Policy." Wall Street Journal, October 30, p. A7.

Burnley, Malcolm. 2012. "For the Amish, Big Agribusiness is Destroying a Way of Life." The Atlantic (August 20).

Burns, Melinda. 2010. "Workfare and the Low-Wage Woman." Miller-McClune (November–December):76–81.

Butler, Daniel Allen. 1998. "Unsinkable": The Full Story. Mechanicsburg, PA: Stackpole Books.

Byrd-Bredbenner, Carol, and Jessica Murray. 2003. "Comparison of the Anthropometric Measurements of Idealized Female Body Images in Media Directed to Men, Women, and Mixed Gender Audiences." Topics in Clinical Nutrition 18 (2):117–129.

C

Côté, James E. 2000. Arrested Adulthood: The Changing Nature of Identity and Maturity in the Late World. New York: New York University.

Calhoun, Craig. 2003. "Belonging in the Cosmopolitan Imaginary." Ethnicities 3 (December):531–553.

Cali, Billie E., Jill M. Coleman, and Catherine Campbell. 2013. "Stranger Danger? Women's Self-Protection Intent and the Continuing Stigma of Online Dating." Cyberpsychology, Behavior, and Social Networking 16 (December):853–857.

Campbell, Frances, Gabriella Conti, James J. Heckman, Seong Hyeok Moon, Rodrigo Pinto Elizabeth Pungello, and Yi Pan. 2014. "Early Childhood Investments Substantially Boost Adult Health." Science (March 28). Accessible at http://science.sciencemag.org/.

Campo-Flores, Arian. 2013. "Street Vendors Battle Limits." Wall Street Journal, January 22, p. A3.

Camponeschi, Chiaara, and Hillete Warner. 2015. "How to Start a Social Street." July 20. Accessible at shareable.net.

Caplan, Ronald L. 1989. "The Commodification of American Health Care." Social Science and Medicine 28 (11):1139–1148.

Caplow, Theodore, and Louis Hicks. 2002. Systems of War and Peace. 2nd ed. Lanham, MD: University Press of America.

Carbon Trust. 2015. "About the Carbon Trust." Accessed December 17 (www.carbontrust.co.uk/about-carbon-trust/pages/default.aspx).

Carden, Maren Lockwood. 1969. Oneida: Utopian Community to Modern Corporation. Baltimore: Johns Hopkins University Press.

Carey, Anne R., and Karl Gelles. 2010. "What Viewers Enjoy Most about Watching the Super Bowl on TV." USA Today, February 5, p. A1; Gallup Poll (May):3.

Carlton-Ford, Steve. 2010. "Major Armed Conflicts, Militarization, and Life Chances." Armed Forces and Society 36 (October):864–899.

Carr, Nicholas. 2010. "Tracking Is an Assault on Liberty, with Real Dangers." Wall Street Journal, August 7, pp. W1, W2.

Carr, Patrick J., and Maria J. Kefalas. 2009. "The Rural Brain Drain." Chronicle of Higher Education (September 25):B7-B9.

Carroll, Joseph. 2006. "Public National Anthem Should Be Sung in English." Gallup Poll (May):3.

Carty, Victoria. 2015. Social Movements and New Technology. Boulder CO: Westview Press.

Caruso, Eugene M., Dobromir A. Rahnev, and Mahzarin R. Banaji. 2009. "Using Conjoint Analysis to Detect Discrimination: Revealing Covert Preferences from Overt Choices." Social Cognition 27 (1):128–137.

Castells, Manuel. 2001. The Internet Galaxy: Reflections on the Internet, Business, and Society. New York: Oxford University Press.

———. 2010a. The Rise of the Network Society. 2nd ed. With a new preface. Malden, MA: Wiley-Blackwell.

———. 2010b. The Power of Identity. 2nd ed. With a new preface. Malden, MA: Wiley-Blackwell.

———. 2015. Networks of Outrage and Hope: Social Movements in the Internet Age. 2nd edition. Cambridge, UK: Polity.

Cauchon, Dennis. 2009. "Women Gain in Historic Job Shift." USA Today, September 3, p. A1.

CBS News. 1979. Transcript of Sixty Minutes segment, "I Was Only Following Orders." March 31, pp. 2–8.

Center for Community Initiatives. 2012. "Northeast Florida Center for Community Initiatives (CCI)." Accessed January 3 (www.unf.edu/coas/cci/).

———. 2014. "Northeast Florida Center for Community Initiatives (CCI)." Accessed January 20, 2016 (www.unf.edu).

Centers for Diseases Control and Prevention. 2015a. "National Marriage and Divorce Rate Trends." November 23. Accessible at www.cdc.gov.

Center on Budget and Policy Priorities. Policy. 2015. Basics: An Introduction to TANF. June 15. Accessible at www.cbpp.org.

———. 2016. The Earned Income Tax Credit. January 15. Accessible at www.cbpp.org.

Centers for Disease Control and Prevention. 2010. "Binge Drinking among High School Students and Adults—United States, 2009." Washington, DC: CDC. Accessible at www.cdc.gov/mmwr/preview/mmwrhtml/mm5939a4.htm?s_cid=mm5939a4_w.

———. 2012a. Vital Signs: Binge Drinking. January 2012. Accessible at www.cdc.gov/vitalsigns/BingeDrinking.

———. 2012b. "National Marriage and Divorce Rate Trends." Accessed February 24 (www.cdc.gov/nchs/nvss/marriage_divorce_tables.htm).

———. 2013. "CDC Health Disparities and Inequalities Report-United States, 2013." Morbidity and Mortality Report 62 (November 22).

———. 2015. "Understanding School Violence Fact Sheet." Accessible at www.cdc.gov.

Centers for Medicare and Medicaid Services. 2013a. "NHE Historical and Projections 1965–2022." Accessible at http://www.cms.gov/ Research-Statistics-Data-and-Systems/Statistics-Trends-and-Reports/NationalHealthExpendData/index.html.

Chalfant, H. Paul, Robert E. Beckley, and C. Eddie Palmer. 1994. *Religion in Contemporary Society.* 3rd ed. Itasca, IL: F. E. Peacock.

Chambliss, William. 1973. "The Saints and the Roughnecks." *Society* 11 (November–December): 24–31.

Charles, Susan T., and Laura L. Carstensen. 2009. "Social and Emotional Aging." *Annual Review of Psychology* 61:383–409.

Charness, Gary, and Marie-Claire Villeval. 2009. "Cooperation and Competition in International Experiments in the Field and the Laboratory." *American Economic Review* 99 (3): 956–978.

Charrad, Mounira M. 2011. "Gender in the Middle East: Islam, State, Agency." *Annual Review of Sociology* 37:417–437

Chase, Randall. 2010. "O'Donnell: 'I'm Not a Witch.'" *Washington Times,* October 4. Accessed March 23 (http://http://www. washingtontimes.com/news/2010/oct/4/ odonnell-im-not-witch/?page52) .

Chase-Dunn, Christopher, and Peter Grimes. 1995. "World-Systems Analysis." Pp. 387–417 in *Annual Review of Sociology,* 1995, edited by John Hagan. Palo Alto, CA: Annual Reviews.

———, Yukio Kawano, and Benjamin D. Brewer. 2000. "Trade Globalization Since 1795: Waves of Integration in the World System." *American Sociological Review* 65 (February):77–95.

Chen, Liyan. 2015. "New York to Hong Kong with the Most Billionaires in 2015." March 4. Forbes/ Lists. Accessible at www.forbes.com.

Cheng, Shu-Ju Ada. 2003. "Rethinking the Globalization of Domestic Service." *Gender and Society* 17 (2):166–186.

Cherlin, Andrew J. 2003. "Should the Government Promote Marriage?" *Contexts* 2 (Fall):22–29

———. 2006. "On Single Mothers 'Doing' Family." *Journal of Marriage and Family* 68 (November):800–803.

———. 2009. *The Marriage-Go-Round: The State of Marriage and the Family in America Today.* New York: Knopf.

———. 2010. *Public and Private Families: An Introduction.* 6th ed. New York: McGraw-Hill.

———. 2011. "The Increasing Complexity of Family Life in the United States." September 8. Accessible at www.prb.org/Articles/2011/us-complex-family-life.aspx?p=1.

Chicago Tribune. 1997. "In London, Prince Meets a Pauper, an Ex-Classmate." December 5, p. 19.

Child Care Aware. 2015. *Child Care in America: 2015 State Fact Sheets.* Accessible at usa.child-careaware.org.

Child Welfare Information. 2011. *How Many Children Were Adopted in 2007 and 2008?* Washington, DC: U.S. Government Printing Office.

China Labor Watch. 2015. "Analyzing Labor Conditions of Pegatron and Foxconn: Apple's Low-Cost Reality." February 11. Accessible at www.chinalaborwatch.com.

Chliova, Myrto, Jan Brinckmann, and Nina Rosenbusch. 2015. "Is Microcredit a Blessing for the Poor? A Meta-analysis Examining Development Outcomes and Contextual Considerations." *Journal of Business Venturing* 30 (Issue 3, May): 467–487.

Choi, Sujin. 2015. "The Two-Step Flow of Communication in Twitter-Based Public Forums." *Social Science Computer Review* 33 (6): 696–711.

Chrisafis, Angelique. 2013. "Faith War Enters Private Spheres." *The Guardian Weekly* (September 8):30–31.

Christakis, Nicholas A., and James H. Fowler. 2007. "The Spread of Obesity in a Large Social Network over 32 Years." *New England Journal of Medicine* 357 (July 26):370–379.

———, and ———. 2009. *Connected: The Amazing Power of Social Networks and How They Shape Our Lives.* New York: Harper.

Chu, Henry. 2005. "Tractors Crush Heart of a Nation." *Los Angeles Times,* July 10, p. A9.

Chung, Esther K., Leny Mathew, Amy C. Rothkopf, Irma T. Elo, James C. Cayne, and Jennifer F. Culhane. 2009. "Parenting Attitudes and Infant Spanking: The Influence of Childhood Experiences." *Pediatrics* 124 (August):278–286.

Clark, Burton, and Martin Trow. 1966. "The Organizational Context." Pp. 17–70 in *The Study of College Peer Groups,* edited by Theodore M. New-comb and Everett K. Wilson. Chicago: Aldine.

Clark, Kim. 2010. "Can School Reform Even Really Work?" *US News and World Report* (January): 23–26, 30–31.

Clarke, Adele E., Janet K. Shim, Laura Maro, Jennifer Ruth Fusket, and Jennifer R. Fishman. 2003. "Bio Medicalization: Technoscientific Transformations of Health, Illness, and U.S. Biomedicine." *American Sociological Review* 68 (April):161–194.

Clarke, Lee. 2002. "Panic: Myth or Reality?" *Contexts* 1 (Fall):21–26.

Clayton, Mark. 2011. "The New Cyber Arms Race." *Christian Science Monitor,* March 7, pp. 26–71.

Cleek, Elizabeth N., Matt Wofsy, Nancy Boyd-Franklin, Brian Mundy, and Tamika J. Howell. 2012. "The Family Empowerment Program: An Interdisciplinary Approach to Working with Multi-Stressed Urban Families." *Family Process* 51(June): 207–217.

Clemmitt, Marcia. 2005. "Intelligent Design." CQ Researcher (July 29), 95: 637–660.

Clifford, Stephanie. 2009b. "Online 'A Reason to Keep On Going.' " *New York Times,* June 2, pp. D5–D6.

Clinard, Marshall B., and Robert F. Miller. 1998. *Sociology of Deviant Behavior.* 10th ed. Fort Worth, TX: Harcourt Brace.

Coates, Rodney. 2008. "Covert Racism in the USA and Globally." *Sociology Compass* 2:208–231.

Coates, Ta-Nehisi. 2014. "The Case for Reparations." *The Atlantic* (June).

Cockerham, William C. 2012. *Medical Sociology.* 12th ed. Upper Saddle River, NJ: Prentice Hall.

Coffman, Katherine B., Lucas C. Coffman, Keith M. Marzilli Ericson. 2013. "The Size of the LGBT Population and the Magnitude of Anti-Gay Sentiment Are Substantially Underestimated." NBER Working Paper No. 19508. Accessible at http://www.nber.org/papers/w19508.

Cohen, Morris. 2015. "Is the Reshoring of U.S. Manufacturing a Myth?" *Knowledge@Wharton.* May 5. Accessible at www.knowledge.wharton. upenn.edu.

Cohen, Patricia. 2012. "At 9/11 Museum, Talking Through an Identity Crisis." *New York Times* (June 3):1, 14, 21.

Cohen, Philip. 2014. "Family Diversity is the New Normal for America's Children." Council on Contemporary Families. November 4. Accessible at https://contemporaryfamilies.org/ the-new-normal/.

Cohen, Thomas H. 2013. *Pretrial Deletion and Misconduct in Federal District Courts.* February. Special Report of the Bureau of Justice Statistics. Accessible at bjs.gov.

Cohn, Nate. 2014. "Why Hispanics Don't Have a Larger Political Voice." *New York Times,* June 17, p. A3.

Colby, Sandra L., and Jennifer M. Ortman. 2015. "Projections of the Size and Composition of U.S. Population: 2014 to 2060." *Current Population Reports* P25-1153. March. Washington DC: U.S. Government Printing Office. Accessible at www. census.gov.

Cole, Nicki Lisa, and Keith Brown. 2014. "The Problem with Fair Trade Coffee." *Contexts* 13 (Winter): 51–55.

Coleman, James William. 2006. *The Criminal Elite: Understanding White-Collar Crime.* 6th ed. New York: Worth.

———, and Donald R. Cressey. 1980. *Social Problems.* New York: Harper and Row.

Collins, Daryl, Jonathan Morduch, Stuart Rutherford, and Orlanda Ruthven. 2009. *Portfolios of the Poor: How the World's Poor Live on $2 a Day.* Princeton, NJ: Princeton University Press.

Collins, James. 2009. "Social Reproduction in Classrooms and Schools." *Annual Review of Anthropology* 38:33–48.

Collins, Patricia Hill. 2000. *Black Feminist Thought: Knowledge, Consciousness, and the Politics of Empowerment.* Revised 10th anniv. 2nd ed. New York: Routledge.

———. 2015. "Intersectionality's Definitional Dilemmas." *Annual Review of Sociology* 41:1–20

Collins, Randall. 1975. *Conflict Sociology: Toward an Explanatory Sociology.* New York: Academic Press.

Collins, Randall. 1980. "Weber's Last Theory of Capitalism: A Systematization." *American Sociological Review* 45 (December):925–942.

———. 1986. *Weberian Sociological Theory.* New York: Cambridge University Press.

———. 1995. "Prediction in Macrosociology: The Case of the Soviet Collapse." *American Journal of Sociology* 100 (May):1552–1593.

Collins, Rebecca L. 2011. "Content Analysis of Gender Roles in Media: Where Are We Now and Where Should We Go?" *Sex Roles* 64 (February): 290–298.

Colucci, Jim. 2008. "All the World's a Screen." *Watch!* (June):50–53.

Commission on Civil Rights. 1981. *Affirmative Action in the 1980s: Dismantling the Process of Discrimination.* Washing, DC: U.S. Government Printing Office.

Commoner, Barry. 1971. *The Closing Circle.* New York: Knopf.

Commoner, Barry. 1990. *Making Peace with the Planet.* New York: Pantheon.

———. 2007. "At 90, an Environmentalist from the 70's Still Has Hope." *New York Times,* June 19, p. D2.

Conley, Dalton et al. 2015. "Big Data, Big Obstacles." *Chronicle of Higher Education* (February 6): B4-B5.

Connell, R. W. 1987. *Gendered Power: Society, the Person, and Sexual Politics.* Stanford, CA: Stanford University Press.

———. 2002. *Gender.* Cambridge, UK: Polity Press.

———. 2005. *Masculinities.* 2nd ed. Berkeley: University of California Press.

Conrad, Peter, ed. 2009. *The Medicalization of Society: On the Transformation of Human Conditions into Treatable Disorders.* 11th ed. Baltimore, MD: Johns Hopkins University.

———, and Kristin K. Barker. 2010. "The Social Construction of Illness: Key Insights and Policy Implications." *Journal of Health and Social Behavior* 51 (5):567–579.

———, and Valerie Leiter. 2013. *The Sociology of Health and Illness: Critical Perspectives.* 9th ed. New York: Worth.

Cooky, Cheryl, and Nicole M. LaVoi. 2012. "Playing but Losing." *Contexts* (Winter): 42–46.

———, Michael Messner, and Michele Mustro. 2015. "It's Dude Time! A Quarter Century of Excluding Women's Sports in Televised News and Highlight Shows." *Communication and Sport* 3 (September): 261–287.

Cooley, Charles. H. 1902. *Human Nature and the Social Order.* New York: Scribner.

Coontz, Stephanie. 2012. "The Myth of Male Decline."*New York Times,* September 30 (Section SR), pp. 1, 8.

Cooper, K., S. Day, A. Green, and H. Ward. 2007. "Maids, Migrants and Occupational Health in the London Sex Industry."*Anthropology and Medicine* 14 (April):41–53.

Cooper, Thia. 2015. "Liberation Theology in Latin America: Dead or Alive?." In *The Changing World Religion Map,* pp. 1955–1969. Springer Netherlands, 2015.

Coser, Lewis A. 1977. *Masters of Sociological Thought: Ideas in Historical and Social Context.* 2nd ed. New York: Harcourt, Brace and Jovanovich.

Coser, Rose Laub. 1984. "American Medicine's Ambiguous Progress." *Contemporary Sociology* 13 (January):9–13.

Couch, Carl J. 1968. "Collective Behavior: An Examination of Some Stereotypes." *Social Problems* 15:310–322.

———, 1996. *Information Technologies and Social Orders.* Edited with an introduction by David R. Maines and Shing-Ling Chien. New York: Aldine de Gruyter.

Council on Ethical and Judicial Affairs, American Medical Association. 1992. "Decisions Near the End of Life," *Journal of the American Medical Association,* 267(April 22–29): 2229–2333.

Counts, Dorothy Ayers, and David Counts. 2012. "The good, the bad, and the unresolved death in Kaliai." *Social Science and Medicine* 58 (No. 5): 887–897.

Cox, Gerry R. 2010. *Death and the American Indian.* Omaha, NE: Grief Illustrated Press.

Cox, Oliver C. 1948. *Caste, Class, and Race: A Study in Social Dynamics.* Detroit: Wayne State University Press.

Cox, Rachel S. 2003. "Home Schooling Debate." *CQ Researcher* 13 (January 17):25–48.

Crabtree, Steve. 2010. *Religiosity Highest in World's Poorest Nations.* August 31. Accessible at www.gallup.com.

CREDO. 2013. *National Charter School Study 2013.* Center for Research on Education Outcomes, Stanford University. Accessible at www.credo.stanford.edu.

Crenshaw, Kimberle. 1991. "Mapping the Margins: Intersectionality, Identity Politics, and Violence against Women of Color." *Stanford Law Review* 43 (July):1241–1299.

Crockett, Zachary. 2014. "The Great Toilet Paper Scare of 1973." July 9, Pricenomics. Accessed June 13, 2016 at www.pricenomics.com.

Crofting Commission. 2016. "Facts & Figures." Accessed July 7 at www.crofting.scotland.gov.uk/facts-and-figures.

Cromartie, John. 2013. "How is Rural America Changing?" May 24. Accessible at www.census.gov.

Crosnoe, Robert. 2011. *Fitting in, Standing out: Navigating the Social Challenges of High School to Get an Education.* New York: Cambridge University Press.

Cross, Simon, and Barbara Bagilhole. 2002. "Girls' Jobs for the Boys? Men, Masculinity and Non-Traditional Occupations." *Gender, Work, and Organization* 9 (April):204–226.

Croteau, David, and William Hoynes. 2006. *The Business of the Media: Corporate Media and the Public Interest.* 2nd ed. Thousand Oaks, CA: Pine Forge Press.

———, and William Hoynes. 2014. *Media/Society: Industries, Images, and Audiences.* 5th ed. Los Angeles: Sage.

———, William Hoynes, and Stefania Milan. 2012. *Media/Society: Industries, Images, and Audiences.* 4th ed. Thousand Oaks CA: Sage.

Crouse, Kelly. 1999. "Sociology of the Titanic." *Teaching Sociology Listserv.* May 24.

Crowe, Jerry, and Valli Herman. 2005. "NBA Lists Fashion Do's and Don'ts." *Los Angeles Times,* October 19, pp. A1, A23.

Cuff, E. C., W. W. Sharrock, and D. W. Francis, eds. 1990. *Perspectives in Sociology.* 3rd ed. Boston: Unwin Hyman.

Cumming, Elaine, and William E. Henry. 1961. *Growing Old: The Process of Disengagement.* New York: Basic Books.

Currie, Elliot. 1985. *Confronting Crime: An American Challenge.* New York: Pantheon.

———. 1998. *Crime and Punishment in America.* New York: Metropolis Books.

Cushing-Daniels, Brenda, and Sheila R. Zedlewski. 2008. "Tax and Spending Policy and Economic Mobility." Washington, DC: Economic Mobility Project. Also accessible at www.economic-mobility.org/reports_and_research/literature_reviews?id=0004.

d

Dade, Corey. 2012. "Battles Over Voter ID Laws Intensify." Accessible at www.npr.org.

Dahl, Robert A. 1961. *Who Governs?* New Haven, CT: Yale University Press.

Dahrendorf, Ralf. 1958. "Toward a Theory of Social Conflict." *Journal of Conflict Resolution* 2 (June):170–183.

———. 1959. *Class and Class Conflict in Industrial Society.* Stanford, CA: Stanford University Press.

Daigle, Katy. 2015. "Legal Limbo Awaits Millions of Future 'Climate Refugees.'" *Washington Post* (December 7). Accessible at www.washington-post.com.

Daitz, Ben. 2011. "Navajos Confront Life's End with Poem." *New York Times* (January 25): D5, D6.

Daley, Suzanne. 2013. "Danes Rethink a Welfare State Ample to a Fault." *New York Times,* April 12, pp. 1, 13.

Dalla, Rochelle L., and Wendy C. Gamble. 2001. "Teenage Mothering and the Navajo Reservation: An Examination of Intergovernmental Perceptions and Beliefs." *American Indian Culture and Research Journal* 25 (1):1–19.

Danziger, Sandra K. 2010. "The Decline of Cash Welfare and Implications for Social Policy and Poverty." *Annual Review of Sociology* 36:523–545.

Darlin, Damon. 2006. "It's O.K to Fall Behind the Technology Curve." *New York Times,* December 30, p. B6

Davenport, Coral. 2015. "In France, Consensus on a Need to Lower Carbon Emissions." *New York Times,* December 13, pp. A1, A19.

David, Gary. 2004. "Scholarship on Arab Americans Distorted Past 9/11." *Al Jadid* (Winter–Spring):26–27.

———. 2008. "Arab Americans." Pp. 84–87, vol. 1, in *Encyclopedia of Race, Ethnicity, and Society,* edited by Richard T. Schaefer. Thousand Oaks, CA: Sage.

Davidson, Paul. 2012. "More U.S. Service Jobs Go Overseas." *USA Today,* December 7, p. B1.

Davies, Christie. 1989. "Goffman's Concept of the Total Institution: Criticisms and Revisions." *Human Studies* 12 (June):77–95.

Davies, Harry and Danny Yadron, 2016. "How Facebook Tracks and Profits from Voters in a $10bn US Election." *The Guardian* (January 28).

Davis, Darren W., and Brian D. Silver. 2003. "Stereotype Threat and Race of Interviewer

Knowledge." *American Journal of Political Science* 47 (January):33–45.

Davis, Gerald. 2004. "American Cronyism: How Executive Networks Inflated the Corporate Bubble." *Contexts* (Summer): 34–40.

Davis, Kingsley. 1947. "A Final Note on a Case of Extreme Isolation." *American Journal of Sociology* 52 (March):432–437.

———. [1949] 1995. *Human Society.* Reprint. New York: Macmillan.

———, and Wilbert E. Moore. 1945. "Some Principles of Stratification." *American Sociological Review* 10 (April):242–249.

Davis, Martha F. 2010. "Abortion Access in the Global Marketplace." *North Carolina Law Review* 88:1657–1685.

Davis, Mike. 2005. *Planet of Slums.* London: Verso.

De Pento, Jennifer, Sarah Durton, Anthony Salvanto, and Fred Backus. 2014. "CBS News Poll on Police, Profiling, and Race Relations." Accessed November 12, 2015 at www.cbsnews.com.

Death Penalty Information Center. 2016. "Facts about the Death Penalty." February 3, 2016. Accessible at ww.death penaltyinformation center.org.

Deegan, Mary Jo, ed. 1991. *Women in Sociology: A Bio-Biographical Sourcebook.* Westport, CT: Greenwood.

Deflem, Mathieu. 2005. "'Wild Beasts without Nationality': The Uncertain Origins of Interpol, 1898–1910." Pp. 275–285 in *Handbook of Transnational Crime and Justice,* edited by Philip Rerchel. Thousand Oaks, CA: Sage.

Deibert, Ronald J., John Palfrey, Rafal Rohozinski, and Jonathan Zittrain. 2008. *Access Denied: The Practice and Policy of Global Internet Filtering.* Cambridge, MA: MIT Press.

Delaney, Kevin J. 2005. "Big Mother Is Watching." *Wall Street Journal,* November 26, pp. A1, A6.

Della Porta, Donatella, and Sidney Tarrow, eds. 2005. *Transnational Protest and Global Activism.* Lanham, MD: Rowman and Littlefield.

DellaPergola, Sergio. 2012. "Jewish Population of the World." Accessible at www.jewishvirtual-library.org.

DeNavas-Walt, Carmen, and Bernadette D. Proctor. 2015. "Income and Poverty in the United States: 2014." Accessible at census.gov.

Denzin, Norman K. 2004. "Postmodernism." Pp. 581–583 in *Encyclopedia of Social Theory,* edited by George Ritzer. Thousand Oaks, CA: Sage.

DeParle, Jason. 2009. "The 'W' Word, Re-Engaged." *New York Times,* February 8, Week in Review, p. 1.

Department of Agriculture. 2016. "Racial/ethnic diversity in America is increasing." June 7. Accessible at www.usda.gov.

Department of Education. 2016. *Working to Keep Schools and Communities Safe.* Accessible at www.ed.gov.

Department of Health and Human Services. 2013. "TANF: Total Number of Families." Accessed December 27 at http://www.acf.hhs.gov/sites/default/files/main/2013_family_tan.pdf.

———. 2015. "TANF: Average Monthly Number of Families. Fiscal and Calendar Year 2015. As of 10/06/2015." Accessed November 3 at www.acf.hhs.gov.

Department of Homeland Security. 2010. *Haiti Social Media: Disaster Monitoring Initiative.* January 21. Washington, DC: U.S. Department of Homeland Security.

———. 2016. "School Safety." Accessible at www.dhe.gov.

Department of Justice. 2000. The Civil Liberties Act of 1988: Redress for Japanese Americans. Accessed June 29 (www.usdoj.gov/crt/ora/main.html).

———. 2008. "Hate Crime Statistics, 2007." Accessible at www.Fbi.gov/ucr/ucr.htm.

———. 2014. "Crime in the United States, 2014." Accessed October 15, 2015 (www.fbi.gov).

Department of Labor. 2015a. Wage and Hour Division: "Minimum Wage Laws in the United States (January 1)." Assessed October 30, 2015, dol.gov.

Department of State. 2015. *Trafficking in Persons Report.* July. Washington: U.S. Government Printing Office. Accessible at www.state.gov.

Desilver, Drew. 2015. "Refugee Surge Brings Youth to an Aging Europe." October 8. Accessible at prwresearch.org.

Deutsch, Francine M. 2007. "Undoing Gender." *Gender and Society* 21 (February):106–127.

Devitt, James. 1999. *Framing Gender on the Campaign Trail: Women's Executive Leadership and the Press.* New York: Women's Leadership Conference.

Dews, Fred. 2014. "Two Charts that Show the Growth of Student Loan Debt." May 12. Accessible at www.brookings.edu.

Dickler, Jessica. 2011. "Dig Deep to Buy Titanic Visit." *Chicago Tribune,* June 3, p. 25.

Dickson, Martin. 2013. "Lunch with the FT Muhammad Yunnus: Micro-financial Times." *Financial Times,* October 27, p. 3.

Diefenbach, Donald L., and Mark D. West. 2007. "Television and Attitudes toward Mental Health Issues: Cultivation Analysis and the Third Person Effect." *Journal of Community Psychology* 35 (2):181–195.

Diehl, David, and Daniel A. McFarland. 2015. "The Organization of Schools and Classrooms." *Emerging Trends in the Social and Behavioral Sciences: An Interdisciplinary, Searchable, and Linkable Resource:* 1–15.

Dillon, Sam. 2004. "Education Can Be Long, Hard Haul for Nation's Rural Kids." *Chicago Tribune,* May 28, p. 13.

———. 2008. "Under 'No Child' Law, Even Solid Schools Falter." *New York Times,* October 1, pp. A1, A14.

Dinovitzer, Ronit, Nancy Reichman, and Joyce Sterling. 2009. "The Differential Valuation of Women's Work: A New Look at the Gender Gap in Lawyers' Incomes." *Social Forces* 88(2):819–864.

DiPrete, Thomas A., Gregory M. Eirich, and Matthew Pittinsky. 2010. "Compensation Benchmarking, Leapfrogs, and the Surge in Executive Pay." *American Journal of Sociology* 115 (May): 1671–1712.

Disaster Research Center. 2016. "Quick Response Studies." Accessible at www.drc.udel.edu.

Dobbin, Frank, and Jiwook Jung. 2010. "Corporate Board Gender Diversity and Stock Performance: The Competence Gap on Institutional Investor Bias?" *North Carolina Law Review* 89.

Dodds, Klaus. 2000. *Geopolitics in a Changing World.* Harlow, UK: Pearson Education.

Domhoff, G. William. 1978. *Who Really Rules? New Haven and Community Power Reexamined.* New Brunswick, NJ: Transaction.

———. 2014. *Who Rules America? The Triumph of the Corporate Rich.* 7th ed. New York: McGraw-Hill.

———. 2014a. *Who Rules America? The Triumph of the Corporate Rich.* 7th ed. New York: McGraw-Hill.

———. 2014b. "Is the Corporate Elite Fractured, or Is There Continuing Corporate Dominance? Two Contrasting Views." *Class, Race and Corporate Power* 3(Issue 1): Article 1.

Domi, Tanya L. 2013. "Women in Combat: Policy Catches up with Reality." *New York Times,* February 8.

Donnelly, Sally B. 2007. "Growing Younger." *Time* (January bonus section): A13–A14.

Donohue, Elizabeth, Vincent Schiraldi, and Jason Ziedenberg. 1998. *School House Hype: SchoolShootings and Real Risks Kids Face in America.* New York: Justice Policy Institute.

Doress, Irwin, and Jack Nusan Porter. 1977. *Kids in Cults: Why They Join, Why They Stay, Why They Leave.* Brookline, MA: Reconciliation Associates.

Dotson, Floyd. 1991. "Community." P. 55 in *Encyclopedic Dictionary of Sociology.* 4th ed. Guilford, CT: Dushkin.

Dougherty, Conor. 2011. "Population Leaves Heartland Behind." *Wall Street Journal,* April 11, p. A6.

Downey, Allen B. 2014. Religious affiliation, education and Internet use. March 21. arXiv:1403.5534. Access at www.arxiv.org.

Dredge, Stuart. 2014. "Upworthy's Founder Talked at SXSW . . . and You'll Never Guess What He said." *The Guardian.* March 10. Accessible at theguardian.com.

DuBois, W. E. B. [1899] 1995. *The Philadelphia Negro: A Social Study.* Philadelphia: University of Pennsylvania Press.

———. [1900] 1969. "To the Nations of the World." Pp. 19–23 in *An ABC of Color,* edited by W. E. B. DuBois. New York: International Publishers.

———. [1903] 1961. *The Souls of Black Folks. Essays and Sketches.* New York: Fawcett.

———. [1903] 2003. *The Negro Church.* Walnut Creek, CA: AltaMira Press.

———. [1909] 1970. *The Negro American Family.* Atlanta University. Reprinted 1970. Cambridge, MA: MIT Press.

———. [1935] 1962. *Black Reconstruction in America 1860–1880.* New York: Athenaeum.

———. [1940] 1968. *Dusk of Dawn.* New York: Harcourt, Brace. Reprint. New York: Schocken Books.

Dugan, Andrew. 2015. "Solid Majority Continues to Support Death Penalty." October 15. Accessible at gallup.com.

Duhigg, Charles, and Keith Bradsher. 2012. "How U.S. Lost Out on iPhone Work." *New York Times,* January 22, p. A1.

Duke P., R.M. Frankel, and S. Reis. 2013. "How to Integrate the Electronic Health Record and Patient-Centered Communication into the Medical Visit: A Skills-Based Approach."*Teaching and Learning in Medicine* 25(4):358–65.

Dukić, Vanja, Hedibert F. Lopes, and Nicholas G. Polson. 2011. "Tracking Flu Epidemics Using Google Flu Trends and Particle Learning." Accessible athttp://faculty.chicagobooth.edu/nicholas.polson/research/papers/Track.pdf.

Duncan, Greg J. and Richard J. Murnane. 2014. "Growing Income Inequality Threatens American Education." March 28. *Phi Delta Kappan.* Accessible at www.edweek.org.

Duneier, Mitchell. 1994a. "On the Job, but Behind the Scenes." *Chicago Tribune,* December 26, pp. 1, 24.

———. 1994b. "Battling for Control." *Chicago Tribune,* December 28, pp. 1, 8.

Dunlap, Riley E. 2010. "At 40, Environmental Movement Endures with Less Consensus." April 22. Accessed April 27 (www.gallup.com/poll/127487/Environmental-Movement-Endures-Less-Consensus.aspx?version=print).

———, and Angela G. Mertig. 1991. "The Evolution of the U.S. Environmental Movement from 1970 to 1990: An Overview." *Society of National Resources* 4 (July–September): 209–218.

DuPuis, Nicole, and Brooks Rainwater. 2014. *The Sharing Economy: An Analysis of Current Sentiment Surrounding Homesharing and Ridesharing.* Washington DC: National League of Cities. Accessible at www.nlc.org.

Durex. 2007. "The Face of Global Sex 2007—First Sex: An Opportunity of a Lifetime." Accessible athttp://www.durexnetwork.org/SiteCollection-Documents/Research%20%20Face%20of%20Global%20Sex%202007.pdf.

Durkheim, Émile. [1893] 1933. *Division of Labor in Society.* Translated by George Simpson. Reprint. New York: Free Press.

———. [1912] 2001. *The Elementary Forms of Religious Life.* A new translation by Carol Cosman. New York: Oxford University Press.

———. [1895] 1964. *The Rules of Sociological Method.* Translated by Sarah A. Solovay and John H. Mueller. Reprint. New York: Free Press.

———. [1897] 1951. *Suicide.* Translated by John A. Spaulding and George Simpson. Reprint. New York: Free Press.

Dutta, Soumitra, Thierry Geiger, and Bruno Lanvin (eds.). 2015. *The Global Information Technology Report 2015: ICTs for Inclusive Growth.* Geneva: World Economic Forum. Accessible at http://reports.weforum.org/global-information-technology-report-2015/.

Eagan, Kevin, Ellen Bara Stolzenberg, Abigail K. Bates, Melissa C. Aragon, Maria Ramirez Suchard, and Cecilia Rios-Arguilar. 2016. *The American Freshman: National Norms Fall 2015.* Los Angeles: Higher Education Research Institute.

Eaton, Leslie. 2007. "Urban to Care, Storm Evacuees Give Farm a Try." *New York Times,* April 28, pp. A1, A9.

Ebaugh, Helen Rose Fuchs. 1988. *Becoming an Ex: The Process of Role Exit.* Chicago: University of Chicago Press.

Eby, Lillian T., Charleen P. Maher, and Marcus M. Butts. 2010. "The Intersection of Work and Family Life: The Role of Affect." *Annual Review of Psychology* 61:599–622.

Economic Mobility Project. 2009. *Findings from a National Survey and Focus Groups on Economic Mobility.* Washington, DC: Pew Charitable Trusts.

The Economist. 2005a. "The Mountain Man and the Surgeon." December 24: 24–26.

———. 2005b. "We Are Tous Québécois." (January 8):39.

———. 2008b. "Following the Crowd." (September 6):10–11.

———. 2011b. "China's Population: The Most Surprising Demographic Crisis." (May 7): 43–44.

———. 2011c. "Digging for Victory." (September 24):60.

———. 2012. "Digital Diplomacy: Virtual Relations." (September 22):69.

———. 2013a. "Romania: The Nanny State." (August 17):51–52.

———. 2013b. "A Giant Cage." (April 6):S1–S16.

———. 2013e. "Game, Sex and Match." (September 7):61–62.

———. 2013f. "Here, There and Everywhere." (January 19):S1–S20.

———. 2014a. "Let's Set the World on Fire." (October 18): 30–31.

———. 2015a. "Gambling and Poverty: Of Slots and Sloth." (January 17): 17.

———. 2015b. "Final Certainty." (July 27): 20.

Eggen, Dan. 2009. "AARP's Dual Role." *Washington Post National Weekly Edition* 27 (November 2): 11.

Ehrenreich, Barbara. 2001. *Nickel and Dimed: On (Not) Getting By in America.* New York: Metropolitan.

Ehrlich, Paul R. and Katherine Ellison. 2002. "A Looming Threat We Won't Face."*Los Angeles Times,* January 20, p. M6.

Eitzen, D. Stanley. 2009. *Fair and Foul: Beyond the Myths and Paradoxes of Sport.* 4th ed. Lanham, MD: Rowman and Littlefield.

El Nasser, Haya, and Paul Overberg. 2011. "Recession Reshapes Life in the USA." *USA Today,* September 12, p. 3A.

Electronic Frontier Foundation. 2016. "Do Not Track." Accessed February 11 at www.eff.org.

Elgan, Mike. 2011. "How to Pop Your Internet 'Filter Bubble.'" *Computer World* (May 7). Accessed November 11 (www.computerworld.com/s/article/9216484/Elgan_How_to_pop_your_Internet_filter_bubble).

Eligon, John. 2016. "A Question of Environmental Racism in Flint." *New York Times* (January 22), pp. A1, A16.

Ellis, Renee R., and Tavia Simmons. 2014. "Coresident Grandparents and Their Grandchildren: 2012." *Current Population Reports* P20-576. Accessible at www.census.gov.

Ellison, Charles D. 2015. "Racism in the Air You Breathe: When Where You Live Determines How Fast You Die." August 17. Accessible at WWW.theroot.com.

Ellison, Nicole B., Jeffrey T. Hancock, and Catalina L. Toma. 2012. "Profile as Promise: A Framework for Conceptualizing the Veracity of Self Presentation in Online Dating Profiles."*New Media and Society,* 14 (February):45–62.

Ellison, Ralph. 1952. *Invisible Man.* New York: Random House.

Engels, Friedrich [1884] 1959. "The Origin of the Family, Private Property, and the State." Pp. 392–394, excerpted in*Marx and Engels: Basic Writings on Politics and Philosophy,* edited by Lewis Feuer. Garden City, NY: Anchor Books.

Ennis, Sharon R., Merarys Rios-Vargas, and Nora G. Albert. 2011. *The Hispanic Population: 2010.* 2010 Census Brief BR-04. Washington, DC: U.S. Government Printing Office.

Environmental Justice Foundation. 2015. "Climate justice: Protecting climate refugees." Accessed December 17 at www.ejfoundation.org.

Environmental Protection Agency. 2012. Global Greenhouse Gas Data. Accessible at http://epa.gov/climatechange/emissions/globalghg.html.

Epstein, Robert. 2009. "The Truth about Online Dating."*Scientific American* (Special Edition).

Erikson, Kai. 1966. *Wayward Puritans: A Study in the Sociology of Deviance.* New York: Wiley.

Erlanger, Steven. 2015. "As China Seeks More Births, Higher Limit May Not Be the Answer." *New York Times,* November 10, p. A9.

Etaugh, Claire. 2003. "Witches, Mothers and Others: Females in Children's Books." *Hilltopics* (Winter):10–13.

Etzioni, Amitai. 1964. *Modern Organization.* Englewood Cliffs, NJ: Prentice Hall.

———. 1965. *Political Unification.* New York: Holt, Rinehart and Winston.

Eurostat. 2015. "People at Risk of Poverty or Social Exclusion." *European Union.* October 25. Accessible at www.ec.euroipa.eu.

Evergeti, Venetia, and Elisabetta Zontini. 2006. "Introduction: Some Critical Reflections on Social Capital, Migration and Transnational Families."*Ethnic and Racial Studies* 29 (November):1025–1039.

Ewing, Maura. 2015. "Punished for Being Poor." *Pacific Standard Magazine* (September/October):16–17.

Fagge, Nick. 2015. "Picks, Pans and Bare Hands: How Miners in the Heart of Africa Toil in Terrible Conditions to Extract the Rare Minerals

That Power Your iPhone." *Daily Mail* (October 22). Accessible at www.dailymail.co.uk.

Faiola, Anthony. 2005. "Their Husbands Made Them Sick." *Washington Post National Weekly Edition* 23 (October 24): 18.

———. 2006. "Japan's Vulnerable Elderly." Washington Post National Weekly Edition 23 (February 27):18.

Farley, Melissa, and Victor Malarek. 2008. "The Myth of the Victimless Crime." *New York Times,* March 12, p. A27.

Farr, Grant M. 1999. *Modern Iran.* New York: McGraw-Hill.

Farrell, Amy, and Jack McDevitt. 2010. "Identifying and Measuring Racial Profiling by the Police." *Sociology Compass* 4:77–88.

Farrell, Jane, and Sarah Jane Glynn. 2013. "The FAMILY Act: Facts and Frequently Asked Questions." December 12. Accessible at www.americanprogress.com.

Feagin, Joe R. 1989. *Minority Group Issues in Higher Education: Learning from Qualitative Research.* Norman: Center for Research on Minority Education, University of Oklahoma.

———, Harnán Vera, and Nikitah Imani. 1996. *The Agony of Education: Black Students at White Colleges and Universities.* New York: Routledge.

Featherman, David L., and Robert M. Hauser. 1978. *Opportunity and Change.* New York: Aeodus.

Federal Bureau of Investigation. 2015. "Bias Breakdown." November 6. News Release. Accessible at www.fbi.gov.

———. 2016. *2015 Hate Crime Statistics.* Accessible at www.fbi.gov.

Felson, David, and Akis Kalaitzidis. 2005. "A Historical Overview of Transnational Crime." Pp. 3–19 in *Handbook of Transnational Crime and Justice,* edited by Philip Reichel. Thousand Oaks, CA: Sage.

Ferber, Abby L., and Michael S. Kimmel. 2008. "The Gendered Face of Terrorism." *Sociology Compass* 2:870–887.

Ferdinand Tönnies. [1887]1988. *Community and Society.* Rutgers, NJ: Transaction.

Ferrera, Jesse. 2015. "Canada Voter Turnout in this Election was the Highest in 2 Decades." *Huffington Post.* October 20. Accessible at www.huffingpost.ca.

Feuer, Lewis S. 1989. *Marx and Engels: Basic Writings on Politics and Philosophy.* New York: Anchor Books.

Fields, Gary, and Erica E. Phillips. 2013. "The New Asylums: Jails Swell with Mentally Ill." *Wall Street Journal,* September 20, pp. A1, A12.

Fiji TV. 2012. Home Page. Accessed January 10 (www.fijitv.com.fj).

File, Thom. 2013. "The Diversifying Electorate-Voting Rates by Race and Hispanic Origin in 2012 (and Other Recent Elections)." Current Population Survey P20-568. Accessible at http://www.census.gov.

Fine, Gary Alan, and Bill Ellis. 2011. *The Global Grapevine: Why Rumors of Terrorism, Immigration, and Trade Matter.* New York: Oxford University Press.

———, and Nicholas DiFonzo. 2011. "Uncertain Knowledge."*Contexts* (November):16–21.

Fine, Gary C. 1987. With the Boys: Little League Baseball and Preadolescent Culture. Chicago: University of Chicago Press.

———. 2008. "Robbers Cave." Pp. 1163–4, vol. 3, in *Encyclopedia of Race, Ethnicity, and Society,* edited by Richard T. Schaefer. Thousand Oaks, CA: Sage.

Fishman, Ted C. 2010a. *Shock of Gray.* New York: Scribner.

———. 2010b. "The Old World." *New York Times Magazine* (October 17): 48–53.

Fiss, Peer C., and Paul M. Hirsch. 2005. "The Discourse of Globalization: Framing of an Emerging Concept." *American Sociological Review* (February):29–52.

Fjellman, Stephen M. 1992. *Vinyl Leaves: Walt Disney World and America.* Boulder, CO: Westview Press.

Flacks, Richard. 1971. *Youth and Social Change.* Chicago: Markham.

Fletcher, Connie. 1995. "On the Line: Women Cops Speak Out." *Chicago Tribune Magazine,* February 19, pp. 14–19.

Flora, Cornelia Butter, and Jan L. Flora, with Susan Fey. 2004. *Rural Communities: Legacy and Change.* 2nd ed. Boulder, CO: Westview Press.

Flores, Glenn, M. Abreu, C. P. Barone, R. Bachur, and H. Lin. 2012. "Errors of Medical Interpretation and Their Potential Clinical Consequences: A Comparison of Professional versus Ad Hoc versus No Interpreters." *Annals of Emergency Medicine* 60 (5):545–553.

Foladare, Irving S. 1969. "A Clarification of 'Ascribed Status' and 'Achieved Status.'" *The Sociological Quarterly* 10, No. 1 (Winter, 1969), 53–61.

Foley, Douglas. 2011. "The Rise of Class Culture in Theory in Educational Anthropology." Chapter 6 in Bradley Lester and Mica Pollock (eds.) *A Companion to the Anthropology of Education.* New York: John Wiley.

Fonseca, Felicia. 2008. "Dine College on Quest to Rename Navajo Cancer Terms." *News from Indian Country* 22 (January 7):11.

Foucault, Michel. 1978. *The History of Sexuality.* Vol. 1, *An Introduction.* New York: Vintage.

Fox, Porter. 2014. "The End of Snow?" *New York Times,* February 9 (Section SR), pp. 1, 6.

Francis, David. 2010. "Homeschoolers Seek Asylum in US." *Christian Science Monitor,* March 8, p. 12.

Frank, Arthur W. 2015. "From Sick Role to Narrative Subject: An Analytic Memoir." *Health* (London). November 18. pii: 1363459315615395. [Epub ahead of print].

Frank, Robert H. 2010. "A Remedy Worse than the Disease." *Pathways* (Summer): 17–21. Thurm, Scott. 2010. "Oracle's Ellison: Pay King." *Wall Street Journal* (July 27), pp. A1, A16.

Frank, Robert. 2015. "More Millionaires Than Ever Are Living in the U.S." March 10. Accessible at www.cnbc.com.

Franke, Richard Herbert, and James D. Kaul. 1978. "The Hawthorne Experiments: First Statistical Interpretation."*American Sociological Review* 43 (October):623–643.

Franklin, John Hope, and Evelyn Brooks Higginbotham. 2011. *From Slavery to Freedom.* 9th ed. New York: McGraw-Hill.

Freedman, Des. 2014. *The Contradictions of Media Power.* London: Bloomsbury.

Freese, Jeremy. 2008. "Genetics and the Social Science Explanation of Individual Outcomes." *American Journal of Sociology* 114 (Suppl.): 51–535.

Freidson, Eliot. 1970. *Profession of Medicine.* New York: Dodd, Mead.

Freudenburg, William R. 2005. "Seeing Science, Courting Conclusions: Reexamining the Intersection of Science, Corporate Cash, and the Law."*Sociological Forum* 20 (March):3–33.

Freudenheim, Milt. 2005. "Help Wanted: Oldest Workers Please Apply." *New York Times,* March 23, pp. A1, C3.

Frey, Benedikt, and Michael Osborne. 2013. "The Future of Employment: How Susceptible Are Jobs to Computerisation?" September 17, 2013. Working paper accessible at http://www.oxfordmartin.ox.ac.uk/downloads/academic/The_Future_of_Employment.pdf.

Frey, William H. 2011. *A Demographic Tipping Point among America's Three-Year-Olds.* February 7. Accessible at http://www.brookings.edu/opinions/2011/0207_population_frey.aspx?p=1.

———. 2015. "Racial Minorities and the 'Suburban Dream.'" March 30. Accessible at www.brookings.edu.

Fridlund, Alan J., Paul Erkman, and Harriet Oster. 1987. "Facial Expressions of Emotion; Review of Literature 1970–1983." Pp. 143–224 in *Non-verbal Behavior and Communication,* 2nd ed., edited by Aron W. Seigman and Stanley Feldstein. Hillsdale, NJ: Erlbaum.

Friedan, Betty. 1963. *The Feminine Mystique.* New York: Dell.

Friedman, Richard A. 2012. "In Gun Debate, a Misguided Focus on Mental Illness." *New York Times,* December 18, p. D6.

Friedrich, Alena, Barbara Flunger, Benjamin Nagengast, Kathrin Jonkmann, and Ulrich Trautwein. 2015. "Pygmalion Effects in the Classroom: Teacher Expectancy Effects on Students' Math Achievement." *Contemporary Educational Psychology* 41 (April 2015):1–12.

Fry, Erica. 2015. "Here's How Many Fortune 500 Board Seats Women Will Hold in 2016." November 19. Accessible at www.fortune.com.

Fukase, Atsuko, and Kana Inagaki. 2012. "Japan Insider Penalty: $600." *Wall Street Journal,* March 22, p. C2.

g

Gabriel, Trip. 2010. "Despite Push, Success at Charter Schools Is Mixed. *New York Times* (May 1).

Galbraith, John Kenneth. 1977. *The Age of Uncertainty.* Boston: Houghton Mifflin.

Galea, Sandro, Melissa Tracy, Katherine J. Hoggatt, Charles DiMaggio, and Adam Karpati. 2011. "Estimated Deaths Attributed to Social Factors in the United States." *American Journal of Public Health* 101 (August):1456–1465.

Gans, Herbert J. 1991. *People, Plans, and Policies: Essays on Poverty, Racism, and Other National Urban Problems.* New York: Columbia University Press and Russell Sage Foundation.

———. 1995. *The War against the Poor: The Underclass and Antipoverty Policy.* New York: Basic Books.

———. 2013. "Public opinion polls do not always report public opinion." *Neiman Journalism Lab* (April 29). Accessed April 30, 2014 at www.niemanlab.org.

Garfinkel, Harold. 1956. "Conditions of Successful Degradation Ceremonies." *American Journal of Sociology* 61 (March):420–424.

Garner, Roberta. 1996. *Contemporary Movements and Ideologies.* New York: McGraw-Hill.

———. 1999. "Virtual Social Movements." Presented at Zaldfest: A conference in honor of Mayer Zald. September 17, Ann Arbor, MI.

Garreau, Joel. 1991. *Edge City: Life on the New Frontier.* New York: Doubleday.

Garrett-Peters, Raymond. 2009. "'If I Don't Have to Work Anymore, Who Am I?': Job Loss and Collaborative Self-Concept Repair." *Journal of Contemporary Ethnography* 38 (5):547–583.

Gasparro, Annie, and Julie Jargon. 2012. "McDonald's to Go Vegetarian India." *Wall Street Journal,* September 5, p. B7.

Gates, Gary J. 2012. "LGBT VOTE 2012." Los Angeles: The Williams Institute. Accessible at www.law.ucla.edu/williamsinstitute.

Gaudin, Sharon. 2009. "Facebook Has Whopper of a Problem with Burger King Campaign." *Computerworld,* January 15.

Gay, Lesbian and Straight Education Network. 2016. "About GLSEN." Accessed February 26 (www.glsen.org).

Gecas, Viktor. 2004. "Socialization, Sociology of." Pp. 14525–14530 in *International Encyclopedia of the Social and Behavioral Sciences,* edited by Neil J. Smelser and Paul B. Baltes. Cambridge, MA: Elsevier.

Gelles, David. 2011. "It's All About the Algorithm." *Financial Times* (July 30).

Gengler, Amanda M., and Megan V. Jarrell. 2015. "What Difference Does Difference Make? The Persistence of Inequalities in Healthcare Delivery." *Sociology Compass* 10:718–730.

Gentleman, Amelia. 2006. "Bollywood Captivated by the Call Centre Culture." *Guardian Weekly,* June 2, p. 17.

Gerth, H. H., and C. Wright Mills. 1958. *From Max Weber: Essays in Sociology.* New York: Galaxy.

Gertner, Jon. 2005. "Our Ratings, Ourselves." *New York Times Magazine,* April 10, pp. 34–41, 56, 58, 64–65.

Gibbs, Nancy. 2009. "What Women Want Now." *Time* 174 (16):24–33.

Giddens, Anthony. 1991. *Modernity and Self-Identity: Self and Society in the Late Modern Age.* Cambridge, UK: Polity.

Giddings, Paul J. 2008. *Ida: A Sword among Lions.* New York: Amistad.

Gillespie, C., and K. Hurvitz. 2013. "Prevalence of Hypertension and Controlled Hypertension—United States, 2007–2010." *Morbidity and Mortality Weekly Report (MMWR)* 62(03): 144–148.

Gilley, Brian Joseph. 2006. *Becoming Two-Spirit: Gay Identity and Social Acceptance in Indian Country.* Lincoln: University of Nebraska Press.

Gillum, Jack. 2011. "How *USA Today* Analyzed Border Crime Trends." *USA Today,* July 16, p. 7A.

Giordano, Peggy C. 2003. "Relationships in Adolescence." Pp. 257–281 in *Annual Review of Sociology,* 2003, edited by Karen S. Cook and John Hagan. Palo Alto, CA: Annual Reviews.

Giroux, Henry A. 1988. *Schooling and the Struggle for Public Life: Critical Pedagogy in the Modern Age.* Minneapolis: University of Minnesota Press.

Gitlin, Todd. 2002. *Media Unlimited: How the Torrent of Images and Sounds Overwhelms Our Lives.* New York: Henry Holt.

Gladstone, Rick. 2015. "Many Ask, Why Not Call It Terrorism?" *New York Times,* June 19, p. A15.

Gladwell, Malcolm. 2015. "Starting Over." *New Yorker* (August 24). 2

Glazer, Sarah. 2013. "Plagiarism and Cheating: Are They Becoming More Acceptable to the Internet Age?" *CQ Researcher* 23 (January 4).

Glazer, Susan. 2010. "Evaluating Microfinance." *EQ Global Research* 4 (April).

Goffman, Erving. 1959. *The Presentation of Self in Everyday Life.* New York: Doubleday.

———. 1961. *Asylums: Essays on the Social Situation of Mental Patients and Other Inmates.* Garden City, NY: Doubleday.

———. 1963. *Stigma: Notes on Management of Spoiled Identity.* Englewood Cliffs, NJ: Prentice Hall.

———. 1979. *Gender Advertisements.* Cambridge, MA: Harvard University Press.

Golann Joanne W. 2015. "The Paradox of Success at a No-Excuses School." *Sociology of Education* 88 (April, no. 2): 103–119.

Goldman, David. 2012. "Are Landlines Doomed?" CNN Money. April 10. Accessed April 11 (http://money.cnn.com/2012/04/10/technology/att-verizon-landlines/index.htm).

Goldstein, Greg. 1998. "World Health Organization and Housing." Pp. 636–637 in *The Encyclopedia of Housing,* edited by Willem van Vliet. Thousand Oaks, CA: Sage.

Goldstein, Melvyn C., and Cynthia M. Beall. 1981. "Modernization and Aging in the Third and Fourth World: Views from the Rural Hinterland in Nepal." *Human Organization* 40(Spring):48–55.

Gomez, Alan, Jack Gillum, and Kevin Johnson. 2011. "On U.S. Side, Cities Are Havens from Drug Wars." *USA Today,* July 15, pp. 1A, 6A–7A.

Gorney, Cynthia. 2014. "Far from Home." *National Geographic* (February):7–95.

Gottdiener, Mark, and Joe R. Feagin, Ray Hutchison, and Mikael T. Ryan. 2015. *The New Urban Sociology.* 5th ed. Boulder, CO: Westview Press.

Gottfredson, Michael, and Travis Hirschi. 1990. *A General Theory of Crime.* Palo Alto, CA: Stanford University Press.

Gough, Margaret, and Alexandra Killewald. 2011. "Unemployment in Families: The Case of Housework." *Journal of Marriage and Family* 73 (October):1085–1100.

Gould, Kenneth A. and Tammy L. Lewis (eds.). 2015. *Twenty Lessons in Environmental Sociology.* Second ed. New York: Oxford University Press.

Gould, Larry A. 2002. "Indigenous People Policing Indigenous People: The Potential Psychological and Cultural Costs." *Social Science Journal* 39:171–188.

Government Accountability Office. 2003. "Women's Earnings: Work Patterns Partially Explain Difference between Men's and Women's Earnings." Washington, DC: U.S. Government. Printing Office.

Grady, John. 2007. "Visual Sociology." In Clifton D. Bryant and Dennis L. Peck (eds.), *21st Century Sociology: A Reference Handbook,* Vol. II. Thousand Oaks CA: Sage.

Graells-Garrido, Eduardo, Mounia Lalmas, and Daniele Quercia. 2013. "Data Portraits: Connecting People of Opposing Views." Submitted November 19. Accessed December 1 at http://arxiv.org/abs/1311.4658.

Grall, Timothy. 2013. "Custodial Mothers and Fathers and Their Child Support: 2011." *Current Population Reports* P60-246. Accessible at www.census.gov.

Grameen Bank. 2016. "Monthly Report in USD." October. Accessed February 27 at www.grameen.com.

Gramsci, Antonio. 1929. *Selections from the Prison Notebooks.* Edited and translated by Quintin Hoare and Geoffrey Nowell Smith. London: Lawrence and Wishort.

Grant, Tobin. 2015. "Hawai'i telescope stalled because of indigenous rights, not 'superstition.'" December 7. *Religion News Service.* Accessible at www.religionnews.com.

Grattet, Ryken. 2011. "Societal Reactions to Deviance." *Annual Review of Sociology* 37:185–204.

Grauerholz, Liz, and Marc Settembrino. 2016. "Teaching Inequalities: Using Public Transportation and Visual Sociology to make it Real." *Teaching Sociology* 44 (July): 200–211.

Greeley, Andrew M. 1989. "Protestant and Catholic: Is the Analogical Imagination Extinct?" *American Sociological Review* 54 (August):485–502.

Greenhalgh, Susan. 2008. *Just One Child: Science and Policy in Deng's China.* Berkeley, CA: University of California Press.

Greenhouse, Steven. 2008a. "Unions Look for New Life in the World of Obama." *New York Times,* December 29:B6.

———. 2009. "In America, Labor Has an Unusually Long Fuse." *New York Times,* April 5, Week in Review, p. 3.

Greenstone, Michael, Adam Looney, Jeremy Patashnik, and Muxin Yu. 2013. "Thirteen Economic Facts about Social Mobility and the Role of Education." June. Accessible at www.brookings.edu.

Gregor, Alison. 2013. "A NORC, Up Close and Personal." *New York Times,* May 5, p. 8.

Gross, Lynne Schaefer. 2013. *Electronic Media: An Introduction.* 11th ed. New York: McGraw-Hill.

Groza, Victor, Daniela F. Ileana, and Ivor Irwin. 1999. *A Peacock or a Crow: Stories, Interviews, and Commentaries on Romanian Adoptions.* Euclid, OH: Williams Custom Publishing.

Gruenert, Steve, and Todd Whitaker. 2015. *School Culture Rewired: How to Define, Assess, and Transition It.* Alexandra VA: ASCD.

Grundberg, Sven, and Jens Hansegard. 2014. "Women Now Up Almost Half of Gamers." *Wall Street Journal,* August 20. Accessible at www.wsj.com.

Guedel, W. Gregory. 2014. "Sovereignty, Economic Development, and Human Security in Native American Nations." *American Indian Law Journal* 3(Fall): 17–39.

Guenther, Julia, and Eswarappa Kasi. 2015. "Globlaization and People at the Margins: Experiences from the Global South." *Journal of Developing Societies* 31 (1):1–7.

Guest, Robert. 2011. "Tribes Still Matter." *The Economist* (January 22):17–18.

Guillermo, Emil. 2015. "Model Minority? In St. Paul, Asian-American Test Scores Lag." *NBC News.* May 5. Accessible at www.nbcnews.com.

Guo, Guang, Michael E. Roettger, and Tianji Cai. 2008. "The Integration of Genetic Propensities into Social-Control Models of Delinquency and Violence among Male Youths." *American Sociological Review* 73 (August):543–568.

Gutiérrez, Gustavo. 1990. "Theology and the Social Sciences." Pp. 214–225 in *Liberation Theology at the Crossroads: Democracy or Revolution?* edited by Paul E. Sigmund. New York: Oxford University Press.

Guttmacher Institute. 2008. *Facts on Induced Abortion Worldwide.* New York: Guttmacher.

———. 2016. "State Policies in Brief as of February 1, 2016: An Overview of Abortion Laws." Accessible www.guttmacher.org.

h

Haas, Steven A., David R. Schaefer, and Olga Kornienko. 2010. "Health and the Structure of Adolescent Social Networks." *Journal of Health and Social Behavior* 5 (4):424–439.

Hacker, Andrew. 1964. "Power to Do What?" Pp. 134–146 in *The New Sociology,* edited by Irving Louis Horowitz. New York: Oxford University Press.

Hacker, Helen Mayer. 1951. "Women as a Minority Group." *Social Forces* 30 (October):60–69.

———. 1974. "Women as a Minority Group, Twenty Years Later." Pp. 124–134 in *Who Discriminates against Women?* edited by Florence Denmark. Beverly Hills, CA: Sage.

Hallinan, Maureen T. 1997. "The Sociological Study of Social Change." *American Sociological Review* 62 (February):1–11.

Hamel, Liz, Jamie Firth, and Mollyann Brodie. 2015. *New Orleans Ten Years After the Storm.*

Washington DC: Kaiser Family Foundation. Accessible at www.kf.org.

Hamilton, Martha. 2014. "Why Walk-in Health Care Is a Fast-Growing Profit Center for Retail Chains." April 4. Accessible at www.washingtonpost.com.

Hamm, Katie, and Carmel Martin. 2015. *A New Vision for Child Care in the United States.* Washington DC: Center for American Progress.

Hamm, Steve. 2007. "Children of the Web." *BusinessWeek,* July 2, pp. 50–56, 58.

Hamman, Robin. 1997. "Introduction to Virtual Communities Research." *Cybersociology Magazine,* Number Two. Accessible at www.cybersociology.com.

Hani, Yoko. 1998. "Hot Pots Wired to Help the Elderly." *Japan Times Weekly International Edition* (April 13), p. 16.

Haq, Husna. 2011. "How Marriage Is Faring." *Christian Science Monitor,* February 14, p. 21.

Harlow, Harry F. 1971. *Learning to Love.* New York: Ballantine.

Harman, Donna. 2009. "Dubai's Glitz Lost in Grim Life." *Christian Science Monitor,* May 3, p. 8.

Harmon, Katherine. 2011. "How Obesity Spreads in Social Networks." May 5. Accessible at http://www.scientificamerican.com/article.cfm?id=social-spread-obesity.

Harper, Douglas. 1988. "Visual Sociology: Expanding Sociological Vision." *American Sociologist* (Spring): 54–70.

Harrell, Erika. 2015. *Victims of Identity Theft, 2014.* September 27. Washington DC: U.S. Government Printing Office.

Harrington, Michael. 1962. *The Other America: Poverty in the United States.* Penguin Books, Inc.: Baltimore.

———. 1980. "The New Class and the Left." Pp. 123–138 in *The New Class,* edited by B. Bruce Briggs. Brunswick, NJ: Transaction.

Harris, Chauncy D., and Edward Ullman. 1945. "The Nature of Cities." *Annals of the American Academy of Political and Social Science* 242 (November):7–17.

Harris, Scott. 2015. "Returning to Homeland, Vietnamese Americans Make Their Mark." *Los Angeles Times* (August 30). Accessible at www.latimes.com.

Harrisinteractive. 2008. "Cell Phone Usage Continues to Increase." Accessed January 13 (www.harrisinteractive.com).

Hartocollis, Anemona, and Jess Bidgood. 2015. "Racial Discrimination Protests Ignite at Colleges Across the U.S." *New York Times* (November 11):A16.

Haub, Carl. 2010. "2010 World Population Data Sheet." Washington, DC: Population Reference Bureau.

———. 2013. "Were the Population Alarmists Right or Wrong?" Washington, DC: Population Reference Bureau. Accessed April 24 at demographicsrevealed.org/2013/03/26/were-the-population-alarmists-right-or-wrong/.

Hauser, Orlee. 2011. "'We Rule the Base Because We're Few': 'Lone Girls' in Israel's Military." *Journal of Contemporary Ethnography* 40 (6):623–651.

Haviland, William A., Harald E. L. Prins, Dana Walrath, and Bunny McBride. 2015. *Cultural*

Anthropology—The Human Challenge. 14th ed. Boston, MA: Cengage.

Hay, Andrew. 2009. "Spain's New Middle Classes Slip into Poverty." Reuters. April 8. Accessed May 11, 2011 (http://uk.reuters.com/article/email/ioUKTRE537029200904).

Hayden, H. Thomas. 2004. "What Happened at Abu Ghraib." Accessed August 7 (www.military.com).

He, Wan, Daniel Goodkind, and Paul Kowal. March. 2016. "An Aging World: 2015." *International Population Reports* P95/16-1. Washington DC: U.S. Government Reports.

Health Cost Institute. 2013. "The Impact of the Mental Health Parity and Addiction Equity Act on Inpatient Admissions." February. Issue Brief #5. Accessed May 15 at http://www.healthcostinstitute.org/files/HCCI-Mental-Health-Parity-Issue-Brief.pdf.

Healthy Families Act. 2015. "H.R. 932 – Healthy Families Act." Accessed December 3 at www.congress.gov.

Hebel, Sara. 2006. "In Rural America, Few People Harvest 4-Year Degrees." *Chronicle of Higher Education* 53 (November 3):A21–A24.

Heckert, Druann, and Amy Best. 1997. "Ugly Duckling to Swan: Labeling Theory and the Stigmatization of Red Hair." *Symbolic Interaction* 20 (4):365–384.

Hedley, R. Alan. 1992. "Industrialization in Less Developed Countries." Pp. 914–920, vol. 2, in *Encyclopedia of Sociology,* edited by Edgar F. Borgatta and Marie L. Borgatta. New York: Macmillan.

Heilman, Madeline E. 2001. "Description and Prescription: How Gender Stereotypes Prevent Women's Ascent up the Organizational Ladder." *Journal of Social Issues* 57 (4):657–674.

Heisig, Jan Paul. 2011. "Who Does More Housework: Rich or Poor? A Comparison of 33 Countries." *American Sociological Review* 76 (1):74–99.

Hellmich, Nanci. 2001. "TV's Reality: No Vast American Waistlines." *USA Today,* October 8, p. D7.

Helman, Ruth, Mathew Greenwald, Craig Copeland, and Jack VanDerhel. 2012. "The 2012 Retirement Confidence Survey: Job Security, Debt Weigh on Retirement Confidence, Savings." *Employee Benefit Research Institute* Notes 33 (March).

Henderson, Carter. 1997. *Funny, I Don't Feel Old.* San Francisco: ICS Press.

Hendrickson, Brett. 2015. "Neo-shamans, *Curanderismo* and Scholars." *Nova Religio: The Journal of Alternative and Emergent Religions* 19 (No. 1): 25–44.

Hengeveld, Rob. 2012. *Wasted World: How Our Consumption Challenges the Planet.* Chicago: University of Chicago Press.

Herman, Max Arthur. 2005. *Fighting in the Streets: Ethnic Succession and Urban Unrest in Twentieth-Century America.* New York: Peter Lang.

Hernandez, Elaine M., and Christopher Uggen. 2012. "Institutions, Politics, and Mental Health Parity." *Society and Mental Health* 2 (3):154–171.

Herrera, Giaconda. 2013. "Gender and International Migration: Contributions and Cross-Fertilization." *Annual Review of Sociology* 39:471–489.

Hersch, Patricia. 1998. *A Tribe Apart: A Journey into the Heart of the American Adolescence.* New York: Fawcett Books.

Hewlett, Sylvia Ann, and Carolyn Buck Luce. 2005. "Off-Ramps and On-Ramps: Keeping Talented Women on the Road to Success." *Harvard Business Review* (March):43–53.

Heymann, Jody, with Kristen McNeill. 2013. *Children's Chances: How Countries Can Move from Surviving to Thriving.* Cambridge, MA: Harvard University Press.

Higgins, Andrew. 2015. "German Village of 102 Braces for 750 Asylum Seekers." *New York Times.* October 31, pp. 1, 10.

Higgins, Chris A., Linda E. Duxbury, and Sean T. Lyons. 2010. "Coping with Overload in Stress: Men and Women in Dual-Earner Families." *Journal of Marriage and Family* 72 (August):847–859.

Hill, Michael R., and Susan Hoecker-Drysdale, eds. 2001. *Harriet Martineau: Theoretical and Methodological Perspectives.* New York: Routledge.

Hillery, George A. 1955. "Definitions of Community: Areas of Agreement." *Rural Sociology* (2):111–123.

Himes, Christine L. 2001. "Elderly Americans." *Population Bulletin* 56 (December).

Hinduja, Sameer, and Justin W. Patchin. 2015. "Cyberbulying Legislation and Case Law." Updated January. Accessible at www.cyberbullying.org.

Hira, Ron. 2008. "An Overview of the Offshoring of U.S. Jobs." In Marlene A. Lee and Mark Mather, "U.S. Labor Force Trends." *Population Bulletin* 63 (June).

Hirschi, Travis. 1969. *Causes of Delinquency.* Berkeley: University of California Press.

Hirst, Paul, and Grahame Thompson. 1996. *Globalization in Question: The International Economy and the Possibilities of Governance.* Cambridge, UK: Polity Press.

Hitlin, Steven, and Jane Allyn Piliavin. 2004. "Values: Reviving a Dormant Concept." Pp. 359–393 in *Annual Review of Sociology, 2004,* edited by Karen S. Cook and John Hagan. Palo Alto, CA: Annual Reviews.

Hixson, Lindsay, Bradford B. Hepler, and Myoung Ouk Kim. 2012. I*slander Population: 2010.* May 2012. C2010BR-12. Washington, DC: U.S. Government Printing Office.

Hochschild, Arlie Russell. 1990. "The Second Shift: Employed Women Are Putting in Another Day of Work at Home." *Utne Reader* 38 (March – April):66–73.

———. 2005. *The Commercialization of Intimate Life: Notes from Home and Work.* Berkeley: University of California Press.

———, with Anne Machung. 2012. *The Second Shift: Working Parents and the Revolution at Home.* Revised with a new Afterword. New York: Penguin.

Hoeffel, Elizabeth M., Sonya Rastogi, Myoung Ouk Kim, and Hasan Shahid. 2012. *The Asian Population: 2010.* C2101BR-11. Washington, DC: U.S. Government Printing Office.

Holden, Constance. 1980. "Identical Twins Reared Apart." *Science* 207 (March 21):1323–1328.

———. 1987. "The Genetics of Personality." *Science* 257 (August 7):598–601.

Holguin, Robert. 2013. "LAPD monitors social media for flash mob crime sprees." July 18. Accessed June 13, 2016 at www.abc7.com (Los Angeles affiliate).

Hollingshead, August B. 1975. *Elmtown's Youth and Elmtown Revisited.* New York: Wiley.

Holmes, Mary. 2009. "Commuter Couples and Distance Relationships: Living Apart Together." Sloan Work and Family Research Network. Accessible at http://wfnetwork.bc.edu/encyclopedia_entry.php?id=15551&area=all.

Homans, George C. 1979. "Nature versus Nurture: A False Dichotomy."*Contemporary Sociology* 8 (May):345–348.

Home School Legal Defense Association. 2016. "My State: Laws." Accessed February 26 at www.hslda.org.

Hooks, bell. 1994. *Feminist Theory: From Margin to Center.* 2nd ed. Boston: South End Press.

Horgan, John. 1993. "Eugenics Revisited." *Scientific American* 268 (June):122–128, 130–133.

Horkheimer, Max, and Theodore Adorno. [1944] 2002. *Dialectic of Enlightenment.* Palo Alto, CA: Stanford University Press.

Horner, James. 2015. "Speak Out: Should students and faculty be allowed to carry guns on college campuses?" *Annenberg Classroom.* Accessed October 23 at annenbergclassroom.org.

Horowitz, Helen Lefkowitz. 1987. *Campus Life.* Chicago: University of Chicago Press.

Horwitz, Allan V. 2002. *Creating Mental Illness.* Chicago: University of Chicago Press.

Hosokawa, William K. 1969. *Nisei: The Quiet Americans.* New York: Morrow.

Hossain, Ziarat, Soyoung Lee, Ashley Martin-Cuellar. 2015. "Latino Mothers' and Fathers' Caregiving with Their School-Age Children." *Hispanic Journal of Behavioral Sciences* (May, No. 2): 186–203.

Housing and Urban Development. 2010. *The Annual Homeless Assessment Report to Congress.* Washington DC: U.S. Government Printing Office.

Howard, Judith A. 1999. "Border Crossings between Women's Studies and Sociology." *Contemporary Sociology* 28 (September):525–528.

Howard, Michael C. 1989. *Contemporary Cultural Anthropology.* 3rd ed. Glenview, IL: Scott, Foresman.

Howard, Michael. 2009. *Modern Wicca: A History from Gerald Gardner to the Present.* St. Paul, MN: Llewellyn Books.

Howard, Russell D., and Reid L. Sawyer. 2003. *Terrorism and Counterterrorism: Understanding the New Security Environment.* Guilford, CT: McGraw-Hill/Dushkin.

Hu, Winnie. 2010. "In a New Role, Teachers Move to Run Schools." *New York Times,* September 7, pp. A1, A20.

Huang, Gary. 1988. "Daily Addressing Ritual: A Cross-Cultural Study." Presented at the annual meeting of the American Sociological Association, Atlanta.

Huelsman, Mark. 2015. "The Debt Divide: The Racial and Class Bias Behind the 'New Normal' of Student Borrowing." May 19. Accessible at www.demos.org.

Hughes, Everett. 1945. "Dilemmas and Contradictions of Status." *American Journal of Sociology* 50 (March):353–359.

Human Genome Project. 2015. "All About The Human Genome Project (HGP)." Accessed January 4, 2016, at www.genome.gov.

Humes, Karen R., Nicholas A. Jones, and Roberto R. Ramirez. 2011. *Overview of Race and Hispanic Origin: 2010.* 2010 Census Brief BR-02. Accessible at www.census.gov/prod/cen2010/briefs/c2010br-02.pdf.

Hunter, Herbert M., ed. 2000. *The Sociology of Oliver C. Cox: New Perspectives: Research in Race and Ethnic Relations,* vol. 2. Stamford, CT: JAI Press.

Hunter, James Davison. 1991. *Culture Wars: The Struggle to Define America.* New York: Basic Books.

Hunter, Lori M., Jessie K. Luna, and Rachel M. Norton. 2015. "Environmental Dimensions of Migration." *Annual Review of Sociology* 41: 377–397.

Huntington, Samuel P. 1993. "The Clash of Civilizations?" *Foreign Affairs* 72 (Summer):22–49.

Hur, Song-Woo. 2011. "Mapping South Korean Women's Movements During and After Democratization: Shifting Identities." *East Asian Social Movements,* edited by J. Broadbent and V. Brockman.

Hurn, Christopher J. 1985. *The Limits and Possibilities of Schooling,* 2nd ed. Boston: Allyn and Bacon.

Hurwitz, Heather McKee, and Verta Taylor. 2012. "Women's Cultures and Social Movements in Global Context." *Sociology Compass* 6 (October): 808–822.

Hussar, William J., and Tabitha M. Bailey. 2011. *Projections of Education Statistics to 2019.* Washington, DC: National Center for Education Statistics.

———, and Tabitha M. Bailey. 2013. Projection of Education Statistics to 2021. Washington, DC: U.S. Government Printing Office. Accessible at http://nces.ed.gov/programs/projections/projections2021/.

———, and Tabitha M. Bailey. 2014. "Projections of Education Statistics to 2022." Accessible at nced.ed.gov.

Hutson, Matthew. 2014. "Espousing Equality, but Embracing a Hierarchy." *New York Times* (June 22), sect. BU, p. 3.

———. 2015. "Tall Tales."*The Atlantic* (November): 38.

I

Igo, Sarah E. 2007. *The Average American: Surveys, Citizens, and the Making of a Mass Public.* Cambridge, MA: Harvard University Press.

Immervoll, Herwig, and David Barber. 2005. *Can Parents Afford to Work? Childcare Costs, Tax-Benefit Policies and Work Incentives.* Paris: Organisation for Economic Co-Operation and Development.

India, Government of. 2009. *India: Urban Poverty Report 2009.* February 3. New Delhi: Ministry of Housing and Urban Poverty Alleviation., Accessible at www.in.undp.org.

Inglehart, Ronald, and Wayne E. Baker. 2000. "Modernization, Cultural Change, and the Persistence of Traditional Values." *American Sociological Review* 65 (February):19–51.

Innocence Project. 2015. "The Innocent and the Death Penalty." Accessed October 28 at innocenceproject.org.

Inoue, Sachiko, Takashi Yorifuji, Soshi Takao, Hiroyuki Doi, and Ichiro Kawachi. 2013. "Social Cohesion and Mortality: A Survival Analysis of Older Adults in Japan." *American Journal of Public Health* 103 (December):e60-e66.

Institute for Economics and Peace. 2015a. "Global Peace Index 2015." Accessible at www.economicsandpeace.org.

Institute for Economics and Peace. 2015b. "Global Terrorism Index 2015." Accessible at www.economics and peace.org.

Institute for Policy Studies. 2015. "Wealth Inequality." Accessed October 30 at inequality.org, a Project of the Institute for Policy Studies.

Inter-Parliamentary Union. 2015. "Women in National Parliaments." November 1. Accessed December 7 at www.ipu.org.

Interbrand. 2015. "Best Global Brands 2013." Accessible at www.interbrand.com/en/best-global-brands/2013/Best-Global-Brands-2013.aspx.

International Center for Academic Integrity. 2015. "Statistics." Accessed February 11, 2016 at www.academicintegrity.org.

International Federation of Robotics. 2015a. *World Robotics 2015: Executive Summary.* Accessible at www.ifr.org.

———. 2015b. "World Robotics Survey: Industrial robots are conquering the world." IPA Press Release. September 30. Accessible at www.ifr.org.

International Institute for Democracy and Electoral Assistance. 2013. *Atlas of Electoral Gender quotas.* Stockholm: IDEA. Accessible at www.ipu.org.

———. 2015. *Databases and Networks.* Accessed December 7 at www.idea.int.

International Monetary Fund. 2000. "World Economic Outlook: Asset Prices and the Business Cycle." Washington, DC: International Monetary Fund.

International Survey Social Programme. 2014. "ISSP 2012- Family and Changing Gender Roles IV Variable Report." October 29. Cologne Germany: GESIS Leibniz Institute for Social Sciences.

International Telecommunication Union. 2012. Global Technology Development Figures. October 11. Accessed November 14, 2013 at http://www.itu.int/net/pressoffice/press_releases/2012/70.aspx#.UoUJgKW50pE.

International Trade Union Confederation. 2009. "Davos: World Unions Call for Action against Corporate Grand Theft." Accessed January 31 at www.ituc-csi.org/spip.php?article2736.

———. 2014. *ITUC Global Poll 2014.* Accessible at www.ituc-csi.org.

International Visual Sociology Association. 2016. "About IVSA." Accessible at www.visual sociology.org.

Internet World Stats. 2015. "Usage and Population Statistics" and "Internet World Users by Language." Updated on March 29. Accessed March 29 (www.internetworldstats.com).

Ironside, Virginia. 2011. "Romania's Orphanages: Locking the Past Away." *The Independent (UK)* (November 29). Accessed September 25, 2012 at http://www.independent.co.uk/life-style/health-and-families/features/romanias-orphanages-locking-the-past-away-6269173.html.

Isaacs, Julia B. 2007b. *Economic Mobility of Men and Women.* Washington, DC: Economic Mobility Project.

Isaacs, Julia B., Isabel V. Sawhill, and Ron Haskins. 2008. *Getting Ahead or Losing Ground: Economic Mobility in America.* Washington, DC: Pew Charitable Trusts.

Ishak, Adam. 2013. "The new media in post-revolution Egypt." January 21. Accessible at Roskilde University; http://rudar.ruc.dk/handle/1800/9886.

ITOPF. 2006. "Statistics: International Tanker Owners Pollution Federation Limited." Accessed May 2 (www.itopf.com/stats.html).

j

Jäntti, Markus. 2009. "Mobility in the United States in Comparative Perspectives." *Focus* 26 (Fall).

Jackson, Philip W. 1968. *Life in Classrooms.* New York: Holt.

Jacobs, Andres. 2010. "As China's Economy Grows, Pollution Worsens Despite New Efforts to Control It." *New York Times,* July 29, p. A4.

Jacobs, Anna W., and Irene Padavic. 2015. "Hours, Scheduling and Flexibility for Women in the US Low-Wage Labour Force." *Gender, Work and Organization* 22 (No. 1 January).

Jacobsen, Linda A., May Kent, Marlene Lee, and Mark Mather. 2011. "America's Aging Population." *Population Bulletin* 66 (February).

Jain, Saranga, and Kathleen Kurz. 2007. *New Insights on Preventing Child Marriage: A Global Analysis of Factors and Programs.* Washington, DC: International Center for Research on Women.

James, Selma. 2012. *Sex, Race and Class: The Perspective of Winning: A Selection of Writings 1952–2011.* Oakland CA: PM Press.

Janta, Barbara. 2014. *Caring for Children in Europe.* Brussels: RAND Europe. delete Domeij and Klein, L. King.

Japan Aisaika Organization. 2012. "Aisaika Organization Prospectus." Accessed January 15 (www.aisaika.org/en/prospectus.html).

Jasper, James M. 2014. *Protest: A Cultural Introduction to Social Movements.* Cambridge UK: Polity Books.

Jenkins, Henry. 2006. *Convergence Culture: Where Old and New Media Collide.* New York: New York University Press.

Jensen, Gary F. 2005. "Social Organization Theory." In *Encyclopedia of Criminology,* edited by Richard A. Wright and J. Mitchell Miller. Chicago: Fitzrog Dearborn.

Jensen, Todd, and Matthew O. Howard. 2015. "Perceived Stepparent–Child Relationship Quality: A Systematic Review of Stepchildren's Perspectives." *Marriage and Family Review* 51 (No. 2): 99–153.

Joas, Hans, and Wolfgang Knöbl. 2009. *Social Theory: Twenty Introductory Lectures.* Cambridge: Cambridge University Press.

Johannes, Laura. "2014. AARP Faces Competition from Conservative-Leaning Groups." *Wall Street Journal,* March 30. Accessible at www.wsj.com.

John, Robert. 2012. "The Native American Family." Pp. 361–410 in *Ethnic Families in America: Patterns and Variations.* 5th ed., edited by Roosevelt Wright, Jr., Charles H. Mindel, Thanh Van Tran, and Robert W. Halsenstein. Upper Saddle River, NJ: Pearson.

Johnson, Bobbie. 2010. "Privacy No Longer a Social Norm, Says Facebook Founder." January 10. Accessed December 2, 2013 at http://www.theguardian.com/technology/2010/jan/11/facebook-privacy.

Johnson, Ian. 2012. "A Promise to Tackle China's Problems, but Few Hints of a Shift in Path." *New York Times,* November 16, p. A19.

Jones, Jeffrey M. 2013. "Americans Still Divided on Energy-Environment Trade-Off." April 10. Accessible at www.gallup.com.

———. 2015. "Perceptions of Tax Fairness Diverging by Income in U.S." April 14. Accessible at www.gallup.com.

———. 2015a. "In U.S., New Record 43% Are Political Independents." January 7. Accessible at www.gallup.com.

———. 2015b. "Democrats Regain Edge in Party Affiliation." July 2. Accessible at www.gallup.com.

———, and Gary J. Gates. 2015. "Same-Sex Marriages Up After Supreme Court Ruling." November 5. Accessible at www.gallup.com.

Jones, Jeff, and Lydia Saad. 2014. Gallup Poll Social Series: Crime. Final Topline. Timberline: 937008. October 12–15, 2014. Accessible at gal-lup.com.

Jones, Maggie. 2015. "Her Choice Was No Choice at All." *New York Times Magazine* (January 18): 30–37, 51.

Jones-Puthoff, Alexa. 2013. *Is the U.S. Population Getting Older and More Diverse?* June 14. Accessible at http://www.census.gov/newsroom/cspan/pop_diverse/.

Jost, Kenneth. 2008. "Women in Politics." *CQ Researcher* 18 (March 21).

Julian, Tiffany, and Robert Kominski. 2011. *Education and Synthetic Work-Life Earnings Estimates.* ACS-14. Washington, DC: U.S. Government Printing Office.

Juniper Research. 2015. *Cybercrime and the Internet of Threats.* Basingstoke England: Juniper Research.

K

Kadlec, Dan. 2015. "1 in 3 Older Workers Likely to be Poor or Near Poor in Retirement." *Time* (April 8). Accessed April 9, 2015, at www.time.com.

Kahlenberg, Richard D. 2015. "The Future of Affirmative Action." *The Atlantic* (December 8). Accessible at www.theatlantic.com.

Kambayashi, Takehiko. 2008. "Japanese Men Shout the Oft-Unsaid 'I love you.'" *Christian Science Monitor,* February 13.

Kampf, Zohar. 2014. "News-Media and Terrorism: Changing Relationship, Changing Definitions." *Sociology Compass* 8 (no. 1).

Kandel, William. 2005. "Rural Hispanics at a Glance." *Economic Information Bulletin* (December).

Kaneda, Toshiko, and Kristin Bietsch. 2015. *2015 World Population Data Sheet.* Washington DC: Population Reference Bureau.

Karides, Marina. 2010. "Theorizing the Rise of Microenterprise Development in Caribbean Context." *Journal of World-Systems Research* 16 (2):192–216.

Karmel, Tom. 2015. "Skills Deepening or Credentialism? Education Qualifications and Occupational Outcomes, 1996–2011." *Australian Journal of Labour Economics* 18 (April, no. 1).

Katovich, Michael A. 1987. Correspondence. June 1.

Katz, Michael. 1971. *Class, Bureaucracy, and the Schools: The Illusion of Educational Change in America.* New York: Praeger.

Kaufman, Sharon R., and Lynn M. Morgan. 2005. "The Anthropology of the Beginnings and Ends of Life." *Annual Review of Anthropology* 34:317–341.

Keeter, Scott, and Courtney Kennedy. 2006. "The Cell Phone Challenge to Survey Research." Washington, DC: Pew Research Center.

Kelleher, Jennifer Sinco. 2011. "23 Arrested for Refusing to Leave Iolani Palace." *News from Indian Country,* November, p. 5.

Kennicott, Philip. 2011. "Review: 9/11 Memorial in New York." Accessed August 26 (www.washingtonpost.com).

Kenny, Charles. 2009. "Revolution in a Box." *Foreign Policy* (November):68–74.

Kephart, William M. 1963. "Experimental Family Organization: An Historic-Cultural Report on the Oneida Community." *Marriage and Family Living* 25 (August): 261–71.

Kerbo, Harold R. 2006. *World Poverty: The Roots of Global Inequality and the World System.* New York: McGraw-Hill.

———. 2012. *Social Stratification and Inequality.* 8th ed. New York: McGraw-Hill.

Kesmodel, David, and Danny Yadron. 2010. "E-Cigarettes Spark New Smoking War." *Wall Street Journal,* August 25, pp. A1, A12.

Kessler, Ronald C., Emil F. Coccaro, Maurizio Fava, Savina Jaeger, Robert Jin, and Ellen Walters. 2006. "The Prevalence and Correlates of DSM-IV Intermittent Explosive Disorder in the National Comorbidity Survey Replication." *Archives of General Psychiatry* 63 (June):669–678.

Khadaroo, Stacy Tericher. 2014. "New Orleans' Bold Test." *Christian Science Monitor* (March 10): 21–24.

Khan, Shamus. 2013. "We Are Not All in This Together." *New York Times,* December 15 (Section SR), p. 4.

Kidder, Jeffrey L. 2012. "Parkour, the Affective Appropriation of Urban Space, and the Real/Virtual Dialectic." *City and Community* 11 (September):229–253.

Kiener, Robert. 2015. "Will Opponents of Capital Punishment Continue to Gain Ground?" *CQ Researcher* (July 7).

Kim, Hyun Sik. 2011. "Consequences of Parental Divorce for Child Development." *American Sociological Review* 76 (3):487–511.

Kim, Jerry W., Bruce Kogut, and Jae-Suk Yang. 2015. "Executive Compensation, Fat Cats, and Best Athletes." *American Sociological Review* 80 (no. 2): 299–328.

Kim, Kwang Chung. 1999. *Koreans in the Hood: Conflict with African Americans.* Baltimore: Johns Hopkins University Press.

Kimmel, Michael S. 2008. *The Gendered Society.* 3rd ed. New York: State University of New York at Stony Brook.

King, Gary. 2011. "Ensuring the Data-Rich Future of the Social Sciences." *Science* (February 11):719–721.

King, Meredith L. 2007. *Immigrants in the U.S. Health Care System.* Washington, DC: Center for American Progress.

Kingsbury, Alex. 2008. "Q and A: Sudhir Venkatesh." *US News and World Report,* January 21, p. 14.

Kinsey, Alfred C., Wardell B. Pomeroy, and Clyde E. Martin. 1948. *Sexual Behavior in the Human Male.* Philadelphia: Saunders.

———, 1953. *Sexual Behavior in the Human Female.* Philadelphia: Saunders.

Kiser, Edgar. 1992. "War." Pp. 2243–2247 in *Encyclopedia of Sociology,* edited by Edgar F. Borgatta and Marie L. Borgatta. New York: Macmillan.

Kitchener, Richard F. 1991. "Jean Piaget: The Unknown Sociologist." *British Journal of Sociology* 42 (September):421–442.

Klein, Lloyd. 1994. "We're Going to Disney World: Consumers Credit and the Consumption of Social Experience." *Free Inquiry in Creative Sociology* 22 (November):117–124.

Klein, Naomi. 1999. *No Logo: Money, Marketing, and the Growing Anti-Corporate Movement.* New York: Picador (St. Martin's Press).

Kleiner, Art. 2003. "Are You In with the In Crowd?" *Harvard Business Review* 81 (July): 86–92.

Klinenberg, Eric. 2015. *Heat Wave: A Social Autopsy of Disaster in Chicago.* Second edition. Chicago: University of Chicago Press.

Kneebone, Elizabeth, and Alan Berube. 2013. *Confronting Suburban Poverty in America.* Washington DC: Brookings Institution Press.

Knudsen, Morten. 2010. "Surprised by Method—Functional Method and System Theory." *Forum: Qualitative Social Research* 11 (September): article 12.

———. 2015. "The American Middle Class Is Losing Ground." Washington, DC: Pew Research Center.

Kochhar, Rakesh, Richard Fry, and Paul. 2011. "Twenty-to-One: Wealth Gaps Rise to Record Highs between Whites, Blacks and Hispanics." July 26. Accessible at http://www.pewsocialtrends.org/files/2011/07/SDT-Wealth-Report_7-26-11_FINAL.pdf.

———. 2014. "Wealth inequality has widened along racial, ethnic lines since end of Great Recession." December 12. Accessible at www.pewreserach,org.

Kochhnar, Rakesh. 2014. "As the population grays, Americans stay upbeat." February 12. Accessed March 8 at www.pewresearch.org.

Kohut, Andrew, et al. 2005. *American Character Gets Mixed Reviews: 16-Nation Pew Global Attitudes Survey.* Washington, DC: Pew Global Project Attitudes.

———. 2007. *Global Unease with Major World Powers: Rising Environmental Concern in 47-Nation Survey.* Washington, DC: Pew Global Project Attitudes.

Kokmen, Leyla. 2008. "Environmental Justice for All." *Utne Reader* (March–April):42–46.

Korean Women's Association United. 2010. "Republic of Korea: Critical Issues on the Seventh Periodical Report on the Convention on the Elimination of All Forms of Discrimination against Women." November 10. Accessed March 27, 2010 (www2.ohchr.org/English/bodies/cedaw/docs/ngos/Korean_Womens_Association_United(PSWG).pdf).

Kornblum, Janet. 2007. "Meet the 'Tech-No's': People Who Reject Plugging into the Highly Wired World." *USA Today,* January 11, pp. A1, A2.

Kosmin, Barry A., and Ariela Keysar. 2009. *American Religious Identification Survey.* Hartford, CT: Trinity College.

Kottak, Conrad. 2015. *Anthropology: Appreciating Human Diversity.* 17th ed. New York: McGraw-Hill.

Krane, Jim. 2009. *Dubai: The Story of the World's City.* London: Atlantic Books.

———. 2010. "To Spend or Not to Spend." Interviewed on Al Jazeera television, March 26. Accessed April 20 (http://english.aljazeera.net/programmes/counting thecost/2010/03/201032510494187263.html).

Kratz, Corinne A., and Iman Karp. 1993. "Wonder and Worth: Disney Museums in World Showcase." *Museum Anthropology* 17 (3):32–42.

Kraybill, Donald. 2001. *The Riddle of Amish Culture.* Rev. ed. Baltimore: Johns Hopkins University Press.

Kreider, Rose M. 2011. "Contexts of Racial Socialization: Are Transracial Adoptive Families More Like Multiracial or White Monoracial Families?" March 1. Accessible at www.census.gov.

Kriesberg, Louis. 1992. "Peace." Pp. 1432–1436 in *Encyclopedia of Sociology,* edited by Edgar F. Borgatta and Marie L. Borgatta. New York: Macmillan.

Kristof, Nicholas D. 1998. "As Asian Economies Shrink, Women Are Squeezed Out." *New York Times,* June 11, pp. A1, A12.

Krogstad, Jens Manuel. 2015. "Cuban Immigration to U.S. Surges as Relations Warm." October 7. Accessible at www.pewresearch.org
———. "What Americans, Europeans think of immigrants." Pew Research Center. September 24. Accessible at www. pewresearch.org.

Kronstadt, Jessica, and Melissa Favreault. 2008. "Families and Economic Mobility." Washington, DC: Economic Mobility Project. Also accessible at www.economicmobility.org/reports_and_research/literature_reviews?id=0004.

Kübler-Ross, Elisabeth. 1969. *On Death and Dying.* New York: Macmillan.

Kunle, Oluyemisi Folashade, Henry Omoregie Egharevba, and Peter Ochogu Ahmadu. 2012. "Standardization of Herbal Medicines—A Review." *International Journal of Biodiversity and Conservation* 4(3): 101–112.

Kunzig, Robert. 2011. "Seven Billion." *National Geographic* (January):40–69.

Ladner, Joyce. 1973. *The Death of White Sociology.* New York: Random Books.

Lahey, Joanna. 2006. *Age, Women, and Hiring: An Experimental Study.* Boston: Center for Retirement Research, Boston College. Accessed at http://escholarship.bc.edu/ 521 retirement_papers/134.

Lajimodiere, Denise K. 2013. "American Indian Females and Stereotypes: Warriors, Leaders, Healers, Feminists; Not Drudges, Princesses, Prostitutes." *Multicultural Perspectives* 15 (Issue 2).

Landtman, Gunnar. [1938] 1968. *The Origin of Inequality of the Social Class.* New York: Greenwood (original edition 1938, Chicago: University of Chicago Press).

Lasswell, Harold D. 1936. *Politics: Who Gets What, When, How.* New York: McGraw-Hill.

Last, Jonathan. 2013. *What to Expect When No One's Expecting: America's Coming Demographic Disaster.* New York: Encounter Books.

Laumann, Edward O., John H. Gagnon, and Robert T. Michael. 1994a. "A Political History of the National Sex Survey of Adults." *Family Planning Perspectives* 26 (February):34–38.
———. 1994b. *The Social Organization of Sexuality: Sexual Practices in the United States.* Chicago: University of Chicago Press.

Lavrakas, Paul J., Charles D. Shuttles, Charlotte Steel, and Howard Fienberg. 2007. "The State of Surveying Cell Phone Numbers in the United States: 2007 and Beyond." *Public Opinion Quarterly* 71 (5):840–854.

Lawson, Sandra. 2008. *Girls Count.* New York: Goldman Sachs.

Lazarsfeld, Paul, and Robert K. Merton. 1948. "Mass Communication, Popular Taste, and Organized Social Action." Pp. 95–118 in *The Communication of Ideas,* edited by Lymon Bryson. New York: Harper and Brothers.

Lazarsfeld, Paul, Bernard Berelson, and H. Gaudet. 1948. *The People's Choice.* New York: Columbia University Press.

Lazer, David, Ryan Kennedy, Gary King, and Alessandro Vespignani. 2014. "The Parable of Google Flu: Traps in Big Data Analysis." *Science* 343 (March 14):1203–1205.

Leavell, Hugh R., and E. Gurney Clark. 1965. *Preventive Medicine for the Doctor in His Community: An Epidemiologic Approach.* 3rd ed. New York: McGraw-Hill.

Ledgerwood, Joanna, ed. 2013. *The New Microfinance Handbook: A Financial Market Perspective.* Washington, DC: World Bank.

Lee, Alfred McClung. 1983. *Terrorism in Northern Ireland.* New York: Rowman & Littlefield.

Lee, Barrett A., Kimberly A. Tyler, and James D. Wright. 2010. "The New Homelessness Revisited." *Annual Review of Sociology* 30:501–521.

Lee, Ji Hyun. 2013. "Modern Lessons from Arranged Marriages." *New York Times,* January 18. Accessible at http://www.nytimes.com/2013/01/20/fashion/weddings/parental-involvement-can-help-in-choosing-marriage-partners-experts-say.html?pagewanted=all.

Lee, Ronald D. and David S. Reher. 2011. "Introduction: The Landscape of Demographic Transition and Its Aftermath." *Population and Development Review* 37 (Supplement): 1–7.

Lehman, Chris. 2012. "Retirement Communities Find Niche with Gay Seniors." February 16. Accessible at http://www.wbur.org/npr/146713531/retirement-communities-find-niche-with-gay-seniors.

Lemert, Charles. Ed. 2013. *Social Theory: The Multicultural, Global, and Classical Readings.* 5th ed. Philadelphia: Westview.

Lengermann, Patricia Madoo, and Jill Niebrugge-Brantley. 1998. *The Women Founders: Sociology and Social Theory, 1830–1930.* Boston: McGraw-Hill.

Lenski, Gerhard. 1966. *Power and Privilege: A Theory of Social Stratification.* New York: McGraw-Hill.

Leonhardt, David 2004 "As Wealthy Fill Top Colleges Concerns Grow Over Fairness." *New York Times* (April 22), pp. A1, A12.

Levin, Jack, and William C. Levin. 1980. *Ageism.* Belmont, CA: Wadsworth.

Levinson, Daniel J. 1978. *On Human Nature.* Cambridge, MA: Harvard University Press.
———. 1996. *The Seasons of a Woman's Life.* With Judy D. Levinson. New York: Knopf.

Levitt, Peggy, and B. Nadya Jaworsky. 2007. "Transnational Migration Studies: Past Developments and Future Trends." *Annual Review of Sociology* 33:129–156.

Levitt, Steven D., and Stephen J. Dubner. 2006. *Freakonomics: A Rogue Economist Explores the Hidden Side of Everything.* Revised and expanded edition. New York: Morrow.
———, and Sudhir Venkatesh. 2000. "An Economic Analysis of a Drug-Selling Gang's Finances." *Quarterly Journal of Economics* (August):775–789.

Li, Jennifer S., Tracie A. Barnett, Elizabeth Goodman, Richard C. Wasserman, and Alex R. Kemper. 2013. "Approaches to the Prevention and Management of Childhood Obesity: The Role of Social Networks and the Use of Social Media and Related Electronic Technologies: A Scientific Statement from the American Heart Association." *Circulation* 127:260–267.

Lichter, Daniel T., Domenico Parisi, and Michael C. Taquino. 2015. "Toward New Macro-Segregation? Decomposing Segregation within and between Metropolitan Cities and Suburbs." *American Sociological Review* 80 (No. 4): 843–873.

Lind-Valdan, Anna Bolette. 2014. *The feminist preschool?* Doctoral dissertation at Rutgers University, Public Administration. Accessible at https://rucore.libraries.rutgers.edu/rutgers-lib/43987/PDF/1/.

Lindner, Eileen. 2012. *Yearbook of American and Canadian Churches.* Nashville, TN: Abingdon Press.

Linn, Susan, and Alvin F. Poussaint. 1999. "Watching Television: What Are Children Learning about Race and Ethnicity?" *Child Care Information Exchange* 128 (July):50–52.

Lino, Mark. 2013. *Expenditures on Children by Families, 2012.* Washington, DC: U.S. Department of Agriculture, Center for Nutrition Policy and Promotion.

Linton, Ralph. 1936. *The Study of Man.* New York: Appleton-Century Crofts, Inc.

Liptak, Adam. 2006. "The Ads Discriminate, but Does the Web?" *New York Times,* March 5, p. 16.
———. 2008. "From One Footnote, a Debate over the Tangles of Law, Science and Money." *New York Times,* November 25, p. A13.

Liska, Allen E., and Steven F. Messner. 1999. *Perspectives on Crime and Deviance.* 3rd ed. Upper Saddle River, NJ: Prentice Hall.

Livingstone, Gretchen. 2014a. "Growing Number of Dads Home with the Kids." June 5. Accessible at www.pewsocialtrends.com.
———. 2014b. "Four-in-Ten Couples Say 'I Do,' Again." November 14. Accessible at www.pew-socialtrends.org.

Livingstone, Sonia. 2004. "The Challenge of Changing Audiences." *European Journal of Communication* 19 (March):75–86.

Llana, Sara Miller, and Whitney Eulich. 2013. "Women at War, Worldwide." *Christian Science Monitor Weekly* (February 4):18–20.

Lofland, John. 1985. *Protests: Studies of Collective Behavior and Social Movements.* Rutgers, NJ: Transaction.

Lofland, Lyn H. 1975. "The 'Thereness' of Women: A Selective Review of Urban Sociology." Pp. 144–170 in *Another Voice,* edited by M. Millman and R. M. Kanter. New York: Anchor/Doubleday.

Logan, John R., Richard D. Alba, and Werquan Zhang. 2002. "Immigrant Enclaves and Ethnic Communities in New York and Los Angeles." *American Sociological Review* 67 (April):299–322.

Lohr, Steve. 2008. "For a Good Retirement, Find Work. Good Luck." *New York Times,* June 22, p. 3.

Loomer, Jon. 2014. "Core Audiences: How to Target Facebook Ads Using More Demographics." May 12. Accessed November 5, 2015 at jonloomer.com.

Lopez, Mark Hugo. 2011. *The Latino Electorate in 2010: More Voters, More Non-Voters.* Washington, DC: Pew Hispanic Center.

———, and Ana Gonzalez-Barrera. 2013. "Inside the 2012 Latino Electorate." June 3. Accessible at www.pewhispanic.org.

Lorber, Judith. 2005. *Breaking the Bowls: Degendering and Feminist Change.* New York: Norton.

Loughran, Thomas A., Holly Nguyen, Alex R. Piquero, and Jeffrey Fagan. 2013. "The Returns to Criminal Capital. " *American Sociological Review* 78 (6):925–948.

Lubienski, Christopher A., and Peter C. Weitzel. 2012. *The Charter School Experiment: Expectations, Evidence, and Implications.* Cambridge MA: Harvard Education Press.

Lucas, Edward. 2015. *Cyberphobia.* London: Bloomsbury.

Luhnow, David. 2014. "Most Violent Region in the World: Latin America." *Wall Street Journal* (April 12): A9.

Lukacs, Georg. 1923. *History and Class Consciousness.* London: Merlin.

Luster, Tom, Kelly Rhoades, and Bruce Haas. 1989. "The Relation between Parental Values and Parenting Behavior: A Test of the Kohn Hypothesis." *Journal of Marriage and the Family* 51 (February):139–147.

Lyall, Sarah. 2002. "For Europeans, Love, Yes; Marriage, Maybe." *New York Times,* March 24, pp. 1–8.

Lynn, Barry C. 2003. "Trading with a Low-Wage Tiger."*American Prospect* 14 (February):10–12.

m

MacDorman, Marian F., and T. J. Mathews. 2009. "Behind International Rankings of Infant Mortality: How the United States Compares with Europe." NCHS Date Brief (No. 23, November).

MacFarquhar, Neil. 2008. "Resolute or Fearful, Many Muslims Turn to Home Schooling." *New York Times,* March 26, p. A1.

Machalek, Richard, and Michael W. Martin. 2010. "Evolution, Biology and Society: A Conversation for the 21st-Century Sociology Classroom." *Teaching Sociology* 38 (1):35–45.

Mack, Mick G. 2003. "Does Exercise Status Influence the Impressions Formed by College Students?" *College Student Journal* 37 (December).

Mack, Raymond W., and Calvin P. Bradford. 1979. *Transforming America: Patterns of Social Change.* 2nd ed. New York: Random House.

Mackun, Paul, and Steven Wilson. 2011. *Population Distribution and Change: 2000 to 2010.* March 2011. 2010 Census Brief BR-01.

Madden, Mary, Amanda Lenhart, Sandra Cortesi, Urs Gasser, Maeve Duggan, Aaron Smith, and Meredith Beaton. 2013. "Teens, Social Media, and Privacy." May 21. Accessible at http://pewinternet.org/Reports/2013/Teens-Social-Media-AndPrivacy.aspx.

Magga, Ole Henrik. 2006. "Diversity in Sami Terminology for Reindeer, Snow, and Ice." *International Social Science Journal* 58 (March):25–34.

Magnier, Mark. 2004. "China Clamps Down on Web News Discussion." *Los Angeles Times,* February 26, p. A4.

Magnolia Pictures. 2014. "The Wolf Pack: Final Film Notes." Accessible at www.magpictures.com/thewolfpack/.

Malcolm X, with Alex Haley. [1964] 1999. *The Autobiography of Malcolm X.* Revised with Epilogue by Alex Haley and Afterword by Ossie Davis. New York: One World, Ballantine Books.

Males, Mike, and Meda Chesney-Lind. 2010. "The Myth of Mean Girls." *New York Times,* April 2, p. A21.

Malhotra, Neil, and Yotam Margalit. 2009. "State of the Nation: Anti-Semitism and the Economic Crisis." *Boston Review* (May–June). Accessible at http://bostonreview.net/BR34.3/malhotra_margalit.php.

Mandel, Hadas. 2016. "The Role of Occupational Attributes in Gender Earnings Inequality, 1970–2010. *Social Science Research* 55 (January):122–138.

Manza, Jeff, and Clem Brooks. 2012. "How Sociology Lost Public Opinion: A Genealogy of a Missing Concept in the Study of the Political." *Sociological Theory* 30 (no. 2): 89–113.

Marable, Manning. 2011. *Malcolm X: A Life of Reinvention.* New York: Viking.

Marist Poll. 2015. "PBS NewsHour/Marist Poll: Summary of National Findings." September. Accessible at www.pbs-newshour-marist-poll-sep2015.pdf.

Markson, Elizabeth W. 1992. "Moral Dilemmas." *Society,* 29(July–August): 4–6.

Marshall, Brent K., and J. Steven Picou. 2008. "Postnormal Science, Precautionary Principle, and Worst Cases: The Challenge of Twenty-First-Century Catastrophes." *Sociological Inquiry* 78 (May):230–247.

Martin, Daniel C., and James E. Yankay. 2014. "Refugees and Asylees 2013." Accessible at www.dhs.gov.

Martin, Dominique, Jean-Luc Metzger, and Philippe Pierre. 2006. "The Sociology of Globalization: Theoretical and Methodological Reflections." *International Sociology* 21 (July):499–521.

Martin, Greg. 2015. *Understanding Social Movements.* New York: Palgrave.

Martin, Isaac, and Monica Prasad. 2014. "Taxes and Fiscal Sociology." *Annual Review of Sociology* 40:331–345.

Martin, Jeff. 2012. "Westward ho! for more Amish." *USA Today* (August 15): 3A.

Martin, Joyce A., Brady E. Hamilton, and Michelle J.K. Osterman. 2015. "Births in the United States, 2014." NCHS Data Brief No 216. National Center for Health Statistics. September 2015. Accessible at www.cdc.gov.

Martin, Karin A. 2009. "Normalizing Heterosexuality: Mothers' Assumptions, Talk, and Strategies with Young Children." *American Sociological Review* 74 (April):190–207.

Martin, Marvin. 1996. "Sociology Adapting to Changes." *Chicago Tribune,* July 21, sec. 18, p. 20.

Martin, Susan E. 1994. "Outsider within the Station House: The Impact of Race and Gender on Black Women Politics." *Social Problems* 41 (August):383–400.

Martineau, Harriet. [1837] 1962. *Society in America.* Edited, abridged, with an introductory essay by Seymour Martin Lipset. Reprint. Garden City, NY: Doubleday.

———, [1838] 1989. *How to Observe Morals and Manners.* Philadelphia: Leal and Blanchard. Sesquentennial edition, edited by M. R. Hill, Transaction Books.

Marx, Gary T. 2012. "Looking at Smelser's Theory of Collective Behavior After Almost 50 Years: A Review and Appreciation." *American Sociologist* 43 (June): 135–152.

Marx, Karl. [1844] 1964. "Contribution to the Critique of Hegel's Philosophy of Right." In *On Religion, Karl Marx and Friedrich Engels.* New York: Schocker Books.

———, and Friedrich Engels. [1847] 1955. *Selected Work in Two Volumes.* Reprint. Moscow: Foreign Languages Publishing House.

Maryanski, Alexandra, Richard Machalek, and Jonathan H. Turner. 2015. *Handbook on Evolution and Society: Toward an Evolutionary Social Science.* New York: Palgrave.

Massey, Douglas S., and Nancy A. Denton. 1993. *American Apartheid: Segregation and the Making of the Underclass.* Cambridge, MA: Harvard Un. Press.

———, and Margarita Mooney. 2007. "The Effects of America's Three Affirmative Action Programs on Academic Performance."*Social Problems* 54 (1):99–117.

Masud-Piloto, Felix. 2008. "Cuban Americans." Pp. 357–359, vol. 1, in *Encyclopedia of Race, Ethnicity, and Society,* edited by Richard T. Schaefer. Thousand Oaks, CA: Sage.

Masuda, Takahiko, Phoebe C. Ellsworth, Batja Mesquita, Janxin Leu, Shigehito Tanida, and Ellen Van de Veerdonk. 2008. "Attitudes and Social Cognition: Placing the Face in Context: Cultural Differences in the Perception of Facial Emotion." *Journal of Personality and Social Psychology* 94 (3):365–381.

Mather, Mark, Linda A. Jacobsen, and Kelvin M. Pollard. 2015. "Aging in the United States." *Population Bulletin* 70 (December).

Mayhew, Robert J. 2014. *Malthus: The Life and Legacies of an Untimely Prophet.* Cambridge MA: Harvard University Press.

Mazurczak, Filip. 2014. "Eastern Europe's Christian Awakening." First Things (January 17). Accessible at www.firsthtings.com.

Mazumder, Bhashkar. 2008. *Upward Intergenerational Economic Mobility in the United States.* Washington DC: Economic Mobility Project.

_____. 2013. *The Fracturing of the American Corporate Elite.* Cambridge: Harvard University Press.

McCall, Leslie. 2008. "What Does Class Inequality Among Women Look Like? A Comparison with Men and Families, 1970–2000." In Annette

Lareau and Dalton Conley (eds.), *Social Class, How Does It Work?* pp. 293–325. New York: Russell Sage Foundation.

McCarthy, Justin. 2014. "Seven in 10 Americans Back Euthanasia." June 18. Accessible at www.gallup.com.

_____. 2015. "More Americans Say Crime is Rising in U.S." October 22. Accessible at www.gallup.com.

McCarthy, Lauren A. 2014. "Human Trafficking and the New Slavery." *Annual Review of Law and Society* 10:221–242.

McCormack, Mark. 2010. "Changing Masculinities in Youth Cultures." *Qualitative Sociology* 33:111–115.

McCormick, John. 2015. "Bloomberg Politics Poll." December 9. Accessible at www.bloomberg.com.

McGurty, Eileen Maura. 2000. "Warren County, NC, and the Emergence of the Environmental Justice Movement: Unlikely Coalitions and Shared Meanings in Local Collective Action."*Society and Natural Resources* 13:373–387.

McKenzie, Brian. 2014. "Modes Less Traveled–Bicycling and Walking to Work in the United States: 2008–2012." May. *American Community Survey Reports ACS-25* Accessible at www.census.gov.

McKeown, Janet K.L. "'I Will Not be Wearing Heels Tonight!:' A Feminist Exploration of Singlehood, Dating and Leisure." *Journal of Leisure Research* 4 (4): 485.

McLanahan, Sara, and Christine Percheski. 2008. "Family Structure and the Reproduction of Inequalities." *Annual Review of Sociology* 38:257–276.

McLane, Daisann. 2013. "Getting Off on the Wrong Foot." *National Geographic Traveler* (January):28.

McLuhan, Marshall. 1964. *Understanding Media: The Extensions of Man.* New York: New American Library.

———. 1967. *The Medium Is the Message: An Inventory of Effects.* New York: Bantam Books.

McMurtrie, Beth. 2014. "Why Colleges Haven't Stopped Binge Drinking." *New York Times,* December 14. Accessible at nytimes.com.

McNamara, Keithand, and Jeanne Batalova. 2015. "Filipino Immigrants in the United States. July 21." Accessible at www.migrationpolicy.org.

McNeil, Donald G., Jr. 2002. "W.H.O. Moves to Make AIDS Drugs More Accessible to Poor Worldwide." *New York Times,* August 23, p. D7.

_____. 2004. "When Real Food Isn't an Option." *New York Times,* September 3, pp. A1, A5.

McPhail, Clark. 1991. *The Myth of the Madding Crowd.* New York: De Gruyter.

_____. 1994. "The Dark Side of Purpose in Riots: Individual and Collective Violence." *Sociological Quarterly* 35 (January):i–xx.

_____. 2006. "The Crowd and Collective Behavior: Bringing Symbolic Interaction Back In." *Symbolic Interaction* 29 (Issue 4):433–464.

———, and David Miller. 1973. "The Assembling Process: A Theoretical Empirical Examination." *American Sociological Review* 38 (December):721–735.

Mead, George H. 1934. In *Mind, Self and Society,* edited by Charles W. Morris. Chicago: University of Chicago Press.

_____. 1964a. In *On Social Psychology,* edited by Anselm Strauss. Chicago: University of Chicago Press.

_____. 1964b. "The Genesis of the Self and Social Control." Pp. 267–293 in *Selected Writings: George Herbert Mead,* edited by Andrew J. Reck. Indianapolis: Bobbs-Merrill.

Mead, Margaret. [1935] 2001. *Sex and Temperament in Three Primitive Societies.* New York: Perennial, HarperCollins.

Mee, Kim Eun. 2015. "Realizing the rights of marginalized and disadvantaged women and girls." March 18. Commission on the Status of Women, Fifty-ninth session. Accessible at www.unwomen.org.

Mehan, Hugh. 2015. "Detracking: A Promising Strategy to Increase Social Mobility for Underserved Youth." Pp. 75–82 in *Opening the Doors to Opportunity for All: Setting a Research Agenda for the Future.* Washington DC: American Institutes for Research.

Mehl, Matthias R., Simine Vazire, Nairán Ramírez-Esparza, Richard B. Slatcher, and James W. Pennebaker. 2007. "Are Women Really More Talkative than Men?" *Science* 317 (July 6):82.

Mendez, Jennifer Bickman. 1998. "Of Mops and Maids: Contradictions and Continuities in Bureaucratized Domestic Work." *Social Problems* 45 (February):114–135.

Merton, Robert. 1948. "The Bearing of Empirical Research upon the Development of Social Theory."*American Sociological Review* 13 (October):505–515.

_____. 1968. *Social Theory and Social Structure.* New York Free Press.

_____, and Alice S. Kitt. 1950. "Contributions to the Theory of Reference Group Behavior." Pp. 40–105 in *Continuities in Social Research: Studies in the Scope and Methods of the American Soldier,* edited by Robert K. Merton and Paul L. Lazarsfeld. New York: Free Press.

Messner, Michael A. 2002. "Gender Equity in College Sports: 6 Views." *Chronicle of Higher Education* 49 (December 6):B9–B10.

Meston, Cindy M., and David M. Buss. 2007. "Why Humanoids Have Sex."*Archives of Sexual Behavior* 36 (August).

Michels, Robert. 1915. *Political Parties.* Glencoe, IL: Free Press (reprinted 1949).

Microcredit Finance Summit. 2015. "State of the Campaign Report 2014: Data Reported to the Campaign in 2013." Accessible www.microcreditsummit.org.

Migration Policy Institute. 2016. "Brain Drain & Brain Gain." Accessible at www.migrationpolicy.org.

Milgram, Stanley. 1963. "Behavioral Study of Obedience."*Journal of Abnormal and Social Psychology* 67 (October):371–378.

_____. 1975. *Obedience to Authority: An Experimental View.* New York: Harper and Row.

Miller, Claire C. 2014. "The Divorce Surge Is Over, But the Myth Lives On." *New York Times,* December 2, p. A3.

Miller, David E. 2006. "Rumor: An Examination of Some Stereotypes." *Symbolic Interaction* 28 (4):505–519.

Miller, David L. 2014. *Introduction to Collective Behavior and Collective Action.* 3rd ed. Long Grove, IL: Waveland Press.

_____, and JoAnne DeRoven Darlington. 2002. "Fearing for the Safety of Others: Disasters and the Small World Problem." Paper presented at Midwest Sociological Society, Milwaukee, WI.

Miller, Jacqueline W., Timothy S. Naimi, Robert D. Brewer, and Sherry Everett Jones. 2007. "Binge Drinking and Associated Health Risk Behaviors among High School Students." *Pediatrics* 119 (January):76–85.

Miller, Laura. 2008. "The Rise of the Superclass." Accessed in*Salon,* May 2 (www.salon.com/books/review/2008/03/14/superclass/print.html).

Miller, Lisa. 2015. "Slender Man Is Watching." *New York* (August 24).

Miller, Reuben. 1988. "The Literature of Terrorism."*Terrorism* 11 (1):63–87.

Mills, C. Wright. [1959] 2000a. *The Sociological Imagination.* 40th anniversary edition. New Afterword by Todd Gitlin. New York: Oxford University Press.

_____. [1956] 2000b. *The Power Elite.* New edition. Afterword by Alan Wolfe. New York: Oxford University Press.

Miner, Horace. 1956. "Body Ritual among the Nacirema." *American Anthropologist* 58 (June): 503–507.

Minton, Todd D., and Daniela Golinelli. 2014. *Jail Inmates at Midyear 2013 - Statistical Tables.* Washington, DC: U.S. Department of Justice, Office of Justice Programs, Bureau of Justice Statistics.

Mishel, Lawrence, and Alyssa Davis. 2015. "Top CEOs Make 300 Times More than Typical Workers." June 21. Economic Policy Institute. Accessible at www.epi.org.

Mitra, Aditi. 2013. *Voices of Privilege and Sacrifice from Women Volunteers in India.* Lexington MA: Lexington Books.

Moaveni, Azadeh. 2005a. *Lipstick Jihad. A Memoir of Growing Up Iranian in America and American in Iran.* New York: Public Affairs.

_____. 2005b. "Fast Times in Tehran." *Time* (June 12):38–42.

_____. 2007. "The Unbearable Chic-ness of Jihad." *Time* (April 10).

———. 2009. *Honeymoon in Tehran: Two Years of Love and Danger in Iran.* New York: Random House.

_____. 2015. "Is this Iran's Berlin Wall Moment?" July 14. Accessible at www.theguardian.com.

Moeller, Susan D., Elia Powers, and Jessica Roberts. 2012. "The World Unplugged and 24 Hours without Media: Media Literacy to Develop Self-Awareness Regarding Media." *Comunicar* 20 (39):45–52.

Mohai, Paul, and Robin Saha. 2007. "Racial Inequality in the Distribution of Hazardous Waste: A National-Level Reassessment." *Social Problems* 54 (3):343–370.

Mohai, Paul, David Pellow, and J. Timmons Roberts. 2009. "Environmental Justice."

Annual Review of Environmental Research 34:405–430.

Mollen, Milton. 1992. "A Failure of Responsibility": Report to Mayor David N. Dinkins on the December 28, 1991, Tragedy at City College of New York. New York: Office of the Deputy Mayor forPublic Safety.

Monaghan, Peter. 1993. "Sociologist Jailed Because He 'Wouldn't Snitch' Ponders the Way Research Ought to Be Done."*Chronicle of Higher Education* 40 (September 1):A8, A9.

Monahan, Torin. 2011. "Surveillance as Cultural Practice." *The Sociological Quarterly* 52:495–508.

Moncarz, Roger J., Michael G. Wolf, and Benjamin Wright. 2008. "Service Providing Occupations, Off-Shoring, and the Labor Market. *Monthly Labor Review* (December): 71 -86.

Monson, Tamlyn Jane. 2015. "Collective Mobilization and the Struggle for Squatter Citizenship: Rereading 'Xenophobic' Violence in a South African Settlements.*" International Journal of Conflict and Violence* 9 (1):39–55.

Montgomery, Marilyn J., and Gwendolyn T. Sorell. 1997. "Differences in Love Attitudes across Family Life Stages." *Family Relations* 46:55–61.

Moore, Malcolm. 2012. "China's New Leader X, Jinping Warns Communist Party Forces 'Severe Challenges.'" *Telegraph (London)* (November 15). Accessed at www.telegrapj.co.ul.

Moore, Mignon, and Michael Stambolis-Ruhstorfer. 2013. "LGBT Sexuality and Families at the Start of the Twenty-First Century." *Annual Review of Sociology* 39:491–507.

Moore, Molly. 2006. "Romance, but Not Marriage." *Washington Post National Weekly Edition,* November 27, p. 18.

Moore, Wilbert E. 1967. *Order and Change: Essays in Comparative Sociology.* New York: Wiley.

Morin, Paul. 2014. "Beyond Burqa Bans: U.S. Must Update Laws on Face Veils." *Christian Science Monitor Weekly* (April 7):36.

Morin, Rich, and Seth Motel. 2013. "After a Highly Partisan Election Year, Survey Finds Less Group Conflict." January 10. Accessible at www. pewsocialtrends.org.

Morris, Aldon. 2000. "Reflections on Social Movement Theory: Criticisms and Proposals." *Contemporary Sociology* 29 (May):445–454.

Morris, C. Zawadi. 2015. "Housing Discrimination on Craigslist Prompts Letter from Comptroller to Human Rights Commission." December 2. Accessible at www.bkreader.com.

Morrison, Denton E. 1971. "Some Notes toward Theory on Relative Deprivation, Social Movements, and Social Change." *American Behavioral Scientist* 14 (May–June):675–690.

Moskos, Peter, 2008. *Cop in the Hood: My Year Policing Baltimore's Eastern District.* Princeton, NJ: Princeton University Press, 2008.

Moss, Trefor. 2016. "Call-Center Jobs Start to Lose Human Touch." *Wall Street Journal* (June 22): B1–B2.

Mossaad, Nadwa. "Refugees and Asylees: 2015." January 2016. Accessible at www.dhs.gov.

Mouawad, Jad. 2014. "Once a Humble Refueling Stop, Dubai is Crossroad to the World." *New York Times* (June 19): A1, A4.

Mozur, Pauland Mark Scott. 2016. "Fake News in U.S. Election? Elsewhere, That's Nothing New." *New York Times* (November 17).

Mueller, G. O. 2001. "Transnational Crime: Definitions and Concepts." Pp. 13–21 in *Combating Transnational Crime: Concepts, Activities, and Responses,* edited by P. Williams and D. Vlassis. London: Franklin Cass.

Muench, Ulrike, Jody Sindelar, Susan H. Busch, and Peter I. Buerhaus. 2015. "Salary Differences Between Male and Female Registered Nurses in the United States." *Journal of American Medical Association* 313(12):1265–1267

Mulhere, Kaitlin. 2015. "Momentum for Campus Carry." Inside Higher Education, March 30. Accessible at insidehigher.com.

Mulrine, Anna. 2012. "Up in Arms."*Christian Science Monitor Weekly* (July 2): 26–32.

Murdock, George P. 1945. "The Common Denominator of Cultures." Pp. 123–142 in *The Science of Man in the World Crisis,* edited by Ralph Linton. New York: Columbia University Press.

_____. 1949. *Social Structure.* New York: Macmillan.

———. 1957. "World Ethnographic Sample." *American Anthropologist* 59 (August): 664–687.

Murphy, Dean E. 1997. "A Victim of Sweden's Pursuit of Perfection." *Los Angeles Times,* September 2, pp. A1, A8.

Murray, Velma McBride, Amanda Willert, and Diane P. Stephens. 2001. "The Half-Full Glass: Resilient African American Single Mothers and Their Children." *Family Focus* (June):F4–F5.

n

Nakao, Keiko, and Judith Treas. 1994. "Updating Occupational Prestige and Socioeconomic Scores: How the New Measures Measure Up." *Sociological Methodology* 24:1–72.

Nash, Manning. 1962. "Race and the Ideology of Race." *Current Anthropology* 3 (June):285–288.

National Advisory Commission on Criminal Justice. 1976. *Organized Crime.* Washington, DC: U.S. Government Printing Office.

National Alliance for Caregiving. 2009. *Caregiving in the U.S.: Executive Summary.* Washington, DC: NAC and AARP.

National Alliance for Public Charter Schools. 2015. *The Public Charter Schools Dashboard.* Washington, DC: NAPCS.

National Alliance on Mental Illness. 2008. "What Is Mental Illness?" Accessed May 24, 2011 at www.nami.org.

National Alliance to End Homelessness. 2016. "The State of Homelessness in America." Accessible at www.endhomelessness.org.

National Association for Home Care and Hospice. 2016. "About NAHC." Accessed April 26 at www.nahc.org.

National Center for Education Statistics. 2015a. *Digest of Education Statistics 2013.* Table 330.10. Average undergraduate tuition and fees and room and board rates charged for full-time students in degree-granting postsecondary institutions, by level and control of institution: 1963–64 through 2012–13. Accessible at www.nces.gov.

_____. 2015b. *Digest of Education Statistics 2014* Tables and Figures. Table 203.10. Enrollment in public and elementary and secondary schools, by level and grade: Selected years, fall 1980 through fall 2024. Accessible at wwwnces.gov.

_____. 2015c. *Digest of Education Statistics 2013.* "Tables and figures. Table 206.10. Number and percentage of homeschooled students ages 5 through 17 with a grade equivalent of kindergarten through 12th grade, by selected child, parent, and household characteristics: 2003, 2007, and 2012." Accessible at www.nces.gov.

National Center on Addiction and Substance Abuse at Columbia University. 2007. *Wasting the Best and the Brightest: Substance Abuse at America's Colleges and Universities.* New York: NCASA at Columbia University.

National Coalition for the Homeless. 2012. *Hate Crimes against the Homeless: The Brutality of Violence Unveiled,.* Accessible at www.national-homelessness.org.

National Conference of State Legislatures. 2015. *Guns on Campus: Overview.* October 5. Accessible at ncsl.org.

National Education Association. 2015. *Rankings and Estimates. Rankings of the States 2014 and Estimates of School Statistics 2015.* Accessible at www.nea.org.

National Federation of State High School Associations. 2015. "High School Sports Participation Increases for 26th Consecutive Year." August 13. Accessible at www.nfhs.org.

National Geographic. 2015. "Climate refugees." Accessed December 17 at http://www. education.nationalgeographic.org/encyclopedia/ climate-refugee/.

National Institute on Aging. 1999. *Early Retirement in the United States.* Washington, DC: U.S. Government Printing Office.

National Law Center on Homelessness and Poverty. 2014. "No Safe Place: The Criminalization of Homelessness in U.S. Cities." Accessible at www.nichp.org.

National Low Income Housing Coalition. 2016. *Out of Reach 2016: No Refuge for Low Income Renters.* Accessible at www.nihc.org.

National Oceanic and Atmospheric Administration. 2014. "Climate Information." Accessed February 2, 2014 at http://www.ncdc.noaa.gov/ climate-information.

National Organization for Men Against Sexism. 2016. Home Page. Accessed February 226 (www.nomas.org).

National Science Foundation. 2011. Survey of Earned Doctorates, 2011. Accessed September 12, 2013. Available at www.nsf.gov/statistics/ sed/digest/2011.

Navarro, Mireya. 2005. "When You Contain Multitudes."*New York Times,* April 24, pp. 1, 2.

Needham, Paul. 2011. "9/11 Memorial Review: At Ground Zero, Staying Above Ground Matters." September 9. Accessible at www.huffington post.com.

Nelson, Paul. 2015. "What is the 100RC Network?" July 2. Accessible at www.100resilentcities.org.

Neuman, Lawrence W. 2009. *Understanding Research.* Boston: Allyn and Bacon.

Neuwirth, Robert. 2004. *Shadow Cities: A Billion Squatters, a New Urban World.* New York: Routledge.

Neves, Barbara Barbosa. 2013. "Social Capital and Internet Use: The Irrelevant, the Bad, and the Good." *Sociology Compass* 7/8:599–611.

Newport, Frank. 2012. " Americans Want Federal Gov't Out of State Marijuana Laws; Overall Support for Legalizing Marijuana Use Is Split." December 10. Accessible at www.gallup.com.

New Unionism Network. 2011. "State of the Unions." Accessed February 10, 2011 at http://www.newunionism.net/State_of_the_Unions.htm.

New York Times. 2015. "Shining Sunlight on Executive Pay." August 6. p. A26.

Newman, Katherine S. 2012. *The Accordion Family: Boomerang Kids, Anxious Parents, and the Private Toll of Global Competition.* Boston: Beacon Press.

Newman, William M. 1973. *American Pluralism: A Study of Minority Groups and Social Theory.* New York: Harper and Row.

Newport, Frank. 2010b. "In U.S., Increasing Number Have No Religious Identity." Accessed March 28, 2011 (www.gallup.com).

———. 2012. "Americans Want Federal Gov't Out of State Marijuana Laws; Overall Support for Legalizing Marijuana Use Is Split." December 10. Accessible at www.gallup.com.

———. 2014 "In U.S., 42% Believe Creationist View of Human Origins." June 2. Accessible at www.gallup.com.

———. 2015. "Americans Continue to Say U.S. Wealth Distribution Is Unfair." May 4. Accessible at www.gallup.com.

———. 2016. "Americans Still Say Upper-Income Pay Too Little in Taxes." April 6. Accessible at www.gallup.com.

Newsday. 1997. "Japan Sterilized 16,000 Women." September 18, p. A19.

NICHD. 2007. "Children Who Complete Intensive Early Childhood Program Show Gains in Adulthood: Greater College Attendance, Lower Crime and Depression." Accessed January 7, 2008 (www.nichd.nih.gov/news.releases/early_inter-ventions_082107.cfm).

Nicklett, Emily J., and Sarah Burgard. 2009. "Downward Social Mobility and Major Depressive Episodes Among Latino and Asian-American Immigrants to the United States." *American Journal of Epidemiology,* 170(6): 793–801.

Nielsen Company. 2010. "Most Super Bowl Viewers Tune in for the Commercials Nielsen Says." Accessed February 11 at http://www.nielsen.com/us/en/insights/press-room/2010/most_super_bowl_vieqwers.html.

Nielsen, Joyce McCarl, Glenda Walden, and Charlotte A. Kunkel. 2000. "Gendered Heteronormativity: Empirical Illustrations in Everyday Life." *Sociological Quarterly* 41 (2):283–296.

Niezen, Ronald. 2005. "Digital Identity: The Construction of Virtual Selfhood in the Indigenous Peoples' Movement." *Comparative Studies in Society and History* 47 (3):532–551.

Nixon, Darren. 2009. "'I Can't Put a Smiley Face On': Working-Class Masculinity, Emotional Labor and Service Work in the 'New Economy.'" *Gender, Work and Organization* 16 (3):300–322.

Noack, Rick. 2015. "Sweden Is about to Add a Gender-neutralPpronoun to Its Official Dictionary." April 1. Accessible at washingtonpost.com. https:/

Nocera, Joe. 2012. "Guns and Mental Illness." *New York Times,* December 29, p. A17.

Nolan, Patrick D. 2004. "Ecological-Evolutionary Theory: A Reanalysis and Reassessment of Lenski's Theory for the 21st Century." *Sociological Theory* 22 (June):328–337.

Nolan, Patrick D., and Gerhard Lenski. 2015. *Human Societies: An Introduction to Macrosociology.* 12th ed. New York: Oxford University Press.

Nordrum, Amy. 2015. "Rural Broadband Access Still Lacking in U.S,, Even as Remote Alaska Communities Connect." February 2. Accessible at ibtimes.com.

NORML. 2015. "Main: State Info. United States (map)." Accessed October 22 at norml.org.

———. 2016. "2016 Election: Marijuana Ballot Proposals." Accessible at www.norml.org.

Norris, Tina, Paula L. Vines, and Elizabeth M. Hoeffel. 2012. *The American Indian and Alaska Native Population: 2010.* C2010BR-10. Accessible at www.census.gov.

North Carolina Department of Environmental and Natural Resources. 2008. "Warren County PCB Landfill Fact Sheet." Accessed April 9 (www.wastenotnc.org/WarrenCo_Fact_Sheet.htm).

Northam, Jack. 2014. "As Overseas Costs Rise, More U.S. Companies Are 'Reshoring.'" January 27. Accessed January 28, 2014 at www.wbur.org.

O

O'Harrow, Jr., Robert. 2005. "Mining Personal Data." *Washington Post National Weekly Edition,* February 6, pp. 8–10.

Office for National Statistics. 2013. "Female Male Occupation." Accessed March 3 at www.ons.gov.uk.

Office of Family Assistance. 2015. "Healthy Marriage & Responsible Fatherhood." Accessible at www.acf.hhs.gov.

Office of Immigration Statistics. 2014. "2013 Yearbook of Immigration Statistics." Accessible at www.dhs.gov.

Office of Inspector General. 2016. "Patient Dumping." Accessible at www.ois.hhs.gov.

Office of the United States Trade Representative. 2016. "Benefits of Trade." February 22, 2016. Accessed at www.ustr.gov.

Ogas, Ogi, and Sai Gaddam. 2011. *A Billion Wicked Thoughts: What the World's Largest Experiment Reveals about Human Desire.* New York: Dutton.

Ogburn, William F. 1922. *Social Change with Respect to Culture and Original Nature.* New York: Huebsch (reprinted 1966, New York: Dell).

———, and Clark Tibbits. 1934. "The Family and Its Functions." Pp. 661–708 in *Recent Social Trends in the United States,* edited by Research Committee on Social Trends. New York: McGraw-Hill.

Okano, Kaori, and Motonori Tsuchiya. 1999. *Education in Contemporary Japan: Inequality and Diversity.* Cambridge: Cambridge University Press.

Okun, Barbara, and Joseph Nowinski. 2011, *Saying Goodbye: How Families Can Find Renewal Through Loss.* Cambridge, MA: Harvard Health Publications.

Omi, Michael, and Howard Winant. 2015. *Racial Formation in the United States.* 3rd ed. New York: Routledge.

Orfield, Gary, John Kucsera, and Genevieve Siegel-Hawley. 2012. "E Pluribus . . . Separation: Deepening Double Segregation for More Students." September 19. Accessible at http://civilrightsproject.ucla.edu/research/k-12-education/integration-and-diversity/mlk-national/e-pluribus . . . separation-deepening-double-segregation-for-more-students.

Organisation for Economic Co-Operation and Development. 2008. Growing Unequal? Income Distribution and Poverty in OECD Countries. Geneva: OECD.

———. 2012b. "Gender Equality and Social Institutions in Afghanistan." Accessed February 22 (http://genderindex.org/country/Afghanistan).

———. 2015a. "Poverty rates and poverty gaps." Accessed October 30 at oecd-library.org.

———. 2015b. *Official Development Statistics 2000–2014.* Accessed November 4 at data-oecd.org.

———. 2015c. "At a Glance 2015." *OECD Indicators.* Paris: OECD.

Ormond, James. 2005. "The McDonaldization of Football." Accessed January 23, 2006 (http://courses.essex.ac.uk/sc/sc111).

Ortega, Mariana. 2015. "Latina Feminism, Experience and the Self." *Philosophy Compass* 10 (April):244–254.

Ortman, Jennifer, and Hyon B. Shin. 2011. "Language Projections: 2010 to 2020." Presented at the American Sociological Association.

Ortulay, Barbara. 2013. "Pew: Love Is in the Air and on the Web." Associated Press, October 21, 2013. Accessible at www.pewinternet.org/Media-Mentions/2013.

Orwell, George. 1949. *Nineteen Eighty-Four.* London: Secker and Warburg.

OutRight Action International. 2016. "Home Page." Accessed March 1 at www.outright international.org.

Oxford Poverty and Human Development Initiative. 2012. "Multidimensional Poverty Index." Accessed January 30 (www.ophi.org.uk).

O'Brien, Daniel Tumminelli, Robert J. Sampson, and Christopher Winship. 2013. *Econometrics in the Age of Big Data: Measuring and Assessing 'Brooklyn Windows' Using Administrative Records.* Cambridge, MA: Radcliffe Institute for Advanced Study, Harvard University.

P

Pace, Richard. 1993. "First-Time Televiewing in Amazonia: Television Acculturation in Gurupa, Brazil. *Ethnology* 32:187–205.

———. 1998. "The Struggle for Amazon Town." Boulder, CO: Lynne Rienner.

Padilla, Efren N. 2008. "Filipino Americans." Pp. 493–497 in vol. 1, *Encyclopedia of Race, Ethnicity, and Society,* edited by Richard T. Schaefer. Thousand Oaks, CA: Sage.

Page, Charles H. 1946. "Bureaucracy's Other Face." *Social Forces* 25 (October):89–94.

Pager, Devah. 2007. *Marked: Race, Crime, and Finding Work in an Era of Mass Incarceration.* Chicago: University of Chicago Press.

———, Bruce Western, and Bart Bonikowski. 2009. "Discrimination in a Low-Wage Labor Market: A Field Experiment." American Sociological Review 74 (October): 777–799.

Pariser, Ei. 2011a. *The Filter Bubble. What the Internet Is Hiding from You.* New York: Penguin Press.

———. 2011b. "In Our Own Little Internet Bubbles." *Guardian Weekly,* June 24, p. 32.

Park, Haeyoun, Josh Keller, and Josh Williams. 2016. "The Faces of American Power, Nearly as White as the Oscar Nominees." *New York Times* (February 28):19.

Park, Haeyoun. 2015. "A Trickle of Syrian Refugees Settles Across the United States." *New York Times.* November 3, p. A18.

Park, Robert E. 1916. "The City: Suggestions for the Investigation of Human Behavior in the Urban Environment." *American Journal of Sociology* 20 (March):577–612.

———. 1922. *The Immigrant Press and Its Control.* New York: Harper.

———. 1936. "Succession, an Ecological Concept." *American Sociological Review* 1 (April):171–179.

Parke, Jeanne. 2015. "Europe's Migration Crisis." *Council of Foreign Relations Backgrounder* (September 23). Accessible at cfr.org.

Parker, Ashley. 2015. "Facebook Expands in Politics, and Campaigns Find Much to Like." *New York Times* (July 29).

Parkin, Stephen, and Ross Coomber. 2009. "Value in the Visual: On Public Injecting, Visual Methods and their Potential for Informing Policy (and Change)." *Methodological Innovations Online* 4(2) 21–36.

Parsons, Talcott, and Robert Bales. 1955. *Family: Socialization and Interaction Process.* Glencoe, IL: Free Press.

Parsons, Talcott. 1951. *The Social System.* New York: Free Press.

———. 1975. "The Sick Role and the Role of the Physician Reconsidered." *Milbank Medical Fund Quarterly Health and Society* 53 (Summer):257–278.

Parsons, Talcott. 1966. *Societies: Evolutionary and Comparative Perspectives.* Englewood Cliffs, NJ: Prentice Hall.

Passel, Jeffrey S., and D'Vera Cohn. 2015. "Unauthorized Immigrant Population Stable for Half a Decade." July 22. Accessible at pewresearch.org.

Passero, Kathy. 2002. "Global Travel Expert Roger Axtell Explains Why." *Biography* (July):70–73, 97–98.

Patel, Reena. 2010. *Working the Night Shift: Women in India's Call Center Industry.* Stanford CA: Stanford University Press.

Pattillo-McCoy, Mary. 1999. *Black Picket Fences: Privilege and Peril among the Black Middle Class.* Chicago: University of Chicago Press.

Paul, Brad. 2014. "Dating Questions for Successful Relationships." Accessed January 18, 2014 at http://www.solotopia.com/dating-questions.

Pavlik, John V. 2013. "Trends in New Media Research: A Critical Review of Recent Scholarship." *Sociology Compass* 7 (1):1–12.

PBS Hawaii. 2015. "What Would It Take to Achieve Hawaiian Sovereignty?" July 16. Accessible at www.pbshawaii.org.

Pear, Robert. 1997. "Now, the Archenemies Need Each Other." *New York Times,* June 22, sec. 4, pp. 1, 4.

———. 2009. "Congress Relaxes Rules on Suits over Pay Inequity." *New York Times,* January 28, p. A14.

Pellow, David N., and Hollie Nyseth Brehm. 2013. "An Environmental Sociology for the Twenty-First Century." *Annual Review of Sociology* 39:229–250.

Pennington, Bill. 2008. "College Athletic Scholarships: Expectations Lose Out to Reality." *New York Times,* March 10, pp. A1, A15.

Peralta, Eyder. 2011. "Who Are the 1 Percent? Gallup Finds They're a Lot Like the 99 Percent." December 5. Accessed December 12 (www.wbur.org/npr/143143332/who-are-the-1-percent-gallup-finds-theyre-a-lot-like-the-99-percent).

Perlman, Janice. 2010. *Favela: Four Decades of Living on the Edge in Rio de Janeiro.* London: Oxford University Press.

Perrin, Andrew. 2015. *Social Media-Usage: 2005–2015.* October 8. Accessible at www.pewinternet.org.

Pescosolido, Bernice A., and Jack K. Martin. 2015. "The Stigma Complex." *Annual Review of Sociology* 41:87–116.

Peter, Laurence J., and Raymond Hull. 1969. *The Peter Principle.* New York: Morrow.

Peters, Jeremy W. 2015. "Jeb Bush Visits Puerto Rico in Hopes of Reconnecting with Hispanic Voters." *New York Times,* April 29, p. A15.

Petrášová, Alexandra. 2006. *Social Protection in the European Union.* Brussels: European Union.

Petrie, Michelle, and James E. Coverdill. 2010. "Who Lives and Dies on Death Row? Race, Ethnicity, and Post-Sentence Outcomes in Texas." *Social Problems* 57 (4):630–652.

Pew Charitable Trust. 2012. Pursuing the American Dream: Economic Mobility Across Generations. July. Accessible at www.economicmobility.org.

Pew Research Center for the People and the Press. 2014. "Political Polarization in the American Public." June 12. Accessible at http://www.people-press.org.

Pew Research Center. 2013. "Second-Generation Americans: A Portrait of the Adult Children of Immigrants." February 7. Accessible at www.persocialtrends.org.

———. 2014. "Internet User Demographics." January 24. Accessible at pewinternet.org.

———. 2014b. "Emerging and Developing Economies Much More Optimistic than Rich Countries about the Future." October 9. Accessible at www.pewresearch.org.

———. 2015a. "Teen Voices: Dating in the Digital Age." October 1. Accessible at www.pewinternet.org.

———. 2015b. "America's Changing Religious Landscape." May 12. Accessible at www.pewforum.org.

———. 2015c. "Modern Immigration Wave Brings 59 Million to U.S., Driving Population Growth and Change through 2065: Views of Immigration's Impact on U.S. Society Mixed." September. Accessible at www.pewhispanic.org.

Pew-Templeton. 2015. "The Future of World Religions: Population Growth Projections, 2010–2050." April 2. Accessible at www.pewresearch.org.

Phelan, Jo. C., and Bruce G. Link. 2015. "Is Racism a Fundamental Cause of Inequalities in Health?" *Annual Review of Sociology* 41:311–330.

Phillips, E. Barbara. 1996. *City Lights: Urban–Suburban Life in the Global Society.* New York: Oxford University Press.

Phillips, Susan A. 1999. *Wallbangin': Graffiti and Gangs in L.A.* Chicago: University of Chicago Press.

Piaget, Jean. 1954. *Construction of Reality in the Child.* Translated by Margaret Cook. New York: Basic Books.

Pickert, Kate. 2009. "Getting Well While You Shop." *Time,* June 22, pp. 68–70.

Pincus, Fred L. 2003. *Reverse Discrimination: Dismantling the Myth.* Boulder, CO: Lynne Rienner.

———. 2008. "Reverse Discrimination." Vol. 3, *Encyclopedia of Race, Ethnicity, and Society.* Richard T. Schaefer, ed. Pp. 1159–61. Thousand Oaks, CA: Sage.

Pinderhughes, Dianne. 1987. *Race and Ethnicity in Chicago Politics: A Reexamination of Pluralist Theory.* Urbana: University of Illinois Press.

Pinto, Nick. 2015. "The Bail Trap." *New York Times* (August 13). Accessible at nytimes.com.

Piturro, Marlene. 2012. "NORCs: Some of the Best Retirement Communities Occur Naturally." May 30. Accessed November 14, 2013 at www.nextavenue.org/article/2012-05/norcs-some-best-retirement-communities-occur-naturally.

Piven, Frances Fox, and Richard A. Cloward. 1996. "Welfare Reform and the New Class War." Pp. 72–86 in *Myths about the Powerless: Contesting Social Inequalities,* edited by M. Brinton Lykes, Ali Banuazizi, Ramsay Liem, and Michael Morris. Philadelphia: Temple University Press.

Plüss, Caroline. 2005. "Constructing Globalized Ethnicity." *International Sociology* 20 (June):201–224.

Plomin, Robert. 1989. "Determinants of Behavior." *American Psychologist* 44 (February):105–111.

Poder, Thomas C. 2011. "What Is Really Social Capital? A Critical Review." *American Sociologist* 42:341–367.

Pogash, Carol. 2008. "Poor Students in High School Suffer Stigma from Lunch Aid." *New York Times,* March 1, pp. A1, A14.

Polletta, Francesca, and James M. Jasper. 2001. "Collective Identity and Social Movements." Pp. 283–305 in *Annual Review of Sociology, 2001,* edited by Karen S. Cook and Leslie Hogan. Palo Alto, CA: Annual Reviews.

Pollitt, Katha. 2015. *Pro: Reclaiming Abortion Rights.* With a new afterword. New York: Picador.

Population Reference Bureau. 1996. "Speaking Graphically." *Population Today* 24 (June/July).

Porter, Eduardo. 2013. "In the War on Poverty, a Dogged Adversary." *New York Times,* December 16, pp. B1, B3.

———. 2015. "An Aging Society Changes the Story on Poverty for Retirees." *New York Times* (December 22).

Portes, Alejandro, Cristina Escobar, and Renelinda Arana. 2008. "Bridging the Gap: Transnational and Ethnic Organizations in the Political Incorporation of Immigrants in the United States." *Ethnic and Racial Studies* 31 (September 6):1056–1090.

Portman, Jennifer M., Victoria A. Velkoff, and Howard Hogan. 2014. *An Aging Nation: The Older Population in the United States: Population Estimates and Projections.* P25-1140. Washington DC: U.S. Government Printing Office.

Poushter, Jacob. 2014. "What's Morally Acceptable? It Depends on Where in the World You Live." April 15. Accessible at www.pewresearch.org.

———. 2016. "Pew Research Center Global Attitudes Project: Smartphone Ownership and Internet Usage Continues to Climb in Emerging Economies." February 22. Accessible at www.pewresearch.org.

Powell, Gary N. 2010. *Women and Men in Management.* 4th ed. Thousand Oaks, CA: Sage.

Prehn, John W. 1991. "Migration." Pp. 190–191 in *Encyclopedia of Sociology,* 4th ed. Guilford, CT: Dushkin.

Preston, Jennifer, and Brian Stelter. 2011. "Cellphone Cameras Become World's Eyes and Ears on Protests across the Middle East ." *New York Times,* February 19, p. A7.

Price, Tom. 2013. "Big Data and Privacy." *CQ Researcher* 23 (October 25):909–932. Accessible at http://library.cqpress.com.ezproxy1.lib.depaul.edu/cqresearcher/.

Prince, Martin, Vikram Patel, Shekhar Saxena, Mario Maj, Johanna Maselko, Michael Phillips, and Atif Rahman. 2007. "No Health without Mental Health." *The Lancet* 370 (September 8):859–877.

ProCon. 2016. "Fact Sheet: State-by-State Guide to Physician-Assisted Suicide." Accessible at euthanasia.procon.org.

Proctor, Bernadette D., Jessica J. Smerga, and Melissa A. Kollar. 2016. *Income and Poverty in the United States 2015.* September. Accessible at www.census.gov.

Pryor, John H., Kevin Egan, Laura Palucki Blake, Sylvia Hurtado, Jennifer Berdan, Matthew H. Case, and Linda DeAngelo. 2013. *The American Freshman: National Norms for Fall 2012.* Los Angeles: Higher Education Research Institute, UCLA.

Pryor, John H., Sylvia Hurtado, Victor B. Saenz, José Luis Santos, and William S. Korn. 2007. *The American Freshman: Forty Year Trends.* Los Angeles: Higher Education Research Institute, UCLA.

Putnam, Robert D. 2015. *Our Kids: The American Dream in Crisis.* New York: Simon and Schuster.

q

Quadagno, Jill. 2014. *Aging and the Life Course: An Introduction to Social Gerontology.* 6th ed. New York: McGraw-Hill.

Quarantelli, Enrico L. 1957. "The Behavior of Panic Participants." *Sociology and Social Research* 41 (January):187–194.

Quarantelli, Enrico L., and James R. Hundley, Jr. 1975. "A Test of Some Propositions about Crowd Formation and Behavior." Pp. 538–554 in *Readings in Collective Behavior,* edited by Robert R. Evans. Chicago: Rand McNally.

Quarantelli, Enrico L., and Russell R. Dynes. 1970. "Property Norms and Looting: Their Patterns in Continuity Crises." *Phylon* (Summer):168–182.

Quinney, Richard. 1970. *The Social Reality of Crime.* Boston: Little, Brown.

———. 1974. *Criminal Justice in America.* Boston: Little, Brown.

———. 1979. *Criminology.* 2nd ed. Boston: Little, Brown.

———. 1980. *Class, State and Crime.* 2nd ed. New York: Longman.

r

Rabinovitch, Shelley, and James Lewis, eds. 2004. *The Encyclopedia of Modern Witchcraft and New Paganism.* New York: Citadel Press.

Rainie, Lee. 2015. "Digital Divides." September 22. Accessible at pewinternet.org. Charts 4, 9, 14, 19, 25.

Rajan, Gita, and Shailja Sharma. 2006. *New Cosmopolitanisms: South Asians in the US.* Stanford, CA: Stanford University Press.

Ramnarace, Cynthia. 2015. "Maternity Leave around the World." Accessed December 3 at www.thebump.com.

Ramstad, Evan. 2011. "Studying Too Much Is a New No-No In Upwardly Mobile South Korea." *Wall Street Journal,* October 6, p. A1.

RAND. 2010. "Retail Medical Clinics Perform Well Relative to Other Medical Settings." *RAND Review* (Winter 2009–2010). Accessed January 25 (www.rand.org/publications/randreview/issues/winter2009/news.html#medclinics).

Randolph, Tracey H.., and Mellisa Holtzman. 2010. "The Role of Heritage Camps in Identity Development Among Korean Transnational Adoptees: A Relational Dialectics Approach." *Adoption Quarterly* 13:75–91.

Rangaswamy, Padma. 2005. "Asian Indians in Chicago." In *The New Chicago,* edited by John Koval et al. Philadelphia: Temple University Press.

Rango, Marzia. 2015. "How Big Data Can help Migrants." October 5. World Economic Forum Agenda. Accessible at https://agenda.weforum.org/2015/10/how-big-data-can-help-migrants/.

Rasmussen Reports. 2013. "59% Believe Voter ID Laws Do Not Discriminate." Accessible at http://www.rasmussenreports.com.

Ratnesar, Romesh. 2011. "The Menace Within." *Stanford Magazine* (July/August). Accessible at www.stanfordalumni.org.

Ravitch, Diane. 2010. *The Death and Life of the Great American School System: How Testing and Choice Are Undermining Education.* New York: Basic Books.

Rawlinson, Linnie, and Nick Hunt. 2009. "Jackson Dies, Almost Takes Internet with Him." Accessed July 1 (www.cnn.com/2009/TECH/06/26/michael.jackson.internet/).

Ray, Brian D. 2009. *Homeschool Progress Report 2009: Academic Achievement and Demographics.* Purcellville VA: Home School Legal Defense Association.

Reardon, Sean F. 2016. "School District Socioeconomic Status, Race, and Academic Achievement." Working paper. Stanford CA: Stanford University. Accessible at cepa.standford.edu.

———, Demetra Kalogrides, and Ken Shores. 2016, "The Geography of Racial/Ethnic Test Score Gaps." Working paper. Stanford CA: Stanford University. Accessible at cepa.standford.edu.

Reddy, Sumathi. 2015. "Screen Time for Doctors." *Wall Street Journal,* December 15, pp. D1, D3.

Reeves, Richard V. and Joanna Venator. 2014. "Social Mobility Data: How Much Can the Past Teach Us About the Present?" April 25. Brookings Social Mobility Memos accessible at www.brookings.edu.

Reger, Jo. 2014. "Debating US Contemporary Feminism." *Sociology Compass* (1): 43–51.

Reinharz, Shulamit. 1992. *Feminist Methods in Social Research.* New York: Oxford University Press.

Reitzes, Donald C., and Elizabeth J. Mutran. 2006. "Lingering Identities in Retirement." *Sociological Quarterly* 47:333–359.

Religion News Service. 2003. "New U.S. Guidelines on Prayer in Schools Get Mixed Reaction." *Los Angeles Times,* February 15, p. B24.

Renzulli, Linda A., and Vincent J. Roscigno. 2007. "Charter Schools and Public Good." *Contexts* 6 (Winter):31–36.

Reschovsky, Clara. 2004. *Journey to Work: 2000.* Census 200 Brief C2KBR-23. Washington, DC: US Government Printing Office.

Ribisi-Braley, Jamie. 2015. Interview with Secretary, Board of Directors, Friends of the Shakers, Sabbathday Lake Village, Maine. October 7.

Rich, Motoko, Amanda Cox, and Matthew Bloch. 2016. "In Schools Nationwide, Money Predicts Success." *New York Times* (May 3): A3.

Ridgeway, L. Cecilia. 2011. *Framed by Gender: How Gender Inequality Persists in the Modern World.* New York: Oxford University Press.

Riding, Alan. 1998. "Why 'Titanic' Conquered the World." *New York Times,* April 26, sec. 2, pp. 1, 28, 29.

Rieker, Patricia R.., and Chloe E. Bird. 2000. "Sociological Explanations of Gender Differences in Mental and Physical Health." Pp. 98–113 in *Handbook of Medical Sociology,* edited by Chloe Bird, Peter Conrad, and Allan Fremont. New York: Prentice Hall.

Riffkin, Rebecca. 2014. "Americans Still Prefer a Male Boss to a Female Boss." October 14. Accessible at www.gallup.com.

Rimer, Sara. 1998. "As Centenarians Thrive, 'Old' Is Redefined." *New York Times,* June 22, pp. A1, A14.

Ripley, Amanda. 2011. "Teacher, Leave Those Kids Alone." *Time,* December 5, pp. 46–49.

Ritzer, George. 2015. *The McDonaldization of Society,* 8th Edition. Thousand Oaks CA: Sage.

———, and Paul Dean. 2015. *Globalization: A Basic Text.* 2nd ed. New York: John Wiley.

Rkasnuam, Hataipreuk, and Jeanne Batalova. 2014. "Vietnamese Immigrants in the United States." August 25. Accessible at www.migration policy.org

Robertson, Roland. 1988. "The Sociological Significance of Culture: Some General Considerations." *Theory, Culture, and Society* 5 (February):3–23.

Robinson, Kristopher, and Edward M. Crenshaw. 2010. "Reevaluating the Global Digital Divide: Socio-Demographic and Conflict Barriers to the Internet Revolution." *Sociological Inquiry* 80 (February):34–62.

Robnett, Belinda, and Cynthia Feliciano. 2011. "Patterns of Racial-Ethnic Exclusion by Internet Daters." *Social Forces* 89 (March): 807–828.

Rodman, George. 2011. *Mass Media in a Changing World.* 3rd ed. New York: McGraw-Hill.

Rootes, Christopher. 2007. "Environmental Movements." Pp. 608–640 in *The Blackwell Companion to Social Movements,* edited by David A.Snow, Sarah A. Sovle, and Hanspeter Kriesi. Malden, MA: Blackwell.

Roscigno, Vincent J. 2010. "Ageism in the American Workplace." *Contexts* (Winter): 15–21.

Rose, Arnold. 1951. *The Roots of Prejudice.* Paris: UNESCO.

Rose, Christina. 2015. "8 Reasons Why Feminism Matters in Indian Country." March 4. Accessible at indiancountrytodaynetwork.com.

Rose, Peter I.., MyronGlazer, and Penina Migdal Glazer. 1979. "In Controlled Environments: Four Cases of Intense Resocialization." Pp. 320–338 in *Socialization and the Life Cycle,* edited by Peter I. Rose. New York: St. Martin's Press.

Rosen, Christine. 2015. "They're Out to Get You." *Wall Street Journal,* December 20, p. C7.

Rosen, Eva, and Sudhir Alladi Venkatesh. 2008. "A Perversion of Choice: Sex Work Offers Just Enough in Chicago's Urban Ghetto."

Journal of Contemporary Ethnography (August):417–441.

Rosenberg, H. Douglas. 1991. "Capitalism." Pp. 33–34 in *Encyclopedic Dictionary of Sociology,* 4th ed., edited by Dushkin Publishing Group. Guilford, CT: Dushkin.

Rosenbloom, Stephanie. 2011. "Love, Lies, and What They Learned."*New York Times,* November 13, pp. ST1, ST8.

Rosenfeld, Jake, and Meredith Klegkamp. 2012. "Organized Labor and Racial Wage Inequality in the United States." *American Journal of Sociology* 117 (March):1460–1502.

Rosenfeld, Jake. 2010. "Little Labor." *Pathways* (Summer):4–6.

Rosenfeld, Michael J.., and Reuben J. Thomas. 2012. "Searching for a Mate: The Rise of the Internet as a Social Intermediary."*American Sociological Review* 77 (4):523–547.

Rosenthal, Robert, and Lenore Jacobson. 1968. *Pygmalion in the Classroom.* New York: Holt.

Rosenthal, Robert, and Lenore Jacobson. 1992. *Pygmalion in the Classroom: Teacher Expectations and Pupils' Intellectual Development.* Newly expanded edition. Bancyfelin, UK: Crown House.

Ross, John. 1996. "To Die in the Street: Mexico City's Homeless Population Booms as Economic Crisis Shakes Social Protections." *SSSP Newsletter* 27 (Summer):14–15.

Rossi, Peter H. 1987. "No Good Applied Social Research Goes Unpunished."*Society* 25 (November–December):73–79.

Rossi, S. Alice 1968. "Transition to Parenthood." *Journal of Marriage and the Family* 30 (February): 26–39.

———. 1984. "Gender and Parenthood." *American Sociological Review* 49 (February):1–19.

Rossides, W. Daniel. 1997. *Social Stratification: The Interplay of Class, Race, and Gender.* 2nd ed. Upper Saddle River, NJ: Prentice Hall.

Roszak, Theodore. 1969. *The Making of a Counterculture.* Garden City, NY: Doubleday.

Rothkopf, David. 2008. *Superclass: The Global Power Elite and the World They Are Making.* New York: Farrar, Straus and Giroux.

Rowe, AimeeCarrillo, SheenaMalhotra, and Kimberlee Pérez. 2013. *Answer the Call: Virtual Migration in Indian Call Centers.* Minneapolis: University of Minnesota Press.

Rubin, J. Alissa. 2003. "Pat-Down on the Way to Prayer." *Los Angeles Times,* November 25, pp. A1, A5.

Rudel, Thomas K., J. Timmons Roberts, and Jo Ann Carmin. 2011. "Political Economy of the Environment." *Annual Review of Sociology* 37:221–238.

Rueb, Emily S. 2015. "The Battle of the Birdmen." *New York Times,* August 2, pp. 20–21.

Rugh, Jacob S., Len Albright, and Douglas S. Massey. 2015. "Race, Space, and Cumulative Disadvantage: A Case Study of the Subprime Lending Collapse." *Social Problems* 62: 186–218.

Ryan, Camille. 2013. *Language Use in the United States.* ACS-22. Washington, DC: U.S. Government Printing Office.

Ryan, Patrick. 2015. "Now Is Prime Time for Dialogue about Asians on TV."*USA Today* (November 17): 2D.

Ryan, William. 1976. *Blaming the Victim.* Rev. ed. New York: Random House.

S

Saad, Lydia. 2012. "In U.S., Half of Women Prefer a Job Outside the Home." September 7. Accessible at www.gallup.com.

———. 2015. "Americans Choose 'Pro-Choice' for First Time in Seven Years." May 29. Accessible at www.gallup.com.

Sacks, Peter. 2007. *Tearing Down the Gates: Confronting the Class Divide in American Education.* Berkeley: University of California Press.

SAGE. 2016. "What We Do." Accessible at www. sageusa.org.

Saguy, Abigail, and Rene Almeling. 2008. "Fat in the Fire? Science, the News Media, and the 'Obesity Epidemic.'" *Sociological Forum* 23 (March):53–83.

Said, W. Edward. 2001. "The Clash of Ignorance." *Nation,* October 22.

Salem, Richard, and Stanislaus Grabarek. 1986. "Sociology B.A.s in a Corporate Setting: How Can They Get There and of What Value Are They?" *Teaching Sociology* 14 (October):273–275.

Sampson, Robert. 2011 . *Great American City: Chicago and the Enduring Neighborhood Effect.* Chicago: University of Chicago Press.

———, and W. Byron Graves. 1989. "Community Structure and Crime: Testing Social-Disorganization Theory." *American Journal of Sociology* 94 (January):774–802.

Samuel, Alexandra. 2015. "The Asset Too Many Companies Ignore." *Wall Street Journal,* October 14, p. R6.

Samuelson, Paul A., and William D. Nordhaus. 2010. *Economics.* 19th ed. New York: McGraw-Hill.

Sandberg, Sheryl. 2015. *Lean In: Women, Work, and the Will to Lead.* New York: Knopf.

Sanderson, Stephen K.., Seth A. Abrutyn, and Kristopher R. Proctor. 2011. "Testing the Protestant Ethic Thesis with Quantitative Historical Data: A Research Note." *Social Forces* 89 (March):905–912.

Sanderson, Warren, and Sergei Scherbov. 2008. "Rethinking Age and Aging." *Population Bulletin* 63 (December).

Sanua, R. Marianne. 2007. "AJC and Intermarriage: The Complexities of Jewish Continuity, 1960–2006." Pp. 3–32 in *American Jewish Yearbook 2007,* edited by David Singer and Lawrence Grossman. New York: American Jewish Committee.

Sapir, Edward. 1929. "The State of Linguistics as a Science." *Language* 5 (4):207–214.

Satel, Sally. 2013. "Why the Fuss over the D.S.M.-5?" *New York Times,* May 12, Week in the News, p. 5.

Sauerbrey, Anne. 2013. "Paris Changes Everything." *New York Times,* November 17, p. A23.

Sawhill, Isabel, and John E. Morton. 2007. *Economic Mobility: Is the American Dream Alive and Well?* Washington, DC: Economic Mobility Project, Pew Charitable Trusts.

Sawhill, Isabel, and Ron Haskins. 2009. "If You Can Make It Here . . ." *Washington Post National Weekly Edition,* November 9, p. 27.

Scarce, Rik. 2005. *Contempt of Court: A Scholar's Struggle for Free Speech Behind Bars.* Walnut Creek, CA: Alta Mira Press.

Schaefer, Peter. 2008. "Digital Divide." Pp. 388–389, vol. 1, in *Encyclopedia of Race, Ethnicity, and Society in the United States,* edited by Richard T. Schaefer. Thousand Oaks, CA: Sage.

Schaefer, Richard, and William Zellner. 2015. *Extraordinary Groups.* 9th ed. Long Grove, IL: Waveland Press.

Schaefer, Richard T. 1998. "Differential Racial Mortality and the 1995 Chicago Heat Wave." Presentation at the annual meeting of the American Sociological Association, August, San Francisco.

———. 2008b. "'Power' and 'Power Elite.'" In *Encyclopedia of Social Problems,* edited by Vincent Parrillo. Thousand Oaks, CA: Sage.

———. 2015. *Racial and Ethnic Groups.* 14th ed. Upper Saddle River, NJ: Pearson.

Scharfenberg, David. 2013. "Big Data Comes to Boston's Neighborhoods." Accessed athttp://www.wbur.org/2013/07/03/big-data-boston.

Scharnberg, Kirsten. 2007. "Black Market for Midwives Defies Bans." *Chicago Tribune,* November 25, pp. 1, 10.

Scheid, L. Teresa. 2013. "A Decade of Critique: Notable Books in the Sociology of Mental Health." *Contemporary Sociology* 42 (2): 177–183.

Scherer, Michael. 2011. "Introduction: Taking It to the Streets." Pp. 5–12 in *Occupy: What Is Occupy?* New York: Time Books.

Scherer, Ron. 2009. "Job Migration to Suburbs: An Unstoppable Flow?" *New York Times,* April 6.

———. 2010a. "A Long Struggle to Find Jobs." *Christian Science Monitor,* January 31, pp. 18–19.

———. 2010b. "For Jobless, Online Friends Can Be Lifelines." *Christian Science Monitor,* March 25, p. 21.

———. 2010c. "Jim Bunning Delays Vote; Unemployed Face First Week Without Check." *Christian Science Monitor,* March 2.

Schlesinger, Jacob M., and Alexander Martin. 2015. "Graying Japan Looks for a Silvery Lining." 2015. *Wall Street Journal* (November 30): A1, A14.

Schnaiberg, Allan. 1994. *Environment and Society: The Enduring Conflict.* New York: St. Martin's Press.

Schneider, Friedrich. 2010. "Dues and Don'ts." *The Economist* (August 14):62.

Schrad, Mark Lawrence. 2014. "Ukraine and ISIS Are Not Justifications of a 'Clash of Civilizations.'" *Washington Post* (September 22): Op-Ed at washingtonpost.com.

Schram, Sanford F., Richard C. Fording, Joe Soss, and Linda Houser. 2009. "Deciding to Discipline: Race, Choice and Punishment at the Frontlines of Welfare Reform." *American Sociological Review* 74 (June):398–422.

Schreiber, Noam, and Stephanie Strom. 2015. "Labor Board Ruling Eases Way for Fast-Food Unions' Efforts." *New York Times* (August 24): A1, A3.

Schulman, I. Gary. 1974. "Race, Sex, and Violence: A Laboratory Test of the Sexual Threat of the Black Male Hypothesis." *American Journal of Sociology* 79 (March):1260–1272.

Schur, M. Edwin. 1965. *Crimes without Victims: Deviant Behavior and Public Policy.* Englewood Cliffs, NJ: Prentice Hall.

———. 1968. *Law and Society: A Sociological View.* New York: Random House.

———. 1985. "'Crimes without Victims': A 20-Year Reassessment." Paper presented at the annual meeting of the Society for the Study of Social Problems.

Schwartz, A. Brad. 2015. *Broadcast Hysteria.* New York: Hill &16973 Wang.

Schwartz, Felicia, and Gordon Lubold. 2015. "U.S. Opening All Military Combat Roles to Women." *Wall Street Journal,* December 4, pp. A1, A2.

Schwartz, H. Shalom, and Anat Bardi. 2001. "Value Hierarchies across Cultures: Taking a Similarities Perspective." *Journal of Cross-Cultural Perspective* 32 (May):268–290.

Scott, Alan. 1990. *Ideology and the New Social Movements.* London: Unwin Hyman.

Scott, Gregory. 2001. "Broken Windows behind Bars: Eradicating Prison Gangs through Ecological Hardening and Symbolic Cleansing." *Corrections Management Quarterly* 5 (Winter):23–36.

Scott, W. Richard, and Gerald F. Davis. 2007. *Organizations and Organizing: Rational, Natural and Open Systems Perspectives.* New York: Pearson.

Scottish Government. 2015. "Future of Crofting." January 14. Accessible at www.ruralpayments.org.

Scoville, David. 2010. "Disneyland Deconstructed: Postmodernism Revealed." April 16. Accessible at http://davidscoville.blogspot.com/2010/04/Disneyland-deconstructed-postmodernism.html.

Searcey, Dionne, and Robert Gebeloff. 2015. "U.S. Seniors Prosper, Finding 'Sweet Spot' in Middle Class." *New York Times* (June 15): A1, B8.

Sedgwick, Eve Kosofsky. 1990. *Epistemology of the Closet.* Berkeley: University of California Press.

Seetharaman, Deepa. 2015. "The Answer Is in the Stars." *Wall Street Journal* (October 14): R1-R2.

Sefiha, Ophir. 2012. "Bad Sports: Explaining Sport Related Deviance." *Sociology Compass* 6:949–961.

Segal, L. Nancy. 2012. *Born Together—Reared Apart. O Brother, Who Art Thou.* Cambridge, MA: Harvard University Press.

Sellers, Frances Stead. 2004. "Voter Globalization." *Washington Post National Weekly Edition,* November 29, p. 22.

Selod, Saher Farooq. 2008a. "Muslim Americans." Pp. 920–923, vol. 2, in *Encyclopedia of Race, Ethnicity, and Society,* edited by Richard T. Schaefer. Thousand Oaks, CA: Sage.

Selod, Saher Farooq. 2008b. "Veil." Pp. 1359–1360, vol. 3, in *Encyclopedia of Race, Ethnicity, and Society,* edited by Richard T. Schaefer. Thousand Oaks, CA: Sage.

Sengupta, Somini. 2009. "An Empire for Poor Working Women, Guided by a Gandhian Approach." *New York Times,* March 7, p. A6.

Sengupta, Somini. 2015. "Europe Tries Incentives and Persuasion to Keep Migrants at Home." *New York Times.* September 12, p. A12.

Sernau, Scott. 2001. *Worlds Apart: Social Inequalities in a New Century.* Thousand Oaks, CA: Pine Forge Press.

Settersten, Richard, and Barbara Ray. 2011. *Not Quite Adults: Why 20-Somethings Are Choosing a Slower Path to Adulthood, and Why It's Good for Everyone.* New York: Bantam.

Shachtman, Tom. 2006. *Rumspringa: To Be or Not to Be Amish.* New York: North Point Press.

Shahrani, M. Nazif. 1981. "Growing in Respect: Aging among the Kirghiz of Afghanistan." Pp. 175 -192 in *Other Ways of Growing Old,* edited by P. Amoss and S. Harrell. Stanford CA: Stanford University Press.

Shane, Scott. 2010. "Wars Fought and Wars Googled." *New York Times,* June 27, pp. PWK1–5.

Shankland, Stephen. 2015. "Like It or Not, Europe's Quota System Puts Women on Boards." *CNET.* May 7. Accessible at www.cnet.com.

Shapiro, P. Joseph. 1993. *No Pity: People with Disabilities Forging a New Civil Rights Movement.* New York: Times Books.

Shapley, Dan. 2010. "4 Dirty Secrets of the Exxon Valdez Oil Spill." Accessed May 3 (www.thedailygreen.com).

Sharp, Jeff S., and Jill K. Clark. 2008. "Between the Country and the Concrete: Rediscovering the Rural-Urban Fringe." *City and Community* 7 (March):61–77.

Sharp, M. Ansel, Charles A. Register, and Paul W. Grimes. 2013. *Economics of Social Issues.* 20th ed. New York: McGraw Hill.

Shaw, R. Clifford, and Henry D. McKay. 1942. *Juvenile Delinquency and Urban Areas.* Chicago: University of Chicago Press.

Shea, Andrea. 2013. "Facebook Envy: How the Social Work Affects Our Self-Esteem." February 20. Accessed at www.wbur.org.

Shear, Michael D. 2016. "Obama Bans Federal Solitary Confinement for Youths." *New York Times* (January 26): A18.

Sheehan, Charles. 2005. "Poor Seniors Take On Plans of Condo Giant." *Chicago Tribune,* March 22, pp. 1, 9.

Sherman, Arloc. 2007. *Income Inequality Hits Record Levels, New CBO Data Show.* Washington, DC: Center on Budget and Policy Priorities.

Sherman, Jennifer, and Elizabeth Harris. 2012. "Social Class and Parenting: Classic Debates and New Understandings." *Sociology Compass* 6:60–71.

Sheskin, Ira, and Arnold Dashefsky. 2015. "Jewish Population in the United States, 2014." Reprinted from the *American Jewish Year Book 2014.*

Dashefsky, Sergo DellaPergola, and Ira Sheskin (eds.). New York: Jewish Federation of North America.

Shipler, David. 2005. *The Working Poor: Invisible in America.* New York: Alfred A. Knopf.

Shirahase, Sawako. 2015. "Income inequality among older people in rapidly aging Japan." *Research in Social Stratification and Mobility.*

Short, Kathleen. 2015. *The Research Supplemental: Poverty Measure 2014.* Current Population Reports. P60–254. Washington, DC: U.S. Government Printing Office.

Shostak, B. Arthur. 2002. "Clinical Sociology and the Art of Peace Promotion: Earning a World without War." Pp. 325–345 in *Using Sociology: An Introduction from the Applied and Clinical Perspectives,* edited by Roger A. Straus. Lanham, MD: Rowman and Littlefield.

Shuttleworth, Jay. 2015. "Teaching the Social Issues of a Sustainable Food Supply." *The Social Studies* 106 (4): 159–169.

Sieber, E. Renée, DanielSpitzberg, HannahMuffatt, KristenBrewer, Blanka Füleki, and Naomi Arbit. 2006. *Influencing Climate Change Policy: Environmental Non-Governmental Organizations (ENGOs) Using Virtual and Physical Activism.* Montreal: McGill University.

Silva, M. Jennifer. 2012. "Constructing Adulthood in an Age of Uncertainty." *American Sociological Review* 77 (4):505–522.

Silver, Ira. 1996. "Role Transitions, Objects, and Identity." *Symbolic Interaction* 10 (1):1–20.

Silverman, Rachel Emma. 2009. "As Jobs Grow Scarce, Commuter Marriages Rise." Accessed March 31, 2010 (http://blogs.wsj.com/juggle/2009/01/16/as-jobs-grow-scarce-commuter-marriages-rise/).

———. 2013. "Tracking Sensors Invade the Workplace." *Wall Street Journal,* March 7, pp. B1, B2.

Simmons, Alicia D., and Lawrence D. Bobo. 2015. "Can Non-Full-Probability Internet Surveys Yield Useful Data? A Comparison with Full-Probability Face-to-Face Surveys in the Domain of Race and Social Inequality Attitudes." *Sociological Methodology* 1–31.

Simpson, S. Sally. 2013. "White-collar Crime: A Review of Recent Developments and Promising Directions for Future Research." *Annual Review of Sociology* 39:309–331.

Sjoberg, Gideon. 1960. *The Preindustrial City: Past and Present.* Glencoe, IL: Free Press.

Skocpol, Theda, and Vanessa Williamson. 2012. *The Tea Party and the Remaking of Republican Conservatism.* New York: Oxford University Press.

Slackman, Michael. 2008. "9/11 Rumors That Harden into Conventional Wisdom." *New York Times,* September 9, p. A16.

Slavin, Barbara. 2007. "Child Marriage Rife in Nations Getting U.S. Aid." *USA Today,* July 17, p. 6A.

Sloan, Allan. 2009. "What's Still Wrong with Wall Street." *Time,* November 9, pp. 24–29.

Sloop, M. John. 2009. "Queer: Approaches to Communication." Pp. 90–100 in *21st Century Communication,* edited by Bill Eadie. Thousand Oaks, CA: Sage.

Slug-Lines.com. 2016. "What's New." Accessed January 20, 2016. (www.slug-lines.com).

Smart, Barry. 1990. "Modernity, Postmodernity, and the Present." Pp. 14–30 in *Theories of Modernity and Postmodernity,* edited by Bryan S. Turner. Newbury Park, CA: Sage.

Smelser, Neil. 1962. *Theory of Collective Behavior.* New York: Free Press.

———. 1963. *The Sociology of Economic Life.* Englewood Cliffs, NJ: Prentice Hall.

———. 1997. *Problematics of Sociology.* Berkeley: University of California Press.

———. 1981. *Sociology.* Englewood Cliffs, NJ: Prentice Hall.

Smith, Aaron. 2013. "Online Dating & Relationships." October 21, 2013. Accessible at http://www.pewinternet.org/Reports/2013/Online-Dating/Summary-of-Findings.aspx.

———. 2014. Cell Phones, Social Media and Campaign 2014. November 3. Accessible at www.pewinternet.org.

———, and Maeve Duggan. 2012. "Presidential Campaign Donations in the Digital Age." October 25. Accessible at http://www.pewinternet.org/Reports/2012/Election-2012-Donations/Key-Findings/Presidential-Campaign-Donations-in-the-Digital-Age.aspx.

Smith, Bethany. 2015. "The Existence of a Hidden Curriculum in Sex and Relationships Education in Secondary Schools." *Transformations* 1 (No. 1): 42–55.

Smith, C. Lawrence. 2011. *The World in 2050: Four Forces Shaping Civilizations Northern Future.* New York: A Plume Book.

Smith, Christian. 2007. "Getting a Life: The Challenge of Emerging Adulthood." *Books and Culture: A Christian Review* (November–December).

———. 2008. "Future Directions in the Sociology of Religion." *Social Forces* 86 (June):1564–1589.

Smith, Dan. 1999. *The State of the World Atlas.* 6th ed. London: Penguin.

Smith, David A. 1995. "The New Urban Sociology Meets the Old: Rereading Some Classical Human Ecology." *Urban Affairs Review* 20 (January):432–457.

Smith, David A., and Michael Timberlake. 1993. "World Cities: A Political Economy/Global Network Approach." Pp. 181–207 in *Urban Sociology in Transition,* edited by Ray Hutchison. Greenwich CT: JAI Press.

Smith, Denise, and Hava Tillipman. 2000. "The Older Population in the United States." *Current Population Reports,* ser. P-20, no. 532. Washington, DC: U.S. Government Printing Office.

Smith, Jessica C., and Carla C. Medalia. 2015. "Insurance Coverage in the United States 2014." *Current Population Reports* P60-23. Accessible at www.census.gov.

Smith, Michael Peter. 1988. *City, State, and Market.* New York: Basil Blackwell.

Smith, S. Craig. 2006. "Romania's Orphans Face Widespread Abuse, Group Says." *New York Times,* May 10, p. A3.

Smith, Stacy L. et al. 2015. *Inequality in 700 Popular Films: Examining Portrayals of Gender, Race, & LGBT Status from 2007 to 2014.*

University of Southern California: Annenberg Center.

Smith, W. Tom. 2003. *Coming of Age in 21st Century America: Public Attitudes toward the Importance and Timing of Transition to Adulthood.* Chicago: National Opinion Research Center.

———. 2009. *Religious Change around the World.* Chicago: NORC/University of Chicago.

Smith, Tom W.; Peter V. Marsden; Michael Hout. 2015. *General Social Surveys, 1972–2014.* Chicago: National Opinion Research Center.

Smith, Wesley J. 2011. "Euthanasia Spreads in Europe." *National Review,* October 26. Accessible at http://nationalreview.com.

Snow, David A., Louis A. Zurcher, and Robert Peters. 1981. "Victory Celebrations as Theater: A Dramaturgical Approach to Crowd Behavior." *Symbolic Interaction* 4 (Spring): 21–42.

Soffel, Jenny. 2011. "Gender Bias Fought at Egalia Preschool in Stockholm, Sweden." June 26. Accessible at www.huffingtonpost.com.

Somaskanda, Sumi. 2012. "European Pensions Targeted." *USA Today,* September 20, p. 2B.

Sorokin, A. Pitirim. [1927] 1959. *Social and Cultural Mobility.* New York: Free Press.

Southern Poverty Law Center. 2010. "Active 'Patriot' Groups in the United States in 2009." Accessed November 5 (www.splcenter.org/patriot).

———. 2015. "Active Antigovernment Groups in the United States." Accessed November 5, 2015 (www.splcenter.org).

Spalter-Roth, Roberta, Nicole Van Vooren, and Mary S. Senter. 2013. "Using the Bachelor's and Beyond Project to Help Launch Students in Careers." Accessed November 1 at www.asanet.org/documents/research/docs/B%26BLaunchingCareers.pptx.

Spencer, Nancy. 2008. "Title IX." Pp. 1308–1310, vol. 3, in *Encyclopedia of Race, Ethnicity, and Society,* edited by Richard T. Schaefer. Thousand Oaks, CA: Sage.

Sperber, Murray. 2000. *Beer and Circus: How Big-Time College Sports Is Crippling Undergraduate Education.* New York: Henry Holt & Co.

Spiegel, Peter, Alex Barker, and Claire Jones. "Killings Inflame Debate over Migrants and Borders." *Financial Times* (November 16): 4.

Sprague, Joey. 2005. *Feminist Methodologies for Critical Research: Bridging Differences.* Lanham, MD: AltaMira Press.

Squires, Gregory D., ed. 2002. *Urban Sprawl: Causes, Consequences and Policy Responses .* Washington, DC: Urban Institute.

Stablen, Timothy, Joseph Lorenzo Hall, Chauna Pervis, and Denise L. Anthony. 2015. "Negotiating stigma in health care: disclosure and the role of electronic health records." *Health Sociology Review* 24 (Issue 3).

Stansell, Christine. 2011. *The Feminist Promise: 1792 to the Present.* New York: The Modern Library.

Stark, Rodney, and William Sims Bainbridge. 1979. "Of Churches, Sects, and Cults: Preliminary Concepts for a Theory of Religious Movements." Journal for the Scientific Study of Religion 18 (June):117–131.

——, and ——. 1985. *The Future of Religion.* Berkeley: University of California Press.

Stark, Rodney. 2004. *Exploring the Religious Life.* Baltimore: Johns Hopkins University Press.

Staton, Ron. 2004. "Still Fighting for National Hawaiian Recognition." *Asian Week,* January 22, p. 8.

Steffen, Alex, ed. 2008. *World Changing: A User's Guide for the 21st Century.* New York: Harry N. Abrams.

Stenning, Derrick J. 1958. "Household Viability among the Pastoral Fulani," in John R. Goody (ed.), *The Developmental Cycle in Domestic Groups.* Cambridge, Eng.: Cambridge University Press, pp. 92–119.

Stevenson, Betsey, and Justin Wolfers. 2007. "Marriage and Divorce: Changes and their Driving Forces." National Bureau of Economic Research. Working Paper No. 12944. Accessible at www.nber.org.

Stevick, A. Richard. 2007. *Growing Up Amish: The Teenage Years.* Baltimore: Johns Hopkins University Press.

Stokes, Bruce, Richard Wilke, and Jill Carle. 2015. "Global Concern about Climate Change, Broad Support for Limiting Emissions: U.S., China Less Worried; Partisan Divides in Key Countries." December 5. Accessible at www.pewglobal.com.

Stoner, Madeleine R. 2008. "Homelessness." pp. 641–644, vol. 2, in *Encyclopedia of Race, Ethnicity, and Society,* edited by Richard T. Schaefer. Thousand Oaks, CA: Sage.

Strauss, Gary. 2011. "$228, 000 for a Part-time Job? Apparently, That's Not Enough." *USA Today* (March 4), p. A1.

Stray, Jonathan. 2012. "Are We Stuck in Filter Bubbles? Here Are Five Potential Paths out." July 12. Accessed December 1 at http://www.niemanlab.org/2012/07/are-we-stuck-in-filter-bubbles-here-are-five-potential-paths-out/.

Stryker, Roy Emerson, and Nancy Wood. 1973 [1935–1943]. *In This Proud Land.* Greenwich: New York Graphic Society .

Subramaniam, Mangala. 2006. *The Power of Women's Organization: Gender, Caste, and Class in India.* Lanham, MD: Lexington Books.

Subramanian, Ram, Ruth Delaney, Stephen Roberts, Nancy Fishman, Peggy McGarry. 2015. *Incarceration's Front Door: The Misuse of Jails in America.* New York: The Vera Institute.

Suchar, Charles S. 1997. "Grounding Visual Sociology Research in Shooting Scripts." *Qualitative Sociology* 20 (1): 33–55.

Suh, Michael. 2014. "2013 Survey of LGBT Adults." September 18. Accessible at www.pew-sociatrends.org.

Suitor, J. Jill, Staci A. Minyard, and Rebecca S. Carter. 2001. "'Did You See What I Saw?' Gender Differences in Perceptions of Avenues to Prestige among Adolescents."*Sociological Inquiry* 71 (Fall):437–454.

Sullivan, Harry Stack. [1953] 1968. *The Interpersonal Theory of Psychiatry.* Edited by Helen Swick Perry and Mary Ladd Gawel. New York: Norton.

Sumner, William G. 1906. *Folkways.* New York: Ginn.

Sunstein, Cass. 2002. *Republic.com.* Rutgers, NJ: Princeton University Press.

Survival International. 2016. " The Uncontacted Indians of Brazil." Accessed February 11 (www.survivalinternational.org/tribes/Brazilian).

Sutherland, Anna. 2015. "What's Behind the Reversal of the Gender Gap in Higher Education?" October 12. Accessible at www.family-studies.org.

Sutherland, H. Edwin. 1937. *The Professional Thief.* Chicago: University of Chicago Press.

——. 1940. "White-Collar Criminality." *American Sociological Review* 5 (February):1–11.

——. 1949. *White Collar Crime.* New York: Dryden.

——. 1983. *White Collar Crime: The Uncut Version.* New Haven, CT: Yale University Press.

——, Donald R. Cressey, and David F. Luckenbill. 1992. *Principles of Criminology.* 11th ed. New York: Rowman and Littlefield.

Swanson, Emily. 2013. "Poll: Few Identify as Feminists, but Most Believe in Equality of Sexes." *Huffington Post,* April 15. Accessible at www.huffingtonpost.com.

Swarns, Rachel L. 2015. "Biased Lending Evolves, and Blacks Face Trouble Getting Mortgages." October 30. *New York Times.* Accessible at nytimes.com.

Swartz, Jon. 2012. "Google's Personalized Search Charges Set Off Uproar." *USA Today,* January 12, p. B1.

Swatos, H. William, Jr., ed. 1998. *Encyclopedia of Religion and Society.* Lanham, MD: AltaMira.

Sweet, Kimberly. 2001. "Sex Sells a Second Time."*Chicago Journal* 93 (April):12–13.

Swidler, Ann. 1986. "Culture in Action: Symbols and Strategies." *American Sociological Review* 51 (April):273–286.

Szasz, Andrew. 2007. *Shopping Our Way to Safety: How We Changed from Protecting the Environment to Protecting Ourselves.* Minneapolis: University of Minnesota Press.

Szasz, Thomas. 2010. *The Myth of Mental Illness: Foundations of a Theory of Personal Conduct.* 50th Anniversary Edition. New York: Harper Perennial.

t

Tabuchi, Hiroko. 2013. "Desperate Hunt for Day Care." *New York Times,* February 27, pp. A4, A9.

Takei, Isao, and Arthur Sakamoto. 2011. "Poverty Among Asian Americans in the 21st Century." *Sociological Perspectives* 54 (Summer):251–276.

Talev, Margaret. 2015. "Bloomberg Politics Poll: Most Americans Oppose Syrian Refugee Resettlement." November 18. Accessible at www.bloomberg.com.

Tanielian, Terri. 2009. "Assessing Combat Exposure and Post-Traumatic Stress Disorder in Troops and Estimating the Costs to Society." Testimony presented before the House Veterans' Affairs Committee, Subcommittee on Disability Assistance and Memorial Affairs (March 24).

Tannen, Deborah. 1990. *You Just Don't Understand: Women and Men in Conversation.* New York: Ballantine.

Tarricone, Barbara. 2014. "Being Social." *The American/In Italia.* May 2. Accessible at theamericanmag.com.

Tatchell, Jo. 2009. *A Diamond in the Desert: Behind the Scenes in the World's Richest City.* London: Hodder and Stoughton.

Taylor, Keeanga-Yamahtta. 2016. *From #BlackLivesMatter to Black Liberation.* Chicago:Haymarket Books.

Taylor, Paul, Ana Gonzalez-Barrera, Jeffrey S. Passel, and Mark Hugo Lopez. 2012. "An Awakened Giant: The Hispanic Electorate is Likely to Double by 2030." November 14. Accessible at www.pewhispanic.org.

Taylor, Verta, Leila J. Rupp, and Nancy Whittier. 2009. *Feminist Frontiers.* 8th ed. New York: McGraw-Hill.

Teaching Tolerance. 2012. "LGBT Content Access Denied." Accessed March 29 (www.tollerance.org/blog/lgbt-content-access-denied).

Tedeschi, Bob. 2006. "Those Born to Shop Can Now Use Cellphones." *New York Times,* January 2.

Teranishi, Robert T. 2010. *Asians in the Ivory Tower: Dilemmas of Racial Inequity in American Higher Education.* New York: Teachers College Press.

Tett, Gillian. 2015 *The Silo Effect: The Peril of Expertise and the Promise of Breaking Down Barriers.* New York: Simon & Schuster.

Tharoor, Ishaan. 2015. "What Americans Thought of Jewish refugees on the Eve of World War II." *Washington Post,* November 17. Accessible at washingtonpost.com.

The Liman Program, Yale Law School Association of State Correctional Administrators. 2015. *Time-in Cell: The ASCA-Liman 2014 National Survey of Administrative Segregation in Prison.* Available at law.yale.edu.

The Week. 2015. "Why Jurassic World Has a Starbucks." June 26:32.

The Week. 2014. "A New Way of Doing Business." September 4: 11.

Themed Entertainment Association. 2015. *Global Attractions Attendance Report 2014.* Burbank, CA: TEA.

Thomas Jr., Landon. 2011. "Money Troubles Take Personal Toll in Greece." *New York Times,* May 16, pp. A1, A2. Accessible at www.nytimes.com/2011/05/16/business/global/16drachma.html?pagewanted=all.

Thomas, R. Murray. 2003. "New Frontiers in Cheating." In *Encyclopaedia Britannica 2003 Book of the Year.* Chicago: Encyclopaedia Britannica.

Thomas, William I. 1923. *The Unadjusted Girl.* Boston: Little, Brown.

Thomasrobb.com. 2007. "WhitePride TV." Accessed May 7 (http://thomasrobb.com).

Thompson, Tony. 2005. "Romanians Are Being Paid to Play Computer Games for Westerners." *Guardian Weekly,* March 25, p. 17.

Threadcraft, Shatema. 2008. "Welfare Queen." In *Encyclopedia of Race, Ethnicity and Society,* edited by Richard T. Schaefer. Thousand Oaks, CA: Sage.

Thurm, Scott. 2010. "Oracle's Ellison: Pay King." *Wall Street Journal* (July 27), pp. A1, A16.

———. 2012. *Virtually Religious: Technology and Internet Use in American Congregations.* Hartford Institute. Accessible at http://www. hartfordinstitute.org/research/religion_web_ articles.html

Thurow, Lester. 1984. "The Disappearance of the Middle Class." *New York Times,* February 5, sec. 5, p. 2.

Tibbles, Kevin. 2007. "Web Sites Encourage Eating Disorders." *Today,* February 18. Accessed May 7 (www.msabc.msn.com).

Tierney, John. 1990. "Betting the Planet." *New York Times Magazine* (December 2):52–53, 80–81, 76, 78, 71, and 74.

Tierney, Kathleen J. 1980. "Emergent Norm Theory as 'Theory': An Analysis and Critique of Turner's Formulation." Pp. 42–53 in *Collective Behavior: A SourceBook,* edited by Meredith David Pugh. St. Paul, MN: West.

———. 2007. "From the Margins to the Mainstream? Disaster Research at the Crossroads."*Annual Review of Sociology* 33:503–525.

Tigay, Chanan. 2011. "Women and Sports." *CQ Researcher* 21 (March 25).

Tilly, Charles. 1980. "The Old New Social History and the New Old Social History." October. Center for Research on Social Organization Working Paper No. 218. Accessed December 1, 2013 at http://deepblue.lib.umich.edu/ bitstream/handle/2027.42/50992/218. pdf?sequence=1.

———. 1993. *Popular Contention in Great Britain 1758–1834.* Cambridge, MA: Harvard University Press.

———. 2004. *Social Movements, 1768–2004.* Boulder, CO: Paradigm.

———. 2007. "Trust Networks in Transnational Migration." *Sociological Forum* 22 (March):3–24.

Time. 2015. "See Women's Progress in the U.S. Military." September 8. Accessible at http://time. com/4022143/women-in-military/.

Timmerman, Kelsey. 2009. *Where Am I Wearing?* Hoboken NJ: Wiley.

Toensing, Gale Country. 2009. "Akaka Bill Gets Obama Approval."*Indian Country Today* (August 19):1, 2.

Toma, Catalina L., and Jeffrey T. Hancock. 2010. "Looks and Lies: The Role of Physical Attractiveness in Online Dating Self-Presentation and Deception."*Community Research* 37 (3):335–351.

Toma, Catalina L., Jeffrey T. Hancock, and Nicole B. Ellison. 2008. "Separating Fact from Fiction: An Examination of Deceptive Self-Presentation in Online Dating Profiles."*Personality and Social Psychology Bulletin* 34:1023–1036.

Tonkinson, Robert. 1978. *The Mardudjara Aborigines.* New York: Holt.

Tönnies, Ferdinand. [1887] 1988. *Community and Society.* Rutgers, NJ: Transaction.

Tonry, Michael (ed.). 2014. Why Crime Rates Fall and Why They Don't. Special Issue of *Crime and Justice* 43 (No.1).

Toossi, Mitra. 2009. "Employment Outlook: 2008– 2018." *Monthly Labor Review* (November): 30–51.

———. 2012. "Labor Force Projections to 2020: A More Slowly Growing Labor Force." *Monthly Labor Review* (January):43–64.

———. 2012. "Projections of the labor force to 2050: a visual essay." *Monthly Labor Review* (October): 3–16. Accessible at http://www.bls. gov.

Toppo, Greg. 2011. "The Search for a New Way to Test Schoolkids." *USA Today,* March 18, p. A4.

Toro, Paul A. 2007. "Toward an International Understanding of Homelessness." *Journal of Social Issues* 63 (3):461–481.

Touraine, Alain. 1974. *The Academic System in American Society.* New York: McGraw-Hill.

Tracey, Paul. 2012. "Religion and Organization: A Critical Review of Current Trends and Future Directions."*The Academy of Management Annals* 6(1): 87–134.

Transactional Records Access Clearinghouse. 2015. "Justice Department Data Reveal 29 Percent Drop in Criminal Prosecutions of Corporations." October 13. Accessible at www.trac.syr.edu.

Trimble, Charles. 2008. "Itheska: Notes from Mixed Blood Country." *Indian Country Today* (May 7):5

Trimble, Lindsey B., and Julie A. Kmec. 2011. "The Role of Social Networks in Getting a Job." *Sociology Compass* 5 (2):165–178.

Truman, Jennifer L., and Lynn Langton. 2015. *Criminal Victimization, 2014.* August, revised September. Accessible at bjs.gov.

Trumbull, Mark. 2006. "America's Younger Workers Losing Ground on Income." *Christian Science Monitor,* February 27.

Tuan, Mia, and Jiannbin Lee Shiao. 2011. *Choosing Ethnicity, Negotiating Race: Korean Adoptees in America.* New York: Russell Sage Foundation.

Tuchman, Gaye. 1992. "Feminist Theory." Pp. 695–704 in *Encyclopedia of Sociology,* vol. 2, edited by Edgar F. Borgatta and Marie L. Borgatta. New York: Macmillan.

Tucker, Robert C. (ed.) 1978. *The Marx-Engels Reader.* 2nd ed. New York: Norton.

Tukachinsky, Rita, Dana Mastro, and Moran Yarchi. 2015. "Documenting Portrayals of Race/ Ethnicity on Primetime Television over a 20-Year Span and Their Association with National-Level Racial/Ethnic Attitudes." *Journal of Social Issues* 71 (No. 1): 17–38.

Ture, Kwame, and Charles Hamilton. 1992. *Black Power: The Politics of Liberation.* With new Afterword by authors. New York: Vintage Books.

Turkle, Sherry. 2004. "How Computers Change the Way We Think." *Chronicle of Higher Education* 50 (January 30):B26–B28.

———. 2011. *Alone Together: Why We Expect More from Technology and Less from Each Other.* New York: Basic Books.

Turner, Bryan S., ed. 1990. *Theories of Modernity and Postmodernity.* Newbury Park, CA: Sage.

Turner, Ralph, and Lewis M. Killian. 1987. *Collective Behavior.* 3rd ed. Englewood Cliffs, NJ: Prentice Hall.

U

U.S. English. 2016. "Making English the Official Language." Accessed February 11 (www. usenglish.org/inc/).

U.S. Surgeon General. 1999. *Surgeon General's Report on Mental Health.* Washington, DC: U.S. Government Printing Office.

UN High Commissioner for Refugees. 2015. "'Refugee' or 'migrant'-- Which is right?" August 28. Accessed November 12 at www. unrefugees.org.

UN Women. 2015. *Progress of the World's Women 2015–2016. Transforming Economics. Realizing Rights.* Accessible at www.unwomen.org

UNAIDS. 2013. *AIDS by the Numbers.* Geneva Switzerland: UNAIDS/SIDA.

UNHCR. 2010. *UNHCR Statistical Yearbook 2009.* Geneva: UNHCR.

UNICEF. 2009. *Progress for Children: A Report Card on Child Protection.* September. Vienna: UNICEF.

———. 2014. Child marriage in 2005–2014. Accessed February 9, 2016 at www.unicef.org.

Unionwiki. 2015. *The Global Union Database Project.* Accessed September 11 at unionwiki. net.

United Nations Development Programme. 2000. *Poverty Report 2000: Overcoming Human Poverty.* Washington, DC: UNDP.

———. 2009. *Overcoming Barriers: Human Mobility and Development.* New York: Palgrave Macmillan.

United Nations Economic and Social Council. 2010. "Review of the Implementation of the Beijing Declaration." New York: Economic and Social Council.

United Nations Office on Drugs and Crime. 2015. "Factsheets: Transnational Organized Crime: Let's Put Them out of Business." Accessed October 26 at unodc.org.

———. 2015b. *Crime and Criminal Justice Statistics.* Accessed October 26 at unodc.org.

United Nations Population Division. 2014. A World of Cities. *Population Facts.* No. 2014/2. August. New York: Department of Economic and Social Affairs, Population Division.

———. 2014. "Despite Overall Expansion in the Legal Grounds for Abortion, Policies Remain Restrictive in Many Countries." *Population Facts* No. 2014/1. Accessible at www.un.org.

United Nations Secretary General. 2014. *The World Survey on the Role of Women in Development.* New York: United Nations. Accessible at unwomen.org.

United Nations Statistics Division. 2013. "Marriage and Divorce." Accessible at www.unstats.org.

United Nations. 2013. "Number of International Migrants Rises above 232 Million, UN Reports." September 11. United Nations News Centre. Accessible at www.un.org.

———. 2015. "Population, Consumption and the Environment. Wall Chart." Accessible at www.un.org.

University of Michigan. 2003. Information on Admissions Lawsuits. Accessed August 8 (www.umich.edu/urel/admissions).

Urban Dictionary. 2016. "Urban Amish." Accessed March 5 at www.urbandictionary.com.

V

van den Berghe, Pierre L. 1978. *Race and Racism: A Comparative Perspective.* 2nd ed. New York: Wiley.

Van Gennep, Arnold. [1909] 1960. *The Rites of Passage.* Translated by Monika B. Vizedom and Gabrielle L. Caffee. Chicago: University of Chicago Press.

van Vucht Tijssen, Lieteke. 1990. "Women between Modernity and Postmodernity." Pp. 147–163 in *Theories of Modernity and Postmodernity,* edited by Bryan S. Turner. London: Sage.

Vaughan, R. M. 2007. "Cairo's Man Show." *Utne Reader* (March–April):94–95.

Veblen, Thornstein, 1914. *The Instinct of Workmanship and the State of the Industrial Arts.* New York: Macmillan.

———. [1899] 1964. *Theory of the Leisure Class.* New York: Macmillan. New York: Penguin.

Venkatesh, Sudhir Alladi. 2006. *Off the Books: The Underground Economy of the Urban Poor.* Cambridge, MA: Harvard University Press.

———. 2008. *Gang Leader for a Day: A Rogue Sociologist Takes to the Streets.* New York: Penguin Press.

Vergeer, Maurice. 2015. "Twitter and Political Campaigning." *Sociology Compass* 99: 745–760.

Vernon, Glenn. 1962. *Sociology and Religion.* New York: McGraw-Hill.

Viramontes, Helena Maria. 2007. "Loyalty Spoken Here." *Los Angeles Times,* September 23, p. R7.

Visser, Jelle. 2006. "Union Membership Statistics in 24 Countries." *Monthly Labor Review* (January):38–49.

Volti, Rudi. 2013. *Society and Technological Change.* 7th ed. New York: Worth Publishers.

W

Wachtendorf, Tricia. 2002. "A Changing Risk Environment: Lessons Learned from the 9/11 World Trade Center Disaster." Presentation at the Sociological Perspectives on Disasters, Mt. Macedon, Australia, July.

Wagley, Charles, and Marvin Harris. 1958. *Minorities in the New World: Six Case Studies.* New York: Columbia University Press.

Wagner, Paul. 2011. "Pay Czar's Rules Had Few Lasting Effects, Watchdog Says." February 10. Accessible at www.huffingtonpost.com.

Waitzkin, Howard. 1986. *The Second Sickness: Contradictions of Capitalist Health Care.* Chicago: University of Chicago Press.

Walder, Andrew, and Giang Hoang Nguyen. 2008. "Ownership, Organization, and Income Inequality; Market Transition in Rural Vietnam." *American Sociological Review* 73 (April):251–269.

Waldinger, Roger. 2015. *The Cross-Border Connection: Immigrants, Emigrants, and Their Homelands.* Cambridge MA: Harvard University Press.

Walker, Andrea C., and David E. Balk. 2007. "Bereavement Rituals in the Muscogee Creek Tribe." *Death Studies* 31:633–652.

Walker, Edward. 2010. "Activism Industry-Driven."*Contexts (*Spring):43–49.

Wallerstein, Immanuel. 1974. *The Modern World System.* New York: Academic Press.

———. 1979a. *Capitalist World Economy.* Cambridge: Cambridge University Press.

———. 1979b. *The End of the World as We Know It: Social Science for the Twenty-First Century.* Minneapolis: University of Minnesota Press.

———. 2000. *The Essential Wallerstein.* New York: New Press.

———. 2012. "Reflections on an Intellectual Adventure." *Contemporary Sociology* 41 (1):6–12.

Wallis, Claudia. 2008. "How to Make Great Teachers." *Time* 171 (February 25):28–34.

Walsh, Anthony. 2000. "Behavior Genetics and Anomie/Strain Theory." *Criminology* (November):1075–1107.

Wan, Daniel Goodkind, and Paul Kwai. 2016. *An Aging World: 2015.* Washington DC: U.S. Government Printing Office.

Wang, Esther. 2013. "As Wal-Mart Swallows China's Economy, Workers Fight Back." April 23. Accessed November 16 at http://prospect.org/article/wal-mart-swallows-chinas-economy-workers-fight-back.

Wang, Wendy. 2012. "The Rise of Intermarriage: Rates, Characteristics Vary by Race and Gender." Washington, DC: Pew Social and Demographic Trends.

———. 2015. "Interracial Marriage. Who Is 'Marrying Out'?" June 12. Accessible at pewresearch.org.

Warrell, Helen. 2013. "Cost of Malnutrition to Global Economy Put at $125bn by 2030." *Financial Times* (May 28):3.

Wasik, Bill. 2012. "Crowd Control." *Wired* (January): 76–83, 112–113.

Wayland-Smith, Ellen. 2016. *Oneida: From Free Love Utopia to the Well-Set Table.* New York: Picador.

Weatherall, Ann. 2015. "Sexism in Language and Talk-in-Interaction." *Journal of Language and Social Psychology* 34(4).

Webb, Lynne M., and Brittany Lee. 2012. "Blogs and Blogging." Pp. 24–26 in *Encyclopedia of Gender in the Media,* edited by Mary Kosut. Los Angeles: Sage Reference.

Weber, Max. [1904] 1949. *Methodology of the Social Sciences.* Translated by Edward A. Shils and Henry A. Finch. Glencoe, IL: Free Press.

———. [1904] 2011. *The Protestant Ethic and the Spirit Capitalism.* The Revised 1920 Edition. Translation by Stephen Kalberg. New York: Oxford University Press.

———. [1913–1922] 1947. *The Theory of Social and Economic Organization.* Translated by A Henderson and T. Parsons. New York: Free Press.

———. [1916] 1958. *The Religion of India: The Sociology of Hinduism and Buddhism.* New York: Free Press.

Wechsler, Henry, J. E. Lee, M. Kuo, M. Seibring, T. F. Nelson, and H. Lee. 2002. "Trends in College Binge Drinking during a Period of Increased Prevention Efforts: Findings from Four Harvard School of Public Health College Alcohol Surveys: 1993–2001." *Journal of American College Health* 50 (5):203–217.

Wechsler, Henry, Mark Seibring, I-Chao Liu, and Marilyn Ahl. 2004. "Colleges Respond to Student Binge Drinking: Reducing Student Demand or Limiting Access." *Journal of American College Health* 52 (4):159–168.

Weeks, John R. 2012. *Population: An Introduction to Concepts and Issues.* 11th ed. Belmont, CA: Cengage.

Weinberg, Daniel H. 2004. "Evidence from Census 2000 About Earnings by Detailed Occupation for Men and Women." CENSR-15. Washington, DC: U.S. Government Printing Office.

———. 2007. "Earnings by Gender: Evidence from Census 2000." *Monthly Labor Review* (July–August):26–34.

Weinraub, Bernard. 2004. "UPN Show Is Called Insensitive to Amish." *New York Times,* March 4, pp. B1, B8.

Welch, William M. 2011. "More Hawaii Residents Identify as Mixed Race." *USA Today,* February 28.

Wells-Barnett, Ida B. 1970. *Crusade for Justice: The Autobiography of Ida B. Wells.* Edited by Alfreda M. Duster. Chicago: University of Chicago Press.

Wentling, Tre, Elroi Windsor, Kristin Schilt, and Betsy Lucal. 2008. "Teaching Transgender." *Teaching Sociology* 36 (January):49–57.

Wesolowski, Amy, Nathan Eagle, Andrew J. Tatem, David L. Smith, Abdisalam M. Noor, Robert W. Snow, and Caroline O. Buckee. 2012. "Quantifying the Impact of Human Mobility on Malaria." *Science* (October 12):267–270.

Wessell, David, and Stephanie Banchero. 2012. "Education Slowdown Threatens U.S." *Wall Street Journal,* April 26, p. A1.

Wessell, David. 2011. "Untangling the Long-Term-Unemployment Crisis." *Wall Street Journal,* October 20, p. A6.

West, Candace, and Don H. Zimmerman. 1987. "Doing Gender."*Gender and Society* 1 (June):125–151.

West, Candace, and Don H. Zimmerman. 2009. "Accounting for Doing Gender." *Gender & Society* 23:112–122.

Western, Bruce, and Jake Rosenfeld. 2011. "Unions, Norms, and the Rise in U.S. Wage Inequality." *American Sociological Review* 70 (4):513–537.

White, Gillian. 2015. "In the Sharing Economy, No One's an Employee." June 15. Accessible at www.theatlantic.com.

Whitlock, Craig. 2005. "The Internet as Bully Pulpit." *Washington Post National Weekly Edition* 22 (August 22):9.

Whittaker, Stephanie. 2006. "Who Would You Prefer to Work For?" *Gazette* (Montreal), November 4, p. 1.

Whyte, John. 2010. "Media Portrayal of People Who Are Obese." *Journal of Medical Ethics* 12 (April): 320–323.

Whyte, William Foote. 1981. *Street Corner Society: Social Structure of an Italian Slum.* 3rd ed. Chicago: University of Chicago Press.

WIEGO. 2016. "About the Informal Economy." *Women in Informal Employment: Globalizing and Organizing.* Accessed February 26 at www.wiego.org.

Wildsmith, Elizabeth, Nicole R. Steward-Streng, and Jennifer Manlove. 2011. "Childbearing Outside of Marriage: Estimates and Trends in the United States." *Child Trends Research Brief* #2011–29. Accessible at www.child trends.org.

Wilford, John Noble. 1997. "New Clues Show Where People Made the Great Leap to Agriculture." *New York Times,* November 18, pp. B9, B12.

Wilgoren, Jodi. 2005. "In Kansas, Darwinism Goes on Trial Once More." *New York Times,* May 6, p. A14.

Wilkins, Amy C. "Becoming Black Women: 2012. Intimate Stories and Intersectional Identities." Social Psychological Quarterly 75 (2):173–196.

Williams, Audra. 2015. "Stop Shaming Syrian Refuges for Using Their Cellphones." *The Daily Dot.* September 11. Accessible at www.dailydot.com/opinion/ syria-refugees-cell-phone-use/.

Williams, Carol J. 1995. "Taking an Eager Step Back." *Los Angeles Times,* June 3, pp. A1, A14.

Williams, Gregory P. 2013. "Special Contribution: Interview with Immanuel Wallerstein Retrospective on the Origins of World-Systems Analysis." *Journal of World-Systems Research* 19 (No. 1):202–210).

Williams, J. Allen, Christopher Podeschi, Nathan Palmer, Philip Schwadel, and Deanna Meyler. 2012. "The Human-Environment Dialog in Award-winning Children's Picture Books." *Sociological Inquiry* 82 (February): 145–159.

Williams, Kristine N., Ruth Herman, Byron Gajewski, and Kristel Wilson. 2009. "Elderspeak Communication: Impact on Dementia Care." *American Journal of Alzheimer's Disease and Other Dementias* 24 (March):11–20.

Williams, Robin M., Jr. 1970. *American Society.* 3rd ed. New York: Knopf.

Williams, Robin M., Jr., with John P. Dean and Edward A. Suchman. 1964. *Strangers Next Door: Ethnic Relations in American Communities.* Englewood Cliffs, NJ: Prentice Hall.

Wilson, Edward O. 1975. *Sociobiology: The New Synthesis.* Cambridge, MA: Harvard University Press.

———. 2000. *Sociobiology: The New Synthesis.* Cambridge, MA: Belknap Press, Harvard University Press.

———. 1978. *On Human Nature.* Cambridge, MA: Harvard University Press.

Wilson, John. 1973. *Introduction to Social Movements.* New York: Basic Books.

Wilson, William Julius. 1996. *When Work Disappears: The World of the New Urban Poor.* New York: Knopf.

———. 1999. *The Bridge over the Racial Divide: Rising Inequality and Coalition Politics.* Berkeley: University of California Press.

———. 2009. *More Than Just Race: Being Black and Poor in the Inner City.* New York: Norton.

———. 2012a. *The Declining Significance of Race: Blacks and Changing American Institutions.* 3rd ed. Chicago: University of Chicago Press.

———. 2012b. *The Truly Disadvantaged: The Inner City, the Underclass and Public Policy.* 2nd ed. Chicago: University of Chicago Press.

———, J. M. Quane, and B. H. Rankin. 2004. "Underclass." In *International Encyclopedia of Social and Behavioral Sciences.* New York: Elsevier.

Wimmer, Andreas. 2014. "War." *Annual Review of Sociology* 40:173–197.

Winant, Howard B. 2006. "Race and Racism: Towards a Global Future." *Ethnic and Racial Studies* 29 (September):986–1003.

Winickoff, Jonathan P., Joan Friebely, Susanne E. Tanski, Cheryl Sherrod, George E. Matt, Melbourne F. Hovell, and Robert C. McMillen. 2009. "Beliefs about the Health Effects of 'Thirdhand' Smoke and Home Smoking Bans." *Pediatrics* 123 (January):74–79.

Winter, J. Allen. 2008. "Symbolic Ethnicity." Pp. 1288–1290, vol. 3, in *Encyclopedia of Race, Ethnicity, and Society,* edited by Richard T. Schaefer. Thousand Oaks, CA: Sage.

Wirth, Louis. 1928. *The Ghetto.* Chicago: University of Chicago Press.

———. 1931. "Clinical Sociology." *American Journal of Sociology* 37 (July):49–60.

———. 1938. "Urbanism as a Way of Life." *American Journal of Sociology* 44 (July): 1–24.

Witte, Griff. 2005. "The Vanishing Middle Class." *Washington Post National Weekly Edition,* September 27, pp. 6–9.

Wolf, Naomi. 1992. *The Beauty Myth: How Images of Beauty Are Used against Women.* New York: Anchor Books.

Wong, Morrison G. 2006. "Chinese Americans." Pp. 110–145 in *Asian Americans: Contemporary Trends and Issues,* 2nd ed., edited by Pyong Gap Min. Thousand Oaks, CA: Sage.

Working Women's Forum. 2016. Home Page. Accessed January 4 (www.workingwomens forum.org).

World Bank 2015a. *2015 World Development Indicators.* Accessible at worldbank.org.

———. 2015b. "World Bank Data: Income share held by highest 20% and lowest 20%." Accessible at data.worldbank.org.

———. 2015b. "Migration and Remittances: Recent Developments and Outlook." April 13. Accessible at www.worldbank.org.

———. 2015c. *World Bank Indicators 2015.* Accessible at www.worldbank.org.

———. 2015c. "Update of World Bank Group Gender Strategy: Consultations" Accessed November 23 at www.worldbank,org.

———. 2015c. "World Development Indicators: Size of the economy." Accessible at data.worldbank.org.

———. 2015d. "Poverty Home: Overview." Accessible at www.worldbank.org.

———. 2015f. "World Bank Data: Health expenditure, public (% of total health expenditure)." Accessible at data.worldbank.org.

———. 2016. "Education." Accessed February 25 at www.worldbank.org.

World Development Forum. 1990. "The Danger of Television." 8 (July 15):4.

World Health Organization Media Centre. 2014. "Children: Reducing Mortality." Fact Sheet 178. Updated September 2014. Accessible at www.who.int.

World Health Organization. 2000. *The World Health Report 2000. Health Systems: Improving Performance.* Geneva: WHO.

———. 2010. "Suicide Prevention." Accessed October 31 (http://www.who.int/mental_health/ prevention/en/).

Worth, Robert F. 2008. "As Taboos Ease, Saudi Girl Group Dares to Rock." *New York Times,* November 24, pp. A1, A9.

Wortham, Robert A. 2008. "DuBois, William Edward Burghardt." Pp. 423–427, vol. 1, in *Encyclopedia of Race, Ethnicity, and Society,* edited by Richard T. Schaefer. Thousand Oaks CA: Sage.

Wray, Matt, Cynthia Colen, and Bernice Pescosolido, 2011. "The Sociology of Suicide." *Annual Review of Sociology* 37:505–528.

Wray, Matt, Matthew Miller, Jill Gurvey, Joanna Carroll, and Ichiro Kawachi. 2008. "Leaving Las Vegas: Exposure to Las Vegas and Risk of Suicide." *Social Science and Medicine* 67:1882–1888.

Wright II, Earl. 2012. "Why, Where, and How to Infuse the Atlanta Sociological Laboratory into the Sociology Curriculum." *Teaching Sociology* 40 (43):257–270.

Wright, Charles R. 1986. *Mass Communication: A Sociological Perspective.* 3rd ed. New York: Random House.

Wright, Eric R., William P. Gronfein, and Timothy J. Owens. 2000. "Deinstitutionalization, Social Rejection, and the Self-Esteem of Former Mental Patients." *Journal of Health and Social Behavior* (March).

Wright, Erik O. 2011. "The Classical Marxist Theory of the History of Capitalism's Future." October 3. Accessed January 20, 2012 (www. ssc.wisc.edu/~wright/621-2011/lecture%208%20 2011%20–%20Classical%20Theory%20of%20 Capitalisms%20future.pdf).

Wright, Erik O., David Hachen, Cynthia Costello, and Joey Sprague. 1982. "The American Class Structure." *American Sociological Review* 47 (December):709–726.

X

Xu, Jun, and Jennifer Lee. 2013. "The Marginalized 'Model' Minority: An Empirical Examination of the Racial Triangulation of Asian Americans." *Social Forces* 91 (4): 1363–1397.

Y

Yap, Kioe Sheng. 1998. "Squatter Settlements." Pp. 554–556 in *The Encyclopedia of Housing*, edited by Willem van Vliet. Thousand Oaks, CA: Sage.

Yavorsky, Jill E., Claire M. Kamp Dush, and Sarah J. Schoppe-Sullivan. 2015. "The Production of Inequality: The Gender Division of Labor Across the Transition to Parenthood." *Journal of Marriage and Family* 77 (3): 662–679.

Yellen, Janet L. 2014. "Perspectives on Inequality and Opportunity from the Survey of Consumer Finances." Remarks by the Chair, Board of Governors of the Federal Reserve System, at the Conference on Economic Opportunity and Inequality, Federal Reserve Bank of Boston. Accessible at federalreserve.gov.

Yemma, John. "Teaching the freedom to believe." 2013. *Christian Science Monitor* (June 17): 5.

Yinger, J. Milton. 1970. *The Scientific Study of Religion*. New York: Macmillan.

York, Richard, Eugene A. Rosa, and Thomas Dietz. 2010. "Ecological Modernization Theory: Theoretical and Empirical Challenges." Pp. 77–90 in *The International Handbook and Environmental Sociology*, 2nd ed., edited by Michael R. Redclift and Graham Woodgate. Cheltenham, UK: Edward Elgar.

Young, Kevin, ed. 2004. *Sporting Bodies, Damaged Selves*. New York: Elsevier.

Yuhas, Alan. 2015. "Colony, State or Independence: Puerto Rico's Status Anxiety Adds to Debt Crisis." July 7. Accessible at www.theguardian.com.

Yunus, Muhammad. 2010. *Building Social Business*. New York: Perseus.

Z

Zarembo, Alan. 2004a. "A Theater of Inquiry and Evil." *Los Angeles Times,* July 15, pp. A1, A24, A25.

Zellner, William M. 1995. *Counter Cultures: A Sociological Analysis*. New York: St. Martin's Press.

Zernike, Kate. 2002. "With Student Cheating on the Rise, More Colleges Are Turning to Honor Codes." *New York Times,* November 2, p. A10.

Zerouala, Faiza. 2014. "Headscarf Ban Turns France's Muslim Women towards Homeworking." October 3. Accessible at www.theguardian.com.

Zhang, Xiaodan. 2009. "Trade Unions under the Modernization of Paternalists Rule in China." *Journal of Labor and Society* 12 (June): 193–218.

Zi, Jui-Chung Allen. 2007. *The Kids Are OK: Divorce and Children's Behavior Problems*. Santa Monica, CA: RAND.

Zimbardo, Philip G. 1972. "Pathology of Imprisonment." *Society* 9 (April):4, 6, 8.

———. 2004. "Power Turns Good Soldiers into 'Bad Apples.'"*Boston Globe,* May 9. Also accessible at www.prisonexp.org.

———. 2007a. "Revisiting the Stanford Prison Experiment: A Lesson in the Power of the Situation." *Chronicle of Higher Education* 53 (March 20):B6, B7.

———. 2015. "Philip Zimbardo Thinks We All Can Be Evil." Interview by Jon Ronson. *New York Times Magazine* (July 19), 58.

———, Robert L. Johnson, and Vivian McCann Hamilton. 2009. *Psychology: Core Concepts*. 6th ed. Upper Saddle River, NJ: Pearson.

Zimmerman, Seth. 2008a. "Globalization and Economic Mobility." Washington, DC: Economic Mobility Project. Also accessible at www.economicmobility.org/reports_and_research/literature_reviews?id=0004.

———. 2008b. *Labor Market Institutions and Economic Mobility*. Washington, DC: Pew Charitable Trusts.

Zirin, Dave. 2008. "Calling Sports Sociology off the Bench." *Contexts* (Summer):28–31.

Zogby. 2010. "Zogby Interactive: 54% Support Ethnic & Religious Profiling; 71% Favor Full-Body Scans." February 4. Accessed July 2, 2011 (http://www.zogby.com/news/2010/02/04/zogby-interactive-54-support-ethnic-religious-profiling-71-favor-full-body-scans/).

Zola, Irving K. 1972. "Medicine as an Institution of Social Control." *Sociological Review* 20 (November):487–504.

———. 1983. *Socio-Medical Inquiries*. Philadelphia: Temple University Press.

Zong, Jie, and Jeanne Batalova. 2015. "Korean Immigrants in the United States." December 3. Accessible at www.migrationpolicy.org.

Zorthian, Julia. 2015. "Facebook Expanding Worldwide Parental Leave to Four Months." *Time,* November 29. Accessible at www.time.com.

Zweigenhaft, Richard L., and G. William Domhoff. 2006. *Diversity in the Power Elite: How It Happened, Why It Matters*. 2nd ed. New York: Rowman and Littlefield.

———. 2006. "Japan's Vulnerable Elderly." *Washington Post National Weekly Edition* 23 (February 27): 18.

———. 2010b. "The Old World." *New York Times Magazine* (October 17): 48–53.

name index

subject index

Apple, Inc., 215*f*, 388–389
applied sociology, 19–20, 23
Arab Americans
  homeschooling by, 342
  negative stereotyping of, 157
  racial and ethnic inequality and,
    248–249, *249*
  racial profiling of, 165, 239, 249
  religious affiliations of, 249, 249*f*
Arabic language, 248, 455*f*
Arab Spring (2011), 380, 433, 446
Argentina, *92*, 211*f*
argot, 70
Arkansas, 295
Armenia, 211*f*
arranged marriages, 311, 312
"artificial mothers," 79
Arunta people (Australia), 9
ASA. *See* American Sociological
  Association
ascending fellowship, 308
ascribed status(es), 100, 100*f*, 106
  achieved status compared, 100*f*,
    100–101, *101*, 106
  in formal organizations, 116
  in preindustrial societies, 110
  race and ethnicity as, 101, 228
  in stratification systems, 182–185,
    200, 204
Ashe, Arthur, 101
Asia. *See also specific Asian countries*
  asylees from, 254
  attitudes toward divorce in, 319
  immigration from, 253, 253*f*
  impact of globalization in, 213
  Internet domination by, 455, 455*f*
  South Asia tsunami (2004), 21–22, 89
Asian Americans
  Asian Indians, 245*f*, 247
  Chinese Americans, 238, 245*f*,
    246–247, 376
  demographics, 229, 229*t*, 230*f*,
    245, 245*f*
  earnings of, 233, 233*f*
  Filipino Americans, 247–248
  interracial marriage among, 311
  Japanese Americans, 238, 245*f*, 248
  Korean Americans, 248, 351
  lifetime earnings of, 332*f*
  as "model minority," 245–246,
    246, 256
  oppression of women, 267
  racial inequality and, 230*f*, 245*f*,
    245–248
  strong social networks of, 286
  Vietnamese Americans, 233, 248
Asian Indians, 245*f*, 247
assembling perspective, 434, *434*, 440
assimilation, 241*f*, 241–242, 460
asylees, 254, 256, 342
Atlanta Sociological Laboratory, 11, 19
attention-deficit/hyperactivity disorder
  (ADHD), 342
audience, 142–143
Australia, 48*f*, 121*f*, 211*f*, 313*f*, 330*f*
  Aboriginal people of, 245, *245*
  Arunta people of, 9
  economy of, 382*f*

family leave law (2010), 322
foreign aid per capita, 214*f*
poverty rate in, 196*f*
voter turnout, 376*f*
Austria, 121*f*, 211*f*, 215*f*
authority, 368–369, 375. *See also* power
  charismatic, 369, *369*, 375
  hierarchy of. *See* hierarchy of
    authority
  institutionalized, 405
  obedience to, 154–155, 166, 333
  patterns of, in families, 306–307
  rational-legal, 369
  social movements and, 443
  traditional, 369
  Weber's classification of,
    368–369, *369*
authority figures, 154
automation, job loss and, 456, 456*f*
Avatar (film), *441*
Azerbaijan, 211*f*

b

baby boom, 416
baby boomers, 297
"Baby Mama" (song), 317
Baghdad, Iraq, looting in, 435
Bahrain, 133
Baltimore (Md.) Police Department,
  152–153
Bangladesh, 57*f*, 208–209, 211*f*, 215*f*
  economic optimism in, *220*
  microfinancing in, 389–391, *390*
  natural disaster in, 421
  paid family leave in, 322*f*, 323*f*
  television in, 144
basic (pure) sociology, 20, 23
beauty myth, 159, *160*, 273
behavioral continuum, 411
Belarus, 211*f*
Belgium, 211*f*, 300
belief, religious, 356–357, 358, 358*t*
"believer's church," 359
Bell v. Maryland (1964), 251
Beloved Wives Day, 99
benevolence, 64
Benin, 211*f*
bereavement practices, 294
"bereavement symptoms," 410
Betsileo people (Madagascar), 305
Bhutan, 57*f*, 211*f*
BIA (Bureau of Indian Affairs), 244
bias, 231, 233
bias crimes, 170, 170*f*
Big Brother (TV series), 135
big data, 145–146
Big Toe Crew, *67*
bilateral descent, 306, 310
bilingualism, 71–73, 331, 377
Bill and Melinda Gates Foundation,
  343–344
binge drinking, 156, *156*
bin Laden, Osama, 117
biology, 56–57, 447
biotechnology, 451, 457–458, *458*, 461
bioterrorism, tracking, 402

bipolar disorder, *410*
birthrates, 413–414
bisexuality, 270
Blackish (TV series), 135
#BlackLivesMatter, 434, 441
Black Lives Matter movement, 239,
  241, 374
Black power ideology, 243
Blacks. *See* African Americans
"blaming the victim," 164, 198, 232
blended families, 318
blogging, 137–138
Bluefish, 198
B'nai B'rith, 252
body image, 159, 160, *160*, 262
"Body Ritual among the Nacirema"
  (Miner), 54
Boko Haram, 374
Bolivia, 211*f*
"boomerang kids," 305
born again Christians, 358
"Born This Way" (song), *270*
Bororo people (Brazil), 68
Bosnia-Herzegovina, 211*f*, 413
Botswana, 102, 211*f*
boundary maintenance, 161
Bourdieu, Pierre, 12
bourgeoisie, 187
BP (British Petroleum), 134, 215*f*
brain drain, 399
"brand casting," *130*, 130–131
brand loyalty, 144
brass ceiling, 264
Brazil, 48*f*, 211*f*, 218*f*, 313*f*, 376*f*
  cultural survival in, 68
  economy of, 382*f*, 419
  environment in, 419
  growth of middle class in, 219
  native people of, 68, 305
  paid family leave in, 322*f*, 323*f*
  Portuguese spoken in, 251
  skin color gradients in, 229
  social inequality in, *450*
  tanning beds banned in, 450
  television in, *144*, 144–145
Breaking Bad (TV series), 135
British Airways, 384
British Empire, 210, 212
British Petroleum (BP), 134, 215*f*
Brown v. Board of Education
  (2014), 333
Buddhism, 355*t*, 356, 356*f*, 359
Bulgaria, 211*f*, 289*f*, 413*f*
bureaucracies, 117–120, 118*t*, 123
  bureaucratization process, 119–120
  division of labor in, 117, 118*t*, 119
  formal organizations and, 116
  hierarchy of authority in, 117–118,
    118*t*, 119, *120*, 121
  impersonality of, 118, 118*t*, 119,
    337–338, 406
  McDonaldization. *See*
    McDonaldization
  oligarchies, 120, 122
  organizational culture and, 120–121
  qualifications for employment in, 118,
    118*t*, 119, 338
  small-group bureaucracies, 119–120

social control by, 153
  written rules and regulations in, 118,
    118*t*, 119
bureaucracy's other face, 120
bureaucratization
  process of, 119–120
  of schools, 333, 337–338, *338*, 345
Bureau of Indian Affairs (BIA), 244
Bureau of Justice Statistics, 171
Bureau of Labor Statistics, 36
Bureau of the Census, 24, 33–34, 195,
  249, 249*f*, 274–275
Burger King, 138–139
Burj Khalifa, 453
Burkina Faso, 57*f*, 211*f*
Burundi, 211*f*, 383–384, *384*

C

California Civil Rights Initiative
  (Proposition 209) of 1996, 387
call center subcultures, *69*, 70
Cambodia, 211*f*, 376*f*
Cameroon, 211*f*
Canada, 48*f*, 211*f*, 313*f*, 330*f*, 399*f*
  economy of, 382*f*
  First Nations, education of, 235
  foreign aid per capita, 214*f*
  global brands of, 132*f*
  government health expenditures, 222
  labor unions in, 121*f*
  physician-assisted suicide in, 300
  population growth rate in, 413*f*
  poverty rate in, 196*f*
  religious participation in, 357*f*
  women in combat, 264
  women in workforce, 274*f*
capitalism, 382–384, 385, 385*t*
  as cause of environmental
    problems, 420
  conflict perspective on, 352, 403
  educational inequalities in, 334
  laissez-faire, 383
  Marxist view of, 187, *187*, 189–190,
    352, 379, 403, 418
  Protestant ethic and, 352, *352*
  in Rwanda, 383–384, *384*
  "spirit of," 353
  Weber on, 10*f*, 352, *353*
career criminals, 168
careers in sociology, 23–25, 24*f*
  academic careers, 24, 339, *339*
  entrepreneurship, 114, *114*
  in military, *372, 372*
  in post-secondary education, 235, *235*
  program administration, 91, *91*
  requirements for, 23–25
  research, 42, *42*
  social media consulting, 137
  with U.S. Secret Service, 173
Carnegie Mellon University
  (CMU), *39*
castes *(varnas)*, 183–184, 191
categories, groups distinguished
  from, 113
cattle (zebu), 13–14, 56
causal logic, 30*f*, 31, 33*f*

interactionist perspective on, 336
labeling of Latino children in, 250
recession and, 4
rise in formal education, 432
social policy: charter schools, 342, 343f, 343–345, *344*
social policy: religion in schools, *362,* 362–363
sociological perspectives on, 330f, 330–337, 336t
status bestowed by, 334
Title IX (Education Act of 1972), 335
U.S. school system, 329
use of Internet and, 141f, 338
of women, 337
Education Act of 1972, 305, 335
efficiency studies, 120
Egalia preschool, 269
egalitarian family, 307, 309, 310
egocasting, 139
Egypt, 59–60, 133, 211f, 422
eHarmony (Web site), 312
Eighth Amendment (1791), 158
EITC (Earned Income Tax Credit), 191
elderly persons, 290, 295. *See also* aging; retirement
age as ascribed status, 100
age as master status, 285, 288
collective consciousness of, 298, *298*
declining poverty among, 297
health care system and, 404–405
health of, 286, *286,* 296
impact of Medicare on, 408
LGBT, organizations for, 298
negative stereotypes of, 285
social involvement of, 286–287
volunteer work by, 287
wealth of, 295–296
women, 295, 296
in workforce, 287, *287,* 292, 296–298, 297f
elderspeak, 287, *287,* 296
electrocutions, *175*
electronic church, 361, 363
Electronic Communications Privacy Act of 1986, 146, 457
Electronic Media (Gross), 128
Elementary and Secondary Education Act (ESEA) of 1965, 72–73
Elementary Forms of Religious Life (Durkheim), 10f
elite model of power relations, 378, 381
"Elmtown" study, 340
El Salvador, 172, 211f
Emergency Management Center, 436
emergent norm perspective
on collective behavior, 432–433, *433,* 434, 440
on panics, 438
on urban rioting, 435
emigrants, 413
Emirates Golf Club (Dubai), *453*
Empire (TV series), 135
employment
degree requirements for, 333
effects of technology on, 456, 456f
employer opposition to unions, 122

globalization and, *212*
labor unions: social policy, 121f, 121–123
men in "female" occupations, 263, *263,* 275
at minimum wage, 190, 195, 196f
occupational prestige, 192–193, 193t, 339
occupational segregation, 273–274
part-time or temporary, 122, 186, *186,* 388
qualifications for, in bureaucracies, 118, 118t, 119, 338
racial discrimination in hiring, 232–233, 233f
resocialization and, 91
restrictive leave practices, 235
during retirement, 287, *287,* 292, 296–298, 297f
rewards for dangerous work, 189, *189*
self-employment, 202
status and, 102
of women. *See* women in U.S. workforce
for young job seekers, 304
Endangered Species Act, 424
end-of-life care, 293
endogamy, 311, 318
Engels, Friedrich, 9–10, 21, 117
England. *See* Great Britain
Engle v. Vitale (1962), 362
English language, 235, 455, 455f
environment (environmental issues), 427
air pollution, *395,* 422
climate change, *420,* 422–424, 423f
conflict perspective on, 419–420, 424, 427
destruction of, in Congo, 383–384, *384*
ecological modernization approach, 420, *420*
ecotourism, *420*
effects of consumption on, 453
environmental justice, 420–421, *421,* 427
hazards in, 396, 422
human ecology view of, 414t, 419, 427, 447
natural disasters, 436
population and, 424
social policy: environmentalism, 424–426, 425f, 427
sociological perspectives on, 419–427, *420*
water pollution, 422, *422*
world systems analysis view of, 419, 424
environmentalism (environmental movement)
as new social movement, 443
social policy on, 424–426, 425f, 427
environmental justice, 420–421, *421,* 427
Environmental Protection Agency (EPA), 396, 424
environmental refugees, 421
environmental sociology, 20

EPA (Environmental Protection Agency), 396, 424
equilibrium model of social change, 447, 449
Eritrea, 57f, 140, 211f
ESEA (Elementary and Secondary Education Act) of 1965, 72–73
Essays on the Principle of Population (Malthus), 412
established sect, 359
estate system (feudalism), 184, 191
esteem, 192
Estonia, 211f
ethics
of biotechnology, 458
confidentiality, 41
conflict of interest, 41–43, *42*
Protestant ethic, 10f, 352, *353,* 354
of sociological research, 41–43
value neutrality, 43
Ethiopia, 57f, 210, 211f
ethnic groups, 228, 229t, 230f, 237
expulsion or secession of, 240, *240*
racial groups distinguished from, 230–231
segregation of, 240–241, 241f
social networks and, 104, 286
spectrum of intergroup relations, 240–242, 241f
in U.S. workforce, 386–389
ethnicity. *See also* racial and ethnic inequality
aging and, 295, 295f, 296
as ascribed status, 101, 228
college subcultures, 341, 342f
differences in families, 314f, *314,* 314–315
health and, 408
income and, 233f
interethnic marriage, 252, 311
in matrix of domination, 267, 267f, 268t
role in social mobility, 202
shown on television, *247*
social epidemiology and, 403–404
symbolic ethnicity, 252
urban ethnic neighborhoods, 242, 246–247
White ethnics, 252, *252*
women oppressed by, 267
ethnic succession, 169
ethnocentrism, 56, 58, 216, 232
ethnography, 37–39, 40, 40t
Europe, 289, 455, 455f. *See also specific countries*
European Union, 240, 417
euthanasia, 299f, 299–300
"evacuation camps," 248
evolution, teaching of, 362
evolutionary theory, 56–57, 447, 450t, 452, 453
"exception culturelle", 135
executive compensation, 202–203, *203*
executive summary of report, 30
exogamy, 311, 318
Expedia, 202
experience, religious, 358, 358t, *358*
experiment(s), 39, *39,* 40, 40t

experimental groups, 39
exploitation
economic, in colonialism, 209, 212
history of, 449
of women in developing nations, 219
of women in workforce, 272
of working class, 22, 187, *187,* 218
exploitation theory, 238, 242
expressiveness, 266
expulsion of ethnic groups, 240, *240*
extended families, *285,* 306, 310, 314
ExxonMobil, 213f
Exxon *Valdez* oil spill, 41–43, *42,* 422

f

Facebook, 138–139, 142, 143, 270, 324, *324*
"Facebook envy," 188
face-to-face interaction, 108, *108, 400*
between physician and patient, 400
face-work, 83, 85t
fads, 437–438, 440, 440t
fair trade coffee, 22
false consciousness, 187, 277, 442
familismo (familism), 314
family(ies), 303–325. *See also* child-rearing patterns
as agent of socialization, 87–89, *89*
alternative. *See* nontraditional families
in Asian Indian culture, 247
authority patterns in, 306–307
conflict perspective on, 306–307, 309, 310t
distribution of family wealth, 194f, 194–195
diverse lifestyles, 321–322
divorce and, 313, 319f, 319–320
egalitarian family, 307, 309, 310
extended families, *285,* 306, 310, 314
female-headed households, 314, 314f
feminist perspective on, 309–310
functionalist perspective on, 307–309, 310, 310t
global view of, 305–310
interactionist perspective on, 307, 309, *309,* 310t
kinship patterns in, 306
lesbian and gay relationships, 320, *320*
loyalty to *(sa pamilya),* 247
major trends in, 304–305
male domination of, 267, 307, 309
marriage and. *See* marriage
racial and ethnic differences in, 314f, *314,* 314–315
single-parent families, 314f, 317–318, 321
size of, culture and, 414–415
social class differences in, 313
social policy: family leave, 322f–324f, 322–325
sociological perspectives on, 307–309
stepfamilies, 309, 318
variations in composition of, 305f, 305–306
variations in family life, 313–315

high schools, 336
  shootings, 114, 133–134
  stigmatization in, 336
  subcultures, 340–341
hijab, 273, *273*
Hill-Burton Act of 1946, 407
Hinduism, 353, 355*t*, 356, 356*f*
  caste system under, 184
  cow as sacred in, 13–14, 56
hiring, racial discrimination in,
  232–233, 233*f*
"Hispandering", 377
Hispanics. *See* Latinos/Hispanics
history, 4, 441, 449
HIV/AIDS, 47, 101, 402, 403*f*
holistic medicine, 407, 408
Holocaust, 155, 240, 351
Homeland (TV series), 135
homeschooling, 342, 343, 345
homicide, 172, 219
homogamy, 312, 318
homophobia, 262
homosexuality
  labeled as mental disorder, 270,
    400, 410
  lesbian and gay relationships, 320, *320*
  LGBT persons. *See* lesbian, gay,
    bisexual, and transgender persons
  prejudice against, 262
  queer theory on, 135
Honduras, 172, 211*f*
honeymoon phase of retirement, 291
Hong Kong, *92,* 211*f*
Hopi tribe, 293
horizontal (flat) hierarchy of authority,
  120, *120*
horizontal social mobility, 200
horticultural societies, 110
hospice care, 293
housework, 268, 272–273, 275
housing issues, 44–45, 45*f,* 233,
  234, 241
Hudson City Savings Bank, 234
Hull House, 11
human behavior
  conforming v. deviant, 159
  crowds. *See* collective behavior;
    crowds
  discriminatory, 232–233, 233*f*
  early explanations for, 161
  inequality as determinant of, 209–210
  influence of culture on, 55
  learning of, 162–163
  mass media and, 142
  mental illness and. *See* mental illness
  norms of, 61–63
  political. *See* politics (political
    behavior)
  sexual. *See* human sexuality
  small-group behavior, 120
  social behavior, 106, 400
  stigmatization of, 160
human ecology, 414*t,* 419, 427, 447
human relations approach, 120
human rights movement, 443–444
human sexuality
  bisexuality, 270
  celibacy, 105

definitions of deviance, *270,* 270–271
gender and, 269–270
heterosexuality, 61
homosexuality. *See* homosexuality
labeling and, 269–271
in Oneida Community, 308
premarital cohabitation, 63
regulation of, as function of
  family, 308
role of mass media in, 130
romantic relationships, 104
sex education, *332*
sexual expression on Internet, 139
sexual norms, 308
sociological research on, 37, 37*t,* 47*f,*
  47–48, 48*f*
human trafficking, 44, *44,* 183, 183*t*
Human Trafficking Report, 183*t*
Hungary, 211*f,* 215*f,* 218*f,* 330*f*
hunting-and-gathering societies, *109,*
  109–110, 190
Hurricane Katrina (2005), 21, 135, 198,
  344, 421
  disaster response following,
    436–437, *437*
  study of, 5–6
Hutterites, 359
hyperconsumerism, 111, 130
hyper-local media, 135–136
hypertension, 403
hypotheses
  contact hypothesis, 239–240, 242
  formulating, 30*f,* 31–33, 35
  Sapir-Whorf hypothesis, 59
  support for, 34, 34*f*

i

Iceland, 63*f,* 321, 372
Ice Road Truckers (TV series), *189*
ID (intelligent design), 362, *362*
ideal minorities, 245–246, *246,* 256
ideal types, 9, 117, 118, 360, 360*t*
identity theft, 169, *169*
Ikebukuro Honcho, 290
illegal abortions, 279
illegal immigration, 253, 461
IMDb (Internet Movie Database), 131*t*
immigrant(s), 413
  children, socialization through
    education, 331
  early Chinese immigrants, 246–247
  effect of globalization on, 459–460
  illegal, 253, 461
  importance of religion to, 351
  in organized crime, 169
  refugees contrasted with, 254
  workers, 21, 453, 460
immigration. *See also* migration
  from Asia, 253, 253*f*
  assimilation and, 460
  conflict perspective on, 242, 253
  controversy over, 254–255, 256
  functionalist perspective on, 253
  illegal, 253, 461
  from Latin America, 229, 253, 253*f*
  Muslims, ban on, 239

population growth and, 416–417
restrictions on, 459
social mobility and, 202
U.S. policies on, 253, 253*f*
Immigration Act of 1965, 247
Immigration and Naturalization Service,
  247, 342
Immigration Reform and Control Act of
  1986, 253
impersonality, bureaucratic, 118, 118*t,*
  119, 337–338, 406
impression management, 83, 84, 85*t,*
  87, 312
incest taboo, 311–312
inclusion, 449
income, 181, 218*f*
  aging and, 295–296
  distribution of, 186, *186,* 195,
    218, 218*f*
  dual-income families, 310, 317, *317*
  effects of education on, 31, 32*f*–34*f,*
    331, 332*f*
  gross national income, 211*f,* 213,
    214*f,* 215*f*
  lifetime earnings, 332*f*
  mean household income, 194, 194*f*
  national, per capita, 211*f*
  by race, ethnicity, and gender, 233*f*
  stratification by, 193–195, 194*f*
  use of Internet and, 139, 141*f*
  of women, increase in, 202
income inequality, 193–195, 223
  causes of, 180–181
  mean household income, 194, 194*f*
  racial discrimination in hiring and,
    232–233, 233*f*
independent variable, 31
index crimes, 171, 171*t*
India, 57*f,* 144*f,* 211*f,* 242, 313*f*
  acceptance of parental leave, 324*f*
  call center subcultures in, *69,* 70
  CO_2 emissions in, 423*f*
  Dongria Kondh people, *441*
  economy of, 382*f*
  female infanticide in, 219
  growth of middle class in, 219
  human sexual behavior in, 48*f*
  infant mortality rates, 399*f*
  microfinancing in, 389
  partitioning of (1947), 240
  population growth in, 413*f,* 416*f*
  premarital cohabitation in, 63*f*
  religious violence in, 351
  social mobility in, 219
  television in, 144
  voter turnout, 376*f*
  women in government, 378*f*
  women's social movements in,
    443, 444
Indian Gambling Regulatory Act of
  1988, 244
Indonesia, 211*f,* 322*f,* 323*f,* 460
industrialized nations
  child care in, 94
  consumption in, 420
  deindustrialization, 386, *388,* 391
  demographic transition in, 414
  internal migration in, 418

occupational segregation in, 273–274
organized labor in, 216
secularization in, 357
social mobility in, 218–219
Industrial Revolution, 110, 121, 382, 385
industrial societies, 9, 110, 110*t,*
  382, 385
industry(ies)
  deindustrialization, 386, *388,* 391
  in developing nations, 437, *438*
  "global office," 214–215, 388
  government-owned, 384
  resistance to regulation of, 450
  service industries, 214–215, 386–388
inequality
  in access to Internet, 454
  as determinant of human behavior,
    209–210
  educational, 334
  gender inequality. *See* gender
    inequality
  in income. *See* income inequality
  by race or ethnicity. *See* racial and
    ethnic inequality
  in social institutions. *See* social
    inequality
  worldwide. *See* global inequality
infanticide, female, 219
infant mortality rates, 399, 399*f,*
  403, 413
influence, 368, 375
informal economy, 384–385, 385*t,* 389
informal groups, 120
informal norms, 61, 62*t,* 65
informal social control, 155–156
in-groups, 114, 116
innovation, 66, 69, 162, 162*t,* 163
innovators, 12
inpatient treatment of mental illness,
  410, 410–411
Instagram, 143
institutional discrimination, 105–106,
  237, *237*
  preferential admissions as, 235, 237
  racial, 234–235
  slavery and, 243
  voting rights, 236, *236*
  against women, 271–272, 280
in-store health clinics, 406, *406*
instrumentality, 266
intelligent design (ID), 362, *362*
interactionist perspective, 16, 17*t,* 18–19
  on adoption, 315
  on aging, *286,* 286–287, 288*t*
  on charismatic authority, 369
  on child care, 93
  on collective behavior, 434
  on culture, 55, 65*t*
  on deviance, 162–164, 166, 166*t,* 167
  on digital surveillance, 146
  on education, 336, 336*t*
  on family, 307, 309, *309*
  on family leave, 323
  on gender stratification, 268
  on health, 399–400, *400,* 401*t*
  on international migration, 460
  on mass media, 138–139, 139*f,*
    139*t,* 142

to define sick role, 400
distributive, 367
as element of stratification, 188, 190, 191
male domination, 442
in male-female relations, 266
of mass media, 133
pluralist model of, 380, *380,* 381
in political systems, 368
power elite models, 378–379, *379f,* 381
structural, 367
unequal distribution of, 367, 368
The Power Elite (Mills), 378
power elite models, 378–379, 381
Domhoff's model, *379f,* 379–380
Mills's model, 378–379, *379f*
power structure of U.S., 378–381
pluralist model, 380, *380*
power elite models, 378–380
precarious work, 388
precipitating factor, 433–434
predatory lending, 389, 391
preferential admissions practices, 235
preindustrial societies, *109,* 109–110, 110*t,* 382
prejudice, *231,* 231–232, 237
economically motivated, 238
homophobia, 262
racial discrimination and, 231–237
rooted in stereotypes, 232
preoperational stage of development, 84
preparatory stage of self, 82, *83t*
preretirement, 291
presentation of self, 83–84
preservation of order, 105
prestige, occupational, 192–193, 193*t,* 339
primary groups, 113, 113*t,* 116
primate studies, 79
PRISM operation of NSA, 145, 147
prisons
Abu Ghraib, 155, 372
debtors' jails, 158
inmate gangs in, 11
mental patients confined in, 411
mock prison experiment, 98, 164, 372
solitary confinement in, 157
privacy
data collection and, 46
of medical records, 400
new technologies and, 456–457, *457*
privacy rights, *145,* 145–147, *147*
private schools, *336,* 337
product placement, *130,* 130–131
profane realm, 350
professional criminals, *168*
profiteering in microfinancing, 389
Project Head Start, 331
proletariat, 10, 187, *187*
pro-life activists, 277–278
property crimes, 172
Proposition 209 (California Civil Rights Initiative) of 1996, 387
prostitution, 167
protective function of family, 307

Protestant ethic, 10*f,* 352, *352, 354*
The Protestant Ethic and the Spirit of Capitalism (Weber), 10*f,* 352, *353*
protests. *See also* activism
antiwar protesters, *434*
for environmental justice, 420, 421
against institutional discrimination, 235
resource mobilization in, *443*
role of audiences, 143
social media and, 432
by social movements, 441
psychoanalysis, 85*t*
psychological approaches to self, 84–85, 85*t*
psychology, 4
public opinion, 381, 439, 440*t*
economic optimism, 220, *220*
on environmental issues, 425
on physician-assisted suicide, 299
publics, 439, 440*t*
Pueblo tribes, 293
Puerto Ricans, 249, 249*f,* 250, *250*
Puerto Rico, 211*f,* 250
pure (basic) sociology, 20
Puritans, 161
purpose, sense of, 105
Pygmalion in the Classroom (Rosenthal & Jacobson), 336

q

Quakers, 238
qualitative research, 37
quantitative research, 37
quasi-religions, 361, *361*
Québec, 72
queer theory, 15–16, 17*t,* 19, 320
on homosexuality, 135
research methodology, 44
on self-injury, 29
on sports, 18
questionnaires, 35, 37, 40, 44
quinceañera, 85
quotas, 274, 378
Qur'an (Koran), 248, *378*

r

race, 21–22. *See also specific races*
aging and, 295, 296
as ascribed status, 101, 228
college subcultures, 310, 342*f*
contact hypothesis of race relations, 239–240, 242
cultural assumptions regarding, 88
differences in families, 314*f, 314,* 314–315
health and, 408
income and, 233*f*
interracial marriage, 62, 241, 311, *311*
in matrix of domination, 267, 267*f,* 268*t*
Milgram experiment and, 154
in modern education, 332–333

multiple identities, 229–230
multiracial people, 227, 229–230, 251
online dating and, 312
racial groups, 228–231, 237
role in political behavior, 376–377, 378*f,* 378
role in social mobility, 201–202
social construction of, 228–229, 230*f*
social epidemiology and, 403–404
transracial adoption, 316, *316*
use of Internet and, 139, 141*f*
women oppressed by, 267
race neutrality, 232
racial and ethnic inequality, 226–256. *See also* ethnicity; race; *specific ethnicities*
Arab Americans and, 248–249, *249*
conflict perspective on, 238
ethnicity, 230–231
functionalist perspective on, 238
immigration and, 253, 253*f*
interactionist perspective on, 239–240
labeling perspective on, 238–239, *239*
Latinos/Hispanics and, 249*f,* 249–251
minority groups, 228, 229*t*
Native Americans and, 230*f,* 243*f,* 244, *244,* 245
prejudice and discrimination, 231–237
social policy: global refugee crisis, 254*t,* 254–255, *255*
sociological perspectives on, 238–242, 240*t*
spectrum of intergroup relations. *See* intergroup relations
in United States, 230*f,* 243*f,* 243–256
racial discrimination, 256
in death penalty, 174–175
in hiring, 232–233, 233*f*
institutional, 234–235
prejudice and, 231–237
racial formation, 229
racial groups, 228–231, 237
racial profiling, 242
of African Americans, 238–239, *239*
of Muslims, 165, 239, 249
racism, 232
color-blind, 232, 237, 387
functions of prejudiced beliefs, 238
in health care, 403–404
social institutions and, 105
random sample, 33
rape, 166, 171
rational-legal authority, 369, 375
Reagan, Ronald, 122
rebellion, 162, 162*t*
recreational function of family, 309
Red Crescent, 373
Red Cross, 373, 421, 436
redlining, 234
reference groups, 114–115, *115,* 116
fashions and, 437–438
in relative deprivation, 442
"Reflecting Absence" (Arad), 60, *60*
refugees, 254*t,* 254–255, *255,* 256

relationship(s)
in families, analysis of, 309, *309*
as function of family, 307–308
lesbian and gay relationships, 320, *320*
love relationship, 312
romantic, among teens, 104
relationship marketing, 138–139, 139*f*
relative deprivation approach, 442, 445*t,* 446
relative poverty, 196
reliability, ensuring, 33–34, 35
religion, 348–363, *354. See also specific religions and churches*
as agent of socialization, 91, 94
Arab American affiliations, 249, 249*f*
components of, 356–358, 358*t*
conflict perspective on, 350, 353, 354*t*
denominations, 359, 360*t*
Durkheim's approach to, 350, 351, *351,* 354, 354*t,* 362
ecclesiae, 359, 360*t*
electronic church, 361, 363
feminist perspective on, 353–354, *354*
functionalist perspective on, 351, *352,* 354*t*
fundamentalism, 357, 362, 363
impact of Internet on, 361
levels of adherence to, 355, 355*t*
liberation theology, 352
Marxist perspective on, 353, 354
new religious movements, 360, 360*t,* 363
organizational view of, 360*t,* 360–361
Protestant ethic, 10*f,* 352, *352, 354*
quasi-religions, 361, *361*
religion-based clothing, 261, 273, *273*
religious conversion, 355
religious toys, 349, *349, 351*
sects, 359, 360*t*
social change and, 352, 353, *353*
social policy: religion in schools, *362,* 362–363
social support function of, 351–352, *352*
sociological perspectives on, 350–354
value to society, 10–11
world religions, 355*t,* 355–358, 356*f*
religious activism, 352
religious beliefs, 356–357, 358, 358*t*
religious experience, 358, 358*t*
religious norms, 357
religious organization, 359–363
basic forms of, 359–361, 360*t*
comparison of forms, 360–361
denominations, 359
ecclesiae, 359
sects, 359
religious rituals, 357–358, 358*t*
religious toys, 349, *349, 351*
remittances, 247, 253
reorientation phase of retirement, 291
reparations, 243, 248
replacement of personnel, 105
report writing, 50
representative democracy, 370
reproductive function of family, 307
Republican Party, 377

research designs, 35–40, 40t
  ethnography, 37–39
  experiments, 39, 39
  secondary analysis, 39, 39t, 40t
  surveys. See surveys
  visual sociology, 38, 38, 137
researchers, rights of, 41
reshoring, 389
resistance to social change, 450–451,
    451, 461
resistance to technology, 451, 451
resocialization, 91, 318
resource allocation, 105, 190, 212, 412
resource management, 208–209
resource mobilization, 442, 443,
    445t, 446
"retired-husband syndrome," 290
retirement
  adjusting to, 291–292, 294
  anticipatory socialization for, 292
  employment during, 287, 287, 292,
    296–298, 297f
  NORCs, 292
  phases of, 291–292, 292
retirement homes for LGBT
    persons, 298
retreatism, 162, 162t
"reverse discrimination," 387
review of literature, 30f, 31, 35, 50
Rhode Island, 295
right to die, social policy on, 299f,
    299–300
rioting, 241, 435
rites of passage, 85, 85–86, 87
ritual
  Native American death rituals, 293
  religious, 357–358, 358t
ritualism, in deviance, 162, 162t
robotics, 454, 456f
Roe v. Wade (1973), 277, 278
role conflict, 101–102, 103
role exit, 102–103, 103
role expectations, 101
role strain, 102
role taking, 82, 83t
role transitions
  death and dying, 292–294, 294
  retirement, adjusting to, 291–292
  sandwich generation, 290–291, 291
  through life course, 290–294
Rolling Stone magazine, 131t
Roma (Gypsies), 240, 240
Roman Catholic Church, 247, 351, 359
  disapproval of birth control, 451
  indifference to Cuban Americans, 251
  liberation theology and, 352
  Native American converts, 293, 293
  resistance to birth control, 450–451
  women and, 267, 354
Romania, 79, 79, 211f
romantic relationships, 104
Roommates.com, 233
Royal Dutch Shell, 215f
ruling class, 380
rumors, 438–439, 439, 440, 440t
rum springa, 88
rural life, 109
Russia, 211f, 218f, 313f, 382f, 423f

acceptance of parental leave, 324f
growth of middle class in, 219
media penetration in, 144f
population growth rate in, 413f
premarital cohabitation in, 63f
religious participation in, 357f
Russian language, 455f
Rwanda, Republic of
  capitalism and, 383–384, 384
  women in government, 377–378, 378f

S

sacred realm, 350
SAGE (Services and Advocacy for
    GLBT Elders), 298
same-sex marriage, 305, 306, 320,
    320, 325
Sami people (Norway), 58
sample selection, 33, 35
Samsung, 215f
sanctions, 61, 62t, 65, 153, 222
"sandwich generation," 284, 290–291,
    291, 294
sa pamilya, 247
Sapir-Whorf hypothesis, 59
Saudi Arabia, 59, 211f, 219, 357, 358
Scarce, Rik, 41
"scheduled castes," 184
school(s), 219. See also education
  as agent of socialization, 89, 94
  "apartheid schools," 333
  bureaucratization of, 333, 337–338,
    338, 345
  charter schools, social policy on, 342,
    343f, 343–344, 344, 345
  conflict perspective on, 89, 343
  "cram schools," 63
  as formal organizations, 337–345
  homeschooling, 342, 343, 345
  religion in, social policy on, 362,
    362–363
  roles of teachers in, 338–339,
    339, 341f
  sex education in, 332
  shootings in, 114, 133–134, 160, 409
  social control in, 331
  student subcultures in, 339–341, 342f
  U.S. school system, 329
school choice programs, 338
school prayer, social policy on, 362–363
science, 3
scientific management approach, 120
scientific method, 30f, 30–35
  data collection and analysis, 30f,
    33–34, 35
  defining problem, 30–31, 35
  developing conclusions, 30f, 34,
    34f, 35
  formulating hypothesis, 30f, 31–33, 35
  modern education and, 332
  review of literature, 30f, 31, 35, 50
SCLC (Southern Christian Leadership
    Conference), 243
SEC (Securities and Exchange
    Commission), 116, 203
secession of ethnic groups, 240

secondary analysis, 39, 39t, 40, 40t
secondary groups, 113, 113t, 114, 116
Second Life, 2
The Second Sex (de Beauvoir), 276
second shift, 275
Secret Service, 173
sects, religious, 359, 360t, 363
secularization, 350, 357
Securities and Exchange Commission
    (SEC), 116, 203
Security Council, U.N., 374
segmented audience, 142–143
segregation, 235, 237, 333
  of ethnic groups, 240–241, 241f
  by gender, 219
  occupational, 273–274
Seinfeld (TV series), 247
self, 82–87
  looking-glass self, 82, 85t
  Mead's stages of, 82, 83t, 85t
  Mead's theory of, 82–83
  presentation of, 83–84
  psychological approaches to,
    84–85, 85t
  sociological approaches to, 82–84, 85t
self-employment, 202
self-identity, 460
  developing, 82
  labeling and, 269, 270, 270–271
self-injury, 29, 44, 446
semiperiphery nations, 212, 212f
Seneca Falls Convention (1848),
    276–277
Senegal, 211f, 220, 220
senilicide, 299
sensorimotor stage of development, 84
September 11, 2001 terrorist
    attacks, 171
  bureaucratic dysfunction and, 117
  economic effects of, 21
  Internet reaction to, 133
  media and, 129–130, 134
  racial profiling following, 239, 249
  rumors concerning, 439
  social control following, 156–157
  USA Patriot Act of 2001, 146,
    374, 457
  World Trade Center collapse, 436,
    436, 437
Serbia, 211f
serial monogamy, 306
service industries, 214–215, 386–388
service occupations, 110, 245, 263
Services and Advocacy for GLBT Elders
    (SAGE), 298
SES. See socioeconomic status
Seventh-Day Adventists, 359
sex discrimination, 271–272, 275, 280,
    335–336
sex education, 332
sexism, 105, 335–336
  in coverage of female athletes, 137
  in health care and research, 404
  sex discrimination, 271–272, 275, 280,
    335–336
sex offender registries, 160
sexual harassment, 102, 264, 265
sexual identity, 271

high school subcultures and, 340–341
labeling and, 270, 270–271
social movements and, 442–443
stratification by, 268, 270
study of society and. See queer theory
Sexual Politics (Millett), 276
Shakers, 105, 354
Shanghai Stock Exchange, 384
sharing economy, 386–388, 391
Sherpa people (Nepal), 285
Shia (Shiite) Muslims, 351
shootings
  Charleston S.C. church shootings
    (2015), 133, 133
  Columbine High School (1999),
    114, 134
  mental illness as factor in, 160
  Newtown, Conn. elementary school
    (2012), 160, 409
  Trayvon Martin, 434
  Virginia Tech shootings (2007), 4,
    113, 133–134, 168
Shopping Our Way to Safety (A. Szasz),
    396, 426
Shoshit, Setkari, Kashtakari, Kamgar,
    Mukti Sangharsh (SSKKMS), 444
Shout Your Love from the Middle of a
    Cabbage Patch Day, 99
sick role, 397–398, 402
Sierra Leone, 57f, 211f
significant others, 83, 87
"silo effect," 117
"silver collar economy," 296
"silver surfers," 286
Singapore, 155, 211f
singlehood as lifestyle, 321–322
single mothers, 197
single-parent families, 314f,
    317–318, 321
Sinopec, 215f
"16 Days of Activism Against Gender
    Based Violence," 219
Sixteenth Amendment (1916), 191
skin color, 228–229, 238–239, 239, 400
slave reparations, 243
slavery
  Africans defined as sick, 400
  Anti-Slavery Union, 229
  demands for reparations, 243
  as stratification system, 183, 183t, 191
  as transnational crime, 170
Slender Man, 438–439
Slovakia, 92, 211f
Slovenia, 211f
"slugging," 16
smoking, 34, 34, 160, 165
SNAP (Supplemental Nutrition Assis-
    tance Program), 196
Snapchat, 143
"snowball" samples, 33
Snowden, Edward, 145
snowfall, reduced, 422–423
social behavior, 106, 400
social capital, 12, 138
social change, 430–461, 449f
  anticipating, 452–453
  conflict perspective on, 449, 450t,
    450, 452

in Dubai, *453,* 453–454, 460, 461
education as agent of, 331–332, 332*f, 332*
evolutionary theory of, 447, 453
functionalist perspective on, 447, 449, 453
in *Gesellschaft,* 108
global, 452–461
religion and, 352, 353, *353*
resistance to, 450–451, *451,* 461
social movements and. *See* social movements
social policy: transnationals, 458–461, 459*f*
theories of, 447, 448*f,* 449*f,* 449–452, 450*t*
social class. *See also* class system
family and, 313
gender and, 192
impact on elderly persons, 288
inequalities preserved by schools, 334
labeling and, 164
life chances and, 198
objective method of measuring, 192–193, 193*t,* 195
occupational prestige and, 192, 193*t*
social epidemiology and, 402–403
socioeconomic status (SES) and, 193
stratification by, 184–186, 192–195
underclass, 197–198
social construction
of gender, 261–268
of race, 228–229, 230*f*
social constructionist perspective, 165, 166*t*
social control, *153,* 153–159
agents of, 165
of binge drinking, 156
collective behavior and, 433, 434
by Communist Party, 433
conformity and obedience, 153–159
control theory, 158
education and, 331
formal and informal, *155,* 155–157
of gender roles, 265
law as, 157–158
medicine as, 398
Milgram experiment in, 154, *154*
religion and, 353, 354*t*
social policy: death penalty, 173–175, 174*f, 175*
social customs, 70–71
social disorganization theory, 163–164, *164,* 166*t,* 167
social epidemiology, 402–408, 403*f*
social factors in gender stratification, 267, 267*f,* 268*t*
social impact of religion, 350
social indicators of modernization, 217
social inequality, 21, 180–181, 191, *450*
attitudes toward, 190*t*
credentialism and, 333
functionalist perspective on, 189, *189*
minority groups, 228
open displays of, *214*
preserved by schools, 334
social institutions, 1–6, 104–106, 118*t*
conflict perspective on, 105–106

education as. *See* education; school(s)
feminist perspective on, 105–106
functionalist perspective on, 105
interactionist perspective on, 105–106
social integration, 331
social interaction(s), 98
as key to development, 84–85
media-free days and, 92, *92*
micro-level analysis of, 59
reality and, 99–100
social structure and, 99–106
social interactions, 106
social involvement, aging and, 286–287
socialism, 384, 385, 385*t*
socialization, 76–94, *81*
agents of. *See* agents of socialization
anticipatory, 86–87, 102–113, 115, 292, 315
of children, 78–79, *79,* 331
to conforming behavior, 158
as function of education, 331
as function of family, 307
to gender roles, 261–262, 263, 331
occupational, 90–91
role of, *78–81*
self and, 82–87, 85*t*
social policy: child care, *93,* 93–94
throughout life course, 85–86
social meanings, 59–60, 99, 100, 232
social media
careers in, 137
collective behavior and, 433
physician-assisted suicide and, 300
politicking on, 142–143, 381
protests and, 432
social movements and, 431, 445
social networks and, 138–139, 139*f*
use by terrorists, 374
social media consulting, 137
social mobility, 199–202, 204
in developing nations, *219,* 219–221
education and, 198, 201
gender and, *201,* 202, 219–221, 223
globally, 220, *220*
in industrialized nations, 218–219
occupational mobility, 201
in open v. closed systems, 200
poverty and, 195–204, 196*f,* 220, *220,* 223
roles of race and ethnicity in, 201–202
types of, 200, 200*f*
social movements, 440*t, 441,* 441–446, 445*t*
bureaucratization of, 120
communications technologies and, 431, 445, *445,* 446
ecofeminist movement, 426
emergence of, 441–444, 445*t*
environmentalism, 424–426, 425*f,* 427, 443
gender and, 442–443
Internet and, 445
new social movements, 443–444, 445*t,* 446
relative deprivation approach to, 442, 445*t,* 446
resource mobilization approach to, 442, *443,* 445*t*

role of communication in, 445, *445,* 446
transnationals in, 460
women's, 443, 444, *444*
Social Movements and New Technology (Carty), 431, 432
social networks, 12, 104, 106
communal bonds and, 164
of corporate executives, 203
ethnicity and, 104, 286
in formal organizations, 120
online marketing through, 138–139, 139*f*
women's use of, 104, 137–138
social policy, 22
on abortion, 277–279, 279*f,* 280
bilingualism, 71–73
charter schools, 342, 343*f,* 343–344, *344,* 345
child care, *93,* 93–94
death penalty, 173–175, 174*f, 175*
environmentalism, 424–426, 425*f,* 427
on executive compensation, 202–203, *203*
family leave, 322*f*–324*f,* 322–325
global refugee crisis, 254*t,* 254–255, *255*
labor unions, 121*f,* 121–123
microfinancing, 389–391, *390, 391*
religion in schools, *362,* 362–363
right to die, 299*f,* 299–300
right to privacy, 145–147, *147*
studying human sexuality, 47*f,* 47–48, 48*f*
toward immigrant laborers, 21
transnationals, 458–461, 459*f*
welfare, *221,* 221–223
social reality, 99–100
social reformers, 11–12
social roles, 101–103, 106
role conflict, 101–102, *103*
role exit, 102–103, *103*
role strain, 102
social sciences, 3–6, 5*t,* 7
Social Security Administration, 297
Social Security benefits, 288, 291, 297
social service programs, 384
social status, 193, 290, 309
"social street," 108, *108*
social structure, 98, 100–106
Gemeinschaft and *Gesellschaft,* 107–108, 109*t*
global perspective on, 107–112
groups. *See* group(s)
mechanical and organic solidarity, 107, 112
social institutions. *See* social institutions
social networks. *See* social networks
social policy: labor unions, 121*f,* 121–123
social roles, 101–103, 106
sociocultural evolution approach, 109–112, 110*t*
statuses. *See* status(es)
social support, religion as, 351–352, *352*
social welfare, 221–223
social work, 23–24

societal-reaction approach. *See* labeling theory
society(ies), 55, 57. *See also specific stages of society*
aging and, 285–288
analysis of, 12
contradictory nature of, 449
extinction of, 105
growth rate of, 413
law and, 157–158
McDonaldization of, 66–67, 119, *119*
medicalization of, 398, *398*
Society for the Study of Social Problems, 12
Society in America (Martineau), 8
sociobiology, 56–57, 447
sociocultural evolution, 109–112, 110*t*
industrial societies, 110
postindustrial and postmodern societies, 110–112
preindustrial societies, *109,* 109–110
socioeconomic status (SES), 193, 195
of child's family, 309
in matrix of domination, 267, 267*f,* 268*t*
Sociological Abstracts, 50
sociological imagination, 3, 7, 20–22
sociological perspectives
on aging, 285–289, 288*t*
on culture, 55, 63*f,* 65, 65*t*
on deviance, 161–166, 166*t*
on education, 330*f,* 330–337, 336*t*
on environmental issues, 419–427, *420*
on families, 307–309
on gender, 265–268
on global inequality, 217*t*
global view of family, 307–310
on health, 397–400, 401*t*
on mass media, 129–142, 139*t*
on poverty, 197, 198
on racial and ethnic inequality, 238–242, 240*t*
on religion, 350–354
on stratification, 187–188, 190*t*
sociological research, 28–50
on affirmative action, 387, *387*
on age stratification, 284
on aging and declining poverty, 297
on Amish subculture, 88, *88*
attitudes toward marijuana, 49*f,* 49–50
on automation, 456, 456*t*
careers in, 42, *42*
content analysis, 39–40
cross-cultural, 100, 219, 265
on demographics, 412–413
on disability as master status, 102
on elderspeak, 287, *287*
"Elmtown" study, 340
ethics of, 41–43
feminist. *See* feminist perspective
on housing issues in Boston, 44–45, 45*f*
on human sexuality, 37, 37*t,* 47*f,* 47–48, 48*f*
on institutional discrimination, 236, *236*
on Latino political activity, 377, *377*
Milgram experiment, 154, *154*

upper-middle class, 185
"urban Amish," 451
urban life
    changes in caste system and, 184
    ethnic neighborhoods, 242, 246–247
    Gesellschaft, 107, 108
    migration to cities, 219, *219*
    underclass in, 197–198
Uruguay, 211*f*, 322*f*, 323*f*
USA Patriot Act of 2001, 146, 374, 457
USS *New York,* 60
Uzbekistan, 211*f*, 311

V

validity, 33, 35
value-added perspective, 433–434, 440
value generalization, 449
value neutrality, 43
values, 62–63, 63*f*
vandalism, 170, 435
variables, 28, 31, 34, *34*
varnas (castes), 183–184, 191
veil(s), 273
"veiled reporting" technique, 44
Venezuela, 63*f*, 172, 211*f*, 324*f*
verstehen, 9
vertical social mobility, 200
vested interests, 450, 452
victimization surveys, 171, 171*t*
victimless crimes, 167, 176
video gaming, 137
Viet Kieu, 248
Vietnam, 211*f*, 240, 384
Vietnamese Americans, 233, 245*f*, 248
Vietnam War, 248
Village (Grameen) Bank, 389, *390,* 391
A Vindication of the Rights of Women
    (Wollstonecraft), 266
violence
    association with mental illness, 409
    domestic violence, 309
    ethnic riots in France, 241
    female infanticide, 219
    gender-based, action against, 219
    rape, 166, 171
    religion-based, 351
    shootings. *See* shootings
    study of, 4
    against women, 265
violent crime
    in border areas, 6
    homicide, 172
    rioting, 241, 435
    shootings. *See* shootings
    Slender Man murder, 439
    in U.S., 171*t,* 172
Virginia Tech shootings (2007), 4, 113,
    133–134, 168
visual sociology, 38, *38,* 137
vital statistics, 413
vocational subculture, 341
Volkswagen, 215*f*
volunteer work, by elderly persons, 287
voter ID cards, 236, *236,* 377

voting
    eligibility of transnationals, 460
    by Latinos, 250
    mental illness and, 409
    participation and apathy,
        375–376, 376*f*
voting rights, 235, 236, *236*

W

wage inequality
    gender-based, 116, 274–275
    labor unions and, 122
wages/salaries
    executive compensation, 202–203, *203*
    gender-based wage gap, 116, 274–275
    migration to cities and, 219
    for teachers, 339, 341*f*
    unemployment compensation, 190
    of women in U.S. workforce, 116,
        274–275
Walgreens, 406
Walk Free Foundation, 183
"wallet biopsies," 408
Walmart, 122, 215*f*, 406, 432, 433, *433*
Walt Disney World, 111, *111*
war, 371–372, 375. *See also specific*
        wars
    decision to declare, 371
    over resources, 383–384, *384*
    women in combat, 264, *264,* 372
The War of the Worlds (radio
        broadcast), 438
water pollution, 422, *422*
wealth, 181. *See also* income; poverty
    analysis of wealthy, 190*t*
    in China, 384
    distribution of family wealth, 194*f,*
        194–195
    of elderly persons, 295–296
    gender inequality among wealthy,
        272–273
    stratification by, 194*f,* 194–195
    unequal distribution of, 195
web-based surveys, 36
Weber, Max, 9, 10*f,* 12
    on bureaucracies, 117, 118, 120, 123
    classification of authority,
        368–369, *369*
    power as element of
        stratification, 188
    on Protestant ethic, 10*f,* 352,
        353, 354
    view of stratification, 188, 191
weblining, 147
welfare
    social policy on, *221,* 221–223
    stigma associated with, 191
"welfare scapegoating," 222
wellness clinics, 407
Wells-Barnett, Ida, 11–12, 15, *15,* 17*t*
West Bank, 211*f*
Western Electric Company, 39
West Virginia, 295
Whirlpool Corporation, 389

white-collar crime, *169,* 169–170, 176
White ethnics, 252, *252*
White privilege, 233–234
Whites
    demographics, 229*t,* 230*f*
    in environmental movements, 426
    health of, 408
    influence in pluralism, 380
    lifetime earnings of, 332*f*
    single-parent families among, 317
WHO (World Health Organization),
    397, 407
The Who, 432, 433
Who Rules America? The Triumph of
        the Corporate Rich (Domhoff),
    367, 368
Who Wants to be a Millionaire
        (TV series), 135
Wicca, 353, 361, *361*
WikiLeaks, 146
The Wolf Pack (film), 77
women. *See also* men (males)
    activism of, 220, 444, *444*
    as athletes, *17,* 17–18
    bloggers, 138–139
    child care issues, *93,* 93–94
    collective consciousness of, 276–277
    in combat, 264, *264,* 372
    coverage of women's sports, 40, 137
    disenfranchised, 376
    as economic support of family, 313
    education of, 337
    effects of disasters on, 21–22, 89
    elderly, 295, 296
    female infanticide, 219
    feminization of poverty, 197, 197*t,*
        272, 313
    gender roles of, *262,* 262–263
    gender wage inequality, 116, 274–275
    health care system and, 404
    in informal economy, 385
    institutional discrimination against,
        271–272, 280
    in Iran, lives of, 260–261
    microfinancing and, 389, 390
    Muslim, wearing of *hijab,* 273, *273*
    occupational prestige and, 192–193
    as oppressed majority, 271–280
    in politics, 271, 272, 377–378, 378*f*
    post-war pressure for marriage, 416
    sexism and sex discrimination,
        271–272, 275, 280, 335–336
    sexualization in motion pictures,
        47, 47*f*
    shortage of, in China, 415
    social mobility of, *201,* 202
    social movements by, 443, 444, *444*
    social networks and, 104, 137–138
    as sociologists, *7,* 8, *11,* 11–12,
        15, *15*
    status of, 43, 272–273
    stereotyped, 137, 335
    subordination of, in Christianity,
        353–354, *354*
    superior academic performance of,
        335–336

treatment of, in Afghanistan,
    265, 336
trend toward single lifestyle, 321–322
value of women's unpaid labor, 192
women in U.S. workforce,
    273–275, 280
    affirmative action and, 387
    compensation of, 116, 274–275
    exploitation of, 272, 282
    impact on family, 309–310
    labor force participation, 273–274,
        274*f,* 275*t*
    marriage and, 275
    preference for male bosses, 276, *276*
    reasons for leaving employment,
        275, 277*f*
    self-employment, 202
    social consequences of employment,
        272*f,* 275, 277*f*
Women's Day (S. Korea), 444, *444*
Women's Sports Foundation, 335
work
    consequences of, 8
    decline in walking to work, 447, 449*f*
    substandard, impact of, 195
    women's work devalued, 266
workers
    dysfunctions of informal
        economy, 385
    immigrant, in Dubai, 453, 460
    migrants. *See* migrant laborers
    transnationals, 458–461, 459*f*
    women as. *See* women in U.S.
        workforce
Worker's Party of Korea, *370*
workforce. *See also* migrant laborers
    affirmative action in, 387
    automation and, 456
    changing face of, 386–389
    competition from elderly in, 287, *287,*
        292, 296–298, 297*f*
    exploitation of workers, 22, 187, *187,*
        217, 218
    temporary employment, 122, 186,
        186, 388
    women in. *See* women in U.S.
        workforce
working class, 21, 185
    exploitation of, 22, 187, *187,* 218
    old age and, 288
workplace
    as agent of socialization, 90–91, 94
    pro-child practices in, 322
    secondary groups in, 113, 113*t*
    social norms in, 106
World Bank, 213
World Changing (Steffen), 445
World Economic Forum, 138
World Health Organization (WHO),
    397, 407
world religions, 355*t,* 355–358, 356*f*
world systems analysis, 437
world systems analysis view
    of environmental issues, 419, 424
    of global development
        inequalities, 421

of global inequality, 212*f*, 212–213, 217, 217*t*

of microfinancing, 390

World Trade Center, 436, *436*, 437

World Trade Center memorial, 60, *60*

World Trade Organization, 441

World War II, 248

baby boom following, 416

"death control" following, 414

genocide during, 155, 240, 351

written rules and regulations

in bureaucracies, 118, 118*t*, 119

in schools, 337

X

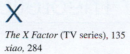

The X Factor (TV series), 135

xiao, 284

y

Yanomami people (Brazil & Venezuela), 305

Yemen, *80, 211f*

young people

attitudes toward privacy issues, 456–457

job seekers, 304

political apathy of, 376, 381

YouTube, flash mobs on, 435

Yule, Jack, 80

Yunus, Muhammad, 389, *390,* 391

Z

Zambia, 57*f*, 211*f,* 213

Zapatistas (Mexico), 445

zebu (cattle), 13–14, 56

zero population growth (ZPG), 417

Zimbabwe, 211*f*

ZPG (zero population growth), 417

Zuni tribe, 293

Applications of *Sociology's* Major Theoretical Approaches

Sociology in Modules provides comprehensive coverage of the major sociological perspectives. This summary table includes a sample of the topics in the text that have been explored using the major approaches. "M" indicates the module and the numbers in parentheses indicate the pertinent chapters.

FUNCTIONALIST PERSPECTIVE

- M3 Defined and explained (1)
- M40 Adoption (13)
- M24 Anomie theory of deviance (7)
- M12 Bilingualism (3)
- M43 Bureaucratization of schools (14)
- M44 Charter schools (14)
- M3 Cow worship in India (1)
- M10 M43 Culture (3, 14)
- M26 Davis and Moore's view of stratification (8)
- M23 Death penalty (7)
- M23 Debtors' prisons (7)
- M37 Disengagement theory of aging (12)
- M9 Dominant ideology (3)
- M24 Durkheim's view of deviance (7)
- M32 Dysfunctions of racism (10)
- M9 Ethnocentrism (3)
- M28 Executive compensation (8)
- M40 Family (13)
- M42 Family leave policies (13)
- M19 Formal organizations (5)
- M32 Functions of racism (10)
- M28 Gans's functions of poverty (8)
- M42 Gay marriage (13)
- M34 Gender stratification (11)
- M33 Global immigration (10)
- M37 Global refugee crisis (10)
- M52 Health and illness (17)
- M53 Human ecology (17)
- M27 Income tax (8)
- M18 In-groups and out-groups (5)
- M45 Integrative function of religion (15)
- M22 Internet privacy (6)
- M20 Media and social norms (6)
- M20 Media and socialization (6)
- M20 Media and status conferral (6)
- M22 Media concentration (6)
- M20 Media promotion of consumption (6)
- M29 Modernization theory (9)
- M29 Multinational corporations (9)
- M24 Narcotizing effect of the media (6)
- M51 Offshoring (16)
- M32 Racial prejudice and discrimination (10)
- M45 Religion as a source of social support (15)
- M43 M57 Social change (14, 18)
- M23 M43 Social control (7, 14)
- M16 Social institutions (5)
- M45 Socialization function of religion (15)
- M15 M43 Socialization in schools (4, 14)
- M3 Sports (1)
- M11 Subcultures (3)
- M60 Transnationals (18)

CONFLICT PERSPECTIVE

- M3 Defined and explained (1)
- M36 Abortion (11)
- M53 Access to health care (17)
- M60 Access to technology (18)
- M51 Affirmative action (16)
- M37 Age stratification (12)
- M12 Bilingualism (3)
- M44 Bureaucratization of schools (14)
- M50 Capitalism (16)
- M44 Charter schools (14)
- M28 Corporate welfare (8)
- M43 Correspondence principle (14)
- M43 Credentialism (14)
- M10 Culture (3)
- M15 Day care funding (4)
- M25 Death penalty (7)
- M24 Deviance (7)
- M16 Disability as a master status (5)
- M9 M20 M26 Dominant ideology (3, 6, 8)
- M51 Downsizing (16)
- M49 Elite model of the U.S. power structure (16)
- M56 Environmental issues (17)
- M56 Environmentalism (17)
- M28 Executive compensation (8)
- M32 Exploitation theory of discrimination (10)
- M40 Family (13)
- M42 Gay marriage (13)
- M43 Gender equity in education (13)
- M34 Gender stratification (11)
- M33 Global immigration (10)
- M37 Global refugee crisis (10)
- M25 Gun control (7)
- M43 Hidden curriculum (14)
- M19 Iron Law of Oligarchy (5)
- M26 Marx's view of stratification (8)
- M34 Matrix of domination (11)
- M22 Media concentration (6)
- M20 Media gatekeeping (6)
- M20 Media stereotypes (6)

- M52 Medicalization of society (17)
- M51 Microfinancing (16)
- M28 Minimum wage laws (8)
- M30 Mobility (9)
- M33 Model minority (10)
- M29 Multinational corporations (9)
- M28 Poverty (8)
- M38 Poverty among the elderly (12)
- M60 Privacy and technology (18)
- M53 Racism and health (17)
- M45 Religion and social control (15)
- M59 Social change (18)
- M23 Social control (7)
- M16 Social institutions (5)
- M15 Socialization in schools (4)
- M3 Sports (1)
- M12 Subcultures (3)
- M43 Tracking (14)
- M60 Transnationals (18)
- M24 Victimless crimes (7)
- M25 White-collar crime (7)
- M29 M56 World systems analysis (9, 18)

INTERACTIONIST PERSPECTIVE

- M3 Defined and explained (1)
- M36 Activity theory of aging (12)
- M41 Adoption (13)
- M51 Affirmative action (16)
- M48 Charismatic authority (16)
- M3 Commuter behavior (1)
- M26 Conspicuous consumption (8)
- M32 Contact hypothesis (10)
- M10 Culture (3)
- M24 Differential association (7)
- M52 Doctor-patient interaction (17)
- M14 M48 Dramaturgical approach (4, 16)
- M20 Electronic communication (6)
- M28 Executive compensation (8)
- M40 Family relationships (13)
- M42 Family leave policies (13)
- M42 Gay marriage (13)
- M34 Gender stratification (11)
- M52 Health and illness (17)
- M19 Human relations approach (5)
- M49 Influence of social media sites on politics (16)
- M22 Media concentration (6)
- M51 Microfinancing (16)
- M28 Minimum wage laws (8)
- M23 Obedience (7)
- M14 Presentation of the self (4)
- M24 Routine activities theory (7)
- M24 Social disorganization theory (7)
- M16 Social institutions (5)

- M3 Sports (1)
- M16 Tattoos and social reality (5)
- M43 Teacher-expectancy effect (14)
- M40 Teenage pregnancy (13)
- M60 Transnationals (18)
- M59 Vested interests in NASA's Constellation Project (18)
- M34 Women in combat (11)

FEMINIST PERSPECTIVE

- M3 Defined and explained (1)
- M15 Day care funding (4)
- M24 Deviance (7)
- M9 Dominant ideology (3)
- M8 Ethnographic research (2)
- M40 Family (13)
- M42 Family leave policies (13)
- M43 Gender gap in education (14)
- M34 Gender stratification (11)
- M10 Language (3)
- M34 Matrix of domination (1)
- M20 Media stereotypes (6)
- M51 Microfinancing (16)
- M39 Oneida community (13)
- M20 Pornography (6)
- M24 Rape (7)
- M45 Religion and socialization (15)
- M6 Research methodology (2)
- M5 Self-injury (2)
- M3 Sports (1)
- M60 Transnationals (18)
- M24 Victimless crimes (7)
- M19 Wage inequality (5)
- M8 Women in film (2)
- M36 Women's movement (11)

LABELING THEORY

- M3 Defined and explained (1)
- M16 Disabilities and labeling (5)
- M52 Health and illness (17)
- M35 Human sexuality (12)
- M32 Profiling at airports (10)
- M24 Racial profiling (7)
- M24 Sexual deviance (7)
- M24 Societal reaction approach (7)
- M43 Teacher-expectancy effect (14)
- M24 Victimless crimes (7)

QUEER THEORY

- M9 Child rearing (3)
- M35 Gay marriage (12)
- M20 Homosexuality in the mass media (6)
- M35 LGBT households (12)
- M8 Research methodology (2)
- M3 Sports (1)